Less managing. More teaching. Greater learning.

 INSTRUCTORS...

Would you like your **students** to show up for class **more prepared**?
(Let's face it, class is much more fun if everyone is engaged and prepared...)

Want an **easy way to assign** homework online and track student **progress**?
(Less time grading means more time teaching...)

Want an **instant view** of student or class performance?
(No more wondering if students understand...)

Need to **collect data and generate reports** required for administration or accreditation?
(Say goodbye to manually tracking student learning outcomes...)

Want to **record and post your lectures** for students to view online?
(The more students can see, hear, and experience class resources, the better they learn...)

With **McGraw-Hill's Connect,™**

INSTRUCTORS GET:

- Simple **assignment management**, allowing you to spend more time teaching.
- **Auto-graded** assignments, quizzes, and tests.
- **Detailed visual reporting** where student and section results can be viewed and analyzed.
- Sophisticated **online testing** capability.
- A **filtering and reporting** function that allows you to easily assign and report on materials that are correlated to learning objectives and Bloom's taxonomy.
- An easy-to-use **lecture capture** tool.
- The option to **upload course documents** for student access.

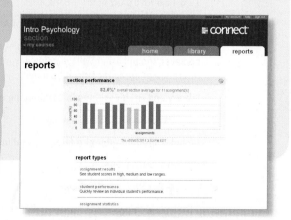

The *McGraw-Hill* Companies

McGraw-Hill Ryerson
Connect. Learn. Succeed.™

Canadian Edition

PsychSmart

Editorial Director: *Rhondda McNabb*
Senior Sponsoring Editor: *Marcia Siekowski*
Marketing Manager: *Margaret Janzen*
Senior Developmental Editor: *Jennifer Cressman*
Supervising Editor: *Cathy Biribauer*
Photo/Permissions Researcher: *Derek Capitaine, www.mrmassociates.ca*
Senior Editorial Associate: *Marina Seguin*
Copy Editor: *Cat Haggert*
Production Coordinator: *Tammy Mavroudi*
Cover and Interior Design: *Mark Cruxton, type+image*
Composition: *Michelle Losier*
Cover Photo: *©John Molloy/Getty Images*
Printer: *Quad Graphics*

ISBN-13: 978-0-07-105674-8
ISBN-10: 0-07-105674-2

1 2 3 4 5 6 7 8 9 0 QG 1 9 8 7 6 5 4 3

Printed and bound in the United States of America

Library and Archives Canada Cataloguing in Publication Data

PsychSmart. -- Canadian ed.

Includes bibliographical references and index.

ISBN 978-0-07-105674-8

1. Psychology--Textbooks.

BF121.P86 2012   150   C2012-902211-X

Ch. 5
HOW WE LEARN

Ch. 10
LIFESPAN AND
FAMILIES

Ch. 1 >
THE ROOTS OF
PSYCHOLOGY

< Ch. 11
WHERE DOES
PERSONALITY
COME FROM?

Canadian Edition

PsychSmart

BRIEF CONTENTS

1 Introduction to Psychology 2

2 Neuroscience and Behaviour 30

3 Sensation & Perception 58

4 States of Consciousness 86

5 Learning 110

6 Memory 134

7 Thinking, Language, and Intelligences 160

8 Motivation and Emotion 190

9 Social Psychology 216

10 Development 242

11 Personality 280

12 Psychological Disorders and Treatments 302

13 Health Psychology: Stress, Coping, and Well-Being 338

About the Canadian Author

Barbara Bond is a Professor of Psychology at both Sir Sandford Fleming College and Trent University in Peterborough, Ontario. Bond completed a Law and Justice diploma at Fleming College prior to completing a MSc in Psychology at Trent University. Recipient of the Charles E. Pascal Award for Excellence in Teaching at Fleming College, twice nominated for the Award of Excellence in Part-time Teaching at Trent University, and once nominated for the Distinguished Teaching Award for Educational Leadership and Innovation in Instruction at Trent University, Bond has published several articles and presented at numerous conferences on her research interests, emotional intelligence and academic success.

About the Contributors

Tanya Renner, Professor of Psychology at Kapiʻolani Community College, earned a PhD in developmental psychology from the University of California at Berkeley. In addition to teaching introductory psychology, Renner studies effective teaching and learning practices and ways to develop critical thinking skills. A strong advocate for problem-based learning, both as an educator and as a researcher, she also actively supports the use of ePortfolio software as a teaching-learning strategy and participated in a national project headed by the American Council on Education to develop specific strategies for using ePortfolios and for assessing the student learning demonstrated in an ePortfolio.

Robert S. Feldman is a Professor of Psychology and Dean of the College of Social and Behavior Sciences at the University of Massachusetts at Amherst. A winner of the College Distinguished Teacher award and a Fellow of both the American Psychological Association and the Association for Psychological Science, Feldman has written more than 100 books, book chapters, and scientific articles. For much of his career, Feldman has studied lying and deception, culminating in the recent publication of *The Liar in Your Life: The Way to Truthful Relationships*. He holds a PhD from the University of Wisconsin-Madison.

Joe Morrissey, a product of Rutgers University and Boston University, is a cognitive psychologist who studies face recognition and teaches a variety of psychology courses, including introductory psychology, statistics, research methods, learning, neuroscience, and industrial/organizational psychology. He is a frequent contributor to textbook supplements.

Lynda Mae holds a PhD in Social Psychology from Purdue University. She teaches psychology at Arizona State University in Tempe and does trial consulting. She specializes in the creation of multimedia lectures and courtroom presentations using engaging imagery, film clips, music, and other media.

Mike Majors, Assistant Professor of Psychology at Delgado Community College, prepared the supplements for *PsychSmart* (available at www.mhhe.com/psychsmart1e2011). Majors has a bachelor's degree from Auburn University and a master's degree in psychology from Mississippi State University. He currently teaches both traditional face-to-face classes and online classes in general psychology. In addition, he is the author of several introductory psychology study guides. Majors is a member of the Association for Psychological Science (APS), the Society for the Teaching of Psychology (American Psychological Association Division 2), and Psi Chi, the National Honor Society in Psychology.

1 > Introduction to Psychology 2

Could you live without social media? 3

WHAT IS PSYCHOLOGY? 4
Modern Perspectives of Psychology 5
Key Issues in Psychology 8
The Subfields of Psychology 10
Working at Psychology 11

A SCIENCE EVOLVES 13
The Roots of Psychology 14
Founding Mothers of Psychology 15
Psychology's Future 16

THE RESEARCH PROCESS IN PSYCHOLOGY 16
The Scientific Method 16
Theories: Broad Explanations 17
Hypotheses: Testable Predictions 17
Psychological Research Methods 17
Descriptive Research 18
Experimental Research 21

RESEARCH CHALLENGES 24
Experimental Bias 24
The Ethics of Research 26
Should Animals Be Used in Research? 26

2 > Neuroscience and Behaviour 30

The fallen athlete 31

NEURONS: THE BASIC UNITS OF THE NERVOUS SYSTEM 33
Structure of the Neuron 33
How Neurons Fire 34
Bridging the Gap Between Neurons 35
Neurotransmitters: Chemical Couriers 37

THE NERVOUS SYSTEM: LINKING NEURONS 39
Central and Peripheral Nervous Systems 40
Behavioural Genetics 42

THE BRAIN 43
Spying on the Brain 43
The Central Core: Our "Old Brain" 45
The Limbic System: Beyond the Central Core 46
The Cerebral Cortex: Our "New Brain" 47
The Adaptable Brain 49
Two Brains or One? 50
Human Diversity and Brain Lateralization 51
The Split Brain: Exploring the Two Hemispheres 52
Controlling Your Heart—and Mind—Through Biofeedback 53

THE ENDOCRINE SYSTEM: HORMONES AND GLANDS 54

3 > Sensation & Perception 58

Kari cannot recognize her own family 59

SENSATION AND PERCEPTION: TWO SIDES OF THE SAME COIN 60

SENSING THE WORLD AROUND US 60

Absolute Thresholds 62

Difference Thresholds 62

Sensory Adaptation 63

PERCEPTION: CONSTRUCTING OUR IMPRESSIONS OF THE WORLD 64

Perceptual Sets 64

Top-Down and Bottom-Up Processing 64

The Gestalt Laws of Organization 65

Perceptual Constancy 66

Depth Perception 66

Perceptual Illusions 67

Culture and Perception 68

VISION: SHEDDING LIGHT ON THE EYE 69

Illuminating the Eye 70

Colour Vision and Colour Blindness 73

HEARING AND THE OTHER SENSES 75

Sensing Sound 75

Smell and Taste 77

The Skin Senses: Touch, Pressure, Temperature, and Pain 78

Pain Management 81

How Our Senses Interact 81

4 > States of Consciousness 86

Midnight receiver 87

SLEEP AND DREAMS 88

Circadian Rhythms 89

The Stages of Sleep 89

REM Sleep: The Paradox of Sleep 91

Why Do We Sleep and How Much Sleep Is Necessary? 92

The Impact of Electronics on Sleep 93

The Function and Meaning of Dreaming 93

Sleep Disturbances 95

HYPNOSIS AND MEDITATION 97

Hypnosis: A Trance-Forming Experience? 97

Meditation: Regulating Our Own Consciousness 98

Cross-Cultural Routes to Altered States of Consciousness 99

DRUG USE: THE HIGHS AND LOWS OF CONSCIOUSNESS 100

Stimulants: Drug Highs 101

Depressants: Drug Lows 104

Narcotics 106

Identifying Drug and Alcohol Problems 107

5 > Learning 110

A four-legged co-worker 111

CLASSICAL CONDITIONING 113

What Is Classical Conditioning? 113

How Do Conditioning Principles Apply to Human Behaviour? 115

Extinction of a Conditioned Response 116

Generalization and Discrimination 116

OPERANT CONDITIONING 117

How Operant Conditioning Works 118

Behaviour Analysis and Behaviour Modification 126

COGNITIVE APPROACHES TO LEARNING 127

Latent Learning 127

Observational Learning: Learning Through Imitation 129

Violence in Television and Video Games: Does the Media's Message Matter? 130

6 > Memory 134

I wish my memory was perfect so I wouldn't have to study so much! 135

THE FOUNDATIONS OF MEMORY 137
Sensory Memory 138
Short-Term Memory 139
Long-Term Memory 141
Long-Term Memory Modules 142
Semantic Networks 143

RECALLING LONG-TERM MEMORIES 144
Retrieval Cues 144
Levels of Processing 145
Explicit and Implicit Memory 146
Flashbulb Memories 147
Constructive Processes in Memory 148

FORGETTING: WHEN MEMORY FAILS 152
Why We Forget 154
Proactive and Retroactive Interference 155
Memory Dysfunctions 155
The Neuroscience of Memory 156

7 > Thinking, Language, and Intelligences 160

Solving lottery fraud 161

THINKING AND REASONING 162
Mental Images 162
Concepts 162
Algorithms and Heuristics 163
Solving Problems 164
Creativity and Problem Solving 169
Learning to Be a Better Thinker 170

LANGUAGE 171
Grammar: The Rules of Language 172
Language Development 173
Theories of Language Acquisition 174

INTELLIGENCE 175
Theories of Intelligence 176
Measuring Intelligence 180
Variations in Intellectual Ability 184
Group Differences in Intelligence 186
Nature, Nurture, and IQ 186

8 > Motivation and Emotion 190

She would not give up 191

EXPLAINING MOTIVATION 192
Instinct Approaches 192
Drive-Reduction Approaches 193
Arousal Approaches 193
Incentive Approaches 194
Cognitive Approaches 195
Maslow's Hierarchy of Needs 195
Applying Motivation Approaches 196

HUMAN NEEDS AND MOTIVATION 197
The Needs for Achievement, Affiliation, and Power 197
Measuring Achievement Motivation 197
Hunger and Eating 198
Sexual Motivation 204

UNDERSTANDING EMOTIONAL EXPERIENCES 208
The Functions of Emotions 208
Determining the Range of Emotions 209
The Roots of Emotion s 209
Cultural Differences in Expressions of Emotion 212

9 > Social Psychology 216

Sexual assault posted on Facebook 217

ATTITUDES AND SOCIAL COGNITION 218
Persuasion: Changing Attitudes 218
Social Cognition: Understanding Others 222

SOCIAL INFLUENCE AND GROUPS 225
Conformity: Following What Others Do 226
Compliance: Submitting to Direct Social Pressure 227

STEREOTYPES, PREJUDICE, AND DISCRIMINATION 231
The Foundations of Prejudice 231
Measuring Prejudice and Discrimination: The Implicit Association Test 232
Reducing Prejudice and Discrimination 233

POSITIVE AND NEGATIVE SOCIAL BEHAVIOUR 233
Liking and Loving: Interpersonal Attraction and the Development of Relationships 233
Aggression and Prosocial Behaviour 235

10 > Development 242

A 624 gram miracle 243

NATURE AND NURTURE 244
Developmental Research Techniques 246

PRENATAL DEVELOPMENT 247
Basic Genetics 247
Earliest Development 247

INFANCY AND CHILDHOOD 250
The Extraordinary Newborn 250
Infancy Through Middle Childhood 251
Development of Social Behaviour 252

ADOLESCENCE 263
Physical Changes 263
Moral and Cognitive Development 264
Adolescent Social Development 265

ADULTHOOD 269
The Peak of Health 270
Adult Social Development 271
Growing Old 273
Adjusting to Death 276

11 > Personality 280

Perfect husband or serial killer? 281

WHAT IS PERSONALITY? 282

PSYCHODYNAMIC APPROACHES TO PERSONALITY 282
Freud's Psychoanalytic Theory: Mapping the Unconscious Mind 283
The Neo-Freudian Psychoanalysts 287

TRAIT APPROACHES TO PERSONALITY 288
Allport's Trait Theory 289
Factor Analysis 289
The Big Five Factors of Personality 289
Evaluating Trait Approaches to Personality 290

LEARNING APPROACHES TO PERSONALITY 290
Skinner's Behaviourist Approach 291
Social Cognitive Approaches 291
Evaluating Learning Approaches to Personality 292

BIOLOGICAL AND EVOLUTIONARY APPROACHES TO PERSONALITY 293

HUMANISTIC APPROACHES TO PERSONALITY 294

Rogers and the Need for Self-Actualization 294

Evaluating Humanistic Approaches 295

COMPARING APPROACHES TO PERSONALITY 296

ASSESSING PERSONALITY 296

Self-Report Measures of Personality 296

Projective Methods 297

Behavioural Assessment 299

12 > Psychological Disorders and Treatment 302

Chris Coles 303

DEFINING AND DIAGNOSING ABNORMAL BEHAVIOUR 304

Perspectives on Abnormality: From Superstition to Science 304

Classifying Abnormal Behaviour: The *DSM* 305

MAJOR CATEGORIES OF PSYCHOLOGICAL DISORDERS 307

Anxiety Disorders 307

Mood Disorders 311

Schizophrenia 313

Personality Disorders 316

Dissociative Disorders 317

Other Disorders 318

Psychological Disorders in Perspective 319

The Social and Cultural Context of Psychological Disorders 320

TREATMENT OF PSYCHOLOGICAL DISORDERS 321

Biomedical Therapy 322

Psychotherapies 325

Behavioural Approaches to Therapy 327

Cognitive Approaches to Therapy 330

Humanistic Therapy 330

Interpersonal Therapy 331

Group Therapy and Family Therapy 332

Evaluating Psychotherapy 332

Deciding When You Need Help 335

13 > Health Psychology: Stress, Coping, and Well-Being 338

School daze 339

STRESS AND COPING 340

The Nature of Stressors: My Stress Is Your Pleasure 340

Coping with Stress 345

PSYCHOLOGICAL ASPECTS OF ILLNESS AND WELL-BEING 348

The As, Bs, and Ds of Coronary Heart Disease 348

Psychological Aspects of Cancer 349

Smoking 350

PROMOTING HEALTH AND WELLNESS 352

Healthy Eating 352

Sport and Exercise 353

Yoga and Meditation 353

Well-Being and Happiness 354

GLOSSARY 359

REFERENCES 371

CREDITS 411

INDEX 415

Meet PsychSmart. ^{Canadian Edition}

More current, more portable, more captivating.

we listen

Barbara Bond — Canadian Edition

PsychSmart

Stressed out?
How you can cope with it all.

DON'T BELIEVE EVERYTHING
YOU THINK!

Are you addicted
to social media?
Some students can't quit... can you?

Study smarter,
not harder!
Memory techniques can
improve your grades!

Want to live
to be 100?
Find out how.

We listened to students.

We conducted extensive ethnographic student research, examining the workflow of today's student. Students told us they wanted a briefer, more portable text with more visual appeal.

We also listened to instructors.

We used our tried and true market-driven research process and found that instructors need a dynamic and engaging solution for their course needs—but without sacrificing currency, quality, and academic content.

We responded.

PsychSmart blends core content and psychological research with a wealth of real-world examples plus media and online interactivities to create a complete learning resource.

⌄ What's Inside? »

As You Read »

- What is memory?
- Why do we recall some memories better than others?
- Why do we forget information?
- What is the neuroscience of memory?
- How can learning about the concepts in this chapter make you a better student?

For Review »

What is memory?
Memory is the process by which we encode, store, and retrieve information. Memory can be thought of as a three-stage process. Sensory memories are very brief, but they are precise, storing a nearly exact replica of a stimulus. Roughly seven (plus or minus two) chunks of information can be transferred and held in short-term memory for 15 to 25 seconds; if they are not transferred to long-term memory, they are then lost. Memories are transferred into long-term storage by encoding the information for meaning and other strategies, such as elaborative rehearsal. Long-term memory includes declarative memory and procedural memory. Declarative memory is divided into episodic memory and semantic memory.

Why do we recall some memories better than others?
Retrieval cues, such as emotions, sights, and sounds, are a major strategy for recalling information successfully. The levels-of-processing approach to memory suggests that the way in which information is initially perceived and

analyzed determines the success with which it is recalled; the deeper the initial processing, the greater the recall. Flashbulb memories are memories centred on a specific, important event. The more distinctive a memory is, the more easily it can be retrieved. Memory is a constructive process, such that our memories are influenced by the meaning we give to events. Eyewitnesses are apt to make substantial errors when they try to recall the details of crimes. The problem of memory reliability becomes even more acute when the witnesses are children.

Why do we forget information?
Several processes account for memory failure, including decay, interference (both proactive and retroactive), and cue-dependent forgetting, as well as Alzheimer's disease and amnesia. Alzheimer's disease is an illness characterized in part by a progressive loss of memory. Amnesia, another type of memory loss that occurs without other mental difficulties, can take two forms: retrograde amnesia and anterograde amnesia.

⌃
⌃

Learning objectives, listed under the *As You Read* title, help students preview chapter content and study effectively.

‹‹ A summary of each learning objective is provided in the *For Review* section.

Psych Think questions prompt students to think critically about and apply the information discussed in the text. Suggested answers are provided on the last page of each chapter.

⌄
⌄

Study tip

Remember that *d*endrites *d*etect messages from other neurons; *a*xons carry signals *a*way from the cell body.

‹‹ *Study Tips* call attention to important concepts and suggest effective strategies for learning and studying.

Psych think

> > > Use the five elements of classical conditioning to explain why someone who was in a car accident in the past year now feels anxiety and slows down cautiously when driving through an intersection.

BUY IT?

The Lunar Effect: Does a Full Moon Mean More Violent Behaviour?

Are you one of the many people who believe that weird things happen on nights of a full moon? People have reported an increase in traffic accidents, births, casino payouts, and assaults and violent behaviour during a full moon. This is referred to as the lunar effect because many people believe that the full moon has an effect on people's behaviour. As a good critical thinker, hopefully you said that while you have heard of this phenomenon, you will suspend your belief until consulting the empirical research! Good thing you did, because research has not found a significant relationship between full moons and violent behaviour (Kelly, Rotton, & Culver, 1985; Owen, Tarantello, Jones, & Tennant, 1998).

Why do you think so many people believe in the lunar effect? We can explain this using some of the heuristics and biases you've learned about in this chapter. The media tends to report anecdotal evidence of the full moon's impact on human behaviour, which makes this information readily available in reader's minds, thus, the availability heuristic is at work here. Moreover, when people believe in the full moon they will more likely notice the moon's impact on people's behaviour, which confirms their belief in the lunar effect. This of course is an example of confirmation bias, because people are confirming their own belief (The Skeptics Dictionary, 2011).

<< Buy It? sections prompt students to become critical consumers of information.

Psych at the Movies boxes suggest feature-length movies related to the chapter's topics.

∨
∨

Psych
At The Movies

Memento
The main character of this movie suffers from anterograde amnesia. He cannot form new short-term memories and relies on sticky notes and tattoos to carry information from day to day.

The Bourne Identity
A CIA assassin suffers from a form of amnesia in which he has lost all memory of self-identifying information, but he retains procedural memory for such things as hand-to-hand combat skills.

Eternal Sunshine of the Spotless Mind
Are we better off with or without our more difficult memories? Would you erase memories if you could? The main characters in this movie are faced with this decision.

DID YOU KNOW?

One study has suggested that high ceilings may prompt thinking outside the box (free style, broader thinking), and low ceilings may encourage thinking inside the box (more detail-focused thinking) (Meyers-Levy & Zhu, 2007).

Get Involved!

You can do your own observational study of how people react to broken social norms.
How do others react if you face the back or side of the elevator? If you wear your pyjamas to class? If you read out loud in a coffee shop? If you offer small coins to someone on a downtown street (Hey, buddy, here's some extra change)?

<< Get Involved sections extend the study of psychology beyond the classroom by encouraging students to participate in activities that help illustrate concepts in the text.

∧
∧

Did You Know? boxes provide short, interesting nuggets of information relevant to the chapter's topics.

From the Perspective of… questions explore the impact of psychology on different professions, such as policing, medicine, marketing, and education.

∨
∨

Try It! exercises offer students a chance to apply psychology concepts by answering self-assessment questionnaires.

∨
∨

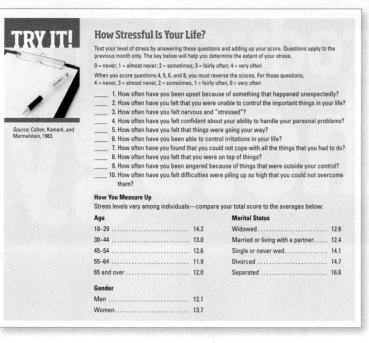

TRY IT!

How Stressful Is Your Life?

Test your level of stress by answering these questions and adding up your score. Questions apply to the previous month only. The key below will help you determine the extent of your stress.

0 = never; 1 = almost never; 2 = sometimes; 3 = fairly often; 4 = very often
When you score questions 4, 5, 6, and 8, you must reverse the scores. For those questions, 4 = never, 3 = almost never, 2 = sometimes, 1 = fairly often, 0 = very often

_____ 1. How often have you been upset because of something that happened unexpectedly?
_____ 2. How often have you felt that you were unable to control the important things in your life?
_____ 3. How often have you felt nervous and "stressed"?
_____ 4. How often have you felt confident about your ability to handle your personal problems?
_____ 5. How often have you felt that things were going your way?
_____ 6. How often have you been able to control irritations in your life?
_____ 7. How often have you found that you could not cope with all the things that you had to do?
_____ 8. How often have you felt that you were on top of things?
_____ 9. How often have you been angered because of things that were outside your control?
_____ 10. How often have you felt difficulties were piling up so high that you could not overcome them?

How You Measure Up
Stress levels vary among individuals—compare your total score to the averages below:

Age		Marital Status	
18–29	14.2	Widowed	12.6
30–44	13.0	Married or living with a partner	12.4
45–54	12.6	Single or never wed	14.1
55–64	11.9	Divorced	14.7
65 and over	12.0	Separated	16.6
Gender			
Men	12.1		
Women	13.7		

Source: Cohen, Kamark, and Mermelstein, 1983.

From the perspective of …

AN EARLY CHILDHOOD EDUCATOR What advice would you give to families about children's exposure to violent media and video games?

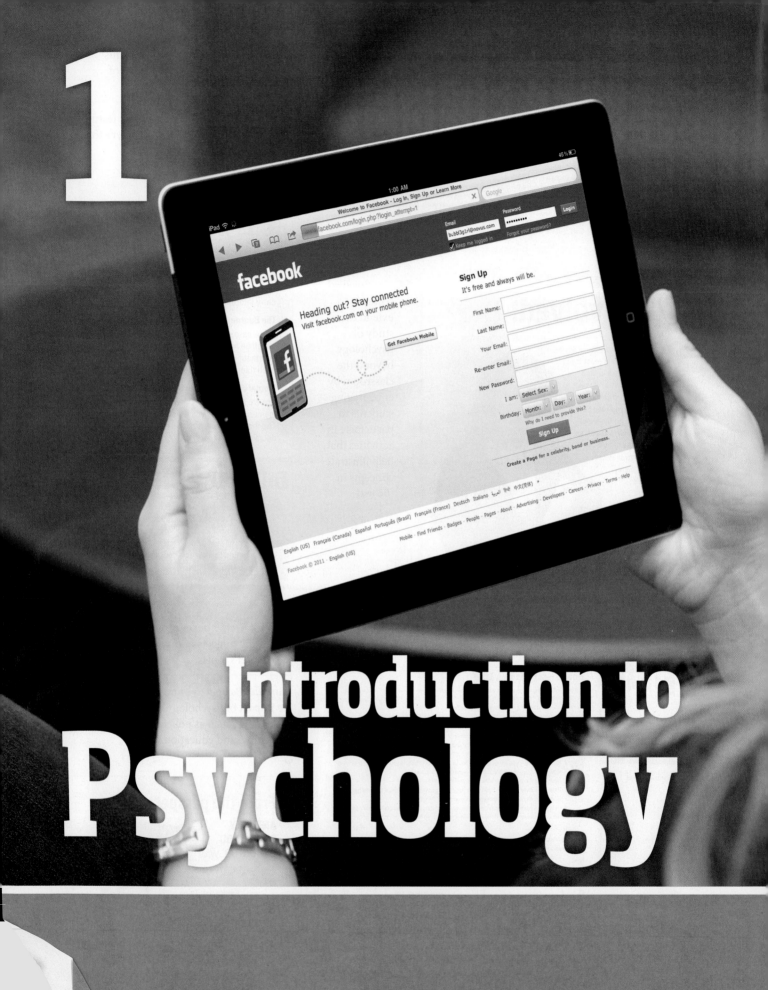

1

Introduction to Psychology

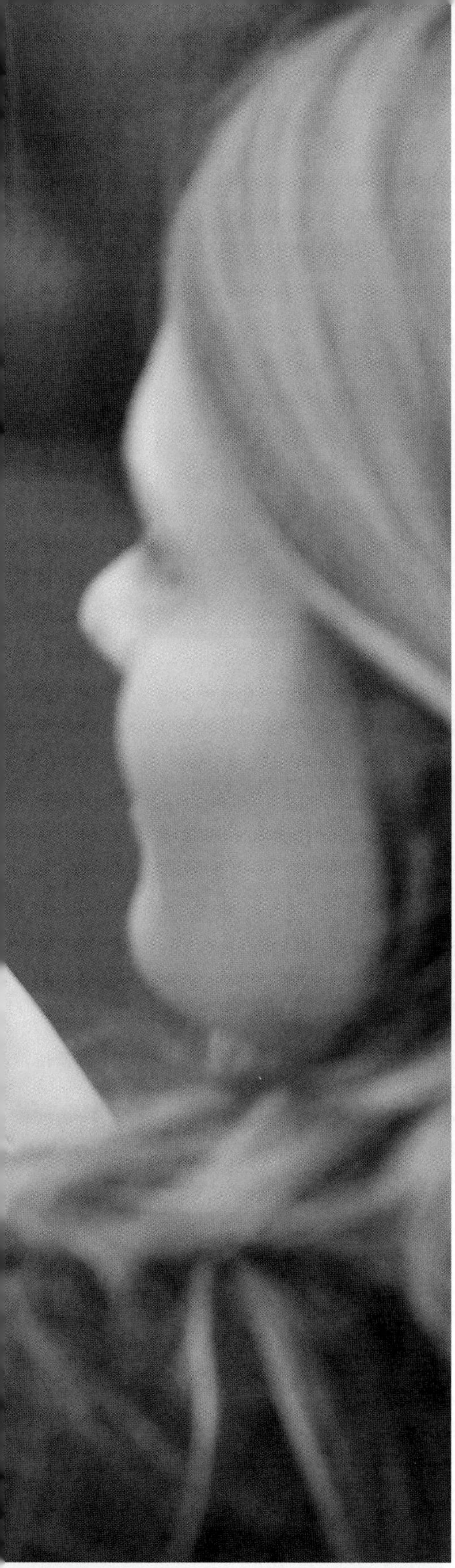

WHAT'S TO COME

What Is Psychology?

A Science Evolves

The Research Process in Psychology

Research Challenges

Could you live without social media?

How often do you text your friends? How often do you update your Facebook page or Twitter? Do you spend a considerable amount of your day using social media (texting, Twitter, instant messaging, Facebook, and YouTube)? If so, could you go 24 hours without it? What about one week? A whole semester? If the very thought of going without your social media for even one day causes anxiety, you are not alone!

S tudents in a media class at the University of Maryland were given a homework assignment to go without all social media (including their iPods and television) for 24 hours. What do you think happened? Students reported feeling isolated, lonely, and anxious (ICMPA, 2010). Similarly, but a little more extreme, university students in Pennsylvania withstood a one week blackout on all social media on campus. However, they still had access to social media on their smartphones, which resulted in behaviour similar to those who have been banned from smoking indoors—they snuck outside to check their Facebook accounts and text their friends! Some students were angry, arguing that their human rights had been violated, and some just went along with it. The most fascinating part was hearing how much time some students spent on social media. One student reported checking Facebook up to 21 hours a day (Hurdle, 2010)! If you think one week sounds scary, imagine being a student in Professor Robert Doede's Philosophy class at Trinity Western University in British Columbia. Professor Doede offered a 5 percent bonus in their grade for students who withdrew from all social and traditional media for an entire semester. The students had to journal about their experience. Approximately one-third of the class accepted the challenge, but only about 17 percent lasted the entire semester. Students who did last reported feeling less anxious as the semester continued. They also reported that their grades improved, they lost weight, and they had more time for other activities in their lives (Mussolum, 2009).

Why do many students find it so difficult to "unplug" social media? Why are their reports of how they felt when they no longer had access to social media remarkably similar to reports of addicts who no longer have access to drugs or alcohol? Is it an addiction? Should doctors and psychologists classify it as an addiction and treat it as such? Is there enough scientific evidence to suggest that students are in fact addicted to social media or are reports to date just anecdotal?

The field of psychology addresses such questions as these—and many, many more. In this chapter, we begin our examination of psychology—the different areas of psychology, what makes the study of behaviour a science, and many of the various explanations for human behaviour and thought that psychologists have put forward.

Explaining why people seem to be addicted to social media is an example of the type of question that psychologists attempt to answer.

- What is the definition of psychology and why is psychology considered a science?
- What are the goals of psychology?
- What are the major perspectives used by psychologists?
- What are the major subfields in the field of psychology?
- What is the scientific method, and how do psychologists use theory and research to answer questions of interest?
- What research methods do psychologists use?
- What are the ethics of research?

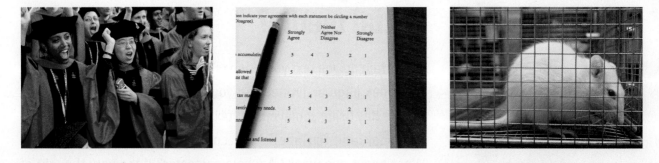

What Is Psychology?

Why can you almost instantly remember the name of your first-grade teacher after years of not thinking about this person? Why are some people afraid to fly in airplanes? Why do some people think bungee jumping is exhilarating while others find it terrifying? Why do you spend so much time on Facebook? Why do babies cry when their mothers leave the room? Why does drinking Red Bull make you feel more alert? Why do you have that recurring dream? How can you get your partner or spouse to help out more at home? As you try to answer each of these questions, you are doing what psychologists do—trying to describe, explain, predict, and/or control behaviour!

Psychology is the scientific study of behaviour and mental processes. It's not just about what people do but also about their thoughts, emotions, perceptions, reasoning processes, memories, and even the biological activities that help them function. Although many people think psychology is just common sense, psychology is a science because it uses the scientific method to find answers (we will discuss this more at the end of the chapter). This is far more reliable than relying on intuition, speculation, and common sense, which are often inaccurate and biased.

The **goals of psychology** are simple: psychologists try to describe, explain, predict, and control or change human behaviour and mental processes. You can remember these goals using the mnemonic device DEP-C!

The first goal of psychology is to *describe* behaviour. Psychologists try to do this as objectively as possible in a "Just the facts, Jack" kind of manner. Many of you will enter a profession where you will need to write reports on daily behaviour or write case notes, so you will use this goal on a regular basis. To do so, you will need to describe your observations in an objective manner, free from biases or personal opinion. For example, we might describe eight-year-old Jokiem's behaviour like this, "Jokiem struck the other child using an open palm." You will notice that we did not use any biased or judgmental language here; we simply described the behaviour as it was observed.

The second goal of psychology is to *explain* behaviour. In this goal, psychologists attempt to clarify why the behaviour occurred. This is an important goal because without it, psychologists would not be able to control or change the behaviour (the last goal of psychology). For example, why did Jokiem strike the other child? Perhaps he observed someone else do it? Perhaps he has some difficulties at home and is acting out? Perhaps he has poor impulse control? Perhaps he gets attention from his peers for doing so? Each of these is a different explanation and will therefore require a different way of managing the behaviour.

The third goal is to *predict* behaviour, where psychologists attempt to identify when the behaviour will happen. If we know when the behaviour is likely to happen, we can take steps to control or manage this (the last goal of psychology). For example, if we have determined that Jokiem is likely to strike other children after school when there is little supervision, we can control this situation by making sure Jokiem is involved in an activity after school.

The final goal of psychology is to *control or change* behaviour. Sometimes students find the word "control" a little oppressive. Instead of thinking of it in negative terms, you can interchange the word "control" with manage, treat, or intervene. In this goal, psychologists attempt to manage or change behaviour if necessary. Before doing this, it is important to first determine the cause of the behaviour (the second goal). Once the actual explanation is determined (usually through a rigorous scientific process) a plan can be put in place to control or change the behaviour.

psychology The scientific study of behaviour and mental processes.

goals of psychology To describe, explain, predict, and control behaviour and mental processes.

Psychological Truths?

To test your knowledge of psychology, try to answer the following questions:

1. Infants love their mothers primarily because their mothers fulfill their basic biological needs, such as providing food. True or false? _____
2. Geniuses generally have poor social adjustment. True or false? _____
3. The best way to ensure that a desired behaviour will continue after training is completed is to reward that behaviour every single time it occurs during training rather than rewarding it only periodically. True or false? _____
4. People with schizophrenia have at least two distinct personalities. True or false? _____
5. Parents should do everything they can to ensure children have high self-esteem and a strong sense that they are highly competent. True or false? _____
6. Children's IQ scores have little to do with how well they do in school. True or false? _____
7. Frequent masturbation can lead to mental illness. True or false? _____
8. Once people reach old age, their leisure activities change radically. True or false? _____
9. Most people would refuse to give painful electric shocks to other people. True or false? _____
10. People who talk about suicide are unlikely to try to kill themselves. True or false? _____

Source: Adapted from Lamal, 1979.

Scoring: The truth about each of these items: they are all false. Based on psychological research, each of these "facts" has been proven untrue. You will learn the reasons why as we explore what psychologists have discovered about human behaviour.

For example, if we determined that Jokiem is acting out because he is experiencing difficulties at home, we can attempt to intervene by providing Jokiem a place to talk about his feelings.

MODERN PERSPECTIVES OF PSYCHOLOGY

One issue students often struggle with when learning about psychology is that there are multiple ways of explaining any given behaviour (just like in the Jokiem example). Think about a behaviour you exhibit on a regular basis; perhaps you procrastinate, bite your nails, or have trouble sleeping. Each of these behaviours can be explained (and then controlled or changed) in many different ways. For example, maybe you procrastinate because you are anxious that your work is not good enough or because you receive some sort of reward for waiting until the last minute to start something. Maybe you procrastinate because you think you produce a better product when you work under pressure. Maybe your parents were procrastinators and you inherited this behaviour from them. In this example, the cause of a single behaviour (procrastination) was explained from many different perspectives.

The field of psychology approaches behaviour in much the same way. There are seven major perspectives of psychology and you will notice that each approaches the goals of behaviour (describe, explain, predict, and control/change) differently. To help you understand how each perspective explains behaviour, we will use depression as an example. Notice that while depression is described the same way by each perspective below, the explanation for its cause is quite different!

neuroscience perspective The approach that explains behaviour from the perspective of the brain, the nervous system, genes, and other biological functions.

The Neuroscience Perspective The **neuroscience perspective** explains behaviour and mental processes from a biological approach, such as how the brain, nervous system, genes, and other biological functions influence behaviour. Another aspect of this approach is how the inheritance of certain characteristics from parents

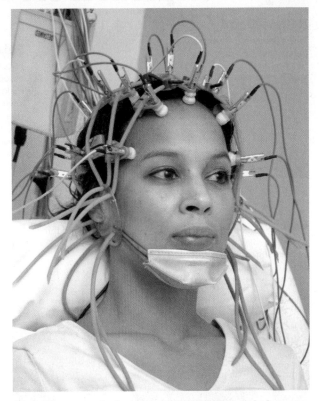

One technique neuroscientists use to study activity in the brain is electroencephalography (EEG). In this painless procedure, electrodes are attached to the scalp and changes in electrical activity are recorded while the person performs specific tasks.

and other ancestors influences behaviour. If psychologists were to explain depression from the neuroscience perspective, they might say it is caused by heredity, or by differences in a structure of the brain called the hippocampus (Sheline et al., 2004). For example, Stephen Ferguson from the University of Western Ontario, Hymie Anisman from Carlton University, and their colleagues found a biological link between stress, depression, and anxiety by identifying how stress- and depression-related molecules in the brain interact to influence depression (Magalhaes et al., 2010).

Psychologists who subscribe to the neuroscience perspective have made major contributions to the understanding and betterment of human life, ranging from cures for certain types of deafness to drug treatments for people with severe mental disorders. Furthermore, advances in methods for examining the anatomy and functioning of the brain have permitted the neuroscientific perspective to extend its influence across a broad range of subfields in psychology.

The Psychodynamic Perspective To many people who have never taken a psychology course, psychology is all about the **psychodynamic perspective**. Proponents of the psychodynamic perspective argue that behaviour can be explained by inner forces and conflicts that we have repressed into our unconscious because they are too difficult to cope with. Instead, we use dreams and slips of the

> **psychodynamic perspective** The approach based on the view that behaviour is motivated by unconscious inner forces over which the individual has little control.
>
> **behavioural perspective** The approach that focuses on observable, measurable behaviour and ways to change problem behaviours.

tongue to reveal what we are truly feeling. According to the psychodynamic perspective, early childhood experiences are most important in explaining our behaviour. If someone from the psychodynamic perspective were to try to explain depression for example, she might say that the cause was due to traumatic experiences during childhood that the person with depression has repressed into his unconscious. Notice how very different this explanation of depression is from how the neuroscience approach would have explained it?

The origins of the psychodynamic view are linked to one person: Sigmund Freud, who originally called it the psychoanalytic approach. Freud was a Viennese physician in the early 1900s whose ideas about unconscious determinants of behaviour had a revolutionary effect on twentieth-century thinking, not just in psychology but also in related fields.

The Behavioural Perspective In contrast to the neuroscience and psychodynamic approaches, the **behavioural perspective** grew out of a rejection of psychology's

Figure 1.1
Major Perspectives of Psychology

Neuroscience
Views behaviour from the perspective of biological functioning

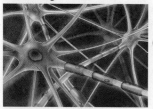

Behavioural
Focuses on the associations we make in our environment, such as the effect of rewards and punishments on behaviour

Cognitive
Examines how people understand and think about the world

Psychodynamic
Believes behaviour is motivated by inner, unconscious forces over which a person has little control

Humanistic
Contends that people can control their behaviour and that they naturally try to reach their full potential

Socio-cultural
Focuses on the social and cultural influences on behaviour

Evolutionary
Focuses on how behaviour is adaptive for our survival

Sigmund Freud

The Cognitive Perspective This perspective explains behaviour as a result of how people think, understand, and reason about the world. The emphasis is on learning how people internally perceive and understand the outside world and how our ways of thinking about the world influence our behaviour.

Psychologists who rely on the **cognitive perspective** ask questions ranging from how people make decisions to whether a person can watch television and study at the same time. The common elements that link cognitive approaches are an emphasis on how people understand and think about the world and an interest in describing the patterns and irregularities in the operation of their minds. For example, someone from this approach might explain depression as being due to faulty thoughts or perceptions. If the person with depression thinks he is worthless and that life is not worth living, this will influence his depressive behaviour.

From the perspective of …

A NURSE How would someone's thoughts about how much a needle hurt impact the perception of pain? How could the cognitive approach be helpful in answering this question?

The Humanistic Perspective Rejecting the view that behaviour is determined largely by automatically unfolding biological forces, unconscious processes, or the environment, the **humanistic perspective** instead suggests that all individuals naturally strive to grow, develop, and be in control of their lives and behaviour. Humanistic psychologists maintain that each of us has the capacity to seek and reach fulfillment.

According to Carl Rogers and Abraham Maslow, who were central figures in the development of the humanistic perspective, people will strive to reach their full potential if they are given the opportunity to do so. The emphasis of the humanistic perspective is on **free will**, the ability to freely make decisions about one's own behaviour and life. The notion of free will stands in contrast to **determinism**, which sees behaviour as caused, or determined, by things beyond a person's control.

early emphasis on the inner workings of the mind. Instead, behaviourists suggested that the field should focus on observable behaviour that can be measured objectively.

John B. Watson was one of the first psychologists to advocate a behavioural approach. Working in the 1920s, Watson was adamant in his view that one could gain a complete understanding of behaviour by studying and modifying the environment in which people operate. In fact, Watson believed that it was possible to bring forth any desired type of behaviour by controlling a person's environment.

The behavioural perspective was championed by B. F. Skinner, a pioneer in the field. According to this approach our behaviours can be explained as a result of what happens in our environment. This might be due to associations we make between two events (such as salivating when you read the word lemon…. Did you just salivate?) or associations we make between our behaviours and the rewards or punishments that follow. For example, the behavioural approach might explain someone's depressive behaviour as a result of the attention she receives from others or as a means to avoid unpleasant activities such as school or work. Someone from the behaviourist approach is not at all interested in biological or early childhood explanations of behaviour. Remember, this approach is about what can be observed in the environment!

As you will see, the behavioural perspective is involved in many areas of psychology. Along with its influence in the area of learning processes, this perspective has made contributions in such diverse areas as treating mental disorders, curbing aggression, resolving sexual problems, and ending drug addiction.

cognitive perspective The perspective that suggests that people's thoughts and beliefs are a central component of normal and abnormal behaviour.

humanistic perspective The approach that suggests that all individuals naturally strive to grow, develop, and be in control of their lives and behaviour.

free will The idea that behaviour is caused primarily by choices that are made freely by the individual.

determinism The idea that people's behaviour is produced primarily by factors outside of their wilful control.

socio-cultural perspective This perspective explains behaviour as being due to social and cultural influences.

evolutionary perspective The evolutionary perspective explains our behaviour as functional to natural selection; that we have adapted our behaviours over time to ensure our survival as a species.

The humanistic perspective assumes that people have the ability to make their own choices about their behaviour rather than relying on societal standards. More than any other approach, it stresses the role of psychology in enriching people's lives and helping them achieve self-fulfillment. The humanistic approach to depression may take many forms. For example, a psychologist from the humanistic perspective might explain the depressive behaviour as being due to poor self-esteem or a failure to reach self-actualization.

The Socio-cultural Perspective This perspective explains behaviour as being due to social and cultural influences. A psychologist from the **socio-cultural perspective** would examine the differences in human behaviour and thinking across various cultures. On the issue of depression, the socio-cultural perspective would examine how depression may be influenced by cultural background, religious beliefs, social pressures, or family systems.

The Evolutionary Perspective Are you afraid of spiders? The **evolutionary perspective** would explain your fear as being adaptive for your survival. The problem is that while this fear was once adaptive, it is not really necessary anymore, especially in Canada! The evolutionary perspective explains our behaviour as functional to natural selection; that we have adapted our behaviours over time to ensure our survival as a species. This theory draws on Darwin's theory of natural selection, but applies it to psychological phenomena. If this approach were to explain depression, they might say that this behaviour has evolved to warn us that we need to slow down so we can think about how to change some aspect of our behaviour.

Study tip

Make sure you can describe the four goals of psychology and the seven perspectives of psychology! Complete the PSYCH think section on this page to help you with the perspectives.

KEY ISSUES IN PSYCHOLOGY

As you consider the many topics and perspectives that make up psychology, you might find yourself thinking that the discipline of psychology lacks consistency. However, the field is more unified than a first glimpse might suggest. For one thing, no matter what topical area a psychologist specializes in, he or she will rely primarily on one of the seven major perspectives. For example, a health psychologist who specializes in the study of health and wellness can make use of the cognitive perspective or the behavioural perspective.

Psych think

> > > Think of a behaviour that you exhibit on a regular basis (i.e., procrastinating, nail biting, smoking, anxiety, trouble sleeping, etc.). Try to explain the cause of your behaviour from each of the major perspectives of psychology (i.e., neuroscience, psychodynamic, behavioural, cognitive, humanistic, socio-cultural, and evolutionary). Notice that while each perspective describes your behaviour the same way, they explain it quite differently.

Psychologists also agree on what the key issues of the field are. Although there are differences about how best to address them, psychology is a unified science, because psychologists of all perspectives agree that the key issues must be addressed if the field is going to advance. As you contemplate these issues, try not to think of them in "either/or" terms. Instead, consider the opposing viewpoints on each issue as the opposite ends of a continuum, with the positions of individual psychologists typically falling somewhere between the two ends.

- Is David Suzuki so intelligent about the environment because his parents were intelligent? Is it because his father got him interested in nature and took him camping as a young child? Is it both?

David Suzuki

Figure 1.2
Key Issues in Psychology

Issue	Neuroscience	Cognitive	Behavioural	Humanistic	Psychodynamic	Socio-cultural	Evolutionary
Nature (heredity) vs. nurture (environment)	Nature (heredity)	Both	Nurture (environment)	Nurture (environment)	Nature (heredity)	Nurture (environment)	Both
Conscious vs. unconscious determinants of behaviour	Unconscious	Both	Conscious	Conscious	Unconscious	Conscious	Both
Observable behaviour vs. internal mental processes	Internal emphasis	Internal emphasis	Observable emphasis	Internal emphasis	Internal emphasis	Internal emphasis	Internal emphasis
Free will vs. determinism	Determinism	Free will	Determinism	Free will	Determinism	Determinism	Determinism
Individual differences vs. universal principles	Universal emphasis	Individual imphasis	Both	Individual imphasis	Universal emphasis	Universal emphasis	Internal emphasis

Nature (heredity) versus nurture (environment) is one of the major issues that psychologists address. How much of behaviour is due to an individual's genetically determined nature (heredity), and how much is due to nurture, the influences of the physical and social environment in which a child is raised? And what is the interplay between heredity and environment? These questions have deep philosophical and historical roots, and they permeate many topics in psychology.

- After trying on a dress that was two sizes too small, Alina asked Lila how she looked. Wanting to be polite, Lila meant to say "You look great," but unfortunately for both of them, she accidentally said "You look fat."

A second major question of interest to psychologists concerns *conscious versus unconscious causes of behaviour.* How much of our behaviour is produced by forces of which we are fully aware, and how much is due to unconscious activity—mental processes that are not accessible to the conscious mind? For example, clinical psychologists adopting a psychodynamic perspective argue that psychological disorders are brought about by unconscious factors, whereas psychologists employing the cognitive perspective suggest that psychological disorders largely are the result of faulty thinking processes.

- Cole could swear that his dog, Lady, decides whether to obey a command. Although sometimes she eagerly comes when she is called, other times she seems to think it over first.

A third issue is *observable behaviour versus internal mental processes.* Should psychology concentrate solely on behaviour that can be seen by outside observers, or should it focus on undetected thinking processes?

Some psychologists, especially those relying on the behavioural perspective, contend that the only legitimate source of information for psychologists is behaviour that can be observed directly. Other psychologists, building on the cognitive perspective, argue that what goes on inside a person's mind is critical to understanding behaviour.

- Shirley and Lorraine come from a family with a history of depression. When Shirley starts to feel depressed, she claims she can talk herself out of it. When her sister, Lorraine, begins feeling depressed, she claims she is powerless to stop it.

Free will versus determinism is a fourth key issue. How much of our behaviour is a matter of free will (choices made freely by an individual), and how much is subject to determinism, the notion that behaviour is largely produced by factors beyond a person's wilful control? For example, some psychologists who specialize in psychological disorders argue that people make intentional choices and that those who display so-called abnormal behaviour should be considered responsible for their actions. Other psychologists disagree and contend that such individuals are the victims of forces beyond their control.

- Anyone from anywhere in the world can recognize anger in a person's face. Yet people behave quite differently from one another when riled up. Some start fist fights, some keep their anger inside, and some yell at the dog.

The fifth key issue concerns *individual differences versus universal principles.* How much of our behaviour is a consequence of our unique and special qualities, and how much reflects the culture and society in which we live? How much of our behaviour is universally human? Psychologists who take the neuroscience perspective tend to look for universal principles of behaviour, such as how the nervous system operates, concentrating on the similarities in our behavioural destinies despite vast differences in our upbringing. In contrast, humanistic psychologists focus more on the uniqueness of every individual. They consider every person's behaviour a reflection of distinct and special individual qualities.

> **Nature (heredity) versus nurture (environment) is one of the major issues that psychologists address.**

THE SUBFIELDS OF PSYCHOLOGY

As the study of psychology has grown, it has given rise to a number of subfields. One way to identify the key subfields is to look at some of the basic questions about behaviour that they address. You will notice that the subfields of psychology employ one or a variety of the major psychological perspectives discussed earlier. As you read about the subfields of psychology, try to think of what perspective that subfield likely adheres to.

Behavioural Neuroscience In the most fundamental sense, people are biological organisms. *Behavioural neuroscience* is the subfield of psychology that mainly examines how the brain and the nervous system—and other biological processes—determine behaviour. Thus, neuroscientists consider how our bodies influence our behaviour. For example, behavioural neuroscientists might want to know what physiological changes occur in the brain when listening to music.

Experimental Psychology If you have ever wondered why you are susceptible to optical illusions, how your body registers pain, or how to make the most of your study time, an experimental psychologist can answer your questions. *Experimental psychology* is the branch of psychology that studies the processes of sensing, perceiving, learning, and thinking about the world. (The term *experimental psychologist*, however, is somewhat misleading: Psychologists in every specialty area use experimental techniques.)

Several subspecialties of experimental psychology have become specialties in their own right. One is *cognitive psychology*, which focuses on higher mental processes, including thinking, memory, reasoning, problem solving, judging, decision making, and language. For example, a cognitive psychologist might be interested in what the survivors of the Dawson College shooting in Montreal remember about their experience.

Developmental Psychology A baby producing her first smile . . . taking her first steps . . . saying her first word.

These universal milestones in development are also singularly special and unique for each person. *Developmental psychology* studies how people grow and change from the moment of conception through death. *Personality psychology* focuses on the consistency in people's behaviour over time and the traits that differentiate one person from another. Developmental and personality psychologists draw on a number of different perspectives in their practice.

Clinical Psychology Frequent depression, stress, and fears that prevent people from carrying out their normal activities are topics that would interest a health psychologist, a clinical psychologist, and a counselling psychologist. *Health psychology* explores the relationship between psychological factors and physical ailments or disease. For example, health psychologists are interested in assessing how long-term stress (a psychological factor) can affect physical health and in identifying ways to promote behaviour that brings about good health.

Clinical psychology deals with the study, diagnosis, and treatment of psychological disorders. Clinical psychologists are trained to diagnose and treat problems that range from the crises of everyday life, such as unhappiness over the breakup of a relationship, to more extreme conditions, such as profound, lingering depression.

Like clinical psychologists, counselling psychologists deal with people's psychological problems, but the problems they deal with are more specific. *Counselling psychology* focuses primarily on educational, social, and career adjustment problems. Almost every college has a centre staffed with counselling psychologists. This is where students can get advice on the kinds of jobs they might be best suited for, on methods of studying effectively, and on strategies for resolving everyday difficulties, such as problems with roommates or relationships.

Social Psychology Our complex networks of social interrelationships are the focus for a number of subfields of psychology. *Social psychology* is the study of how people's thoughts, feelings, and actions are affected by others. Social psychologists concentrate on such diverse topics as human aggression, liking and loving, persuasion, and conformity.

Cross-cultural psychology investigates the similarities and differences in psychological functioning in and across various cultures and ethnic groups. For example, cross-cultural psychologists examine how cultures differ in their use of punishment during child rearing. Did you guess that these psychologists would use the socio-cultural approach in their practice? If so, you are correct!

Evolutionary Psychology *Evolutionary psychology* considers how behaviour is influenced by our genetic inheritance from our ancestors. The evolutionary approach suggests that the chemical coding of information in our cells not only determines traits such as hair colour and race, but also holds the key to understanding a broad variety of behaviours that helped our ancestors survive and reproduce.

Behavioural Genetics *Behavioural genetics* seeks to understand how we might inherit certain behavioural traits and how the environment influences whether we actually display such traits (Bjorklund & Ellis, 2005; Moffitt & Caspi, 2007; Rende, 2007).

Clinical Neuropsychology *Clinical neuropsychology* unites the areas of neuroscience and clinical psychology. Building on advances in our understanding of the structure and chemistry of the brain, this specialty has already led

to promising new treatments for psychological disorders as well as debates over the use of medication to control behaviour.

WORKING AT PSYCHOLOGY

Psychologists are employed in a variety of settings. Many psychologists are employed by universities and colleges or are self-employed, usually working as private practitioners treating clients. Other work sites include hospitals, clinics, mental health centres, counselling centres, government human-services organizations, criminal justice facilities, and schools (CPA, 2010).

Psychologists: A Portrait Although there is no "average" psychologist in terms of personal characteristics, we can draw a statistical portrait of the profession. Today, close to 16,000 psychologists work in Canada. In every province the number of women psychologists outweighs the number of men (CIHI, 2011). Issues such as our aging population, increased mental health problems, pathological gambling, and child and youth behavioural problems have resulted in an increase in the number of psychologists in Canada over the past few years (CIHI, 2011).

Megamind
This cartoon movie nicely demonstrates the role of nurture when Megamind and Metro Man, two infant extraterrestrials, arrive on Earth. Megamind becomes a villain after growing up in a prison while Metro Man, who grows up in a normal middle-class family, becomes a conservative nice guy.

The Sixth Sense
The psychologist portrayed in this movie is sane, compassionate, and ethical. This is an accurate and realistic portrayal of the profession.

The Boy in the Striped Pyjamas
This movie illustrates determinism, where the tragedy experienced by the main characters—two boys in a forbidden friendship—is caused by factors outside their control.

DID YOU KNOW?

What can psychology majors do after graduation? Lots of things! For example, graduates with a bachelor's degree in psychology may find entry-level opportunities in advertising, publishing, business management, law enforcement, and social services, to name a few occupations. For information on what psychologists do and where they work, visit the Canadian Psychological Association (CPA) Web site at www.cpa.ca/public/whatisapsychologist/.

The Education of a Psychologist How do people become psychologists? The most common route is to obtain a doctorate, either a *PhD* (Doctor of Philosophy) or, less frequently, a *PsyD* (Doctor of Psychology). The PhD is a research degree that requires a dissertation based on an original investigation. Although some students think they are similar, psychologists are different from psychiatrists. Psychiatrists are medical doctors who also specialize in the treatment of psychological disorders. It takes 12 years of post-secondary education to become a psychiatrist (a four-year Bachelor of Science degree, four years of medical school, and four years of psychiatry training). The PsyD is obtained by psychologists who wish to focus on clinical psychology but who may not produce original research. PsyD programs are relatively rare in Canada. Up until recently, there were only two PsyD programs in Canada, and both were in Quebec (University of Quebec and Laval University). Memorial University in Newfoundland has only recently offered a PsyD program.

Both the PhD and the PsyD typically take four to six years of education past the bachelor's level. Some fields of psychology involve education beyond the doctorate. For instance, doctoral-level clinical psychologists, who work with people with psychological disorders, typically spend an additional year doing an internship.

About a quarter of people working in the field of psychology have a master's degree as their highest degree, which they earn after two or three years of graduate study. These psychologists teach, provide therapy, conduct research, or work in specialized programs dealing with drug abuse or crisis intervention. Some work in universities, government, and business, collecting and analyzing data.

Careers for Psychology Majors Although some psychology majors head for graduate school in psychology or an unrelated field, the majority join the workforce immediately after graduation. Most report that the jobs they take after graduation are related to their psychology

Figure 1.4
Milestones in Psychology

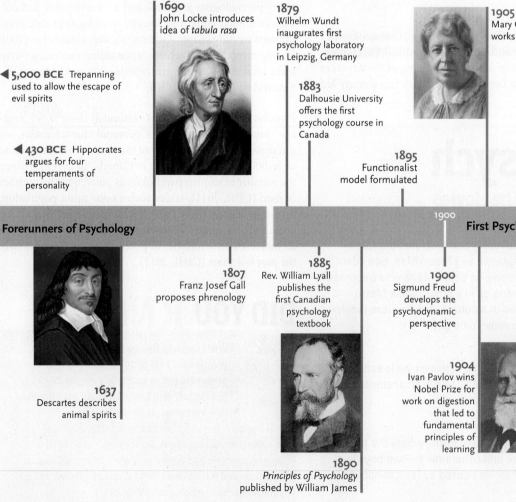

1690
John Locke introduces idea of *tabula rasa*

1879
Wilhelm Wundt inaugurates first psychology laboratory in Leipzig, Germany

1905
Mary Calkins works on memory

◀ **5,000 BCE** Trepanning used to allow the escape of evil spirits

1883
Dalhousie University offers the first psychology course in Canada

◀ **430 BCE** Hippocrates argues for four temperaments of personality

1895
Functionalist model formulated

1915
Strong emphasis on intelligence testing

Forerunners of Psychology

1900 **First Psychologists**

1807
Franz Josef Gall proposes phrenology

1885
Rev. William Lyall publishes the first Canadian psychology textbook

1900
Sigmund Freud develops the psychodynamic perspective

1920
Gestalt psychology becomes influential

1637
Descartes describes animal spirits

1904
Ivan Pavlov wins Nobel Prize for work on digestion that led to fundamental principles of learning

1890
Principles of Psychology published by William James

Figure 1.3
Where Psychologists Work

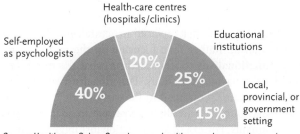

Self-employed as psychologists **40%**

Health-care centres (hospitals/clinics) **20%**

Educational institutions **25%**

Local, provincial, or government setting **15%**

Source: Healthcare Salary Canada, www.healthcaresalarycanada.com/psychologist_salary.html.

background. An undergraduate major in psychology provides excellent preparation for a variety of occupations. Because undergraduates who specialize in psychology develop good analytical skills, are trained to think critically, and are able to synthesize and evaluate information well, employers in business, industry, and the government value their preparation (Kuther, 2003).

A Science Evolves

- Seven thousand years ago, people assumed that psychological problems were caused by evil spirits. To allow those spirits to escape from a person's body, ancient healers chipped a hole in a patient's skull with crude instruments—a procedure called trepanning.

- According to the seventeenth-century philosopher Descartes, nerves were hollow tubes through which "animal spirits" conducted impulses in the same way that water is transmitted through a pipe. When a person put a finger too close to a fire, heat was transmitted to the brain through the tubes.

- Franz Josef Gall, an eighteenth-century physician, argued that a trained observer could discern intelligence, moral character, and other basic personality characteristics from the shape and the number of bumps on a person's skull. His theory gave rise to the field of phrenology, employed by hundreds of practitioners in the nineteenth century.

1924 McGill University develops the first psychology department in Canada

1924 John B. Watson, an early behaviourist, publishes *Behaviorism*

1953 B. F. Skinner publishes *Science and Human Behavior*, advocating the behavioural perspective

1934 Katharine M. Banham is the first woman to be awarded a PhD from the University of Montreal

1939 The establishment of the Canadian Psychological Association (CPA)

1959 Mary J. Wright becomes the first female director of the CPA

1969 Arguments regarding the genetic basis of IQ fuel lingering controversies

1970 Mary Salter Ainsworth uses the Strange Situation Test to assess attachment

1980 Jean Piaget, an influential developmental psychologist, dies

1990 Greater emphasis on multiculturalism and diversity

2010 New subfields develop such as clinical neuropsychology and evolutionary psychology

1950

Modern Psychology

2000

1928 Leta Stetter Hollingworth publishes work on adolescence

1951 Carl Rogers publishes *Client-Centered Therapy*, helping to establish the humanistic perspective

1942 Magda B. Arnold receives a PhD and a lecturer position at the University of Toronto

1961 Albert Bandura starts conducting research on childhood aggression using the Bobo Dolls

1957 Leon Festinger publishes *A Theory of Cognitive Dissonance*, producing a major impact on social psychology

1974 Elizabeth Loftus discovers that leading questions after a traffic accident can distort memories

1985 Increasing emphasis on cognitive perspective

1981 David Hubel and Torsten Wiesel win Nobel Prize for work on vision cells in the brain

1934 Wilder Penfield founds McGill University's Montreal Neurological Institute

1954 Abraham Maslow publishes *Motivation and Personality*, developing the concept of self-actualization

Although these practices might sound far-fetched, in their own times they represented the most advanced thinking about behaviour and the brain. Psychology has come a long way since the eighteenth century, but most of the advances have been recent. As sciences go, psychology is relatively young.

THE ROOTS OF PSYCHOLOGY

The formal beginning of psychology as a scientific discipline is generally considered to be in the late nineteenth century, when, in Leipzig, Germany, Wilhelm Wundt established the first experimental laboratory devoted to psychological phenomena. When Wundt set up his laboratory in 1879, his aim was to study the building blocks of the mind. He considered psychology to be the study of conscious experience. His perspective, which came to be known as **structuralism**, focused on uncovering the fundamental mental components of perception, consciousness, thinking, emotions, and other kinds of mental states and activities.

To determine how basic sensory processes shape our understanding of the world, Wundt and other structuralists used a procedure called **introspection**, in which they presented people with a stimulus—such as a bright green object or a sentence printed on a card—and asked them to describe, in their own words and in as much detail as they could, what they were experiencing. Wundt argued that by analyzing their reports, psychologists could come to a better understanding of the structure of the mind.

Over time, psychologists challenged Wundt's approach. They became increasingly dissatisfied with the assumption that introspection could reveal the structure of the mind. Introspection was not a truly scientific technique, because there were few ways an outside observer could confirm the accuracy of others' introspections. Moreover, people had difficulty describing some kinds of inner experiences, such as emotional responses. Those drawbacks led to the development of a new approach, which largely replaced structuralism.

The perspective that replaced structuralism is known as functionalism. Rather than focusing on the mind's structure, **functionalism** concentrated on what the mind *does* and how behaviour functions. Functionalists, whose perspective became prominent in the early 1900s, asked what role behaviour plays in allowing people to adapt to their environments. For example, a functionalist might examine the function of the emotion of fear in preparing us to deal with emergency situations.

Led by William James, the functionalists examined how behaviour allows people to satisfy their needs and how our "stream of consciousness" permits us to adapt to our environment. The American educator John Dewey drew on functionalism to develop the field of school psychology, proposing ways to best meet students' educational needs.

Another important reaction to structuralism was the development of gestalt psychology in the early 1900s. **Gestalt psychology** emphasizes how perception is organized. Instead of considering the individual parts that make up thinking, gestalt psychologists took the opposite approach, studying how people consider individual elements together as units or wholes. Gestalt psychologists proposed that "The whole is different from the sum of its parts"—that is, our perception, or understanding, of objects is greater and more meaningful than the individual elements that make up our perceptions. Gestalt psychologists have made substantial contributions to our understanding of perception.

John B. Watson was an early psychologist who disagreed with the approaches of the structuralists and the functionalists. We discussed John B. Watson earlier in the chapter when we discussed the modern perspective of behaviourism. Remember that the behaviourists believe that behaviour should be studied objectively based on what one can observe. Behaviourism is one of two current perspectives that have developed from a historical approach; the other was the psychoanalytic approach. As you will recall, Sigmund Freud was more interested in the unconscious and early childhood experiences than observable behaviours. In fact, Freud believed that sexual and aggressive impulses unconsciously influenced our behaviours, over which we had little control. While many of Freud's theories are no longer accepted, the current psychodynamic perspective still focuses on the role of the unconscious in our behaviour.

FOUNDING MOTHERS OF PSYCHOLOGY

As in many scientific fields, social prejudices hindered women's participation in the early development of psychology. Many universities would not even admit women to their graduate psychology programs in the early 1900s.

Despite the hurdles they faced, women made notable contributions to psychology, although their impact on the field was largely overlooked until recently. For example, Margaret Floy Washburn (1871–1939) was the first woman to receive a doctorate in psychology, and she did important work on animal behaviour. Leta Stetter Hollingworth (1886–1939) was one of the first psychologists to focus on child development and on women's issues. She collected data to refute the view, popular in the early 1900s, that women's abilities periodically declined during parts of the menstrual cycle (Denmark & Fernandez, 1993; Furumoto & Scarborough, 2002; Hollingworth, 1943/1990).

Mary Calkins (1863–1930), who studied memory in the early part of the twentieth century, became the first female president of the American Psychological Association. Karen Horney (pronounced "HORN-eye") (1885–1952) focused on the social and cultural factors behind personality, and June Etta Downey (1875–1932) spearheaded the study of personality traits and became the first woman to head a psychology department at a state university. Anna Freud (1895–1982), the daughter of Sigmund Freud, also made notable contributions to the treatment of abnormal behaviour, and Mamie Phipps Clark (1917–1983) carried out pioneering work on how children of colour grew to recognize racial differences (Horney, 1937; Lal, 2002; Stevens & Gardner, 1982).

Canadian women did not start attaining PhDs in psychology until almost a generation after American women did (not until the late 1920s and 1930s). This is in part because psychology was not recognized as a separate discipline in Canada until the 1920s and because women were not entering many professional fields at that time, especially those in male-dominant fields (Keats & Stam, 2009). Canadian women did not face the educational barriers and discrimination that their US counterparts did a generation earlier, which appears to be in part because when they entered the field, many men were away at war (Keats & Stam, 2009). Some prominent Canadian women psychologists are Katharine M. Banham (1897–1995), Magda B. Arnold (1903–2002), Mary L. Northway (1909–1987), Brenda Milner (1918–present), Mary D. Salter Ainsworth (1913–1999), and Mary J. Wright (1915–present). Mary Ainsworth is well known for her work in attachment theory and Mary Wright, who studied women in Canadian psychology, became the first female president of the Canadian Psychological Association (Keats & Stam, 2009). Do you want to learn more about women in psychology? Visit www.feministvoices.com/history-of-women-in-psychology/.

In 2004 and 2005, nearly 78 percent of doctoral graduates of psychology were women (King, 2008).

PSYCHOLOGY'S FUTURE

What does the future hold for the discipline of psychology? Although the course of scientific development is difficult to predict, several trends seem likely:

- As its knowledge base grows, psychology will become increasingly specialized, and new perspectives will evolve. For example, our growing understanding of the brain and the nervous system, combined with scientific advances in genetics and gene therapy, will allow psychologists to focus on *prevention* of psychological disorders rather than only on their treatment.

- The evolving sophistication of neuroscientific approaches is likely to have an increasing influence over other branches of psychology. For instance, social psychologists are already increasing their understanding of social behaviours such as persuasion by using brain scans as part of an evolving field known as *social neuroscience* (Bunge & Wallis, 2008; Harmon-Jones & Winkielman, 2007).

- Psychology's influence on issues of public interest also will grow. The major problems of our time—such as violence, terrorism, racial and ethnic prejudice, poverty, and environmental and technological disasters—have important psychological aspects (Hobfoll, Hall, & Canetti-Nisim, 2007; Marshall et al., 2007; Zimbardo, 2004a).

- Finally, as the population becomes more multicultural, issues of diversity—embodied in the study of racial, ethnic, linguistic, and cultural factors—will become more important to psychologists who provide services and research. The result will be a field that can provide an understanding of *human* behaviour in its broadest sense (Chang & Sue, 2005; Leong & Blustein, 2000; Quintana, Aboud, & Chao, 2006).

The Research Process in Psychology

Birds of a feather flock together.

Opposites attract.

Which of these statements is more accurate? It is hard to say, because we can come up with successful examples of friends and romantic partners who seem to be very similar to each other. We can also come up with examples of friends and partners who seem to be from different planets. Both statements make sense when considered independently.

THE SCIENTIFIC METHOD

If we were to rely on common sense to understand behaviour, we'd have considerable difficulty—especially because commonsense views are often contradictory. Psychologists

Figure 1.5
The Scientific Method

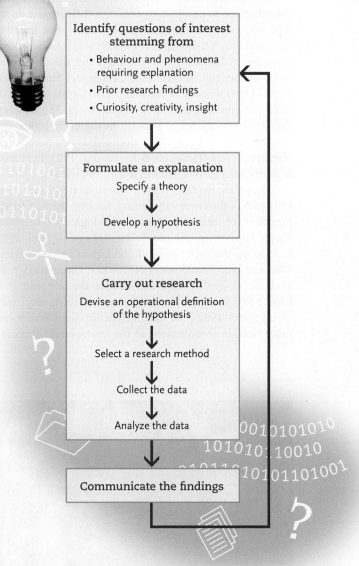

Identify questions of interest stemming from
- Behaviour and phenomena requiring explanation
- Prior research findings
- Curiosity, creativity, insight

Formulate an explanation
Specify a theory
Develop a hypothesis

Carry out research
Devise an operational definition of the hypothesis
Select a research method
Collect the data
Analyze the data

Communicate the findings

and other scientists meet the challenge of posing appropriate questions and properly answering them by relying on the scientific method. The **scientific method** is the approach used by psychologists to systematically acquire knowledge and understanding about behaviour and other phenomena of interest. The scientific method consists of four steps: (1) identifying questions of interest, (2) formulating a hypothesis, (3) carrying out research designed to support or refute the explanation, and (4) communicating the findings.

scientific method The approach through which psychologists systematically acquire knowledge and understanding about behaviour and other phenomena of interest.

> The scientific method is the approach used by psychologists and other scientists to systematically acquire knowledge and understanding about behaviour and other phenomena of interest. "

THEORIES: BROAD EXPLANATIONS

Psychologists ask questions about the nature and the causes of behaviour. They may wish to explore explanations for everyday behaviours or for various phenomena. They may also pose questions that build on findings from their previous research or from research carried by other psychologists. Or they may produce new questions that are based on curiosity, creativity, or insight.

Once a question has been identified, the next step in the scientific method is to develop a theory to explain the observed phenomenon. **Theories** are broad explanations and predictions concerning phenomena of interest. They provide a framework for understanding the relationships among a set of otherwise unorganized facts or principles.

All of us have developed our own informal theories of human behaviour, such as "People are basically good" or "People's behaviour is usually motivated by self-interest." However, psychologists' theories are more formal and focused. They are established on the basis of a careful study of the psychological literature to identify earlier relevant research and previously formulated theories, as well as psychologists' general knowledge of the field (McGuire, 1997; Sternberg & Beall, 1991).

HYPOTHESES: TESTABLE PREDICTIONS

Once a theory is formed, the next step is to carry out research that is designed to test the theoretical explanation. For this step, psychologists need to create a hypothesis. A **hypothesis** is a prediction that can be tested. Hypotheses stem from theories; they help test the underlying soundness of theories.

A hypothesis must be stated in a way that will allow it to be tested, which involves creating an operational definition. An **operational definition** is the translation of a hypothesis into specific, testable procedures that can be measured and observed. It is essentially how the researcher defines and measures her variables.

There is no single way to go about devising an operational definition for a hypothesis; it depends on logic, the equipment and facilities available, the psychological perspective being employed, and ultimately the creativity of the researcher. For example, one researcher might develop a hypothesis in which she uses as an operational definition of "fear" as an increase in heart rate. In contrast, another psychologist might use as an operational definition of "fear" as a self-report written response to the question "How much fear are you experiencing at this moment?"

Hypotheses and the theories behind them help psychologists to pose appropriate questions. With properly stated questions in hand, psychologists proceed to step 3 of the scientific method: research.

Psych think

> > > Look before you leap. He who hesitates is lost. Absence makes the heart grow fonder. Our world is full of commonsense ideas like these contradictory adages. How would you apply the scientific method to determine the answer?

PSYCHOLOGICAL RESEARCH METHODS

Research—systematic inquiry aimed at the discovery of new knowledge—is a central component of the scientific method. Research indicates the degree to which hypotheses are accurate. Psychologists can select from a number of alternative research methods. These methods fall into two broad categories: descriptive research and experimental research.

THEORIES OF EVERYTHING

Everything's gone downhill since 1964.

Everything is my fault.

Everything IS your fault.

Everything would be perfect if I had a dirt bike.

theories Broad explanations and predictions concerning phenomena of interest.

hypothesis A prediction, stemming from a theory, stated in a way that allows it to be tested.

operational definition The translation of a hypothesis into specific, testable procedures that can be measured and observed.

DESCRIPTIVE RESEARCH

Broadly speaking, descriptive research is the systematic collection of information about a person, group, or patterns of behaviour. Descriptive research methods include naturalistic observation, survey research, and case studies.

Naturalistic Observation Do boys play more aggressively than girls? One way to research this question would be through naturalistic observation. In **naturalistic observation**, the investigator observes some naturally occurring behaviour and does not make a change in the situation. For example, a researcher investigating differences in aggressive behaviour among boys and girls might observe them on the playground during recess. The important point to remember about naturalistic observation is that the researcher simply records what occurs, making no modification in the situation that is being observed (Moore, 2002; Rustin, 2006; Schutt, 2001).

Although the advantage of naturalistic observation is obvious—we get a sample of what people do in their "natural habitat"—there is also an important drawback, namely, the inability to control any aspect of the situation. Because naturalistic observation prevents researchers from making changes in a situation, the researchers must wait until the appropriate conditions occur. Furthermore, if people know they are being watched, they may not behave naturally.

Survey Research Are students addicted to social media as we explored in the opening vignette? There is no more straightforward way of finding out what people think, feel, and do than asking them directly. For this reason, surveys are an important research method. In **survey research**, a *sample* of people chosen to represent a larger group of interest (a *population*) is asked a series of questions about their behaviour, thoughts, or attitudes. There are many ways a researcher can conduct survey research. For example, a researcher might use paper and pencil, computerized, telephone, or Internet surveys. When we conduct research we do not need to study every single person in the population (this would be impossible!). Instead, we choose a sample that represents the population. Therefore, a good sample is *representative* of the population. This simply means that the sample is like the population. For example, the population is full of many different kinds of people (different gender, ethnicity, intelligence, personality, religious beliefs, attitudes

etc.) and our sample should also include an equal mix of people (this holds true for many of the research methods, not just surveys).

Imagine we wanted to conduct a survey on attitudes towards abortion and we needed many people to complete the survey. Since we know that we can find many people at church on Sunday, we decide to conduct our survey there. Do you see any problem with this? Hopefully you realized that this would potentially be a biased sample and therefore not very representative of the population. If we want a **representative sample** we need to make sure that we choose our participants randomly. We might choose every fourth person in the telephone directory or randomly ask people on the street at various hours of the day. This is called a **random sample**, in which every member has an equal chance of being chosen. This helps researchers generalize what they learned from the sample to the greater population. Survey methods have become so sophisticated that even with a very small sample researchers are able to infer with great accuracy how a larger group would respond.

Different types of surveys share similar advantages and disadvantage. One advantage of surveys is that a large number of people can be studied at one time, which is both time and cost effective. For example, by having students at one college complete a questionnaire about Internet use, a researcher could learn whether one group uses the Internet more than the other. Survey research has several potential pitfalls, however. For one thing, if the sample of people who are surveyed (students at one college, for example) is not representative of the broader population of interest (say, all Canadian college students), the results of the survey will have little meaning. In addition, survey respondents may not want to admit to holding socially undesirable attitudes. (Most racists know they are racists and might not want to admit it.) And in some cases, people may not even be consciously aware of what their true attitudes are, or why they hold them.

naturalistic observation Research in which an investigator simply observes some naturally occurring behaviour and does not make a change in the situation.

survey research Research in which people chosen to represent a larger population are asked a series of questions about their behaviour, thoughts, or attitudes.

representative sample The sample chosen represents the greater population so that the results can be generalized from the sample to the population.

random sample A sample that is representative because it was chosen randomly and every member of the population had an equal chance of being included.

Internet surveys have potential disadvantages that other types do not. For one thing, it is difficult to obtain informed consent and to provide proper debriefing to participants. The other major challenge is that samples on the Internet may not be representative of the population. Only a portion of the population has access to the Internet, so some portion of the population cannot be included in the sample. Moreover, some people who do have access may not have high speed Internet (as many in rural areas of Canada experience) and use their computers primarily for email. Internet samples may also not be representative of all age groups, as some older people do not use computers. This is changing of course, but for now, researchers must acknowledge the limitations of this research method.

The Case Study What can a serial killer such as Russell Williams tell us about why he killed? In contrast to a survey, in which many people are studied, a **case study** is an in-depth, intensive investigation of a single individual or a small group. When case studies are used as a research technique, the goal is often not only to learn about the few individuals being examined but also to use the insights gained from the study to improve our understanding of people in general. By interviewing serial killers, for example, psychologists can gain insights into the mechanisms that have led to this disturbing behaviour.

One way that psychologists learn about uncommon or unusual behaviour is through the case study.

What are the drawbacks to case studies? If the individuals examined are unique in certain ways, we cannot make valid generalizations to a larger population. Just because something applies to one person, does not mean it will apply to everyone else! Still, such studies sometimes lead the way to new theories and to new treatments for psychological disorders.

Correlational Research In using the descriptive research methods we have discussed, researchers often want to determine the relationship between two variables. **Variables** are behaviours, events, or other characteristics that can change, or vary, in some way. For example, in a study to determine whether the amount of studying makes a difference in test scores, the variables would be study time and test scores.

In **correlational research**, two variables are examined to determine whether they are associated, or "correlated." The strength and the direction of the relationship between the two variables are represented by a mathematical statistic known as a *correlation* (or, more formally, a *correlation coefficient*), which can range from +1.0 to −1.0.

A *positive correlation* indicates that as the value of one variable increases, we can predict that the value of the other variable will also increase. For example, if we predict that the more time students spend studying for a test, the higher their grades on the test will be, and that the less they study, the lower their test scores will be, we are expecting to find a positive correlation. Positive does not mean "good" here—remember that it means that as one variable increases, so does the other. For example, higher values of the variable "amount of study time" would be associated with higher values of the variable "test score," and lower values of "amount of study time" would be associated with lower values of "test score." The correlation, then, would

case study An in-depth, intensive investigation of an individual or small group of people.

variables Behaviours, events, or other characteristics that can change, or vary, in some way.

correlational research Research in which the relationship between two sets of variables is examined to determine whether they are associated, or related.

Figure 1.6
Positive and Negative Correlations

A positive correlation is a relationship in which two factors vary in the same direction, as shown in the two graphs on the left. A negative correlation is a relationship in which two factors vary in opposite directions, as shown in the two graphs on the right.

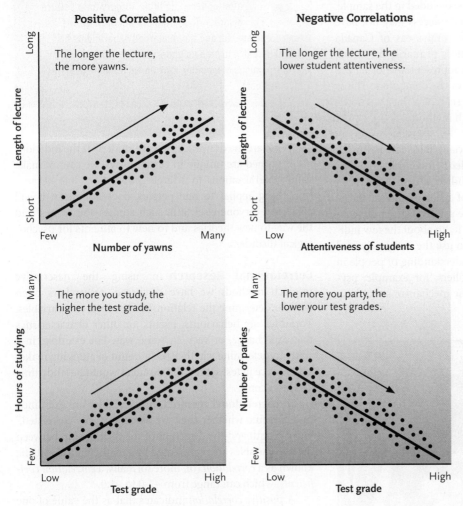

Positive Correlations

The longer the lecture, the more yawns.

Length of lecture (Short → Long) / *Number of yawns* (Few → Many)

The more you study, the higher the test grade.

Hours of studying (Few → Many) / *Test grade* (Low → High)

Negative Correlations

The longer the lecture, the lower student attentiveness.

Length of lecture (Short → Long) / *Attentiveness of students* (Low → High)

The more you party, the lower your test grades.

Number of parties (Few → Many) / *Test grade* (Low → High)

Source: Santrock & Mitterer, *Psychology*, 3rd Canadian Ed. © 2006. Figure 2.3, p. 53.

be indicated by a positive number, and the stronger the association between studying and test scores, the closer the number would be to +1.0. For example, we might find a correlation of +.85 between test scores and amount of study time, indicating a strong positive association.

In contrast, a *negative correlation* tells us that as the value of one variable increases, the value of the other decreases. For instance, we might predict that as the number of hours spent partying increases, final grades will decrease. Here we are expecting a negative correlation, ranging between 0 and –1.0. More partying is associated with lower grades, and lower grades are associated with more partying. It does not matter which way we say this because we are not saying that one variable causes the other. We are only saying that there is a negative correlation; as one variable increases the other decreases, and vice versa. The stronger the association between partying and final grades is, the closer the correlation will be to –1.0. For instance, a correlation of –.85

would indicate a strong negative association between partying and final grades.

Of course, it's quite possible that two variables are unrelated or only slightly related. For instance, we would probably not expect to find a relationship between number of study hours and height. Lack of a relationship would be indicated by a correlation close to 0. For example, if we found a correlation of –.02 or +.03, it would indicate that there is virtually no association between the two variables; knowing how much someone studies does not tell us anything about how tall he or she is.

When two variables are strongly correlated with each other, we are tempted to assume that one variable causes the other. For example, if we find that more study time is associated with higher grades, we might guess that more studying *causes* higher grades. Although this is not a bad guess, it remains just a guess—because finding that two variables are correlated does not mean that there is a causal relationship between them. The strong correlation suggests that knowing how much a person studies can help us *predict* how that person will do on a test, but it does not mean that the studying causes the test performance. There may be many other variables that influence studying and test performance. It might be, for instance, that people who are more interested in the subject matter tend to study more than do those who are less interested, and that the amount of interest, not the number of hours spent studying, predicts test performance.

Psych think

> > > Try to come up with a variable that is positively correlated with exercise (for example, the more you exercise, the more...); a variable that is negatively correlated with exercise (for instance, the more you exercise, the less...); and a variable that is not correlated at all with exercise (for example, the amount of exercise you do is not related to...).

Figure 1.7
Research Strategies

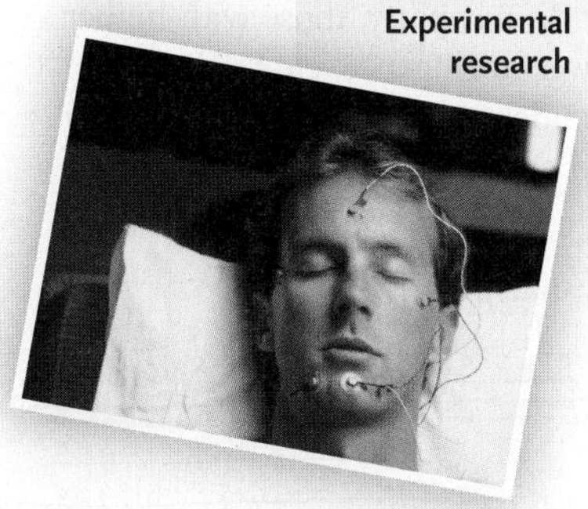

Research Method	Description	Advantages	Shortcomings
Correlational research	Researcher observes a previously existing situation but does not make a change in the situation	Offers insight into relationships between variables	Cannot determine causality
Naturalistic observation	Observation of naturally occurring behaviour, without making a change in the situation	Provides a sample of people in their natural environment	Cannot control the "natural habitat" being observed
Survey research	A sample is chosen to represent a larger population and asked a series of questions	A small sample can be used to infer attitudes and behaviour of a larger population	Sample may not be representative of the larger population; participants may not provide accurate responses to survey questions
Case study	Intensive investigation of an individual or small group	Provides a thorough, in-depth understanding of participants	Results may not be generalizable beyond the sample
Experimental research	Investigator produces a change in one variable to observe the effects of that change on other variables	Experiments offer the only way to determine cause-and-effect relationship	To be valid, experiments require random assignment of participants to conditions, well-conceptualized independent and dependent variables, and other careful controls

Source: Based on a study by Kaplan & Manuck.

The mere fact that two variables occur together does not mean that one causes the other.

The inability to demonstrate cause-and-effect relationships is a crucial drawback of correlational research. To establish causality, scientists rely on an alternative technique: the experiment.

EXPERIMENTAL RESEARCH

The *only* way psychologists can establish if one variable caused another is by carrying out an **experiment**. In a formal experiment, the researcher investigates whether one variable (or more than one variable) caused an effect in another variable. The researchers determine this by deliberately manipulating (i.e., changing) one variable in a controlled situation and observing the effects of that change on another variable. In an experiment, the conditions are created and controlled by the researcher, who deliberately makes a change in those conditions to observe the effects of that change on some kind of outcome variable. The change that the researcher deliberately makes in an experiment is called the **experimental manipulation**.

The Five Steps of an Experiment Several steps are involved in carrying out an experiment, but the process typically begins with the development of one or more hypotheses for the experiment to test. Experimenters must manipulate at least one variable to observe the effects of the manipulation on another variable while keeping other factors in the situation the same. Students sometimes struggle with the definition of "manipulation." What this means is that one variable is changed or modified in some way. For example, think back to the example at the beginning of the chapter where some students said they felt anxious after giving up social media. If we were to test this using an experiment, we would "manipulate" one variable (i.e., some students would give up social media and another group would not) and then we would measure the

> **experiment** The investigation of the effect of one (or more) variables on another by deliberately producing a change in one variable and observing the effects of that change on another variable.
>
> **experimental manipulation** The change that an experimenter deliberately produces in an experiment.

outcome to see if there were any differences (i.e., were the students who gave up social media more anxious?).

"The only way psychologists can research cause-and-effect relationships is by carrying out an experiment."

Step 1: Hypothesis As you may remember from the figure of the scientific method on p. 16, after researchers consult the scientific literature to see what kind of research has been done in their area of interest, they will develop a hypothesis. In this first step of the experiment, the researcher must start with a specific prediction about what will happen. This prediction is based on what the previous research found. For example, let's say we are researchers and we have read in the scientific literature that students who party more tend to have lower final grades. Unfortunately, the research to date has been correlational, which tells us the variables are related, but not whether one variable caused the other. To test this, we must conduct our experiment! Our hypothesis will be that students who party more will have lower final grades at the end of the semester.

Remember that we introduced the concept of operationalizing your variables? This means we need to be very specific about how we will define each of our variables. We will operationalize partying as "going to a social event or social establishment and consuming at least four or more alcoholic beverages on three or more occasions in a one week period." Notice that we were very specific in our definition. This is so that other researchers can replicate our research if they want to. It also allows other people to critique our research. We must also operationalize our other variable, final grades. We will define this as "final grades after first semester."

Step 2: Determine the Independent and Dependent Variables In the second step of the experiment the researcher must identify the independent and dependent variables. The **independent variable (IV)** is the condition that is manipulated by an experimenter. (You can think of the independent variable as being independent of the actions of those taking part in an experiment; it is controlled by the experimenter). The **dependent variable (DV)** is the variable that is measured and is expected to change as a result of how the researcher manipulated the independent variable. The dependent variable is dependent on what happens to the independent variable. Students often struggle with the concept of the IV and the DV, which makes sense because these are difficult terms to understand. It sometimes helps to think of the independent variable as "the cause" and the dependent variable as "the effect." For example, in our study, our hypothesis was that students who party more will have lower final grades at the end of the semester. What do you think is the "cause" (the IV) and what do you think is the effect (the DV)? You are correct if you said that the amount of partying is like the cause (and therefore the IV) and the final grades are the effect (the DV).

Step 3: Choose the Participants The next step in the experiment is to choose the participants. We need to be very careful how we do this because we want to make sure that our sample is representative of the population. Just as we discussed in the section on survey research, we need to use *random sampling* to ensure our sample is representative. For example, in our experiment on student partying and final grades, we want to randomly select the students so that we don't have one type of student (i.e., those who regularly party, those who regularly do not party, those with higher intelligence, those with lower intelligence, etc.). We want a sample that represents all students, which will include many different kinds of behaviour and intelligence levels.

"What if these guys in white coats who bring us food are, like, studying us and we're part of some kind of big experiment?"
© The New Yorker Collection 2004 Mike Twohy from cartoonbank.com. All Rights Reserved.

Step 4: Random Assignment of Participants to the Experimental and Control Groups The fourth step in the experiment is assigning the participants to either an experimental group or a control group. The **experimental group** receives some special **treatment** (the manipulation implemented by the experimenter) and the **control group** receives no treatment, a different treatment, or a **placebo** (a false or simulated treatment). In some experiments there are multiple experimental and control groups, each of which is compared with another group.

independent variable (IV) The variable that is manipulated by an experimenter.

dependent variable (DV) The variable that is measured and is expected to change as a result of changes caused by the experimenter's manipulation of the independent variable.

experimental group Any group participating in an experiment that receives a treatment (e.g., intervention, medicine, etc.).

treatment The manipulation (or change) implemented by the experimenter.

control group A group participating in an experiment that receives no treatment. This group often receives a placebo instead.

placebo A false treatment, such as a pill, "drug," or other substance, that has no significant chemical properties or active ingredient.

By including both experimental and control groups in an experiment, researchers are able to rule out the possibility that something other than the experimental manipulation produced the results observed in the experiment. Researchers call those **confounding variables** because they have the potential to impact the results. Without a control group, we couldn't be sure that some other confounding variable, such as the temperature at the time we were running the experiment, the participant's mood, or even the mere passage of time, wasn't causing the changes observed.

For example, consider a medical researcher who thinks she has invented a pill that cures the common cold. To test her claim, she gives the pill to a group of 20 people who have colds and finds that 10 days later all of them are cured.

Eureka? Not so fast. A good consumer of research (and a good critical thinker) might reasonably argue that in this flawed study the people may have improved even without the medicine. What the researcher obviously needed was a control group consisting of people with colds who *didn't* get the medicine and whose health is also checked 10 days later. The researcher can only assess the effectiveness of the medicine if there is a significant difference between the experimental and control groups. This is why researchers use control groups; they can isolate specific causes for their finding and draw cause-and-effect conclusions.

To make an experiment a valid test of the hypothesis, the participants must be *randomly assigned* to the experimental and control groups. The significance of this step becomes clear when we examine various alternative procedures. For example, the experimenters might have assigned just males to the experimental group and just females to the control group. If they had done this, however, any differences they found between the two groups could not be attributed with any certainty solely to the independent variable, because the differences might just as well have been due to gender. A more reasonable procedure would be to ensure that each group had the same composition in terms of gender; then the researchers would be able to make comparisons across groups with considerably more accuracy.

Participants in each of the experimental groups ought to be comparable, and it is easy enough to create groups that are similar in terms of gender. The problem becomes a bit trickier, though, when we consider other participant characteristics. How can we ensure that participants in each experimental group will be equally intelligent, extroverted, cooperative, and so forth, when the list of characteristics—any one of which could be important—is potentially endless?

Just as researchers have to be careful to use random sampling when choosing their sample, they also have to make sure they use **random assignment to condition** when they assign their sample to either the experimental or control group. For example, in our study we might randomly assign half the participants to the "party group" (the experimental group) and half to the "non–party group" (the control group). To do this, we might, for instance, flip a coin for each participant and assign a participant to one group when "heads" came up and to the other group when "tails" came up. The advantage of this technique is that there is an equal chance that participant characteristics will be distributed across the various groups. When a researcher uses random assignment—which in practice is usually carried out using computer-generated random numbers—chances are that each of the groups will have approximately the same proportion of people who regularly party, people who do not regularly party, people with higher intelligence, and people with lower intelligence, etc.

All experiments include the following set of key elements, which are important to keep in mind as you consider whether a research study is truly an experiment:

- A hypothesis that predicts the effect that the independent variable will have on the dependent variable

- An independent variable; the variable that is manipulated by the experimenter (like the cause)

- A dependent variable; the variable that is measured by the experimenter and that is expected to change as a result of the manipulation of the independent variable (like the effect)

- A procedure that randomly assigns participants to different experimental groups, or "conditions," of the independent variable

Only if each of these elements is present can a research study be considered a true experiment in which cause-and-effect relationships can be determined.

confounding variables Variables that might influence the outcome (or dependent variable) of the study. These can be avoided by using random sampling and by having a control group.

random assignment to condition A procedure in which participants are assigned to different experimental groups or "conditions" on the basis of chance and chance alone.

Figure 1.8

Design of an Experiment of Memory Consolidation in Different Sleep Stages

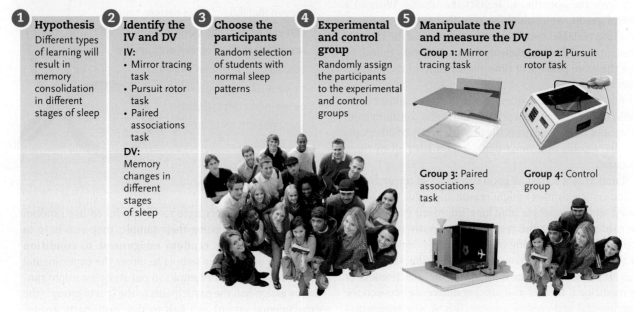

1 Hypothesis
Different types of learning will result in memory consolidation in different stages of sleep

2 Identify the IV and DV
IV:
• Mirror tracing task
• Pursuit rotor task
• Paired associations task

DV:
Memory changes in different stages of sleep

3 Choose the participants
Random selection of students with normal sleep patterns

4 Experimental and control group
Randomly assign the participants to the experimental and control groups

5 Manipulate the IV and measure the DV
Group 1: Mirror tracing task
Group 2: Pursuit rotor task
Group 3: Paired associations task
Group 4: Control group

Source: Fogel, S. M., Smith, C. T., & Cote, K. A. (2007). Dissociable learning-dependent changes in REM and non-REM sleep in declarative and procedural memory systems. *Behavioural Brain Research, 180,* 48–61.

Step 5: Manipulate the Independent Variable and Measure the Outcome After the researcher has randomly assigned the participants to the experimental and control groups he can manipulate the independent variable and see what effect it had on the dependent variable. Even when the results of an experiment seem straightforward, the researcher cannot be sure that the results were truly meaningful until he determines whether the results represented a **significant outcome**. Using statistical analysis, researchers can determine whether a numeric difference is a real difference or is due merely to chance. Only when differences between groups are large enough that statistical tests show them to be significant is it possible for researchers to support a hypothesis (Cohen, 2002; Cwikel, Behar, & Rabson-Hare, 2000).

Moving Beyond the Study Of course, one experiment does not resolve forever the question of cause and effect. Psychologists—like other scientists—require that findings be **replicated**, or repeated, sometimes using other procedures, in other settings, with other groups of participants, before full confidence can be placed in the results of any single experiment. A procedure called *meta-analysis* permits psychologists to combine the results of many separate studies in one overall conclusion (Peterson & Brown., 2005; Tenenbaum & Ruck, 2007).

In addition to replicating experimental results, psychologists need to test the limitations of their theories and hypotheses to determine under which specific circumstances they do and do not apply. It is critical to continue carrying out experiments to understand the conditions in which exceptions occur and those in which the rule holds (Aronson, 1994; Garcia et al., 2002).

Research Challenges

You probably realize by now that psychologists must make choices about the type of study to conduct, the measures to take, and the most effective way to analyze the results. Even after they have made these essential decisions, they must still consider several critical issues. We turn first to the issue of *experimental bias*.

EXPERIMENTAL BIAS

Even the best-laid experimental plans are susceptible to **experimental bias**—factors that distort the way the independent variable affects the dependent variable in an experiment. One of the most common forms of experimental bias is *experimenter expectations*: An experimenter

significant outcome Meaningful results that make it possible for researchers to feel confident that they have supported their hypotheses.

replication The repetition of research, sometimes using other procedures, settings, and groups of participants, to increase confidence in prior findings.

experimental bias Factors that distort how the independent variable affects the dependent variable in an experiment.

unintentionally transmits cues to participants about the way they are expected to behave in a given experimental condition. The danger is that those expectations will bring about an "appropriate" behaviour—one that otherwise might not have occurred (Rosenthal, 2002, 2003).

A related problem is *participant expectations* about appropriate behaviour. If you have ever been a participant in an experiment, you know that you quickly develop guesses about what is expected of you. In fact, it is typical for people to develop their own hypotheses about what the experimenter hopes to learn from the study. If participants form their own hypotheses, they, rather than the experimental manipulation, may produce the effect.

Psych think

> > > A researcher strongly believes that college professors tend to show female students less attention and respect in the classroom than they show male students. She sets up an experimental study involving observations of classrooms in different conditions. In explaining the study to the professors and students who will participate, what steps should the researcher take to eliminate experimental bias based on both experimenter expectations and participant expectations?

To guard against participant expectations that may bias the results of an experiment, the experimenter may try to disguise the true purpose of the experiment. Participants who do not know that helping behaviour is being studied, for example, are more apt to act in a "natural" way than they would if they knew.

Sometimes it is impossible to hide the actual purpose of research; when that is the case, other techniques are available to prevent bias. Suppose you were interested in testing the ability of a new drug to alleviate the symptoms of severe depression. If you simply gave the drug to half your participants and not to the other half, the participants who were given the drug might report feeling less depressed merely because they knew they were getting a drug. Similarly, the participants who got nothing might report feeling no better because they knew that they were in a no-treatment control group.

To solve this problem, psychologists typically use a placebo. Because members of both groups are kept in the dark about whether they are getting a real or a false treatment, any differences in outcome can be attributed to the quality of the drug and not to the possible psychological effects of being administered a pill or other substance (Crum & Langer, 2007; Rajagopal, 2006).

However, there is one more safeguard that a careful researcher must apply in an experiment such as this one. To overcome the possibility that *experimenter expectations* will affect the participant, the person who administers the drug shouldn't know whether it is the true drug or the placebo. By keeping both the participant and the experimenter who interacts with the participant "blind" to the nature of the drug that is being administered, researchers can more accurately assess the effects of the drug. This method is known as the *double-blind procedure*.

Because the field of psychology is based on an accumulated body of research, psychologists must scrutinize the methods, results, and claims of researchers. Several basic questions can help us sort through what is valid and what is not. Among the most important questions to ask are these:

1. *What was the purpose of the research?* Research studies should evolve from a clearly specified theory.

Get Involved!

Do you want to take part in ongoing psychological research? There are hundreds of Web-based studies on everything from "humour in relationships" to "workplace bullying" to "food affecting mood." Hanover College's psych department (http://psych.hanover.edu/research/exponnet.html#top) maintains a list of participatory online studies conducted by psychological researchers at reputable academic institutions— maybe even yours! Oh, and if you can't get enough— wait a week and go back, because the Web site is updated very frequently.

Furthermore, we must take into account the specific hypothesis that is being tested. Unless we know what hypothesis is being examined, we cannot judge how successful a study has been.

2. *How well was the study conducted?* Consider who the participants were, how many were involved, what methods were employed, and what problems the researcher encountered in collecting the data. There are important differences, for example, between a case study that reports the anecdotes of a handful of respondents and a survey that collects data from several thousand people.

3. *Are the results presented fairly?* Assess statements on the basis of the actual data they reflect and their logic. For instance, that a manufacturer of car X boasts that "no other car has a better safety record than car X" does not mean that car X is safer than every other car. It just means that no other car has been proven safer, although many other cars could be just as safe as car X. Expressed in the latter fashion, the statement doesn't seem worth bragging about.

These three questions can help you assess the validity of research findings—both within and outside the field of psychology. The more you know about how to evaluate research in general, the stronger consumer of information you will be!

THE ETHICS OF RESEARCH

Another important research consideration is ethics. Because research has the potential to violate the rights of participants, psychologists are expected to adhere to a strict set of ethical guidelines aimed at protecting participants (APA, 2002; CPA, 2000)

The guidelines involve these safeguards:
- Protection of participants from physical and mental harm
- The right of participants to privacy regarding their behaviour
- The assurance that participation in research is completely voluntary
- The necessity of informing participants about the nature of procedures before their participation in the experiment

All experiments, including the minority of studies that involve deception, must be reviewed by an independent panel before being conducted (Fisher et al., 2002; Fisher, 2003; Smith, 2003). One of psychologists' key ethical principles is **informed consent**. Before participating in an experiment, the participants must sign a document affirming that they have been told the basic outlines of the study and are

informed consent A document signed by participants affirming that they have been told the basic outlines of the study and are aware of what their participation will involve.

debriefing After the study is completed, participants receive an explanation of the study and the procedures that were involved.

aware of what their participation will involve, what risks the experiment may hold, and the fact that their participation is purely voluntary and they may terminate it at any time. Furthermore, after participation in a study, they must be given a **debriefing** in which they receive an explanation of the study and the procedures that were involved. The only time informed consent and a debriefing can be eliminated is in experiments in which the risks are minimal, as in a purely observational study in a public place (Barnett et al., 2007; Fallon, 2006; Koocher, Norcross, & Hill, 2005). This is the type of research that many social psychologist conduct.

SHOULD ANIMALS BE USED IN RESEARCH?

Like those who work with humans, researchers who use non-human animals in experiments have their own set of exacting guidelines to safeguard the animals. Specifically, researchers must make every effort to minimize discomfort, illness, and pain. Procedures that subject animals to distress are permitted only when an alternative approach is unavailable and when the research is justified by its prospective value (Canadian Council on Animal Care, 2007). Along with avoiding causing physical discomfort, researchers are required to promote the *psychological* well-being of some species of research animals, such as primates (Auer et al., 2007; Lutz & Novak, 2005; Rusche, 2003).

Research involving animals is controversial but, when conducted within ethical guidelines, can yield significant benefits for humans.

But why should animals be used for research in the first place? Is it really possible to learn about human behaviour from research on rats, gerbils, and pigeons? The answer is that psychological research that does employ non-humans is designed to answer questions different from those posed in research with humans. For example, the shorter life span of animals (rats live an average of two years) allows researchers to learn about the effects of aging in a relatively short time frame. It is also possible to provide greater experimental control over non-humans and to carry out procedures that might not be possible with people. For example, some studies require large numbers of participants who share similar backgrounds or who have been exposed to particular environments—conditions that could not practically be met with human beings.

Research with animals has provided psychologists with information that has profoundly benefited humans. For instance, it furnished the keys to detecting eye disorders in children early enough to prevent permanent damage, to communicating more effectively with severely retarded children, and to reducing chronic pain in people. Still, the use of research using non-humans is controversial, involving complex moral and philosophical concerns.

Consequently, all research involving non-humans must be carefully reviewed beforehand to ensure that it is conducted ethically (Hackam, 2007; Herzog, 2005; Plous & Herzog, 2000; Saucier & Cain, 2006).

From the perspective of ...

A RESEARCH ANALYST AT STATISTICS CANADA You are hired to study people's attitudes toward Facebook by circulating a questionnaire via the Internet. Is this study likely to accurately reflect the views of the general population? Why or why not?

BUY IT?

Being a Good Consumer of Information

Imagine you are online and an ad popped up that showed an image of someone who took a weight loss pill and lost 10 pounds in less than two weeks. You close the ad, but it pops up again the next day and it gets you thinking, "Should I try this? It's only $19.99, what do I have to lose?" But you tell yourself no! What if they had several people provide testimonials that the weight loss pill worked? Still no? Good—hopefully you said that there are many reasons why people might say the product worked. First, you need to question whether the people in the commercial actually lost the weight or whether they were paid to say so. But even if they actually lost weight, there may be other explanations for why they lost the weight. Can you think of any? Maybe they changed their diet or maybe they started to exercise more?

The only way to really find out if the weight loss pill is worth buying is to see if there were any valid experiments conducted that demonstrated that the experimental group that used the weight loss pill lost weight while the control group who used a placebo did not (and both groups would have the same kind of diet and exercise regime). Of course the experimenter would also make sure that he used random sampling and random assignment to the experimental and control groups to ensure the study generalized to the general population!

For Review ››

What is the definition of psychology and why is psychology considered a science?

Psychology is the scientific study of behaviour and mental processes, encompassing not just what people do but also their biological activities, feelings, perceptions, memory, reasoning, and thoughts.

What are the goals of psychology?

The goals of psychology are to describe, explain, predict, and control/change (DEP-C).

What are the major perspectives used by psychologists?

The major perspectives are the evolutionary, psychodynamic, socio-cultural, humanistic, behavioural, neuroscientific, and cognitive perspectives. You can remember these using the acronym "Every Psychologist Studies Human Behaviour 'N Cognition"! (We will discuss other memory devices in the chapter on memory!)

What are the major subfields in the field of psychology?

Behavioural neuroscience, experimental psychology, cognitive psychology, developmental psychology, personality psychology, clinical and counselling psychology, health psychology, social psychology, and cross-cultural psychology.

What is the scientific method, and how do psychologists use theory and research to answer questions of interest?

The scientific method is the approach psychologists use to understand behaviour. It consists of four steps: identifying questions of interest, formulating an explanation, carrying out research that is designed to support or refute the explanation, and communicating the findings. Research in psychology is guided by theories (broad explanations and predictions regarding phenomena of interest) and hypotheses (theory-based predictions stated in a way that allows them to be tested).

What research methods do psychologists use?

In survey research, people are asked a series of questions about their behaviour, thoughts, or attitudes. The case study is an in-depth interview and examination of one person or group. In naturalistic observation, researchers observe people in their natural environment, but in experimental research people are often observed in a laboratory where their behaviour can be more easily controlled.

What are the ethics of research?

All participants in research must be protected from harm. Moreover, participants of research must always sign a document showing that they have provided informed consent and they must be debriefed by the researcher after the study is over about what the study was about.

Psych think answers

Psych think 1 On p. 8 we asked you to think of a behaviour that you exhibit on a regular basis (i.e., procrastinating, nail biting, smoking, anxiety, trouble sleeping, etc.) and to explain the cause of your behaviour from each of the major perspectives of psychology (i.e., neuroscience, psychodynamic, behavioural, cognitive, humanistic, sociocultural, and evolutionary). See the chart below for how each of the approaches would explain procrastination. Notice that while each perspective describes your behaviour the same way, they explain it quite differently.

Neuroscience	Cognitive	Behavioural	Humanistic	Psychodynamic	Socio-cultural	Evolutionary
Genetics may influence procrastination.	Thoughts of potential failure will influence procrastination.	The reward of other more exciting activities will influence procrastination	One may delay meeting one need (procrastinating) until another need is met.	Early childhood experiences of failure have been repressed into the unconscious, which influence current levels of procrastination	One may come from a culture that values fun and leisure rather than work or less exciting activities.	It may have been adaptive to wait before hunting to ensure survival.

Psych think 2 In the PSYCH think on p. 17 we asked you how you would apply the scientific method to one of the commonsense ideas such as "Look before you leap. He who hesitates is lost. Absence makes the heart grow fonder."

You could use the five steps to an experiment from p. 16 to test the theory that absence makes the heart grow fonder!

Step 1: State the hypothesis. Couples who live apart for eight weeks will have higher rates of marital satisfaction than couples who live together full time.

Step 2: Determine the IV and the DV. The independent variable will be living away from each other for eight weeks and the dependent variable will be marital satisfaction.

Step 3: Choose the participants. We want to make sure we have a representative sample of married couples so we must use random selection of our sample. We will do this by putting an advertisement in newspapers in major cities such as Toronto, Vancouver, Montreal, and Halifax as well as in one smaller city in four other provinces. We will randomly select 60 couples for our study.

Step 4: Randomly assign participants to the experimental and control group. Remember that the experimental group always receives the independent variable. In this case, the experimental group will be the group who lives away from each other for eight weeks. The control group will be the group that lives together full time.

Step 5: Manipulate the independent variable and measure the outcome. In this step we will separate our experimental group for eight weeks (i.e., ensure those couples live apart during that time). At the end of the eight weeks we will have all couples complete a marital satisfaction survey and then measure whether couples who lived apart had stronger relationships than couples who lived together (i.e., Does absence make the heart grow fonder?). We would then use statistical analysis to determine if the differences between our two groups are statistically significant. If so, we can then confirm that the commonsense idea is in fact true.

Psych think 3 In the PSYCH think on p. 20 we asked you to try to come up with a variable that is positively correlated with exercise (for example, the more you exercise, the more...); a variable that is negatively correlated with exercise (for instance, the more you exercise, the less...); and a variable that is not correlated at all with exercise (for example, the amount of exercise you do is not related to...). You may have said something like "the more you exercise, the better you feel" for a positive correlation. For a negative correlation you may have said "the less you exercise the more you weigh," and for a zero correlation (i.e., no correlation) you may have said "the amount you exercise is not related to your shoe size."

Psych think 4 In the PSYCH think on p. 25 we described a situation in which a researcher strongly believed that college professors tend to show female students less attention and respect in the classroom than they showed male students. We indicated that the professor set up an experimental study involving observations of classrooms in different conditions. We asked what steps the researcher should take to eliminate experimental bias based on both experimenter expectations and participant expectations? The answer would be to use a double-blind study where the researcher and the participants are unaware of what condition they are in.

Neuroscience
and Behaviour

WHAT'S TO COME

Neurons: The Basic Units of the Nervous System

The Nervous System: Linking Neurons

The Brain

The Endocrine System: Hormones and Glands

The fallen athlete

Marc Savard, from Peterborough, Ontario, played junior hockey for the Oshawa Generals, and had a very successful career in the National Hockey League (NHL) with the Calgary Flames and the Atlanta Thrashers before signing on with the Boston Bruins in 2006. The Boston Bruins were Stanley Cup champions in 2011, but unfortunately for Savard, he was not able to live the dream of hoisting the Stanley Cup above his head with his teammates. He did not play the 2011 season because of post-concussion symptoms.

avard received a dangerous blindside hit to the side of head by an opponent during a hockey game in March, 2010. One moment Mark Savard was carrying the puck down the ice toward the opposing net, and the next moment he was lying on the ice unconscious before being carried out on a stretcher. His concussion was diagnosed as severe and he was out for the rest of the regular season. Savard played part of the 2010–2011 season, but suffered another moderate concussion after receiving a check into the end boards by an opposing player.

Savard's post-concussion symptoms included what one might expect after experiencing a major blow to the head (i.e., headaches and dizziness), but his other symptoms such as short-term memory loss, irritability, fatigue, slower motor skills, and depression speak to the impact that the human brain has on behaviour. As you may recall, the neuroscience perspective explains behaviour and mental processes as being influenced by the brain, nervous system, genes, and other biological processes. In this chapter you will learn more specifically how this happens and see why Marc Savard's career ended at the age of 34 because of two significant hits to his brain.

Former Canadian Olympian Clara Hughes exemplifies the exquisite coordination between the brain and the body.

As You Read >>

- Why do psychologists study the brain and nervous system?
- What are the basic units of the nervous system, and what are their functions?
- What are the major parts of the brain, and what are their functions?
- How do the two halves of the brain specialize, and how do they work together?
- How does the endocrine system affect behaviour?

behavioural neuroscientists (or biopsychologists)
Psychologists who specialize in considering the ways in which the biological structures and functions of the body affect behaviour.

Because the nervous system plays the leading role in controlling behaviour and because humans at their most basic level are biological beings, many researchers in psychology and other fields as diverse as computer science, zoology, and medicine have made biological explanations of behaviour their specialty. These experts collectively are called *neuroscientists* (Beatty, 2000; Cartwright, 2006; Gazzaniga, Ivry, & Mangun, 2002; Posner & DiGiorlamo, 2000).

Psychologists who specialize in considering the ways in which the biological structures and functions of the body affect behaviour are known as **behavioural neuroscientists** (or biopsychologists). Their research on the brain and other parts of the nervous system enhances our understanding of sensory experiences, states of consciousness, motivation and emotion, development throughout the life span, and physical and psychological health. Moreover, advances in behavioural neuroscience have led to the creation of drugs and other treatments for psychological and physical disorders (Compagni & Manderscheid, 2006; Kosslyn et al., 2002; Plomin, 2003a, b).

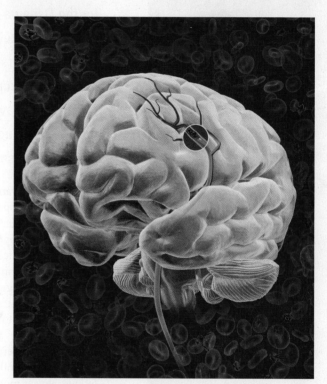

A stroke disrupts normal brain function by cutting off the supply of oxygen and nutrients to the affected area.

DID YOU KNOW?

A stroke occurs when the blood supply to part of the brain is suddenly cut off by a blood clot or when a blood vessel in the brain bursts. Stroke symptoms vary, depending on the location of the stroke, and may include paralysis on one side of the body or the inability to speak.

Neurons: The Basic Units of the Nervous System

Watching Sidney Crosby effortlessly score a goal or Steve Nash dribble a basketball past guys twice his size reminds us of the complexity—and wondrous abilities—of the human body. But even the most everyday tasks, such as pouring a cup of coffee or humming a tune, depend on a sophisticated sequence of events in the body. The nervous system is the pathway for the instructions that permit our bodies to carry out such precise activities. Neurons, the cells that make up the nervous system, convey messages throughout the body, enabling us to move, think, experience emotion, and engage in a wide range of other behaviours.

STRUCTURE OF THE NEURON

Imagine that you are driving down the road when suddenly your friend, who is sitting next to you, shouts: "Watch out for that truck!" Immediately you experience strong anxiety, step on the brake, and look around in every direction. This process might seem automatic—but think about it for a moment. How did that information get from your ears into your head and trigger these emotions and behaviours?

Driving a car, texting, or playing the piano depends on exact muscle coordination. But if we consider how the muscles can be activated so precisely, we find that it is up to the brain to communicate and coordinate the complex movements that make up meaningful physical activity.

The brain not only controls movement and other behaviour by sending messages to cells throughout the body, but it also receives messages about the body's status on a continuous basis. These messages pass through specialized cells called neurons. **Neurons**, or nerve cells, are the basic units of the nervous system. Their quantity is staggering—perhaps as many as 1 trillion neurons are involved in the control of behaviour (Boahen, 2005).

Unlike most other cells, neurons have the ability to communicate with other cells and transmit information across relatively long distances. Many of the body's neurons receive signals from our physical surroundings or relay the nervous system's messages to muscles and other cells, but the vast majority of neurons communicate only with other neurons in the elaborate information system that regulates behaviour. Neurons are how our body communicates with itself. Information flows from neuron to neuron to neuron. When all is working well, this information flows seamlessly. We need this information to feel, to think, and to act.

Although there are several types of neurons, they all have a similar structure. Like most cells, neurons have a cell body and a nucleus. The nucleus incorporates the hereditary material that determines how a cell functions. Neurons are physically held in place by glial cells. Glial cells provide nourishment to neurons, insulate them, help repair damage, and generally support neural functioning (Bassotti et al., 2007; Fields, 2004; Kettenmann & Ransom, 2005).

At one end of the neuron's cell body is a cluster of branching fibres called **dendrites**, which receive messages from other neurons. On the opposite side of the cell body is a long, slender extension called an **axon**. The axon carries messages received by the dendrites to other neurons. The axon is considerably longer than the rest of the neuron. Although most axons are several millimetres in length, some are almost a metre long. Axons end in small bulges called **terminal buttons** (sometimes called **end bulbs** or **axon terminals**), which send messages forward to other neurons.

neurons Nerve cells, the basic elements of the nervous system.

dendrite A cluster of fibres at one end of a neuron that receive messages from other neurons.

axon The part of the neuron that carries messages destined for other neurons.

terminal buttons Small bulges at the end of axons that send messages to other neurons. (Sometimes called end bulbs or axon terminals.)

Figure 2.1
Structure of a Neuron

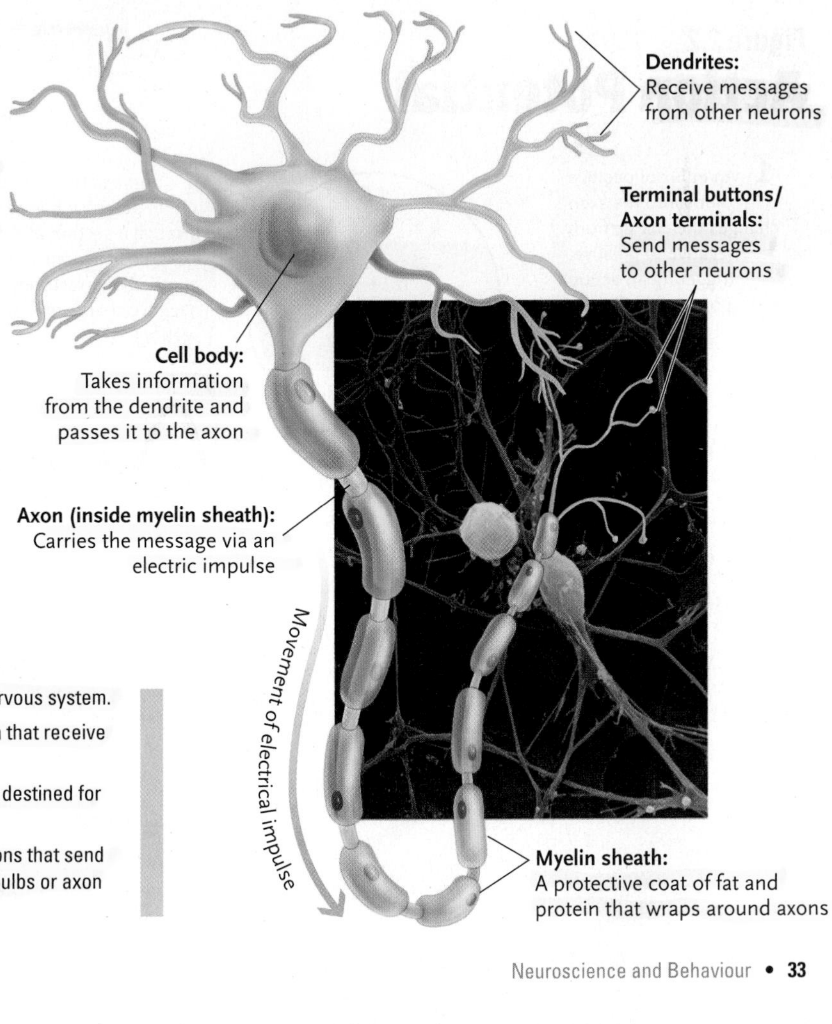

Dendrites: Receive messages from other neurons

Terminal buttons/ Axon terminals: Send messages to other neurons

Cell body: Takes information from the dendrite and passes it to the axon

Axon (inside myelin sheath): Carries the message via an electric impulse

Movement of electrical impulse

Myelin sheath: A protective coat of fat and protein that wraps around axons

Messages travel through a neuron in the form of electrical impulses. Generally those impulses move across neurons in one direction only, as if they were travelling on a one-way street. Impulses follow a route that begins with the dendrites, continues into the cell body, and leads ultimately along the axon to adjacent neurons.

To prevent messages from veering off course, most axons are insulated, just as electrical wires must be insulated to prevent current from escaping. The axon insulation, known as a **myelin sheath**, is a protective coating of fat and protein that wraps the axon like a sausage casing. Myelination, the process by which neurons become encased in a myelin sheath, begins before birth and continues into young adulthood (Fields, 2008). The myelin sheath has a very important function in protecting the axon. Sometimes the myelin sheath can become damaged, which means an axon cannot send its message properly. For example, in multiple sclerosis (MS) the immune system destroys an individual's own myelin sheath and the neuron can no longer carry that important information to tell the body what it needs to do (Frohman, Racke, & Raine, 2006). What's interesting is that while there is a known biological

cause of MS, other environmental factors play a role as well. Dr. Ruth Anne Marrie from the University of Manitoba has completed a significant amount of research on this very issue. Marrie (2004) indicated that factors such as diet, physical and emotional stress, infections, exposure to toxins, and hepatitis B vaccinations also interact with biological factors to influence the risk of developing MS (Marrie, 2004). Marrie's research is another reminder that much of our behaviour is influenced by multiple causes.

HOW NEURONS FIRE

Like a gun, neurons either fire—that is, transmit an electrical impulse along the axon—or don't fire. There is no in between stage. Similarly, neurons follow an **all-or-none law**: they are either on or off, with nothing in between the on state and the off state. Once there is enough stimulation, a neuron fires.

Before a neuron fires—that is, when it is in a **resting state**—it has a negative electrical charge of about –70 millivolts (a millivolt is one one-thousandth of a volt). When a message arrives at a neuron, gates along the cell membrane open briefly to allow positive ions (electrically charged

> **myelin sheath** A protective coat of fat and protein that wraps around axons.
>
> **all-or-none law** The rule that neurons are either on or off.
>
> **resting state** The state in which there is a negative electrical charge of about negative 70 millivolts within a neuron.

Figure 2.2

Action Potential

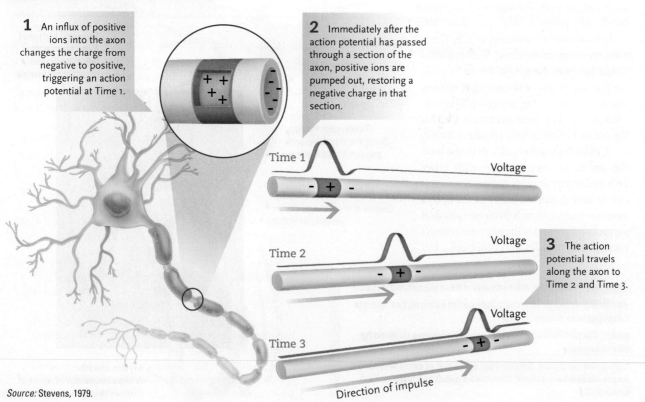

1 An influx of positive ions into the axon changes the charge from negative to positive, triggering an action potential at Time 1.

2 Immediately after the action potential has passed through a section of the axon, positive ions are pumped out, restoring a negative charge in that section.

3 The action potential travels along the axon to Time 2 and Time 3.

Time 1   Voltage

Time 2   Voltage

Time 3   Voltage

Direction of impulse

Source: Stevens, 1979.

subatomic particles) to rush in at rates as high as 100 million ions per second. The sudden arrival of these positive ions causes the charge within the nearby part of the cell to change momentarily from negative to positive. When the positive charge reaches a critical level, the "trigger" is pulled, and an electrical impulse, known as an action potential, travels along the axon of the neuron.

The **action potential** moves from one end of the axon to the other like a flame travelling along a fuse. As the impulse is transmitted along the axon, the movement of ions causes a change in charge from negative to positive in successive sections of the axon. After the impulse has passed through a particular section of the axon, positive ions are pumped out of that section, and its charge returns to negative while the action potential continues to move along the axon.

Just after an action potential has passed through a section of the axon, the cell membrane in that region cannot admit positive ions again for a fraction of a second, and so a neuron cannot fire again immediately no matter how much stimulation it receives. This is called negative after-potential, and is similar to a "gun" having to be reloaded after each shot. There then follows a period in which, although it is possible for the neuron to fire, a stronger stimulus is needed than would be needed if the neuron had reached its normal resting state. Eventually, however, the normal resting state is restored, and the neuron is ready to fire once again.

Neurons vary not only in terms of how quickly an impulse moves along the axon but also in their potential rate of firing. Some neurons are capable of firing as many as a thousand times per second; others fire at much slower rates. The intensity of a stimulus determines how much of a neuron's potential firing rate is reached. A strong stimulus, such as a bright light or a loud sound, leads to a higher rate of firing than a less intense stimulus does. Thus, even though all impulses move at the same strength or speed through a particular axon—because of the all-or-none law—there is variation in the frequency of impulses, providing a mechanism by which we can distinguish the tickle of a feather from the weight of someone standing on our toes.

BRIDGING THE GAP BETWEEN NEURONS

If you have ever looked inside a computer, you've seen that each part is physically connected to another part. In contrast, evolution has produced a neural transmission system that at some points has no need for a structural connection between its components. Instead, a chemical connection bridges the gap between two neurons—this is called the synapse. The **synapse** is the space between two neurons where the axon of a sending neuron communicates with the dendrites of a receiving neuron by using chemical messages (Dean & Dresbach, 2006; Fanselow & Poulos, 2005).

> Just as a jigsaw puzzle piece can fit in only one place in a puzzle, each kind of neurotransmitter has a distinctive configuration that allows it to fit into a specific type of receptor site on the receiving neuron.

When a nerve impulse comes to the end of the axon and reaches a terminal button, the terminal button releases a chemical courier called a neurotransmitter. **Neurotransmitters** are chemicals that carry messages across the synapse to receptor sites on a receiving neuron. Like a boat that ferries passengers across a river, neurotransmitters move across the synapse toward other neurons. The chemical mode of message transmission that occurs between neurons is strikingly different from the means by which communication occurs inside neurons: Although messages are transmitted as electrical impulses within a neuron, they are transmitted chemically between neurons.

There are several types of neurotransmitters, and not all neurons are capable of receiving the chemical message carried by a particular neurotransmitter. In the same way that a jigsaw puzzle piece can fit in only one specific location in a puzzle, each kind of neurotransmitter has a distinctive configuration that matches a specific type of receptor site on the receiving neuron. Only when a neurotransmitter fits

Figure 2.3

Changes in Electrical Charge in a Neuron During an Action Potential

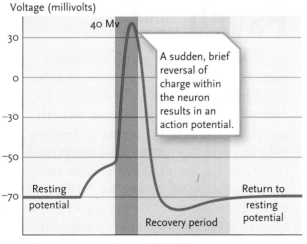

Voltage (millivolts)

40 Mv

A sudden, brief reversal of charge within the neuron results in an action potential.

Resting potential

Recovery period

Return to resting potential

Time →

action potential An electric nerve impulse that travels through a neuron's axon when it is set off by a "trigger," changing the neuron's charge from negative to positive.

synapse The space between two neurons where the axon of a sending neuron communicates with the dendrites of a receiving neuron by using chemical messages.

neurotransmitters Chemicals that carry messages across the synapse to the dendrite (and sometimes the cell body) of a receiving neuron.

Figure 2.4
How Synapses and Neurotransmitters Work

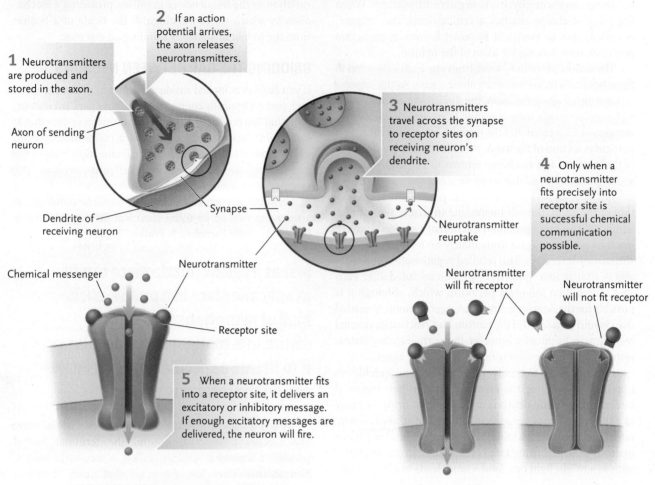

1 Neurotransmitters are produced and stored in the axon.

2 If an action potential arrives, the axon releases neurotransmitters.

3 Neurotransmitters travel across the synapse to receptor sites on receiving neuron's dendrite.

4 Only when a neurotransmitter fits precisely into receptor site is successful chemical communication possible.

Axon of sending neuron

Dendrite of receiving neuron

Synapse

Neurotransmitter

Neurotransmitter reuptake

Chemical messenger

Receptor site

Neurotransmitter will fit receptor

Neurotransmitter will not fit receptor

5 When a neurotransmitter fits into a receptor site, it delivers an excitatory or inhibitory message. If enough excitatory messages are delivered, the neuron will fire.

precisely into a receptor site is successful chemical communication possible.

When someone knocks at your door, you may not always hear it. For instance, if you are waiting for a pizza delivery, you may be especially sensitive to door knocking sounds. However, if you are studying and expecting no visitors, you are much less likely to hear the rap, rap, rap. Your state of mind primes or inhibits your door-knock-sensing ability. Neurotransmitters work in much the same way. If a neurotransmitter matches a receptor site on the receiving neuron, the chemical message it delivers is either excitatory or inhibitory. **Excitatory messages** make it more likely that a receiving neuron will fire and an action potential will travel down its axon. **Inhibitory messages**, in contrast, do just the opposite; they provide chemical information that prevents or decreases the likelihood that the receiving neuron will fire.

excitatory message A chemical message that makes it more likely that a receiving neuron will fire and an action potential will travel down its axon.

inhibitory message A chemical message that prevents or decreases the likelihood that a receiving neuron will fire.

Because the dendrites of a neuron receive both excitatory and inhibitory messages simultaneously, the neuron must integrate the messages by using a kind of chemical calculator. Put simply, if the excitatory messages ("fire!") outnumber the inhibitory ones ("don't fire!"), the neuron

Psych think

> > > One helpful way to remember the parts of the neuron is to think of the neuron as being like something you know well. For example, if we think of the neuron as being like a tree, we might say that the roots of the tree are like the dendrites of the neuron and the root ball is like the cell body of a neuron. The trunk of the tree is like the axon and the bark surrounding the trunk is like the myelin sheath. The branches and leaves therefore, are like the terminal buttons. Can you think of some other examples that might be relevant to your life?

Figure 2.5
Major Neurotransmitters

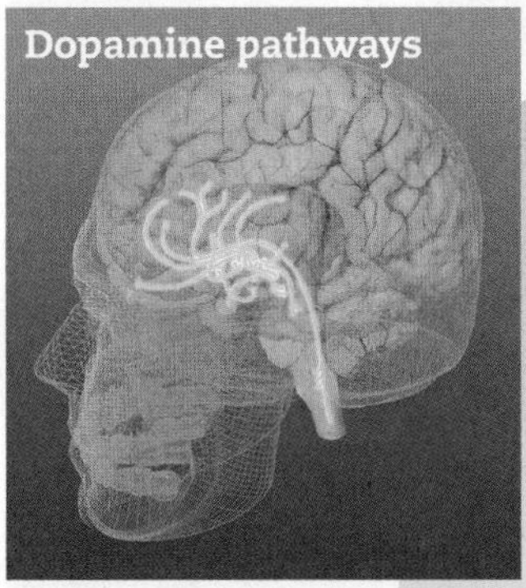

Dopamine pathways

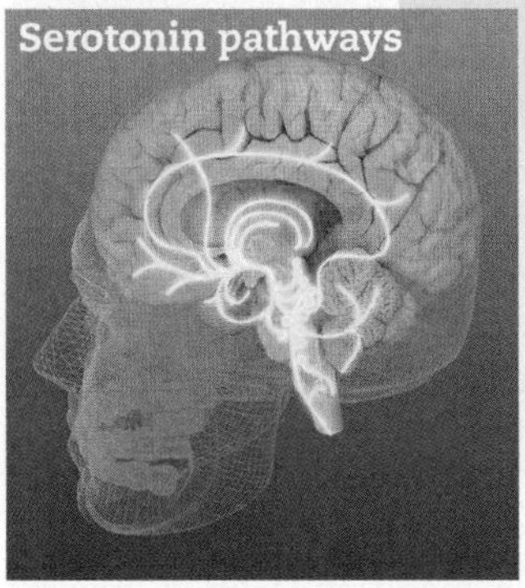

Serotonin pathways

Name	Location	Effect	Function
Acetylcholine (ACh)	Brain, spinal cord, peripheral nervous system, especially some organs of the parasympathetic nervous system	Excitatory in brain and autonomic nervous system; inhibitory elsewhere	Muscle movement, cognitive functioning
Glutamate	Brain, spinal cord	Excitatory	Memory
Gamma-amino butyric acid (GABA)	Brain, spinal cord	Main inhibitory neurotransmitter	Eating, aggression, sleeping
Dopamine (DA)	Brain	Inhibitory or excitatory	Movement control, pleasure and reward, attention
Serotonin	Brain, spinal cord	Inhibitory	Sleeping, eating, mood, pain, depression
Endorphins	Brain, spinal cord	Primarily inhibitory, except in hippocampus	Pain suppression, pleasurable feelings, appetites, placebos

fires. In contrast, if the inhibitory messages outnumber the excitatory ones, nothing happens, and the neuron remains in its resting state (Flavell et al., 2006; Mel, 2002).

If neurotransmitters remained in the synapse, receiving neurons would be awash in a continual chemical bath, producing constant stimulation or constant inhibition of the receiving neurons. In this situation, effective communication across the synapse would not be possible. To solve this problem, neurotransmitters are either deactivated by enzymes or—more commonly—reabsorbed by the terminal button in a recycling process called **reuptake**. Like a vacuum cleaner sucking up dust, neurons reabsorb the neurotransmitters that are clogging the synapse. The activities involved in reuptake occur at lightning speed, with the process taking just several milliseconds (Holt & Jahn, 2004).

NEUROTRANSMITTERS: CHEMICAL COURIERS

Neurotransmitters are a particularly important link between the nervous system and behaviour. They are vital for normal brain and body functions—so vital, in fact, that a deficiency or an excess of a neurotransmitter can produce severe behaviour disorders. More than a hundred chemicals have been found to act as neurotransmitters, and neuroscientists believe that more may ultimately be identified (Penney, 2000; Schmidt, 2006).

reuptake The reabsorption of neurotransmitters by a terminal button.

The effects of a particular neurotransmitter vary, depending on the area of the nervous system in which it is produced. The same neurotransmitter can act as an

Psych
At The Movies

What the Bleep Do We Know?
This film questions concepts that we often take for granted, such as reality, and includes a fascinating video clip of neurotransmitter activity in the brain.

The Aviator
Leonardo DiCaprio plays Howard Hughes, a man with obsessive-compulsive disorder. After playing this role, DiCaprio noticed that it took effort to stop exhibiting OCD behaviours. Brain scanning evidenced plasticity—his brain had actually started to rewire similar to one with OCD.

The Hitchhiker's Guide to the Galaxy
The Vogons practice a unique form of torture on their captured enemies. Note the signs of sympathetic nervous system arousal when Arthur is restrained and subjected to a Vogon poetry reading.

excitatory message to a neuron located in one part of the brain and can inhibit firing in neurons located in another part.

One important neurotransmitter, acetylcholine (or ACh, its chemical symbol), is found throughout the nervous system. ACh is involved in our every move, because—among other things—it transmits messages to our skeletal muscles. ACh is also involved in memory capabilities, and diminished production of ACh may be related to Alzheimer's disease (Bazalakova et al., 2007; Mohapel et al., 2005). If you travel, you may want to be careful about a chance meeting with the Widow spider! This highly venomous spider is found in various areas of the world, but has a high concentration in Australia. When the Widow spider bites, it causes a quick release of ACh in its victim which can cause painful muscle contractions and sometimes temporary muscle paralysis (Jelinek, 1997).

Another major neurotransmitter is dopamine (DA), which is involved in movement, attention, and learning. The discovery that certain drugs can have a significant effect on dopamine release has led to the development of effective treatments for a wide variety of physical and mental ailments. For instance, Parkinson's disease, which Michael J. Fox has, is a progressive disorder marked by muscle tremors and impaired coordination, and is caused by a deficiency of dopamine in the brain. Techniques for increasing the production of dopamine in Parkinson's patients are proving effective (Iversen & Iversen, 2007; Kaasinen & Rinne, 2002; Willis, 2005).

*Over*production of dopamine also produces negative consequences. For example, researchers have suggested that schizophrenia and some other severe mental disturbances are affected or perhaps even caused by unusually high levels of dopamine. Drugs that block the reception of dopamine

After being diagnosed with Parkinson's disease, Michael J. Fox became an ardent advocate for research leading to a cure for this disorder of the nervous system.

reduce the symptoms displayed by some people diagnosed with schizophrenia (Baumeister & Francis, 2002; Bolonna & Kerwin, 2005; Olijslagers, Werkman, & McCreary, 2006). Another neurotransmitter, serotonin, is associated with the regulation of sleep, eating, mood, and pain. A growing body of research suggests that serotonin also plays a role in such diverse behaviours as alcoholism, depression, suicide, impulsivity, aggression, and coping with stress (Addolorato et al., 2005; Montgomery, 2006; Zalsman & Apter, 2002). Endorphins, another class of neurotransmitters, are chemicals produced by the brain that are similar in structure to

The runner's high has been attributed to endorphins—neurotransmitters produced in response to stress or pain.

painkilling drugs such as morphine. The production of endorphins reflects the brain's effort to deal with pain as well as to elevate mood. This explains why someone who was injured during a sporting event may be able to play through that injury.

Endorphins also may produce the euphoric feelings that runners sometimes experience after long runs. The exertion and perhaps the pain involved in a long run may stimulate the production of endorphins, ultimately resulting in what has been called "runner's high" (Kolata, 2002; Pert, 2002; Stanojevic, Mitic, & Vujic, 2007).

The Nervous System: Linking Neurons

In light of the complexity of individual neurons and the neurotransmission process, it should come as no surprise that the connections and the structures formed by the neurons are complicated. Each neuron can be connected to 80,000 other neurons, so the total number of possible connections is astonishing. Estimates of the number of neural connections in the brain alone fall in the neighbourhood of 10 quadrillion—a 1 followed by 16 zeros—and some experts put the number even higher (Boahen, 2005; Forlenza & Baum, 2004; Kandel, Schwartz, & Jessell, 2000).

Whatever the actual number of neural connections, the human nervous system has both logic and elegance. We turn now to a discussion of its basic structures.

DID YOU KNOW?

Do you crack your knuckles? Don't worry, it does not cause arthritis, but it does release endorphins. Knuckle cracking may be addictive, because a small amount of endorphins is released each time you crack a knuckle.

Figure 2.6

Parts of the Nervous System

The Nervous System
Consists of the brain and the neurons extending throughout the body

Central Nervous System
Consists of the brain and spinal cord

Brain
An organ roughly half the size of a loaf of bread that constantly controls behaviour

Spinal Cord
A bundle of nerves that leaves the brain and runs down the length of the back; transmits messages between the brain and the body

Peripheral Nervous System
Made up of long axons and dendrites, it contains all parts of the nervous system other than the brain and spinal cord

Somatic Division (voluntary)
Specializes in the control of voluntary movements and the communication of information to and from the sense organs

Autonomic Division (involuntary)
Concerned with the parts of the body that function involuntarily without our awareness

Sympathetic Division
Acts to prepare the body in stressful emergency situations, engaging resources to respond to a threat

Parasympathetic Division
Acts to calm the body after an emergency situation has engaged the sympathetic division; provides a means for the body to maintain storage of energy sources

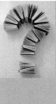

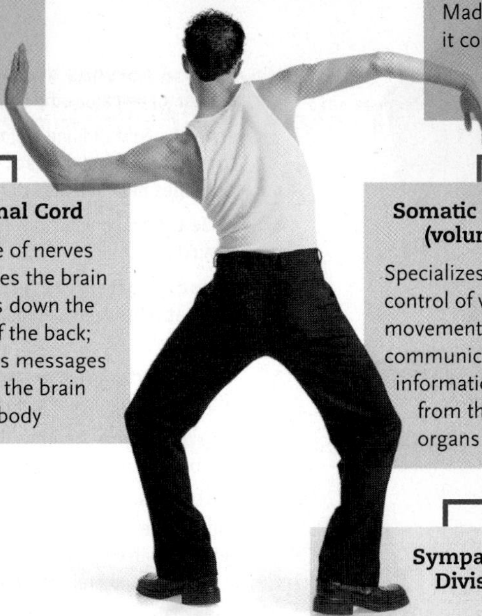

CENTRAL AND PERIPHERAL NERVOUS SYSTEMS

The nervous system consists of the central nervous system and the peripheral nervous system. The **central nervous system (CNS)** includes the brain and the spinal cord. The **spinal cord**, a bundle of neurons about the thickness of a pencil, runs from the brain down the length of the back. The spinal cord is the primary means for transmitting messages between the brain and the rest of the body.

However, the spinal cord is not just a communication channel. It also controls some simple behaviours on its own, without any help from the brain. An example is the way the knee jerks forward when it is tapped with a rubber hammer. This behaviour is a type of **reflex**, an automatic, involuntary response to an incoming stimulus. A reflex is also at work when you touch a hot stove and immediately withdraw your hand. Although the brain eventually analyzes and reacts to the situation ("Ouch—hot stove—pull away!"), the initial withdrawal is directed only by neurons in the spinal cord.

Three kinds of neurons are involved in reflexes. **Sensory (afferent) neurons** transmit information from the perimeter of the body to the central nervous system (you can remember this by "A to B"—afferent nerves go to the brain!). **Motor (efferent) neurons** communicate information from the nervous system to muscles and glands. **Interneurons** connect sensory and motor neurons, carrying messages between the two.

As suggested by its name, the **peripheral nervous system** branches out from the spinal cord and brain and reaches the extremities (the periphery) of the body. Made up of neurons with long axons and dendrites, the peripheral nervous system encompasses all the parts of the nervous system other than the brain and the spinal cord. There are two major divisions—the somatic division and the autonomic division—both of which connect the central nervous system with the sense organs, muscles, glands, and other organs. The **somatic division** specializes in the control of voluntary movements—such as the motion of the eyes to read this sentence or those of the hand to turn this page—and the communication of information to and from the sense organs. In contrast, the **autonomic division** controls the parts of the body that keep us alive—heart, blood vessels, glands, lungs, and other organs that function involuntarily without our awareness (you can remember this by thinking about autonomic as "automatic"—We don't have to think about it, it just happens!). At this moment, the autonomic division of the peripheral nervous system is pumping blood through your body, pushing your lungs in and out, and overseeing the digestion of your last meal, automatically!

The autonomic division plays a particularly crucial role during emergencies. Suppose that as you are reading you suddenly sense that a stranger is watching you through the window. As you look up, you see the glint of something that might be a knife. As confusion clouds your mind and fear overcomes your attempts to think rationally, what happens to your body? If you are like most people, you react immediately on a physiological level. Your heart rate increases, you begin to sweat, and you develop goose bumps all over your body.

Figure 2.7

Central and Peripheral Nervous Systems

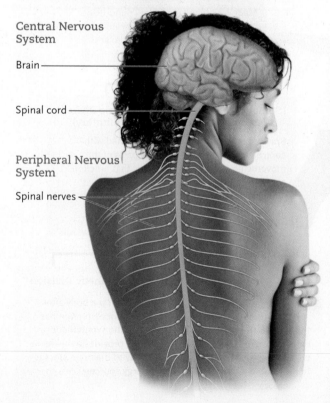

Central Nervous System

Brain

Spinal cord

Peripheral Nervous System

Spinal nerves

central nervous system (CNS) The part of the nervous system that includes the brain and spinal cord.

spinal cord A bundle of neurons that leaves the brain and runs down the length of the back and is the main means for transmitting messages between the brain and the body.

reflex An automatic, involuntary response to an incoming stimulus

sensory (afferent) neurons Neurons that transmit information from the perimeter of the body to the central nervous system.

motor (efferent) neurons Neurons that communicate information from the nervous system to muscles and glands.

interneurons Neurons that connect sensory and motor neurons, carrying messages between the two.

peripheral nervous system The part of the nervous system that includes the autonomic and somatic subdivisions; made up of neurons with long axons and dendrites, it branches out from the spinal cord and brain and reaches the extremities of the body.

somatic division The part of the peripheral nervous system that specializes in the control of voluntary movements and the communication of information to and from the sense organs.

autonomic division The part of the peripheral nervous system that controls involuntary movement of the heart, glands, lungs, and other organs.

Figure 2.8
Major Functions of the Autonomic Nervous System

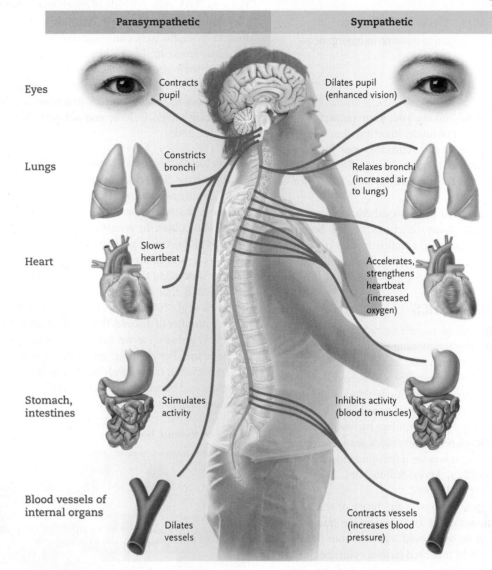

Parasympathetic	Sympathetic

Eyes — Contracts pupil / Dilates pupil (enhanced vision)

Lungs — Constricts bronchi / Relaxes bronchi (increased air to lungs)

Heart — Slows heartbeat / Accelerates, strengthens heartbeat (increased oxygen)

Stomach, intestines — Stimulates activity / Inhibits activity (blood to muscles)

Blood vessels of internal organs — Dilates vessels / Contracts vessels (increases blood pressure)

Get Involved!

Confused about the division of labour in the nervous system? Get in touch with your inner child and listen to some Schoolhouse Rock! At www.schoolhouserock.tv/Telegraph.html you can play "Telegraph Line" and hear a catchy song about the various parts of the nervous system. You will have a hard time getting it out of your head, but that may come in handy during exam time.

The physiological changes that occur during a crisis result from the activation of one of the two parts of the autonomic nervous system: the **sympathetic division**. The sympathetic division acts to prepare the body for action in stressful situations by engaging all of the organism's resources to run away or to confront the threat. This response is often called the "fight-or-flight" response.

In contrast, the **parasympathetic division** acts to calm the body after the emergency has ended. When you find, for instance, that the stranger at the window is actually your roommate, who has lost his keys and is climbing in

sympathetic division The part of the autonomic division of the nervous system that acts to prepare the body for action in stressful situations, engaging all the organism's resources to respond to a threat.

parasympathetic division The part of the autonomic division of the nervous system that acts to calm the body after an emergency has ended.

Psych think

> > > In what ways is the "fight-or-flight" response helpful to humans in emergency situations?

the window to avoid waking you, your parasympathetic division begins to predominate, lowering your heart rate, stopping your sweating, and returning your body to the state it was in before you became alarmed. The parasympathetic division also directs the body to store energy for use in emergencies.

The sympathetic and parasympathetic divisions work together to regulate many functions of the body. For instance, sexual arousal is controlled by the parasympathetic division, but sexual orgasm is a function of the sympathetic division.

BEHAVIOURAL GENETICS

Our evolutionary heritage manifests itself not only through the structure and the functioning of the nervous system but also through our behaviour. In the view of a growing area of study, people's personality and behavioural habits are affected in part by their genetic heritage. **Behavioural genetics** studies the effects of heredity on behaviour. Behavioural genetics researchers are finding increasing evidence that cognitive abilities, personality traits, sexual orientation, and psychological disorders are determined to some extent by genetic factors (Ilies, Arvey, & Bouchard, 2006; Reif & Lesch, 2003; Viding et al., 2005).

Behavioural genetics lies at the heart of the nature–nurture question, one of the key issues in the study of psychology. Although no one would argue that our behaviour is determined solely by inherited factors, evidence collected by behavioural geneticists does suggest that our genetic inheritance predisposes us to respond in particular ways to our environment, and even to seek out particular kinds of environments. For instance, research indicates that genetic factors may be related to such diverse behaviours as level of family conflict, schizophrenia, learning disabilities, and general sociability (Harlaar et al., 2005; Moffitt & Caspi, 2007).

Furthermore, important human characteristics and behaviours are related to the presence (or absence) of particular genes, the inherited material that controls the transmission of traits. For example, researchers have found evidence that novelty-seeking behaviour is determined, at least in part, by a certain gene.

As we will consider later in the book when we discuss human development, researchers have identified some

25,000 individual genes, each of which appears in a specific sequence on a particular chromosome, a rod-shaped structure that transmits genetic information across generations. In 2003, after a decade of effort, researchers identified the sequence of the 3 billion chemical pairs that make up human DNA, the basic component of genes. Understanding the basic structure of the human genome—the "map" of humans' total genetic makeup—brings scientists a giant step closer to understanding the contributions of individual genes to specific human structures and functioning (Andreasen, 2005; Dale & von Schantz, 2007; Plomin & McGuffin, 2003).

Behavioural Genetics, Gene Therapy, and Genetic Counselling Behavioural genetics also holds the promise of developing new diagnostic and treatment techniques for genetic deficiencies that can lead to physical and psychological difficulties. In *gene therapy*, scientists inject into a patient's bloodstream genes meant to cure a particular disease. When the genes arrive at the site of defective genes that are producing the illness, they trigger the production of chemicals that can treat the disease (Jaffé et al., 2006; Lymberis et al., 2004; Rattazzi, LaFuci, & Brown, 2004).

The number of diseases that can be treated through gene therapy is growing, as we will see when we discuss human development. For example, gene therapy is now being used in experimental trials involving people with certain forms of cancer and blindness (Hirschler, 2007; Nakamura, 2004; Wagner et al., 2004).

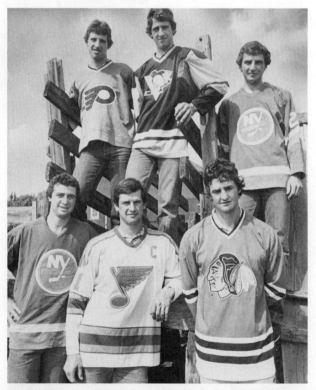

The Sutter family from Alberta had six brothers (Brent, Brian, Darryl, Rich, Duanne, and Ron) who played in the National Hockey League between 1970 and the mid-1980s. Behavioural geneticists would be interested in the hereditary factors that might have contributed to their success as hockey players.

behavioural genetics The study of the effects of heredity on behaviour.

Advances in behavioural genetics also have led to the development of a profession that did not exist several decades ago: genetic counselling. Genetic counsellors help people deal with issues related to inherited disorders. For example, genetic counsellors provide advice to prospective parents about the potential risks in a future pregnancy, based on their family history of birth defects and hereditary illnesses. In addition, the counsellor considers the parents' age and problems with children they already have. They also can take blood, skin, and urine samples to examine specific chromosomes.

Scientists have already developed genetic tests to determine whether someone is susceptible to certain types of cancer or heart disease, and it may not be long before analysis of a drop of blood can indicate whether a child—or potentially an unborn fetus—is susceptible to certain psychological disorders. How such knowledge will be used is a source of considerable speculation and controversy, controversy that is certain to grow as genetic testing becomes more common (Etchegary, 2004).

From the perspective of . . .

A GENETIC COUNSELLOR How would you explain the pros and cons of genetic counselling to someone who was interested in receiving genetic screening for various diseases and disorders?

The Brain

It is not much to look at. Soft, spongy, mottled, and pink-ish-grey in colour, weighing about 1.4 kilograms, it hardly can be said to possess much in the way of physical beauty. Despite its physical appearance, however, it ranks as the greatest natural marvel that we know and has a beauty and sophistication all its own. This is the brain.

The brain is responsible for our loftiest thoughts—and our most primitive urges—as well as overseeing the intricate workings of the human body. It would be nearly impossible to design a computer to perform the full range of the brain's capabilities. In fact, it has proved difficult even to come close. The sheer quantity of nerve cells in the brain—numbering in the billions in the average adult—is enough to discourage even the most ambitious computer engineer. Even more astounding than the number of neurons in the brain is the brain's ability to orchestrate complex interconnections among neurons, guiding behaviour and giving rise to thoughts, hopes, dreams, and emotions.

We turn now to a consideration of the particular structures of the brain and the primary functions to which they are related. However, a caution is in order. Although we'll discuss specific areas of the brain in relation to specific behaviours, this approach is an oversimplification. No straightforward one-to-one correspondence exists between a distinct part of the brain and a particular behaviour.

SPYING ON THE BRAIN

Do you think you are affectionate? Do you have a special poetic ability? Do you have a heightened sense of colour? Are you particularly witty? In the nineteenth century, you could go see your local phrenologist to gain insight into your personality and other psychological attributes. During your office visit, the phrenologist would feel the bumps on your head to assess your psychological strengths and weaknesses. Phrenologists believed that the shape of your skull was related to the shape of your brain, and the size of various areas of the brain indicated the presence (or absence) of a variety of moral and intellectual facilities. In other words, bigger bumps meant "more" of a particular trait or behaviour.

Although phrenology is no longer considered valid in any way, it shows a desire to link parts of the brain with specific behaviours at a time when the only way to look inside the brain was to cut it open, generally after an individual had died. Although informative, this procedure could hardly tell us much about the functioning of the healthy brain.

Today, brain-scanning techniques provide a window into the living brain. Using these techniques, researchers can take a "snapshot" of the internal workings of the brain without having to open a person's skull. For psychologists, the most important scanning techniques are the electro-encephalogram (EEG), positron emission tomography (PET), magnetic resonance imaging (MRI), functional magnetic resonance imaging (fMRI), and transcranial magnetic stimulation imaging (TMS).

One of the oldest imaging techniques, the *electroen-cephalogram (EEG)*, records electrical activity in the brain through electrodes placed on the head. Although traditionally the EEG produced only a graph of electrical wave patterns, new techniques are now used to transform the brain's

Figure 2.9
Brain-Scanning Techniques

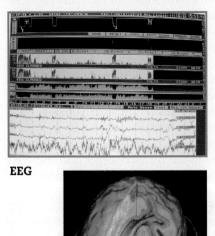

EEG

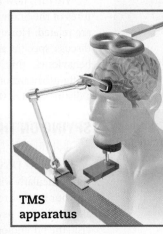

TMS apparatus

fMRI scan

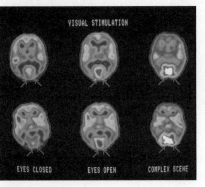

PET scan

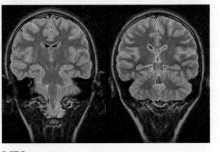

MRI

electrical activity into a pictorial representation of the brain that allows more precise diagnosis of such disorders as epilepsy and learning disabilities.

Magnetic resonance imaging (MRI) scans use magnets and radio waves to receive very clear images of the structure of the brain and body. An MRI test involves placing the part of the body for study into a large machine. If the patient must be fully inside the MRI and has fears of confined spaces, the MRI test can cause some anxiety. However, doctors will sometimes prescribe medication to help calm the patient down. The MRI can be used for various parts of the body, but a common area related to neuroscience is of course, the brain. The MRI can be used to detect tumours, aneurysms, nerve damage, or injuries due to a stroke. Once the images have been taken, they can be stored digitally for later study.

Functional magnetic resonance imaging (fMRI) scans are similar to MRI scans in that they also provide detailed, three-dimensional computer-generated images of brain structures and activity by aiming a powerful magnetic field at the body. With fMRI, it is possible to produce vivid, detailed images of the functioning of the brain.

Using fMRI scans, researchers can see features of less than a millimetre in size and view changes occurring at intervals of one-tenth of a second. For example, fMRI scans can show the operation of individual bundles of nerves by tracing the flow of blood, opening the way for improved diagnosis of ailments ranging from chronic back pain to certain nervous system disorders such as stroke, multiple sclerosis, and Alzheimer's disease (a progressive disorder in

which neurons die). Scans using fMRI are routinely used in planning brain surgery because they can help surgeons distinguish areas of the brain involved in normal and disturbed functioning (D'Arcy, Bolster, & Ryner, 2007; Mazard et al., 2005; Quenot et al., 2005). In addition to acting as a diagnostic tool, the fMRI is also used quite often in neuroscience research. For example, Jodie Gawryluk and colleagues from the Institute for Biodianostics in Atlantic Canada have used fMRIs to study white matter disease in the brain (Gawryluk et al., 2011) .

Positron emission tomography (PET) scans show biochemical activity within the brain at a given moment. PET scans begin with the injection of a radioactive (but safe) liquid into the bloodstream, which carries it to the brain. By locating radiation within the brain, a computer can pinpoint the more active regions, providing a striking picture of the brain at work. One application of this technique is to search for brain tumours in people with memory problems (Gronholm et al., 2005; McMurtray et al., 2007).

Transcranial magnetic stimulation (TMS) is one of the newest brain-scanning techniques. By exposing a tiny region of the brain to a strong magnetic field, TMS briefly disrupts electrical activity. Researchers then are able to note the effects of this interruption on normal brain functioning. This procedure is sometimes called a "virtual lesion," because it produces effects similar to what would occur if areas of the brain were physically cut. The enormous advantage of TMS, of course, is that the virtual cut is only temporary. In addition to identifying areas of the brain that are responsible for particular functions, TMS has been found to be useful in the treatment of certain kinds of psychological disorders, such as depression and schizophrenia (Fregni & Pascual-Leone, 2007; Sampson, Solvason, & Husain, 2007; Simons & Dierick, 2005).

THE CENTRAL CORE: OUR "OLD BRAIN"

Although the capabilities of the human brain far exceed those of the brain of any other species, humans share some basic functions, such as breathing, eating, and sleeping, with more primitive animals. Not surprisingly, those activities are directed by a relatively primitive part of the brain. A portion of the brain known as the **central core** is quite similar in all vertebrates (species with backbones). The central core is sometimes referred to as the "old brain," because its evolution can be traced back some 500 million years to primitive structures found in non-human species. Situated atop the spinal cord at the base of the skull, the central core of the brain houses the hindbrain, the midbrain

central core The "old brain," which controls basic functions such as eating and sleeping and is common to all vertebrates.

cerebellum (ser uh BELL um) The part of the brain that controls bodily balance.

(which contains the reticular formation), the thalamus, and the hypothalamus.

The Hindbrain The hindbrain contains the medulla, the pons, and the cerebellum. The medulla controls a number of critical body functions, the most important of which are breathing and heartbeat. The pons lies above the medulla, joining the two halves of the cerebellum. Made up of large bundles of nerves, the pons acts as a transmitter of motor information, coordinating muscles and integrating movement between the right and the left halves of the body. It also plays a role in regulating sleep.

The **cerebellum** is found just above the medulla and behind the pons. Without the cerebellum, we would be unable to walk a straight line without staggering and lurching forward, because it is the job of the cerebellum to control balance. It constantly monitors feedback from the muscles to coordinate their placement, movement, and tension. Drinking too much alcohol seems to depress the activity of the cerebellum, leading to the unsteady gait and movement characteristic of drunkenness. The cerebellum is also involved in several intellectual functions, ranging from the analysis and coordination of sensory information

Figure 2.10
Major Structures in the Brain

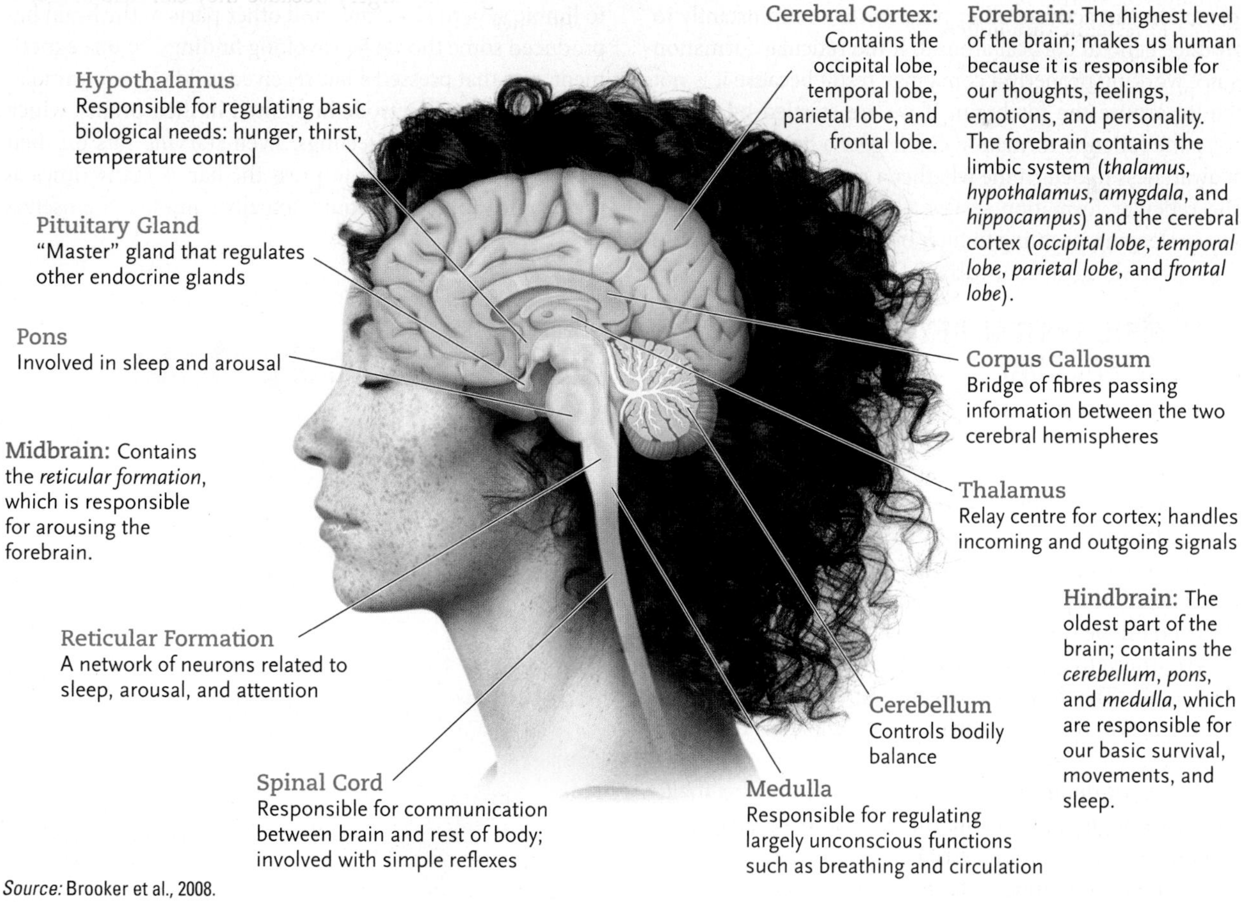

Hypothalamus
Responsible for regulating basic biological needs: hunger, thirst, temperature control

Pituitary Gland
"Master" gland that regulates other endocrine glands

Pons
Involved in sleep and arousal

Midbrain: Contains the *reticular formation*, which is responsible for arousing the forebrain.

Reticular Formation
A network of neurons related to sleep, arousal, and attention

Spinal Cord
Responsible for communication between brain and rest of body; involved with simple reflexes

Cerebral Cortex:
Contains the occipital lobe, temporal lobe, parietal lobe, and frontal lobe.

Forebrain: The highest level of the brain; makes us human because it is responsible for our thoughts, feelings, emotions, and personality. The forebrain contains the limbic system (*thalamus, hypothalamus, amygdala,* and *hippocampus*) and the cerebral cortex (*occipital lobe, temporal lobe, parietal lobe,* and *frontal lobe*).

Corpus Callosum
Bridge of fibres passing information between the two cerebral hemispheres

Thalamus
Relay centre for cortex; handles incoming and outgoing signals

Hindbrain: The oldest part of the brain; contains the *cerebellum, pons,* and *medulla,* which are responsible for our basic survival, movements, and sleep.

Cerebellum
Controls bodily balance

Medulla
Responsible for regulating largely unconscious functions such as breathing and circulation

Source: Brooker et al., 2008.

Figure 2.11
The "Old" and "New" Brain

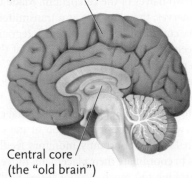

Cerebral cortex
(the "new brain")

Central core
(the "old brain")

Source: Seeley, Stephens, & Tate, 2000.

to problem solving (Bower & Parsons, 2007; Paquier & Mariën, 2005; Vandervert, Schimpf, & Liu, 2007).

The Midbrain The midbrain contains the **reticular formation**, which extends from the medulla through the pons, passing through the middle section of the brain—or midbrain—and into the front-most part of the brain, called the forebrain. Like an ever-vigilant guard, the reticular formation can activate other parts of the brain instantly to produce general cortical arousal. If the reticular formation is not working properly a coma may result because it is not able to arouse the forebrain. If we are startled by a loud noise the reticular formation can trigger a heightened state of awareness to determine whether a response is necessary. The reticular formation serves a different function when we are sleeping, seeming to filter out background stimuli to allow us to slumber undisturbed.

THE LIMBIC SYSTEM: BEYOND THE CENTRAL CORE

The **limbic system** consists of a series of doughnut-shaped structures that include the *thalamus, hypothalamus, amygdala,* and the *hippocampus.* It borders the top of the central core and has connections with the cerebral cortex.

The **thalamus** acts primarily as a relay station for information about the senses. We like to think of it as an old-time telephone operator who transfers calls by means of a switchboard, because messages from the eyes, the ears, and the skin travel to the thalamus to be relayed to higher parts of the brain. The thalamus also integrates information from higher parts of the brain, sorting it out before sending it on to the cerebellum and medulla.

The **hypothalamus** is located just below the thalamus. Although tiny—about the size of a fingertip—the hypothalamus plays an extremely important role. One of its major functions is to maintain a steady internal

reticular formation The part of the brain extending from the medulla through the pons and made up of groups of nerve cells that can immediately activate other parts of the brain to produce general cortical arousal.

limbic system The part of the brain that controls eating, aggression, and reproduction.

thalamus The part of the brain located in the middle of the central core that acts primarily to relay information about the senses.

hypothalamus A tiny part of the brain, located below the thalamus, that maintains the body's internal environment and regulates such vital behaviour as eating, self-protection, and sex.

environment for the body. The hypothalamus helps keep the body's temperature constant and monitors the amount of nutrients stored in the cells. Equally important, the hypothalamus produces and regulates behaviour that is critical to the survival of the species, such as eating, self-protection, and sex.

The limbic system controls a variety of functions relating to emotions and self-preservation, such as eating, aggression, and reproduction. Injury to the limbic system can produce striking changes in behaviour. For example, injury to the amygdala, which is involved in fear and aggression, can turn animals that are usually docile and tame into belligerent savages. Conversely, animals that are usually wild and uncontrollable may become meek and obedient following injury to the amygdala (Bedard & Persinger, 1995; Gontkovsky, 2005).

Research examining the effects of mild electric shocks to limbic system structures and other parts of the brain has produced some thought-provoking findings. In one experiment, rats that pressed a bar received mild electric stimulation through an electrode implanted in their brains, which produced pleasurable feelings. Even starving rats on their way to food would stop to press the bar as many times as they could. Some rats would actually stimulate themselves

Figure 2.12
The Limbic System

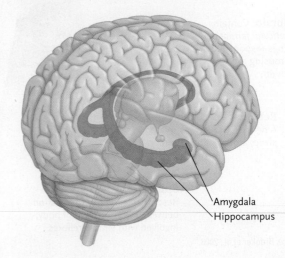

Amygdala
Hippocampus

literally thousands of times an hour—until they collapsed with fatigue (Fountas & Smith, 2007; Olds & Fobes, 1981; Routtenberg & Lindy, 1965).

The extraordinarily pleasurable quality of certain kinds of stimulation has also been experienced by humans who received electrical stimulation to the limbic system as part of their treatment for brain disorders. Although at a loss to describe just what it feels like, these people report the experience to be intensely pleasurable and similar in some respects to sexual orgasm.

The limbic system generally and the hippocampus in particular play an important role in learning and memory, a finding demonstrated in individuals with epilepsy. In an attempt to stop their seizures, surgeons have occasionally removed portions of the limbic system from epileptic patients. One unintended consequence of the surgery is that the patients sometimes have difficulty learning and remembering new information. In one case, a patient who had undergone surgery was unable to remember where he lived, although he had resided at the same address for eight years. Further, even though the patient was able to carry on animated conversations, he was unable, a few minutes later, to recall what had been discussed (Milner, 1966; Rich & Shapiro, 2007).

Functions performed by the limbic system, including self-preservation, learning, memory, and the experience of pleasure, are hardly unique to humans. In fact, the limbic system is sometimes referred to as the "animal brain," because its structures and functions are so similar to those of other mammals. The part of the brain that provides the complex and subtle capabilities that are distinctly human is the cerebral cortex.

THE CEREBRAL CORTEX: OUR "NEW BRAIN"

Although the central core, or "old brain," and the limbic system, or "animal brain," provide essential functions, the structure responsible for the uniquely human ability to think, evaluate, and make complex judgments—indeed, the very capabilities that allow you to read this sentence—resides in the **cerebral cortex**.

The cerebral cortex is referred to as the "new brain" because of its relatively recent evolution. It consists of a mass of deeply folded, rippled, convoluted tissue. Although only about 1/12 of an inch thick, the cortex, if flattened out, would cover an area more than two feet square. The folded configuration allows the surface area of the cortex to be considerably greater than it would be if it were smooth and solid. The uneven shape also permits a high level of integration of neurons, allowing sophisticated information processing.

The Forebrain The forebrain contains the cerebral cortex and has four major sections called **lobes**. If we take a side view of the brain, the frontal lobes lie at the front centre of the cortex, and the parietal lobes lie behind them. The temporal lobes occupy the lower centre portion of the cortex, with the occipital lobes behind them. These four sets of lobes are physically separated by deep grooves called sulci.

The **frontal lobes** are directly behind the forehead and are responsible for controlling voluntary movements, intelligence, and personality. The frontal lobe is often referred to as the "executive" because it is responsible for some of your higher order functioning. The frontal lobes contain the motor area of the cortex, which is responsible for your movements (we will discuss the motor cortex in more detail below).

The **parietal lobes** lie behind the frontal lobes and are responsible for all of our bodily sensations. For example, the parietal lobe senses pressure and pain. The parietal lobes also help you in your spatial world. For example, when you get up in the middle of night and work your way in the dark to the washroom it is your parietal lobe that helps you get a sense of where you are in the dark.

The temporal lobes are located in an area right behind your ears and near your temple (which will help you remember what their function is)! The **temporal lobes** help you process auditory information such as understanding what other people are saying to you. There is actually a very special area in the temporal lobe called **Wernicke's area** that allows you to understand the spoken word. Once you have understood the word, the information then moves to **Broca's area** in the frontal lobe, which allows you to speak. In addition to processing auditory information, the temporal lobes also assist with your long-term memories. In fact, early proof for the physical basis of memory came from the work of Wilder Penfield (Penfield & Steelman, 1947) from McGill University in Montreal. Penfield was interested in understanding the cause and treatment of epilepsy, so he developed a technique called the "Montreal Procedure" in which patients were administered a local anaesthetic during brain surgery. By physically stimulating different areas of the cortex, Penfield could more accurately target his surgery, reducing the subsequent side effects. Penfield was initially interested in seeing what parts of the brain were responsible for specific functions. One thing Penfield noticed was that when the temporal lobe was stimulated, the patient was able to recall specific memories (Feinel & Penfield, 1954).

The **occipital lobes** help you process visual information and are located at the back of the brain. You may have had

cerebral cortex The "new brain," contained in the forebrain, is responsible for the most sophisticated information processing in the brain; contains four lobes.

lobes The four major sections of the cerebral cortex: frontal, parietal, temporal, and occipital.

frontal lobes The lobes responsible for controlling voluntary movements, intelligence, and personality.

parietal lobes The lobes responsible for all of our bodily sensations such as temperature, touch, and taste.

temporal lobes The lobes that help you process auditory information and hold long-term memories.

Wernicke's area An area in the temporal lobe that allows you to understand the spoken word.

Broca's area An area in the frontal lobe that allows you to speak.

occipital lobes The lobes that help you process visual information.

Figure 2.13
The Cerebral Cortex

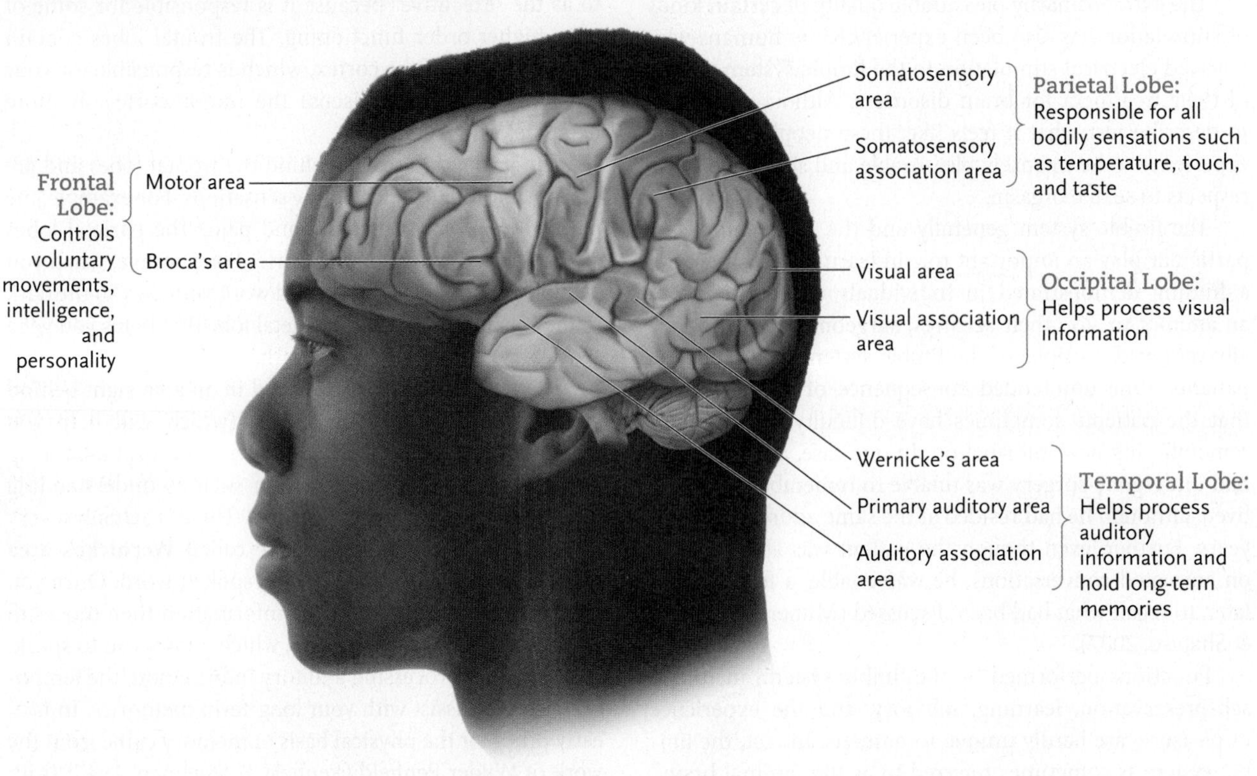

Frontal Lobe: Controls voluntary movements, intelligence, and personality

Motor area

Broca's area

Somatosensory area

Somatosensory association area

Parietal Lobe: Responsible for all bodily sensations such as temperature, touch, and taste

Visual area

Visual association area

Occipital Lobe: Helps process visual information

Wernicke's area

Primary auditory area

Auditory association area

Temporal Lobe: Helps process auditory information and hold long-term memories

---

an experience of "seeing stars" after falling and hitting your head. This is because the neurons in your occipital lobe have been activated by the impact of the fall.

Another way to describe the brain is in terms of the functions associated with a particular area. Three major functional areas are known: the motor area, the sensory area, and the association area. Although we will discuss these areas as though they were separate and independent, remember that behaviour is influenced simultaneously by several structures and areas within the brain, operating interdependently.

The Motor Area of the Cortex What part of your brain causes your hand to go up when you want to speak in class? The **motor area** of the cortex (located in the frontal lobes) is largely responsible for voluntary body movements. When Marc Savard received the hit to the side of his head, his motor cortex would have been impacted, which resulted in his slower movements after his concussion. Every portion of the motor area corresponds to a specific locale within the body. If we were to insert an electrode into a particular part of the motor area of the cortex and apply mild electrical stimulation, there would be involuntary movement in the

---

motor area The part of the cortex that is largely responsible for the body's voluntary movement.

sensory area The brain tissue that corresponds to the different senses, with the degree of sensitivity related to the amount of tissue.

---

corresponding part of the body. If we moved to another part of the motor area and stimulated it, a different part of the body would move.

The motor area is so well mapped that researchers have identified the amount and relative location of brain tissue used to produce movement in specific parts of the human body. For example, the control of movements that are relatively large scale and require little precision, such as the movement of a knee or a hip, is centred in a very small space in the motor area. In contrast, movements that must be precise and delicate, such as facial expressions and finger movements, are controlled by a considerably larger portion of the motor area.

> Every portion of the motor area corresponds to a specific part of the body.

The Sensory Area of the Cortex How does your brain know when your nose itches? Sensory neurons in your nose send a message to a region of the brain known as the sensory area for processing. Given the one-to-one correspondence between the motor area and body location, it is not surprising to find a similar relationship between a specific portion of the cortex and the senses.

The **sensory area** of the cortex includes three regions of the lobes: one that corresponds primarily to body sensations (including touch; in the parietal lobes), one relating to

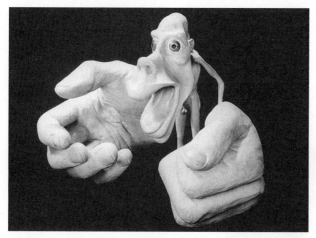

The greater the amount of tissue in the somatosensory area of the brain that is related to a specific body part, the more sensitive is that body part. If the size of our body parts reflected the corresponding amount of brain tissue, we would look like this strange creature.

sight (in the occipital lobes), and one relating to sound (in the temporal lobes). For instance, the somatosensory area processes sensations of touch and pressure on the skin. As with the motor area, the greater the amount of brain tissue devoted to a specific area of the body, the more sensitive that area of the body.

The senses of sound and sight are also represented in specific areas of the cerebral cortex. An auditory area located in the temporal lobe is responsible for hearing. If the auditory area is stimulated electrically, a person will report hearing sounds such as clicks or hums. It also appears that particular locations within the auditory area respond to specific pitches (Brown & Martinez, 2007; Hudspeth, 2000).

The visual area in the cortex, located in the occipital lobe, responds in a similar way to electrical stimulation. Stimulation by electrodes produces the experience of flashes of light or colours, suggesting that the raw sensory input from the eyes is received in this area of the brain and transformed into meaningful images (Stenbacka & Vanni, 2007; Wurtz & Kandel, 2000).

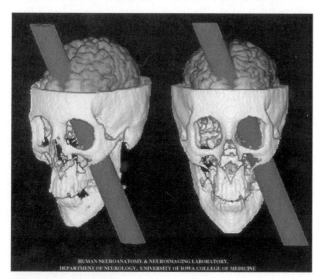

Phineas Gage injury model.

The Association Areas of the Cortex In a freak accident in 1848, an explosion drove a three-foot-long iron bar completely through the skull of railroad worker Phineas Gage, where it remained after the accident. Amazingly, Gage survived, and, despite the rod lodged through his head, a few minutes later he seemed to be fine. But he wasn't. Before the accident, Gage was hard-working and cautious. Afterward, he became irresponsible, drank heavily, and drifted from one wild scheme to another. In the words of one of his physicians, "he was 'no longer Gage' " (Harlow, 1869, p. 14).

What had happened to the old Gage? Although there is no way of knowing for sure, we can speculate that the accident may have damaged the region of Gage's cerebral cortex known as the **association areas**, which generally are considered to be the site of higher mental processes such as thinking, language, memory, and speech (Rowe et al., 2000).

The association areas make up a large portion of the cerebral cortex and consist of the sections that are not directly involved in either sensory processing or directing movement. The association areas control executive functions, abilities that relate to planning, goal setting, judgment, and impulse control.

Much of our understanding of the association areas comes from individuals who, like Phineas Gage, have suffered some type of brain injury. These people undergo personality changes that affect their ability to make moral judgments and process emotions, and yet they can still be capable of reasoning logically, performing calculations, and recalling information (Damasio et al., 1994). In addition to examining individuals with brain injuries, knowledge of how the brain works comes from neuroscientists who spend their lifetime studying the brain. Another prominent Canadian neuroscientist was Donald Hebb from McGill University in Montréal. Hebb published an influential book called *The Organization of Behaviour* in 1949 in which he discussed the role of neurons in learning and memory. Hebb proposed that cognitive processes such as learning and memory originated in the cerebral cortex and were influenced by groups of neurons called the Hebb synapse (Klein, 1999).

THE ADAPTABLE BRAIN

Shortly after he was born, Jacob Stark's arms and legs started jerking every 20 minutes. Weeks later he could not focus his eyes on his mother's face. The diagnosis: uncontrollable epileptic seizures involving his entire brain.

His mother, Sally Stark, recalled: "When Jacob was 2½ months old, they said he would never learn to sit up, would never be able to feed himself. . . . They told us to take him home, love him, and find an institution." (Blakeslee, 1992, p. C3)

association areas One of the major regions of the cerebral cortex; the site of the higher mental processes, such as thought, language, memory, and speech.

Instead, when Jacob was five months old surgeons removed 20 percent of his brain. The operation was a complete success. Three years later Jacob seemed normal in every way, with no sign of seizures.

The surgery that helped Jacob was based on the premise that neurons in part of his brain were misfiring and producing seizures throughout the brain. Surgeons reasoned that if they removed the faulty portion, the remaining parts of the brain, which appeared normal in PET scans, would take over. They correctly bet that Jacob could lead a normal life after surgery, particularly because the surgery was done at so young an age.

The success of Jacob's surgery illustrates that the brain has the ability to shift functions to different locations after injury to a specific area or after surgery. But equally encouraging are some new findings about the regenerative powers of the brain and nervous system.

Scientists have learned in recent years that the brain continually reorganizes itself in a process termed **neuroplasticity**. For many years, conventional wisdom held that no new brain cells are created after childhood, but recent research has found otherwise: The interconnections between neurons not only become more complex throughout life, but new neurons apparently also develop in certain areas of the brain during adulthood—a process called neurogenesis. In fact, new neurons may become integrated with existing neural connections after some kinds of brain injury during adulthood (Bhardwaj et al., 2006; Jang, You, & Ahn, 2007; Poo & Isaacson, 2007).

Psych think

> > > How many parts of the brain are active during simple tasks? To get an idea, read the following sentence aloud: "Multiple brain areas are active in reading a simple sentence aloud." Try to think of all the brain areas that might be involved in reading the previous sentence. Keep in mind that you had to see the individual letters, recognize the words they spelled, understand what the words mean, speak the words aloud, and listen as you spoke. Not as simple as you might have guessed!

The ability of neurons to renew themselves during adulthood has significant implications for the treatment of disorders of the nervous system. For example, drugs that trigger the development of new neurons might be used to counter such diseases as Alzheimer's disease (Steiner, Wolf, & Kempermann, 2006; Tsai, Tsai, & Shen, 2007). We will discuss Alzheimer's disease in more detail in the chapter on memory.

Furthermore, specific experiences can modify the way in which information is processed. For example, if you learn to read Braille, the amount of tissue in your cortex related to sensation in the fingertips will expand. Similarly, if you take up the violin, the area of the brain that receives messages from your fingers will grow—but relating only to the fingers that actually move across the violin's strings (Kolb, Gibb, & Robinson, 2003; Schwartz & Begley, 2002).

TWO BRAINS OR ONE?

You may have heard people say they are right-brained, because they have a special appreciation for art, or left-brained, because they can solve Sudoku puzzles really quickly. What are they talking about? Do people really favour one side of their brain? Do the different halves of the brain really do different things?

To answer these questions, you need to know about the most recent development, at least in evolutionary terms, in the organization and operation of the human brain: a specialization of the functions controlled by the left and the right sides of the brain. This change probably occurred within the last million years (McManus, 2004; Sun, Patoine, et al., 2005).

The brain is divided into two roughly mirror-image halves. Just as we have two arms, two legs, and two lungs, we have a left brain and a right brain. Because of the way nerves in the brain are connected to the rest of the body, these symmetrical left and right halves, called **hemispheres**, control motion in—and receive sensation from—the side of the body opposite their location. The left hemisphere of the brain, then, generally controls the right side of the body, and the right hemisphere controls the left side of the body. Thus, damage to the right side of the brain is typically indicated by functional difficulties in the left side of the body.

Despite the appearance of similarity between the two hemispheres of the brain, they control somewhat different functions, and they control them in somewhat different ways. Certain behaviours are more likely to reflect activity in one hemisphere than in the other and are said to be **lateralized**.

For example, for most people, language processing occurs mainly on the left side of the brain. In general, the left hemisphere concentrates more on tasks that require verbal competence, such as speaking, reading, thinking, and reasoning. In addition, the left hemisphere tends to

neuroplasticity Changes in the brain that occur throughout the lifespan relating to the addition of new neurons, new interconnections between neurons, and the reorganization of information-processing areas.

hemispheres Symmetrical left and right halves of the brain that control the side of the body opposite to their location.

lateralization The dominance of one hemisphere of the brain in specific functions, such as language.

TRY IT!

Source: Adapted in part from Morton, B. E. (2003). Asymmetry questionnaire outcomes correlate with several hemisphericity measures. *Brain and Cognition*, 51, 372–374.

Assessing Brain Lateralization

To get a rough sense of your own preferences in terms of brain lateralization, complete this questionnaire.

1. I often talk about my and other's feelings of emotion. True or false? _____
2. I am an analytical person. True or false? _____
3. I methodically solve problems. True or false? _____
4. I'm usually more interested in people and feelings than objects and things. True or false? _____
5. I see the big picture, rather than thinking about projects in terms of their individual parts. True or false? _____
6. When planning a trip, I like every detail in my itinerary worked out in advance. True or false? _____
7. I tend to be independent and work things out in my head. True or false? _____
8. When buying a new car, I prefer style over safety. True or false? _____
9. I would rather hear a lecture than read a textbook. True or false? _____
10. I remember names better than faces. True or false? _____

Scoring: Give yourself one point for each of the following responses: 1. False; 2. True; 3. True; 4. False; 5. False; 6. True; 7. True; 8. False; 9. False; 10. True. Maximum score is 10, and minimum score is 0.

The higher your score, the more your responses are consistent with people who are left-brain oriented, meaning that you have particular strength in tasks that require verbal competence, analytic thinking, and processing of information sequentially, one bit of information at a time.

The lower your score, the more your responses are consistent with a right-brain orientation, meaning that you have particular strengths in non-verbal areas, recognition of patterns, music, and emotional expression, and process information globally.

Remember, though, that this is only a rough estimate of your processing preferences and that all of us have strengths in both hemispheres of the brain.

process information sequentially, one bit at a time (Banich & Heller, 1998; Hines, 2004; Turkewitz, 1993).

The right hemisphere has its own strengths, particularly in nonverbal areas such as the understanding of spatial relationships, recognition of patterns and drawings, music, and emotional expression. The right hemisphere tends to process information globally, considering it as a whole (Ansaldo, Arguin, & Roch-Locours, 2002; Holowka & Petitto, 2002).

Nonetheless, differences in specialization between the hemispheres of the brain are not great, and the degree and the nature of lateralization vary from one person to another. Furthermore, the two hemispheres function in tandem, working to decipher, interpret, and react to the world.

Moreover, people who suffer damage to the left side of the brain and lose linguistic capabilities often recover the ability to speak, because the right side takes over some of the functions of the left side, especially in young children. The extent of recovery increases the earlier the injury occurs (Gould et al., 1999; Johnston, 2004; Kempermann & Gage, 1999).

HUMAN DIVERSITY AND BRAIN LATERALIZATION

Brain lateralization patterns and brain structure appear to differ in males and females, and even from one culture to another. Let's consider sex differences first. Accumulating evidence points to intriguing gender differences in brain

lateralization and brain weight (Boles, 2005; Clements et al., 2006).

For instance, most males tend to show greater lateralization of language in the left hemisphere. For them, language is clearly a left brain function. In contrast, women display less lateralization, with language abilities apt to be more evenly divided between the two hemispheres. These differences may account, in part, for the superiority often displayed by females on certain measures of verbal skills, such as the beginning of and the fluency of speech (Frings et al., 2006; Petersson et al., 2007).

Other research suggests that men's brains are somewhat bigger than women's brains are, even after taking differences in body size into account. In contrast, part of the corpus callosum, a bundle of fibres that connects the hemispheres

From the perspective of ...

AN EDUCATOR According to evidence of female–male brain lateralization differences, how might you use different techniques to teach children to read?

of the brain, is proportionally larger in women than in men (Cahill, 2005; Luders et al., 2006; Smith et al., 2007).

Men and women also may process information differently. For example, in one study, fMRI brain scans of men making judgments that discriminate real from false words showed activation of the left hemisphere of the brain, whereas women used areas on both sides of the brain (Rossell et al., 2002).

The meaning of sex differences in brain lateralization is far from clear. Consider one hypothesis related to differences in the proportional size of the corpus callosum. Its greater size in women may permit stronger connections to develop between the parts of the brain that control speech. In turn, this would explain why speech tends to emerge slightly earlier in girls than in boys.

> **Physical brain differences may be a *reflection* of social and environmental influences rather than a *cause* of differences in men's and women's behaviour.**

Before we rush to such a conclusion, however, we must consider an alternative hypothesis: The reason verbal abilities emerge earlier in girls may be that infant girls receive greater encouragement to talk than do infant boys. In turn, this greater early experience may foster the growth of certain parts of the brain. If so, physical brain differences may be a reflection of social and environmental influences rather than a cause of differences in men's and women's behaviour. At this point, it is impossible to know which of these alternative hypotheses might be correct (Hamberg, 2005).

Culture also gives rise to differences in brain lateralization. Native speakers of Japanese, for instance, seem to process information regarding vowel sounds primarily in the left hemisphere. In contrast, North and South Americans, Europeans, and individuals of Japanese ancestry who learn Japanese later in life handle vowel sounds principally in the right hemisphere. One explanation proposed for this difference is that certain characteristics of the Japanese language, such as the ability to express complex ideas by using only vowel

Figure 2.14

The Split Brain

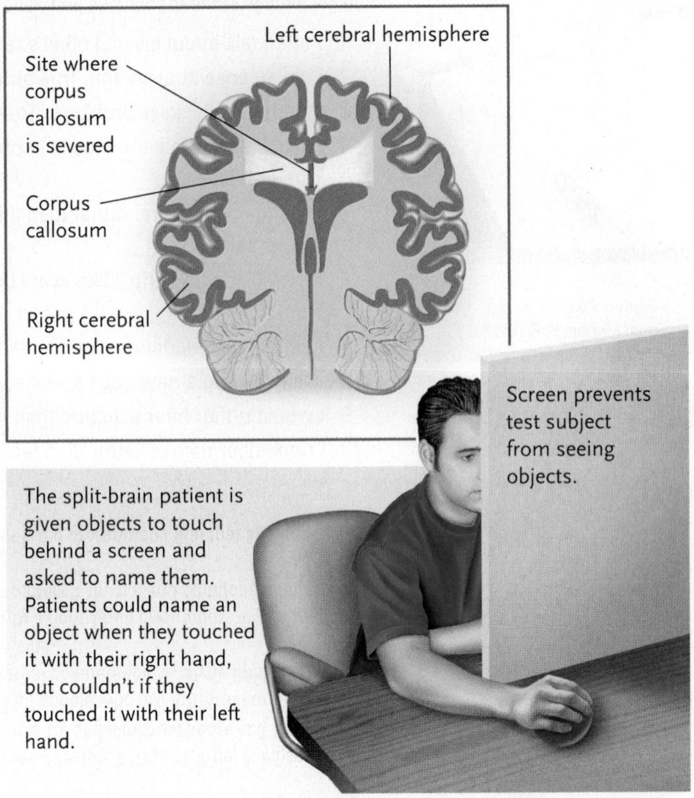

Left cerebral hemisphere

Site where corpus callosum is severed

Corpus callosum

Right cerebral hemisphere

Screen prevents test subject from seeing objects.

The split-brain patient is given objects to touch behind a screen and asked to name them. Patients could name an object when they touched it with their right hand, but couldn't if they touched it with their left hand.

Source: Brooker et al., 2008, p. 943.

sounds, result in the development of a specific type of brain lateralization in native speakers (Kess & Miyamoto, 1994; Lin, Y. Y., et al., 2005).

THE SPLIT BRAIN: EXPLORING THE TWO HEMISPHERES

The patient, V. J., had suffered severe seizures. By cutting her corpus callosum, the fibrous portion of the brain that carries messages between the hemispheres, surgeons hoped to create a firebreak to prevent the seizures from spreading. The operation did decrease the frequency and severity of V. J.'s attacks. But V. J. developed an unexpected side effect: She lost the ability to write at will, although she could read and spell words aloud. (Strauss, 1998, p. 287)

People such as V. J., whose corpus callosum has been surgically cut to stop seizures and who are called split-brain patients, offer a rare opportunity for researchers investigating the independent functioning of the two hemispheres of the brain. Psychologist Roger Sperry—who won the Nobel Prize in medicine for his work—developed a number of ingenious techniques for studying how each hemisphere operates (Gazzaniga, 1998; Savazzi et al., 2007; Sperry, 1982).

In one experimental procedure, blindfolded patients touched an object with their right hand and were asked to name it. Because the right side of the body corresponds

Psych think

> > > If someone had a stroke in their left hemisphere, what would the effects be?

to the language-oriented left side of the brain, split-brain patients were able to name the object. However, if blind-folded patients touched the object with their left hand, they were unable to name it aloud, even though the information had registered in their brains. When the blindfold was removed, patients could identify the object they had touched. Information can be learned and remembered, then, using only the right side of the brain. (By the way, unless you've had a split-brain operation, this experiment won't work with you, because the bundle of fibres connecting the two hemispheres of a normal brain immediately transfers information from one hemisphere to the other.)

It is clear from experiments like this one that the right and the left hemispheres of the brain specialize in different sorts of information. At the same time, we must realize that both hemispheres are capable of understanding, knowing, and being aware of the world. The two hemispheres, then, should be regarded as different in terms of the efficiency with which they process certain kinds of information, rather than as two entirely separate brains. The hemispheres work together to allow the full range and richness of thought possible for humans.

CONTROLLING YOUR HEART—AND MIND—THROUGH BIOFEEDBACK

When Tammy DeMichael was involved in a horrific car accident that broke her neck and crushed her spinal cord, experts told her that she was doomed to be a quadriplegic for the rest of her life, unable to move from the neck down. But they were wrong. Not only did she regain the use of her arms, but she also learned to walk 60 feet with a cane (Morrow & Wolff, 1991).

The key to DeMichael's astounding recovery: biofeed-back. **Biofeedback** is a procedure in which a person learns to control through conscious thought internal physiological processes such as blood pressure, heart and respiration rate, skin temperature, sweating, and the constriction of particular muscles. Although it traditionally had been thought that heart rate, respiration rate, blood pressure, and other bodily functions are under the control of parts of the brain over which we have no influence, psychologists have discovered that these responses are actually susceptible to voluntary control (Cho, Holyoak, & Cannon, 2007; Nagai et al., 2004).

In biofeedback, a person is hooked up to electronic devices that provide continuous feedback relating to the physiological response in question. For instance, a person interested in controlling headaches through biofeedback might have electronic sensors placed on certain muscles on her head and learn to control the constriction and relaxation of those muscles. Later, when she felt a headache

> **biofeedback** A procedure in which a person learns to control through conscious thought internal physiological processes such as blood pressure, heart and respiration rate, skin temperature, sweating, and the constriction of particular muscles.

BUY IT?

Biofeedback for Stress Reduction

Can biofeedback help you relax when you're tense or stressed? Although control of physiological processes using biofeedback techniques is not easy to learn, biofeedback has been applied successfully to a variety of ailments, including emotional problems (such as anxiety, depression, phobias, tension headaches, insomnia, and hyperactivity), physical illnesses with a psychological component (such as asthma, high blood pressure, ulcers, muscle spasms, and migraine headaches), and physical problems (such as spinal cord injuries, strokes, cerebral palsy, and curvature of the spine) (Cho et al., 2007; Morone & Greco, 2007).

Stress reduction is another application of biofeedback, one that can benefit individuals experiencing severe stress or chronic pain (Vitiello, Bonello, & Pollard, 2007). But is biofeedback useful for people

dealing with occasional stress caused by the pressures of everyday life, such as exams, a bad day at work, or the end of a romantic relationship?

If you search the Internet for information on stress reduction, you'll find Web sites marketing biofeedback products to consumers for just this purpose. They may claim to be "clinically proven," and they may be effective for some people, such as individuals with stressful occupations or those with a lot of anxiety or high blood pressure. Before you spend $100 or more on one of these devices, however, you might want to consider less expensive alternatives for dealing with stress, such as spending time with friends, exercise, meditation (see p. 98), or any of the strategies recommended on p. 346 (Benight, 2004; Lee, S. H. et al., 2007; Yesilyaprak, Kisac, & Sanlier, 2007).

starting, she could relax the relevant muscles and abort the pain (Andrasik, 2007).

In DeMichael's case, biofeedback was effective because not all of the nervous system's connections between the brain and her legs were severed. Through biofeedback, she learned how to send messages to specific muscles, "ordering" them to move. Although it took more than a year, DeMichael successfully regained a large degree of her mobility.

endocrine system A chemical communication network that sends messages through the bloodstream to all parts of the body.

hormone Substance produced by a gland or tissue and circulated through the blood to regulate the functioning or growth of the body.

The Endocrine System: Hormones and Glands

Another of the body's communication systems, the **endocrine system**, is a chemical communication network that sends messages throughout the body via the bloodstream. Its job is to secrete **hormones**, chemicals that circulate through the blood and regulate the functioning and growth of the body. The endocrine system also influences—and is influenced by—the functioning of the nervous system. Although the endocrine system is not part of the brain, it is closely linked to the hypothalamus.

Figure 2.15
Major Endocrine Glands

Despite its designation as the "master gland," the pituitary is actually a servant of the brain, because the brain is ultimately responsible for the endocrine system's functioning. The brain maintains the internal balance of the body through the hypothalamus.

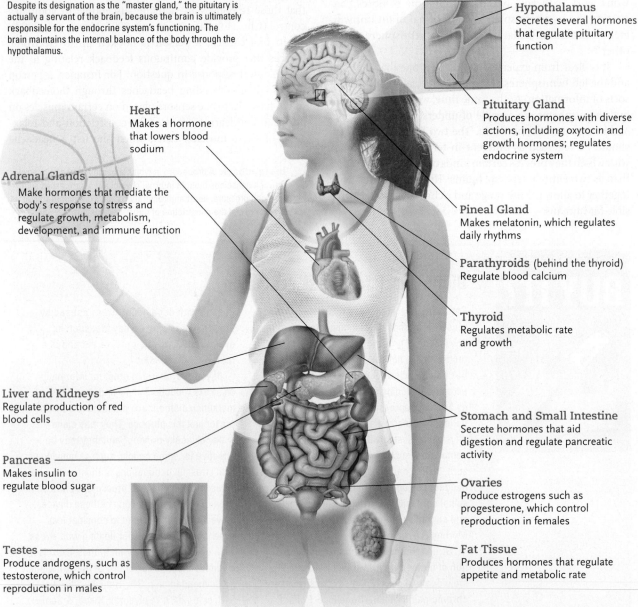

Heart
Makes a hormone that lowers blood sodium

Adrenal Glands
Make hormones that mediate the body's response to stress and regulate growth, metabolism, development, and immune function

Liver and Kidneys
Regulate production of red blood cells

Pancreas
Makes insulin to regulate blood sugar

Testes
Produce androgens, such as testosterone, which control reproduction in males

Hypothalamus
Secretes several hormones that regulate pituitary function

Pituitary Gland
Produces hormones with diverse actions, including oxytocin and growth hormones; regulates endocrine system

Pineal Gland
Makes melatonin, which regulates daily rhythms

Parathyroids (behind the thyroid)
Regulate blood calcium

Thyroid
Regulates metabolic rate and growth

Stomach and Small Intestine
Secrete hormones that aid digestion and regulate pancreatic activity

Ovaries
Produce estrogens such as progesterone, which control reproduction in females

Fat Tissue
Produces hormones that regulate appetite and metabolic rate

As chemical messengers, hormones are like neurotransmitters, although their speed and mode of transmission are quite different. Whereas neural messages are transmitted in thousandths of a second, hormonal communications may take minutes to reach their destination. Furthermore, neural messages move through neurons in specific lines (like a signal carried by wires strung along telephone poles), whereas hormones travel throughout the body, in a manner similar to the way radio waves are transmitted across the entire landscape. Just as radio waves evoke a response only when a radio is tuned to the correct station, hormones flowing through the bloodstream activate only those cells that are receptive and "tuned" to the appropriate hormonal message.

A key component of the endocrine system is the tiny **pituitary gland**, which is found near—and regulated by—the hypothalamus. The pituitary gland has been called the "master gland," because it controls the functioning of the rest of the endocrine system. But the pituitary gland has important functions in its own right. For instance, hormones secreted by the pituitary gland control growth. Extremely short people and unusually tall ones usually have pituitary gland abnormalities. Other endocrine glands affect emotional reactions, sexual urges, and energy levels.

> **pituitary gland** The major component of the endocrine system, or "master gland," which secretes hormones that control growth and other parts of the endocrine system.

For Review ››

Why do psychologists study the brain and nervous system?

Fully understanding human behaviour requires knowledge of the biological influences on behaviour, especially those originating in the nervous system. Psychologists who study the effects of biological structures and functions on behaviour are known as behavioural neuroscientists.

What are the basic units of the nervous system, and what are their functions?

Neurons, the most basic structural units of the nervous system, carry nerve impulses within the brain and from one part of the body to another. Information generally enters a neuron via the dendrites, moves into the cell body, and ultimately travels down the tube-like extension called the axon.

What are the major parts of the brain, and what are their functions?

The brain is divided into three key parts: the hindbrain, the midbrain, and the forebrain. The central core, or "old brain," consists of the hindbrain. This is made up of the medulla (which controls functions such as breathing and the heartbeat), the pons (which coordinates the muscles and the two sides of the body), and the cerebellum (which controls balance). The midbrain includes the reticular formation (which acts to heighten awareness in emergencies).

The forebrain contains the cerebral cortex and has four major sections called lobes. The *frontal lobes* lie at the front centre of the cortex, and the parietal lobes lie behind them. The *temporal lobes* occupy the lower centre portion of the cortex, with the *occipital lobes* behind them. The cerebral cortex, or "new brain," has areas that control voluntary movement (the motor area); the senses (the sensory area); and thinking, reasoning, speech, and memory (the association areas).

The limbic system borders on the "old" and "new" brains and is associated with eating, aggression, reproduction, and the experiences of pleasure and pain. It includes the thalamus (which communicates sensory messages to and from the brain), and the hypothalamus (which maintains the body's internal equilibrium and regulates behaviour related to basic survival).

How do the two halves of the brain specialize, and how do they work together?

The brain is divided into left and right halves, or hemispheres, each of which generally controls the opposite side of the body. The left hemisphere specializes in verbal tasks, such as logical reasoning, speaking, and reading, whereas the right hemisphere specializes in non-verbal tasks, such as spatial perception, pattern recognition, and emotional expression. Nevertheless, both hemispheres are capable of understanding, knowing, and being aware of the world and operate interdependently.

How does the endocrine system affect behaviour?

The endocrine system secretes hormones, chemicals that regulate the functioning of the body, via the bloodstream. The pituitary gland secretes growth hormones and influences the release of hormones by other endocrine glands, and in turn is regulated by the hypothalamus.

Psych <u>think</u> answers

Psych think 1 In the first PSYCH think on p. 36 we provided an example of how the neuron is similar to a tree and we asked if you could think of some other examples that might be relevant to your life. You may have also said that the neuron is like working at Tim Hortons. For example, as the person receiving the order, you are like the dendrites. The computer where you enter the order is like the cell body, and the cable that runs back to the screen that the other workers use behind the counter is like the axon, which is surrounded by a coating which is like the myelin sheath. The information runs along the cable to the screen, which is like the terminal buttons, sending the information to the workers in the back so they know what to prepare.

Psych think 2 In the PSYCH think on p. 42 we asked you in what ways is the "fight-or-flight" response was helpful to humans in emergency situations. Remember that it is the sympathetic nervous system that is activated when you are in your fight-or-flight response. When the sympathetic nervous system is activated your body gets ready for action. It does this by priming you. For example, your pupils dilate, your heart rate increases, your blood pressure increases and there is a release of adrenaline throughout your body that allows you to either fight or flee (i.e., run away for safety). Once you realize that you are safe, your parasympathetic nervous system is activated, which helps calm you down.

Psych think 3 In the PSYCH think on p. 50 we asked you how many parts of the brain are active during simple tasks. More specifically, we asked you to read the following sentence aloud: "Multiple brain areas are active in reading a simple sentence aloud" and then to try to think of all the brain areas that might be involved in reading that sentence. When you looked at the individual letters you used your occipital lobes. When you looked at the words that were spelled and understood what the words meant you used your temporal lobes.

Psych think 4 In the PSYCH think on p. 53 we asked you what the effects would be if someone was to have a stroke in their left hemisphere. To answer this question you have to remember about lateralization. Remember that the left side of the brain is responsible for functions such as language, so a stroke to the left hemisphere would make it difficult for someone to understand language. Also remember that the left hemisphere controls the right side of the body, so if the stroke affected the left frontal lobe the individual would have difficulty controlling voluntary movement of the right side of the body.

McGraw-Hill
Ryerson
Connect. Learn. Succeed.

Get Connected.

Stay Connected.

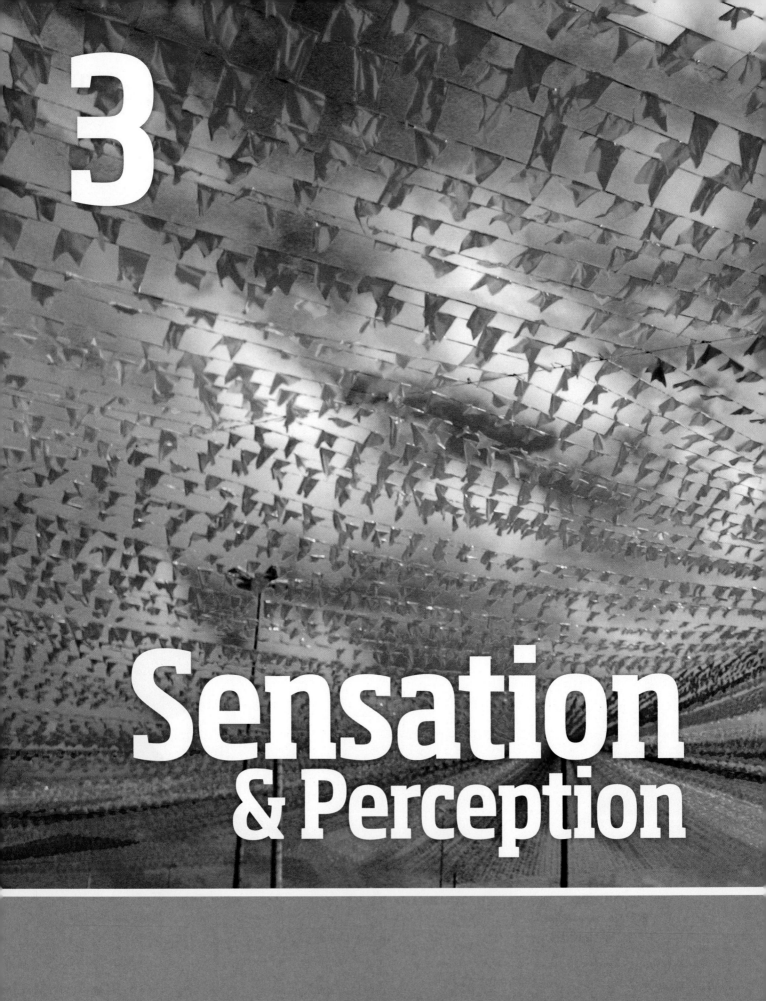

3

Sensation
& Perception

Sensation and perception together allow us to "see" the vivid colours of these flags receding in the distance.

WHAT'S TO COME

Sensation and Perception: Two Sides of the Same Coin

Sensing the World Around Us

Perception: Constructing Our Impressions of the World

Vision: Shedding Light on the Eye

Hearing and the Other Senses

Kari cannot recognize her own family

Kari (who does not want her last name published), a young woman from New Brunswick, is unable to recognize the faces of people she knows, even people close to her such as her parents and her younger brother. Kari has face blindness.

It wasn't always this way. Kari used to be able to recognize people just as most of us can. Things started to change after Kari underwent brain surgery for severe epileptic seizures. While the seizures improved after the surgery, Kari soon realized that she could no longer see people's faces. While astonishing, this face blindness happens to other people as well. The technical name for this is prosopagnosia, and can be a result of some kind of stroke, head trauma, or as in Kari's case, brain surgery. Individuals with prosopagnosia have normal eyesight and memory but cannot remember human faces, even those of family members they see on a daily basis.

Conditions such as face blindness illustrate how much we depend on our senses to function normally. Our senses offer a window to the world, not only providing us with awareness, understanding, and appreciation of the world's beauty, but also alerting us to its dangers. Our senses enable us to feel the gentlest of breezes, see flickering lights kilometres away, and hear the soft music of distant songbirds. But sensations such as these lack meaning until they have been received and interpreted by the brain—called perception. In this chapter, we explore both sensation and perception, which work together to give us an integrated understanding of our surroundings.

- What's the difference between sensation and perception?
- How do we respond to the characteristics of physical stimuli?
- How does perception turn sensory stimuli into meaningful information?
- How do our sense organs process stimuli?

Sensation and Perception: Two Sides of the Same Coin

If you are, or someone you know is, a runner, this situation might be familiar to you: When Kyle prepares for a run, he turns on his iPod. He quickly searches for something upbeat to motivate him. After turning down the volume, he skips the first few songs—too slow, too sad. Finally, 50 Cent's "In da Club" starts to play. Perfect! Kyle is able to hear the music because sensation takes the physical stimulus of air pressure from the headset and sends it to Kyle's brain so that he detects sounds. Perception is the process that allows us to distinguish the sounds of one song from another.

In other words, sensation is an organism's first encounter with a raw sensory stimulus, whereas perception is the process by which the brain interprets, analyzes, and integrates that stimulus with other sensory information. Imagine a ringing fire alarm, for instance. If we were considering sensation, we might ask about the loudness of the fire alarm. If we were considering perception, we might ask whether someone recognizes the ringing sound as an alarm and identifies its meaning.

Psychologists who study sensation and perception deal with a wide range of questions, including the ones at the beginning of the chapter and others such as "Why do visual illusions fool us?" and "How do we distinguish one person from another?" We address all these questions and more in this chapter. Let's look first at how our sense organs respond to stimuli.

Sensing the World Around Us

As Isabel sat down to her birthday dinner, her father carried her extra large pizza with double cheese and pepperoni in on a tray and placed it squarely in the centre of the table. The noise level, already high from the talking and laughter of family members, grew louder still. The smell of the pizza reached Isabel and she felt her stomach growl hungrily. The sight and sounds of her family around the table, along with the smells and tastes of the birthday meal, made Isabel feel more relaxed than she had since starting school in the fall.

Put yourself in this setting, and consider how different it might be if any one of your senses were not functioning. What if you were blind and unable to see Aunt Mary's latest tattoo? What if you had no sense of hearing and could not listen to Grandpa and Grandma's annual argument over who would get the largest piece? What if you were unable to feel your stomach growl, smell the dinner, or taste the food? Clearly, you would experience the dinner very differently than would someone who's sensory apparatus was intact.

Moreover, the sensations mentioned above barely scratch the surface of sensory experience. Although you might have been taught, as we were, that there are just five senses—sight, sound, taste, smell, and touch—that list is incomplete. Human sensory capabilities go well beyond the basic five senses. For example, we are sensitive not merely to touch but also to a considerably wider set of stimuli—pain, pressure, temperature, and vibration, to name a few. In addition, vision has two subsystems—relating to day and night

sensation The activation of the sense organs by a source of physical energy.

perception The sorting out, interpretation, analysis, and integration of stimuli by the sense organs in the brain.

stimulus Energy that produces a response in a sense organ.

transduction The process of converting physical energy to an electrical impulse

psychophysics The study of the relationship between the physical aspects of stimuli and our psychological experience of them.

vision—and the ear is responsive to information that allows us not only to hear but also to keep our balance.

To consider how psychologists understand the senses and, more broadly, sensation and perception, we first need a basic working vocabulary. In formal terms, **sensation** is the activation of the sense organs by a source of physical energy. Sensations are passive in the sense that information arrives via the sense organs (eyes, ears, nose, tongue, skin, etc.). **Perception** is more active because it involves the brain sorting, interpreting, analyzing, and integrating stimuli received by the sense organs. A **stimulus** is any passing source of physical energy that produces a response in a sense organ.

Remember that in the neuroscience chapter we discussed the four lobes of the cerebral cortex? These lobes play a role in your ability to perceive information. It all starts with our sensory receptors being activated in some way. This might be the neurons in our eyes when we see something or the neurons in our ears when we hear something (or the other many sensory receptors we will discuss later in the chapter). When your sensory receptors are activated, the physical energy (such as light or sound waves) is changed into electrical impulses so they can be carried via your neurons to the particular area in the brain responsible for perceiving that particular sense. The process of converting the physical energy to an electrical impulse is

Like this gymnast, we rely on our ears to keep our balance.

Study tip Remember that sensation refers to the activation of the sense organs (a physical response), whereas perception refers to how stimuli are interpreted (a psychological response).

called **transduction**. For example, when you see something, the light waves enter your eye (sensation) and the information is transduced into a neural impulse that travels to the visual association area of your occipital lobe so that you can process what you see (perception).

Stimuli vary in both type and intensity. Different types of stimuli activate different sense organs. For instance, we can differentiate light stimuli (which activate the sense of sight and allow us to see the colours of a tree in autumn) from sound stimuli (which, through the sense of hearing, permit us to hear the sounds of an orchestra). In addition, stimuli differ in intensity, relating to how strong a stimulus needs to be before it can be detected.

The area of psychology that examines stimulus type and intensity is known as psychophysics. **Psychophysics** is the

This classic picture represents a good example of the differences between sensation and perception. Sensation allows us to see the black-and-white splotches of ink. Perception allows us to recognize the pattern as a picture of a…Can you figure out what you're looking at?

Psych think

> > > Do you think it is possible to have sensation without perception? Is it possible to have perception without sensation?

study of the relationship between the physical aspects of stimuli and our psychological experience of them. Psychophysics played a central role in the development of the field of psychology (Chechil, 2003; Gardner, 2005; Hock & Ploeger, 2006).

ABSOLUTE THRESHOLDS

How do we even detect a sight, a smell, or a sound? Think about all the auditory sensory information affecting you at the moment. You may be listening to music; your room-mate may be talking on her cellphone; the laptop on your desk may be buzzing; the lights overhead may be humming. Although we are immersed in sensory information, we thrive. Our bodies seem well prepared to deal with an abundance of stimuli.

What is the least amount of stimulation that our senses can detect? The answer to this question lies in the concept of absolute threshold. An **absolute threshold** is the smallest intensity of a stimulus that must be present for our senses to detect it (Aazh & Moore, 2007).

Our senses are extremely responsive to stimuli. For example, the sense of touch is so keen that we can feel a bee's wing fall on our cheek when the wing is dropped from a distance of one centimetre. Moreover, we can see a candle 48 kilometres away on a clear night and we can smell a single drop of perfume in a house with three rooms. We can also taste one teaspoon of sugar in nine litres of water and hear a watch ticking up to six metres away!

In fact, we might have problems if our senses were any more acute than they are. If our ears were slightly more responsive to noise, for instance, we would be able to hear the sound of air molecules in our ears knocking into the eardrum—a phenomenon that would surely prove distracting and might even prevent us from hearing sounds outside our bodies.

Absolute thresholds are measured under ideal conditions. Normally, noise prevents our senses from detecting stimulation at the absolute thresholds. As defined by

absolute threshold The smallest intensity of a stimulus that must be present for the senses to detect it.

difference threshold (just noticeable difference) The smallest level of added or reduced stimulation required to sense that a change in stimulation has occurred at least 50% of the time.

Weber's law A basic law of psychophysics stating that a just-noticeable difference is a constant proportion of the intensity of an initial stimulus.

psychophysicists, *noise* is background stimulation that interferes with the perception of other stimuli. Noise, then, refers not just to auditory stimuli, as the word suggests, but also to any unwanted stimuli that interfere with other senses.

For example, think back to the last time you were at a party in someone's dorm room or apartment. Picture a crowd of talkative people crammed into a small room while loud music plays on the stereo. The din of the crowd and the music make it hard to hear individual voices. In this case, the crowded conditions would be considered "noise," because they prevent sensation at more discriminating levels.

> " The sense of touch is so acute that we can feel a bee's wing fall on our cheek when the wing is dropped from a distance of one centimetre. "

DIFFERENCE THRESHOLDS

Suppose you are making spaghetti for your best friend who is visiting from out of town. You don't cook much, and you are trying to spice up the can of tomato sauce you bought at the grocery store. You taste your sauce and note that it needs more salt, so you sprinkle some salt in and stir. You taste the sauce again, but can't taste any difference so you sprinkle in more salt and stir. You taste it one more time and the sauce finally tastes a bit saltier.

You have just demonstrated the **difference threshold**, defined by psychologists as the lowest level of added (or reduced) stimulation required to sense that a *change* in stimulation has occurred at least 50% of the time. Because the difference threshold is the minimum change in stimulation required to detect the difference between two stimuli, it also is called a **just-noticeable difference** (Nittrouer & Lowenstein, 2007).

The stimulus value that constitutes a just-noticeable difference depends on the initial intensity of the stimulus. This relationship between changes in the original value of a stimulus and the degree to which a change will be noticed forms one of the basic laws of psychophysics, Weber's law. **Weber's law** (Weber is pronounced vay-bear) states that a just-noticeable difference is a *constant proportion* of the intensity of an initial stimulus.

For example, the just-noticeable difference for weight is 1:50. Consequently, it takes a 1-gram increase in a 50-gram weight to produce a noticeable difference, and it would take a 10-gram increase to produce a noticeable difference if the initial weight were 500 grams. In both cases, the same proportional increase is necessary to produce a just-noticeable difference—1:50 = 10:500. Similarly, the just-noticeable difference for changes in loudness is greater for sounds that are initially loud than it is for sounds that are initially soft, but the *proportional* increase remains the same.

TRY IT!

How Sensitive Are You?

To test your awareness of the capabilities of your senses, answer the following questions:

1. How far can a candle flame be seen on a clear, dark night?
   a. From a distance of 16 kilometres_____
   b. From a distance of 48 kilometres_____
2. How far can the ticking of a watch be heard under quiet conditions?
   a. From 2 metres away_____
   b. From 6 metres away_____
3. How much sugar is needed to allow it to be detected when dissolved in 9 litres of water?
   a. 30 grams (2 tablespoons) _____
   b. 5 grams (1 teaspoon) _____
4. Over what area can a drop of perfume be detected?
   a. A 1.5-metre by 1.5-metre area_____
   b. A 3-room apartment_____

Source: Adapted from Galanter, 1962.

Scoring: In each case, the answer is b, illustrating the tremendous sensitivity of our senses.

Study tip

Remember that Weber's law holds for every type of sensory stimulus, including taste and smell.

Weber's law helps explain why a person in a quiet room is more startled by the ringing of a telephone than is a person in an already noisy room. To produce the same amount of reaction in a noisy room, a telephone ring might have to approximate the loudness of a car alarm. Similarly, when the moon is visible during the late afternoon, it appears relatively dim—yet against a dark night sky, it seems quite bright.

adaptation An adjustment in sensory capacity after prolonged exposure to unchanging stimuli.

SENSORY ADAPTATION

You enter a movie theatre and immediately are aware of the popcorn aroma. A few minutes later, you barely notice the smell. The reason you acclimate to the odour is sensory adaptation. **Adaptation** is an adjustment in sensory capacity after prolonged exposure to unchanging stimuli. Adaptation occurs as people become accustomed to a stimulus and change their frame of reference. In a sense, the brain reduces our sensitivity to the stimulation that it's experiencing (Calin-Jageman & Fischer, 2007).

Adaptation also occurs after repeated exposure to a strong stimulus. If you were to hear a loud tone over and over again, for example, eventually it would begin to sound softer. Similarly, although jumping into a cold lake may be temporarily unpleasant, eventually you probably would become accustomed to the temperature.

This apparent decline in sensitivity to sensory stimuli is due to the inability of the sensory nerve receptors to fire off messages to the brain indefinitely. Because these receptor

Going for a swim on a cold winter's day isn't for everyone, but after the initial plunge, sensory adaptation helps the body adjust to the frigid water—at least for a little while.

cells are most responsive to *changes* in stimulation, constant stimulation is not effective in producing a sustained reaction.

Perception: Constructing Our Impressions of the World

We turn now from a focus on the initial response to a stimulus (sensation) to what our minds make of that stimulus—perception. Perception is a constructive process by which we go beyond the stimuli that are presented to us and attempt to construct a meaningful situation.

One of the most important points you should keep in mind about perception is that there is not a 1:1 correspondence between our perceptual representation of the world and the physical reality of the world. Perception takes the physical information in the world and interprets it. Why? Because physical information is typically ambiguous. We take the available information provided by our senses and interpret physical stimuli based on what we know about the world.

PERCEPTUAL SETS

In the chapter on memory we discuss how our mood, the context, our personality, our previous experiences, and our expectations impact what we are able to remember. This

also holds true for what we perceive. Imagine you are someone with a firm belief in the possibility that aliens could visit Earth from another planet. Imagine then, that you are out for a nice evening stroll when you see something fly overhead in the sky. You are quite certain that it was not an airplane, or a bird, or a bat, or anything else recognizable. Given your firm belief in alien visits, you may have an expectation then that this unidentified flying object is an alien spaceship.

The expectations and beliefs that impact what we see are called a **perceptual set**. This may also explain why some people believe they have witnessed a Sasquatch or a picture of a religious icon on a grilled cheese sandwich. Often times, when we expect to see something we think we saw it. Consider how this may impact someone working in the field of law and justice. If a police officer enters an area of town that is known to house gang members and that officer is confronted by someone holding something in their hand, the officer is likely to perceive the "something" as a gun. The officer's perceptual set may very well result in either saving his or her own life if it is in fact a gun, or harming an innocent person who was holding a cell phone. This may also have implications for eyewitness testimony, something we discuss in more detail in the chapter on memory.

> " **Perception is a constructive process by which we go beyond the stimuli that are presented to us and attempt to construct a meaningful situation.** "

TOP-DOWN AND BOTTOM-UP PROCESSING

Ca- yo- re-d t-is -en-en-e, w-ic- ha- ev-ry -hi-d l-tt-r m-ss-ng? It probably won't take you too long to figure out that it says, "Can you read this sentence, which has every third letter missing?"

If perception were based primarily on breaking down a stimulus into its most basic elements, understanding the sentence, as well as other ambiguous stimuli, would not be possible. The fact that you were probably able to recognize such an imprecise stimulus illustrates that perception proceeds along two different avenues, called top-down processing and bottom-up processing.

Picture an adult and a five-year-old boy watching the popular game show *Wheel of Fortune*. Each works very hard at trying to solve the puzzles, but the adult always wins, not because she is smarter than the child but because she uses the clue (for example, "famous person") and the various letters to decipher B E - - - - E as "Beyoncé." The boy, who is just beginning to read, can't read the clue yet, so he can rely only on recognizing the letters as they are revealed. He sounds out the revealed letters and comes up with words

When the usual cues we use to distinguish figure from ground are absent, we may shift back and forth between different views of the same figure. If you look at each of these objects long enough, you'll probably experience a shift in what you're seeing.

Vase-Face Illusion
Is it a vase or the profiles of two people?

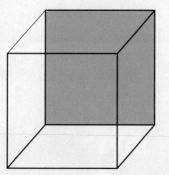

Necker Cube
Is the colour portion of the cube the front side or the back?

perceptual set The expectations and beliefs that impact what we (think we) see.

Top-Down Processing
The power of context helps us perceive the letter B in the top line and the same figure as the number 13 in the bottom line.

Source: Coren & Ward, 1989.

like "beehive." Psychologists would argue that the adult solves the puzzle first because she relies on both top-down processing and bottom-up processing, whereas the child relies much more on bottom-up processing.

In **top-down processing**, perception is guided by higher-level knowledge, experience, expectations, and motivations. You were able to figure out the meaning of the sentence with the missing letters at the beginning of this section because of your prior reading experience and because written English contains redundancies. Not every letter of each word is necessary to decode its meaning. Moreover, your expectations played a role in your being able to read the sentence. You were probably expecting a statement that had *something* to do with psychology, not the lyrics to an Eminem song.

Top-down processing is illustrated by the importance of context in determining how we perceive objects. However, top-down processing cannot occur on its own. Even though top-down processing allows us to fill the gaps in ambiguous and out-of-context stimuli, we would be unable to perceive the meaning of such stimuli without bottom-up processing. **Bottom-up processing** consists of the progression of recognizing and processing information from individual components of a stimulus and moving to the perception of the whole. We would make no headway in our recognition of the sentence without being able to perceive the individual shapes that make up the letters. Some perception, then, occurs at the level of the patterns and features of each of the separate letters.

Top-down and bottom-up processing occur simultaneously and interact with each other in perception. Bottom-up processing permits us to process the fundamental characteristics of stimuli, whereas top-down processing allows us to bring our experience to bear on perception. As psychologists learn more about the complex processes involved in perception, they are developing a better understanding of how the brain continually interprets information from the

top-down processing Perception that is guided by higher-level knowledge, experience, expectations, and motivations.

bottom-up processing Perception that consists of the progression of recognizing and processing information from individual components of a stimuli and moving to the perception of the whole.

Gestalt laws of organization A series of principles that describe how we organize bits and pieces of information into meaningful wholes.

senses and permits us to make responses appropriate to the environment (Buschman & Miller, 2007).

THE GESTALT LAWS OF ORGANIZATION

Some of the most basic perceptual processes can be described by a series of principles that focus on the ways we organize bits and pieces of information into meaningful wholes. Known as **Gestalt laws of organization**, these principles were set forth in the early 1900s by a group of German psychologists who studied patterns, or *Gestalten* (Wertheimer, 1923). Those psychologists discovered a number of principles that are valid for visual—and auditory—stimuli: closure, proximity, similarity, and simplicity.

> **Study tip**
> The Gestalt laws of organization are classic principles in the field of psychology. Use the four figures at the bottom of this page to help you remember them.

In *closure*, we group elements to form enclosed or complete figures rather than open ones. We use *proximity* by perceiving elements that are closer together as grouped together. Elements that are *similar* in appearance we perceive as grouped together. Finally, in a general sense, the overriding Gestalt principle is *simplicity*: When we observe a pattern, we perceive it in the most basic, straightforward manner that we can. If we have a choice of interpretations, we generally opt for the simpler one.

Although Gestalt psychology no longer plays a prominent role in contemporary psychology, its legacy endures. One fundamental Gestalt principle that remains influential is that two objects considered together form a whole that is different from the simple combination of the objects. Gestalt psychologists argued that the perception of stimuli in our environment goes well beyond the individual elements that we sense. Instead, it represents an active, constructive process carried out within the brain (Humphreys & Müller, 2000; Lehar, 2003; van der Helm, 2006).

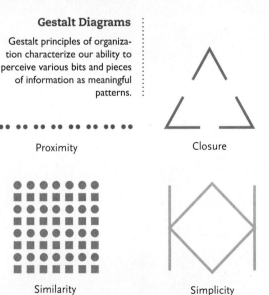

Gestalt Diagrams

Gestalt principles of organization characterize our ability to perceive various bits and pieces of information as meaningful patterns.

Proximity

Closure

Similarity

Simplicity

"I'm turning into my mother"
Understanding this cartoon involves the separation of the figure and ground. If you're having trouble appreciating the humour, stare at the woman on the right and you will see her transformed.

PERCEPTUAL CONSTANCY

Consider what happens as you finish a conversation with a friend and she begins to walk away from you. As you watch her walk down the street, the image on your retina becomes smaller and smaller. Do you wonder why she is shrinking? Of course not. Despite the very real change in the size of the retinal image, you factor into your thinking the knowledge that your friend is moving farther away from you because of perceptual constancy. **Perceptual constancy** is a phenomenon in which physical objects are perceived as unvarying and consistent despite changes in their appearance or in the physical environment.

Perceptual constancy applies not just to size but to shape and colour as well. For example, despite the varying images on the retina as an airplane approaches, flies overhead, and disappears, we do not perceive the airplane as changing shape (Redding, 2002; Wickelgren, 2004). Because of colour constancy we also know that even though our blue car looks black in the evening, someone has not come along and painted the car without our knowledge!

DEPTH PERCEPTION

As sophisticated as the retina is, the images projected onto it are flat and two-dimensional. Yet the world around us is three-dimensional, and we perceive it that way. How do we make the transformation from 2D to 3D?

The ability to view the world in three dimensions and to perceive distance—a skill known as **depth perception**—is due largely to the fact that we have two eyes. Because there is a certain distance between the eyes, a slightly different image reaches each retina. The brain integrates the two images into one composite view, but it also recognizes the difference in images and uses it to estimate the distance of an object from us. The difference in the images seen by the left eye and the right eye is known as *binocular disparity*.

To get a sense of binocular disparity, hold a pencil at arm's length and look at it first with one eye and then with the other. There is little difference between the two views relative to the background. Now bring the pencil just 15 centimetres away from your face, and try the same thing. This time you will perceive a greater difference between the two views.

The fact that the discrepancy between the images in the two eyes varies according to the distance of objects that we view provides us with a means of determining distance. If we view two objects and one is considerably closer to us

> **perceptual constancy** Phenomenon in which physical objects are perceived to have constant shape, colour, and size, despite changes in their appearance or in the physical environment.

> **depth perception** The ability to view the world in three dimensions and to perceive distance.

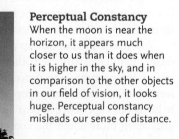

Perceptual Constancy
When the moon is near the horizon, it appears much closer to us than it does when it is higher in the sky, and in comparison to the other objects in our field of vision, it looks huge. Perceptual constancy misleads our sense of distance.

Depth Perception
Railroad tracks that seem to join together in the distance illustrate linear perspective.

than the other is, the retinal disparity will be relatively large, and we will have a greater sense of depth between the two. However, if the two objects are a similar distance from us, the retinal disparity will be minor, and we will perceive them as being a similar distance from us.

In some cases, certain cues permit us to obtain a sense of depth and distance with just one eye. These cues are known as *monocular cues*. One monocular cue—*motion parallax*—is the change in position of an object on the retina caused by movement of your body relative to the object. For example, suppose you are a passenger in a moving car, and you focus your eye on a stable object such as a tree. Objects that are closer than the tree will appear to move backward, and the nearer the object is, the more quickly it will appear to move. In contrast, objects beyond the tree will seem to move at a slower speed, but in the same direction as you are going. Your brain is able to use these cues to calculate the relative distances of the tree and other objects.

Similarly, experience has taught us that if two objects are the same size, the one that makes a smaller image on the retina is farther away than is the one that provides a larger image—an example of the monocular cue of *relative size*. But it's not just size of an object that provides information about distance; the quality of the image on the retina helps us judge distance. The monocular cue of *texture gradient* provides information about distance because the details of things that are far away are less distinct (Proffitt, 2006).

Finally, anyone who has ever seen railroad tracks that seem to join together in the distance knows that distant objects appear to be closer together than nearer ones, a phenomenon called linear perspective. People use *linear perspective* as a monocular cue in estimating distance, allowing the two-dimensional image on the retina to record the three-dimensional world (Bruce, Green, & Georgeson, 1997; Bruggeman, Yonas, & Konczak, 2007; Dobbins et al., 1998; Shimono & Wade, 2002).

PERCEPTUAL ILLUSIONS

If you look carefully at the Parthenon, one of the most famous buildings of ancient Greece, still standing at the top of an Athens hill, the Acropolis, you'll see that it was built with a bulge on one side. If it didn't have that bulge—and quite a few other architectural "tricks" like it, such as columns that incline inward—it would look as if it were crooked and about to fall down. Instead, it appears to stand completely straight, at right angles to the ground.

The fact that the Parthenon appears to be completely upright is the result of a series of visual illusions. **Visual illusions** are physical stimuli that consistently produce errors in perception. In the case of the Parthenon, the building appears to be completely square. However, if it had been built that way, it would look curved. The reason for this is an illusion that makes right angles placed above a line appear as if they were bent. To offset the illusion, the Parthenon was constructed with a slight upward curvature.

Another visual illusion, the *Franz Carl Müller-Lyer illusion*, has fascinated psychologists for decades. It consists of two lines that are the same length, but one has arrow tips pointing inward and appears to be longer than the other one, which has the arrow tips pointing outward.

Although all kinds of explanations for visual illusions have been suggested, most concentrate either on the physical operation of the eye or on our misinterpretation of the visual stimulus. For example, one explanation for the Müller-Lyer illusion is that eye movements are greater when the arrow tips point inward, making us perceive the line as longer than it is when the arrow tips face outward. In contrast, a different explanation for the illusion suggests that we unconsciously attribute particular significance to each of the lines (Gregory, 1978; Redding & Hawley, 1993).

visual illusions Physical stimuli that consistently produce errors in perception.

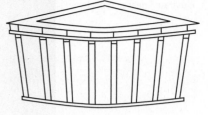

If the Parthenon had been built with completely true right angles, it would look like this:

To compensate for this illusion, it was designed to have a slight upward curvature, as illustrated here:
Source: Coren & Ward, 1989, p. 5.

Visual Illusion

The Parthenon on the Acropolis in Athens, Greece, is an architectural wonder that looks perfectly straight in the photo.

Müller-Lyer Illusion

In the Müller-Lyer illusion the left vertical line appears shorter than the one at the right even though they're the same length.

One explanation for the Müller-Lyer illusion suggests that the line with arrow points directed outward is perceived as the relatively close corner of a rectangular object, such as the outside corner of a building. The line with arrow points directed inward is interpreted as the inside corner of a rectangular object, such as a room extending away from us. Our previous experience with distance cues leads us to assume that the outside corner, (left) is closer than the inside corner, (right) and that the inside corner must therefore be longer.

We tend to perceive one line as if it were the relatively close outside corner of a rectangular object, such as the outside corner of a room. In contrast, when we view the other line, we perceive it as the relatively more distant inside corner of a rectangular object, such as the inside corner of a room. Because previous experience leads us to assume that the outside corner is closer than the inside corner, we make the further assumption that the inside corner must be larger.

Study tip

The explanation for the Müller-Lyer illusion is complicated. The drawing on this page will help you master it.

Despite the complexity of the latter explanation, a good deal of evidence supports it. For instance, cross-cultural studies show that people raised in areas where there are few right angles—such as the Zulu in Africa—are much less susceptible to the illusion than are people who grow up where most structures are built using right angles and rectangles (Segall, Campbell, & Herskovits, 1966).

CULTURE AND PERCEPTION

In the late 1950s, anthropologist Colin Turnbull studied the life of the Bambuti pygmies, who lived their entire lives in dense forests. One afternoon, Turnbull asked a pygmy named Kenge to accompany him on a trip to the mountains. This trip required a long drive across the vast plains of Congo. Kenge had never stepped out of the forest, so he tentatively accepted Turnbull's offer. As they were driving, Turnbull pointed out some buffalo in the far distance. Kenge could not believe these brown specks were buffalo and forcefully argued they must be insects. As they drove closer to the buffalo, the images of the buffalo gradually increased in size. Kenge thought Turnbull was performing witchcraft to make these animals grow. After several similar experiences that day, Kenge began to accept that objects in the distance look smaller than they do close up and started to reconsider his ideas about perceptual constancy. Kenge did, however, return to the forest claiming that the plains were a "bad country" (Turnbull, 1961).

Kenge's experience demonstrates that the culture in which we are raised has clear consequences for how we perceive the world. Consider, for instance, the so-called devil's tuning fork, a mind-boggling drawing in which the centre tine of the fork alternates between appearing and disappearing.

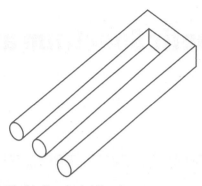

The "devil's tuning fork" has three prongs—or does it have two?

Try to make your own drawing of the devil's tuning fork on a piece of paper. Chances are that the task is nearly impossible for you—unless you are a member of an African culture that has had little exposure to Western cultures. Westerners automatically interpret the drawing as something that cannot exist in three dimensions, and they therefore are inhibited from reproducing it. Some African peoples, in contrast, do not make the assumption that the figure is "impossible" and instead view it in two dimensions, a perception that enables them to copy the figure with ease (Deregowski, 1973).

Kenge's experiences also demonstrate that cultural differences are also reflected in depth perception. A Western viewer of the drawing of the hunter above would interpret the hunter as aiming for the antelope in the foreground, while an elephant stands under the tree in the background. In contrast, in one study in which the drawing was used, members of an isolated African tribe interpreted the scene very differently by assuming that the hunter is aiming at the elephant. Westerners use the difference in sizes between the two animals as a cue that the elephant is farther away than the antelope (Hudson, 1960).

Ultimately, then, the misinterpretations created by visual illusions are due to errors in both fundamental visual processing and the way the brain interprets the information it receives. But visual illusions, by illustrating something fundamental about perception, become more than mere psychological curiosities. There is a basic connection between our prior knowledge, needs, motivations, and expectations about how the world is put together and the way we perceive it. Our view of the world is very much an outcome of fundamental psychological factors. Furthermore, each person perceives the environment in a way that is unique and special (Knoblich & Sebanz, 2006; Repp & Knoblich, 2007).

Vision: Shedding Light on the Eye

If, as poets say, the eyes provide a window to the soul, they also provide us with a window on the world. The ability to see permits us to admire and to react to the beauty of a sunset, the configuration of a lover's face, or the words in a book.

Vision starts with light, the physical energy that stimulates the eye. Light is a form of electromagnetic radiation, which is measured in wavelengths. Different wavelengths correspond to different types of energy. The range of wavelengths to which humans are sensitive is called the *visible spectrum*.

Light waves coming from some object outside the body, such as a butterfly, are sensed by the only organ that is capable of responding to the visible spectrum: the eye. Our eyes convert light to a form that can be used by the neurons linking the eyes and the brain. The neurons themselves take up a relatively small percentage of the total eye. Most of the

Is the man aiming for the elephant or the antelope? Westerners assume that the differences in size between the two animals indicate that the elephant is farther away, and therefore the man is aiming for the antelope. In contrast, members of some African tribes, not used to depth cues in two-dimensional drawings, assume that the man is aiming for the elephant.

Source: From Fig. 1 (p. 186) of W. Hudson (1960). Pictorial depth perception in sub-cultural groups in Africa. *Journal of Social Psychology,* 52, 183-208. Reprinted by permission.

Figure 3.1
The Electromagnetic Spectrum and the Visible Spectrum

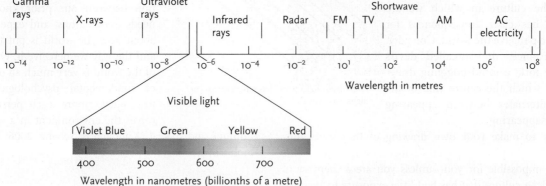

Gamma rays | X-rays | Ultraviolet rays | Infrared rays | Radar | FM | TV | Shortwave | AM | AC electricity

10^{-14} 10^{-12} 10^{-10} 10^{-8} 10^{-6} 10^{-4} 10^{-2} 10^{1} 10^{2} 10^{4} 10^{6} 10^{8}

Wavelength in metres

Visible light

Violet Blue | Green | Yellow | Red

400   500   600   700

Wavelength in nanometres (billionths of a metre)

eye is a mechanical device that is similar in many respects to a non-electronic camera that uses film.

Despite the similarities between the eye and a camera, vision involves processes that are far more complex and sophisticated than those of any camera. Furthermore, once an image reaches the neuronal receptors of the eye, the eye/camera analogy ends, because the processing of the visual image in the brain is more reflective of a computer than it is of a camera.

ILLUMINATING THE EYE

The ray of light reflected by an object such as a butterfly first travels through the *cornea*, a transparent, protective window. The cornea, because it is curved, bends (or *refracts*) light as it passes through to sharpen its focus. After moving through the cornea, the light traverses the pupil. The *pupil* is a dark hole in the center of the *iris*, the coloured part of the eye, which in humans ranges from a light blue to a dark brown. The size of the pupil depends on the amount of light in the environment. The dimmer the surroundings are, the more the pupil opens to allow more light to enter.

Once light passes through the pupil, it enters the lens, which is directly behind the pupil. The lens bends the rays of light so that they are properly focused on the rear of the eye. The lens focuses light by changing its own thickness, a process called *accommodation*: It becomes flatter when viewing distant objects and rounder when looking at closer objects. Have you noticed that your parents (or yourself if you are a mature student!) are starting to hold their menus at arm's length when ordering food at a restaurant? The

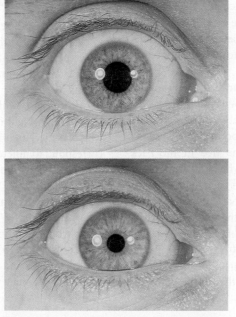

Like the automatic lighting system on a camera, the pupil in the human eye expands to let in more light (top) and contracts to block out light (bottom).

ability of our lenses to accommodate decreases with age and makes it harder to focus on close objects. For this reason, people start needing reading glasses, bifocal lenses, or longer arms as early as their 40s.

Striking the Retina Having travelled through the pupil and the lens, the image of the butterfly reaches the **retina**, a thin layer of nerve cells at the back of the eye. The retina converts the electromagnetic energy of light to electrical impulses (transduction) for transmission to the brain. There are two kinds of light-sensitive receptor cells in the retina; their names describe their shapes: rods and cones. **Rods** are thin, cylindrical receptor cells that are highly sensitive to light. **Cones** are cone-shaped, light-sensitive receptor cells that are responsible for sharp focus and colour perception, particularly in bright light. The rods and cones are distributed unevenly throughout the retina. Cones are concentrated on the part of the retina called the *fovea*. The fovea is a particularly sensitive region of the retina. If you want to focus on something specific, you will automatically try to centre the image on the fovea to see it more sharply.

retina The part of the eye that converts the electromagnetic energy of light to electrical impulses for transmission to the brain.

rods Thin, cylindrical receptor cells in the retina that are highly sensitive to light.

cones Cone-shaped, light-sensitive receptor cells in the retina that are responsible for sharp focus and colour perception, particularly in bright light.

Figure 3.2
Similarities Between the Human Eye and a Camera

A camera's lens focuses the inverted image on the film in the same way the eye's lens focuses images on the retina

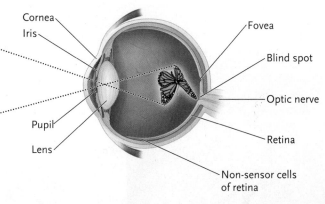

Cornea
Iris
Fovea
Blind spot
Optic nerve
Pupil
Lens
Retina
Non-sensor cells of retina

The rods and cones not only are structurally dissimilar, but they also have different functions. Cones are primarily responsible for the sharply focused perception of colour (you can remember this by thinking cones=colour), particularly in brightly lit situations; rods are helpful in dimly lit situations and are largely insensitive to colour and details. The rods play a key role in *peripheral vision*—seeing objects that are outside the main centre of focus—and in night vision.

Rods and cones also are involved in *dark adaptation*, the phenomenon of adjusting to dim light after being in brighter light. (Think of the experience of walking into a dark movie theatre and groping your way to a seat but a few minutes later seeing the seats quite clearly.) The speed at which dark adaptation occurs is a result of the rate of change in the chemical composition of the rods and cones. Although the cones reach their greatest level of adaptation in just a few minutes, it takes the rods 20 to 30 minutes to reach their maximum level. The opposite phenomenon—*light adaptation*, or the process of adjusting to bright light after exposure to dim light—occurs much more quickly, taking only a minute or so.

Sending an Image to the Brain When light energy strikes the rods and cones, it starts a chain of events that transforms light into neural impulses that can be communicated to the brain. Even before the neural message reaches the brain, however, some initial coding of the visual information takes place.

Stimulation of the nerve cells in the eye triggers a neural response that is transmitted to other nerve cells in the

DID YOU KNOW?

Light conditions are not the only factor that controls the size of the pupil. When we are aroused, our pupils dilate, or widen. Is it useful to look deeply into your partner's eyes and know her intentions? Although early research suggested that pupil dilation occurred only during sexual arousal, recent research has demonstrated that any type of emotional arousal, such as anger, fear, or surprise, can cause our pupils to dilate. (Bradley et al., 2008; Hess & Polt, 1960).

Study tip Cones are responsible for colour vision. Rods are highly sensitive to light but not to colours. Rods help us to see better at night.

Figure 3.3
Receptor Cells–Rods and Cones–in the Eye

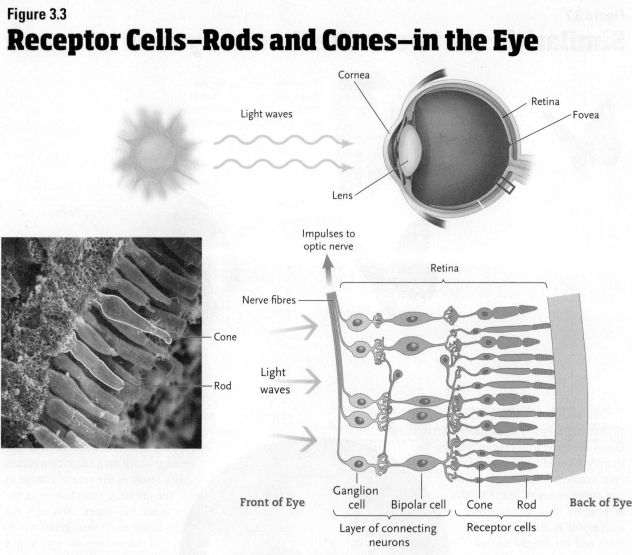

Cornea

Retina

Fovea

Light waves

Lens

Impulses to optic nerve

Retina

Nerve fibres

Cone

Rod

Light waves

Ganglion cell

Bipolar cell

Cone

Rod

Front of Eye

Back of Eye

Layer of connecting neurons

Receptor cells

Source: Shier, Butler, & Lewis, 2000.

retina called bipolar cells and *ganglion cells*. Bipolar cells receive information directly from the rods and cones and communicate that information to the ganglion cells. The ganglion cells collect and summarize visual information, which is then moved out the back of the eyeball and sent to the brain through a bundle of ganglion axons that make up the **optic nerve**.

Because the opening for the optic nerve passes through the retina, no rods or cones exist in that area, and their absence produces a blind spot, an area roughly in the middle of your field of vision where you can't see anything. Normally, however, the blind spot does not interfere with vision, because you automatically compensate for what you can't see.

Once they have left the eye itself, neural impulses relating to the image move through the optic nerve. As the optic nerve leaves the eyeball, it does not take the most direct route to the part of the brain right behind the eye. Instead,

optic nerve A bundle of ganglion axons that carry visual information to the brain.

the optic nerves from each eye meet in the brain at a point roughly between the two eyes—called the *optic chiasm* (pronounced *ki-asm*)—where each optic nerve then splits.

When the optic nerves split, the nerve impulses coming from the right half of each retina travel to the right side of the brain, and the impulses arriving from the left half of each retina go to the left side of the brain. Because the image on the retinas is reversed and upside down, however, images coming from the right half of each retina actually originated in the field of vision to the person's left, and the images coming from the left half of each retina originated in the field of vision to the person's right.

Processing the Visual Message By the time a visual message reaches the brain, it has already passed through several stages of processing. The ultimate processing of visual images takes place in the visual cortex of the brain, and it is here that the most complex kinds of processing occur. Psychologists David Hubel and Torsten Wiesel won the Nobel Prize in 1981 for their discovery that many neurons in the cortex are extraordinarily specialized to respond

To find your blind spot, close your right eye and look at the haunted house with your left eye. You will see the ghost on the periphery of your vision. Now, while staring at the house, move the page toward you. When the book is about 30 centimetres from your eye, the ghost will disappear. At this moment, the image of the ghost is falling on your blind spot. But also note how, when the page is at that distance, not only does the ghost seem to disappear, but the line seems to run continuously through the area where the ghost used to be. This simple experiment shows how we automatically compensate for missing information by using nearby material to complete what is unseen. That's the reason you never notice the blind spot. What is missing is replaced by what is seen next to the blind spot.

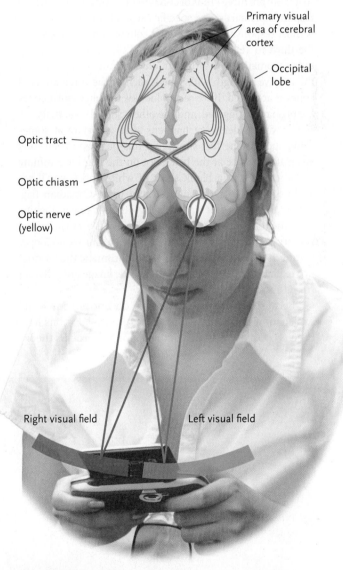

only to visual stimuli of a particular shape or pattern—a phenomenon known as **feature detection**. They found that some cells are activated only by lines of a particular width, shape, or orientation. Other cells are activated only by moving, as opposed to stationary, stimuli (Hubel & Wiesel, 2004; Pelli, Burns, & Farell, 2006).

More recent work has added to our knowledge of the complex ways in which visual information coming from individual neurons is combined and processed. Different parts of the brain process nerve impulses in several individual systems simultaneously. For instance, one system relates to shapes, one to colours, and others to movement, location, and depth. Furthermore, different parts of the brain are involved in the perception of specific *kinds* of stimuli, showing distinctions, for example, between the perception of human faces, animals, and inanimate stimuli (Brady, Campbell, & Flaherty, 2005; Werblin & Roska, 2007; Winston et al., 2006). For example, Kari, the woman with face blindness that we discussed at the beginning of the chapter, was not able to perceive or remember human faces, even though she could perceive other stimuli.

COLOUR VISION AND COLOUR BLINDNESS

Back in elementary school you probably memorized the colours of the rainbow using the mnemonic device: ROYG-BIV. Can you recall what each letter represents? ROYGBIV stands for the order of hues in the visual spectrum (red, orange, yellow, green, blue, indigo, violet). Although the range of wavelengths to which humans are sensitive is relatively narrow in comparison with the entire electromagnetic spectrum, the portion to which we are capable of responding allows us great flexibility in sensing the world. Nowhere is this clearer than in terms of the number of colours we can discern. A person with normal colour vision is capable of distinguishing no less than seven million different colours (Bruce, Green, & Georgeson, 1997; Rabin, 2004).

Although the variety of colours that people are generally able to distinguish is vast, some individuals have a limited ability to perceive colour; they are colour-blind. Interestingly, the study of colour blindness has provided some of the most

feature detection The activation of neurons in the cortex by visual stimuli of specific shapes or patterns.

Figure 3.4
Hemispheric Differences in the Right and Left Visual Field

Primary visual area of cerebral cortex

Occipital lobe

Optic tract

Optic chiasm

Optic nerve (yellow)

Right visual field

Left visual field

Because the optic nerve coming from each eye splits at the optic chiasm, the image to a person's right is sent to the left side of the brain, and the image to the person's left is transmitted to the right side of the brain.
Source: Mader, 2000.

important clues to understanding how colour vision operates (Bonnardel, 2006; Neitz, Neitz, & Kainz, 1996).

Approximately 7% of men and 0.4% of women are colour-blind. For most people with colour blindness, the world looks quite dull. Red fire engines appear yellow, green grass seems yellow, and the three colours of a traffic light all look yellow. In fact, in the most common form of colour blindness, all red and green objects are seen as yellow. There are other forms of colour blindness as well, but they are quite rare. In yellow-blue blindness, people are unable to tell the difference between yellow and blue, and in the most extreme case an individual perceives no colour at all. To such a person the world looks something like the picture on a black-and-white television set.

Explaining Colour Vision To understand why some people are colour blind, we need to consider the two processes of colour vision. The first process is explained by the **trichromatic theory of colour vision**. This theory suggests that there are three kinds of cones in the retina, each of which responds primarily to a specific range of wavelengths. One is most responsive to blue-violet colours, one to green, and the third to yellow-red (Brown & Wald, 1964). According to trichromatic theory, perception of colour is influenced by the relative strength with which each of the three kinds of cones is activated. If we see a blue sky, the blue-violet cones are primarily triggered, and the others show less activity.

Now consider what happens after you stare at something such as the flag shown on this page and then look away. If you stare at the black dot on the flag for a minute and then look at a blank sheet of white paper, you'll see an image of the traditional red and white Canadian flag. Where there was green and black, you'll see red and white. This phenomenon is called an *afterimage*. It occurs because activity in the retina continues even when you are no longer staring at the original picture. The trichromatic theory does not explain why the colours in the afterimage are different from those in the original.

Because trichromatic processes do not provide a full explanation of colour vision, alternative explanations have been proposed. According to the **opponent-process theory**

Get Involved!

What would the world look like if you were colour-blind? At the Web site Vischeck.com, you can upload a picture of a loved one, your dorm room, or even yourself and select the type of colour blindness you want to experience. Vischeck will transform your picture so that you can see it from the perspective of a person with colour blindness (www.vischeck.com/vischeck/vischeckImage.php).

of colour vision, receptor cells are linked in pairs, working in opposition to each other. Specifically, there are a blue-yellow pairing, a red-green pairing, and a black-white pairing. If an object reflects light that contains more blue than yellow, it will stimulate the firing of the cells sensitive to blue, simultaneously discouraging or inhibiting the firing of receptor cells sensitive to yellow—and the object will appear blue. If, in contrast, a light contains more yellow than blue, the cells that respond to yellow will be stimulated to fire while the blue ones are inhibited, and the object will appear yellow (Robinson, D. N., 2007).

The opponent-process theory provides a good explanation for afterimages. When we stare at the green in the figure, for instance, our receptor cells for green become

> **trichromatic theory of colour vision** The theory that there are three kinds of cones in the retina, each of which responds primarily to a specific range of wavelengths.
>
> **opponent-process theory of colour vision** The theory that receptor cells for colour are linked in pairs, working in opposition to each other.

Stare at the dot in this flag for about a minute and then look at a piece of plain white paper. What do you see? Most people see an afterimage that converts the colours in the figure into the traditional red and white of the Canadian flag. If you have trouble seeing it the first time, blink once and try again.

fatigued and are less able to respond to green stimuli. In contrast, the receptor cells for the red part of the red-green pair are not tired, because they are not being stimulated. When we look at a white surface, the light reflected by it would normally stimulate both the yellow and the blue receptors equally. But the fatigue of the yellow receptors prevents this from happening. They temporarily do not respond to the yellow, causing the white light appear to be blue. Because the other colours in the figure do the same thing relative to their specific opponents, the afterimage produces the opponent colours—for a while. The afterimage lasts only a short time, because the yellow receptors soon recover from their fatigue and begin to perceive the white light more accurately.

Study tip Know the distinctions between the two explanations for colour vision—the trichromatic and opponent-process theories.

Both opponent-processes and trichromatic mechanisms are at work in allowing us to see colour. However, they operate in different parts of the visual sensing system. Trichromatic processes work within the retina itself, whereas opponent mechanisms operate both in the retina and at later stages of neuronal processing (Baraas, Foster, & Amano, 2006; Chen, Zhou, & Gong, 2004; Gegenfurtner, 2003).

As our understanding of the processes that permit us to see has increased, some psychologists have begun to develop new techniques to help those with serious vision problems to overcome their impairments. For example,

Psych think

> > > Repairing faulty sensory organs through devices such as personal guidance systems and eyeglasses is the goal of much ongoing research. Should researchers also try to improve normal sensory capabilities beyond their "natural" range, so that human visual or audio capabilities are more sensitive than normal? What benefits might this ability bring? What problems might it cause?

one technology allows light-sensitive chips to be surgically implanted under the retina, such chips detect light entering the eye and striking them; they then send electrical impulses to the ganglion cells that normally convey visual information from the retina to the nervous system. They therefore function in much the same way as natural photoreceptors would, although the visual information that they can capture and relay to the brain is still limited to simple patterns formed by dots of light (Wickelgren, 2006).

Hearing and the Other Senses

The blast-off was easy compared with what the astronaut was experiencing now: space sickness. The constant nausea and vomiting were enough to make him wonder why he had worked so hard to become an astronaut. Even though he had been warned that there was a two-thirds chance that his first experience in space would cause these symptoms, he wasn't prepared for how terribly sick he really felt.

Whether or not the astronaut wishes he could head right back to earth, his experience, a major problem for space travellers, is related to a basic sensory process: the sense of motion and balance. This sense allows people to navigate their bodies through the world and keep themselves upright without falling. Along with hearing—the process by which sound waves are translated into understandable and meaningful forms—the sense of motion and balance resides in the ear.

SENSING SOUND

Although many of us think primarily of the outer ear when we speak of the ear, that structure is only one simple part of the whole. The outer ear acts as a reverse megaphone to collect and bring sounds into the internal portions of the ear. The location of the outer ears on different sides of the head helps with *sound localization*, the process by which we identify the direction from which a sound is coming. Wave patterns in the air enter each ear at a slightly different time, and the brain uses the discrepancy as a clue to the sound's point of origin.

Sound is the movement of air molecules set off by a source of vibration. Sounds, arriving at the outer ear in the form of wavelike vibrations, are funnelled into the *auditory canal*, a tubelike passage that leads to the eardrum. The **eardrum** is aptly named, because it operates as a miniature drum, vibrating when sound waves hit it. The more intense the sound, the more the eardrum vibrates. These vibrations are transferred into the *middle ear*, a tiny chamber containing three bones (the *hammer*, the *anvil*, and the *stirrup*), which in turn transmit vibrations to the oval window, a thin membrane leading to the inner ear. Because the hammer,

sound The movement of air molecules brought about by a source of vibration.

eardrum The part of the ear that vibrates when sound waves hit it.

cochlea (KOKE-le-uh) A coiled tube in the ear filled with fluid that vibrates in response to sound.

basilar membrane A vibrating structure that runs through the centre of the cochlea, dividing it into an upper chamber and a lower chamber and containing sense receptors for sound.

hair cells Tiny cells covering the basilar membrane that, when bent by vibrations entering the cochlea, transmit neural messages to the brain.

place theory of hearing The theory that different areas of the basilar membrane respond to different frequencies.

anvil, and stirrup act as a set of levers, they not only transmit vibrations but also increase their strength. Moreover, because the opening into the middle ear (the eardrum) is considerably larger than the opening out of it (the *oval window*), the force of sound waves on the oval window becomes amplified. The middle ear, then, acts as a tiny mechanical amplifier.

The *inner ear* is the portion of the ear that changes sound waves into a form in which they can be transmitted to the brain. (As you will see, it also contains the organs that allow us to locate the position of the body and determine how we are moving through space.) When sound enters the inner ear through the oval window, it moves into the **cochlea**, a coiled tube that looks something like a snail and is filled with fluid that vibrates in response to sound. Inside the cochlea is the **basilar membrane**, a structure that runs through the centre of the cochlea, dividing it into an upper chamber and a lower chamber. The basilar membrane is covered with **hair cells**. When the hair cells are bent by the vibrations entering the cochlea, the cells send a neural message to the brain (Cho, 2000; Zhou, Liu, & Davis, 2005). Do you remember what part of the brain processes auditory information? If you said the temporal lobe, you are correct!

Sorting Out Theories of Sound How does the brain sort out wavelengths of different frequencies and intensities? That is, how do we differentiate Kermit the Frog's voice from Darth Vader's voice or screams at a rock concert from

Figure 3.5
Parts of the Ear

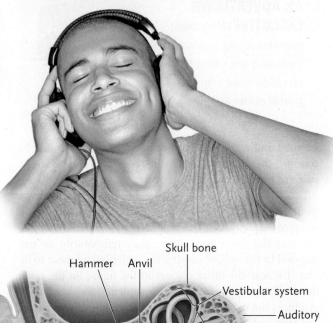

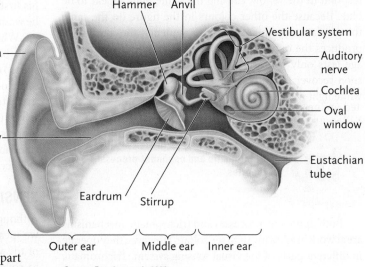

Source: Brooker et al., 2008.

whispers in the library? One clue comes from studies of the basilar membrane, the area in the cochlea that translates physical vibrations into neural impulses. It turns out that sounds affect different areas of the basilar membrane, depending on the frequency of the sound wave. The part of the basilar membrane nearest to the oval window is most sensitive to high-frequency sounds, and the part nearest to the cochlea's inner end is most sensitive to low-frequency sounds. This finding has led to the **place theory of hearing**, which states that different areas of the basilar membrane respond to different frequencies.

Place theory does a good job at explaining how we differentiate various high pitched sounds (for instance, distinguishing Kermit's voice from Miss Piggy's voice), but it does not tell the full story of hearing, because very low frequency sounds (for example, Darth Vader's voice) trigger neurons across such a wide area of the basilar membrane that no single site is involved. Consequently, an additional explanation for hearing has been proposed: frequency

DID YOU KNOW?

Did you know that our outer ears help us locate the source of a sound? Humans have evolved so that one ear is slightly higher on the head than the other ear, and this difference helps us locate sounds from above and below. Look in the mirror. Can you tell which of your ears is higher? On some people, glasses look slightly crooked when this difference is large. If you are one of those people with crooked glasses, don't think of your ears as lopsided but rather as highly evolved!

frequency theory of hearing The theory that the entire basilar membrane acts like a microphone, vibrating as a whole in response to a sound.

semicircular canals Three tubelike structures of the inner ear containing fluid that sloshes through them when the head moves, signalling rotational or angular movement to the brain.

otoliths Tiny, motion-sensitive crystals within the semicircular canals that sense body acceleration.

through a complex series of neural interconnections. As the message is transmitted, it is communicated through neurons that respond to specific types of sounds. Within the auditory cortex itself, there are neurons that respond selectively to very specific sorts of sound features, such as clicks and whistles. Some neurons respond only to a specific pattern of sounds, such as a steady tone but not an intermittent one. Furthermore, specific neurons transfer information about a sound's location through their particular pattern of firing (Middlebrooks et al., 2005; Tervaniemi, Jacobsen, & Röttger, 2006; Wang et al., 2005).

Study tip

Know the difference between the place theory and the frequency theory of hearing.

theory. The **frequency theory of hearing** suggests that the entire basilar membrane acts as a microphone, vibrating as a whole in response to a sound. According to this explanation, the nerve receptors send out signals that are tied directly to the frequency (the number of wave crests per second) of the sounds to which we are exposed, with the number of nerve impulses being a direct function of a sound's frequency. Thus, the higher the pitch of a sound (and therefore the greater the frequency of its wave crests), the greater the number of nerve impulses that are transmitted up the auditory nerve to the brain.

Neither place theory nor frequency theory provides the full explanation for hearing. Place theory provides a better explanation for the sensing of high-frequency sounds, whereas frequency theory explains what happens when low-frequency sounds are encountered. Medium-frequency sounds incorporate both processes (Hirsh & Watson, 1996; Hudspeth, 2000).

After an auditory message leaves the ear, it is transmitted to the auditory cortex of the temporal lobes of the brain

Balance: The Ups and Downs of Life Several structures in the ear are related more to our sense of balance than to our hearing. The **semicircular canals** of the inner ear consist of three tubes containing fluid that sloshes through them when the head moves, signalling rotational or angular movement to the brain. The pull on our bodies caused by the acceleration of forward, backward, or up-and-down motion, as well as the constant pull of gravity, is sensed by the **otoliths**, tiny, motion-sensitive crystals in the semicircular canals. When we move, these crystals shift like grains of sand on a windy beach. The brain's inexperience in interpreting messages from the weightless otoliths is the cause of the space sickness commonly experienced by two-thirds of all space travellers (Flam, 1991; Stern & Koch, 1996).

SMELL AND TASTE

Until he bit into a piece of raw cabbage on that February evening . . . , Raymond Fowler had not thought much about the sense of taste. The cabbage, part of a pasta dish he was preparing for his family's dinner, had an odd, burning taste, but he did not pay it much attention. Then a few minutes later, his daughter handed him a glass of pop, and he took a swallow. "It was like sulfuric acid," he said. "It was like the hottest thing you could imagine boring into your mouth." (Goode, 1999, pp. D1–D2)

The weightlessness of the ear's otoliths produces space sickness in most astronauts.

It was evident that something was very wrong with Fowler's sense of taste. After extensive testing, it became clear that he had damaged the nerves involved in his sense of taste, probably because of a viral infection or a medicine he was taking. (Luckily, a few months later his sense of taste returned to normal.)

Smell Even without disruptions in our ability to perceive the world such as those experienced by Fowler, we all know how important the chemical senses of taste and smell are. Although many animals have keener abilities to detect odours than we do, the human sense of smell (*olfaction*) permits us to detect more than 10,000 separate smells. We also have a good memory for smells, and long-forgotten events and memories—good and bad—can be brought back with the mere whiff of cotton candy, baby powder, or the disinfectant used to clean the restrooms in elementary school (DiLorenzo & Youngentob, 2003; Stevenson & Case, 2005; Willander & Larsson, 2006).

The sense of smell is activated when the molecules of a substance enter the nasal passages and meet *olfactory cells*, the receptor neurons of the nose, which are spread across the nasal cavity. More than 1,000 separate types of receptors have been identified on those cells so far. Each of these receptors is so specialized that it responds only to a small number of different odours. The responses of the separate olfactory cells are transmitted to the brain, where they are combined into recognition of a particular smell (Marshall, Laing, & Jinks, 2006; Murphy et al., 2004).

Taste We are so lucky that we can enjoy the sweetness of jelly beans, the tartness of lemonade, and the saltiness of French fries. We don't consider ourselves as lucky when the bitter aftertaste of certain medicines leaves us longing for a different flavour. The sense of taste (*gustation*) involves receptor cells that respond to four basic qualities: sweet, sour, salty, and bitter. A fifth category, called *umami*, also exists, although there is controversy about whether it qualifies as a fundamental taste. *Umami* is difficult to translate from Japanese, although the English words *meaty* and *savoury* come close. Chemically, umami characterizes food that contains amino acids (the substances that make up proteins) (McCabe & Rolls, 2007; Shi, Huang, & Zhang, 2005).

Although the receptor cells for taste are specialized to respond most strongly to a particular type of taste, they also are capable of responding to other tastes as well. Ultimately, every taste is simply a combination of the basic flavour qualities, in the same way that the primary colours blend into a vast variety of shades and hues (Dilorenzo & Youngentob, 2003; Yeomans, Tepper, & Ritezschel, 2007).

The receptor cells for taste are located in roughly 10,000 *taste buds* distributed across the tongue and other parts of the mouth and throat. The taste buds wear out and are replaced every 10 days or so. Otherwise we would lose the ability to taste.

The sense of taste differs significantly from one person to another, largely as a result of genetic factors. Some people, dubbed "supertasters," are highly sensitive to taste; they have twice as many taste receptors as "non-tasters," who are relatively insensitive to taste. Supertasters (who, for unknown reasons, are more likely to be female than male) find sweets sweeter, cream creamier, and spicy dishes spicier, and weaker concentrations of flavour are enough to satisfy any cravings they may have. In contrast, because they aren't so sensitive to taste, non-tasters may seek out relatively sweeter and fattier foods to maximize the taste. As a consequence, they may be prone to obesity (Bartoshuk, 2000; Pickering & Gordon, 2006; Snyder, Fast, & Bartoshuk, 2004).

THE SKIN SENSES: TOUCH, PRESSURE, TEMPERATURE, AND PAIN

It started innocently when Jennifer Darling hurt her right wrist during gym class. At first it seemed like a simple sprain. But even though the initial injury healed, the excruciating, burning pain accompanying it did not go away. Instead, it spread to her other arm and then to her legs. The pain, which Jennifer described as similar to "a hot iron on your arm," was unbearable—and never stopped.

The source of Darling's pain turned out to be a rare condition known as "reflex sympathetic dystrophy syndrome," or RSDS. For a victim of RSDS, a stimulus as mild as a gentle breeze or the touch of a feather can produce agony. Even bright sunlight or a loud noise can trigger intense pain.

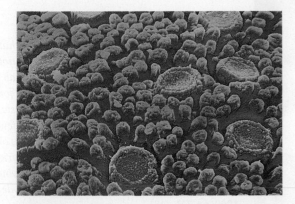

Taste buds may not be much to look at, but they are important for survival. Why do you think the sense of taste might be adaptive?

TRY IT!

Average tasters lie in between supertasters and non-tasters. Bartoshuk and Lucchina lack the data at this time to rate salt reliability, but you can compare your results to others taking the test.

Source: Bartoshuk & Lucchina (1997). Reprinted by permission of Dr. Linda Bartoshuk.

Take a Taste Test

1. **Taste Bud Count**
   Punch a hole with a standard hole punch in a square of wax paper. Paint the front of your tongue with a cotton swab dipped in blue food colouring. Put the wax paper on top of your tongue, just to the right of centre. With a flashlight and magnifying glass, count the number of pink unstained circles. They contain taste buds.

2. **Sweet Taste**
   Rinse your mouth with water before tasting each sample. Put 1/2 cup sugar in a measuring cup, and then add enough water to make 1 cup. Mix. Coat the front half of your tongue, including the tip, with a cotton swab dipped in the solution. Wait a few moments. Rate the sweetness according to the scale below.

3. **Salt Taste**
   Put 2 teaspoons of salt in a measuring cup and add enough water to make 1 cup. Repeat the steps listed above, rating how salty the solution is.

4. **Spicy Taste**
   Add 1 teaspoon of Tabasco sauce to 1 cup of water. Apply with a cotton swab to first half inch of the tongue, including the tip. Keep your tongue out of your mouth until the burn reaches a peak, then rate the burn according to the scale.

Taste Scale

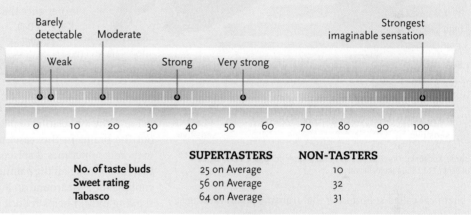

	SUPERTASTERS	NON-TASTERS
No. of taste buds	25 on Average	10
Sweet rating	56 on Average	32
Tabasco	64 on Average	31

Pain like Darling's can be devastating, yet a lack of pain can be equally bad. If you never experienced pain, for instance, you might not notice that your arm had brushed against a hot pan, and you would suffer a severe burn. Similarly, without the warning sign of abdominal pain that typically accompanies an inflamed appendix, your appendix might eventually rupture, spreading a fatal infection throughout your body.

In fact, all our **skin senses**—touch, pressure, temperature, and pain—play a critical role in survival, making us aware of potential danger to our bodies. Most of these senses operate through nerve receptor cells located at various depths throughout the skin, distributed unevenly throughout the body. For example, some areas, such as the fingertips, have many more receptor cells sensitive to touch and as a consequence are notably more sensitive than other areas of the body (Gardner & Kandel, 2000).

Probably the most extensively researched skin sense is pain, and with good reason: About 1.5 million Canadians

skin senses The senses of touch, pressure, temperature, and pain.

between the ages of 12 and 44 experience chronic pain (Statistics Canada, 2010).

Pain is a response to a great variety of different kinds of stimuli. A light that is too bright can produce pain, and sound that is too loud can be painful. One explanation is that pain is an outcome of cell injury; when a cell is damaged, regardless of the source of damage, it releases

Figure 3.6
Skin Sensitivity

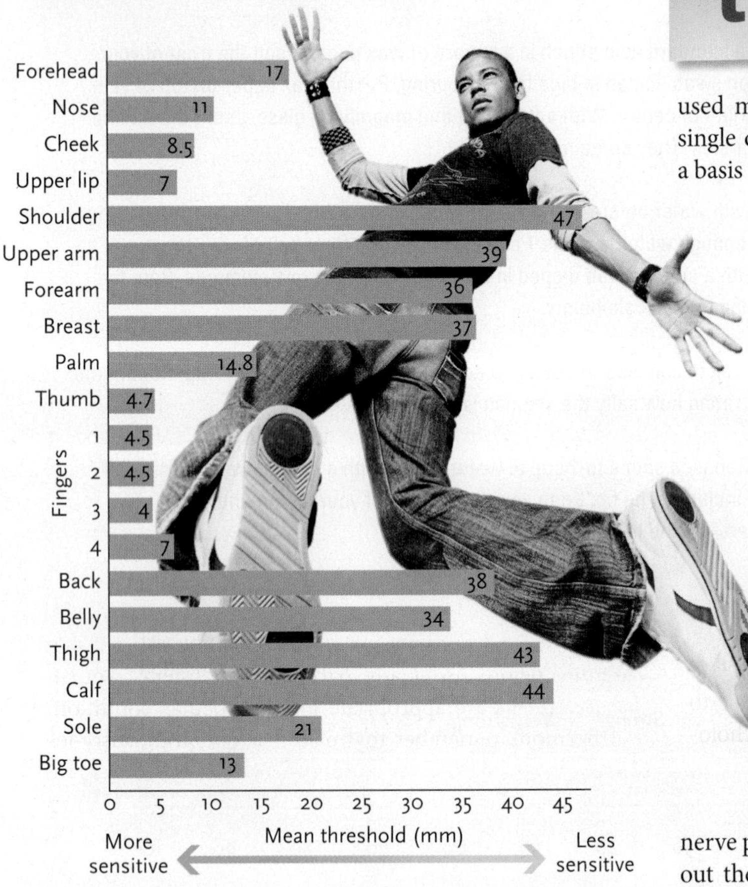

Study tip Remember that there are multiple skin senses, including touch, pressure, temperature, and pain.

Body part	Mean threshold (mm)
Forehead	17
Nose	11
Cheek	8.5
Upper lip	7
Shoulder	47
Upper arm	39
Forearm	36
Breast	37
Palm	14.8
Thumb	4.7
Fingers 1	4.5
Fingers 2	4.5
Fingers 3	4
Fingers 4	7
Back	38
Belly	34
Thigh	43
Calf	44
Sole	21
Big toe	13

0 5 10 15 20 25 30 35 40 45
Mean threshold (mm)

More sensitive ← → Less sensitive

Source: Kenshalo, *The Skin Senses*, 1968. Courtesy of Charles C Thomas, Publisher, Ltd., Springfield, Illinois.

a chemical called *substance P* that transmits pain messages to the brain.

Some people are more susceptible to pain than others. For example, women experience painful stimuli more intensely than men. These gender differences are associated with the production of hormones related to menstrual cycles. In addition, certain genes are linked to the experience of pain—thus we may inherit our sensitivity to pain (Apkarian et al., 2005; Edwards & Fillingim, 2007).

Dr. Ronald Melzack from McGill University in Montreal is a prominent pain researcher and was one of the early researchers who proposed that pain was not simply a "one-dimensional sensation" (Melzack, 2005, p. 201). Instead, Melzack thought that pain involved many other psychological variables, such as motivations and emotions. Melzack developed his theories after visiting patients at a pain clinic. One of his patients, Mrs. Hull, had phantom limb pains after having her leg amputated. Phantom limb is a condition where individuals report feeling pain and burning in the limb that was amputated. Melzack found that Mrs. Hull

used many descriptions of her pain that went beyond a single description of intensity. Melzack used the words as a basis for his research on a new measure of pain, called the McGill Pain Questionnaire. This measure was different than any other pain measurement before it because it not only assessed the sensory aspect of pain, but also the emotional and cognitive aspects of pain (Melzack, 2005). Melzack was also famous for his work on another theory of pain called the gate-control theory.

According to the **gate-control theory of pain**, particular nerve receptors in the spinal cord lead to specific areas of the brain related to pain. When these receptors are activated because of an injury or problem with a part of the body, a "gate" to the brain is opened, allowing us to experience the sensation of pain (Melzack & Katz, 2004).

However, another set of neural receptors can, when stimulated, close the "gate" to the brain, thereby reducing the experience of pain. The gate can be shut in two different ways. First, other impulses can overwhelm the nerve pathways relating to pain, which are spread throughout the brain. In this case, non-painful stimuli compete with and sometimes displace the neural message of pain, thereby shutting off the painful stimulus. This explains why rubbing the skin around an injury (or even listening to distracting music) helps reduce pain. The competing stimuli can overpower the painful ones (Villemure, Slotnick, & Bushnell, 2003).

Psychological factors account for the second way a gate can be shut. Depending on an individual's current emotions, interpretation of events, and previous experience, the brain can close a gate by sending a message down the spinal cord to an injured area, producing a reduction in or relief from pain. Thus, soldiers who are injured in battle may experience no pain—the surprising situation in more than half of all combat injuries. The lack of pain probably occurs because a soldier experiences such relief at still being alive that the brain sends a signal to the injury site to shut down the pain gate (Gatchel & Weisberg, 2000; Pincus & Morley, 2001; Turk, 1994).

Gate-control theory also may explain the effectiveness of *acupuncture*, an ancient Chinese technique in which sharp needles are inserted into various parts of the body. The sensation from the needles may close the gateway to the brain, reducing the experience of pain. It is also possible that the body's own painkillers—called endorphins—as well as positive and negative emotions play a role in opening and closing the gate (Daitz, 2002; Fee et al., 2002; Witt, Jena, & Brinkhaus, 2006).

gate-control theory of pain The theory that particular nerve receptors in the spinal cord lead to specific areas of the brain related to pain.

Psych
At The Movies

Chocolat
This French film conveys sensory experience so well that you can almost smell and taste the chocolate.

At First Sight
After surgery restores a man's eyesight he has trouble making sense of what he sees.

The Illusionist
A magician uses his skills in optical illusions to pursue the love of his life.

The Matrix
A sci-fi adventure in a world where machines control our perceptions, and nothing is what it really seems.

PAIN MANAGEMENT

Are you one of the 1.5 million people in the Canada who suffer from persistent pain? What options are available to help people who live with pain on a daily basis? Psychologists and medical specialists have devised several strategies to fight pain. Among the most important approaches are these:

- *Medication.* Painkilling drugs are the most popular treatment in fighting pain. Medication can be in the form of pills, patches, injections, or liquids. (Kalb, 2003; Pesmen, 2006).

- *Nerve and brain stimulation.* Pain can sometimes be relieved by applying a low-voltage electric current to the painful area. In cases of severe pain, electrodes can be implanted surgically into the brain, or a handheld

The ancient practice of acupuncture is still used as a treatment for pain. How does the gate-control theory of pain explain how acupuncture works?

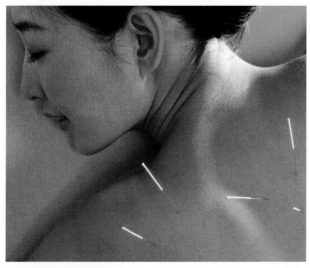

battery pack can stimulate nerve cells to provide direct relief (Campbell & Ditto, 2002; Ross, 2000; Tugay et al., 2007).

- *Light therapy.* Exposure to specific wavelengths of red or infrared light increases the production of enzymes that may promote healing (Evcik et al., 2007; Underwood, 2003).

- *Biofeedback and relaxation techniques.* Using *biofeedback*, people learn to control "involuntary" functions, such as heartbeat and respiration. If the pain involves muscles, as in tension headaches or back pain, sufferers can be trained to relax their bodies systematically (Vitiello, Bonello, & Pollard, 2007).

- *Cognitive restructuring.* Cognitive treatments are effective for people who believe that "This pain will never stop," "The pain is ruining my life," or "I can't take it anymore" and are thereby likely to make their pain even worse. By substituting more positive ways of thinking, people can increase their sense of control—and actually reduce the pain they experience (Bogart et al., 2007; Spanos, Barner, & Lang, 2005).

Of course, it's important to investigate these methods carefully before using any particular treatment. Not all the treatments are appropriate for a particular condition. Furthermore, remember that pain is a symptom of something that is amiss. You need to identify the underlying cause of pain before treating it, so seek professional help to discover its source.

DID YOU KNOW?

Pain relief may come at a cost, literally. Dan Ariely, a behavioural economist who studies pain, had people take a placebo (fake) pain relief pill while enduring electric shocks. Those who were told that each pill cost $2.50 thought the pill worked better at reducing the pain from the shocks than did those who were informed that each pill cost $.10 (Waber et al., 2008).

HOW OUR SENSES INTERACT

When Matthew Blakeslee shapes hamburger patties with his hands, he experiences a vivid bitter taste in his mouth. Esmerelda Jones (a pseudonym) sees blue when she listens to the note C sharp played on the piano; other notes evoke different hues—so much so that the piano keys are actually colour-coded, making it easier for her to remember and play musical scales (Ramachandran, Hubbard, & Butcher, 2004, p. 53).

The explanation? Both of these people have a rare condition known as *synesthesia*, in which exposure to one sensation (such as sound) evokes an additional one (such as vision).

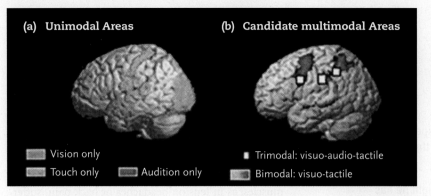

(a) **Unimodal Areas**   (b) **Candidate multimodal Areas**

Vision only
Touch only   Audition only

Trimodal: visuo-audio-tactile
Bimodal: visuo-tactile

Participants in a study examining sensory interaction were exposed to visual, touch, and auditory stimuli. Although some parts of the brain responded to these stimuli independently (a), other parts responded to the three types of stimuli in an integrated fashion (b). The results illustrate the ways in which various sensory stimuli are integrated.

Source: Macaluso & Driver, 2005, Figure 1(a).

The origins of synesthesia are a mystery. It is possible that people with synesthesia have unusually dense neural linkages between the different sensory areas of the brain. Another hypothesis is that they lack neural controls that usually inhibit connections between sensory areas (Pearce, 2007; Ramachandran & Hubbard, 2001; Ramachandran, Hubbard, & Butcher, 2004).

Whatever the reason for synesthesia, it is a rare condition. Even so, everyone's senses interact and integrate in a variety of ways. For example, the taste of food is influenced by its texture and temperature. We perceive food that is warmer as sweeter (think of the sweetness of steamy hot chocolate compared with cold chocolate milk). Spicy foods stimulate some of the same pain receptors that are also stimulated by heat—making the use of "hot" as a synonym for "spicy" quite accurate (Balaban, McBurney, & Affeltranger, 2005; Cruz & Green, 2000; Green & George, 2004).

It's important, then, to think of our senses as interacting with one another. For instance, increasing evidence from brain imaging studies show that the senses work in tandem to build our understanding of the world (Macaluso & Driver, 2005).

Moreover, despite the fact that very different sorts of stimuli activate our individual sensory systems, the senses all react according to the same basic principles that we discussed at the start of this chapter. For example, our responses to visual, auditory, and taste stimuli all follow Weber's law describing our sensitivity to changes in the strength of stimuli.

In short, in some ways our senses are more similar to one another than they are different. Each of them is designed to pick up information from the environment and translate it into useable information. Individually and collectively, our senses help us to understand the complexities of the world, allowing us to navigate through it effectively and intelligently.

BUY IT?

ESP and Subliminal Persuasion

Good consumers of information should question claims of extrasensory perception (ESP) and subliminal perception. ESP may take several different forms such as telepathy (the claimed ability to read other's minds), clairvoyance (the claimed ability to perceive events or objects in out of sight places), precognition (the claimed ability to predict future events), and psychokinesis (the claimed ability to be able to move objects without touching them). As a good critical thinker and consumer of information, the first question you want to ask is "What does the scientific evidence tell us"? Although many people claim to have ESP, the scientific evidence does not support these claims (Milton & Wiseman, 1999). Most of the claims of ESP are anecdotal and cannot be replicated by valid scientific experiments. Remember that good research must be reliable, which means the results must be able to be replicated across several different studies. Even without knowledge of the scientific support, a good critical thinker would ask logical questions such as, "If someone had the ability to predict the future, why wouldn't they have warned people about 9/11, the tsunami on the Indian Ocean in 2004, or the massive earthquake in Japan in 2011"?

Subliminal perception is the ability to perceive information that is below our conscious awareness. Subliminal *persuasion* goes a little further to suggest that our behaviour can be *influenced* by information that is below our conscious awareness. While there is evidence to suggest that we perceive information that is below our conscious awareness (Overgaard & Timmermans, 2010), this is not the same as saying that our behaviour can be influenced by this information. Knowing this, would you spend your money on a download of a subliminal audio file that purported to help you quit smoking or lose weight? While it would be nice if all we had to do to quit smoking or lose weight was to listen to music with embedded subliminal messages, unfortunately research indicates that we cannot be influenced by subliminal persuasion. For example, Greenwald, Spangengerg, Pratanis, and Eskenazi (1991) used a double blind design to test whether participants could improve their memory or increase their self esteem using subliminal audio tapes. The researchers did not find any increase in memory or self-esteem in the groups that listened to the subliminal audio tapes; however they did find that the groups who thought they were listening to a subliminal tape, when it was in fact a placebo tape, did show an increase in self-esteem and memory. This is further evidence of the powerful effect of the placebo, but does not confirm that subliminal persuasion works!

For Review »

What's the difference between sensation and perception?

Sensation is the activation of the sense organs by any source of physical energy. In contrast, perception is the process by which we sort out, interpret, analyze, and integrate stimuli to which our senses are exposed.

How do we respond to the characteristics of physical stimuli?

The absolute threshold is the smallest amount of physical intensity at which a stimulus can be detected. The difference threshold, or just noticeable difference, is the smallest change in the level of stimulation required to sense that a change has occurred. According to E. H. Weber, a just-noticeable difference is a constant proportion of the intensity of an initial stimulus. Sensory adaptation occurs when we become accustomed to a constant stimulus and change our evaluation of it. Repeated exposure to a stimulus results in an apparent decline in sensitivity to it.

How does perception turn sensory stimuli into meaningful information?

Perception is a constructive process in which people try to construct a meaningful interpretation. The Gestalt laws of organization describe the way in which we organize bits and pieces of information into meaningful wholes. In top-down processing, perception is guided by higher-level knowledge, experience, expectations, and motivations. In bottom-up processing, perception consists of the progression of recognizing and processing information from individual components of a stimuli and moving to the perception of the whole. Perceptual constancy permits us to perceive stimuli as unvarying in size, shape, and colour despite changes in the environment or the appearance of the objects being perceived.

How do our sense organs process stimuli?

Vision depends on sensitivity to light, electromagnetic waves in the visible part of the spectrum that are either reflected off objects or produced by an energy source. The eye shapes the light into an image that is transformed into nerve impulses and interpreted by the brain.

Sound, motion, and balance are centred in the ear. Sounds, in the form of vibrating air waves, enter through the outer ear and travel through the auditory canal and the eardrum into the middle ear. In the inner ear, hair cells on the basilar membrane change the sound waves into nerve impulses that are transmitted to the brain.

The skin senses are responsible for the experiences of touch, pressure, temperature, and pain.

Psych think answers

Psych think 1 In the first PSYCH think on p. 62 we asked you if it would be possible to have sensation without perception or perception without sensation? The answer is no! The process starts with sensation when your sensory receptors are activated and the physical energy is transduced into the electrical impulse that is carried to your brain where the information can be perceived. Sensation and perception work together— you cannot have one without the other.

Psych think 2 In the PSYCH think on p. 64 we asked how evolutionary psychologists would explain adaptation. Remember that evolutionary psychologists study how our behaviour has adapted for our survival. When we talk about adaptation in sensation and perception, adaptation means that we start to get used to the sensation that we perceive. When we adapt to a sensation we don't have to think about it anymore so that we can move on to other things. For example, when we walk out into a field in June after the farmer has spread manure the stench is quite strong at first, however it doesn't take long for us to become used to that smell so that we can then move on to doing other things. From an evolutionary point of view this adaptation is adaptive because it has allowed us to put our energy into something else.

Psych think 3 In the PSYCH think on p. 75 we asked if researchers should try to improve normal sensory capabilities beyond their "natural" range, so that human visual or audio capabilities are more sensitive than normal. What did you think? Some potential benefits is that if we had improved vision we would be better drivers, we could recognize people at a greater distance, and surgeons could perform surgery without having to use microscopes. The benefits of having improved audio capabilities would be being able to hear if someone was calling for help and not having to have our iPods on so loud. The downside of improved vision may be that we would have sensitivity to light or sunlight and that driving at night may feel bothersome because of the headlights. The downside of improved audio capabilities would be that we would hear everything. All of the noises and stimulation that already interfere in our daily lives would be amplified.

This is your brain

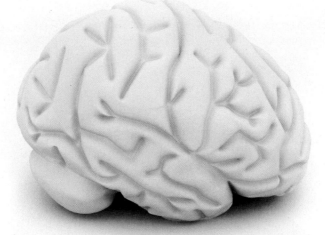

This is your brain on
McGraw Hill connect™

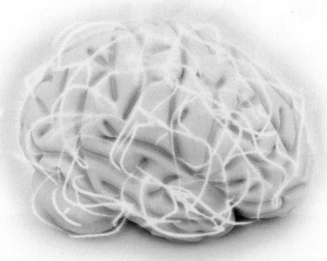

4

States
of Consciousness

WHAT'S TO COME

Sleep and Dreams

Hypnosis and Meditation

Drug Use: The Highs and Lows of Consciousness

Midnight receiver

The crowd roared as running back Donald Dorff, age 67, took the pitch from his quarterback and accelerated smoothly across the artificial turf. As Dorff braked and pivoted to cut back over a tackle, a huge defensive lineman loomed in his path. One hundred twenty pounds of resolve, Dorff did not hesitate. But let the retired grocery merchandiser tell it:

There was a 280-pound tackle waiting for me, so I decided to give him my shoulder. When I came to, I was on the floor in my bedroom. I had smashed into the dresser and knocked everything off it and broke the mirror and just made one heck of a mess. It was 1:30 a.m. (Long, 1987, p. 787).

Dorff, it turned out, was suffering from a rare condition (called REM sleep behaviour disorder), in which the mechanism that usually shuts down bodily movement during dreams does not function properly. People with the malady have been known to hit others, smash windows, punch holes in walls—all while fast asleep.

Luckily, Dorff's problem had a happy ending. With the help of clonazepam, a drug that suppresses movement during dreams, his malady vanished, permitting him to sleep through the night undisturbed.

In this chapter, we consider a range of topics about sleep and, more broadly, states of consciousness. Among these, sleeping and dreaming occur naturally for most of us. In contrast, drug use, hypnosis, and meditation are methods of deliberately altering our subjective understanding of both our physical surroundings and our private internal world.

There are many different ways to understand consciousness. Did you know, for example, that while you are asleep you are still monitoring your environment?

What is consciousness?

As You Read >>

- What is consciousness?
- What happens when we sleep, and what do dreams mean?
- What are the major sleep disturbances?
- What kind of consciousness do hypnotized people experience?
- How do different drugs affect consciousness?

Consciousness is the awareness of the sensations, thoughts, and feelings we experience at a given moment. In *waking consciousness*, we are awake and fully aware of our thoughts, emotions, and perceptions. All other states of consciousness are considered *altered states of consciousness*, although psychologists make a distinction between altered states of consciousness that occur naturally, such as sleep and dreaming, and those that result from the use of alcohol and other drugs.

Sleep and Dreams

Mike Trevino, 29, slept 9 hours in 9 days in his quest to win a 3,000-mile, cross-country bike race. For the first 38 hours and 646 miles, he skipped sleep entirely. Later he napped—with no dreams he can remember—for no more than 90 minutes

▌**consciousness** The awareness of the sensations, thoughts, and feelings we experience at a given moment.

Figure 4.1
Circadian Rhythms

7:00 A.M.
- Hay fever symptoms are worst

6:00 A.M.
- Onset of menstruation is most likely
- Insulin levels in the bloodstream are lowest
- Blood pressure and heart rate begin to rise
- Levels of the stress hormone cortisol increase
- Melatonin levels begin to fall

4:00 A.M.
- Asthma attacks are most likely to occur

2:00 A.M.
- Levels of growth hormone are highest

1:00 A.M.
- Pregnant women are most likely to go into labour
- Immune cells called helper T lymphocytes are at their peak

8:00 A.M.
- Risk for heart attack and stroke is highest
- Symptoms of rheumatoid arthritis are worst
- Helper T lymphocytes are at their lowest daytime level

Noon
- Level of hemoglobin in the blood is at its peak

3:00 P.M.
- Grip strength, respiratory rate, and reflex sensitivity are highest

4:00 P.M.
- Body temperature, pulse rate, and blood pressure peak

6:00 P.M.
- Urinary flow is highest

9:00 P.M.
- Pain threshold is lowest

11:00 P.M.
- Allergic responses are most likely

Source: Young, 2000.

circadian rhythms Physiological fluctuations that occur on approximately a 24-hour cycle.

seasonal affective disorder (SAD) A form of seasonal depression resulting from a disruption in circadian rhythms.

a night. Soon he began to imagine that his support crew was part of a bomb plot. "It was almost like riding in a movie. I thought it was a complex dream, even though I was conscious," says Trevino, who finished second (Springen, 2004, p. 47).

Trevino's case is unusual—in part because he was able to function with so little sleep for so long—and it raises many questions about sleep and dreams. Can we live without sleep? What *is* sleep anyway? And what are dreams?

CIRCADIAN RHYTHMS

Cycling back and forth between wakefulness and sleep is an example of the body's circadian rhythms. **Circadian rhythms** (from the Latin *circa diem*, or "about a day") are physiological fluctuations that take place on a daily basis. Sleeping and waking, for instance, occur naturally to the beat of an internal pacemaker that works on a cycle of about 24 hours. Several other bodily functions, such as body temperature, hormone production, and blood pressure, also follow circadian rhythms (Beersma & Gordijn, 2007; Blatter & Cajochen, 2007; Saper et al., 2005).

Our circadian rhythms are influenced by many environmental factors, such as our Canadian seasons and travelling across time zones. Our shorter Canadian days in the late fall and winter and our longer days in the summer disrupt our circadian rhythms and for some this can result in a form of seasonal depression called **seasonal affective disorder (SAD)**. Individuals with this disorder report feeling excessively tired with increased appetites.

Circadian rhythms can also be influenced by flying across time zones. Imagine flying across Canada from west (e.g., Victoria, British Columbia) to east (e.g., St. John's, Newfoundland). In doing so, you will cross six different time zones and lose 4.5 hours from your day! For example, if you fly from Victoria and arrive in St. John's at 11:00 p.m. it will be dark and close to bedtime. However, for you, it's only 6:30 p.m., which is dinner time. If you stay up to your "regular" 11:00 p.m. bedtime (i.e., Victoria time), it will be 3:30 a.m. in St. John's—and the sun will rise in approximately three hours (depending on the time of year, of course). When the sun rises, it influences your biological clock by stimulating a part of your hypothalamus called the suprachiasmatic nuclei (SCN), which helps control the release of melatonin, a sleep-related chemical in your pineal gland. When you are exposed to light, the SCN decreases the amount of melatonin, making you feel more awake. When you are exposed to darkness, the SCN increases the amount of melatonin, allowing you to feel sleepier. Luckily for you, if you spend a few days in St. John's, you will become used to the new time zone and your circadian rhythms will adjust!

Circadian cycles involve a variety of behaviours. For instance, sleepiness occurs throughout the day in regular patterns, with most of us getting drowsy in mid-afternoon—regardless of whether we have eaten a heavy lunch. By making an afternoon siesta part of their everyday habit, people in several cultures take advantage of the body's natural inclination to sleep at this time (Reilly & Waterhouse, 2007; Takahashi et al., 2004; Wright, 2002).

For long-term problems with sleep, you might consider visiting a sleep disorders centre. For information on accredited clinics, consult the Canadian Sleep Society at www.canadiansleepsociety.ca.

THE STAGES OF SLEEP

Many people consider sleep a time of tranquility, when we set aside the tensions of the day and spend the night in uneventful slumber. However, a scientific look at sleep shows that a good deal of brain and physical activity occurs throughout the night (Gorfine & Zisapel, 2009).

While we sleep, our mental and physical states change all night long. Measures of electrical activity in the brain show that the brain is active throughout the night. It produces electrical signals with systematic, wavelike patterns that change in height (or amplitude) and speed (or frequency). There is also significant physical activity in muscle and eye movements.

As the wavelike electrical patterns change, we move through a series of distinct stages of sleep during a night's rest. There are five stages, known as *stage 1* through *stage 4* and *REM sleep*. We move through these stages in cycles lasting about 90 minutes. (Actually, these 90-minute cycles are typical only of young, healthy adults who do not abuse drugs.) Each of these sleep stages is associated with a unique pattern of brain waves. What is interesting is the way we cycle through sleep. For example, our sleep cycle starts with stage 1 then stage 2, stage 3, stage 4 and then back to stage 3, stage 2, and then REM sleep. We always enter REM from stage 2 sleep and then go back to stage 2 sleep from REM. Let's now discuss what happens in each of the stages of sleep.

Figure 4.2

The Stages of Sleep

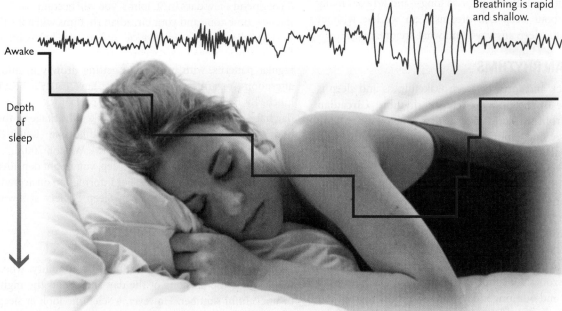

Stage 1
Light sleep. Muscle activity slows. Occasional muscle twitching. Theta waves.

Stage 2
Breathing and heart rate slows down. Slight decrease in body temperature. Sleep spindles present.

Stage 3
Deep sleep begins. Brain begins to generate slow delta waves.

Stage 4
Very deep sleep. Rhythmic breathing. Limited muscle activity. Brain produces delta waves.

Rapid eye movement (REM)
Brainwaves speed up and dreaming occurs. Muscles relax and heart rate increases. Breathing is rapid and shallow.

Awake

Depth of sleep

Source: Hobson, 1989.

When people first go to sleep, they move from a waking state in which they are relaxed with their eyes closed into **stage 1 sleep**, which has relatively rapid, low-amplitude brain waves. This stage is a transition between wakefulness and sleep and lasts only a few minutes. During stage 1, images sometimes appear, as if we were viewing still photos, although this is not true dreaming. Stage 1 occurs only when we first fall asleep.

As sleep becomes deeper, we enter **stage 2 sleep**. Young adults in their early 20s spend about half of their sleep time in this stage. Stage 2 is characterized by a slower,

more regular wave pattern with momentary interruptions of sharply pointed wave spikes called sleep spindles. It becomes increasingly difficult to awaken a person from sleep as stage 2 progresses. Drs. Stuart Fogel and Carlyle Smith from Trent University in Peterborough, Ontario, conducted an experiment on the changes in the amount of stage 2 sleep and the number of sleep spindles after learning a simple tracing task. The researchers found that the experimental group (who completed the simple motor learning tasks) had longer periods of stage 2 sleep as well as a significant increase in the number of sleep spindles following the learning compared to the control group. The researchers concluded that sleep spindles are important for simple procedural motor memories (Fogel & Smith, 2006).

In **stage 3 sleep**, the brain waves become slower, with higher peaks and lower valleys in the wave pattern. By the time sleepers arrive at **stage 4 sleep**, the pattern is even slower and more regular. In stage 4, we are least responsive to efforts to wake us up and are quite possibly aggravated if the attempt is successful.

stage 1 sleep The state of transition between wakefulness and sleep, characterized by relatively rapid, low-amplitude brain waves.

stage 2 sleep A sleep deeper than that of stage 1, characterized by a slower, more regular wave pattern, along with momentary interruptions of "sleep spindles."

stage 3 sleep A sleep characterized by slow brain waves, with greater peaks and valleys in the wave pattern than in stage 2 sleep.

stage 4 sleep The deepest stage of sleep, during which we are least responsive to outside stimulation.

Sleep Quiz

Although sleeping is something we all do for a significant part of our lives, myths and misconceptions about the topic abound. To test your own knowledge of sleep and dreams, try answering the following questions before reading further.

1. Some people never dream. True or false? _____
2. Most dreams are caused by body sensations such as an upset stomach. True or false? _____
3. It has been proved that people need eight hours of sleep to maintain mental health. True or false? _____
4. When people do not recall their dreams, it is probably because they are secretly trying to forget them. True or false? _____
5. Depriving someone of sleep will inevitably cause the individual to become mentally imbalanced. True or false? _____
6. If we lose some sleep we will eventually make up all the lost sleep the next night or another night. True or false? _____
7. No one has been able to go more than 48 hours without sleep. True or false? _____
8. Everyone is able to sleep and breathe at the same time. True or false? _____
9. Sleep enables the brain to rest because little brain activity takes place during sleep. True or false? _____
10. Drugs have been proved to provide a long-term cure for sleeplessness. True or false? _____

Source: Palladino & Carducci (1984).

Stage 4 sleep typically occurs during the early part of the night. In the first half of the night, sleep is dominated by stages 3 and 4. In the second half, we spend more time in stage 2—as well as a fifth stage, REM, when dreaming occurs.

REM SLEEP: THE PARADOX OF SLEEP

Several times a night, when sleepers have cycled back to a shallower state of sleep in stage 2, something curious happens. The heart rate increases and becomes irregular, blood pressure rises, breathing rate increases, and males—even male infants—have erections. Most characteristic of this period is the back-and-forth movement of the eyes, as if the sleeper were watching an action-filled movie. This period of sleep is called **rapid eye movement**, or **REM, sleep** and it contrasts with stages 1 through 4, which are collectively labelled *non-REM* (or *NREM*) sleep. REM sleep occupies a little over 20% of adults' total sleeping time.

rapid eye movement (REM) sleep Sleep occupying 20% of an adult's sleeping time, characterized by increased heart rate, blood pressure, and breathing rate; erections; eye movements; and the experience of dreaming.

Figure 4.3
The Sleep Cycle

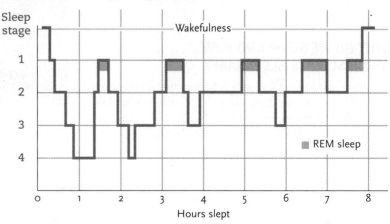

Source: From Ernest Hartmann, *The Biology of Dreaming* (1967), p. 6. Courtesy of Charles C. Thomas Publisher, Ltd., Springfield, Illinois.

DID YOU KNOW?

Although mammals and birds display REM sleep, reptiles do not. So you may notice your dog or cat in REM sleep by the way their eyes dart back and forth under their eyelids, but you will not see this in your pet lizard!

Paradoxically, while all this activity is occurring, the major muscles of the body appear to be paralyzed. In addition, and most important, REM sleep correlates positively with dreaming. In other words, REM is usually accompanied by dreams, which—whether or not people remember them—are experienced by *everyone* during some part of the night. Although some dreaming occurs in non-REM stages of sleep, dreams are most likely to occur in the REM period, when they are the most vivid and most easily remembered (Conduit, Crewther, & Coleman, 2004; Titone, 2002). Most people enter REM about every 90 minutes, which means that we average four to five REM periods (i.e., dream periods) a night, with the first one being the shortest and the latter few being the longest.

There is good reason to believe that REM sleep plays a critical role in everyday human functioning. People deprived of REM sleep—by being awakened every time they begin to display the physiological signs of that stage—show a *rebound effect* when allowed to rest undisturbed. With this rebound effect, REM-deprived sleepers spend significantly more time in REM sleep than they normally would (Villablanca, de Andrés, & Garzón, 2003).

Study tip

Remember the five stages of sleep (stage 1, stage 2, stage 3, stage 4, and REM sleep), which produce different brain-wave patterns. Also remember that we cycle through the stages from stage 1-4, and then back to stage 2 before we enter REM. For example, we cycle from stage 1-2-3-4-3-2-REM-2-3-4-3-2-REM, etc.

WHY DO WE SLEEP AND HOW MUCH SLEEP IS NECESSARY?

Sleep is a requirement for normal human functioning. Surprisingly, though, we don't know exactly what sleep does or why it is necessary. It seems reasonable that our bodies would require a tranquil "rest and relaxation" period to become revitalized. Indeed, experiments with rats show that total sleep deprivation results in death (Rechtschaffen et al., 2002). Further, studies of sleep deprivation in humans show that we experience weakened immune systems, difficulty concentrating, and are more easily irritated when deprived of sleep (Hui et al., 2007; Palma et al., 2007). But why?

Some researchers, using an evolutionary perspective, have suggested that sleep permitted our ancestors to conserve energy at night, a time when food was relatively hard to come by. Others have proposed that the reduced activity of the brain during non-REM sleep may give neurons in the brain a chance to repair themselves. Another hypothesis suggests that the onset of REM sleep stops the release of neurotransmitters called *monoamines*, and so permits receptor cells to rest so that their sensitivity will be greater during periods of wakefulness. Still, these explanations remain speculative (McNamara, 2004; Porkka-Heiskanen et al., 1997; Siegel, 2003; Steiger, 2007).

Airlines whose pilots fly for many hours with little sleep put the safety of their flight crews and passengers at risk.

Figure 4.4

Working More Means Sleeping Less

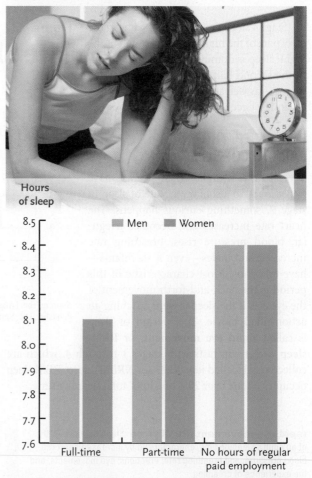

Hours of sleep

Source: Statistics Canada, General Social Survey, 2005. *More Time Working Means Less Sleep.* http://www41.statcan.gc.ca/2008/0075/ceb0075_001-eng.htm.

Scientists have also been unable to establish just how much sleep we need. Most people sleep between seven and eight hours each night. In addition, there is wide variability among individuals, with some people needing as little as three hours of sleep. Sleep requirements also vary over the course of a lifetime: As they age, people generally need less and less sleep (Gangwisch et al., 2008). This is why you often see people your grandparent's age out walking early in the morning!

People who participate in sleep deprivation experiments, in which they are kept awake for stretches as long as 200 hours, show no lasting effects. It's no fun—they feel weary and irritable, can't concentrate, and show a loss of creativity, even after only minor deprivation. They also show a decline in logical reasoning ability. However, after being allowed to sleep uninterruptedly, they bounce back and are able to perform normally after just a few days (Dinges et al., 1997; McClelland & Pilcher, 2007; Veasey et al., 2002).

In short, as far as we know, most people suffer no permanent consequences of temporary sleep deprivation. But even a temporary lack of sleep can make us feel edgy, slow our reaction time, and lower our performance on academic and physical tasks. In addition, we put ourselves, and others, at serious risk when we do routine activities, such as driving, when we're very sleepy (Anderson & Home, 2006; Philip et al., 2005; Stickgold, Winkelman, & Wehrwein, 2004).

THE IMPACT OF ELECTRONICS ON SLEEP

Statistics Canada has shown that working longer hours and looking after children significantly impacts the amount of sleep that Canadians get (see Figure 4.4). But work and childcare are not the only impediments to a good night's sleep. More and more young people are becoming sleep deprived because of their use of electronics at bedtime or while they are supposed to be sleeping (Paddock, 2010).

Watching television, surfing the Internet, texting, or listening to music has become a regular nighttime activity for many adolescents and young adults (Cain & Gradisar, 2010). Recent research has shown that use of electronic devices at bedtime or during the night is related to anxiety, depression, irritability, and extreme tiredness during the day, and sleep disturbances such as insomnia during the night (Cain & Gradisar, 2010; Paddock, 2010).

THE FUNCTION AND MEANING OF DREAMING

The average person experiences 150,000 dreams by the age of 70. Although dreams tend to be subjective to the person having them, there are some common elements that frequently occur in everyone's dreams. Typically, people dream about everyday events, such as going to the supermarket, working, and preparing a meal. Students dream about going to class; professors dream about teaching. Dental patients dream of getting their teeth drilled; dentists dream of drilling the wrong tooth (Domhoff, 1996; Schredl, & Piel, 2005; Taylor & Bryant, 2007).

What, if anything, do dreams mean? Whether dreams have a specific significance and function is a question that scientists have considered for many years. To address this question, they have developed alternative theories.

Do Dreams Have Hidden Meaning? The Psychoanalytic Approach Sigmund Freud viewed dreams as a guide to the unconscious (Freud, 1900). In his **unconscious wish fulfillment theory**, he proposed that dreams represent unconscious wishes that dreamers desire to see fulfilled. However, because these wishes are threatening to the dreamer's conscious awareness, the

> **unconscious wish fulfillment theory** Sigmund Freud's theory that dreams represent unconscious wishes that dreamers desire to see fulfilled.

Figure 4.5
What Do People Dream About?

Percentage of respondents reporting at least one thematic event

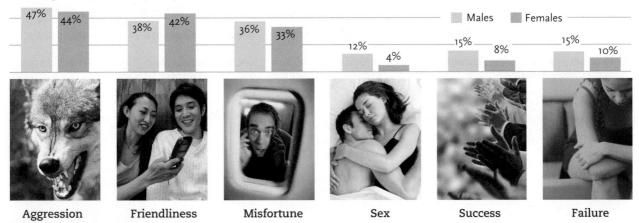

| Aggression | Friendliness | Misfortune | Sex | Success | Failure |

Males 47% — Females 44% (Aggression); Males 38% — Females 42% (Friendliness); Males 36% — Females 33% (Misfortune); Males 12% — Females 4% (Sex); Males 15% — Females 8% (Success); Males 15% — Females 10% (Failure)

Source: Schneigler & Domhoff, 2002.

actual wishes—called the **latent content of dreams**—are disguised. The true subject and meaning of a dream has little to do with its apparent storyline, which Freud called the **manifest content of dreams**.

To Freud, interpreting a dream's manifest content was necessary to understand the true (latent) meaning of the dream. As people described their dreams to him, Freud tried to associate symbols in the manifest content with the latent content. He argued that certain symbols and their meanings were universal. For example, to Freud, dreams in which a person is flying symbolized a wish for sexual intercourse.

Many psychologists reject Freud's view that dreams typically represent unconscious wishes and that particular objects and events in a dream are symbolic. Instead, they consider the direct, overt action of a dream to be the dream's meaning. For example, a dream in which we are walking down a long hallway to take an exam for which we haven't studied does not relate to unconscious, unacceptable wishes. Instead, it may just mean that we are concerned about an impending test (Cartwright, Agargum, & Kirkby, 2006; Nikles et al., 1998; Picchioni et al., 2002).

Dreams-for-Survival Theory: The Cognitive Approach According to the **dreams-for-survival theory**, dreams permit us to reconsider information that is critical for our daily survival. In this view, dreaming

latent content of dreams According to Freud, the "disguised" meanings of dreams, hidden by more obvious subjects.

manifest content of dreams According to Freud, the apparent storyline of dreams.

dreams-for-survival theory The theory suggesting that dreams permit information that is critical for our daily survival to be reconsidered and reprocessed during sleep.

activation-synthesis theory Hobson's theory that the brain produces random electrical energy during REM sleep that stimulates memories lodged in various portions of the brain.

is an inheritance from our animal ancestors, whose small brains were unable to sift through all the information they received during waking hours. Consequently, dreaming provided a mechanism for processing information 24 hours a day.

According to this theory, dreams represent concerns about our daily lives, illustrating our uncertainties, indecisions, ideas, and desires. Dreams are seen as consistent with everyday living and represent key concerns growing out of our daily experiences (Ross, 2006; Winson, 1990).

Research supports the dreams-for-survival theory, suggesting that certain dreams permit people to focus on and consolidate memories, particularly those related to motor skills. For example, rats seem to dream about mazes that they learned to run through during the day, at least according to the patterns of brain activity produced while they are sleeping (Kenway & Wilson, 2001; Kuriyama, Stickgold, & Walker, 2004; Smith, 2006; Stickgold et al., 2001).

Activation-Synthesis Theory: The Biological Approach According to psychiatrist J. Allan Hobson, who proposed **activation-synthesis theory**, the brain produces

Study **tip**

Figure 4.6 summarizes the differences between the three main explanations of dreaming.

Figure 4.6
Three Theories of Dreams

Theory	Approach	Basic Explanation	Meaning of Dreams	Is Meaning of Dream Disguised?
Unconscious wish fulfillment theory (Freud)	Psychoanalytic approach	Dreams represent unconscious wishes the dreamer wants to fulfill	Latent content reveals unconscious wishes	Yes, by manifest content of dreams
Dreams-for-survival theory	Cognitive approach	Information relevant to daily survival is reconsidered and reprocessed	Clues to everyday concerns about survival	Not necessarily
Activation-synthesis theory	Biological approach	Dreams are the result of random activation of various memories, which are tied together in a logical story line	Dream scenario that is constructed is related to dreamer's concerns	Not necessarily

random electrical energy during REM sleep, possibly as a result of changes in neurotransmitter production. In theory, this electrical energy randomly stimulates memories lodged in various portions of the brain. Because we have a need to make sense of our world even while asleep, the brain takes these chaotic memories and weaves them into a logical story line, filling in the gaps to produce a rational scenario (Hobson, 2005; Porte & Hobson, 1996).

However, Hobson does not entirely reject the view that dreams reflect unconscious wishes. He suggests that the particular scenario a dreamer produces is not random but instead is a clue to the dreamer's fears, emotions, and concerns. What starts out as a random process, then, culminates in something meaningful. For example, suppose your visual memory of a horse is stimulated, and your auditory memory of a cat's meow is stimulated, and your emotional memory of sadness is stimulated. And let's say that your biggest worry right now is your mother's health. Your brain's attempt to make sense of these sensations and your anxiety might result in a storyline like this: You dream you are walking a horse toward your mother but the horse meows and turns into a cat, which makes you very sad.

Psych think

> > > Suppose that a new "miracle pill" allows a person to function with only one hour of sleep per night. However, because a night's sleep is so short, a person who takes the pill will never dream again. Knowing what you do about the functions of sleep and dreaming, what would be some advantages and drawbacks of such a pill?

SLEEP DISTURBANCES

Sleep disturbances fall under two major categories: *dysomnias* and *parasomnias*. Dysomnias result in problems with the quality of your sleep, such as the timing and amount you sleep and include insomnia, narcolepsy, and sleep apnea. The parasomnias on the other hand, result in abnormal disturbances while you sleep and include nightmares, night terrors, sleep walking, sleep talking, and REM sleep behaviour disorder.

BUY IT?

Getting a Good Night's Sleep

Do you have trouble sleeping? You're not alone. According to Statistics Canada, 3.3 million Canadians have problems falling asleep. If you are one of those people, should you run out and buy a "white noise" CD to help you sleep? Being the good consumer that you are, of course you said that you would first see if there is any valid research supporting the use of such a device! In fact, researchers LeAnne Forquer and C. Merle Johnson recently investigated the use of a white noise generator to decrease night waking in college students (Forquer & Johnson, 2007). Although the study only had a sample size of four students, the researchers found that using a white noise generator did result in less night waking for the college students. However, once students stopped using the white noise generator, their sleep problems returned. Knowing this, you might want to consider some free alternatives to a white noise generator. Psychologists studying sleep disturbances have a number of suggestions for overcoming insomnia (Benca, 2005; Edinger et al., 2001; Finley & Cowley, 2005). Here are some ideas:

• *Exercise during the day (at least six hours before bedtime) and avoid naps.* Not

surprisingly, it helps to be tired before going to sleep!

• *Choose a regular bedtime and stick to it.* Going to sleep at the same time every day helps your natural internal rhythms regulate your body.

• *Avoid drinks with caffeine after lunch.* The effects of beverages such as coffee, tea, and some soft drinks can linger for as long as 8 to 12 hours after they are consumed.

• *Drink a glass of warm milk at bedtime.* Milk contains the chemical tryptophan, which helps people fall asleep.

• *Try not to sleep.* This approach works because people often have difficulty falling asleep because they are trying so hard. A better strategy is to go to bed only when you feel tired. If you don't get to sleep within 10 minutes, leave the bedroom and do something else, returning to bed only when you feel sleepy. Continue this process all night if necessary. But get up at your usual hour in the morning, and don't take any naps during the day. After three or four weeks, most people become conditioned to associate their beds with sleep—and fall asleep rapidly at night (Sloan et al., 1993; Smith, 2001; Ubell, 1993).

Dysomnias: Poor Sleep Quality At one time or another, almost all of us have difficulty sleeping—a condition known as *insomnia*. It could be due to a particular situation, such as the breakup of a relationship, concern about an upcoming test, or the loss of a job. Some cases of insomnia, however, have no obvious cause. Some people are simply unable to fall asleep easily, or they go to sleep readily but wake up frequently during the night. About one in three people will experience insomnia at some point in their lives (American Insomnia Association, 2005; Bains, 2006; Cooke & Ancoli-Israel, 2006).

Insomnia can have many negative effects, such as an increase in irritability, a lack of attention, poor memory, and sleepiness through the day. Researchers from Laval University in Quebec found that severely fatigued participants with insomnia had a lower quality of life (i.e., more depression and anxiety, reduced motivation, and more bodily pains) than participants who were less fatigued (Fortier-Brochu et al., 2010).

People who fall asleep uncontrollably for short periods while they are awake have *narcolepsy*. No matter what the activity—holding a heated conversation, exercising, or driving—a narcoleptic will suddenly fall asleep. People with narcolepsy go directly from wakefulness to REM sleep, skipping the other stages. The causes of narcolepsy are not known, although there could be a genetic component, because narcolepsy runs in families (Ervik, Abdelnoor, & Heier, 2006; Mahmood & Black, 2005).

Other sleep problems are less common than insomnia, although they are still widespread. For instance, some 20 million people suffer from *sleep apnea*, a condition in which a person has difficulty breathing while sleeping. The result is disturbed sleep, because the person is constantly reawakened when the lack of oxygen becomes great enough to trigger a waking response. Some people with sleep apnea wake as many as 500 times during the course of a night, although they may not even be aware that they woke up. Not surprisingly, sleep disrupted by apnea results in extreme fatigue the next day. Sleep apnea also may play a role in *sudden infant death syndrome (SIDS)*, a mysterious killer of seemingly normal infants who die while sleeping (Aloia, Smith, & Arendt, 2007; Gami et al., 2005; Rambaud & Guilleminault, 2004).

Parasomnias: Abnormal Disturbances During Sleep Waking up suddenly from a really scary dream is not uncommon, no matter what your age. If you remember your scary dream in vivid detail and feel the emotions associated with that scary dream, you have likely experienced a *nightmare*. Nightmares usually occur towards the end of your sleep cycle and happen during REM sleep. Unlike nightmares, *night terrors* typically occur in younger children and in stages 3 and 4 earlier in the sleep cycle. Small children who have night terrors may scream, bringing terrified parents running. But typically these children will not understand why the parents have come and will not recall why they screamed.

Another one of the parasomnias is *sleepwalking*. Sleepwalkers usually have a vague consciousness of the world around them, and they may be able to walk with agility around obstructions in a crowded room. Unless a sleepwalker wanders into a dangerous environment, sleepwalking typically poses little risk (Baruss, 2003; Guilleminault et al., 2005; Lee-Chiong, 2006). Sleepwalking happens in stage 3 or 4 (when there is no sleep paralysis so the person is able to walk around) and although they have a vague consciousness, the individual typically has no recollection of sleepwalking when they awake the next morning. Similar to sleepwalking, *sleep talking* typically occurs in stages 3 or 4, but can occur in all stages of sleep. The sleep talker is usually unaware that he or she is talking, and does not recall what was said when waking in the morning. Sleep talking is harmless and usually is more disruptive to others who may be disturbed by the sounds as they try to sleep.

Get Involved!

You can start your own dream study group. Have members set their alarms for random times throughout the night and keep a dream journal. If you happen to be awakened during REM, you can usually remember what you were dreaming, and if you act quickly, you can record your dream. Before meeting, have each member pick one dream to share with the group and exchange interpretation ideas. Often members' interpretations are off-track, but occasionally someone may come up with a helpful insight. Most interesting are those interpretations that you quickly dismiss but that come back to haunt you.

Donald Dorff, the gentleman we described at the beginning of the chapter, had a parasomnia called *REM sleep behaviour disorder*. Individuals with this disorder, such as Donald Dorff, act out their dreams while they sleep because their muscles have failed to become paralyzed during REM sleep. This disorder can be very dangerous for the individual, but also for anyone else who may be sharing the individual's bed. It tends to be more common among men over the age of 50, and may be caused by use of antidepressants or by some sort of neurological disorder.

Hypnosis and Meditation

You are feeling relaxed and drowsy. You are getting sleepier. Your body is becoming limp. Your eyelids are feeling heavier. Your eyes are closing; you can't keep them open anymore. You are totally relaxed. Now, place your hands above your head. But you will find they are getting heavier and heavier—so heavy you can barely keep them up. In fact, although you are straining as hard as you can, you will be unable to hold them up any longer.

An observer watching this scene would notice a curious phenomenon. Many of the people listening to the voice are dropping their arms to their sides. The reason for this strange behaviour? These people have been hypnotized.

HYPNOSIS: A TRANCE-FORMING EXPERIENCE?

People under **hypnosis** appear to be in a trancelike state of heightened susceptibility to the suggestions of others. In some respects, it appears that they are asleep. Yet other aspects of their behaviour contradict this notion, because they are attentive to the hypnotist's suggestions and may carry out bizarre or silly suggestions.

Despite their compliance when hypnotized, people do not lose all will of their own. They will not perform antisocial behaviours, and they will not carry out self-destructive acts if they realize the acts are destructive. People will not reveal hidden truths about themselves, and they are capable of lying. Moreover, despite popular misconceptions, people cannot be hypnotized against their will (Gwynn & Spanos, 1996; Raz, 2007).

DID YOU KNOW?

Imagine that your dentist suggests that you may experience a sour taste in your mouth and/or hear yourself being paged over a speaker while in the dental chair. How vulnerable do you think you would be to the power of suggestion? A creative and humorous study found dental patients to be more suggestible to such hallucinations while in a state of consciousness induced by nitrous oxide (laughing gas).

Source: Whalley & Brooks, 2009

There are wide variations in people's susceptibility to hypnosis. About 5% to 20% of the population cannot be hypnotized at all, and some 15% are very easily hypnotized. Most people fall somewhere in between. Moreover, the ease with which a person is hypnotized correlates with a number of other characteristics. People who are readily hypnotized are also easily absorbed while reading books or listening to music, becoming unaware of what is happening around them, and they often spend an unusual amount of time daydreaming. In sum, then, they show a high ability to concentrate and to become completely focused on what they are doing (Benham, Woody, & Wilson, 2006; Kirsch & Braffman, 2001; Rubichi et al., 2005).

> **People cannot be hypnotized against their will.**

A Different State of Consciousness? Some psychologists consider hypnosis a state of consciousness that differs significantly from other states. In this view, the high suggestibility, increased ability to recall and construct images, and acceptance of suggestions that clearly contradict reality suggest that hypnosis is a different state, one that involves dissociation (a splitting of consciousness into separate parts). Moreover, changes in electrical activity in the brain during hypnosis support the position that hypnosis is distinctly different from normal waking consciousness (Fingelkurts, Fingelkurts, & Kallio, 2007; Hilgard, 1992; Kallio & Revonsuo, 2003). Not everyone agrees with this position.

On the other side of this controversial issue are psychologists who believe that hypnosis occurs during normal waking consciousness. They argue that altered brain-wave patterns are not sufficient to demonstrate a qualitative

hypnosis A trancelike state of heightened susceptibility to the suggestions of others.

meditation A learned technique for refocusing attention that brings about an altered state of consciousness.

Kihlstrom, 2005b; Lynn et al., 2000). As arguments about the true nature of hypnosis continue, though, one thing is clear: Hypnosis has been used successfully to solve practical human problems. In fact, psychologists working in many different areas have found hypnosis to be a reliable, effective tool for pain control, smoking reduction, improvement of athletic performance, and treatment of psychological disorders.

MEDITATION: REGULATING OUR OWN CONSCIOUSNESS

When traditional practitioners of the Eastern religion of Zen Buddhism want to achieve greater spiritual insight, they turn to meditation, a technique that has been used for centuries to alter consciousness. **Meditation** is a learned technique for focusing attention that brings about an altered state of consciousness. A popular meditation practice is to repeat a *mantra*—a sound, word, or syllable—over and over. In other forms of meditation, the focus may be on a picture, flame, or specific part of the body. Still other forms of meditation, including some styles of yoga, engage the body and mind in mutual, concentrated focus. Regardless of the type, the key to meditation is to concentrate so thoroughly that the meditator reaches a different state of consciousness.

After meditation, people often report feeling thoroughly relaxed. They sometimes relate that they have gained new insights into themselves and their problems. The long-term practice of meditation may even improve health because of the physiological changes it produces. For example, during meditation, oxygen usage decreases, heart rate and blood pressure decline, and brain-wave patterns change (Arambula et al., 2001; Barnes et al., 2004; Lee, Kleinman, & Kleinman, 2007).

Anyone can achieve relaxation through meditation by following a simple procedure. The fundamentals include sitting in a quiet room with the eyes closed, breathing deeply and rhythmically, and repeating a word or sound—such as the word *one*—over and over. Practiced twice a day for 20 minutes, the technique is effective in bringing about relaxation (Aftanas & Golosheykin, 2005; Benson et al., 1994).

Another common form of meditation is called mindful meditation. In this type of meditation the individual tries to be in the present moment while meditating. To do so individual focuses on the breath and acknowledges any thoughts that may arise but then ignores the thoughts and refocuses on the breath. Some researchers believe that mindfulness meditation can help with academic success.

difference, because no other specific physiological changes occur when people are in trances. Nick Spanos (now deceased) was a professor at Carleton University in Ottawa who argued against the notion that hypnosis involved a splitting of consciousness. Instead, Spanos used the experimental method to demonstrate that people under hypnosis were highly motivated to act as they thought they were expected to (i.e., they were playing the role of someone who had been hypnotized) (Spanos et al., 1996).

Moreover, little support exists for the contention that adults can recall memories of childhood events accurately while hypnotized. That lack of evidence suggests that there is nothing qualitatively special about the hypnotic trance (Hongchun & Ming, 2006; Lynn et al., 2003; Lynn, Fassler, & Knox, 2005).

More recent models suggest that the hypnotic state may best be viewed as involving normal waking consciousness, but with some important differences (Jamieson, 2007;

Study tip

The question of whether hypnosis represents a different state of consciousness or is similar to normal waking consciousness is an unresolved issue in psychology.

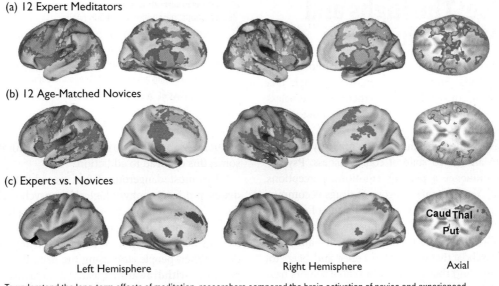

(a) 12 Expert Meditators

(b) 12 Age-Matched Novices

(c) Experts vs. Novices

Caud Thal
Put

Left Hemisphere   Right Hemisphere   Axial

To understand the long-term effects of meditation, researchers compared the brain activation of novice and experienced meditators. These fMRI brain scans show the regions of brain activation in (a) expert meditators, who had between 10,000 and 54,000 hours of practice in meditating; (b) novice meditators, who had no experience mediating; and (c) the comparison between the two. In (c), red hues show greater activation in the experts, and blue hues show greater activation for the novices. The findings suggest that long-term meditation produces significant changes in regions of the brain related to concentration and attention.

For example, Roudan Shao and Daniel Skarlicki from the University of British Columbia wanted to determine if mindfulness was associated with higher academic performance in an MBA program. The researchers used a correlational study and found that there was a significant positive relationship for mindfulness and academic performance in women, however performance was not found to be significant in men (Shao & Skarlicki, 2009).

From the perspective of ...

A PHYSICIAN Would you recommend meditation to your patients as a way to help them with stress? Why or why not?

CROSS-CULTURAL ROUTES TO ALTERED STATES OF CONSCIOUSNESS

A group of Canadian Aboriginal people sit in a steaming sweat lodge as water is thrown on sizzling rocks to send billows of scalding steam into the air.

Aztec priests smear themselves with a mixture of crushed poisonous herbs, hairy black worms, scorpions, and lizards. Sometimes they drink the potion.

During the sixteenth century, a devout Hasidic Jew lies across the tombstone of a celebrated scholar. As he murmurs the name of God repeatedly, he seeks to be possessed by the soul of the dead wise man's spirit. If successful, he will attain a mystical state, and the deceased's words will flow out of his mouth.

Each of these rituals has a common goal: suspension from the bonds of everyday awareness and access to an altered state of consciousness. These rituals represent an apparently universal effort to alter consciousness (Bartocci, 2004; Fine, 1994; Irwin, 2006). Some scholars suggest that the quest to alter consciousness represents a basic human desire (Siegel, 1989). Whether or not we accept this view, it is clear that variations in states of consciousness share several characteristics across a variety of cultures. Alterations in states of consciousness can lead to changes in thinking, people's sense of time can become disturbed, and their perceptions of the physical world and of themselves may change. They may lose self-control and do things that they would never do otherwise. Finally, they may feel a sense of *ineffability*—the inability to understand an experience rationally or describe it in words (Finkler, 2004; Martindale, 1981; Travis, 2006).

Of course, recognizing that efforts to produce altered states of consciousness are widespread throughout the world's societies does not answer a fundamental question: Is the experience of unaltered states of consciousness similar across different cultures?

Because humans are pretty much alike in the ways our brains and bodies are wired, we might assume that the basic experience of consciousness is similar across cultures. However, the ways in which certain aspects of consciousness are interpreted and viewed vary widely among different cultures. For example, the passage of time is experienced differently by people in various cultures. For instance, Arabs perceive time as moving more slowly than do North Americans, who tend to be more hurried (Alon & Brett, 2007).

Drug Use: The Highs and Lows of Consciousness

Drugs of one sort or another are a part of almost everyone's life in Canada. From infancy on, many people take vitamins, aspirin, or cold-relief medicine; nonetheless, these drugs rarely produce an altered state of consciousness (Dortch, 1996).

In contrast, some substances, known as psychoactive drugs, lead to an altered state of consciousness. **Psychoactive drugs** influence a person's emotions, perceptions, and behaviour. Yet even this category of drugs is common in most of our lives. If you have ever had a cup of coffee or sipped a beer, you have taken a psychoactive drug. A large number of individuals have used more potent—and more dangerous—psychoactive drugs than coffee and beer; for instance, surveys find that 41% of high school seniors have used an illegal drug in the last year. In addition, 30% report having been drunk on alcohol. The figures for the adult population are even higher (Johnston et al., 2007).

Of course, the effects of drugs vary widely, in part because they affect the nervous system in very different ways. Some drugs alter the limbic system, and others affect the operation of specific neurotransmitters. For example, some drugs block or enhance the release of neurotransmitters, others block the receipt or the removal of a neurotransmitter, and still others mimic the effects of a particular neurotransmitter. One reason many people use psychoactive drugs is because of the effect drugs have on the reward pathways in the limbic system. Psychoactive drugs bypass the association areas of the brain and instead go directly to the reward centre, resulting in feelings of immediate pleasure. Drugs such as methamphetamine, for example, get the neurons to release large doses of dopamine, which result in the user having instant elation. As we will learn more in the chapter on learning, when things

psychoactive drugs Drugs that influence a person's emotions, perceptions, and behaviour.

addictive drugs Drugs that produce a physiological or psychological dependence in the user.

tolerance When people use a drug for a period of time, they need increasing amounts to achieve the same feelings.

withdrawal A craving for the drug that, in some cases, may be nearly irresistible.

feel good, we are likely to do them again! Unfortunately, for some, this can lead to addiction.

The most dangerous drugs are addictive. **Addictive drugs** produce a physiological or psychological dependence in the user. When people use a drug for a period of time, they need increasing amounts to achieve the same feelings because they have developed a **tolerance** for the drug. When people stop using the drug they often have a period of **withdrawal** that leads to a craving for the drug that, in some cases, may be nearly irresistible. In *biologically based* addictions, the body becomes so accustomed to functioning in the presence of a drug that it cannot function without it. *Psychologically based* addictions are those in which people believe that they need the drug to cope with the stresses of daily living. Although we generally associate addiction with drugs such as heroin, everyday sorts of drugs, such as caffeine (found in coffee and some colas) and nicotine (found in cigarettes), have addictive aspects as well (Li, Volkow, & Baler, 2007).

Why do people take drugs in the first place? There are many reasons, ranging from the perceived pleasure of the experience itself, to the escape that a drug-induced high affords from the everyday pressures of life, to an attempt to achieve a religious or spiritual state. However, other factors having little to do with the nature of the experience itself also lead people to try drugs (McDowell & Spitz, 1999).

For instance, highly publicized drug use by role models such as movie stars and professional athletes, the easy availability of some illegal drugs, and peer pressure all play a role in the decision to use drugs. In some cases, the motive is simply the thrill of trying something new. Finally, genetic factors may predispose some people to be more susceptible to drugs and to become addicted to them. Regardless of the forces that lead a person to begin using drugs, drug addiction is among the most difficult of all behaviours to modify, even with extensive treatment (Lemonick, 2000; Mosher & Akins, 2007; Ray & Hutchison, 2007).

The 2009 Canadian alcohol and drug use monitoring

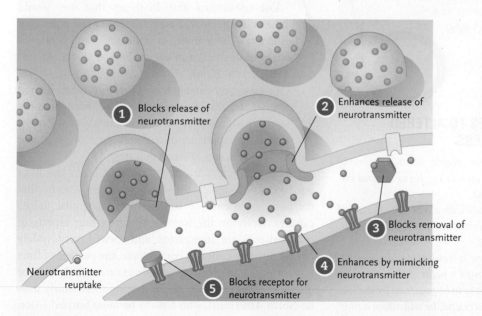

① Blocks release of neurotransmitter

② Enhances release of neurotransmitter

③ Blocks removal of neurotransmitter

④ Enhances by mimicking neurotransmitter

⑤ Blocks receptor for neurotransmitter

Neurotransmitter reuptake

Different drugs affect different parts of the nervous system and brain and function in one of these specific ways.

Figure 4.7
Drug Use by High School Students

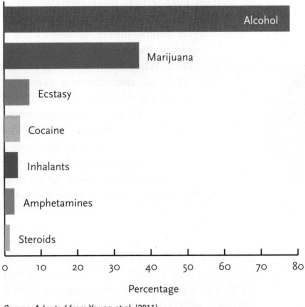

Percentage

Source: Adapted from Young et al. (2011).

survey (CADUMS) conducted by Health Canada found that drug use by youth aged 15–24 years is almost five times higher than those 25 years and older (Health Canada, 2010c). However, illicit drug use (i.e., heroin, hallucinogens, speed, cocaine, or crack) by those between 15 and 24 years old declined 5% in the past five years (Health Canada, 2010c).

> Drug addiction is among the most difficult of all behaviours to modify, even with extensive treatment.

Because of the difficulty in treating drug problems, there is little disagreement that the best hope for dealing with the overall societal problem of substance abuse is to prevent people from becoming involved with drugs in the first place. However, there is little accord on how to accomplish this goal (Clayton, Segress, & Caudill, 2008; D'Amico et al., 2009).

STIMULANTS: DRUG HIGHS

It's one o'clock in the morning, and you still haven't finished reading the last chapter of the text on which you will be tested in the morning. Feeling exhausted, you turn to the one thing that may help you stay awake for the next two hours: a cup of strong black coffee.

If you have ever found yourself in this situation, you have resorted to a major *stimulant*, caffeine, to stay awake. *Caffeine* is one of a number of **stimulants**, drugs whose

stimulants Drugs that have an arousal effect on the central nervous system, causing a rise in heart rate, blood pressure, and muscular tension.

effect on the central nervous system causes a rise in heart rate, blood pressure, and muscular tension. Caffeine is present not only in coffee, but it is also an important ingredient in energy drinks, tea, soft drinks, and chocolate.

Caffeine produces several reactions. The major behavioural effects are an increase in attentiveness and improved reaction time. Caffeine can also brighten one's mood, most likely by mimicking the effects of a natural brain chemical, adenosine. Too much caffeine, however, can result in nervousness and insomnia. People can develop a physiological dependence on the drug. Regular users who suddenly stop drinking coffee may experience headaches or depression. Many people who drink large amounts of coffee on weekdays have headaches on weekends because of a sudden drop in the amount of caffeine they are consuming (Juliano & Griffiths, 2004; Kendler, Gatz, & Gardner, 2006; Satel, 2006).

What about energy drinks? Not to be confused with sports drinks such as Gatorade or Powerade, which help hydrate the user, energy drinks actually dehydrate the user. Energy drinks contain large amounts of caffeine, carbohydrates, and sugar and are purported to increase attention, concentration, and cognitive function, but research has shown that overuse of these types of drinks can be very dangerous (Kaminer, 2010). Some energy drinks contain as much as 500 mg of caffeine, where an average cup of coffee has about 100 to 150 mg of caffeine. The risk of using too much of these types of drinks is caffeine intoxication, which can result in the user having increased anxiety, nervousness, upset stomach, insomnia, and in severe cases, death (Reissig, Strain, & Griffiths, 2009). These drinks can be even more hazardous when mixed with alcohol because

Coffee is an integral part of social rituals in cultures around the world.

Figure 4.8
Levels of Caffeine in Common Beverages and Drugs

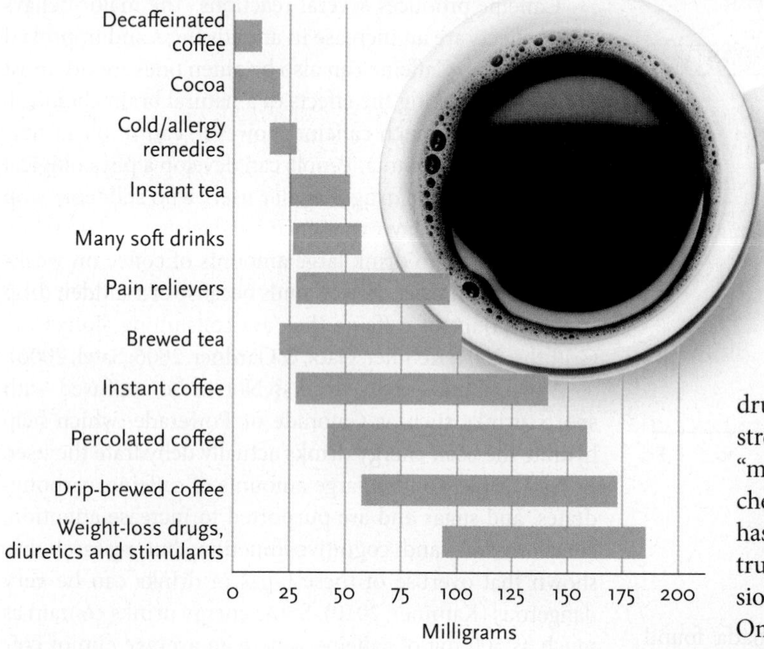

Beverage/Drug	Milligrams
Decaffeinated coffee	
Cocoa	
Cold/allergy remedies	
Instant tea	
Many soft drinks	
Pain relievers	
Brewed tea	
Instant coffee	
Percolated coffee	
Drip-brewed coffee	
Weight-loss drugs, diuretics and stimulants	

Milligrams: 0 25 50 75 100 125 150 175 200

Source: New York Times Graphics.

the user does not fully feel the effects of the alcohol when it is mixed with the energy drink. This may lead to alcohol-related consequences such as personal injury, driving while intoxicated, or sexual assault (Reissig, Strain, & Griffiths, 2009). Health Canada suggests that users should consume no more than two 8.3 oz cans of energy drinks per day, and suggests that it should not be mixed with alcohol (Health Canada, 2010e).

Nicotine, found in cigarettes, is another common stimulant. Besides stimulating the central nervous system, nicotine increases levels of the neurotransmitter dopamine in the brain, making the smoker feel good. This effect helps explain why cigarette smoking is addictive. Smokers become dependent on nicotine, and those who suddenly stop smoking develop a strong craving for the drug. This mechanism is similar to the ones activated by cocaine and heroin, which are also highly addictive (Collins & Izenwasser, 2004; Haberstick, Timberlake, & Ehringer, 2007).

Amphetamines Dexedrine and Benzedrine, also known as uppers, speed, black beauties, bumble bees, co-pilots, and bennies, belong to a class of strong stimulants known as *amphetamines*. In small quantities, amphetamines—which stimulate the central nervous system—produce a sense of energy and alertness, talkativeness, heightened confidence, and a mood "high." They increase concentration and reduce fatigue. Amphetamines also cause a loss of appetite, increased anxiety, and irritability. When taken over long periods of time, amphetamines can cause feelings of being persecuted and a general sense of suspiciousness. People taking amphetamines may lose interest in sex. If taken in too large a quantity, amphetamines overstimulate the central nervous system to such an extent that they may cause convulsions and death (Carhart-Harris, 2007).

Methamphetamine is a white, crystalline drug that police now say is the most dangerous street drug. Commonly known as "ice," "crank," or "meth," this drug is highly addictive and relatively cheap, and it produces a strong, lingering high. It has made addicts of people across the social spectrum, ranging from soccer moms to urban professionals to poverty-stricken inner-city residents. Once addicted, users take it more and more frequently and in increasing doses. Long-term use of this drug can lead to brain damage (Sharma, Sjoquist, & Ali, 2007; Thompson et al., 2004).

Psych think

> > > Knowing the pros and many cons of energy drinks, would you still choose to use them?

Cocaine Although the use of cocaine has declined over the last decade, this stimulant and its derivative, crack, still represent a serious concern. Cocaine is inhaled or "snorted" through the nose, smoked, or injected directly into the bloodstream. It is rapidly absorbed into the body and takes effect almost immediately.

When used in relatively small quantities, cocaine produces feelings of profound psychological well-being, increased confidence, and alertness. Cocaine produces this "high" through the neurotransmitter dopamine, which is one of the chemicals that are related to ordinary feelings of pleasure. Normally when dopamine is released, excess amounts of the neurotransmitter are reabsorbed by the releasing neuron. However, when cocaine enters the brain, it blocks reabsorption of leftover dopamine. As a result, the brain is flooded with dopamine-produced pleasurable sensations (Jarlais, Arasteh, & Perlis, 2007; Redish, 2004).

However, there is a steep price to be paid for the pleasurable effects of cocaine. The brain may become permanently rewired, triggering a psychological and physical

Study tip Refer back to the summary in Figure 4.9 when you're studying the effects of specific drugs.

Figure 4.9
Drugs and Their Effects

Drugs	Effects	Withdrawal Symptoms	Risks
Stimulants			
Cocaine Amphetamines	Increased confidence, mood elevation, sense of energy and alertness, decreased appetite, anxiety, irritability, insomnia, transient drowsiness, delayed orgasm	Apathy, general fatigue, prolonged sleep, depression, disorientation, suicidal thoughts, agitated motor activity, irritability, bizarre dreams	Elevated blood pressure, increase in body temperature, face picking, suspiciousness, bizarre and repetitive behaviour, vivid hallucinations, convulsions, possible death
Depressants			
Alcohol Sedatives	Anxiety reduction, impulsiveness, dramatic mood swings, bizarre thoughts, suicidal behaviour, slurred speech, disorientation, slowed mental and physical functioning, limited attention span	Weakness, restlessness, nausea and vomiting, headaches, nightmares, irritability, depression, acute anxiety, hallucinations, seizures, possible death	Confusion, decreased response to pain, shallow respiration, dilated pupils, weak and rapid pulse, coma, possible death
Rohypnol	Anxiety reduction, muscle relaxation, amnesia, sleep	Seizures	Seizures, coma, incapacitation, inability to resist sexual assault
Narcotics			
Heroin Morphine	Anxiety and pain reduction, apathy, difficulty in concentration, slowed speech, decreased physical activity, drooling, itching, euphoria, nausea	Anxiety, vomiting, sneezing, diarrhea, lower back pain, watery eyes, runny nose, yawning, irritability, tremors, panic, chills and sweating, cramps	Depressed levels of consciousness, low blood pressure, rapid heart rate, shallow breathing, convulsions, coma, possible death
Hallucinogens			
Cannabis	Euphoria, relaxed inhibitions, increased appetite, disoriented behaviour	Hyperactivity, insomnia, decreased appetite, anxiety	Severe reactions rare but include panic, paranoia, fatigue, bizarre and dangerous behaviour, decreased testosterone over long-term; immune-system effects
MDMA (Ecstasy)	Heightened sense of oneself and insight, feelings of peace, empathy, energy	Depression, anxiety, sleeplessness	Increase in body temperature, memory difficulties
LSD	Heightened aesthetic responses; vision and depth distortion; heightened sensitivity to faces and gestures; magnified feelings; paranoia, panic, euphoria	Not reported	Nausea and chills; increased pulse, temperature, and blood pressure; slow, deep breathing; loss of appetite; insomnia; bizarre, dangerous behaviour

depressants Drugs that slow down the nervous system.

addiction in which users grow obsessed with obtaining the drug. Over time, users deteriorate mentally and physically. In extreme cases, cocaine can cause hallucinations; a common one is of insects crawling over one's body. Ultimately, an overdose of cocaine can lead to death (George & Moselhy, 2005; Nestler, 2001; Paulozzi, 2006).

DEPRESSANTS: DRUG LOWS

In contrast to the initial effect of stimulants—increased arousal of the central nervous system—the effect of **depressants** is to impede the nervous system by inhibiting the firing of neurons. Small doses of depressants result in at least temporary feelings of *intoxication*—drunkenness—along with a sense of euphoria and joy. When large amounts are taken, however, speech becomes slurred and muscle control becomes disjointed, making motion difficult. Ultimately, heavy users may lose consciousness entirely.

Alcohol The most common depressant in Canada is alcohol, which is used by more Canadians than any other drug. In fact, Canadians spent 18 billion dollars on beer and liquor in the year 2007 alone (CBC News, 2008). Although alcohol consumption has declined steadily over the last decade, surveys of college students show that more than three-fourths of them have had a drink within the last 30 days (Jung, 2002; Midanik, Tam, & Weisner, 2007).

One of the more disturbing trends is the high frequency of binge drinking among college students. For men, binge drinking is defined as having five or more drinks in one sitting. For women, who generally weigh less than men and

Figure 4.10
Drinking Habits of Students Aged 15-24

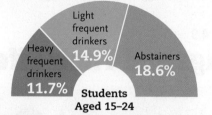

Source: Health Canada. *Canadian Alcohol and Drug Use Monitoring Survey.* Table 6. www.hc-sc.gc.ca/hc-ps/drugs-drogues/stat/_2009/tables-tableaux-eng.php#t6 (accessed January 23, 2012).

whose bodies absorb alcohol less efficiently, binge drinking is defined as having four or more drinks at one sitting (Mokdad, Brewer, & Naimi, 2007).

Around 50% of male college students and 40% of female college students say they engaged in binge drinking at least once within the previous two weeks. Some 17% of female students and 3% of male students admitted drinking on 10 or more occasions during the previous 30 days. Furthermore, even light drinkers were affected by the high rate of alcohol use: Two-thirds of lighter drinkers said that they had had their studying or sleep disturbed by drunk students, and a quarter of the women said they had been the target of an unwanted sexual advance by a drunk classmate (Park & Grant, 2005; Wechsler et al., 1994, 2000, 2002).

It used to be that women were somewhat lighter drinkers than men, but the gap between the sexes is narrowing for

Consider Your Drinking Style

If you drink alcohol, do you have a style of use that is safe and responsible? Read the statements below and rate the extent to which you agree with them, using the following scale:

1 = Strongly disagree   2 = Disagree   3 = Neutral   4 = Agree   5 = Strongly agree

	1	2	3	4	5
1. I usually drink alcohol a few times a week					
2. I sometimes go to class after I've been drinking alcohol					
3. I frequently drink when I'm alone					
4. I have driven while under the influence of alcohol					
5. I've used a fake ID card to purchase alcohol					
6. I'm a totally different person when I'm drinking alcohol					
7. I often drink so much that I feel drunk					
8. I wouldn't want to go to a party where alcohol wasn't being served					
9. I avoid people who don't like to drink alcohol					
10. I sometimes urge others to drink more alcohol					

Do you want to see how your drinking habits compare to other college and university students in Canada? Check out the Web site at www.checkyourdrinkingu.net.

Scoring: The lower your score (that is, the more 1s and 2s), the better able you are to control your alcohol consumption and the more likely it is that your alcohol use is responsible. The higher your score (that is, the more 4s and 5s), the greater is your use and reliance on alcohol, and the more likely it is that your alcohol consumption may be reckless. If your score is over 40, you may have an alcohol problem and should seek professional help to control your alcohol usage.

In a study of more than 800 rape victims, 20% of the rapes were conducted while the victim was in an altered state of consciousness induced by drugs or alcohol. One date rape drug (Rohypnol) can cause loss of muscle control, sleepiness, difficulty speaking, amnesia for the event, and other hypnotic effects.

older men and women and there is no difference between genders for teenagers. Women are more susceptible to the effects of alcohol, and alcohol abuse may harm the women's brains more than men's (Mancinelli, Binetti, & Ceccanti, 2007; Mann et al., 2005; Wuethrich, 2001).

Although alcohol is a depressant, most people claim that it increases their sense of sociability and well-being. The discrepancy between the actual and the perceived effects of alcohol lies in the initial effects it produces in the majority of individuals who use it: the release of tension and stress, feelings of happiness, and loss of inhibitions (Sayette, 1993; Steele & Josephs, 1990).

As the dose of alcohol increases, however, the depressive effects become more pronounced. People may feel emotionally and physically unstable. They also show poor judgment and may act aggressively. Moreover, memory is impaired, brain processing of spatial information is diminished, and speech becomes slurred and incoherent. Eventually they may fall into a stupor and pass out. If they drink enough alcohol in a short time, they may die of alcohol poisoning (Murphy, Monahan, & Miller, 1998; Thatcher & Clark, 2006; Zeigler et al., 2005).

> **The average person over the age of 14 drinks 9.5 litres of pure alcohol over the course of a year.**

Although most Canadians fall into the category of casual users, 4 to 5 million Canadians are estimated to be high risk drinkers (Health Canada, 2010c). *Alcoholics* are people with alcohol-abuse problems, who come to rely on alcohol and continue to drink even though it causes serious health and other life problems. In addition, they develop a tolerance to alcohol and become increasingly immune to the intoxicating effect. Consequently, alcoholics must drink progressively more to experience the initial positive feelings that alcohol produces.

Some alcoholics must drink constantly to feel well enough to function in their daily lives. Others drink inconsistently, but occasionally go on binges in which they consume large quantities of alcohol.

It is not clear why certain people become alcoholics and develop a tolerance for alcohol, while others do not. There may be a genetic cause, although the question whether there is a specific inherited gene that produces alcoholism is controversial. What is clear is that the chances of becoming an alcoholic are considerably higher if alcoholics are present in earlier generations of a person's family. However,

Figure 4.11
Effects of Alcohol

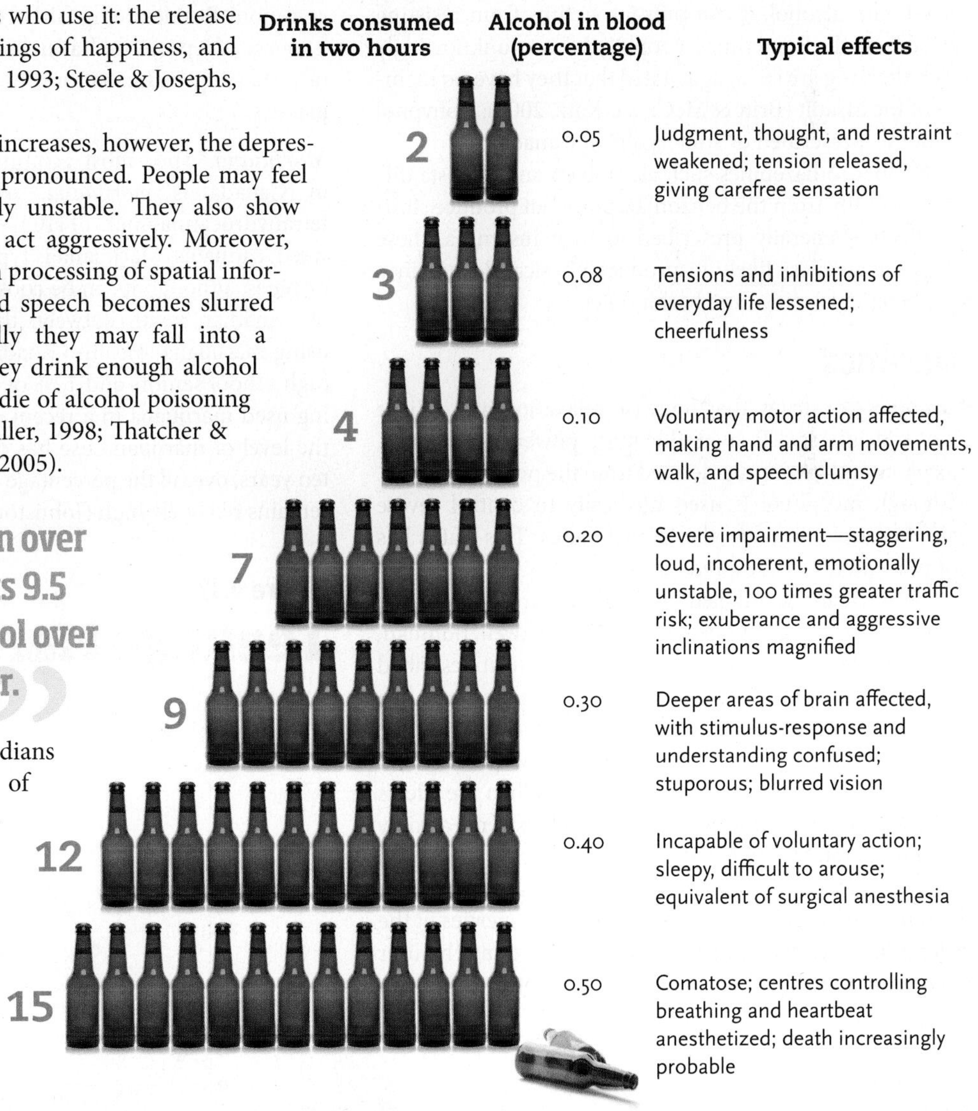

Drinks consumed in two hours	Alcohol in blood (percentage)	Typical effects
2	0.05	Judgment, thought, and restraint weakened; tension released, giving carefree sensation
3	0.08	Tensions and inhibitions of everyday life lessened; cheerfulness
4	0.10	Voluntary motor action affected, making hand and arm movements, walk, and speech clumsy
7	0.20	Severe impairment—staggering, loud, incoherent, emotionally unstable, 100 times greater traffic risk; exuberance and aggressive inclinations magnified
9	0.30	Deeper areas of brain affected, with stimulus-response and understanding confused; stuporous; blurred vision
12	0.40	Incapable of voluntary action; sleepy, difficult to arouse; equivalent of surgical anesthesia
15	0.50	Comatose; centres controlling breathing and heartbeat anesthetized; death increasingly probable

Note: A drink refers to a typical 355 ml (12 ounce) bottle of beer, a 50 ml (approximately 1.5 ounce) shot of hard liquor, or a 150 ml (approximately 5 ounce) glass of wine. These quantities are only rough benchmarks. The effects vary significantly depending on an individual's height, recent food intake, genetic factors, and even psychological state.

not all alcoholics have close relatives who are alcoholics. In these cases, environmental stressors are suspected of playing a larger role (Nurnberger & Bierut, 2007; Whitfield et al., 2004; Zimmermann, Blomeyer, & Laucht, 2007).

Sedatives Sedatives, including barbiturates, benzodiazepines, and nonbenzodiazepines, are depressant drugs that reduce irritability and have a calming effect. Barbiturates, such as Nembutal, Seconal, and phenobarbital, are older prescription drugs that have a high potential for addiction. Prescribed to induce sleep or reduce stress, barbiturates, such as Seconal and phenobarbital, produce a sense of relaxation. They have a high potential for abuse and overdose.

A newer class of drugs, benzodiazepines, have largely replaced barbiturates for short-term treatment of anxiety, insomnia, seizures, and alcohol withdrawal. Like barbiturates, benzodiazepines, which include Xanax and Valium, are prescription drugs to be used only under a doctor's supervision.

Another benzodiazepine, Rohypnol, is a short-acting sedative that is sometimes called the "date rape drug." When mixed with alcohol, it can prevent victims from resisting sexual assault. Sometimes people who are unknowingly given the drug are so incapacitated that they have no memory of the assault (Britt & McCance-Katz, 2005). Rohypnol cannot be prescribed or sold legally in Canada.

Nonbenzodiazepines such as Ambien and Lunesta differ chemically from the benzodiazepines but produce similar effects. Generally prescribed to treat insomnia, these drugs are also less likely to produce physical dependence than benzodiazepines and barbiturates.

NARCOTICS

Narcotics are drugs that increase relaxation and relieve pain and anxiety. Two of the most powerful narcotics, *morphine* and *heroin*, are derived from the poppy seed pod. Although morphine is used medically to control severe pain, heroin is illegal in the United States. This status has not prevented its widespread use.

Heroin can be inhaled or injected directly into the bloodstream with a hypodermic needle (Maxwell, Bohman, & Spense, 2004). The immediate effect has been described as a "rush" of positive feeling, similar in some respects to a sexual orgasm—and just as difficult to describe. After the rush, a heroin user experiences a sense of well-being and peacefulness that lasts three to five hours. When the effects of the drug wear off, however, the user feels extreme anxiety and a desperate desire to repeat the experience. Moreover, larger amounts of heroin are needed each time to produce the same pleasurable effect. These last two properties fit the criteria for physical and psychological addiction: The user is constantly either shooting up or attempting to obtain

ever-increasing amounts of the drug. Eventually, the life of the addict revolves around heroin.

Because of the powerful feelings of physical pleasure the drug produces, heroin addiction is particularly difficult to cure (van den Brink & van Ree, 2003). One treatment that has shown some success is replacing heroin with methadone. *Methadone* is a synthetic chemical that satisfies a heroin user's physiological cravings for the drug without providing the "high" that accompanies heroin. When heroin users receive regular doses of methadone, they may be able to function relatively normally. The use of methadone has one significant drawback, however: It replaces the addiction to heroin with an addiction to methadone. Researchers are attempting to identify non-addictive chemical substitutes for heroin as well as substitutes for other addictive drugs that do not replace one addiction with another (Amato et al., 2005; Joe, Flynn, & Broome, 2007; Verdejo, Toribio, & Orozco, 2005).

Hallucinogens: Psychedelic Drugs What do some mushrooms, jimsonweed, and morning glories have in common? Besides being fairly common plants, each can be a source of a powerful **hallucinogen**, a drug that is capable of producing hallucinations, or changes in the perceptual process.

Marijuana. The most commonly used hallucinogen in Canada is *marijuana*, whose active ingredient—tetrahydrocannabinol (THC)—is found in a common weed, cannabis. Marijuana is typically smoked in cigarettes or pipes, although it can be cooked and eaten. Almost 11% of Canadian youth between the age of 15–24 indicated using marijuana (Health Canada, 2010c). Just over 31% of high school seniors and 12% of eighth-graders report having used marijuana in a recent one-year period. Although the level of marijuana use has declined slightly in the last ten years, overall the percentage of teenagers using the drug remains relatively high (Johnston et al., 2007).

Figure 4.12
Teenage Marijuana Use

2008
Percentage of users

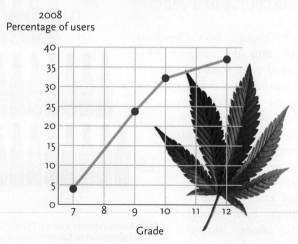

Grade

Source: Adapted from Young et al. (2011).

narcotics Drugs that increase relaxation and relieve pain and anxiety.

hallucinogen A drug that is capable of producing hallucinations, or changes in the perceptual process.

The effects of marijuana vary from person to person, but they typically consist of feelings of euphoria and general well-being. Sensory experiences seem more vivid and intense, and a person's sense of self-importance seems to grow. Memory may be impaired, causing users to feel pleasantly "spaced out." However, the effects are not universally positive. Individuals who use marijuana when they feel depressed can end up even more depressed, because the drug tends to magnify both good and bad feelings.

There are clear risks associated with long-term, heavy marijuana use. Although marijuana does not seem to produce addiction by itself, some evidence suggests that there are similarities in the way marijuana and drugs such as cocaine and heroin affect the brain. Furthermore, there is some evidence that heavy use at least temporarily decreases the production of the male sex hormone testosterone, potentially affecting sexual activity and sperm count (Block et al., 2000; Iverson, 2000; Lane Cherek, & Tcheremissine, 2007).

In addition, marijuana smoked during pregnancy may have lasting behavioural effects on children who are exposed prenatally, although the results are inconsistent. Heavy use also affects the ability of the immune system to fight off germs and increases stress on the heart, although it is unclear how strong these effects are. There is one unquestionably negative consequence of smoking marijuana: The smoke damages the lungs much the way cigarette smoke does, producing an increased likelihood of developing cancer and other lung diseases (Cornelius et al., 1995; Julien, 2001).

Despite the risks associated with it, marijuana has several medical uses. It helps to prevent nausea from chemotherapy, treat some AIDS symptoms, and relieve muscle spasms for people with spinal cord injuries. Health Canada allows individuals with debilitating diseases legal access to medicinal marijuana (Health Canada, 2010d).

MDMA (Ecstasy) and LSD. Two powerful hallucinogens are *MDMA* ("Ecstasy") and *lysergic acid diethylamide* (LSD, or "acid"). Both drugs affect the operation of the neurotransmitter serotonin in the brain, causing an alteration in brain-cell activity and perception (Aghajanian, 1994; Buchert et al., 2004; Cloud, 2000).

Ecstasy users report a sense of peacefulness and calm. People on the drug report experiencing increased empathy and connection with others, as well as feeling more relaxed, yet energetic. Although the data are not conclusive, some researchers have found declines in memory and performance on intellectual tasks associated with Ecstasy use, and such findings suggest that there may be long-term changes in serotonin receptors in the brain (El-Mallakh & Abraham, 2007; Montgomery et al., 2005; Parrott, 2002).

LSD, which is structurally similar to serotonin, produces vivid hallucinations. Perceptions of colours, sounds, and shapes are altered so much that even the most mundane experience—such as looking at the knots in a wooden table—can seem moving and exciting. Time perception is distorted, and objects and people may be viewed in a new

From the perspective of ...

A CLINICAL PSYCHOLOGIST How would you explain why people start using drugs to the family members of someone who is addicted?

way. Some users report that LSD increases their understanding of the world. For others, the experience brought on by LSD can be terrifying, particularly if users have had emotional difficulties in the past. Furthermore, people occasionally experience flashbacks, in which they hallucinate long after they initially used the drug (Baruss, 2003; Wu, Schlenger, & Galvin, 2006).

IDENTIFYING DRUG AND ALCOHOL PROBLEMS

In a society bombarded with commercials for drugs that are guaranteed to do everything from curing the common cold to giving new life to "tired blood," it is no wonder that drug-related problems are a major social issue. Yet many people with drug and alcohol problems deny they have them, and even close friends and family members may fail to realize when occasional social use of drugs or alcohol has turned into abuse.

Certain signs indicate when use becomes abuse (Archambault, 1992; National Institute on Drug Abuse, 2000). Among them are these:

- Always getting high to have a good time
- Being high more often than not
- Getting high to get oneself going
- Going to work or class while high
- Missing or being unprepared for class or work because you were high

Psych think

> > > Think of someone you know who may have (or definitely has) a drug or alcohol problem. How do you know this person has a problem? What are the indicators?

Help for drug and alcohol problems is available from national hotlines. You can call 1-855-224-7574 to speak to someone directly or you can visit the Web site for the Centre for Addiction and Mental Health (CAMH) at www.camh.ca (link from the home page to Care Programs and Services, then Addictions Program) to see links for various addictions programs.

- Feeling badly later about something you said or did while high
- Driving a car while high
- Coming in conflict with the law because of drugs
- Doing something while high that you wouldn't do otherwise
- Being high in non-social, solitary situations
- Being unable to stop getting high
- Feeling a need for a drink or a drug to get through the day

- Becoming physically unhealthy
- Failing at school or on the job
- Thinking about liquor or drugs all the time
- Avoiding family or friends while using liquor or drugs

Any combination of these symptoms indicates the possibility of a serious drug problem. Because drug and alcohol dependence are almost impossible to cure on one's own (Room, Babor, & Rehm, 2005), people who suspect that they have a problem should seek immediate attention from a psychologist, physician, or counsellor.

For Review »

What is consciousness?

Consciousness is a person's awareness of the sensations, thoughts, and feelings at a given moment. Waking consciousness can vary from active to passive states. Altered states of consciousness include naturally occurring sleep, dreaming, and drug-induced states.

What happens when we sleep, and what do dreams mean?

The brain is active throughout the night, and sleep proceeds through a series of stages identified by unique patterns of brain waves. REM (rapid eye movement) sleep is characterized by an increase in heart rate, a rise in blood pressure, an increase in the rate of breathing, and, in males, erections. Dreams occur during this stage. According to Freud, dreams have both a manifest content (an apparent story line) and a latent content (a true but hidden meaning). The dreams-for-survival theory suggests that information relevant to daily survival is reconsidered in dreams. The activation-synthesis theory proposes that dreams are a result of random electrical energy that haphazardly stimulates different memories, which then are woven into a coherent story line.

What are the major sleep disturbances?

Sleep disturbances fall under two major categories: *dysomnias* and *parasomnias*. Dysomnias result in problems with the quality of your sleep, such as the timing and amount you sleep and include insomnia, narcolepsy, and sleep apnea. Parasomnias, on the other hand, result in abnormal disturbances while you sleep and include nightmares, night terrors, sleep walking, sleep talking, and REM sleep behaviour disorder.

What kind of consciousness do hypnotized people experience?

Hypnosis produces significant behavioural changes, including increased concentration and suggestibility, heightened ability to recall and construct images, lack of initiative, and acceptance of suggestions that clearly contradict reality.

How do different drugs affect consciousness?

Stimulants cause arousal in the central nervous system. Two common stimulants are caffeine and nicotine. More dangerous are cocaine and amphetamines, which in large quantities can lead to convulsions and death. Alcohol and other depressants decrease arousal in the central nervous system. They can cause intoxication along with feelings of euphoria. Alcohol's initial effects of released tension and positive feelings yield to depressive effects as the dose of alcohol increases. Morphine and heroin are narcotics, drugs that produce relaxation and relieve pain and anxiety. Because of their addictive qualities, morphine and heroin are particularly dangerous. Hallucinogens are drugs that produce hallucinations or other changes in perception. The most frequently used hallucinogen is marijuana, which has several long-term risks. Two other hallucinogens are LSD and Ecstasy.

Psych think answers

Psych think 1 In the first PSYCH think on p. 95 we asked you what would be some advantages and drawbacks of taking a pill that eliminated your ability to dream from a personal standpoint, knowing what you do about the functions of sleep and dreaming. If you indicated that you would take such a pill to eliminate your dreams, you may be in trouble depending on the psychological approach to dreaming you adhere to! For example, Freud's psychoanalytic approach argues that dreams represent unconscious wishes that we desire to see fulfilled. If you no longer dreamt, you would not have any way to work out these unconscious desires. If you adhere to the cognitive approach's dreams-for-survival theory, which states that dreams allow you to process information that you did not have time to process during the day, your lack of dreams would deny you the opportunity to work out this information. If you adhere to the biological approach's activation-synthesis theory of dreaming, it wouldn't matter if you never dreamt again because your dreams are meaningless bits of random neuronal firing!

Psych think 2 In the PSYCH think on p. 102 we asked you to consider whether you would use energy drinks now that you know the pros and cons. Of course we cannot answer this for you, but we can remind you that the dangers of these drinks (increased anxiety, caffeine intoxication, etc), especially when mixed with alcohol, may not be worth the immediate feelings of energy. Moreover, many of these drinks also have a high amount of sugar that may lead to potential unwanted weight gain. There are other ways to get a quick burst of energy without adding robust amounts of caffeine and sugar to your diet, such as a brisk walk outside, a lukewarm/cold shower, or some quick and deep breaths.

Psych think 3 In the PSYCH think on p. 107 we asked you to discuss the indicators of a drug or alcohol problem of someone you know. Some of the signs are listed below:

- Always getting high to have a good time
- Being high more often than not
- Getting high to get oneself going
- Going to work or class while high
- Missing or being unprepared for class or work because they were high
- Feeling badly later about something they said or did while high
- Driving a car while high
- Coming in conflict with the law because of drugs
- Doing something while high that they wouldn't do otherwise
- Being high in non-social, solitary situations
- Not being able to stop getting high
- Feeling a need for a drink or a drug to get through the day
- Becoming physically unhealthy
- Failing at school or on the job
- Thinking about liquor or drugs all the time
- Avoiding family or friends while using liquor or drugs

5

Learning

WHAT'S TO COME

Classical Conditioning

Operant Conditioning

Cognitive Approaches to Learning

Skills, abilities, and behaviours are acquired through learning.

A four-legged co-worker

Declan lies on his back wanting his belly scratched. The 8-year-old Labrador swings his legs in the air for a few minutes before resigning himself to chewing on someone's shoe. . . . In the office he behaves like any pet dog, but in the field he is like a tornado—focused on finding illegal drugs being smuggled. Declan is a drug-detector dog for the Customs Service and has been busting drug smugglers with his handler, Kevin Hattrill, for many years.

irport passengers look on with curiosity as Declan darts around people and their luggage. Within minutes he sniffs out a person of interest, who is taken away and questioned by airport authorities.

Dogs like Declan are trained to detect illegal drugs, such as cannabis, methamphetamine and cocaine, or explosives. Hattrill said the dogs were dual response-trained when they detected something. "If the odour is around a passenger, they are trained to sit beside them. If it's around cargo, they are trained to scratch. When they detect something, their whole temperament changes. The dogs can screen up to 300 people within 10 to 15 minutes at the airport. Nothing else can do that" (McKenzie-McLean, 2006, p. 7).

Declan's expertise did not just happen, of course. It is the result of painstaking training procedures—the same ones that are at work in humans, illustrated by our ability to read a book, drive a car, play poker, study for a test, or perform any of the numerous activities that make up our daily routine. Like Declan, each of us must acquire and then refine our skills and abilities through learning.

As You Read >>

- What is learning?
- What is the role of reward and punishment in learning?
- How can the information from this chapter be used to change undesired behaviours?
- Does thinking matter at all in learning?

The Eaton Centre is a favourite destination for tourists in downtown Toronto. Visitors to the city can't help but notice the large neon signs, crowded streets, noise, and unfamiliar smells, all stimuli to which long-time residents are habituated.

Learning is a relatively permanent change in behaviour that is brought about by experience. From the beginning of life, humans are primed for learning. Infants exhibit a primitive type of learning called *habituation*, defined by psychologists as the decrease in response to a stimulus that occurs after repeated presentations of the same stimulus. Young infants, for example, may initially show interest in a novel stimulus, such as a brightly coloured toy, but they will soon lose interest if they see the same toy over and over. Habituation permits us to ignore things that have stopped providing new information. Adults exhibit habituation, too: newlyweds soon stop noticing that they are wearing a wedding ring.

Most learning is considerably more complex than habituation, and the study of learning has been at the core of the field of psychology. Psychologists have approached the study of learning from several directions. Among the most fundamental are studies that focus on what is observable in our environment, such as the type of learning that is illustrated in responses ranging from a dog salivating when it hears its owner opening a can of dog food to the emotions we feel when our national anthem is played. Other theories consider how learning is a consequence of rewarding circumstances, which is studied by individuals who adhere to the behaviourist approach that we learned about in the first chapter. Other approaches to learning focus on the cognitive aspects, that is, the thought processes that underlie learning and are studied by individuals who favour the cognitive approach. We will discuss these in the latter part of the chapter.

Although philosophers have speculated on the foundations of learning since the time of Aristotle, the first systematic research on learning in the West was done at the beginning of the twentieth century, when Ivan Pavlov (does

learning A relatively permanent change in behaviour brought about by experience.

the name ring a bell?) developed a framework for learning called classical conditioning.

Classical Conditioning

For many of us just the thought of having lemon squeezed directly onto our tongue will result in us salivating. Is there another word or phrase or event that makes you salivate? Maybe the thought of homemade chocolate chip cookies, or pub night, makes you salivate! If so, you are displaying a basic form of learning called classical conditioning. *Classical conditioning* helps explain such diverse phenomena as shivering when you look outside at night and see snow, and getting sweaty palms and a racing heart while watching a movie that has scary music, dark scenes, and sudden scene changes.

WHAT IS CLASSICAL CONDITIONING?

Ivan Pavlov (1849–1936), a Russian physiologist, never intended to do psychological research. In 1904 he won the Nobel Prize for his work on digestion, a testament to his contribution to that field. Yet Pavlov is remembered not for his physiological research but for his experiments on learning—work that he began quite accidentally (Marks, 2004; Samoilov & Zayas, 2007).

Pavlov had been studying the secretion of stomach acids and salivation in dogs in response to the ingestion of varying amounts and kinds of food. While doing that, he observed a curious phenomenon: Sometimes stomach secretions and salivation would begin in the dogs when they had not yet eaten any food. The mere sight of the experimenter who normally brought the food, or even the sound of the experimenter's footsteps, was enough to produce salivation in the dogs. Pavlov's genius lay in his ability to recognize the implications of this discovery. He saw that the dogs were responding not only on the basis of a biological need (hunger) but also as a result of learning—or, as it came to be called, classical conditioning. **Classical conditioning** is a type of learning in which a neutral stimulus (such as the experimenter's footsteps) comes to elicit a response after being paired with a stimulus (such as food) that naturally brings about that response.

To demonstrate classical conditioning, Pavlov (1927) attached a tube to a dog's mouth so that he could measure precisely the dog's salivation. He then rang a bell and, just a few seconds later, allowed the dog to eat its food. This pairing occurred repeatedly and was carefully planned so

classical conditioning A type of learning in which a neutral stimulus comes to bring about a response after it is paired with a stimulus that naturally brings about that response.

neutral stimulus (NS) A stimulus that, before conditioning, does not naturally bring about the response of interest.

unconditioned stimulus (UCS) A stimulus that naturally brings about a particular response without having been learned.

unconditioned response (UCR) A response that is natural and needs no training (for example, salivation at the smell of food).

For many of us, just the thought of having lemon squirted into our mouths will make us salivate.

that, each time, exactly the same amount of time elapsed between the presentation of the bell and the food. At first the dog would salivate only when the food was in its mouth, but soon it began to salivate at the sound of the bell. In fact, even when Pavlov stopped giving the food to the dog, the dog still salivated after hearing the sound. The dog had been classically conditioned to salivate to the bell.

The basic processes of classical conditioning that underlie Pavlov's discovery are straightforward, although the terminology he chose is not simple. Before conditioning, there are two unrelated stimuli: the ringing of a bell and food. We know that normally the ringing of a bell does not lead to salivation, although it may lead to some other type of response, such as pricking up the ears. The bell is therefore called the **neutral stimulus**, or **NS**, because it is a stimulus that, before conditioning, does not naturally bring about the response in which we are interested. We also have food, which naturally causes a dog to salivate when it is placed on the tongue—the response we want to condition. The food on the tongue is considered an **unconditioned stimulus**, or **UCS**, because food placed in a dog's mouth automatically causes salivation to occur. The reflexive response that the food elicits (salivation) is called an **unconditioned response**, or **UCR**. This is a natural, inborn, reflexive response that is not associated with previous learning.

One way to tell if a stimulus is an UCS (unconditioned stimulus) is to consider whether every normal human would experience the UCR (unconditioned response). If the answer is yes, then it is likely a UCS. For example, would any healthy human experience sweating in extremely hot and humid weather? The answer is yes. So extreme heat and humidity are the UCS and sweating is the UCR.

Figure 5.1
Classical Conditioning

1 **Before conditioning** The ringing bell does not bring about salivation, making it a neutral stimulus.

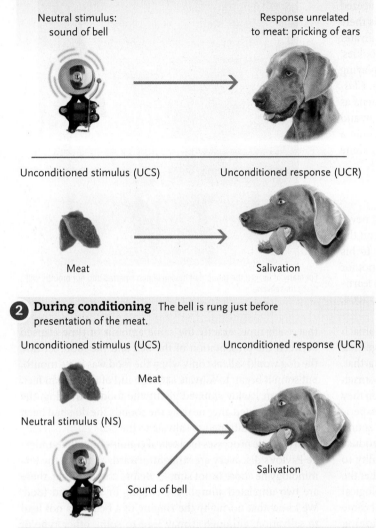

Neutral stimulus: sound of bell

Response unrelated to meat: pricking of ears

Unconditioned stimulus (UCS)

Unconditioned response (UCR)

Meat

Salivation

2 **During conditioning** The bell is rung just before presentation of the meat.

Unconditioned stimulus (UCS)

Unconditioned response (UCR)

Meat

Neutral stimulus (NS)

Salivation

Sound of bell

3 **After conditioning** The ringing bell alone stimulates salivation, making it a conditioned stimulus and salivation the conditioned response.

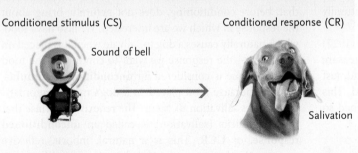

Conditioned stimulus (CS)

Conditioned response (CR)

Sound of bell

Salivation

Study tip

To understand the process of classical conditioning, you need to know the difference between the UCS (unconditioned stimulus) and the CS (conditioned stimulus) and their relationship to the UCR (unconditioned response) and the CR (conditioned response). Also, remember that the NS (neutral stimulus) always becomes the CS!

Unconditioned responses are always brought about by the presence of unconditioned stimuli.

Returning to Pavlov's study, the bell is rung each time the dog is about to receive food. The goal of conditioning is for the dog to associate the bell with the unconditioned stimulus (meat) and therefore to bring about the same response as the unconditioned stimulus. After a number of pairings of the bell and meat, the bell alone causes the dog to salivate. When conditioning is complete, the bell is no longer a neutral stimulus but has become a **conditioned stimulus**, or **CS**. At this point, salivation in response to the conditioned stimulus (bell) is considered a **conditioned response**, or **CR**. After conditioning, then, the conditioned stimulus evokes the conditioned response.

The reason classical conditioning occurs is because the dogs anticipated that the presentation of the food (UCS) would reliably lead to the presentation of the bell (the NS which then becomes the CS). Pavlov suggested that the UCS should precede the NS within at least five seconds so the organism learns that the UCS will lead to the NS (which then becomes the CS).

Although the terminology Pavlov used to describe classical conditioning may seem confusing, the following summary can help make the relationships between stimuli and responses easier to understand and remember:

- Conditioned = learned
- Unconditioned = not learned (inborn, genetically programmed)
- An *unconditioned* (unlearned) stimulus leads to an *unconditioned* (unlearned) response.
- *Unconditioned* stimulus–*unconditioned* response pairings are *un*learned and *un*trained.
- During conditioning, a previously neutral stimulus is transformed into the conditioned stimulus.
- A conditioned stimulus leads to a conditioned response, and a conditioned stimulus–conditioned response pairing is a consequence of learning and training.
- An unconditioned response and a conditioned response are similar (such as salivation in Pavlov's experiment), but the unconditioned response occurs naturally and is typically stronger, whereas the conditioned response is learned and usually less intense.

conditioned stimulus (CS) A once-neutral stimulus that has been paired with an unconditioned stimulus to bring about a response formerly caused only by the unconditioned stimulus.

conditioned response (CR) A response that, after conditioning, follows a previously neutral stimulus (for example, salivation at the ringing of a bell).

HOW DO CONDITIONING PRINCIPLES APPLY TO HUMAN BEHAVIOUR?

Although the first conditioning experiments were carried out with animals, classical conditioning principles were soon found to explain many aspects of everyday human behaviour. Recall, for instance, the earlier illustration of how people may salivate at the thought of having lemon squeezed into their mouths. The cause of this reaction is classical conditioning: The previously neutral lemon has become associated with the sour lemon that has been experienced on previous occasions (the unconditioned stimulus), causing the lemons to become a conditioned stimulus that brings about the conditioned response of salivation.

Emotional responses are especially likely to be learned through classical conditioning processes. For instance, how do some of us develop fears of mice, spiders, and other creatures that are typically harmless? In a now infamous case study, psychologist John B. Watson and colleague Rosalie Rayner (1920) showed that classical conditioning could be one cause of such fears by conditioning an 11-month-old infant named Albert to be afraid of rats. "Little Albert," like any healthy infant with normal hearing, initially was frightened by loud noises (UCS) but had no fear of rats (neutral stimulus).

In the study, the experimenters went behind Albert and made a very loud, sudden noise just as they showed Little Albert a rat. The noise (the unconditioned stimulus) evoked fear (the unconditioned response). After just a few pairings of noise and rat, Albert began to show fear of the rat by itself, bursting into tears when he saw it. The rat, then, had become a CS that brought about the CR, fear. Furthermore, the conditioning effects lingered: Five days later, Albert reacted with fear not only when shown a rat but also when shown objects that looked similar to the white, furry rat, including a rabbit, a sealskin coat, and even a Santa Claus mask. (By the way, we don't know what happened to the unfortunate Little Albert. Watson, the experimenter, has been condemned for using ethically questionable procedures that would not be permitted today.)

While Watson and Raynor showed that classical conditioning could be used to evoke fear, more recently, researchers from McGill University have found that classical conditioning can impact our self-esteem. Baccus, Baldwin, and Packer (2004) wanted to know if participants who viewed a smiling face (a neutral stimulus) at the same time as they read statements about themselves (the unconditioned stimulus) would show improvements in their implicit self-esteem (the automatic and unconscious aspect of self-esteem). The researchers used the experimental method to test this research question. Each participant completed a measure of self-esteem and then was randomly placed in the experimental or the control group. The experimental group viewed smiling faces as they read statements about themselves (the independent variable), while the control group viewed images of various types of faces (including smiling, frowning, and neutral faces). All participants then completed a test to measure their implicit self-esteem (the dependent variable). The researchers found that the participants who were exposed to the smiling faces had higher levels of implicit self-esteem compared to the participants who were not exposed to the smiling faces (Baccus, Baldwin, & Packer, 2004).

Learning through classical conditioning occurs throughout our lives. For example, you may be one of many people who do not go to a dentist as often as you should because of prior associations of dentists with pain. In this case, the UCS would be the drill hitting a nerve in your tooth, and the UCR would be pain. The NS would be the sound of the drill. What is the CS? (If you said the sound of the drill, you are correct! Remember that the NS always becomes the CS). In extreme cases, classical conditioning can lead to the development of *phobias*, which are intense, irrational fears that we will consider later in the book.

Classical conditioning also accounts for pleasant experiences. That is, certain events trigger the release of neurotransmitters that help us feel pleasure. The runner's high, for example, occurs when endorphins are released in response to jogging a long distance. The UCS is the extended jogging, and the UCR is the release of endorphins. The CS could be any number of things, including the smell or sight of running clothes or shoes. Classical conditioning,

From the perspective of ...

A PRACTICAL NURSE How could knowledge of classical conditioning be useful in addressing patients' anxieties about visits to the doctor? What are some changes a nurse could make when dealing with a patient who has a phobia about visiting the doctor?

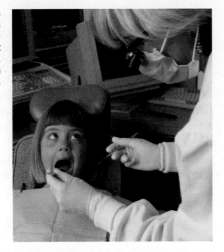

Avoiding all dentists because of a previous unpleasant experience at one dentist isn't uncommon. That's how stimulus generalization works.

extinction A basic phenomenon of learning that occurs when a previously conditioned response decreases in frequency and eventually disappears.

spontaneous recovery The re-emergence of an extinguished conditioned response after a period of rest and with no further conditioning.

stimulus generalization Occurs when a conditioned response follows a stimulus that is similar to the original conditioned stimulus; the more similar the two stimuli are, the more likely generalization is to occur.

then, may explain many of the reactions we have to stimuli in the world around us.

Classical conditioning is also very prevalent in advertising (in fact, John Watson worked in advertising after leaving the university where he conducted the Little Albert experiments). When you think about your favourite product, do you associate it with some sort of pleasant response? Perhaps it reminds you of something funny, or sexy, or refreshing, or cute? If so, you have been classically conditioned by the advertisers of your product. For example, remember when Coca Cola used the cute polar bears in their commercials? Can you identify the five elements of classical conditioning in this example? The product itself (the Coke) is the NS, which is presented with the very cute polar bears (UCS) which produces the automatic pleasant response of "awwww, aren't they cute" response (UCR). After pairing the cute polar bears (UCS) with the product (NS), you soon start to associate the product (now the CS) with pleasant feelings. Can you think of how classical conditioning works in some other commercials?

EXTINCTION OF A CONDITIONED RESPONSE

What would happen if a dog that had become classically conditioned to salivate at the ringing of a bell never again received food when the bell was rung? The answer lies in one of the basic phenomena of learning: extinction. **Extinction** occurs when a previously conditioned response decreases in frequency and eventually disappears.

To produce extinction, one needs to end the association between conditioned stimuli and unconditioned stimuli. For instance, if we had trained a dog to salivate (CR) at

the ringing of a bell (CS), we could produce extinction by repeatedly ringing the bell but not pairing it with food. At first the dog would continue to salivate when it heard the bell, but after a few such instances, the amount of salivation would probably decline, and the dog would eventually stop responding to the bell altogether. At that point, we could say that the response had been extinguished. In sum, extinction occurs when the conditioned stimulus is presented repeatedly without the unconditioned stimulus.

Once a conditioned response has been extinguished, has it vanished forever? Not necessarily. Pavlov discovered this phenomenon when he returned to his dog a few days after the conditioned behaviour had seemingly been extinguished. If he rang a bell, the dog once again salivated—an effect known as **spontaneous recovery**, or the re-emergence of an extinguished conditioned response after a period of rest and with no further conditioning.

Spontaneous recovery helps explain why it is so hard to overcome drug addictions. For example, cocaine addicts who are thought to be "cured" can experience an irresistible impulse to use the drug again if they are subsequently confronted by a stimulus with strong connections to the drug, such as seeing a white powder (DiCano & Everitt, 2002; Plowright, Simonds, & Butler, 2006; Rodd et al., 2004).

GENERALIZATION AND DISCRIMINATION

Despite differences in colour and shape, to most of us a rose is a rose. The pleasure we experience at the beauty, smell, and grace of the flower is similar for different types of roses. Pavlov noticed a similar phenomenon. His dogs often salivated not only at the ringing of the bell that was used during their original conditioning but also at the sound of a buzzer as well.

Such behaviour is called **stimulus generalization**. Stimulus generalization occurs when a conditioned response follows a stimulus that is similar to the original conditioned stimulus. The greater the similarity between two stimuli, the greater the likelihood of stimulus generalization. Little Albert, who, as we mentioned earlier, was conditioned to be fearful of white rats, grew afraid of other furry white things as well (such as white beards). However, according to the principle of stimulus generalization, it is unlikely that he would have been afraid of a black dog, because its colour would have differentiated it sufficiently from the original fear-evoking stimulus.

The conditioned response elicited by the new stimulus is usually not as intense as the original conditioned response, although the more similar the new stimulus is to the old one, the more similar the new response will be. It is unlikely, then, that Little Albert's fear of the Santa Claus mask was as great as his learned fear of a rat. Still, stimulus generalization is the reason drivers know, for example, that they ought to brake at all red lights, even if there are minor variations in the size, shape, and shade of the traffic signal.

> "Stimulus generalization is the reason drivers know that they should brake at all red lights, even if there are minor variations in the size, shape, and shade of the traffic signal."

Stimulus discrimination, in contrast, occurs if two stimuli are sufficiently distinct from each other that one evokes a conditioned response but the other does not. Stimulus discrimination is the ability to differentiate between stimuli. For example, a dog might come running into the kitchen when she hears the sound of the electric can opener, which she has learned is used to open her dog food when her dinner is about to be served. But she does not race into the kitchen at the sound of the food processor, which is similar. In other words, the dog discriminates between the stimuli of can opener sound and food processor sound. Similarly, our ability to discriminate between the behaviour of a growling dog and that of one whose tail is wagging can lead to adaptive behaviour—avoiding the growling dog and petting the friendly one. (Can you remember what approach to psychology would explain this behaviour as adaptive? If you said the evolutionary approach, you are correct!).

Psych think

> > > Use the five elements of classical conditioning to explain why someone who was in a car accident in the past year now feels anxiety and slows down cautiously when driving through an intersection.

Operant Conditioning

Very good . . . What a clever idea . . . Fantastic . . . I agree . . . Thank you . . . Excellent . . . Super . . . Right on . . . This is the best paper you've ever written; you get an A . . . You are really getting the hang of it . . . I'm impressed . . . You're getting a raise . . . Have a cookie . . . You look great . . . I love you . . .

Few of us mind being the recipient of any of these comments. But what is especially noteworthy about them is that each of these simple statements can be used, through a process known as operant conditioning, to bring about powerful changes in behaviour and to teach the most complex tasks. Operant conditioning is the basis for many of the most important kinds of human, and animal, learning.

Operant conditioning is learning in which a voluntary response becomes more likely to occur again or less likely, depending on its favourable or unfavourable consequences. For example, if some money fell down out of the sky every time you finished reading a page in your textbook, would you be more likely to read more pages in your book? If so, the money would be considered a favourable consequence that led to the strengthening of your reading response.

Unlike classical conditioning, in which the original behaviours are the natural, involuntary biological responses to the presence of a stimulus such as food, water, or pain, operant conditioning applies to *voluntary* responses, which an organism performs deliberately to produce a desirable outcome. The term *operant* emphasizes this point: The organism *operates* on its environment to produce a desirable result. Operant conditioning is at work when we learn that working industriously can bring about a raise or that studying hard results in good grades. It is also at work when we learn that partying all night results in poor grades!

As with classical conditioning, the basis for understanding operant conditioning was laid by work with animals. We turn now to some of that early research.

> **stimulus discrimination** The process that occurs if two stimuli are sufficiently distinct from each other that one evokes a conditioned response but the other does not; the ability to differentiate between stimuli.
>
> **operant conditioning** Learning in which a voluntary response is strengthened or weakened, depending on its favourable or unfavourable consequences.

HOW OPERANT CONDITIONING WORKS

B. F. Skinner (1904–1990), one of the twentieth century's most influential psychologists, inspired a whole generation of psychologists studying operant conditioning. Skinner became interested in specifying how behaviour varies as a result of alterations in the environment. To illustrate, let's consider what happens to a rat in the typical Skinner box, a chamber with a highly controlled environment that Skinner designed to study operant conditioning processes with laboratory animals (Pascual & Rodríguez, 2006).

Suppose you want to teach a hungry rat to press a lever that is in its box. At first the rat will wander around the box, exploring the environment in a relatively random fashion. At some point, however, it will probably press the lever by chance, and when it does, you have set up the box so that the rat will receive a food pellet. The first time this happens, the rat will not learn the connection (contingency) between pressing a lever and receiving food and will continue to explore the box. Sooner or later the rat will press the lever again and receive a pellet, and in time the frequency of the pressing response will increase. Eventually, the rat will press the lever continually until it satisfies its hunger, thereby demonstrating that it has learned that receiving food is contingent on pressing the lever. Declan, the drug sniffing dog from the opening paragraph learned in much the same way. Once he was able to respond to the target stimulus (i.e., the drug) but not other kinds of odours, he would receive some sort of treat. He then learned getting the treat was contingent on indicating when he sniffed the drug and ignored other odours.

Reinforcement: The Central Concept of Operant Conditioning

Skinner called the process that leads the rat to continue pressing the key "reinforcement" (just as the treat Declan received was reinforcement). **Reinforcement** is the process by which a stimulus increases the probability that a preceding behaviour will be repeated. In other words, pressing the lever is more likely to occur again because of the stimulus of food.

B.F. Skinner devised the Skinner box to condition rats to press a lever to obtain food.

In a situation such as this one, the food is called a reinforcer. A **reinforcer** is any stimulus that increases the probability that a preceding behaviour will occur again. Hence, food is a reinforcer, because it increases the probability that the behaviour of pressing (formally referred to as the *response* of pressing) will take place.

What kind of stimuli can act as reinforcers? Bonuses, toys, good grades, and food can serve as reinforcers—if they strengthen the probability of the response that occurred before their introduction. What makes something a reinforcer depends on individual preferences. Although a chocolate bar can act as a reinforcer for one person, an individual who dislikes chocolate may find 75 cents more desirable. The only way we can know if a stimulus is a reinforcer for a particular organism is to observe whether the frequency of a previously occurring behaviour increases after the presentation of the stimulus.

Of course, we are not born knowing that 75 cents can buy a candy bar. Rather, through experience we learn that money is a valuable commodity because of its association with stimuli (such as food and drink) that are naturally reinforcing. This fact suggests a distinction between primary reinforcers and secondary reinforcers. A *primary reinforcer* satisfies some biological need and works naturally, regardless of a person's prior experience. Food for a hungry person, warmth for a cold person, and relief for a person in pain all would be classified as primary reinforcers. A *secondary reinforcer*, in contrast, is a stimulus that becomes reinforcing because of its association with a primary reinforcer. For instance, we know that money is valuable because we have learned that it allows us to obtain other desirable objects, including primary reinforcers such as food and shelter. Money thus becomes a secondary reinforcer.

Positive Reinforcers, Negative Reinforcers, and Punishment

In many respects, reinforcers can be thought of in terms of rewards; both a reinforcer and a reward increase the probability that a preceding response will occur again. But the term *reward* is limited to *positive* occurrences, and this is where it differs from a reinforcer—for it turns out that reinforcers can be positive or negative. One important point to remember is that when we refer to positive and negative we do not mean good and bad. Think

DID YOU KNOW?

Skinner actually taught pigeons to bowl and play table tennis, and dogs to climb walls using *operant conditioning*.

reinforcement The process by which a stimulus increases the probability that a preceding behaviour will be repeated.

reinforcer Any stimulus that increases the probability that a preceding behaviour will occur again.

We learn the value of money as a secondary reinforcer at a young age.

of positive as meaning something will be added, and negative to mean something will be taken away.

A **positive reinforcer** is a desirable stimulus that is *added* to the environment that brings about an increase in a preceding response. If desirable food, water, money, or praise is provided after a response, it is more likely that that response will occur again in the future. The pay cheques that workers get at the end of the week, for example, increase the likelihood that they will return to their jobs the following week.

In contrast, a **negative reinforcer** refers to an unpleasant (or undesirable) stimulus whose removal leads to an increase in the probability that a preceding response will be repeated in the future. This can be a confusing concept for students, so if you are feeling a bit confused right now, don't worry! Think of this example and see if it makes a bit more sense. For example, if you have an itchy rash (an unpleasant stimulus) that is relieved (removed) when you use a certain brand of ointment, you are more likely to use that ointment the next time you have an itchy rash. In this example you have been negatively reinforced to use the ointment. You removed the unpleasant stimulus (itching) using the ointment, which felt good—so next time, you are more likely to use the ointment (that's the reinforcement part). Similarly, if your iPod volume is so loud that it hurts your ears when you first turn it on, you are likely to reduce the volume level. Lowering the volume is negatively reinforcing, and you are more apt to repeat the action in the future when you first turn it on. Negative reinforcement, then, teaches the individual that taking an action removes a negative condition that exists in the environment. But remember—just like positive reinforcers, negative reinforcers also increase the likelihood that preceding behaviours will be repeated. That's why they are called reinforcers!

> **Reinforcement** *increases* **the frequency of the behaviour preceding it; punishment** *decreases* **the frequency of the behaviour preceding it.**

Note that negative reinforcement is not the same as punishment. **Punishment** refers to a stimulus that *decreases* the probability that a prior behaviour will occur again. Unlike negative reinforcement, which produces an *increase* in behaviour, punishment *reduces* the likelihood of a prior response.

Let's consider something unpleasant that might happen in your environment: nagging by your housemates or parents. Your mother nagging you to clean your room could be an unpleasant stimulus. If you clean your room to make the nagging stop, you are more likely to repeat this behaviour in the future (by the way, this is an example of negative reinforcement, do you know why?). In this way your room-cleaning behaviour has been strengthened (reinforced) by removing the annoying nagging (removal of the unpleasant stimulus).

There are two types of punishment: positive punishment and negative punishment, just as there are positive reinforcement and negative reinforcement. In both cases, "positive" means adding something, and "negative" means removing something. *Positive punishment* weakens a response through the application of an unpleasant stimulus. For instance, spanking a child for misbehaving, or receiving an F on your test because you did not study are examples of positive punishment. In contrast, *negative punishment* consists of the removal of something pleasant. For instance, when a teenager is told she is "grounded" and will no longer be able to use the family car because of her poor grades, or when an

positive reinforcer A stimulus added to the environment that brings about an increase in a preceding response.

negative reinforcer An unpleasant stimulus whose removal leads to an *increase* in the probability that a preceding response will be repeated in the future (if the response will be repeated in the future, it is reinforcement).

punishment A stimulus that *decreases* the probability that a previous behaviour will occur again (if the response is not likely to occur again, it is punishment).

employee is informed that he has been demoted with a cut in pay because of a poor job evaluation, negative punishment is being administered. Both positive and negative punishment result in a decrease in the likelihood that a previous behaviour will be repeated. Another example relates to a new law in Ontario in which a person caught driving 50 kilometres over the posted speed limit will receive a large fine (positive punishment—because the unpleasant large fine was added to decrease the speeding behaviour). The person will also have his or her licence suspended for a period of time, which is an example of negative punishment because the pleasant stimulus (the right to drive) has been removed to decrease the speeding behaviour next time.

These rules can help you distinguish among the concepts of positive and negative reinforcement and punishment:

- Reinforcement *increases* the frequency of the behaviour preceding it; punishment *decreases* the frequency of the behaviour preceding it.
- The *application* of a *positive* stimulus brings about an increase in the frequency of behaviour and is referred to as positive reinforcement; the *application* of a *negative* stimulus decreases or reduces the frequency of behaviour and is called positive punishment.
- The *removal* of a *negative* stimulus that results in an increase in the frequency of behaviour is negative reinforcement; the *removal* of a *positive* stimulus that decreases the frequency of behaviour is negative punishment.

Study tip

The differences between positive reinforcement, negative reinforcement, positive punishment, and negative punishment are trickier than you might think, so pay special attention to the list you just read and the summary in Figure 5.2.

The Pros and Cons of Punishment: Why Reinforcement Beats Punishment Is punishment an effective way to modify behaviour? Punishment often presents the quickest route to changing behaviour that, if allowed to continue, might be dangerous to an individual. For instance, a parent may not have a second chance to warn a child not to run into a busy street, and so punishing the first incidence of this behaviour may prove to be wise. Moreover, the use of punishment to suppress behaviour, even temporarily, provides an opportunity to reinforce a person for subsequently behaving in a more desirable way. Remember, punishment only teaches what not to do. If you want someone to learn a particular behaviour, you must reinforce the behaviour you want to see!

Punishment has several disadvantages that make its routine use questionable. For one thing, punishment is frequently ineffective, particularly if it is not delivered shortly after the undesired behaviour or if the individual is able to leave the setting in which the punishment is being given.

Figure 5.2
Reinforcement and Punishment

Intended Result	When stimulus is added, the result is . . .	When stimulus is removed or terminated, the result is . . .
Reinforcement (increase in behaviour)	**Positive reinforcement** Example: Giving a raise for good performance Result: *Increase* in response of good performance	**Negative reinforcement** Example: Applying ointment to relieve an itchy rash leads to a higher future likelihood of applying the ointment Result: *Increase* in response of using ointment
Punishment (decrease in behaviour)	**Positive punishment** Example: Yelling at a teenager when she steals a bracelet Result: *Decrease* in frequency of response of stealing	**Negative punishment** Example: Teenager's access to car restricted by parents due to teenager's breaking curfew Result: *Decrease* in response of breaking curfew

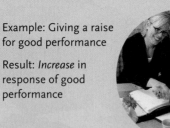
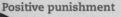
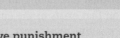

An employee who is reprimanded by the boss may quit; a teenager who loses the use of the family car may borrow a friend's car instead. In such instances, the initial behaviour that is being punished may be replaced by one that is even less desirable.

Even worse, physical punishment can convey to the recipient the idea that physical aggression is permissible and perhaps even desirable. A father who yells at and hits his son for misbehaving teaches the son that aggression is an appropriate, adult response. The son soon may copy his father's behaviour by acting aggressively toward others. In addition, physical punishment is often administered by people who are themselves angry or enraged. It is unlikely that individuals in such an emotional state will be able to think through what they are doing or control carefully the degree of punishment they are inflicting. Ultimately, those who resort to physical punishment run the risk that they will grow to be feared. Punishment can also reduce the self-esteem of recipients unless they can understand the reasons for it (Baumrind, Larzelere, & Cowan, 2002; Sorbring, Deater-Deckard, & Palmerus, 2006).

Finally, punishment does not convey any information about what an alternative, more appropriate behaviour might be. To be useful in bringing about more desirable behaviour in the future, punishment must be accompanied by specific information about the behaviour that is being punished, along with specific suggestions concerning a more desirable behaviour. As we mentioned earlier, we must

In what ways is punishment ineffective?

Psych think

> > > Provide an example of how each of the different elements of operant conditioning (positive reinforcement, negative reinforcement, positive punishment, and negative punishment) could be applied in your life.

reinforce the behaviour we want to see. Punishing a child for staring out the window in school could merely lead her to stare at the floor instead. Unless we teach her appropriate ways to respond, we have merely managed to substitute one undesirable behaviour for another. If punishment is not followed up with reinforcement for subsequent behaviour that is more appropriate, little will be accomplished.

In short, reinforcing desired behaviour is a more effective technique for modifying behaviour than using punishment. Both in and out of the scientific arena, reinforcement usually beats punishment (Hiby, Rooney, & Bradshaw, 2004; Pogarsky & Piquero, 2003; Sidman, 2006).

Schedules of Reinforcement The world would be a different place if people who played the lottery never bought a ticket again after losing, fishermen returned to shore as soon as they missed a catch, or telemarketers never made another phone call after their first hang-up. The fact that such unreinforced behaviours continue, often with great frequency and persistence, illustrates that reinforcement does not need to be continually received for behaviour to be learned and maintained. In fact, behaviour that is reinforced only occasionally can ultimately be learned better than can behaviour that is always reinforced.

When we refer to the frequency and timing of reinforcement that follows desired behaviour, we are talking about **schedules of reinforcement**. Behaviour that is reinforced every time it occurs is said to be on a **continuous reinforcement schedule**; if it is reinforced some but not all of the time, it is on a **partial (or intermittent) reinforcement schedule**. Continuous reinforcement works really well for new behaviours because learning occurs more rapidly when the behaviour is continuously reinforced. Imagine, for example, that you are trying to teach your cat to greet you every time you come home. The cat will learn much more quickly that it is going to get a reward when it greets you if you give it a reward every single time it greets

> **schedules of reinforcement** Different patterns of frequency and timing of reinforcement following desired behaviour.
>
> **continuous reinforcement schedule** Reinforcing of a behaviour every time it occurs; good for new behaviours.
>
> **partial (or intermittent) reinforcement schedule** Reinforcing of a behaviour sometimes but not all of the time.

you. Later, once a behaviour is learned, it will last longer if you stop giving reinforcement all the time. If you reinforce the cat's greeting only sometimes, that is, if you use a partial reinforcement schedule to maintain its behaviour, it will be more likely to keep on greeting you long after you stop giving it a reward (Casey, Cooper-Brown, & Wacher, 2006; Gottlieb, 2004; Staddon & Cerutti, 2003).

Why should intermittent reinforcement result in stronger, longer-lasting learning than continuous reinforcement does? We can answer the question by examining how we might behave when using a candy vending machine compared with a slot machine. When we use a vending machine, prior experience has taught us that every time we put in the appropriate amount of money, the reinforcement, a candy bar, ought to be delivered. In other words, the schedule of reinforcement is continuous. In comparison, a slot machine offers intermittent reinforcement. People who use these machines learn that after putting in their cash, most of the time they will not receive anything in return. At the same time, though, they know that they will occasionally win something.

Now suppose that, unknown to us, both the candy vending machine and the slot machine are broken, and so neither one is able to dispense anything. It would not be very long before we stopped depositing coins into the broken candy machine. Probably at most we would try only two or three times before leaving the machine in disgust. But the story would be quite different with the broken slot machine. Here, money might be dropped into the machine for a considerably longer time, even though there would be no payoff, because we know that at some point there must be reinforcement (unfortunately, some people spend a considerable amount of money waiting for the reinforcement that does not come to them).

In formal terms, we can see the difference between the two reinforcement schedules: partial reinforcement schedules (such as those provided by slot machines) maintain performance longer than do continuous reinforcement

People keep adding money to slot machines because of variable-ratio schedules of reinforcement.

fixed-ratio schedule A schedule by which reinforcement is given only after a specific or set number of responses are made.

variable-ratio schedule A schedule by which reinforcement occurs after a varying number of responses rather than after a fixed number.

fixed-interval schedule A schedule that provides reinforcement for a response only if a fixed time period has elapsed, making overall rates of response relatively low.

schedules (such as those established in candy vending machines) before *extinction*—the disappearance of the conditioned response—occurs.

Certain kinds of partial reinforcement schedules produce stronger and lengthier responding before extinction than do others. Although many different partial reinforcement schedules have been examined, they can most readily be put into two categories: schedules that consider the *number of responses* made before reinforcement is given, called *fixed-ratio* and *variable-ratio schedules*, and those that consider the *amount of time* that elapses before reinforcement is provided, called *fixed-interval* and *variable-interval schedules* (Gottlieb, 2006; Pellegrini et al., 2004; Svartdal, 2003).

In a **fixed-ratio schedule**, reinforcement is given only after a specific or set number of responses. For instance, a rat might receive a food pellet every tenth time it pressed a lever; here, the ratio would be 1:10. Similarly, garment workers are generally paid on fixed-ratio schedules: They receive a specific number of dollars for every blouse they sew. Because a greater rate of production means more reinforcement (i.e., more money!), people on fixed-ratio schedules are apt to work as quickly as possible.

In a **variable-ratio schedule**, reinforcement occurs after a varying number of responses rather than after a fixed number. Although the specific number of responses necessary to receive reinforcement varies, the number of responses usually hovers around a specific average. A good example of a variable-ratio schedule is a slot machine. People who play the slots do not know the number of coins they will need to deposit before they receive the reinforcement (i.e., the payout), but they do know that there will be a reinforcement after some number of responses. This schedule of reinforcement is very strong because it leads to a high rate of response and resistance to extinction, which is one reason why so many people have an addiction to gambling.

In contrast to fixed-ratio and variable-ratio schedules, in which the crucial factor is the number of responses (you can remember this by remembering that ratios involve numbers), fixed-*interval* and variable-*interval* schedules focus on the amount of time that has elapsed since a person or animal was reinforced. One example of a fixed-interval schedule is a weekly pay cheque. For people who receive regular, weekly pay cheques, it typically makes relatively little difference exactly how much they produce in a given week.

Because a **fixed-interval schedule** provides reinforcement for a response only if a fixed time period has elapsed, overall rates of response are relatively low. This is especially true in the period just after reinforcement, when the

Do your study habits follow a fixed-interval schedule?

wait time before another reinforcement is relatively long. Students' study habits often exemplify this reality. If the periods between exams are relatively long (meaning that the opportunity for reinforcement for good performance is given fairly infrequently), students often study minimally or not at all until the day of the exam draws near. Just before the exam, however, students begin to cram for it, signalling a rapid increase in the rate of their studying response. As you might expect, immediately after the exam there is a rapid decline in the rate of responding, with few people opening a book the day after a test.

One way to decrease the delay in responding that occurs just after reinforcement, and to maintain the desired behaviour more consistently throughout an interval, is to use a

variable-interval schedule. In a **variable-interval schedule**, the time between reinforcements varies around some average rather than being fixed. For example, a professor who gives surprise quizzes that vary from one every three days to one every three weeks, averaging one every two weeks, is using a variable-interval schedule. Compared to the study habits we observed with a fixed-interval schedule, students' study habits under such a variable-interval schedule would most likely be very different. Students would be apt to study more regularly, because they would never know when the

Psych think

> > > How might operant conditioning be applied in the classroom to increase the likelihood that students will complete their homework more frequently?

variable-interval schedule A schedule by which the time between reinforcements varies around some average rather than being fixed.

Figure 5.3

Four Schedules of Reinforcement

Fixed-ratio schedule	**Variable-ratio schedule**	**Fixed-interval schedule**	**Variable-interval schedule**
Reinforcement is given only after a predictable or set number of responses are made, such as getting paid $20.00 for every four tires you make.	Reinforcement occurs after an unpredictable or varying number of responses are made, such as winning at the slot machine after an unpredictable number of coins are put in it.	Reinforcement for a response after a predictable or fixed time period has elapsed, making overall rates of response relatively low. For example, getting paid every two weeks.	Reinforcement occurs after an unpredictable or varying amount of time has elapsed, such as a parent picking up a crying child—the child does not know how long he or she needs to cry before he or she is picked up.

next surprise quiz was coming. Variable-interval schedules, in general, are more likely to produce relatively steady rates of responding than are fixed-interval schedules, with responses that take longer to extinguish after reinforcement ends.

Discrimination and Generalization in Operant Conditioning It does not take a child long to learn that sharing toys gets rewarded with a cookie and refusing to share results in a time out. The same operant conditioning principles account for the way that a pigeon can learn to peck a key when a green light goes on, but not when a red light appears. Just as in classical conditioning, then, operant learning involves the phenomena of discrimination and generalization.

The process by which people learn to discriminate stimuli is known as stimulus control training. In *stimulus control training*, a behaviour is reinforced in the presence of a specific stimulus, but not in its absence. For example, one of the most difficult discriminations many people face is determining when someone's friendliness is not mere friendliness but a signal of romantic interest. People learn to make the discrimination by observing the presence of certain non-verbal cues—such as increased eye contact and touching—that indicate romantic interest. When such cues are absent, people learn that no romantic interest is indicated. In this case, the non-verbal cue acts as a discriminative stimulus, one to which an organism learns to respond during stimulus control training. A *discriminative stimulus* signals the likelihood that reinforcement will follow a response. For example, if you wait until your roommate is in a good mood before you ask to borrow her iPad, your behaviour can be said to be under stimulus control because you can discriminate among her moods.

Just as in classical conditioning, the phenomenon of stimulus generalization, in which an organism learns a response to one stimulus and then exhibits the same response to slightly different stimuli, occurs in operant conditioning. If you have learned that being polite helps you to get your way in a certain situation (reinforcing your politeness), you are likely to generalize your response to other situations. Sometimes, though, generalization can have unfortunate consequences, as when people behave negatively toward all members of a racial group because they have had an unpleasant experience with one member of that group, creating stereotypes which we will discuss in more detail in the Social Psychology chapter.

Shaping: Reinforcing What Doesn't Come Naturally Consider the difficulty of using only operant conditioning to teach people to repair an automobile transmission. You would have to wait until they performed a desired behaviour before providing reinforcement. It would probably take them a very long time to accidentally stumble on the correct behaviour.

There are many complex behaviours, ranging from auto repair to zoo management, that we would not expect to occur naturally as part of anyone's spontaneous behaviour. Since these behaviours would never occur naturally, there would be no opportunity to reinforce them. However, there is a procedure, known as shaping, that can be used

BUY IT?

Should You Spend Your Money on Lottery Tickets?

Do you buy lottery tickets? If so, why do you spend your money on lottery tickets when the probability of winning is so low? Dr. Jeffery Rosenthal from the University of Toronto argues that the odds of you winning Lotto 649 are just 1 in 14 million, and that if you purchased a lottery ticket every week, your chances of winning would be once every 250,000 years (Rosenthal, 2006). In fact, Rosenthal suggests that you are more likely to be killed in a car accident on the way to purchase your lottery ticket than you are to win the actual lottery. Admit it; you are probably thinking right now, "Well, someone has to win!" It's this type of thinking that makes lottery corporations so rich. When people think they have a chance to win, they are likely to spend their money, even if they cannot afford it. Can you think of what learning principle is at work here? Money is a secondary reinforcer, and winning money (especially the thought of winning lots of money) is positive reinforcement. The problem is that lottery winnings are not on a continuous schedule of reinforcement. Imagine winning every time you played! As we discussed earlier, lottery winnings, like slot machine payouts, are on a variable-ratio schedule of reinforcement. This means that the number of tickets you have to buy before you win is unpredictable. You might win, but you do not know when (however, keep in mind Rosenthal's odds of your winning). Variable schedules of reinforcement are very powerful in influencing our behaviour, and they are difficult to extinguish. Keep these points in mind before spending your hard-earned money on lottery tickets.

Figure 5.4
Classical and Operant Conditioning Compared

Concept	Classical Conditioning	Operant Conditioning
Basic principle	Building associations between a conditioned stimulus and conditioned response.	Reinforcement *increases* the frequency of the behaviour preceding it; punishment *decreases* the frequency of the behaviour preceding it.
Nature of behaviour	Based on involuntary, natural, innate behaviour. Behaviour is elicited by the unconditioned or conditioned stimulus.	An organism voluntarily operates on its environment to produce a desirable result. After behaviour occurs, the likelihood of the behaviour occurring again is increased or decreased by the behaviour's consequences.
Order of events	Before conditioning, an unconditioned stimulus leads to an unconditioned response. After conditioning, a conditioned stimulus leads to a conditioned response.	Reinforcement leads to an increase in behaviour; punishment leads to a decrease in behaviour.
Example	After a physician gives a child a series of painful injections (an unconditioned stimulus) that produce an emotional reaction (an unconditioned response), the child develops an emotional reaction (a conditioned response) whenever she sees the physician (the conditioned stimulus).	A student who, after studying hard for a test, earns an A (the positive reinforcer), is more likely to study hard in the future. A student who, after going out drinking the night before a test, fails the test (punishment) is less likely to go out drinking the night before the next test.

to guide someone toward the desired behaviour. **Shaping** is the process of teaching a complex behaviour by rewarding closer and closer approximations of the desired behaviour. In shaping, you start by reinforcing any behaviour that is at all similar to the behaviour you want the person to learn. Later, you reinforce only responses that are closer to the behaviour you ultimately want to teach. Finally, you reinforce only the desired response. Each step in shaping, then, moves only slightly beyond the previously learned behaviour, permitting the person to link the new step to the behaviour learned earlier.

Shaping allows other species to learn complex responses that would never occur naturally, ranging from lions jumping through hoops, dolphins rescuing divers lost at sea, or rodents finding hidden land mines. Shaping also underlies the learning of many complex human skills. For instance, the ability to participate in a college psychology class is shaped from the first childhood experiences in a classroom. Behaviours such as attention and concentration, for example, are much less apparent in a preschool than they are in a college classroom. Over the years, we are rewarded for closer and closer approximations of desirable attention and concentration behaviours.

shaping The process of teaching a complex behaviour by rewarding closer and closer approximations of the desired behaviour.

Psych think

> > > In light of what you've learned about classical and operant conditioning, do you think that Declan, the drug-and-bomb-sniffing dog described at the beginning of this chapter, learned his particular skills primarily by classical conditioning or by operant conditioning? Why? If you've ever had a puppy, what conditioning techniques did you use to train it?

Comparing Classical and Operant Conditioning
We've considered classical conditioning and operant conditioning as two completely different processes. Further, there are a number of key distinctions between the two forms of learning. For example, the key concepts in classical conditioning are the associations between stimuli and the *reflexive* responses we experience, whereas in operant conditioning the key concept is making a *voluntary* response to obtain reinforcement. In classical conditioning the reflexive behaviour is elicited by a signal in the environment *before* the behaviour occurs, whereas in operant conditioning the reinforcement or punishment is given *after* the voluntary behaviour occurs.

BEHAVIOUR ANALYSIS AND BEHAVIOUR MODIFICATION

Two people who had been living together for three years began to fight frequently. The issues of disagreement ranged from who was going to do the dishes to the quality of their love life. Disturbed, the couple went to a *behaviour analyst*, a psychologist who specializes in behaviour-modification techniques. He asked both partners to keep a detailed written record of their interactions over the following two weeks.

When they returned with the data, he carefully reviewed the records with them. In doing so, he noticed a pattern: each of their arguments had occurred just after one or the other had left a household chore undone, such as leaving dirty dishes in the sink or draping clothes on the only chair in the bedroom.

Using the data the couple had collected, the behaviour analyst asked both partners to list all the chores that could possibly arise and assign each one a point value depending on how long it took to complete. Then he had them divide the chores equally and agree in a written contract to fulfill the ones assigned to them. If either failed to carry out one of the assigned chores, he or she would have to place $1 per point in a fund for the other to spend. They also agreed to a program of verbal praise, promising to reward each other verbally for completing a chore.

Both partners agreed to try the program for a month and to keep careful records of the number of arguments they had during that period. To their surprise, the number declined rapidly.

This case provides an illustration of **behaviour modification**, a formalized technique for promoting the frequency of desirable behaviours and decreasing the incidence of unwanted ones. Using the basic principles of learning theory, behaviour-modification techniques have proved to be helpful in a variety of situations. For example, people with severe mental retardation (intellectual disabilities) have started dressing and feeding themselves for the first time in their lives as a result of behaviour modification. Behaviour modification has also helped people lose weight, give up smoking, and behave more safely (Delinsky, Latner, & Wilson, 2006; Ntinas, 2007; Wadden, Crerand, & Brock, 2005).

The techniques used by behaviour analysts are as varied as the list of processes that modify behaviour. They include reinforcement scheduling, shaping, generalization training, and extinction. Participants in a behaviour-change program do, however, typically follow a series of similar basic steps:

- *Identifying goals and target behaviours.* The first step is to define *desired behaviour*. Is it an increase in time spent studying? A decrease in weight? An increase in the use of language? A reduction in the amount of aggression displayed by a child? The goals must be stated in observable terms and must lead to specific targets. For instance, a goal might be "to increase study

behaviour modification A formalized technique for promoting the frequency of desirable behaviours and decreasing the incidence of unwanted ones.

Psych
At The Movies

A Clockwork Orange
An ultraviolent, young, British man, imprisoned for rape and murder, volunteers to participate in an experimental program in which classical conditioning and aversion therapy are used in an attempt to rehabilitate him.

The Manchurian Candidate
The effects of classical conditioning and hypnosis in this movie are so powerful they turn a loyal soldier into a dangerous assassin.

What About Bob?
Bob uses shaping strategies (reinforcing "baby steps") from his psychologist's book in an attempt to overcome his irrational fears and anxieties.

Rounders
Casinos capitalize on the power of intermittent schedules of reinforcement. The main character in this movie battles a gambling addiction that keeps pulling him back in.

time," whereas the target behaviour would be "to study at least two hours per day on weekdays and an hour on Saturdays."

- *Designing a data-recording system and recording preliminary data.* To determine whether behaviour has changed, one must collect data before any changes are made in the situation. This information provides a baseline against which future changes can be measured.

- *Selecting a behaviour-change strategy.* The most crucial step is to select an appropriate strategy. Because all the principles of learning can be employed to bring about behaviour change, a "package" of treatments is normally used. This might include the systematic use of positive reinforcement for desired behaviour (verbal praise or something more tangible, such as food), as well as a program of extinction for undesirable behaviour (ignoring a child who throws a tantrum). Selecting the right reinforcers is critical, and it may be necessary to experiment a bit to find out what is important to a particular individual.

- *Implementing the program.* Probably the most important aspect of program implementation is consistency. It is also important to reinforce the intended behaviour. For example, suppose a mother wants her daughter to spend more time on her homework, but as soon as the child sits down to study, she asks for a snack. If the mother gets a snack for her, she is likely to be reinforcing her daughter's delaying tactic, not her studying.

- *Keeping careful records after the program is implemented.* Another crucial task is record keeping. If the target behaviours are not monitored, there is no way of knowing whether the program has actually been successful.
- *Evaluating and altering the ongoing program.* Finally, the results of the program should be compared with baseline, pre-implementation data to determine the program's effectiveness. If the program has been successful, the procedures employed can be phased out gradually. For instance, if the program called for reinforcing every instance of picking up one's clothes from the bedroom floor, the reinforcement schedule could be modified to a fixed-ratio schedule in which every third instance was reinforced. However, if the program has not been successful in bringing about the desired behaviour change, consideration of other approaches might be advisable.

Behaviour-change techniques based on these general principles have enjoyed wide success and have proved to be one of the most powerful means of modifying behaviour. Clearly, it is possible to employ the basic notions of learning theory to improve our lives.

Cognitive Approaches to Learning

Consider what happens when someone learns to drive a car. They don't just get behind the wheel and stumble around until they randomly put the key into the ignition and, later, after many false starts, accidentally manage to get the car to move forward, thereby receiving positive reinforcement. This is how it would work if conditioning were the only type of learning. In real life, however, conditioning is only part of how we learn complex behaviours. For example, we already know the basic elements of driving from prior experience as passengers, when we likely noticed how the key was inserted into the ignition, the car was put in drive, and the gas pedal was pressed to make the car go forward.

Learning to drive a car is an example of a cognitive approach to learning.

Clearly, not all learning can be explained by operant and classical conditioning paradigms. In fact, activities like learning to drive a car imply that some kinds of learning must involve higher-order processes in which people's thoughts and memories and the way they process information account for their responses. Such situations argue against regarding learning as the unthinking, mechanical, and automatic acquisition of associations between stimuli and responses, as in classical conditioning, or the presentation of reinforcement, as in operant conditioning.

Some psychologists view learning in terms of the thought processes, called *cognitions*, that underlie it—an approach known as **cognitive learning theory**. Although psychologists working from the cognitive learning perspective do not deny the importance of classical and operant conditioning, they have developed approaches that focus on the unseen mental processes that occur during learning, rather than concentrating solely on external stimuli, responses, and reinforcements. For example, two types of learning that cannot be explained by operant or classical conditioning concepts are latent learning and observational learning.

LATENT LEARNING

Early evidence for the importance of cognitive processes comes from a series of animal experiments that revealed a type of cognitive learning called latent learning. In **latent learning**, a new behaviour is learned but not demonstrated until some incentive is provided for displaying it (Tolman & Honzik, 1930). In short, latent learning occurs without reinforcement.

In the studies demonstrating latent learning, psychologists examined the behaviour of rats in a maze such as the one shown on the next page. In one experiment, rats were randomly assigned to one of three experimental conditions. One group of rats was allowed to wander around the maze once a day for 17 days without ever receiving a reward. Understandably, those rats made many errors and spent a relatively long time reaching the end of the maze. A second group, however, was always given food at the end of the maze. Not surprisingly, those rats learned to run quickly and directly to the food box, making few errors.

cognitive learning theory An approach to the study of learning that focuses on the thought processes that underlie learning.

latent learning Learning in which a new behaviour is acquired but is not demonstrated until some incentive is provided for displaying it.

A third group of rats started out in the same situation as the unrewarded rats, but only for the first 10 days. On the 11th day, a critical experimental manipulation was introduced: from that point on, the rats in this group were given food for completing the maze. The results of this manipulation were dramatic. The previously unrewarded rats, which had earlier seemed to wander about aimlessly, showed such reductions in running time and declines in error rates that their performance almost immediately matched that of the group that had received rewards from the start.

To cognitive theorists, it seemed clear that the unrewarded rats had learned the layout of the maze early in their explorations; they just never displayed their latent learning until the reinforcement was offered. Instead, those rats seemed to develop a cognitive map of the maze—a mental representation of spatial locations and directions.

Latent learning occurs without reinforcement.

People, too, develop cognitive maps of their surroundings. For example, latent learning may permit you to know the location of a kitchenware store at a local mall you've frequently visited, even though you've never entered the store and don't even like to cook.

The possibility that we develop our cognitive maps through latent learning presents something of a problem for strict operant conditioning theorists. If we consider the results of the maze-learning experiment, for instance, we cannot clearly see what reinforcement permitted the rats that initially received no reward to learn the layout of the maze, because there was no obvious reinforcer present. Instead, the results support a cognitive view of learning,

Figure 5.5

Latent Learning in Rats

Once a day for 17 days rats were allowed to run through a maze. Rats that were never rewarded (unrewarded control condition) consistently made the most errors. Those that received food for finishing the maze each time (rewarded control condition) made far fewer errors. The experimental group was initially unrewarded but began to be rewarded on the tenth day. Soon their error rate fell to about the same level as that of the rewarded controls. Apparently, this group had developed a cognitive map of the maze and demonstrated their latent learning when they were rewarded for completing the maze successfully. Rats learned the layout of the maze early in their explorations but they did not display their latent learning until reinforcement was offered.

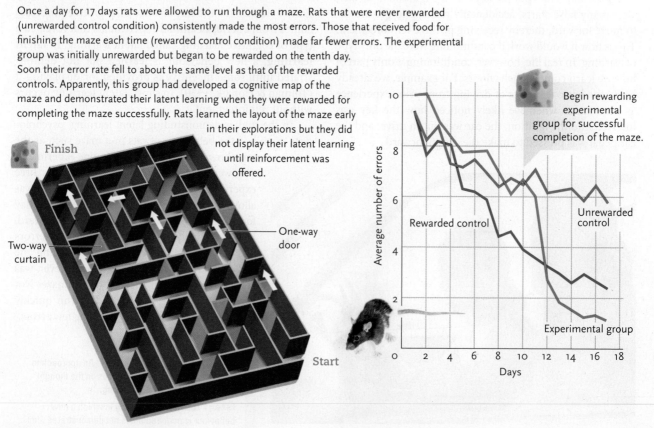

Source: Tolman & Honzik, 1930.

in which changes occur in unobservable mental processes (Beatty, 2002; Frensch & Rünger, 2003; Stouffer & White, 2006; Voicu & Schmajuk, 2002).

OBSERVATIONAL LEARNING: LEARNING THROUGH IMITATION

Let's return for a moment to the case of a person learning to drive. How can we account for instances in which an individual with no direct experience in carrying out a particular behaviour learns the behaviour and then performs it? To answer this question, psychologists have focused on another aspect of cognitive learning: observational learning.

According to psychologist Albert Bandura and colleagues, a major part of human learning consists of **observational learning**, which is learning by watching the behaviour of another person, or *model*. Because of its reliance on observation of others—a social phenomenon—the perspective taken by

observational learning Learning by observing the behaviour of another person or model.

Albert Bandura demonstrated that much of our learning occurs through observation.

Bandura is often referred to as a *social cognitive* approach to learning (Bandura, 1999, 2004).

Bandura dramatically demonstrated the ability of models to stimulate learning in a classic experiment. In the study, young children saw a film of an adult wildly hitting a 1.5-metre-tall inflatable punching toy called a Bobo doll (Bandura, Ross, & Ross, 1963a, 1963b). Later the children were given the opportunity to play with the Bobo doll themselves, and, sure enough, most displayed the same kind of behaviour, in some cases mimicking the aggressive behaviour almost identically.

Observational learning is particularly important in acquiring skills in which the operant conditioning technique of shaping is inappropriate. Piloting an airplane and performing brain surgery, for example, are behaviours that could hardly be learned by using trial-and-error methods without grave cost—literally—to those involved in the learning process.

Not all behaviour that we witness is learned or carried out, of course. One crucial factor that determines whether we later imitate a model is whether the model is rewarded for his or her behaviour. If we observe a friend being rewarded for putting more time into her studies by receiving higher grades, we are more likely to imitate her behaviour than we would if her behaviour resulted only in being stressed and tired. Models who are rewarded for behaving in a particular way are more apt to be mimicked than are models who receive punishment. Observing the punishment of a model, however, does not necessarily stop observers from learning the behaviour. Observers can still describe the model's behaviour—they are just less apt to perform it (Bandura, 1977, 1986, 1994).

Children often learn by observing and imitating their parents.

Study tip

A key point of observational learning approaches is that the behaviour of models who are rewarded for a given behaviour is more likely to be imitated than behaviour in which the model is punished for the behaviour.

From the perspective of ...

AN EARLY CHILDHOOD EDUCATOR What advice would you give to families about children's exposure to violent media and video games?

Observational learning provides a framework for understanding a number of important issues relating to the extent to which people learn simply by watching the behaviour of others. For instance, does watching violence on television cause us to become more violent?

VIOLENCE IN TELEVISION AND VIDEO GAMES: DOES THE MEDIA'S MESSAGE MATTER?

In an episode of *The Sopranos* television series, fictional mobster Tony Soprano murdered one of his associates. To make identification of the victim's body difficult, Soprano and one of his henchmen dismembered the body and dumped the body parts.

A few months later, two real-life half brothers in Riverside, California, strangled their mother and then cut her head and hands from her body. Victor Bautista, 20, and Matthew Montejo, 15, were caught by police after a security guard noticed that the bundle they were attempting to throw into a dumpster had a foot sticking out of it. They told police that the plan to dismember their mother was inspired by the *Sopranos* episode (Martelle, Hanley, & Yoshino, 2003).

Like other "media copycat" killings, the brothers' cold-blooded brutality raises a critical issue: Does observing violent and antisocial acts in the media lead viewers to behave in similar ways? Because research on modelling shows that people frequently learn and imitate the aggression that they observe, this question is among the most important issues being addressed by psychologists.

Certainly, the amount of violence in the mass media is enormous. By the time of elementary school graduation, the average child will have viewed more than 8,000 murders and more than 800,000 violent acts on network television (Huston et al., 1992; Mifflin, 1998).

Some experts argue that watching high levels of media violence makes viewers more susceptible to acting aggressively, and one recent study supports this claim. For example, a survey of serious and violent young male offenders showed that one-fourth of them had attempted to commit a media-inspired copycat crime (Surette, 2002). A significant proportion of those teenage offenders noted that they paid close attention to the media.

Violent video games have also been linked with actual aggression. In one of a series of studies by psychologist Craig Anderson and his colleagues, for example, college students who frequently played violent video games, such as *Postal* or *Doom*, were more likely to have been involved in delinquent behaviour and aggression than were their peers. Frequent players also had lower academic achievement (Anderson &

Dill, 2000; Anderson et al., 2004; Bartholow & Anderson, 2002).

Several aspects of media violence may contribute to real-life aggressive behaviour (Bushman & Anderson, 2001; Johnson et al., 2002). For one thing, experiencing violent media content seems to lower inhibitions against carrying out aggression—watching television portrayals of violence or using violence to win a video game makes aggression seem a legitimate response to particular situations. Exposure to media violence also may distort our understanding of the meaning of others' behaviour, predisposing us to view even non-aggressive acts by others as aggressive. Finally, a continuous diet of aggression may leave us desensitized to violence, and what previously would have repelled us now produces little emotional response. Our sense of the pain and suffering brought about by aggression may be diminished (Bartholow, Bushman, & Sestir, 2006; Carnagey, Anderson, & Bushman, 2007; Weber, Ritterfeld, & Kostygina, 2006).

> When you hear reports that media violence causes aggression, make sure you read the original research (don't rely on someone else's summary). Remember that correlational studies on media violence and aggression only tell us there is a link; they do not account for other variables that might influence violent behaviour.

While some evidence suggests a correlation or link between observing media violence and acting aggressively, a good critical thinker would question the assumption that watching media violence *causes* aggressive behaviour. Remember, correlations only tell us that there is a link between two variables; they do not take into account any other variables that may be influencing one, or both of the two initial variables. For example, we don't know if the individual was violent before watching the violent media or if other personality, social, or biological variables may have influenced the behaviour. Jonathan Freedman from the University of Toronto argues that exposure to media violence does not result in violent behaviour (Freedman, 2002). Freedman asserts that much of the research in this area has been misinterpreted and that a careful reading of the primary research demonstrates that watching violent television or playing violent video games does not cause violent behaviour. This is a good reminder that we should always read the original research ourselves rather than relying on someone else's summary because the research may be misinterpreted, even by credible sources.

For Review »

What is learning?

Learning is a relatively permanent change in behaviour resulting from experience. Classical conditioning is a form of learning that occurs when a neutral stimulus—one that normally brings about no relevant response—is repeatedly paired with a stimulus (called an unconditioned stimulus) that brings about a reflexive, untrained response. By studying salivation in dogs, Pavlov determined that conditioning occurs when the neutral stimulus is repeatedly presented just before the unconditioned stimulus. After repeated pairings, the neutral stimulus elicits the same response that the unconditioned stimulus brings about. When this occurs, the neutral stimulus has become a conditioned stimulus, and the response a conditioned response. Watson applied Pavlov's principles to condition a human infant called "Little Albert" to fear a white rat. Little Albert also came to fear other white furry objects, demonstrating stimulus generalization. Learning is not always permanent. Extinction occurs when a previously learned response decreases in frequency and eventually disappears.

What is the role of reward and punishment in learning?

In operant conditioning, a voluntary behaviour is strengthened or weakened through reinforcement or punishment. Skinner's work with animals showed that reinforcing or rewarding behaviour increases the probability that the behaviour will be repeated. Reinforcers can be positive or negative, which means that something is added (positive) or something is removed (negative). Reinforcement is most effective when it is on a variable schedule where the person (or animal) is unsure of exactly when the reinforcement will be received. In contrast to reinforcement, positive and negative punishment decreases or suppresses a target behaviour.

How can the information from this chapter be used to change undesired behaviours?

Behaviour modification is a method for applying the principles of learning theory to promote the frequency of desired behaviours and to decrease or eliminate unwanted ones.

Does thinking matter at all in learning?

Cognitive approaches to learning consider learning in terms of thought processes, or cognition. Latent learning and the apparent development of cognitive maps support cognitive approaches. Learning also occurs when we observe the behaviour of others, as in observational learning. The major factor that determines whether an observed behaviour will actually be performed is the nature of the reinforcement or punishment a model receives.

Psych _think_ answers

Psych think 1 In the first PSYCH think on p. 117 we asked you to use the five elements of classical conditioning to explain why someone who was in a car accident last year now feels anxiety and slows down cautiously when driving through an intersection. To answer this, you needed to consider what happened when the person was initially in the car accident. Given that the person drives slowly through the intersection you can assume that the accident happened at an intersection. If so, the car crash was the UCS (unconditioned stimulus) and the anxiety was the UCR (unconditioned response). The intersection was initially the NS (neutral stimulus) that became the CS (conditioned stimulus) because the individual now feels anxiety (now the CR, conditioned response) when driving through intersections (NS).

Psych think 2 In the PSYCH think on p. 121 we asked you to provide an example of how each of the different elements of operant conditioning (positive reinforcement, negative reinforcement, positive punishment, and negative punishment) could be applied in your life. Remember that reinforcement means that the behaviour will increase. For example, many of us learned how to potty train through positive reinforcement. Our parents or guardians would provide some sort of reinforcer (i.e., praise, candy, or stickers) whenever we used the toilet. Now, it's not likely that your parents still reinforce this behaviour (hopefully!), so they moved from using a continuous schedule of reinforcement to an intermittent schedule of reinforcement, to not reinforcing the behaviour at all. A more recent example in your life for negative reinforcement might be the last time you took pain medication for a headache. In this case, taking the pain medication was reinforced because it removed the unpleasant stimulus (the headache). An example of positive punishment may have been when you received a spanking for hitting your sister or brother. This is an example of positive punishment because something unpleasant was added (the spanking) to decrease the behaviour (hitting your sibling). An example of negative punishment might be receiving a 5% deduction for handing in your assignment a day late. In this case, something pleasant (good grades) is removed to decrease the late behaviour the next time. In both of these examples the goal was to decrease the chance the behaviour would happen again, so they were examples of punishment.

Psych think 3 In the PSYCH think on p. 123 we asked how operant conditioning could be applied in the classroom to increase the likelihood that students would complete their homework more frequently. As the teacher or educational assistant, you could initially set up a continuous reinforcement schedule using positive reinforcement. For example, every day the students come to school with their homework complete they are provided extra time on the computer. After the completed homework becomes more regular, you could move the students to a partial schedule of reinforcement, in particular, a variable-interval schedule. For example, you might offer extra time on the computer some days but not others so the students do now know which day they will be rewarded. Remember that variable schedules are very effective at maintaining behaviour so this should help with the frequency that the homework is complete.

Psych think 4 In the PSYCH think on p. 125 we asked if you thought Declan, the drug-and-bomb-sniffing dog described at the beginning of this chapter, learned his particular skills primarily by classical conditioning or by operant conditioning. If you said operant conditioning, you are correct! Dogs learn to discriminate between the odour of the drug and other odours the dog may encounter through reinforcement. When the dog responds to the odour of the drug, it receives a positive reinforcer (e.g., praise or a treat) but when it responds to any other odours, the dog's behaviour is ignored.

6

Memory

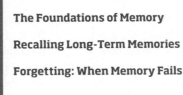

WHAT'S TO COME

The Foundations of Memory

Recalling Long-Term Memories

Forgetting: When Memory Fails

I wish my memory was perfect so I wouldn't have to study so much!

Sound familiar? Many students make this statement, but in truth, "perfect" memory is extremely rare. For example, a photographic memory (actually called eidetic memory) involves being able to recall information, images, and sounds in immense detail, but there is controversy about whether eidetic memory actually exists, and if it does, there currently are not any known individuals with true eidetic memory. Another rare type of "perfect" memory is called hyperthymestic syndrome, in which one has exceptional memories for the details of his or her life. Hyperthymesia was relatively unknown until a woman referred to as A. J. (now known to be Jill Price) contacted Dr. James McGaugh at the Center for the Neurobiology of Learning and Memory at the University of California, Irvine. Jill Price wrote McGaugh a letter describing her condition,

My first memories are of being a toddler in the crib (circa 1967) however I can take a date, between 1974 and today, and tell you what day it falls on, what I was doing that day and if anything of great importance (e.g., the Challenger explosion, Tuesday, January 28, 1986) occurred on that day I can describe that to you as well. I do not look at calendars beforehand and I do not read twenty-four years of my journals either. Whenever I see a date flash on the television (or anywhere else for that matter) I automatically go back to that day and remember where I was, what I was doing, what day it fell on and on and on and on and on. It is non-stop, uncontrollable, and totally exhausting (Parker, Cahill, & McGaugh, 2006, p. 35).

While hyperthymesia may sound good to some students, Jill Price's exceptional autobiographical memory does not mean she has superior memory for other information (such as test taking). For example, she told McGaugh that she needed to make lists to help her remember things and at times she had difficulty remembering what key is used for what on her key ring. Moreover, when asked to recall what her interviewers were wearing during an interview a few hours prior, Jill Price was not able to recall (Parker, Cahill, & McGaugh, 2006).

Memory is very important in many areas of our life, and knowing how your memory works and how to improve it can make you a better student!

Individuals with superior memory typically rely on memory strategies and practice (not innate abilities), which is actually good news for students because it means that you do not have to be born with superior memory to do better in school, it can be learned. We have provided a quick list of some strategies to get you started. You will find more detail about some of these strategies throughout the chapter (especially how effective elaborative rehearsal and deep levels of processing can be in helping you remember the material from your lectures and text readings).

- **Organization cues.** To help recall material you read in textbooks, try organizing the material in memory the first time you read it. Organize your reading on the basis of any advance information you have about the content and about its arrangement. You will then be able to make connections and see relationships among the various facts and process the material at a deeper level, which in turn will later aid recall.

- **Keywords.** If you are studying a foreign language, try the *keyword technique* of pairing a foreign word with a common English word that has a similar sound. This English word is known as the *keyword*. For example, to learn the Spanish word for duck (*pato*, pronounced *pot-o*), you might choose the keyword *pot*; for the Spanish word for horse (*caballo*, pronounced *cob-eye-yo*), the keyword might be *eye*. Once you have thought of a keyword, imagine the Spanish word "interacting" with the English keyword. You might envision a duck taking a bath in a pot to remember the word *pato*, or a horse with a large, bulging eye in the centre of its head to recall *caballo* (Carney & Levin, 1998; Wyra, Lawson, & Hungi, 2007).

- **Elaborative rehearsal.** Although practice does not necessarily make perfect, it helps. Making meaningful connections provides a framework for remembering. By studying and rehearsing material after mastering it—a process called *overlearning*—people show better long-term recall than they show if they stop practicing after their initial learning of the material. We will talk more about this useful technique.

- **Effective note taking.** "Less is more" is perhaps the best advice for taking lecture notes that facilitate recall. Rather than trying to jot down every detail of a lecture, it is better to listen and think about the material, and take down the main points. In effective note taking, thinking about the material when you first hear it is more important than writing it down. This is one reason why borrowing someone else's notes is a bad idea; you will have no framework in memory that you can use to understand them (Feldman, R. S., 2009).

- **Read information out loud.** Professor Colin MacLeod and colleagues from the University of Waterloo examined the production effect—studying information aloud compared to studying information silently. The researchers found that studying by reading information aloud resulted in much better memory (MacLeod, et al., 2010).

We turn now to the scientific study of memory. First, we define some essential terms that describe basic memory processes. Next, we consider the major theories that have been proposed to explain how memory works and the research that has been done to investigate their validity. The topics we cover include the ways in which information is stored and retrieved, the problems of retrieving information from memory, the accuracy of memories, and the reasons information is sometimes forgotten. We also consider the biological foundations of memory and discuss some practical means of increasing memory capacity.

As You Read »

- What is memory?
- Why do we recall some memories better than others?
- Why do we forget information?
- What is the neuroscience of memory?
- How can learning about the concepts in this chapter make you a better student?

The Foundations of Memory

You are sitting in the classroom writing your final test. You spent hours studying the night before and you were confident that you knew it all last night. Now you're racking your brain trying to figure out the answer to the question "What are the goals of psychology"? As you rack your brain for the answer, several fundamental processes relating to memory come into play. You know you were exposed to the information regarding the goals of psychology because you read the chapter and you attended the first lecture. But now that you think of it, you remember that your friend sent you a text message right when your professor was describing the four goals of psychology and you were distracted trying to respond. This means that even though you were exposed to it, it may simply not have registered in a meaningful way. In other words, the information might not have been recorded in your memory. The initial process of recording information in a form usable to memory, a process called *encoding*, is the first stage in remembering something.

Even if you had been exposed to the information and originally knew the goals of psychology, you may still be unable to recall it during the test because of a failure to retain it. Memory specialists call this *storage*, the maintenance of material saved in memory. If the material is not stored adequately, it cannot be recalled later.

Memory also depends on the process of *retrieval*: Material in memory storage has to be located and brought into awareness to be useful. Your failure to recall the goals of psychology, then, may rest on your inability to retrieve information that you learned earlier.

In sum, psychologists consider **memory** to be the process by which we encode, store, and retrieve information. Each of the three parts of this definition—encoding, storage, and retrieval—represents a different process. You can think of these processes as being analogous to a computer's keyboard (encoding), hard drive (storage), and software that accesses the information for display on the screen

memory The process by which we encode, store, and retrieve information.

Figure 6.1
Three Basic Processes of Memory

Encoding

Initial recording of information

Storage

Information saved for future use

Retrieval

Recovery of stored information

(retrieval). Only if all three processes have operated will you successfully recall the goals of psychology (describe, explain, predict, and control/change).

Recognizing that memory involves encoding, storage, and retrieval gives us a start in understanding the concept. But how does memory actually function? How do we explain what information is initially encoded, what gets stored, and how it is retrieved?

According to the *three-system approach to memory* that dominated memory research for several decades, there are different memory storage systems or stages through which information must travel if it is to be remembered (Atkinson & Shiffrin, 1968, 1971). Historically, the approach has been extremely influential in the development of our understanding of memory, and—although new theories have augmented it—it still provides a useful framework for understanding how information is recalled.

The three-system memory theory focuses on storage and proposes three separate stages of memory storage. **Sensory memory** refers to the initial, momentary storage of sensory information that lasts only an instant. If the information is noticed or the individual pays attention to it, it will move to the second stage, short-term memory. **Short-term memory** holds information for up to 25–30 seconds and stores it according to its meaning rather than as mere sensory stimulation. The third type of storage system is **long-term memory**. Information is stored in long-term memory on a relatively permanent basis, although it may be difficult to retrieve.

SENSORY MEMORY

Imagine you are sitting in the lecture hall during your Introduction to Psychology lecture. There are many things going on in the lecture hall as you're trying to attend to the material your professor is presenting. Someone might be typing on the keyboard, the lights might be flashing, someone may cough or tap a pen, your cellphone may vibrate to indicate a text coming in, or you may feel a kick from the person sitting behind you. Even though all of these stimuli are available while you are trying to pay attention to the lecture,

A momentary flash of lightning leaves a visual memory, a fleeting but exact replica of the sensory stimulus.

you likely don't remember very many because they represent only brief sensations. Such stimuli are initially—and fleetingly—stored in sensory memory, the first storehouse of the information the world presents to us. Actually, there are several types of sensory memories, each related to a different source of sensory information. For instance, *iconic memory* reflects information from the visual system, like what you see on the PowerPoint during the lecture. *Echoic memory* stores auditory information, like what you hear as your professor speaks.

Sensory memory can store information for only a very short time. If sensory information does not pass into short-term memory, it is lost for good. For instance, iconic memory seems to last less than a second and echoic memory typically fades within two or three seconds. Have you ever

sensory memory The initial, momentary storage of information, lasting only an instant; and includes both echoic and iconic memory.

short-term memory The second stage of memory that holds information for 15 to 30 seconds.

long-term memory Memory that stores information on a relatively permanent basis, although it may be difficult to retrieve.

Figure 6.2
Three-System Approach to Memory

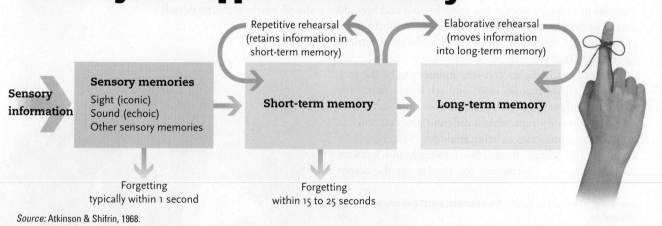

Source: Atkinson & Shifrin, 1968.

asked someone to repeat something they asked you but then answered the question they asked you before they repeated it? This is because of your echoic memory. The question still "echoed" in your sensory memory and you were actually able to answer even though at first you were not aware of it. Sensory memory is highly precise and can store an almost exact replica of each stimulus to which it is exposed (Darwin, Turvey, & Crowder, 1972; Deouell, Parnes, & Pickard, 2006; Long & Beaton, 1982; Sams et al., 1993). Too bad it doesn't last longer!

In sum, sensory memory operates as a kind of snapshot that stores information—which may be of a visual (iconic), auditory (echoic), or other sensory nature—for a brief moment in time. But it is as if each snapshot, immediately after being taken, is destroyed and replaced with a new one. Unless the information in the snapshot is transferred to some other type of memory, it is lost. To make this transfer you must pay attention to that sensory memory. This is why it is really important to try to pay attention to your professor during your lectures (even when it's not that exciting!), otherwise that auditory sensory memory is lost and the information will not move to the next stage of memory, short-term memory.

> **Sensory memory operates as a kind of snapshot that stores sensory information for a brief moment in time. If you do not pay attention, it is lost. This means that if you do not pay attention in your lectures, the content will be lost!**

SHORT-TERM MEMORY

Because the information that is stored briefly in sensory memory consists of representations of raw sensory stimuli, it is not meaningful to us. If we are to make sense of it and possibly retain it, the information must be encoded so that it can be transferred to the next stage of memory: short-term memory. Short-term memory is the memory store in which information first has meaning; although the maximum length of retention there is relatively short (Hamilton & Martin, 2007).

The specific processes by which sensory memories are transformed into short-term memories are not clear. Some theorists suggest that the information is first translated into graphical representations or images, and others hypothesize that the transfer occurs when the sensory stimuli are changed to words (Baddeley & Wilson, 1985). What is clear, however, is that unlike sensory memory, which holds a relatively full and detailed—if short-lived—representation of the world, short-term memory has incomplete representational capabilities. Apparently, short-term memory needs to reduce the incoming information to the parts that are meaningful and important. For example, if you look up from your book, you will

chunk A meaningful grouping of stimuli that can be stored as a unit in short-term memory.

experience a lot of visual stimulation. As soon as you pay attention to and think about part of it, that information will enter your short-term memory.

In fact, the specific amount of information that can be held in short-term memory has been identified as about seven items, or "chunks," of information, with variations up to plus or minus two chunks. A **chunk** is a meaningful grouping of stimuli that can be stored as a unit in short-term memory. According to George Miller (1956), a chunk can be individual letters or numbers, permitting us to hold a seven-digit phone number (such as 226–4610) in short-term memory.

But a chunk also may consist of larger categories, such as words or other meaningful units. For example, consider the following list of 23 letters:

C B C L O L E S L M T V C A A T B F F D E P C

Because the list exceeds seven chunks, it is difficult to recall the letters after one exposure. But suppose they were presented as follows:

CBC LOL ESL MTV CAAT BFF DEP-C

In this case, even though there are still 23 letters, you'd be able to store them in short-term memory, since they represent only seven chunks. Remembering the four lobes of the cerebral cortex by using the acronym F-TOP (frontal, temporal, occipital, parietal) is a special memory device that also uses chunking.

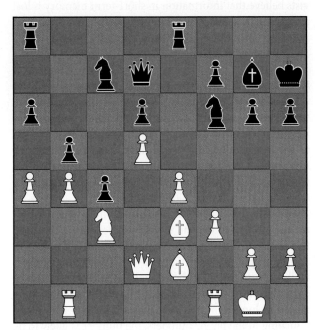

Look at this chessboard for about five seconds, and then, after covering up the board, try to draw the position of the pieces on a blank chessboard or a piece of paper. Unless you are an experienced chess player, you are likely to have great difficulty with this task. Yet chess masters do this quite well (deGroot, 1966). They can reproduce correctly 90% of the pieces on the board, not because they have superior memories but because they see the board in terms of chunks, or meaningful units, and reproduce the positions of the chess pieces by using those units.

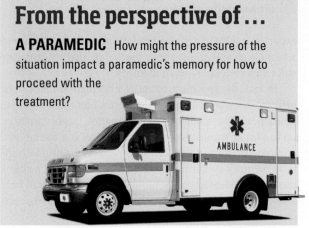

Chunks can vary in size from single letters or numbers to categories that are far more complicated. The specific nature of what constitutes a chunk varies according to one's past experience. For example, expert chess players are able to remember larger configurations of chess pieces than inexperienced players can, because the experts chunk pieces in different (and larger) ways (deGroot, 1978; Oberauer, 2007; Ross, 2006).

Although it is possible to remember seven or so relatively complicated sets of information entering short-term memory, the information cannot be held there very long. Just how brief is short-term memory? If you've ever learned the name of a new person you met, repeated the name to them in the conversation, but forgot their name by the end of the conversation, you know that information does not remain in short-term memory very long. Most psychologists believe that information in short-term memory is lost after about 30 seconds—unless it is transferred to long-term memory (Buchsbaum & D'Esposito, 2009; Jonides et al., 2008; Ranganath & Blumenfeld, 2005).

Rehearsal The transfer of material from short- to long-term memory proceeds largely on the basis of **rehearsal**, the repetition of information that has entered short-term memory. Rehearsal accomplishes two things. First, as long as the information is repeated, it is maintained in short-term memory. More important, however, rehearsal allows us to transfer the information into long-term memory (Kvavilashvili & Fisher, 2007).

Whether the transfer is made from short- to long-term memory seems to depend largely on the kind of rehearsal that is carried out. If the information is simply repeated over and over again—as we might do with a telephone number while we rush from the phone book to the phone—it is kept current in short-term memory, but it will not necessarily be placed in long-term memory. Instead, as soon as we stop punching in the phone numbers, the number is likely to be replaced by other information and completely forgotten. This is why simply repeating your test material over and over again is not a good study strategy. It might work at the moment you are studying, but by the time you write the test, that information is likely forgotten.

In contrast, if the information in short-term memory is rehearsed using a process called elaborative rehearsal, it is much more likely to be transferred into long-term memory. *Elaborative rehearsal* occurs when the information is considered and organized in some fashion. The organization might include expanding the information to make it fit with something you already know, linking it to another memory, turning it into an image, or transforming it in some other way like a metaphor. For example, you might remember the seven modern approaches you learned in the first chapter (neuroscience, psychodynamic, behavioural, cognitive, humanistic, socio-cultural, and evolutionary) by linking each approach with a keyword. For example, for the neuroscience approach you might think about the brain or parts of the body. For the psychodynamic approach you might think of Freud and the unconscious, and for the cognitive approach you might think of the word "thoughts." Can you think of keywords for the other four approaches? You might also use an acronym to help you remember the seven modern approaches of psychology. For example, you could use the first letter of each word to form the sentence "Every Psychologist Studies Human Behaviour 'N Cognition" (evolutionary, psychodynamic, socio-cultural, humanistic, behavioural, neuroscience, and cognitive).

Working Memory Rather than seeing short-term memory as an independent stop into which memories arrive, either to fade or to be passed on to long-term memory, many contemporary memory theorists conceive of short-term memory as far more active. In this view, short-term memory is like an information processing system that

---

rehearsal The repetition of information that has entered short-term memory.

working memory A set of active, temporary memory stores that actively manipulate and rehearse information.

manages both new material gathered from sensory memory and older material that is constantly being drawn from long-term storage. In this increasingly influential view, short-term memory is referred to as **working memory** and is defined as a set of temporary memory stores that actively manipulate and rehearse information (Bayliss et al., 2005a, 2005b; Unsworth & Engle, 2005).

Working memory is thought to contain a *central executive* processor that is involved in reasoning and decision making. The central executive coordinates three distinct storage-and-rehearsal systems: the *visual store*, the *verbal store*, and the *episodic buffer*. The visual store specializes in visual and spatial information, whereas the verbal store holds and manipulates material relating to speech, words, and numbers. The episodic buffer contains information that represents episodes or events (Baddeley, 2001; Bröder & Schiffer, 2006; Martin, 2005).

Working memory permits us to keep information in an active state briefly so that we can do something with the information. For instance, we use working memory when we're doing a multistep arithmetic problem in our heads, storing the result of one calculation while getting ready to move to the next stage. (For example, you might make use of your working memory when you figure a 20% tip in a restaurant by first calculating 10% of the total bill and then doubling it.) Although working memory aids in the recall of information, it uses a significant amount of cognitive resources during its operation. This can make us less aware of our surroundings—which has implications for the debate about using cellphones while driving (or texting during a lecture). If a phone conversation requires thinking, it will burden working memory and leave drivers dangerously less

aware of their surroundings, even when using hands-free devices (Sifrit, 2006; Strayer & Drews, 2007).

> Simply repeating your test material over and over again is not a good study strategy. It might work at the moment you are studying, but by the time you write the test, that information is likely forgotten.

LONG-TERM MEMORY

Material that makes its way from short-term memory to long-term memory enters a storehouse of almost unlimited capacity (Jonides et al., 2008). Like a new file we save on a hard drive, the information in long-term memory is filed and coded so that we can retrieve it when we need it.

Evidence of the existence of long-term memory, as different from short-term memory, comes from a number of sources. For example, people with certain kinds of brain damage have no lasting recall of new information received after the damage occurred, although people and events stored in memory before the injury remain intact (Milner, 1966). Because information that was encoded and stored before the injury can be recalled and because short-term memory after the injury appears to be operational—new material can be recalled for a very brief period—we can infer that there are two distinct types of memory storage: one for short-term and one for long-term storage.

The distinction between short- and long-term memory is also supported by the *serial position effect*, in which the ability to recall information in a list depends on where in the list an item appears. For instance, often a *primacy effect* occurs, in which items presented early in a list are remembered better. This is because people have time to rehearse this material when they're presented with it first and it can be encoded into long-term memory. There is also a *recency effect*, in which items presented late in a list are remembered best. This information is remembered best because less time has passed between when they learned it and when they need to remember it. Information in the middle tends to be lost because it is not able to be encoded into long-term memory and it is no longer in short-term memory when the person is trying to remember. For example, the first time you were presented with the seven modern approaches to psychology (neuroscience, psychodynamic, behavioural, cognitive, humanistic, socio-cultural, and evolutionary) you would remember the first couple (neuroscience and psychodynamic) and the last couple (socio-cultural and evolutionary) the best. This is because when you were trying to remember the neuroscience and psychodynamic approach you had more time to rehearse this information and

Figure 6.3
Model of Working Memory

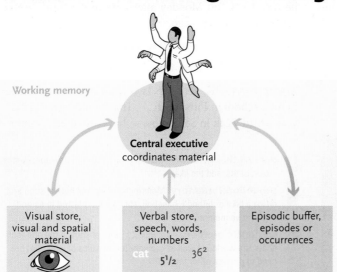

Working memory

Central executive
coordinates material

Visual store, visual and spatial material

Verbal store, speech, words, numbers
cat 5¹/₂ 36²

Episodic buffer, episodes or occurrences

Source: Adapted from Baddeley, Chincotta, & Adlam, 2001

encode it into long-term memory, but while you were doing this you are not able to attend to the middle items (behavioural, cognitive, and humanistic) and this information was lost. You were able to remember the socio-cultural and evolutionary approach because these were presented last and were still in your short-term memory.

LONG-TERM MEMORY MODULES

Just as short-term memory is often conceptualized in terms of working memory, many contemporary researchers now regard long-term memory as having several different components, or *memory modules*. Each of these modules represents a different memory system in the brain (Jonides et al., 2003).

One major distinction within long-term memory is that between declarative memory and procedural memory. **Declarative memory** is memory for factual information: names, faces, dates, and facts, such as "correlation does not mean causation." In contrast, **procedural memory** (or *nondeclarative memory*) refers to memory for skills and habits, such as how to ride a bike or use a smartphone. Information about *things* is stored in declarative memory; information about *how to do things* is stored in procedural memory (Eichenbaum, 2004; Feldhusen, 2006; Schacter, Wagner, & Buckner, 2000).

Declarative memory can be subdivided into semantic memory and episodic memory. **Semantic memory** is memory for general knowledge and facts about the world, as well as memory for the rules of logic that are used to deduce other facts. Because of semantic memory, we remember that the capital of Canada is Ottawa, that British Columbia uses the Pacific time zone while Ontario uses the Eastern time zone, and that *memoree* is the incorrect spelling of *memory*. Thus, semantic memory is somewhat like a mental almanac of facts (Nyberg & Tulving, 1996; Tulving, 2002).

In contrast, **episodic memory** is memory for events that occur in a particular time, place, or context. For example, remembering who helped you balance when you were learning to ride a bike, or a first kiss, or arranging a surprise 19th birthday party for someone is based on episodic memories. Jill Price, the woman from the opening story who had hyperthymesia, had an exceptional episodic memory! Episodic memories relate to particular

The ability to remember specific skills and the order in which they are used is called procedural memory. If driving a car involves procedural memory, is texting while driving safe?

Psych think

> > > It is said that you never forget how to ride a bicycle. Why might this be so? In what type of memory is information about bicycle riding stored?

contexts. For example, remembering *when* and *how* we learned that $2 \times 2 = 4$ would be an episodic memory; the fact itself (that $2 \times 2 = 4$) is a semantic memory.

Episodic memories can be surprisingly detailed. Consider, for instance, how you'd respond if you were asked to identify what you were doing on a specific day two years ago. Impossible? You may think otherwise as you read the following exchange between a researcher and a participant in a study who was asked, in a memory experiment, what he was doing "on Monday afternoon in the third week of September two years ago."

PARTICIPANT: Come on. How should I know?

EXPERIMENTER: Just try it anyhow.

PARTICIPANT: OK. Let's see: Two years ago . . . I would be in high school in Pittsburgh . . . That would be my senior year. Third week in September—that's just after summer—

declarative memory Memory for factual information: names, faces, dates, and the like.

procedural memory Memory for skills and habits, such as riding a bike or hitting a baseball, sometimes referred to as non-declarative memory.

semantic memory Memory for general knowledge and facts about the world, as well as memory for the rules of logic that are used to deduce other facts.

episodic memory Memory for events that occur in a particular time, place, or context.

Figure 6.4

Subcategories of Long-Term Memory

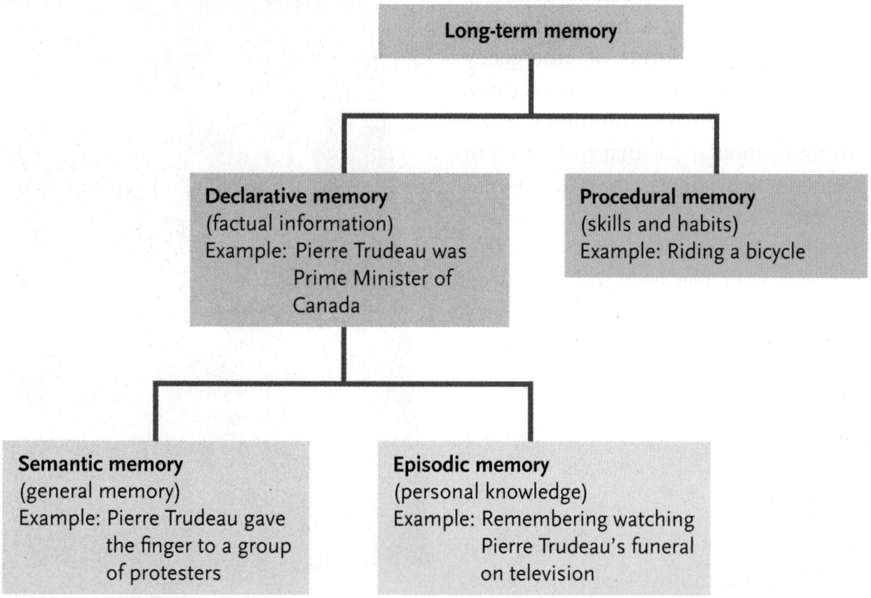

```
                    ┌──────────────────────┐
                    │   Long-term memory   │
                    └──────────┬───────────┘
              ┌────────────────┴────────────────┐
   ┌──────────────────────┐          ┌──────────────────────┐
   │ Declarative memory   │          │ Procedural memory    │
   │ (factual information)│          │ (skills and habits)  │
   │ Example: Pierre      │          │ Example: Riding a    │
   │ Trudeau was          │          │ bicycle              │
   │ Prime Minister of    │          └──────────────────────┘
   │ Canada               │
   └──────────┬───────────┘
       ┌──────┴───────────────────────┐
┌──────────────────────┐   ┌──────────────────────┐
│ Semantic memory      │   │ Episodic memory      │
│ (general memory)     │   │ (personal knowledge) │
│ Example: Pierre      │   │ Example: Remembering │
│ Trudeau gave         │   │ watching             │
│ the finger to a group│   │ Pierre Trudeau's     │
│ of protesters        │   │ funeral              │
└──────────────────────┘   │ on television        │
                           └──────────────────────┘
```

that would be the fall term . . . Let me see. I think I had chemistry lab on Mondays. I don't know. I was probably in chemistry lab. Wait a minute—that would be the second week of school. I remember he started off with the atomic table—a big fancy chart. I thought he was crazy trying to make us memorize that thing. You know, I think I can remember sitting . . . (Lindsay & Norman, 1977)

Episodic memory, then, can provide information about events that happened long in the past (Reynolds & Takooshian, 1988). But semantic memory is no less impressive, permitting us to dredge up tens of thousands of facts ranging from the date of our birthday to the knowledge that $1 is less than $5.

SEMANTIC NETWORKS

Try to recall, for a moment, as many things as you can think of that are the colour red. Now pull from your memory the names of as many fruits as you can recall.

Did the same item appear on both tasks? For many Westerners, an apple comes to mind in both cases, since it fits equally well in each category. And the fact that you might have thought of an apple on the first task makes it even more likely that you'll think of it when doing the second task.

It's actually quite amazing that we're able to retrieve specific material from the vast store of information in our long-term memories. According to some memory researchers, one key organizational tool that allows us to recall detailed information from long-term memory is the associations that we build

between different pieces of information. In this view, knowledge is stored in **semantic networks**, mental representations of clusters of interconnected information (Collins & Loftus, 1975; Collins & Quillian, 1969; Cummings, Ceponiene, & Koyama, 2006).

Figure 6.5

Semantic Memory Networks for Fire Engine

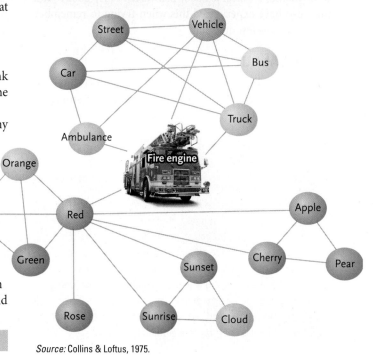

Source: Collins & Loftus, 1975.

semantic networks Mental representations of clusters of interconnected information.

If you grew up in Canada, for example, consider the associations in your memory relating to fire engines, the colour red, and a variety of other semantic concepts. Thinking about a particular concept leads to recall of related concepts. For example, seeing a fire engine may activate our recollections of other kinds of emergency vehicles, such as an ambulance, which in turn may activate recall of the related concept of a vehicle. And thinking of a vehicle may lead us to think about a bus that we've seen in the past. Activating one memory triggers the activation of related memories in a process known as *spreading activation* (Mace, 2007; Roediger, Balota, & Watson, 2001). This may have happened to you while you were trying to sleep one night. Did you ever notice how one thought or memory can quickly lead to another memory?

Recalling Long-Term Memories

An hour after his job interview, Ricardo was sitting in a coffee shop, telling his friend Laura how well it had gone, when the woman who had interviewed him walked in. "Well, hello, Ricardo. How are you doing?" Trying to make a good impression, Ricardo began to make introductions but suddenly realized he could not remember the name of the interviewer. Stammering, he desperately searched his memory, but to no avail. "I *know* her name," he thought to himself, "but here I am, looking like a fool. I can kiss this job good-bye."

Have you ever tried to remember someone's name, convinced that you knew it but were unable to recall it no matter how hard you tried? This common occurrence—known as the **tip-of-the-tongue phenomenon**—exemplifies how difficult it can be to retrieve information stored in long-term memory (Cleary, 2006; Schwartz, 2001, 2002). You may also have experienced this when trying to remember an answer to a test question!

RETRIEVAL CUES

Perhaps recall of names and other memories is not perfect because there is so much information stored in

If someone asked you to name the members of your soccer team from 10 years ago, you might not be able to remember them off the top of your head. But a photo would probably be enough of a retrieval cue to enable you to recall most of the other players' names.

long-term memory. Because the material that makes its way to long-term memory is relatively permanent, the capacity of long-term memory is vast (Anderson, 2000). For instance, if you are like the average college student, your vocabulary includes some 50,000 words, you know hundreds of mathematical "facts," and you are able to conjure up images with no trouble at all. In fact, simply cataloguing all your memories would probably take years of work. Given this enormous amount of information, it is amazing that you can immediately recall the way your childhood home looked.

How do we sort through this vast array of material and retrieve specific information at the appropriate time? One way is through retrieval cues. A *retrieval cue* is a stimulus that allows us to more easily recall information that is in long-term memory. It may be a word, an emotion, or a sound; whatever the specific cue, a memory will suddenly come to mind when the retrieval cue is present. For example, the smell of roasting turkey may evoke memories of Thanksgiving or family gatherings.

Retrieval cues guide people through the information stored in long-term memory in much the same way that a search engine such as Google or Yahoo! guides people through the Internet (Noice & Noice, 2002; Schneider & Logan, 2009). They are particularly important when we are making an effort to *recall* information, as opposed to being

DID YOU KNOW?

"Wait, wait—don't tell me!" If you have experienced the tip-of-the-tongue phenomenon, research suggests that you *should* let someone tell you (or you should look it up) instead of straining to remember a word, because the longer you try, the more likely you will forget it again in the future. It is likely that you will think of many incorrect words while trying to come up with the right one and these can become associated with, and thus clutter, your memory pathway to the word (Warriner & Humphreys, 2008).

tip-of-the-tongue phenomenon The inability to recall information that one realizes one knows—a result of the difficulty of retrieving information from long-term memory.

asked to *recognize* material stored in memory. In **recall**, a specific piece of information must be retrieved—such as that needed to remember what you wore to your sister's wedding or to write an essay or short answer on a test. In contrast, **recognition** occurs when people are presented with a stimulus and asked whether they have been exposed to it previously, or are asked to identify it from a list of alternatives, such as on a multiple-choice test.

As you might guess, recognition is generally a much easier task than recall. Recall is more difficult, because it consists of a series of processes: a search through memory, retrieval of potentially relevant information, and then a decision regarding whether the information you have found is accurate. If the information appears to be correct, the search is over, but if it does not, the search must continue. In contrast, recognition is simpler, because it involves fewer steps (Leigh, Zinkhan, & Swaminathan, 2006; Miserando, 1991). This is why many students think a multiple-choice test is easier—they have only to recognize which choice is the correct one. Do you agree?

Study tip Remember the distinction between recall (in which specific information must be retrieved like in an essay question) and recognition (in which information is presented and must be identified or distinguished from other material like in a multiple-choice question).

LEVELS OF PROCESSING

One determinant of how well memories are recalled is the way in which material is first perceived, processed, and understood. The **levels-of-processing theory** emphasizes the degree to which new material is mentally analyzed. It suggests that the amount of information processing that occurs when material is initially encountered is central in determining how much of the information is ultimately remembered. According to this approach, the depth of information processing during exposure to material—meaning the degree to which it is analyzed and considered—is critical; the greater the intensity of its initial processing is, the more likely we are to remember it (Craik, 1990; Troyer, Häfliger, & Cadieux, 2006).

Because we do not pay close attention to much of the information to which we are exposed, very little mental processing typically takes place, and we forget new material almost immediately (like in your sensory memory). However, information to which we pay greater attention is processed more thoroughly. Therefore, it enters memory at a deeper level—and is more likely to be remembered than information processed at shallower levels.

recall Memory task in which specific information must be retrieved.

recognition Memory task in which individuals are presented with a stimulus and asked whether they have been exposed to it in the past or to identify it from a list of alternatives, such as on a multiple-choice test.

levels-of-processing theory The theory of memory that emphasizes the degree to which new material is mentally analyzed.

Psych think

> > > Based on the levels-of-processing theory, what study tips come to mind for improving your own study habits?

The theory goes on to suggest that there are considerable differences in the ways in which information is processed at various levels of memory. At shallow levels, information is processed merely in terms of its physical and sensory aspects. For example, we may pay attention only to the fact that our professor told us that correlation does not mean cause but not really have an understanding of why. Trying to simply remember the basic fact would be a shallow level of processing. At an intermediate level of processing, we might remember that correlations are used for determining relationships and experiments are used for determining cause.

At the deepest level of processing, information is analyzed in terms of its meaning. We may see it in a wider context and draw associations between the meaning of the information and broader networks of knowledge. For instance, we may think about the experiment and the fact the experiment uses a control group which is why it allows the experimenters to rule out all other possible variables that might impact the results. We may tie this to an example from our own lives, such as whether studying more improves grades. According to the levels-of-processing approach, the deeper the initial level of processing of specific information is, the longer the information will be retained.

There are considerable practical implications to the notion that recall depends on the degree to which information is initially processed. For example, the depth of information processing is critical when learning and studying course material. Rote memorization (i.e., repeating the information over and over again) of a list of key terms for a test is not likely to produce a lasting memory, because processing occurs at a shallow level. In contrast, thinking about the meaning of the terms and reflecting on how they relate to information that one currently knows results in far more effective long-term retention (Conway, 2002; Wenzel, Zetocha, & Ferraro, 2007). This is why if you study by simply repeating the information over and over again you are likely not to remember this the following day when you actually write the test.

> **Rote memorization of a list of key terms for a test is unlikely to produce a lasting memory, because processing occurs at a shallow level. You are likely to do better on your tests if you use a deep level of processing.**

EXPLICIT AND IMPLICIT MEMORY

If you've ever had surgery, you probably hoped that the surgeons were focused completely on the surgery and gave you their undivided attention while slicing into your body. The reality in most operating rooms is quite different, though. Surgeons may be chatting with nurses about a new restaurant or something else unrelated to your surgery.

If you are like most patients, you are left with no recollection of the conversation that occurred while you were under anaesthesia. However, it is very possible that, although you had no conscious memories of the discussions on the merits of the restaurant, on some level you probably did recall at least some information. In fact, careful studies have found that people who are anesthetised during surgery sometimes demonstrate later that they have memories of snippets of conversations they heard during surgery, but they have no *conscious* recollection of when they were exposed to the information (Kihlstrom et al., 1990; Sebel, Bonke, & Winogard, 1993).

The discovery that people have memories about which they are unaware has been an important one. It has led to speculation that two forms of memory, explicit and implicit, may exist side by side. **Explicit memory** refers to intentional or conscious recollection of information. When we try to remember a name or date we have encountered or learned about previously, we are searching our explicit memory.

In contrast, **implicit memory** refers to memories of which people are not consciously aware but that can affect subsequent performance and behaviour. Skills that operate automatically and without thinking, such as jumping out of the path of an automobile coming toward us as we walk down the side of a road, are stored in implicit memory. Similarly, a feeling of vague dislike for an acquaintance, without knowing why we have that feeling, may be a reflection of implicit memories. Perhaps the person reminds us of someone else in our past that we didn't like, even though we are not aware of the memory of that other individual

Explicit memory, or conscious recall of information, benefits from frequent rehearsal.

> **explicit memory** Intentional or conscious recollection of information.
>
> **implicit memory** Memories of which people are not consciously aware but that can affect subsequent performance and behaviour.
>
> **priming** A phenomenon in which exposure to a word or concept (called a *prime*) later makes it easier to recall related information, even when there is no conscious memory of the word or concept.

(Coates, Butler, & Berry, 2006; Tulving, 2000; Uttl, Graf, & Consentino, 2003).

Implicit memory is closely related to the prejudice and discrimination people exhibit toward members of minority groups (Banaji & Greenwald, 1994). As we first discussed in the chapter about conducting psychological research, even though people may say and even believe they harbour no prejudice, assessment of their implicit memories may reveal that they have negative associations about members of minority groups. Such associations can influence people's behaviour without their being aware of their underlying beliefs (Greenwald, Nosek, & Banaji, 2003; Greenwald, Nosek, & Sriram, 2006).

One way that memory specialists study implicit memory is through experiments that use priming. **Priming** is a phenomenon in which exposure to a word or a concept (called a *prime*) later makes it easier to recall related information. Priming effects occur even when people have no conscious memory of the original word or concept (Schacter & Badgaiyan, 2001; Schacter, Dobbins, & Schnyer, 2004; Toth & Daniels, 2002).

The typical experiment designed to illustrate priming helps clarify the phenomenon. In priming experiments, participants are rapidly exposed to a stimulus such as a word, an object, or perhaps a drawing of a face. The second phase of the experiment is done after an interval ranging from several seconds to several months. At that point, participants are exposed to incomplete perceptual information that is related to the first stimulus, and they are asked whether they recognize it. For example, the new material may consist of the first letter of a word that had been presented earlier or a part of a face that had been shown earlier. If participants are able to identify the stimulus more readily than they identify stimuli that have not been presented earlier, priming has taken place (Fazio & Olson, 2003). Clearly, the earlier stimulus has been remembered—although the material resides in implicit memory, not explicit memory.

The same thing happens to us in our everyday lives. Suppose several months ago you watched a documentary on the planets, and the narrator described the moons of Mars, focusing on its moon named Phobos. You promptly forget the name of the moon, at least consciously. Then, several months later, you're completing a crossword puzzle that you have partially filled in, and it includes the letters *obos*. As soon as you look at the set of letters, you think of Phobos and suddenly recall for the first time since your initial exposure to the information that it is one of the moons of Mars. The sudden recollection occurred because your memory was primed by the letters *obos*.

In short, when information that we are unable to consciously recall affects our behaviour, implicit memory is at work. Our behaviour may be influenced by experiences of which we are unaware—an example of what has been called "retention without remembering" (Horton et al., 2005).

FLASHBULB MEMORIES

Where were you on September 11, 2001? You probably have little trouble recalling your exact location and a variety of other trivial details that occurred when you heard about the terrorist attacks, even though the incident happened several years ago. Your ability to remember details about this fatal event illustrates a phenomenon known as flash-bulb memory. **Flashbulb memories** are memories related to a specific, important, or surprising event that are so vivid they represent a sort of snapshot of the event.

Several events that can lead to flashbulb memories are common among college students. For example, involvement in a car accident, meeting one's roommate for the first time, and the night of high school graduation are all typical flashbulb memories (Bohn & Berntsen, 2007; Davidson & Glisky, 2002; Romeu, 2006).

Of course, flashbulb memories do not contain every detail of an original scene. You might remember how you

flashbulb memories Memories centred on a specific, important, or surprising event that are so vivid it is as if they represented a snapshot of the event.

felt when you heard the news of the terrorist attacks and where you were when you watched the scene on television, but you may not remember what clothes you were wearing on that day.

Furthermore, the details recalled in flashbulb memories are often inaccurate. For example, when you remembered when the World Trade Center was struck by the airplanes, do you remember watching television that morning and seeing images of the first plane, and then the second plane, striking the towers?

If you do, you are among the many people who recall viewing the initial television images of both planes on September 11. However, that recollection is wrong: in fact, television broadcasts showed images only of the second plane on September 11. No video of the first plane was available until early the following morning, September 12, when it was shown on television (Begley, 2002).

> **The more distinctive a stimulus is, and the more personal relevance the event has, the more likely we are to recall it later.**

Flashbulb memories illustrate a more general phenomenon about memory: Memories that are exceptional are more easily retrieved (although not necessarily accurately) than are those relating to events that are commonplace. The more distinctive a stimulus is, and the more personal relevance the event has, the more likely we are to recall it later (Berntsen & Thomsen, 2005; Shapiro, 2006).

Where were you the night Sidney Crosby scored the overtime goal for Team Canada in the Vancouver 2010 Olympics? Do you have a flashbulb memory for this event?

CONSTRUCTIVE PROCESSES IN MEMORY

As we have seen, although it is clear that we can have detailed recollections of significant and distinctive events, it is difficult to gauge the accuracy of such memories. In fact, it is apparent that our memories reflect, at least in part, **constructive processes**, processes in which memories are influenced by the meaning we give to events. When we retrieve information, the memory that is produced is affected not just by the direct prior experience we have had with the stimulus but also by the meaning we assign it.

The notion that memory is based on constructive processes was first put forward by Frederic Bartlett, a British psychologist. He suggested that people tend to remember information in terms of **schemas**, organized bodies of information stored in memory that bias the way new information is interpreted, stored, and recalled (Bartlett, 1932). We have schemas for all sorts of things. For example, when you think of the word "dog," what comes to mind? You likely thought of a four-legged furry animal with a wagging tail that barks. In addition to how the dog looks, you also have a schema for how to react to the dog. If you have had positive experiences with dogs in the past, your schema for dog is friendly. If you have had negative or scary experiences with dogs in the past, your schema for dog is unfriendly. Your schema for dog will then influence how you react to a dog when you see one in the future, whether the dog is friendly or not. Our reliance on schemas means that memories often consist of a general reconstruction of previous experience. Bartlett argued that schemas are based not only on the specific material to which people are exposed but also on their understanding of the situation, their expectations about the situation, and their awareness of the motivations underlying the behaviour of others.

Study tip

A key fact about memory is that it is a constructive process, in which memories are influenced by the meaning given to what is being recalled.

One of the earliest demonstrations of schemas came from a classic study that involved a procedure similar to a common children's game, "telephone," in which information from memory is passed sequentially from one person to another. In the study, a participant viewed a drawing in which there were a variety of people of differing racial and ethnic backgrounds on a subway car, one of whom—a white person—was shown with a razor in his hand (Allport & Postman, 1958). The first participant was asked to describe the drawing to someone else without looking back at it. Then that person was asked to describe it to another person (without looking at the drawing), and then the process was repeated with still one more participant.

The report of the last person differed in significant, yet systematic, ways from the initial drawing. Many people described the drawing as depicting an African American with a knife—an incorrect recollection, given that the

drawing showed a razor in the hand of a Caucasian person. The transformation of the Caucasian's razor into an African American's knife clearly indicates that the participants held a schema that included the unwarranted prejudice that African Americans are more violent than Caucasians and thus more likely to be holding a knife. In short, our expectations and knowledge—and prejudices—affect the reliability of our memories (McDonald & Hirt, 1997; Newby-Clark & Ross, 2003).

Memory in the Courtroom For David Milgaard, the inadequate memories of several people cost him more than two decades of his life. Milgaard was the victim of wrongful conviction when his friend, Albert Cadrain, said Milgaard had blood on his clothes the day a young woman, Gayle Miller, was raped and murdered in Saskatoon, Saskatchewan, in 1969. On that basis, he was tried, convicted, and sentenced to life in prison. More than two-and-a-half decades later, DNA testing showed that Milgaard was innocent (MacCallum, 2006). Unfortunately, Milgaard is not the only victim to whom apologies have had to be made; many cases of mistaken identity have led to unjustified legal actions. Thomas Sophonow faced a similar fate in 1981 when he was accused of murdering Barbara Stoppel in Winnipeg based on the testimony of an informant in jail. Sophonow was acquitted in 1985 by the Manitoba Court of Appeal after spending four years in prison. In 2001, the province of Manitoba released an inquiry report with recommendations for future use of eyewitnesses (Province of Manitoba, 2011). Many of the recommendations in the Thomas Sophonow case were based on the findings of some leading Canadian researchers. John Turtle from Ryerson University in Toronto and Rod Lindsay from Queens University in Kingston have conducted numerous studies on the problems with eyewitness testimony. They recently teamed with Gary Wells, an American researcher, to publish a report on best practices for eyewitness evidence procedures. Some of the areas Turtle and his colleagues focused on were the composition

constructive processes Processes in which memories are influenced by the meaning we give to events.

schemas Organized bodies of information stored in memory that bias the way new information is interpreted, stored, and recalled.

of lineups, how to instruct witnesses before they viewed a lineup, how to conduct identification procedures, and how to record identification results (Turtle, Lindsay, & Wells, 2003).

Research on eyewitness identification of suspects, as well as on memory for other details of crimes, has shown that eyewitnesses are apt to make significant errors when they try to recall details of criminal activity—even if they are highly confident about their recollections (MacCallum, 2006; Province of Manitoba, 2011; Thompson, 2000; Wells, Olson, & Charman, 2002; Zaragoza, Belli, & Payment, 2007).

One reason is the effect of the weapons used in crimes. When a criminal perpetrator displays a gun or a knife, it acts as a perceptual magnet, attracting the eyes of the witnesses. As a consequence, witnesses pay less attention to other details of the crime and are less able to recall what actually occurred (Belli & Loftus, 1996; Steblay et al., 2003; Zaitsu, 2007).

Turtle and his colleagues suggest that poor eyewitness identification may be due to memory acquisition, storage, and retrieval (Turtle et al., 2003). For example, in the acquisition stage, eyewitnesses may be in a state of stress which limits their ability to perceive and attend to the information. Eyewitnesses may also have difficulty storing the information because of interference from other information in their long-term memory (e.g., information from

Psych think

> > > Research shows that an eyewitness's memory for details of crimes can contain significant errors. What factors might influence an eyewitness's ability to remember?

other eyewitnesses or reports they heard in the media). Even if eyewitnesses are able to retain the information, they may not be able to retrieve the level of detail needed to identify a suspect (Turtle et al., 2003).

One reason eyewitnesses are prone to memory-related errors is that the specific wording of questions posed to them by police officers or attorneys can affect the way they recall information, as a number of experiments illustrate. For example, in one experiment the participants were shown a film of two cars crashing into each other. Some were then asked the question, "About how fast were the cars going when they *smashed* into each other?" On average, they estimated the speed to be 40.8 miles per hour. In contrast, when another group of participants was asked, "About how fast were the cars going when they *contacted* each other?" the average estimated speed was only 31.8 miles per hour (Loftus & Palmer, 1974).

The problem of memory reliability becomes even more acute when children are witnesses, because increasing evidence suggests that children's memories are highly vulnerable to the influence of others (Douglas Brown, Goldstein, & Bjorklund, 2000; Loftus, 1993; Loftus & Cahill, 2007). For instance, in one experiment, five- to seven-year-old girls who had just had a routine physical examination were shown an anatomically explicit doll. The girls were shown the doll's genital area and asked, "Did the doctor touch you here?" Three of the girls who did not have a vaginal or anal exam said that the doctor had in fact touched them in the genital area, and one of those three made up the detail "The doctor did it with a stick" (Saywitz & Goodman, 1990).

Children's memories are especially susceptible to influence when the situation is highly emotional or stressful. For example, in trials in which there is significant pre-trial publicity or in which alleged victims are questioned repeatedly, often by untrained interviewers, the memories of the alleged victims may be influenced by the types of questions they are asked (Lamb & Garretson, 2003; Quas, Malloy, & Melinder, 2007; Scullin, Kanaya, & Ceci, 2002). This appeared to have happened in Martensville, Saskatchewan, in 1992, when a mother of a two-year-old girl noticed a red rash on her daughter's genitals after she returned from the babysitter's house. The mother called the police and an investigation resulted in nine people being arrested (including five police officers) for participating in a satanic cult that performed ritualistic sexual abuse. Many of the arrests were based on the testimony of the children, who experts believed were provided with praise when they provided the

Figure 6.6

Accuracy of Eyewitness Testimony Affected by Interviewer's Word Choice

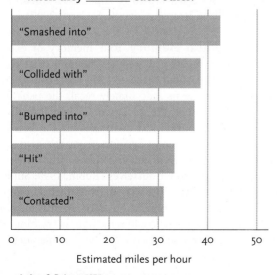

About how fast were the cars going when they _____ each other?

Source: Loftus & Palmer, 1974.

"right" answers after being given leading questions by the police. The children were also shown pictures of the "Devil Church," where the abuse was alleged to have happened; experts suggested images of the building and its contents were incorporated into the children's memories (a forensic investigation of the Devil Church did not result in any evidence). An investigation concluded that there was no satanic cult and eight of the nine charged were found not guilty (CBC News, 2003).

Also consider the case of George Franklin, Sr., a man charged with murdering his daughter's playmate. The entire case was based on memories of Franklin's daughter, who claimed that she had repressed the memories until she began to have flashbacks of the event two decades later. Gradually, the memories became clearer, until she recalled her father lifting a rock over his head and then seeing her friend covered with blood. On the basis of her memories, her father was convicted—but later was cleared of the crime after an appeal of the conviction.

There is good reason to question the validity of *repressed memories*, recollections of events that are initially so shocking that the mind responds by pushing them into the unconscious. Supporters of the notion of repressed memory (based on Freud's psychoanalytic theory) suggest that such memories may remain hidden, possibly throughout a person's lifetime, unless they are triggered by some current circumstance, such as the probing that occurs during psychological therapy (Sabbagh, 2009).

However, memory researcher Elizabeth Loftus maintains that some repressed memories may well be inaccurate or even wholly false—representing a *false memory*. For example, false memories develop when people are unable to recall the source of a memory of a particular event about which they have only vague recollections. When the source of the memory becomes unclear or ambiguous, people may become confused about whether they actually experienced the event or whether it was imagined. Ultimately, people come to believe that the event actually occurred (Lewandowsky et al., 2005; Loftus, 2004; Wade, Sharman, & Garry, 2007).

Stephen Lindsay, from the University of Victoria in British Columbia, collaborated with some colleagues from England on an interesting research project on distorting memories after viewing altered videos (Nash, Wade, & Lindsay, 2009). Lindsay and colleagues had 47 psychology students from the University of Victoria copy some simple acts such as flipping a coin or putting on a hat while being videotaped. Unbeknownst to the participants, the videos were doctored by the researchers and additional actions were added. Two weeks later, the participants were asked to watch the doctored videos, and many of the participants indicated that they remembered performing those acts, even when this did not actually happen (Nash, Wade, & Lindsay, 2009). Lindsay and colleagues concluded that video evidence may provide imagery that can lead to false memories. Furthermore, the researchers cautioned that using false evidence [as some countries do] may lead innocent people to falsely remember having committed a crime they did not commit (Nash, Wade, & Lindsay, 2009).

There is great controversy regarding the legitimacy of repressed memories (Geraerts et al., 2007; Ost, 2006; Sabbagh, 2009). Many therapists give great weight to the authenticity of repressed memories, and their views are supported by research showing that specific regions of the brain help keep unwanted memories out of awareness. On the other side of the issue are researchers who maintain that there is insufficient scientific support for the existence of such memories. There is also a middle ground: memory researchers who suggest that false memories are a result of normal information processing. The challenge for those on all sides of the issue is to distinguish truth from fiction (Anderson et al., 2004; Brown & Pope, 1996; Roediger & McDermott, 2000; Strange, Clifasefi, & Garry, 2007).

Autobiographical Memory Your memory of experiences in your own past may well be a fiction—or at least a distortion of what actually occurred. The same constructive processes that make us inaccurately recall the behaviour of others also reduce the accuracy of autobiographical memories. **Autobiographical memories** are our recollections of circumstances and episodes from our own lives. Autobiographical memories encompass the episodic memories we have about ourselves (Rubin, 1999; Sutin & Robins, 2007). Jill Price, the woman from the beginning of the chapter, had a phenomenal autobiographical memory, but this did not mean she could remember everything. She still needed cues or practice for other types of memory.

autobiographical memories Our recollections of circumstances and episodes from our own lives.

From the perspective of ...

A LAWYER According to what you've learned about repressed memories, should this type of testimony be allowed in court?

Figure 6.7
Autobiographical Memories of Grades Recalled by College Students

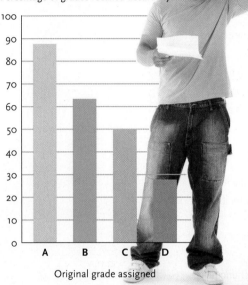

Percentage of grades recalled accurately

Original grade assigned

Source: Bahrick et al., 1996.

For example, we tend to forget information about our past that is incompatible with the way in which we currently see ourselves. One study found that adults who were well adjusted but who had been treated for emotional problems during the early years of their lives tended to forget important but troubling childhood events, such as being in foster care. College students misremember their bad grades—but remember their good ones (Kemps & Tiggemann, 2007; Walker, Skowronski, & Thompson, 2003).

Similarly, when a group of 48-year-olds were asked to recall how they had responded on a questionnaire they had completed when they were high school freshman, their accuracy was no better than chance. For example, although 61% of the questionnaire respondents said that playing sports and other physical activities was their favourite pastime, only 23% of the adults recalled it accurately (Offer et al., 2000).

It is not just certain kinds of events that are distorted; particular periods of life are remembered more easily than others are. For example, when people reach late adulthood, they remember periods of life in which they experienced major transitions, such as attending college and working at their first job, better than they remember their middle-age years (Cordnoldi, De Beni, & Helstrup, 2007).

Cultural Influences on Memory Travellers who have visited areas of the world in which there is no written language often return with tales of people with phenomenal memories. For instance, storytellers in some preliterate cultures can recount long chronicles that recall the names and activities of people over many generations. Those feats led experts to argue initially that people in preliterate societies develop a different, and perhaps better, type of memory than do those in cultures that employ a written language. They suggested that in a society that lacks writing, people are motivated to recall information with accuracy, especially information relating to tribal histories and traditions that would be lost if they were not passed down orally from one generation to another (Berntsen & Rubin, 2004; Daftary & Meri, 2002).

Today, memory researchers dismiss that view. For one thing, preliterate peoples don't have an exclusive claim to amazing memory feats. Some Hebrew scholars memorize thousands of pages of text and can recall the locations of particular words on the page. Similarly, poetry singers in the Balkans can recall thousands of lines of poetry. Even in cultures in which written language exists, then, astounding feats of memory are possible (Rubin et al., 2007; Strathern & Stewart, 2003).

Memory researchers now suggest that there are both similarities and differences in memory across cultures. One current theory says that basic memory processes such as short-term memory capacity and the structure of long-term memory—the "hardware" of memory—is universal and operates similarly in people in all cultures. In contrast, cultural differences can be seen in the way information is acquired and rehearsed—the "software" of memory. Culture determines how people frame information initially, how much they practice learning and recalling it, and the strategies they use to try to recall it (Mack, 2003; Wang & Conway, 2006).

Storytellers in many cultures can recount hundreds of years of history in vivid detail. This amazing ability is due less to basic memory processes than to the ways in which storytellers acquire and retain information.

TRY IT!

What's Your Memory Style?

What's your dominant memory style? Do you most easily remember sounds, sights, or the way things feel? Or perhaps you easily remember all of these? Read the statements below and circle the response choice that most closely describes your habits.

To help recall lectures, I . . .

   V. Read the notes I took during class.

   A. Close my eyes and try to hear what the instructor said.

   K. Try to place myself back in the lecture room and feel what was going on at the time.

To remember a complex procedure, I . . .

   V. Write down the steps I have to follow.

   A. Listen carefully and repeatedly to the instructions.

   K. Do it over and over again.

To learn sentences in a foreign language, I do best if I . . .

   V. Read them on paper to see how they're written.

   A. Hear them in my head until I can say them aloud.

   K. See someone speaking them and then practice moving my mouth and hands the way the speaker did.

If I have to learn a dance move, I like . . .

   V. To see a diagram of the steps before trying it.

   A. Someone to coach me through it while I try it.

   K. To watch it once and then give it a try.

When I recall a very happy moment, I tend to . . .

   V. Visualize it in my head.

   A. Hear the sounds that I heard when experiencing it.

   K. Feel with my hands and rest of my body what I felt at the time.

When I have to remember driving directions, I usually . . .

   V. See a map of the route in my mind.

   A. Repeat the directions aloud to myself.

   K. Feel my hands steering and the car driving along the correct route.

Answer Key: If you chose mostly Vs, your main memory style is visual; your preference is to remember things in terms of the way they appear. If you chose mostly As, your main memory style is auditory; your preference is to recall material in terms of sound. If you chose mostly Ks, your main memory style is kinaesthetic; your preference is to remember using your sense of touch. Keep in mind that this questionnaire gives only a rough idea of how we usually use our memories. Remember: all of us use all of the memory styles during the course of each day.

Forgetting: When Memory Fails

Known in the scientific literature by the alias of H. M., he could remember, quite literally, nothing—nothing, that is, that had happened following experimental surgery to reduce epileptic seizures. Until that time, H. M.'s memory had been quite normal. But after the operation he was unable to recall anything for more than a few minutes, and then the memory was seemingly lost forever. He did not remember his address, or the name of the person to whom he was talking. H. M. would read the same magazine over and over again. According to his own description, his life was like waking from a dream and being unable to know where he was or how he got there (Milner, 1966, 2005). You will learn more about what areas of the brain were responsible for H. M.'s memory loss in the neuroscience and memory section at the end of the chapter.

As the case of H. M. illustrates, a person without a normal memory faces severe difficulties. All of us who have experienced even routine instances of forgetting—such as not remembering an acquaintance's name or a

DID YOU KNOW?

Clinicians recently documented the first case of a memory disorder they call *confabulatory hyperamnesia*. Instead of answering "I don't know" when asked questions outside the boundaries of normal memory (for example, what you were doing on March 13, 1995?), their patient, referred to only as "L. M.," appeared compelled to answer with surprisingly detailed fabrications (Dalla Barba & Decaix, 2009).

fact on a test—understand the very real consequences of memory failure.

Yet memory failure is also essential to remembering important information. The ability to forget inconsequential details about experiences, people, and objects helps us avoid being burdened and distracted by trivial stores of meaningless data. Forgetting permits us to form general impressions and recollections. For example, the reason our friends consistently look familiar to us is because we're able to forget their clothing, facial blemishes, and other transient features that change from one occasion to the next. Instead, our memories are based on a summary of various critical features—a far more economical use of our memory capabilities.

In the late nineteenth century, German psychologist Hermann Ebbinghaus (1885/1913) conducted research on forgetting that laid the foundation for many future studies in memory. Using himself as the only participant in his study, Ebbinghaus memorized lists of three-letter nonsense syllables—meaningless sets of two consonants with a vowel in between, such as FIW and BOZ. By measuring how easy it was to relearn a given list of the nonsense syllables after varying periods of time had passed since the initial learning, he found that forgetting occurs systematically. The most rapid forgetting occurs in the first nine hours, particularly in the first hour. After nine hours, the rate of forgetting slows and declines little, even after the passage of many days.

Figure 6.8
Ebbinghaus's Forgetting Curve

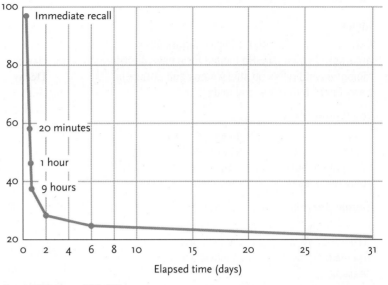

Percentage of retention

Source: Ebbinghaus, 1885, 1913.

Despite his primitive research methods, Ebbinghaus's basic conclusions have been upheld. There is almost always a strong initial decline in memory, followed by a more gradual drop over time. Furthermore, relearning of previously mastered material is almost always faster than starting from scratch, whether the material is academic information or a motor skill such as serving a tennis ball (Wixted & Carpenter, 2007).

A Pill to Forget?

Many of us have at least one bad memory that we relive on a regular basis. For some people, this memory is so vivid they also relive the physiological responses to the event (e.g., increased heart rate and sweating). When the memory is this strong, it is often due to post-traumatic stress disorder (we will talk more about PTSD in the later chapters of the text). Even if you do not have PTSD, if you had a chance to buy a pill that would help get rid of the feelings associated with one of your painful memories, would you buy it? Hopefully you are a good consumer of information, and the first question you just asked yourself was "is there scientific evidence to suggest that a pill could do that"? Interestingly enough, there is! Alain Brunet and Karim Nader from McGill University teamed with some colleagues at Harvard and found that the drug propranolol could reduce the stressful physiological responses participants experienced when they described their traumatic memory (Brunet et al., 2008). Another study found propranolol reduced the abilities of participants to remember traumatic events (Cahill et al., 1994). However, although there is evidence to support the use of propranolol in reducing traumatic memories, there are some who think it is unethical to use medication to suppress memories because of the potential to lose one's episodic memories, and more importantly, one's sense of self (see the President's Council on Bioethics, 2003). What do you think? Do you buy that argument or would you buy propranolol if you had the opportunity?

Psych
At The Movies

Memento
The main character of this movie suffers from anterograde amnesia. He cannot form new short-term memories and relies on sticky notes and tattoos to carry information from day to day.

The Bourne Identity
A CIA assassin suffers from a form of amnesia in which he has lost all memory of self-identifying information, but he retains procedural memory for such things as hand-to-hand combat skills.

Eternal Sunshine of the Spotless Mind
Are we better off with or without our more difficult memories? Would you erase memories if you could? The main characters in this movie are faced with this decision.

WHY WE FORGET

Why do we forget? One reason is that we may not have paid attention to the material in the first place—a failure of *encoding*. For example, if you grew up in Canada, you probably have been exposed to thousands of pennies during your life. Despite this experience, you may not have a clear sense of the details of the coin. Consequently, the reason for your memory failure is that you probably never encoded the information into long-term memory initially. Obviously, if information was not placed in memory to start with, there is no way the information can be recalled (Nickerson & Adams, 1979).

But what about material that has been encoded into memory and yet can't be remembered later (such as when you knew the material the night before the quiz but seemed

decay The loss of information in memory through its non-use.

interference The phenomenon by which information in memory disrupts the recall of other information.

cue-dependent forgetting Forgetting that occurs when there are insufficient retrieval cues to rekindle information that is in memory.

to have lost it all on the day you were writing)? Several processes account for memory failures, including decay, interference, and cue-dependent forgetting.

Decay is the loss of information through non-use. This explanation for forgetting assumes that *memory traces*, the physical changes that take place in the brain when new material is learned, simply fade away over time (Grann, 2007).

Although there is evidence that decay does occur, it doesn't completely explain forgetting. Often there is no relationship between how long ago a person was exposed to information and how well that information is recalled. If decay was responsible for all forgetting, we would expect that the more time that has elapsed between the initial learning of information and our attempt to recall it, the harder it would be to remember it, because there would be more time for the memory trace to decay. Yet people who take several consecutive tests on the same material often recall more of the initial information when taking later tests than they did on earlier tests. If decay were operating, we would expect the opposite to occur (Payne, 1986).

Because decay does not fully account for forgetting, memory specialists have proposed an additional mechanism: **interference**. In interference, information in memory disrupts the recall of other information (Naveh-Benjamin, Guez, & Sorek, 2007). This may explain why you may forget some of the information you studied the night before. Most students take between five and seven courses at any one time, making it quite easy for some information from other courses to interfere with information you need to remember for your quiz.

Finally, forgetting may occur because of **cue-dependent forgetting**, forgetting that occurs when there are insufficient retrieval cues to rekindle information that is in memory

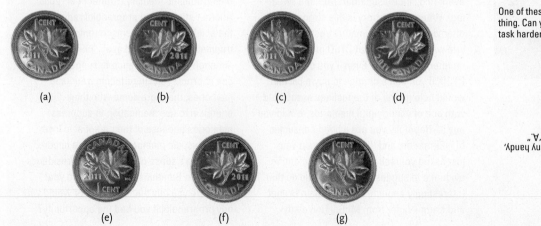

(a)   (b)   (c)   (d)

(e)   (f)   (g)

One of these pennies is the real thing. Can you find it? Why is this task harder than it seems at first?

If you don't have a penny handy, the correct answer is "A."

Figure 6.9
Proactive and Retroactive Interference

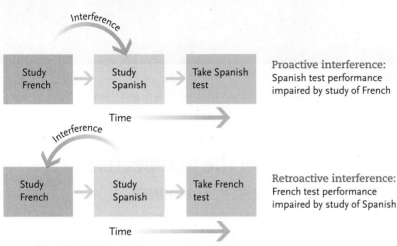

Proactive interference: Spanish test performance impaired by study of French

Retroactive interference: French test performance impaired by study of Spanish

(Tulving & Thompson, 1983). For example, you may not be able to remember where you lost a set of keys until you mentally walk through your day, thinking of each place you visited. When you think of the place where you lost the keys—say, the library—the retrieval cue of the library may be sufficient to help you recall that you left them on the desk in the library. Without that retrieval cue, you might be unable to recall the location of the keys. This may also explain why you cannot remember the material on the day of your quiz. If you simply use maintenance rehearsal and repeat your notes over and over again, you are not giving yourself a cue to help you remember. Using acronyms or a deeper level of processing gives you a cue for that material so you can help remember it during the quiz.

Most research suggests that interference and cue-dependent forgetting are key processes in forgetting (Bower, Thompson, & Tulving, 1994; Mel'nikov, 1993). We forget things mainly because new memories interfere with the retrieval of old ones or because appropriate retrieval cues are unavailable, not because the memory trace has decayed.

Study tip Memory loss through decay comes from non-use of the memory; memory loss through interference is due to the presence of other information in memory.

PROACTIVE AND RETROACTIVE INTERFERENCE

There are actually two sorts of interference that influence forgetting: proactive and retroactive. In **proactive interference**, information learned earlier disrupts the recall of newer material. Suppose, as a student of foreign languages, you first learned French in the tenth grade, and then in the

eleventh grade you took Spanish. When in the twelfth grade you take a college achievement test in Spanish, you may find you have difficulty recalling the Spanish translation of a word because all you can think of is its French equivalent (Bunting, 2006).

In contrast, **retroactive interference** refers to difficulty in the recall of information because of later exposure to different material. If, for example, you have difficulty on a French achievement test because of your more recent exposure to Spanish, retroactive interference is to blame. One way to remember the difference between proactive and retroactive interference is to keep in mind that *pro*active interference progresses in time—the past interferes with the present—whereas *retro*active interference retrogresses in time, working backward as the present interferes with the past (Jacoby et al., 2007).

Although the concepts of proactive and retroactive interference illustrate how material may be forgotten, they do not explain whether forgetting is caused by the actual loss or modification of information or by problems in the retrieval of information. Most research suggests that material that has apparently been lost because of interference can eventually be recalled if appropriate stimuli are presented (Anderson, 1981; Tulving & Psotka, 1971; Wixted, 2005), but the question has not been fully answered.

MEMORY DYSFUNCTIONS

First you notice that you're always misplacing things, or that common nouns are evading you as stubbornly as the names of new acquaintances. Pretty soon you're forgetting appointments and getting flustered when you drive in traffic. On bad days you find you can't hold numbers in your mind long enough to dial the phone. You try valiantly to conceal your lapses, but they become ever more glaring. You crash your car. You spend whole mornings struggling to dress yourself properly. And even as you lose the ability to read or play the piano, you're painfully aware of what's happening to you (Cowley, 2000, p. 46).

These memory problems are symptomatic of **Alzheimer's disease**, an illness characterized in part by severe memory problems. Alzheimer's is the leading cause of disability among Canadians aged 65 and older, affecting approximately 500,000 people (Alzheimer Society,

proactive interference Interference in which information learned earlier disrupts the recall of newer material.

retroactive interference Interference in which there is difficulty in the recall of information learned earlier because of later exposure to different material.

Alzheimer's disease A progressive brain disorder that leads to a gradual and irreversible decline in cognitive abilities.

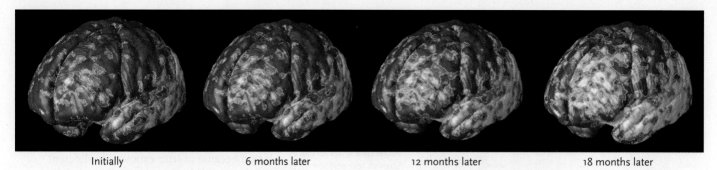

| Initially | 6 months later | 12 months later | 18 months later |

This series of brain images clearly show the changes caused by Alzheimer's disease over 18 months, with the normal tissue (in purple) retreating during that time.

2010). In the beginning, Alzheimer's symptoms appear as simple forgetfulness of things such as appointments and birthdays. As the disease progresses, memory loss becomes more profound, and even the simplest tasks—such as using a telephone—are forgotten. Ultimately, victims may lose their ability to speak or comprehend language, and physical deterioration sets in, leading to death.

The causes of Alzheimer's disease are not fully understood. Increasing evidence suggests that Alzheimer's results from an inherited susceptibility to a defect in the production of the protein beta amyloid, which is necessary for normal nerve cell function. When the synthesis of beta amyloid goes awry, large clumps of cells form, triggering inflammation and the deterioration of neurons in the brain (Detoledo-Morrell, Stoub, & Wang, 2007; Horínek, Varjassyová, & Hort, 2007).

Alzheimer's disease is one of a number of memory dysfunctions. Another is **amnesia**, memory loss that occurs without other mental difficulties. The type of amnesia immortalized in countless Hollywood films involves a victim who receives a blow to the head and is unable to remember anything from his or her past. In reality, amnesia of this type, known as retrograde amnesia, is quite rare. In **retrograde amnesia** memory is lost for occurrences prior to a certain event. Usually, lost memories gradually reappear, although full restoration may take as long as several years. In certain cases, some memories are lost forever. But even in cases of severe memory loss, the loss is generally selective. For example, although people suffering from retrograde amnesia may be unable to recall friends and family members, they still may be able to play complicated card games or knit a sweater quite well (Bright, Buckman, & Fradera, 2006; Verfaellie & Keane, 2002).

A second type of amnesia—*anterograde amnesia*—is exemplified by people who cannot make new long-term memories and therefore remember nothing of their current activities. In **anterograde amnesia** loss of memory occurs for events that follow an injury. Information cannot

amnesia Memory loss that occurs without other mental difficulties.

retrograde amnesia Amnesia in which memory is lost for occurrences prior to a certain event.

anterograde amnesia Amnesia in which memory is lost for events that follow an injury.

From the perspective of ...

A NURSE PRACTITIONER
Alzheimer's disease and amnesia are two of the most pervasive memory dysfunctions. What sorts of activities might health care providers offer their patients to help them combat memory loss?

be transferred from short-term to long-term memory, resulting in the ability to remember only short-term memories in the present for about 20 seconds, and what was in long-term storage before the accident (Gilboa, Winocur, & Rosenbaum, 2006).

THE NEUROSCIENCE OF MEMORY

Chapter 2 focused on neuroscience and behaviour in more detail, but we will touch a little bit more on that here on the neuroscience of memory. Can we pinpoint a location in the brain where sensory, short-term, and long-term memories reside? Is there a single site that corresponds to a particular memory, or is memory distributed in different regions across the brain? Do memories leave an actual physical trace that scientists can view?

The search for the *engram*, the term for the physical memory trace that corresponds to a memory, has proved to be a major puzzle to psychologists and other neuroscientists interested in memory. Using advanced brain scanning procedures in their efforts to determine the neuroscientific basis of memory formation, investigators have learned that certain areas and structures of the brain specialize in different types of memory-related activities. Brenda Milner, from McGill University in Montreal, was one of the first people to find out that the *hippocampus*, a part of the brain's limbic system, plays a central role in the consolidation of memories. Milner was called in to consult on the case we discussed earlier in the chapter, H. M., a man whose hippocampus was partly removed in surgery to help control his epilepsy. After the surgery, H. M. suffered from anterograde amnesia (he could not form new long-term memories). Milner was able to determine that it was the hippocampus that was responsible for the formation of new memories and for memories that were consolidated a few years before the damage. Located within the brain's *medial temporal lobes*, just behind the eyes, the hippocampus aids in the initial encoding of information, acting as a kind of neurological email system. That information is subsequently passed along to the cerebral cortex of the brain, where it is actually stored (Govindarajan, Kelleher, & Tonegawa, 2006; Peters et al., 2007; Wilson, 2002).

The *amygdala*, another part of the limbic system, also plays an important role in memory. The amygdala is especially involved with memories involving emotion (Buchanan & Adolphs, 2004; Hamann, 2001). For example, if you are frightened by a large Doberman, you're likely to remember the event vividly—an outcome related to the functioning of the amygdala. Encountering the Doberman or any large dog in the future is likely to reactivate the amygdala and bring back the unpleasant memory, for a while, at least.

Figure 6.10
Memory Consolidation in the Brain

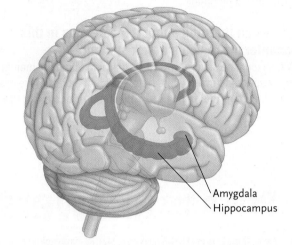

Amygdala
Hippocampus

Source: Van De Graff, 2000.

For Review »

What is memory?

Memory is the process by which we encode, store, and retrieve information. Memory can be thought of as a three-stage process. Sensory memories are very brief, but they are precise, storing a nearly exact replica of a stimulus. Roughly seven (plus or minus two) chunks of information can be transferred and held in short-term memory for 15 to 25 seconds; if they are not transferred to long-term memory, they are then lost. Memories are transferred into long-term storage by encoding the information for meaning and other strategies, such as elaborative rehearsal. Long-term memory includes declarative memory and procedural memory. Declarative memory is divided into episodic memory and semantic memory.

Why do we recall some memories better than others?

Retrieval cues, such as emotions, sights, and sounds, are a major strategy for recalling information successfully. The levels-of-processing approach to memory suggests that the way in which information is initially perceived and analyzed determines the success with which it is recalled; the deeper the initial processing, the greater the recall. Flashbulb memories are memories centred on a specific, important event. The more distinctive a memory is, the more easily it can be retrieved. Memory is a constructive process, such that our memories are influenced by the meaning we give to events. Eyewitnesses are apt to make substantial errors when they try to recall the details of crimes. The problem of memory reliability becomes even more acute when the witnesses are children.

Why do we forget information?

Several processes account for memory failure, including decay, interference (both proactive and retroactive), and cue-dependent forgetting, as well as Alzheimer's disease and amnesia. Alzheimer's disease is an illness characterized in part by a progressive loss of memory. Amnesia, another type of memory loss that occurs without other mental difficulties, can take two forms: retrograde amnesia and anterograde amnesia.

What is the neuroscience of memory?

Certain areas and structures of the brain specialize in different types of memory-related activities. For example, the hippocampus helps to formulate and consolidate new memories and the amygdala is involved in storing memories with strong emotions.

How can learning about the concepts in this chapter make you a better student?

We discussed several ways that learning about the memory concept could make you a better student. For one, we provided a list at the beginning of the chapter of some helpful tips such as organizing your text and lecture notes in a way that will help you remember or using elaborative rehearsal to tie the new information you learned in your courses with information you already have stored in your memory. We also talked about the levels-of-processing theory, which proposes that you will remember information better if you think about it on a deeper level. You may do this by asking yourself questions about what you just read, using metaphors or associations to information you already know, or simply putting the information into your own words rather than copying down direct quotes.

Psych think answers

Psych think 1 In the PSYCH think on p. 142 we said that "you never forget how to ride a bicycle" and asked why this might be so. We also asked what type of memory stores information about bicycle riding. Riding a bike is a procedural memory that is permanently stored in your long-term memory, which is why you never forget how to do it.

Psych think 2 In the PSYCH think on p. 145 we asked you what study tips come to mind for improving your own study habits based on levels-of-processing theory. Remember that the levels-of-processing theory states that you will remember much more when you are initially presented with information if you try to process it on a deep level rather than a more shallow level. To use the levels-of-processing theory to improve your study habits, there are several things that you may do. For example, you need to start by paying attention while in your lectures and while reading your textbook. However, just paying attention is only a shallow level of processing. To go deeper you must make associations between the new material that you are learning and information you already know. When reading your textbook you should stop after each section and ask yourself what you just read. Putting the information into your own words in a way that you understand will greatly improve your study habits.

Psych think 3 In the PSYCH think on p. 149 we indicated that research shows that an eyewitness's memory for details of crimes can contain significant errors. We then asked you what factors might influence an eyewitness's ability to remember. There are several factors that might influence an eyewitness's ability to remember. The stress of the situation, or if a weapon is used may make it difficult for the eyewitness to remember the details of the situation. Other factors, such as interference from other sources of information (e.g., other eyewitnesses or media reports), or the way in which questions are asked of the eyewitness, may make it difficult for the eyewitness to retain that information.

Connect with classmates.

7

Thinking,
Language, and Intelligences

Solving lottery fraud

Bob Edwards, from the small town of Coboconk, Ontario, bought a lottery ticket using his regular numbers made up from a combination of his birthday and the birthdays of his wife and son. Imagine his surprise when he found out that the clerk at the convenience store where he went to check his ticket had stolen his ticket and claimed the $250,000 dollar prize as her own.

fter a long investigation, the Ontario Lottery and Gaming Corporation (OLG) finally settled with Bob Edwards for $150,000. This led the CBC television show *The Fifth Estate* to hire University of Toronto statistics professor Jeffery Rosenthal to use his problem-solving abilities to investigate whether there might be more cases of store clerks stealing winning lottery tickets (Royal Canadian Mounted Police, 2008; CBC News, 2007).

As you will learn in this chapter, the first step in problem solving is preparation, where one attempts to understand and diagnose the problem. Dr. Rosenthal knew that 200 (3.5%) convenience store clerks had won the lottery between 1999 and 2006, but he did not know if this number was higher than what could be expected by chance. After diagnosing the problem, the second step in problem solving is the production stage, where one generates a solution (or solutions) to the problem. Rosenthal used a statistical technique called probability to generate a solution. He calculated the total number of retail lottery sellers and how much money they spent on lottery tickets compared to the general population. He discovered that lottery ticket sellers should have won about 57 major lottery prizes between 1999 and 2006, which was far lower than the 200 actual claims lottery ticket sellers made during that period. He concluded that the probability of lottery ticket sellers winning 200 major lotteries was so improbable that it was not conceivable. It seemed that some lottery ticket sellers were telling their customers that the winning lottery ticket was not a winner, and instead they claimed it for themselves. Rosenthal's use of probability guaranteed a solution to the problem, so he did not need to spend very much time of the final stage of problem solving called judgment, where one evaluates the solution. A rule that guarantees a solution is called an algorithm, which you will learn more about in this chapter.

Major reforms have been made to the way lottery tickets are claimed since *The Fifth Estate* aired Rosenthal's findings. Ticket holders must now sign the back of their tickets and self-checker machines have been placed in convenience stores so customers can check themselves to see if they won. Moreover, other provinces such as British Columbia and Nova Scotia conducted similar investigations into lottery fraud in their provinces because of Rosenthal's findings.

Rosenthal's process of solving the problem of lottery fraud would be of interest to individuals who adhere to a cognitive approach to psychology. Hopefully you remember that *cognitive psychology* is one of the modern approaches to psychology we discussed in the first chapter, and that it focuses on the study of higher mental processes, including thinking, language, problem solving, knowing, reasoning, judging, and decision making. We cover these topics in this chapter, along with intelligence, intelligence testing, and factors associated with creativity. Memory, the subject of Chapter 6, is another cognitive process that cognitive psychologists would be interested in.

As You Read »

- What is thinking?
- How do people approach and solve problems?
- How does language develop?
- How is intelligence defined and conceptualized?
- What are the major approaches to measuring intelligence in the West, and what do intelligence tests measure?
- What are the variations in intelligence?

Thinking and Reasoning

What are you thinking about at this moment?

The mere ability to pose such a question underscores the distinctive nature of the human capacity for thinking. No other species contemplates, analyzes, recollects, or plans the way humans do. Psychologists define **thinking** as the manipulation of mental representations of information. A representation may take the form of a word, a visual image, a sound, or any other type of sensory data stored in memory. Thinking transforms a specific representation of information into new and different forms, allowing us to answer questions, solve problems, and reach goals.

Although a clear sense of what exactly occurs when we think remains elusive, an understanding of the nature of the fundamental elements involved in thinking is growing. We begin by considering our use of mental images and concepts, the building blocks of thought.

MENTAL IMAGES

Think of your best friend.

Chances are that some kind of visual image comes to mind when you are asked to think of her or him, or any other person or object, for that matter. To some cognitive psychologists, such mental images constitute a major part of thinking.

Mental images are representations in the mind of an object or an event. They are not just visual representations; our ability to "hear" a tune in our heads is also considered a mental image. In fact, every sensory modality (seeing, hearing, smelling, etc.) may produce a corresponding mental image (De Beni, Pazzaglia, & Gardini, 2007; Kosslyn, 2005).

Research has found that our mental images have some of the properties of the actual stimuli they represent. For example, it takes the mind longer to scan mental images of large objects than of small ones, just as the eye takes longer to scan an actual large object than an actual small one. Similarly, we are able to manipulate and rotate mental images of objects, just as we are able to manipulate and rotate them in the real world (Iachini & Giusberti, 2004; Mast & Kosslyn, 2002; Shepard et al., 2000).

Some experts see the production of mental images as a way to improve various skills. For instance, many athletes use mental imagery in their training. Basketball players may try to produce vivid and detailed images of the court, the basket, the ball, and the noisy crowd. They may visualize themselves taking a foul shot, watching the ball, and hearing the swish as it goes through the net. And it works: the use of mental imagery can lead to improved performance in sports (MacIntyre, Moran, & Jennings, 2002; Mamassis & Doganis, 2004).

CONCEPTS

If someone asks you what is in your kitchen cabinet, you might answer with a detailed list of items ("a jar of peanut butter, a bag of white rice, six unmatched dinner plates, four

thinking The manipulation of mental representations of information.

mental images Representations in the mind that resemble the object or event being represented.

bowls," and so forth). More likely, though, you would respond by naming some broader categories, such as "food" and "dishes."

Using such categories reflects the operation of concepts. **Concepts** are categorizations of objects, events, or people that share common properties. Concepts enable us to organize complex phenomena into simpler, and therefore more easily usable, cognitive categories (Connolly, 2007; Goldstone & Kersten, 2003; Murphy, 2005).

Many athletes, such as Mike Weir, use mental imagery to focus on a task, a process they call "getting in the zone." What other occupations might require the use of strong mental imagery?

Concepts help us classify newly encountered objects on the basis of our past experience. For example, we can surmise that someone tapping a handheld screen is probably using some kind of tablet, even if we have never encountered that specific model before. Ultimately, concepts influence behaviour; we would assume, for instance, that it might be appropriate to pet an animal after determining that it is a dog, whereas we would behave differently after classifying the animal as a wolf.

When cognitive psychologists first studied concepts, they focused on those that were clearly defined by a unique set of properties or features. For example, an equilateral triangle is a closed shape that has three sides of equal length. If an object has these characteristics, it is an equilateral triangle; if it does not, it is not an equilateral triangle.

Other concepts—often those with the most relevance to our everyday lives—are more ambiguous and difficult to define. For instance, broader concepts such as "table" and "bird" have a set of general, relatively loose characteristic features, rather than unique, clearly defined properties that distinguish an example of the concept from a non-example. When we consider these more ambiguous concepts, we usually think in terms of examples called **prototypes**. Prototypes are typical, highly representative examples of a concept that correspond to our mental image or best example of the concept. For instance, although a robin and an ostrich are both examples of birds, those who grew up around robins and not around ostriches are more likely to think of a robin when asked for an example of a bird. Consequently, for those people who think that robin is the best example of a bird, we would say that robin is a prototype of the concept "bird." Similarly, when we think of the concept of a table, those of us who are likely to think of a coffee table before we think of a drafting table, would have "coffee table" closer to our prototype of a table.

ALGORITHMS AND HEURISTICS

When faced with making a decision, we often turn to various kinds of cognitive shortcuts, known as algorithms and heuristics, to help us. An **algorithm** is a rule that, if applied appropriately, guarantees a solution to a problem. We can use an algorithm even if we cannot understand why it works. For example, you may know that you can find the length of the third side of a right triangle by using the formula $a^2 + b^2 = c^2$, although you may not have the foggiest notion of the mathematical principles behind the formula. Dr. Rosenthal, from the beginning of the chapter, used algorithms to determine the probability of lottery ticket sellers winning the lottery.

concepts Categorizations of objects, events, or people that share common properties.

prototypes Typical, highly representative examples of a concept.

algorithm A rule that, if applied appropriately, guarantees a solution to a problem.

Which one of these two images matches your prototype for "phone"? The one on the left is the first telephone, invented by Alexander Graham Bell.

A **heuristic** is a cognitive shortcut that may lead to a correct solution. Unlike algorithms, heuristics enhance the likelihood of success in coming to a solution but they cannot ensure it. For example, when some people play tic-tac-toe, they follow the heuristic of placing an X in the centre square when they start the game. This tactic doesn't guarantee that they will win, but experience might teach them that it will increase the chances of success. Similarly, some students follow the heuristic of preparing for a test by ignoring the assigned textbook reading and studying only their lecture notes—a strategy that may or may not pay off.

Although heuristics often help people to solve problems and to make decisions, certain kinds of heuristics may lead to inaccurate conclusions. For example, we sometimes use the *representativeness heuristic*, a rule we apply when we judge people by the degree to which they represent a certain category or group of people. Suppose, for instance, you are the owner of a fast-food store that has been robbed many times by teenagers. Using the concept of a prototype discussed above, we could guess that you have developed over time a prototype for the appearance and age of a person who is going to rob your store. The representativeness heuristic (that is, using your prototype category) would lead you to raise your guard each time someone of this age group enters your store (even though, statistically, it is unlikely that any given teenager will rob the store) (Fisk, Bury, & Holden, 2006).

> **Some students follow the heuristic of preparing for a test by ignoring the assigned textbook reading and studying only their lecture notes–a strategy that may or may not pay off.**

The *availability heuristic* involves judging the probability of an event on the basis of how easily the event can be recalled from memory. According to this heuristic, we assume that events we remember easily are likely to have occurred more frequently in the past—and are more likely to occur in the future—than events that are harder to remember.

For instance, the availability heuristic makes us more afraid of dying in a plane crash than in an auto accident, despite statistics clearly showing that airplane travel is much safer than auto travel. Similarly, although ten times more people die from falling out of bed than from lightning strikes, we're more afraid of being hit by lightning than we are getting into bed at night. The reason is that plane crashes

heuristic A cognitive shortcut that may lead to a solution.

Although you might not realize it, you use heuristics every day.

and lightning strikes receive far more publicity, and they are therefore more easily remembered (Fox, 2006; Kluger, 2006; Oppenheimer, 2004; Vaughn & Weary, 2002).

Psych think

> > > How might the availability heuristic contribute to prejudice?

SOLVING PROBLEMS

According to an old legend, a group of Vietnamese monks guard three towers on which sit 64 golden rings. The monks believe that if they succeed in moving the rings from the first tower to the third according to a series of rigid rules, the world as we know it will come to an end. (Should you prefer that the world remain in its present state, there's no need for immediate concern: it would take $2^{64} - 1$ moves to solve the problem, and if we assume that each move takes 1 second, the solution would take close to 600 billion years.)

In the Tower of Hanoi puzzle, a simpler version of the task facing the monks, three disks are placed on three posts (as in Figure 7.1). The goal of the puzzle is to move all three disks to the third post, arranged in the same order, by using as few moves as possible. There are two restrictions: Only one disk can be moved at a time, and no disk can ever cover a smaller one during a move.

Why are cognitive psychologists interested in the Tower of Hanoi problem? Because the way people go about solving such puzzles helps illuminate how people solve complex, real-life problems. Psychologists have found that problem solving typically involves three steps: preparing to create solutions, producing solutions, and evaluating the solutions that have been generated.

Figure 7.1
Tower of Hanoi Puzzle

Can you solve the Tower of Hanoi puzzle? The goal of the puzzle is to move all three disks from the first post to the third and still preserve the original order of the disks, using the fewest number of moves possible while following the rules that only one disk at a time can be moved and no disk can cover a smaller one during a move. The solution lists the moves in sequence.

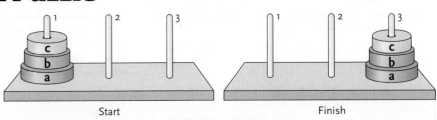

Start   Finish

Solution: Move C to 3, B to 2, C to 2, A to 3, C to 1, B to 3, and C to 3.

Preparation: Understanding and Diagnosing Problems When approaching a problem like the Tower of Hanoi, most people begin by trying to understand the problem thoroughly. If the problem is an unusual one, they probably will pay special attention to any restrictions placed on coming up with a solution—such as the rule about moving only one disk at a time in the Tower of Hanoi problem. If, by contrast, the problem is a familiar one, they are apt to spend considerably less time in this preparation stage.

Problems vary from well defined to ill defined (Arlin, 1989; Evans, 2004; Reitman, 1965). In a *well-defined problem*—such as a mathematical equation or the solution to a jigsaw puzzle—both the nature of the problem itself and the information needed to solve it are available and clear. Thus, we can make straightforward judgments about whether a potential solution is appropriate. With an *ill-defined problem*, such as how to increase morale on an assembly line or how to improve your test taking, not only may the specific nature of the problem be unclear, but the information required to solve the problem may be even less obvious.

Typically, a problem falls into one of the three categories: arrangement, inducing structure, and transformation, as shown in Figure 7.2. Solving each type requires somewhat different kinds of psychological skills and knowledge (Chronicle, MacGregor, & Ormerod, 2004; Spitz, 1987).

Arrangement problems require the problem solver to rearrange or recombine elements in a way that will satisfy a certain criterion. Usually, several different arrangements can be made, but only one or a few of the arrangements will produce a solution. Anagram problems and jigsaw puzzles are examples of arrangement problems (Coventry et al., 2003).

In *problems of inducing structure*, a person must identify the existing relationships among the elements presented and then construct a new relationship among them. In such a problem, the problem solver must determine not only the relationships among the elements but also the structure and size of the elements involved. In the example shown in Figure 7.2, a person must first determine that the solution requires the numbers to be considered in pairs (14-24-34-44-54-64). Only after identifying that part of the problem can a person determine the solution rule (the first number of each pair increases by one, while the second number remains the same).

The Tower of Hanoi puzzle represents the third kind of problem—*transformation problems*—which consist of an initial state, a goal state, and a method for changing the initial state into the goal state. In the Tower of Hanoi problem, the initial state is the original configuration, the goal state is to have the three disks on the third peg, and the method is the rules for moving the disks (Emick & Welsh, 2005; Majeres, 2007; Mataix-Cols & Bartres-Faz, 2002).

> **Eliminating non-essential information is often a critical step in the preparation stage of problem solving.**

Whether the problem is one of arrangement, inducing structure, or transformation, the preparation stage of understanding and diagnosing is critical in problem solving, because it allows us to develop our own cognitive representation of the problem and to place it within a personal framework. We may divide the problem into subparts or ignore some information as we try to simplify the task. Eliminating non-essential information is often a critical step in the preparation stage of problem solving.

Our ability to represent a problem—and the kind of solution we eventually come to—depends on the way a problem is phrased, or framed. Consider, for example, if you were a cancer patient having to choose between surgery and radiation and were given the two sets of treatment options shown in the image on p. 167 (Chandran & Menon, 2004; Tversky & Kahneman, 1987). When the options are framed in terms of the likelihood of survival, only 18% of participants in a study chose radiation over surgery. However, when the choice was framed in terms of the likelihood of dying, 44% chose radiation over surgery—even though the outcomes are identical in both sets of framing conditions.

DID YOU KNOW?

If you want to convince someone to use sunscreen, the odds of succeeding are higher if you use positive framing ("It helps keep your skin looking young") compared to negative framing ("If you don't, you could develop skin cancer") (APA, 1999).

Figure 7.2
Categories of Problems

Arrangement problems

1. Anagrams: Rearrange the letters in each set to make an English word:

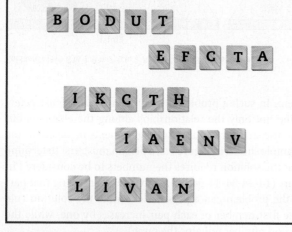

2. Two strings hang from a ceiling but are too far apart to allow a person to hold one and walk to the other. On the floor are a book of matches, a screwdriver, and a few pieces of cotton. How could the strings be tied together?

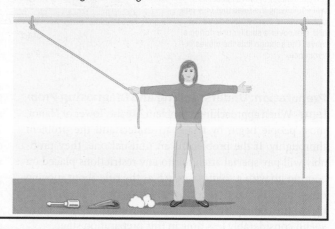

Problems of inducing structure

1. What number comes next in the series?

1 4 2 4 3 4 4 4 5 4 6 4

2. Complete these analogies:

baseball is to bat as tennis is to _____

merchant is to sell as customer is to _____

Transformation problems

1. Water jars: A person has three jars with the following capacities:

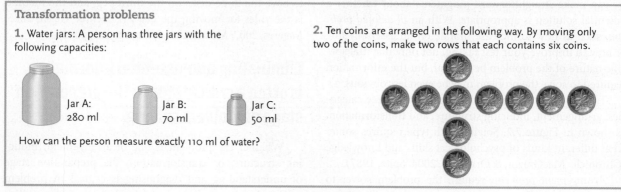

Jar A: 280 ml   Jar B: 70 ml   Jar C: 50 ml

How can the person measure exactly 110 ml of water?

2. Ten coins are arranged in the following way. By moving only two of the coins, make two rows that each contains six coins.

(Answers can be found on p. 168.)

Sources: Bourne, Dominowski, & Loftus, *Cognitive Processes*, 1st ed., © 1979 by Prentice-Hall.

Production: Generating Solutions The second step in problem solving is the production of possible solutions. If a problem is relatively simple, we may already have a direct solution stored in long-term memory, and all we need to do is retrieve the appropriate information. If we cannot retrieve or do not know the solution, we must generate possible solutions and compare them with information in long- and short-term memory.

When all else fails, we can solve problems through trial and error, but we tend to resist this approach in favour of any possible heuristics. Wouldn't you get frustrated if forced to try solving a problem by trial and error instead of using shortcuts? Thomas Edison invented the light bulb only because he tried thousands of different kinds of materials for a filament before he found one that worked

(carbon). Another difficulty with trial and error is that some problems are so complicated that it would take a lifetime to try out every possibility. For example, according to some estimates, there are some 10^{120} possible sequences of chess moves (10^{120} is equal to 1 followed by 120 zeros) (Fine & Fine, 2003).

In place of trial and error, complex problem solving often involves the use of heuristics, cognitive shortcuts that can generate solutions. Probably the most frequently applied heuristic in problem solving is a **means-ends analysis**, figuring out the goal and breaking down the actions needed into small steps. Each step will bring you closer to the goal

means-ends analysis Repeated testing for differences between the desired outcome and what currently exists.

Problem: Surgery or radiation?

Survival Frame

Surgery: Of 100 people having surgery, 90 live through the post-operative period, 68 are alive at the end of the first year, and 34 are alive at the end of five years.

Radiation: Of 100 people having radiation therapy, all live through the treatment, 77 are alive at the end of one year, and 22 are alive at the end of five years.

Far more patients choose surgery

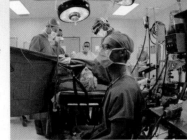

Mortality Frame

Surgery: Of 100 people having surgery, 10 die during surgery, 32 die by the end of the first year, and 66 die by the end of five years.

Radiation: Of 100 people having radiation therapy, none die during the treatment, 23 die by the end of one year, and 78 die by the end of five years.

Far more patients choose radiation

(Chrysikou, 2006; Huber, Beckmann, & Herrmann, 2004; Newell & Simon, 1972). Consider this simple example: I want to take my dog to the vet. What's the difference between what I have and what I want? One of distance. What changes distance? My automobile. My automobile won't work. What is needed to make it work? A new battery. What has new batteries? An auto repair shop . . .

In a means-end analysis, each step brings the problem solver closer to a resolution. Although this approach is often effective, if the problem requires indirect steps that temporarily *increase* the discrepancy between a current state and the solution, means-ends analysis can be counterproductive. For example, sometimes the fastest route to the summit of a mountain requires a mountain climber to backtrack temporarily; a means-end approach—which implies that the mountain climber should always forge ahead and upward—is ineffective in such instances.

Another heuristic commonly used to generate solutions is to divide a problem into intermediate steps, or *subgoals*, and solve each of those steps. For instance, in our modified Tower of Hanoi problem, we could choose several obvious subgoals, such as moving the largest disk to the third post.

If solving a subgoal is a step toward the ultimate solution to a problem, identifying subgoals is an appropriate strategy. In some cases, however, forming subgoals is not all that helpful and may actually increase the time needed to find a solution. For example, some mathematics problems are so complex that it takes longer to identify the appropriate subdivisions than to solve the problems by other means (Fishbach, Dhar, & Zhang, 2006; Kaller et al., 2004; Reed, 1996).

Judgment: Evaluating the Solutions The final stage in problem solving is judging the adequacy of a solution.

Often this is a simple matter: If the solution is clear—as in the Tower of Hanoi problem—we will know immediately whether we have been successful (Varma, 2007).

If the solution is less concrete or if there is no single correct solution, evaluating solutions becomes more difficult. In such instances, we must decide which alternative solution is best. Unfortunately, we often quite inaccurately estimate the quality of our own ideas. For instance, a team of drug researchers working for a specific company may consider their remedy for an illness to be superior to all others, overestimating the likelihood of their success and downplaying the approaches of competing drug companies (Eizenberg & Zaslavsky, 2004).

Theoretically, we can make accurate choices among alternative solutions by relying on heuristics and valid information. Yet, as we see next, several kinds of obstacles and biases in problem solving affect the quality of the decisions and judgments we make.

Study tip

You can use the three steps of problem solving to organize your studying: preparation, production, and judgment (PPJ).

Obstacles to Problem Solving Consider the following problem-solving test (Duncker, 1945):

You are given a set of tacks, candles, and matches, each in a small box, and told your goal is to place three candles at eye level on a nearby door, so that wax will not drip on the floor as the candles burn. How would you approach this challenge?

Figure 7.3
Three-Candle Problem

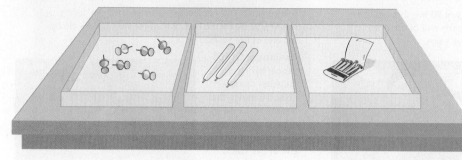

The problem here is to place three candles at eye level on a nearby door so that the wax will not drip on the floor as the candles burn—using only the materials in the figure. The solution appears on p. 170.

If you have difficulty solving the problem, you are not alone. Most people cannot solve it when it is presented with the objects shown *inside* the boxes. However, if the objects were presented *beside* the boxes, just resting on the table, chances are that you would solve the problem much more readily.

The difficulty you probably encountered in solving this problem stems from its presentation, which is misleading at the initial preparation stage. Actually, significant obstacles to problem solving can exist at each of the three major stages. Although cognitive approaches to problem solving suggest that thinking proceeds along fairly rational, logical lines as a person confronts a problem and considers various solutions, several factors can hinder the development of creative, appropriate, and accurate solutions.

- *Functional Fixedness.* The difficulty most people experience with the candle problem is caused by **functional fixedness**, the tendency to think of an object only in terms of its typical use. For instance, functional fixedness probably leads you to think of this book as something to read, instead of its potential use as a doorstop or as kindling for a fire. In the candle problem, because the objects are first presented inside the boxes, functional fixedness leads most people to see the boxes simply as containers for the objects they hold rather than as a potential part of the solution. They do not envision another function for the boxes.

- *Mental Set.* Functional fixedness is an example of a broader phenomenon known as **mental set**, the tendency for old patterns of problem solving to persist. A classic experiment (Luchins, 1946) demonstrated this phenomenon. As you can see in Figure 7.4, the object of the task is to use the jars in each row to measure out the designated amount of liquid. (Try it to get a sense of the power of mental set before moving on.)

If you have tried to solve the problem, you know that the first five rows are all solved in the same way: First fill the largest jar (B), and then from it fill the middle-size jar (A) once and the smallest jar (C) two times. What is left in B is the designated amount. (Stated as a formula, the designated amount is B–A–2C.) The demonstration of mental set comes in the sixth row of the problem, a point at which you probably encountered some difficulty. If you are like most people, you tried the formula and were perplexed when it failed. Chances are, in fact, that you missed the simple (but different) solution to the problem, which involves merely subtracting C from A. Interestingly, people who were given the problem in row 6 *first* had no difficulty with it at all.

- *Inaccurate Evaluation of Solutions.* When the nuclear power plant at Three Mile Island in Pennsylvania malfunctioned in 1979, a disaster that almost led to a nuclear meltdown, the plant operators immediately had

(Answers to problems in Figure 7.2)

Arrangement problems

1. DOUBT, FACET, THICK, NAIVE, ANVIL
2. The screwdriver is tied to one of the strings. This makes a pendulum that can be swung to reach the other string.

Problems of inducing structure

1. 7
2. racket, buy

Transformation problems

1. Fill jar A; empty into jar B once and into jar C twice. What remains in jar A is 110 ml.

2.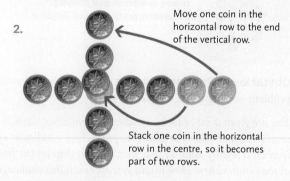

Move one coin in the horizontal row to the end of the vertical row.

Stack one coin in the horizontal row in the centre, so it becomes part of two rows.

functional fixedness The tendency to think of an object only in terms of its typical use.

mental set The tendency for old patterns of problem solving to persist.

Figure 7.4
A Classic Mental Set

Given jars with these capacities (in ml):

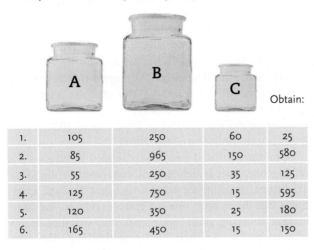

	A	B	C	Obtain:
1.	105	250	60	25
2.	85	965	150	580
3.	55	250	35	125
4.	125	750	15	595
5.	120	350	25	180
6.	165	450	15	150

In this classic demonstration of mental set, the goal is to use the jars in each row to measure out the designated amount of liquid. After you've figured out the solution for the first five rows, you'll probably have trouble with the sixth row—even though the solution is actually easier. In fact, if you had tried to solve the problem in the sixth row first, you probably would have solved it right away.

to solve a problem of the most serious kind. Several monitors gave contradictory information about the source of the problem: One suggested that the pressure was too high, leading to the danger of an explosion; others indicated that the pressure was too low, which could lead to a meltdown. Although the pressure was, in fact, too low, the supervisors on duty relied on the one monitor—which turned out to be faulty—that suggested that the pressure was too high. Once they had made their decision and acted on it, they ignored the contradictory evidence from the other monitors (Wickens, 1984).

The operators' mistake exemplifies **confirmation bias**, in which problem solvers favour initial hypotheses and ignore contradictory information that supports alternative hypotheses or solutions. Even when we find evidence that contradicts a solution we have chosen, we are apt to stick with our original hypothesis.

Confirmation bias occurs for several reasons. For one thing, because rethinking a problem that appears to be solved already takes extra cognitive effort, we are apt to stick with our first solution. For another, we give greater weight to subsequent information that supports our initial position than to information that is not supportive of it (Evans & Feeney, 2004; Gilovich, Griffin, & Kahneman, 2002).

confirmation bias The tendency to favour information that supports one's initial hypotheses and ignore contradictory information that supports alternative hypotheses or solutions.

creativity The ability to generate original ideas or solve problems in novel ways.

CREATIVITY AND PROBLEM SOLVING

Despite obstacles to problem solving, many people adeptly discover creative solutions to problems. One enduring question that cognitive psychologists have sought to answer is what factors underlie **creativity**, the ability to generate original ideas or solve problems in novel ways.

Although identifying the stages of problem solving helps us understand how people approach and solve problems, it does little to explain why some people come up with better solutions than others do. For instance, even the possible solutions to a simple problem often show wide discrepancies. Consider, for example, how you might respond to the question "How many uses can you think of for a newspaper?"

Now compare your solution with this one proposed by a 10-year-old boy:

You can read it, write on it, lay it down and paint a picture on it . . . You could put it in your door for decoration, put it in the garbage can, put it on a chair if the chair is messy. If you have a puppy, you put newspaper in its box or put it in your backyard for the dog to play with. When you build something and you don't want anyone to see it, put newspaper around it. Put newspaper on the floor if you have no mattress, use it to pick up something hot, use it to stop bleeding, or to catch

Psych
At The Movies

The Lookout

Chris suffers memory deficiencies as a result of brain damage. His friend teaches him to use means-end analysis to keep his focus on his goal and figure out the appropriate next step toward its achievement.

Benny & Joon

Sam is not locked into a functional fixedness box. He uses forks and rolls in this movie to choreograph a dance for Joon to win her affection.

The Cuckoo

In this film, fate brings three characters together who do not speak one another's languages. Note the strength of the drive to use language even when it is not functional, the numerous misunderstandings, and the exaggerated non-verbal communication.

The Gods Must Be Crazy

Bushmen of the Kalahari Desert would judge you to be of low intelligence indeed if you didn't know how to keep yourself hydrated by strategically placing collection leaves and extracting water from tubers, as illustrated in the opening scene of this film.

Solution to the three-candle problem in Figure 7.3.

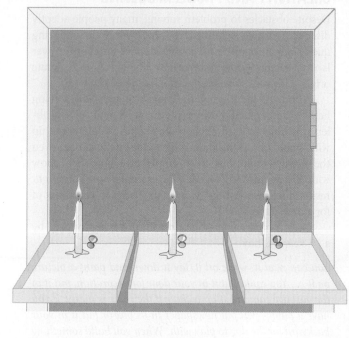

the drips from drying clothes. You can use a newspaper for curtains, put it in your shoe to cover what is hurting your foot, make a kite out of it, shade a light that is too bright. You can wrap fish in it, wipe windows, or wrap money in it . . . You put washed shoes in newspaper, wipe eyeglasses with it, put it under a dripping sink, put a plant on it, make a paper bowl out of it, tie it on your feet for slippers. You can put it on the sand if you had no towel, use it for bases in baseball, make paper airplanes with it, use it as a dustpan when you sweep, ball it up for the cat to play with, wrap your hands in it if it is cold. (Ward, Kogan, & Pankove, 1972)

This list shows extraordinary creativity. Unfortunately, it is much easier to identify examples of creativity than to

"*I'll be happy to give you innovative thinking. What are the guidelines?*"

determine its causes. Several factors, however, seem to be associated with creativity (Kaufman & Baer, 2005; Schepers & van den Berg, 2007; Simonton, 2003).

One of these factors is **divergent thinking**, the ability to generate unusual, yet appropriate, responses to problems or questions. This type of thinking contrasts with **convergent thinking**, which produces responses that are based primarily on knowledge and logic. For instance, in reply to the question "What can you do with a newspaper?" someone relying on convergent thinking might say "You read it." In contrast, "You use it as a dustpan" is a more divergent—and creative—response (Baer, 1993; Cropley, 2006; Finke, 1995; Ho, 2004; Runco, 2006; Runco & Sakamoto, 1993; Sternberg, 2001).

One factor that is *not* closely related to creativity is intelligence, as it is defined and measured in the West. Traditional intelligence tests, which ask focused questions that have only one acceptable answer, tap convergent thinking skills. Such tests may penalize highly creative people for their divergent thinking. This may explain why researchers consistently find that creativity is only slightly related to school grades and intelligence when intelligence is measured using traditional intelligence tests (Hong, Milgram, & Gorsky, 1995; Sternberg & O'Hara, 2000).

Study tip Remember, divergent thinking produces different and diverse kinds of responses, whereas convergent thinking produces more commonsense kinds of responses.

LEARNING TO BE A BETTER THINKER

Critical and creative thinkers are made, not born, according to cognitive researchers. Consider, for instance, these suggestions for increasing critical thinking and creativity (Burbach, Matkin, & Fritz, 2004; Kaufman & Baer, 2006):

- *Redefine problems.* We can modify boundaries and assumptions by rephrasing a problem at either a more abstract or a more concrete level.

- *Use subgoals.* By developing subgoals, we can divide a problem into intermediate steps. This process, known as fractionation, allows us to examine each part for new possibilities and approaches, leading to a novel solution for the problem as a whole.

- *Adopt a critical perspective.* Rather than passively accepting assumptions or arguments, we can evaluate

divergent thinking The ability to generate unusual, yet nonetheless appropriate, responses to problems or questions.

convergent thinking The ability to produce responses that are based primarily on knowledge and logic.

material carefully, consider its implications, credibility and relevance, and think about possible exceptions and contradictions.

- *Consider the opposite.* By considering the opposite of a concept we're seeking to understand, we can sometimes make progress. For example, to define "good mental health," it may be useful to consider what "bad mental health" means.

- *Think divergently.* Instead of the most logical or common use for an object, consider how you might use the object if you were forbidden to use it in the usual way.

- *Experiment with various solutions.* Don't be afraid to use different routes to find solutions for problems (verbal, mathematical, graphic, even dramatic). For instance, try to come up with every conceivable idea

you can, no matter how wild or bizarre it may seem at first. After you've come up with a list of wild and crazy solutions, review each one and try to think of ways to make what initially appeared impractical seem more feasible.

Language

Pldfse prss tpe sglt. Even though there were many spelling errors in this sentence, were you still able to figure out that it said *"Please pass the salt?"*

Our ability to make sense out of nonsense, if the nonsense follows typical rules of language, illustrates the complexity of both human language and the cognitive processes that underlie its development and use. The use of **language**—the communication of information through symbols arranged according to systematic rules—is an important cognitive ability, one that is indispensable if we

> **language** The communication of information through symbols arranged according to systematic rules.

From the perspective of ...

A BUSINESS EXECUTIVE You have the challenge of figuring out how to encourage a team of employees to find a creative solution for getting people to use more paper towels. Can you think of any strategies that would help them think outside the box?

BUY IT?

The Lunar Effect: Does a Full Moon Mean More Violent Behaviour?

Are you one of the many people who believe that weird things happen on nights of a full moon? People have reported an increase in traffic accidents, births, casino payouts, and assaults and violent behaviour during a full moon. This is referred to as the lunar effect because many people believe that the full moon has an effect on people's behaviour. As a good critical thinker, hopefully you said that while you have heard of this phenomenon, you will suspend your belief until consulting the empirical research! Good thing you did, because research has not found a significant relationship between full moons and violent behaviour (Kelly, Rotton, & Culver, 1985; Owen, Tarantello, Jones, & Tennant, 1998).

Why do you think so many people believe in the lunar effect? We can explain this using some of the heuristics and biases you've learned about in this chapter. The media tends to report anecdotal evidence of the full moon's impact on human behaviour, which makes this information readily available in reader's minds, thus, the availability heuristic is at work here. Moreover, when people believe in the full moon they will more likely notice the moon's impact on people's behaviour, which confirms their belief in the lunar effect. This of course is an example of confirmation bias, because people are confirming their own belief (The Skeptics Dictionary, 2011).

are to communicate with one another. Not only is language central to communication, it is also closely tied to the very way in which we think about and understand the world. No wonder psychologists have devoted considerable attention to studying language (Fitch & Sanders, 2005; Hoff, 2008; Stapel & Semin, 2007).

GRAMMAR: THE RULES OF LANGUAGE

To understand how language develops and relates to thought, we first need to review some of the formal elements of language. The basic structure of language rests on **grammar**, the system of rules that determine how our thoughts can be expressed in words.

Grammar deals with three major components of language: phonology, syntax, and semantics. **Phonology** is the study of the smallest basic units of speech, called **phonemes**, that affect meaning, and of the way we use those sounds to form words and produce meaning. For instance, the *a* sound in *fat* and the *a* sound in *fate* represent two different phonemes in English (Hardison, 2006).

Linguists have identified more than 800 different phonemes among all the world's languages. Although English speakers use just 52 phonemes to produce words, other languages use from as few as 15 to as many as 141. Differences in phonemes are one reason people have difficulty learning other languages. For example, to a Japanese speaker, whose native language does not have an *r* phoneme, pronouncing such English words as *roar* presents some difficulty (Gibbs, 2002; Iverson et al., 2003). Similarly, for a native English speaker, it is difficult to hear the difference between the two sounds made by the letter "*p*." Consider the way the *p* sounds in the word *pull*. It you say *pull* while holding a candle in front of your mouth, the flame will be moved by your breath. Now say the word *spell*. Notice that the flame does not move. If you grew up speaking Thai, you are familiar with both of these sounds. Even more challenging than hearing the difference for native English speakers is the problem of making the sound of the *p* in *spell* without using a preceding *s*. Try it. You know you are getting close when you can say *pull* with a lit candle in front of your mouth and the flame is not pushed by the air leaving your mouth.

Syntax refers to the rules that indicate how words and phrases can be combined to form sentences. Every language has intricate rules that guide the order in which words may be strung together to communicate meaning. English speakers have no difficulty recognizing that "TV down the turn" is not a meaningful sequence, whereas "Turn down the TV" is. To understand the effect of one type of syntax

rule in English, consider the changes in meaning caused by the different word orders in the following three utterances: "John kidnapped the boy," "John, the kidnapped boy," and "The boy kidnapped John" (Eberhard, Cutting, & Bock, 2005). In other languages, such as Russian, changing the word order does not change the basic meaning of a sentence. They use prefixes, suffixes, and other devices to change our understanding of who does an action and who/what received an action.

A **morpheme** is the smallest element of a word that can still have meaning. For example, the word *dogs* has the morpheme *dog* and the morpheme *s* to indicate it is plural. A morpheme that can stand on its own, such as the word *dog*, is called a free morpheme. Johanne Paradis from the University of Alberta found that children who spoke only English had better knowledge of English morphology compared to children who were bilingual (children who spoke English and French). One reason for this was that English-only speaking children received more input of the English language than bilingual children, who received input from both languages (Paradis, 2010).

The third major component of language is **semantics**, the meanings of words and sentences. Semantic rules allow us to use words to convey the subtlest nuances. In English, we can again use word order to make the distinction between "The truck hit Laura" (which we would be likely to say if we had just seen the vehicle hitting Laura) and "Laura was hit by a truck" (which we would probably say if someone asked why Laura was missing class while she recuperated) (Pietarinen, 2006; Richgels, 2004). Frequently, the shading of meanings is accomplished in English by the use of words that are similar in meaning, but not identical. Consider, for example, the difference in these two sentences: "Mary loved John." "Mary adored John."

grammar The system of rules that determines how our thoughts can be expressed in words.

phonology The study of the smallest units of speech, called phonemes.

phonemes The smallest units of speech.

syntax Ways in which words and phrases can be combined to form sentences.

morpheme The smallest unit of speech that can still have meaning.

semantics The rules governing the meaning of words and sentences.

Despite the complexities of language, most of us acquire the basics of grammar without even being aware that we have learned its rules. (And our knowledge of these rules likely remains unconscious, which is why most of us probably did not enjoy classes in grammar when we were in school.) Moreover, even though we may have difficulty explicitly stating the rules of grammar, our linguistic abilities are so sophisticated that we can utter an infinite number of different statements. How do we acquire these abilities?

LANGUAGE DEVELOPMENT

To parents, the sounds of their infant babbling and cooing are music to their ears (except, perhaps, at three o'clock in the morning). These sounds also serve an important function. They mark the first step on the road to the development of language.

Babbling Children **babble**—make speechlike but meaningless sounds—from around the age of three months through one year. While babbling, babies may produce, at one time or another, sounds found in all languages, not just the one to which they are exposed. Even infants who are unable to hear but who are exposed to sign language from birth "babble," using their hands (Locke, 2006; Pettito, 1993).

An infant's babbling increasingly resembles the specific language spoken in the infant's environment. Young infants can distinguish among all 869 phonemes that have been identified across the world's languages. However, after the age of six to eight months, that ability begins to decline. Infants begin to "specialize" in the language to which they are exposed as neurons in their brains reorganize to respond only to the specific phonemes the infants routinely hear.

> While babbling, babies may produce sounds found in all languages.

Some theorists argue that a *critical period* exists for language development early in life, in which a child is especially sensitive to language cues and most easily acquires language. In fact, if children are not exposed to language during this critical period, later they will have great difficulty overcoming this deficit (Bates, 2005; Shafer & Garrido-Nag, 2007).

Cases in which abused children have been isolated from contact with others support the theory of such critical periods. In one case, for example, a girl named Genie was exposed to virtually no language from the age of 20 months until she was rescued at age 13 years. She was unable to speak at all. Despite intensive instruction, she learned only some words and was never able to master the complexities of language (Rymer, 1994; Veltman & Browne, 2001).

babble Meaningless, speechlike sounds made by children from around the age of three months through one year.

telegraphic speech Sentences in which words not critical to the message are left out.

Producing Language By the time children are approximately one year old, they stop producing sounds that are not in the language to which they have been exposed. It is then a short step to the production of actual words. In English, these are typically short words that start with a consonant sound such as *b*, *d*, *m*, *p*, and *t*—this helps explain why *mama* and *dada* are so often among babies' first words. Of course, even before they produce their first words, children can understand a fair amount of the language they hear. Language comprehension precedes language production.

After the age of one year, children begin to learn more complicated forms of language. Their vocabulary increases sharply and, by age two, the average child has a vocabulary of more than 50 words. Just six months later, that vocabulary has grown to several hundred words. At first, they produce two-word combinations, called **telegraphic speech**, because these primitive sentences sound as if they were part of a telegram, in which words not critical to the message are left out. Rather than saying, "I showed you the book," a child using telegraphic speech may say, "Show book," and "That's my sister's shoe" may become "Sissy shoe." Gradually, children use less telegraphic speech and produce increasingly complex sentences (Volterra et al., 2003).

By age three, many children have learned to make plurals by adding *s* to nouns and to form the past tense by adding *-ed* to verbs. These skills also lead to errors, because

From the perspective of ...

A DEVELOPMENTAL PSYCHOLOGIST A worried father has brought his 30-month-old child to see you. The father tells you that his child speaks ungrammatically, sometimes using only two words and sometimes adding weird endings to words. For example, just last night the child said, "Two childs finded it." What would you tell this father, and how would you encourage him to maximize his child's language abilities?

Young children master the basic rules of grammar in their native language without being taught them and acquire a large enough vocabulary by age five to hold up their end of a simple conversation.

children carefully apply rules they have just figured out. They **overgeneralize** these rules, using them even when doing so results in an error. Thus, although it is correct to say "he walked" for the past tense of *walk*, the *-ed* rule doesn't work quite so well when children say "he runned" for the past tense of *run* (Gershkoff-Stowe, Connell, & Smith, 2006; Howe, 2002; Rice et al., 2004).

By age five, children have acquired the basic rules of language. However, not until later do they attain a full vocabulary and the ability to comprehend and use subtle grammatical rules. For example, a five-year-old boy who sees a blindfolded doll and is asked, "Is the doll easy or hard to see?" would have great trouble answering the question. In fact, if he were asked to make the doll easier to see, he would probably try to remove the doll's blindfold. By the time they are eight years old, however, children have little difficulty understanding this question, because they realize that the doll's blindfold has nothing to do with an observer's ability to see the doll (Chomsky, 1968; Hoff, 2003).

THEORIES OF LANGUAGE ACQUISITION

Humans make enormous strides in language development during childhood. However, the reasons for this rapid growth are far from obvious. Psychologists have offered two major explanations, one based on learning theory and the other based on innate processes.

Learning-Theory Approaches The **learning-theory approach** suggests that language acquisition follows the principles of reinforcement and conditioning discovered by psychologists who study learning. For example, a child who says "mama" receives hugs and praise from her mother, which reinforces the behaviour of saying "mama" and makes its repetition more likely. This view suggests that children first learn to speak by being rewarded for making sounds that approximate speech. Ultimately, through a process of shaping, language becomes more and more like adult speech (Ornat & Gallo, 2004; Skinner, 1957).

In support of the learning-theory approach to language acquisition, the more that parents speak to their young children, the more proficient the children become in language use. In addition, by the time they are three years old, children who hear higher levels of linguistic sophistication in their parents' speech show a greater rate of vocabulary growth, vocabulary use, and even general intellectual achievement than do children whose parents' speech is more simple (Hart & Risley, 1997).

The learning-theory approach is less successful in explaining how children acquire language rules. Children are reinforced not only when they use language correctly but also when they use it incorrectly. For example, parents' answer a child's "Why the dog won't eat?" as readily as they do the correctly phrased question, "Why won't the dog eat?" Listeners understand both sentences equally well. In this example, learning theory has difficulty fully explaining language acquisition.

DID YOU KNOW?

The ability to read facial expressions is so central to verbal comprehension that over 900 digital emoticons (smiley face, wink, and so on) have been developed for use when communicating by text messaging. =:o

Nativist Approaches Pointing to such problems with learning-theory approaches to language acquisition, linguist Noam Chomsky (1968, 1978, 1991) provided a groundbreaking alternative. Chomsky argued that humans are born with an innate linguistic capability that emerges primarily as a function of maturation. According to his **nativist approach** to language, all the world's languages share a common underlying structure called a **universal grammar**. Chomsky suggested that the human brain has a neural system, the **language-acquisition device**, that not only lets us understand the structure that language provides but also gives us strategies and techniques for learning the unique characteristics of our native language (Lidz & Gleitman, 2004; McGilvray, 2004; White, 2007).

overgeneralization The phenomenon by which children apply language rules even when the application results in an error.

learning-theory approach (to language development) The theory suggesting that language acquisition follows the principles of reinforcement and conditioning.

nativist approach (to language development) The theory that a genetically determined, innate mechanism directs language development.

universal grammar Noam Chomsky's theory that all the world's languages share a common underlying structure.

language-acquisition device As hypothesized by Noam Chomsky, a neural system of the brain that permits understanding of language.

How do we acquire language?

Chomsky used the concept of the language-acquisition device as a metaphor, and he did not identify a specific area of the brain in which it resides. However, evidence collected by neuroscientists suggests that the ability to use language, which was a significant evolutionary advance in human beings, is tied to specific neurological developments (Sahin, Pinker, & Halgren, 2006; Sakai, 2005; Willems & Hagoort, 2007).

For example, scientists have discovered a gene related to the development of language abilities that may have emerged as recently—in evolutionary terms—as 100,000 years ago. Furthermore, it is clear that specific sites within the brain are closely tied to language and that the shape of the human mouth and throat are tailored to the production of speech. And there is evidence that features of some languages, such as Chinese, Vietnamese, Navajo, and other tonal languages in which pitch is used to convey meaning, are tied to specific genes (Chandra, 2007; Dediu & Ladd, 2007; Hauser, Chomsky, & Fitch, 2002).

Still, Chomsky's view has its critics. For instance, learning theorists contend that the apparent ability of certain animals, such as chimpanzees, to learn the fundamentals of human language contradicts the innate linguistic capability view.

interactionist approach (to language development) The view that language development is produced through a combination of genetically determined predispositions and environmental circumstances that help teach language.

Interactionist Approaches To reconcile the differing views, many theorists take an **interactionist approach** to language development. The interactionist approach suggests that language development is produced through a combination of genetically determined predispositions and environmental circumstances that help teach language.

Specifically, proponents of the interactionist approach suggest that the brain's hardwired language-acquisition device that Chomsky and geneticists point to provides the hardware for our acquisition of language, whereas the exposure to language in our environment that learning theorists observe allows us to develop the appropriate software. But the issue of how language is acquired remains hotly contested (Hoff, 2008; Lana, 2002; Pinker & Jackendoff, 2005).

Study tip It's important to understand the different theories that contribute to our understanding of a complex phenomenon, such as language acquisition. Make sure you know the difference between the learning-theory, nativist, and interactionist approaches.

Intelligence

Members of the Trukese tribe in the South Pacific often sail a hundred miles in open ocean waters. Although their destination may be just a small dot of land less than a mile wide, the Trukese are able to navigate precisely toward it without the aid of a compass, chronometer, sextant, or any of the other sailing tools that are used by Western navigators. They are able to sail accurately, even when the winds do not allow a direct approach to the island and they must take a zigzag course (Gladwin, 1964; Mytinger, 2001).

How are the Trukese able to navigate so effectively? If you asked them, they could not explain it. They might tell you that they use a process that takes into account the rising and setting of the stars and the appearance, sound, and feel of the waves against the side of the boat. But at any given moment as they are sailing along, they could not identify their position or say why they are doing what they are doing in terms that would make sense to someone with a Western understanding of navigation. Similarly, they could not explain to us the navigational theory underlying their sailing technique.

If we gave Trukese sailors a Western standardized test of navigational knowledge and theory or, for that matter, a traditional test of intelligence, they might do poorly on it, but it wouldn't be very smart on our part to think that meant that the Trukese were unintelligent: despite their inability to explain to us how they do it, they are able to navigate successfully through open ocean waters. From their perspective, we might be the unintelligent ones, because we cannot understand their explanations and we cannot, therefore, accomplish navigation without all sorts of unnecessary gadgets, such as sextants and computers.

For years psychologists have grappled with the issue of devising a general definition of intelligence that takes cultural differences into account. Laypersons have fairly clear ideas of what intelligence is, although their ideas are grounded in their cultures. Westerners commonly view intelligence as the ability to problem solve, form categories, and debate rationally. In contrast, people in Eastern cultures and some African communities often view intelligence more in terms of understanding and relating to one another (Brislin, Worthley, & MacNab, 2006; Nisbett, 2003; Sternberg & Grigorenko, 2005).

The definition of intelligence that psychologists employ contains some of the same elements found in the layperson's conception. To psychologists, **intelligence** is the capacity to understand the world, think rationally, and use resources effectively when faced with challenges. Although psychologists recognize that intelligence occurs in a specific context, as demonstrated by the examples above and this definition, research lags behind this understanding; it is not yet clear exactly what intelligence is and how it can be measured.

Do you see yourself as a good writer, but you're not really good at math? Are you more comfortable writing a computer program than taking a dance class? Do your friends, parents, and teachers tell you that you are really smart in many different areas?

One basic issue regarding intelligence is this: If you are an intelligent person, are you generally better at most things than someone who would not be considered intelligent? Or, is it the case that we can be brilliant in a few areas

What does the Trukese people's method of navigation, without maps or instruments, tell us about the nature of intelligence?

and pretty slow in others? As you read this next section, try to keep an open mind, because when there are various theories that get a lot of attention, typically they all turn out to have some truth in them.

THEORIES OF INTELLIGENCE

The g-Factor of Intelligence Charles Spearman, an early psychologist interested in intelligence, hypothesized that there was a single, general factor for mental ability, which he called *g*, or the *g*-**factor**. This general intelligence factor was thought to underlie performance in every aspect of intelligence, and it was the g-factor that was presumably being measured on tests of intelligence (Colom, Jung, & Haier, 2006; Gottfredson, 2004; Spearman, 1927).

intelligence The capacity to understand the world, think rationally, and use resources effectively when faced with challenges.

g or g-factor The single, general factor for mental ability assumed to underlie intelligence in some early theories of intelligence.

fluid intelligence Intelligence that reflects information-processing capabilities, reasoning, and memory.

crystallized intelligence The accumulation of information, skills, and strategies that are learned through experience and can be applied in problem-solving situations.

More recent theories see intelligence in a different light. Rather than viewing intelligence as a unitary entity, they consider it to be a multi-dimensional concept that includes different types of intelligence (Stankov, 2003; Sternberg & Pretz, 2005; Tenopyr, 2002).

Fluid and Crystallized Intelligence Some psychologists study two different kinds of intelligence: fluid intelligence and crystallized intelligence. **Fluid intelligence** reflects information-processing capabilities, reasoning, and memory. If we were asked to solve an analogy, group a series of letters according to some criterion, or remember a set of numbers, we would be using fluid intelligence. We use fluid intelligence when we're trying to rapidly solve a puzzle (Cattell, 1998; Kane & Engle, 2002; Saggino, Perfetti, & Spitoni, 2006).

In contrast, **crystallized intelligence** is the accumulation of information, skills, and strategies that people have learned through experience and that they can apply or generalize in problem-solving situations. It reflects our ability to call up information from long-term memory. We would be likely to rely on crystallized intelligence, for instance, if we were asked to participate in a discussion about the solution to the causes of poverty, a task that allows us to draw on our own past experiences and knowledge of the world. In contrast to fluid intelligence, which reflects a more general kind of intelligence, crystallized intelligence is more a reflection of the culture in which a person is raised. The differences between fluid intelligence and crystallized intelligence become especially evident in the elderly, who show declines in fluid, but not crystallized, intelligence (Aartsen, Martin, & Zimprich, 2002; Buehner, Krumm, & Ziegler, 2006; Schretlen et al., 2000).

Piloting a helicopter requires both fluid intelligence and crystallized intelligence. Which of the two kinds of intelligence do you think is more important for this line of work?

Sternberg's Triarchic Theory

An employee who reports to one of your subordinates has asked to talk with you about waste, poor management practices, and possible violations of both company policy and the law on the part of your subordinate. You have been in your present position only a year, but in that time you have had no indications of trouble about the subordinate in question. Neither you nor your company has an "open door" policy, so it is expected that employees should take their concerns to their immediate supervisors before bringing a matter to the attention of anyone else. The employee who wishes to meet with you has not discussed this matter with her supervisors because of its delicate nature. (Sternberg, 1998, p. 17)

Your response to this situation has a lot to do with your future success in a business career, according psychologist Robert Sternberg. The question is one of a series designed to evaluate your practical intelligence. **Practical intelligence** is intelligence related to overall success in living (Muammar, 2007; Sternberg, 2000, 2002b; Sternberg & Hedlund, 2002; Wagner, 2002).

Traditional intelligence tests were developed to predict academic performance, not success in one's career. Sternberg points to evidence showing that most of these traditional measures of intelligence do not, in fact, do a very good job of predicting *career* success (McClelland, 1993). Specifically, although successful business executives usually score at least moderately well on intelligence tests, the rate at which they advance and their ultimate business

practical intelligence According to Sternberg, intelligence related to overall success in living.

analytical intelligence Part of Sternberg's theory; focuses on abstract but traditional types of problems measured on IQ tests.

creative intelligence Part of Sternberg's theory; the generation of novel ideas and products.

achievements are only minimally associated with traditional measures of their intelligence.

Sternberg argues that career success requires a very different type of intelligence from that needed for academic success. Whereas academic success is based on knowledge of a specific information base obtained from reading and listening, practical intelligence is learned mainly through observation of others' behaviour. People who are high in practical intelligence are able to learn general norms and principles and apply them appropriately. Consequently, practical intelligence tests measure the ability to employ broad principles in solving everyday problems (Polk, 1997; Stemler & Sternberg, 2006; Sternberg & Pretz, 2005).

Sternberg's theory is referred to as the triarchic theory of intelligence. In addition to practical intelligence, Sternberg argues there are two other basic, interrelated types of successful intelligence: **analytical intelligence** and **creative intelligence**. Analytical intelligence focuses on abstract but traditional types of problems measured on IQ tests, whereas creative intelligence involves the generation of novel ideas and products (Benderly, 2004; Sternberg, Grigorenko, & Kidd, 2005).

Information-Processing Approach One of the newer contributions to understanding intelligence comes from the work of cognitive psychologists who take an *information-processing approach*. They assert that the way people store material in memory and use that material to solve intellectual tasks provides the most accurate measure of intelligence. Consequently, rather than focusing on the structure of intelligence or its underlying content or dimensions, information-processing approaches examine the processes involved in producing intelligent behaviour (Hunt, 2005; Neubauer & Fink, 2005; Pressley & Harris, 2006). This can be tied back to the material you learned in the chapter on memory.

For example, research shows that people with high scores on tests of intelligence spend more time on the initial encoding stages of problems, identifying the parts of

"To be perfectly frank, I'm not nearly as smart as you seem to think I am."
© The New Yorker Collection 1983 W.B. Park from cartoonbank.com. All Rights Reserved.

a problem and retrieving relevant information from long-term memory, than do people with lower scores. This initial emphasis on recalling relevant information pays off in the end; those who use this approach are more successful in finding solutions than are those who spend relatively less time on the initial stages (Deary & Der, 2005; Hunt, 2005; Sternberg, 1990).

Other information-processing approaches examine the sheer speed of processing. For example, research shows that the speed with which people are able to retrieve information from memory is related to verbal intelligence. In general, people with high scores on measures of verbal intelligence react more quickly on a variety of information-processing tasks, ranging from reactions to flashing lights to distinguishing between letters. The speed of information processing, then, may underlie some differences in intelligence (Deary & Der, 2005; Gontkovsky & Beatty, 2006; Jensen, 2005).

Gardner's Multiple Intelligences Psychologist Howard Gardner has taken an approach very different from traditional thinking about intelligence. Gardner argues that rather than asking "How smart are you?" we should be asking a different question: "How are you smart?" In answering the latter question, Gardner has developed a **theory of multiple intelligences** (Gardner, 1999).

Gardner argues that we have at a minimum eight different forms of intelligence, each relatively independent of the others: musical, bodily kinesthetic, logical-mathematical, linguistic, spatial, interpersonal, intrapersonal, and naturalist. In Gardner's view, each of the multiple intelligences is linked to an independent system in the brain. Jeffery Rosenthal from the beginning of the chapter is likely high in logical-mathematical intelligence because he was able to use probability and statistics to find out how many lottery ticket sellers would likely also be lottery ticket winners. Rosenthal's exceptional mathematical ability allowed the RCMP to convict lottery sellers who had stolen winning tickets from their customers. Gardner suggests that there may be even more types of intelligence, such as *existential intelligence*, which involves identifying and thinking about the fundamental questions of human existence. The Dalai Lama might exemplify this type of intelligence (Gardner, 1999).

Although Gardner illustrates his conception of the specific types of intelligence with descriptions of well-known people, each person has the same eight kinds of

intelligence—in different degrees. Moreover, although the eight basic types of intelligence are presented individually, Gardner suggests that these separate intelligences do not operate in isolation. Normally, any activity encompasses several kinds of intelligence working together.

The concept of multiple intelligences has led to the development of intelligence test questions for which more than one answer can be correct; these provide an opportunity for test takers to demonstrate different kinds of intelligence. In addition, many educators, embracing the concept of multiple intelligences, have designed classroom curricula that are meant to draw on different aspects of intelligence (Armstrong, 2000, 2003; Kelly & Tangney, 2006).

Study tip Gardner's theory suggests that each individual has every kind of intelligence, but in different degrees.

Emotional Intelligence Emotional intelligence includes a set of skills related to an ability to effectively express, understand, and control emotions while also being able to cope and adapt to changes in one's environment (Humphrey, Curran, & Morris, 2007; Mayer, Salovey, & Caruso, 2004; Parker, Summerfeldt, et al., 2004; Zeidner, Matthews, & Roberts, 2004). The notion of emotional intelligence reminds us that there are many ways to demonstrate intelligent behaviour—just as there are multiple views of the nature of intelligence (Barrett & Salovey, 2002; Fox & Spector, 2000).

Emotional intelligence underlies the ability to get along well with others. It provides us with an understanding of what other people are feeling and experiencing and permits us to respond appropriately to others' needs. Abilities in emotional intelligence may help explain why people with only modest scores on traditional intelligence tests can be quite successful. For example, research has found a link between emotional intelligence and academic success in college and university (Parker, Creque, Barnhart, Harris, Majeski, Wood, Bond, & Hogan, 2004; Parker et al., 2004).

James Parker and colleagues from Trent University in Peterborough, Ontario, conducted a study on emotional intelligence and academic success in a group of first-year students at Trent University. Parker and his colleagues assessed the student's emotional intelligence at the beginning of the semester and matched these scores with student's grades at the end of the semester. The students were divided into two groups based on their academic success. One group included students with an average of 80% or higher at the end of the semester, while the other group

Psych think

> > > Use Gardner's theory of multiple intelligence to "assess" how you are intelligent. For example, which of the intelligences are you higher in? Which one would be your lowest?

theory of multiple intelligences Gardner's intelligence theory that proposes that there are eight distinct spheres of intelligence.

emotional intelligence The set of skills that underlie the accurate assessment, evaluation, expression, and regulation of emotions.

Figure 7.5 Gardner's Multiple Intelligences

Musical intelligence ●1

Skills in tasks involving music. Case example:

Avril Lavigne, from Napanee, Ontario, signed a music contract at age 16 worth over two million dollars.

Bodily kinesthetic intelligence ●2

Skills in using the body or various in the solution of problems or in the construction of products or displays, exemplified by dancers, athletes, actors, and surgeons. Case example:

Patrick Chan began skating at age 5. He won the World Figure Skating Championship in 2001 at the age of 21.

Logical-mathematical intelligence ●3

Skills in problem solving and scientific thinking. Case example:

Astronaut Roberta Bondar was the first Canadian woman to visit space. She used her problem solving and scientific reasoning to examine how the human body could best recover after a mission in space.

Linguistic intelligence ●4

Skills involved in the production and use of language. Case example:

Writer Margaret Atwood displays her linguistic abilities in the many novels she has written and in the many literary awards she has received.

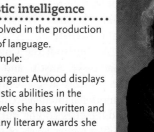

Spatial intelligence ●5

Skills involving spatial configurations, such as those used by artists and architects. Case example:

Canadian Indigenous people display their superior spatial intelligence by navigating through dense forests to locate and hunt food sources.

Interpersonal intelligence ●6

Skills in interacting with others, such as sensitivity to the moods, temperaments, motivations, and intentions of others.

Case example:

The late Jack Layton, leader of the NDP party, had a remarkable ability to connect with others.

Intrapersonal intelligence ●7

The knowledge of the internal aspects of oneself; access to one's own feelings and emotions. Case example:

Member of Parliament (MP) Justin Trudeau is a politician who recognizes that his emotions are an important component of his political philosophy.

Naturalist intelligence ●8

The ability to identify and classify patterns in nature. Case example:

David Suzuki is co-founder of the David Suzuki Foundation whose vision "is that within a generation, Canadians act on the understanding that we are all interdependent with nature" (www.davidsuzuki.org/about/).

Source: Adapted from *Multiple Intelligences: New Horizons* by H. Gardner. © 2006 by Howard Gardner.

consisted of students with an average of 59% or lower at the end of the semester. The researchers found that academically successful students (those with an average of 80% or higher) had higher levels of emotional intelligence at the beginning of the school year than students whose average was 59% or lower, even though both groups had similar grade point averages in high school. What was particularly interesting is that students with higher grades were higher in their intrapersonal abilities (knowledge of oneself), their stress management, and their ability to adapt to their new environment (Parker et al., 2004).

The results of this study suggest a link between emotional intelligence and academic success at college and university. This is consistent with more recent research by Don Saklofske and Sarah Mastoras from the University of Calgary, and Elizabeth Austin from the University of Edinburgh in Scotland. Saklofske, Austin, and Mastoras found that undergraduate students at the University of Calgary who were low in emotional intelligence had higher levels of stress and more difficulties coping during exam time than their peers who had higher levels of emotional intelligence (Austin, Saklfske, & Mastoras, 2010).

MEASURING INTELLIGENCE

Given the variety of approaches to the components of intelligence, we should not be surprised that measuring intelligence has proved challenging. Psychologists who study intelligence have focused much of their attention on the development of **intelligence tests** and have relied on such tests to quantify a person's level of intelligence. These

Healthcare is one field where high emotional intelligence can be a valuable asset. In what other fields might emotional intelligence be beneficial?

intelligence tests Tests devised to quantify a person's level of intelligence.

tests have proved to be of great benefit in identifying students in need of special attention in school, diagnosing cognitive difficulties, and helping people make optimal educational and vocational choices. At the same time, their use has proved controversial and raised important social and educational issues.

Historically, the first effort at intelligence testing in the West was based on an uncomplicated, but completely wrong, assumption: that the size and shape of a person's head could be used as an objective measure of intelligence. The idea was put forward by Sir Francis Galton (1822–1911), an eminent English scientist whose ideas in other domains proved to be considerably better than his notions about intelligence.

Galton's motivation to identify people of high intelligence stemmed from personal prejudices. He sought to demonstrate the natural superiority of people of high social class (including him) by showing that intelligence is inherited. He hypothesized that head configuration, being genetically determined, is related to brain size and therefore is related to intelligence.

Study tip

Traditional intelligence measures relate purely to cognitive performance, while practical intelligence and emotional intelligence are predictive of success in life.

Figure 7.6
Major Approaches to Intelligence

Approach	Characteristics
Fluid and crystallized intelligence	Fluid intelligence relates to reasoning, memory, and information-processing capabilities; crystallized intelligence refers to information, skills, and strategies learned through experience
Sternberg's triarchic theory	Practical intelligence: Intelligence related to overall success in living
	Analytical intelligence: Abstract but traditional types of problems measured on IQ tests
	Creative intelligence: The generation of novel ideas and products
Information-processing approaches	Intelligence is reflected in the ways people store and use material to solve intellectual tasks
Gardner's multiple intelligences	Eight independent forms of intelligence
Emotional intelligence	Intelligence that provides an understanding of what other people are feeling and experiencing, and permits us to respond appropriately to others' needs

Galton's theories were proven wrong on virtually every count. Head size and shape do not correlate with intellectual performance, and subsequent research has found little relationship between brain size and intelligence. However, Galton's work did have at least one desirable result: he was the first person to suggest that intelligence could be quantified and measured in an objective manner (Jensen, 2002).

The Development of IQ Tests The intelligence tests developed by the French psychologist Alfred Binet (1857–1911) provided the foundation for modern intelligence tests. His tests followed from a simple premise: If performance on certain tasks or test items improved with *chronological*, or physical, age, performance could be used to distinguish more intelligent people from less intelligent ones within a particular age group. On the basis of this principle, Binet devised the first formal intelligence test, which was designed to identify the "dullest" students in the Paris school system in order to provide them with remedial aid.

Binet began by presenting tasks to same-age students who had been labelled "bright" or "dull" by their teachers. If a task could be completed by the bright students but not by the dull ones, he retained that task as a proper test item; otherwise it was discarded. In the end he came up with a test that distinguished between the bright and dull groups, and—with further work—one that distinguished among children in different age groups (Binet & Simon, 1916; Sternberg & Jarvin, 2003).

On the basis of the Binet test, children were assigned a score relating to their **mental age**, the average age of individuals who achieved a specific level of performance on a test. For example, if the average eight-year-old answered, say, 45 items correctly on a test, anyone who answered 45 items correctly would be assigned a mental age of eight years. Consequently, whether the person taking the test had a chronological age of twenty years or five years, he or she would have the same mental age of eight years (Cornell, 2006).

Assigning a mental age to students provided an indication of their general level of performance. However, it did not allow for adequate comparisons among people of different chronological ages. By using mental age alone, for instance, we might assume that a 20-year-old responding at an 18-year-old's level would be as bright as a 5-year-old answering at a 3-year-old's level, when actually the 5-year-old would be displaying a much greater *relative* degree of slowness.

A solution to the problem came in the form of the **intelligence quotient**, or **IQ**, a score that takes into account an individual's mental *and* chronological ages. Historically, the first IQ scores employed the following formula, in which *MA* stands for mental age and *CA* for chronological age:

$$\text{IQ score} = (MA/CA) \times 100$$

Using this formula, we can return to the earlier example of 20-year-old performing at a mental age of 18 and

mental age The average age of individuals who achieve a particular level of performance on a test.

intelligence quotient (IQ) A score that takes into account an individual's mental and chronological ages.

calculate an IQ score of $(18/20) \times 100 = 90$. In contrast, the five-year-old performing at a mental age of three comes out with a considerably lower IQ score: $(3/5) \times 100 = 60$.

As a bit of trial and error with the formula will show you, anyone who has a mental age equal to his or her chronological age will have an IQ equal to 100 (this is average intelligence). Moreover, people with a mental age that is greater than their chronological age will have IQs that exceed 100.

Although the basic principles behind the calculation of an IQ score still hold, today IQ scores are figured in a different manner and are known as *deviation IQ scores*. First, the average test score for everyone of the same age who takes the test is determined, and that average score is assigned an IQ of 100. Then, with the aid of statistical techniques that calculate the differences (or "deviations") between each score and the average, IQ scores are assigned.

Study tip

The traditional formula for IQ scores is the ratio of mental age divided by chronological age, multiplied by 100, but the actual calculation of IQ scores today is done in a more sophisticated manner.

When IQ scores from large numbers of people are plotted on a graph, they form a *bell-shaped curve*. Approximately two-thirds of all individuals fall within 15 IQ points of the average score of 100. As scores increase or fall beyond that range, the percentage of people in a category falls considerably (Figure 7.7).

Get Involved!

Remember, there are different types of intelligence. Your IQ score doesn't provide a clue about your level of *emotional* intelligence. You can test your emotional intelligence for free online at queendom.com (a subsidiary of PsychTests AIM Inc.), but keep in mind that tests on the Internet may not be as reliable and valid as psychological tests administered by a trained professional.

Figure 7.7
Distribution of Intelligence

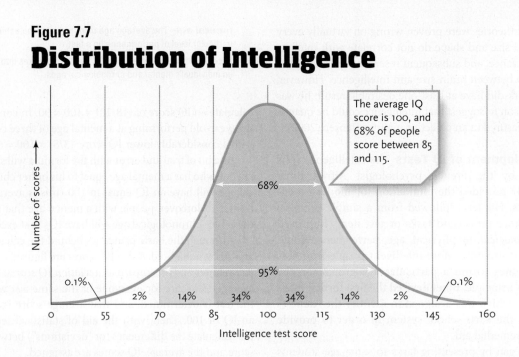

The average IQ score is 100, and 68% of people score between 85 and 115.

Contemporary IQ Tests Remnants of Binet's original intelligence test are still with us, although the test has been revised significantly. Now in its fifth edition and called the *Stanford-Binet Intelligence Scale*, the test consists of a series of items that vary in nature according to the age of the person being tested (Roid, Nellis, & McLellan, 2003). For example, young children are asked to copy figures or answer questions about everyday activities. Older people are asked to solve analogies, explain proverbs, and describe similarities that underlie sets of words.

The test is administered orally. An examiner begins by finding a mental age level at which a person is able to answer all the questions correctly and then moves on to successively more difficult problems. When a mental age level is reached at which no items can be answered, the test is over. By studying the pattern of correct and incorrect responses, the examiner is able to compute an IQ score for the person being tested.

The IQ test most frequently used in North America was devised by psychologist David Wechsler and is known as the *Wechsler Adult Intelligence Scale–III*, or, more commonly, the *WAIS-III*. There is also a children's version, the *Wechsler Intelligence Scale for Children–IV*, or *WISC-IV*. Both the WAIS-III and the WISC-IV have two major parts: a verbal scale and a performance (or non-verbal) scale.

The verbal and performance scales include questions of very different types. Verbal tasks consist of more traditional kinds of problems, including vocabulary definition and comprehension of various concepts. In contrast, the performance (non-verbal) part involves the timed

assembly of small objects and the arrangement of pictures in a logical order. Although an individual's scores on the verbal and performance sections of the test are generally within close range of each other, the scores of a person with a language deficiency or a background of severe environmental deprivation or brain injury may show a relatively large discrepancy between the two sections. By providing separate scores, the WAIS-III and WISC-IV give a more precise picture of a person's specific abilities compared with other IQ tests (Kaufman & Lichtenberger, 1999, 2000).

Achievement and Aptitude Tests IQ tests are not the only kind of tests that you might have taken during the course of your schooling. Two other kinds of tests, related to intelligence but intended to measure somewhat different phenomena, are achievement tests and aptitude tests. An **achievement test** is a test designed to determine a person's level of knowledge in a specific subject area. Rather than measuring general ability, as an intelligence test does, an achievement test concentrates on the specific material a person has learned. For example, your next psychology test will assess your knowledge of the concepts you learned in your psychology course. Your psychology test is an achievement test. Lawyers must pass an achievement test called the Law School Admission Test (LSAT) to study law, and the Canadian Adult Achievement Test (CAAT) is a measure of one's math, reading, and language abilities and may be used by mature students who are pursuing admission to college or university. An **aptitude test** is designed to predict a person's ability in a particular area or line of work. For example, graduate students in psychology may have to take a specialized aptitude test called the Graduate Record Exam (GRE) in Psychology while students interested in dentistry may have to take the Dental Aptitude Test (DAT).

achievement test A test designed to determine a person's level of knowledge in a given subject area.

aptitude test A test designed to predict a person's ability in a particular area or line of work.

Figure 7.8
Sample Items from the Wechsler Adult Intelligence Scale (WAIS-III)

Name	Goal of Item	Example
Verbal scale		
Information	Assess general information	Who wrote *Tom Sawyer*?
Comprehension	Assess understanding and evaluation of social norms and past experience	Why is copper often used for electrical wires?
Arithmetic	Assess math reasoning through verbal problems	Three women divided 18 golf balls equally among themselves. How many golf balls did each person receive?
Similarities	Test understanding of how objects or concepts are alike, tapping abstract reasoning	In what way are a circle and a triangle alike?
Performance scale		
Digit symbol	Assess speed of learning	Test-taker must learn what symbols correspond to what digits and then must replace a multidigit number with the appropriate symbols. 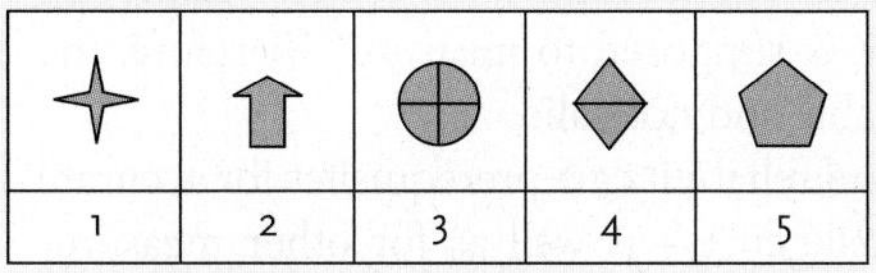
Matrix reasoning	Test spatial reasoning	Test-taker must decide which of the five possibilities replaces the question mark and completes the sequence. 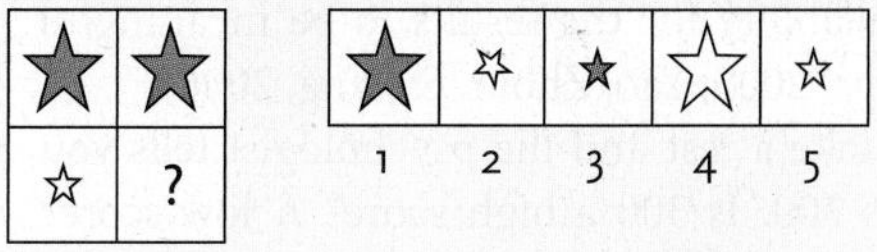
Block design item	Test understanding of relationship of parts to whole	Problems require test-taker to reproduce a design in fixed amount of time. 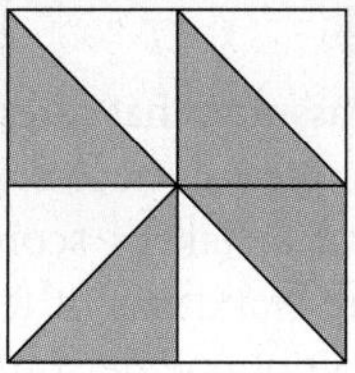

Although in theory the distinction between aptitude tests and achievement tests is precise, it is difficult to develop an aptitude test that does not rely at least in part on past achievement. For example, intelligence tests have been strongly criticized for being less an aptitude test than an achievement test that assesses prior performance.

Reliability and Validity of Tests When we use a ruler, we expect to find that it measures a centimetre in the same way it did the last time we used it. When we weigh ourselves on the bathroom scale, we hope that the variations we see on the scale are due to changes in our weight and not to errors on the part of the scale (unless the change in weight is in an unwanted direction!).

In the same way, we want psychological tests to have **reliability**—to measure consistently what they are trying to measure. Each time a test is administered, a test taker should achieve the same results—assuming that nothing about the person has changed relevant to what is being measured.

Suppose, for instance, that when you first took an IQ test, you scored in the average range. Then, after taking the test again a few months later, you scored in the gifted range. Upon receiving your new score, you might well stop celebrating for a moment to question whether the test

reliability The property by which tests measure consistently what they are trying to measure.

is reliable, for it is unlikely that your abilities could have changed enough to raise your intelligence into the gifted range.

But suppose your score changed hardly at all, and both times you received a similar average score. You couldn't complain about a lack of reliability. However, if you knew your verbal skills were above average, you might be concerned that the test did not adequately measure what it was supposed to measure. In sum, the question has now become one of validity rather than reliability. A test has **validity** when it actually measures what it is supposed to measure.

Knowing that a test is reliable is no guarantee that it is also valid. For instance, Sir Francis Galton assumed that skull size is related to intelligence, and he was able to measure skull size with great reliability. However, the measure of skull size was not valid—it had nothing to do with intelligence. In this case we have reliability without validity.

Generally, if a test is unreliable, it cannot be valid. Given the assumption that all other factors—motivation to score well, knowledge of the material, health, and so forth—are similar, if a person scores high the first time he or she takes a specific test and low the second time, the test cannot be measuring what it is supposed to measure. Therefore, the test is both unreliable and not valid.

Test validity and reliability are prerequisites for accurate assessment of intelligence—as well as for other measurement tasks carried out by psychologists. For example, personality psychologists' measures of personality and social psychologists' measures of attitudes must meet the tests of validity and reliability for the results to be meaningful (Feldt, 2005; Phelps, 2005; Yao, Zhour, & Jiang, 2006).

Suppose you take a test and the psychologist tells you that your score is 300. Is 300 a high score? A low score? Is it average? What do you need to know to answer these questions?

If we assume that a test is both valid and reliable, one additional step is necessary to interpret the meaning of a specific test taker's score: the establishment of norms. **Norms** are standards of test performance that permit the comparison of one person's score on a test to the scores of others who have taken the same test. For example, a norm permits test takers to know that they have scored, say, in the top 15% of those who have taken the test previously. Tests for which norms have been developed are known as *standardized tests*. So let's suppose that the average score on the test you took is 450. What does that tell you?

Test designers develop norms by calculating the average score achieved by a specific group of people for whom the test has been designed. Then the test designers can determine the extent to which each person's score differs from the scores of the other individuals who have taken the test in the past and provide future test takers with a qualitative sense of their performance.

The samples of test takers who are employed in the establishment of norms are critical to the norming process. The people used to determine norms must be representative of the individuals to whom the test is directed. In other words, say for example all the test takers were geniuses with IQs over 200. *Their* average score was 450. You might not feel so bad about your score of 300 because they were not a representative group of college students.

VARIATIONS IN INTELLECTUAL ABILITY

While many people fall within the normal range of intelligence (85–115) some individuals fall at either end of that spectrum. For example, some individuals score an IQ below 70 (people with mental retardation or intellectual disabilities) and some score unusually high IQs (the intellectually gifted).

Mental Retardation (Intellectual Disabilities) Although sometimes thought of as a rare phenomenon, mental retardation occurs in 1% to 3% of the population. There is wide variation in the characteristics of people with mental retardation, in part because of the breadth of the definition. **Mental retardation** (or **intellectual disabilities**) is a disability characterized by significant limitations both in intellectual functioning and in conceptual, social, and practical adaptive skills (American Association of Mental Retardation, 2002).

Although below-average intellectual functioning can be measured in a relatively straightforward manner—using standard IQ tests—gauging limitations in adaptive behaviour is more difficult. Ultimately, this imprecision leads to a lack of uniformity in how experts apply the label *mental retardation*. Furthermore, it has resulted in significant variation in the definition of abilities of people who are categorized as mentally retarded, ranging from those who can be taught to work and function with little special attention to those who virtually cannot be trained and must receive institutional treatment throughout their lives (Detterman, Gabriel, & Ruthsatz, 2000; Greenspan, 2006).

Most people with mental retardation have relatively minor deficits and are classified as having *mild retardation*. These individuals, who have IQ scores ranging from 55

> > > Imagine you took an IQ test that asked you to draw a snowman on three different trials, would this IQ test be reliable and valid, only reliable, only valid, or neither reliable nor valid?

validity The property by which tests actually measure what they are supposed to measure.

norms Standards of test performance that permit the comparison of one person's score on a test with the scores of other individuals who have taken the same test.

mental retardation (intellectual disabilities) A condition characterized by significant limitations both in intellectual functioning and in conceptual, social, and practical adaptive skills.

to 69, constitute some 90% of all people with mental retardation. Although their development is typically slower than that of their peers, they can function independently by adulthood and are able to hold jobs and have families of their own (Bates et al., 2001; Beirne Smith, Patton, & Kim, 2006).

At greater levels of retardation—*moderate retardation* (IQs of 40 to 54), *severe retardation* (IQs of 25 to 39), and *profound retardation* (IQs below 25)—the difficulties are more pronounced. For people with moderate retardation, deficits are obvious early, with language and motor skills lagging behind those of peers. Although these individuals can hold simple jobs, they need to have a moderate degree of supervision throughout their lives. Individuals with severe and profound mental retardation are generally unable to function independently and typically require care for their entire lives (Garwick, 2007).

Most individuals with Down syndrome have mild to moderate mental retardation. Like this student, they can be productive members of society.

> **The most common biological cause of mental retardation is fetal alcohol syndrome, caused by a mother's use of alcohol while pregnant.**

What are the causes of mental retardation? In nearly one-third of the cases, there is an identifiable biological reason. A major biological cause is **fetal alcohol syndrome**, caused by a mother's use of alcohol while pregnant. Increasing evidence shows that even small amounts of alcohol intake can produce intellectual deficits (Manning & Hoyme, 2007; West & Blake, 2005).

Down syndrome, another major biological cause of mental retardation, results from the presence of an extra chromosome. In other cases of mental retardation, an abnormality occurs in the structure of a chromosome. Birth complications, such as a temporary lack of oxygen, may also cause retardation. In some cases, mental retardation occurs after birth or following a head injury, a stroke, or infections such as meningitis (Bittles, Bower, & Hussain, 2007; Plomin & Kovas, 2005).

However, the majority of cases of mental retardation are classified as **familial retardation**, meaning that no apparent biological defect exists but there is a history of retardation in the family. Whether the family background of retardation is caused by environmental factors, such as extreme

continuous poverty leading to malnutrition, or by some underlying genetic factor is usually impossible to determine (Zigler, Finn-Stevenson, & Hall, 2002).

Important advances in the care and treatment of those with retardation have been made in the last three decades. Much of this change was instigated in the United States by the Education for All Handicapped Children Act of 1975 (Public Law 94-142). In this federal law, Congress stipulated that people with retardation are entitled to a full education and that they must be educated and trained in the *least restrictive environment*. The law increased the educational opportunities for individuals with mental retardation, facilitating their integration into regular classrooms as much as possible—a process known as *mainstreaming* (Aussilloux & Baghdadli, 2006; Gibb et al., 2007; Katsiyannis, Zhang, & Woodruff, 2005). In Canada, the process is more often referred to as *integration*, and while it has not had the same federal law influence as in the United States, Canada has committed to providing developmentally delayed children with the same educational opportunities as other children (Bowd, 1992).

Study tip Remember that in most cases of intellectual disability there is no apparent biological deficiency, but a history of mental retardation exists in the family.

The Intellectually Gifted Another group of people—the intellectually gifted—differ from those with average intelligence as much as do individuals with mental retardation, although in a different manner. Accounting for 2%–4% of the population, the **intellectually gifted** have IQ scores greater than 130.

Although the stereotype associated with the gifted suggests that they are awkward, shy social misfits who are

fetal alcohol syndrome A major cause of mental retardation in newborns, occurring when the mother uses alcohol during pregnancy.

familial retardation Mental retardation in which no apparent biological defect exists, but there is a history of retardation in the family.

intellectually gifted The 2% to 4% of the population who have IQ scores greater than 130.

unable to get along well with peers, most research indicates that just the opposite is true. The intellectually gifted are most often outgoing, well adjusted, healthy, popular people who are able to do most things better than the average person can (Gottfredson & Deary, 2004; Lubinski et al., 2006; Winner, 2003).

For example, in a famous study by psychologist Lewis Terman that started in the early 1920s, 1,500 children who had IQ scores above 140 were followed for the rest of their lives. From the start, the members of this group were more physically, academically, and socially capable than their non-gifted peers. In addition to doing better in school, they also showed better social adjustment than average. All these advantages paid off in terms of career success: as a group, the gifted received more awards and distinctions, earned higher incomes, and made more contributions in art and literature than typical individuals did. Perhaps most important, they reported greater satisfaction in life than did the non-gifted (Hegarty, 2007).

Of course, not every member of the group Terman studied was successful. Furthermore, high intelligence is not a homogeneous quality; a person with a high overall IQ is not necessarily gifted in every academic subject but may excel in just one or two. A high IQ is not a universal guarantee of success (Clemons, 2006; Shurkin, 1992; Winner, 2003).

GROUP DIFFERENCES IN INTELLIGENCE

Kwang is often washed with a pleck tied to a

(a) rundel.

(b) flink.

(c) pove.

(d) quirj.

If you found this kind of item on an intelligence test, you would probably complain that the test was totally absurd and had nothing to do with your intelligence or anyone else's—and rightly so. How could anyone be expected to respond to items presented in a language that was so unfamiliar?

Yet to some people, even more reasonable questions may appear just as nonsensical. Consider the example of a child raised in a city who is asked about procedures for milking cows, or someone raised in a rural area who is asked about subway ticketing procedures. Obviously, the previous experience of the test takers would impact their ability to answer correctly. And if such types of questions were included on an IQ test, a critic could rightly contend that the test had more to do with prior experience than with intelligence.

Although IQ tests do not include questions that are so clearly dependent on prior knowledge as questions about cows and subways, the background and experiences of test takers do have the potential to affect results. In fact, the issue of devising fair intelligence tests that measure knowledge unrelated to culture and family background and experience is central to explaining an important and persistent finding: members of certain racial and cultural groups consistently score lower on traditional intelligence tests than do members

of other groups. For example, as a group, African American and African Canadians tend to average 10 to 15 IQ points lower than Caucasians. Does this variation reflect a true difference in intelligence, or are the questions biased in regard to the kinds of knowledge they test? Clearly, if white people perform better because of their greater familiarity with the kind of information that is being tested, their higher IQ scores are not necessarily an indication that they are more intelligent than members of other groups (Fagan & Holland, 2007; Jensen, 2003; Templer & Arikawa, 2006).

> **Efforts to produce culture-fair measures of intelligence relate to a lingering controversy over differences in intelligence between members of minority and majority groups.**

There is good reason to believe that some standardized IQ tests contain elements that discriminate against minority-group members whose experiences differ from those of the white majority. Consider the question "What should you do if another child grabbed your hat and ran off with it?" Most white middle-class children answer that they would tell an adult, and this response is scored as correct. However, a reasonable response might be to chase the person and fight to get the hat back, the answer that is chosen by many urban African American children—but one that is scored as incorrect (Aiken, 1997; Miller-Jones, 1991; Reynolds & Ramsay, 2003).

NATURE, NURTURE, AND IQ

In an attempt to produce a **culture-fair IQ test**, one that does not discriminate against the members of any minority group, psychologists have tried to devise test items that assess experiences common to all cultures or emphasize questions that do not require language usage. However, test-makers have found this difficult to do, because past

culture-fair IQ test A test that does not discriminate against the members of any minority group.

experiences, attitudes, and values almost always affect respondents' answers.

For example, children raised in Western cultures group things on the basis of what they *are* (such as putting *dog* and *fish* into the category of *animal*). In contrast, members of the Kpelle tribe in Africa see intelligence demonstrated by grouping things according to what they *do* (grouping *fish* with *swim*). Similarly, children in the West asked to memorize the position of objects on a chessboard perform better than do African children living in remote villages if household objects familiar to the Western children are used. But if rocks are used instead of household objects, the African children do better. In short, it is difficult to produce a truly culture-fair IQ test (Sandoval et al., 1998; Serpell, 2000; Valencia & Suzuki, 2003).

The efforts of psychologists to produce culture-fair measures of intelligence relate to a lingering controversy over differences in intelligence between members of minority and majority groups. In attempting to identify whether there are real intellectual differences between such groups, psychologists have had to confront the broader issue of determining the relative contribution to intelligence of genetic factors (heredity) and experience (environment)— the nature–nurture issue that is one of the basic issues of psychology.

Richard Herrnstein, a psychologist, and Charles Murray, a sociologist, fanned the flames of the debate with the publication of their book *The Bell Curve* in the mid-1990s (Herrnstein & Murray, 1994). They argued that an analysis of IQ differences between whites and blacks demonstrated

heritability A measure of the degree to which a characteristic is related to genetic, inherited factors.

that although environmental factors played a role, there were also basic genetic differences between the two races. They based their argument on a number of findings. For instance, on average, Caucasian's score 15 points higher than do African Americans on traditional IQ tests even when socio-economic status (SES) is taken into account. According to Herrnstein and Murray, middle- and upper-SES African Americans score lower than do middle- and upper-SES whites, just as lower-SES African Americans score lower on average than do lower-SES whites. Intelligence differences between African Americans and whites, they concluded, could not be attributed to environmental differences alone.

Study tip

Remember that there is much more variation in IQ scores among individuals than in scores among different racial/ethnic groups.

Moreover, intelligence in general shows a high degree of **heritability**, a measure of the degree to which a characteristic can be attributed to genetic, inherited factors (Grigorenko, 2000; Miller & Penke, 2007; Petrill, 2005; Plomin, 2003a). The closer the genetic link between two related people, the greater the association of IQ scores. For example, the correlation for spouses, who are genetically unrelated and have

Figure 7.9

Relationship Between IQ and Closeness of Genetic Relationship

Relationship	Genetic overlap	Rearing	Correlation
Monozygotic (identical) twins	100%	Together	0.86
Dizygotic (fraternal) twins	50%	Together	0.62
Siblings	50%	Together	0.41
Siblings	50%	Apart	0.24
Parent-child	50%	Together	0.35
Parent-child	50%	Apart	0.31
Adoptive parent-child	0%	Together	0.16
Unrelated children	0%	Together	0.25
Spouses	0%	Apart	0.29

The difference between these two correlations shows the impact of the environment.

The relatively low correlation for unrelated children raised together shows the importance of genetic factors.

Source: Adapted from Henderson, 1982.

been reared apart, is relatively low, whereas the correlation for identical twins reared together is high. Using data such as these, Herrnstein and Murray argued that differences between races in IQ scores were largely caused by genetically based differences in intelligence.

Many psychologists strongly refuted the arguments laid out in *The Bell Curve*. One criticism is that even when attempts are made to hold socio-economic conditions constant, wide variations remain among individual households. Furthermore, no one can convincingly assert that the living conditions of African Americans and whites are identical even when their socio-economic status is similar. In addition, as we discussed earlier, there is reason to believe that traditional IQ tests may discriminate against lower-SES urban African Americans by asking for information pertaining to experiences they are unlikely to have had (American Psychological Association Task Force on Intelligence, 1996; Hall, 2002; Horn, 2002; Nisbett, 2007).

Moreover, African Americans who are raised in economically enriched environments have similar IQ scores to whites in comparable environments. For example, a study by Sandra Scarr and Richard Weinberg (1976) examined African American children who had been adopted at an early age by white middle-class families of above-average intelligence. The IQ scores of those children averaged 106—about 15 points above the average IQ scores of unadopted African American children in the study. Other research shows that the racial gap in IQ narrows considerably after a

college education and cross-cultural data demonstrate that when racial gaps exist in other cultures, it is the economically disadvantaged groups that typically have lower scores. In short, there is not compelling evidence that genetic factors play the major role in determining racial differences in IQ (Fagan & Holland, 2007; Sternberg, Grigorenko, & Kidd, 2005; Winston, 2004).

Furthermore, drawing comparisons between different races on any dimension, including IQ scores, is an imprecise, potentially misleading, and often fruitless venture. By far, the greatest discrepancies in IQ scores occur among all *individuals*, not among different racial/ethnic *groups* of people. There are African Americans and African Canadians who score high on IQ tests and whites who score low, just as there are whites who score high and African Americans and African Canadians who score low. For the concept of intelligence to aid in the betterment of society, we must examine how *individuals* perform, not the groups to which they belong (Angoff, 1988; Fagan & Holland, 2002, 2007).

The more critical question to ask is not whether hereditary or environmental factors primarily underlie intelligence, but whether there is anything we can do to maximize the intellectual development of each individual. If we can find ways to do this, we will be able to make changes in the environment—which may take the form of enriched home and school environments—that can lead each person to reach his or her potential.

For Review »

What is thinking?

Thinking is the manipulation of mental representations of information. Thinking transforms such representations into novel and different forms, permitting people to answer questions, solve problems, and reach goals. Mental images, concepts, and prototypes enable us to think about and understand the complex world in which we live.

How do people approach and solve problems?

Problem solving typically involves three stages: preparation, production of solutions, and evaluation of solutions. Strategies for solving problems include simple trial and error and, for more complex problems, algorithms and heuristics. Factors that hinder effective problem solving include mental set, inappropriate use of algorithms and heuristics, and confirmation bias.

How does language develop?

Infants understand their native language before they begin speaking it. Babbling is the first stage of language production, followed by one-word utterances. After one year of age, children use two-word combinations, increase their vocabulary, and use telegraphic speech. By age five, acquisition of language rules is relatively complete. Learning theorists suggest that language is acquired through reinforcement and conditioning. In contrast, the nativist approach suggests that an innate language-acquisition device guides language development. The interactionist approach argues that language development stems from a combination of genetically determined predispositions for language and environmental circumstances.

How is intelligence defined and conceptualized?

Because intelligence can take many forms, defining it is challenging. One commonly accepted view is that intelligence is the capacity to understand the world, think rationally, and use resources effectively when faced with challenges. Among the various conceptions of intelligence proposed by researchers are fluid and crystallized intelligence, Gardner's eight spheres of intelligence, information-processing models, practical intelligence, and emotional intelligence.

What are the major approaches to measuring intelligence in the West, and what do intelligence tests measure?

Intelligence tests have traditionally compared a person's mental age and chronological age to yield an IQ, or intelligence quotient, score. Specific tests of intelligence include the Stanford-Binet test, the Wechsler Adult Intelligence Scale–III (WAIS-III), and the Wechsler Intelligence Scale for Children–IV (WISC-IV). Achievement tests and aptitude tests are other types of standardized tests.

What are the variations in intelligence?

Most people fall within the normal range of intelligence (85–115) but some individuals fall at either end of that spectrum. Examples are individuals scoring an IQ below 70 (people with intellectual disabilities) as well as those with high IQs above 130 (the intellectually gifted). While some have argued that there are variations in intelligence based on ethnicity or culture, drawing comparisons between different races on intelligence can be misleading. The greatest discrepancies in IQ scores occur among all *individuals*, not among different racial/ethnic *groups* of people.

Psych think answers

Psych think 1 In the PSYCH think on p. 164 we asked how the availability heuristic might contribute to prejudice. Remember that the availability heuristic means making a decision based on what information readily comes to your mind. If people have a negative viewpoint of those from a different ethnicity, it may be because they use information that is readily available in their minds to form an opinion. For example, when some people think of Irish people, they readily think about pubs and alcohol, which may lead them to stereotype all Irish people as those who drink too much alcohol.

Psych think 2 In the PSYCH think on p. 178 we asked you to use Gardner's theory of multiple intelligence to "assess" how you are intelligent. For example, which of the intelligences are you higher in? Which one would be your lowest? Of course, the answer here would be individual; however, as an example; one of the authors of this text would describe herself as being higher in Gardner's interpersonal and bodily kinesthetic intelligences. The author is a teacher who is often interacting with others, so it is important that she is sensitive to the mood, temperaments, motivations, and intentions of others. Moreover, the author plays on three different hockey teams, competes in triathlons and running races, and regularly practices yoga. These examples would certainly fit with the description of bodily kinesthetic intelligence where one uses the body in the solution of problems or in the construction of products or displays. While high in interpersonal and bodily kinesthetic intelligence, the author would describe herself as lowest in spatial intelligence. She often needs to use a compass for directions and easily becomes lost while out in the countryside on her bike!

Psych think 3 In the PSYCH think on p. 184 we asked you to imagine you took an IQ test that asked you to draw a snowman on three different trials. We then asked if this IQ test would be reliable and valid, only reliable, only valid, or neither reliable nor valid? To answer this question you first must remind yourself of the definition of reliability and validity. A test is reliable if the test taker gets a similar score each time he or she takes it. A test is valid if it measures what the test intends to measure. For example, a valid psychology test would not ask questions about chemistry! So, the answer to the question is that the IQ test would be reliable but not valid. Your drawings of the snowman were likely similar across all three trials, and if you took the test again, you would likely draw the snowmen in a similar way. However, the test was definitely not a valid measure of intelligence! Drawing snowmen might assess one very small aspect of your intelligence, but not your total IQ. Moreover, there is a cultural bias to this test—what if the test taker grew up in an area without snow and has never seen a snowman before? This person would score very low on this IQ test, but this would not be a fair assessment of his or her intelligence.

8

Motivation
and Emotion

She would not give up

British Columbia resident Rita Chretien, age 56, survived 49 days alone in the Nevada wilderness after her van became stranded on an old logging road. Rita and husband Albert Chretien, age 59, became stuck in the mud when their GPS unit directed their van down an unused road.

After several attempts to dig themselves out and the realization that they did not have cell phone coverage, Albert Chretien set out to get help with the GPS unit while Rita Chretien stayed in the van with an injured knee. Albert never returned with help (he is still missing) and Rita Chretien survived the 49 days on bits of trail mix, candy, and water from a nearby stream. She said she passed the time by writing in her journal and praying, knowing that she would never give up. After 49 days she had lost 30 pounds, but was otherwise reasonably healthy.

Issues of motivation—that is, what moves us—and emotion are central to any explanation of Rita's extraordinary courage and will to live. Psychologists who investigate motivation try to discover what our goals are and how these goals guide various behaviours. For example, if you drink a glass of water because you are thirsty, we would say your goal was to quench your thirst and you drank a glass of water to satisfy your goal. In Rita's case, the goal was survival, and by rationing her food, writing in her journal, and refusing to give up, she achieved her goal.

The study of emotions focuses on our internal experiences at any given moment. All of us feel a variety of emotions: happiness at succeeding at a difficult task, sadness over the death of a loved one, anger at being treated unfairly. Psychologists who research emotions have developed a number of different theories about the nature of emotions and how they function.

We begin this chapter by examining the major conceptions of motivation and discussing how different motives and needs jointly affect behaviour. We consider motives that are biologically based and universal in the animal kingdom, such as hunger, as well as motives that appear to be unique to humans, such as the need for achievement.

We then turn to emotions. We consider the roles and the functions that emotions play in people's lives and discuss several approaches that explain how people understand their emotions. Finally, we look at how non-verbal behaviour communicates emotions.

How do different motives affect behaviour?

- What is motivation and how does it influence behaviour?
- What are our needs for achievement? For affiliation? For power?
- What factors affect hunger and sexual behaviour?
- What are the theories of emotion?
- Does everyone experience emotions in the same way?
- How do we communicate our feelings non-verbally?

Explaining Motivation

Motivation includes the factors that direct and energize the behaviour of humans and other organisms. It explains why we do what we do, such as why Rita Chretien survived almost seven weeks alone in her van in the wilderness. Motivation has biological, cognitive, and social aspects, and the complexity of the concept has led psychologists to develop a variety of approaches. All seek to explain the energy that guides people's behaviour in specific directions. We will discuss the major theories of motivation in the next several pages. As you read, think about how these theories might apply to your own behaviour. What motivates you?

What factors motivated Terry Fox to run across Canada to raise money for cancer research?

INSTINCT APPROACHES

When psychologists first tried to explain motivation, they turned to **instincts**, inborn patterns of behaviour that are biologically determined rather than learned. According to instinct approaches to motivation, people and animals are born pre-programmed with sets of behaviours essential to their survival. Those instincts provide the energy that channels behaviour in appropriate directions. Hence, sexual behaviour may be a response to an instinct to reproduce, and exploratory behaviour may be motivated by an instinct to examine one's territory. These explanations would fit well with the evolutionary approach to psychology that we introduced in the first chapter. Remember that the evolutionary approach explains our behaviour in terms of adaptation, that is, our behaviour served the purpose of survival at some point and we have adapted as a result of this.

By definition, instinctual behaviours are rigid patterns of behaviour that every member of a species (or all females and all males in the case of sexual behaviour) will carry out in exactly the same way. Salmon provide a famous example: They all choose practically the same moment to swim back to the river where they were born. They then swim upstream to reproduce, even though these behaviours result in their death. The problem is that humans don't do *anything* in exactly the same way, even when we try!

So a major problem with trying to use the concept of instinct to explain motivation is that human behaviours are far more complex than those of many other animal species, and we don't appear to have any true instincts. As a result, newer explanations have replaced conceptions of motivation based on instincts.

motivation The factors that direct and energize the behaviour of humans and other organisms.

instincts Inborn patterns of behaviour that are biologically determined rather than learned.

The seasonal migration of birds is instinctual behaviour. In contrast, the motivation underlying human behaviour is complex and can be difficult to explain.

DRIVE-REDUCTION APPROACHES

After rejecting instinct theory, psychologists first proposed simple drive-reduction theories of motivation to take its place (Hull, 1943). **Drive-reduction approaches** suggest that a lack of some basic biological requirement such as water produces a drive to obtain that requirement (in this case, the thirst drive).

In drive-reduction theories, **drive** is defined as motivational tension, or arousal, that energizes behaviour to fulfill a need. Many basic drives, such as hunger, thirst, sleep, and sex, are related to biological needs of the body or of the species as a whole. These are called *primary drives*. Primary drives contrast with secondary drives, in which behaviour fulfills no obvious biological need. In *secondary drives*, prior experience and learning bring about needs. For instance, some people have strong needs to achieve academically and professionally. We can say that their achievement need is reflected in a secondary drive that motivates their behaviour (Seli, 2007).

We usually try to satisfy a primary drive by reducing the underlying need. For example, we become hungry after not eating for a few hours and may raid the refrigerator. Rita Chretien would have tried to reduce her need of hunger by eating the small amounts that she had in the van, but she

also knew that she needed to ration her food, so the underlying need could not be completely reduced.

If the weather turns cold, we put on extra clothing or raise the setting on the thermostat to keep warm. If our bodies need liquids to function properly, we experience thirst and seek out water. In each of these examples, we have reduced the drive by fulfilling the need. Another way to think about this is to think about a time when you were sitting at home studying. You started to get that gnawing feeling in your stomach telling you that you need to do something to satisfy this need. You then have a drive to do something about this so you order a pizza! You have reduced the drive by fulfilling the need. When we fulfill the need we bring our body back to a state of homeostasis, or balance, which the drive-reduction theorists suggest is a large part of this motivation.

Although drive-reduction theories provide a good description of how primary drives motivate behaviour, they cannot address behaviours for which the goal is not to reduce a drive but rather to maintain or even to increase the level of excitement or arousal. For instance, some behaviour seems to be motivated by nothing more than curiosity, such as rushing down the street to watch firefighters investigate an alarm. Similarly, many people pursue thrilling activities such as riding a roller coaster or steering a raft down the rapids of a river. Such behaviours contradict the idea that people seek to reduce all drives, as drive-reduction approaches would indicate (Begg & Langley, 2001; Rosenbloom & Wolf, 2002). It also does not explain why we continue to fulfill a need when it clearly has already been fulfilled. For example, why do we find room for the dessert bar after already gorging ourselves on numerous trips to the all-you-can-eat buffet?

What motivates people to engage in thrill-seeking behaviour, such as skydiving?

Both curiosity and thrill-seeking behaviour, then, shed doubt on drive-reduction approaches as a complete explanation for motivation. In both cases, rather than seeking to reduce an underlying drive, people appear to be motivated to increase their overall level of stimulation and activity. To explain this phenomenon, psychologists have devised yet a third theoretical perspective: arousal approaches to motivation.

AROUSAL APPROACHES

Arousal theories seek to explain behaviour in which the goal is to maintain or to increase excitement. According to **arousal approaches to motivation**, each person tries to maintain a certain level of stimulation and activity. As with the drive-reduction model, this model suggests that if our stimulation and activity levels become too high, we try to reduce them. But, in contrast to the drive-reduction model, the arousal model also suggests that if levels of stimulation

drive-reduction approaches to motivation Theories suggesting that a lack of a basic biological requirement (such as water) produces a drive to obtain that requirement (in this case, the thirst drive).

drive Motivational tension, or arousal, that energizes behaviour to fulfill a need.

arousal approaches to motivation The belief that we try to maintain certain levels of stimulation and activity, increasing or reducing them as necessary.

Do You Seek Out Sensation?

How much stimulation do you crave in your everyday life? You will have an idea after you complete the following questionnaire, which lists some items from a scale designed to assess your sensation-seeking tendencies. Circle either A or B in each pair of statements. If neither A nor B accurately describes you, choose the one that better describes your inclination. Try to answer all items.

1. A I would like a job that requires a lot of travelling.
   B I would prefer a job in one location.
2. A I am invigorated by a brisk, cold day.
   B I can't wait to get indoors on a cold day.
3. A I get bored seeing the same old faces.
   B I like the comfortable familiarity of everyday friends.
4. A I would prefer living in an ideal society in which everyone was safe, secure, and happy.
   B I would have preferred living in the unsettled days of our history.
5. A I sometimes like to do things that are a little frightening.
   B A sensible person avoids activities that are dangerous.
6. A I would not like to be hypnotized.
   B I would like to have the experience of being hypnotized.
7. A The most important goal of life is to live it to the fullest and to experience as much as possible.
   B The most important goal of life is to find peace and happiness.
8. A I would like to try parachute jumping.
   B I would never want to try jumping out of a plane, with or without a parachute.
9. A I enter cold water gradually, giving myself time to get used to it.
   B I like to dive or jump right into the ocean or a cold pool.
10. A When I go on a vacation, I prefer the comfort of a good room and bed.
    B When I go on a vacation, I prefer the change of camping out.
11. A I prefer people who are emotionally expressive, even if they are a bit unstable.
    B I prefer people who are calm and even-tempered.
12. A A good painting should shock or jolt the senses.
    B A good painting should give one a feeling of peace and security.
13. A People who ride motorcycles must have some kind of unconscious need to hurt themselves.
    B I would like to drive or ride a motorcycle.

Source: "Do you seek out sensation?" questionnaire from Marvin Zuckerman, "The Search for High Sensation," *Psychology Today*, February 1978, pp. 30–46.

Scoring: Give yourself one point for each of the following responses: 1A, 2A, 3A, 4B, 5A, 6B, 7A, 8A, 9B, 10B, 11A, 12A, 13B. Find your total score by adding up the number of points and then use the following scoring key:

0–2 very low sensation seeking
4–5 low
6–9 average
10–11 high
12–13 very high

Keep in mind that this questionnaire provides only a rough estimate of your sensation-seeking tendencies. Moreover, as people get older, their sensation-seeking scores tend to decrease. Still, the questionnaire will at least give you an indication of how your sensation-seeking tendencies compare with those of others.

---

and activity are too low, we will try to increase them by seeking stimulation.

People vary widely in the optimal level of arousal they seek out, with some people looking for especially high levels of arousal. For example, people who participate in daredevil sports, high-stakes gamblers, and criminals who pull off high-risk robberies may be exhibiting a particularly high need for arousal (Cavenett & Nixon, 2006; Zuckerman, 2002; Zuckerman & Kuhlman, 2000).

INCENTIVE APPROACHES

When we head to the dessert bar after our numerous trips to the buffet, its appeal has little or nothing to do with the biological need for more food, the reduction of the drive, or the maintenance of arousal. Rather, if we choose to eat the dessert, such behaviour is motivated by the external stimulus of the dessert itself, which acts as an anticipated reward. This reward, in motivational terms, is an *incentive.*

Incentive approaches to motivation suggest that motivation stems from the desire to obtain valued external goals, or incentives. In this view, the desirable properties of external stimuli—whether grades, money, affection, or food—account for a person's motivation. Can you think of what approach to psychology this sounds like? If we are motivated to do something based on the incentive, which is really a reward or reinforcement, this behaviour can be explained from a behavioural approach. Remember that the behavioural approach explains behaviour in terms of reinforcements and punishments.

One problem with the incentive theory is that although it seeks to explain why we may succumb to an incentive (such as a mouth-watering dessert) even when

incentive approaches to motivation Theories suggesting that motivation stems from the desire to obtain valued external goals, or incentives.

we lack internal cues (such as hunger), it does not provide a complete explanation of motivation, because sometimes we seek to fulfill needs even when incentives are not apparent. In other words, we sometimes behave as if we're being motivated only by biological drives. Consequently, many psychologists believe that the internal drives proposed by drive-reduction theory work in tandem with the external incentives of incentive theory to "push" and "pull" behaviour, respectively. Thus, at the same time that we seek to satisfy our underlying hunger needs (the push of drive-reduction theory), we may be drawn to food that appears very appetizing (the pull of incentive theory). Rather than contradicting each other, then, drives and incentives may work together in motivating behaviour (Berridge, 2004; Lowery, Fillingim, & Wright, 2003; Pinel, Assanand, & Lehman, 2000). In other words, as with most behaviour, there may be more than one approach to explaining it!

COGNITIVE APPROACHES

Cognitive approaches to motivation suggest that motivation is a product of our thoughts, expectations, and goals—our cognitions. The cognitive approach can also help explain some of the shortcomings of the incentive approach. One of the other problems with the incentive theory is that it does not explain why people sometimes are not motivated by the incentive. Consider students—some students find that getting an "A" is incentive enough to study and attend class while other students are motivated by simply passing the course.

The cognitive approach differentiates between **extrinsic motivation** where one is motivated by external factors such as rewards or personal recognition, and **intrinsic motivation** where one is motivated by internal factors such as personal satisfaction or interest. Some students are motivated to study for hours and hours, which may be explained by intrinsic motivation (e.g., curiosity and interest in the subject) or by extrinsic motivation (e.g., a desire for the "A"). Rita Chretien may have been motivated intrinsically to prove to herself that she could and would survive in the wilderness until someone found her.

MASLOW'S HIERARCHY OF NEEDS

Abraham Maslow devised a model of motivation that places motivational needs in a hierarchy and suggests that before more sophisticated, higher-order needs can be met, certain primary needs must be satisfied (Maslow, 1970, 1987). Using a pyramid to represent the model, Maslow placed the more fundamental, lower-order needs at the base and the higher-level needs at the top. For a specific higher-order need to guide behaviour, a person must first fulfill the more basic needs in the hierarchy.

The basic needs in Maslow's model are primary physiological drives: needs for water, food, sleep, sex, and the like. Safety needs come next in the hierarchy; Maslow suggests that people need a safe, secure environment to function effectively. After meeting these basic lower-order needs, a person can consider satisfying higher-order needs, such as the needs for love and a sense of belonging, esteem, and self-actualization.

Imagine, for a moment, that you live in a war-torn country. Your village experiences the rapid fire of automatic weapons on a fairly regular basis, your water has been poisoned, and your crops have been destroyed. Which of the following are you going to be most motivated to do: find a place to be safe from the bullets, find true love, or get a haircut? Maslow's assumption would be that we would seek safety before we could focus on higher–level needs such as love and self-esteem. In another example, imagine a child living with his mother in her car. When this child goes to school each morning, his primary motivation will be finding food, not trying to make friends or learn new material in class that day.

Love and belongingness needs include the needs to obtain and to give affection and to be a contributing member of some group or society. After fulfilling these needs, a person strives for esteem. In Maslow's thinking, esteem relates to the need to develop a sense of self-worth by recognizing that others know and value one's competence.

From the perspective of . . .

AN EARLY CHILDHOOD EDUCATOR

The focus on giving students grades may serve to decrease intrinsic motivation for learning the subject matter. What would you recommend to help students reconnect with their intrinsic motivation?

cognitive approaches to motivation Theories suggesting that motivation is a product of people's thoughts and expectations—their cognitions.

extrinsic motivation Part of the cognitive approach to motivation where one is motivated by external factors such as rewards or personal recognition.

intrinsic motivation Part of the cognitive approach to motivation where one is motivated by internal factors such as personal satisfaction or interest.

Figure 8.1
Maslow's Hierarchy of Needs

Higher-order needs

Self-actualization
A state of self-fulfillment

Esteem
The need to develop a sense of self-worth

Love and belongingness
The need to obtain and give affection

Safety needs
The need for a safe and secure environment

SECURITY

Physiological needs
The primary drives: needs for water, food, sleep, and sex

Lower-order needs

Source: After Maslow, 1970.

for two reasons: it highlights the complexity of human needs, and it emphasizes the idea that until more basic biological needs are met satisfactorily, people will be relatively unconcerned with higher-order needs. So if people are starving, their first interest will be in obtaining food (Hanley & Abell, 2002; Samantaray, Srivastava, & Misra, 2002).

APPLYING MOTIVATION APPROACHES

The various theories of motivation give several different perspectives on motivation. Which provides the fullest account of motivation? Actually, many of the approaches we've considered are complementary, rather than contradictory. Employing more than one approach can help us understand motivation in a particular instance.

Consider, for example, Aron Ralston, a hiker who needed to cut off his own arm to save himself from starvation after becoming trapped in a cave in the desert (the movie *127 Hours* highlights this extraordinary story). His interest in climbing in an isolated and potentially dangerous area may be explained by arousal approaches to motivation. From a cognitive perspective, we recognize his careful consideration of various strategies to extricate himself from the boulder. Maslow might point out that his basic needs were not being met while he was

Once these four sets of needs have been fulfilled—no easy task—a person can strive for the highest-level need, self-actualization. **Self-actualization** is a state of self-fulfillment in which people realize their highest potentials, each in his or her own unique way. The important thing is that people feel at ease with themselves and satisfied that they are using their talents to the fullest. In a sense, the goal of self-actualization is to reduce the striving and yearning for greater fulfillment that mark most people's lives and find a sense of satisfaction with life (Laas, 2006; Piechowski, 2003; Reiss & Havercamp, 2005).

Study tip

Review the distinctions between the different explanations for motivation (instinct, drive reduction, arousal, incentive, cognitive, and Maslow's hierarchy of needs).

Although research has not validated the specific order of Maslow's stages, and although it is difficult to measure self-actualization objectively, Maslow's model is important

Where on Maslow's pyramid would you place these Jain monks, whose spiritual beliefs require an ascetic lifestyle, including a limited diet and detachment from people and possessions?

How might different motivation approaches explain a young person's decision to volunteer for military service?

trapped, so he made choices based on the motivation to satisfy food, water, and shelter needs.

In short, applying multiple approaches to motivation in a given situation provides a broader understanding than we might obtain with a single approach. We'll see this again when we consider specific motives—such as the needs for achievement, affiliation, power, and food—and draw on several of the theories for the fullest account of what motivates behaviour.

Psych think

> > > Try to find a story in the media about someone who committed a crime and then explain this person's behaviour from as many of the theories of motivation that you can.

Human Needs and Motivation

THE NEEDS FOR ACHIEVEMENT, AFFILIATION, AND POWER

Powerful secondary drives that have as yet no clear biological basis also motivate us. Among the more prominent of these is the need for achievement.

The Need for Achievement The **need for achievement** is a stable, learned characteristic in which a person obtains satisfaction by striving for and attaining a level of excellence (McClelland et al., 1953). People with a high need for achievement seek out situations in which they can compete against some standard—be it grades, money, or winning at a game—and prove themselves successful. But they are not indiscriminate when it comes to picking their challenges: They tend to avoid situations in which success will come

need for achievement A stable, learned characteristic in which a person obtains satisfaction by striving for and attaining a level of excellence.

too easily (which would be unchallenging) and situations in which success is unlikely. Instead, people high in achievement motivation generally choose tasks that are of intermediate difficulty (Speirs-Neumeister & Finch, 2006).

In contrast, people with low achievement motivation tend to be motivated primarily by a desire to avoid failure. As a result, they seek out easy tasks, being sure to avoid failure, or seek out very difficult tasks for which failure has no negative implications, because almost anyone would fail at them. People with a high fear of failure stay away from tasks of intermediate difficulty, because they may fail where others have been successful (Martin & Marsh, 2002; Morrone & Pintrich, 2006; Puca, 2005).

A high need for achievement generally produces positive outcomes, at least in success-oriented cultures in Western society. For instance, people motivated by a high need for achievement are more likely to attend college than are their low-achievement counterparts; and once they are in college, they tend to receive higher grades in classes that are related to their future careers. Furthermore, high achievement motivation indicates future economic and occupational success (McClelland, 1985; Thrash & Elliot, 2002).

Study tip

A key feature of people with a high need for achievement is that they prefer tasks of *moderate* difficulty.

MEASURING ACHIEVEMENT MOTIVATION

How can we measure a person's need for achievement? The measuring instrument used most frequently is the *Thematic Apperception Test (TAT)* (Spangler, 1992). In the TAT, an examiner shows a series of ambiguous pictures. The examiner tells participants to write a story that describes what is happening, who the people are, what led to the situation, what the people are thinking or wanting, and what will happen next. Researchers then use a standardized scoring system to determine the amount of achievement imagery in people's stories. For example, someone who writes a story in which the main character strives to beat an opponent, studies in order to do well at some task, or works hard to get a promotion shows clear signs of an achievement orientation. The inclusion of such achievement-related imagery in the participants' stories is assumed to indicate an unusually high degree of concern with—and therefore a relatively strong need for—achievement (Tuerlinckx, DeBoeck, & Lens, 2002).

The Need for Affiliation Few of us choose to lead our lives as hermits. Why? One reason is that most people have a **need for affiliation**, an interest in establishing and maintaining relationships with other people. Individuals with a high need for affiliation write TAT stories that emphasize the desire to maintain or reinstate friendships and show concern over being rejected by friends.

People who have higher affiliation needs are particularly sensitive to relationships with others. They desire to be with their friends more of the time, and alone less often, compared with people who are lower in the need for affiliation. However, gender is a greater determinant of how much time is actually spent with friends: Regardless of their affiliative orientation, female students spend significantly more time with their friends and less time alone than male students do (Cantwell & Andrews, 2002; Johnson, 2004; Semykina & Linz, 2007).

How is gender correlated with the need for affiliation?

The Need for Power If your fantasies include becoming the prime minister of Canada or being CEO of a large company such as Apple, your dreams may reflect a high need for power. The **need for power**, a tendency to seek impact, control, or influence over others and to be seen as a powerful individual, is an additional type of motivation (Lee-Chai & Bargh, 2001; Winter, 2007; Zians, 2007).

The need for power is a type of motivation that may explain why people pursue politics.

As you might expect, people with strong needs for power are more apt to belong to organizations and seek office than are those low in the need for power. They also tend to work in professions in which their power needs may be fulfilled, such as business management and—you may or may not be surprised—teaching (Jenkins, 1994). In addition, they seek to display the material trappings of power. Even in college, they are more likely to collect prestigious possessions, such as electronic equipment and sports cars.

From the perspective of . . .

A CAREER ADVISOR How might you use characteristics such as the need for achievement, need for power, and need for affiliation to advise students about successful career choices? What additional criteria would you have to consider?

HUNGER AND EATING

According to the 2002 Canadian Community Health Survey on mental health and well-being, approximately 360,000 women and 64,000 men are at risk of developing an eating disorder (Statistics Canada, 2004). These disorders, which usually appear during adolescence, can bring about extraordinary weight loss and other forms of physical deterioration. Extremely dangerous, they sometimes result in death.

need for affiliation An interest in establishing and maintaining relationships with other people.

need for power A tendency to seek impact, control, or influence over others, and to be seen as a powerful individual.

Why are some people subject to such disordered eating, which revolves around the motivation to avoid weight gain at all costs? And why do so many other people engage in overeating, which leads to obesity? To answer such questions as these, we must consider some of the specific needs that underlie behaviour.

Approximately one-third of Canadians are overweight, and almost a quarter are so heavy that they have **obesity**, body weight that is more than 20% above the average weight for a person of a particular height. The most widely used measure of obesity is the *body mass index (BMI)*, which is based on a ratio of weight to height. People with a BMI greater than 30 are considered obese, whereas those with a BMI between 25 and 30 are overweight. The *Canadian Guidelines for Body Weight Classification in Adults* assesses health risks for individuals over the age of 18 based on BMI and waist circumference (WC). Men who have a WC of approximately 102 cm (40 inches), and women who have a WC of approximately 88 cm (35 inches) are at increased risk of a variety of health issues such as high blood pressure, diabetes, and heart disease (for more information, search for *Canadian Guidelines for Body Weight Classification in Adults* on the Health Canada Web site at www.hc-sc.gc.ca).

The percentage of obesity in Canada has risen from 13.8% in 1979 to 32.1% in 2004 (Statistics Canada, 2004), and the rest of the world is not far behind: A billion people around the globe are overweight or obese. According to the World Health Organization, worldwide obesity has reached epidemic proportions, accompanied by increases in heart disease, diabetes, cancer, and premature deaths (Hill, Catenacci, & Wyatt, 2005; Stephenson & Banet-Weiser, 2007).

Biological Factors in the Regulation of Hunger In contrast to human beings, most other species are unlikely to become obese (unless they are raised by humans!). Internal mechanisms regulate not only the quantity of food they take in but also the kind of food they desire. For example, rats that have been deprived of particular foods seek out alternatives that contain the specific nutrients their diet is

lacking, and many species, given the choice of a wide variety of foods, select a well-balanced diet (Bouchard & Bray, 1996; Jones & Corp, 2003; Woods et al., 2000).

Complex mechanisms tell organisms whether they require food or should stop eating. It's not just a matter of an empty stomach causing hunger pangs and a full one alleviating those pangs. (Even individuals who have had their stomachs removed still experience the sensation of hunger.) One important factor is changes in the chemical composition of the blood. For instance, changes in levels of glucose, a kind of sugar, regulate feelings of hunger. In addition, the hormone *ghrelin* communicates to the brain feelings of hunger (Chapelot et al., 2004; Teff, Petrova, & Havel, 2007; Wren & Bloom, 2007).

The brain's *hypothalamus* monitors glucose levels. Increasing evidence suggests that the hypothalamus carries the primary responsibility for monitoring food intake. Injury to the hypothalamus has radical consequences for eating behaviour, depending on the site of the injury. For example, rats whose *lateral hypothalamus* is damaged may literally starve to death. They refuse food when it is offered, and unless they are force-fed, they eventually die. Rats with an injury to the *ventromedial hypothalamus* display the opposite problem: extreme overeating. Rats with this injury can increase in weight by as much as 400%. Similar phenomena occur in humans who have tumours of the hypothalamus (Seymour, 2006; Woods & Seeley, 2002; Woods et al., 1998).

Although the important role that the hypothalamus plays in regulating food intake is clear, the exact way this organ operates is still unclear. One hypothesis suggests that injury to the hypothalamus affects the **weight set point**, or the particular level of weight that the body strives to maintain, which in turn regulates food intake. Acting as a kind of internal weight thermostat, the hypothalamus calls for either greater or less food intake (Berthoud, 2002; Capaldi, 1996; Woods et al., 2000).

In most cases, the hypothalamus does a good job. Even people who are not deliberately monitoring their weight show only minor weight fluctuations in spite of substantial day-to-day variations in how much they eat and exercise. However, injury to the hypothalamus can alter the weight set point, and a person then struggles to meet the internal

obesity Body weight that is more than 20% above the average weight for a person of a particular height.

weight set point The particular level of weight that the body strives to maintain.

goal by increasing or decreasing food consumption. Even temporary exposure to certain drugs can alter the weight set point (Cabanac & Frankhan, 2002; Hallschmid et al., 2004).

Genetic factors determine the weight set point, at least in part. People seem destined, through heredity, to have a particular **metabolism**, the rate at which food is converted to energy and expended by the body. People with a high metabolic rate can eat virtually as much as they want without gaining weight, whereas others, with low metabolism, may eat literally half as much yet gain weight readily (Jequier, 2002; Westerterp, 2006).

> **People with a high metabolic rate can eat virtually as much as they want without gaining weight, whereas others, with low metabolism, may eat literally half as much yet gain weight readily.**

Social Factors in Eating You're having dinner with relatives at your aunt's home and you've just emptied your plate. You feel completely stuffed. Suddenly your aunt passes you the roast beef platter and encourages you to have another helping. Even though you are full and don't like roast beef very much, you take another serving and eat it all.

Along with internal biological factors, external social factors, based on societal rules and on what psychologists have learned about appropriate eating behaviour, also play an important role in when and how much we eat. Take, for example, the simple fact that some people customarily eat breakfast, lunch, and dinner at approximately the same times every day. Because they tend to eat on schedule every day, they feel hungry as the usual hour approaches, sometimes quite independently of what their internal cues are telling them. Similarly, they put roughly the same amount of food on their plates every day, even though the amount of exercise they may have had, and consequently their need for energy replenishment, varies from day to day.

Other social factors relate to our eating behaviour as well. The behavioural approach would explain our eating behaviour as a result of classical and operant conditioning. For example, after a difficult day some of us head for the refrigerator to seek solace in a large bowl of ice cream. Why? Perhaps when we were children, our parents gave us food when we were upset. Eventually, we may have learned, through the basic mechanisms of classical and operant conditioning, to associate food with comfort and consolation. Similarly, we may learn that eating, which focuses our attention on immediate pleasures, provides an escape from unpleasant thoughts. Consequently, we may eat when we feel distressed (Bulik et al., 2003; Elfhag, Tynelius, & Rasmussen, 2007; O'Connor & O'Connor, 2004).

You may have heard of the "freshman fifteen"—this refers to the amount of weight that many first-year college and university students gain when living on campus. This weight gain is often attributed to an increase in alcohol consumption (for example, an average bottle of beer has between 80 and 150 calories—the same amount as a small chocolate bar!) and the high-fat, high-carbohydrate, and high-calorie diet associated with cafeteria food. Not only do first-year

metabolism The rate at which food is converted to energy and expended by the body.

students tend to eat more unhealthy food, they also do not eat enough fruit and vegetables for a well-balanced diet. Researchers from the University of Lethbridge in Alberta have been working on ways to improve the eating behaviours of college and university students (Deshpande, Basil, & Basil, 2009). The researchers used a correlational analysis to test their hypothesis that healthy eating intentions would be positively related to healthy eating behaviour. The data supported their hypothesis because it was found that students who made an intention to eat healthier food tended to also have healthier eating behaviour. Deshpande et al. (2009) suggested that college and university cafeterias can help motivate students to have a healthier diet by offering meal plans with healthier choices.

The Roots of Obesity Given that both biological and social factors influence eating behaviour, determining the causes of obesity has proved to be a challenging task. Researchers have followed several paths.

Some psychologists suggest that oversensitivity to external eating cues based on social factors, coupled with insensitivity to internal hunger cues, produces obesity. Others argue that overweight people have higher weight set points than other people do. Because their set points are unusually high, their attempts to lose weight by eating less may make them especially sensitive to external, food-related cues and therefore more apt to overeat, perpetuating their obesity (Tremblay, 2004; West, Harvey-Berino, & Raczynski, 2004).

But why may some people's weight set points be higher than those of others? One biological explanation has to do with the hormone *leptin*, which provides a signal to the brain that the body is satiated (i.e., had enough to eat). Although obese individuals appear to have higher levels of leptin, they also seem to be resistant to the satiety cues that leptin provides other individuals. From an evolutionary approach, the body's weight-regulation system appears to be designed more to protect against losing weight than to protect against gaining it. Therefore, it's easier to gain weight than to lose it (Ahiima & Osei, 2004; Levin, 2006; Zhang et al., 2005).

Another biologically based explanation for obesity relates to fat cells in the body. Starting at birth, the body stores fat either by increasing the number of fat cells or by increasing the size of existing fat cells. Furthermore, any loss of weight past infancy does not decrease the number of fat cells; it affects only their size. Consequently, people are stuck with the number of fat cells they inherit from an early age, and the rate of weight gain during the first four months of life is related to being overweight during later childhood (Stettler et al., 2005).

According to the weight-set-point hypothesis, the presence of too many fat cells from earlier weight gain may result in the set point's becoming "stuck" at a higher level than is desirable. In such circumstances, losing weight becomes a difficult proposition, because one is constantly at odds with one's own internal set point when dieting (Freedman, 1995; Leibel, Rosenbaum, & Hirsch, 1995).

Not everyone agrees with the set-point explanation for obesity. Pointing to the rapid rise in obesity over the last several decades in North America, some researchers suggest that the body does not try to maintain a fixed weight set point. Instead, they suggest, the body has a *settling point*, determined by a combination of our genetic heritage and the nature of the environment in which we live. If high-fat/high-sugar foods are prevalent in our environment and we are genetically predisposed to obesity, we settle into an equilibrium that maintains a relatively high weight. In contrast, if our environment is nutritionally healthier, a genetic predisposition to obesity will not be triggered, and we settle into an equilibrium in which our weight is lower (Comuzzie & Allison, 1998; Pi-Sunyer, 2003).

Eating Disorders Eating disorders are among the 10 most frequent causes of disability in young women. One devastating weight-related disorder is **anorexia nervosa**. In this severe eating disorder, people may refuse to eat while denying that their behaviour and appearance—which can become skeleton-like—are unusual. Some 10% of people with anorexia literally starve themselves to death (Striegel-Moore & Bulik, 2007).

Anorexia nervosa mainly afflicts females between the ages of 12 and 40, although both men and women of any age may develop it. People with the disorder typically come

Until recently, school cafeterias served a lot of foods that are high in fat and calories. This situation no doubt contributed to an epidemic of childhood obesity. Now schools are required to offer fresher, healthier options.

anorexia nervosa A severe eating disorder in which people may refuse to eat while denying that their behaviour and appearance—which can become skeleton-like—are unusual.

Brazilian fashion model Ana Carolina Reston died at age 21 of anorexia complications. Following the deaths of Reston and other models, the fashion industry began changing its standards to promote a healthier image. Spain's Madrid fashion show now requires models to have a body mass index of at least 18 to participate.

from stable homes, and they are often successful, attractive, and relatively affluent. The disorder often occurs after serious dieting, which somehow gets out of control. Life begins to revolve around food: Although people with the disorder eat little, they may cook for others, go shopping for food frequently, or collect cookbooks (Myers, 2007; Polivy, Herman, & Boivin, 2005; Reijonen et al., 2003).

A related problem is **bulimia**, a disorder in which an individual binges on large quantities of food, for instance by consuming an entire litre of ice cream and a whole pie in a single sitting. After such a binge, the person experiences guilt and depression and often induces vomiting or takes laxatives to eliminate the food—behaviour known as purging. Though the weight of a person with bulimia often remains normal, constant binging-and-purging cycles and the use of drugs to induce vomiting or diarrhea can cause health problems and may lead to heart failure. (Couturier & Lock, 2006; Mora-Giral et al., 2004).

Exercising to excess in an attempt to become thinner is an eating disorder known as *exercise bulimia*. Unlike people with anorexia, people with exercise bulimia don't control their weight by refusing to eat. Instead, they focus on purging the calories that they do consume; but whereas individuals with bulimia purge by vomiting or using laxatives, those with exercise bulimia purge by monitoring and working off every calorie they eat. As with other eating disorders, people with exercise bulimia can acquire a frail, sickly, and even skeletal appearance while still seeing themselves as overweight and being preoccupied with the fear of eating more calories than they are burning (Abraham et al., 2007; Heywood & McCabe, 2006).

bulimia A disorder in which a person binges on large quantities of food, followed by efforts to purge the food through vomiting or other means.

Since exercise is usually beneficial to health and many people such as competitive athletes exercise very frequently or for long periods of time, when does exercising become a disorder? One indicator is exercise that goes beyond the point of benefit or where the excessive activity starts doing more harm than good. For example, a person with exercise bulimia may sustain sports injuries such as muscle sprains or joint injuries, yet nevertheless continue working out despite the pain (Hrabosky et al., 2007).

Psych think

> > > Which of the modern approaches to psychology would explain anorexia and bulimia as being influenced by societal expectations, through television shows and commercials?

Another indicator is a compulsion to exercise—people with exercise dependency tend to feel anxious and guilty about missing a workout and let their exercise activities interfere with their work and with their social lives. One study suggests that it is this compulsion rather than the actual quantity of exercise that indicates the presence of a disorder (Adkins & Keel, 2005; Hausenblas & Downs, 2002).

Eating disorders represent a growing problem: Estimates show that between 1% and 4% of high school-age and college-age women have either anorexia nervosa or bulimia. As many as 10% of women suffer from bulimia at some point in their lives. Furthermore, an increasing number of men are diagnosed with eating disorders; an estimated 10% to 13% of all cases occur in males (Kaminski et al., 2005; Park, 2007; Swain, 2006).

Brain scans from people with eating disorders show that they process information about food differently than healthy individuals do.

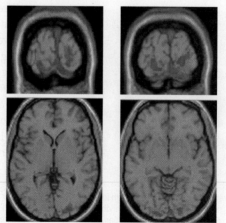

In a study comparing patients with anorexia and healthy individuals, participants viewed images of different foods so researchers could observe their cognitive processing. Comparison of fMRI scans of patients with anorexia (left column) and healthy participants (right column) showed significant differences in their reactions to the food stimuli. The differences suggest that patients with anorexia respond differently to food stimuli than do healthy people, which in turn may be related to restrictions in their eating behaviour.
Source: Santel et al., 2006, Figure 4.

BUY IT?

Losing Weight Successfully

Do you buy into the idea that you can quickly lose weight by depriving yourself of some particular food group? Well, believe it or not, you can… but at a potential cost to your health. Moreover, many fad diets result in rapid initial weight loss but the weight is put back on almost as rapidly.

Although many people say they want to lose weight, it is still an uphill struggle for most of them. Most people who diet eventually regain the weight they have lost, and so they try one weight loss plan after another, getting caught in a seemingly endless cycle of weight loss and gain (Cachelin & Regan, 2006; Newport & Carroll, 2002; Parker-Pope, 2003).

If you want to lose weight, you should keep several things in mind (Gatchel & Oordt, 2003; Heshka et al., 2003):

- *There is no easy route to weight control.* You will have to make permanent changes in your life to lose weight without gaining it back. The most obvious strategy—cutting down on the amount of food you eat—is just the first step toward a lifetime commitment to changing your eating habits.

- *Keep track of what you eat and what you weigh.* Unless you keep careful records, you won't really know how much you are eating and whether any diet is working.

- *Eat "big" foods.* Eat foods that are bulky and heavy but low in calories, such as grapes and soup. Such foods trick your body into thinking you've eaten more and thus decrease hunger.

- *Exercise.* Exercise for at least 30 consecutive minutes three times each week. When you exercise, you use up fat stored in your body as fuel for muscles, which is measured in calories. As you use up this fat, you will probably lose weight. Almost any activity helps burn calories.

- *Decrease the influence of external, social stimuli on your eating behaviour.* Serve yourself smaller portions of food, and leave the table before you see what is being served for dessert. Don't even buy snack foods such as nachos and potato chips; if they're not readily available in the kitchen cupboard, you're not apt to eat them.

- *Avoid fad diets or diet pills.* No matter how popular they are at a particular time, extreme diets, including liquid diets, usually don't work in the long run and can be dangerous to your health.

- *Set reasonable goals.* Know how much weight you want to lose before you start to diet. Don't try to lose too much weight too quickly or you may doom yourself to failure. Even small changes in behaviour—such as walking 15 minutes a day or eating a few less bites at each meal—can prevent weight gain (Hill et al., 2003).

What are the causes of anorexia nervosa and bulimia? Some researchers suspect a biological cause such as a chemical imbalance in the hypothalamus or pituitary gland, perhaps brought on by genetic factors. Furthermore, brain scans from people with eating disorders show that they process information about food differently than healthy individuals do (Polivy & Herman, 2002; Santel et al., 2006).

Other reasons may be explained from the socio-cultural approach, as some believe that the cause has roots in society's valuation of slenderness and the parallel notion that obesity is undesirable. These researchers maintain that people with anorexia nervosa and bulimia become preoccupied with their weight and take to heart the cliché that one can never be too thin. This may explain why, as countries become more developed and Westernized and dieting becomes more popular, eating disorders increase. Finally, some psychologists suggest that the disorders result from overly demanding parents or other family problems (Couturier & Lock, 2006; Grilo et al., 2003; Nagel & Jones, 1992).

The complete explanations for anorexia nervosa and bulimia remain elusive. These disorders most likely stem from both biological and socio-cultural causes, and successful treatment probably encompasses several strategies,

DID YOU KNOW?

You don't have to work out at the gym to benefit from moderate exercise. Washing and waxing your car (45–60 minutes), gardening (30–45 minutes), washing windows (45–60 minutes), and shovelling snow (15 minutes) are a few activities that can take the place of your workout. For more options and recommendations, visit the Public Health Agency of Canada Web site (www.phac-aspc.gc.ca) and link from the homepage to Health Promotion, Physical Activity, and Tips to Get Active.

including therapy and dietary changes (O'Brien & LeBow, 2007; Richard, 2005; Wilson, Grilo, & Vitousek, 2007).

If you or a family member needs advice or help with an eating problem, contact the National Eating Disorder Information Centre at www.nedic.ca or call toll free 1-866-NEDIC-20 (1-866- 633-4220). You can also find more information at www.nlm.nih.gov/medlineplus/eatingdisorders.html.

SEXUAL MOTIVATION

Compared to the sexual behaviour of other species, human sexual behaviour is rather complicated, although the underlying biology is not all that different from that of related species. In males, for example, the *testes* begin to secrete **androgens** at puberty. Androgens are sex hormones that occur in higher levels in males. Not only do androgens produce secondary sex characteristics, such as the growth of body hair and a deepening of the voice, they also increase the sex drive. Because the level of androgen production by the testes is fairly constant, men are capable of (and interested in) sexual activities without any regard to biological

> **androgens** Male sex hormones secreted by the testes.
>
> **estrogens** Class of female sex hormones.
>
> **progesterone** A female sex hormone secreted by the ovaries.
>
> **ovulation** The point at which an egg is released from the ovaries.
>
> **masturbation** Sexual self-stimulation.

cycles. Given the proper stimuli leading to arousal, men can engage in sexual behaviour at any time (Goldstein, 2000).

Women show a different pattern. When they reach maturity at puberty, the two female ovaries begin to produce **estrogens** and **progesterone**, sex hormones that occur in higher levels in females. However, those hormones are not produced consistently; instead, their production follows a cyclical pattern. The greatest output occurs during **ovulation**, when an egg is released from the ovaries, making the chances of fertilization by a sperm cell highest. While in non-humans the period around ovulation is the only time the female is receptive to sex, people are different. Although there are variations in reported sex drive, women are receptive to sex throughout their cycles (Leiblum & Chivers, 2007).

William Masters and Virginia Johnson were the most influential researchers of human sexuality. Masters and Johnston began studying the human sexual response in the late 1950s and they continued their research well into the late 1900s. Keep in mind that Masters and Johnston were studying and reporting on sexual behaviour at a time when most people did not speak of such topics. Alfred Kinsey was also studying human sexual behaviour in the 1950s; however, Masters and Johnson were the first to use laboratory observation of masturbation and sexual intercourse as part of their research. After observing approximately 700 couples, Masters and Johnson discovered that there are four stages of the human sexual response (excitement, plateau, orgasm, and then resolution) (Masters & Johnson, 1966).

Masturbation If you listened to physicians 75 ago, you would have been told that **masturbation**, sexual self-stimulation, often using the hand to rub the genitals, would lead to a wide variety of physical and mental disorders, ranging from hairy palms to insanity. If those physicians had been correct, however, most of us would be wearing gloves to hide the sight of our hair-covered palms—for masturbation is one of the most frequently practiced sexual activities. Some 94% of males and 63% of females have masturbated at least once, and among college and university students, the frequency ranges from "never" to "several times a day" (Hunt, 1974; Laqueur, 2003; Michael et al., 1994; Polonsky, 2006).

Despite the high incidence of masturbation, attitudes toward it still reflect some of the negative views of yesteryear. For instance, one survey found that approximately 10% of people who masturbated experienced feelings of guilt, and 5% of the males and 1% of the females considered their behaviour perverted (Arafat & Cotton, 1974). Despite these negative attitudes, however, most experts on sex view masturbation as a healthy and legitimate—and

Figure 8.2

Cutaway Side Views of the Female and Male Sex Organs

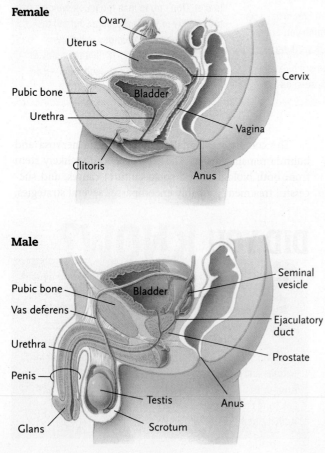

Female

Ovary
Uterus
Cervix
Pubic bone
Bladder
Urethra
Vagina
Clitoris
Anus

Male

Pubic bone
Bladder
Seminal vesicle
Vas deferens
Ejaculatory duct
Urethra
Prostate
Penis
Glans
Testis
Anus
Scrotum

Masters and Johnson were the first to use laboratory observation of masturbation and sexual intercourse as part of their research.

intercourse carried out in the 1940s showed an incidence of 84% across males of all ages; recent figures put the figure at closer to 95%. Moreover, the average age of males' first sexual experience has been declining steadily. Almost half of males have had sexual intercourse by the age of 18, and by the time they reach age 20, 88% have had intercourse. In a 2005 survey of Canadian adolescents, 8% had sexual intercourse before the age of 15 and 43% of 15–19 year olds reported having sexual intercourse on at least one occasion (Statistics Canada, 2008).

Not only are many young people engaging in premarital sex, many are engaging in unprotected sex despite a knowledge of the risks associated with this (O'Sullivan, Udell, Montrose, Antoniello, & Hoffman, 2010). Lucia O'Sullivan from the University of New Brunswick examined the reasons for this risky behaviour and found that less than 25% of their sample (31 men and 32 women) used condoms consistently. The main reason the students used condoms was to prevent pregnancy (without thought of the risks of sexually transmitted infections (STIs). Reasons for not using a condom included: (1) the lack of immediate negative consequences which led them to believe it was a healthy practice; (2) alternative prevention (e.g., withdrawal); (3) a belief that condom use results in a loss of physical sensation; (4) a belief of immunity towards risks or strategies to deal with the potential risks (e.g., abortion or the morning after pill); and (5) disregarding potential risks altogether.

Marital Sex To judge by the number of articles about sex in heterosexual marriages, one would think that sexual behaviour was the number one standard by which marital bliss is measured. Married couples are often concerned that

harmless—sexual activity. In addition, masturbation is seen as providing a means of learning about one's own sexuality and a way of discovering changes in one's body such as the emergence of precancerous lumps (Coleman, 2002; Levin, 2007).

Premarital Sex Until fairly recently, premarital sexual intercourse, at least for women, was considered one of the major taboos in our society. Traditionally, women in Western societies have been warned that "nice girls don't do it"; men have been told that although premarital sex is okay for them, they should marry virgins. This view that premarital sex is permissible for males but not for females is called the **double standard** (Liang, 2007; Treas, 2004).

Although many adults once believed that premarital sex was always wrong, since that time there has been a dramatic change in public opinion. For example, the percentage of middle-aged people who say sex before marriage is "not wrong at all" has increased considerably, and overall 60% of adults say premarital sex is okay. More than half say that living together before marriage is morally acceptable (Thornton & Young-DeMarco, 2001).

Changes in attitudes toward premarital sex were matched by changes in actual rates of premarital sexual activity. For instance, the most recent figures show that just over one-half of women between the ages of 15 and 19 have had premarital sexual intercourse. These figures are close to double the number of women in the same age range who reported having intercourse in 1970. Clearly, the trend over the last several decades has been toward more women engaging in premarital sexual activity (Jones, Darroch, & Singh, 2005).

Among males, there has also been an increase in the incidence of premarital sexual intercourse, although change has not been as dramatic as it has been for females—probably because the rates for males were higher to begin with. For instance, the first surveys of premarital

double standard The view that premarital sex is permissible for males but not for females.

Get Involved!

You can do your own test of the double standard in judgments of sexual behaviour. Type up a description of an individual named Pat and Pat's promiscuous behaviour. Use female pronouns when referring to Pat. Make another version changing only the pronouns (to male). Have an equal number of people read the male and female versions and rate Pat on a number of traits (1 meaning "not at all" to 10 meaning "very much so"), including the trait promiscuity. Compare the promiscuity mean judgments for male Pat and female Pat when engaged in the same behaviour.

they are having too little sex, too much sex, or the wrong kind of sex (Harvey, Wenzel, & Sprecher, 2005).

Although there are many different dimensions along which sex in marriage is measured, one is certainly the frequency of sexual intercourse. What is typical? As with most other types of sexual activities, there is no easy answer to the question, because there are such wide variations in patterns between individuals. We do know that 43% of married couples have sexual intercourse a few times a month and 36% of couples have it two or three times a week. With increasing age and length of marriage, the frequency of intercourse declines. Still, sex continues into late adulthood, with almost half of people reporting that they engage in sexual activity at least once a month and that its quality is high (Michael et al., 1994; Powell, 2006).

Although early research found sexual activity between a married person and someone who is not their spouse, or **extramarital sex**, to be widespread, the current reality appears to be otherwise. According to a survey by the Decima Research group that was published in *Maclean's* magazine in 1995, 80% of Canadians said it was never OK to have an extramarital affair (Macleans/CTV Poll, 1995). Moreover, additional research also shows a high, consistent degree of disapproval of extramarital sex, with nine of ten people saying that it is "always" or "almost always" wrong (Allan, 2004; Daines, 2006; Michael et al., 1994).

However, some may find this surprising given the popularity of the Ashley Madison Web site, developed by Toronto's Noel Biderman, where people in existing marriages can meet to have an affair. According to a *Globe and Mail* interview with Noel Biderman in 2009, there were over 4.5 million members using the site to have an affair. Moreover, Biderman suggests that infidelity may be the best way to save some marriages (Bielski, 2011).

extramarital sex Sexual activity between a married person and someone who is not his or her spouse.

heterosexuality Sexual attraction and behaviour directed to the other sex.

homosexuals Persons who are sexually attracted to members of their own sex.

bisexuals Persons who are sexually attracted to people of the same sex and the other sex.

Heterosexuality People often believe that the first time they have sexual intercourse they have achieved one of life's major milestones. However, **heterosexuality**, sexual attraction and behaviour directed to the other sex, consists of far more than male-female intercourse. Kissing, petting, caressing, massaging, and other forms of sex play are all components of heterosexual behaviour. Still, the focus of sex researchers has been on the act of intercourse, especially in terms of its first occurrence and its frequency (Holtzman & Kulish, 1996; Janssen, 2007).

Homosexuality and Bisexuality **Homosexuals** are sexually attracted to members of their own sex, whereas **bisexuals** are sexually attracted to people of the same sex and the other sex. Many male homosexuals prefer the term *gay* and female homosexuals the label *lesbian*, because these terms refer to a broader array of attitudes and lifestyles than the term *homosexual*, which focuses on the sexual act.

BUY IT?

Should People in a Committed Relationship Continue to Use Condoms?

What do you think? Is it safe to stop using condoms once a relationship becomes exclusive? If you said yes, you are not alone in this opinion. Melissa Bolton and Margaret Schneider from the University of Toronto worked with colleague Alexander McKay from the Sex Information and Education Council of Canada to assess young women's attitudes about condom use while in a dating relationship (Bolton, McKay, Schneider, 2010). The researchers found that many college-aged individuals start using oral contraceptives (i.e., the pill) and stop using condoms once they are in a more committed relationship, despite the fact that they are still at risk of transmitting a sexually transmitted infection (STI). The young women stopped using condoms because they made an assumption that they were not at risk of developing an STI while in a committed relationship. Part of their assumption was based on a belief that the relationship was monogamous and that their partner was STI-free. Many of the young women viewed condoms as a way to prevent pregnancy, not as a means to prevent STIs, which is why they used oral contraception instead. As a good critical thinker, one must be cautious about making assumptions such as these. STIs are a very real risk, especially when having intercourse with multiple partners. Even when you are in a committed monogamous relationship, both you and your partner may have had previous partners who have been infected. Condoms will help prevent STIs, even in committed relationships!

The number of people in a same-sex union at one time or another is considerable. For example, the Statistics Canada 2006 census found that there were over 90 thousand same-sex unions (which included dating, common-law, and married couples) (Statistics Canada, 2006). Keep in mind that this is only the number of people who disclosed their sexual orientation on the census. While attitudes towards gay and lesbian individuals have improved dramatically over the past decade, some people are still reluctant to disclose their sexual orientation.

Although people often view homosexuality and heterosexuality as two completely distinct sexual orientations, the issue is not that simple. Pioneering sex researcher Alfred Kinsey acknowledged this when he considered sexual orientation along a scale or continuum, with "exclusively homosexual" at one end and "exclusively heterosexual" at the other. In the middle were people who showed both homosexual and heterosexual behaviour. Kinsey's approach suggests that sexual orientation is dependent on a person's sexual feelings and behaviours and romantic feelings (Weinberg, Williams, & Pryor, 1991).

What determines whether people become homosexual or heterosexual? Although there are a number of theories, none has proved completely satisfactory.

Some explanations for sexual orientation are biological in nature, suggesting that there are genetic causes. Evidence for a genetic origin of sexual orientation comes from studies of identical twins, which have found that when one twin identified himself or herself as homosexual, the occurrence of homosexuality in the other twin was higher than it was in the general population. Such results occur even for twins

"*Frankly, I've repressed my sexuality so long I've actually forgotten what my orientation is.*"
© The New Yorker Collection 1997 Robert Mankoff cartoonbank.com.
All Rights Reserved.

who have been separated early in life and who therefore are not necessarily raised in similar social environments (Gooren, 2006; Hamer et al., 1993; Kirk, Bailey, & Martin, 2000; Turner, 1995).

Some evidence suggests that differences in brain structures may be related to sexual orientation. For instance, the structure of the anterior hypothalamus, an area of the brain that governs sexual behaviour, differs in male homosexuals and heterosexuals. Similarly, other research shows that, compared with heterosexual men or women, gay men have a larger anterior commissure, which is a bundle of neurons connecting the right and left hemispheres of the brain (Byne, 1996; LeVay, 1993).

DID YOU KNOW?

Homosexuals are more likely to be left-handed than heterosexuals. Whether we are left-handed or right-handed is influenced by our genes, so the finding of a correlation between handedness and a homosexual orientation suggests that there's some biological basis for homosexuality (Lalumiére, Blanchard, & Zucker, 2000).

However, research suggesting that biological causes are at the root of homosexuality is not conclusive, because most findings are based on only small samples of individuals. Still, the possibility is real that some inherited or biological factor exists that predisposes people toward homosexuality, if certain environmental conditions are met (Rahman, Kumari, & Wilson, 2003; Teodorov et al., 2002; Veniegas, 2000).

Little evidence suggests that sexual orientation is brought about by child-rearing practices or family dynamics. Although proponents of psychoanalytic theories once argued that the nature of the parent-child relationship can produce homosexuality (for example, Freud, 1922/1959), research evidence does not support such explanations (Isay, 1994; Roughton, 2002).

Because of the difficulty in finding a consistent explanation, we can't answer the question of what determines sexual orientation. It does seem unlikely that any single factor orients a person toward homosexuality or heterosexuality. Instead, it seems reasonable to assume that a combination of biological and environmental factors is involved (Bem, 1996; Hyde & Grabe, 2008).

Although we don't know at this point exactly why people develop a certain sexual orientation, one thing is clear: There is no relationship between sexual orientation and psychological adjustment. Gays, lesbians, and bisexuals generally enjoy the same quality of mental and physical health that heterosexuals do, although the discrimination they experience may produce higher rates of some disorders, such as depression (Poteat & Espelage, 2007). Heterosexuals, bisexuals, and homosexuals also hold similar kinds of attitudes about themselves, independent of sexual orientation. For such reasons, the American Psychological

Association, the Canadian Psychological Association, and most other mental health organizations have endorsed efforts to reduce discrimination against gays and lesbians (Cochran, 2000; Morris, Waldo, & Rothblum, 2001; Perez, DeBord, & Bieschke, 2000).

Study tip The determinants of sexual orientation have proven difficult to pinpoint. It is important to know the variety of explanations that have been put forward.

Transsexualism **Transsexuals** are people who believe they were born with the body of the opposite gender and who either live as the opposite gender or have a desire to (Heath, 2006; Meyerowitz, 2004). Transsexuals report feeling as though they are trapped in the wrong body and sometimes seek sex-change operations in which their existing genitals are surgically removed and the genitals of the desired sex are fashioned. Several steps, including intensive counselling and hormone injections, along with living as a member of the desired sex for several years, precede surgery, which is, not surprisingly, highly complicated. The outcome, though, can be quite positive (Lobato, Koff, & Manenti, 2006; O'Keefe & Fox, 2003; Stegerwald & Janson, 2003).

Transsexualism is part of a broader category known as transgenderism. The term *transgenderism* encompasses not only transsexuals but also people who view themselves as a third gender, transvestites (who dress in the clothes of the other gender), and others who believe that traditional male-female gender classifications inadequately characterize them (Hyde & Grabe, 2008; Prince, 2005).

Understanding Emotional Experiences

At one time or another, all of us have experienced the strong feelings that accompany both very pleasant and very negative experiences. Perhaps we have felt the thrill of getting a sought-after job, the joy of being in love, the sorrow over someone's death, or the anguish of inadvertently hurting someone. Moreover, we experience such reactions on a less intense level throughout our daily lives: the pleasure of a friendship, the enjoyment of a movie, and the embarrassment of breaking a borrowed item.

Despite the varied nature of these examples, they all represent emotions. Although everyone has an idea of what an emotion is, formally defining the concept has proved to be an elusive task. Here, we'll use a general definition: **emotions** are feelings that generally have both physiological and cognitive elements and that influence behaviour.

transsexuals Persons who believe they were born with the body of the other gender.

emotions Feelings that generally have both physiological and cognitive elements and that influence behaviour.

Think, for example, about how it feels to be happy. First, we obviously experience a feeling that we can differentiate from other emotions. We likely also experience some identifiable physical changes in our bodies: perhaps the heart rate increases, or we find ourselves "jumping for joy." Finally, the emotion probably encompasses cognitive elements: our understanding and evaluation of the meaning of what is happening prompts our feelings of happiness.

We can, however, also experience an emotion without the presence of cognitive elements. For instance, we may react with fear to an unusual or novel situation (such as coming into contact with an erratic, unpredictable individual), or we may experience pleasure over sexual excitation without having cognitive awareness or understanding of just what it is about the situation that is exciting.

THE FUNCTIONS OF EMOTIONS

Imagine what it would be like if we didn't experience emotion—no depths of despair, no depression, no remorse—but at the same time no happiness, joy, or love. Obviously, life would be considerably less satisfying, even dull, if we lacked the capacity to sense and express emotion.

But what purpose do emotions serve beyond making life interesting? Psychologists have identified several key functions that emotions play in our daily lives (Frederickson & Branigan, 2005; Frijda, 2005; Gross, 2006; Siemer, Mauss, & Gross, 2007). Among the most important are these:

- *Preparing us for action.* Emotions act as a link between events in our environment and our responses. If you saw an angry dog charging toward you, your emotional reaction (fear) would be associated with physiological arousal of the sympathetic division of the autonomic nervous system, the activation of the "fight-or-flight" response.

- *Shaping our future behaviour.* Emotions promote awareness that helps us make appropriate responses. For instance, your emotional response to unpleasant events teaches you to avoid similar circumstances in the future.

- *Helping us interact more effectively with others.* We often communicate the emotions we experience through our verbal and non-verbal behaviours, making our emotions obvious to observers. These behaviours can act as a signal to observers, allowing them to understand better what we are experiencing and to help them predict our future behaviour.

DETERMINING THE RANGE OF EMOTIONS

If we were to list the words in the English language that have been used to describe emotions, we would end up with at least 500 examples (Averill, 1975). The list would range from such obvious emotions as *happiness* and *fear* to less common ones, such as *adventurousness* and *pensiveness*.

One challenge for psychologists has been to sort through this list to identify the most important, fundamental emotions. Theorists have hotly contested the issue of cataloguing emotions and have come up with different lists, depending on how they define the concept of emotion. In fact, some reject the question entirely, saying that *no* set of emotions should be singled out as most basic, and that emotions are best understood by breaking them down into their component parts. Other researchers argue for looking at emotions in terms of a hierarchy, dividing them into positive and negative categories, and then organizing them into increasingly narrower subcategories (Dillard & Shen, 2007; Manstead, Frijda, & Fischer, 2003).

Still, most researchers suggest that a list of basic emotions would include, at a minimum, happiness, anger, fear, sadness, and disgust. Other lists are broader, including emotions such as surprise, contempt, guilt, and joy (Ekman, 1994a; Shweder & Heidt, 1994; Tracy & Robins, 2004).

One difficulty in defining a basic set of emotions is that significant differences exist in the ways various cultures experience and express emotion. For instance, Germans talk of *Schadenfreude*, a feeling of pleasure over another person's difficulties, and the Japanese experience *hagaii*, a mood of vulnerable heartache coloured by frustration. In Tahiti, *musu* refers to a feeling of reluctance to yield to unreasonable demands made by one's parents.

Finding *Schadenfreude*, *hagaii*, or *musu* in a particular culture doesn't mean that the members of other cultures are incapable of experiencing such emotions. It does suggest, though, that fitting a particular emotion into a linguistic category to describe that emotion may make it easier to discuss, contemplate, and perhaps experience (Kuppens et al., 2006; Li, Wang, & Fischer, 2004; Russell & Sato, 1995).

THE ROOTS OF EMOTIONS

I've never been so angry before; I feel my heart pounding, and I'm trembling all over . . . I don't know how I'll get through the performance. I feel like my stomach is filled with butterflies . . . That was quite a mistake I made! My face must be incredibly red . . . When I heard the footsteps in the night, I was so frightened that I couldn't catch my breath.

If you examine our language, you will find that there are literally dozens of ways to describe how we feel when we experience an emotion. The language we use to describe emotions is, for the most part, based on the physical symptoms that are associated with a particular emotional experience (Kobayashi, Schallert, & Ogren, 2003; Manstead & Wagner, 2004; Spackman, Fujiki, & Brinton, 2006).

Consider, for instance, the experience of fear. Imagine that it is late on New Year's Eve. You are walking down a dark road, and you hear footsteps behind you. It is clear that the person approaching you is not trying to hurry by but is following directly behind you. You think about what you will do if the stranger attempts to rob you or, worse, hurt you in some way.

While these thoughts are running through your head, something dramatic will be happening to your body. The most likely reactions, which are associated with activation

Figure 8.3
Hierarchy of Emotions

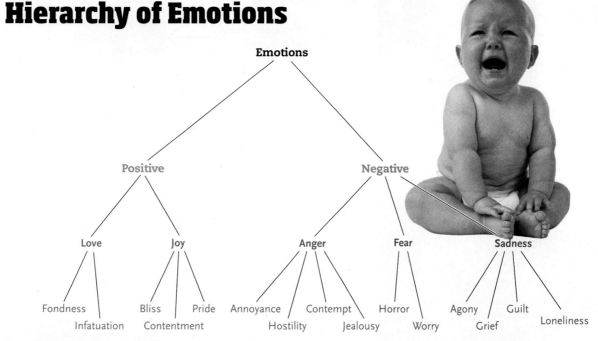

Source: Adapted from Shaver et al., 1987.

of the autonomic nervous system, include an increase in your rate of breathing, an acceleration of your heart rate, a widening of your pupils (to increase visual sensitivity), and a dryness in your mouth as the functioning of your salivary glands, and in fact of your entire digestive system, slows dramatically. At the same time, though, your sweat glands probably become more active, because increased sweating helps you rid yourself of the excess heat produced in response to any emergency activity.

Of course, all these physiological changes are likely to occur without your awareness. At the same time, though, the emotional experience accompanying them will be obvious to you: you most surely would report being fearful.

Although it is easy to describe the general physical reactions that accompany emotions, defining the specific role that those physiological responses play in the experience of emotions has proved to be a major puzzle for psychologists. As we shall see, some theorists suggest that specific bodily reactions cause us to experience a particular emotion—we experience fear, for instance, because the heart is pounding and we are breathing deeply. In contrast, other theorists suggest that the physiological reaction results from the experience of an emotion. In this view, we experience fear, and as a result the heart pounds and our breathing rate increases.

The James-Lange Theory of Emotion William James and Carl Lange were two of the first researchers to explore the nature of emotions. James and Lange characterized emotional experience as a reaction to bodily events that occur in response to some situation or event in the environment. This view is summarized in James's statement, "we feel sorry because we cry, angry because we strike, afraid because we tremble" (James, 1890).

James and Lange suggested that crying at a loss leads us to feel sorrow, that striking out at someone who frustrates us results in our feeling anger, that trembling at a menacing threat causes us to feel fear. In their view, for every major emotion there is an accompanying physiological or "gut" reaction by our internal organs—called a *visceral experience*. It is this specific pattern of visceral response that leads us to label the emotional experience.

In sum, James and Lange proposed that we experience emotions as a result of physiological changes that produce specific sensations. The brain interprets these sensations as specific kinds of emotional experiences. This view has come to be called the **James-Lange theory of emotion** (Cobos et al., 2002; Laird & Bresler, 1990).

The James-Lange theory has some serious drawbacks. For the theory to be valid, visceral changes would have to occur relatively quickly, because we experience some emotions—such as fear when hearing a stranger rapidly approaching on a dark night—almost instantaneously. Yet emotional experiences frequently occur even before certain physiological changes can be set into motion. If while crossing the street you were nearly hit by a car running a stop sign, for example, the increased heartbeat and rapid respiration that accompany fear might not occur until after you jumped out of the way and the incident ended. Because of

Figure 8.4
Three Theories of Emotion

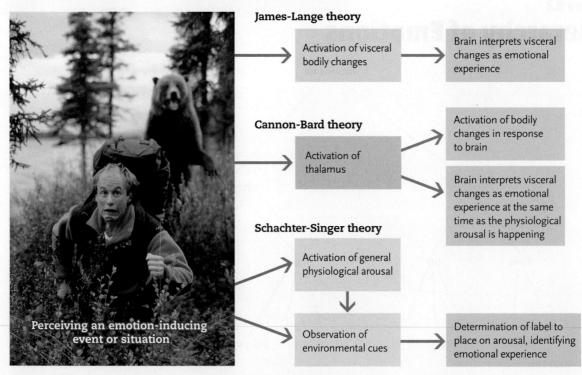

Psych
At The Movies

Touching the Void

Joe is injured while tied to Simon during their descent of Siula Grande in Peru. Simon has to cut the rope to prevent both of them from dying. He believes Joe died, but this is the story of Joe's incredible motivation to survive.

What's Eating Gilbert Grape?

Gilbert's mother suffers prejudice, discrimination, and psychological problems as a result of her obesity.

The Bicentennial Man

A household robot receives an "upgrade" and learns about the complexity of human emotion.

127 Hours

The story of Aaron Ralston's 127 hours trapped under a large boulder and the extraordinary measures he takes to free himself.

the slowness with which some visceral changes take place, it is hard to see how they could be the source of immediate emotional experience.

The James-Lange theory poses another difficulty: Physiological arousal does not invariably produce emotional experience. For example, a person who is jogging has an increased heartbeat and respiration rate, as well as many of the other physiological changes associated with certain emotions. Yet joggers typically do not think of such changes in terms of emotions. There cannot be a one-to-one correspondence, then, between visceral changes and emotional experience. Visceral changes by themselves may not be sufficient to produce emotion.

Finally, our internal organs produce a relatively limited range of sensations. Although some types of physiological changes are associated with specific emotional experiences, it is difficult to imagine how each of the myriad emotions that people are capable of experiencing could be the result of a unique visceral change. Many emotions actually are associated with relatively similar sorts of visceral changes, a fact that contradicts the James-Lange theory (Cameron, 2002; Davidson, Deuser, & Sternberg, 1994).

James-Lange theory of emotion The idea that emotional experience is a reaction to bodily events occurring as a result of an external situation ("I feel sad because I am crying").

Cannon-Bard theory of emotion The view that both physiological arousal and emotional experience are produced simultaneously by the same nerve stimulus.

Schachter-Singer theory of emotion The idea that emotions are determined jointly by a non-specific kind of physiological arousal and its interpretation, based on environmental cues.

The Cannon-Bard Theory In response to the difficulties inherent in the James-Lange theory, Walter Cannon, and later Philip Bard, suggested an alternative view. In what has come to be known as the **Cannon-Bard theory of emotion** (Cannon, 1929), they rejected the view that physiological arousal alone leads to the perception of emotion. Instead, the theory assumes that both physiological arousal *and* the emotional experience are produced simultaneously by the same nerve stimulus, which Cannon and Bard suggested emanates from the thalamus in the brain.

The theory states that after we perceive an emotion-producing stimulus, the thalamus is the initial site of the emotional response. Next, the thalamus sends a signal to the autonomic nervous system, thereby producing a visceral response. At the same time, the thalamus also communicates a message to the cerebral cortex regarding the nature of the emotion being experienced. It is not necessary for different emotions to have unique physiological patterns associated with them, then, as long as the message sent to the cerebral cortex differs according to the specific emotion.

The Cannon-Bard theory seems to have been accurate in rejecting the view that physiological arousal alone accounts for emotions. But more recent research has led to some important modifications of the theory. For one thing, we now understand that the hypothalamus and the limbic system, not the thalamus, play a major role in emotional experience. In addition, the simultaneous occurrence of the physiological and emotional responses, which is a fundamental assumption of the Cannon-Bard theory, has yet to be demonstrated conclusively. This ambiguity has allowed room for yet another theory of emotions: the Schachter-Singer theory.

Study tip

Distinguish the three classic theories of emotion (James-Lange, Cannon-Bard, and Schachter-Singer).

The Schachter-Singer Theory Suppose that, as you are being followed down that dark street on New Year's Eve, you notice a man on the other side of the street being followed by another suspicious-looking figure. The man turns and sees his pursuer. Now assume that instead of reacting with fear, the man begins to laugh and seems gleeful. Would his reactions make you less fearful? Might you decide there is nothing to fear, and start feeling jovial yourself?

According to an explanation that focuses on the role of cognition, the **Schachter-Singer theory of emotion**, this might very well happen. This approach to explaining emotions emphasizes that we identify the emotion we are experiencing by observing our environment and comparing ourselves with others (Schachter & Singer, 1962).

Schachter and Singer's classic experiment found evidence for this hypothesis. In the study, half of the participants were told that they would receive an injection of a vitamin and the other half was told that they would receive an injection of epinephrine. In reality, they were all given

From the perspective of …

A MARKETING STUDENT How might you use the findings by Schachter and Singer on arousal labelling to create interest in a product? Can you think of other ways to manipulate people's arousal level to evoke different emotional responses?

epinephrine, a drug that causes an increase in physiological arousal, including higher heart and respiration rates and a reddening of the face; responses that typically occur during strong emotional reactions. The members of both groups were then placed individually in a situation in which a confederate of the experimenter acted in one of two ways. In one condition he acted as if he was angry and hostile, and in the other condition he behaved as if he were exuberantly happy.

The purpose of the experiment was to determine how the participants would react emotionally to the confederate's behaviour. When they were asked to describe their own emotional state at the end of the experiment, the participants who believed they were given vitamins and who were exposed to the angry confederate tended to report that they felt angry, while those exposed to the happy confederate tended to report feeling happy. Those who were told they received epinephrine tended to report simply feeling the effects of the injection. In sum, the results suggest that participants who thought they were given vitamins turned to the environment and the behaviour of others for an explanation of the physiological arousal they were experiencing.

The results of the Schachter-Singer experiment, then, supported a cognitive view of emotions, in which emotions are determined jointly by a relatively non-specific kind of physiological arousal *and* the labelling of that arousal on the basis of cues from the environment. Later research has found that arousal is not as non-specific as Schachter and Singer assumed. When the source of physiological arousal is unclear, however, we may look to our surroundings to determine just what we are experiencing.

Making Sense of the Multiple Perspectives on Emotion As new approaches to emotion continue to develop, it is reasonable to ask why so many theories of emotion exist and, perhaps more important, which one provides the most complete explanation. Actually, we have only scratched the surface. There are almost as many explanatory theories of emotion as there are individual emotions (for example, DeCoster, 2003; Frijda, 2005; Manstead, Frijda, & Fischer, 2003; Prinz, 2007).

Why are theories of emotion so plentiful? For one thing, emotions are not a simple phenomenon but are intertwined closely with motivation, cognition, neuroscience, and other related branches of psychology. For example, evidence from brain imaging studies shows that even when people come to supposedly rational, non-emotional decisions—such as moral or philosophical judgments—emotions come into play (Greene et al., 2001).

In short, emotions are complex phenomena, encompassing both biological and cognitive aspects, and, at this time, no single theory fully explains all the facets of emotional experience. Furthermore, contradictory evidence of one sort or another challenges each approach, and so no theory has proved invariably accurate in its predictions.

> "At this time, no single theory fully explains all the facets of emotional experience."

This abundance of perspectives on emotion is not a cause for despair—or unhappiness, fear, or any other negative emotion. It simply reflects the fact that psychology is an evolving, developing science. As we gather more evidence, the specific answers to questions about the nature of emotions will become clearer.

CULTURAL DIFFERENCES IN EXPRESSIONS OF EMOTION

Consider, for a moment, the six photos displayed on the following page. Can you identify the emotions being expressed by the person in each of the photos? You don't have to be an expert on facial expressions to see that these expressions display six of the basic emotions: happiness, anger, sadness, surprise, disgust, and fear. Hundreds of studies of non-verbal behaviour show that these emotions are consistently distinct and identifiable, even by untrained observers (Ekman & O'Sullivan, 1991).

Interestingly, these six emotions are not unique to Western cultures; rather, they constitute the basic human emotions that are expressed universally, regardless of where individuals have been raised and what learning experiences they have had. Psychologist Paul Ekman convincingly demonstrated this point when he studied the members of an isolated New Guinea jungle tribe who had had almost

Psych think

> > > If researchers learned how to control emotional responses so that specific emotions such as fear could be prevented, would you sign up for this? How would your life change if you lived without fear?

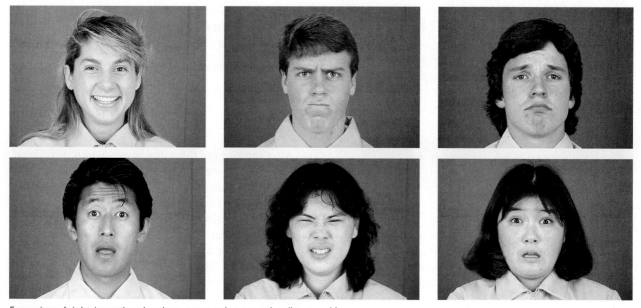

Expressions of six basic emotions: happiness, anger, sadness, surprise, disgust, and fear.

no contact with Westerners (Ekman, 1972). The people of the tribe did not speak or understand English, had never seen a movie, and had had very limited experience with Caucasians before Ekman's arrival. Yet their non-verbal responses to emotion-evoking stories, as well as the ways in which they identified basic emotions, were quite similar to those of Westerners.

Being so isolated, the New Guineans could not have learned from Westerners to recognize or produce similar facial expressions. Instead, their similar abilities and manner of responding emotionally appear to have been innate. Although one could argue that similar experiences in both cultures led the members of each one to learn similar types of non-verbal behaviour, this appears unlikely, because the two cultures are so very different. The expression of basic

emotions, then, seems to be universal (Ekman, 1994b; Izard, 1994; Matsumoto, 2002).

Why do people across cultures express emotions similarly? A hypothesis known as the **facial-affect program** gives one explanation. The facial-affect program—which is assumed to be universally present at birth—is analogous to a computer program that turns on when a particular emotion is experienced. When set in motion, the "program" activates a set of nerve impulses that make the face display an appropriate expression. Each primary emotion produces a unique set of muscular movements, forming different kinds of expressions. For example, the emotion of happiness is universally displayed by movement of a muscle that raises the corners of the mouth—forming what we would call a smile (Ekman, 2003; Ekman, Davidson, & Friesen, 1990; Kim, Kim, & Kim, 2007; Kohler et al., 2004).

The importance of facial expressions is illustrated by an intriguing idea known as the **facial-feedback hypothesis**. According to this hypothesis, facial expressions not only *reflect* emotional experience but also help *determine* how people experience and label emotions (Izard, 1990). Basically, "wearing" an emotional expression provides muscular feedback to the brain that helps produce an emotion congruent with that expression. For instance, the muscles activated when we smile may send a message to the brain indicating the experience of happiness—even if there is nothing in the environment that would produce that particular emotion. Some theoreticians have gone further, suggesting that facial expressions are *necessary* for an emotion to be experienced (Rinn, 1984, 1991). According to this view in its extreme form, if no facial expression is present, the emotion cannot be felt.

"And just exactly what is that expression intended to convey?"

facial-affect program Activation of a set of nerve impulses that make the face display the appropriate expression.

facial-feedback hypothesis The hypothesis that facial expressions not only reflect emotional experience but also help determine how people experience and label emotions.

Support for the facial-feedback hypothesis comes from a classic experiment carried out by psychologist Paul Ekman and colleagues (Ekman, Levenson, & Friesen, 1983). In the study, professional actors were asked to follow very explicit instructions regarding the movements of muscles in their faces. You might try this example yourself:

- Raise your brows and pull them together.

- Raise your upper eyelids.

- Now stretch your lips horizontally back toward your ears.

After carrying out these directions—which, as you may have guessed, are meant to produce an expression of fear—the actors' heart rates rose and their body temperatures fell, physiological reactions that characterize fear. Overall, facial expressions representing the primary emotions produced physiological effects similar to those accompanying the genuine emotions in other circumstances (Keillor et al., 2002; Soussignan, 2002).

For Review »

What is motivation and how does it influence behaviour?

Motivation relates to the factors that direct and energize behaviour. Drive is the motivational tension that energizes behaviour to fulfill a need. Arousal approaches suggest that we try to maintain a particular level of stimulation and activity. Incentive approaches focus on the positive aspects of the environment that direct and energize behaviour. Cognitive approaches focus on the role of thoughts, expectations, and understanding of the world in producing motivation. Maslow's hierarchy of needs include physiological, safety, love and belongingness, esteem, and self-actualization needs. Only after the more basic needs are fulfilled can a person strive to satisfy higher-order needs.

What are our needs for achievement? For affiliation? For power?

Need for achievement refers to the stable, learned characteristic of striving for excellence. The need for affiliation is a concern with establishing and maintaining relationships with others, whereas the need for power is a tendency to seek to exert influence on others.

What factors affect hunger and sexual behaviour?

Eating behaviour is motivated by biological and social factors. The hypothalamus in the brain appears to regulate food intake. Social factors, such as mealtimes, cultural food preferences, and other learned habits, also play a role in the regulation of eating, determining when, what, and how much one eats. An oversensitivity to social cues and an insensitivity to internal cues may contribute to obesity. In addition, obesity may be caused by an unusually high weight set point—the weight the body attempts to maintain—and genetic factors. Sexual behaviour has a biological basis, but almost any kind of stimulus can produce sexual arousal, depending on a person's previous experience. Self-stimulation, or masturbation, is one of the most frequently practiced sexual activities. Attitudes toward masturbation have traditionally been negative even though no negative consequences have been detected. Heterosexuality is the most common sexual orientation, although the number of people who choose same-sex sexual partners at one time or another is considerable. No explanation for why some people are heterosexual and others are homosexual has been confirmed; among the possibilities are genetic or biological factors, childhood and family influences, and previous learning experiences and conditioning.

What are the theories of emotion?

The James-Lange theory, Cannon-Bard theory, and Schacter-Singer theory are three major theories of emotion. The James-Lange theory is based on the idea that emotional experience is a reaction to bodily events occurring as a result of an external situation ("I feel sad because I am crying"). The Cannon-Bard theory of emotion takes the view that both physiological arousal and emotional experience are produced simultaneously by the same nerve stimulus, while the Schachter-Singer theory of emotion is based on the idea that emotions are determined jointly by a nonspecific kind of physiological arousal and its interpretation, based on environmental cues.

Does everyone experience emotions in the same way?

Emotions are broadly defined as feelings that may affect behaviour and generally have both a physiological component and a cognitive component. Emotions prepare us for action, shape future behaviour, and help us interact more effectively with others. Although numerous theories of emotion have been proposed, none of them alone provides a clear-cut explanation that is fully supported by research.

How do we communicate our feelings non-verbally?

A person's facial expressions reveal emotions. Expressions of emotion are universal and can be recognized by people from different cultures. One explanation for this similarity is that an innate facial-affect program activates specific muscle movements representing the emotion being experienced. The facial-feedback hypothesis suggests that facial expressions not only reflect, but also produce, emotional experiences.

Psych think answers

Psych think 1 In the PSYCH think on p. 197 we asked you to find a story in the media about someone who committed a crime and then we asked you to explain the person's behaviour from as many of the theories of motivation that you could. One example of a media story is of a 12-year-old girl from Medicine Hat, Alberta, who killed her parents and younger brother while they were sleeping. The 12-year-old committed the crime with her 23-year-old boyfriend because they felt the girl's parents were trying to break up their relationship. Remember that the theories of motivation include instinct theory, drive-reduction theory, arousal theory, incentive theory, intrinsic and extrinsic motivation, Maslow's hierarchy of needs, and the need for achievement, affiliation, and power. We can use several of the theories of motivation to explain the girl's behaviour. For example, instinct theory may explain her motivation to kill her parents as being due to her instinct to procreate with her boyfriend and her parents were preventing this. Arousal theory may explain her motivation as a need for a high level of arousal that she felt while in the process of killing, and cognitive theories such as extrinsic motivation

might explain it as a need for approval from her boyfriend (the external reward). The incentive to maintain her relationship with her boyfriend may also have acted as motivation for her behaviour, or she may have been seeking love and belonging according to Maslow's hierarchy of needs. Finally, her behaviour may also be explained as a need for affiliation or power. As you can see, there are many possible motivations for her behaviour!

Psych think 2 In the PSYCH think on p. 202 we asked you which of the modern approaches to psychology would explain anorexia and bulimia as being influenced by societal expectations through television shows and commercials. Hopefully you answered the socio-cultural approach, which explains behaviour as being due to social and cultural influences. In the case of anorexia and bulimia, some individuals may see the abundance of thin and underweight people as being a norm to aspire to.

Psych think 3 In the PSYCH think on p. 212 we asked you if you would sign up to have researchers remove your emotional response of fear and if so, how your life

would change if you lived without fear. If you said yes, you may behave in a similar manner to S. M., a woman in her mid-forties who was born without a part of her brain called the amygdala. You learned about the amygdala in the neuroscience chapter when we discussed the parts of the brain. Remember that the amygdala is located in the core of the forebrain in an area called the limbic system. The amygdala is responsible for emotions such as fear and self control. S. M. behaves quite normally in all areas of her life, except she does not experience the emotion of fear. While initially this may sound good because we assume fear is a negative emotion, keep in mind that feeling fear helps protect us from danger. S. M. often puts herself and her children into dangerous situations because she does not feel fear. For example, she lives in a big city and often goes alone to dangerous areas, which has resulted in her being mugged and attacked at knife point. While at first it may sound appealing to have researchers remove your fear response, you may want to reconsider after learning about S. M.!

9

Social Psychology

WHAT'S TO COME

Attitudes and Social Cognition

Social Influence and Groups

Stereotypes, Prejudice, and Discrimination

Positive and Negative Social Behaviour

Sexual assault posted on Facebook

A 16-year-old girl was drugged and sexually assaulted by several teenage males at a rave party at a rural property in Vancouver. Several other people witnessed the assaults but chose not to help. In fact, some of the people took photos with their cell phones and then posted to them to Facebook so others could view them.

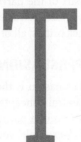

The RCMP tried to have the photos removed from Facebook but others continued to repost them. Eventually, two of the young men who posted the photos to Facebook were charged with production and distribution of child pornography. The police had several other suspects under suspicion but others would not come forward to testify because of a "code of silence." While many people supported the girl by speaking out about the assault and the re-victimization when the photos were posted to Facebook, several others used Facebook as a way to anonymously post disparaging comments. The girl decided to leave her school after the incident because of the ridicule and bullying she received.

This is a shocking story. What made the young men participate in such aggressive group behaviour? Why would they post these photos to Facebook for others to see? Why wouldn't people speak out about who else was involved? Why did some people support the young woman while others bullied her on Facebook? The answers to these questions can be found in this chapter on social psychology, which summarizes how our thoughts, feelings. and behaviour are affected by other people.

How do we influence one another's attitudes and behaviour?

As You Read »

- What are attitudes, how do they influence behaviour, and how can they be changed?
- How do we influence one another?
- Where do stereotypes come from?
- Why are we attracted to certain people? How do relationships develop?
- What makes some people aggressive, and others helpful?
- Why do we help others?

Social psychology is the scientific study of how people's thoughts, feelings, and actions are affected by others. Social psychologists consider the kinds and causes of the behaviour of the individual in social situations. They examine how the nature of situations in which we find ourselves influences our behaviour in important ways.

The broad scope of social psychology is conveyed by the kinds of questions social psychologists ask, such as: How can we convince people to change their attitudes or adopt new ideas and values? In what ways do we come to understand what others are like? How are we influenced by what others do and think? Why do some people display so much violence, aggression, and cruelty toward others that people throughout the world live in fear of annihilation at their hands? And why, in comparison, do some people place their own lives at risk to help others? In exploring these and other questions, we also discuss strategies for confronting and solving a variety of problems and issues that all of us face—ranging from achieving a better understanding of persuasive tactics to forming more accurate impressions of others.

We begin with a look at how our attitudes shape our behaviour and how we form judgments about others. We discuss how we are influenced by others, and we consider prejudice and discrimination, focusing on their roots and the ways in which we can reduce them. After examining what social psychologists have learned about the ways in which people form friendships and relationships, we'll conclude with a look at the determinants of aggression and helping—two opposing sides of human behaviour.

social psychology The scientific study of how people's thoughts, feelings, and actions are affected by others.

attitudes Evaluations of a particular person, behaviour, belief, or concept.

Attitudes and Social Cognition

What do athletes Clara Hughes and Steve Nash have in common?

Each has appeared in advertisements designed to mould or change our thinking about something. Commercials are part of the barrage of messages we receive each day from sources as varied as politicians, sales staff in stores, and celebrities, all of which are meant to influence us.

PERSUASION: CHANGING ATTITUDES

Persuasion is the process of changing attitudes, one of the central concepts of social psychology. **Attitudes** are evaluations of a particular person, behaviour, belief, or concept. For example, you probably hold attitudes toward the Prime Minister (a person), abortion (a behaviour), affirmative action (a belief), or architecture (a concept) (Brock & Green, 2005; Hegarty & Massey, 2007; Perloff, 2003).

The ease with which we can change our attitudes depends on a number of factors, including:

- *Message source.* The characteristics of a person who delivers a persuasive message, known as an *attitude communicator*, have a major impact on the effectiveness of that message. Communicators who are physically and socially attractive produce greater attitude change than those who are less attractive. Moreover, the expertise and trustworthiness of a communicator are related to the effectiveness of a message—except in situations in which the audience believes the communicator has an ulterior motive (Ariyanto, Hornsey, & Gallois, 2006; McClure, Sutton, & Sibley, 2007; Ziegler, Diehl, & Ruther, 2002). This might explain why Jack Layton of the NDP was so successful in the 2011 Federal election

Companies such as Tim Hortons and Gatorade use hockey star Sydney Crosby to persuade us to buy their products. Can celebrities really affect the purchasing habits of consumers?

persuasion: central route and peripheral route processing (Cacioppo & Petty, 1989; Petty et al., 2005). **Central route processing** occurs when the recipient thoughtfully considers the issues and arguments involved in persuasion. In central route processing, people are swayed in their judgments by the logic, merit, and strength of arguments.

In contrast, **peripheral route processing** occurs when people are persuaded on the basis of factors unrelated to the nature or quality of the content of a persuasive message. Instead, factors that are irrelevant or extraneous to the issue influence them, such as who is providing the message, how long the arguments are, or the emotional appeal of the arguments (Petty et al., 2005; Warden, Wu, & Tsai, 2006; Wegener et al., 2004).

Study tip

_C_entral route processing involves the _c_ontent of the message; _p_eripheral route processing involves how the message is _p_rovided.

In general, people who are highly involved and motivated use central route processing to comprehend a message. However, if a person is uninvolved, unmotivated, bored, or distracted, the nature of the message becomes less important, and peripheral factors become more critical. Although both central route and peripheral route processing lead to attitude change, central route processing generally leads to stronger, more lasting attitude change.

compared to the Liberal leader, Michael Ignatieff, who some people had difficulty relating to.

- *Characteristics of the message.* It is not just who delivers a message that affects attitudes but also what the message is like. Generally, two-sided messages—which include both the communicator's position and the one he or she is arguing against—are more effective than one-sided messages, given the assumption that the arguments for the other side can be effectively refuted and the audience is knowledgeable about the topic. In addition, fear-producing messages ("If you don't practice safer sex, you'll get AIDS") are generally effective when they provide the audience with a means for reducing the fear. However, if the fear that is aroused is too strong, messages may evoke people's defence mechanisms and be ignored (Perloff, 2003).

- *Characteristics of the target.* Once a communicator has delivered a message, characteristics of the target of the message may determine whether the message will be accepted. For example, intelligent people are more resistant to persuasion than are those who are less intelligent (Cacioppo et al., 1986; Cacioppo, Petty & Morris, 1983).

Routes to Persuasion Recipients' receptiveness to persuasive messages depends on the type of information-processing they use. Social psychologists have used a model called the Elaboration Likelihood Model to demonstrate two primary information-processing routes to

Figure 9.1

Two Routes to Persuasion

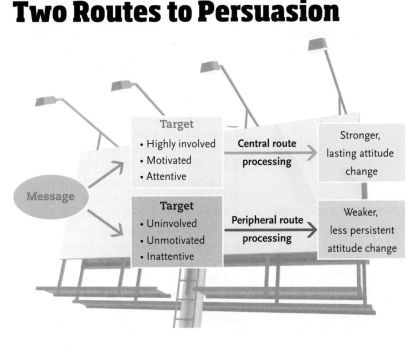

Mark Zanna and colleagues from the University of Waterloo wanted to see if people who watched a movie where the main character smoked would report more favourable thoughts towards smoking when they identified with the main character (Dal Cin et al., 2007). After the participants watched a film where the main character smoked, they were tested using explicit tests of their beliefs about the image of smoking. Participants were also given an Implicit Attitudes Test (we will explain how this test is used to assess prejudice later in the chapter) to determine how much they associated themselves with smoking. The researchers found that both smokers and non-smokers implicitly associated themselves with smoking, and that smokers had a higher intention to smoke after identifying with the main character who smoked in the film. It seems that attitudes and behaviour can be changed simply by watching the message and identifying with the main character. Do you think this would fit better with the central route or peripheral route to persuasion?

Are some people more likely than others to use central route processing rather than peripheral route processing? The answer is yes. People who have a high *need for cognition*, a person's habitual level of thoughtfulness and cognitive activity, are more likely to employ central route processing (Cacioppo, Berntson, & Crites Jr., 1996; Dai & Wang, 2007).

People who have a high need for cognition enjoy thinking, philosophizing, and reflecting on the world. Consequently, they tend to reflect more on persuasive messages by using central route processing and are likely to be persuaded by complex, logical, and detailed messages. In contrast, those who have a low need for cognition become impatient when forced to spend too much time thinking about an issue. Consequently, they usually use peripheral route processing and are persuaded by factors other than the quality and detail of messages (Dollinger, 2003; Van Overwalle & Siebler, 2005).

From the perspective of . . .

A MARKETING STUDENT Suppose you were working on an assignment to develop a full advertising campaign for a product, including television, radio, and print ads. How might theories of persuasion guide your strategy to suit the different media?

The Link Between Attitudes and Behaviour Not surprisingly, attitudes influence behaviour. The strength of the link between particular attitudes and behaviour varies, of course, but generally people strive for consistency between their attitudes and their behaviour. Furthermore, people hold fairly consistent attitudes. For instance, you would probably not hold the attitude that eating meat is immoral and still have a positive attitude toward hamburgers (Ajzen, 2002; Conner et al., 2003; Levi, Chan, & Pence, 2006).

> ❝Sometimes our behaviour shapes our attitudes.❞

Ironically, the consistency that leads attitudes to influence behaviour sometimes works the other way around—sometimes it is our behaviour that shapes our attitudes. Consider, for instance, the following incident:

You've just spent what you feel is the most boring hour of your life, turning pegs for a psychology experiment. Just

TRY IT!

The Need for Cognition

This simple questionnaire will give you a general idea of the level of your need for cognition. Which of the following statements apply to you?

1. I really enjoy a task that involves coming up with new solutions to problems.
2. I would prefer a task that is intellectual, difficult, and important to one that is somewhat important but does not require much thought.
3. Learning new ways to think doesn't excite me very much.
4. The idea of relying on thought to make my way to the top does not appeal to me.
5. I think only as hard as I have to.
6. I like tasks that require little thought once I've learned them.
7. I prefer to think about small, daily projects rather than long-term ones.
8. I would rather do something that requires little thought than something that is sure to challenge my thinking abilities.
9. I find little satisfaction in deliberating hard and for long hours.
10. I don't like to be responsible for a situation that requires a lot of thinking.

Source: Cacioppo, Berntson, & Crites, Jr. (1996).

Scoring: The more you agree with statements 1 and 2, and disagree with the rest, the greater the likelihood that you have a high need for cognition.

as you finally finish and are about to leave, the experimenter asks you to do him a favour. He tells you that he needs a helper for future experimental sessions to introduce subsequent participants to the peg-turning task. Your specific job will be to tell them that turning the pegs is an interesting, fascinating experience. Each time you tell this tale to another participant, you'll be paid $1.

If you agree to help the experimenter, you may be setting yourself up for a state of psychological tension called cognitive dissonance. According to social psychologist Leon Festinger (1957), **cognitive dissonance** occurs when a person holds two contradictory attitudes or thoughts (referred to as *cognitions*).

If you participate in the situation just described, you are left with two contradictory thoughts: (1) I believe the task is boring, but (2) I said it was interesting with little justification ($1). These two thoughts should arouse dissonance. How can you reduce cognitive dissonance? You cannot deny having said that the task is interesting without breaking with reality. Relatively speaking, it is easier to change your attitude toward the task—and thus the theory predicts that participants will reduce dissonance by adopting more positive attitudes toward the task (Cooper, 2007; Cooper, Mirabile, & Scher, 2005).

A classic experiment (Festinger & Carlsmith, 1959) confirmed this prediction. The experiment followed essentially the same procedure outlined earlier, in which a participant was offered $1 to describe a boring task as interesting. In addition, in a comparison condition, some participants were offered $20 to say that the task was interesting. The reasoning behind this condition was that $20 was enough money to give participants in this condition a good reason to convey incorrect information; dissonance would not be aroused, and less attitude change would be expected. The results supported this notion. More of the participants who were paid $1 changed their attitudes (becoming more

Figure 9.2
Cognitive Dissonance and Smoking

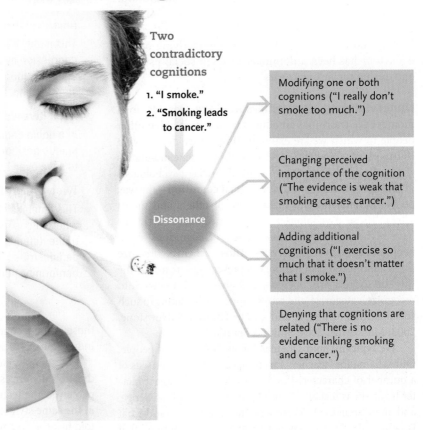

Two contradictory cognitions

1. "I smoke."
2. "Smoking leads to cancer."

Dissonance

Modifying one or both cognitions ("I really don't smoke too much.")

Changing perceived importance of the cognition ("The evidence is weak that smoking causes cancer.")

Adding additional cognitions ("I exercise so much that it doesn't matter that I smoke.")

Denying that cognitions are related ("There is no evidence linking smoking and cancer.")

cognitive dissonance The conflict that occurs when a person holds two contradictory attitudes or thoughts (referred to as cognitions).

positive toward the peg-turning task) than did participants who were paid $20.

We now know that cognitive dissonance theory accounts for many everyday events involving attitudes and behaviour. For example, smokers who know that smoking leads to lung cancer hold contradictory cognitions: (1) I smoke, and (2) smoking leads to lung cancer. The theory predicts that these two thoughts will lead to a state of cognitive dissonance. More important, it predicts that—assuming that they don't change their behaviour by quitting smoking—smokers will be motivated to reduce their dissonance by one of the following methods: (1) modifying one or both of the cognitions, (2) changing the perceived importance of one cognition, (3) adding cognitions, or (4) denying that the two cognitions are related to each other. Hence, a smoker may decide that he really doesn't smoke all that much or that he'll quit soon (modifying the cognition), that the evidence linking smoking to cancer is weak (changing the importance of a cognition), that the amount of exercise he gets compensates for the smoking (adding cognitions), or that there is no evidence linking smoking and cancer (denial). Whichever techniques the smoker uses result in reduced dissonance.

SOCIAL COGNITION: UNDERSTANDING OTHERS

When we meet someone for the first time, we tend to form an impression of that person. What we think of a stranger may or may not be positive, and it may or may not be accurate, but that first impression tends to influence our interpretation of that individual's behaviour from then on. Learning how we come to understand what others are like and how we explain the reasons underlying others' behaviour has been a dominant focus in social psychology during the last few years.

Understanding What Others Are Like Consider for a moment the enormous amount of information about other people to which we are exposed. How do we decide what is important and what is not? How do we make judgments about the characteristics of others? Social psychologists interested in this question study **social cognition**—the way people understand and make sense of others and themselves. Those psychologists have learned that individuals have highly developed schemas, sets of cognitions about people and social experiences. Those schemas organize information stored in memory, represent in our minds the way the social world operates, and give us a framework to recognize, categorize, and recall information relating to such social stimuli as people and groups (Brewer & Hewstone, 2003; Moskowitz, 2004; Smith & Semin, 2007).

We typically hold schemas for specific types of people. Our schema for "teacher," for instance, generally consists of a number of characteristics: knowledge of the subject matter he or she is teaching, a desire to impart that knowledge, and an awareness of the student's need to understand what is being said. Or we may hold a schema for "mother" that includes the characteristics of warmth, nurturance, and caring. Regardless of their accuracy, schemas are important, because they organize the way in which we recall, recognize, and categorize information about others. Moreover, they help us predict what others are like on the basis of relatively little information, because we tend to fit people into schemas even when we do not have much concrete evidence to go on (Bargh & Chartrand, 2000; Ruscher, Fiske, & Schnake, 2000).

Impression Formation How do we decide that Sayreeta is a flirt, Jacob is obnoxious, or Hector is a really nice guy? The earliest work on social cognition examined *impression formation*, the process by which an individual organizes information about another person to form an overall impression of that person.

In a classic early study, students learned that they were about to hear a guest lecturer (Kelley, 1950). Students were randomly assigned to two groups. Those in the first group were told that the lecturer was "a rather warm person, industrious, critical, practical, and determined," while

social cognition The cognitive processes by which people understand and make sense of others and themselves.

central traits The major traits considered in forming impressions of others.

Psych
At The Movies

American History X
This highly disturbing film illuminates the frustration-aggression hypothesis and how it can result in a feedback loop that often perpetuates prejudice, stereotyping, and discrimination.

Hotel Rwanda
In a noble demonstration of altruism, a man uses his unique position and relative wealth and risks his life to save over 1,000 people from genocide.

Twelve Angry Men
This timeless classic depicts a jury deliberation wherein one man attempts to convince 11 others of the defendant's innocence. This classic film demonstrates many social influences, such as conformity, persuasion, and leadership skills.

those in the second group that he was "a rather cold person, industrious, critical, practical, and determined."

The simple substitution of "cold" for "warm" caused drastic differences in the way the students in each group perceived the lecturer, even though he gave the same talk in the same style in each condition. Students who had been told he was "warm" rated him considerably more positively than students who had been told he was "cold."

The findings from this experiment led to additional research on impression formation that focused on the way in which people pay particular attention to certain unusually important traits—known as **central traits**—to help them form an overall impression of others. According to this work, the presence of a central trait alters the meaning of other traits (Jussim, 1989; Neuberg, 1989). Hence, the description of the lecturer as "industrious" presumably meant something different when it was associated with the central trait "warm" than it meant when it was associated with "cold" (Glicksohn & Nahari, 2007; Widmeyer & Loy, 1988).

We make such impressions remarkably quickly. In just a few seconds, using what have been called "thin slices of behaviour" (Ambady & Rosenthal, 1992), we are able to make judgments of people that are often very accurate and that match those of people who make judgments based on longer snippets of behaviour (Choi, Gray, & Ambady, 2004; Pavitt, 2007).

Of course, as we gain more experience with people and see them exhibiting behaviour in a variety of situations, our impressions of them become more complex. However, because our knowledge of others usually has gaps, we still tend to fit individuals into personality schemas that represent particular "types" of people. For instance, we may hold a "gregarious person" schema, made up of the traits of

attribution theory The theory of personality that seeks to explain how we decide, on the basis of samples of an individual's behaviour, what the specific causes of that person's behaviour are.

friendliness, aggressiveness, and openness. The presence of just one or two of those traits may be sufficient for us to assign a person to a particular schema.

Even when schemas are not entirely accurate, they serve an important function: They allow us to develop expectations about how others will behave. Those expectations permit us to plan our interactions with others more easily and serve to simplify a complex social world (Wang & Ross, 2007).

Attribution Processes At one time or another, most of us have puzzled over the reasons behind someone's behaviour. Perhaps it was interpreting the sudden change in mood of a college roommate, or it may have been in more formal circumstances, such as being a judge on a student judiciary board in a cheating case. In contrast to theories of social cognition, which describe how people develop an overall impression of others' personality traits, **attribution theory** seeks to explain how we decide, on the basis of samples of an individual's behaviour, what the *specific* causes of that person's behaviour are.

The general process we use to determine the causes of behaviour and other social occurrences proceeds in several steps. After first noticing that something unusual has happened—for example, golf star Tiger Woods has played a terrible round of golf—we try to interpret the meaning of the event. This leads us to formulate an initial explanation (maybe Woods stayed up late the night before the match). Depending on the time available, the cognitive resources on hand (such as the attention we can give to the matter), and our motivation (determined in part by how important the event is), we may choose to accept our initial explanation or seek to modify it (Woods was sick, perhaps). If we have the time, cognitive resources, and motivation, the event triggers deliberate problem solving as we seek a fuller explanation. During the problem formulation and resolution stage, we may try out several possibilities before we reach a final explanation that seems satisfactory to us (Brown, J., 2006; Malle, 2004).

Figure 9.3
The Process We Use to Explain the Behaviour of Others

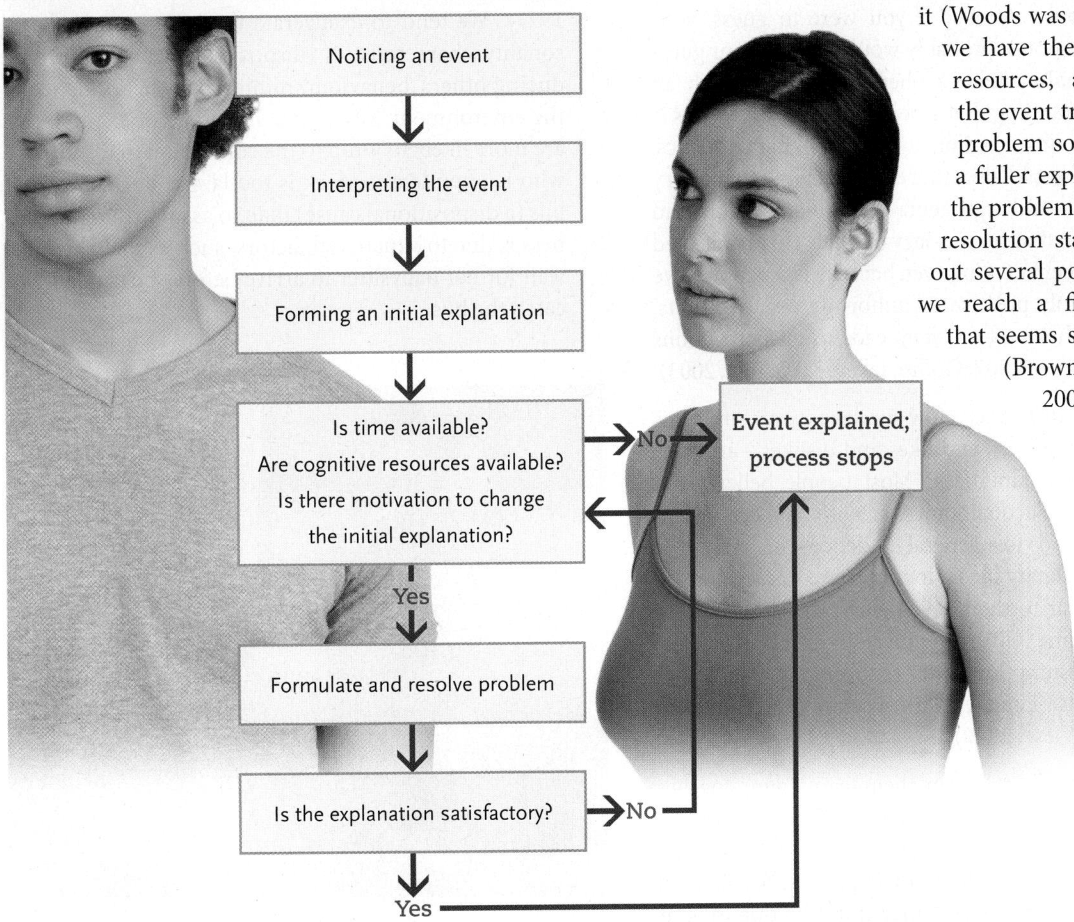

Noticing an event
↓
Interpreting the event
↓
Forming an initial explanation
↓
Is time available? Are cognitive resources available? Is there motivation to change the initial explanation? →No→ Event explained; process stops
↓ Yes
Formulate and resolve problem
↓
Is the explanation satisfactory? →No
↓ Yes

Source: Adapted from Anderson, Krull, & Weiner, 1996.

In seeking an explanation for behaviour, we try to answer the question: Is the cause situational or dispositional? **Situational causes** originate in the environment. For instance, someone who knocks over a litre of milk and then cleans it up probably does the cleaning not because he or she is necessarily a neat person but because the situation requires it. In contrast, a person who spends hours shining the kitchen floor probably does so because he or she is a neat person. In this case, the behaviour has a **dispositional cause**, prompted by the person's disposition (his or her internal traits or personality characteristics).

The central question in making an attribution is whether the cause of behaviour is due to situational (external) or dispositional (internal) factors.

Attribution Biases: To Err Is Human If we always processed information in the rational manner that attribution theory suggests, the world might run a lot more smoothly. Unfortunately, although attribution theory generally makes accurate predictions, people do not always process information about others in as logical a fashion as the theory seems to suggest. In fact, research reveals consistent biases in the ways people make attributions. Typical ones include these:

- *The halo effect.* Harry is intelligent, kind, and loving. Is he also conscientious? If you were to guess, your most likely response probably would be yes. Your guess reflects the **halo effect**, a phenomenon in which an initial understanding that a person has positive traits is used to infer other uniformly positive characteristics. The opposite would also hold true. Learning that Harry was unsociable and argumentative would probably lead you to assume that he was lazy as well. This is referred to as the **horn effect**. However, because few people have either uniformly positive or uniformly negative traits, the halo and horn effect often leads to misperceptions of others (Dennis, 2007; Goffin, Jelley, & Wagner, 2003).

- *Assumed-similarity bias.* How similar to you—in terms of attitudes, opinions, and likes and dislikes—are your friends and acquaintances? Most people believe that their friends and acquaintances are similar to them. But this belief extends to a general tendency—known as the **assumed-similarity bias**—for people to think of others as being similar to them, even when they are meeting for the first time. Given the diversity of people in the world, this assumption often reduces the accuracy of our judgments (Lemay, Clark, Feeney, 2007; Watson, Hubbard, & Wiese, 2000).

- *The self-serving bias.* When their teams win, coaches usually feel that the success is due to their coaching. But when they coach a losing team, coaches may think it's due to the poor skills of their players. Similarly, if you get an A on a test, you may think it's due to your hard work, but if you get a poor grade, it's due to the

situational causes (of behaviour) Perceived causes of behaviour that are based on environmental factors.

dispositional causes (of behaviour) Perceived causes of behaviour that are based on internal traits or personality factors.

halo effect A phenomenon in which an initial understanding that a person has positive traits is used to infer other uniformly positive characteristics.

horn effect Opposite of the halo effect, where a person's negative traits are used to infer other uniformly negative traits.

assumed-similarity bias The tendency to think of people as being similar to oneself, even when meeting them for the first time.

self-serving bias The tendency to attribute personal success to personal factors (skill, ability, or effort) and to attribute failure to factors outside oneself.

fundamental attribution error A tendency to over-attribute others' behaviour to dispositional causes and the corresponding minimization of the importance of situational causes.

professor's inadequacies. The reason is the **self-serving bias**, the tendency to attribute success to personal factors (skill, ability, or effort) and attribute failure to external factors (Bergeron, 2006; Spencer et al., 2003).

- *The fundamental attribution error.* One of the more common attribution biases is the tendency to over-attribute others' behaviour to dispositional causes (internal) and the corresponding failure to recognize the importance of situational (external) causes. Known as the **fundamental attribution error**, this tendency is prevalent in Western cultures (Miller, 1984; Ross, 1977). We tend to exaggerate the importance of personality characteristics (dispositional causes) in producing others' behaviour, minimizing the influence of the environment (situational factors). For example, we are more likely to jump to the conclusion that someone who is often late to work is too lazy to take an earlier bus (a dispositional cause) than to assume that the lateness is due to situational factors, such as that she must wait for her babysitter to arrive before she can leave to catch the bus.

The assumed-similarity bias leads us to believe that others hold similar attitudes, opinions, and likes and dislikes.

Attributions in a Cultural Context Attribution biases do not affect all of us in the same way. Proponents of the socio-cultural approach know that the culture in which we are raised clearly plays a role in how we attribute others' behaviour.

Take, for example, the fundamental attribution error, the tendency to overestimate the importance of personal, dispositional factors and under-attribute situational factors in determining the causes of others' behaviour. The error is pervasive in Western cultures and not in Eastern societies. For instance, adults in India were more likely to use situational attributions than dispositional ones in explaining events. These findings are the opposite of those for North America, and they contradict the fundamental attribution error (Lien et al., 2006; Miller, 1984).

One reason for the difference may lie in the norms and values of Eastern society, which emphasize social responsibility and societal obligations to a greater extent than in Western societies. Cultural differences in attributions may have profound implications. For example, parents in Asia tend to attribute good academic performance to effort and hard work (situational factors). In contrast, parents in Western cultures tend to de-emphasize the role of effort and attribute school success to innate ability (a dispositional factor). As a result, Asian students in general may strive harder to achieve and ultimately outperform North American students in school (Lien et al., 2006; Stevenson, Lee, & Mu, 2000).

The difference in thinking between people in Asian and Western cultures is a reflection of a broader difference in the way the world is perceived. Asian societies generally have a *collectivistic orientation*, a worldview that promotes the notion of interdependence. People with a collectivistic orientation generally see themselves as parts of a larger, interconnected social network and as responsible to others. In contrast, people in Western cultures are more likely to hold an *individualist orientation* that emphasizes personal identity and the uniqueness of the individual. They focus more on what sets them apart from others and what makes them special (Markus & Hamadani, 2007; Markus & Kitayama, 2003; Wang, 2004).

Social Influence and Groups

You have just transferred to a new college and are attending your first class. When the professor enters, the students all immediately begin singing as they fall to their knees and sway side to side. You've never encountered such behaviour, and it makes no sense to you. Is it more likely that you will (1) jump up to join the rest of the class or (2) remain seated?

On the basis of what research has told us about **social influence**, the process by which the actions of an individual or group affect the behaviour of others, a person would almost always choose the first option. As you undoubtedly know from your own experience, pressures to conform can be painfully strong and can bring about changes

Children in Asian societies may perform exceptionally well in school because their culture emphasizes academic success and perseverance.

in behaviour that otherwise never would have occurred (Brehm, Kassin, & Fein, 2005).

Why can conformity pressures in groups be so strong? For one reason, groups, and other people generally, play a central role in our lives. As defined by social psychologists, a **group** consists of two or more people who (1) interact with one another; (2) perceive themselves as part of a group, and (3) are interdependent—that is, the events that affect one group member affect other members, and the behaviour of members has significant consequences for the success of the group in meeting its goals (Brehm et al., 2005).

When groups try to make decisions, two very interesting things happen. While it may seem logical that when people are in a group they would be more moderate about their decisions, the opposite often happens. Sometimes groups make decisions that are more extreme (either more cautious or more risky) than when people make decisions on their own; this is called **group polarization**. This tendency sometimes happens because of another phenomenon, called **group think**. Group think occurs when a highly cohesive group filters out unwanted (although often important) input to reach a consensus. This means that when a group gets along very well and wants to avoid any type of conflict, they are more likely to ignore important information so that they can quickly come to agreement.

social influence The process by which the actions of an individual or group affect the behaviour of others.

group Two or more people who interact with one another; perceive themselves as part of a group, and are interdependent.

group polarization The tendency for groups to make decisions that are more extreme than when people make decisions on their own

group think When a highly cohesive group filters out unwanted (although often important) input to reach a consensus.

Groups develop and hold *norms*, expectations regarding behaviour appropriate to the group. Furthermore, we understand that not adhering to group norms can result in retaliation from other group members, ranging from being ignored to being overtly derided or even being rejected or excluded by the group. Thus, people conform to meet the expectations of the group (Baumeister, Twenge, & Nuss, 2002; Jetten, Hornsey, & Adarves-Yorno, 2006).

Groups exert considerable social influence over individuals, ranging from the mundane, such as the decision to wear a certain kind of jeans, to extreme cases, such as the cruelty of guards at the Abu Ghraib prison in Iraq. We'll consider three types of social pressure: conformity, compliance, and obedience.

CONFORMITY: FOLLOWING WHAT OTHERS DO

Conformity is a change in behaviour or attitudes brought about by a desire to follow the beliefs or standards of other people. Subtle or even unspoken social pressure results in conformity.

The classic demonstration of pressure to conform comes from a series of studies carried out in the 1950s by Solomon Asch (Asch, 1951). In the experiments, the participants thought they were taking part in a test of perceptual skills with six other people. The experimenter showed the participants one card with three lines of varying length and a second card that had a fourth line that matched one of the first three. The task was seemingly straightforward: Each of the participants had to announce aloud which of the first three lines was identical in length to the "standard" line on the second card. Because the correct answer was always obvious, the task seemed easy.

Indeed, the participants all agreed on the first few trials. But then something odd began to happen. From the perspective of the participant in the group who answered last on each trial, all the answers of the first six participants seemed to be wrong—unanimously wrong. And this pattern persisted. Over and over again, the first six participants provided answers that contradicted what the last participant believed to be correct. The last participant faced the dilemma of whether to follow his own perceptions or follow the group by repeating the answer everyone else was giving.

As you might have guessed, this experiment was more contrived than it appeared. The first six participants were actually confederates (paid employees of the experimenter) who had been instructed to give unanimously erroneous answers in many of the trials. And the study had nothing to do with perceptual skills. Instead, the issue under investigation was conformity.

Asch found that in about one-third of the trials, the participants conformed to the unanimous but erroneous group answer, with about 75% of all participants conforming at least once. However, he found strong individual differences. Some participants conformed nearly all the time, whereas others never did.

Since Asch's pioneering work, literally hundreds of studies have examined conformity, and we now know a great deal about the phenomenon. Significant findings focus on:

- *The characteristics of the group.* The more attractive a group is to its members, the greater is its ability to produce conformity. Furthermore, a person's relative **status**, the social rank held within a group, is critical: The lower a person's status in the group, the greater the power of the group over that person's behaviour (Hogg & Hains, 2001).

- *The situation in which the individual is responding.* Conformity is considerably higher when people must respond publicly than it is when they can do so privately.

- *The kind of task.* People working on ambiguous tasks and questions (ones having no clear answer) are more susceptible to social pressure. Asked to give an opinion, such as what type of clothing is fashionable, a person will more likely yield to conformist pressures than he or she will if asked a question of fact. In addition, tasks at which an individual is less competent than others in the group make conformity more likely. For example, a person who is an infrequent computer user may feel

| Standard line | Comparison lines | Which of the three comparison lines is the same length as the "standard" line? |
| 1 2 3 | |

conformity A change in behaviour or attitudes brought about by a desire to follow the beliefs or standards of other people.

status The social rank held within a group.

pressure to conform to an opinion about computer brands when in a group of experienced computer users.

- *Unanimity of the group.* Groups that unanimously support a position show the most pronounced conformity pressures. But what of the case in which people with dissenting views have an ally in the group, known as a **social supporter**, who agrees with them? Having just one person present who puts forward the minority point of view is sufficient to reduce conformity (Goodwin, Costa, & Adonu, 2004; Levine & Moreland, 2006; Prislin, Brewer, & Wilson, 2002).

Conformity to Social Roles Another way in which conformity influences behaviour is through social roles. *Social roles* are the behaviours that are associated with people in a given position. For example, the role of "student" comprises such behaviours as studying, listening to an instructor, and attending class (and perhaps going to the gym, going to the pub, etc.!). Like theatrical roles, social roles tell us what behaviour is associated with a given position.

" Conforming to a social role can have powerful consequences for behaviour. "

Sometimes, though, social roles influence us so profoundly that we engage in behaviour in entirely atypical—and damaging—ways. This fact was brought home in an influential experiment conducted by Philip Zimbardo and colleagues (Zimbardo, 1973). In the study, the researchers set up a mock prison, complete with cells, solitary confinement cubicles, and a small recreation area. The researchers then advertised for students who were willing to spend two weeks in a study of prison life. Once they identified the study participants, the students were randomly assigned by a flip of a coin to be either a prisoner or a prison guard. Neither prisoners nor guards were told how to fulfill their roles (Zimbardo, 1973, 2007; Zimbardo, Maslach, & Haney, 2000).

After just a few days in this mock prison, the students assigned to be guards became abusive to the prisoners, waking them at odd hours and subjecting them to arbitrary punishment. They withheld food from the prisoners and forced them into hard labour. In contrast, the students assigned to the prisoner role soon became docile and submissive to the guards. They became extremely demoralized, and one slipped into a depression so severe he was released after just a few days. In fact, after only six days of captivity, the remaining prisoners' reactions became so extreme that the study was ended (although it was initially intended to last two weeks). If you would like to learn more about the Stanford Prison experiment, visit www.prisonexp.org.

The experiment (which, it's important to note, drew criticism on both methodological and ethical grounds) provided a clear lesson: conforming to a social role can have a powerful consequence on the behaviour of even normal,

social supporter A group member whose dissenting views make nonconformity to the group easier.

deindividuation Feeling less personally responsible and self-conscious when in a group.

well-adjusted people, inducing them to change their behaviour in sometimes undesirable ways. This phenomenon may explain how members of the Canadian Airborne Regiment (CAR) on a peacekeeping mission in Somalia came to torture and murder a 16–year-old boy they thought was trying to steal from the CAR base (Shorey, 2000).

The Stanford Prison experiment also demonstrates **deindividuation**, a feeling one has of being less personally responsible and self-conscious when in a group. The presence of a group can increase arousal and make individuals feel less personally responsible for their actions. Deindividuation can help explain why more damage to property occurs on Halloween when people are dressed in costume. The presence of others increases arousal and makes them feel less personally responsible, and the costume provides a feeling of anonymity, a combination of factors that sometimes increases the chances of bad things happening. Deindividuation may also explain the role of the Canadian Airborne Regiment on the torture of the Somalia boy, and the behaviour of the guards at Abu Ghraib in Iraq.

COMPLIANCE: SUBMITTING TO DIRECT SOCIAL PRESSURE

When we refer to conformity, we usually mean a phenomenon in which the social pressure is subtle or indirect. But in some situations social pressure is much more obvious, with direct, explicit pressure to endorse a particular point of

Get Involved!

You can do your own observational study of how people react to broken social norms.

How do others react if you face the back or side of the elevator? If you wear your pyjamas to class? If you read out loud in a coffee shop? If you offer small coins to someone on a downtown street (Hey, buddy, here's some extra change)?

Study tip

To differentiate among the three types of social pressure—conformity, compliance, and obedience—you need to know the nature and the strength of the social pressure brought to bear on a person.

view or behave in a certain way. Social psychologists call the type of behaviour that occurs in response to direct social pressure **compliance**.

Several specific techniques represent attempts to gain compliance, including these:

- *Foot-in-the-door technique.* A salesperson comes to your door and asks you to accept a small sample. You agree, thinking you have nothing to lose. A little later comes a larger request, which, because you have already agreed to the first one, you have a hard time turning down (Beaman, 1983; Freedman & Fraser, 1966).

  The salesperson in this case is using a tried-and-true strategy that social psychologists call the **foot-in-the-door technique**. In this technique, you ask a person to agree to a small request and later ask that person to comply with a more important one. It turns out that compliance with the more important request increases significantly when the person first agrees to the smaller favour.

  Why does the foot-in-the-door technique work? One theoretical explanation suggests that involvement with the small request leads to an interest in an issue, and taking an action—any action—makes the individual more committed to the issue, thereby increasing the likelihood of future compliance (Beaman, 1983). Another explanation revolves around people's self-perceptions. By complying with the initial request, individuals may come to see themselves as people who provide help when asked. Then, when confronted with the larger request, they agree to avoid cognitive dissonance, as described earlier. Although we don't know if either of these two explanations is more accurate or if another theory might provide better answers, it is clear that the foot-in-the-door strategy is effective (Bloom, McBride, & Pollak, 2006; Burger & Caldwell, 2003).

- *Door-in-the-face technique.* A fundraiser asks for a $500 contribution. You laughingly refuse, telling her that the amount is way out of your league. She then asks for a $10 contribution. What do you do? If you are like most people, you'll probably be a lot more compliant than you would be if she hadn't asked for the huge contribution first. In this tactic, called the **door-in-the-face** technique, someone makes a large request, expecting it to be refused, and follows it with a smaller one. This strategy, which is the opposite of the foot-in-the-door approach, has also proved to be very effective (Millar, 2002; Pascual & Gueguen, 2005, 2006).

  The use of this technique is widespread. You may have tried it at some point, perhaps by asking your parents for a large increase in your allowance and later settling for less. Similarly, television writers, by sometimes sprinkling their scripts with obscenities that they know will be cut out by network censors, hope to keep key phrases intact (Cialdini & Sagarin, 2005).

- *The low-ball technique.* Have you ever purchased a car from a dealership? If so, you have likely experienced the **low-ball technique**. After having taken the car for a test drive you decide that you want the car and you negotiate a deal with the salesperson. She has you sign the papers and tells you to wait while she has her manager sign off on the deal. While she is gone you are imagining yourself driving your new car, visualizing all the looks you will get cruising downtown. Just then, the salesperson comes back into the office and says the manager will not agree to that price, but you can have it for just $1,000 more. While you may initially consider walking away from the deal, you will likely still purchase the car because you have already made a commitment in your own mind that you will do so and you will feel cognitive dissonance if you do not. The low-ball technique involves someone first offering something for a low price to gain agreement and then increasing the price after the buyer has made a commitment to purchase.

- *That's-not-all technique.* In this technique, a salesperson offers you a deal at an inflated price. But immediately after the initial offer, the salesperson offers an incentive, discount, or bonus to clinch the deal. This is a common tactic used by late-night television advertisements for products not often available in stores.

  Although it sounds transparent, the **that's-not-all technique** can be quite effective. In one study, the experimenters set up a booth and sold cupcakes for 75 cents each. In one condition, the experimenters directly told customers that the price was 75 cents. But in another condition, they told customers that the price was originally $1 but had been reduced to 75 cents. As we might predict, more people bought cupcakes at the "reduced" price—even though it was identical to the price in the other experimental condition (Burger, Reed, & DeCesare, 1999; Pratkanis, 2007).

- *Not-so-free sample.* If you ever receive a free sample, keep in mind that it comes with a psychological cost. Although they may not couch it in these terms, salespeople who provide samples to potential customers do so to instigate the norm of reciprocity. The *norm of*

compliance Behaviour that occurs in response to direct social pressure.

foot-in-the-door technique Asking a person to agree to a small request, and then later asking that person to comply with a larger, more important one.

door-in-the-face technique Making a large request, expecting it to be refused, and following it with a smaller one.

low-ball technique First offering something for a low price to gain agreement, and then increasing the price after the buyer has made a commitment to purchase.

that's-not-all technique Offering a deal at an inflated price, and then immediately after the initial offer, offering an incentive, discount, or bonus to clinch the deal.

Can You Resist Persuasion?

As a consumer of information you are faced with advertisements written by talented individuals who are experts at persuading you to purchase their products. Advertisers would not spend millions of dollars for a 30-second commercial or a page in a magazine if they were not effective! Knowing this information, as well as knowing the different techniques of persuasion, you may feel like you are not able to resist these persuasive advertisements. But you can! You can use information from social psychology to help combat these persuasive techniques. One social psychology theory that would be most helpful is called inoculation theory (McGuire & Papageorgis, 1961). This theory is based on the analogy of a medical inoculation, where you would receive immunizations to

protect you from diseases. Inoculation theory states that you must first strengthen your own attitudes and beliefs so you can ward off the persuasive attack. One way to do this is by being forewarned about the persuasive tactics that advertisers use. For example, we explained several of these tactics in this chapter such as the *not-so-free sample*, *that's-not-all technique*, and *foot-in-the-door technique*. Having information about these tactics is your first defence! The other important part of inoculation theory is to develop counterarguments to refute the persuasive attack. Thinking about the other side of the issue will make you more effective at counterarguing, and therefore, more effective at resisting persuasion!

reciprocity is the well-accepted societal standard dictating that we should treat other people as they treat us. Receiving a **not-so-free sample**, then, suggests the need for reciprocation—in the form of a purchase, of course (Cialdini, 2006; Park & Antonioni, 2007; Spiller & Wymer, 2001).

Obedience Compliance techniques are used to gently lead people toward agreement with a request. In some cases, however, requests aim to produce **obedience**, a change in behaviour in response to the commands of others. Although obedience is considerably less common than conformity and compliance, it does occur in several specific kinds of relationships (Nowak, Vallacher & Miller, 2003). For example, we may show obedience to our bosses, teachers, or parents merely because of the power they hold to reward or punish us.

To acquire an understanding of obedience, consider for a moment how you might respond if a stranger said to you:

I've devised a new way of improving memory. All I need is for you to teach people a list of words and then give them a test. The test procedure requires only that you give learners a shock each time they make a mistake on the test. To administer the shocks you will use a "shock generator" that gives shocks ranging from 15 to 450 volts. You can see that the switches are labelled from "slight shock" through "danger: severe shock" at the top level, where there are three red Xs. But don't worry; although the shocks may be painful, they will cause no permanent damage.

not-so-free sample Offering a free sample to instigate the norm of reciprocity (i.e., that we should treat other people as they treat us).

obedience A change in behaviour in response to the commands of others.

Presented with this situation, you would be likely to think that neither you nor anyone else would go along with the stranger's unusual request. Clearly, it lies outside the bounds of what we consider good sense.

Or does it? Suppose the stranger asking for your help were a psychologist conducting an experiment. Or suppose the request came from your teacher, your employer, or your military commander—all people in authority with a seemingly legitimate reason for the request.

If you still believe it's unlikely that you would comply—think again. The situation presented above describes a classic experiment conducted by social psychologist Stanley Milgram in the 1960s. In the study, an experimenter told participants to give increasingly stronger shocks to another person as part of a study on learning. In reality, the experiment had nothing to do with learning; the real issue under consideration was the degree to which participants would comply with the experimenter's requests. In fact, the "learner" supposedly receiving the shocks was a confederate who never really received any punishment (Milgram, 2005).

Most people who hear a description of Milgram's experiment feel that it is unlikely that any participant would give the maximum level of shock—or, for that matter, any shock at all. Even a group of psychiatrists to whom the situation was described predicted that fewer than 2% of the participants would fully comply and administer the strongest shocks (Milgram, 1963, 1974).

However, the actual results contradicted both experts' and non-experts' predictions. Some 65% of the participants eventually used the highest setting on the shock generator—450 volts—to shock the learner. This obedience occurred even though the learner, who had mentioned at the start of the experiment that he had a heart condition, demanded to be released, screaming, "Let me out of here!

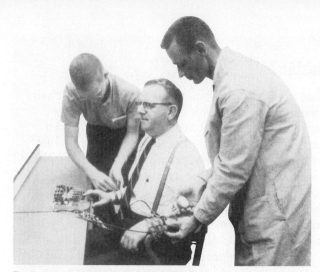

The "learner" in Milgram's experiment was connected to a "shock generator" by electrodes attached to the skin—or so the study participants were led to believe.

Source: Copyright 1965 by Stanley Milgram. From the film *Obedience*, distributed by the New York University Film Library and Pennsylvania State University, PCR.

Let me out of here! My heart's bothering me. Let me out of here!" Despite the learner's pleas, most participants continued to administer the shocks.

Why did so many individuals comply with the experimenter's demands? The participants, who were extensively interviewed after the experiment, said they obeyed primarily because they believed that the experimenter would be responsible for any potential ill effects that befell the learner. The participants accepted the experimenter's orders, then, because they thought that they personally could not be held accountable for their actions—they could always blame the experimenter (Blass, 1996, 2004).

> ## Milgram's experiment forces us to ask ourselves this question: Would we be able to withstand the intense power of authority?

Although most participants in the Milgram experiment later agreed that the knowledge gained from the study outweighed the discomfort they may have felt, the experiment has been criticized for creating an extremely trying set of circumstances for the participants, thereby raising serious ethical concerns. (For ethical reasons the experiment could not be conducted today.) Other critics have suggested that Milgram's methods were ineffective in creating a situation that actually mirrored real-world obedience. For example, how often are people placed in a situation in which someone orders them to continue hurting a victim, while the victim's protests are ignored (Blass, 2000, 2004)?

Despite these concerns, Milgram's research remains the strongest laboratory demonstration of obedience. We need only consider actual instances of obedience to authority to witness some frightening real-life parallels.

For instance, after World War II, the major defence that Nazi officers gave to excuse their participation in atrocities during the war was that they were "only following orders." Milgram's experiment, which was motivated in part by his desire to explain the behaviour of everyday Germans during World War II, forces us to ask ourselves this question: Would we be able to withstand the intense power of authority?

One question that remains is whether people would still obey today as they did back in the 1960s. Some have argued that people today would not blindly follow authority as they would have back then (Burger, 2009). Jerry Burger, a social psychologist from Santa Clara University in California, replicated Milgrim's obedience study (Burger, 2009). One of the major issues in replicating the original study is to do so without violating any ethical concerns. One way that Burger dealt with this issue was to stop the level of shocks at 150 V rather than the extreme 450 V that Milgram used in his study. Burger was also very cautious about how he chose his participants; individuals were removed from the study if they had a previous knowledge of psychology or if they had any psychological disorders or medical conditions. They were also told on several occasions that they could stop the study at any time. Burger hypothesized that participants would behave very similarly to how they behaved in the 1960s and this hypothesis was supported in his replication of the study. Burger found that participants administered shocks up to the 150 V level at a rate that was only slightly below the participants in Milgram's original study. Burger thought this may have been slightly lower because the participants in his study were told on several occasions that they could stop the study at any moment, unlike Milgram's original study. Although a complete replication of Milgrim's study was not possible, Burger was able to demonstrate that people today will obey the orders of an authority figure even if it means another person will be hurt.

From the perspective of ...

A POLICE OFFICER Getting some suspects to comply can be a major issue for many police officers. How might you promote obedience when out in the community? What are some of the potentially harmful ways that police officers could use their social influence to elicit obedience?

Psych <u>think</u>

> > > If you were a participant in a replication of Milgrim's study today, but had no knowledge of the results of the study, do you think you would administer shocks to another individual that were potentially dangerous?

Stereotypes, Prejudice, and Discrimination

What do you think when someone says, "He's African Canadian," "She's Chinese," "That's a woman driver," "He's a white guy"?

If you're like most people, you'll probably automatically form some sort of impression of what each person is like. Most likely your impression is based on a **stereotype**, a set of generalized beliefs and expectations about a specific group and its members. Stereotypes, which may be negative or positive, grow out of our tendency to categorize and organize the vast amount of information we encounter in our everyday lives. All stereotypes share the common feature of oversimplifying the world: We view individuals not in terms of their unique, personal characteristics but in terms of characteristics we attribute to all the members of a particular group.

Stereotypes can lead to **prejudice**, a negative (or positive) evaluation of a group and its members. For instance, racial prejudice occurs when a member of a racial group is evaluated in terms of race and not because of his or her own characteristics or abilities. Although prejudice can be positive ("I love the Irish"), social psychologists have focused on understanding the roots of negative prejudice ("I hate immigrants").

Common stereotypes and forms of prejudice involve racial, religious, gender, and ethnic groups. Over the years, various groups have been called "lazy" or "shrewd" or "cruel" with varying degrees of regularity by those who are not members of that group. Even today, despite major progress toward reducing legally sanctioned forms of prejudice, such as school segregation, stereotypes remain (Eberhardt et al., 2004; Hunt, Seifert, & Armenta, 2006; Pettigrew, 2004b).

stereotype A set of generalized beliefs and expectations about a particular group and its members.

prejudice A negative (or positive) evaluation of a particular group and its members.

discrimination Behaviour directed toward individuals on the basis of their membership in a particular group.

Although usually backed by little or no evidence, stereotypes can have harmful consequences. Acting on negative stereotypes results in **discrimination**—behaviour directed toward individuals on the basis of their membership in a particular group. Discrimination can lead to exclusion from jobs, neighbourhoods, and educational opportunities and may result in lower salaries and benefits for members of specific groups. Discrimination can also result in more favourable treatment to favoured groups, as when an employer hires a job applicant of her own racial group because of the applicant's race.

Stereotyping not only leads to overt discrimination but also can cause members of stereotyped groups to behave in ways that reflect the stereotype through a phenomenon known as the *self-fulfilling prophecy*. Self-fulfilling prophecies are expectations about the occurrence of a future event or behaviour that act to increase the likelihood that the event or behaviour will occur. For example, if people think that members of a specific group lack ambition, they may treat them in a way that actually brings about a lack of ambition (Madon, Willard, & Guyll, 2006; Oskamp, 2000; Seibt & Förster, 2005).

Study tip Remember that *prejudice* relates to *attitudes* about a group and its members, whereas *discrimination* relates to *behaviour* directed to a group and its members.

THE FOUNDATIONS OF PREJUDICE

No one has ever been born disliking a specific racial, religious, or ethnic group. People learn to hate, in much the same way that they learn the alphabet.

According to *observational learning approaches* to stereotyping and prejudice, the behaviour of parents, other adults, and peers shapes children's feelings about members of various groups. For instance, bigoted parents may commend their children for expressing prejudiced attitudes. Likewise, young children learn prejudice by imitating the behaviour of adult models. Such learning starts at an early age: children as young as three years of age begin to show preferences for members of their own race (Dovidio & Gaertner, 2006; Nesdale, Maass, & Durkin, 2005; Schneider, 2003).

The mass media also provide information about stereotypes, not just for children but also for adults. When inaccurate portrayals are the primary source of information about minority groups, they can lead to the development and maintenance of unfavourable stereotypes (Coltraine & Messineo, 2000; Do, 2006; Ward, 2004).

Other explanations of prejudice and discrimination focus on how being a member of a specific group helps to magnify one's sense of self-esteem. According to *social identity theory*, we use group membership as a source of pride and self-worth. Social identity theory suggests that

According to observational learning approaches to stereotyping and prejudice, the behaviour of parents, other adults, and peers shapes children's feelings about members of various groups.

people tend to be *ethnocentric*, viewing the world from their own perspective and judging others in terms of their group membership. Slogans such as "gay pride" and "black is beautiful" illustrate that the groups to which we belong furnish us with a sense of self-respect (Hogg, 2006; Rowley et al., 1998; Tajfel & Turner, 2004).

However, the use of group membership to provide social respect produces an unfortunate outcome. In an effort to maximize our sense of self-esteem, we may come to think that our own group (our *ingroup*) is better than groups to which we don't belong (our *outgroups*). Consequently, we inflate the positive aspects of our ingroup—and, at the same time, devalue outgroups. Ultimately, we come to view members of outgroups as inferior to members of our ingroup (Tajfel & Turner, 2004). The end result is prejudice toward members of groups of which we are not a part.

For example, Stephen Wright from Simon Fraser University and others completed two studies that looked at whether or not members of ethnic minority groups (Asians, Latinos, and Blacks) would differ in their level of trust and acceptance when interacting with majority groups (Whites) (Tropp, Stout, Boatswain, Wright, & Pettigrew, 2006). The researchers told hypothetical stories about interactions with outgroups of people to a group of university students. The students had to rate their feeling of trust and acceptance when the outgroup referred to his/her ethnicity. Results determined that members of an ingroup reported more feelings of trust and acceptance with members of their own group compared to the feelings of trust and acceptance they felt with members of an outgroup.

In another study, Michael Schmitt from Simon Fraser University and his American colleagues looked at racial attitudes of privileged white Americans to test how social identity might impact racism (Branscombe, Schmitt, & Schiffhauer, 2007). The researchers found that those who were highly identified as white Americans and who

admitted to being the privileged race were more likely to justify their superior outcomes by promoting modern racists beliefs.

MEASURING PREJUDICE AND DISCRIMINATION: THE IMPLICIT ASSOCIATION TEST

Could you be prejudiced and not even know it? The answer, according to the researchers who developed the Implicit Association Test (IAT), is probably yes. People are often careful about revealing their true attitudes about members of various groups, not only to others but also to themselves. Even though they may truly believe that they are unprejudiced, the reality is that they actually routinely differentiate between people on the basis of race, ethnicity, and sexual orientation.

> "People are often careful about revealing their true attitudes about members of various groups, not only to others but also to themselves."

The IAT is an ingenious measure of prejudice that permits a more accurate assessment of people's discrimination between members of different groups. It was developed, in part, as a reaction to the difficulty in finding a questionnaire that would reveal prejudice. Direct questions such as "Would you prefer interacting with a member of Group X rather than Group Y?" typically identify only the most blatant prejudices, because people try to censor their responses (Greenwald, Nosek, & Sriram, 2006; Rudman & Ashmore, 2007).

In contrast, the IAT makes use of the fact that people's automatic reactions often provide the most valid indicator of what they actually believe. Having grown up in a culture that teaches us to think about members of particular groups in specific ways, we tend to absorb associations about those groups that are reflective of the culture (Lane et al., 2007).

The results of the IAT show that almost 90% of the people who take the test have a pro-white implicit bias, and more than two-thirds of non-Arab, non-Muslim test-takers display implicit biases against Arab Muslims. Moreover, more than 80% of heterosexuals display an implicit bias against gays and lesbians (Wittenbrink & Schwarz, 2007).

Of course, having an implicit bias does not mean that people will overtly discriminate, a criticism that has been made of the test. Yet it does mean that the cultural lessons to which we are exposed have a considerable unconscious influence on us. (Interested in how you would perform on the IAT? Go to this Web site to take the test: https://implicit.harvard.edu/implicit.)

REDUCING PREJUDICE AND DISCRIMINATION

How can we diminish the effects of prejudice and discrimination? Psychologists have developed several strategies that have proved effective.

- *Increasing contact between the target of stereotyping and the holder of the stereotype.* Research has shown consistently that increasing the amount of interaction between people can reduce negative stereotyping. But only certain kinds of contact are likely to reduce prejudice and discrimination. Situations in which contact is relatively intimate, the individuals are of equal status, or participants must cooperate with one another or are dependent on one another are more likely to reduce stereotyping (Dovidio, Gaertner, & Kawakami, 2003; Pettigrew & Tropp, 2006; Tropp & Pettigrew, 2005).

- *Making values and norms against prejudice more conspicuous.* Sometimes just reminding people about the values they already hold regarding equality and fair treatment of others is enough to reduce discrimination. Similarly, people who hear others making strong, vehement anti-racist statements are subsequently more likely to strongly condemn racism (Czopp & Monteith, 2005; Tropp & Bianchi, 2006).

- *Providing information about the targets of stereotyping.* Probably the most direct means of changing stereotypical and discriminatory attitudes is education: teaching people to be more aware of the positive characteristics of targets of stereotyping. For instance, when the meaning

From the perspective of …

A CORRECTIONS OFFICER How might overt forms of prejudice and discrimination toward disadvantaged groups be reduced in a correctional facility?

of behaviour is explained to people who hold stereotypes, they may come to appreciate the significance of the behaviour (Banks, 2006; Isbell & Tyler, 2003; Nagda, Tropp, & Paluck, 2006).

Positive and Negative Social Behaviour

Are people basically good or bad? Is it human nature to be loving, considerate, unselfish, and noble, or is humankind essentially violent and cruel?

Social psychologists have taken different approaches to try to answer these questions. Here we consider what they have learned about what attracts us to others and about two conflicting sides of human behaviour—aggression and helping.

LIKING AND LOVING: INTERPERSONAL ATTRACTION AND THE DEVELOPMENT OF RELATIONSHIPS

Nothing is more important in most people's lives than their feelings for others (McAdams, 1989). Unsurprisingly, then, liking and loving have become a major focus of interest for social psychologists. Known more formally as the study of **interpersonal attraction**, or **close relationships**, this area addresses the factors that lead to positive feelings for others.

How Do I Like Thee? Let Me Count the Ways By far the greatest amount of research has focused on liking, probably because it is easier and infinitely less expensive for investigators to conduct short-term experiments to produce states of liking in strangers who have just met than to instigate and observe loving relationships over long periods. Consequently, research has given us a good deal of knowledge about the factors that initially attract two people to each other. The important factors considered by social psychologists are the following:

- *Proximity.* If you live in residence or an apartment, consider the friends you made when you first moved in. Chances are that you became friendliest with those who lived geographically closest to you. In fact, this is one of the more firmly established findings in the literature on interpersonal attraction: Proximity leads to liking (Burgoon et al., 2002; Smith & Weber, 2005).

- *Mere exposure.* Repeated exposure to a person is often sufficient to produce attraction. Interestingly, repeated exposure to any stimulus—a person, picture, compact disc, or virtually anything—usually makes us like the stimulus more. Becoming familiar with a person can evoke positive feelings; we then transfer the positive feelings stemming from familiarity to the person (Butler & Berry, 2004; Zajonc, 2001).

interpersonal attraction (or close relationship)
Positive feelings for others; liking and loving.

- *Similarity.* Folk wisdom tells us that birds of a feather flock together. However, it also maintains that opposites attract. Social psychologists have come up with a clear verdict regarding which of the two statements is correct: we tend to like those who are similar to us. Discovering that others have similar attitudes, values, or traits promotes our liking for them. Furthermore, the more similar others are, the more we like them (Bates, 2002; Umphress, Smith-Crowe, & Brief, 2007).

- *Physical attractiveness.* For most people, the equation *beautiful = good* is true. As a result, physically attractive people are more popular than are physically unattractive ones, if all other factors are equal. This finding, which contradicts the values that most people say they hold, is apparent even in childhood—with nursery-school-age children rating their peers' popularity on the basis of attractiveness—and continues into adulthood. Indeed, physical attractiveness may be the single most important element promoting initial liking in college dating situations, although its influence eventually decreases when people get to know each other better (Dion, Berscheid & Walster, 1972; Langlois et al., 2000; Little, Burt, & Perrett, 2006; Zebrowitz & Montepare, 2005).

DID YOU KNOW?

Men show much higher consensus than women when judging physical attractiveness. No wonder to achieve celebrity in our culture, women must all look like J Lo, but Lyle Lovett's, Jason Alexander's, and Jack Nicholson's looks didn't block their climb to the top.

These factors alone, of course, do not account for liking. For example, in one experiment that examined the desired qualities in a friendship, the top-rated qualities in a same-sex friend included sense of humour, warmth and kindness, expressiveness and openness, an exciting personality, and similarity of interests and leisure activities (Sprecher & Reagan, 2002).

How Do I Love Thee? Let Me Count the Ways Whereas our knowledge of what makes people like one another is extensive, our scientific understanding of romantic love is more limited in scope and recently acquired. As a first step, researchers tried to identify the characteristics that distinguish between liking and loving. They discovered that love is not simply a greater quantity of liking, but a qualitatively different psychological state. For instance, at least in its early stages, romantic love includes relatively intense physiological arousal, an all-encompassing interest in another individual, fantasizing about the other, and relatively rapid swings of emotion. Similarly, romantic love, unlike liking, includes elements of passion, closeness, fascination, exclusiveness, sexual desire, and intense caring. We idealize partners by exaggerating their good qualities and

passionate (or romantic) love A state of intense absorption in someone that includes intense physiological arousal, psychological interest, and caring for the needs of another.

companionate love The strong affection we have for those with whom our lives are deeply involved.

minimizing their imperfections (Garza-Guerrero, 2000; Murray, Holmes, & Griffin, 2004).

Other researchers have theorized that there are two main types of love: passionate love and companionate love. **Passionate (or romantic) love** represents a state of intense absorption in someone. It includes intense physiological arousal, psychological interest, and caring for the needs of another. In contrast, **companionate love** is the strong affection we have for those with whom our lives are deeply involved. The love we feel for our parents, other family members, and some close friends falls into the category of companionate love (Hendrick & Hendrick, 2003; Masuda, 2003; Regan, 2006).

Psychologist Robert Sternberg makes an even finer differentiation between types of love. He proposes that love consists of three parts:

- *Decision/commitment*, the initial thoughts that one loves someone and the longer-term feelings of commitment to maintain love

- *Intimacy component*, feelings of closeness and connectedness

- *Passion component*, the motivational drives relating to sex, physical closeness, and romance.

According to Sternberg, these three components combine to produce the different types of love. He suggests that different combinations of the three components vary over the course of relationships. For example, in strong, loving relationships the level of commitment peaks and then

Figure 9.4
Sternberg's Three Types of Love

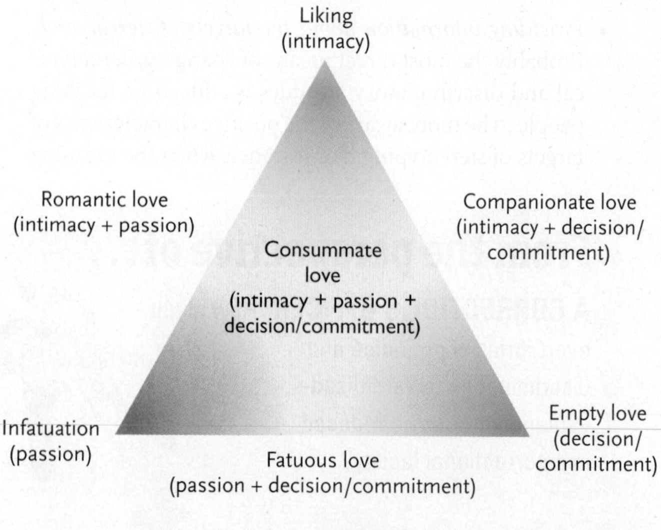

Liking
(intimacy)

Romantic love
(intimacy + passion)

Companionate love
(intimacy + decision/
commitment)

Consummate
love
(intimacy + passion +
decision/commitment)

Infatuation
(passion)

Empty love
(decision/
commitment)

Fatuous love
(passion + decision/commitment)

remains stable. Passion, in contrast, peaks quickly and then declines and levels off relatively early in most relationships. In addition, relationships are happiest in which the strengths of the various components are similar for both partners (Sternberg, Hojjat, & Barnes, 2001; Sternberg, 2004a, 2006).

Liking and loving clearly show a positive side of human social behaviour. Now we turn to behaviours that are just as much a part of social behaviour: aggression and helping behaviour.

AGGRESSION AND PROSOCIAL BEHAVIOUR

Drive-by shootings, carjackings, and abductions are just a few examples of the violence that seems all too common today. Yet we also find examples of generous, unselfish, thoughtful behaviour that suggest a more optimistic view of humankind. Rigoberta Menchú Tum, an indigenous Guatemalan who campaigns tirelessly for civil rights on behalf of indigenous peoples and who won the Nobel Peace Prize in 1992, may epitomize this type of behaviour. Or contemplate the simple kindnesses of life: lending a valued compact disc, stopping to help a child who has fallen off her bicycle, or merely sharing a candy bar with a friend. Such instances of helping are no less characteristic of human behaviour than are the distasteful examples of aggression.

Hurting Others: Aggression We need look no further than the daily paper or the nightly news to be bombarded with examples of aggression, both on a societal level (war, terrorist attacks, assassination) and on an individual level (crime, child abuse, and the many petty cruelties humans are capable of inflicting on one another). Is such aggression an inevitable part of the human condition? Or is aggression primarily a product of particular circumstances that, if changed, could lead to its reduction?

The difficulty of answering such knotty questions becomes apparent as soon as we consider how best to define the term *aggression*. Depending on the way we define the word, many examples of inflicted pain or injury may or may

Source: Benjamin (1985).

Is This Aggression?

To see for yourself the difficulties involved in defining aggression, consider each of the following acts and determine whether it represents aggressive behaviour—according to your own definition of aggression.

1. A spider eats a fly. Yes_____ No_____
2. Two wolves fight for the leadership of the pack. Yes_____ No_____
3. A soldier shoots an enemy at the front line. Yes_____ No_____
4. The warden of a prison executes a convicted criminal. Yes_____ No_____
5. A man viciously kicks a cat. Yes_____ No_____
6. A man, while cleaning a window, knocks over a flower pot, which, in falling, injures a pedestrian. Yes_____ No_____
7. Mr. X, a notorious gossip, speaks disparagingly of many people of his acquaintance. Yes_____ No_____
8. A man mentally rehearses a murder he is about to commit. Yes_____ No_____
9. An angry son purposely fails to write to his mother, who is expecting a letter and will be hurt if none arrives. Yes_____ No_____
10. An enraged boy tries with all his might to inflict injury on his antagonist, a bigger boy, but is not successful in doing so. His efforts simply amuse the bigger boy. Yes____ No_____
11. A senator does not protest the escalation of bombing to which she is normally opposed. Yes____ No_____
12. A farmer beheads a chicken and prepares it for supper. Yes ____ No _____
13. A hunter kills an animal and mounts it as a trophy. Yes_____ No_____
14. A physician gives a flu shot to a screaming child. Yes_____ No_____
15. A boxer gives his opponent a bloody nose. Yes_____ No_____
16. A Girl Scout tries to assist an elderly woman but trips her by accident. Yes____ No____
17. A bank robber is shot in the back while trying to escape. Yes_____ No_____
18. A tennis player smashes her racket after missing a volley. Yes_____ No_____
19. A person commits suicide. Yes_____ No_____
20. A cat kills a mouse, parades around with it, and then discards it. Yes____ No_____

aggression The intentional injury of, or harm to, another person.

catharsis The process of discharging built-up aggressive energy.

not qualify as aggression. For instance, a rapist is clearly acting with aggression toward his victim. It is less certain that a physician carrying out an emergency medical procedure without an anaesthetic, thereby causing incredible pain to the patient, should be considered aggressive.

Most social psychologists define aggression in terms of the intent and the purpose behind the behaviour. **Aggression** is intentional injury or harm to another person (Anderson, 2004). By this definition, the rapist is clearly acting aggressively, whereas the physician causing pain during a medical procedure is not (Berkowitz, 2001).

Social psychologists have developed several approaches to the scientific study of aggressive behaviour, including instinct, frustration-aggression, and observational learning theories.

Instinct Approaches If you have ever punched an adversary in the nose, you may have experienced a certain satisfaction, despite your better judgment. Instinct theories, noting the prevalence of aggression not only in humans but also in animals, propose that aggression is primarily the outcome of innate—or inborn—urges.

Sigmund Freud (1920) was one of the first to suggest, as part of his theory of personality, that aggression is a primary instinctual drive. Konrad Lorenz, an ethologist (a scientist who studies animal behaviour), expanded on Freud's notions by arguing that humans, along with members of other species, have a fighting instinct, which in earlier times ensured protection of food supplies and weeded out the weaker of the species (Lorenz, 1966, 1974). Lorenz's instinct approach led to the controversial notion that aggressive energy constantly builds up within an individual until the person finally discharges it in a process called **catharsis**. The longer the energy builds up, says Lorenz, the greater will be the amount of the aggression displayed when it is discharged.

However, little research has found evidence for the existence of a pent-up reservoir of aggression that needs to be released. In fact, some studies flatly contradict the notion of catharsis, leading psychologists to look for other explanations for aggression (Bushman & Anderson, 2002; Bushman, Wang, & Anderson, 2005; Scheele & DuBois, 2006).

Frustration-Aggression Approaches Frustration-aggression theory suggests that *frustration* (the reaction to the thwarting or blocking of goals) produces anger, leading to a readiness to act aggressively. Whether actual aggression occurs depends on the presence of *aggressive cues*, stimuli that have been associated in the past with actual aggression or violence and that will trigger aggression again (Berkowitz, 2001).

What kinds of stimuli act as aggressive cues? They can range from the most explicit, such as the presence of

weapons, to more subtle cues, such as the mere mention of the name of an individual who behaved violently in the past. For example, angered participants in experiments behave significantly more aggressively when in the presence of a gun than a comparable situation in which no guns are present. Similarly, frustrated participants who view a violent movie are more physically aggressive toward a confederate with the same name as the star of the movie than they are toward a confederate with a different name. It appears, then, that frustration does lead to aggression, at least when aggressive cues are present (Berkowitz, 2001; Marcus-Newhall, Pederson, & Carlson, 2000).

Study tip

Understand the distinction between the instinctual, frustration-aggression, and observational learning approaches to aggression.

Observational Learning Approaches Do we learn to be aggressive? The observational learning (sometimes called social learning) approach to aggression says that we do. Taking an almost opposite view from instinct theories, which focus on innate explanations of aggression, observational learning theory emphasizes that social and environmental conditions can teach individuals to be aggressive. The theory sees aggression not as inevitable, but rather as a learned response that can be understood in terms of rewards and punishments.

Observational learning theory pays particular attention not only to direct rewards and punishments that individuals themselves receive but also to the rewards and punishments that models—individuals who provide a guide to appropriate behaviour—receive for their aggressive behaviour. According to observational learning theory, people observe the behaviour of models and the subsequent consequences of that behaviour. If the consequences are positive, the behaviour is likely to be imitated when observers find themselves in a similar situation (Askew & Field, 2008; Green & Osborne, 1985).

From the perspective of . . .

A HOCKEY COACH How would checking someone into the boards be interpreted by proponents of the three main approaches to the study of aggression: instinct approaches, frustration-aggression approaches, and observational learning approaches? Do you think any of these approaches fits this example better than the others?

BUY IT?

Dealing Effectively with Anger

At one time or another, almost everyone feels angry. The anger may result from a frustrating situation, or it may be due to the behaviour of another individual. The way we deal with anger may determine the difference between a promotion and a lost job or a broken relationship and one that mends itself. How can we manage our anger? Social psychologists who have studied the topic suggest several good anger management strategies that maximize the potential for positive consequences (Nelson & Finch, 2000). Among the most useful strategies are the following:

- *Look again at the anger-provoking situation from the perspective of others.* By taking others' points of view, you may be able to understand the situation better, and with increased understanding you may become more tolerant of the apparent shortcomings of others.

- *Minimize the importance of the situation.* Does it really matter that someone is driving too slowly and that you'll be late to an appointment as a result? Reinterpret the situation in a way that is less bothersome.

- *Fantasize about getting even—but don't act on it.* Fantasy provides a safety valve. In your fantasies, you can yell at that unfair professor all you want and suffer no consequences at all. However, don't spend too much time brooding: fantasize, but then move on.

- *Relax.* By teaching yourself the kinds of relaxation techniques used in systematic desensitization (discussed in Chapter 12, psychological disorders), you can help reduce your reactions to anger. In turn, your anger may dissipate.

No matter which of these strategies you try, above all, don't ignore your anger. People who always try to suppress their anger may experience a variety of consequences, such as self-condemnation, frustration, and even physical illness (Burns, Quartana, & Bruehl, 2007; Finney, Stoney, & Engebretson, 2002; Quartana & Burns, 2007).

Suppose, for instance, a girl hits her younger brother when he damages one of her new toys. Whereas instinct theory would suggest that the aggression had been pent up and was now being discharged and frustration-aggression theory would examine the girl's frustration at no longer being able to use her new toy, observational learning theory would look to previous situations in which the girl had viewed others being rewarded for their aggression. For example, perhaps she had watched a friend get to play with a toy after he painfully twisted it out of the hand of another child.

Observational learning theory has received wide research support. For example, nursery-school-age children who have watched an adult model behave aggressively and then receive reinforcement for it later display similar behaviour themselves if they have been angered, insulted, or frustrated after exposure.

Helping Others Turning away from aggression, we move now to the opposite—and brighter—side of human nature: helping behaviour. Helping behaviour, or **prosocial behaviour** as it is more formally known, has been considered

prosocial behaviour Helping behaviour.

bystander effect (or **bystander apathy effect**) A phenomena that happens in emergency situations when many people are present, but nobody tries to help the victim.

under many different conditions. However, the question that psychologists have looked at most closely relates to bystander intervention in emergency situations (Latané & Darley, 1968, 1970; Latané & Nida, 1981; Levine & Crowther, 2008). Why does someone help a person in need?

In 1964, a young woman named Kitty Genovese was sexually assaulted and then murdered in the parking lot of her apartment in Queens, New York. Winston Mosely stabbed Kitty Genovese in the back as she screamed for help. Mosely left the scene but returned 10 minutes later and stabbed her to death on the doorstep of her apartment. The story gained widespread attention because several neighbours (some reports say as many as 38 people) heard the screams of Genovese, but nobody tried to help her. This led social psychologists John Darley and Bibb Latané to study why people do not receive help when many other people are present. Their research led to a theory called the **bystander effect**, a phenomena that happens in emergency situations when many people are present, but nobody tries to help the victim. This phenomenon is sometimes also called the **bystander apathy effect**. The bystander effect was also at work in the opening story at the beginning of the chapter about the girl who was sexually assaulted while others stood by and watched (and took photos on their cellphones). The bystanders in this instance did nothing to help the girl.

Why does the bystander apathy effect happen? One critical factor is the number of other people present. When more than one person witnesses an emergency situation, a sense of **diffusion of responsibility** can arise among the bystanders. Diffusion of responsibility is the tendency for people to feel that responsibility for acting is shared, or diffused, among those present. The more people who are present in an emergency, the less personally responsible each individual feels—and therefore the less help he or she provides (Barron & Yechiam, 2002; Blair, Thompson, & Wuensch, 2002; Gray, 2006). This may also have explained why other teenagers in the group did not help the girl.

> **The more people who are present in an emergency, the less personally responsible each individual feels–and therefore the less help he or she provides.**

Although most research on helping behaviour supports the diffusion-of-responsibility explanation, other factors are clearly involved in helping behaviour. According to a model of the helping process, the decision to give aid involves four basic steps (Garcia et al., 2002; Latané and Darley, 1970):

1. *Noticing a person, event, or situation that may require help.*

2. *Interpreting the event as one that requires help.* Even if we notice an event, it may be sufficiently ambiguous for us to interpret it as a non-emergency situation. It is here that the presence of others first affects helping behaviour. The presence of inactive others may indicate to us that a situation does not require help—a judgment we do not necessarily make if we are alone.

3. *Assuming responsibility for helping.* It is at this point that diffusion of responsibility is likely to occur if others are present. Moreover, a bystander's particular expertise is likely to play a role in determining whether he or she helps. For instance, if people with training in medical aid or lifesaving techniques are present, untrained bystanders are less likely to intervene, because they feel they have less expertise.

4. *Deciding on and implementing the form of helping.* After we assume responsibility for helping, we must decide how to provide assistance. Helping can range from very indirect forms of intervention, such as calling the police, to more direct forms, such as giving first aid or

diffusion of responsibility The tendency for people to feel that responsibility for acting is shared, or diffused, among those present.

altruism Helping behaviour that is beneficial to others but clearly requires self-sacrifice.

egoism Helping behaviour where the ultimate goal is to benefit one's self.

principlism Helping behaviour to help others to uphold moral principles.

Figure 9.5
The Helping Process

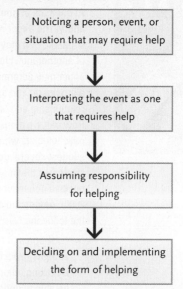

Source: Bibb Latané & John M. Darley. *The Unresponsive Bystander: Why Doesn't He Help?* 1st ed., © 1970. Reproduced in print and electronic formats by permission of Pearson Education, Inc., Upper Saddle River, New Jersey.

taking the victim to a hospital. Most social psychologists use a *rewards-costs approach* for helping to predict the nature of the assistance a bystander will choose to provide. The general notion is that the rewards for helping, as perceived by the bystander, must outweigh the costs if helping is to occur, and most research tends to support this notion (Bartlett & DeSteno, 2006; Koper & Jaasma, 2001; Lin & Lin, 2007).

After determining the nature of the assistance needed, the actual help must be implemented. Social psychologist Daniel Batson has spent the last thirty years trying to find out what motivates people to help others. He outlined four motivations for acting for the public good, which are based on the individual's ultimate goal in helping (Batson, 1994). One motivation is **altruism**, in which the ultimate goal is to benefit others, such as by volunteering to donate blood. Another motivation is **egoism**, where the ultimate goal is to benefit one's self, such as when a politician volunteers at a food bank for a photo opportunity. **Principlism** is another motivation, where the ultimate goal is to uphold moral principles, such as by volunteering each week at church.

> > > How would Batson's four motivations for acting for the public good apply if you volunteered your time as part of a school project on service learning?

Altruism is often the only bright side of a natural disaster.

The last motivation is **collectivism**, where the ultimate goal is to benefit the welfare of a particular group, such as by participating in the Relay for Life to raise money for cancer research.

People sometimes behave altruistically, even when it clearly involves a level of self-sacrifice that might lead to one's own harm. For example, people who helped strangers escape from the burning World Trade Center towers during the 9/11 terrorist attack, putting themselves at mortal risk, would be considered altruistic (Batson & Powell, 2003; Krueger, Hicks, & McGue, 2001; Manor & Gailliot, 2007). However, some argue that true altruism such as this is contrary to the evolutionary perspective that states we behave in ways that ensure survival of our species. The evolutionary perspective would explain altruistic behaviour towards one's family members as a means of protecting the genes and survival of the family. But what about non-family members? Why would someone risk their own survival to help others? One theory, **reciprocal altruism**, might help explain this. This theory suggests that we help others because we expect that others will help us out in return. This is a form of egoism, where we are actually helping others in order to benefit ourselves in the future (either directly by the person we helped, or indirectly when someone else helps us when we need it). Another theory, the **empathy-altruism hypothesis**, suggests that we help others when we feel empathy and compassion toward them and their situation.

Study tip

The distinction between *prosocial behaviour* and *altruism* is important. Prosocial behaviour need not have a self-sacrificing component; altruism, by definition, contains an element of self-sacrifice.

For Review ››

What are attitudes, how do they influence behaviour, and how can they be changed?

Attitudes are evaluations of a particular person, behaviour, belief, or concept. Attitudes can be changed by others, through persuasion. The two primary information-processing routes—central route processing and peripheral route processing—determine our receptiveness to persuasion. When an individual simultaneously holds two cognitions—attitudes or thoughts—that contradict each other, cognitive dissonance occurs. To resolve the contradiction, we either change our thinking or deny there's a contradiction, thereby reducing cognitive dissonance.

Our attitudes about other people are part of social cognition. Often the impressions we form of people influence the way we interpret their behaviour. Attribution theory suggests that we use situational or dispositional factors to understand the causes of behaviour. Attribution biases are the errors we make when making attributions about others, and include the halo effect, the horn effect, the assumed-similarity bias, the self-serving bias, and the fundamental attribution error.

How do we influence one another?

Social influence is the area of social psychology concerned with situations in which the actions of an individual or group affect the behaviour of others. Conformity refers to changes in behaviour or attitudes that result from a desire to follow the beliefs or standards of others. Compliance is behaviour that results from direct social pressure. Obedience is a change in behaviour in response to the commands of others.

Where do stereotypes come from?

Stereotypes are generalized beliefs and expectations about a specific group and its members. Stereotyping can lead to prejudice and self-fulfilling prophecies. Prejudice is the negative (or positive) evaluation of a particular group and its members. Stereotyping and prejudice can lead to discrimination, behaviour directed toward individuals on the basis of their membership in a particular group. According to observational learning approaches, children learn stereotyping and prejudice by observing the behaviour of parents, other adults, and peers. Social identity theory suggests that group membership is used as a source of pride and self-worth, and this may lead people to think of their own group as better than others.

Why are we attracted to certain people? How do relationships develop?

The primary determinants of liking include proximity, exposure, similarity, and physical attractiveness. Loving is distinguished from liking by the presence of intense physiological arousal, an all-encompassing interest in another, fantasies about the other, rapid swings of emotion, fascination, sexual desire, exclusiveness, and strong feelings of caring. Love can be categorized as passionate or companionate. In addition, love has several components: intimacy, passion, and decision/commitment.

What makes some people aggressive and others helpful?

Aggression is intentional injury of or harm to another person. Explanations of aggression include instinct approaches, frustration-aggression theory, and observational learning. Helping behaviour in emergencies is determined in part by the phenomenon of diffusion of responsibility, which results in a lower likelihood of helping when more people are present. Deciding to help is the outcome of a four-stage process consisting of noticing a possible need for help, interpreting the situation as requiring aid, assuming responsibility for taking action, and deciding on and implementing a form of assistance.

Why do we help others?

Sometimes we help others altruistically, which means we simply want to benefit them without any benefit to ourselves, even if it requires some sort of self-sacrifice. Evolutionary theory would say that we help our own family members to ensure survival of the species, while the empathy-altruism hypothesis would say we help because we feel empathy and compassion for others, whether they are family members or not. Reciprocal altruism is a form of egoism, where we help others in order to benefit ourselves at some point in the future.

Psych think answers

Psych think 1 In the PSYCH think on p. 223, we asked you about Annette, a new co-worker, who you saw act in a way that seems abrupt and curt. You conclude that Annette is unkind and unsociable. The next day you see Annette acting kindly toward another worker. We asked if you would be likely to change your impression of Annette. To answer this question, you need to consider your *impression formation*, the process by which you would organize information about Annette to form an overall impression of her. You would likely not change your impression because of the fundamental attribution error, where you would likely assess Annette's initial behaviour as being due to her disposition, rather than the situation.

Psych think 2 In the PSYCH think on p. 231 we asked if you were a participant in a replication of Milgrim's study today, but had no knowledge of the results of the study, would you administer shocks to another individual that were potentially dangerous. Your first inclination is likely to say that you do not think you would, as many people predicted in Milgram's original study. However you need to keep in mind the powerful effect that others can have on your behaviour. Moreover, several factors in Milgram's study would make it more likely that you would obey. For example we tend to obey when the person giving the orders is physically close to us. It's harder to say no face-to-face. We also tend to obey when the person giving the orders as an authority figure, and when the victim is kept at a distance from us so that we cannot see them. It is also important to look at other research when thinking about how you would answer this question. Perhaps you thought you would not behave the same way as someone would in 1960, but Burger replicated Milgram's study in 2006 and found that many participants continued to obey the authority figure and administered shocks that they believed to be hurtful. So while we would like to think that we would never behave in such a way, we have to keep in mind the power of the situation.

Psych think 3 In the PSYCH think on p. 238 we asked you how Batson's four motivations for acting for the public good would apply if you volunteered your time as part of a school project on service learning. Remember the first motivation is *altruism*, in which the ultimate goal is to benefit others. If you volunteered solely to help others then you could say you did this to be altruistic, but given that you did this for an assignment, your behaviour was probably not solely altruistic. Another motivation is *egoism*, where the ultimate goal is to benefit one's self. This motivation probably fits the best because you are ultimately benefitting yourself by volunteering in order to get a grade. *Principlism* is another motivation, where the ultimate goal is to uphold moral principles. If you chose to volunteer at your church because you felt this was morally right then this motivation would be a good fit. The last motivation is *collectivism*, where the ultimate goal is to benefit the welfare of a particular group. This motivation may apply if you chose to volunteer where many people would benefit, such as participating in a hike for hospice where the money would be used to help families living with a family member who is dying.

10

Development

WHAT'S TO COME

Nature and Nurture

Prenatal Development

Infancy and Childhood

Adolescence

Adulthood

A 624 gram miracle

"She looked like a little old man," says Elizabeth Thatcher of her daughter, Hattie, who was born at 25 weeks, weighing 624 grams. "She wasn't plump like a baby should be. She was skin and bones."

Hattie, Elizabeth and husband Brad's firstborn, faced tough odds, but couple held out hope. A friend's baby born at 23 weeks was doing fine—so, too, the Thatchers prayed, would their little girl. . . .

The Thatchers visited Hattie every day, singing and talking to her. Preemies can't handle much stimulation, so instead of holding her, they lovingly cupped her head and body with their hands.

A fighter from the start, today Hattie, 6, is an outgoing little girl who loves pretending to be a lion. She's eagerly looking forward to Valentine's Day, busy making paper hearts for everyone in her family and "all my neighbours." "On February 14, my mom will get a Valentine under her pillow," she says. Hattie plays soccer every Monday. "I like kicking the ball," she says.

At a recent five-year reunion for NICU (neonatal intensive care unit) babies from Roosevelt Hospital, Hattie bounced around the room, happily hugging her former nurses.

Some children came in wheelchairs. "It made us realize how lucky we really are," says Brad gratefully. (Kelly, 2006, p. 26)

Infants are not supposed to be born as early as Hattie was. Yet, she was far from alone: over 10% of all babies are born prematurely. And, with the help of medical advances, the prospects for those born early are improving significantly.

Hattie's story serves as an introduction to one of the broadest and most important areas of psychology, developmental psychology. Developmental psychology is the branch of psychology that studies the patterns of growth and change that occur throughout life; it includes topics as diverse as finding new ways to conceive children, learning how to raise children most sensibly, and understanding the milestones of life that we all face.

Developmental psychologists study the interaction between the unfolding of biologically predetermined patterns of growth and a constantly changing, dynamic environment. They ask how our genetic background affects our behaviour throughout our lives and how environmental influences, events, and experiences work with—or against—genetic capabilities to shape us throughout our lives.

We grow and change physically, cognitively, and socially throughout the lifespan.

As You Read »

- What methods do psychologists use to conduct developmental research?
- How do infants grow and develop before birth?
- What do newborn babies actually know, and how can we tell?
- How do children learn to get along with and understand other people?
- What are the moral, cognitive, and social challenges of adolescence?
- In what ways do people continue to develop and to grow after they reach adulthood?

Nature and Nurture

How many bald, six-foot-six, 250-pound volunteer firefighters in who live in the same city wear droopy mustaches, aviator-style eyeglasses, and a key ring on the right side of the belt?

The answer is two: Gerald Levey and Mark Newman. They are twins who were separated at birth. Each twin did not even know the other existed until they were reunited—in a fire station—by a fellow firefighter who knew Newman and was startled to see his double, Levey, at a firefighters' convention.

The lives of the twins, although separate, took remarkably similar paths. Levey went to college, studying forestry; Newman planned to study forestry in college but instead took a job trimming trees. Both had jobs in supermarkets. One had a job installing sprinkler systems; the other installed fire alarms.

Both men are unmarried and find the same kind of woman attractive: "tall, slender, long hair." They share similar hobbies, enjoying hunting, fishing, going to the beach, and watching old John Wayne movies and professional wrestling. Both like Chinese food and drink the same brand of beer. Their mannerisms are also similar—for example, each one throws his head back when he laughs. And, of course, there is one more thing: They share a passion for fighting fires.

The similarities we see in twins Gerald Levey and Mark Newman vividly raise one of the fundamental questions posed by **developmental psychology**, the study of the patterns of growth and change that occur throughout life. The question is this: how can we distinguish between the

Gerald Levey and Mark Newman, identical twins raised apart.

environmental causes of behaviour (the influence of parents, siblings, family, friends, schooling, nutrition, and all the other experiences to which a child is exposed) and *hereditary* causes (those based on the genetic makeup of an individual that influence growth and development throughout life)? This question sums up the **nature–nurture issue**. In this context, nature refers to hereditary factors, and nurture to environmental influences.

Although the question was first posed as a nature-*versus*-nurture issue, developmental psychologists today agree that both nature and nurture interact to produce specific developmental patterns and outcomes. Consequently, the question has evolved to *How and to what degree do environment and heredity both produce their effects?* No one grows up free of environmental influences, nor does anyone develop without being affected by his or her inherited *genetic makeup.* However, the debate over the relative influence of the two factors remains active, with different approaches and different theories of development emphasizing the environment or heredity to a greater or lesser

developmental psychology The branch of psychology that studies the patterns of growth and change that occur throughout life.

nature–nurture issue The issue of the degree to which environment and heredity influence behaviour.

Study tip

Psychologists agree that nature and nurture act together to shape behaviour. Today researchers ask *how and to what degree* environment and heredity influence a person's development and behaviour.

degree (Gottesman & Hanson, 2005; Pinker, 2002; Rutter, 2006).

For example, some developmental theories rely on basic psychological principles of learning and stress the role that learning plays in producing changes in behaviour in a developing child. Such theories emphasize the role of the environment in development. In contrast, other developmental theories emphasize the influence of one's physiological makeup and functioning on development. These theories stress the role of heredity and *maturation*—the unfolding of biologically predetermined patterns of behaviour—in producing developmental change. Maturation can be seen, for instance, in the development of sex characteristics (such as breasts and body hair) that occurs at the start of adolescence. Furthermore, behavioural geneticists, who study the effects of heredity on behaviour by looking for genetic commonalities among families and corresponding behaviours, and evolutionary psychologists, who look for behaviour patterns over large groups of people that may result from the genetic inheritance of our ancestors, have highlighted the importance of heredity in influencing human behaviour (Buss, 2003a, 2003b; Ilies, Arvey, & Bouchard, 2006; Reif & Lesch, 2003).

Despite their differences over theory, developmental psychologists agree on some points. They agree that genetic factors not only provide the potential for specific behaviours or traits to emerge but also place limitations on the emergence of such behaviour or traits. For instance, heredity defines people's general level of intelligence, setting an upper limit that—regardless of the quality of the environment—people cannot exceed. Heredity also places limits on physical abilities; humans simply cannot run at a speed of 80 kilometres per hour, nor will they grow as tall as 2 metres, no matter what the quality of their environment (Dodge, 2004; Pinker, 2004).

Developmental psychologists also agree that in most instances environmental factors play a critical role in enabling people to reach the potential capabilities that their genetic background makes possible. If Albert Einstein had received no intellectual stimulation as a child and had not been sent to school, it is unlikely that he would have reached his genetic potential. Similarly, a great athlete such as Team Canada hockey star Hayley Wickenheiser would have been unlikely to display much physical skill if she had not been raised in an environment that nurtured her innate talent and gave her the opportunity to train and perfect her natural abilities.

Psych think

> > > When researchers find similarities in development between very different cultures, what implications might such findings have for the nature–nurture issue?

Clearly, the relationship between heredity and environment is far from simple. As a consequence, developmental psychologists typically take an *interactionist* position on the nature–nurture issue, suggesting that a combination of hereditary and environmental factors influences development. Developmental psychologists face the challenge of identifying the relative strength of each of these influences on the individual, as well as that of identifying the specific changes that occur over the course of development (McGregor & Capone, 2004; Moffitt, Caspi, & Rutter, 2006).

Developmental psychologists use several approaches to determine the relative influence of genetic and environmental factors on behaviour. In one approach, researchers can experimentally control the genetic makeup of laboratory animals by carefully breeding them for specific traits. For instance, by observing animals

Figure 10.1

Characteristics Strongly Influenced by Heredity

Physical Characteristics	Intellectual Characteristics	Emotional Characteristics and Disorders
Height	Memory	Shyness
Weight	Intelligence	Extraversion
Obesity	Age of language acquisition	Emotionality
Tone of voice	Reading disability	Neuroticism
Blood pressure	Mental retardation (intellectual disabilities)	Schizophrenia
Tooth decay		Anxiety
Athletic ability		Alcoholism
Alcoholism		
Firmness of handshake		
Age of death		
Activity level		

with identical genetic backgrounds placed in varied environments, researchers can learn the effects of specific kinds of environmental stimulation. Although researchers must be careful when generalizing the findings of non-human research to a human population, findings from animal research provide important information that they cannot obtain, for ethical reasons, by using human participants.

Non-human research helps us better understand the influences of nature and nurture.

Human twins serve as another important source of information about the relative effects of genetic and environmental factors. If **identical twins** (those who are genetically identical) display different patterns of development, those differences have to be attributed to variations in the environment in which the twins were raised. The most useful data come from identical twins (such as Gerald Levey and Mark Newman) who are adopted at birth by different sets of adoptive parents and raised apart in differing environments. Studies of non-twin siblings who are raised in totally different environments also shed some light on the issue. Because they have relatively similar genetic backgrounds, siblings who show similarities as adults provide strong evidence for the importance of heredity (Gottesman, 1997; Sternberg, R. J., 2002a).

Researchers can also take the opposite approach. Instead of concentrating on people with similar genetic backgrounds who are raised in different environments, they may consider people raised in similar environments who have totally dissimilar genetic backgrounds. If they find similar courses of development in, for example, two adopted children who have different genetic backgrounds and have been raised in the same family; they have evidence for the importance of environmental influences on development. Moreover, psychologists can carry out research involving animals with dissimilar genetic backgrounds; by experimentally varying the environment in which they are raised, they can determine the influence of environmental factors (independent of heredity) on development (Petrill & Deater-Deckard, 2004).

DEVELOPMENTAL RESEARCH TECHNIQUES

Because of the demands of measuring behavioural change across different ages, developmental researchers use several unique methods. The most frequently used, **cross-sectional research**, compares people of different ages at the same point in time. Cross-sectional studies provide information about differences in development among different age groups (Creasey, 2005; Huijie, 2006).

Suppose, for instance, we are interested in the development of intellectual ability in adulthood. To carry out a cross-sectional study, we might compare a sample of 25-, 45-, and 65-year-olds who all take the same IQ test. We then can determine whether average IQ test scores differ in each age group.

Cross-sectional research has limitations, however. For instance, we cannot be sure that the differences in IQ scores we might find in our example are due to age differences alone. Instead, the scores may reflect differences in the educational attainment of the cohorts represented. A *cohort* is a group of people who grow up at similar times, in similar places, and in similar conditions. In the case of IQ differences, any age differences we find in a cross-sectional study may reflect educational differences among the cohorts studied: people in the older age group, for example, may belong to a cohort that was less likely to attend college than were the people in the younger groups.

A longitudinal study, the second major research strategy used by developmental psychologists, provides one way around this problem. **Longitudinal research** traces the behaviour of one or more participants as the participants age. Longitudinal studies assess *change* in behaviour over time, whereas cross-sectional studies assess *differences* among groups of people.

Study tip

Be sure you can distinguish between the three types of developmental research—cross-sectional, longitudinal, and sequential.

For instance, consider how we might investigate intellectual development during adulthood by using a longitudinal research strategy. First, we might give an IQ test to a group of 25-year-olds. We'd then come back to the same people 20 years later and retest them at age 45. Finally, we'd return to them once more when they were 65 years old and test them again.

By examining changes at several points in time, we can clearly see how individuals develop. Unfortunately, longitudinal research requires an enormous expenditure of time (as the researcher waits for the participants to get older), and participants who begin a study at an early age may drop out, move away, or die as the research continues. Moreover, participants who take the same test at several points in time may become "test-wise" and perform better each time they take it, having become more familiar with the test.

identical twins Twins who are genetically identical.

cross-sectional research A research method that compares people of different ages at the same point in time.

longitudinal research A research method that investigates behaviour as participants age.

sequential research A research method that combines cross-sectional and longitudinal research by considering a number of different age groups and examining them at several points in time.

To make up for the limitations in both cross-sectional and longitudinal research, investigators have devised an alternative strategy. Known as **sequential research**, it combines cross-sectional and longitudinal approaches by taking a number of different age groups and examining them at several points in time. For example, investigators might use a group of 3-, 5-, and 7-year-olds, examining them every six months for a period of several years. This technique allows a developmental psychologist to tease out the specific effects of age changes from other possibly influential factors.

Prenatal Development

Our increasing understanding of the first stirrings of life spent inside a mother's womb has permitted significant medical advances, such as those that help infants like Hattie, born more than 10 weeks ahead of schedule, to survive the first critical weeks after birth and to go on to become healthy, energetic individuals. Yet our knowledge of the biology of *conception*—when a male's sperm penetrates a female's egg—and its aftermath makes the start of life no less remarkable.

Let's consider how an individual is created by looking first at the genetic endowment that the fertilized cell receives at the moment of conception.

BASIC GENETICS

The one-cell entity established at conception contains 23 pairs of **chromosomes**, rod-shaped structures that contain all basic hereditary information. One member of each pair is from the mother, and the other is from the father. Each chromosome contains thousands of **genes**—the basic units through which genetic information is transmitted. Either individually or in combination, genes produce the specific characteristics of each person. Composed of sequences of *DNA (deoxyribonucleic acid) molecules*, genes are the biological equivalent of "software" that programs the future development of all parts of the body's hardware.

Study tip

Know the basic building-blocks of genetics: chromosomes, which contain genes, which in turn are composed of DNA.

Humans have some 25,000 different genes. Some genes control the development of systems common to all members of the human species—the heart, circulatory system, brain, lungs, and so forth; others shape the characteristics that make each human unique, such as facial configuration, height, and eye colour. The child's sex is also determined by a specific combination of genes. Specifically, a child usually inherits an X chromosome from its mother and either an X or a Y chromosome from its father. When it receives an XX combination, it develops as a female; with an XY combination, it develops as a male. Male development is triggered by a single gene on the Y chromosome, and without the presence of that specific gene (or when it malfunctions), the individual will develop as a female.

As behavioural geneticists have discovered, genes are also at least partially responsible for a wide variety of personal characteristics, including intelligence, personality traits, and psychological disorders. Of course, few of these characteristics are determined by a single gene. Instead, most traits result from a combination of genes, which operate together and interact with environmental influences (Haberstick et al., 2005; Plomin & McGuffin, 2003; Ramus, 2006).

Most traits result from a combination of genes, which operate together and interact with environmental influences.

EARLIEST DEVELOPMENT

When an egg becomes fertilized by the sperm, the resulting one-celled entity, called a **zygote**, immediately begins to develop. The zygote starts out as a microscopic speck. Three days after fertilization, though, the zygote increases to around 32 cells, and within a week it has grown to 100–150 cells. These first two weeks are known as the *germinal period*.

Two weeks after conception, the developing individual enters the *embryonic period*, which lasts from week 2 through week 8, and he or she is now called an **embryo**. As an embryo develops through an intricate, preprogrammed process of cell division, it grows 10,000 times larger by 4 weeks of age, attaining a length of about one-fifth of an inch. At this point, it has developed a beating heart, a brain, an intestinal tract, and a number of other organs. Although all these organs are at a primitive stage of development, they are clearly recognizable. Moreover, by week 8, the embryo is about an inch long, and has discernible arms and legs and a face.

From week 8 and continuing until birth, the developing individual enters the *fetal period* and is called a **fetus**. At the start of this period, it begins to respond to touch. At 16 to

Conception occurs when a male's sperm cell penetrates a female's egg cell.

---

chromosomes Rod-shaped structures that contain all basic hereditary information.

genes The parts of the chromosomes through which genetic information is transmitted.

zygote The new cell formed by the union of an egg and sperm.

embryo A developed zygote that has a heart, a brain, and other organs.

fetus A developing individual, from 8 weeks after conception until birth.

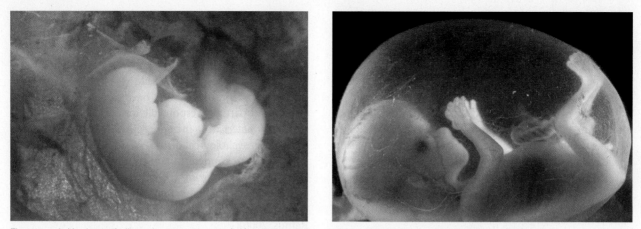

These remarkable photos of a live embryo at age 4 weeks (left) and a fetus at 15 weeks (right) illustrate the degree of physical development that occurs in 11 weeks.

18 weeks, its movements become strong enough for the mother to sense them. About the same time, hair may begin to grow on the fetus's head, and the facial features become similar to those the child will display at birth. The major organs begin functioning, although the fetus could not survive outside the mother's womb. In addition, a lifetime's worth of brain neurons are produced—although it is unclear whether the brain is capable of thinking at this early stage.

By week 24, a fetus has many of the characteristics it will display as a newborn. In fact, when an infant is born prematurely at this age, it can open and close its eyes; suck; cry; look up, down, and around; and even grasp objects placed in its hands, although it is still unable to survive for long outside the mother.

The fetus continues to develop before birth. It begins to grow fatty deposits under the skin, and it gains weight. At prenatal age 28 weeks, the fetus weighs less than 1,361 grams and is about 41 centimetres long. It may be capable of learning: one study found that the infants of mothers who had repeatedly read aloud the Dr. Seuss story *The Cat in the Hat* before giving birth preferred the sound of that story to other stories after they were born (Spence & DeCasper, 1982).

Before birth, a fetus passes through several *sensitive periods*. A sensitive period is the time when organisms are exceptionally receptive to certain kinds of stimuli. For example, fetuses are especially affected by their mothers' use of drugs at certain times before birth. If they are exposed to a specific drug before or after a sensitive period, the drug may have relatively little effect, but if exposure comes during a sensitive period, the effect will be significant (Konig, 2005; Uylings, 2006; Werker & Tees, 2005).

Sensitive periods can also occur after birth. For instance, some language specialists suggest that there is a period in which children are especially receptive to developing language. If children are not exposed to appropriate linguistic stimuli, their language development may be impaired (Innocenti, 2007; Sohr-Preston & Scaramella, 2006).

In the final weeks of pregnancy, the fetus continues to gain weight and grow. At the end of the normal 38 weeks of pregnancy the fetus typically weighs 3.2 kilograms and is about 50 centimetres in length. However, the story is different for *preterm infants*, who are born before week 38. Because they have not been able to develop fully, they are at higher risk for illness, future problems, and death. For infants who have been in the womb for more than 30 weeks, the prospects are relatively good. However, for those born before week 30, the story is often less positive. Such newborns, who may weigh as little as 907 grams at birth, are in grave danger; because they have immature organs they have less than a 50:50 chance of survival. If they do survive—and it takes extraordinary medical intervention to assure this—they may later experience significant developmental delays.

Genetic Influences on the Fetus The process of fetal growth that we have just described reflects normal development, which occurs in 95% to 98% percent of all pregnancies. In the other 2% to 5% of cases, children are born with serious birth defects. A major cause of such defects is faulty genes or chromosomes. Here are some of the more common genetic and chromosomal difficulties.

- *Phenylketonuria (PKU)*. A child born with the inherited disease phenylketonuria cannot produce an enzyme that is required for normal development. This deficiency results in an accumulation of poisons that eventually cause profound mental retardation (intellectual disabilities). The disease is treatable, however, if it is caught early. Most infants today are routinely tested for PKU, and children with the disorder can be placed on a special diet that allows them to develop normally (Christ et al., 2006; Ievers-Landis et al., 2005).

- *Sickle-cell anemia*. Children with this disease may have episodes of pain, yellowish eyes, stunted growth, and vision problems. Heart problems can lead to premature death in middle age (Selove, 2007; Taras & Potts-Datema, 2005).

- *Tay-Sachs disease*. Children born with Tay-Sachs disease, a disorder most often found in Jews of eastern European ancestry, usually die by age three or four because of the body's inability to break down fat. If both parents carry the genetic defect that produces the fatal illness, their child has a one in four chance of being born with the disease (Leib et al., 2005).

- *Down syndrome.* Down syndrome, one of the causes of mental retardation (intellectual disabilities), occurs when the zygote receives an extra chromosome on the 21st pair at the moment of conception. Down syndrome is related to the mother's age; mothers over 35 and younger than 18 stand a higher risk than other women do of having a child with the syndrome (Roizen & Patterson, 2003).

Prenatal Environmental Influences Genetic factors are not the only causes of difficulties in fetal development. Environmental influences—the *nurture* part of the nature–nurture equation—also affect the fetus. Some of the more profound consequences are brought about by a **teratogen**, an environmental agent such as a drug, chemical, or virus that produces a birth defect. Among the major prenatal environmental influences on the fetus are these:

- *Mother's nutrition.* What a mother eats during her pregnancy can have important implications for the health of her baby. Seriously undernourished mothers cannot provide adequate nutrition to a growing fetus, and they are likely to give birth to underweight babies. Poorly nourished babies are also more susceptible to disease, and a lack of nourishment may have an adverse effect on their mental development (Adams & Parker, 1990; Najman et al., 2004; Ricciuti, 1993; Sigman, 1995; Zigler, Finn-Stevenson, & Hall, 2002).

- *Mother's illness.* Several diseases that have a relatively minor effect on the health of a mother can have

teratogen An environmental agent such as a drug, chemical, virus, or other factor that produces a birth defect.

devastating consequences for a developing fetus if they are contracted during a sensitive period of embryonic or fetal development. For example, rubella (German measles), syphilis, diabetes, and high blood pressure may each produce a permanent effect on the fetus.

- *Mother's use of drugs.* Mothers who take physically addictive drugs such as cocaine run the risk of giving birth to babies who are similarly addicted. Their newborns suffer painful withdrawal symptoms and sometimes show permanent physical and mental impairment as well. Even legal drugs, such as the acne medication, accutane, can have a tragic effect when taken by a pregnant woman (who may not know that she has become pregnant) (Ikonomidou et al., 2000; Schecter, Finkelstein, & Koren, 2005).

- *Alcohol.* Alcohol is extremely dangerous to fetal development. One out of every 750 infants is born with fetal alcohol syndrome (FAS), a condition resulting in below-average intelligence, growth delays, and facial deformities. FAS is now the primary preventable cause of mental retardation (intellectual disabilities). Even mothers who use small amounts of alcohol during pregnancy place their child at risk. *Fetal alcohol effects (FAE)* is a condition in which children display some, although not all, of the problems of FAS owing to their mother's

Figure 10.2
Environment and Prenatal Development

Environmental Factor	Possible Effect on Prenatal Development
Rubella (German measles)	Blindness, deafness, heart abnormalities, stillbirth
Syphilis	Mental retardation (intellectual disabilities), physical deformities, maternal miscarriage
Addictive drugs	Low birth weight, addiction of infant to drug, with possible death after birth from withdrawal
Nicotine	Premature birth, low birth weight and length
Alcohol	Mental retardation (intellectual disabilities), lower-than-average birth weight, small head, limb deformities
Radiation from X rays	Physical deformities, mental retardation (intellectual disabilities)
Inadequate diet	Reduction in growth of brain, smaller-than-average weight and length at birth
Mother's age—younger than 18 at birth of child	Premature birth, increased incidence of Down syndrome
Mother's age—older than 35 at birth of child	Increased incidence of Down syndrome
DES (diethylstilbestrol)	Reproductive difficulties and increased incidence of genital cancer in children of mothers who were given DES during pregnancy to prevent miscarriage
AIDS	Possible spread of AIDS virus to infant; facial deformities; growth failure
Accutane	Mental retardation (intellectual disabilities) and physical deformities

consumption of alcohol during pregnancy (Henderson, Kesmodel, & Gray, 2007; Niccols, 2007; Wass, Mattson, & Riley, 2004).

Several other environmental factors have an impact on the child before and during birth. Keep in mind, however, that although we have been discussing the influences of genetics and environment separately, neither factor works alone. Furthermore, despite the emphasis here on some of the ways in which development can go wrong, the vast majority of births occur without difficulty. And in most instances, subsequent development also proceeds normally.

Infancy and Childhood

His head was moulded into a long melon shape and came to a point at the back. . . . He was covered with a thick greasy white material known as "vernix," which made him slippery to hold, and also allowed him to slip easily through the birth canal. In addition to a shock of black hair on his head, his body was covered with dark, fine hair known as "lanugo." His ears, his back, his shoulders, and even his cheeks were furry. . . . His skin was wrinkled and quite loose, ready to scale in creased places such as his feet and hands. . . . His ears were pressed to his head in unusual positions—one ear was matted firmly forward on his cheek. His nose was flattened and pushed to one side by the squeeze as he came through the pelvis (Brazelton, 1969, p. 3).

What kind of creature is this? Although the description hardly fits that of the adorable babies seen in baby food ads, it depicts a normal, completely developed child just after the moment of birth. The newborn arrives in the world in a form that hardly meets the standards of beauty by which we typically measure babies.

THE EXTRAORDINARY NEWBORN

Several factors cause a newborn's strange appearance. The trip through the mother's birth canal may have squeezed the incompletely formed bones of the skull together and squashed the nose into the head. The skin secretes vernix, a white, greasy covering, for protection before birth, and the baby may have *lanugo*, a soft fuzz, over the entire body for a similar purpose. The infant's eyelids may be puffy with an accumulation of fluids because of the upside-down position during birth. All these features change during the first two weeks of life, as the newborn takes on a more familiar appearance. Even more impressive are the capabilities a newborn begins to display right after birth—capabilities that grow at an astounding rate over the ensuing months.

Reflexes A newborn enters the world with a number of *reflexes*—unlearned, involuntary responses that occur automatically in the presence of certain stimuli. Critical for survival, many of these reflexes unfold naturally as part of an infant's ongoing maturation. The *rooting reflex*, for instance, causes newborns to turn their heads toward things that touch their cheeks—such as the mother's nipple or a bottle. Similarly, a *sucking reflex* prompts infants to suck

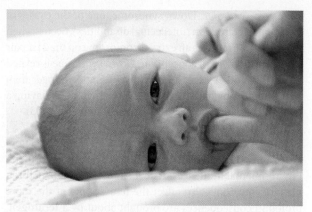

The sucking reflex is one of several innate responses that are critical to a newborn's survival.

at things that touch their lips. Among other reflexes are a *gag reflex* (to clear the throat), the *startle reflex* (a series of movements in which an infant flings out the arms, fans the fingers, and arches the back in response to a sudden noise), and the *Babinski reflex* (a baby's toes fan out when the outer edge of the sole of the foot is stroked).

Study tip

Newborns exhibit several reflexes—unlearned, involuntary responses—including rooting, sucking, gag, startle, and Babinski reflexes.

Infants lose these primitive reflexes after the first few months of life, replacing them with more complex and organized behaviours. Although at birth a newborn is capable of only jerky, limited voluntary movements, during the first year of life the ability to move independently grows enormously. The typical baby rolls over by the age of about 3 months, sits without support at about 6 months, stands alone at about 11 months, and walks at just over a year old. Not only does the ability to make large-scale movements (such as moving an arm or leg) improve during this time, fine-muscle movements (for example, using a finger to push a toy) become increasingly sophisticated.

Development of the Senses When parents peer into the eyes of their newborn, is the child able to return their gaze? Although it was thought for some time that newborns can see only a hazy blur, most current findings indicate that the capabilities of newborns are far more impressive. Although their eyes have a limited capacity to focus on objects that are not within a 17- to 22-centimetre distance from the face, newborns can follow objects moving within their field of vision. They also show the rudiments of depth perception, as they react by raising their hands when an object appears to be moving rapidly toward the face (Gelman & Kit-Fong Au, 1996; Maurer et al., 1999).

You might think that it would be hard to figure out just how well newborns can see, because their lack of both language and reading ability clearly prevents them from saying what direction the E on a vision chart is facing. However,

habituation The decrease in response to a stimulus that occurs after repeated presentations of the same stimulus.

researchers have devised a number of ingenious methods to test perceptual skills, relying on the newborn's biological responses and innate reflexes.

For instance, infants who see a novel stimulus typically pay close attention to it, and, as a consequence, their heart rates increase. But if they repeatedly see the same stimulus, their attention to it decreases, and the heart rate returns to a slower rate. This phenomenon is known as **habituation**, the decrease in the response to a stimulus that occurs after repeated presentations of the same stimulus. By studying habituation, developmental psychologists can tell when a child who is too young to speak can detect and discriminate a stimulus (del Rosal, Alonso, & Moreno, 2006; Grunwald et al., 2003; Hannon & Johnson, 2005).

Through the use of such research techniques, we now know that infants' visual perception is remarkably sophisticated from the start of life. At birth, babies prefer patterns with contours and edges over less distinct patterns, indicating that they can respond to the configuration of stimuli. Furthermore, even newborns are apparently born with the understanding that objects stay the same size even when the image on the retina changes size as the object moves closer and farther away (Moore, Goodwin, & George, 2007; Norcia et al., 2005).

In fact, newborns can discriminate facial expressions—and even imitate them. Newborns who see an adult with a happy, sad, or surprised facial expression can produce a good imitation of the adult's expression. Even very young infants, then, can respond to the emotions and moods that their caregivers' facial expressions reveal. This capability provides the foundation for social interaction skills in children (Grossman, Striano, & Friederici, 2007; Lavelli & Fogel, 2005; Meltzoff, 1996).

Other visual abilities grow rapidly after birth. By the end of their first month, babies can distinguish some colours from others, and after four months they can focus on near or far objects. By age four or five months they are able to recognize two- and three-dimensional objects, and they can perceive the gestalt organizing principles discovered by psychologists who study perception. By the age of

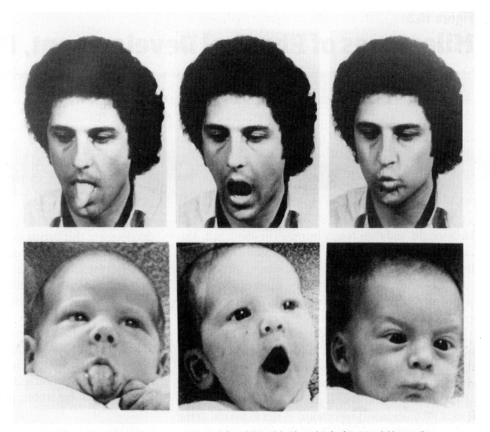

The young infant is clearly imitating the expressions of the adult model, rehearsing for future social interactions. (*Source:* Courtesy of Dr. Tiffany Field.)

seven months, neural systems related to the processing of information about facial expressions show a high degree of sophistication, causing babies to respond differently to specific facial expressions (Johnson, 2004; Leppanen et al., 2007; Striano & Vaish, 2006).

In addition to vision, infants display other impressive sensory capabilities. Newborns can distinguish different sounds to the point of being able to recognize their own mothers' voices at the age of three days. They can also make subtle perceptual distinctions that underlie language abilities.

INFANCY THROUGH MIDDLE CHILDHOOD

During infancy and childhood, until the start of adolescence, around age 11 or 12, development proceeds rapidly in physical, social, and cognitive domains. Physical growth provides the most obvious sign of children's development. During the first year of life, children typically triple their

DID YOU KNOW?

Children who learn to ride a bike at ages six or seven suffer fewer bicycle-related injuries than do children who learn at an earlier age. This suggests that this is the age range at which motor skills are appropriately developed for bicycling.

Figure 10.3

Milestones of Physical Development, Birth to Age 2

| 3.2 months: Rolling over | 3.3 months: Grasping rattle | 5.9 months: Sitting without support | 7.2 months: Standing while holding on | 8.2 months: Grasping with thumb and finger |

birth weight, and their height increases by about half. This rapid growth slows down as the child gets older—think how gigantic adults would be if that rate of growth were constant—and from age 3 to the beginning of adolescence at around age 13, growth averages a gain of about 2.3 kilograms and 7.6 centimetres a year.

The physical changes that occur as children develop are not just a matter of increasing height and weight. The relationship of the size of the various body parts to one another changes dramatically as children age. For example, the head of a fetus (and a newborn) is disproportionately large, but it soon becomes more proportional in size to the rest of the body as growth occurs mainly in the trunk and legs (see Figure 10.4).

DEVELOPMENT OF SOCIAL BEHAVIOUR

Anyone who has seen an infant smiling at the sight of his or her mother can guess that at the same time that infants grow physically and hone their perceptual abilities, they also develop socially. The nature of a child's early social development provides the foundation for social relationships that will last a lifetime.

Relationships with Caregivers **Attachment**, the positive emotional bond that develops between a child and a specific individual, is the most important form of social development that occurs during infancy. The earliest studies of attachment, carried out by animal ethologist Konrad Lorenz (1966), focused on newborn goslings. Under normal circumstances, goslings instinctively follow their mother, the first moving object they perceive after birth. Lorenz found that goslings whose eggs were raised in an incubator and who viewed him immediately after hatching would follow his every movement, as if he were their mother. He labelled this process *imprinting*, behaviour that takes place during a critical period and involves attachment to the first moving object that is observed.

From the perspective of . . .

A PRACTICAL NURSE Consider what factors might determine why a child is not learning to walk at the same pace as his peers. What kinds of environmental influences might be involved? What kinds of genetic influences might be involved?

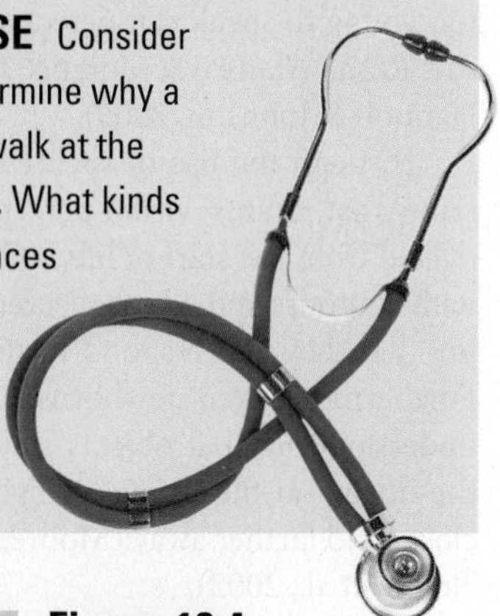

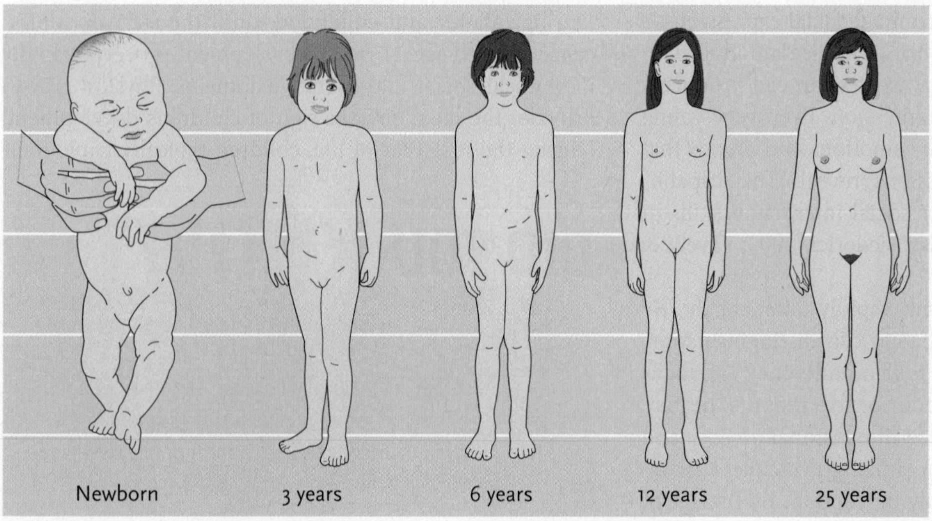

Figure 10.4

Head Size Relative to Body Size, Birth to Age 25

Newborn   3 years   6 years   12 years   25 years

Source: Adapted from Figure 5 from W. J. Robbins, *Growth.* Copyright 1928 Yale University Press. Used by permission of Yale University Press.

| 11.5 months: Standing alone well | 12.3 months: Walking well | 14.8 months: Building tower of two cubes | 16.6 months: Walking up steps | 23.8 months: Jumping in place |

Source: Frankenburg et al., 1992.

DID YOU KNOW?

Animals can become imprinted to any conspicuous moving object—even a rolling ball or wind-up-toy (Cardoso & Sabbatini, 2001)!

Our understanding of attachment progressed when psychologist Harry Harlow developed a classic study. Harlow rejected the ideas of Freud and others, who thought attachment was based solely on food. Harlow gave infant monkeys the choice of cuddling a wire "monkey" that provided milk or a soft, terry-cloth "monkey" that was warm but did not provide milk. Their choice was clear: they spent most of their time clinging to the warm cloth "monkey," although they made occasional forays to the wire monkey to nurse. The cloth monkey provided greater comfort to the infants than did milk alone (Blum, 2002; Harlow & Zimmerman, 1959).

Building on this pioneering work with non-humans, developmental psychologists have suggested that human

In Harlow's classic study, baby monkeys preferred the soft, terry-cloth "mother" even though the wire "mother" provided their food. (Source: Harry Harlow Primate Laboratory / University of Wisconsin.)

attachment grows through the responsiveness of infants' caregivers to the signals the babies provide, such as crying, smiling, reaching, and clinging. The greater the responsiveness of the caregiver to the child's signals, the more likely it is that the child will become securely attached. Full attachment eventually develops as a result of the complex series of interactions between caregiver and child. In the course of these interactions, the infant plays as critical and active a role as the caregiver in the formation of the bond. Infants who respond positively to a caregiver produce more positive behaviour on the part of the caregiver, which in turn produces an even stronger degree of attachment in the child. Developmental psychologists have devised a quick and direct way to measure attachment. Developed by Canadian Mary Ainsworth, the *Ainsworth strange situation* consists of a sequence of events involving a child and (typically) his or her mother. Initially, the mother and the baby enter an unfamiliar room, and the mother permits the baby to explore while she sits down. An adult stranger then enters the room, after which the mother leaves. The mother returns, and the stranger leaves. The mother once again leaves the baby alone, and the stranger returns. Finally, the stranger leaves, and the mother returns (Ainsworth et al., 1978; Combrink-Graham & McKenna, 2006; Izard & Abe, 2004).

Babies' reactions to the experimental situation vary drastically, depending, according to Ainsworth, on the baby's degree of attachment to the mother. One-year-old children who are *securely attached* employ the mother as a kind of home base, exploring independently but returning to her occasionally. When she leaves, they exhibit distress, and they go to her when she returns. *Avoidant* children do not cry when the mother leaves, and they seem to avoid her when she returns, as if they were indifferent to her. *Ambivalent* children display anxiety before they are separated and are upset when the mother leaves, but they may show ambivalent reactions to her return, such as seeking close contact but simultaneously hitting and kicking her. A fourth reaction is *disorganized-disoriented*; these children show inconsistent, often contradictory behaviour.

attachment The positive emotional bond that develops between a child and a specific individual.

In the strange situation procedure, a stranger attempts to play with the child after the primary caretaker leaves the room.

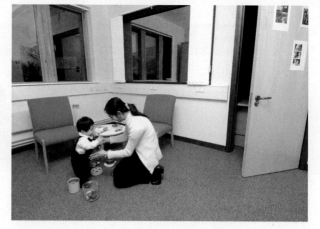

In the final stage of the strange situation procedure, the primary caretaker returns to the room and attempts to comfort the child. The child's attachment style is based on the reaction to the caretaker when she returns to the room.

The nature of attachment between children and their mothers has far-reaching consequences for later development. For example, children who are securely attached to their mothers tend to be more socially and emotionally competent than are their less securely attached peers, and others find them more cooperative, capable, and playful. Furthermore, children who are securely attached at age one show fewer psychological difficulties when they grow older compared with avoidant and ambivalent youngsters. As adults, children who are securely attached tend to have more successful romantic relationships. However, being securely attached at an early age does not guarantee good adjustment later, and, conversely, children who lack secure attachment do not always have difficulties later in life (Hardy, 2007; Mikulincer & Shaver, 2005; Roisman et al., 2005).

Keep in mind that Ainsworth and her colleagues used primarily North American caregivers and children from middle-class families in the research, so there may be some differences in how children from different cultures or socioeconomic statuses react in the strange situation test. For example, German mothers encourage independence in their children while Japanese mothers spend a considerable amount of time with their children, which results in differences in how these children respond in the strange situation compared to North American children. Overall, however, research has found that while there are differences in the levels of non-secure attachment styles, many countries (such as North America, Germany, Japan, and Sweden) had similar levels of secure attachment (Sagi, Van Ijzendoorn, & Koren-Kari, 1991). There were cultural differences in the level of secure attachment for children living in a kibbutz in Israel (a rural communal settlement), which isn't surprising given that the kibbutz children do not interact with strangers very often (Sagi, Van Ijzendoorn, & Koren-Kari, 1991).

Although early developmental research focused largely on the mother-child relationship, more recent research has highlighted the father's role in parenting, and with good reason: The number of fathers who are primary caregivers for their children has grown significantly, and fathers play an increasingly important role in their children's lives. For example, in almost 13% of families with children, the father is the parent who stays at home to care for preschoolers (Day & Lamb, 2004; Halford, 2006; Parke, 2004).

The close attachment bond that forms between infants and their primary caregiver is the most important social relationship of an individual's early life.

Fathers today are more likely to be the primary caregivers for their young children than was the case when psychologists started studying attachment. More recent studies show that the nature of attachment between fathers and children can be similar to that of mothers and children.

When fathers interact with their children, their play often differs from that of mothers. Fathers engage in more physical, rough-and-tumble sorts of activities, whereas mothers play more verbal and traditional games, such as peekaboo. Despite such behavioural differences, the nature of attachment between fathers and children compared with that between mothers and children can be similar. In fact, children can form multiple attachments simultaneously (Borisenko, 2007; Paquette, Carbonneau, & Dubeau, 2003; Pellis & Pellis, 2007).

Kim Bartholomew, from Simon Fraser University in British Columbia, has conducted numerous studies on adult attachment, relationship styles, and parenting over the past two decades. In one study, she collaborated with colleagues from Israel to examine how parenting role reversal, where children take on the role of the parent, might be related to parenting style and later attachment in adulthood (Mayseless, Bartholomew, Henderson, & Trinke, 2004). Bartholomew and colleagues found that parenting role reversal was related to growing up in families with more neglect, rejection, and little comfort. Moreover, they found that girls tended to take on this role more than boys did; however, boys did take on a parenting role more in situations of divorce. The good news was that although the children needed to take on the role of parent while they were children, this did not result in poor adult attachment or overly caretaking behaviour as adults.

Relationships with Peers By the time they are two years old, children have become less dependent on their parents and more self-reliant, increasingly preferring to play with friends. Initially, play is relatively independent: Even though they may be sitting side by side, two-year-olds pay more attention to toys than to one another when playing. They soon begin to actively interact, however, modifying one another's behaviour and later exchanging roles during play (Colwell & Lindsey, 2005; Lindsey & Colwell, 2003).

Cultural factors also affect children's styles of play. For example, Korean children engage in a higher degree of parallel play—playing independently even when they are next to each other—than do their Caucasian counterparts, while Caucasian preschoolers are involved in more pretend play (Bai, 2005; Drewes, 2005; Suizzo & Bornstein, 2006).

As children reach school age, their social interactions begin to follow set patterns, as well as becoming more frequent. Children may engage in elaborate games involving teams and rigid rules. This play serves purposes other than mere enjoyment. It allows children to become increasingly competent in their social interactions with others. Through play they learn to take the perspective of other people and to infer others' thoughts and feelings, even when those thoughts and feelings are not directly expressed (Royzman, Cassidy, & Baron, 2003).

In short, social interaction helps children to interpret the meaning of others' behaviour and to develop the capacity to respond appropriately. Furthermore, children learn physical and emotional self-control: they learn to avoid hitting a playmate who beats them at a game, to be polite, and to control their emotional displays and facial expressions (for example, smiling even when receiving a disappointing gift). Situations that provide children with opportunities for social interaction, then, may enhance their social development (Feldman, 1993; Lengua & Long, 2002; Talukdar & Shastri, 2006).

Parenting Styles Parents' child-rearing practices are critical in shaping their children's social competence. According to classic research by developmental psychologist Diana Baumrind, there are four main categories of parenting styles. Rigid and punitive, **authoritarian parents** value unquestioning obedience from their children. They have strict standards and discourage expressions of disagreement. **Permissive parents** give their children relaxed or inconsistent direction and, although warm, require little of the children. In contrast, **authoritative parents** are firm, setting limits for their children. As the children get older, these parents try to reason and explain things to them. They also set clear goals and encourage their children's independence. This is in contrast to **uninvolved parents**, who show

authoritarian parents Parents who are rigid and punitive and value unquestioning obedience from their children.

permissive parents Parents who give their children relaxed or inconsistent direction and, although they are warm, require little of the children

authoritative parents Parents who are firm, set clear limits, reason with their children, and explain things to them.

uninvolved parents Parents who show little interest in their children and are emotionally detached.

little interest in their children. Emotionally detached, they view parenting as nothing more than providing food, clothing, and shelter for children. At their most extreme, uninvolved parents are guilty of neglect, a form of child abuse (Baumrind, 2005; Lagacé-Séguin & d'Entremont, 2006; Winsler, Madigan, & Aquilino, 2005).

As you might expect, the four kinds of child-rearing styles seem to produce very different kinds of behaviour in children (with many exceptions, of course). Children of authoritarian parents tend to be unsociable, unfriendly, and relatively withdrawn. In contrast, permissive parents' children show immaturity, moodiness, dependence, and low self-control. The children of authoritative parents fare best. With high social skills, they are likable, self-reliant, independent, and cooperative. Parental monitoring, an aspect of authoritative parenting, involves both solicitation of information about the child's activities and control or limits on the child's behaviour. Teena Wiloughby and Chloe Hamza from Brock University found that higher levels of parental monitoring are associated with a decrease in behaviour problems (Wiloughby & Hamza, 2011). Worst off are the children of uninvolved parents; they feel unloved and emotionally detached, and their physical and cognitive development is impeded. Children with low social skills face peer rejection that can have lasting results (Berk, 2005; Saarni, 1999; Snyder, Cramer, & Afrank, 2005).

Study tip

Know the four major types of child-rearing practices—authoritarian, permissive, authoritative, and uninvolved—and how they impact the child's behaviour.

Psych think

> > > Which of Baumrind's parenting styles (authoritarian, permissive, authoritative, and uninvolved) is most effective?

Before we congratulate authoritative parents and condemn authoritarian, permissive, and uninvolved ones, we should note that in many cases non-authoritative parents also produce perfectly well-adjusted children. Moreover, children are born with a particular **temperament**—a basic, innate disposition. Some children are naturally easy-going and cheerful, whereas others are irritable and fussy, or pensive and quiet. The kind of temperament a baby is born with may in part bring about specific kinds of parental child-rearing styles (Lengua & Kovacs, 2005; Majdandzic & van den Boom, 2007; Porter & Hsu, 2003).

Erikson's Theory of Psychosocial Development In tracing the course of social development, some theorists have considered how the challenges of society and culture change as an individual matures. Following this path, psychoanalyst Erik Erikson developed one of the more comprehensive theories of social development. Erikson (1963) viewed the developmental changes occurring throughout life as a series of eight stages of psychosocial development,

temperament The basic, innate disposition that emerges early in life.

Figure 10.5
Baumrind's Four Styles of Parenting

Parenting Style	Parent Behaviour	Type of Behaviour Produced in Child
Authoritarian	Rigid, punitive, strict standards (example: "If you don't clean your room, I'm going to take away your iPod for good and ground you.")	Unsociable, unfriendly, withdrawn
Permissive	Lax, inconsistent, undemanding (example: "It might be good to clean your room, but I guess it can wait.")	Immature, moody, dependent, low self-control
Authoritative	Firm, sets limits and goals, uses reasoning, encourages independence (example: "You'll need to clean your room before we can go out to the restaurant. As soon as you finish, we'll leave.")	Good social skills, likable, self-reliant, independent
Uninvolved	Detached emotionally, sees role only as providing food, clothing, and shelter (example: "I couldn't care less if your room is a pigsty.")	Indifferent, rejecting behaviour

of which four occur during childhood. **Psychosocial development** involves changes in the way in which people understand themselves, one another, and the world around them over the course of a lifetime.

Erikson suggests that passage through each of the stages necessitates the resolution of a crisis or conflict. Accordingly, Erikson represents each stage as a pairing of the most positive and most negative aspects of the crisis of that period. Although each crisis is never resolved entirely—life becomes increasingly complicated as we grow older—it has to be resolved sufficiently to equip us to deal with demands made during the stages of development that follow. Refer to Figure 10.10 for a summary of Erikson's stages of psychosocial development.

Erikson's theory of psychosocial development is one of the few theories that encompass the entire lifespan.

In the first stage of psychosocial development, the **trust-versus-mistrust stage** (ages birth to one-and-a-half years), infants develop feelings of trust if their physical requirements and psychological needs for attachment are consistently met and their interactions with the world are generally positive. In contrast, inconsistent care and unpleasant interactions with others can lead to mistrust and leave an infant unable to meet the challenges required in the next stage of development.

In the second stage, the **autonomy-versus-shame-and-doubt stage** (ages one-and-a-half to three years), toddlers develop independence and autonomy if exploration and freedom are encouraged, or they experience shame, self-doubt, and unhappiness if they are overly restricted and protected. As you can imagine, it will be difficult for children to feel free to explore in safety if they have not developed basic trust with one or more of their primary caregivers. According to Erikson, the key to the development of autonomy during this period is that the child's caregivers provide the appropriate amount of control. If parents provide too much control, children cannot assert themselves and develop their own sense of control over their environment; if parents provide too little control, the children become overly demanding and controlling.

Next, children face the crises of the **initiative-versus-guilt stage** (ages three to six). In this stage, children's desire to act independently conflicts with the guilt that comes from the unintended and unexpected consequences of such behaviour. Children in this period come to understand that they are persons in their own right, and they begin to make decisions about their behaviour. If parents

psychosocial development Development of individuals' interactions and understanding of one another and of their knowledge and understanding of themselves as members of society.

trust-versus-mistrust stage According to Erikson, the first stage of psychosocial development, occurring from birth to age one-and-a-half years, during which time infants develop feelings of trust or lack of trust.

autonomy-versus-shame-and-doubt stage The period during which, according to Erikson, toddlers (ages one-and-a-half to three years) develop independence and autonomy if exploration and freedom are encouraged, or shame and self-doubt if they are restricted and overprotected.

initiative-versus-guilt stage According to Erikson, the period during which children ages three to six years experience conflict between independence of action and the sometimes negative results of that action.

industry-versus-inferiority stage According to Erikson, the last stage of childhood, during which children age six to twelve years may develop positive social interactions with others or may feel inadequate and become less sociable.

react positively to children's attempts at independence, they will help their children resolve the initiative-versus-guilt crisis positively.

The fourth and last stage of childhood is the **industry-versus-inferiority stage** (ages six to twelve). During this period, increasing competency in all areas, whether social interactions or academic skills, characterizes successful psychosocial development. In contrast, difficulties in this stage lead to feelings of failure and inadequacy.

Erikson's theory suggests that psychosocial development continues throughout life, and he proposes four more crises that are faced after childhood (described on p. 266). Although his theory has been criticized on several grounds (for example, some of the concepts are vague and/or not easy to measure), it remains influential and is one of the few theories that encompass the entire life span.

According to Erikson, children develop autonomy between the ages of one-and-a-half to three years if their caregivers give them an opportunity to explore without too many restrictions.

Study tip

Four of Erikson's stages of psychosocial development occur during childhood: trust-versus-mistrust, autonomy-versus-shame-and-doubt, initiative-versus-guilt, and industry-versus-inferiority.

Cognitive Development: Children's Thinking About the World Suppose you are at a restaurant and you and your friend order the same drink but the server brings them in two different glasses—one short and broad and one tall and thin. It appears at first as though your friend who received the tall and thin glass received more, but you quickly determine that the glasses hold the exact same amount. However, if you were a four-year-old, you would probably start crying because you perceived your friend was getting more.

Why are young children confused by this problem? The reason is not immediately obvious. Anyone who has observed preschoolers must be impressed by how far they have progressed from the early stages of development. They speak with ease, know the alphabet, count, play complex games, use computers, tell stories, and communicate ably. Yet despite this seeming sophistication, there are deep gaps in children's understanding of the world. Some theorists have suggested that children cannot understand certain ideas and concepts until they reach a certain stage of **cognitive development**—the process by which a child's understanding of the world changes as a function of age and experience. In contrast to Erikson's theory of psychosocial development discussed previously, theories of cognitive development seek to explain the intellectual advances that occur during development. These advances include quantitative and qualitative changes. Quantitative development refers to growth that adds more to what already is in place. In physical development, for example, children grow taller as they develop. In intellectual development, children tend to develop longer attention spans as they grow.

Children's cognitive development advances as their attention spans increase.

Qualitative development refers to changes that instead of adding more abilities result in different ones. For example, walking is a physical development that occurs after crawling, but walking is not simply more crawling. Qualitative changes in intellectual development enhance the ability to think.

Now stop reading for a moment, and consider what you are planning to do this weekend. How many items did you hold in your mind while thinking about your plans? As we will see in the following discussion of Piaget's theory, children's ability to think about different concepts depends on how many items they can hold in mind. At first, they can't hold any!

cognitive development The process by which a child's understanding of the world changes as a function of age and experience.

assimilation Attempting to fit new information into existing schemas.

accommodation Modifying or changing existing schemas to fit new information.

sensorimotor stage According to Piaget, the stage from birth to two years, during which a child has little competence in representing the environment by using images, language, or other symbols.

object permanence The awareness that objects—and people—continue to exist even if they are out of sight.

Piaget's Theory of Cognitive Development No theory of cognitive development has been more influential than that of Swiss psychologist Jean Piaget. Piaget was interested in how children's thinking developed as they grew older and experienced more of their world. By observing children's mental errors, he noticed that children needed to constantly make mental adaptations as they interacted with their world. Two ways that children adapt is by assimilation and accommodation. **Assimilation** is when the child fits new knowledge into his or her existing schemas (how he or she organizes the categories of information he or she already knows). For example, suppose three-year-old Carson has a golden retriever named Chico. His schema for dogs will be golden retrievers and when he sees another animal that resembles his schema for dogs, he will assimilate this information into his existing schema for dogs. So if Carson sees a cat (four legged furry animal that fits his schema for dog) he will say "doggy." After being nicely corrected by his parents, Carson will learn that cats and dogs are different and will subsequently develop a new schema for cats. When Carson does this, he has gone through the process of **accommodation**, which means he has modified or changed his existing schema.

> ## No theory of cognitive development has been more influential than that of Swiss psychologist Jean Piaget.

Piaget (1970) suggested that children around the world proceed through a series of four stages in a fixed order. He maintained that these stages differ not only in the *quantity* of information acquired at each stage but also in the *quality* of knowledge and understanding as well. Taking an interactionist point of view, he suggested that movement from one stage to the next occurs when a child reaches an appropriate level of maturation *and* is exposed to relevant types of experiences. Piaget assumed that, without having such experiences, children could not reach their highest level of cognitive growth.

Piaget proposed four stages: sensorimotor, preoperations, concrete operations, and formal operations. During the **sensorimotor stage**, from birth to age two, children base their understanding of the world primarily on touching, sucking, chewing, shaking, and manipulating objects. In the initial part of the stage, children have a limited ability to think about the world using images, language, or other kinds of symbols. Consequently, infants lack what Piaget calls **object permanence**, the ability to hold in mind

Figure 10.6
Piaget's Theory of Cognitive Development

Sensorimotor Stage

Development of object permanence, development of motor skills, little or no capacity for symbolic representation

Birth to 2 Years

Preoperational Stage

Development of language and symbolic thinking, egocentric thinking

2 to 7 Years

Concrete Operational Mastery Stage

Development of conservation, of concept of reversibility

7 to 12 Years

Formal Operational Stage

Development of logical and abstract thinking

12 Years Through Adulthood

a mental representation of things and ideas. Without this ability, infants cannot have the awareness that objects—and people—continue to exist even if they are out of sight.

How do we know that children lack object permanence? Although we cannot ask infants, we can observe their reactions when a toy they are playing with is hidden under a blanket. Until the age of about nine months, children will make no attempt to locate the hidden toy. However, soon after that age they will begin an active search for the missing object, indicating that they have developed a mental representation of the toy. Object permanence, then, is a critical development during the sensorimotor stage.

The most important development during the **preoperational stage**, beginning about age two and lasting till age seven, is the use of language. Children develop internal representational systems that allow them to describe people, events, and feelings. They even use symbols in play, pretending, for example, that a book pushed across the floor is a car.

Although children use more advanced thinking in this stage than they did in the earlier sensorimotor stage, their thinking is still qualitatively different to that of adults. We see this when we observe a preoperational child using **egocentric thought**, a way of thinking in which the child views the world entirely from his or her own perspective.

Children who have not mastered the principle of conservation assume that the volume of a liquid increases when it is poured from a short, wide container into a tall, thin one.

Preoperational children do not understand that other people have a different perspective and knowledge. Thus, children's stories and explanations to adults can be maddeningly uninformative, as they are delivered without any context. For example, a preoperational child may start a story with "He wouldn't let me go," neglecting to mention who "he" is or where the storyteller wanted to go. We also see egocentric thinking when children at the preoperational stage play hiding games. For instance, three-year-olds frequently hide with their faces against a wall, covering their eyes—although they are still in plain view. It seems to them that if *they* cannot see, then no one else will be able to see them.

In addition, preoperational children have not yet developed the ability to understand the **principle of conservation**, which is the knowledge that quantity is unrelated to the arrangement and physical appearance of objects. Children who have not mastered this

preoperational stage According to Piaget, the period from two to seven years of age that is characterized by language development.

egocentric thought A way of thinking in which a child views the world entirely from his or her own perspective.

principle of conservation The knowledge that quantity is unrelated to the arrangement and physical appearance of objects.

Figure 10.7
Principles of Conservation

Conservation of...	Modality	Change in physical appearance	Average age at full mastery
Number	Number of elements in a collection	Rearranging or dislocating elements	6–7 years
Substance (mass)	Amount of a malleable substance (e.g., clay or liquid) 	Altering shape	7–8 years
Length	Length of a line or object	Altering shape or configuration	7–8 years
Area	Amount of surface covered by a set of plane figures 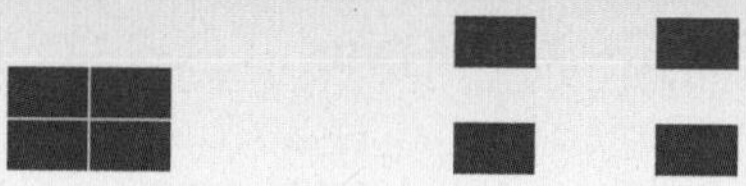	Rearranging the figures	8–9 years
Weight	Weight of an object	Altering shape	9–10 years
Volume	Volume of an object (in terms of water displacement) 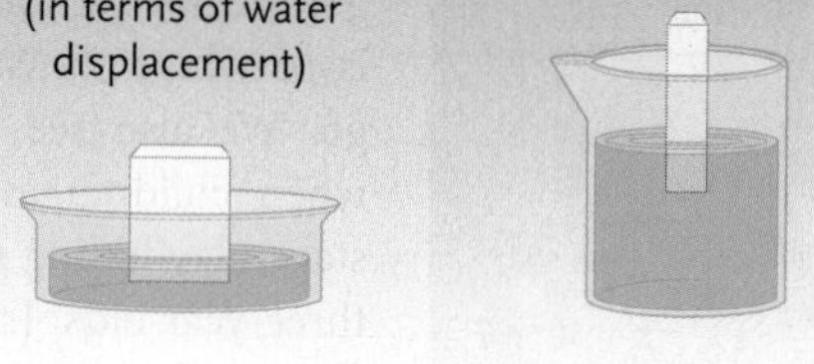	Altering shape	14–15 years

concept do not know that the amount, volume, or length of an object does not change when its shape or configuration changes. The question about the two glasses—one short and broad and the other tall and thin—with which we began our discussion of cognitive development illustrates this point clearly. Children who do not understand the principle of conservation invariably state that the amount of liquid changes as it is poured back and forth. They cannot comprehend that a transformation in appearance does not imply a transformation in amount. Instead, it seems as reasonable to the child that there is a change in quantity as it does to the adult that there is no change.

In a number of other ways, some quite startling, the failure to understand the principle of conservation affects children's responses. Research demonstrates that principles that are obvious to and unquestioned by adults may

be completely misunderstood by children during the preoperational period.

Mastery of the principle of conservation, at around age seven, marks the beginning of Piaget's **concrete operational stage**, although children do not fully understand some aspects of conservation, such as conservation of weight and volume, until they are older.

During the concrete operational stage, which spans the ages of 7 to 12, children develop the ability to think in a more logical manner and begin to overcome some of the egocentrism of the preoperational period. One of the major principles children learn during this stage is reversibility, the idea that some changes can be undone by reversing an earlier action. For example, they can understand that when someone rolls a ball of clay into a long sausage shape, that person can re-create the original ball by reversing the action. Children can even conceptualize this principle in their heads, without having to see the action performed before them; at this point, they can hold two ideas in mind simultaneously.

Although children make important advances in their logical capabilities during the concrete operational stage, their thinking still displays one major limitation: They are largely bound to the concrete, physical reality of the world. For the most part, they have difficulty understanding questions of an abstract or hypothetical nature.

Piaget's **formal operational stage** produces a new kind of thinking that is abstract, formal, and logical. During the period from age 12 to adulthood, thinking is no longer tied to events that individuals observe in the environment but incorporates logical techniques for resolving problems.

The way in which children approach the "pendulum problem" devised by Piaget (Inhelder & Piaget, 1958) illustrates the emergence of formal operational thinking. The problem solver is asked to figure out what determines how fast a pendulum swings. Is it the length of the string, the

concrete operational stage According to Piaget, the period from 7 to 12 years of age that is characterized by logical thought and a loss of egocentrism.

formal operational stage According to Piaget, the period from age 12 to adulthood that is characterized by abstract thought.

weight of the pendulum, or the force with which the pendulum is pushed? (For the record, the answer is the length of the string.)

Children in the concrete operational stage approach the problem haphazardly, without a logical or rational plan of action. For example, they may simultaneously change the length of the string and the weight on the string and the force with which they push the pendulum. Because they are varying all the factors at once, they cannot tell which factor is the critical one. In contrast, people in the formal operational stage approach the problem systematically. Acting as if they were scientists conducting an experiment, they examine the effects of changes in one variable at a time. This ability to rule out competing possibilities characterizes formal operational thought.

Although formal operational thought emerges during the teenage years, some individuals use this type of thinking only infrequently. Moreover, it appears that many individuals never reach this stage at all; most studies show that only 40% to 60% of college students and adults fully reach it, with some estimates running as low as 25% of the general population (Keating & Clark, 1980).

No other theorist has given us as comprehensive a theory of cognitive development as Piaget did. In general, most developmental psychologists agree that Piaget provided us with a fairly accurate account of age-related changes in cognitive development. Still, many contemporary theorists suggest that stage theories such as Piaget's do not accurately predict children's cognitive development. For instance, children are not always consistent in their performance of tasks that—if Piaget's theory is accurate—ought to be performed equally well at a specific stage (Feldman, 2003, 2004).

Piaget also underestimated the age at which infants and children can understand specific concepts and principles. In fact, they seem to be more sophisticated in their cognitive abilities than Piaget believed. For instance, some evidence suggests that infants as young as five months have a rudimentary understanding of arithmetic (Wynn, 1995, 2000; Wynn, Bloom, & Chiang, 2002).

Furthermore, some developmental psychologists suggest that cognitive development proceeds in a more continuous fashion than Piaget's stage theory implies. They propose that cognitive development is primarily

Psych
At The Movies

Thirteen

This is a study of the vulnerability of adolescence when a stable identity is not yet established and peer pressure can be particularly powerful.

Schindler's List

An Austrian businessman evidences the highest level of moral reasoning by risking his life to save Jews destined for the gas chambers during World War II.

My First Mister

A cynical young goth woman forms an unlikely friendship with a middle-aged, relatively conservative man. Watch for stages of dying and grieving as the young woman deals with her friend's impending death.

quantitative in nature, rather than qualitative. In this view, although there are differences in when, how, and to what extent a child can use specific cognitive abilities—reflecting quantitative changes—the underlying cognitive processes change relatively little with age (Case & Okamoto, 1996; Gelman & Baillargeon, 1983).

Information-Processing Approaches: Charting Children's Mental Programs If cognitive development does not proceed as a series of stages, as Piaget suggested, how can we explain the enormous growth in children's cognitive abilities? Many developmental psychologists attribute cognitive development to changes in **information processing**, the way in which people take in, use, and store information (Cashon & Cohen, 2004; Lacerda, von Hofsten, & Heimann, 2001; Munakata, 2006).

According to this approach, quantitative changes occur in children's ability to organize and manipulate information. From this perspective, children become increasingly adept at information processing, much as a computer program may become more sophisticated as a programmer modifies it on the basis of experience. Information-processing approaches consider the kinds of "mental programs" that children invoke when approaching problems.

Several significant changes occur in children's information-processing capabilities. The speed at which children can scan, recognize, and compare stimuli increases with age. As they grow older, children can pay attention to stimuli longer and discriminate among different stimuli more readily, and they are less easily distracted (Myerson et al., 2003; Van den Wildenberg & Van der Molen, 2004).

Psych think

> > > Imagine you are speaking on the telephone with three-year-old Palmer. At one point in the conversation he says to you "look at the fort I made out of pillows" and you hear him move the telephone from the side of his head to in front of his fort. Why would Palmer think that you could see what he could see?

information processing The way in which people take in, use, and store information.

Both short-term and long-term memory also improve dramatically with age. Preschoolers can hold only two or three chunks of information in short-term memory, five-year-olds can hold four, and seven-year-olds can hold five. (Adults are able to keep seven, plus or minus two, chunks in short-term memory.) The size of chunks held in short-term memory also grows with age, as does the sophistication and organization of knowledge stored in long-term memory. Still, long-term memory capabilities are impressive at a very early age: even before they can speak, infants can remember for months events in which they actively participated (Bayliss et al., 2005b; Cowan et al., 2003).

Finally, improvement in information processing relates to advances in **metacognition**, an awareness and understanding of one's own cognitive processes. Metacognition involves the planning, monitoring, and revising of cognitive strategies. Younger children, who lack an awareness of their own cognitive processes, often do not realize their incapabilities. Thus, when they misunderstand others, they may fail to recognize their own errors. It is only later, when metacognitive abilities become more sophisticated, that children are able to know when they don't understand. Such increasing sophistication reflects a change in children's *theory of mind*, their knowledge and beliefs about the way the mind operates (Bernstein, Loftus, & Meltzoff, 2005; Matthews & Funke, 2006; McCormick, 2003).

Vygotsky's Socio-Cultural View of Cognitive Development According to Russian developmental psychologist Lev Vygotsky, the culture in which we are raised significantly affects our cognitive development; we cannot understand cognitive development without taking into account the social aspects of learning. Vygotsky argues that cognitive development occurs as a consequence of social interactions in which children work with others to jointly solve problems. Through such interactions, children's cognitive skills increase, and they gain the ability to function intellectually on their own. More specifically, he suggests that children's cognitive abilities increase when they encounter information that they are ready to learn. He called this readiness to learn the **zone of proximal development (ZPD)**, the level at which a child can almost, but not fully, comprehend or perform a task on his or her own. When children receive information that falls within the ZPD, they can increase their understanding or master a new task. In contrast, if the information lies outside children's ZPD, the children will not be able to master it (Maynard & Martini, 2005; Rieber & Robinson, 2006; Vygotsky, 1926/1997).

In short, cognitive development occurs when parents, teachers, or skilled peers assist a child by presenting information that is both new and within the ZPD. This type of assistance, called *scaffolding*, provides support for learning

Adults and older children promote cognitive development in young children by helping them to complete new tasks. Vygotsky called this kind of support scaffolding.

and problem solving that encourages independence and growth. For example, suppose five-year-old Maria is ready to learn that subtraction is the reverse of addition. Her older brother could give her some apples and encourage her to use them to do some addition problems. Then he could provide scaffolding for subtraction, perhaps by demonstrating a few times, until Maria could do the subtraction problems on her own. Vygotsky claims that scaffolding not only promotes the solution of specific problems but also aids in the development of overall cognitive abilities (Schaller & Crandall, 2004).

More than other approaches to cognitive development, Vygotsky's theory considers how an individual's specific cultural and social context affects intellectual growth. The way in which children understand the world grows out of interactions with parents, peers, and other members of a specific culture (John-Steiner & Mahn, 2003; Kozulin et al., 2003).

From the perspective of...

AN ELEMENTARY SCHOOL TEACHER

How would you put Vygotsky's ideas to practical use in the classroom?

metacognition An awareness and understanding of one's own cognitive processes.

zone of proximal development (ZPD) According to Vygotsky, the level at which a child can almost, but not fully, comprehend or perform a task on his or her own.

Vygotsky's approach compliments Piaget's theory and the information-processing perspectives. These theories contribute in different ways to our understanding of the complex and intriguing process of cognitive development and its biological and environmental underpinnings.

Adolescence

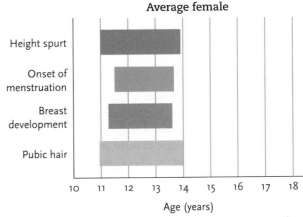

Joseph Charles, Age 13: Being 13 is very hard at school. I have to be bad in order to be considered cool. I sometimes do things that aren't good. I have talked back to my teachers and been disrespectful to them. I do want to be good, but it's just too hard. (Gibbs, 2005, p. 51)

Trevor Kelson, Age 15: "Keep the Hell Out of my Room!" says a sign on Trevor's bedroom wall, just above an unmade bed, a desk littered with dirty T-shirts and candy wrappers, and a floor covered with clothes. Is there a carpet? "Somewhere," he says with a grin. "I think it's gold." (Fields-Meyer, 1995, p. 53)

Lauren Barry, Age 18: "I went to a National Honour Society induction. The parents were just staring at me. I think they couldn't believe someone with pink hair could be smart. I want to be a high-school teacher, but I'm afraid that, based on my appearance, they won't hire me."

Although Joseph, Trevor, and Lauren have never met, they share anxieties that are common to adolescence—concerns about friends, parents, appearance, independence, and their futures. **Adolescence**, the developmental stage between childhood and adulthood, is a crucial period. It is a time of profound changes and, occasionally, turmoil. Adolescence is not the same thing as puberty, when sexual maturation occurs. Puberty is defined by biology while adolescence is defined more by society. For example, in earlier times the transition between childhood and adulthood was virtually non-existent. Children reached adulthood when they were biologically capable of bearing children. Because many years of schooling precede most people's entry into the workforce in Western societies, the stage of adolescence is fairly long, beginning just before the teenage years and ending just after them. No longer children but considered by our society to be not quite adults, adolescents must cope with a period of rapid physical, cognitive, and social change. Adolescence is a period of considerable biological changes as adolescents attain sexual and physical maturity. At the same time, and

rivalling these physiological changes, important social, emotional, and cognitive changes occur as adolescents strive for independence and move toward adulthood.

PHYSICAL CHANGES

If you think back to the start of your own adolescence, the changes you probably remember best are physical ones. A spurt in height, the growth of breasts in girls, deepening voices in boys, the development of body hair, and intense sexual feelings cause curiosity, interest, and sometimes embarrassment for young adolescents.

The physical changes that occur at the start of adolescence result largely from the secretion of various hormones, and they affect virtually every aspect of an adolescent's life. Not since infancy has development been so dramatic. Weight and height increase rapidly, owing to a growth spurt that typically begins around age 10 for girls and age 12 for boys. Adolescents may grow as much as 13 centimetres in one year.

Puberty, the period when the sexual organs mature, begins at about age 11 or 12 for girls, when menstruation starts. There are wide variations, however. Some girls experience *menarche*, the onset of menstruation, as early

Figure 10.8
Physical Development in Adolescence

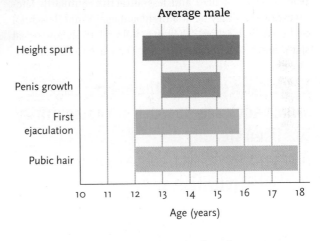

Source: Based on Tanner, 1978.

---

adolescence The developmental stage between childhood and adulthood.

puberty The period at which maturation of the sexual organs occurs, beginning about age 11 or 12 for girls and 13 or 14 for boys.

as age 8 or 9 or as late as age 16. In Western cultures, the average age at which adolescents reach sexual maturity has been steadily decreasing over the last century, most likely as a result of improved nutrition and medical care (Finlay, Jones, & Coleman, 2002; Tanner, 1990).

For boys, the onset of puberty is marked by their first ejaculation, known as *spermarche*. Spermarche usually occurs around the age of 13. At first, relatively few sperm are produced during an ejaculation, but the amount increases significantly within a few years.

The age at which puberty begins has implications for the way adolescents feel about themselves—as well as the way others treat them. Early-maturing boys have a distinct advantage over later-maturing boys. They do better in athletics, are generally more popular with peers, and have more positive self-concepts (Becker & Luthar, 2007; Ge et al., 2003).

The picture differs for girls. Although early-maturing girls are more sought after as dates and have better self-esteem than do later-maturing girls, some consequences of early physical maturation may be less positive. For example, early breast development may set them apart from their peers and be a source of ridicule (Franko & Striegel-Moore, 2002; Nadeem & Graham, 2005; Olivardia & Pope, 2002).

Late physical maturation may produce certain psychological difficulties for both boys and girls. Boys who are smaller and less coordinated than their more mature peers tend to feel ridiculed and less attractive. Similarly, late-maturing girls may be at a disadvantage in middle school and early high school. They may hold relatively low social status and be overlooked in dating (Lanza & Collins, 2002).

> **In Western cultures, the average age at which adolescents reach sexual maturity has been steadily decreasing over the last century, most likely as a result of improved nutrition and medical care.**

Clearly, the rate at which physical changes occur during adolescence can affect the way in which people are viewed by others and the way they view themselves. Just as important as physical changes, however, are the psychological and social changes that unfold during adolescence.

MORAL AND COGNITIVE DEVELOPMENT

In a European country, a woman is near death from a special kind of cancer. The one drug that the doctors think might save her is a medicine that a medical researcher has recently discovered. The drug is expensive to make, and the researcher is charging 10 times the cost, or $5,000, for a small dose. The sick woman's husband, Henry, approaches everyone he knows in hopes of borrowing money, but he can get together only about $2,500. He tells the researcher that his wife is dying and asks him to lower the price of the drug or let him pay later. The

researcher says, "No, I discovered the drug, and I'm going to make money from it." Henry is desperate and considers stealing the drug for his wife.

What would you tell Henry to do?

Kohlberg's Theory of Moral Development In the view of psychologist Lawrence Kohlberg, the advice you give Henry reflects your level of moral development. According to Kohlberg, people pass through a series of stages in the evolution of their sense of justice and in the kind of reasoning they use to make moral judgments (Kohlberg, 1984). Largely because of the various cognitive limitations that Piaget described, preadolescent children tend to think either in terms of concrete, unvarying rules ("It is always wrong to steal" or "I'll be punished if I steal") or in terms of the rules of society ("Good people don't steal" or "What if everyone stole?").

Adolescents, however, can reason on a higher plane, having typically reached Piaget's formal operational stage of cognitive development. Because they are able to comprehend broad moral principles, they can understand that morality is not always black and white and that conflict can exist between two sets of socially accepted standards.

Kohlberg (1984) suggests that the changes in moral reasoning can be understood best as a three-level sequence. The first level is called *preconventional morality*, where one focuses on the rewards or punishments associated with the behaviour. The second level is called *conventional morality*, where one considers how the behaviour would reflect on his or her ability to be a good member of society. The last and highest level is called the *postconventional morality*, and at this stage the individual is able to use moral reasoning that goes beyond the needs of society.

Kolberg's theory assumes that people move through the levels in a fixed order and that they cannot reach the highest level, postconventional, until about age 13—primarily because of limitations in cognitive development before that age. However, many people never reach the highest level of moral reasoning. In fact, Kohlberg found that only a relatively small percentage of adults rise above the second level of his model (Hedgepeth, 2005; Kohlberg & Ryncarz, 1990; Powers, 2006).

Although Kohlberg's theory has had a substantial influence on our understanding of moral development, the research support is mixed. One difficulty with the theory is that it pertains to moral *judgments*, not moral *behaviour*. Knowing right from wrong does not mean that we will

Figure 10.9

Kohlberg's Three Levels of Moral Development

Sample Moral Reasoning of Subjects

Level	In Favour of Stealing the Drug	Against Stealing the Drug
Level 1 Preconventional morality: At this level, the concrete interests of the individual are considered in terms of rewards and punishments.	"If you let your wife die, you will get in trouble. You'll be blamed for not spending the money to save her, and there'll be an investigation of you and the druggist for your wife's death."	"You shouldn't steal the drug because you'll be caught and sent to jail if you do. If you do get away, your conscience will bother you thinking how the police will catch up with you at any minute."
Level 2 Conventional morality: At this level, people approach moral problems as members of society. They are interested in pleasing others by acting as good members of society.	"If you let your wife die, you'll never be able to look anybody in the face again."	"After you steal the drug, you'll feel bad thinking how you've brought dishonour on your family and yourself; you won't be able to face anyone again."
Level 3 Postconventional morality: At this level, people use moral principles which are seen as broader than those of any particular society.	"If you don't steal the drug, and if you let your wife die, you'll always condemn yourself for it afterward. You won't be blamed and you'll have lived up to the outside rule of the law, but you won't have lived up to your own conscience and standards of honesty."	"If you steal the drug, you won't be blamed by other people, but you'll condemn yourself because you won't have lived up to your own conscience and standards of honesty."

Source: D. Goslin (ed.), *Handbook of Socialization and Research.* © 1969 by Rand McNally.

always act in accordance with our judgments. In addition, the theory applies primarily to Western societies and their moral codes; cross-cultural research conducted in cultures with different moral systems suggests that Kohlberg's theory is not necessarily applicable to them (Barandiaran, Pascual, & Samaniego, 2006; Coles, 1997; Damon, 1999; Nucci, 2002).

One glaring shortcoming of Kohlberg's research is that he primarily used male participants. Psychologist Carol Gilligan (1996) argues that, because of men's and women's distinctive socialization experiences, a fundamental difference exists in the way each gender views moral behaviour. According to Gilligan, men view morality primarily in terms of broad principles, such as justice and fairness. In contrast, women see it in terms of responsibility toward individuals and willingness to make sacrifices to help a specific individual within the context of a particular relationship. Compassion for individuals is a more salient factor in moral behaviour for women than it is for men.

Because Kohlberg's model defines moral behaviour largely in terms of abstract principles such as justice, Gilligan finds that it inadequately describes the moral development of females. She suggests that women's morality centres on individual well-being and social relationships—a morality of *caring*. In her view, compassionate

concern for the welfare of others represents the highest level of morality.

The fact that Gilligan's conception of morality differs greatly from Kohlberg's suggests that gender plays an important role in determining what a person sees as moral. Although the research evidence is not definitive, it seems plausible that their differing conceptions of what constitutes moral behaviour may lead men and women to regard the morality of a specific behaviour in different ways (Jorgensen, 2006; Lippa, 2005; Weisz & Black, 2002).

Study tip

The difference between Kohlberg's theory and Gilligan's approach to moral development is significant, with Kohlberg's theory focusing on stages of development in males and Gilligan's resting on gender differences.

ADOLESCENT SOCIAL DEVELOPMENT

"Who am I?" "How do I fit into the world?" "What is life all about?"

Questions such as these assume special significance during the teenage years, as adolescents seek to find their place in the broader social world. As we will see, this quest takes adolescents along several routes.

THE WORLD'S FIRST GENETICALLY ENGINEERED HUMAN HITS ADOLESCENCE

We buy you the best genes in the world— FOR THIS?

So, I got my nose pierced. So what, man.

I remember checking "genius" on the order form— AND NOW LOOK!

Erikson's Theory of Psychosocial Development

Erikson's theory of psychosocial development emphasizes the search for identity during the adolescent years. As was noted earlier, psychosocial development encompasses the way people's understanding of themselves, of one another, and of the world around them changes during the course of development (Erikson, 1963).

The fifth stage of Erikson's theory, **identity-versus-role-confusion**, encompasses adolescence. During this stage, a time of major testing, people try to determine what is unique about themselves. They attempt to discover who they are,

identity-versus-role-confusion stage According to Erikson, a time in adolescence of major testing to determine one's unique qualities.

identity The distinguishing character of the individual: who each of us is, what our roles are, and what we are capable of.

what their strengths are, and what kinds of roles they are best suited to play for the rest of their lives—in short, their **identity**. Unsuccessful navigation of this stage leaves a person confused about the most appropriate role to play in life. He or she may lack a stable identity, adopt an unacceptable role such as that of a social deviant, and/or have difficulty maintaining close personal relationships later in life (Goldstein, 2006; Updegraff et al., 2004; Vleioras & Bosma, 2005).

Part of the successful navigation of identity formation is a positive and supportive social environment. This may take the form of parental support or support from the adolescent's peers or academic environment. This was evident in the research of Tara Dumas from the University of Western Ontario, who worked with colleagues from Wilfred Laurier University to examine how identity development and was associated with parenting style. The researchers found that adolescents who perceived their parents to have an authoritative style of parenting (i.e., emotionally supportive and involved in their lives) were emotionally well adjusted and had a positive sense of identity in adulthood (Dumas, Lawford, Tieu, & Pratt, 2009).

Other Canadian researchers have also been interested in the factors that influence positive identity formation. For example, Marie Good from Brock University and colleague Gerard Adams from Guelph University looked at the influence of a positive university experience on identity formation, psychological strength, and academic success. The

Figure 10.10

Erikson's Stages of Psychosocial Development

1 Trust-Versus-Mistrust

Approximate age: Birth–1¹/₂ years

Positive outcomes: Feelings of trust from environmental support

Negative outcomes: Fear and concern regarding others

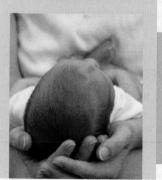

2 Autonomy-Versus-Shame-and-Doubt

Approximate age: 1¹/₂–3 years

Positive outcomes: Self-sufficiency if exploration is encouraged

Negative outcomes: Doubts about self, lack of independence

3 Initiative-Versus-Guilt

Approximate age: 3–6 years

Positive outcomes: Discovery of ways to initiate actions

Negative outcomes: Guilt from actions and thoughts

4 Industry-Versus-Inferiority

Approximate age: 6–12 years

Positive outcomes: Development of sense of competence

Negative outcomes: Feelings of inferiority, no sense of mastery

researchers found that students who had a positive relationship with faculty tended to do better academically and that identity formation was positively related to psychological strength (Good & Adams, 2008).

The identify-versus-role confusion period can be particularly challenging because adolescents feel pressured to decide what to do with their lives. Because this pressure comes at a time of major physical changes as well as important changes in what society expects of them, adolescents can find the period to be an especially difficult one. The identity-versus-role-confusion stage has another important characteristic: declining reliance on adults for information, with a shift toward using the peer group as a source of social judgments. The peer group becomes increasingly important, enabling adolescents to form close, adult-like relationships and helping them clarify their personal identities. According to Erikson, the identity-versus-role-confusion stage marks a pivotal point in psychosocial development, paving the way for continued growth and the future development of personal relationships.

During early adulthood, people enter the **intimacy-versus-isolation stage**. Spanning the period of early adulthood (from post-adolescence to the early 30s), this stage focuses on developing close relationships with others. Difficulties during this stage result in feelings of loneliness and a fear of close relationships, whereas successful resolution of the crises of the stage results in the possibility of forming relationships that are intimate on a physical, intellectual, and emotional level.

Development continues during middle adulthood as people enter the **generativity-versus-stagnation stage**. Generativity is the ability to contribute to one's family, community, work, and society, and to assist the development

intimacy-versus-isolation stage According to Erikson, a period during early adulthood that focuses on developing close relationships.

generativity-versus-stagnation stage According to Erikson, a period in middle adulthood during which we take stock of our contributions to family and society.

ego-integrity-versus-despair stage According to Erikson, a period from late adulthood until death during which we review life's accomplishments and failures.

of the younger generation. Success in this stage results in a person's feeling positive about the continuity of life, whereas difficulties lead a person to feel that his or her activities are trivial or stagnant and have done nothing for upcoming generations. In fact, if a person has not successfully resolved the identity crisis of adolescence, he or she may still be foundering in identifying an appropriate career, for example.

Finally, the last stage of psychosocial development, the **ego-integrity-versus-despair stage**, spans later adulthood and continues until death. Now a sense of accomplishment signifies success in resolving the difficulties presented by this stage of life; failure to resolve the difficulties results in regret over what might have been achieved but was not.

Notably, Erikson's theory suggests that development does not stop at adolescence but continues throughout adulthood, a view that a significant amount of research now confirms. For instance, a 22-year study by psychologist Susan Whitbourne found considerable support for the fundamentals of Erikson's theory, determining that psychosocial development continues through adolescence and adulthood. In sum, adolescence is not an end point but rather a way station on the path of psychosocial development (McAdams et al., 1997; Whitbourne et al., 1992).

5 Identity-Versus-Role-Confusion	6 Intimacy-Versus-Isolation	7 Generativity-Versus-Stagnation	8 Ego-Integrity-Versus-Despair
Approximate age: Adolescence	**Approximate age:** Early adulthood	**Approximate age:** Middle adulthood	**Approximate age:** Late adulthood
Positive outcomes: Awareness of uniqueness of self, knowledge of role to be followed	**Positive outcomes:** Development of loving, sexual relationships and close friendships	**Positive outcomes:** Sense of contribution to continuity of life	**Positive outcomes:** Sense of unity in life's accomplishments
Negative outcomes: Inability to identify appropriate roles in life	**Negative outcomes:** Fear of relationships with others	**Negative outcomes:** Trivialization of one's activities	**Negative outcomes:** Regret over lost opportunities of life

Psychologist Carol Gilligan suggests that women may develop identity through the construction of caring networks among themselves and others.

Although Erikson's theory provides a broad outline of identity development, critics have pointed out that his approach is anchored in male-oriented concepts of individuality and competitiveness. In an alternative conception, psychologist Carol Gilligan suggests that women may develop identity through the establishment of relationships. In her view, a primary component of women's identity is the construction of caring networks among themselves and others (Gilligan, 2004).

Adolescent Suicide Although the vast majority of teenagers pass through adolescence without major psychological difficulties, some experience unusually severe psychological problems. Sometimes those problems become so extreme that adolescents take their own lives. In fact, suicide is the second leading cause of death for young men and young women in Canada (Statistics Canada, 2008a) and male adolescents are five times more likely to commit suicide than are females, although females *attempt* suicide more often than males do.

Compared to other countries, Canada scored above average on suicide rate, and has continued to have a slightly higher rate of suicide than the United States since the 1970s (Conference Board of Canada, 2007). Moreover, the rate of adolescent suicide is significantly greater (five to seven times higher) among First Nation and Inuit youth in Canada (Health Canada, 2006). These statistics are alarming, but keep in mind that the reported rate of suicide may actually be understated, because medical personnel hesitate to report suicide as a cause of death. Instead, they frequently label a death as an accident in an effort to protect the survivors.

Although the question of why so many adolescents commit suicide remains unanswered, several factors put adolescents at risk. One factor is depression, characterized by unhappiness, extreme fatigue, and—a variable that seems especially important—a profound sense of hopelessness. In other cases, adolescents who commit suicide are perfectionists, inhibited socially, and prone to extreme anxiety when they face any social or academic challenge (Caelian, 2006; Centers for Disease Control, 2004b; Richardson et al., 2005).

Family background and adjustment difficulties are also related to suicide. A long-standing history of conflicts

Figure 10.11

Suicide Rates, 2007 or Most Recent Year: Canada Ranks 9th out of 16 Peer Countries

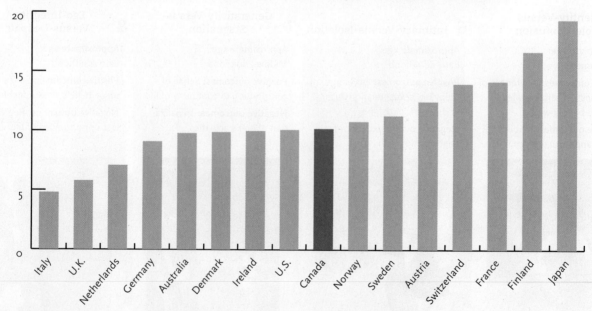

Source: The Conference Board of Canada, www.conferenceboard.ca/hcp/details/society/suicides.aspx.

between parents and children may lead to adolescent behaviour problems, such as delinquency, dropping out of school, and aggressive tendencies. In addition, teenage alcoholics and abusers of other drugs have a relatively high rate of suicide (Stronski, Ireland, & Michaud, 2000; Winstead & Sanchez, 2005).

Several warning signs indicate when a teenager's problems may be severe enough to warrant concern about the possibility of a suicide attempt. They include these signs:

- School problems, such as missing classes, truancy, and a sudden change in grades
- Frequent incidents of self-destructive behaviour, such as careless accidents
- Loss of appetite or excessive eating
- Withdrawal from friends and peers
- Sleeping problems
- Signs of depression, tearfulness, or overt indications of psychological difficulties, such as hallucinations
- A preoccupation with death, an afterlife, or what would happen "if I died"
- Putting affairs in order, such as giving away prized possessions or making arrangements for the care of a pet
- An explicit announcement of thoughts of suicide

If you know someone who shows signs that he or she is suicidal, urge that person to seek professional help. You may need to take assertive action, such as enlisting the assistance of family members or friends. Talk of suicide is a serious signal for help, not a confidence to be kept.

To find a crisis centre near you, visit the Canadian Association for Suicide Prevention Web site at www.suicideprevention.ca (link to In Crisis Now? and Find a Crisis Centre). For immediate help with a suicide-related problem, call the National Suicide Prevention Lifeline toll-free at 1-800-273-TALK (or visit the Web site at www.suicidepreventionlifeline.org). Based in the United States, this 24-hour confidential hotline is also available nationwide in Canada.

Rites of Passage: Coming of Age Around the World It is not easy for male members of the Awa tribe in New Guinea to make the transition from childhood to adulthood. First come whippings with sticks and prickly branches, both for the boys' own past misdeeds and in honour of those tribesmen who were killed in warfare. In the next phase of the ritual, adults jab sharpened sticks into the boys' nostrils. Then they force a 5-foot length of vine into the boys' throats, until they gag and vomit. Finally, tribesmen cut the boys' genitals, causing severe bleeding.

Although the rites that mark the coming of age of boys in the Awa tribe might horrify insulated Westerners, the Awa isn't the only culture that practices coming-of-age rituals. Other cultures have less fearsome, but no less important, ceremonies marking the passage from childhood to adulthood. For instance, when a girl first menstruates in traditional Apache tribes, the event is marked by dawn-to-dusk chanting. Western religions, too, have several types

of celebrations, including bar and bat mitzvahs at age 13 for Jewish boys and girls and confirmation ceremonies for children in many Christian denominations (Magida, 2006). The Turtle Lodge in Sagkeeng First Nation, Manitoba, offers ancient rites of passage to both young males and females over the age of 12 to initiate them into adulthood. Young women take part in the Makoose Ka Win, and young men in the Vision Quest. In the Makoose Ka Win ceremony, young women who have had their first menses (moon time) gather with a group of grandmothers, elders, and mentors to learn the sacredness of being a woman. In the Vision Quest, young men will spend three days alone in the wilderness without food or water to seek a vision from Mother Earth to help initiate them into manhood (The Turtle Lodge, 2011).

In most societies, males, but not females, are the focus of coming-of-age ceremonies. The renowned anthropologist Margaret Mead remarked, only partly in jest, that the preponderance of male ceremonies might reflect the fact that "the worry that boys will not grow up to be men is much more widespread than that girls will not grow up to be women" (1949, p. 195). It may be, however, that most cultures place greater emphasis on male rites than on female ones because, for females, the transition from childhood is marked by a definite, biological event: menstruation. For males, in contrast, no single event can be used to pinpoint entry into adulthood. Thus, men are forced to rely on culturally determined rituals to acknowledge their arrival into adulthood.

Adulthood

Psychologists generally agree that early adulthood begins around age 20 and lasts until about age 40 to 45, with middle adulthood beginning then and continuing until around age 65. Perhaps because the physical changes that occur during these periods are less apparent and more gradual than are those at other times during the life span and the diverse social changes that arise during adulthood defy simple categorization, researchers have not paid as much attention to adulthood as to earlier life stages. Recently, however, developmental psychologists have begun to focus on this period, particularly on the social changes in the family and in women's careers.

THE PEAK OF HEALTH

For most people, early adulthood marks the peak of physical health. From about 18 to 25 years of age, people's strength is greatest, their reflexes are quickest, and their chances of dying from disease are slim. Moreover, reproductive capabilities are at their highest level.

Around age 25, the body becomes slightly less efficient and more susceptible to disease. Overall, however, ill health remains the exception; most people stay remarkably healthy during early adulthood. (Can you think of any machine other than the body that can operate without pause for so long a period?)

During middle adulthood people gradually become aware of changes in their bodies. People often experience weight gain, as their eating habits continue unchanged while they begin to get less exercise. Furthermore, the sense organs gradually become less sensitive, and reactions to stimuli are slower. But generally, the physical declines that occur during middle adulthood are minor and often unnoticeable (DiGiovanna, 1994).

One important biological change that occurs to both women and men during middle adulthood pertains to reproductive capabilities. On average, during their late 40s or early 50s, women approach **menopause**, at which point

Physically, most individuals reach their peak in young adulthood.

they stop menstruating and are no longer fertile. Because menopause is accompanied by a significant reduction in the production of estrogen, a female hormone, women sometimes experience symptoms such as hot flashes, sudden sensations of heat. Sometimes, in industrialized cultures, these symptoms are treated through *hormone therapy (HT)*, in which menopausal women take synthetic hormones.

Menopause was once blamed for a variety of psychological symptoms, including depression and memory loss.

> **menopause** The period during which women stop menstruating and are no longer fertile.

BUY IT?

Can Acupuncture Make People Look Younger?

There are many claims on the Internet and elsewhere that acupuncture can make one's face look younger by reducing wrinkles, sags, and frown lines. The procedure, called cosmetic acupuncture (or acupuncture facial rejuvenation), involves placing tiny needles on various points of the face, which is claimed to increase blood flow, collagen, and qi (i.e., the body's energy, which is pronounced "chee"). Some people are turning to cosmetic acupuncture in place of more expensive and invasive procedures like cosmetic surgery and Botox injections; however, cosmetic acupuncture is still reasonably expensive, ranging from $80–$120 per session, with many clinics recommending a minimum of 10 sessions to start. The initial price and follow up appointments do not seem to deter people. Many claim that the benefits outweigh the price, and they state that it is safer and less expensive than cosmetic surgery or Botox injections. Users of cosmetic acupuncture indicate that it makes them look younger and feel better overall.

As a critical thinker and good consumer of information, would you buy it? Hopefully the first thing you asked is whether there is any scientific evidence to demonstrate that it actually works! While some studies have shown that acupuncture can be effective in pain management (Daitz, 2002; Fee et al., 2002; Witt, Jena, S. & Brinkhaus, 2006), there is not enough scientific evidence to show that cosmetic acupuncture is effective. As a critical thinker you must also consider other reasons that people claim it works (remember what you learned about testimonials in Chapter 1?). People may be experiencing the placebo effect or expectancy effects, or it may be that the increased blood flow to the face initially makes it appear as though wrinkles and lines have disappeared, but once the blood settles back to normal levels, so does the skin. The point is that just because someone provides a personal testimonial that something works for them, you do not have to buy it!

However, it is not yet clear how the erratic changes in hormonal levels that characterize menopause are related to such difficulties. Current cross-cultural research shows that women's reactions to menopause vary significantly across cultures, and suggests that the more a society values old age, the less difficulty its women have during menopause (Beven, Gillis, & Lee, 2007; Elliot, Berman, & Kim, 2002). Without more information, however, we can only speculate as to the cause-and-effect relationship between these two variables.

For men, the aging process during middle adulthood is somewhat subtler. There are no physiological signals of increasing age equivalent to the end of menstruation in women; that is, no male menopause exists. In fact, men remain fertile and are capable of fathering children until well into late adulthood. However, some gradual physical decline occurs: Sperm production decreases and the frequency of orgasm tends to decline. Once again, though, any psychological difficulties associated with these changes are usually brought about not so much by physical deterioration as by the inability of an aging individual to meet the exaggerated standards of youthfulness.

ADULT SOCIAL DEVELOPMENT

Social developmental transitions in adulthood are qualitative and profound. During this period, people typically launch themselves into careers, marriage, and families, all of which require significant adjustment.

Entry into early adulthood is usually marked by leaving one's childhood home and entering the world of work. People envision life goals and make career choices. Their lives often centre on their careers, which form an important part of their identity (Levinson, 1990, 1992; Vaillant & Vaillant, 1990).

In their early 40s, people may begin to question their lives as they enter a period called the *mid-life transition*. The idea that life will end at some point becomes increasingly influential in their thinking, and they may question their past accomplishments (Gould, 1978). Facing signs of physical aging and feeling dissatisfaction with their lives, some individuals experience what has been popularly labelled a *mid-life crisis*.

Early adulthood is when most individuals focus on their jobs and careers.

Psych think

> > > Do you think the fact that many couples are waiting to have children until they are in their thirties will impact the mid-life crisis?

In most cases, though, the passage into middle age is relatively calm, and not the crisis it was once believed to be. Most 40-year-olds view their lives and accomplishments positively enough to proceed relatively smoothly through mid-life, and the 40s and 50s are often a particularly rewarding period. Rather than looking to the future, people concentrate on the present, and their involvement with their families, friends, and other social groups takes on new importance (Whitbourne, 2000).

> "Most 40-year-olds view their lives and accomplishments positively enough to proceed relatively smoothly through mid-life, and the 40s and 50s are often a particularly rewarding period."

Finally, during the last stages of adulthood, people become more accepting of others and of their own lives and are less concerned about issues or problems that once bothered them. People come to accept the fact that death is inevitable, and they try to understand their accomplishments in terms of the broader meaning of life. Although people may begin, for the first time, to label themselves as "old," many also develop a sense of wisdom and feel freer to enjoy life (Baltes & Kunzmann, 2003; Miner-Rubino, Winter, & Stewart, 2004; Ward-Baker, 2007).

Marriage, Children, and Divorce In the typical fairy tale, a dashing young man and a beautiful young woman marry, have children, and live happily ever after. However, that scenario does not match the realities of love and marriage in the twenty-first century. Today, it is just as likely that the man and the woman would first live together, then marry and have children, but ultimately divorce. (Or the partners could be same-sex.)

The percentage of households made up of unmarried couples has increased dramatically over the last two decades. At the same time, the average age at which marriage takes place is higher than at any time since the turn of the twentieth century. These changes have been dramatic, and they suggest that the institution of marriage has changed considerably from earlier historical periods.

When people do marry, the probability of divorce is high, especially for younger couples. Even though divorce rates have been declining since they peaked in 1981, about half of all first marriages end in divorce. Before they are

Young adulthood is a time of developmental transitions, when many people begin careers, marry, and start a family.

18 years old, two-fifths of children will experience the breakup of their parents' marriages. Moreover, the rise in divorce is not just a Western phenomenon: The divorce rate has accelerated over the last several decades in most industrialized countries. In some countries, the increase has been enormous. In South Korea, for example, the divorce rate quadrupled from 11% to 47% in the 12-year period ending in 2002 (Lankov, 2004; Olson & DeFrain, 2005; Schaefer, 2000).

Changes in marriage and divorce trends have doubled the number of single-parent households over the last two decades. Almost 25% of all family households are now headed by one parent, compared with 13% in 1970. If present trends continue, almost 75% of children will spend some portion of their lives in a single-parent family before they turn 18. For children in minority households, the numbers are even higher.

What are the economic and emotional consequences for children living in homes with only one parent? Single-parent families are often economically less well off, and this economic disadvantage has an effect on children's opportunities. Over a third of single-mother families with children have incomes below the poverty line. In addition, good child care at an affordable price is often hard to find. Furthermore, for children of divorce, the parents' separation is often a painful experience that may result in obstacles to their establishing close relationships later in life. Children may blame themselves for the breakup or feel pressure to take sides (Liu, He, & Wu, 2007; U.S. Bureau of the Census, 2000; Wallerstein et al., 2000).

Nevertheless, most evidence suggests that children from stable, single-parent families are no less well adjusted than are those from stable, two-parent families. In fact, children may be more successful growing up in a harmonious single-parent family than in a two-parent family that engages in continuous conflict (Clarke-Stewart et al., 2000; Harold et al., 1997; Kelly, 2000; Olson & DeFrain, 2005).

Changing Roles of Men and Women One of the major changes in family life in the last two decades has been the evolution of men's and women's roles. More women than ever before act simultaneously as wives, mothers, and wage earners—in contrast to women in traditional marriages, in which the husband is the sole wage earner and the wife assumes primary responsibility for care of the home and children.

In spite of the increasing involvement of men in family life, women who work outside the home typically also manage most homemaking and childcare responsibilities.

Close to 75% of all married women with children under age 16 are now employed outside the home. In the mid-1970s, only 28% of mothers with children under age three worked full-time; now, more than approximately 65% under age three are in the labour force (Almey, 2005).

Most married working women are not free of household responsibilities. Even in marriages in which the spouses hold jobs that have similar status and require similar hours, the distribution of household tasks between husbands and wives has not changed substantially. Working wives are still more likely than husbands to feel responsible for traditional homemaking tasks such as cooking and cleaning. In contrast, husbands still view themselves as responsible primarily for household tasks such as repairing broken appliances and doing yard work (Ganong & Coleman, 1999; Juster, Ono, & Stafford, 2002).

GROWING OLD

I've always enjoyed doing things in the mountains—hiking or, more recently, active cliff-climbing. The more difficult the climb, the more absorbing it is. The climbs I really remember are the ones I had to work on. Maybe a particular section where it took two or three tries before I found the right combination of moves that got me up easily—and, preferably, elegantly. It's a wonderful exhilaration to get to the top and sit down and perhaps have lunch and look out over the landscape and be so grateful that it's still possible for me to do that sort of thing. (Lyman Spitzer, age 74, quoted in Kotre & Hall, 1990, pp. 358–359)

If you can't quite picture a 74-year-old man rock-climbing, some rethinking of your view of late adulthood may be in order. In spite of the societal stereotype of "old age" as a time of inactivity and physical and mental decline, gerontologists, specialists who study aging, are beginning to paint a very different portrait of late adulthood.

By focusing on the period of life that starts at around age 65, gerontologists are making important contributions to clarifying the capabilities of older adults. Their work is demonstrating that significant developmental processes continue even during old age. And as life expectancy increases, the number of people who reach older adulthood will continue to grow substantially. Consequently, developing an understanding of late adulthood has become a critical priority for psychologists (Birren, 1996; Moody, 2000, Schaie, 2005).

Olivia Patricia "Pat" Thomas celebrates after blowing out her candles at her 112th birthday party. In June 2009, Thomas turned 114. As increasing numbers of people are living into their 90s and beyond, the study of late adulthood has become a priority for psychologists.

The Aging Body Napping, eating, walking, and conversing. It probably doesn't surprise you that these relatively non-strenuous activities represent the typical pastimes of late adulthood. But it is striking that these activities are identical to the most common leisure activities reported in a survey of college students (Harper, 1978). Although the students cited more active pursuits—such as sailing and playing basketball—as their favourite activities, in actuality they engaged in such sports relatively infrequently, spending most of their free time napping, eating, walking, and conversing.

Although the leisure activities in which older adults engage may not differ all that much from the ones that younger people pursue, many physical changes are, of course, brought about by the aging process. The most obvious are those of appearance—hair thinning and turning grey, skin wrinkling and folding, and sometimes a slight loss of height as the thickness of the disks between vertebrae in the spine decreases—but subtler changes also occur in the body's biological functioning. For example, sensory capabilities decrease as a result of aging: vision, hearing, smell, and taste become less sensitive. Reaction time slows, and physical stamina changes (Madden, 2007; Schieber, 2006; Stenklev & Laukli, 2004).

What are the reasons for these physical declines? **Genetic preprogramming theories of aging** suggest that human cells have a built-in time limit to their reproduction. These theories suggest that after a certain time cells stop dividing or become harmful to the body—as if a kind of automatic self-destruct button had been pushed. In contrast, **wear-and-tear theories of aging** suggest that

Get Involved!

A great active way to learn more about people of different ages is to work and interact with such individuals. Many colleges and universities have offices or Web sites listing diverse volunteer opportunities within the local communities. You may want to investigate volunteering (and simultaneously building your résumé) at a daycare centre, youth organization, assisted living home, or another agency in your community. Such organizations often offer a variety of volunteer opportunities, such as assistance with recreational activities, food service, and clerical tasks.

the mechanical functions of the body simply work less efficiently as people age. Waste by-products of energy production eventually accumulate, and mistakes are made when cells divide. Eventually the body, in effect, wears out, just as an old automobile does (Hayflick, 2007; Ly et al., 2000; Miquel, 2006).

It may be that both the genetic preprogramming and the wear-and-tear views contribute to natural aging. It is clear, however, that physical aging is not a disease but a natural biological process. Many physical functions do not decline with age. For example, sex remains pleasurable well into old age (although the frequency of sexual activity decreases), and some people report that the pleasure they derive from sex increases during late adulthood (DeLamater & Sill, 2005; Gelfand, 2000).

Study tip Two major theories of aging—genetic preprogramming and wear-and-tear—explain some of the physical changes that take place in older adults.

Thinking in Late Adulthood At one time, many gerontologists would have agreed with the popular view that older adults are forgetful and confused. Most research today indicates that this assessment is far from accurate, however.

When older people are compared with young adults, differences can be exaggerated if the older ones have health problems that may affect cognitive functioning. Older people are often less healthy than younger ones, and when only *healthy* older adults are compared to healthy younger adults, intellectual differences are far less evident. Furthermore, the average number of years in school is often lower in older adults (for historical reasons) than in younger ones, and older adults may be less motivated to perform well on intelligence tests than younger people. Finally, traditional IQ tests may be inappropriate measures of intelligence in late adulthood. Older adults sometimes perform better on tests of practical intelligence than do younger individuals (Dixon & Cohen, 2003; Willis & Schaie, 1994).

Still, some declines in intellectual functioning during late adulthood do occur, although the pattern of age differences is not uniform for different types of cognitive abilities. In general, skills relating to *fluid intelligence* (which involves information-processing skills such as speed of memory retrieval, calculations, and analogy solving) show declines in late adulthood. In contrast, skills relating to *crystallized intelligence* (intelligence based on the accumulation of knowledge, skills, and strategies learned through experience) remain steady and in some cases even improve (Rozencwajg et al., 2005; Stankov, 2003; van Hooren, Valentijn, & Bosma, 2007).

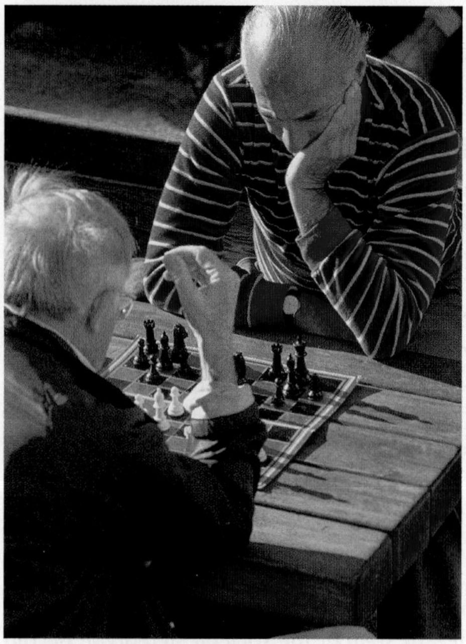

Some decline in cognitive functioning occurs in late adulthood, but abilities based on accumulated knowledge and experience may actually improve as people age.

Even when changes in intellectual functioning do occur during late adulthood, people often are able to compensate for any decline. They can still learn; they may just need more

Figure 10.12

Age-Related Changes in Intellectual Skills

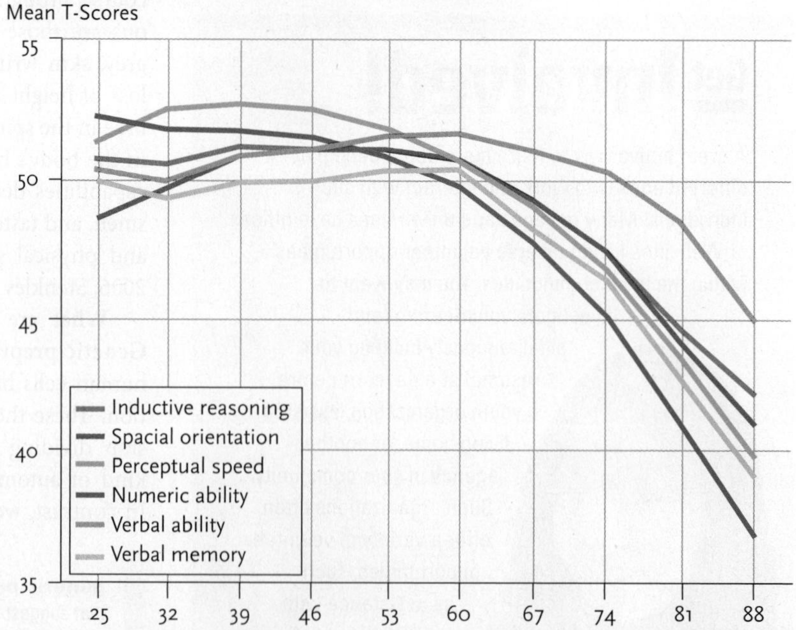

Mean T-Scores
55
50
45
40
35
25
32
39
46
53
60
67
74
81
88
Age
Inductive reasoning
Spacial orientation
Perceptual speed
Numeric ability
Verbal ability
Verbal memory

Source: Schaie, K. W. (2005). Longitudinal studies. In *Developmental influences on adult intelligence: The Seattle Longitudinal Study,* Figure 5.7a (p. 127). Copyright © 2005 by Oxford University Press, Inc. By permission of Oxford University Press, Inc. www.oup.co.uk.

time to master what they choose to learn. Furthermore, teaching older adults strategies for dealing with new problems can prevent declines in performance (Cavallini, Pagnin, & Vecchi, 2003; Peters et al., 2007; Saczynski, Willis, & Schaie, 2002).

Are Older Adults Forgetful?

One of the characteristics we commonly associate with late adulthood is forgetfulness. How accurate is this assumption?

Most evidence suggests that memory deficits are not an inevitable part of the aging process. For instance, research shows that older people in cultures in which older adults are held in high esteem, such as mainland China, are less likely to show memory losses than are those living in cultures in which the expectation is that memory will decline. Similarly, when older people in Western societies are reminded of the advantages of age (for example, "age brings wisdom"), they tend to do better on tests of memory (Dixon, Rust, & Feltmate, 2007; Hess, Hinson, & Statham, 2004; Levy, 1996).

In the past, older adults with severe cases of memory decline, accompanied by other cognitive difficulties, were said to suffer from senility. *Senility* is a broad, imprecise term typically applied to older adults who experience progressive deterioration of mental abilities, including memory loss, disorientation to time and place, and general confusion. Once thought to be an inevitable state that accompanies aging, senility is now viewed by most gerontologists as a label that has outlived its usefulness. Rather than senility being the cause of certain symptoms, the symptoms are deemed to be caused by some other factor.

Some cases of memory loss are caused by disease. For instance, *Alzheimer's disease*, which was introduced in the memory chapter, is a progressive brain disorder that leads to a gradual and irreversible decline in cognitive abilities. As was discussed in the memory chapter, Alzheimer's is the leading cause of disability among Canadians aged 65 and older, affecting approximately 500,000 people (Alzheimer's Society of Canada, 2010).

Alzheimer's occurs when production of the *beta amyloid precursor protein* goes awry, producing large clumps of cells that trigger inflammation and deterioration of nerve cells. The brain shrinks, neurons die, and several areas of the hippocampus and frontal and temporal lobes deteriorate. So far, there is no cure for Alzheimer's (Blennow &

Vanmechelen, 2003; Lanctot, Herrmann, & Mazzotta, 2001; Medeiros et al., 2007; Wolfe, 2006).

In other cases, cognitive declines may be caused by temporary anxiety and depression, which can be treated successfully, or may even be due to overmedication. The danger is that people with such symptoms may receive no treatment, thereby continuing their decline (Sachs-Ericsson et al., 2005; Selkoe, 1997).

In sum, declines in cognitive functioning in late adulthood, for the most part, are not inevitable. The key to maintaining cognitive skills may lie in intellectual stimulation. Like most people, older adults need a stimulating environment to hone and to maintain their skills (Bosma et al., 2003; Glisky, 2007).

The Social World of Late Adulthood

Just as the view that old age predictably means mental decline has proved to be wrong, so has the view that late adulthood inevitably brings loneliness. People in late adulthood most often see themselves as functioning members of society, with only a small number of them reporting that loneliness is a serious problem (Binstock & George, 1996; Jylha, 2004).

From the perspective of . . .

A PRACTICAL NURSE What sorts of recommendations would you make to older people about how to deal with aging? What would you say to someone who believed that getting older has only negative consequences?

Certainly, late adulthood brings significant challenges. People who retire after having worked all of their adult lives experience a major shift in the role they play. Moreover, many older people must face the death of their spouse or partner. The death of a spouse or partner means the loss of a companion, confidante, and lover. It can also bring about changes in economic well-being.

People approach aging in different ways. According to the **disengagement theory of aging**, aging is accompanied by a gradual withdrawal from the world on physical, psychological, and social levels. Such disengagement serves an important purpose, providing an opportunity for increased reflection and decreased emotional investment in others at a time of life when social relationships will inevitably be ended by death (Adams, 2004; Wrosch, Bauer, & Scheier, 2005).

disengagement theory of aging A theory that suggests that aging produces a gradual withdrawal from the world on physical, psychological, and social levels.

DID YOU KNOW?

 Mandatory retirement age for air traffic controllers in the United States is 56, but in Canada there is not a mandatory age of retirement. Canada may be on the right track, because research suggests that retirement-aged air traffic controllers prevent mid-air collisions as well as younger ones. They effectively use their experience (crystallized intelligence) to make up for cognitive losses associated with aging (Nunes & Kramer, 2009).

The **activity theory of aging** presents an alternative view of aging, holding that the people who age most successfully are those who maintain the interests, activities, and level of social interaction they experienced during middle adulthood. According to activity theory, late adulthood should reflect a continuation, as much as possible, of the activities in which people participated during the earlier part of their lives (Crosnoe & Elder, 2002; Nimrod & Kleiber, 2007).

Both disengagement and activity can lead to successful aging. But not all people in late adulthood need a life filled with activities and social interaction to be happy. Like some people in every stage of life, some older adults are satisfied leading a relatively inactive, solitary existence. What may be more important than social interaction is how people view the aging process: Evidence shows that positive self-perceptions of aging are associated with increased longevity (Levy et al., 2002; Levy & Myers, 2004).

Regardless of how people approach aging, most engage in a process of **life review**, in which they examine and evaluate their lives. Remembering and reconsidering what has occurred in the past, people in late adulthood often come to a better understanding of themselves, sometimes resolving lingering problems and conflicts, and facing their lives with greater wisdom and serenity.

ADJUSTING TO DEATH

At some time in our lives, we all face death—not only our own demise but also the deaths of friends and loved ones. Although there is nothing more inevitable in life, for many people death remains a frightening, emotion-laden topic. Certainly, little is more stressful than the death of a loved one or the contemplation of our own imminent death, and preparing for death is one of our most crucial developmental tasks (Aiken, 2000a).

activity theory of aging A theory that suggests that the elderly who are most successful while aging are those who maintain the interests and activities they had during middle age.

life review The process by which people examine and evaluate their lives.

A generation ago, talking about death was taboo. The topic was never mentioned to dying people, and gerontologists had little to say about it. That changed, however, with the pioneering work of Elisabeth Kübler-Ross (1969), who brought the subject of death into the open with her observation that those facing their own impending death tend to move through five broad stages:

- *Denial.* In this stage, people resist the idea that they are dying. Even if told that their chances for survival are small, they refuse to admit that they are facing death.

- *Anger.* After moving beyond the denial stage, dying people become angry—angry at people around them who are in good health, angry at medical professionals for being ineffective, angry at God.

- *Bargaining.* Anger leads to bargaining, in which the dying try to think of ways to postpone death. They may decide to dedicate their lives to religion if God saves them; they may say, "If only I can live to see my son married, I will accept death then."

- *Depression.* When dying people come to feel that bargaining is of no use, they move to the next stage: depression. They realize that their lives really are coming to an end, leading to what Kübler-Ross calls "preparatory grief" for their own deaths.

- *Acceptance.* In this stage, people accept impending death. Usually they are unemotional and uncommunicative; it is as if they have made peace with themselves and are expecting death with no bitterness.

Keep in mind that not everyone and not every culture experiences each of these stages in the same way. In fact, Kübler-Ross's stages pertain only to people who are fully aware that they are dying and have the time to evaluate their impending death. Furthermore, vast differences occur in the way individuals react to impending death. The specific cause and duration of dying, as well as the person's culture, sex, age, and personality and the type of support received from family and friends, all have an effect on how people respond to death (Carver & Scheier, 2002).

TRY IT!

How Do You Feel About Death?

To assess your feelings about death, complete the following questionnaire. For statements 1 through 11, use these scale labels:

1 = never; 2 = rarely; 3 = sometimes; 4 = often

1. I think about my own death. _____
2. I think about the death of loved ones. _____
3. I think about dying young. _____
4. I think about the possibility of my being killed on a busy road. _____
5. I have fantasies of my own death. _____
6. I think about death just before I go to sleep. _____
7. I think of how I would act if I knew I were to die within a given period of time. _____
8. I think of how my relatives would act and feel upon my death. _____
9. When I am sick, I think about death. _____
10. When I am outside during a lightning storm, I think about the possibility of being struck by lightning. _____
11. When I am in a car, I think about the high incidence of traffic fatalities. _____

For statements 12 through 30, use these scale labels:

0 = strongly disagree 1 = disagree 2 = neutral 3 = agree 4 = strongly agreee

12. I think people should first become concerned about death when they are old. _____
13. I am much more concerned about death than those around me. _____
14. Death hardly concerns me. _____
15. My general outlook just doesn't allow for morbid thoughts. _____
16. The prospect of my own death arouses anxiety in me. _____
17. The prospect of my own death depresses me. _____
18. The prospect of the death of my loved ones arouses anxiety in me. _____
19. The knowledge that I will surely die does not in any way affect the conduct of my life. _____
20. I envisage my own death as a painful, nightmarish experience. _____
21. I am afraid of dying. _____
22. I am afraid of being dead. _____
23. Many people become disturbed at the sight of a new grave, but it does not bother me. _____
24. I am disturbed when I think about the shortness of life. _____
25. Thinking about death is a waste of time. _____
26. Death should not be regarded as a tragedy if it occurs after a productive life. _____
27. The inevitable death of humanity poses a serious challenge to the meaningfulness of human existence. _____
28. The death of the individual is ultimately beneficial because it facilitates change in society. _____
29. I have a desire to live on after death. _____
30. The question of whether or not there is a future life worries me considerably. _____

Source: Dickstein, 1972.

Scoring: If you rated any of these items—13, 16, 17, 18, 20, 21, 22, 24, 27, 29, and 30—as 1, change these ratings to 4; those you rated as 2, change to 3; those you rated as 3, change to 2; and those you rated as 4, change to 1. Add up your ratings.

Average scores on the scale typically range from about 68 to 80. If you scored about 80, death is something that seems to produce some degree of anxiety. Scores lower than 68 suggest that you experience little fear of death.

For Review >>

What methods do psychologists use to conduct developmental research?

Researchers often use cross-sectional or longitudinal research to study development. In cross-sectional research the researcher compares people of different ages at one point in time, while in longitudinal research they follow one age group over a long period of time. Sequential research combines both of these approaches and takes a number of different age groups and examines them at several points in time.

How do infants grow and develop before birth?

At conception, a male sperm and a female egg unite, with each contributing to the new individual's genetic makeup. A newborn baby normally enters the world after 38 weeks of pregnancy. Genes affect a wide array of personal characteristics as well as physical characteristics. Genetic abnormalities produce birth defects such as phenylketonuria (PKU), sickle-cell anemia, Tay-Sachs disease, and Down syndrome. Among the environmental influences on fetal growth are the mother's nutrition, illnesses, and drug intake.

What do newborn babies actually know, and how can we tell?

Newborns infants have reflexes, which are unlearned, involuntary responses that occur automatically in the presence of certain stimuli. These reflexes disappear a few months after birth. Sensory abilities develop rapidly in infants. Relatively soon after birth infants can distinguish colour, depth, sound, tastes, and smells.

How do children learn to get along with and understand other people?

Attachment—the positive emotional bond between a child and a specific individual—is central to social development in infancy. Measured in the laboratory by means of the Ainsworth strange situation, attachment relates to later social and emotional adjustment. As children become older, the nature of their social interactions with peers changes. Initially play occurs relatively independently, but it becomes increasingly cooperative. According to Erikson,

eight stages of psychosocial development involve people's changing interactions and understanding of themselves and others over the course of their lifetime. During childhood, the four stages are trust-versus-mistrust (birth to one-and-a-half years), autonomy-versus-shame-and-doubt (one-and-a-half to three years), initiative-versus-guilt (three to six years), and industry-versus-inferiority (six to twelve years).

What are the moral, cognitive, and social challenges of adolescence?

Adolescence, the developmental stage between childhood and adulthood, begins with the onset of puberty, the point at which sexual maturity occurs. The age at which puberty begins has implications for the way people view themselves and the way others see them. Moral judgments during adolescence increase in sophistication, according to Kohlberg. Although Kohlberg's model adequately describes males' moral development, Gilligan suggests that women view morality in terms of caring for individuals rather than in terms of broad, general principles of justice. According to Erikson's model of psychosocial development, adolescence may be accompanied by an identity crisis. Adolescence is followed by three more stages of psychosocial development that cover the remainder of the life span.

In what ways do people continue to develop and grow after they reach adulthood?

Early adulthood marks the peak of physical health. Physical changes occur relatively gradually in men and women as they age. One major physical change occurs at the end of middle adulthood for women: they begin menopause, after which they are no longer fertile. During middle adulthood, people typically experience a mid-life transition in which the notion that life is not unending becomes more important. In some cases this may lead to a mid-life crisis. People in their 50s realize that their lives and accomplishments are fairly well set, and they try to come to terms with them. Among the important developmental milestones during adulthood are marriage, family changes, and divorce. Another important determinant of adult development is work.

Psych think answers

Psych think 1 In the PSYCH think on p. 245 we asked you what the implications might be for the nature–nurture issue when researchers find similarities in development between very different cultures. First of all, remember that researchers who are interested in the differences of behaviour across cultures are from the socio-cultural approach. If the behaviour of people across cultures is similar it would suggest that there is a biological/genetic (nature) explanation for the behaviour because people are behaving the same way despite very different environmental influences (nurture).

Psych think 2 In the PSYCH think on p. 256 we asked you which of Baumrind's parenting styles (authoritarian, permissive, authoritative, and uninvolved) is most effective. Let's first review the four parenting styles. Authoritarian parents are more punitive and value obedience, while permissive parents are warm, but inconsistent and lenient. Uninvolved parents are emotionally detached and show little interest other than providing the basic needs (food, clothing, shelter), and authoritative parents are firm but fair and encourage independence in their children. While it appears that authoritative parenting may be most effective, you also have to keep in mind what type of temperament the child has. A difficult child may require more authoritarian parenting than a child who is more fearful of reprimand.

Psych think 3 In the PSYCH think on p. 261 we asked you to imagine you were speaking on the telephone with three-year-old Palmer. We said that at one point in the conversation he says to you "look at the fort I made out of pillows" and you hear him move the telephone from the side of his head to in front of his fort.

We then asked you why you thought Palmer would think that you could see what he could see. To answer this question you must consider what level Palmer is at in Piaget's stages of cognitive development. Knowing that Palmer is three years old, you know that he is at the preoperational stage and he is engaging in egocentric thinking, where he thinks that you can see what he can see. He is not able to take your perspective and understand that you cannot see through the telephone!

Psych think 4 In the PSYCH think on p. 271 we asked you if the fact that many couples are waiting to have children until they are in their thirties would impact the mid-life crisis. First of all, the mid-life crisis is not nearly as much of a crisis as was once believed. Even people who had children earlier in life and who are entering mid-life with their children in college or university find mid-life to be a rewarding time. People are usually more financially secure at this point in their lives and they are at a point in their life where they have a good sense of who they are. It would be reasonable then to assume that people who are having children later in life would also avoid the "crisis" of mid-life!

11

Personality

Humans share many traits, and yet our personalities are incredibly diverse.

WHAT'S TO COME

What Is Personality?

Psychodynamic Approaches to Personality

Trait Approaches to Personality

Learning Approaches to Personality

Biological and Evolutionary Approaches to Personality

Humanistic Approaches to Personality

Comparing Approaches to Personality

Assessing Personality

Perfect husband or serial killer?

Russell Williams was a Colonel in the Canadian Forces and commander of Canadian Forces Base Trenton, Ontario, where he had the honour of piloting several important dignitaries on the Canadian Forces VIP aircraft, such as the Governor General of Canada, Queen Elizabeth II, and Prince Phillip. To his wife, Russell Williams was a dedicated and devoted husband who drove 16 hours round trip to visit her while they were courting. People who lived on their street called the couple "wonderful neighbours" and warmly described his obvious dedication to his wife and their cat (the couple did not have children). Russell Williams was so devoted to his cat that when it was time for his cat to be euthanized, he paid extra for the veterinarian to come to their house so the cat would be in a familiar place when it was put down. His friends noted how quickly he would become emotional when he spoke of the cat's death.

Russell Williams sounds like a pretty stand-up guy. But to the police, prosecutors, and victims, Williams was a predator and serial killer. He was charged with breaking and entering, forcible confinement, sexual assault, and murder. He broke into the homes of his neighbour and stole their 12-year-old daughter's underwear, the same girl that taught him to play cribbage at the family dining room table. In fact, he broke into a total of 82 homes stealing underwear of young girls and lingerie of young women. He photographed himself wearing this lingerie while masturbating and catalogued all of these photos on his home computer. He also kept bags and bags of the underwear and lingerie that he stole, hidden in various places in his home and cottage so his wife would not see. His break and enters soon escalated to sexual assault and murder. He was charged with the murders of Marie-France Comeau, whom he worked with, and Jessica Lloyd, a young woman from Belleville, Ontario. Both women were sexually assaulted and tortured before he watched them die. His old friend, Jeffery Manney, spoke about Russell Williams, "I ask myself: 'How did I befriend someone who could have done these things?'…He loved his wife, he was always a nice guy, and I just don't know how. I can't put the two people together. I can't." (Friscolanti, Gulli, & Patriquin, 2011).

Who is the real Russell Williams? The "nice guy" or the cold predator described by prosecutors? Many people, like Williams, have different sides to their personalities, appearing one way to some people and quite differently to others. But generally, people have stable personalities. We tend to behave in ways consistent with our personalities over time and from one situation to the next. As we'll see, personality psychology is the study of the psychological makeup of individuals and how it influences their interactions with others and with their physical environment.

As You Read »

- How do psychologists think about personality?
- What are the major features of the different psychological approaches to personality?
- How can psychologists most accurately measure personality?
- What are the major types of personality measures?

What Is Personality?

How would you describe your best friend to someone you've just met? Apart from describing her physical characteristics (maybe she's 170 cm tall and has brown hair and green eyes), would you add some personal qualities, such as happy and easy-going, or sympathetic and conscientious but shy?

Most of us would agree that individuals have certain lasting characteristics, such as a happy disposition, that make their behaviour fairly predictable from one day to the next. Indeed, psychologists define **personality** as the pattern of enduring characteristics that produce consistency and individuality in a given person. Personality encompasses the behaviours that make each of us unique and that differentiate us from others. It is also personality that leads us to act consistently in different situations and over extended periods of time.

Like other areas of psychology, personality psychology includes several different perspectives or approaches. Here we consider a number of them. We begin with psychodynamic theories of personality, which emphasize the role of the unconscious mind. Next, we consider approaches that focus on personality traits (including sociability and conscientiousness); theories that view personality as a set of learned behaviours; biological and evolutionary perspectives on personality; and approaches, known as humanistic theories, that highlight the uniquely human aspects of personality. We end with a discussion of personality measurement and applications of personality tests.

DID YOU KNOW?

Animals have personalities too. Birds, mice, and spiders are some of the creatures that have shown evidence of individual differences, which may have evolved because different personalities contribute to a species' survival (Wolf et al., 2007).

Psychodynamic Approaches to Personality

The college student was intent on making a good first impression on an attractive woman he had spotted across the room at a party. As he walked toward her, he mulled over a line he had heard in an old movie the night before: "I don't believe

personality The pattern of enduring characteristics that produce consistency and individuality in a given person.

we've been properly introduced yet." To his horror, what came out was a bit different. After threading his way through the crowded room, he finally reached the woman and blurted out, "I don't believe we've been properly seduced yet."

Although this student's error may seem to be merely an embarrassing slip of the tongue, according to some personality theorists such a mistake is not an error at all (Motley, 1987). Instead, *psychodynamic personality theorists* might argue that the error illustrates one way in which behaviour is triggered by inner forces that are beyond our awareness. These hidden drives, shaped by childhood experiences, play an important role in energizing and directing everyday behaviour.

Psychodynamic approaches to personality are based on the idea that personality is motivated by inner forces and conflicts about which people have little awareness and over which they have no control. The most important pioneer of the psychodynamic approach was Sigmund Freud. A number of Freud's followers, including Carl Jung, Karen Horney, and Alfred Adler, refined Freud's theory and developed their own psychodynamic approaches.

FREUD'S PSYCHOANALYTIC THEORY: MAPPING THE UNCONSCIOUS MIND

Sigmund Freud, an Austrian physician, developed **psychoanalytic theory** in the early 1900s. According to Freud's theory, conscious experience is only a small part of our psychological makeup and experience. He argued that much of our behaviour is motivated by the **unconscious**, a part of the personality that contains the memories, knowledge, beliefs, feelings, urges, drives, and instincts of which the individual is not aware.

Like the unseen mass of a floating iceberg, the contents of the unconscious far surpass in quantity the information in our conscious awareness. Freud maintained that

Figure 11.1
Freud's Model of Personality

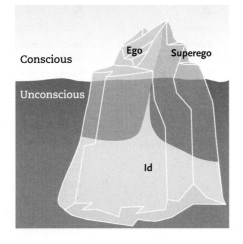

psychodynamic approaches to personality Approaches that assume that personality is motivated by inner forces and conflicts about which people have little awareness and over which they have no control.

psychoanalytic theory Freud's theory that unconscious forces act as determinants of personality.

unconscious A part of the personality that contains the memories, knowledge, beliefs, feelings, urges, drives, and instincts of which the individual is not aware.

id The raw, unorganized, inborn part of personality whose sole purpose is to reduce tension created by primitive drives related to hunger, sex, aggression, and irrational impulses.

to understand personality, we must expose what is in the unconscious. But because the unconscious disguises the meaning of the material it holds, the content of the unconscious cannot be observed directly. It is therefore necessary to interpret clues to the unconscious—slips of the tongue, fantasies, and dreams—to understand the unconscious processes that direct behaviour. A slip of the tongue such as the one quoted earlier (sometimes termed a *Freudian slip*) may be interpreted as revealing the speaker's unconscious sexual desires.

To Freud, much of our personality is determined by our unconscious. Some of the unconscious is made up of the *preconscious*, which contains material that is not threatening and is easily brought to mind, such as the knowledge that 2 + 2 = 4. But deeper in the unconscious are instinctual drives, the wishes, desires, demands, and needs that are hidden from conscious awareness because of the conflicts and pain they would cause if they were part of our everyday lives. The unconscious provides a "safe haven" for our recollections of threatening events.

Structuring Personality: Id, Ego, and Superego To describe the structure of personality, Freud developed a comprehensive theory that held that personality consists of three separate but interacting components: the id, the ego, and the superego. Freud suggested that the three structures can be diagrammed to show how they relate to the conscious and the unconscious.

Although the three components of personality described by Freud may appear to be actual physical structures in the nervous system, they are not. Instead, they represent abstract conceptions of a general *model* of personality that describes the interaction of forces that motivate behaviour.

If personality consisted only of primitive, instinctual cravings and longings, it would have just one component: the id. The **id** is the raw, unorganized, inborn part of personality. From the time of birth, the id attempts to reduce tension created by primitive drives related to hunger, sex, aggression, and irrational impulses. Those drives are fuelled by "psychic energy," which we can think of as a limitless energy source constantly putting pressure on the various parts of the personality.

The id operates according to the *pleasure principle*, in which the goal is the immediate reduction of tension and the maximization of satisfaction. However, in most cases reality prevents the fulfillment of the demands of the pleasure principle: We cannot always eat when we are hungry, and we can discharge our sexual drives only when the time and the place are appropriate. To account for this fact of life, Freud suggested a second component of personality, which he called the ego.

The **ego**, which begins to develop soon after birth, strives to balance the desires of the id and the realities of the objective, outside world. In contrast to the pleasure-seeking id, the ego operates according to the *reality principle*, in which instinctual energy is restrained to maintain the safety of the individual and to help integrate the person into society. In a sense, then, the ego is the "executive" of personality: it makes decisions, controls actions, and allows thinking and problem solving of a higher order than the id's capabilities permit.

The **superego**, the final personality structure to develop in childhood, represents the rights and wrongs of society as taught and modelled by a person's parents, teachers, and other significant individuals. The superego includes the *conscience*, which prevents us from behaving in a morally improper way by making us feel guilty if we do wrong. The superego helps us to control impulses coming from the id, making our behaviour less selfish and more virtuous. What would Freud say about Russell Williams from the opening vignette? It would appear from the psychoanalytic perspective, that Russell Williams did not develop a strong superego.

ego The part of the personality that provides a buffer between the id and the outside world.

superego According to Freud, the final personality structure to develop; it represents the rights and wrongs of society as handed down by a person's parents, teachers, and other important figures.

psychosexual stages Developmental periods that individuals pass through during which they encounter conflicts between the demands of society and their own sexual urges.

fixations Conflicts or concerns that persist beyond the developmental period in which they first occur.

Both the superego and the id are unrealistic in that they do not consider the practical realities imposed by society. The superego, if left to operate without restraint, would create perfectionists unable to make the compromises that life requires. An unrestrained id would create a primitive, pleasure-seeking, thoughtless individual seeking to fulfill every desire without delay. As a result, the ego must mediate between the demands of the superego and the demands of the id.

Study **tip**

Remember that the three parts of personality in Freud's theory—the id, the ego, and the superego—are abstract conceptions and *not* physical structures in the brain.

Developing Personality: Psychosexual Stages

Freud also provided us with a view of how personality develops through a series of five **psychosexual stages**, during which individuals encounter conflicts between the demands of society and their own sexual urges. The five psychosexual stages of personality development in Freud's theory—oral, anal, phallic, latency, and genital—suggest how personality develops as people age. Refer to Figure 11.2 for a description of each of these stages.

The sequence Freud proposed is noteworthy because it explains how experiences and difficulties during a particular childhood stage may predict specific characteristics in the adult personality. This theory is also unique in associating each stage with a major biological function, which Freud assumed to be the focus of pleasure in a given period.

According to Freud, failure to resolve the conflicts at a particular stage can result in **fixation**, the persistence of conflicts or concerns beyond the developmental period in which they first occur. Such conflicts may be due to having

Figure 11.2
Freud's Psychosexual Stages of Personality Development

1 **Oral Stage**	2 **Anal Stage**	3 **Phallic Stage**	4 **Latency Stage**	5 **Genital Stage**
Age: Birth to 12–18 months	**Age:** 12–18 months to 3 years	**Age:** 3 to 5–6 years	**Age:** 5–6 years to adolescence	**Age:** Adolescence to adulthood
Source of pleasure: Interest in oral gratification from sucking, eating, mouthing, biting	**Source of pleasure:** Gratification from expelling and withholding feces; coming to terms with society's controls relating to toilet training	**Source of pleasure:** Interest in the genitals, coming to terms with Oedipal conflict leading to identification with same-sex parent	**Source of pleasure:** Sexual concerns largely unimportant	**Source of pleasure:** Re-emergence of sexual interests and establishment of mature sexual relationships
Adult fixation: Smoking, eating, talking, sarcasm	**Adult fixation:** Unusual rigidity, orderliness, or extreme sloppiness	**Adult fixation:** Attraction to people like one's opposite-sex parent	**Adult fixation:** Does not apply	**Adult fixation:** Does not apply
Erogenous zone: Mouth	**Erogenous zone:** Anus	**Erogenous zone:** Genitals	**Erogenous zone:** None	**Erogenous zone:** Genitals

In the oral stage of Freud's psychosexual stages, the source of pleasure is oral gratification.

needs ignored or (conversely) being overindulged during the earlier period.

According to Freud, one of the most important hurdles of personality development, the **Oedipal conflict**, arises during the phallic stage (ages three to five or six). Freud thought that during this stage children unconsciously develop a sexual interest in their mother and see their father as a rival. Freud reasoned that little boys in the phallic stage would think that little girls do not have a penis because it was cut off (castrated) by their fathers, causing the little boys to think the fathers could do the same thing to them if they desired their mothers. To resolve such unacceptable feelings, little boys come to identify with their fathers. Freud defined **identification** as the process of wanting to be like another person as much as possible, imitating that person's behaviour and adopting similar beliefs and values. Freud did not apply the Oedipal conflict to little girls in the same way he did with little boys. He thought that little girls must be envious of the fact that boys had a penis, resulting in what he called "penis envy." It was Carl Jung (pronounced "yoong"), who developed the theory of the **Electra complex**, where little girls unconsciously wish to have a relationship with their fathers while rivalling their mothers.

Although Freud did not agree to using the term Electra complex, he did believe that the superego of both boys and girls would start to emerge during the phallic stage and their personality would be fully formed by about age five or six. Freud also believed that the defence mechanisms people used would also help shape their personality development. We will discuss defence mechanisms in the next section.

Defence Mechanisms Freud's efforts to describe and theorize about the underlying dynamics of personality and its development were motivated by very practical problems that his patients faced in dealing with *anxiety*, an intense, negative emotional experience. According to Freud, anxiety is a danger signal to the ego. Although anxiety can arise from realistic fears—such as seeing a poisonous snake about to strike—it can also occur in the form of *neurotic*

anxiety, in which irrational impulses emanating from the id threaten to burst through and become uncontrollable.

Because anxiety, obviously, is unpleasant, Freud believed that people develop a range of defence mechanisms to deal with it. Defence mechanisms are *unconscious* strategies that people use to reduce anxiety by concealing the source from themselves.

> ## According to Freud, anxiety is a danger signal to the ego.

The primary defence mechanism is **repression**, in which unacceptable or unpleasant id impulses are pushed back into the unconscious. Repression is the most direct method of dealing with anxiety; instead of handling an anxiety-producing impulse on a conscious level, we simply ignore it. For example, a college student who feels hatred for her mother may repress those personally and socially unacceptable feelings. The feelings remain lodged within the unconscious, because acknowledging them would provoke anxiety. Similarly, memories of childhood abuse may be repressed. Although such memories may not be consciously recalled, according to Freud they can affect later behaviour, and they may be revealed through dreams or slips of the tongue or symbolically in some other fashion.

If repression is ineffective in keeping anxiety at bay, we might use other defence mechanisms. Freud, and later his daughter Anna Freud (who became a well-known psychoanalyst), formulated an extensive list of potential defence mechanisms. (Conte, Plutchik, & Draguns, 2004; Cramer, 2007; Hentschel et al., 2004). Refer to Figure 11.3 for a description of each of the defence mechanisms.

Do men and women rely on different defence mechanisms? Johnathan Petraglia and colleagues from McGill University and the University of Montreal (Petraglia, Thygeses, Lecours, & Drapeau, 2009) found that men tend to rely more on intellectualization and sublimation than women do. Gender differences aside, all of us employ defence mechanisms to some degree, according to Freudian theory, and they can serve a useful purpose by protecting us from unpleasant information. Yet some people fall prey to them to such an extent that they must constantly direct a large amount of psychic energy toward hiding and rechanneling unacceptable impulses. When this occurs, everyday living becomes difficult. In such cases, the result is a mental disorder produced by anxiety—what Freud

Oedipal conflict A child's sexual interest in his or her mother, typically resolved through identification with the mother.

identification The process of wanting to be like another person as much as possible, imitating that person's behaviour and adopting similar beliefs and values.

Electra complex Where little girls unconsciously wish to have a relationship with their fathers while rivalling their mothers.

repression The primary defence mechanism in which unacceptable or unpleasant id impulses are pushed back into the unconscious.

Figure 11.3
Freud's Defence Mechanisms

Defense Mechanism	Explanation	Example
Repression	Unacceptable or unpleasant impulses are pushed back into the unconscious.	A woman is unable to recall that she was raped.
Regression	People behave as if they were at an earlier stage of development.	A boss has a temper tantrum when an employee makes a mistake.
Displacement	The expression of an unwanted feeling or thought is redirected from a more threatening powerful person to a weaker one.	A brother yells at his younger sister after a teacher gives him a bad grade.
Rationalization	People provide self-justifying explanations in place of the actual, but threatening, reason for their behaviour.	A student who goes out drinking the night before a big test rationalizes his behaviour by saying the test isn't all that important.
Denial	People refuse to accept or acknowledge an anxiety-producing piece of information.	A student refuses to believe that he has flunked a course.
Projection	People attribute unwanted impulses and feelings to someone else.	A man who is unfaithful to his wife and feels guilty suspects that his wife is unfaithful.
Sublimation	People divert unwanted impulses into socially approved thoughts, feelings, or behaviours.	A person with strong feelings of aggression becomes a soldier.
Reaction formation	Unconscious impulses are expressed as their opposite in consciousness.	A mother who unconsciously resents her child acts in an overly loving way toward the child.

Psych think

> > > What is the difference between the defence mechanisms sublimation and reaction formation?

called "neurosis" (a term rarely used by psychologists today, although it endures in everyday conversation).

Evaluating Freud's Legacy Freud's theory has had a significant effect on the field of psychology—and even more broadly on Western philosophy and literature. The ideas of the unconscious, defence mechanisms, and childhood roots of adult psychological difficulties have been accepted by many people (Noland, 1999).

However, many contemporary personality psychologists have levelled significant criticisms against psychoanalytic theory. Among the most important is the lack of compelling scientific data to support it. Although individual case studies *seem* supportive, we lack conclusive evidence showing that the personality is structured and operates along the lines Freud laid out. The lack of evidence is due, in part, to the fact that Freud's conception of personality is built on unobservable abstract concepts. Moreover, it is not clear that the stages of personality that Freud laid out provide an

accurate description of personality development. We also know now that important changes in personality can occur in adolescence and adulthood—something that Freud did not believe happened. Instead, he argued that personality largely is set by adolescence (Hayslip et al., 2006).

The vague nature of Freud's theory also makes it difficult to predict how certain developmental difficulties will be displayed in an adult. For instance, if a person is fixated at the anal stage, according to Freud, he or she may be unusually messy—or unusually neat. Freud's theory offers no way to predict how the difficulty will be exhibited (Crews, 1996; Macmillan, 1996). Furthermore, Freud can be faulted for arguing that women have weaker superegos than men do and in some ways unconsciously yearn to be men (the concept of penis envy).

Finally, Freud made his observations and derived his theory from a limited population. His theory was based almost entirely on case studies of upper-class Austrian women living in the strict, puritanical era of the early 1900s who had come to him seeking treatment for psychological and physical problems. How far one can generalize beyond this population is a matter of considerable debate.

Still, Freud generated an important method of treating psychological disturbances called *psychoanalysis*. As we will see when we discuss treatment approaches to psychological disorder, psychoanalysis remains in use today (Heller, 2005; Messer & McWilliams, 2003; Riolo, 2007).

Moreover, Freud's emphasis on the unconscious has been partially supported by current research on dreams and implicit memory. As we first noted when we discussed dreaming, advances in neuroscience are not inconsistent with some of Freud's arguments. Furthermore, cognitive and social psychologists have found increasing evidence that unconscious processes help us think about and evaluate our world, set goals, and choose a course of action (Derryberry, 2006; Litowitz, 2007).

THE NEO-FREUDIAN PSYCHOANALYSTS

Freud laid the foundation for important work done by a series of successors who were trained in traditional Freudian theory but later rejected some of its major points. These theorists are known as **neo-Freudian psychoanalysts**.

The neo-Freudians placed greater emphasis than Freud had on the functions of the ego, suggesting that it has more control than does the id over day-to-day activities. They focused more on the social environment and minimized the importance of sex as a driving force in children and adults' lives. They also paid greater attention to the effects of society and culture on personality development.

Jung's Collective Unconscious

One of the most influential neo-Freudians, Carl Jung, rejected Freud's view of the primary importance of unconscious sexual urges. Instead, he looked at the primitive urges of the unconscious more positively, arguing that they represented a more general and positive life force, one that that encompassed an inborn drive that motivated creativity and more positive resolution of conflict (Cassells, 2007; Lothane, 2005).

In terms of Jung's theory, Batman and the Joker represent archetypes of good and evil.

> Jung rejected Freud's view of the primary importance of unconscious sexual urges.

Jung suggested that we have a universal **collective unconscious**, a common set of ideas, feelings, images, and symbols that we inherit from our relatives, the whole human race, and even non-human animal ancestors from the distant past. This collective unconscious is shared by everyone and is displayed in behaviour that is common across diverse cultures—such as love of mother, belief in a supreme being, and even behaviour as specific as fear of snakes (Drob, 2005; Hauke, 2006; Oehman & Mineka, 2003).

neo-Freudian psychoanalysts Psychoanalysts who were trained in traditional Freudian theory but who later rejected some of its major points.

collective unconscious According to Jung, a common set of ideas, feelings, images, and symbols that we inherit from our ancestors, the whole human race, and even animal ancestors from the distant past.

archetypes According to Jung, universal symbolic representations of a particular person, object, or experience (such as good and evil).

Jung went on to propose that the collective unconscious contains **archetypes**, universal symbolic representations of a particular person, object, or experience. For instance, a mother archetype, which contains reflections of our ancestors' relationships with mother figures, is suggested by the prevalence of mothers in art, religion, literature, and mythology. (Think of the Virgin Mary, the Earth Mother, wicked stepmothers in fairy tales, Mother's Day, and so forth.) Jung also suggested that an unconscious feminine archetype affects how men behave, whereas a male archetype influences women's behaviour (Bair, 2003; Jung, 1961; Smetana, 2007).

To Jung, archetypes play an important role in determining our day-to-day reactions, attitudes, and values. For example, Jung might explain the popularity of the *Star Wars* movies as being due to their use of broad archetypes of good (Luke Skywalker) and evil (Darth Vader).

Although no reliable research evidence confirms the existence of the collective unconscious—and even Jung acknowledged that such evidence would be difficult to produce—Jung's theory has had significant influence in areas beyond psychology, including business and the arts (Furnham & Crump, 2005; Gladwell, 2004).

From the perspective of...

A MARKETING STUDENT How might you use Jung's concept of archetypes in designing your advertisements? Which of the archetypes would you use?

Karen Horney was one of the earliest proponents of women's issues in psychology.

Horney's Feminist Perspective Karen Horney (pronounced "HORN-eye") was one of the earliest western psychologists to champion women's issues and is sometimes called the first feminist psychologist. Horney suggested that personality develops in the context of social relationships and depends particularly on the relationship between parents and child and how well the child's needs are met. She rejected Freud's suggestion that women have penis envy, asserting that what women envy most in men is not their anatomy but the independence, success, and freedom that women often are denied (Horney, 1937; Miletic, 2002; Smith, 2007).

Horney was also one of the first to stress the importance of cultural factors in the determination of personality. For example, she suggested that society's rigid gender roles for women lead them to experience ambivalence about success, fearing that they will lose their friends. Her conceptualizations, developed in the 1930s and 1940s, laid the groundwork for many of the central ideas of feminism that emerged decades later (Eckardt, 2005; Jones, 2006).

Adler and the Other Neo-Freudians Alfred Adler, another important neo-Freudian psychoanalyst, also considered Freudian theory's emphasis on sexual needs misplaced. Instead, Adler proposed that the primary human motivation is a striving for superiority, not in terms of superiority over others but in a quest for self-improvement and perfection (Hjertaas, 2004; Rosov, 1993).

Adler used the term **inferiority complex** to describe situations in which adults have not been able to overcome the feelings of inferiority they developed as children, when they were small and limited in their knowledge about the world. Early social relationships with parents have an important

inferiority complex According to Adler, a problem affecting adults who have not been able to overcome the feelings of inferiority that they developed as children, when they were small and limited in their knowledge about the world.

traits Consistent personality characteristics and behaviours displayed in different situations.

trait theory A model of personality that seeks to identify the basic traits necessary to describe personality.

effect on children's ability to outgrow feelings of personal inferiority and instead to orient themselves toward attaining more socially useful goals, such as improving society.

Other neo-Freudians included Erik Erikson, whose theory of psychosocial development we discussed in the chapter on human development, and Freud's daughter, Anna Freud. Like Adler and Horney, Erikson and Anna Freud focused less than Freud did on inborn sexual and aggressive drives and more on the social and cultural factors behind personality (Salzman, 1964).

Trait Approaches to Personality

If someone asked you to characterize another person, you would probably come up with a list of that individual's personal qualities, as you see them. In fact, much of our own understanding of others' behaviour is based on the premise that people possess certain traits that are consistent across different situations. For example, we generally assume that if someone is outgoing and sociable in one situation, he or she is outgoing and sociable in other situations (Gilbert et al., 1992; Gilbert, Miller, & Ross, 1998; Mischel, 2004). But how would you know which of those qualities are most important to an understanding of that person's behaviour?

DID YOU KNOW?

We tend to be more accurate at guessing personal information about our casual acquaintances than we are about our close friends (Gershoff & Johar, 2006).

Personality psychologists have asked similar questions. To answer them, some have developed a model of personality centred on traits. **Traits** are consistent personality characteristics and behaviours displayed in different situations. **Trait theories** attempt to identify the consistencies in individuals' behaviour.

Trait theorists do not assume that some people have a trait and others do not; rather, they propose that all people possess certain traits, but that the degree to which a particular trait applies to a specific person varies and can be quantified (Olson, 2006). For instance, you may be relatively friendly, whereas your friend may be relatively unfriendly. But you both have a "friendliness" trait, although your degree of "friendliness" is higher than your friend's. The major challenge for trait theorists taking this approach has been to identify the specific primary traits necessary to describe personality.

Study tip

All trait theories explain personality in terms of traits (consistent personality characteristics and behaviours), but they differ in terms of which and how many traits are seen as fundamental.

ALLPORT'S TRAIT THEORY

Personality psychologist Gordon Allport was faced with a problem crucial to all trait approaches: identifying the principal traits. Allport eventually suggested that there are three fundamental categories of traits: cardinal, central, and secondary (Allport, 1961, 1966). A *cardinal trait* is a single characteristic that directs most of a person's activities. For example, a totally selfless person may direct all her energy toward humanitarian activities; an intensely power-hungry person may be driven by an all-consuming need for control.

Most people, however, do not develop a single, comprehensive cardinal trait. Instead, they possess a handful of central traits that make up the core of personality. *Central traits*, such as honesty and sociability, are the major characteristics of an individual. According to Allport, they usually number from five to ten in any one person. Finally, *secondary traits* are characteristics that affect behaviour in fewer situations and are less influential than central or cardinal traits. For instance, a mild reluctance to eat meat and a casual interest in modern art might be considered secondary traits (Glicksohn & Nahari, 2007; Nicholson, 2003). *Common traits* are those we share in common with others in our culture. For example, speaking loudly and talking with one's hands is a common trait to people who are Italian.

FACTOR ANALYSIS

Later attempts to identify primary personality traits have centred on a statistical technique known as factor analysis (Kim & Mueller, 1978; Lee & Ashton, 2007). *Factor analysis* is a statistical method of identifying associations among a large number of variables to reveal more general patterns. For example, a personality researcher might administer a questionnaire to many participants, asking them to describe themselves by referring to an extensive list of traits. By statistically combining responses and computing which traits are associated with one another in the same person, a researcher can identify the most fundamental patterns or combinations of traits—called *factors*—that underlie participants' responses.

Using factor analysis, personality psychologist Raymond Cattell (1965) suggested that 16 pairs of *source traits* represent the basic dimensions of personality. Using those source traits, he developed the Sixteen Personality Factor Questionnaire, or 16 PF, a measure that provides scores for each of the source traits (Cattell, Cattell, & Cattell, 1993, 2000). The source traits include abstractedness, apprehension, dominance, emotional stability, liveliness, openness to change, perfectionism, privateness, reasoning, rule consciousness, self-reliance, sensitivity, social boldness, tension, vigilance, and warmth. Cattell (1965) argued that we all fall somewhere on the continuum of these traits.

Another trait theorist, psychologist Hans Eysenck (1995), also used factor analysis to identify patterns of traits, but he came to a very different conclusion about the nature of personality. He found that personality could best be described in terms of just three major dimensions: *extraversion*, *neuroticism*, and *psychoticism*. The extraversion

Figure 11.4
Eysenck's Three Dimensions of Personality

Extraversion	Neuroticism	Psychoticism
Sociable	Anxious	Aggressive
Lively	Depressed	Cold
Active	Guilt feelings	Egocentric
Assertive	Low self-esteem	Impersonal
Sensation-seeking	Tense	Impulsive

Source: Eysenck, 1990.

dimension relates to the degree of sociability, whereas the neurotic dimension encompasses emotional stability. Finally, psychoticism refers to the degree to which reality is distorted. By evaluating people along these three dimensions, Eysenck was able to predict behaviour accurately in a variety of situations (Eysenck, 1991).

THE BIG FIVE FACTORS OF PERSONALITY

For the last two decades, the most influential trait approach contends that five traits or factors—called the "Big Five"— lie at the core of personality. Using modern factor analytic statistical techniques, a host of researchers have identified a similar set of five factors that underlie personality. The five factors are *openness to experience, conscientiousness, extraversion, agreeableness,* and *neuroticism* (emotional stability) (Costa & McCrae, 2008; John & Srivastava, 1999; McCrae & Costa, 1990). When listed in this order the first letters of each word spell the word OCEAN—a nice mnemonic device to help you remember the five factors! You can see each factor and some sample traits in Figure 11.5.

The "Big Five" traits are found in a number of areas. For example, the "Big Five" are descriptive of different populations of people, including children, college students, older adults, and speakers of different languages. Cross-cultural research conducted in areas ranging from Europe to the Middle East to Africa also has been supportive (McCrae et al., 2005a, 2005b; Rossier, Dahourou, & McCrae, 2005; Schmitt, Allik, & McCrae, 2007).

DID YOU KNOW?

The firmness of your handshake can reveal aspects of your personality. Individuals who are extroverted and open to experience tend to have firmer handshakes. Handshakes of neurotic individuals are generally more limp (Chaplin et al., 2000).

Figure 11.5

The Big Five Personality Factors and Dimensions of Sample Traits

Openness to experience
Independent—Conforming
Imaginative—Practical
Preference for variety—
Preference for routine

Conscientiousness
Careful—Careless
Disciplined—Impulsive
Organized—Disorganized

Extraversion
Talkative—Quiet
Fun-loving—Sober
Sociable—Retiring

Agreeableness
Sympathetic—Fault-finding
Kind—Cold
Appreciative—Unfriendly

Neuroticism
(Emotional Stability)
Stable—Tense
Calm—Anxious
Secure—Insecure

Source: Adapted from Pervin, 1990, Chapter 3, and McCrae & Costa, 1986, p. 1002.

Udi Blankstein and colleagues from the University of Toronto completed some interesting research on personality traits and brain structure in a group of adolescents (Blankstein et al., 2009). The researchers found that neuroticism and extraversion impacted the frontal lobe and limbic area of the brains of adolescents, and that these structural differences related to how young men and women reported feelings of pain and depression. Blankstein et al. (2009) found that young women had more brain grey matter volume in the frontal-limbic area of the brain which was related to higher levels of neuroticism and more chronic pain and depression; the opposite was true for young men.

The growing consensus is that the "Big Five" currently represent the best description of personality traits (Costa & McCrae, 2008). Still, the debate over the specific number and kinds of traits—and even the usefulness of trait approaches in general—remains a lively one (Fleeson, 2004).

EVALUATING TRAIT APPROACHES TO PERSONALITY

Trait approaches have several virtues. They provide a clear, straightforward characterization of people's behavioural consistencies. Furthermore, traits allow us to readily compare one person with another. Because of these advantages, trait approaches to personality have had an important influence on the development of several useful personality measures (Funder, 1991; Larsen & Buss, 2006; Wiggins, 2003).

However, trait approaches also have some drawbacks. For example, we have seen that various trait theories describing personality come to very different conclusions about which traits are the most fundamental and descriptive. The difficulty in determining which of the theories is the most accurate has led some personality psychologists to question the validity of trait conceptions of personality in general. Even if we can identify a set of primary traits, we are left with little more than a label or description of personality rather than an explanation of behaviour. In the view of some critics, then, traits do not provide explanations for behaviour; they merely describe it (Fleeson, 2004).

Study tip

You can remember the "Big Five" set of personality traits by using the acronym OCEAN (*O*penness to experience, *C*onscientiousness, *E*xtraversion, *A*greeableness, and *N*euroticism).

Learning Approaches to Personality

The psychodynamic and trait approaches concentrate on the "inner" person—the fury of an unobservable but powerful id or a hypothetical set of traits. In contrast, early behavioural approaches to personality focused on the "outer" person. To a strict behaviourist, personality was simply the sum of learned responses to the external environment. Internal events such as thoughts, feelings, and motivations

Psych
At The Movies

Paprika
A machine that allows psychologists to enter a patient's unconscious through his or her dreams is stolen and falls into the wrong hands.

The Closet
A man tries to save his job by pretending to be gay. Note the reaction formation displayed by his co-worker Felix, who believes the story.

The Incredibles
In this creative, animated film, Mr. Incredible's boss displays an anal retentive personality with his rigid thinking and excessively orderly office and desktop.

Little Children
Residents of a quiet, suburban neighbourhood are unsettled when a prior sex offender comes to live with his mother, with whom he has a pseudo-Oedipal conflict. Watch how the Oedipal conflict unfolds.

were ignored, because they were irrelevant. Although the existence of personality was not denied, these theorists said that personality was best understood by looking at features of a person's environment.

SKINNER'S BEHAVIOURIST APPROACH

According to the most influential learning theorist, B. F. Skinner (who carried out pioneering work on operant conditioning), personality was a collection of learned behaviour patterns (Skinner, 1975). Similarities in responses across different situations were caused by similar patterns of reinforcement that had been received in such situations in the past. If one is sociable both at parties and at meetings, it is because he or she has been reinforced for displaying social behaviours—not because he or she is fulfilling an unconscious wish based on experiences during childhood or because of an internal trait of sociability.

Psych think

> > > How would the behaviourist approach explain the personality development of singer Lady Gaga?

SOCIAL COGNITIVE APPROACHES

Modern approaches of personality that are grounded in behaviourist theories have found it necessary to stop rejecting the importance of what is "inside" a person and to stop focusing solely on the "outside." These theories, called collectively **social cognitive approaches**, emphasize the influence of cognition—thoughts, feelings, expectations, and values—as well as observation of others' behaviour, on personality. They also recognize that even though people may have a set of traits that are relatively stable, their behaviour can still change when they are in different situations. The interaction between the individual and the situation/environment can be explained by the term **reciprocal determinism**. This term explains the interaction as being two-way, which means that the individual impacts the situation or environment, and the situation or environment impacts the individual. Social cognitive theorists

social cognitive approaches to personality Theories that emphasize the influence of a person's cognitions—thoughts, feelings, expectations, and values—as well as observation of others' behaviour, in determining personality.

reciprocal determinism The two-way interaction between the individual and the situation or environment, where the individual impacts the situation or environment, and the situation or environment impacts the individual.

self-efficacy Belief in one's personal capabilities. Self-efficacy underlies people's faith in their ability to carry out a particular behaviour or produce a desired outcome.

believe that personality develops based on this reciprocal determinism.

Another aspect of the social cognitive approach to personality is *observational learning*. According to Albert Bandura, people can foresee the possible outcomes of certain behaviours in a specific setting without actually having to carry them out. This understanding comes primarily through *observational learning*—viewing the actions of others and observing the consequences (Bandura, 1986, 1999).

For instance, children who view a model behaving in an aggressive manner tend to copy the behaviour if the consequences of the model's behaviour are seen to be positive. If, in contrast, the model's aggressive behaviour has resulted in no consequences or negative consequences, children are considerably less likely to act aggressively (Bandura, 1986, 1992). According to social cognitive approaches, then, personality develops through repeated observation and imitation of the behaviour of others.

Self-Efficacy Bandura's approach places particular emphasis on **self-efficacy**, belief in one's personal capabilities. Self-efficacy underlies people's faith in their ability to carry out a specific behaviour or produce a desired outcome. People with high self-efficacy have higher aspirations and greater persistence in working to attain goals and ultimately achieve greater success than do those with lower self-efficacy (Bandura, 2001; Bandura & Locke, 2003; Glickler, 2006).

For example, someone who has studied hard while in college and has gotten high grades is likely to have a high sense of self-efficacy with regard to succeeding in college. In contrast, someone who studied a lot but did not get good grades probably would not have a strong sense of self-efficacy for college success.

"I Think I Can!": Improving Your Self-Efficacy Knowing that people with a higher level of self-efficacy tend to have greater success than people with lower self-efficacy, it is important to be aware that you can improve your self-efficacy (Bandura, 2001; Bandura & Locke, 2003; Glickler, 2006). The following tips can help you do this:

- *Try to enhance your self-efficacy by choosing one small achievement that you feel confident you can make.* The great thing about self-efficacy is that simply making achievements can start the process of raising your level of self-efficacy. Once you achieve your first goal, work on another achievable goal.

> **People with high self-efficacy have higher aspirations and greater persistence in working to attain goals, and ultimately achieve greater success than do those with lower self-efficacy.**

- *Think about situations in the past where you were successful and draw on the strength of the memory that you have done this before.* Think specifically about what aspects made you successful and use those skills/attributes for current situations.

- *Use visualization to "practice" in your mind before trying.* Athletes use visualization all of the time and it has proven to be very helpful in allowing them to succeed when they need it.

- *Find a role model you identify with and who you feel somewhat equal to.* Knowing that this person is able to achieve will help you feel confident that you can be successful too.

- *Having a good system of social support can be very helpful.* Surround yourself with people who believe in you and who can encourage you to be successful. If you have friends who doubt you, avoid discussing your goals with them because they can be too discouraging.

- *Improving your mood can lead to more success.* Know what makes you happy and use these techniques to help elevate your mood. This can ultimately help boost your belief in success.

- *Acknowledging your own doubt is important.* Think about it for a moment, but then remind yourself that you are capable of achieving by using the points above to help you!

Self-Esteem Our behaviour also reflects the view we have of ourselves and the way we value the various parts of our personalities. **Self-esteem** is the component of personality that encompasses our positive and negative self-evaluations. Unlike self-efficacy, which focuses on our views of whether we are able to carry out a task, self-esteem relates to how we feel about ourselves.

Although people have a general level of self-esteem, it is not one dimensional. We may see ourselves positively in one domain but negatively in others. For example, a good student may have high self-esteem in academic domains but lower self-esteem in sports (Crocker & Park, 2004; Salmela-Aro & Nurmi, 2007; Swann, Chang-Schneider, & Larsen McClarty, 2007).

self-esteem The component of personality that encompasses our positive and negative self-evaluations.

Almost everyone goes through periods of low self-esteem (after, for instance, an undeniable failure), but some people are chronically low in self-esteem. For them, failure seems to be an inevitable part of life. In fact, low self-esteem may lead to a cycle of failure in which past failure breeds future failure.

Consider, for example, students with low self-esteem who are studying for a test. Because of their low self-esteem, they expect to do poorly on the test. In turn, this belief raises their anxiety level, making it increasingly difficult to study and perhaps even leading them not to work as hard. Because of these attitudes, the ultimate outcome is that they do, in fact, perform badly on the test, and this outcome has a negative effect on their sense of self-efficacy. Failure reinforces their low self-esteem, and the cycle is perpetuated. In short, low self-esteem and low self-efficacy can lead to a cycle of failure that is self-destructive.

From the perspective of . . .

A POLICE OFFICER
What role does self-esteem and self-efficacy play in a person developing competencies for a law enforcement career?

EVALUATING LEARNING APPROACHES TO PERSONALITY

Because they ignore the internal processes that are uniquely human, early learning theorists such as Skinner were accused of oversimplifying personality to such an extent that the concept became meaningless. In the eyes of their critics, reducing behaviour to a series of stimuli and responses, and excluding thoughts and feelings from the realm of personality, left behaviourists practicing an unrealistic and inadequate form of science.

Nonetheless, learning approaches had a major impact on the study of personality. For one thing, they offered a strategy for gathering evidence that helped make personality psychology an objective, scientific venture by focusing on observable behaviour and the environment. In addition, they produced important, successful means of treating a variety of psychological disorders. The degree of success of these treatments is a testimony to the merits of learning theory approaches to personality.

Biological and Evolutionary Approaches to Personality

Approaching the question of what determines personality from a different direction, **biological and evolutionary approaches to personality** suggest that important components of personality are inherited. Building on the work of behavioural geneticists, researchers using biological and evolutionary approaches argue that personality is determined at least in part by our genes, in much the same way that our height is largely a result of genetic contributions from our ancestors. The evolutionary perspective assumes that personality traits that led to the reproductive success of our ancestors are more likely to be preserved and passed on to subsequent generations (Buss, 2001).

The importance of genetic factors in personality is illustrated by studies of twins. For instance, personality psychologist Auke Tellegen and colleagues examined the personality traits of pairs of twins who were genetically identical but were raised apart from each other (Tellegen et al., 1988, 2004). In the study, each twin was given a battery of personality tests, including one that measured 11 key personality characteristics.

The results of the personality tests indicated that in major respects the twins were quite similar in personality,

biological and evolutionary approaches to personality Theories that suggest that important components of personality are inherited.

despite having been separated at an early age. Moreover, certain traits were more heavily influenced by heredity than were others. For example, social potency (the degree to which a person assumes mastery and leadership roles in social situations) and traditionalism (the tendency to follow authority) had particularly strong genetic components, whereas achievement and social closeness had relatively weak genetic components.

Some researchers contend that specific genes are related to personality. For example, people with a longer dopamine-4 receptor gene are more likely to be thrill seekers than are those without such a gene. These thrill seekers tend to be extroverted, impulsive, quick-tempered, and always in search of excitement and novel situations (Golimbet et al., 2007; Robins, 2005; Zuckerman & Kuhlman, 2000).

Does the identification of specific genes linked to personality mean that we are destined to have certain types of personalities? Hardly. First, it is unlikely that any single gene is linked to a specific trait. For instance, the dopamine-4 receptor accounts for only around 10% of the variation in novelty seeking between different individuals. In other words, there are many reasons why people might be thrill

Figure 11.6
Genetic Influences on Personality

Percentage (degree to which heredity influences each characteristic)

61%	**Social potency**	Is masterful; a forceful leader who likes to be the centre of attention
60%	**Traditionalism**	Follows rules and authority; endorses high moral standards and strict discipline
55%	**Stress reaction**	Feels vulnerable and sensitive; is given to worrying and easily upset
55%	**Absorption**	Has a vivid imagination readily captured by rich experience; relinquishes sense of reality
55%	**Alienation**	Feels mistreated and used, that "the world is out to get me"
54%	**Well-being**	Has a cheerful disposition; feels confident and optimistic
51%	**Harm avoidance**	Shuns the excitement of risk and danger; prefers the safe route even if it is tedious
48%	**Aggression**	Is physically aggressive and vindictive; has taste for violence; is "out to get the world"
46%	**Achievement**	Works hard; strives for mastery; puts work and accomplishment ahead of other things
43%	**Control**	Is cautious and plodding; is rational and sensible; likes carefully planned events
33%	**Social closeness**	Prefers emotional intimacy and close ties; turns to others for comfort and help

Source: Tellegan et al., 1988.

People are born with particular temperaments, dispositions that are consistent throughout childhood.

Biological and evolutionary approaches to personality seek to explain the consistencies in personality that are found in some families.

seekers, and most of them appear to be environmental and/or due to other genes (Keltikangas-Järvinen et al., 2004; Lahti et al., 2005).

More importantly, genes interact with the environment, and it is impossible to completely divorce genetic factors from environmental factors. For this reason, although studies of identical twins raised in different environments are helpful, they are not definitive. To fully control environmental factors, we would have to take identical twins away from their natural parents at birth and randomly assign them to grow up together or grow up as an only child. They might be raised by robot parents whose programming could be adjusted as needed to study the effects of different parenting styles, and their environments might be arranged so that they would have the exact experiences that the researchers were interested in studying. Clearly this is not possible or even remotely desirable. But without these controls in place, psychologists cannot be sure when environmental factors have more influence than genetic factors and what kinds of affects they have. Furthermore, estimates of the influence of genetics are just that—estimates—and apply to groups, not individuals.

Study tip

Remember that biological and evolutionary approaches focus on the way in which people's genetic heritage affects personality.

Although an increasing number of personality theorists are taking biological and evolutionary factors into account, no comprehensive, unified theory that considers biological and evolutionary factors is widely accepted. Still, it is clear that certain personality traits have significant genetic components and that heredity and environment interact to determine personality (Bouchard, 2004; Ebstein, Benjamin, & Belmaker, 2003; Plomin et al., 2003).

Humanistic Approaches to Personality

Where, in all the approaches to personality that we have discussed, is an explanation for the selflessness of a Nelson Mandela, the creativity of a Michelangelo, or the brilliance and perseverance of an Einstein? An understanding of such unique individuals—as well as more ordinary sorts of people who have some of the same attributes—comes from humanistic theory. **Humanistic approaches to personality** emphasize people's inherent goodness and their tendency to move towards higher levels of functioning. It is this conscious, self-motivated ability to change and improve, along with people's unique creative impulses, that humanistic theorists argue make up the core of personality (Pennington, D., 2003).

ROGERS AND THE NEED FOR SELF-ACTUALIZATION

The major proponent of the humanistic point of view is Carl Rogers (1971). Along with other humanistic theorists, such as Abraham Maslow, Rogers maintains that all people have a fundamental need to move in the direction of *self-actualization*, a way of living in which people realize their highest potential, each in a unique way.

Becoming self-actualizing may be a lifelong process for some individuals; others may never reach that condition. A more basic need, according to Rogers, is peoples' need for positive regard, which reflects the desire to be loved and respected. Because others provide this positive regard, we grow dependent on them. We begin to see and judge ourselves through the eyes of other people, relying on their values and being preoccupied with what they think of us.

According to Rogers, one outgrowth of placing importance on the opinions of others is that a conflict may grow between people's experiences and their *self-concepts*, the set of beliefs they hold about what they are like as individuals. If the discrepancies are minor, so are the consequences. But if the discrepancies are great, they will lead to psychological disturbances in daily functioning, such as the experience of frequent anxiety.

For example, suppose you believe that you are a generous person. If you occasionally observe that others think your contributions are less than generous, you might count this as a minor discrepancy. But suppose everyone criticized you for being greedy and stingy. This would be a large discrepancy. If you continued to believe you were generous in the face of all that evidence to the contrary, you might develop serious anxiety.

Rogers suggests that one way of overcoming the discrepancy between experience and self-concept is through the receipt of unconditional positive regard from another

humanistic approaches to personality Theories that emphasize people's innate goodness and desire to achieve higher levels of functioning.

unconditional positive regard An attitude of acceptance and respect on the part of an observer, no matter what a person says or does.

person—a friend, a spouse, or a therapist. **Unconditional positive regard** refers to an attitude of acceptance and respect on the part of an observer, no matter what a person says or does. This acceptance, says Rogers, gives people the opportunity to evolve and grow both cognitively and emotionally and to develop more realistic self-concepts. You may have experienced the power of unconditional positive regard when you confided in someone, revealing embarrassing secrets, because you knew the listener would still love and respect you, even after hearing the worst about you (Marshall, 2007; Snyder, 2002).

In contrast, *conditional positive regard* depends on your behaviour. In such cases, others withdraw their love and acceptance if you do something of which they don't approve. The result is that you experience a discrepancy between who you are and what others wish you would be, and this can lead to anxiety and frustration.

EVALUATING HUMANISTIC APPROACHES

Although humanistic theories suggest the value of providing unconditional positive regard toward people, unconditional positive regard toward humanistic theories has been less forthcoming. The criticisms have centred on the difficulty of verifying the basic assumptions of the approach, as well as on the question of whether unconditional positive regard does, in fact, lead to greater personality adjustment.

Figure 11.7

The Need for Unconditional Positive Regard

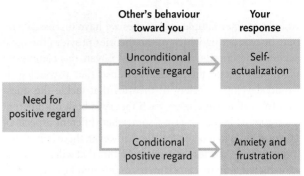

Humanistic approaches have also been criticized for making the assumption that people are basically "good"—a notion that is unverifiable—and, equally important, for using non-scientific values to build supposedly scientific theories. Is Russell Williams, the serial killer introduced at the beginning of the chapter, basically good? Some would argue that it is difficult to provide unconditional positive regard for people who commit such horrific crimes. Still, humanistic theories have been important in highlighting the

Figure 11.8

Summary of the Five Approaches to Personality

Theoretical Approach and Major Theorists	Conscious Versus Unconscious Determinants of Personality	Hereditary Factors (Nature) Versus Environmental Factors (Nurture)	Free Will Versus Determinism	Stability Versus Modifiability
Psychodynamic (Freud, Jung, Horney, Adler)	Emphasizes the unconscious	Stresses innate, inherited structure of personality while emphasizing importance of childhood experience	Stresses determinism, the view that behaviour is directed and caused by factors outside one's control	Emphasizes the stability of characteristics throughout a person's life
Trait (Allport, R. B. Cattell, Eysenck)	Disregards both conscious and unconscious	Approaches vary	Stresses determinism, the view that behaviour is directed and caused by factors outside one's control	Emphasizes the stability of characteristics throughout a person's life
Learning (Skinner, Bandura)	Disregards both conscious and unconscious	Focuses on the environment	Stresses determinism, the view that behaviour is directed and caused by factors outside one's control	Stresses that personality remains flexible and resilient throughout one's life
Biological and evolutionary (Tellegen)	Disregards both conscious and unconscious	Stresses the innate, inherited determinants of personality	Stresses determinism, the view that behaviour is directed and caused by factors outside one's control	Emphasizes the stability of characteristics throughout a person's life
Humanistic (Rogers, Maslow)	Stresses the conscious more than the unconscious	Stresses the interaction between both nature and nurture	Stresses the freedom of individuals to make their own choices	Stresses that personality remains flexible and resilient throughout one's life

uniqueness of human beings and guiding the development of a significant form of therapy designed to alleviate psychological difficulties (Bauman & Kopp, 2006; Cain, 2002).

Comparing Approaches to Personality

In light of the multiple approaches we have discussed, you may be wondering which of the theories provides the most accurate description of personality. Given the complexity of human personality, it makes sense that psychologists would develop a variety of theories that tackle the question from different angles. Each theory is built on different assumptions and focuses on somewhat different aspects of personality. When taken together, however, these apparently independent theories show us the factors that will need to be explained before we can claim to understand how personality works, how it is developed, and how it may be changed.

Psych think

> > > Think of a cartoon character. Now use three theories of personality to explain the personality of that cartoon character.

Assessing Personality

Psychologists interested in assessing personality must be able to define the most meaningful ways of discriminating between one person's personality and another's. To do this, they use **psychological tests**, measures devised to assess behaviour objectively. With the results of such tests, psychologists can help people better understand themselves and make decisions about their lives. Psychological tests are also employed by researchers interested in the causes and the consequences of personality (Aiken, 2000b; Hambleton, 2006; Kaplan & Saccuzzo, 2001).

Like the assessments developed to measure intelligence, all psychological tests must have reliability and validity. *Reliability* refers to the measurement consistency of a test. If a test is reliable, it yields the same result each time it is

psychological tests Standard measures devised to assess behaviour objectively; used by psychologists to help people make decisions about their lives and understand more about themselves.

self-report measures A method of gathering data about people by asking them questions about a sample of their behaviour.

Minnesota Multiphasic Personality Inventory-2 (MMPI-2) A widely used self-report test that identifies people with psychological difficulties and is employed to predict some everyday behaviours.

test standardization A technique used to validate questions in personality tests by studying the responses of people with known diagnoses.

administered to a specific person or group. In contrast, unreliable tests give different results each time they are administered.

For meaningful conclusions to be drawn, tests also must be valid. Tests have *validity* when they actually measure what they are designed to measure. If a test is constructed to measure sociability, for instance, we need to know that it actually measures sociability, not some other trait.

Study tip The distinction between reliability and validity is important. For instance, a test that measures cheerfulness is reliable if it yields the same results each time it is administered, and it would be valid if it measures cheerfulness accurately.

Suppose you took a test and were told you had earned a 325. Is that a good score? Is it very low? Average? To address this issue, psychological tests are given to samples of people to establish *norms*, that is, standards of test performance that permit the comparison of one person's score on a test with the scores of others who have taken the same test. For example, a norm permits test takers who have received a certain score on a test to know that they have scored in the top 10% of all those who have taken the test.

SELF-REPORT MEASURES OF PERSONALITY

Psychologists use **self-report measures** to ask people about a small sample of their behaviour. This sampling of self-report data is then used to infer the presence of particular personality characteristics.

One of the best examples of a self-report measure, and one of the most frequently used personality tests (Sellbom & Ben-Porath, 2006), is the **Minnesota Multiphasic Personality Inventory-2 (MMPI-2)**. Although the original purpose of this measure was to identify people with specific sorts of psychological difficulties, the MMPI-2 has been found to predict a variety of other behaviours. For instance, MMPI scores have been shown to be good predictors of whether college students will marry within 10 years and will get an advanced degree. Police departments use the test to measure whether police officers are likely to use their weapons (Butcher, 2005; Sellbom & Ben-Porath, 2006; Weis, Crockett, & Vieth, 2004).

The test consists of a series of 567 items to which a person responds "true," "false," or "cannot say." The questions cover a variety of issues, ranging from mood ("I feel useless at times") to opinions ("People should try to understand their dreams") to physical and psychological health ("I am bothered by an upset stomach several times a week" and "I have strange and peculiar thoughts").

There are no right or wrong answers. Instead, interpretation of the results rests on the pattern of responses. The test yields scores on ten separate scales, plus three scales meant to measure the validity of the respondent's answers (Bacchiochi, 2006; Butcher, 2005; Stein & Graham, 2005). The authors of the MMPI used a procedure known as **test standardization** to determine what specific patterns of responses indicate. To create the test, the authors asked

BUY IT?

Do Personality Tests on the Internet Assess Personality in a Reliable and Valid Way?

Assessments of personality are used routinely in the workplace to help with hiring decisions. Online dating services also require applicants to take a "personality test." And many Web sites offer free personality analysis and personality-based career tests. How can you evaluate these assessments and their results? First and foremost, remember that many validated personality tests have a fee associated with them. If someone is offering a personality test and results on the Internet, a good consumer of information will ask why they are offering the test for free. Regardless of the source, keep several points in mind:

- *Understand what the test claims to measure.* Standard personality measures are accompanied by information that discusses how the test was developed, to whom it is most applicable, and how the results should be interpreted. Read any explanations of the test; they will help you understand the results.

- *Base no decision only on the results of any one test.* Test results should be interpreted in the context of other information—academic records, social interests, and home and community activities.

- *Remember that test results are not always accurate.* The results may be in error; the test may be unreliable or invalid. You may, for example, have had a "bad day" when you took the test, or the person scoring and interpreting the test may have made a mistake. You should not place too much significance on the results of a single administration of any test.

In sum, remember that human behaviour—particularly your own—is complex. Just as there is currently no single, all-encompassing theory of personality, no single test provides an understanding of the intricacies of someone's personality (Gladwell, 2004; Hogan, Davies, & Hogan, 2007; Paul, 2004).

---

groups of psychiatric patients with a specific diagnosis, such as depression or schizophrenia, to complete a large number of items. They then determined which items best differentiated members of those groups from a comparison group of normal participants, and included those specific items in the final version of the test.

Another popular self-report test used in the world of business (and sometimes dating services!) is called the **Myers-Briggs Type Indicator**. This test measures people's preferences for thinking and behaving across 16 different types, such as a preference for extraversion vs. introversion, sensing vs. intuition, thinking vs. feeling, and judgment vs. perception (Gladwell, 2004). Researchers then use people's preferences to make predictions about their behaviour. For example, Robert Baudouin from the University of Moncton in New Brunswick found that students with a preference for extroversion coupled with a focus on sensation are more likely to withdraw from university than those with preferences for other personality traits (Baudouin & Uhl, 1998).

One issue with any personality test is the issue of faking. When prospective employees are highly motivated to get a job, they may not be completely honest when answer questions on a personality test such as the Myers-Briggs. Richard Goffin and Alison Boyd from the University of Western Ontario have studied faking behaviour on personality assessments and suggest that although it is prevalent, it does not undermine the importance of using personality assessments to select personnel (Goffin & Boyd, 2009). These researchers suggest that employers should be aware of potential faking and try to understand the process prospective employees go through when faking.

PROJECTIVE METHODS

In a **projective personality test** a person is shown an ambiguous stimulus and asked to describe it or tell a story about it. The responses are considered to be "projections" of the individual's personality.

The best-known projective test is the **Rorschach test**. Devised by Swiss psychiatrist Hermann Rorschach (1924),

Get Involved!

You can learn more about your personality by taking one of the free online tests on the Psychology Today Web site at www.psychologytoday.com (link from the home page to Tests and Personality).

TRY IT!

The Life Orientation Test

Use the following scale to answer the items below:

0 = strongly disagree   1 = disagree   2 = neutral   3 = agree   4 = strongly agree

1. In uncertain times, I usually expect the best.
2. It's easy for me to relax.
3. If something can go wrong for me, it will.
4. I'm always optimistic about my future.
5. I enjoy my friends a lot.
6. It's important for me to keep busy.
7. I hardly ever expect things to go my way.
8. I don't get upset too easily.
9. I rarely count on good things happening to me.
10. Overall, I expect more good things to happen to me than bad.

Scoring: First, reverse your answers to questions 3, 7, and 9. Do this by changing a 0 to a 4, a 1 to a 3, a 3 to a 1, and a 4 to a 0 (answers of 2 stay as 2). Then sum the reversed scores, and add them to the scores you gave to questions 1, 4, and 10. (Ignore questions 2, 5, 6, and 8, which are filler items.)

The total score you get is a measure of a particular orientation to life: your degree of optimism. The higher your score, the more positive and hopeful you generally are about life. For comparison purposes, the average score for college students is 14.3, according to the results of a study by Scheier, Carver, and Bridges (1994). People with a higher degree of optimism generally deal with stress better than do those with lower scores.

---

the test involves showing people a series of symmetrical stimuli, or "inkblots," and asking what the figures represent to them. Their responses are recorded, and through a complex set of clinical judgments on the part of the examiner, people are classified by their personality type. For instance, respondents who see a bear in one inkblot are thought to have a strong degree of emotional control, according to the scoring guidelines developed by Rorschach (Silverstein, 2007; Weiner, 2004b).

The **Thematic Apperception Test (TAT)** is another well-known projective test. The TAT consists of a series of pictures about which a person is asked to write a story. The stories are then used to draw inferences about the writer's personality characteristics (Langan-Fox & Grant, 2006; Weiner, 2004b).

Study tip

In projective tests such as the Rorschach and Thematic Apperception Test (TAT), researchers present an ambiguous stimulus and ask a person to describe or tell a story about it, and use the responses to make inferences about personality.

Tests with stimuli as ambiguous as those used in the Rorschach and TAT require particular skill and care in their interpretation—too much, critics say. The Rorschach in particular has been criticized for requiring too much inference on the part of the examiner, and attempts to standardize scoring have frequently failed. The argument is that the projections of the examiner may interfere with getting valid results. Furthermore, many critics question the validity of the information provided by the Rorschach about underlying personality traits. Despite such problems, both the Rorschach and the TAT are widely used, especially in clinical settings, and their proponents suggest that their reliability and validity are good enough to provide useful inferences about personality (Garb et al., 2005; Society for Personality Assessment, 2005; Wood et al., 2003).

From the perspective of . . .

A POLITICIAN Imagine you had to vote on a law that would require companies and other organizations to hire people only after giving them a standardized performance test and using the results to make employment decisions. Would you support such a law? Why or why not?

Myers-Briggs Type Indicator A self-report test that measures people's preferences for thinking and behaviour.

projective personality test A test in which a person is shown an ambiguous stimulus and asked to describe it or tell a story about it.

Rorschach test A test that involves showing a series of symmetrical visual stimuli to people who then are asked what the figures represent to them.

Thematic Apperception Test (TAT) A test consisting of a series of pictures about which a person is asked to write a story.

BEHAVIOURAL ASSESSMENT

If you were a psychologist subscribing to a learning approach to personality, you would be likely to object to the inferential nature of projective tests. Instead, you would be more apt to use **behavioural assessment**—direct observational measures of an individual's behaviour designed to describe personality characteristics. An effort is made to ensure that behavioural assessment is carried out objectively, quantifying behaviour as much as possible. For example, an observer may record the number of social contacts that a person initiates, the number of questions asked, or the number of aggressive acts. Another method is to measure the duration of events: the duration of a temper tantrum in a child, the length of a conversation, the amount of time spent working, or the time spent in coop-

behavioural assessment Direct measures of an individual's behaviour used to describe personality characteristics.

erative behaviour. While some may argue that behavioural assessment may not be valid, Meanne Chan and colleagues from the University of British Columbia found that people are quite accurate in assessing other people's personalities, either after only a brief first meeting or by watching a brief video clip (Chan et al., 2011).

Behavioural assessment is particularly appropriate for observing—and eventually remedying—specific behavioural difficulties, such as profound shyness in children. It provides a means of assessing the specific nature and incidence of a problem and subsequently allows psychologists to determine whether intervention techniques have been successful.

For Review »

How do psychologists think about personality?

Personality is defined as the pattern of enduring characteristics that produce consistency and individuality in a given person.

What are the major features of the different psychological approaches to personality?

The psychodynamic approaches focus on the unconscious foundations of personality. Freud's psychoanalytic theory laid the foundation for the psychodynamic approaches. Freud proposed that personality consists of the pleasure-seeking id, the realistic ego, and the superego, or conscience. In addition, Freud suggested that personality develops through a series of psychosexual stages, each of which is associated with a primary biological function. Defence mechanisms, according to Freudian theory, are unconscious strategies with which people reduce anxieties relating to impulses from the id. Neo-Freudian psychoanalytic theorists built on Freud's work, although they placed greater emphasis on the role of the ego and paid more attention to the role of social factors in determining behaviour.

Trait approaches have been used to identify relatively enduring dimensions along which people differ from one another—dimensions known as traits. Learning approaches to personality concentrate on observable behaviour. To a strict learning theorist, personality is the sum of learned responses to the external environment. Biological and evolutionary approaches to personality focus on the way in which personality characteristics are inherited. Humanistic approaches emphasize the inherent goodness of people. They consider the core of personality in terms of a person's ability to change and improve.

How can psychologists most accurately measure personality?

Psychological tests such as the MMPI-2 and the Myers-Briggs are standard assessment tools that measure behaviour objectively. They must be reliable (measuring what they are trying to measure consistently) and valid (measuring what they are supposed to measure).

What are the major types of personality measures?

Self-report measures ask people about a sample range of their behaviours. These reports are used to infer the presence of particular personality characteristics. Projective personality tests (such as the Rorschach and the Thematic Apperception Test) present an ambiguous stimulus, and the test administrator infers information about the test taker from his or her responses. Behavioural assessment is based on the principles of learning theory. It employs direct measurement of an individual's behaviour to determine characteristics related to personality.

Psych think answers

Psych think 1 In the PSYCH think on p. 286 we asked you what the difference is between the defence mechanisms sublimation and reaction formation. Students sometimes confuse these two defence mechanisms; however, they are quite different. Sublimation is when someone takes an unacceptable impulse and diverts it to something that is socially acceptable. For example, someone who enjoys reading sexually explicit material might work for the government censoring reading material or someone who has aggressive tendencies might become a boxer. Reaction formation is acting in a way that is opposite of how one really feels. For example, if someone is homosexual but is afraid to come out to others, he or she may speak forcefully against homosexuality. In another example, someone who really dislikes his mother-in-law may treat her with excessive kindness instead.

Psych think 2 In the PSYCH think on p. 291 we asked how the behaviourist approach would explain the personality development of singer Lady Gaga. If you are not familiar with Lady Gaga, she is a pop singer who often dresses in outrageous costumes, and on one occasion, wore clothing made out of raw meat. Skinner, from the behaviourist approach, would explain Lady Gaga's outgoing and outrageous behaviour as a result of what she learned from her environment. She likely received attention for her behaviour, which acts as positive reinforcement for her outrageous personality.

Psych think 3 In the PSYCH think on p. 296 we asked you to think of a cartoon character and then use three of the theories of personality to explain the personality of the cartoon character you chose. If you chose a character like Bart Simpson, you could apply the psychodynamic, trait theorist, and humanistic approaches to his behaviour. For example, the psychodynamic approach would say that Bart Simpson's reckless and defiant behaviour is due to a weakly formed superego. He may not have had his needs met during the anal stage of his life and as such he is the opposite of one who would be called "anal retentive." The trait theorists would say that Bart Simpson is high on the extraversion dimension of personality and low on the conscientious and agreeable dimensions of personality. The humanistic approach would say that while Bart's behaviour may be considered bad, he still needs unconditional positive regard and we should still love him as a person.

Study wherever and whenever you choose.

12

Psychological
Disorders and Treatment

WHAT'S TO COME

Defining and Diagnosing Abnormal Behaviour

Major Categories of Psychological Disorders

Treatment of Psychological Disorders

Chris Coles

Chris Coles heard the voice in his head for the first time late one evening. The voice told him to meet a friend at that moment, and to apologize to the friend for planning to date the friend's girlfriend.

Although Chris had never thought about dating the girlfriend, he nonetheless did as he was told, arriving at the beach at two o'clock in the morning. No one was there.

Chris put the incident out of his mind, attributing it to a trick of imagination, like something in a dream. However, the voice kept intruding in Chris's thoughts. And then he started to see visions. He would see whales and dolphins swimming up to the beach, and there would be a golden Buddha shining from the bushes. He also began to think he could control nature.

As Chris later said, "I felt that I had power over things in nature, influence over the whales and dolphins and waves. I thought I could make things happen magically in the water." (Begley, 2002, p. 44)

Chris Coles was losing his grip on reality. It turned out that he was suffering from schizophrenia, one of the more severe psychological disorders. Although drug treatments eventually stilled the voices that ran through his head, his experience raises several questions. What caused his disorder? What were the genetic influences and what life experiences, especially stressors, may have contributed? Were there signs that family and friends should have noticed earlier? Could his schizophrenia have been prevented, and how can it be treated?

We address the issues raised by Chris Coles's case in this chapter. We begin by discussing different perspectives on abnormal behaviour and describing categories of psychological disorders. Then we consider ways of evaluating behaviour—one's own and that of others—to determine whether seeking help from a mental health professional is warranted. Finally, we describe the various approaches to therapy.

What makes someone's behaviour abnormal?

As You Read »

- How is abnormal behaviour defined and classified?
- What theories do psychologists use to explain psychological disorders?
- What are the major categories of psychological disorders?
- How can we tell when it's time to get professional help for ourselves or someone else?
- What types of treatment are available for psychological disorders?

Defining and Diagnosing Abnormal Behaviour

Psychologists typically define **abnormal behaviour** broadly, considering it to be behaviour that causes people to experience distress and prevents them from functioning in their daily lives (Nolen-Hoeksema, 2007). Because of the imprecision of this definition, it's best to view abnormal behaviour and normal behaviour as marking two ends of a continuum rather than as absolute states. Behaviour should be evaluated in terms of gradations, ranging from fully normal functioning to extremely abnormal behaviour (Wilmshurst, 2009). Daily behaviour of humans typically falls somewhere between these extremes. Generally, when we try to define what is abnormal, we look to three general criteria: deviant, maladaptive, and personally distressful.

- Deviant: The behaviour is atypical or unlike the behaviour of most other people in one's culture.

- Maladaptive: The behaviour makes it difficult for the person to function in his or her daily life. For example, the behaviour makes it difficult for the individual to go to school or work, or to have relationships with other people.

- Personally distressful: The behaviour causes distress in the individual or to other people who interact with the individual.

"It's best to view abnormal behaviour and normal behaviour as marking two ends of a continuum rather than as absolute states."

PERSPECTIVES ON ABNORMALITY: FROM SUPERSTITION TO SCIENCE

Throughout much of human history, people linked abnormal behaviour to superstition and witchcraft. Particularly in the West, individuals who displayed abnormal behaviour were accused of being possessed by demons. Authorities "treated" abnormal behaviour by attempting to drive out the source of the problem. This typically involved whipping, immersion in hot water, starvation, or other forms of torture in which the cure was often worse than the affliction (Berrios, 1996; Howells & Osborn, 1984).

Contemporary Western approaches to abnormal behaviour are grounded in scientific theory and evidence. The perspectives used to understand psychological disorders today suggest not only different causes of abnormal behaviour but different treatment approaches as well. Some perspectives seem to offer better explanations for specific disorders than others do. Here we survey the biomedical, psychoanalytic, behavioural, and cognitive perspectives.

Biomedical Perspective When people display the symptoms of tuberculosis, medical professionals can generally find tubercular bacteria in their body tissue. Similarly, the **biomedical perspective** suggests that when an individual displays symptoms of abnormal behaviour, the fundamental cause will be found through a physical examination

> **abnormal behaviour** Behaviour that causes people to experience distress and prevents them from functioning in their daily lives.
>
> **biomedical perspective** The perspective that suggests that when an individual displays symptoms of abnormal behaviour, the root cause will be found in a physical examination of the individual, which may reveal a hormonal imbalance, a chemical deficiency, or a brain injury.

Figure 12.1

Perspectives on Psychological Disorders

Perspective	Description
Biomedical perspective	Assumes that physiological causes are at the root of psychological disorders
Psychoanalytic perspective	Argues that psychological disorders stem from childhood conflicts
Behavioural perspective	Assumes that abnormal behaviours are learned responses
Cognitive perspective	Assumes that cognitions (people's thoughts and beliefs) are central to psychological disorders

of the individual, which may reveal a hormonal imbalance, a chemical deficiency, or a brain injury. Indeed, when we speak of mental "illness," "symptoms" of abnormal behaviour, and mental "hospitals," we are using terminology associated with the biomedical perspective.

Psychoanalytic Perspective Whereas the biomedical perspective suggests that biological causes are at the root of abnormal behaviour, the **psychoanalytic perspective**, based on Freud's psychoanalytic theory, holds that abnormal behaviour stems from childhood conflicts over opposing wishes regarding sex and aggression. As we have discussed in earlier chapters, according to Freud, children pass through a series of stages in which sexual and aggressive impulses take different forms and produce conflicts that require resolution. If these childhood conflicts are not dealt with successfully they remain unresolved in the unconscious and eventually bring about abnormal behaviour during adulthood. To uncover the roots of people's disordered behaviour, the psychoanalytic perspective scrutinizes their early life history.

Behavioural Perspective Both the biomedical and the psychoanalytic perspectives look at abnormal behaviours as *symptoms* of an underlying problem. In contrast, the behavioural perspective views the behaviour itself as the problem. Using the basic principles of classical and operant conditioning and social learning, behavioural theorists see both normal and abnormal behaviours as responses to various stimuli, responses that have been learned through past experience and that are guided in the present by stimuli in the individual's environment. To explain why abnormal behaviour occurs, we must analyze how an individual has learned abnormal behaviour and observe the circumstances in which it is displayed. For example, what is reinforcing the behaviour?

Cognitive Perspective Rather than considering only external behaviour, as in traditional behavioural approaches,

the cognitive perspective assumes that *cognitions* (people's thoughts and beliefs) are central to a person's abnormal behaviour. A primary goal of treatment using the cognitive perspective is to explicitly teach new, more adaptive ways of thinking. For instance, suppose that you develop the erroneous belief that, whenever you take an exam, "doing well on this exam is crucial to my entire future." Through therapy, you might learn to hold the more realistic, and less anxiety-producing, thought: "my entire future is not dependent on this one exam." By changing cognitions in this way, psychologists working within a cognitive framework help people free themselves from thoughts and behaviours that are potentially maladaptive (Clark, 2004; Everly & Lating, 2007).

From the perspective of...

AN EMPLOYER Imagine that a well-paid employee was arrested for shoplifting a $15 sweater. What sort of explanation for this behaviour would be provided by the proponents of *each* perspective on abnormality: the biomedical perspective, the psychoanalytic perspective, the behavioural perspective, and the cognitive perspective?

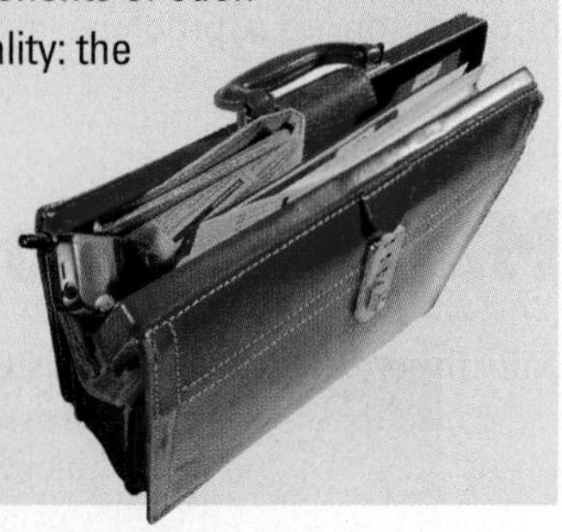

CLASSIFYING ABNORMAL BEHAVIOUR: THE *DSM*

At the beginning of the chapter we discussed three general criteria for defining abnormal behaviour (deviant, maladaptive, and personally distressful). Over the years, mental health professionals have developed many different classification systems that vary in terms of their utility and the degree to which they have been accepted. However, one standard system, devised by the American Psychiatric Association (APA), has emerged and most professionals today use this classification system, known as the ***Diagnostic and Statistical Manual of Mental Disorders, Fourth Edition, Text Revision (DSM-IV-TR)***, to diagnose and classify abnormal behaviour (American Psychiatric Association, 2000).

> **psychoanalytic perspective** The perspective that suggests that abnormal behaviour stems from childhood conflicts over opposing wishes regarding sex and aggression.
>
> ***Diagnostic and Statistical Manual of Mental Disorders, Fourth Edition, Text Revision (DSM-IV-TR)*** A system, devised by the American Psychiatric Association, used by most professionals to diagnose and classify abnormal behaviour.

DSM-IV-TR presents comprehensive and relatively precise definitions for more than 200 disorders, divided into 17 major categories. The intent is that, by following the criteria presented in the DSM-IV-TR classification system, diagnosticians can identify the specific problem that an individual is experiencing. The DSM-IV-TR is organized into five axes (dimensions) that take into account the specific disorders (Axis I and II), any general medical conditions (Axis III), and psychosocial and environmental problems (Axis IV) that may contribute to or have implications for the disorder. The final axis (Axis V) takes into account the individual's current level of social, occupational, or educational functioning.

DSM-IV-TR is designed to be primarily descriptive and avoids suggesting an underlying cause for an individual's behaviour and problems. For instance, the term neurotic—a label that is commonly used by people in their everyday descriptions of abnormal behaviour—is not listed as a DSM-IV-TR category. Because the term neurosis refers to problems associated with a specific cause based in Freud's theory of personality, it is not included in DSM-IV-TR.

DSM-IV-TR has the advantage, then, of providing a descriptive system that does not specify the cause of or reason for a problem. Instead, it paints a picture of the behaviour that is being displayed. Why should this approach be important? For one thing, it allows communication between mental health professionals of diverse backgrounds and theoretical approaches. In addition, precise classification enables researchers to explore the causes of a problem. Without reliable descriptions of abnormal behaviour, researchers would be hard-pressed to find ways to investigate the disorder. Finally, DSM-IV-TR provides a kind of conceptual shorthand with which professionals can describe the behaviours that tend to manifest simultaneously in an individual (Frances, First, & Pincus, 2002; Widiger & Clark, 2000). If you would like to read more about DSM-IV-TR, visit http://dsm.psychiatryonline.org/dsmLibrary.aspx?bookid=22.

The Shortcomings of DSM When clinical psychologist David Rosenhan and eight colleagues conducted a study called "Being Sane in Insane Places" they sought admission to separate mental hospitals in the 1970s, each stating that he or she was hearing voices—"unclear voices" that said "empty," "hollow," and "thud"—and each was immediately admitted to the hospital. However, the truth was that they were conducting a study, and none of them was really hearing voices. Aside from this misrepresentation, *everything*

Figure 12.2

Major Categories of Psychological Disorders

Categories of Disorders	Examples
Anxiety Problems in which anxiety impedes daily functioning	Generalized anxiety disorder, panic disorder, phobic disorder, obsessive-compulsive disorder, post-traumatic stress disorder
Somatoform Psychological difficulties displayed through physical problems	Hypochondriasis, conversion disorder
Dissociative The splitting apart of crucial parts of personality that are usually integrated	Dissociative identity disorder (multiple personality), dissociative amnesia, dissociative fugue
Mood Emotions of depression or euphoria that are so strong they intrude on everyday living	Major depression, bipolar disorder
Schizophrenia and psychotic disorders Declines in functioning, thought and language disturbances, perception disorders, emotional disturbances, residual subtypes and withdrawal from others	Disorganized, paranoid, catatonic, undifferentiated, residual subtypes
Personality Problems that create little personal distress but that lead to an inability to function as a normal member of society	Antisocial (sociopathic) personality disorder, narcissistic personality disorder
Sexual Problems related to sexual arousal from unusual objects or problems related to functioning	Paraphilia, sexual dysfunction
Substance-related Problems related to drug dependence and abuse	Alcohol, cocaine, hallucinogens, marijuana
Dementia, amnesia, and other cognitive disorders	

DIAGNOSTIC AND STATISTICAL MANUAL OF MENTAL DISORDERS

FOURTH EDITION

TEXT REVISION

DSM-IV-TR

AMERICAN PSYCHIATRIC ASSOCIATION

else they did and said represented their true behaviour, including the responses they gave during extensive admission interviews and their answers to the battery of tests they were asked to complete. In fact, as soon as they were admitted, they said they no longer heard any voices. In short, each of the imposters acted in a "normal" way (Rosenhan, 1973).

We might assume that Rosenhan and his colleagues would have been quickly discovered as the impostors they were, but this was not the case. Instead, each of them was diagnosed as severely abnormal on the basis of observed behaviour. Mental health professionals labelled most as suffering from schizophrenia and kept them in the hospital for 3 to 52 days, with the average stay being 19 days. When they were discharged, most of the "patients" left with the label *schizophrenia—in remission*, implying that the abnormal behaviour had only temporarily subsided and could recur at any time. Most disturbing, no one on the hospital staff identified any of the impostors as such—although some of the real patients figured out the ruse.

The results of Rosenhan's classic study illustrate that placing labels on individuals powerfully influences the way mental health workers perceive and interpret their actions. It also points out that determining who is psychologically disordered is not always a clear-cut or accurate process.

Although *DSM-IV-TR* was developed to provide more accurate and consistent diagnoses of psychological disorders, it has not been entirely successful. For instance, critics charge that it relies too much on the medical perspective. Because it was drawn up by psychiatrists—who are physicians—some condemn it for viewing psychological disorders primarily in terms of the symptoms of an underlying physiological disorder, much like a medical issue. Moreover, critics suggest that *DSM-IV-TR* compartmentalizes people into inflexible, all-or-none categories, rather than considering the degree to which a person displays psychologically disordered behaviour (Samuel & Widiger, 2006; Schmidt, Kotov, & Joiner, 2004). If you think about it, many people display "abnormal" behaviour on one occasion or another—does this mean they should receive a diagnosis and treatment?

"First off, you're not a nut, you're a legume."

> > > How do you define abnormal behaviour? What are the pros and cons of having a classification system such as the *DSM-IV-TR*?

Psych think

Other concerns with *DSM-IV-TR* are more subtle, but equally important. For instance, some critics argue that labelling an individual as abnormal provides a dehumanizing, lifelong stigma. (Think, for example, of political contenders whose candidacies have been terminated by the disclosure that they received treatment for psychological disorders.) Furthermore, after an initial diagnosis has been made, mental health professionals, who may concentrate on the initial diagnostic category, could overlook other diagnostic possibilities (Duffy et al., 2002; Quinn, Kahng, & Crocker, 2004; Szasz, 1994).

Despite the drawbacks inherent in any labelling system, *DSM-IV-TR* has significantly influenced the way in which mental health professionals view psychological disorders. It has increased both the reliability and the validity of diagnostic categorization. In addition, it offers a logical way to organize examination of the major types of mental disturbance (Milling, Chau, & Mills-Baxter, 2006; Widiger & Mullins-Sweatt, 2008).

It is important to note that the DSM Task Force has been working on a new edition of the *DSM* called the *DSM-5*, which will be released in May, 2013. If you would like to view some of the changes of the new edition, visit www.dsm5.org.

Major Categories of Psychological Disorders

Now that we understand something about abnormality and the classification of psychological disorders, we can turn our attention to several categories of disorders. Within each category we consider some of the specific disorders, including their major symptoms and some possible causes. Keep in mind that, although we'll be discussing these disorders in an objective manner, each represents a very human set of difficulties that influence, and in some cases considerably disrupt, people's lives. Also keep in mind that the *DSM-IV-TR* describes over 200 disorders and we would need an entire textbook to discuss each of these. Instead, we will focus only on the more commonly occurring disorders that you will likely need to know for your personal or professional life.

ANXIETY DISORDERS

All of us, at one time or another, experience *anxiety*, a feeling of apprehension or tension, in reaction to stressful situations. This type of anxiety is a normal reaction to stress that often helps, rather than hinders, our daily functioning. But some people experience anxiety in situations in which there is no external reason or cause for such distress. When anxiety occurs without external justification and begins to interfere with people's daily functioning, mental health professionals consider it maladaptive. Mental health professionals categorize persistent anxiety that impairs daily functioning as **anxiety disorder**. The major types of anxiety disorders are phobic disorder, panic disorder, generalized anxiety disorder, obsessive-compulsive disorder, and post-traumatic stress disorder.

Many times anxiety disorders are maladaptive because they prevent people from engaging in regular activities in their lives, such as attending classes, going to work, or going to other, potentially anxiety-provoking places that they would otherwise go to. In addition, Laura Summerfeldt and colleagues from Trent University in Peterborough, Ontario, found that individuals with anxiety disorders (specifically social phobia, obsessive-compulsive disorder, and panic disorder) tended to have lower intrapersonal skills than individuals who did not have anxiety disorders (Summerfeldt et al., 2011). Intrapersonal skills include an ability to accurately assess and utilize one's emotional state—people with anxiety disorders tended to have more difficulty regulating their self-focus and were less able to perceive their own emotions (Summerfeldt et al., 2011).

Phobic Disorder *It's not easy moving through the world when you're terrified of electricity. "Donna," 45, a writer, knows that better than most. Get her in the vicinity of an appliance or a light switch or—all but unthinkable—a thunderstorm, and she is overcome by a terror so blinding she can think of nothing but fleeing. That, of course, is not always possible, so over time, Donna has come up with other answers. When she opens the refrigerator door, rubber-sole shoes are a must. If a light bulb blows, she will tolerate the dark until someone else changes it for her. Clothes shopping is done only when necessary, lest static on garments send her running from the store. And swimming at night is absolutely out of the question, lest underwater lights electrocute her* (Kluger, 2001, p. 51).

Donna suffers from a **phobia**, an intense, irrational fear of a specific object or situation. For example, claustrophobia

Acrophobia, the fear of heights, is a relatively common phobia.

Figure 12.3
Types of Phobias

Agoraphobia Fear of places where help might not be available in case of emergency

Example: Person becomes housebound because any place other than the person's home arouses extreme anxiety symptoms.

Specific phobias

Animal type Fear of specific animals or insects
Example: Person has extreme fear of dogs, cats, or spiders.

Natural environment type Fear of events or situations in the natural environment
Example: Person has extreme fear of storms, heights, or water.

Situational type Fear of public transportation, tunnels, bridges, elevators, flying, driving
Example: Person becomes extremely claustrophobic in elevators.

Blood injection-injury type
Fear of blood, injury, injections
Example: Person panics when viewing a child's scraped knee.

Social phobia Fear of being judged or embarrassed by others

Example: Person avoids all social situations and becomes a recluse for fear of encountering others' judgment.

Source: Adapted from Nolen-Hoeksema, 2007.

is a fear of enclosed places, acrophobia is a fear of high places, xenophobia is a fear of strangers, social phobia is the fear of being judged or embarrassed by others, and—as in Donna's case—electrophobia is a fear of electricity.

The objective danger posed by an anxiety-producing stimulus (which can be just about anything) is typically small or non-existent. However, to someone suffering from the phobia, the danger is great, and a full-blown panic attack may follow exposure to the stimulus. Phobic disorders differ from generalized anxiety disorders and panic disorders in that they involve a specific, identifiable stimulus that sets off the anxiety reaction.

anxiety disorder The occurrence of anxiety without an obvious external cause, affecting daily functioning.

phobias Intense, irrational fears of specific objects or situations.

panic disorder Anxiety disorder that takes the form of panic attacks lasting from a few seconds to as long as several hours.

generalized anxiety disorder The experience of long-term, persistent anxiety and worry.

Phobias may have only a minor effect on people's lives if those who suffer from them can avoid the stimuli that trigger fear. Unless they are firefighters or window washers, for example, people with a fear of heights may experience little daily stress from the phobia (although it may prevent them from living on a high floor in an apartment). However, a *social phobia*, or a fear of embarrassing oneself in front of strangers, presents a more serious problem. In one extreme case, a woman left her home just three times in thirty years—once to visit her family, once for a medical operation, and once to purchase ice cream for a dying companion (Adler, 1984; Kimbrel, 2007).

Panic Disorder In another type of anxiety disorder, **panic disorder**, *panic attacks* occur that last from a few seconds to several hours. Unlike phobias, which are stimulated by specific objects or situations, panic disorders do not have any identifiable stimuli. Instead, during an attack, anxiety suddenly—and often without warning—rises to a peak, and an individual feels a sense of impending, unavoidable doom. Although the physical symptoms differ from person to person, they may include heart palpitations, shortness of breath, unusual amounts of sweating, faintness and dizziness, gastric sensations, and sometimes a sense of imminent death. After such an attack, many sufferers understandably tend to feel exhausted (Laederach-Hofmann & Messerli-Buergy, 2007; Rachman & deSilva, 2004).

Panic attacks seemingly come out of nowhere and are not connected to any specific stimulus. Because they don't know what triggers their feelings of panic, victims of panic attacks may become fearful of going places. In fact, some people with panic disorder develop a complication called *agoraphobia*, the fear of being in a situation in which escape is difficult and in which help for a possible panic attack would not be available. In extreme cases, people with agoraphobia never leave their homes (Herrán, Carrera, & Sierra-Biddle, 2006; Marcaurelle, Belanger, & Marchand, 2003, 2005).

In addition to the physical symptoms, panic disorder affects how information is processed in the brain. For instance, people with panic disorder have reduced reactions in the anterior cingulate cortex to stimuli (such as viewing

a fearful face) that normally produce a strong reaction in those without the disorder. It may be that recurring high levels of emotional arousal experienced by individuals with panic disorder desensitizes them to emotional stimuli (Pillay et al., 2006, 2007).

Generalized Anxiety Disorder People with **generalized anxiety disorder (GAD)** experience long-term, persistent anxiety and uncontrollable worry. Sometimes their concerns are about identifiable issues involving family, money, work, or health. In other cases, though, people with the disorder feel that something dreadful is about to

Figure 12.4

Frequency of Symptoms in Generalized Anxiety Disorder

Percentage of cases in which symptom occurs

Actual fainting
Feeling of choking
Diarrhea
Nausea
Hands trembling
Difficulty breathing
Fear of dying
Sweating all over
Speech blocked
Wobbly
Heart racing
Hands sweating
Terrified
Weakness all over
Confusion
Unable to control thoughts
Jumpy
Fear of losing control
Frightened
Tense
Difficulty concentrating
Unable to relax

0 10 20 30 40 50 60 70 80 90 100

Source: Adapted from Beck & Emery, 1985, pp. 87–88.

Psych think

> > > If someone is afraid to leave their house because they have an intense fear of the bugs that might be outside, do they suffer from agoraphobia with panic attacks, a specific phobia of the animal type, or social phobia?

happen but can't identify the reason, experiencing "free-floating" anxiety. Michel Dugas and colleagues from Concordia University in Montreal believe that GAD is related to an inability to tolerate uncertainty, which precipitates the anxiety and sometimes more obsessive-compulsive behaviours (Dugas et al., 2010).

Because of persistent anxiety, people with generalized anxiety disorder cannot concentrate or set their worry and fears aside; their lives become centred on their worry. Furthermore, their anxiety is often accompanied by physiological symptoms such as muscle tension headaches, dizziness, heart palpitations, and insomnia (Starcevic et al., 2007).

Obsessive-Compulsive Disorder In **obsessive-compulsive disorder**, people are plagued by unwanted thoughts, called obsessions, and/or feel that they must carry out actions, termed *compulsions*, against their will.

An **obsession** is a persistent, unwanted thought or idea that keeps recurring. For example, a student may be unable to stop thinking that she has neglected to put her name on a test and may think about it constantly for the two weeks it takes to get the paper back. A man may go on vacation and wonder the whole time whether he locked his house. A woman may hear the same tune running through her head over and over. In each case, the thought or idea is unwanted and difficult to put out of mind. Of course, many people suffer from mild obsessions from time to time, but usually such thoughts persist only for a short period. For people with serious obsessions, however, the thoughts persist for days or months and may consist of bizarre, troubling images (Lee & Kwon, 2003; Lee et al., 2005; Rassin & Muris, 2007).

As part of an obsessive-compulsive disorder, people may also experience **compulsions**, irresistible urges to repeatedly carry out some act that seems strange and unreasonable, even to them. Whatever the compulsive behaviour is, people experience extreme anxiety if they cannot carry it out, even if it is something they want to stop. The acts may be relatively trivial, such as repeatedly checking the stove to make sure all the burners are turned off, or more unusual, such as continually washing oneself (Clark, 2007; Frost & Steketee, 2002).

For example, consider this case report of a 27-year-old woman with a cleaning ritual:

Bess would first remove all of her clothing in a pre-established sequence. She would lay out each article of clothing at specific spots on her bed, and examine each one for any indications of "contamination." She would then thoroughly scrub her body, starting at her feet and working meticulously up to the top of her head, using certain washcloths for certain areas of her body. Any articles of clothing that appeared to have been

obsessive-compulsive disorder A disorder characterized by obsessions or compulsions.

obsession A persistent, unwanted thought or idea that keeps recurring.

compulsion An irresistible urge to repeatedly carry out some act that seems strange and unreasonable.

Canadian comedian Howie Mandel has talked openly about his struggles with obsessive-compulsive disorder (OCD). Although he has developed coping strategies, he still cannot bring himself to shake hands. His alternative is to bump fists.

"contaminated" were thrown into the laundry. Clean clothing was put in the spots that were vacant. She would then dress herself in the opposite order from which she took the clothes off (Meyer & Osborne, 1987, p. 156).

Although such compulsive rituals lead to some immediate reduction of anxiety, in the long term the anxiety returns. In fact, people with severe cases lead lives filled with unrelenting tension (Goodman, Rudorfer, & Maser, 2000; Penzel, 2000).

Causes of Anxiety Disorders We've considered the four major types of anxiety disorders, but there are others as well. For instance, *post-traumatic stress disorder* (in which a person re-experiences a stressful event in vivid flashbacks or dreams, and which is covered in more detail in the chapter on Health Psychology) is classified as an anxiety disorder.

Because there are so many different kinds of anxiety disorders, it is unlikely that any single theory would explain them all. From a biomedical perspective, genetic factors clearly are part of the picture. For example, if one member of a pair of identical twins has panic disorder, there is a 30% chance that the other twin will have it also (Gelernter & Stein, 2009; Hettema, 2005). Furthermore, a person's characteristic level of anxiety is related to a specific gene involved in the production of the neurotransmitter serotonin. This is consistent with findings indicating that certain chemical deficiencies in the brain appear to produce some kinds of anxiety disorder (Beidel & Turner, 2007; Holmes et al., 2003; Rieder, Kaufmann, & Knowles, 1996).

mood disorder A disturbance in emotional experience that is strong enough to intrude on everyday living.

major depression A severe form of depression that interferes with concentration, decision making, and sociability.

Some researchers believe that an overactive autonomic nervous system may be at the root of panic attacks. Specifically, they suggest that poor regulation of the brain's locus ceruleus may lead to panic attacks, which cause the limbic system to become overstimulated. In turn, the overstimulated limbic system produces chronic anxiety, which ultimately leads the locus ceruleus to generate still more panic attacks (Balaban, 2002).

Psychologists who employ the behavioural perspective have taken a different approach that emphasizes environmental factors. They consider anxiety to be a learned response to stress. For instance, suppose a dog bites a young girl. When the girl next sees a dog, she is frightened and runs away—a behaviour that relieves her anxiety and thereby reinforces her avoidance behaviour. After repeated encounters with dogs in which she is reinforced for her avoidance behaviour, she may develop a full-fledged phobia regarding dogs.

Finally, the cognitive perspective suggests that anxiety disorders grow out of inappropriate and inaccurate thoughts and beliefs about circumstances in a person's world. For example, people with anxiety disorders may view a friendly puppy as a ferocious and savage pit bull, or they may see an air disaster looming every moment they are in the vicinity of an airplane. According to the cognitive perspective, people's maladaptive thoughts about the world are at the root of an anxiety disorder (Frost & Steketee, 2002; Wang & Clark, 2002).

Each of these perspectives alone offers part of the answer; however, we know that most behaviour can be explained by more than one perspective. Consider the following example to see how these explanations might work together. According to the neuroscience perspective, the young girl who was bitten by a dog might have a greater tendency to develop an anxiety disorder, in this case a phobia of dogs, because of her genetic heritage and/or because of her brain chemistry. Further, after she has learned to be afraid as described by the behaviourists, she would probably come to view friendly dogs as dangerous, which would be a cognitive issue.

MOOD DISORDERS

From the time I woke up in the morning until the time I went to bed at night, I was unbearably miserable and seemingly incapable of any kind of joy or enthusiasm. Everything— every thought, word, movement—was an effort. Everything that once was sparkling now was flat. I seemed to myself to be dull, boring, inadequate, thick brained, unlit, unresponsive, chill skinned, bloodless, and sparrow drab. I doubted, completely, my ability to do anything well. It seemed as though my mind had slowed down and burned out to the point of being virtually useless (Jamison, 1995, p. 110).

We all experience shifts in mood. Sometimes we are happy, perhaps even euphoric; at other times we feel upset, saddened, or depressed. Such changes in mood are a normal part of everyday life. In some people, however, moods are so pronounced and lingering—like the feelings described above by writer (and psychiatrist) Kay Redfield Jamison— that they interfere with the ability to function effectively. In extreme cases, a mood may become life-threatening, and in others it may cause the person to lose touch with reality. Situations such as these represent **mood disorders**, disturbances in emotional experience that are strong enough to intrude on everyday living.

Major Depression Comedian Jim Carrey, late night talk show host Conan O'Brien, and singer/songwriters Leonard Cohen and Nellie Furtado have all suffered from periodic attacks of **major depression**, a severe psychological disorder that interferes with concentration, decision making, and sociability. Major depression is one of the most common mental disorders. Some 121 million people worldwide suffer from major depression, and one in five Canadians experiences major depression at some point in life. Moreover, 15% of college students have received a diagnosis of depression and the cost of depression is more than $80 billion a year in lost productivity (Scelfo, 2007; Winik, 2006, World Health Organization, 2011).

Study tip

Major depression differs from the normal depression that occasionally occurs during most people's lives; major depression is more intense, lasts longer, and may have no clear trigger.

Women are twice as likely to be diagnosed with major depression as men, with one-fourth of all females apt to encounter it at some point during their lives (Whiffen & Demidenko, 2006). Furthermore, although no one is sure why, the rate of reported depression is going up throughout the world (Bhugra & Mastrogianni, 2004; Compton et al., 2006; Lecrubier, 2001). Results of in-depth interviews conducted in Canada, the United States, Puerto Rico, Taiwan, Lebanon, Italy, Germany, and France indicate that reported incidents of depression have increased significantly over previous rates in each country. In some countries, the likelihood that individuals will have major depression at some point in their lives is three times higher than it was for earlier generations (Kendler, Gatz, & Gardner, 2006; Staley, Sanacora, & Tamagnan, 2006).

When psychologists speak of major depression, they do not mean the sadness that comes from experiencing one of life's disappointments or hardships, something that we all have experienced. Some depression is normal after the breakup of a long-term relationship, the death of a loved one, or the loss of a job. It is normal even after less serious problems, such as losing a favourite possession or not winning the lottery.

A Test for Depression

This is a version of a test distributed by mental health organizations during the annual National Depression Screening Day in the United States, a nationwide event that seeks to identify people who are suffering from depression that is severe enough to warrant psychological intervention. To complete the questionnaire, count the number of statements with which you agree.

1. I feel downhearted, blue, and sad.
2. I don't enjoy the things I used to.
3. I feel that others would be better off if I were dead.
4. I feel that I am not useful or needed.
5. I notice that I am losing weight.
6. I have trouble sleeping through the night.
7. I am restless and can't keep still.
8. My mind isn't as clear as it used to be.
9. I get tired for no reason.
10. I feel hopeless about the future.

Source: Adapted from W. W. K. Zung (1965). A self-rating depression scale. *Archives of General Psychiatry, 12,* 63–70, Table 3 (p. 65). Copyright © 1965, American Medical Association. Reprinted with permission.

Scoring: If you agree with at least five of the statements, including either item 1 or 2, and if you have had these symptoms for at least two weeks, help from a professional is strongly recommended. If you answer yes to number 3, you should get help immediately.

People who suffer from major depression experience similar sorts of feelings as those who are experiencing a normal mood shift, but their feelings are much stronger. They may feel useless, worthless, and lonely and may think the future is hopeless and that no one can help them. They may lose their appetite and have no energy. Moreover, they may experience such feelings for months or even years. They may cry uncontrollably, have sleep disturbances, and be at risk for suicide. The severe depth and the long duration of such behaviour are the hallmarks of major depression (Cadwallader, 1991; Coyne, 1976; Mialet, Pope & Yurgelun, 1996; Tse & Bond, 2004).

Mania and Bipolar Disorder Depression leads to the depths of despair; mania, in contrast, leads to emotional heights. **Mania** is an extended state of intense, wild elation. People experiencing mania feel intense happiness, power, invulnerability, and energy. They may become involved in wild schemes, believing they will succeed at anything they attempt.

Some people sequentially experience periods of mania and depression (Johnson, Fulford, & Eisner, 2009). This alternation of mania and depression is called **bipolar disorder** (a condition previously known as manic-depressive disorder). The swings between highs and lows may occur a few days apart or may alternate over a period of years. In addition, in bipolar disorder, periods of depression are usually longer than periods of mania (Zarate & Manji, 2009). The late Norman Endler, psychologist and former chair of the Psychology from York University, specialized in research on depression, anxiety, coping, and stress. Interestingly, his specialization overlapped with his own personal battles with bipolar disorder. Endler fluctuated between bouts of mania and depression and he was treated

mania An extended state of intense, wild elation.

bipolar disorder A disorder in which a person alternates between periods of euphoric feelings of mania and periods of depression.

using antidepressants and electric convulsive therapy, treatments which are discussed further at the end of the chapter.

Bipolar disorder can be very difficult to live with, as Endler professed on many occasions. While bouts of mania tend to feel much better than the lows of depression, manic behaviour can be both exhausting and sometimes dangerous. Individuals in periods of mania tend to have poor impulse control and take greater risks than at other times in their lives. This may result in risky financial or sexual behaviour. Biopolar disorder can also be very difficult for family members to cope with. Anne-Marie Linnen and colleagues from Concordia and McGill University found that adolescents with parents with bipolar disorder tended to have more behavioural problems than adolescents from parents without the disorder (Linnen et al., 2009).

DID YOU KNOW?

Actors Robert Downey, Jr. and Ben Stiller have dealt with symptoms of bipolar disorder for years. Although there is no cure for this disorder as yet, it can be managed with medication.

Causes of Mood Disorders Because they represent a major mental health problem, mood disorders—and, in particular, depression—have received a great deal of study. Several approaches have been used to explain the disorders.

Some mood disorders have genetic and biochemical roots. In fact, most neuroscience evidence suggests that bipolar disorder has biological origins. For instance, bipolar disorder (and some forms of major depression) clearly runs in some families. Additionally, several neurotransmitters, including serotonin and norepinephrine, have been implicated in depression (Kato, 2007; Plomin & McGuffin, 2003).

Further evidence from the neuroscience perspective comes from brain imaging studies that suggest that people with depression experience a general blunting of emotional reactions. For example, one study found that the brains of people with depression showed significantly less activation when these people viewed photos of human faces displaying strong emotions than did those of people without the disorder (Gotlib et al., 2004).

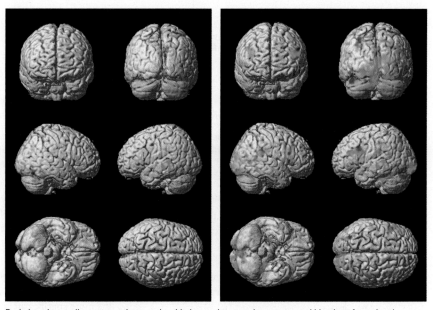

Brain imaging studies suggest that people with depression experience a general blunting of emotional reactions. In one study, represented here, the brains of individuals with depression (left) showed significantly less activation in response to photos of sad, angry, and fearful faces than did those of people without the disorder (right). (*Source:* Ian Gotlib, Stanford Mood and Anxiety Disorders Laboratory, 2004.)

Cognitive explanations of mood disorders have benefited greatly from Martin Seligman's seminal work with dogs (Seligman, 1975; Seligman & Maier, 1967). Based on that work, he suggests that depression is largely a response to learned helplessness. *Learned helplessness* is a learned expectation that events in one's life are uncontrollable and that one cannot escape from the situation. As a consequence, people simply give up fighting aversive events and submit to them, thereby producing depression. Other cognitive theorists go a step further, suggesting that depression results from hopelessness, a combination of learned helplessness and an expectation that negative outcomes in one's life are inevitable (Bjornstad, 2006; Kwon & Laurenceau, 2002; Maier & Watkins, 2000).

The various theories of depression have not provided a complete answer to an elusive question that has dogged researchers: Why is depression diagnosed in approximately twice as many women as men—a pattern that is similar across cultures?

Why is depression diagnosed in approximately twice as many women as men?

One explanation suggests that the stress experienced by women may be greater than that experienced by men at certain points in their lives—such as when a woman must simultaneously earn a living and be the primary caregiver for her children (Stephens & Townsend, 1997). In addition, women have a higher risk for physical and sexual abuse, typically earn lower wages than men, report greater unhappiness with their marriages, and generally experience chronic negative circumstances. Furthermore, women and men may respond to stress with different coping mechanisms. For instance, men may abuse drugs, but women respond with depression (Antonucci et al., 2002; Holden, 2005; Nolen-Hoeksema, 2007).

Biological factors may also explain some women's depression. For example, because the rate of female depression begins to rise during puberty, hormones have been suggested as a factor that causes women to be more vulnerable to the disorder (Hyde, Mezulis & Abramson, 2008). In addition, 25% to 50% of women who take oral contraceptives report symptoms of depression, and depression that occurs after the birth of a child has been linked to hormonal changes (Bloch et al., 2006; Serrano & Warnock, 2007). It is clear, ultimately, that researchers have discovered no definitive solutions to the puzzle of depression, and there are many alternative theories. Most likely, a complex interaction of several factors causes mood disorders.

SCHIZOPHRENIA

I'm a doctor, you know . . . I don't have a diploma, but I'm a doctor. I'm glad to be a mental patient, because it taught me how to be humble. I use Cover Girl creamy natural makeup. Oral Roberts has been here to visit me . . . This place is where Mad magazine is published. The Nixons make Noxon metal polish. When I was a little girl, I used to sit and tell stories to myself. When I was older, I turned off the sound on the TV set and made up dialogue to go with the shows I watched . . . I'm a week pregnant. I have schizophrenia—cancer of the nerves. My body is overcrowded with nerves. This is going to win me the Nobel Prize for medicine. I don't consider myself schizophrenic anymore. There's no such thing as schizophrenia, there's only mental telepathy. I once had a friend named Camilla Costello (Sheehan, 1982, pp. 72–73).

Figure 12.5
Subtypes of Schizophrenia

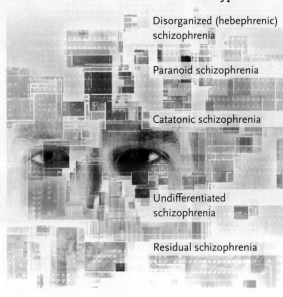

Subtype	Symptoms
Disorganized (hebephrenic) schizophrenia	Inappropriate laughter and giggling, silliness, incoherent speech, infantile behaviour, strange and sometimes obscene behaviour
Paranoid schizophrenia	Delusions and hallucinations of persecution or of greatness, loss of judgment, erratic and unpredictable behaviour
Catatonic schizophrenia	Major disturbances in movement; in some phases, loss of all motion, with patient frozen into a single position, remaining that way for hours and sometimes even days; in other phases, hyperactivity and wild, sometimes violent, movement
Undifferentiated schizophrenia	Variable mixture of major symptoms of schizophrenia; classification used for patients who do not fit into any of the more specific categories
Residual schizophrenia	Minor signs of schizophrenia after a more serious episode

schizophrenia A class of disorders in which severe distortion of reality occurs.

This excerpt illustrates the efforts of a woman with schizophrenia, one of the more severe forms of mental disturbance, to hold a conversation with a clinician. People with schizophrenia account for by far the largest percentage of those hospitalized for mental disorders. They are also in many respects the least likely to recover from their psychological difficulties (Awad & Voruganti, 2007).

Schizophrenia refers to a class of disorders in which severe distortion of reality occurs. Thinking, perception, and emotion may deteriorate; the individual may withdraw from social interaction; and the person may display bizarre behaviour. Chris Coles, the person described in the opening paragraph of the chapter, suffered from schizophrenia. Although there are several types of schizophrenia (see Figure 12.5), the distinctions between them are not always clear-cut. Moreover, the symptoms displayed by persons with schizophrenia may vary considerably over time and people with schizophrenia show significant differences in the pattern of their symptoms even when they are labelled with the same diagnostic category. Nonetheless, *DSM-IV-TR* describes a number of characteristics that reliably distinguish schizophrenia from other disorders. They include the following:

- *Decline from a previous level of functioning.* An individual can no longer carry out activities he or she was once able to do.

- *Disturbances of thought and language.* People with schizophrenia use logic and language in a peculiar way. Their thinking often does not make sense, and their

information processing is frequently faulty. They also do not follow conventional linguistic rules (Penn et al., 1997). Consider, for example, the following response to the question "Why do you think people believe in God?"

Uh, let's, I don't know why, let's see, balloon travel. He holds it up for you, the balloon. He don't let you fall out, your little legs sticking down through the clouds. He's down to the smokestack, looking through the smoke trying to get the balloon gassed up you know. Way they're flying on top that way, legs sticking out. I don't know, looking down on the ground, heck, that'd make you so dizzy you just stay and sleep you know, hold down and sleep there. I used to be sleep outdoors, you know, sleep outdoors instead of going home. (Chapman & Chapman, 1973, p. 3)

As this selection illustrates, although the basic grammatical structure may be intact, the substance of thinking characteristic of schizophrenia is often illogical, garbled, and lacking in meaningful content (Heinrichs, 2005; Holden, 2003).

- *Delusions.* People with schizophrenia often have delusions, which are firmly held, unshakable beliefs with no basis in reality. Among the common delusions experienced by people with schizophrenia are the beliefs that they are being controlled by someone else, they are being persecuted by others, and their thoughts are being broadcast so that others know what they are thinking (Coltheart, Langdon, & McKay, 2007; Stompe et al., 2003).

- *Hallucinations and perceptual disorders.* People with schizophrenia do not perceive the world as most other people do. They also may have *hallucinations,*

Psych think

> > > Take on the role of a psychologist! Morgan is an 18-year-old man in his first semester of college. While riding his bike to school along the bike path he noticed that there were often people in the bushes watching him and saying "I want that bike." He installed three extra locks on his door and barricaded himself in at night because his roommates were stealing from him. He eventually stopped going to school altogether and stayed in his room for two weeks straight. School counsellors called his parents to pick him up but he thought they were going to lock him up in their basement so he ran away. How would you diagnose Morgan?

the experience of perceiving things that do not exist. Furthermore, they may see, hear, or smell things differently than other people do and may not even have a sense of their bodies in the way that others do; they may have difficulty determining where their bodies stop and the rest of the world begins (Botvinick, 2004; Copolov et al., 2003).

- *Emotional disturbances.* People with schizophrenia sometimes show a lack of emotion in which even the most dramatic events produce little or no emotional response. Conversely, they may display emotion that is inappropriate to a situation (Combs et al., 2008; Kring & Earnst, 2003; Kring & Moran, 2008). For example, a person with schizophrenia may laugh uproariously at a funeral or react with anger when being helped by someone.

- *Withdrawal.* People with schizophrenia tend to have little interest in others. They tend not to socialize or hold real conversations with others, although they may talk at another person. In the most extreme cases they do not even acknowledge the presence of other people, appearing to be in their own isolated world (Combs et al., 2008; Combs & Mueser, 2007).

Types of Schizophrenia The symptoms of schizophrenia are classified into two types by *DSM-IV-TR*. Positive-symptom schizophrenia is indicated by the *presence* of disordered behaviour such as hallucinations, delusions, and emotional extremes, as Chris Cole demonstrated. In contrast, negative-symptom schizophrenia shows an *absence or a loss* of normal functioning, such as social withdrawal, blunted emotions, or lack of motivation. George

Foussias and colleagues from the University of Toronto found that of all the negative symptoms, a lack of motivation was the strongest predictor of poor functioning in individuals with schizophrenia (Foussias et al., 2009). Schizophrenia researchers sometimes speak of *Type I schizophrenia*, in which positive symptoms are dominant, and *Type II schizophrenia*, in which negative symptoms are more prominent (Buchanan et al., 2007; Levine & Rabinowitz, 2007). The distinction between Type I and Type II schizophrenia is important, because it suggests that two different processes might trigger schizophrenia, the cause of which remains one of the greatest mysteries facing psychologists who deal with disordered behaviour.

Study tip

In Type I schizophrenia, positive symptoms such as hallucinations, delusions, and emotional extremes are dominant; in Type II schizophrenia, negative symptoms, characterized by an absence or a loss of normal functioning, are dominant.

Solving the Puzzle of Schizophrenia The predominant approach used to explain the onset of schizophrenia today, the *predisposition model of schizophrenia*, incorporates a number of biological and environmental factors. This model suggests that individuals may inherit a predisposition or an inborn sensitivity to schizophrenia that makes them particularly vulnerable to stressful factors in

Figure 12.6

Risk of Developing Schizophrenia, Based on Genetic Relatedness to a Person with Schizophrenia

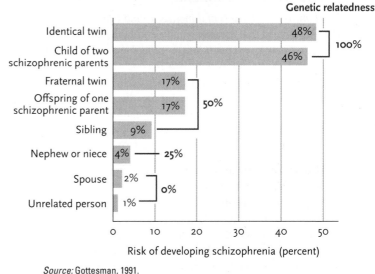

Source: Gottesman, 1991.

the environment, such as social rejection or dysfunctional family communication patterns (Combs et al., 2008). The stressors may vary, but if they are strong enough and are coupled with a genetic predisposition, the result is the onset of schizophrenia. Similarly, a strong genetic predisposition may lead to the onset of schizophrenia even when the environmental stressors are relatively weak.

One indication that genetic factors seem to be involved in producing at least a susceptibility to developing schizophrenia is that schizophrenia is more common in some families than in others. For example, the closer the genetic link between a person with schizophrenia and another individual, the greater the likelihood that the other person will experience the disorder (Brzustowicz et al., 2000; Gottesman & Hanson, 2005; Plomin & McGuffin, 2003).

If genetics alone were responsible for schizophrenia, the chance of both of two identical twins having schizophrenia would be 100% instead of just under 50%, because identical twins have the same genetic makeup. Moreover, attempts to find a link between schizophrenia and a particular gene have been only partly successful. Apparently, genetic factors alone do not produce schizophrenia (Franzek & Beckmann, 1996; Lenzenweger & Dworkin, 1998).

Other theories look toward environmental influences, such as the emotional and communication patterns of the families of people with schizophrenia. For instance, some researchers suggest that schizophrenia results from high levels of expressed emotion (McCleary & Sanford, 2002). *Expressed emotion* is an interaction style characterized by criticism, hostility, and emotional intrusiveness by family members. Other researchers suggest that faulty communication patterns lie at the heart of schizophrenia (Lobban, Barrowclough, & Jones, 2006; Miklowitz & Tompson, 2003). An important point to remember is that the models used today associate schizophrenia with several kinds of biological and environmental factors. It is increasingly clear that no single factor, but a combination of interrelated variables, produces schizophrenia (McDonald & Murray, 2004; Meltzer, 2000).

PERSONALITY DISORDERS

I had always wanted lots of things; as a child I can remember wanting a bullet that a friend of mine had brought in to show the class. I took it and put it into my school bag and when my friend noticed it was missing, I was the one who stayed after school with him and searched the room, and I was the one who sat with him and bitched about the other kids and how one of them took his bullet. I even went home with him to help him break the news to his uncle, who had brought it home from the war for him. (Duke & Nowicki, 1979, pp. 309–310)

This excerpt provides a graphic first-person account of a person with a personality disorder. *DSM-IV-TR* characterizes a **personality disorder** by a set of inflexible, maladaptive behaviour patterns that keep a person from functioning appropriately in society. Personality disorders differ from the other problems we have discussed, because people affected by them often have little sense of personal distress

personality disorder A disorder characterized by a set of inflexible, maladaptive behaviour patterns that keep a person from functioning appropriately in society.

anti-social personality disorder A disorder in which individuals show no regard for the moral and ethical rules of society or the rights of others.

associated with the psychological maladjustment. In fact, people with personality disorders frequently lead seemingly normal lives. However, just below the surface lies a set of rigid, unhealthy personality traits that do not permit these individuals to function as productive members of society (Clarkin & Lenzenweger, 2004; Friedman, Oltmanns, & Turkheimer, 2007; Millon & Davis, 1996).

The best-known type of personality disorder, illustrated by the case above, is classified in *DSM-IV-TR* as **anti-social personality disorder** (sometimes referred to as a sociopathic personality). Individuals with this disturbance show no regard for the moral and ethical rules of society or the rights of others. They may seem at first to be quite intelligent, charming, and highly persuasive. On closer examination, however, they often turn out to be manipulative and deceptive. In fact, some of the best con artists have anti-social personalities. Russell Williams, the serial killer we discussed in the chapter on personality, is a recent Canadian example of someone with anti-social personality disorder.

DID YOU KNOW?

The most common self-mutilation behaviours are cutting and using cigarettes to burn one's own flesh. Self-mutilators report an immediate release of tension and feelings of power and control (Favazza, 1996).

Individuals with anti-social personality disorder may also be impulsive and lack the ability to withstand frustration. Moreover, they lack any guilt or anxiety about their wrongdoing. For example, Russell Williams was concerned that he may have upset his wife when he was charged with sexual assault, forcible confinement, and murder; however, he did not express remorse for his victims. When those with anti-social personality disorder behave in a way that injures someone else, they understand intellectually that they have caused harm but feel no remorse (Goodwin & Hamilton, 2003; Hilarski, 2007; Lykken, 1995).

What causes such an unusual constellation of problem behaviours? A variety of factors have been suggested, ranging from an inability to experience emotions appropriately to problems in family relationships. For example, in many cases of anti-social behaviour, the individual has come from a home in which a parent has died or left, or one in which there is a lack of affection, a lack of consistency in discipline, or outright rejection. Other explanations concentrate on socio-cultural factors, because an unusually high proportion of people with anti-social personalities come from lower socio-economic groups (Millon et al., 1998). Still, no one has been able to pinpoint the specific causes of anti-social personalities, and it is likely that some combination of factors is responsible (Costa & Widiger, 2002; Nigg & Goldsmith, 1994; Rosenstein & Horowitz, 1996).

People diagnosed with **borderline personality disorder** have difficulty developing a secure sense of who they are. Their behaviour is often unstable and emotionally volatile. As a consequence, they tend to rely on relationships with others to define their identity. The problem with this strategy is that rejections are devastating. Furthermore, people with this disorder distrust others and have difficulty controlling their anger. They seem to be highly sensitive to emotional cues in faces, so that they perceive emotions more quickly (and often inaccurately) than most other people. Their emotional volatility can lead to impulsive and self-destructive behaviour, including self-mutilation. Individuals with borderline personality disorder often feel empty and alone. They may form intense, sudden, one-sided relationships, demanding the attention of another person and then feeling angry when they don't receive it. Some cognitive theorists suggest that this disorder may be linked to environments where others have discounted or criticized their emotional reactions, and they may not have learned to regulate their emotions effectively (Linehan, Cochran, & Kehrer, 2001a, 2001b; Links, Eynan, & Heisel, 2007; Trull, Stepp, & Durrett, 2003).

From the perspective of . . .

A PSYCHOLOGIST Personality disorders are often not apparent to others, and many people with these problems seem to live basically normal lives. Because these people often appear from the outside to function well in society, why should they be considered psychologically disordered?

While personality disorders are not often diagnosed in childhood, a diagnosis called borderline pathology of childhood shares many of the same impulsive and emotional volatility features of adult borderline personality disorder and may be a precursor to adult borderline personality disorder (Zelkowitz et al., 2007). To test the theory, Phyllis Zelkowitz and colleagues from McGill University examined the level of functioning of a group of adolescents who had been diagnosed with borderline pathology as children and found that the adolescents continued to have serious behavioural and functioning problems consistent with borderline personality disorder. These results support their theory that borderline pathology of childhood may be a precursor to adult borderline personality disorder, however

DID YOU KNOW?

What does your Facebook profile reveal about you? Research suggests that other people can judge someone's narcissism pretty well just from browsing his or her Facebook profile. Some of the narcissism flags appear to be an abnormally large number of posted friends and the prominent display of a glamorous photo (Buffardi & Campbell, 2008).

they acknowledge that more research is needed in this area (Zelkowitz et al., 2007).

Another example of a personality disturbance is the **narcissistic personality disorder**, which is characterized by an exaggerated sense of self-importance. Those with the disorder expect special treatment from others while at the same time disregarding others' feelings. In some ways, in fact, the main attribute of the narcissistic personality is an inability to experience empathy for other people.

The *DSM-IV-TR* includes several other categories of personality disorder, ranging in severity from individuals who may simply be regarded by others as eccentric, obnoxious, or difficult to people who act in a manner that is criminal and dangerous to others. Although they are not out of touch with reality in the way that people with schizophrenia are, many people with personality disorders lead lives that put them on the fringes of society (Millon, Davis, & Millon, 2000; Trull & Widiger, 2003).

DISSOCIATIVE DISORDERS

The three kinds of dissociative disorders are dissociative amnesia, dissociative fugue, and dissociative identity disorder. Dissociative disorders are generally rare and include a change in identity or sudden memory loss as a result of extreme shock or stress. Individuals with **dissociative amnesia** have sudden memory loss after experiencing some sort of severe psychological stress (such as a traumatic car accident). Individuals with **dissociative fugue** have the amnesia, but they also relocate, leaving the area associated with the stress. Because they do not know who they are, they will often adopt a new identity and are unable to recognize or remember their loved ones until undergoing intensive therapy. The final dissociative disorder is the most controversial.

borderline personality disorder A disorder in which individuals have difficulty developing a secure sense of who they are. Their behaviour is often unstable and emotionally volatile.

narcissistic personality disorder A personality disturbance characterized by an exaggerated sense of self-importance.

dissociative amnesia A dissociative disorder characterized by sudden memory loss after experiencing severe psychological stress.

dissociative fugue A dissociative disorder that combines dissociative amnesia with flight (the individual leaves the area associated with the stress and assumes a new identity).

dissociative identity disorder A disorder (formally termed Multiple Personality Disorder) where the individual has two or more distinct personalities with separate traits, behaviours, mannerisms, and memories.

Individuals with **dissociative identity disorder** (DID; this used to be called Multiple Personality Disorder) have two or more distinct personalities with separate traits, behaviours, mannerisms, and memories. The individual displays only one personality at a time, and often is unaware that other personalities even exist. There are many clinicians who claim that DID is not a real disorder and it does not belong in the *DSM-IV-TR* (Piper, 1997). Harold Merskey, from the University of Western Ontario, has been a vocal opponent to DID for over 20 years (Merskey, 1992). Merskey argues that DID has exploded in popularity largely because of the media and that therapists may be leading their patients to believe they have the disorder. Despite the controversy, DID continues to be classified in the *DSM-IV-TR*.

OTHER DISORDERS

Keep in mind that the various forms of psychological disorders described in *DSM-IV-TR* cover much more ground than we have been able to discuss in this chapter. Some relate to topics previously considered in other chapters. For example, *psychoactive substance-use disorder* relates to prob-lems that arise from the use and abuse of drugs. Further-more, *alcohol-use disorders* are among the most serious and widespread problems (Chanon & Boettiger, 2009; Stimson et al., 2007). Both psychoactive substance-use disorder and alcohol-use disorder co-occur with many other psychologi-cal disorders, such as mood disorders, post-traumatic stress disorder, and schizophrenia, complicating treatment con-siderably (Salgado, Quinlan, & Zlotnick, 2007).

Other disorders are specific to childhood. One of these is *attention-deficit hyperactivity disorder (ADHD)*, a disor-der marked by inattention, impulsiveness, a low tolerance for frustration, and generally a great deal of inappropriate activity. Another is autism, a severe developmental disabil-ity that impairs children's ability to communicate and relate to others. Autism usually appears in the first three years and typically continues throughout life (Barkley, 2005; Smith, Barkley, & Shapiro, 2006; Swanson, Harris, & Graham, 2003).

Another widespread problem is *eating disorders*. They include such disorders as *anorexia nervosa* and *bulimia*, which we considered in the chapter on motivation and emotion, as well as *binge-eating disorder*, characterized by binge eating without behaviours designed to prevent weight gain. Finally, *sexual disorders*, in which one's sexual activity is unsatisfactory, are another important class of problems.

BUY IT?

How Helpful Are Self-Help Books?

Take a walk down the self-help aisle of your local bookstore and you will probably find hundreds of books claiming to help you with a wide range of problems. The advantage to self-help books is their availability, readabil-ity, and their cost. A self-help book may range anywhere from $15 to $50, where one session with a therapist can range from $100 to $160 per hour. The major problem with self-help books is of course, their effectiveness.

A good critical thinker will start by asking about the credentials of the author (i.e., is this person qualified to be offering this advice and does he or she have an affiliation at a college, university, or hospital?). Is the information based on scientifically validated evidence? Unfortunately, many published (and popular) books are not based on any scientific evidence, and many oversimplify the information by offering general advice that is more akin to a pep talk.

This is not to say that all self-help books are a waste of your money! Dr. Richard Redding and colleagues have identified a list of self-help books recommended by expert psychologists based on a set of criteria including usefulness for psychological and behavioural change, scientific and theoreti-cal validity, guidance in self-diagnosis and monitoring progress, promotion of reasonable expectations for improvement, and whether the author's suggest advice that is harmful (Redding et al., 2008). Many of the top-rated self-help books were for anxiety disorders (OCD and social phobia), with a focus on the cognitive-behavioural approach. Moreover, the top-rated books were written by experts in the field with credentials at the doctoral level (i.e., PhD or MD) and they were based on empirically validated research (Redding et al., 2008).

Some of the top-rated self-help books by expert psychologists were as follows:

- *The OCD Workbook: Your Guide to Breaking Free From Obsessive-Compulsive Disorder* by B. M. Hyman and C. Pedrick
- *The Shyness & Social Anxiety Workbook: Proven Techniques for Overcoming your Fears*, by M. M. Antony and R. P. Swinson
- *Bipolar Disorder Demystified*, by L. R. Castle
- *Feeling Good* by D. D. Burns

They include *sexual desire disorders*, *sexual arousal disorders*, and *paraphilias*, atypical sexual activities that may include non-consenting partners.

Organic mental disorders are problems that have a purely biological basis, such as Alzheimer's disease and some types of mental retardation (intellectual disabilities). There are other disorders that we have not mentioned at all, and each of the classes we have discussed can be divided into several subcategories (Kopelman & Fleminger, 2002; Pratt et al., 2003; Reijonen et al., 2003).

PSYCHOLOGICAL DISORDERS IN PERSPECTIVE

How common are the kinds of psychological disorders we've been discussing? Here's one answer: About half of the people you meet are likely to suffer, at some point during their life, from a psychological disorder.

That's the conclusion drawn from a massive study on the prevalence of psychological disorders (Kessler, Berglund, & Demler, 2005). In that study, researchers conducted face-to-face interviews with more than 8,000 men and women between the ages of 15 and 54 years. According to results of the study, 48% of those interviewed had experienced a disorder at some point in their lives. In addition, 30% experienced a disorder in any particular year, and the number of people who experienced simultaneous multiple disorders (known as *comorbidity*) was significant (Merikangas et al., 2007; Welkowitz et al., 2000).

> **About half of the people you meet are likely to suffer, at some point during their life, from a psychological disorder.**

The most common disorder reported in the study was depression, with 17% of those surveyed reporting at least one major episode. Ten percent had suffered from depression during the current year. The next most common disorder was alcohol dependence, which occurred at a lifetime incidence rate of 14%. In addition, 7% of those interviewed had experienced alcohol dependence in the last year. Other frequently occurring psychological disorders were drug dependence, disorders involving panic (such as an overwhelming fear of talking to strangers and terror of heights), and post-traumatic stress disorder.

Although some researchers think the estimates of severe disorders may be too high (Narrow et al., 2002), the findings are consistent with studies of college students and their psychological difficulties. For example, in one study of the problems of students who visited a college counselling centre, more than 40% of students reported being depressed. These figures include only students who sought help from the counselling centre, not those who did not seek treatment. Consequently, the figures are not representative of the entire college population (Benton et al., 2003).

Figure 12.7
Canadians' Self-Perceived Mental Health

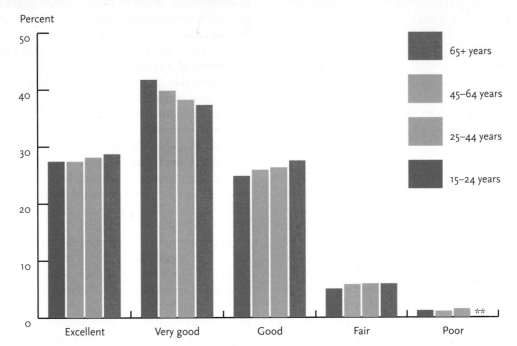

Percent

65+ years
45–64 years
25–44 years
15–24 years

**Insufficient sample size.

Source: Government of Canada. *The Human Face of Mental Health and Mental Illness in Canada.* 2006. © Minister of Public Works and Government Services Canada, 2006. Accessed online at www.phac-aspc.gc.ca/publicat/human-humain06/pdf/human_face_e.pdf (Figure 1-1).

Figure 12.8
Problems Reported by Students Visiting a College Counselling Centre

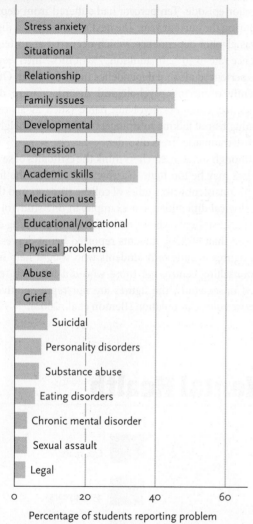

Percentage of students reporting problem

Source: Benton et al., 2003.

depression varies significantly from one culture to another. The probability of having at least one episode of depression is only 1.5% in Taiwan and 2.9% in Korea, compared with 11.6% in New Zealand and 16.4% in France. Such notable differences underscore the importance of considering the cultural context of psychological disorders, the focus of the socio-cultural approach (Horwath & Weissman, 2000; Tseng, 2003; Weissman et al., 1997).

THE SOCIAL AND CULTURAL CONTEXT OF PSYCHOLOGICAL DISORDERS

In considering the nature of the psychological disorders described in *DSM-IV-TR*, keep in mind that the specific disorders reflect turn-of-the-twenty-first-century Western cultures. The classification system provides a snapshot of how its authors viewed mental disorder when it was published. In fact, the development of the most recent version of *DSM* was a source of great debate, in part reflecting issues that divide society.

For example, two disorders caused particular controversy during the revision process. One, known as *self-defeating personality disorder*, was ultimately removed from the appendix, where it had appeared in the previous revision. The term *self-defeating personality disorder* had been applied to cases in which people who were treated unpleasantly or demeaningly in relationships neither left nor took other action. It was typically used to describe people who remained in abusive relationships.

Although some clinicians argued that it was a valid category, one that they observed in clinical practice, the disorder seemed to lack enough research evidence to support its designation as a disorder in *DSM*. Furthermore, some critics complained that use of the label had the effect of condemning targets of abuse for their plight—a blame-the-victim phenomenon—and as a result, the category was removed from the manual.

A second and even more controversial category was "premenstrual dysphoric disorder." That disorder is characterized by severe, incapacitating mood changes or depression related to a woman's menstrual cycle. Some critics argued that the classification simply labels normal female behaviour as a disorder. Former U.S. Surgeon General Antonia Novello suggested that what "in women is called PMS [premenstrual syndrome, a similar classification] in men is called healthy aggression and initiative" (Cotton, 1993, p. 270). Advocates for including the disorder prevailed, however, and "premenstrual dysphoric disorder" appears in the appendix of *DSM-IV-TR* (Hartung & Widiger, 1998).

Such controversies underline the fact that our understanding of abnormal behaviour reflects the society and culture in which we live. Future revisions of *DSM* may include a different catalogue of disorders. Even now, other cultures might include a list of disorders that look very different from the list that appears in the current *DSM*, as we discuss next. If we use the *DSM* to guide our judgments, then a person who hears voices of the recently deceased will probably be considered to be a victim of a psychological disturbance. Yet some Plains Indians routinely hear the

According to the World Health Organization, mental health difficulties are also a global concern. Throughout the world, psychological disorders are widespread. Furthermore, there are economic disparities in treatment, such that more affluent people with mild disorders receive more and better treatment than do poor people who have more severe disorders. In fact, psychological disorders make up 14% of global illness, and 90% of people in developing countries receive no care at all for their disorders (Jacoby et al., 2007; Wang et al., 2007; WHO World Mental Health Survey Consortium, 2004).

Also, keep in mind that the incidence of specific disorders varies significantly in other cultures. For instance, cross-cultural surveys show that the incidence of major

From the perspective of . . .

A COLLEGE COUNSELLOR What kinds of educational materials would you publish for college students about psychological disorders? How would you make your publication sensitive to cultural differences?

and wakefulness. I vaguely recall the anaesthesiologist having had me count to ten, but I never got beyond three or four. I remember Charlie Welch and his ECT [electroconvulsive therapy] team, but am not sure I got the treatment. One clue is a slight headache, which they told me ECT might cause but which could have come from the anaesthesia. Another is the goo on my hair, where they must have attached the electrodes.

There is one more sign that I did in fact have my first session of seizure therapy: I feel good—I feel alive. (From *Shock: The Healing Power of Electroconvulsive Therapy* by Kitty Dukakis and Larry Tye, copyright © 2006 by Kitty Dukakis & Larry Tye. Used by permission of Avery Publishing, an imprint of Penguin Group (USA) Inc.)

The procedure that has brought new life to the former first lady of Massachusetts Kitty Dukakis is just one of many approaches to the treatment of psychological disorders. All the different approaches, ranging from one-meeting informal counselling sessions to long-term drug therapy to more invasive procedures such as ECT, have a common objective: the relief of psychological disorders and the ultimate aim of enabling individuals to achieve richer, more meaningful, and more fulfilling lives within the context of their culture.

Many approaches to treating psychological disorders focus on treating the individual person; others focus on treating the social system (especially family) in which dysfunctional issues have arisen. Despite their diversity, those therapies that focus on individuals tend to fall into two main categories: biologically based and psychologically

voices of the dead calling to them from the afterlife, and this is considered normal in their culture.

This is only one example of the role of culture in labelling behaviour as "abnormal." In fact, among all the major adult disorders included in the *DSM* categorization, just four are found across all cultures of the world: schizophrenia, bipolar disorder, major depression, and anxiety disorders. *All* the rest are specific to North America and Western Europe (Cohen, Slomkowski, & Robins, 1999; Kleinman, 1996; López & Guarnaccia, 2000).

Furthermore, even though disorders such as schizophrenia are found throughout the world, cultural factors influence the specific symptoms of the disorder. Hence, catatonic schizophrenia, in which an individual appears to be frozen in the same position, sometimes for days, is rare in North America and Western Europe. In contrast, in India, 80% of people with schizophrenia are catatonic.

Other cultures have disorders that do not appear in the West. For example, in Malaysia, a behaviour called *amok* is characterized by a wild outburst in which a person, usually quiet and withdrawn, kills or severely injures another. *Koro* is a condition found in Southeast Asian males who develop an intense panic that the penis is about to withdraw into the abdomen. (Cohen, Slomkowski, & Robins, 1999; López & Guarnaccia, 2000).

In sum, we should not assume that the *DSM* provides the final word on psychological disorders. The disorders it includes are very much a creation and function of Western cultures at a particular moment in time, and its categories should not be seen as universally applicable (Tseng, 2003). Moreover, it is important to keep in mind that the disorders listed in the *DSM* change according to social, historical, and political influences.

Treatment of Psychological Disorders

Next thing I know I am waking up. I am back on an upper floor of the hospital, in the unit where I slept last night. I feel light-headed, groggy, the way you do when anaesthesia is wearing off and you are floating in the abyss between sleep

Psych
At The Movies

As Good as It Gets
Melvin has obsessive-compulsive disorder evidenced by obsessions, such as fear of contamination and magical thinking, and related compulsions, such as excessive hand washing and avoiding sidewalk cracks.

The Three Faces of Eve
This timeless classic movie is based on the true story of Eve White, a woman with a rare condition called *dissociative identity disorder* (previously called *multiple personality disorder*), and was written from her actual therapy notes.

The Soloist
A journalist befriends a homeless musical genius who suffers from schizophrenia. The reporter discovers realistic limitations when trying to help a person with a mental disorder, but he also gains rewards from his efforts.

based therapies. **Biomedical therapy** relies on drugs and medical procedures to improve psychological functioning. In contrast, psychologically based therapy, or **psychotherapy**, is treatment in which a trained professional—a therapist—uses psychological techniques to help someone overcome psychological difficulties and disorders, resolve problems in living, or bring about personal growth. In psychotherapy, the goal is to produce psychological change in a person (called a "client" or "patient") through discussions and interactions with the therapist.

As we describe the various approaches to therapy, keep in mind that although the distinctions may seem clear-cut, the classifications and procedures overlap a good deal. In fact, many therapists today use a variety of methods with an individual patient, taking an *eclectic approach to therapy*. Assuming that both psychological and biological processes often produce psychological disorders, eclectic therapists may draw from several perspectives simultaneously to address both the psychological and the biological aspects of a person's problems (Berman, Jobes, & Silverman, 2006; Goin, 2005).

BIOMEDICAL THERAPY

If you get a kidney infection, your doctor gives you an antibiotic, and with luck, about a week later your kidney should be as good as new. If your appendix becomes inflamed, a surgeon removes it and your body functions normally once more. Could a comparable approach, focusing on the body's physiology, be effective for psychological disturbances?

According to biological approaches to treatment, the answer is yes. Therapists routinely use biomedical therapies (Markowitz & Patrick, 2008). This approach suggests that rather than focusing on a client's psychological conflicts

biomedical therapy Therapy that relies on drugs and other medical procedures to improve psychological functioning.

psychotherapy Treatment in which a trained professional—a therapist—uses psychological techniques to help a person overcome psychological difficulties and disorders, resolve problems in living, or bring about personal growth.

drug therapy Control of psychological disorders through the use of drugs.

antipsychotic drugs Drugs that temporarily reduce such psychotic symptoms as agitation, hallucinations, and delusions.

or past traumas, or on environmental factors that may produce abnormal behaviour, focusing treatment directly on brain chemistry and other neurological factors may be more appropriate. To do this, therapists can use drugs, electric shock, or surgery to provide treatment.

Drug Therapy **Drug therapy**, the control of psychological disorders through drugs, works by altering the operation of neurotransmitters and neurons in the brain. Some drugs operate by inhibiting neurotransmitters or receptor neurons, reducing activity at particular synapses, the sites where nerve impulses travel from one neuron to another. Other drugs do just the opposite: They increase the activity of certain neurotransmitters or neurons, allowing particular neurons to fire more frequently.

Probably no greater change has occurred in mental hospitals than the successful introduction in the mid-1950s of **antipsychotic drugs**—drugs used to reduce severe symptoms of disturbance, such as loss of touch with reality and agitation (Stroup, Kraus, & Marder, 2006). Previously, the typical mental hospital wasn't very different from the stereotypical nineteenth-century insane asylum, giving mainly custodial care to screaming, moaning, clawing

Figure 12.9
Drug Treatments for Psychological Disorders

Class of Drug	Effects of Drug	Primary Action of Drug	Examples
Antipsychotic Drugs, Atypical Antipsychotic Drugs	Reduction in loss of touch with reality, agitation	Block dopamine receptors	Antipsychotic: Chlorpromazine (Thorazine), clozapine (Clozaril), haloperidol (Haldol) Atypical Antipsychotic: rizperadine, olanzapine
Antidepressant Drugs			
Tricyclic antidepressants	Reduction in depression	Permit rise in neurotransmitters such as norepinephrine	Trazodone (Desyrel), amitriptyline (Elavil), desipramine (Norpamin)
MAO inhibitors	Reduction in depression	Prevent MAO from breaking down neurotransmitters	Phenelzine (Nardil), tranylcypromine (Parnate)
Selective serotonin reuptake inhibitors (SSRIs)	Reduction in depression	Inhibit reuptake of serotonin	Fluoxetine (Prozac), Luvox, Paxil, Celexa, Zoloft, nefazodone (Serzone)
Mood Stabilizers			
Lithium	Mood stabilization	Can alter transmission of impulses within neurons	Lithium (Lithonate), Depakote, Tegretol
Antianxiety Drugs	Reduction in anxiety	Increase activity of neurotransmitter GABA	Benzodiazepines (Valium, Xanax)

patients who displayed bizarre behaviours. Suddenly, in just a matter of days after hospital staff members administered antipsychotic drugs, the wards became considerably calmer environments in which professionals could do more than just try to get patients through the day without causing serious harm to themselves or others.

This dramatic change came about through the introduction of the drug *chlorpromazine*. Along with other similar drugs, chlorpromazine rapidly became the most popular and successful treatment for schizophrenia. Interestingly, chlorpromazine was initially used as by anaesthesiologists to help patients remain calm during surgery. It was Dr. Ruth Kajander, a psychiatrist still practicing in Thunder Bay, Ontario, who first prescribed chlorpromazine to patients in 1953 (*Waslenki, 2008*). Today, drug therapy is the preferred treatment for most cases of severely abnormal behaviour and, as such, is used for most patients hospitalized with psychological disorders (Sharif et al., 2007). The newest generation of antipsychotics, which are referred to as *atypical antipsychotics* and have fewer side effects, include *risperidone*, *olanzapine*, and *paliperidone* (Anand & Burton, 2003; Lublin, Eberhard, & Levander, 2005; Savas, Yumru, & Kaya, 2007).

How do antipsychotic drugs work? Most block dopamine receptors at the brain's synapses. Atypical antipsychotics affect both serotonin and dopamine levels in certain parts of the brain, such as those related to planning and goal-directed activity (Advokat, 2005; Sawa & Snyder, 2002).

Despite the effectiveness of antipsychotic drugs, they do not produce a "cure" in the same way that an antibiotic cures an infection. Most of the time, when the drug is withdrawn, the symptoms reappear. Furthermore, such drugs can have long-term side effects, such as dryness of the mouth and throat, dizziness, and sometimes tremors and loss of muscle control, which may continue after drug treatments are stopped (Voruganti et al., 2007).

As their name suggests, **antidepressant drugs** are a class of medications used in cases of severe depression to improve the moods of clients. They are also sometimes used for other disorders, such as anxiety disorders and bulimia (Hedges et al., 2007; Walsh et al., 2006).

Most antidepressant drugs work by changing the concentration of specific neurotransmitters in the brain. For example, *tricyclic drugs* increase the availability of norepinephrine at the synapses of neurons, whereas *MAO inhibitors* prevent the enzyme monoamine oxidase (MAO) from breaking down neurotransmitters. Newer antidepressants—such as Lexapro—are *selective serotonin reuptake inhibitors (SSRIs)*. SSRIs target the neurotransmitter serotonin, permitting it to linger at the synapse. Some antidepressants produce a combination of effects. For instance, nefazodone (Serzone) blocks serotonin at some receptor sites but not others, whereas bupropion (Wellbutrin and Zyban) affect

the norepinephrine and dopamine systems (Anand, 2002; Lucki & O'Leary, 2004; Robinson, D. S., 2007).

The overall success rate of antidepressant drugs is good. Unlike antipsychotic drugs, antidepressants can produce lasting, long-term recovery from depression. In many cases, even after clients stop taking the drugs, their depression does not return. Yet antidepressant drugs may produce side effects such as drowsiness and faintness, and there is evidence that SSRI antidepressants can increase the risk of suicide in children and adolescents (Gibbons et al., 2007; Leckman & King, 2007).

Mood stabilizers are used to treat mood disorders. For example, the drug *lithium*, a form of mineral salts, has been used successfully to control bipolar disorder. Although no one knows definitely why, lithium and other mood stabilizers such as divalproex sodium (Depakote) and carbamazepine (Tegretol) effectively reduce manic episodes. But they do not effectively treat depressive phases of bipolar disorder, so antidepressants are usually prescribed during those phases (Abraham & Calabrese, 2007; Dubovsky, 1999; Fountoulakis et al., 2005).

Lithium and similar drugs have a quality that sets them apart from other drug treatments: They can be a *preventive* treatment, blocking future episodes of manic depression. Often, people who have had episodes of bipolar disorder can take a daily dose of lithium to prevent a recurrence of their symptoms. Most other drugs are useful only when symptoms of psychological disturbance occur (Keck & McElroy, 2007; Pary et al., 2006).

Antianxiety drugs, as the name implies, reduce the level of anxiety a person experiences and increase feelings of well-being. They are prescribed not only to reduce general tension in people who are experiencing temporary difficulties but also to aid in the treatment of more serious anxiety disorders (Zito, 1993).

Antianxiety drugs such as Xanax and Valium are among the medications most frequently prescribed by physicians. Although the popularity of antianxiety drugs suggests that they hold few risks, they can produce a number of potentially serious side effects. For instance, they can cause fatigue, and long-term use can lead to dependence. Moreover, when taken in combination with alcohol, some antianxiety drugs can be lethal. But a more important issue concerns their use to suppress anxiety. Almost every therapeutic approach to psychological disturbance views continuing anxiety as a signal of some other sort of problem.

antidepressant drugs Medications that improve mood and promote a feeling of well-being in severely depressed individuals.

mood stabilizers Drugs used to treat mood disorders that prevent manic episodes of bipolar disorder.

antianxiety drugs Drugs that reduce the level of anxiety a person experiences, essentially by reducing excitability and increasing feelings of well-being.

Thus, drugs that mask anxiety may simply be hiding other difficulties. Consequently, rather than confronting their underlying problems, people may be hiding from them through the use of antianxiety drugs (Pandit, Argyropoulos, & Nutt, 2001).

Electroconvulsive Therapy (ECT) First introduced in the 1930s, **electroconvulsive therapy (ECT)** is a procedure used in the treatment of severe depression. In this procedure, an electric current of 70 to 150 volts is briefly administered to a patient's head, causing a loss of consciousness and often causing seizures. Health professionals usually sedate patients and give them muscle relaxants before administering the current, and such preparations help reduce the intensity of muscle contractions produced during ECT. Typically, a patient receives about 10 such treatments in the course of a month, but some patients continue with maintenance treatments for months afterward (Greenberg & Kellner, 2005; Stevens & Harper, 2007).

ECT is a controversial technique. Apart from the obvious distastefulness of a treatment that evokes images of electrocution, side effects are common. For instance, after treatment, patients often experience disorientation, confusion, and sometimes memory loss that may remain for months. Furthermore, ECT often does not produce long-term improvement; one study found that without follow-up medication, depression returned in most individuals who had undergone ECT treatments. Finally, even when ECT does work, we do not know why, and some critics believe it may cause permanent brain damage (Frank, 2002; Sackeim et al., 2001; Valente, 1991).

In light of the drawbacks to ECT, why do therapists use it at all? Basically, in many severe cases of depression, it offers the only quickly effective treatment—as in the case of Kitty Dukakis, whose treatment was described previously in this chapter, or Norman Endler, who we discussed in the section on bipolar disorders. For instance, it may prevent depressed, suicidal individuals from committing suicide, and it can act more quickly than antidepressant medications (Kellner et al., 1997).

The use of ECT has risen in the last decade, with more than 100,000 people undergoing it each year. Still, ECT tends to be used only when other treatments have proved ineffective, and researchers continue to search for alternative treatments (Eranti & McLoughlin, 2003; Fink, 2000; Pandya, Pozuelo, & Malone, 2007).

One new and promising alternative to ECT is **transcranial magnetic stimulation (TMS)**. TMS creates a precise magnetic pulse in a specific area of the brain. By activating particular neurons, TMS has been found to be effective in relieving the symptoms of depression in a number of controlled experiments. However, the therapy can produce side effects, such as seizures and convulsions, and it is still considered experimental (Lefaucheur et al., 2007; Leo & Latif, 2007; Simons & Dierick, 2005).

Psychosurgery If ECT strikes you as a questionable procedure, the use of **psychosurgery**—brain surgery in which

the object is to reduce symptoms of mental disorder—probably appears even more dubious. A technique used only rarely today, psychosurgery was introduced as a "treatment of last resort" in the 1930s.

The initial form of psychosurgery, a *prefrontal lobotomy*, consisted of surgically destroying or removing parts of a patient's frontal lobes, which, surgeons thought, controlled emotionality. In the 1930s and 1940s, surgeons performed the procedure on thousands of people, often with little precision. For example, in one common technique, a surgeon would jab an ice pick under a patient's eyeball and swivel it back and forth (El-Hai, 2005; Ogren & Sandlund, 2007).

Often psychosurgery did improve a patient's behaviour—but not without drastic side effects. Along with remission of the symptoms of the mental disorder, patients sometimes experienced personality changes, becoming bland, colourless, and unemotional. In other cases, patients became aggressive and unable to control their impulses. In the worst cases, the patient died as a result of the surgery (Mashour, Walker, & Martuza, 2005).

With the introduction of effective drug treatments—and the obvious ethical questions regarding the appropriateness of forever altering someone's personality—psychosurgery became nearly obsolete. However, it is still used in very rare cases when all other procedures have failed and the individual's behaviour presents a high risk to himself and others. Today, surgeons sometimes use a more precise form of psychosurgery called a *cingulotomy* in rare cases of obsessive-compulsive disorder. Occasionally, psychosurgery is performed on dying individuals with severe, uncontrollable pain. Still, even these cases raise important ethical issues, and psychosurgery remains a highly controversial treatment (Mashour, Walker, & Martuza, 2005; Steele et al., 2007).

Biomedical Therapies in Perspective In some respects, no greater revolution has occurred in the field of mental health than biological approaches to treatment. As previously violent, uncontrollable individuals have been calmed by the use of drugs, mental hospitals have been able to concentrate more on actually helping them and less on custodial functions. Similarly, people whose lives have been disrupted by depression or bipolar episodes have been able to function normally, and other forms of drug therapy have also shown remarkable results.

The use of biomedical therapy for everyday problems is rising. For example, one survey of users of a college counselling service found that from 1989 to 2001, the proportion of students receiving treatment who were taking medication

electroconvulsive therapy (ECT) A procedure used in the treatment of severe depression in which an electric current of 70 to 150 volts is briefly administered to the head.

transcranial magnetic stimulation (TMS) A depression treatment in which a precise magnetic pulse is directed to a specific area of the brain.

psychosurgery Brain surgery once used to reduce the symptoms of mental disorder but rarely used today.

for psychological disorders increased from 10% to 25% (Benton et al., 2003).

Furthermore, new forms of biomedical therapy are promising. For example, the newest treatment possibility—which remains experimental at this point—is gene therapy. As we discussed when considering behavioural genetics, specific genes may be introduced to particular regions of the brain. These genes then have the potential to reverse or even prevent biochemical events that give rise to psychological disorders (Lymberis et al., 2004; Sapolsky, 2003; Tuszynski, 2007).

Despite their current usefulness and future promise, biomedical therapies do not represent a cure-all for psychological disorders. For one thing, critics charge that such therapies merely provide relief of the *symptoms* of mental disorder; as soon as the drugs are withdrawn, the symptoms return. Although it is considered a major step in the right direction, biomedical treatment may not solve the underlying problems that led to therapy in the first place (Alonso, 2004). Biomedical therapies also can produce side effects, ranging from minor to serious physical reactions to the development of *new* symptoms of abnormal behaviour.

Still, biomedical therapies—sometimes alone and more often in conjunction with psychotherapy—have permitted millions of people to function more effectively (Stroup, Kraus, & Marder, 2006). Furthermore, although biomedical therapy and psychotherapy appear distinct, research shows that biomedical therapies ultimately may not be as different from talk therapies as one might imagine, at least in terms of their consequences.

Specifically, measures of brain functioning as a result of drug therapy compared with psychotherapy show little difference in outcomes. For example, one study compared the reactions of clients with major depression who received either an antidepressant drug or psychotherapy. After six weeks of either therapy, activity in the portion of the brain related to the disorder—the basal ganglia—had changed in similar ways, and that area appeared to function more normally. Although such research is not definitive, it does suggest that at least for some disorders, psychotherapy may be just as effective as biomedical interventions—and vice versa. Research also makes it clear that no single treatment is effective universally, and that each type of treatment has both advantages and disadvantages (DeRubeis, Hollon, & Shelton, 2003; Hollon, Thase, & Markowitz, 2002; Pinquart, Duberstein, & Lyness, 2006).

PSYCHOTHERAPIES

Therapists use some 400 different varieties of psychotherapy, approaches to therapy that focus on psychological factors. Although diverse in many respects, all psychological approaches see treatment as a way of solving psychological problems by modifying individuals' behaviour and helping them gain a better understanding of themselves and their past, present, and future.

psychodynamic therapy Therapy that seeks to bring unresolved past conflicts and unacceptable impulses from the unconscious into the conscious, where clients may deal with the problems more effectively.

Most psychotherapists employ one of four major approaches to therapy (Sampson, McCubbin & Tyrer, 2006): psychodynamic, behavioural, cognitive, and humanistic treatments. These approaches are based on the models of personality and psychological disorders developed by psychologists. Here we'll consider the psychodynamic, behavioural, cognitive, and humanistic approaches, as well as interpersonal psychotherapy and group therapy, and the effectiveness of psychotherapy.

Psychodynamic Approaches to Therapy **Psychodynamic therapy** seeks to bring unresolved past conflicts and unacceptable impulses from the unconscious into the conscious, where clients may deal with the problems more effectively. Psychodynamic approaches are based on Freud's psychoanalytic approach to personality, which holds that individuals employ *defence mechanisms*, psychological strategies to protect themselves from unacceptable unconscious impulses (Gabbard, 2009; Huprich, 2009; Kudler et al., 2009).

The most common defence mechanism is repression, which pushes threatening conflicts and impulses back into the unconscious. However, since unacceptable conflicts and impulses can never be completely buried, some of the anxiety associated with them can produce abnormal behaviour in the form of what Freud called *neurotic symptoms* (Huprich, 2009).

How do we rid ourselves of the anxiety produced by unconscious, unwanted impulses and drives? To Freud, the answer was to confront the conflicts and impulses by bringing them out of the unconscious part of the mind and into the conscious part. Freud assumed that this technique would reduce anxiety stemming from past conflicts and that the client could then participate in his or her daily life more effectively.

In the TV series *In Treatment*, Gabriel Byrne (right) plays a psychotherapist. The fact that the show's writers have gone through therapy lends realism to the fictional sessions.

A psychodynamic therapist, then, faces the challenge of finding a way to assist an individual's attempts to explore and understand the unconscious. The technique that has evolved has a number of components, but basically it consists of guiding clients to consider and discuss their past experiences, in explicit detail, from the time of their first memories. This process assumes that clients will eventually stumble on long-hidden crises, traumas, and conflicts that are producing anxiety in their adult lives. It's the therapist's role to recognize these issues and help the client to "work through"—understand and rectify—those difficulties (Gabbard, 2009; Huprich, 2009).

Study tip To better understand psychodynamic therapy, review Freud's psychoanalytic theory, discussed in the chapter on personality.

Psychoanalysis: Freud's Therapy Classic Freudian psychodynamic therapy, called *psychoanalysis*, tends to be a lengthy and expensive affair. **Psychoanalysis** is Freudian psychotherapy in which the goal is to release hidden unconscious thoughts and feelings to reduce their power in controlling behaviour.

In psychoanalysis, clients may meet with a therapist frequently, sometimes for as much as 50 minutes a day, four to six days a week, for several years. In their sessions, they often use a technique developed by Freud called *free association*. Psychoanalysts using this technique tell clients to say aloud whatever comes to mind, regardless of its apparent irrelevance or senselessness, and the analysts attempt to recognize and label the connections between what a client says and the client's unconscious. Therapists also use *dream interpretation*, examining dreams to find clues to unconscious conflicts and problems. Moving beyond the surface description of a dream (called the *manifest content*), therapists seek its underlying meaning (the *latent content*), thereby revealing the true unconscious meaning of the dream (Auld, Hyman, & Rudzinski, 2005; Bodin, 2006; Galatzer-Levy & Cohler, 1997).

Because of the close interaction between client and psychoanalyst, the relationship between the two often becomes emotionally charged and takes on a complexity unlike most other relationships. Clients may come to think of the analyst as a symbol of a significant other in their past, perhaps a parent or a lover, and apply some of their feelings for that person to the analyst—a phenomenon known as transference. Specifically, **transference** is the unconscious transfer to a psychoanalyst of feelings of love or anger that had been originally directed at parent or other authority figures (Evans, 2007; Van Beekum, 2005). Another issue that may arise in psychoanalysis is called **resistance**, a defence mechanism where the patient unconsciously resists or defends against the possible painful memories that may arise during therapy. The patient may argue with the therapist, show up late for appointments, or talk about less important issues to avoid getting at the real issues.

Contemporary Psychodynamic Approaches Few people have the time, money, or patience to participate in years of traditional psychoanalysis. Moreover, no conclusive evidence shows that psychoanalysis, as originally conceived by Freud in the nineteenth century, works better than other, more recent forms of psychodynamic therapy (de Maat et al., 2009; Huprich, 2009).

Today, psychodynamic therapy tends to be of shorter duration, usually lasting no longer than three months or 20 sessions. The therapist takes a more active role than Freud would have liked, controlling the course of therapy and prodding and advising the client with considerable directness. Finally, the therapist puts less emphasis on a client's past history and childhood, concentrating instead on an individual's current relationships and specific complaints (Charman, 2004; Goode, E., 2003b; Wolitzky, 2006).

Evaluating Psychodynamic Therapy Even with its current modifications, psychodynamic therapy has its critics. In its longer versions, it can be time-consuming and expensive, especially in comparison with other forms of psychotherapy, such as behavioural and cognitive approaches. Furthermore, less articulate clients may not do as well as more verbal ones do (de Maat et al., 2009; Huprich, 2009).

Ultimately, the most important concern about psychodynamic treatment is whether it actually works, and there

psychoanalysis Freudian psychotherapy in which the goal is to release hidden unconscious thoughts and feelings to reduce their power in controlling behaviour.

transference The transfer of feelings of love or anger to a psychoanalyst that had been originally directed to a client's parents or other authority figure.

resistance A defence mechanism where the patient unconsciously resists or defends against the possible painful memories that may arise during therapy.

"And when did you first realize you weren't like other precipitation?"
© The New Yorker Collection 2007 Michael Maslin from cartoonbank.com. All Rights Reserved.

is no simple answer to this question. Psychodynamic treatment techniques have been controversial since Freud introduced them. Part of the problem is the difficulty in establishing whether clients have improved after psychodynamic therapy. Determining effectiveness depends on reports from the therapist or the clients themselves, reports that are obviously open to bias and subjective interpretation (de Maat et al., 2009; Huprich, 2009).

Furthermore, critics have questioned the entire theoretical basis of psychodynamic theory, maintaining that constructs such as the unconscious have not been scientifically confirmed. Despite the criticism, for some people, the psychodynamic treatment approach provides solutions to difficult psychological issues and effective treatment for psychological disturbance. It also permits the potential development of an unusual degree of insight into one's life (Ablon & Jones, 2005; Bond, 2006; Clay, 2000).

BEHAVIOURAL APPROACHES TO THERAPY

Perhaps, when you were a child, your parents rewarded you with an ice cream cone when you were especially good . . . or sent you to your room if you misbehaved. Sound principles back up such a child-rearing strategy: good behaviour is maintained by reinforcement, and unwanted behaviour can be eliminated by punishment, concepts that are explained in the chapter on learning.

These principles represent the underpinnings of **behavioural treatment approaches**. Building on the basic processes of learning, behavioural treatment approaches make this fundamental assumption: both abnormal behaviour and normal behaviour are *learned*. People who act abnormally either have failed to learn the skills they need to cope with the problems of everyday living or have acquired faulty skills and patterns that are being maintained through some form of reinforcement. To modify abnormal behaviour, then, proponents of behavioural approaches propose that people must learn new behaviour to replace the faulty skills they have developed and unlearn their maladaptive behaviour patterns (Agras & Berkowitz, 1996; Bergin & Garfield, 1994; Krijn et al., 2004; Norton & Price, 2007).

Behavioural psychologists do not believe they need to delve into people's pasts or their psyches. Rather than viewing abnormal behaviour as a symptom of an underlying problem, they consider the abnormal behaviour as the problem in need of modification. The goal of therapy is to change people's behaviour to allow them to function more effectively. In this view, then, there is no problem other than the maladaptive behaviour itself, and if one can change that behaviour, treatment is successful.

Behavioural approaches to treatment would seek to modify the behaviour of this couple, rather than focusing on the underlying causes of behaviour.

behavioural treatment approaches Treatment approaches that build on the basic processes of learning, such as reinforcement and extinction, and assume that normal and abnormal behaviour are both learned.

aversive conditioning A form of therapy that reduces the frequency of undesired behaviour by pairing an aversive, unpleasant stimulus with undesired behaviour.

systematic desensitization A behavioural technique in which gradual exposure to an anxiety-producing stimulus is paired with relaxation to extinguish the response of anxiety.

Classical Conditioning Treatments Suppose you bite into your favourite chocolate bar and find that not only is it infested with ants but that you've also swallowed a bunch of them. You immediately become sick to your stomach and throw up. What do you think will happen next time you see that type of chocolate bar? You will likely associate it with feeling nauseous so you avoid eating it. You have learned, through the basic process of classical conditioning, to avoid candy so that you will not get sick and throw up.

This simple example illustrates how a person can be classically conditioned to modify behaviour. Behaviour therapists use this principle when they employ **aversive conditioning**, a form of therapy that reduces the frequency of undesired behaviour by pairing an aversive, unpleasant stimulus with undesired behaviour. For example, behaviour therapists might use aversive conditioning by pairing alcohol with a drug that causes severe nausea and vomiting. After the two have been paired a few times, the person associates the alcohol alone with vomiting and finds alcohol less appealing.

Although aversion therapy works reasonably well in inhibiting substance-abuse problems such as alcoholism and certain kinds of sexual disorder, critics question its long-term effectiveness (Mann, 2004; McLellan & Childress, 1985). Also, important ethical concerns surround aversion techniques that employ such potent stimuli as electric shock, which therapists use only in the most extreme cases, such as client self-mutilation (Kishore & Dutt, 1986). Nonetheless, aversion therapy offers an important procedure for eliminating maladaptive responses for some period of time—a respite that provides, even if only temporarily, an opportunity to encourage more adaptive behaviour patterns (Bordnick et al., 2004; Delgado, Labouliere, & Phelps, 2006).

Another treatment to grow out of classical conditioning is systematic desensitization. In **systematic desensitization**, gradual exposure to an anxiety-producing stimulus is paired with relaxation to extinguish the response of anxiety (Choy, Fyer, & Lipsitz, 2007; McGlynn, Smitherman, & Gothard, 2004; Pagoto, Kozak, & Spates, 2006).

Figure 12.10
How to Achieve the Relaxation Response

Step 1 Pick a focus word or short phrase that's firmly rooted in your personal belief system. For example, a nonreligious individual might choose a neutral word like *one* or *peace* or *love*. A Christian person desiring to use a prayer could pick the opening words of Psalm 23. *The Lord is my shepherd;* a Jewish person could choose *Shalom*.

Step 2 Sit quietly in a comfortable position.

Step 3 Close your eyes.

Step 4 Relax your muscles.

Step 5 Breathe slowly and naturally, repeating your focus word or phrase silently as you exhale.

Step 6 Throughout, assume a passive attitude. Don't worry about how well you're doing. When other thoughts come to mind, simply say to yourself, "Oh, well," and gently return to the repetition.

Step 7 Continue for 10 to 20 minutes. You may open your eyes to check the time, but do not use an alarm. When you finish, sit quietly for a minute or so, at first with your eyes closed and later with your eyes open. Then do not stand for one or two minutes.

Step 8 Practice the technique once or twice a day.

Suppose, for instance, you were extremely afraid of flying. The very thought of being in an airplane would make you begin to sweat and shake, and you couldn't get yourself near enough to an airport to know how you'd react if you actually had to fly somewhere. Using systematic desensitization to treat your problem, you would first be trained in relaxation techniques by a behaviour therapist, learning to relax your body fully.

The next step would involve constructing a *hierarchy of fears*—a list, in order of increasing severity, of the things you associate with your fears. For instance, your hierarchy might resemble this one:

1. Watching a plane fly overhead.
2. Going to an airport.
3. Buying a ticket.
4. Stepping into the plane.
5. Seeing the plane door close.
6. Having the plane taxi down the runway.
7. Taking off.
8. Being in the air.

Once you had developed this hierarchy and had learned relaxation techniques, you would learn to associate the two sets of responses. To do this, your therapist might ask you to put yourself into a relaxed state and then imagine yourself in the first situation identified in your hierarchy. Once you could consider that first step while remaining completely relaxed, you would move on to the next situation, eventually moving up the hierarchy in gradual stages until you could imagine yourself being in the air without experiencing anxiety. Then you would be asked to make a visit to an airport and ultimately would take a flight. A recent type of

> **exposure** A behavioural treatment for anxiety in which people are confronted, either suddenly or gradually, with a stimulus that they fear.

systematic desensitization is virtual reality therapy. It can be costly to go through the process of systematic desensitization at an airport (imagine all the tickets you would have to buy or trying to get through security) so virtual reality therapy can be used to realistically simulate the experience of getting on a plane and taking off for flight. This type of therapy can be used for many different types of phobias, such as a fear of heights, elevators, and spiders.

Although systematic desensitization has proven to be a successful treatment, today it is often replaced with a less complicated form of therapy called exposure. **Exposure** is a behavioural treatment for anxiety in which people are confronted, either suddenly or gradually, with a stimulus that they fear. However, unlike systematic desensitization, relaxation training is omitted. Exposure allows the maladaptive response of anxiety or avoidance to extinguish, and research shows that this approach is generally as effective as systematic desensitization (Havermans et al., 2007; Hoffmann, 2007; Tryon, 2005).

From the perspective of . . .

A TEACHER How might you use systematic desensitization to help children overcome their fears?

In most cases, therapists use *graded exposure* in which clients are exposed to a feared stimulus in gradual steps. For example, an individual who is afraid of dogs might first view a video of dogs. Gradually, as the client becomes comfortable with images of dogs, the exposure escalates to seeing a live, leashed dog across the room and then actually petting and touching the dog (Berle, 2007; Means & Edinger, 2007).

Exposure has proved to be an effective treatment for a number of problems, including phobias, anxiety disorders, and even impotence and fear of sexual contact. Through this technique, people can learn to enjoy the things they once feared (Choy, Fyer, & Lipsitz, 2007; Tryon, 2005).

Operant Conditioning Techniques Some behavioural approaches make use of the operant conditioning principles that we discussed in the learning chapter. These approaches are based on the concept that rewarding people for carrying out desirable behaviour increases the likelihood that they will repeat the behaviour and that punishing or ignoring undesirable behaviour eventually extinguishes it.

One example of the systematic application of operant conditioning principles is the *token system*, which rewards a person for desired behaviour with a token, such as a poker chip or some kind of play money. Although it is most frequently employed in institutional settings for individuals with relatively serious problems, and sometimes with children as a classroom management technique, the system resembles what parents do when they give children money for being well behaved—money that the children can later exchange for something they want. The desired behaviour may range from simple things, such as keeping one's room neat, to personal grooming and interacting with other people. In institutions, patients can exchange tokens for some object or activity, such as snacks, new clothes, or, in extreme cases, being able to sleep in one's own bed rather than in a sleeping bag on the floor (Kadzin, 1988; McKinley et al., 1988).

Contingency contracting, a variant of the token system, has proved quite effective in producing behaviour modification (D'Eramo & Francis, 2004; Francis, 1995). In *contingency contracting*, the therapist and the client (or teacher and student, or parent and child) draw up a written agreement. The contract states a series of behavioural goals the client hopes to achieve. It also specifies the positive consequences for the client if the client reaches goals—usually an explicit reward such as money or additional privileges. Contracts frequently state negative consequences if the client does not meet the goals. For example, clients who are trying to quit smoking might write out a cheque to a cause they have no interest in supporting (for instance, a scholarship fund for the University of Manitoba if they are a graduate of the University of Winnipeg). If the client smokes on a given day, the therapist will mail the cheque.

Behaviour therapists also use *observational learning*, the process in which the behaviour of other people is modelled, to systematically teach people new skills and ways of handling their fears and anxieties. For example, modelling helps when therapists are teaching basic social skills such as maintaining eye contact during conversation and acting assertively. Similarly, children with dog phobias have been able to overcome their fears by watching another child—called the "Fearless Peer"—repeatedly walk up to a dog, touch it, pet it, and finally play with it. Modelling, then, can play an effective role in resolving some kinds of behaviour difficulties, especially if the model receives a reward for his or her behaviour (Bandura, Grusec, & Menlove, 1967; Greer, Dudek-Singer, Gautreaux, 2006).

Evaluating Behaviour Therapy Behaviour therapy works especially well for eliminating anxiety disorders, treating phobias and compulsions, establishing control over impulses, and learning complex social skills to replace maladaptive behaviour. More than any of the other therapeutic techniques, it provides methods that non-professionals can use to change their own behaviour. Moreover, it is efficient, because it focuses on solving carefully defined problems (Barlow, 2007; Richard & Lauterbach, 2006).

Critics of behaviour therapy believe that because this therapy emphasizes changing external behaviour, people do not necessarily gain insight into thoughts and expectations that may be fostering their maladaptive behaviour (Farmer & Chapman, 2008; Miltenberger, 2008). Yet neuroscientific evidence shows that behavioural treatments can produce actual changes in brain functioning, suggesting that behavioural treatments can produce changes beyond external behaviour (Miltenberger, 2008).

A "Fearless Peer" who models appropriate and effective behaviour can help children overcome their fears.

COGNITIVE APPROACHES TO THERAPY

If you assumed that illogical thoughts and beliefs lie at the heart of psychological disorders, wouldn't the most direct treatment route be to teach people new, more adaptive modes of thinking? The answer is yes, according to psychologists who take a cognitive approach to treatment.

Cognitive treatment approaches teach people more adaptive ways of thinking by changing their dysfunctional cognitions about the world and themselves. Unlike behaviour therapists, who focus on modifying external behaviour, cognitive therapists attempt to change the way people think, as well as their behaviour. Because they often use basic principles of learning, their methods are sometimes referred to as the **cognitive-behavioural approach** (Beck & Rector, 2005; Butler et al., 2006; Friedberg, 2006).

Although cognitive treatment approaches take many forms, they all share the assumption that anxiety, depression, and negative emotions develop from maladaptive thinking. For example, Nancy Kocovski and colleagues from York University in Toronto found that a group of individuals with high levels of social anxiety tended to have more negative thoughts and engage in more upward counterfactual thinking (where they think about how a social situation might have been better after it is already over) than individuals with low levels of social anxiety (Kocovski, et al., 2005).

> **Cognitive therapists teach clients more adaptive ways of thinking.**

Accordingly, cognitive treatments seek to change the thought patterns that lead to getting "stuck" in dysfunctional ways of thinking. Therapists systematically teach clients to challenge their assumptions and adopt new approaches to old problems (Freeman et al., 2004; Perkins, Conklin, & Levine, 2008).

Cognitive therapy is relatively short-term, usually lasting a maximum of 20 sessions. Therapy tends to be highly structured and focused on concrete problems. Therapists often begin by teaching the theory behind the approach and then continue to take an active role throughout the course of therapy, acting as teacher, coach, and partner (Freeman et al., 2004).

Another influential form of therapy that builds on a cognitive perspective is that of Aaron Beck (Beck, 1995, 2004). Beck's *cognitive therapy* aims to change people's illogical thoughts about themselves and the world. Playing the role of teacher, the cognitive therapist urges clients to obtain information on their own that will lead them to discard their inaccurate thinking through a process of cognitive appraisal. In *cognitive appraisal*, clients are asked to evaluate situations, themselves, and others in terms of their memories, values, beliefs, thoughts, and expectations. During the course of treatment, therapists help clients discover ways of thinking more appropriately about themselves and others (Beck, Freeman, & Davis, 2004; Moorey, 2007; Rosen, 2000).

DID YOU KNOW?

Mobile devices can be useful therapy tools. They are used to study mood shifts associated with borderline personality disorder. Programmed to beep at random times throughout the day, the device prompt clients to report their immediate moods without requiring them to decide when a mood shift has occurred (Trull, Solhan, & Watson, 2008).

Evaluating Cognitive Approaches to Therapy Cognitive approaches to therapy have proved successful in dealing with a broad range of disorders, including anxiety disorders, depression, substance abuse, and eating disorders. Furthermore, the willingness of cognitive therapists to incorporate additional treatment approaches (for example, combining cognitive and behavioural techniques in cognitive-behavioural therapy) has made this approach a particularly effective form of treatment (Ishikawa et al., 2007; McMullin, 2000; Mitte, 2005).

At the same time, critics have pointed out that the focus on helping people to think more rationally ignores the fact that life is, in reality, sometimes irrational. Changing one's assumptions to make them more reasonable and logical thus may not always be helpful—even assuming that it is possible to bring about true cognitive change. Still, the success of cognitive approaches has made it one of the most frequently employed therapies (Beck, 2005; Newman et al. (2002)).

HUMANISTIC THERAPY

As you know from your own experience, a student cannot master the material covered in a course without some hard work, no matter how good the teacher and the textbook are. *You* must take the time to study, memorize the vocabulary, and learn the concepts. Nobody else can do it for you. If you choose to put in the effort, you'll succeed; if you don't, you'll fail. The responsibility is primarily yours.

Humanistic therapy draws on this philosophical perspective of self-responsibility in developing treatment techniques. The many different types of therapy that fit into this category have a similar rationale: We have control of our own behaviour, we can make choices about the kinds of lives we want to live, and it is up to us to solve the difficulties we encounter in our daily lives.

> **cognitive treatment approaches** Treatment approaches that teach people to think in more adaptive ways by changing their dysfunctional cognitions about the world and themselves.
>
> **cognitive-behavioural approach** A treatment approach that incorporates basic principles of learning to change the way people think.
>
> **humanistic therapy** Therapy in which the underlying rationale is that people have control of their behaviour, can make choices about their lives, and are essentially responsible for solving their own problems.

Instead of acting in the more directive manner of some psychodynamic and behavioural approaches, humanistic therapists view themselves as guides or facilitators. Therapists using humanistic techniques seek to help people to understand themselves and to find ways to come closer to the ideal they hold for themselves. In this view, psychological disorders result from the inability to find meaning in life and from feelings of loneliness and a lack of connection to others (Cain, 2002).

Humanistic approaches have produced many therapeutic techniques. Among the most important is person-centred therapy.

Person-Centred Therapy Consider the following therapy session excerpt:

ALICE: I was thinking about this business of standards. I somehow developed a sort of a knack, I guess, of—well—habit—of trying to make people feel at ease around me, or to make things go along smoothly . . .

THERAPIST: In other words, what you did was always in the direction of trying to keep things smooth and to make other people feel better and to smooth the situation.

ALICE: Yes. I think that's what it was. Now the reason why I did it probably was—I mean, not that I was a good little Samaritan going around making other people happy, but that was probably the role that felt easiest for me to play . . .

THERAPIST: You feel that for a long time you've been playing the role of kind of smoothing out the frictions or differences or whatnot . . .

ALICE: M-hm.

THERAPIST: Rather than having any opinion or reaction of your own in the situation. Is that it? (Rogers, 1951, pp. 152–153)

The therapist does not interpret or answer the questions the client has raised. Instead, the therapist clarifies or reflects what the client has said (for example, "In other words, what you did . . ."; "You feel that . . ."; "Is that it?"). This therapeutic technique, known as *non-directive counselling*, is at the heart of person-centred therapy, which was first practiced by Carl Rogers in the mid-twentieth century (Raskin & Rogers, 1989; Rogers, 1951).

Person-centred therapy (also called *client-centred therapy*) aims to enable people to reach their potential for self-actualization. By providing a warm and accepting environment, therapists hope to motivate clients to air their problems and feelings. In turn, this enables clients to make realistic and constructive choices and decisions about the things that bother them in their current lives (Bohart, 2006; Bozarth, Zimring, & Tausch, 2002; Kirschenbaum, 2004).

person-centred therapy Therapy in which the goal is to reach one's potential for self-actualization.

interpersonal therapy (IPT) Short-term therapy that focuses on the context of current social relationships.

Instead of directing the choices clients make, therapists provide what Rogers calls *unconditional positive regard*—expressing acceptance and understanding, regardless of the feelings and attitudes the client expresses. By providing this support, therapists hope to create an atmosphere that enables clients to come to decisions that can improve their lives (Kirschenbaum & Jourdan, 2005; Vieira & Freire, 2006). We discussed this concept in the chapter on personality as part of the humanistic approach to personality development.

Furnishing unconditional positive regard does not mean that therapists must approve of everything their clients say or do. But they do need to communicate that they are caring and *empathetic*—understanding of a client's emotional experiences (Fearing & Clark, 2000).

Study tip To better remember the concept of unconditional positive regard, try offering it to a friend during a conversation by showing your support, acceptance, and understanding no matter what thought or attitude is being offered.

Person-centred therapy is rarely used today in its purest form. Contemporary approaches tend to be somewhat more directive, with therapists nudging clients toward insights rather than merely reflecting their statements. However, therapists still view clients' insights as central to the therapeutic process (Presbury, McKee, & Echterling, 2007; Raskin & Rogers, 1989; Tudor, 2008).

Evaluating Humanistic Therapies The idea that psychological disorders result from restricted growth potential appeals philosophically to many people (Rice & Greenberg, 1992; Whitton, 2003). In the supportive atmosphere that humanistic therapists create, clients can discover solutions to difficult psychological problems.

However, humanistic treatments lack specificity, a problem that has troubled their critics. Humanistic approaches are not very precise and are probably the least scientifically and theoretically developed type of treatment. Moreover, this form of treatment works best for the same type of highly verbal client who profits most from psychoanalytic treatment.

INTERPERSONAL THERAPY

Interpersonal therapy (IPT) considers therapy in the context of social relationships. Although its roots stem from psychodynamic approaches, interpersonal therapy concentrates more on the here and now with the goal of improving a client's current relationships. It typically focuses on interpersonal issues such as conflicts with others, social skills issues, role transitions (such as divorce), and grief (Weissman, Markowitz, & Klerman, 2007).

Interpersonal therapy is more active and directive than traditional psychodynamic approaches, and sessions are more structured. The approach makes no assumptions about the underlying causes of psychological disorders but focuses on the interpersonal context in which a disorder is developed and maintained. It also tends to be shorter than traditional psychodynamic approaches, typically lasting only 12 to 16 weeks. During those sessions, therapists make concrete suggestions on improving relations with others, offering recommendations and advice.

Because interpersonal therapy is short and structured, researchers have been able to demonstrate its effectiveness more readily than longer-term types of therapy. Evaluations of the approach have shown that interpersonal therapy is especially effective in dealing with depression, anxiety, addictions, and eating disorders (De Mello et al., 2005; Grigoriadis & Ravitz, 2007; Salsman, 2006).

GROUP THERAPY AND FAMILY THERAPY

Although most treatment takes place between a single individual and a therapist, some forms of therapy involve groups of people seeking treatment. In **group therapy**, several unrelated people meet with a therapist to discuss some aspect of their psychological functioning.

Within the group people typically discuss their problems, which often centre on a common difficulty, such as alcoholism or a lack of social skills. The other members of the group provide emotional support and dispense advice on ways in which they have coped effectively with similar problems (Alonso, Alonso, & Piper, 2003; Rigby & Waite, 2007; Scaturo, 2004).

Groups vary greatly in terms of the particular model they employ; there are psychoanalytic groups, humanistic groups, and groups corresponding to the other therapeutic approaches. Furthermore, groups also differ in regard to the degree of guidance the therapist provides. In some, the therapist is quite directive, whereas in others, the members of the group set their own agenda and determine how the group will proceed (Beck & Lewis, 2000; Stockton, Morran, & Krieger, 2004).

Because in group therapy several people are treated simultaneously, it is a much more economical means of

In group therapy, people with psychological problems meet with a therapist to talk about their problems.

treatment than individual psychotherapy. However, critics argue that group settings lack the individual attention inherent in one-to-one therapy and that especially shy and withdrawn individuals may not receive the attention they need in a group setting (Olivares-Olivares, Rosa-Alcazar, & Olivares-Rodriguez, 2008; Takahashi & Washington, 1991).

Family Therapy One specialized form of group therapy is family therapy. As the name implies, **family therapy** involves two or more family members, one (or more) of whose problems led to treatment. But rather than focusing simply on the members of the family who present the initial problem, family therapists consider the family as a unit, to which each member contributes. By meeting with the entire family simultaneously, family therapists try to understand how the family members interact with one another (Cooklin, 2000; Strong & Tomm, 2007).

Many family therapists believe that family members fall into rigid roles or set patterns of behaviour, with one person acting as the scapegoat, another as a bully, and so forth. In their view, that system of roles perpetuates family disturbances. One goal of this type of therapy, then, is to get the family members to adopt new, more constructive roles and patterns of behaviour (Minuchin, 1999; Sori, 2006; Sprenkle & Moon, 1996).

EVALUATING PSYCHOTHERAPY

Is therapy effective? This question requires a complex response. Identifying the most appropriate form of treatment is a controversial, and still unresolved, task for mental health professionals. Even before considering whether one form of therapy works better than another, we need to determine whether therapy in *any* form effectively alleviates psychological disturbances.

"So, would anyone in the group care to respond to what Clifford has just shared with us?

© The New Yorker Collection 2005 Tom Cheney from cartoonbank.com. All Rights Reserved.

group therapy Therapy in which an unrelated group of people meet with a therapist to discuss problems.

family therapy An approach to therapy that focuses on the family and its dynamics.

Until the 1950s, most people simply assumed that therapy was effective. But in 1952, psychologist Hans Eysenck published an influential study in which he concluded that people would go into **spontaneous remission**, recovery without treatment, if they were simply left alone. Eysenck's review stimulated a continuing stream of better controlled, more carefully crafted studies on the effectiveness of psychotherapy, and today most psychologists agree: therapy works (Fraser & Solovey, 2007). Several comprehensive reviews indicate that therapy brings about greater improvement than does no treatment at all, with the rate of spontaneous remission being fairly low (for example, Carr, 2009; Corcoran & Pillai, 2009; de Maat et al., 2009; Moore et al., 2009; Venning et al., 2009). In most cases, then, the symptoms of abnormal behaviour do not go away by themselves if left untreated—although the issue continues to be hotly debated (Lutz et al., 2006; Seligman, 1996; Westen, Novotny, & Thompson-Brenner, 2004).

Other research, relying on *meta-analysis*, in which data from a large number of studies are statistically combined, yields similar general conclusions. Furthermore, a massive survey of 186,000 individuals found that respondents felt they had benefited substantially from psychotherapy. However, there was little difference in "consumer satisfaction" on the basis of the specific type of treatment they had received (*Consumer Reports*, 1995; Malouff, Thorsteinsson, & Schutte, 2007; Nielsen et al., 2004; Seligman, 1995; Strupp, 1996).

In short, converging evidence allows us to draw several conclusions about the effectiveness of psychotherapy (Pachankis & Goldfried, 2007; Seligman, 1996; Strupp & Binder, 1992):

- *For most people, psychotherapy is effective.* This conclusion holds over different lengths of treatment, specific kinds of psychological disorders, and various types of treatment. Thus, the question "Does psychotherapy work?" appears to have been answered convincingly: it does (Seligman, 1996; Spiegel, 1999; Westen, Novotny, & Thompson-Brenner, 2004).

- *However, psychotherapy doesn't work for everyone.* As many as 10% of people treated show no improvement or deteriorate (Boisvert & Faust, 2003; Coffman et al., 2007; Lilienfeld, 2007; Pretzer & Beck, 2005).

- *No single form of therapy works best for every problem, and certain specific types of treatment are better, although not invariably, for specific types of problems.* For example, cognitive therapy works especially well for panic disorders, and exposure therapy relieves specific phobias effectively. However, there are exceptions to

spontaneous remission Recovery without treatment.

Figure 12.11
Reasons Canadians Stopped Going to Psychotherapy

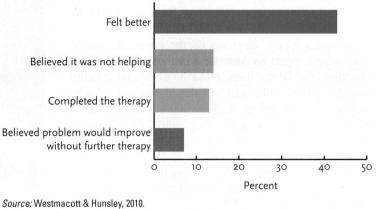

Source: Westmacott & Hunsley, 2010.

these generalizations, and often the differences in success rates for different types of treatment are not substantial (Miller & Magruder, 1999; Westen, Novotny, & Thompson-Brenner, 2004).

- *Most therapies share several basic similar elements.* Despite the fact that the specific methods used in different therapies are very different from one another, there are several common themes that lead them to be effective. These elements include the opportunity for a client to develop a positive relationship with a therapist; an explanation or interpretation of a client's symptoms; and confrontation of negative emotions. The fact that these common elements exist in most therapies makes it difficult to compare one treatment with another (Norcross, 2002; Norcross, Beutler & Levant, 2006).

Because no single type of psychotherapy is invariably effective for every individual, some therapists use an eclectic approach to therapy. As mentioned earlier in the chapter, in this approach therapists use a variety of techniques, integrating several perspectives, to treat a person's problems. By employing more than one approach, therapists can choose the appropriate mix of treatments to match the specific needs of the individual. Furthermore, therapists with certain personal characteristics may work better with particular individuals and types of treatments, and racial and ethnic factors may also be related to the success of treatment (Chambless et al., 2006; Cheston, 2002).

People's environmental and cultural backgrounds are important considerations during treatment for psychological disorders. In particular, members of racial and ethnic minority groups, especially those who are also poor, may behave in ways that help them deal with a society that discriminates against them. As a consequence, behaviour that may signal psychological disorders in middle- and upper-class whites may simply be adaptive in people from other racial and socio-economic groups. For instance, characteristically suspicious and distrustful people may be displaying a survival strategy to protect them from psychological and physical injury, rather than suffering from a psychological disturbance (Paniagua, 2000; Pottick et al., 2007; Tseng, 2003).

In fact, therapists must question some basic assumptions of psychotherapy when dealing with clients who are from a different racial and/or ethnic background than the therapist. For example, Asian and Latino cultures typically place much greater emphasis on the group, the family, and society. When an Asian or a Latino/a faces a critical decision, the family helps make it—a cultural practice suggesting that family members should also play a role in psychological treatment (Leitner, 2007; McCarthy, 2005; Ponterotto, Gretchen, & Chauhan, 2001). Clearly, therapists *cannot* be "colour-blind." Instead, they must take into account the racial, ethnic, cultural, and social class backgrounds of their clients in determining the nature of a psychological disorder and the course of treatment (Aponte & Wohl, 2000; Pedersen et al., 2002).

Community Psychology The approaches to treatments discussed so far have a common element: They are "restorative," aimed at alleviating psychological difficulties that already exist. Unlike those approaches, **community psychology** aims to prevent or minimize the incidence of psychological disorders.

Community psychology came of age in Canada in the 1970s, when university-based community psychology programmes were developed. The community psychology approach in Canada focused on values and ethics, community mental health, health promotion and prevention, social network intervention and mutual aid, promotion of inclusion and diversity, and social intervention and community economic development (Nelson, Lavoie, & Mitchell, 2007).

> Unlike other approaches, community psychology aims to prevent or minimize the incidence of psychological disorders.

In another development, the population of mental hospitals plunged as drug treatments made physical restraint unnecessary (Dixon & Goldman, 2003). This resulted in the transfer of former mental patients out of institutions and into the community—a process known as **deinstitutionalization**. It was encouraged by the growth of the community psychology movement. Proponents of deinstitutionalization wanted to ensure not only that deinstitutionalized individuals received proper treatment but also that their rights were maintained (St. Dennis et al., 2006; Wolff, 2002).

Unfortunately, the promise of deinstitutionalization has not been met, largely because insufficient resources are

While deinstitutionalization has had many successes, it has also contributed to the release of mental patients into the community with little or no support. As a result, many have become homeless.

provided to deinstitutionalized clients. What started as a worthy attempt to move people out of mental institutions and into the community ended, in many cases, with former patients being dumped into the community without any real support. Many became homeless—between a third and a half of all homeless adults are thought to have a major psychological disorder—and some became involved in illegal acts caused by their disorders. In short, many people who need treatment do not get it, and in some cases care for people with psychological disorders has simply shifted from one type of treatment site to another (Doyle, 2002; Lamb & Weinberger, 2005; Shinn et al., 2007).

However, the community psychology movement has had some positive outcomes. Telephone "hot lines" are now

community psychology A branch of psychology that focuses on the prevention and minimization of psychological disorders in the community.

deinstitutionalization The transfer of former mental patients from institutions to the community.

Get Involved!

You can gain valuable training and experience in the mental health field by volunteering to work at a suicide or crisis hotline. Many colleges and universities have offices and Web sites listing diverse volunteer opportunities for students within their communities.

common. At any time of the day or night, people experiencing acute stress can call a trained, sympathetic listener who can provide immediate—although obviously limited—treatment (Cauce, 2007; Paukert, Stagner, & Hope, 2004; Reese, Conoley, & Brossart, 2002).

College and high school crisis centres are another innovation that grew out of the community psychology movement. Modelled after suicide prevention hotline centres (services that enable potential suicide victims to call and speak to someone about their difficulties), crisis centres give callers an opportunity to discuss life crises with a sympathetic listener, who is often a volunteer.

DECIDING WHEN YOU NEED HELP

How do you know when you or someone you know needs the help of a mental health professional? The following list of symptoms offers a rough set of guidelines for determining when the normal problems of everyday living have escalated beyond your ability to deal with them by yourself (Engler & Goleman, 1992):

- Long-term feelings of distress that interfere with your sense of well-being, competence, and ability to function effectively in daily activities

- Occasions in which you experience overwhelmingly high stress, accompanied by feelings of inability to cope with the situation

- Prolonged depression or feelings of hopelessness, especially when they do not have any clear cause (such as the death of someone close)

- Withdrawal from other people

- Thoughts of inflicting harm on oneself or suicide

- A fear or phobia that prevents you from engaging in everyday activities

- Inability to interact effectively with others, preventing the development of friendships and loving relationships

If you decide to seek therapy, you're faced with a daunting task. Choosing a therapist is not a simple matter. One place to begin the process of identifying a therapist is at the "Finding the Psychologist for You" page of the Canadian Psychological Association (CPA) at www.cpa.ca/public/findingapsychologist.

You may also want to visit the Canadian Mental Health Association (CMHA) at www.cmha.ca to learn more about mental illnesses and what to do if you would like help from a CMHA branch near you.

For Review ››

How is abnormal behaviour defined and classified?

Psychologists broadly define behaviour as abnormal if it causes people to experience distress and prevents them from functioning in their daily lives. Part of the classification takes into account whether the behaviour is deviant, maladaptive, and personally distressful. Abnormal behaviour is further classified using the *Diagnostic and Statistical Manual of Mental Disorders*, Fourth Edition, Text Revision (*DSM-IV-TR*). The *DSM-IV-TR* is organized into five axes (dimensions), which take into account the specific disorders (Axis I and II) as well as any general medical conditions (Axis III) or psychosocial and environmental problems (Axis IV) that may contribute to or have implications for the disorder. The final axis (Axis V) takes into account the individual's current level of social, occupational, or educational functioning.

What theories do psychologists use to explain psychological disorders?

The medical perspective views abnormality as a symptom of an underlying disease. Psychoanalytic perspectives suggest that abnormal behaviour stems from childhood conflicts in the unconscious. Behavioural approaches view abnormal behaviour not as a symptom of an underlying problem but as the problem itself. The cognitive approach suggests that abnormal behaviour is the result of faulty cognitions (thoughts and beliefs). In this view, abnormal behaviour can be remedied by changing one's flawed thoughts and beliefs.

What are the major categories of psychological disorders?

Anxiety disorders are present when a person experiences so much anxiety that it affects daily functioning. Mood disorders are characterized by emotional states of depression or euphoria so strong that they intrude on everyday living. Schizophrenia is one of the more severe forms of mental illness. Symptoms of schizophrenia include declines in functioning, thought and language disturbances, perceptual disorders, emotional disturbance, and withdrawal from others. People with personality disorders experience little or no personal distress, but they do suffer from an inability to function as normal members of society. These disorders include anti-social personality disorder, borderline personality disorder, and narcissistic personality disorder.

How can we tell when it's time to get professional help for ourselves or someone else?

The signals that indicate a need for professional help include long-term feelings of psychological distress, feelings of inability to cope with stress, withdrawal from other people, thoughts of inflicting harm on oneself or suicide, prolonged feelings of hopelessness, chronic physical problems with no apparent causes, phobias and compulsions, paranoia, and an inability to interact with others.

What types of treatment approaches are available for psychological disorders?

Drug therapy, the best example of biomedical treatment, can dramatically reduce the symptoms of mental disturbance. Antipsychotic drugs effectively reduce psychotic symptoms. Antidepressant drugs reduce depression so successfully that they are used widely. Antianxiety drugs, or minor tranquilizers, are among the most frequently prescribed medications of any sort. Non-drug biomedical treatments include electroconvulsive therapy (ECT), used in severe cases of depression, and psychosurgery, which typically consists of surgically destroying or removing certain parts of the brain.

Psychoanalytic treatment approaches seek to bring unresolved past conflicts and unacceptable impulses from the unconscious into the conscious, where clients may deal with the problems more effectively. Behavioural approaches to treatment view abnormal behaviour as the problem, rather than as a symptom of some underlying cause. This view suggests that the outward behaviour must be changed by means of aversive conditioning, systematic desensitization, observational learning, or other behavioural therapy. Cognitive treatment approaches consider the goal of therapy to be helping a person restructure a faulty belief system into a more realistic, rational, and logical view of the world. Humanistic therapy is based on the premise that people have control of their behaviour, that they can make choices about their lives, and that it is up to them to solve their problems. Interpersonal therapy focuses on interpersonal relationships and strives for immediate improvement during short-term therapy.

Psych _think_ answers

Psych think 1 In the PSYCH think on p. 307 we asked you how you define abnormal behaviour, and to discuss the pros and cons of having a classification system such as the *DSM-IV-TR*. Defining abnormal behaviour according to the text definition is not difficult, it simply says that it is behaviour that causes people to experience distress and prevents them from functioning in their daily lives. But when you think about this definition, it does not really provide all of the needed information because there are likely days where you have experienced distress and were not able to function in your daily life. Does that mean you were displaying "abnormal behaviour"? It doesn't seem that way. Many people have distress and are not able to function, but they are not abnormal. The *DSM-IV-TR* helps with the definition because it offers specific symptoms and criteria for timelines that must be met before a diagnosis can be made. The *DSM-IV-TR* allows for a common language among clinicians and allows diagnosis so that treatment plans can be put in place. Those are the pros—however, there are some downsides. When someone is labelled with a particular disorder they may experience a stigma associated with the disorder, which prevents them from having some educational or work opportunities. They also may start to have a self-fulfilling prophecy, where their behaviour matches their diagnosis, preventing them from improving. Finally, the *DSM-IV-TR* takes an "all-or-nothing" approach where people are classified or

they are not. It does not take into account the continuum of abnormal behaviour, such as those times when you experience distress and are not able to function, but in a day or so, you are ok.

Psych think 2 In the PSYCH think on p. 309 we asked you if someone is afraid to leave their house because they have an intense fear of the bugs that might be outside, do they suffer from agoraphobia with panic attacks, a specific phobia of the animal type, or social phobia. The answer is a specific phobia of the animal type, which of course would be the bugs the person is so afraid of. People who suffer from agoraphobia have a fear of something dreadful happening that they will not be able to escape from. This is often (but not always) paired with panic attacks, which are intense feelings of panic associated with their fears. Social phobia, on the other hand, is a fear of embarrassing oneself while out in public. People with social phobias often avoid being in situations where they might be observed or where they will be the centre of attention (such as public speaking).

Psych think 3 In the PSYCH think on p. 315 we asked you to diagnosis Morgan. If you said you would give the diagnosis of paranoid schizophrenia, you are correct! Morgan displayed paranoid behaviour (people wanted to steal his bike and his belongings in his residence room), hallucinations (people in the bush), and delusions (he thought his parents would lock him up in the basement.

Psych think 4 In the PSYCH think on p. 329, we asked you to take on the role of a psychiatrist. We told you about your patient Rose and asked if you would recommend that she find another job. As her doctor, your first course of action would be to see if Rose is able to overcome her fears before turning down the job. Anxiety disorders can be treated in a number of ways so you must consider each of these. You may decide to start with the biomedical approach and prescribe Rose an anti-anxiety medication such as one of the benzodiazepines Xanax or Valium, but knowing that anti-anxiety medication can be habit forming you decide to also take a behavioural approach and use systematic desensitization and virtual reality therapy. During your systematic desensitization sessions you first have Rose learn some relaxation techniques. You then systematically have Rose imagine being in the elevator while in a relaxed state. After these sessions, Rose will take part in virtual reality therapy, where she will be in a virtual elevator while remaining in a relaxed state. She will soon start to associate the elevator and higher floors with the relaxed state. After several sessions, it is evident that with medication and behavioural therapy, Rose is able to take her dream job!

13

Health Psychology:
Stress, Coping, and Well-Being

School daze

Louisa Denby's day began badly: She slept through her alarm and had to skip breakfast to catch the bus to campus. Then, when she went to the library to catch up on the reading she had to do before taking a test the next day, the one article she needed was missing. The librarian told her that replacing it would take 24 hours. Feeling frustrated, she walked to the computer lab to print out the paper she had completed at home the night before.

The computer wouldn't read her flash drive. She searched for someone to help her, but she was unable to find anyone who knew any more about computers than she did.

It was only 9:42 a.m., and Louisa had a wracking headache. Apart from that pain, she was conscious of only one feeling: stress.

Have you had days like Louisa's? Are most of your days like hers? Then you're no stranger to stress. It's something that all students experience to varying degrees.

Stress and how we cope with it have long been central topics of interest for psychologists. In recent years, however, the focus has broadened as psychology has come to view stress in the broader context of one of psychology's newer subfields: health psychology. In the pages that follow, we discuss the ways in which psychological factors affect health. We first focus on the causes and consequences of stress, as well as on the means of coping with it. Next, we explore the psychological aspects of several major health problems, including heart disease, cancer, and ailments resulting from smoking. Finally, we examine the ways in which patient–physician interactions influence our health and offer suggestions for increasing people's compliance with recommendations about behaviour that will improve their well-being.

Yoga is a popular approach to managing the stresses of everyday life.

As You **Read** >>

- How is health psychology a union between medicine and psychology?
- What is stress, how does it affect us, and how can we best cope with it?
- How can our attitudes and beliefs affect health-related problems such as coronary heart disease, cancer, and smoking?
- How can you promote health and wellness in your life?
- How does a sense of well-being develop?

Health psychology investigates the psychological factors related to wellness and illness, including the prevention, diagnosis, and treatment of medical problems. Health psychologists investigate the effects of psychological factors such as stress on illness. They examine the psychological principles underlying treatments for disease and illness. They also study prevention: how more healthful behaviour can help people avoid and reduce health problems such as stress and heart disease.

Health psychologists recognize that good health and the ability to cope with illness are affected by psychological factors such as thoughts, emotions, and the ability to manage stress. They have paid particular attention to the *immune system*, the complex of organs, glands, and cells that constitute our bodies' natural line of defence in fighting disease.

In fact, health psychologists are among the primary investigators in a growing field called **psychoneuroimmunology**, or **PNI**, the study of the relationship among psychological factors, the immune system, and the brain. PNI has led to discoveries such as the existence of an association between a person's emotional state and how well the immune system fights disease (Dickerson et al., 2004; Kemeny, 2007).

health psychology The branch of psychology that investigates the psychological factors related to wellness and illness, including the prevention, diagnosis, and treatment of medical problems.

psychoneuroimmunology (PNI) The study of the relationship among psychological factors, the immune system, and the brain.

stress A person's response to events that are threatening or challenging.

Stress and Coping

Most of us need little introduction to the phenomenon of **stress**, people's response to events that threaten or challenge them. Whether it is a paper or an exam deadline, a family problem, or even the ongoing threat of a terrorist attack, life is full of circumstances and events that threaten our well-being. Even pleasant events—such as planning a party or beginning a sought-after job—can produce stress, although negative events often result in greater detrimental consequences than do positive ones.

All of us face stress. Some health psychologists believe that daily life actually involves a series of repeated sequences of perceiving a threat, considering ways to cope with it, and ultimately adapting to the threat, with greater or lesser success. Although adaptation is often minor and occurs without our awareness, adaptation requires a major effort when stress is more severe or longer lasting. Our attempts to overcome extreme or continuing stress may produce biological and psychological responses that result in health problems (Boyce & Ellis, 2005; Dolbier, Smith, & Steinhardt, 2007).

DID YOU **KNOW?**

High maternal stress during pregnancy may increase the chances of the child having schizophrenia later in life.

THE NATURE OF STRESSORS: MY STRESS IS YOUR PLEASURE

Stress is a personal thing. Although certain kinds of events, such as the death of a loved one or participation in military combat, are universally stressful, other situations may or may not be stressful to a specific person.

A person's interpretation of events plays an important role in determining what is stressful. This is called cognitive appraisal.

Consider, for instance, bungee jumping. Some people would find jumping off a bridge while attached to a slender rubber tether extremely stressful. However, there are individuals who see such an activity as challenging and fun-filled. Whether bungee jumping is stressful depends in part, then, on a person's perception of the activity.

For people to consider an event stressful, they must perceive it as threatening or challenging and must not have access to all of the resources needed to deal with it effectively. Consequently, the same event may at some times be stressful and at other times provoke no stressful reaction at all. A young man may experience stress when he is turned down for a date—if he attributes the refusal to his unattractiveness or unworthiness. But if he attributes it to some factor unrelated to his self-esteem, such as a previous commitment by the person he asked, the experience of being refused may create no stress at all. Hence, a person's interpretation of events plays an important role in determining what is stressful (Folkman & Moskowitz, 2000; Friborg et al., 2007; Giacobbi, et al., 2004).

Even positive events can produce significant stress.

Categorizing Stressors What kinds of events tend to be seen as stressful? There are three general types of stressors: cataclysmic events, personal stressors, and daily hassles.

Cataclysmic events are strong stressors that occur suddenly and typically affect many people simultaneously. Disasters such as tornadoes, major floods, plane crashes, and terrorist attacks are examples of cataclysmic events that can affect hundreds or thousands of people simultaneously.

Although it might seem that cataclysmic events would produce potent, lingering stress, in many cases they do not. In fact, cataclysmic events involving natural disasters may produce less stress in the long run than do events that initially are not as devastating. One reason is that natural disasters have a clear resolution. Once they are over, people can look to the future knowing that the worst is behind them. Moreover, the stress induced by cataclysmic events is shared by others who also experienced the disaster. Such sharing permits people to offer one another social support and a first-hand understanding of the difficulties that others are going through (Benight, 2004; Hobfoll et al., 1996; Yesilyaprak, Kisac, & Sanlier, 2007).

Some victims of major catastrophes and severe personal stressors experience *post-traumatic stress disorder*, or *PTSD*, in which a person has experienced a significantly stressful event that has long-lasting effects that may include re-experiencing the event in vivid flashbacks or dreams. An episode of PTSD may be triggered by an otherwise innocent stimulus, such as the sound of a honking horn that leads someone to re-experience a past event that produced considerable stress (Paris, 2000).

Symptoms of post-traumatic stress disorder also include emotional numbing, sleep difficulties, interpersonal problems, alcohol and drug abuse, and—in some cases—suicide. PTSD tends to be slightly higher in Canadian military personal (10.3%) than in the general Canadian population (9.2%). This is similar to, but slightly lower than American data, which found that approximately 16% of soldiers returning from Iraq show symptoms of PTSD (Dohrenwend et al., 2006; McKeever & Huff, 2003; Pole, 2007; Van Ameringen et al., 2008).

The second major category of stressor is the personal stressor. **Personal stressors** include such major life events as the death of a parent or spouse, the loss of one's job, a major personal failure, or even something positive such as getting married. Typically, personal stressors produce an immediate major reaction that soon tapers off. For example, stress arising from the death of a loved one tends to be greatest just after the time of death, but people begin to feel less stress and are better able to cope with the loss over time (Compas & Wagner, 1991).

Daily hassles are the third major category of stressors. Exemplified by standing in a long line at a bank and getting stuck in a traffic jam, daily hassles are the minor irritations of life that most of us face time and time again. Another type of background stressor is a long-term, chronic problem, such as experiencing dissatisfaction with school or a job, being in an unhappy relationship, or living in crowded quarters without privacy (Lazarus, 2000; Weinstein et al., 2004). Louisa Denby, the student described in the opening vignette, had many daily hassles that would contribute to her level of stress. Sleeping through the alarm,

cataclysmic events Strong stressors that occur suddenly, affecting many people at once (for example, natural disasters).

personal stressors Major life events, such as the death of a family member, that have immediate negative consequences that generally fade with time.

daily hassles Everyday annoyances, such as being stuck in traffic, that cause minor irritations and may have long-term ill effects if they continue or are compounded by other stressful events.

missing breakfast, and having the computer crash can be very stressful!

By themselves, daily hassles do not require much coping or even a response on the part of the individual, although they certainly produce unpleasant emotions and moods. Yet they add up—and ultimately they may take as great a toll as a single, more stressful incident does. In fact, the *number* of daily hassles people face is positively correlated with psychological symptoms and health problems such as flu, sore throat, and backaches.

The flip side of hassles is *uplifts*, the minor positive events that make us feel good—even if only temporarily. Uplifts range from relating well to a companion to finding one's surroundings pleasing. What is especially intriguing about uplifts is that they are negatively correlated with people's psychological health: The greater the number of uplifts we experience, the fewer the psychological symptoms we report (Chamberlain & Zika, 1990; Jain, Mills, & Von Känel, 2007; Ravindran et al., 2002).

The High Cost of Stress Stress can produce both biological and psychological consequences. Often the most immediate reaction to stress is a biological one. Exposure to stressors generates a rise in hormone secretions by the adrenal glands, an increase in heart rate and blood pressure, and changes in how well the skin conducts electrical impulses.

Everyone confronts daily hassles such as heavy traffic. At what point do daily hassles become more than mere irritants?

On a short-term basis, these responses may be adaptive, because they produce an "emergency reaction" in which the body prepares to defend itself through activation of the sympathetic nervous system. Those responses may allow more effective coping with the stressful situation (Akil & Morano, 1996; McEwen, 1998).

However, continued exposure to stress results in a decline in the body's overall level of biological functioning

Psych think

> > > Which of the three kinds of stressors can be most negative? How can uplifts help with this?

Figure 13.1
Common Daily Hassles and Uplifts

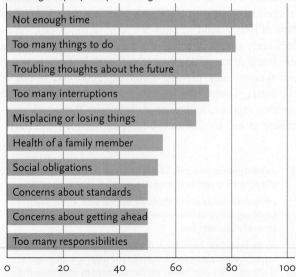

Hassles
Percentage of people experiencing

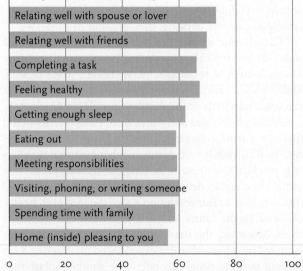

Uplifts
Percentage of people experiencing

Sources: (left) Chamberlain & Zika, 1990; (right) Kanner et al., 1981.

psychophysiological disorders Medical problems influenced by an interaction of psychological, emotional, and physical difficulties.

general adaptation syndrome (GAS) A theory developed by Selye that suggests that a person's response to a stressor consists of three stages: alarm and mobilization, resistance, and exhaustion.

because of the constant secretion of stress-related hormones. Over time, stressful reactions can promote deterioration of body tissues such as blood vessels and the heart. Ultimately, we become more susceptible to disease as our ability to fight off infection is lowered (Brydon et al., 2004; Dean-Borenstein, 2007; Kemeny, 2003).

Furthermore, an entire class of physical problems known as **psychophysiological disorders** often result from or are worsened by stress (Siegel, R., 2005). Once referred to as *psychosomatic disorders* (a term dropped because people assumed that the disorders were somehow unreal), psychophysiological disorders are actual medical problems that are influenced by an interaction of psychological, emotional, and physical difficulties (Siegel & Davis, 2008). The more common psychophysiological disorders range from such major problems as high blood pressure to usually less-serious conditions, such as headaches, backaches, skin rashes, indigestion, fatigue, and constipation. Stress has even been positively correlated with the common cold (Andrasik, 2006; Cohen et al., 2003).

On a psychological level, high levels of stress prevent people from adequately coping with life. Their view of the environment can become clouded (for example, a minor criticism made by a friend is blown out of proportion). Moreover, at the highest levels of stress, emotional responses may be so extreme that people are unable to act at all. People under a lot of stress also become less able to deal with new stressors.

The negative effects of stress have also been observed in children. Hanson and Chen (2010) from the University of British Columbia found that children who experienced daily stressors had higher levels of cortisol and more difficulties with sleep.

In short, stress affects us in multiple ways. It may increase the risk that we will become ill, it may directly cause illness, it may make us less able to recover from a disease, and it may reduce our ability to cope with future stress (Gurunjj & Roethel-Wendorf, 2009).

DID YOU KNOW?

It's no surprise that the top 20 most stressful occupations include police, firefighters, and airline pilots. But did you know that the list also includes unexpected occupations, such as actors, musicians, and assembly line workers?

The General Adaptation Syndrome Model The effects of long-term stress are illustrated in a series of stages proposed by Hans Selye (pronounced "ZELL-yay"), a pioneering stress theorist who conducted much of his research at McGill University and the Université de Montréal (Selye, 1976, 1993). This model, the **general adaptation syndrome (GAS)**, suggests that the physiological response to stress follows the same set pattern regardless of the cause of stress.

The GAS has three phases. The first stage—*alarm and mobilization*—occurs when people become aware of the presence of a stressor. On a biological level, the sympathetic nervous system becomes energized, helping a person cope initially with the stressor.

However, if the stressor persists, people move into the second response stage: *resistance*. During this stage, the body prepares to fight the stressor. During resistance, people use a variety of means to cope with the stressor—sometimes

Figure 13.2
Selye's General Adaptation Syndrome (GAS)

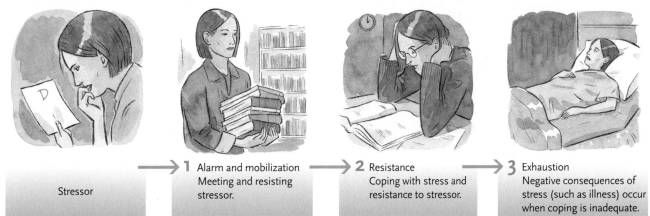

Stressor

1 Alarm and mobilization
Meeting and resisting stressor.

2 Resistance
Coping with stress and resistance to stressor.

3 Exhaustion
Negative consequences of stress (such as illness) occur when coping is inadequate.

Source: Selye, 1976.

successfully but at a cost of some degree of physical or psychological well-being. For example, a student who faces the stress of failing several courses might spend long hours studying, seeking to cope with the stress.

If the coping strategies used in the resistance phase are not enough to resolve the stressor, people enter the last stage of the GAS: *exhaustion*. During the exhaustion stage, a person's ability to adapt to the stressor declines to the point where negative consequences of stress appear: physical illness and psychological symptoms in the form of an inability to concentrate, heightened irritability, or, in severe cases, disorientation and a loss of touch with reality. In a sense, people wear out, and their physical reserves are used up. For example, when people experience a major cataclysmic event such as a major flood to their community, people may respond initially with alarm and quickly move into resistance. However, their best efforts to cope are unlikely to slow down the water, and they will eventually become exhausted.

How do people move out of the exhaustion stage after they have entered it? In some cases, exhaustion allows people to avoid a stressor. For example, people who become ill from overwork may be excused from their duties for a time, giving them a temporary respite from their responsibilities. At least for a time, then, the immediate stress is reduced.

Although the GAS has had a substantial impact on our understanding of stress, Selye's theory has not gone unchallenged. For example, whereas the theory suggests that regardless of the stressor, the biological reaction is similar, some health psychologists disagree. They believe that people's biological responses are specific to the way they appraise a stressful event, something we will discuss more throughout the chapter. If a stressor is seen as unpleasant but not unusual, then the biological response may be different from that if the stressor is seen as unpleasant, out of the ordinary, and unanticipated. This perspective has led to an increased focus on psychoneuroimmunology (Gaab, et al., 2005; Taylor et al., 2000).

Psychoneuroimmunology and Stress Contemporary health psychologists specializing in PNI focus on the outcomes of stress, and have identified three main consequences. First, stress has direct physiological results, including an increase in blood pressure, an increase in hormonal

Source: Cohen, Kamark, and Mermelstein, 1983.

How Stressful Is Your Life?

Test your level of stress by answering these questions and adding up your score. Questions apply to the previous month only. The key below will help you determine the extent of your stress.

0 = never; 1 = almost never; 2 = sometimes; 3 = fairly often; 4 = very often

When you score questions 4, 5, 6, and 8, you must reverse the scores. For those questions, 4 = never, 3 = almost never, 2 = sometimes, 1 = fairly often, 0 = very often

_____ 1. How often have you been upset because of something that happened unexpectedly?
_____ 2. How often have you felt that you were unable to control the important things in your life?
_____ 3. How often have you felt nervous and "stressed"?
_____ 4. How often have you felt confident about your ability to handle your personal problems?
_____ 5. How often have you felt that things were going your way?
_____ 6. How often have you been able to control irritations in your life?
_____ 7. How often have you found that you could not cope with all the things that you had to do?
_____ 8. How often have you felt that you were on top of things?
_____ 9. How often have you been angered because of things that were outside your control?
_____ 10. How often have you felt difficulties were piling up so high that you could not overcome them?

How You Measure Up

Stress levels vary among individuals—compare your total score to the averages below:

Age		Marital Status	
18–29	14.2	Widowed	12.6
30–44	13.0	Married or living with a partner	12.4
45–54	12.6	Single or never wed	14.1
55–64	11.9	Divorced	14.7
65 and over	12.0	Separated	16.6
Gender			
Men	12.1		
Women	13.7		

Figure 13.3
Major Consequences of Stress

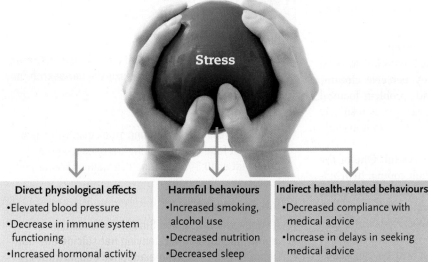

Stress		
Direct physiological effects	**Harmful behaviours**	**Indirect health-related behaviours**
•Elevated blood pressure	•Increased smoking, alcohol use	•Decreased compliance with medical advice
•Decrease in immune system functioning	•Decreased nutrition	•Increase in delays in seeking medical advice
•Increased hormonal activity	•Decreased sleep	•Decrease in likelihood of seeking medical advice
•Psychophysiological conditions	•Increased drug use	

Source: Adapted from Baum, 1994.

activity, and an overall decline in the functioning of the immune system. Second, stress leads people to engage in behaviours that are harmful to their health, including increased nicotine, drug, and alcohol use; poor eating habits; and decreased sleep. Finally, stress produces indirect consequences that result in declines in health: a reduction in the likelihood of obtaining health care and decreased compliance with medical advice when it is sought (Broman, 2005; Lindblad, Lindahl, & Theorell, 2006; Sapolsky, 2003).

Why is stress so damaging to the immune system? One reason is that stress may overstimulate the immune system. Rather than fighting invading bacteria, viruses, and other foreign invaders, it may begin to attack the body itself, damaging healthy tissue. When that happens, it can lead to disorders such as arthritis and an allergic reaction. Stress can also decrease the immune system response, permitting viruses that cause colds to reproduce more easily or allowing cancer cells to spread more rapidly (Cohen, Hamrick, & Rodriguez, 2002; Dougall & Baum, 2004; Segerstrom & Miller, 2004).

COPING WITH STRESS

Stress is a normal part of life—and not necessarily a completely bad part. For example, without stress, we might not be sufficiently motivated to complete the activities we need to accomplish. However, it is also clear that too much stress can take a toll on physical and psychological health. How do people deal with stress? Is there a way to reduce its negative effects?

coping The efforts to control, reduce, or learn to tolerate the threats that lead to stress.

cognitive appraisal The way that people interpret or appraise an event that can impact how stressful it appears.

Efforts to control, reduce, or learn to tolerate the threats that lead to stress is known as **coping**. We habitually use certain coping responses to deal with stress. Most of the time, we're not aware of these responses—just as we may be unaware of the minor stressors of life until they build up to harmful levels (Wrzesniewski & Chylinska, 2007).

The way we interpret or appraise an event can impact how stressful it feels for us. This is called **cognitive appraisal**, and can include two main categories (Folkman & Moskowitz, 2000, 2004):

- *Emotion-focused coping.* In emotion-focused coping, people try to manage their emotions in the face of stress, seeking to change the way they feel about or perceive a problem. Examples of emotion-focused coping include strategies such as accepting sympathy from others and looking at the bright side of a situation.

> **Stress can decrease the immune system response, permitting viruses that cause colds to reproduce more easily or allowing cancer cells to spread more rapidly.**

- *Problem-focused coping.* Problem-focused coping attempts to modify the stressful problem or source of stress. Problem-focused strategies lead to changes in behaviour or to the development of a plan of action to deal with stress. Starting a study group to improve

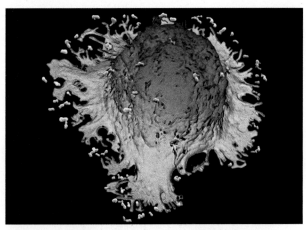

Psychological factors affect the ability to fight off disease. In this highly enlarged view, a cell from the body's immune system engulfs and destroys disease-producing bacteria.

poor classroom performance is an example of problem-focused coping. In addition, one might take a time-out from stress by creating positive events. For example, taking a day off from caring for a relative with a serious, chronic illness to go a health club or spa can bring significant relief from stress.

People often employ several types of coping strategies simultaneously. Furthermore, they use emotion-focused strategies more frequently when they perceive circumstances as being unchangeable and problem-focused approaches more often in situations they see as relatively modifiable (Penley, Tomaka, & Wiebe, 2002; Stanton et al., 2000).

Some forms of coping are less successful. One of the least effective forms of coping is avoidant coping. In *avoidant coping*, a person may use wishful thinking to reduce stress or use more direct escape routes, such as drug use, alcohol use, and overeating. An example of wishful thinking to avoid a test would be to say to oneself, "Maybe it will snow so hard tomorrow that the test will be cancelled." Alternatively, a person might get drunk to avoid a problem. Either way, avoidant coping usually results in a postponement of dealing with a stressful situation, and this often makes the problem even worse (Hutchinson, Baldwin, & Oh, 2006; Roesch et al., 2005).

Effective Coping Strategies How can we deal with the stress in our lives? Effective coping depends on the nature of the stressor and the degree to which it can be controlled, but here are some general guidelines (American Psychological Association, 2007; Aspinwall & Taylor, 1997; Folkman & Moskowitz, 2000):

- *Turn a threat into a challenge.* This type of cognitive appraisal can be very useful. When a stressful situation might be controllable, treat the situation as a challenge, focusing on ways to control it. If your car is always breaking down, you might take a course in auto mechanics and learn to deal directly with the car's problems.

- *Make a threatening situation less threatening.* "Look for the silver lining in every cloud." When a stressful situation seems to be uncontrollable, try changing your appraisal of the situation and modifying your attitude toward it. (Smith & Lazarus, 2001; Cheng & Cheung, 2005).

From the perspective of …

A POLICE OFFICER How would a police officer cope with the stress of the profession?

Psych
At The Movies

Juno

A young, precocious pregnant woman demonstrates high problem-focused coping skills in her search for a good home for her child.

Falling Down

Daily hassles, such as getting stuck in a traffic jam and a fast food restaurant that refuses to serve breakfast at 10:31 a.m., send the main character, Bill Foster, over the edge.

Girl, Interrupted

A young woman named Suzanna spends time at a mental institution after denying her suicide attempt. Denial is a form of the maladaptive coping strategy called avoidance.

Wilby Wonderful

One of the main characters in this quirky Canadian film, a workaholic real estate agent, demonstrates the classic Type A behaviour pattern.

- *Change your goals.* For an uncontrollable situation, adopt new goals that fit the situation. For example, a dancer who has been in an automobile accident and has lost full use of her legs may no longer have a career in dance but might try to become a choreographer instead.

- *Take physical action.* Changing your physiological reaction to stress can help with coping. For example, biofeedback and exercise can be effective in reducing stress (Hamer, Taylor, & Steptoe, 2006; Langreth, 2000).

- *Know yourself.* Understand how you experience stress because we don't all experience it in the same way. Examine how you think and behave in times of stress so you can recognize when you start to feel it. Do you overreact? Do you get more emotional (sad, angry)? Do you eat or drink more? Do you have trouble sleeping?

- *Know the source.* Part of understanding how you experience stress is to know what things are typically stressful for you. Do you worry about money, grades, assignments, family? Knowing will help you predict when you might experience stress.

- *Know how to manage the stress.* Use healthy stress management techniques such as yoga, meditation, exercise, and healthy eating (go to Health Canada's Web site, www.hc-sc.gc.ca, and search for *Canada's Food Guide* to find tips on healthy eating). Having a good network for social support and positive life thoughts can also be helpful.

Taking a course in car repair would be one way to cope with frequent car breakdowns or with the loss of a job in a shrinking company.

- *Know when you need more support.* Friends are great listeners, but sometimes you might need more help than your friends are qualified to offer. If you are feeling too overwhelmed, you may want to consider speaking with a psychologist or counsellor. Most colleges will have counsellors for you to speak to on site.

- *Prepare for stress before it happens.* When possible, practice *proactive coping*, that is, anticipating and preparing for stress. For example, in anticipation of busy test weeks, you can try to arrange your schedule so you have more time to study (Aspinwall & Taylor, 1997; Bode et al., 2007).

Learned Helplessness Have you ever faced an intolerable situation that you just couldn't resolve, and you finally simply gave up and accepted things the way they were? This example illustrates one of the possible consequences of being in an environment in which control over a situation is not possible—a state that produces learned helplessness. This term came from American psychologist Martin Seligman, who observed that dogs who had learned they could not control their escape from pain would later give up trying when placed in other situations where they could escape the pain. **Learned helplessness** occurs when people conclude that unpleasant or aversive stimuli cannot be controlled—a view of the world that becomes so ingrained that they cease trying to remedy the aversive circumstances, even if, at some later point, they actually could exert some influence on the situation (Aujoulat, Luminet, & Deccache, 2007; Seligman, 1975, 2007).

learned helplessness A state in which people conclude that unpleasant or aversive stimuli cannot be controlled—a view of the world that becomes so ingrained that they cease trying to remedy the aversive circumstances, even if they actually can exert some influence.

social support A mutual network of caring, interested others.

Victims of learned helplessness have concluded that there is nothing they can do to change the conditions in their lives that are intolerable. People who perceive that they have little or no control experience more physical symptoms and depression than those who feel a sense of control over a situation (Bjornstad, 2006; Chou, 2005).

Social Support Our relationships with others help us cope with stress. Researchers have found that **social support**, the knowledge that we are part of a mutual network of caring, interested others, enables us to experience lower levels of stress and be better able to cope with the stress we do undergo (Bolger & Amarel, 2007; Cohen, 2004; Martin & Brantley, 2004).

DID YOU KNOW?

Social support from friends and family (in the form of encouraging words, cheering, and so on) could make the difference for a winning performance in sports.

The social and emotional support that people provide one another helps us to deal with stress in several ways. For instance, such support demonstrates that a person is an important and valued member of a social network. Similarly, other people can provide information and advice about appropriate ways of dealing with stress (Day & Livingstone, 2003; Lindorff, 2005).

Finally, people who are part of a social support network can provide actual goods and services to help others in stressful situations. For instance, they can supply temporary living quarters to a person whose house has burned down, or they can offer study help to a student who is experiencing stress because of poor academic performance (Natvig, Albrektsen, & Ovarnstrøm, 2003a, 2003b; Takizawa, Kondo, & Sakihara, 2007).

Get Involved!

Social support helps to buffer stressful events in life, but many people find it difficult to meet others in their area. The Internet has proven to be a valuable resource for many. You can search www.meetup.com by postal code to look for hobby or support groups in your area. You could also use this site to start your own group!

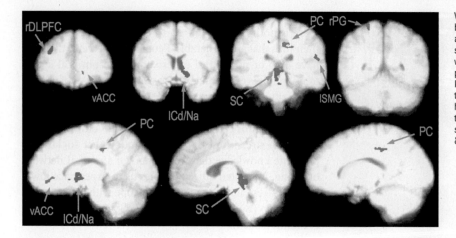

When participants in a study were threatened by being told they would be receiving a shock, activation of the areas of the brain that reflect stress was reduced when social support was provided by having either a stranger or a participant's spouse hold the participant's hand. In this image, green areas highlight brain areas that show reductions in activity with spouse hand-holding; blue clusters highlight brain areas that show reductions in activity with spouse and stranger hand-holding (*Source:* Coan, Schaefer, & Davidson, 2006, Figure 3).

Recent research is also beginning to identify how social support affects brain processing. For instance, one experiment found that activation of the areas of the brain reflecting stress was reduced when social support—simply being able to hold the hand of another person—was available (Coan, Schaefer, & Davidson, 2006).

Psychological Aspects of Illness and Well-Being

Once a week they meet to talk, to cry, sometimes to laugh together. "Is the pain still worse in the mornings?" Margaret asks Kate today.

A petite, graceful woman in her late 40s, Kate shakes her head no. "It's getting bad all the time," she says in a voice raw with worry and fatigue. . . . They nod in tacit understanding, eight women sitting in a loose circle of chairs here in a small, sparely furnished room at their medical centre. They know. All of them have been diagnosed with recurrent breast cancer.

They gather here each Wednesday afternoon to talk with each other and to listen. It's a chance to discuss their fears and find some small comfort, a time to feel they're not alone. And in some way that no one has been able to explain, it may be keeping them alive (Jaret, 1992, p. 87).

As recently as two decades ago, most psychologists and health-care providers would have scoffed at the notion that a discussion group could improve a cancer patient's chances of survival. Today, however, such methods have gained increasing acceptance.

Growing evidence suggests that psychological factors have a substantial effect both on major health problems that were once seen in purely physiological terms and on our everyday sense of health, well-being, and happiness. We'll consider the psychological components of three major health problems—heart disease, cancer, and smoking—and then consider the nature of people's well-being and happiness.

Type A behaviour pattern A cluster of behaviours involving hostility, competitiveness, time urgency, and feeling driven.

Type B behaviour pattern A cluster of behaviours characterized by a patient, cooperative, non-competitive manner.

THE As, Bs, AND Ds OF CORONARY HEART DISEASE

Many of us feel angry, frustrated, or competitive at one time or another, but for some people these feelings represent a pervasive, characteristic set of personality traits known as the Type A behaviour pattern. The **Type A behaviour pattern** is a cluster of behaviours involving hostility, competitiveness, time urgency, and feeling driven. In contrast, the **Type B behaviour pattern** is characterized by a patient, cooperative, non-competitive, and non-aggressive manner. It's important to keep in mind that Type A and Type B represent the ends of a continuum, and most people fall somewhere in between the two endpoints. Few people are purely a Type A or a Type B.

The importance of the Type A behaviour pattern lies in its links to coronary heart disease. Men who display the Type A pattern develop coronary heart disease twice as often and suffer significantly more fatal heart attacks than do those classified as having the Type B pattern. Moreover,

Survivors of natural disasters are at greater risk for heart disease. Not only does stress affect risk-related behaviour such as smoking and poor eating habits, but it can also lead to increased blood pressure, inflammation, and damage to the blood vessels, including the coronary arteries (Underwood, 2005).

the Type A pattern predicts who is going to develop heart disease at least as well as—and independently of—any other single factor, including age, blood pressure, smoking habits, and cholesterol levels in the body (Beresnevaité, Taylor, & Bagby, 2007; Rosenman et al., 1994; Wielgosz & Nolan, 2000).

Hostility is the key component of the Type A behaviour pattern that is related to heart disease. Although competition, time urgency, and feelings of being driven may produce stress and potentially other health and emotional problems, they aren't linked to coronary heart disease in the way that hostility is (Boyle et al., 2005; Ohira et al., 2007; Williams et al., 2000).

Why is hostility so toxic? The key reason is that hostility produces excessive physiological arousal in stressful situations. That arousal, in turn, results in increased production of the hormones epinephrine and norepinephrine, as well as increases in heart rate and blood pressure. Such an exaggerated physiological response ultimately produces an increased incidence of coronary heart disease (Demaree & Everhart, 2004; Eaker et al., 2004; Myrtek, 2007).

Study tip It's important to distinguish between Type A (hostility, competitiveness), Type B (patience, cooperativeness), and Type D (distressed) behaviours.

Keep in mind that not everyone who displays Type A behaviours is destined to have coronary heart disease. For one thing, a firm association between Type A behaviours and coronary heart disease has not been established for women; most findings pertain to males, not to females, in part because until recently, most research was done on men. In addition, other types of negative emotions, besides the hostility found in Type A behaviour, appear to be related to heart attacks. For example, psychologist Johan Denollet has found evidence that what he calls *Type D*—for "distressed"—behaviour is linked to coronary heart disease. In his view, insecurity, anxiety, and the negative outlook displayed by Type Ds puts them at risk for repeated heart attacks (Denollet, 2005; Denollet & Brutsaert, 1998; Schiffer et al., 2005).

PSYCHOLOGICAL ASPECTS OF CANCER

Hardly any disease is feared more than cancer. Many people think of cancer in terms of lingering pain and suffering (Feuerstein, 2007; White & Macleod, 2002). Although a diagnosis of cancer is not as grim as it once was—several kinds of cancer have a high cure rate if detected early enough (Feuerstein, 2007)—it is estimated by the Canadian Cancer Society that in 2012 there will be 186,400 new cases of cancer and 75,700 deaths (Canadian Cancer Society, 2012).

Although the processes involved in the spread of cancer are physiological, accumulating evidence suggests that the emotional responses of cancer patients to their disease may have a critical effect on its course. For example, one experiment found that people who adopt a fighting spirit are more likely to recover than are those who pessimistically suffer and resign themselves to death (Pettingale et al., 1985). The study analyzed the survival rates of women who had undergone the removal of a breast because of cancer (Greer, 1999).

The results suggested that the survival rates were related to the psychological response of the women three months after surgery. Women who stoically accepted their fate, trying not to complain, and those who felt the situation was hopeless and that nothing could be done showed the lowest survival rates; most of those women were dead after 10 years. In comparison, the survival rates of women who showed a fighting spirit (predicting that they would overcome the disease and planning to take steps to prevent its recurrence) and the survival rates of women who (erroneously) denied that they had ever had cancer (saying that the breast removal was merely a preventive step) were significantly higher. In sum, according to this study, cancer patients with a positive attitude were more likely to survive than were those with a more negative one.

Jack Layton, former leader of the NDP party, demonstrated a fighting spirit when he was diagnosed with cancer.

Figure 13.4
Relationship Between Patient Attitude and Cancer Survival

Source: Pettingale et al., 1985.

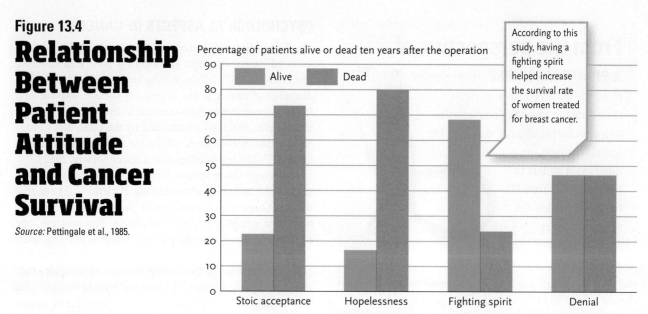

Percentage of patients alive or dead ten years after the operation

According to this study, having a fighting spirit helped increase the survival rate of women treated for breast cancer.

Women's psychological reactions three months after the operation

> **One experiment found that people who adopt a fighting spirit are more likely to recover from cancer than are those who pessimistically suffer and resign themselves to death.**

However, other research contradicts the notion that the course of cancer is affected by patients' attitudes and emotions. For example, some findings show that although a "fighting spirit" leads to better coping, the long-term survival rate is no better than it is for patients with a less positive attitude (Watson et al., 1999).

What is increasingly clear, however, is that certain types of psychological therapy have the potential for extending the lives of cancer patients. For example, the results of one study showed that women with breast cancer who received psychological treatment lived at least a year and a half longer, and experienced less anxiety and pain, than did women who did not participate in therapy. Research on patients with other health problems, such as heart disease, also has found that therapy can be beneficial, both psychologically and medically (Frasure-Smith, Lesperance, & Talajic, 2000; Galavotti et al., 1997; Spiegel, 1993, 1996).

SMOKING

Would you walk into a convenience store and buy an item with a label warning you that its use could kill you? Although most people would probably answer no, millions make such a purchase every day: a pack of cigarettes. Furthermore, they do this despite clear, well-publicized evidence that smoking is linked to cancer, heart attacks, strokes, bronchitis, emphysema, and a host of other serious illnesses. Worldwide, close to five million people die each year from the effects of smoking (Ezzati et al., 2005).

Why People Smoke Why do people smoke despite all the evidence showing that it is bad for their health? For example, in 2009 it was found that 17.5% of Canadians over the age of 15 were current smokers, despite being well aware of the risks (Reid & Hammond, 2011). It is not that they are somehow unaware of the link between smoking and disease; surveys show that most *smokers* agree with the statement "Cigarette smoking frequently causes disease and death." And in 2000, 70% of nearly 47 million smokers said they would like to quit (CDC, 2000; Wetter et al., 1998).

Heredity seems to determine, in part, whether people will become smokers, how much they will smoke, and how easily they can quit. Genetics also influences how susceptible people are to the harmful effects of smoking. However, although genetics plays a role in smoking, most research suggests that environmental factors are the primary cause of the habit (Fernander, Shavers & Hammons, 2007; Morley et al., 2007). Smoking at first may be seen as "cool" or sophisticated, as a rebellious act, or as facilitating calm performance in stressful situations. Greater exposure to smoking in media such as film also leads to a higher risk of becoming an established smoker. In addition, smoking a cigarette is sometimes viewed as a "rite of passage" for adolescents, undertaken at the urging of friends and viewed as a sign of growing up (Sargent et al., 2007; Wagner & Atkins, 2000).

Ultimately, smoking becomes a habit. People begin to label themselves smokers, and smoking becomes part of their self-concept. Moreover, they become dependent physiologically as a result of smoking, because nicotine, a primary ingredient of tobacco, is highly addictive. A complex relationship develops among smoking, nicotine levels, and a smoker's emotional state, in which a certain nicotine level becomes associated with a positive emotional state. As a result, people smoke in an effort to regulate *both* emotional states and nicotine levels in the blood (Amos, Wiltshire, & Haw, 2006; Kassel et al., 2007).

Quitting Smoking Because smoking has both psychological and biological components, it is a difficult habit to break (Dodgen, 2005). Long-term successful treatment typically occurs in just 15% of those who try to stop smoking, and once smoking becomes a habit, it is as hard to stop as an addiction to cocaine or heroin. In fact, some of the biochemical reactions to nicotine are similar to those to cocaine, amphetamines, and morphine. Many people try to quit and fail (Foulds, 2006; Vanasse, Niyonsenga, & Courteau, 2004). However, 60% of Canadians who once smoked have now successfully quit (Reid & Hammond, 2011).

Although smoking is prohibited in an increasing number of places, it remains a significant social problem.

DID YOU KNOW?

Failure may contribute to success! Most ex-smokers didn't succeed in quitting until their third, fourth, or fifth attempts.

Among the most effective tools for ending the smoking habit are drugs that replace the nicotine found in cigarettes, called nicotine replacement therapy (NRT). Whether in the form of gum, patches, nasal sprays, or inhalers, these products provide a dose of nicotine that reduces dependence on cigarettes (Vagg & Chapman, 2005). NRT was used by more than 50% of Canadians who attempted to quit smoking (Reid & Hammond, 2011). Another approach is exemplified by the drugs Zyban and Chantrix, which, rather than replacing nicotine, reduce the pleasure from smoking and suppress withdrawal symptoms that smokers experience when they try to stop (Dalsgaro et al., 2004; Garwood & Potts, 2007; Shiffman, 2007).

Behavioural strategies, which view smoking as a learned habit and concentrate on changing the smoking response, can also be effective. Initial "cure" rates of 60% have been reported, and one year after behavioural treatment more than half of those who quit have not resumed smoking. Counselling, either individually or in groups, also increases the rate of success in breaking the habit. The best treatment seems to be a combination of nicotine replacement and counselling. What doesn't work? Going it alone: Only 5% of smokers who quit cold-turkey on their own are successful (Noble, 1999; Rock, 1999; Woodruff, Conway, & Edwards, 2007).

Psych think

> > > Is it possible for people to quit smoking?

In the long term, the most effective means of reducing smoking may be changes in societal norms and attitudes toward the habit. For instance, in addition to banning smoking from inside many buildings, numerous cities and towns have made smoking in public places illegal (Hamilton, Biener, & Brennan, 2007).

The long-term effect of the barrage of information regarding the negative consequences of smoking on people's health has been substantial; overall, smoking has declined over the last two decades, particularly among males (Druss, 2005; Keltner & Grant, 2006). Still, more than one-fourth of students enrolled in high school are active smokers by the time they graduate, and there is evidence that the decline in smoking is levelling off. Among these students, around 10% become active smokers as early as the eighth grade (Fichtenberg & Glantz, 2006; Johnston et al., 2007).

Promoting Smoking Throughout the World

A Jeep decorated with the Camel logo pulls up to a high school in Buenos Aires. A woman begins handing out free cigarettes to 15- and 16-year-olds during their lunch recess.

At a video arcade in Taipei, free cigarettes are strewn atop each game. At a disco filled with high school students, free packs of Salems are on each table (Ecenbarger, 1993, p. 50).

The Canadian Tobacco Use Survey (Health Canada, 2010b) has reported a decline in the smoking rate of individuals aged 15 and older between 1999 (where 25% smoked) and 2010 (where 15% smoked). As the number of smokers has declined in Canada, cigarette manufacturers have turned to new markets in an effort to increase the number of people who smoke. In the process, they have employed some dubious marketing techniques.

For instance, a few years ago the RJ Reynolds tobacco company developed a line of candy-flavoured Camel Exotic Blend cigarettes with names such as TwistaLime and Warm Winter Toffee. These cigarettes were clearly targeted at the youth market. One study indicated that 17-year-olds made up the largest group of smokers of these cigarettes. Outraged by the manufacturer's blatant efforts to entice teens and young adults to take up smoking, authorities outlawed the sale of flavoured tobacco (except for menthol) in 2009 (Harris, 2009; Klein et al., 2008).

Figure 13.5
Smoking Prevalence in Canada, 1985-2010

Source: Health Canada (2010). Current Smoking Prevalence by Age, Canada, 1985–2010. www.hc-sc.gc.ca/hc-ps/tobac-tabac/research-recher-che/stat/ctums-esutc_2010-eng.php.

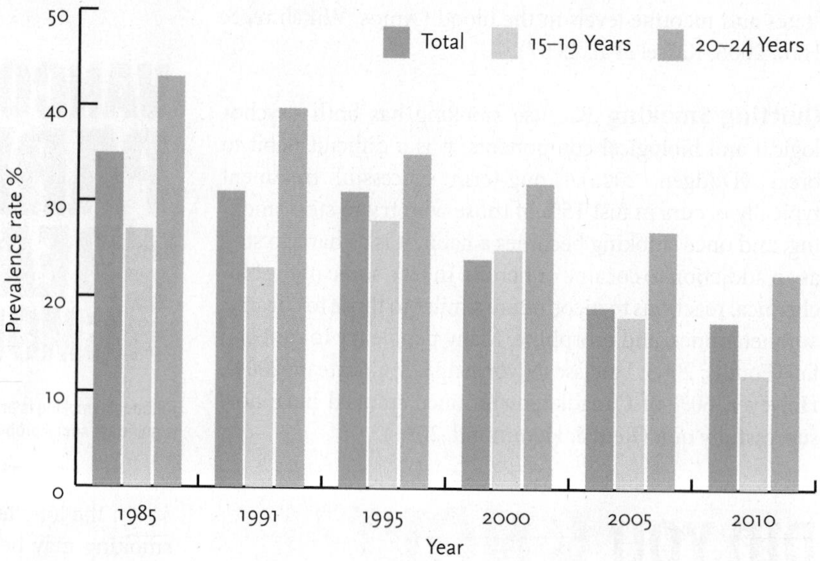

Because of legal constraints on smoking in Canada and the United States, manufacturers have turned their sights to other parts of the world, where they see a fertile market of non-smokers. Although they must often sell cigarettes more cheaply than they do in the North America, the huge number of potential smokers still makes it financially worthwhile for the tobacco companies (Bartecchi, MacKenzie, & Schrier, 1995; Brown, 2001).

Clearly, the push into worldwide markets has been successful. In some Latin American cities, as many as 50% of teenagers smoke. Children as young as age seven smoke in Hong Kong, and 30% of children smoked their first whole cigarette before the age of 10 in India, Ghana, Jamaica, and Poland. The World Health Organization predicts that smoking will prematurely kill some 200 million of the world's children and that ultimately 10% of the world's population will die as a result of smoking. Of everyone alive today, 500 million will eventually die from tobacco use (Mackay & Eriksen, 2002).

> " Because of the decline of smoking in Canada and the United States, manufacturers have turned their sights to other parts of the world. "

Promoting Health and Wellness

Health Canada (2007) would like Canadians to take a more active role in their own health by engaging in healthy living (i.e., healthy eating and physical activity) and by avoiding negative lifestyle practices such as smoking and excessive use of alcohol. Healthy eating, sport and exercise, yoga, meditation, and happiness all contribute to healthy living,

which is a positive way to both mediate and manage stress, particularly the stress you may experience as a student.

HEALTHY EATING

If you found out your body mass index from the chapter on motivation and emotion, you may have found that you are at a healthy weight. However, even if you are at a healthy weight, you may not be getting the necessary vitamins, minerals, and nutrients to live healthily and manage your stress. Using *Canada's Food Guide* is an easy way to make sure your body is getting what it needs to manage the stress in your life (for more information, see www.hc-sc.gc.ca and link to Food & Nutrition, Canada's Food Guide, Food Guide Basics, and How Much Food You Need Every Day). For example, most adults between the ages of 19–50 need daily servings of 7–8 fruits and vegetables, 6–7 grains, 2 milk or milk alternatives, 2 meat or meat alternatives, and 30–45 ml (2 to 3 tablespoons) of unsaturated fats such as olive, peanut, or canola oil (Health Canada, 2007).

The food choices you make are also very important! For example, try to choose the "coloured" vegetables (like sweet potato, broccoli, carrots, and spinach) and try to eat your fruit and vegetables rather than drinking them in the form of juices because juice often has added sugar and salt. Try also to eat whole grains such as bulger, quinoa, and

From the perspective of . . .

A HEALTH-CARE PROVIDER How would you try to encourage your patients to maintain a healthy lifestyle?

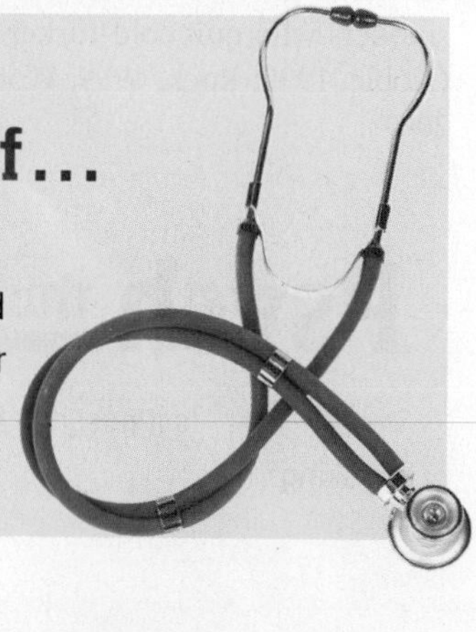

Eat Well and Be Active Every Day

Find related educational tools at: www.health.gc.ca/eatwell-beactive

brown or wild rice rather than white breads and pasta. If you are not used to eating whole grains, you might want to introduce them gradually into your diet because they have a slightly different taste. The meat choices you make should be lean (such as chicken or turkey breast, pork, or fish) and you should try to limit your intake of processed sandwich meats because they contain high levels of sodium and other unhealthy additives (Health Canada, 2007).

DID YOU KNOW?

Despite all the hype about low-carbohydrate diets, a recent study found that participants on low-fat, low-carbohydrate, or high-protein diets all had a similar level of weight loss after a two-year period. It appears that a reduced calorie diet is most beneficial for maintaining weight loss rather than focusing on eliminating or adding major types of food (Sacks, Bray, Carey et al., 2009).

SPORT AND EXERCISE

Sometimes the very thing you need the most is the thing you put on the bottom of the list because you feel far too busy to allow the time for it. It is for this reason that some students claim that they do not have time to exercise, and while this may feel true, it is not impossible to benefit from exercise with only a little of your time. A recent study found that exercising for at least 15 minutes a day can improve health and prolong life (Wen, Pui, Tsai et al., 2011). This does not have to include highly vigorous activity either; moving your body by walking, dancing, and using the stairs instead of the elevator can go a long way in improving your health and helping you manage the stress in your life.

If you can find a little more time, sport is an excellent way to promote health and wellness. Involvement in organized sports provides an easy way to be physically active, which can improve your mood and attitude. Moreover, participating in sports offers an opportunity for you to meet others so that you can create a network of friendship and social support, both of which can help in the management of stress (Davis-Marchand, 2009).

YOGA AND MEDITATION

People in the Eastern part of the world have long known about the benefits of yoga and meditation, but it has taken longer for people in our part of the world to understand how yoga and meditation can be used to manage stress. While many people claim that yoga and meditation improves their mood and helps them feel more relaxed, a good critical thinker would examine the evidence! Trisha daSilva from the Centre for Addiction and Mental Health in Toronto, Ontario, did just that. She worked with two colleagues to conduct a comprehensive review of the scientific studies on the benefit of yoga in coping with anxiety and depression (daSilva, Ravindran, & Ravindran, 2009). daSilva and her colleagues found that while there were very few scientific studies on the benefits of yoga, the studies that had been conducted supported the notion that yoga is effective in coping with anxiety and depression.

The research that daSilva reviewed outlined some important benefits of yoga and deep breathing that would

Psych think

> > > Being a student can be very stressful, especially during weeks when there are many tests and assignments. How can you manage this stress so that you can be more successful on your tests and assignments?

Cody Franson, like many of his Toronto Maple Leaf teammates, practices yoga in the off-season. While Cody understands the benefits of yoga, he also admits, "yoga is friggin hard!" (*Source:* Ulmer, 2011)

also be helpful in the management of stress. For example, yoga has been found to reduce levels of the stress hormone cortisol, which is often released in the alarm stage of the general adaptation syndrome model. Yoga also has been found to increase levels of the neurotransmitter GABA, which is related to mood. Moreover, the deep breathing associated with both yoga and meditation has had positive impacts on emotions, stress, and positive thinking (daSilva, Ravindran, & Ravindran, 2009). In a more recent study, Laura White found that a Mindfulness-based Stress Reduction (MBSR) program that involved both yoga and meditation was very effective in helping a group of school-aged girls improve their cognitive appraisal and their overall ability to cope with stress (White, 2012). Similar benefits were found in a group of firefighters who participated in at least four on-shift yoga classes over a period of six weeks who demonstrated a significant improvement in their flexibility, functional fitness, and their perceived stress (Cowen, 2010).

subjective well-being People's own evaluation of their lives in terms of both their thoughts and their emotions.

WELL-BEING AND HAPPINESS

What makes for a good life?

This is a question that philosophers and theologians have pondered for centuries, and now health psychologists are turning their spotlight on the question. They are doing that by investigating **subjective well-being**, people's evaluations of their lives in terms of both their thoughts and their emotions. Considered another way, subjective well-being is the measure of how happy people are (Diener, Lucas, & Oishi, 2002; Dolan & White, 2007; Tsaousis, Nikolaou, & Serdaris, 2007).

What Are the Characteristics of Happy People?

Research on the subject of well-being shows that happy people share several characteristics (Diener & Seligman, 2002; Myers, 2000; Otake, Shimai, & Tanaka-Matsumi, 2006):

- *Happy people have high self-esteem.* Particularly in Western cultures, which emphasize the importance of individuality, people who are happy like themselves. They see themselves as more intelligent and better able to get along with others than the average person. In fact, they often hold *positive illusions* or moderately inflated views of themselves as good, competent, and desirable (Boyd-Wilson, McClure, & Walkey, 2004; Taylor et al., 2000).

- *Happy people have a firm sense of control.* They feel more in control of events in their lives, unlike those who feel they are the pawns of others and who experience learned helplessness (Myers & Diener, 1995).

- *Happy individuals are optimistic.* Their optimism permits them to persevere at tasks and ultimately to achieve more. Moreover, their health is better (Peterson, 2000).

- *Happy people like to be around other people.* They tend to be extroverted and have a supportive network of close relationships (Diener & Seligman, 2002).

Perhaps most important, most people are at least moderately happy most of the time. In both national and international surveys, people living in a wide variety of circumstances report being happy. Furthermore, life-altering events that one might expect would produce long-term

Faces Scale: "Which face comes closest to expressing how you feel about your life as a whole?"

Most people rate themselves as happy, whereas only a small minority indicate that they are "not too happy."
Source: Myers, 2000, p. 57, drawn from *Social Indicators of Well-being: Americans' Perceptions of Life Quality*, pp. 207 and 306, by F. M. Andrews and S. B. Withey, 1976. New York, Plenum. Copyright 1976 by Plenum.

Can Thinking About Happy Life Events Make You More Satisfied With Your Life?

While this might sound like too simple a solution to be true, psychology professor Sonja Lyubomirsky found that people who thought about a happy life event for three consecutive days had higher levels of life satisfaction after four weeks than they had before they participated in the study (Lyubomirsky, Sousa, & Dickerhoof, 2006). You can help manage your stress by thinking about happy life events! Lyubomirsky (2010) provided further suggestions for improving your happiness. First, regularly write a gratitude journal or gratitude letter. Second, practice thinking positively about yourself by talking or writing about happy moments in your life and your future goals. Third, frequently commit acts of kindness towards others, whether you know them or not. Fourth, set life goals and take small steps to achieve these, and five, try to appreciate the positive experiences in your life.

---

spikes in happiness, such as winning the lottery, probably won't make you much happier than you already are, as we discuss next (Diener & Biswas-Diener, 2008; Tov & Diener, 2007).

Does Money Buy Happiness? If you were to win the lottery, would you be happier?

Probably not. At least that's the implication of health psychologists' research on subjective well-being. That research shows that although winning the lottery brings an initial surge in happiness, a year later winners' level of happiness seems to return to what it was before. The converse phenomenon occurs for people who have had serious injuries in accidents: Despite an initial decline in happiness, in most cases victims return to their prior levels of happiness after the passage of time (Diener & Biswas-Diener, 2002; Nissle & Bschor, 2002; Spinella & Lester, 2006).

Why is the level of subjective well-being so stable? One explanation is that people have a general *set point* for happiness, a marker that establishes the tone for one's life. Although specific events may temporarily elevate or depress one's mood (a surprise promotion or a job loss, for example), ultimately people return to their general level of happiness.

Although the theory doesn't yet include an explanation for how people's happiness set points are initially established, some evidence suggests that the set point is determined at least in part by genetic factors. Specifically, identical twins who grow up in widely different circumstances turn out to have very similar levels of happiness (Diener, Lucas, & Scollon, 2006; Kahneman, Diener, & Schwarz, 1998).

Remember the concept that individuals have a set point (a general, consistent level) for subjective well-being.

Moreover, few differences exist between members of different demographic groups. Men and women report being equally happy and even countries that are not economically prosperous have, on the whole, happy residents (Diener & Clifton, 2002; Myers & Diener, 1995; Suh, 2002; Suhail & Chaudhry, 2004).

The bottom line: money does not seem to buy happiness. Despite the ups and downs of life, most people tend to be reasonably happy, and they adapt to the trials and tribulations—and joys and delights—of life by returning to a steady-state level of happiness. That habitual level of happiness can have profound—perhaps life-prolonging—implications (Diener & Seligman, 2004; Hecht, 2007).

For Review >>

How is health psychology a union between medicine and psychology?
The field of health psychology considers how psychology can be applied to the prevention, diagnosis, and treatment of medical problems.

What is stress, how does it affect us, and how can we best cope with it?
Stress is a response to threatening or challenging environmental conditions. People encounter stressors—the circumstances that produce stress—of both a positive and a negative nature. General classes of events that provoke stress are cataclysmic events, personal stressors, and daily hassles. Stress produces immediate physiological reactions. In the short term those reactions may be adaptive, but in the long term they may have negative consequences, including the development of psychophysiological disorders. Stress can be reduced by developing a sense of control over one's circumstances. Coping with stress can take a number of forms, including the use of emotion-focused or problem-focused coping strategies.

How can our attitudes and beliefs affect health-related problems such as coronary heart disease, cancer, and smoking?
Hostility, a key component of the Type A behaviour pattern, is linked to coronary heart disease. The Type A behaviour pattern is a cluster of behaviours involving hostility, competitiveness, time urgency, and feeling driven. Increasing evidence suggests that people's attitudes and emotional responses affect the course of cancer through links to the immune system. Smoking, the leading preventable cause of health problems, is hard to quit, even though most smokers are aware of the dangerous consequences of the behaviour.

How can you promote health and wellness in your life?
You can promote health and wellness in your life by eating healthily and by engaging in sport and exercise. Practicing yoga and meditation also contribute to wellness and healthy living. In addition to contributing to your health and wellness, all of these behaviours are a positive way to mediate and manage the stress in your life.

How does a sense of well-being develop?
Subjective well-being, the measure of how happy people are, is highest in people with high self-esteem, a sense of control, optimism, and a supportive network of close relationships.

Psych think answers

Psych think 1 In the PSYCH think on p. 342 we asked which of the three kinds of stressors can be most negative and how uplifts can help with this. The three kinds of stressors are cataclysmic stressors (such as natural disasters), personal stressors (such as major life events), and daily hassles (such as waiting in long lines or traffic). While cataclysmic and personal stressors can have a large impact, it is the daily hassles that can really add up to produce negative health effects. Uplifts are small pick-me-ups that include positive relationships with others and enjoying particular places. These small uplifts can help combat the daily hassles!

Psych think 2 In the PSYCH think on p. 351 we asked if it was possible for people to quit smoking. While many people find quitting difficult, it is still possible to quit. Remember that 60% of Canadians who once smoked have now successfully stopped! The most successful tool for quitting appears to be nicotine replacement therapy (such as gum, patches, nasal sprays, or inhalers). Drugs such as Zyban and Chantrix have also been helpful.

Psych think 3 In the PSYCH think on p. 353 we asked how you can manage the stress of being a student so that you can be more successful on your tests and assignments. The first thing you can do is use more effective coping strategies such as turning threats into challenges and making threatening situations less threatening. You can also try to change goals that need to be changed. For example, perhaps you hoped to have four assignments complete in one week but a personal crisis makes this impossible. Changing your goal can be a helpful strategy in coping with that stress. You can also try to prepare for stress before it happens by being more proactive. In addition to using good coping skills, there are some other tips from the American Psychological Association that might be helpful. For example, knowing the typical source of your stress and how you usually react to it can help you make predictions about when it might happen. Using healthy stress management techniques such as yoga, meditation, exercise, and healthy eating will make it easier for you to cope. Finding support from friends or a more qualified counsellor can also help you cope and manage.

A

abnormal behaviour Behaviour that causes people to experience distress and prevents them from functioning in their daily lives.

absolute threshold The smallest intensity of a stimulus that must be present for the senses to detect it.

accommodation Modifying or changing existing schemas to fit new information.

achievement test A test designed to determine a person's level of knowledge in a given subject area.

action potential An electric nerve impulse that travels through a neuron's axon when it is set off by a "trigger," changing the neuron's charge from negative to positive.

activation-synthesis theory Hobson's theory that the brain produces random electrical energy during REM sleep that stimulates memories lodged in various portions of the brain.

activity theory of aging A theory that suggests that the elderly who are most successful while aging are those who maintain the interests and activities they had during middle age.

adaptation An adjustment in sensory capacity after prolonged exposure to unchanging stimuli.

addictive drugs Drugs that produce a physiological or psychological dependence in the user.

adolescence The developmental stage between childhood and adulthood.

aggression The intentional injury of, or harm to, another person.

algorithm A rule that, if applied appropriately, guarantees a solution to a problem.

all-or-none law The rule that neurons are either on or off.

altruism Helping behaviour that is beneficial to others but clearly requires self-sacrifice.

Alzheimer's disease A progressive brain disorder that leads to a gradual and irreversible decline in cognitive abilities.

amnesia Memory loss that occurs without other mental difficulties.

analytical intelligence Part of Sternberg's theory; focuses on abstract but traditional types of problems measured on IQ tests.

androgens Male sex hormones secreted by the testes.

anorexia nervosa A severe eating disorder in which people may refuse to eat while denying that their behaviour and appearance—which can become skeleton-like—are unusual.

anterograde amnesia Amnesia in which memory is lost for events that follow an injury.

antianxiety drugs Drugs that reduce the level of anxiety a person experiences, essentially by reducing excitability and increasing feelings of well-being.

antidepressant drugs Medications that improve mood and promote a feeling of well-being in severely depressed individuals.

antipsychotic drugs Drugs that temporarily reduce such psychotic symptoms as agitation, hallucinations, and delusions.

anti-social personality disorder A disorder in which individuals show no regard for the moral and ethical rules of society or the rights of others.

anxiety disorder The occurrence of anxiety without an obvious external cause, affecting daily functioning.

aptitude test A test designed to predict a person's ability in a particular area or line of work.

archetypes According to Jung, universal symbolic representations of a particular person, object, or experience (such as good and evil).

arousal approaches to motivation The belief that we try to maintain certain levels of stimulation and activity, increasing or reducing them as necessary.

assimilation Attempting to fit new information into existing schemas.

association areas One of the major regions of the cerebral cortex; the site of the higher mental processes, such as thought, language, memory, and speech.

assumed-similarity bias The tendency to think of people as being similar to oneself, even when meeting them for the first time.

attachment The positive emotional bond that develops between a child and a specific individual.

attitudes Evaluations of a particular person, behaviour, belief, or concept.

attribution theory The theory of personality that seeks to explain how we decide, on the basis of samples of an individual's behaviour, what the specific causes of that person's behaviour are.

authoritarian parents Parents who are rigid and punitive and value unquestioning obedience from their children.

authoritative parents Parents who are firm, set clear limits, reason with their children, and explain things to them.

autobiographical memories Our recollections of circumstances and episodes from our own lives.

autonomic division The part of the peripheral nervous system that controls involuntary movement of the heart, glands, lungs, and other organs.

autonomy-versus-shame-and-doubt stage The period during which, according to Erikson, toddlers (ages one-and-a-half to three years) develop independence and autonomy if exploration and freedom are encouraged, or shame and self-doubt if they are restricted and overprotected.

aversive conditioning A form of therapy that reduces the frequency of undesired behaviour by pairing an aversive, unpleasant stimulus with undesired behaviour.

axon The part of the neuron that carries messages destined for other neurons.

B

babble Meaningless, speechlike sounds made by children from around the age of three months through one year.

basilar membrane A vibrating structure that runs through the centre of the cochlea, dividing it into an upper chamber and a lower chamber and containing sense receptors for sound.

behaviour modification A formalized technique for promoting the frequency of desirable behaviours and decreasing the incidence of unwanted ones.

behavioural assessment Direct measures of an individual's behaviour used to describe personality characteristics.

behavioural genetics The study of the effects of heredity on behaviour.

behavioural neuroscientists (or biopsychologists) Psychologists who specialize in considering the ways in which the biological structures and functions of the body affect behaviour.

behavioural perspective The approach that focuses on observable, measurable behaviour and ways to change problem behaviours.

behavioural treatment approaches Treatment approaches that build on the basic processes of learning, such as reinforcement and extinction, and assume that normal and abnormal behaviour are both learned.

biofeedback A procedure in which a person learns to control through conscious thought internal physiological processes such as blood pressure, heart and respiration rate, skin temperature, sweating, and the constriction of particular muscles.

biological and evolutionary approaches to personality Theories that suggest that important components of personality are inherited.

biomedical perspective The perspective that suggests that when an individual displays symptoms of abnormal behaviour, the root cause will be found in a physical examination of the individual, which may reveal a hormonal imbalance, a chemical deficiency, or a brain injury.

biomedical therapy Therapy that relies on drugs and other medical procedures to improve psychological functioning.

bipolar disorder A disorder in which a person alternates between periods of euphoric feelings of mania and periods of depression.

bisexuals Persons who are sexually attracted to people of the same sex and the other sex.

borderline personality disorder A disorder in which individuals have difficulty developing a secure sense of who they are. Their behaviour is often unstable and emotionally volatile.

bottom-up processing Perception that consists of the progression of recognizing and processing information from individual components of a stimuli and moving to the perception of the whole.

Broca's area An area in the in the frontal lobe that allows you to speak.

bulimia A disorder in which a person binges on large quantities of food, followed by efforts to purge the food through vomiting or other means.

bystander effect (or bystander apathy effect) A phenomena that happens in emergency situations when many people are present, but nobody tries to help victim.

C

Cannon-Bard theory of emotion The view that both physiological arousal and emotional experience are produced simultaneously by the same nerve stimulus.

case study An in-depth, intensive investigation of an individual or small group of people.

cataclysmic events Strong stressors that occur suddenly, affecting many people at once (for example, natural disasters).

catharsis The process of discharging built-up aggressive energy.

central core The "old brain," which controls basic functions such as eating and sleeping and is common to all vertebrates.

central nervous system (CNS) The part of the nervous system that includes the brain and spinal cord.

central route processing Message interpretation characterized by thoughtful consideration of the issues and arguments used to persuade.

central traits The major traits considered in forming impressions of others.

cerebellum (ser uh BELL um) The part of the brain that controls bodily balance.

cerebral cortex The "new brain," responsible for the most sophisticated information processing in the brain; contains four lobes.

chromosomes Rod-shaped structures that contain all basic hereditary information.

chunk A meaningful grouping of stimuli that can be stored as a unit in short-term memory.

circadian rhythms Physiological fluctuations that occur on approximately a 24-hour cycle.

classical conditioning A type of learning in which a neutral stimulus comes to bring about a response after it is paired with a stimulus that naturally brings about that response.

cochlea (KOKE-le-uh) A coiled tube in the ear filled with fluid that vibrates in response to sound.

cognitive appraisal The way that people interpret or appraise an event that can impact how stressful it appears.

cognitive approaches to motivation Theories suggesting that motivation is a product of people's thoughts and expectations—their cognitions.

cognitive development The process by which a child's understanding of the world changes as a function of age and experience.

cognitive dissonance The conflict that occurs when a person holds two contradictory attitudes or thoughts (referred to as cognitions).

cognitive learning theory An approach to the study of learning that focuses on the thought processes that underlie learning.

cognitive perspective The perspective that suggests that people's thoughts and beliefs are a central component of normal and abnormal behaviour.

cognitive treatment approaches Treatment approaches that teach people to think in more adaptive ways by changing their dysfunctional cognitions about the world and themselves.

cognitive-behavioural approach A treatment approach that incorporates basic principles of learning to change the way people think.

collective unconscious According to Jung, a common set of ideas, feelings, images, and symbols that we inherit from our ancestors, the whole human race, and even animal ancestors from the distant past.

collectivism Helping behaviour where the ultimate goal is to benefit the welfare of a particular group.

community psychology A branch of psychology that focuses on the prevention and minimization of psychological disorders in the community.

companionate love The strong affection we have for those with whom our lives are deeply involved.

compliance Behaviour that occurs in response to direct social pressure.

compulsion An irresistible urge to repeatedly carry out some act that seems strange and unreasonable.

concepts Categorizations of objects, events, or people that share common properties.

concrete operational stage According to Piaget, the period from 7 to 12 years of age that is characterized by logical thought and a loss of egocentrism.

conditioned response (CR) A response that, after conditioning, follows a previously neutral stimulus (for example, salivation at the ringing of a bell).

conditioned stimulus (CS) A once-neutral stimulus that has been paired with an unconditioned stimulus to bring about a response formerly caused only by the unconditioned stimulus.

cones Cone-shaped, light-sensitive receptor cells in the retina that are responsible for sharp focus and colour perception, particularly in bright light.

confirmation bias The tendency to favour information that supports one's initial hypotheses and ignore contradictory information that supports alternative hypotheses or solutions.

conformity A change in behaviour or attitudes brought about by a desire to follow the beliefs or standards of other people.

confounding variables Variables that might influence the outcome (or dependent variable) of the study. These can be avoided by using random sampling and by having a control group.

consciousness The awareness of the sensations, thoughts, and feelings we experience at a given moment.

constructive processes Processes in which memories are influenced by the meaning we give to events.

continuous reinforcement schedule Reinforcing of a behaviour every time it occurs.

control group A group participating in an experiment that receives no treatment. This group often receives a placebo instead.

convergent thinking The ability to produce responses that are based primarily on knowledge and logic.

coping The efforts to control, reduce, or learn to tolerate the threats that lead to stress.

correlational research Research in which the relationship between two sets of variables is examined to determine whether they are associated, or related.

creative intelligence Part of Sternberg's theory; the generation of novel ideas and products.

creativity The ability to generate original ideas or solve problems in novel ways.

cross-sectional research A research method that compares people of different ages at the same point in time.

crystallized intelligence The accumulation of information, skills, and strategies that are learned through experience and can be applied in problem-solving situations.

cue-dependent forgetting Forgetting that occurs when there are insufficient retrieval cues to rekindle information that is in memory.

culture-fair IQ test A test that does not discriminate against the members of any minority group.

D

daily hassles Everyday annoyances, such as being stuck in traffic, that cause minor irritations and may have long-term ill effects if they continue or are compounded by other stressful events.

debriefing After the study is completed, participants receive an explanation of the study and the procedures that were involved.

decay The loss of information in memory through its non-use.

declarative memory Memory for factual information: names, faces, dates, and the like.

deindividuation Feeling less personally responsible and self-conscious when in a group.

deinstitutionalization The transfer of former mental patients from institutions to the community.

dendrite A cluster of fibres at one end of a neuron that receive messages from other neurons.

dependent variable The variable that is measured and is expected to change as a result of changes caused by the experimenter's manipulation of the independent variable.

depressants Drugs that slow down the nervous system.

depth perception The ability to view the world in three dimensions and to perceive distance.

determinism The idea that people's behaviour is produced primarily by factors outside of their wilful control.

developmental psychology The branch of psychology that studies the patterns of growth and change that occur throughout life.

Diagnostic and Statistical Manual of Mental Disorders, Fourth Edition, Text Revision (DSM-IV-TR) A system, devised by the American Psychiatric Association, used by most professionals to diagnose and classify abnormal behaviour.

difference threshold (just-noticeable difference) The smallest level of added or reduced stimulation required to sense that a change in stimulation has occurred at least 50% of the time.

diffusion of responsibility The tendency for people to feel that responsibility for acting is shared, or diffused, among those present.

discrimination Behaviour directed toward individuals on the basis of their membership in a particular group.

disengagement theory of aging A theory that suggests that aging produces a gradual withdrawal from the world on physical, psychological, and social levels.

dispositional causes (of behaviour) Perceived causes of behaviour that are based on internal traits or personality factors.

dissociative amnesia A dissociative disorder characterized by sudden memory loss after experiencing severe psychological stress.

dissociative fugue A dissociative disorder that combines dissociative amnesia with flight (the individual leaves the area associated with the stress and assumes a new identity).

dissociative identity disorder A disorder (formally termed Multiple Personality Disorder) where the individual has two or more distinct personalities with separate traits, behaviours, mannerisms, and memories.

divergent thinking The ability to generate unusual, yet nonetheless appropriate, responses to problems or questions.

door-in-the-face technique Someone makes a large request, expecting it to be refused, and follows it with a smaller one.

double standard The view that premarital sex is permissible for males but not for females.

dreams-for-survival theory The theory suggesting that dreams permit information that is critical for our daily survival to be reconsidered and reprocessed during sleep.

drive Motivational tension, or arousal, that energizes behaviour to fulfill a need.

drive-reduction approaches to motivation Theories suggesting that a lack of a basic biological requirement (such as water) produces a drive to obtain that requirement (in this case, the thirst drive).

drug therapy Control of psychological disorders through the use of drugs.

E

eardrum The part of the ear that vibrates when sound waves hit it.

ego The part of the personality that provides a buffer between the id and the outside world.

egocentric thought A way of thinking in which a child views the world entirely from his or her own perspective.

ego-integrity-versus-despair stage According to Erikson, a period from late adulthood until death during which we review life's accomplishments and failures.

egoism Helping behaviour where the ultimate goal is to benefit one's self.

Electra complex Where little girls unconsciously wish to have a relationship with their fathers while rivalling their mothers.

electroconvulsive therapy (ECT) A procedure used in the treatment of severe depression in which an electric current of 70 to 150 volts is briefly administered to the head.

embryo A developed zygote that has a heart, a brain, and other organs.

emotional intelligence The set of skills that underlie the accurate assessment, evaluation, expression, and regulation of emotions.

emotions Feelings that generally have both physiological and cognitive elements and that influence behaviour.

empathy-altruism hypothesis Helping others when we feel empathy toward them and their situation.

endocrine system A chemical communication network that sends messages through the bloodstream to all parts of the body.

episodic memory Memory for events that occur in a particular time, place, or context.

estrogens Class of female sex hormones.

evolutionary perspective The evolutionary perspective explains our behaviour as functional to natural selection; that we have adapted our behaviours over time to ensure our survival as a species.

excitatory message A chemical message that makes it more likely that a receiving neuron will fire and an action potential will travel down its axon.

experiment The investigation of the effect of one (or more) variables on another by deliberately producing a change in one variable and observing the effects of that change on another variable.

experimental bias Factors that distort how the independent variable affects the dependent variable in an experiment.

experimental group Any group participating in an experiment that receives a treatment (e.g., intervention, medicine, etc.).

experimental manipulation The change that an experimenter deliberately produces in a situation.

explicit memory Intentional or conscious recollection of information.

exposure A behavioural treatment for anxiety in which people are confronted, either suddenly or gradually, with a stimulus that they fear.

extinction A basic phenomenon of learning that occurs when a previously conditioned response decreases in frequency and eventually disappears.

extramarital sex Sexual activity between a married person and someone who is not his or her spouse.

extrinsic motivation Part of the cognitive approach to motivation where one is motivated by external factors such as rewards or personal recognition.

F

facial-affect program Activation of a set of nerve impulses that make the face display the appropriate expression.

facial-feedback hypothesis The hypothesis that facial expressions not only reflect emotional experience but also help determine how people experience and label emotions.

familial retardation Mental retardation in which no apparent biological defect exists, but there is a history of retardation in the family.

family therapy An approach to therapy that focuses on the family and its dynamics.

feature detection The activation of neurons in the cortex by visual stimuli of specific shapes or patterns.

fetal alcohol syndrome A major cause of mental retardation in newborns, occurring when the mother uses alcohol during pregnancy.

fetus A developing individual, from eight weeks after conception until birth.

fixations Conflicts or concerns that persist beyond the developmental period in which they first occur.

fixed-interval schedule A schedule that provides reinforcement for a response only if a fixed time period has elapsed, making overall rates of response relatively low.

fixed-ratio schedule A schedule by which reinforcement is given only after a specific number of responses are made.

flashbulb memories Memories centred on a specific, important, or surprising event that are so vivid it is as if they represented a snapshot of the event.

fluid intelligence Intelligence that reflects information-processing capabilities, reasoning, and memory.

foot-in-the-door technique Asking a person to agree to a small request and then later asking that person to comply with a larger, more important one.

formal operational stage According to Piaget, the period from age 12 to adulthood that is characterized by abstract thought.

free will The idea that behaviour is caused primarily by choices that are made freely by the individual.

frequency theory of hearing The theory that the entire basilar membrane acts like a microphone, vibrating as a whole in response to a sound.

frontal lobes The lobes responsible for controlling voluntary movements, intelligence, and personality.

functional fixedness The tendency to think of an object only in terms of its typical use.

functionalism An early approach to psychology that concentrated on what the mind does—the functions of mental activity—and the role of behaviour in allowing people to adapt to their environments.

fundamental attribution error A tendency to over-attribute others' behaviour to dispositional causes and the corresponding minimization of the importance of situational causes.

G

g or g-factor The single, general factor for mental ability assumed to underlie intelligence in some early theories of intelligence.

gate-control theory of pain The theory that particular nerve receptors in the spinal cord lead to specific areas of the brain related to pain.

general adaptation syndrome (GAS) A theory developed by Selye that suggests that a person's response to a stressor consists of three stages: alarm and mobilization, resistance, and exhaustion.

generalized anxiety disorder The experience of long-term, persistent anxiety and worry.

generativity-versus-stagnation stage According to Erikson, a period in middle adulthood during which we take stock of our contributions to family and society.

genes The parts of the chromosomes through which genetic information is transmitted.

genetic preprogramming theories of aging Theories that suggest that human cells have a built-in time limit to their reproduction, and that after a certain time they are no longer able to divide.

gestalt (geh-SHTALLT) psychology An approach to psychology that focuses on the organization of perception and thinking in a "whole" sense rather than on the individual elements of perception.

Gestalt laws of organization A series of principles that describe how we organize bits and pieces of information into meaningful wholes.

goals of psychology To describe, explain, predict, and control behaviour and mental processes.

grammar The system of rules that determines how our thoughts can be expressed in words.

group polarization The tendency for groups to make decisions that are more extreme than when people make decisions on their own.

group therapy Therapy in which an unrelated group of people meet with a therapist to discuss problems.

group think When a highly cohesive group filters out unwanted (although often important) input to reach a consensus.

group Two or more people who interact with one another; perceive themselves as part of a group, and are interdependent.

H

habituation The decrease in response to a stimulus that occurs after repeated presentations of the same stimulus.

hair cells Tiny cells covering the basilar membrane that, when bent by vibrations entering the cochlea, transmit neural messages to the brain.

hallucinogen A drug that is capable of producing hallucinations, or changes in the perceptual process.

halo effect A phenomenon in which an initial understanding that a person has positive traits is used to infer other uniformly positive characteristics.

health psychology The branch of psychology that investigates the psychological factors related to wellness and illness, including the prevention, diagnosis, and treatment of medical problems.

hemispheres Symmetrical left and right halves of the brain that control the side of the body opposite to their location.

heritability A measure of the degree to which a characteristic is related to genetic, inherited factors.

heterosexuality Sexual attraction and behaviour directed to the other sex.

heuristic A cognitive shortcut that may lead to a solution.

homosexuals Persons who are sexually attracted to members of their own sex.

hormone Substance produced by a gland or tissue and circulated through the blood to regulate the functioning or growth of the body.

horn effect Opposite of the halo effect, where a person's negative traits are used to infer other uniformly negative traits.

humanistic approaches to personality Theories that emphasize people's innate goodness and desire to achieve higher levels of functioning.

humanistic perspective The approach that suggests that all individuals naturally strive to grow, develop, and be in control of their lives and behaviour.

humanistic therapy Therapy in which the underlying rationale is that people have control of their behaviour, can make choices about their lives, and are essentially responsible for solving their own problems.

hypnosis A trancelike state of heightened susceptibility to the suggestions of others.

hypothalamus A tiny part of the brain, located below the thalamus, that maintains the body's internal environment and regulates such vital behaviours as eating, self-protection, and sex.

hypothesis A prediction, stemming from a theory, stated in a way that allows it to be tested.

I

id The raw, unorganized, inborn part of personality whose sole purpose is to reduce tension created by primitive drives related to hunger, sex, aggression, and irrational impulses.

identical twins Twins who are genetically identical.

identification The process of wanting to be like another person as much as possible, imitating that person's behaviour and adopting similar beliefs and values.

identity The distinguishing character of the individual: who each of us is, what our roles are, and what we are capable of.

identity-versus-role-confusion stage According to Erikson, a time in adolescence of major testing to determine one's unique qualities.

implicit memory Memories of which people are not consciously aware but that can affect subsequent performance and behaviour.

incentive approaches to motivation Theories suggesting that motivation stems from the desire to obtain valued external goals, or incentives.

independent variable The variable that is manipulated by an experimenter.

industry-versus-inferiority stage According to Erikson, the last stage of childhood, during which children age six to twelve years may develop positive social interactions with others or may feel inadequate and become less sociable.

inferiority complex According to Adler, a problem affecting adults who have not been able to overcome the feelings of inferiority that they developed as children, when they were small and limited in their knowledge about the world.

information processing The way in which people take in, use, and store information.

informed consent A document signed by participants affirming that they have been told the basic outlines of the study and are aware of what their participation will involve.

inhibitory message A chemical message that prevents or decreases the likelihood that a receiving neuron will fire.

initiative-versus-guilt stage According to Erikson, the period during which children ages three to six years experience conflict

between independence of action and the sometimes negative results of that action.

instincts Inborn patterns of behaviour that are biologically determined rather than learned.

intellectually gifted The 2% to 4% of the population who have IQ scores greater than 130.

intelligence The capacity to understand the world, think rationally, and use resources effectively when faced with challenges.

intelligence quotient (IQ) A score that takes into account an individual's mental and chronological ages.

intelligence tests Tests devised to quantify a person's level of intelligence.

interactionist approach (to language development) The view that language development is produced through a combination of genetically determined predispositions and environmental circumstances that help teach language.

interference The phenomenon by which information in memory disrupts the recall of other information.

interneurons Neurons that connect sensory and motor neurons, carrying messages between the two.

interpersonal attraction (or close relationship) Positive feelings for others; liking and loving.

interpersonal therapy (IPT) Short-term therapy that focuses on the context of current social relationships.

intimacy-versus-isolation stage According to Erikson, a period during early adulthood that focuses on developing close relationships.

intrinsic motivation Part of the cognitive approach to motivation where one is motivated by internal factors such as personal satisfaction or interest.

introspection A procedure used to study the structure of the mind in which subjects are asked to describe in detail what they are experiencing when they are exposed to a stimulus.

J

James-Lange theory of emotion The idea that emotional experience is a reaction to bodily events occurring as a result of an external situation ("I feel sad because I am crying").

L

language The communication of information through symbols arranged according to systematic rules.

language-acquisition device As hypothesized by Noam Chomsky, a neural system of the brain that permits understanding of language.

latent content of dreams According to Freud, the "disguised" meanings of dreams, hidden by more obvious subjects.

latent learning Learning in which a new behaviour is acquired but is not demonstrated until some incentive is provided for displaying it.

lateralization The dominance of one hemisphere of the brain in specific functions, such as language.

learned helplessness A state in which people conclude that unpleasant or aversive stimuli cannot be controlled—a view of the world that becomes so ingrained that they cease trying to remedy the aversive circumstances, even if they actually can exert some influence.

learning A relatively permanent change in behaviour brought about by experience.

learning-theory approach (to language development) The theory suggesting that language acquisition follows the principles of reinforcement and conditioning.

levels-of-processing theory The theory of memory that emphasizes the degree to which new material is mentally analyzed.

life review The process by which people examine and evaluate their lives.

limbic system The part of the brain that controls eating, aggression, and reproduction.

lobes The four major sections of the cerebral cortex: frontal, parietal, temporal, and occipital.

longitudinal research A research method that investigates behaviour as participants age.

long-term memory Memory that stores information on a relatively permanent basis, although it may be difficult to retrieve.

low-ball technique First offering something for a low price to gain agreement and then increasing the price after the buyer has made a commitment to purchase.

M

major depression A severe form of depression that interferes with concentration, decision making, and sociability.

mania An extended state of intense, wild elation.

manifest content of dreams According to Freud, the apparent storyline of dreams.

masturbation Sexual self-stimulation.

means-ends analysis Repeated testing for differences between the desired outcome and what currently exists.

meditation A learned technique for refocusing attention that brings about an altered state of consciousness.

memory The process by which we encode, store, and retrieve information.

menopause The period during which women stop menstruating and are no longer fertile.

mental age The average age of individuals who achieve a particular level of performance on a test.

mental images Representations in the mind that resemble the object or event being represented.

mental retardation (intellectual disabilities) A condition characterized by significant limitations both in intellectual functioning and in conceptual, social, and practical adaptive skills.

mental set The tendency for old patterns of problem solving to persist.

metabolism The rate at which food is converted to energy and expended by the body.

metacognition An awareness and understanding of one's own cognitive processes.

Minnesota Multiphasic Personality Inventory-2 (MMPI-2) A widely used self-report test that identifies people with psychological difficulties and is employed to predict some everyday behaviours.

mood disorder A disturbance in emotional experience that is strong enough to intrude on everyday living.

mood stabilizers Drugs used to treat mood disorders that prevent manic episodes of bipolar disorder.

morpheme The smallest unit of speech that can still have meaning.

motivation The factors that direct and energize the behaviour of humans and other organisms.

motor area The part of the cortex that is largely responsible for the body's voluntary movement.

motor (efferent) neurons Neurons that communicate information from the nervous system to muscles and glands.

myelin sheath A protective coat of fat and protein that wraps around axons.

Myers-Briggs Type Indicator A self-report test that measures people's preferences for thinking and behaviour.

N

narcissistic personality disorder A personality disturbance characterized by an exaggerated sense of self-importance.

narcotics Drugs that increase relaxation and relieve pain and anxiety.

nativist approach (to language development) The theory that a genetically determined, innate mechanism directs language development.

naturalistic observation Research in which an investigator simply observes some naturally occurring behaviour and does not make a change in the situation.

nature–nurture issue The issue of the degree to which environment and heredity influence behaviour.

need for achievement A stable, learned characteristic in which a person obtains satisfaction by striving for and attaining a level of excellence.

need for affiliation An interest in establishing and maintaining relationships with other people.

need for power A tendency to seek impact, control, or influence over others, and to be seen as a powerful individual.

negative reinforcer An unpleasant stimulus whose removal leads to an increase in the probability that a preceding response will be repeated in the future.

neo-Freudian psychoanalysts Psychoanalysts who were trained in traditional Freudian theory but who later rejected some of its major points.

neurons Nerve cells, the basic elements of the nervous system.

neuroplasticity Changes in the brain that occur throughout the lifespan relating to the addition of new neurons, new interconnections between neurons, and the reorganization of information-processing areas.

neuroscience perspective The approach that views behaviour from the perspective of the brain, the nervous system, genes, and other biological functions.

neurotransmitters Chemicals that carry messages across the synapse to the dendrite (and sometimes the cell body) of a receiving neuron.

neutral stimulus A stimulus that, before conditioning, does not naturally bring about the response of interest.

norms Standards of test performance that permit the comparison of one person's score on a test with the scores of other individuals who have taken the same test.

not-so-free sample Offering a free sample to instigate the norm of reciprocity (i.e., that we should treat other people as they treat us).

O

obedience A change in behaviour in response to the commands of others.

obesity Body weight that is more than 20% above the average weight for a person of a particular height.

object permanence The awareness that objects—and people—continue to exist even if they are out of sight.

observational learning Learning by observing the behaviour of another person or model.

obsession A persistent, unwanted thought or idea that keeps recurring.

obsessive-compulsive disorder A disorder characterized by obsessions or compulsions.

occipital lobes The lobes that help you process visual information.

Oedipal conflict A child's sexual interest in his or her mother, typically resolved through identification with the mother.

operant conditioning Learning in which a voluntary response is strengthened or weakened, depending on its favourable or unfavourable consequences.

operational definition The translation of a hypothesis into specific, testable procedures that can be measured and observed.

opponent-process theory of colour vision The theory that receptor cells for colour are linked in pairs, working in opposition to each other.

optic nerve A bundle of ganglion axons that carry visual information to the brain.

otoliths Tiny, motion-sensitive crystals within the semicircular canals that sense body acceleration.

overgeneralization The phenomenon by which children apply language rules even when the application results in an error.

ovulation The point at which an egg is released from the ovaries.

P

panic disorder Anxiety disorder that takes the form of panic attacks lasting from a few seconds to as long as several hours.

parasympathetic division The part of the autonomic division of the nervous system that acts to calm the body after an emergency has ended.

parietal lobes The lobes responsible for all of our bodily sensations such as temperature, touch, and taste.

partial (or intermittent) reinforcement schedule Reinforcing of a behaviour sometimes but not all of the time.

passionate (or romantic) love A state of intense absorption in someone that includes intense physiological arousal, psychological interest, and caring for the needs of another.

perception The sorting out, interpretation, analysis, and integration of stimuli by the sense organs in the brain.

perceptual constancy Phenomenon in which physical objects are perceived to have constant shape, colour, and size, despite changes in their appearance or in the physical environment.

perceptual set The expectations and beliefs that impact what we (think we) see.

peripheral nervous system The part of the nervous system that includes the autonomic and somatic subdivisions; made up of neurons with long axons and dendrites, it branches out from the spinal cord and brain and reaches the extremities of the body.

peripheral route processing Message interpretation characterized by consideration of the source and related general information rather than of the message itself.

permissive parents Parents who give their children relaxed or inconsistent direction and, although they are warm, require little of the children.

person-centred therapy Therapy in which the goal is to reach one's potential for self-actualization.

personal stressors Major life events, such as the death of a family member, that have immediate negative consequences that generally fade with time.

personality The pattern of enduring characteristics that produce consistency and individuality in a given person.

personality disorder A disorder characterized by a set of inflexible, maladaptive behaviour patterns that keep a person from functioning appropriately in society.

phobias Intense, irrational fears of specific objects or situations.

phonemes The smallest units of speech.

phonology The study of the smallest units of speech, called phonemes.

pituitary gland The major component of the endocrine system, or "master gland," which secretes hormones that control growth and other parts of the endocrine system.

place theory of hearing The theory that different areas of the basilar membrane respond to different frequencies.

placebo A false treatment, such as a pill, "drug," or other substance, without any significant chemical properties or active ingredient.

positive reinforcer A stimulus added to the environment that brings about an increase in a preceding response.

practical intelligence According to Sternberg, intelligence related to overall success in living.

prejudice A negative (or positive) evaluation of a particular group and its members.

preoperational stage According to Piaget, the period from two to seven years of age that is characterized by language development.

priming A phenomenon in which exposure to a word or concept (called a prime) later makes it easier to recall related information, even when there is no conscious memory of the word or concept.

principle of conservation The knowledge that quantity is unrelated to the arrangement and physical appearance of objects.

principlism Helping behaviour to help others to uphold moral principles.

proactive interference Interference in which information learned earlier disrupts the recall of newer material.

procedural memory Memory for skills and habits, such as riding a bike or hitting a baseball, sometimes referred to as non-declarative memory.

progesterone A female sex hormone secreted by the ovaries.

projective personality test A test in which a person is shown an ambiguous stimulus and asked to describe it or tell a story about it.

prosocial behaviour Helping behaviour.

prototypes Typical, highly representative examples of a concept.

psychoactive drugs Drugs that influence a person's emotions, perceptions, and behaviour.

psychoanalysis Freudian psychotherapy in which the goal is to release hidden unconscious thoughts and feelings to reduce their power in controlling behaviour.

psychoanalytic perspective The perspective that suggests that abnormal behaviour stems from childhood conflicts over opposing wishes regarding sex and aggression.

psychoanalytic theory Freud's theory that unconscious forces act as determinants of personality.

psychodynamic approaches to personality Approaches that assume that personality is motivated by inner forces and conflicts about which people have little awareness and over which they have no control.

psychodynamic perspective The approach based on the view that behaviour is motivated by unconscious inner forces over which the individual has little control.

psychodynamic therapy Therapy that seeks to bring unresolved past conflicts and unacceptable impulses from the unconscious into the conscious, where clients may deal with the problems more effectively.

psychological tests Standard measures devised to assess behaviour objectively; used by psychologists to help people make decisions about their lives and understand more about themselves.

psychology The scientific study of behaviour and mental processes.

psychoneuroimmunology (PNI) The study of the relationship among psychological factors, the immune system, and the brain.

psychophysics The study of the relationship between the physical aspects of stimuli and our psychological experience of them.

psychophysiological disorders Medical problems influenced by an interaction of psychological, emotional, and physical difficulties.

psychosexual stages Developmental periods that individuals pass through during which they encounter conflicts between the demands of society and their own sexual urges.

psychosocial development Development of individuals' interactions and understanding of one another and of their knowledge and understanding of themselves as members of society.

psychosurgery Brain surgery once used to reduce the symptoms of mental disorder but rarely used today.

psychotherapy Treatment in which a trained professional—a therapist—uses psychological techniques to help a person overcome psychological difficulties and disorders, resolve problems in living, or bring about personal growth.

puberty The period at which maturation of the sexual organs occurs, beginning about age 11 or 12 for girls and 13 or 14 for boys.

punishment A stimulus that decreases the probability that a previous behaviour will occur again.

R

random assignment to condition A procedure in which participants are assigned to different experimental groups or "conditions" on the basis of chance and chance alone.

random sample A sample that is representative because it was chosen randomly and every member of the population had an equal chance of being included.

rapid eye movement (REM) sleep Sleep occupying 20% of an adult's sleeping time, characterized by increased heart rate, blood pressure, and breathing rate; erections; eye movements; and the experience of dreaming.

recall Memory task in which specific information must be retrieved.

reciprocal altruism Helping others because we expect that others will help us in return.

reciprocal determinism The two-way interaction between the individual and the situation or environment, where the individual impacts the situation or environment, and the situation or environment impacts the individual.

recognition Memory task in which individuals are presented with a stimulus and asked whether they have been exposed to it in the past or to identify it from a list of alternatives, such as a multiple-choice test.

reflex An automatic, involuntary response to an incoming stimulus.

rehearsal The repetition of information that has entered short-term memory.

reinforcement The process by which a stimulus increases the probability that a preceding behaviour will be repeated.

reinforcer Any stimulus that increases the probability that a preceding behaviour will occur again.

reliability The property by which tests measure consistently what they are trying to measure.

replication The repetition of research, sometimes using other procedures, settings, and groups of participants, to increase confidence in prior findings.

representative sample The sample chosen represents the greater population so that the results can be generalized from the sample to the population.

repression The primary defence mechanism in which unacceptable or unpleasant id impulses are pushed back into the unconscious.

resistance A defence mechanism where the patient unconsciously resists or defends against the possible painful memories that may arise during therapy.

resting state The state in which there is a negative electrical charge of about negative 70 millivolts within a neuron.

reticular formation The part of the brain extending from the medulla through the pons and made up of groups of nerve cells that can immediately activate other parts of the brain to produce general bodily arousal.

retina The part of the eye that converts the electromagnetic energy of light to electrical impulses for transmission to the brain.

retroactive interference Interference in which there is difficulty in the recall of information learned earlier because of later exposure to different material.

retrograde amnesia Amnesia in which memory is lost for occurrences prior to a certain event.

reuptake The reabsorption of neurotransmitters by a terminal button.

rods Thin, cylindrical receptor cells in the retina that are highly sensitive to light.

Rorschach test A test that involves showing a series of symmetrical visual stimuli to people who then are asked what the figures represent to them.

S

Schachter-Singer theory of emotion The idea that emotions are determined jointly by a non-specific kind of physiological arousal and its interpretation, based on environmental cues.

schedules of reinforcement Different patterns of frequency and timing of reinforcement following desired behaviour.

schemas Organized bodies of information stored in memory that bias the way new information is interpreted, stored, and recalled.

schizophrenia A class of disorders in which severe distortion of reality occurs.

scientific method The approach through which psychologists systematically acquire knowledge and understanding about behaviour and other phenomena of interest.

seasonal affective disorder (SAD) A form of seasonal depression resulting from a disruption in circadian rhythms.

self-actualization A state of self-fulfillment in which people realize their highest potential, each in a unique way.

self-efficacy Belief in one's personal capabilities. Self-efficacy underlies people's faith in their ability to carry out a particular behaviour or produce a desired outcome.

self-esteem The component of personality that encompasses our positive and negative self-evaluations.

self-report measures A method of gathering data about people by asking them questions about a sample of their behaviour.

self-serving bias The tendency to attribute personal success to personal factors (skill, ability, or effort) and to attribute failure to factors outside oneself.

semantic memory Memory for general knowledge and facts about the world, as well as memory for the rules of logic that are used to deduce other facts.

semantic networks Mental representations of clusters of interconnected information.

semantics The rules governing the meaning of words and sentences.

semicircular canals Three tubelike structures of the inner ear containing fluid that sloshes through them when the head moves, signalling rotational or angular movement to the brain.

sensation The activation of the sense organs by a source of physical energy.

sensorimotor stage According to Piaget, the stage from birth to two years, during which a child has little competence in representing the environment by using images, language, or other symbols.

sensory (afferent) neurons Neurons that transmit information from the perimeter of the body to the central nervous system.

sensory area The brain tissue that corresponds to the different senses, with the degree of sensitivity related to the amount of tissue.

sensory memory The initial, momentary storage of information, lasting only an instant; and includes both echoic and iconic memory.

sequential research A research method that combines cross-sectional and longitudinal research by considering a number of different age groups and examining them at several points in time.

shaping The process of teaching a complex behaviour by rewarding closer and closer approximations of the desired behaviour.

short-term memory The second stage of memory that holds information for 15 to 25 seconds.

significant outcome Meaningful results that make it possible for researchers to feel confident that they have supported their hypotheses.

situational causes (of behaviour) Perceived causes of behaviour that are based on environmental factors.

skin senses The senses of touch, pressure, temperature, and pain.

social cognition The cognitive processes by which people understand and make sense of others and themselves.

social cognitive approaches to personality Theories that emphasize the influence of a person's cognitions—thoughts, feelings, expectations, and values—as well as observation of others' behaviour, in determining personality.

social influence The process by which the actions of an individual or group affect the behaviour of others.

social psychology The scientific study of how people's thoughts, feelings, and actions are affected by others.

social support A mutual network of caring, interested others.

social supporter A group member whose dissenting views make nonconformity to the group easier.

socio-cultural perspective This perspective explains behaviour as being due to social and cultural influences.

somatic division The part of the peripheral nervous system that specializes in the control of voluntary movements and the communication of information to and from the sense organs.

sound The movement of air molecules brought about by a source of vibration.

spinal cord A bundle of neurons that leaves the brain and runs down the length of the back and is the main means for transmitting messages between the brain and the body.

spontaneous recovery The reemergence of an extinguished conditioned response after a period of rest and with no further conditioning.

spontaneous remission Recovery without treatment.

stage 1 sleep The state of transition between wakefulness and sleep, characterized by relatively rapid, low-amplitude brain waves.

stage 2 sleep A sleep deeper than that of stage 1, characterized by a slower, more regular wave pattern, along with momentary interruptions of "sleep spindles."

stage 3 sleep A sleep characterized by slow brain waves, with greater peaks and valleys in the wave pattern than in stage 2 sleep.

stage 4 sleep The deepest stage of sleep, during which we are least responsive to outside stimulation.

status The social rank held within a group.

stereotype A set of generalized beliefs and expectations about a particular group and its members.

stimulants Drugs that have an arousal effect on the central nervous system, causing a rise in heart rate, blood pressure, and muscular tension.

stimulus Energy that produces a response in a sense organ.

stimulus discrimination The process that occurs if two stimuli are sufficiently distinct from each other that one evokes a conditioned response but the other does not; the ability to differentiate between stimuli.

stimulus generalization Occurs when a conditioned response follows a stimulus that is similar to the original conditioned stimulus; the more similar the two stimuli are, the more likely generalization is to occur.

stress A person's response to events that are threatening or challenging.

structuralism Wundt's approach, which focuses on uncovering the fundamental mental components of consciousness, thinking, and other kinds of mental states and activities.

subjective well-being People's own evaluation of their lives in terms of both their thoughts and their emotions.

superego According to Freud, the final personality structure to develop; it represents the rights and wrongs of society as handed down by a person's parents, teachers, and other important figures.

survey research Research in which people chosen to represent a larger population are asked a series of questions about their behaviour, thoughts, or attitudes.

sympathetic division The part of the autonomic division of the nervous system that acts to prepare the body for action in stressful situations, engaging all the organism's resources to respond to a threat.

synapse The space between two neurons where the axon of a sending neuron communicates with the dendrites of a receiving neuron by using chemical messages.

syntax Ways in which words and phrases can be combined to form sentences.

systematic desensitization A behavioural technique in which gradual exposure to an anxiety-producing stimulus is paired with relaxation to extinguish the response of anxiety.

T

telegraphic speech Sentences in which words not critical to the message are left out.

temperament The basic, innate disposition that emerges early in life.

temporal lobes The lobes that help you process auditory information and hold long-term memories.

teratogen An environmental agent such as a drug, chemical, virus, or other factor that produce a birth defect.

terminal buttons Small bulges at the end of axons that send messages to other neurons. (Sometimes called end bulbs or axon terminals.)

test standardization A technique used to validate questions in personality tests by studying the responses of people with known diagnoses.

thalamus The part of the brain located in the middle of the central core that acts primarily to relay information about the senses.

that's-not-all technique Offering a deal at an inflated price, but immediately after the initial offer, offering an incentive, discount, or bonus to clinch the deal.

Thematic Apperception Test (TAT) A test consisting of a series of pictures about which a person is asked to write a story.

theories Broad explanations and predictions concerning phenomena of interest.

theory of multiple intelligences Gardner's intelligence theory that proposes that there are eight distinct spheres of intelligence.

thinking The manipulation of mental representations of information.

tip-of-the-tongue phenomenon The inability to recall information that one realizes one knows—a result of the difficulty of retrieving information from long-term memory.

tolerance When people use a drug for a period of time, they need increasing amounts to achieve the same feelings.

top-down processing Perception that is guided by higher-level knowledge, experience, expectations, and motivations.

trait theory A model of personality that seeks to identify the basic traits necessary to describe personality.

traits Consistent personality characteristics and behaviours displayed in different situations.

transcranial magnetic stimulation (TMS) A depression treatment in which a precise magnetic pulse is directed to a specific area of the brain.

transduction **The process of converting the physical energy to an electrical impulse.**

transference The transfer of feelings of love or anger to a psychoanalyst that had been originally directed to a client's parents or other authority figure.

transsexuals Persons who believe they were born with the body of the other gender.

treatment The manipulation (or change) implemented by the experimenter.

trichromatic theory of colour vision The theory that there are three kinds of cones in the retina, each of which responds primarily to a specific range of wavelengths.

trust-versus-mistrust stage According to Erikson, the first stage of psychosocial development, occurring from birth to age one-and-a-half years, during which time infants develop feelings of trust or lack of trust.

Type A behaviour pattern A cluster of behaviours involving hostility, competitiveness, time urgency, and feeling driven.

Type B behaviour pattern A cluster of behaviours characterized by a patient, cooperative, non-competitive manner.

U

unconditional positive regard An attitude of acceptance and respect on the part of an observer, no matter what a person says or does.

unconditioned response (UCR) A response that is natural and needs no training (for example, salivation at the smell of food).

unconditioned stimulus (UCS) A stimulus that naturally brings about a particular response without having been learned.

unconscious wish fulfillment theory Sigmund Freud's theory that dreams represent unconscious wishes that dreamers desire to see fulfilled.

unconscious A part of the personality that contains the memories, knowledge, beliefs, feelings, urges, drives, and instincts of which the individual is not aware.

uninvolved parents Parents who show little interest in their children and are emotionally detached.

universal grammar Noam Chomsky's theory that all the world's languages share a common underlying structure.

V

validity The property by which tests actually measure what they are supposed to measure.

variable-interval schedule A schedule by which the time between reinforcements varies around some average rather than being fixed.

variable-ratio schedule A schedule by which reinforcement occurs after a varying number of responses rather than after a fixed number.

variables Behaviours, events, or other characteristics that can change, or vary, in some way.

visual illusions Physical stimuli that consistently produce errors in perception.

W

wear-and-tear theories of aging Theories that suggest that the mechanical functions of the body simply stop working efficiently.

Weber's law A basic law of psychophysics stating that a just-noticeable difference is a constant proportion of the intensity of an initial stimulus.

weight set point The particular level of weight that the body strives to maintain.

Wernicke's area An area in the temporal lobe that allows you to understand the spoken word.

withdrawal A craving for the drug that, in some cases, may be nearly irresistible.

working memory A set of active, temporary memory stores that actively manipulate and rehearse information.

Z

zone of proximal development (ZPD) According to Vygotsky, the level at which a child can almost, but not fully, comprehend or perform a task on his or her own.

zygote The new cell formed by the union of an egg and sperm.

A

Aartsen, M. J., Martin, M., & Zimprich, D. (2002). Gender differences in level and change in cognitive functioning: Results from the longitudinal aging study Amsterdam. *Gerontology, 50,* 35–38.

Aazh, H., & Moore, B. C. J. (2007). Dead regions in the cochlea at 4 kHz in elderly adults: Relation to absolute threshold, steepness of audiogram, and pure-tone average. *Journal of the American Academy of Audiology, 18,* 97–106.

Ablon, J. S., & Jones, E. E. (2005). On analytic process. *Journal of the American Psychoanalytic Association, 53,* 541–568.

Abraham, P. F., & Calabrese, J. R. (2007). Review of: *Lithium treatment of mood disorders: A practical guide,* 6th rev. ed. *Bipolar Disorders, 9,* 548.

Abraham, S. F., Boyd, C., Luscombe, G., Hart, S., & Russell, J. (2007). When energy in does not equal energy out: Disordered energy control. *Eating Behaviors, 8,* 350–356.

Adams, B., & Parker, J. D. (1990). Maternal weight gain in women with good pregnancy outcome. *Obstetrics and Gynecology, 76,* 1–7.

Adams, K. B. (2004). Changing investment in activities and interests in elders' lives: Theory and measurement. *International Journal of Aging and Human Development, 58,* 87–108.

Adams, W. L. (2006). The truth about photographic memory. *Psychology Today,* March 1. Accessed from www.psychologytoday.com/articles/pto-20060323-000001.html.

Addolorato, G., Leggio, L., Abenavoli, L., & Gasbarrini, G. (2005). Neurobiochemical and clinical aspects of craving in alcohol addiction: A review. *Addictive Behaviors, 30,* 1209–1224.

Adkins, E., & Keel, P. (2005). Does "excessive" or "compulsive" best describe exercise as a symptom of bulimia nervosa? *International Journal of Eating Disorders, 38,* 24–29.

Adler, J. (1984, April 23). The fight to conquer fear. *Newsweek,* pp. 66–72.

Advokat, C. (2005). Differential effects of clozapine versus other antipsychotics on clinical outcome and dopamine release in the brain. *Essential Psychopharmacology, 6,* 73–90.

Aftanas, L., & Golosheykin, S. (2005). Impact of regular meditation practice on EEG activity at rest and during evoked negative emotions. *International Journal of Neuroscience, 115,* 893–909.

Aghajanian, G. K. (1994). Serotonin and the action of LSD in the brain. *Psychiatric Annals, 24,* 137–141.

Agras, W. S., & Berkowitz, R. I. (1996). Behavior therapy. In R. E. Hales & S. C. Yudofsky (Eds.), *The American Psychiatric Press synopsis of psychiatry.* Washington, DC: American Psychiatric Press.

Ahiima, R. S., & Osei, S. Y. (2004). Leptin signaling. *Physiology and Behavior, 81,* 223–241.

Aiken, L. (1997). *Psychological testing and assessment* (9th ed.). Needham Heights, MA: Allyn & Bacon.

Aiken, L. (2000a). *Dying, death, and bereavement* (4th ed.). Mahwah, NJ: Erlbaum.

Aiken, L. (2000b). *Personality: Theories, assessment, research, and applications.* Springfield, IL: Charles C. Thomas.

Ainsworth, M. D. S., Blehar, M. C., Waters, E., & Wall, S. (1978). *Patterns of attachment: A psychological study of the strange situation.* Hillsdale, NJ: Erlbaum.

Ajzen, I. (2002). Residual effects of past on later behavior: Habituation and reasoned action perspectives. *Personality and Social Psychology Review, 6,* 107–122.

Akil, H., & Morano, M. I. (1996). The biology of stress: From periphery to brain. In S. J. Watson (Ed.), *Biology of schizophrenia and affective disease.* Washington, DC: American Psychiatric Press.

Allan, G. (2004). Being unfaithful: His and her affairs. In J. Duncombe, K. Harrison., G. Allan, & D. Marsden (Eds.), *The state of affairs: Explorations in infidelity and commitment.* Mahwah, NJ: Lawrence Erlbaum Associates Publishers.

Allport, G. W. (1961). *Pattern and growth in personality.* New York: Holt, Rinehart and Winston.

Allport, G. W. (1966). Traits revisited. *American Psychologist, 21,* 1–10.

Allport, G. W., & Postman, L. J. (1958). The basic psychology of rumor. In E. D. Maccoby, T. M. Newcomb, & E. L. Hartley (Eds.), *Readings in social psychology* (3rd ed.). New York: Holt, Rinehart and Winston.

Almey, M. (2005). Women in Canada: Work chapter updates. Statistics Canada. Retrieved on May 17, 2012, from www.statcan.gc.ca/pub/89f0133x/89f0133x2006000-eng.htm.

Aloia, M. S., Smith, K., & Arendt, J. T. (2007). Brief behavioral therapies reduce early positive airway pressure discontinuation rates in sleep apnea syndrome: Preliminary findings. *Behavioral Sleep Medicine, 5,* 89–104.

Alon, I., & Brett, J. M. (2007). Perceptions of time and their impact on negotiations in the Arabic-speaking Islamic world. *Negotiation Journal, 23,* 55–73.

Alonso, A., Alonso, S., & Piper, W. (2003). Group psychotherapy. In G. Stricker & T. A. Widiger, et al. (Eds.), *Handbook of psychology: Clinical psychology* (Vol. 8). New York:

Alonso, Y. (2004, May). The biopsychosocial model in medical research: The evolution of the health concept over the last two decades. *Patient Education and Counseling, 53*(2), 239–244.

Alzheimer Society of Canada. (2010). *Rising tide: The impact of dementia on Canadian society.* Toronto, ON: Alzheimer Society of Canada.

Amato, L., Davoili, M., Perucci, C. A., Ferri, M., Faggiano, F., & Mattick R. P. (2005). An overview of systematic reviews of the effectiveness of opiate maintenance therapies: Available evidence to inform clinical practice and research. *Journal of Substance Abuse Treatment, 28,* 321–329.

Ambady, N., & Rosenthal, R. (1992, March). Thin slices of expressive behavior as predictors of interpersonal consequences: A meta-analysis. *Psychological Bulletin, 111*(2), 256–274.

American Association of Mental Retardation (AAMR). (2002). *Mental retardation: Definition, classification, and systems of supports* (10th ed.). Washington, DC: AAMR.

American Insomnia Association (2005). Causes of insomnia. In L. Vande Creek (Ed.), *Innovations in clinical practice: Focus on adults.* Sarasota, FL: Professional Resource Press/ Professional Resource Exchange.

American Psychiatric Association Task Force on DSM-IV (2000). *Diagnostic and statistical manual of mental disorders* (4th ed. Text Revision). Arlington, VA: American Psychiatric Association.

American Psychological Association (APA). (2007, October). Stress tip sheet. APA offers tips on how to manage your stress. Retrieved from www.apa.org/news/press/releases/2007/10/stress-tips.aspx.

American Psychological Association Task Force on Intelligence. (1996). *Intelligence: Knowns and unknowns.* Washington, DC: American Psychological Association.

Amos, A., Wiltshire, S., & Haw, S. (2006). Ambivalence and uncertainty: Experiences of and attitudes towards addiction and smoking cessation in the mid-to-late teens. *Health Education Research, 21,* 181–191.

Anand, G. (2002). Antidepressants Remain Popular But Often Disappoint Consumers. *The Wall Street Journal.* www.astrocyte-design.com/pseudoscience/wsj.html.

Anand, G., & Burton, T. M. (2003, April 11). Drug debate: New antipsychotics pose a quandary for FDA, doctors. *The Wall Street Journal,* pp. A1, A8.

Anderson, C. (2004). Aggression. In E. Borgatta (Ed.), *The encyclopedia of sociology* (rev. ed.). New York: Macmillan.

Anderson, C. A., & Dill, K. E. (2000). Video games and aggressive thoughts, feelings, and behavior in the laboratory and in life. *Journal of Personality and Social Psychology, 78,* 772–790.

Anderson, C. A., Carnagey, N. L., Flanagan, M., Benjamin, A. J., Jr., Eubanks, J., & Valentine, J. C. (2004). Violent video games: Specific effects of violent content on aggressive thoughts and behavior. In M. P. Zanna (Ed.), *Advances in experimental social psychology* (Vol. 36). San Diego, CA: Elsevier Academic Press.

Anderson, C. A., Krull, D. S., & Weiner, B. (1996). Explanations: Processes and Consequences. In E.T. Higgins & A.W. Kruglanski (Eds.), *Social Psychology: Handbook of Basic Principles* (p. 274). New York: Guilford Press.

Anderson, C., & Home, J. A. (2006). Sleepiness enhances distraction during monotonous task. *Sleep: Journal of Sleep and Sleep Disorders Research, 29,* 573–576.

Anderson, J. (2000). *Learning and memory: An integrated approach* (2nd ed.). Hoboken, NJ: John Wiley & Sons Inc.

Anderson, J. R. (1981). Interference: The relationship between response latency and response accuracy. *Journal of Experimental Psychology: Human Learning and Memory, 7,* 311–325.

Anderson, Q. (2005). Lying faces. ScienCentral. www.sciencentral.com/articles/view.php3?language=english&type=article& article_id=218392481.

Andrasik, F. (2006). Psychophysiological disorders: Headache as a case in point. In F. Andrasik, *Comprehensive handbook of personality and psychopathology: Vol. 2: Adult psychopathology*. Hoboken, NJ: John Wiley & Sons.

Andrasik, F. (2007). What does the evidence show? Efficacy of behavioural treatments for recurrent headaches in adults. *Neurological Science, 28*, Supplement, S70–S77.

Andreasen, N. C. (2005). *Research advances in genetics and genomics: Implications for psychiatry*. Washington, DC: American Psychiatric Publishing.

Angoff, W. H. (1988). The nature-nurture debate, aptitudes, and group differences. *American Psychologist, 43*, 713–720.

Ansaldo, A. I., Arguin, M., & Roch Locours, L. A. (2002). The contribution of the right cerebral hemisphere to the recovery from aphasia: A single longitudinal case study. *Brain Languages, 82*, 206–222.

Antonucci, T. C., Lansford, J. E., Akiyama, H., Smith, J., Baltes, M. M., Takahashi, K., et al. (2002). Differences between men and women in social relations, resource deficits, and depressive symptomatology during later life in four nations. *Journal of Social Issues, 58*, 767–783.

APA (American Psychological Association). (1999, March 21). It's not what you say, it's how you say it: Message framing motivates beach-goers to use sunscreen. Retrieved from www.apa.org/releases/ sunscreen.html.

APA (American Psychological Association). (2002, August 21). APA ethics code, 2002. Washington, DC: American Psychological Association.

Apkarian, A. V., Bushnell, M. C., Treede, R. D., & Zubeita, J. K. (2005). Human brain mechanisms of pain perception and regulation in health and disease. *European Journal of Pain, 9*, 463–484.

Aponte, J. F., & Wohl, J. (2000). *Psychological intervention and cultural diversity*. Needham Heights, MA: Allyn & Bacon.

Arafat, I., & Cotton, W. L. (1974). Masturbation practices of males and females. *Journal of Sex Research, 10*, 293–307.

Arambula, P., Peper, E., Kawakami, M., & Gibney, K. H. (2001). The physiological correlates of Kundalini yoga meditation: A study of a yoga master. *Applied Psychophysiology & Biofeedback, 26*, 147–153.

Archambault, D. L. (1992). Adolescence: A physiological, cultural, and psychological no man's land. In G. W. Lawson & A. W. Lawson (Eds.), *Adolescent substance abuse: Etiology, treatment, and prevention*. Gaithersburg, MD: Aspen.

Ariyanto, A., Hornsey, M. J., & Gallois, C. (2006). Group-directed criticism in Indonesia: Role of message source and audience. *Asian Journal of Social Psychology, 9*, 96–102.

Arlin, P. K. (1989). The problem of the problem. In J. D. Sinnott (Ed.), *Everyday problem solving: Theory and applications*. New York: Praeger.

Armstrong, T. (2000). *Multiple intelligences in the classroom* (2nd ed.). Washington, DC: Association for Supervision & Curriculum Development.

Armstrong, T. (2003). *The multiple intelligences of reading and writing: Making the words come alive* (2nd ed.). Washington, DC: Association for Supervision & Curriculum Development.

Aronson, E. (1994). *The social animal*. New York: Macmillan.

Asch, S. E. (1951). Effects of group pressure upon the modification and distortion of judgments. In H. Guetzkow (Ed.), *Groups, leadership, and men*. Pittsburgh: Carnegie Press.

Askew, C., & Field, A. (2008, October). The vicarious learning pathway to fear 40 years on. *Clinical Psychology Review, 28*(7), 1249–1265.

Aspinwall, L. G., & Taylor, S. E. (1997). A stitch in time: Self-regulation and proactive coping. *Psychological Bulletin, 121*, 417–436.

Atkinson, R. C., & Shiffrin, R. M. (1968). Human memory: A proposed system and its control processes. In K. W. Spence & J. T. Spence (Eds.), *The psychology of learning and motivation: Advances in research and theory* (Vol. 2) (pp. 80–195). New York: Academic Press.

Atkinson, R. C., & Shiffrin, R. M. (1971). The control of short-term memory. *Scientific American, 225*, 82–90.

Auer, J. A., Goodship, A., Arnoczky, S., Pearce, S., Price, J., Claes, L., von Rechenberg, B., Hofmann-Amtenbrinck, M., Schneider, E., Muller-Terpitz, R., Thiele, F., Rippe, K. P., & Grainger, D. W. (2007). Refining animal models in fracture research: Seeking consensus for changing the agenda in optimising both animal welfare and scientific validity for appropriate biomedical use. *BMC Musculoskeletal Disorders, 8*, 72.

Aujoulat, I., Luminet, O., & Deccache, A. (2007). The perspective of patients on their experience of powerlessness. *Quality Health Research, 17*, 772–785.

Auld, F., Hyman, M., & Rudzinski, D. (2005). Theory and strategy of dream interpretation. In F. Auld & M. Hyman (Eds.), *Resolution of inner conflict: An introduction to psychoanalytic therapy* (2nd ed.). Washington, DC: American Psychological Association.

Aussilloux, C., & Baghdadli, A. (2006). Handicap mental et société: Soigner, éduquer, intégrer. Mental handicap and society. *Neuropsychiatrie de l'Enfance et de l'Adolescence, 54*, 336–340.

Austin, E., Saklofske, D., & Mastoras, S. (2010). Emotional intelligence, coping, and exam-related stress in Canadian undergraduate students. *Australian Journal of Psychology, 62*, 42–50.

Averill, J. R. (1975). A semantic atlas of emotional concepts. *Catalog of Selected Documents in Psychology, 5*, 330.

Awad, A., & Voruganti, L. (2007). Antipsychotic medications, schizophrenia and the issue of quality of life. *Quality of life impairment in schizophrenia, mood and anxiety disorders: New perspectives on research and treatment* (pp. 307–319). New York: Springer Science + Business Media.

B

Bacchiochi, J. R. (2006). Development and validation of the Malingering Discriminant Function Index (M-DFI) for the Minnesota Multiphasic Personality Inventory-2 (MMPI-2). *Dissertation Abstracts International: Section B: The Sciences and Engineering, 66*(10-B), 5673.

Baccus, J. R., Baldwin, M. W., & Packer, D. J. (2004). Increasing implicit self-esteem through classical conditioning. *Psychological Science, 15*, 498–502.

Baddeley, A. (2001). Is working memory still working? *American Psychologist, 56*, 849–864.

Baddeley, A., & Wilson, B. (1985). Phonological coding and short-term memory in patients without speech. *Journal of Memory and Language, 24*, 490–502.

Baddeley, A., Chincotta, D., & Adlam, A. (2001). Working memory and the control of action: Evidence from task switching. *Journal of Experimental Psychology: General, 130*, 641–657.

Baer, J. (1993). *Creativity and divergent thinking: A task-specific approach*. Hillsdale, NJ: Erlbaum.

Bahrick, H. P., Hall, L. K., & Berger, S. A. (1996). Accuracy and distortion in memory for high school grades. *Psychological Science, 7*, 265–269

Bai, L. (2005). Children at play: A childhood beyond the Confucian shadow. *Childhood: A Global Journal of Child Research, 12*, 9–32.

Bains, O. S. (2006). Insomnia: Difficulty falling and staying asleep. In N. F. Watson, & B. V. Bradley, *Clinician's guide to sleep disorders*. Philadelphia: Taylor & Francis.

Bair, D. (2003). *Jung: A biography*. New York: Little, Brown, and Company.

Balaban, C. D. (2002). Neural substrates linking balance control and anxiety [Special issue: The Pittsburgh special issue]. *Physiology and Behavior, 77*, 469–475.

Balaban, C. D., McBurney, D. H., & Affeltranger, M. A. (2005). Three distinct categories of time course of pain produced by oral capsaicin. *The Journal of Pain, 6*, 315–322.

Baltes, P. B., & Kunzmann, U. (2003). Wisdom. *Psychologist, 16*, 131–133.

Banaji, M., & Greenwald, A. (1994). Implicit stereotyping and prejudice. *The psychology of prejudice: The Ontario symposium* (Vol. 7) (pp. 55–76). Hillsdale, NJ: Lawrence Erlbaum Associates, Inc.

Bandura, A. (1977). *Social learning theory*. Englewood Cliffs, NJ: Prentice Hall.

Bandura, A. (1986). *Social foundations of thought and action: A social cognitive theory*. Englewood Cliffs, NJ: Prentice Hall.

Bandura, A. (1992). Social cognitive theory. *Six theories of child development: Revised formulations and current issues* (pp. 1:60). London: Jessica Kingsley Publishers.

Bandura, A. (1994). Social cognitive theory of mass communication. In J. Bryant & D. Zillmann (Eds.), *Media effects: Advances in theory and research: LEA's communication series*. Hillsdale, NJ: Erlbaum.

Bandura, A. (1999). Social cognitive theory of personality. In D. Cervone & Y. Shod (Eds.), *The coherence of personality*. New York: Guilford.

Bandura, A. (2001). Social cognitive theory: An agentic perspective. *Annual Review of Psychology, 52*, 1–26.

Bandura, A. (2004). Swimming against the mainstream: The early years from chilly tributary to transformative mainstream. *Behaviour Research and Therapy, 42*, 613–630.

Bandura, A., & Locke, E. A. (2003). Negative self-efficacy and goal effects revisited. *Journal of Applied Psychology, 88*, 87–99.

Bandura, A., Grusec, J. E., & Menlove, F. L. (1967). Vicarious extinction of avoidance behavior. *Journal of Personality and Social Psychology, 5*, 16–23.

Bandura, A., Ross, D., & Ross, S. (1963a). Imitation of film-mediated aggressive models. *Journal of Abnormal and Social Psychology, 66*, 3–11.

Bandura, A., Ross, D., & Ross, S. (1963b). Vicarious reinforcement and imitative learning. *Journal of Abnormal and Social Psychology, 67*, 601–607.

Banich, T., & Heller, W. (1998). Evolving perspectives on lateralization of function. *Current Directions in Psychological Science, 7*, 1–2.

Banks, J. A. (2006). Improving race relations in schools: From theory and research to practice. *Journal of Social Issues, 62*, 607–614.

Baraas, R. C., Foster, D. H., & Amano, K. (2006). Anomalous trichromats' judgments of surface color in natural scenes under different daylights. *Neuroscience, 23*, 629–635.

Barandiaran, A. A., Pascual, A. C., & Samaniego, C. M. (2006). Una aportación crítica a la teoría kohlberiana: El desarrollo moral en adultos e implicaciones educativas. [A criticism of the Kohlberg theory: The moral development in adults and educative implications.] *Revista de Psicología General y Aplicada, 59*, 165–182.

Bargh, J. A., & Chartrand, T. L. (2000). The mind in the middle: A practical guide to priming and automaticity research. In H. T. Reis & C. M. Judd (Eds.), *Handbook of research methods in social and personality psychology.* New York: Cambridge University Press.

Barkley, R. (2005). *ADHD and the nature of self-control.* New York: Guilford.

Barlow, D. H. (2007). *Clinical handbook of psychological disorders: A step-by-step treatment manual* (4th ed.). New York: Guilford Press.

Barnes, V. A., Davis, H. C., Murzynowski, J., & Treiber, F. A. (2004). Impact of meditation on resting and ambulatory blood pressure and heart rate in youth. *Medicine, 66*, 909–914.

Barnett, J. E., Wise, E. H., & Johnson-Greene, D. (2007). Informed consent: Too much of a good thing or not enough? *Professional Psychology: Research and Practice, 38*, 179–186.

Barrett, L. F., & Salovey, P. (Eds.). (2002). *The wisdom in feeling: Psychological processes in emotional intelligence.* New York: Guilford Press.

Barron, G., & Yechiam, E. (2002). Private e-mail requests and the diffusion of responsibility. *Computers in Human Behavior, 18*, 507–520.

Bartecchi, C. E., MacKenzie, T. D., & Schrier, R. W. (1995, May). The global tobacco epidemic. *Scientific American*, 44–51.

Bartholow, B. D., & Anderson, C. A. (2002). Effects of violent video games on aggressive behavior: Potential sex differences. *Journal of Experimental Social Psychology, 38*, 283–290.

Bartholow, B. D., Bushman, B. J., & Sestir, M. A. (2006). Chronic violent video game exposure and desensitization to violence: Behavioral and event-related brain potential data. *Journal of Experimental Social Psychology, 42*, 532–539.

Bartlett, F. (1932). *Remembering: A study in experimental and social psychology.* Cambridge: Cambridge University Press.

Bartlett, M. Y., & DeSteno, D. (2006). Gratitude and prosocial behavior: Helping when it costs you. *Psychological Science, 17*, 319–325.

Bartocci, G. (2004). Transcendence techniques and psychobiological mechanisms underlying religious experience. *Mental Health, Religion and Culture, 7*, 171–181.

Bartoshuk, L. (2000, July/August). The bitter with the sweet. *APS Observer, 11*, 33.

Bartoshuk, L., & Lucchina, L. (1997, January 13). Are you a supertaster? *U.S. News & World Report*, pp. 58–59.

Baruss, I. (2003). *Alterations of consciousness: An empirical analysis for social scientists.* Washington, DC: American Psychological Association.

Bassottdi, G., Villanacci, V., Fisogni, S., Rossi, E., Baronio, P., Clerici, C., Maurer, C. A., Cathomas, G., & Antonelli, E. (2007). Enteric glial cells and their role in gastrointestinal motor abnormalities: Introducing the neurogliopathies. *World Journal of Gastroenterology, 14*, 4035–4041.

Bates, E. (2005). Plasticity, localization, and language development. In S. T. Parker and J. Langer (Eds.), *Biology and knowledge revisited: From neurogenesis to psychogenesis.* Mahwah, NJ: Lawrence Erlbaum Associates.

Bates, P. E., Cuvo, T., Miner, C. A., & Korabek, C. A. (2001). Simulated and community-based instruction involving persons with mild and moderate mental retardation. *Research in Developmental Disabilities, 22*, 95–115.

Bates, R. (2002). Liking and similarity as predictors of multi-source ratings. *Personnel Review, 31*, 540–552.

Batson, C. D., & Powell, A. A. (2003). Altruism and prosocial behavior. In T. Millon & M. J. Lerner (Eds.), *Handbook of psychology: Personality and social psychology* (Vol. 5). New York: Wiley.

Batson, C. D. (1994). Why act for the public good? Four answers. *Personality and Social Psychology Bulletin, 20*, 603–610.

Baudouin, R., & Uhl, N. (1998). The relationship between Jungian type, academic and social integration, and persistence during the freshman year. *Journal of Psychological Type, 45*, 29–35.

Bauman, S., & Kopp, T. G. (2006). Integrating a humanistic approach in outpatient sex offender groups. *Journal for Specialists in Group Work, 31*, 247–261.

Baumeister, A., & Francis, J. L. (2002). Historical development of the dopamine hypothesis of schizophrenia. *Journal of the History of the Neurosciences, 11*, 265–277.

Baumeister, R. F., Twenge, J. M., & Nuss, C. K. (2002). Effects of social exclusion on cognitive processes: Anticipated aloneness reduces intelligent thought. *Journal of Personality and Social Psychology, 83*, 817–827.

Baumrind, D. (2005). Patterns of parental authority and adolescent autonomy. *New Directions for Child and Adolescent Development, 108*, 61–69.

Baumrind, D., Larzelere, R. E., & Cowan, P. A. (2002). Ordinary physical punishment: Is it harmful? Comment on Gershoff (2002). *Psychological Bulletin, 32*, 42–51.

Bayliss, D. M., Jarrold, C., Baddeley, A. D., & Gunn, D. M. (2005a). The relationship between short-term memory and working memory: Complex span made simple? *Memory, 13*, 414–421.

Bayliss, D. M., Jarrold, C., Baddeley, A. D., Gunn, D. M., & Leigh, E. (2005b). Mapping the developmental constraints on working memory span performance. *Developmental Psychology, 41*, 579–597.

Bazalakov, M. H., Wright, J., Schneble, E. J., McDonald, M. P., Hellman, C. J., Levey, A. I., & Blakely, R. D. (2006). Deficits in acetylcholine homeostasis, receptors and behaviors in choline transporter heterozygous mice. *Genes, Brain and Behavior, 6*, 411–424.

Beaman, A. (1983, June). Fifteen years of foot-in-the-door research: A meta-analysis. *Personality and Social Psychology Bulletin, 9*(2), 181–196.

Beatty, J. (2000). *The human brain: Essentials of behavioral neuroscience.* Thousand Oaks, CA: Sage.

Beatty, W. W. (2002). Sex difference in geographical knowledge: Driving experience is not essential. *Journal of the International Neuropsychological Society, 8*, 804–810.

Beck, A. P., & Lewis, C. M. (Eds.). (2000). *The process of group psychotherapy: Systems for analyzing change.* Washington, DC: American Psychological Association.

Beck, A. T. (1995). Cognitive therapy: Past, present, and future. In M. J. Mahoney (Ed.), *Cognitive and constructive psychotherapies: Theory, research, and practice.* New York: Springer.

Beck, A. T. (2004). Cognitive therapy, behavior therapy, psychoanalysis, and pharmacotherapy: A cognitive continuum. In A. Freeman, M. J. Mahoney, P. Devito, & D. Martin (Eds.), *Cognition and psychotherapy* (2nd ed.). New York: Springer.

Beck, A. T., & Emery, G. (1985). *Anxiety disorders and phobias: A cognitive perspective.* New York: Basic Books.

Beck, A. T., & Rector, N. A. (2005). Cognitive approaches to schizophrenia: theory and therapy. *Annual Review of Clinical Psychology, 1*, 577–606.

Beck, A. T., Freeman, A., & Davis, D. D. (2004). *Cognitive therapy of personality disorders* (2nd ed.). New York: Guilford Press.

Beck, J. S. (2005). *Cognitive therapy for challenging problems: What to do when the basics don't work.* New York: Guilford.

Becker, B. E., & Luthar, S. S. (2007). Peer-perceived admiration and social preference: Contextual correlates of positive peer regard among suburban and urban adolescents. *Journal of Research on Adolescence, 17*, 117–144.

Bedard, W. W., & Parsinger, M. A. (1995). Prednisolone blocks extreme intermale social aggression in seizure-induced, brain-damaged rats: Implications for the amygdaloid central nucleus, corticotrophin-releasing factor, and electrical seizures. *Psychological Reports, 77*, 3–9.

Beersma, D. G. M., & Gordijn, M. C. M. (2007). Circadian control of the sleep-wake cycle. *Physiology & Behavior, 90.*

Begg, D., & Langley, J. (2001). Changes in risky driving behavior from age 21 to 26 years. *Journal of Safety Research, 32*, 491–499.

Begley, S. (2002, September 13). The memory of September 11 is seared in your mind; but is it really true? *The Wall Street Journal*, p. B1.

Beidel, D. C., & Turner, S. M. (2007). Etiology of social anxiety disorder. In D. C. Beidel & S. M. Turner, *Shy children, phobic adults: Nature and treatment of social anxiety disorders* (2nd ed.). Washington, DC: American Psychological Association.

Beirne Smith, M., Patton, J. R., & Kim, S. (2006) *Mental retardation* (7th ed.). Columbus, OH: Merrill.

Belli, R. F., & Loftus, E. F. (1996). The pliability of autobiographical memory: Misinformation and the false memory problem. In D. C. Rubin (Ed.), *Remembering our past: Studies in autobiographical memory* (pp. 157–179). New York: Cambridge University Press.

Bem, D. J. (1996). Exotic becomes erotic: A developmental theory of sexual orientation. *Psychological Review, 103*, 320–335.

Benca, R. M. (2005). Diagnosis and treatment of chronic insomnia: A review. *Psychiatric Services, 56*, 332–343.

Benderly, B. L. (2004). Looking beyond the SAT. *American Psychological Society, 17*, 12–18.

Benham, G., Woody, E. Z., & Wilson, K. S. (2006). Expect the unexpected: Ability, attitude, and responsiveness to hypnosis. *Journal of Personality and Social Psychology, 91*, 342–350.

Benight, C. C. (2004). Collective efficacy following a series of natural disasters. *Stress and Coping: An International Journal, 17*, 401–420.

Benjamin, L. T., Jr. (1985). Defining aggression. An exercise for classroom discussion. *Teaching of Psychology, 12*, 40–42, Table 1, 41.

Benson, H., Kornhaber, A., Kornhaber, C., LeChanu, M. N., et al. (1994). Increases in positive psychological characteristics with a new relaxation-response curriculum in high school students. *Journal of Research and Development in Education, 27*, 226–231.

Benton, S. A., Robertson, J. M., Tseng, W. C., Newton, F. B., & Benton, S. L. (2003). Changes in counseling center client problems across 13 years. *Professional Psychology: Research and Practice, 34*, 66–72.

Beresnevaité, M., Taylor, G. J., & Bagby, R. M. (2007). Assessing alexithymia and type A behavior in coronary heart disease patients: A multimethod approach. *Psychotherapy and Psychosomatics, 76*, 186–192.

Bergeron, J. M. (2006). Self-serving bias: A possible contributor of construct-irrelevant variance in high-stakes testing. *Dissertation Abstracts International Section A: Humanities and Social Sciences, 67*(1-A), 88.

Bergin, A. E., & Garfield, S. L. (Eds.). (1994). *Handbook of psychotherapy and behavior change* (4th ed.). New York: Wiley.

Berk, L. E. (2005). Why parenting matters. In S. Olfman (Ed.), *Childhood lost: How American culture is failing our kids* (pp. 19–53). Westport, CT: Praeger Publishers/Greenwood Publishing Group.

Berkowitz, L. (2001). On the formation and regulation of anger and aggression: A cognitive-neoassociationistic analysis. In W. G. Parrott (Ed.), *Emotions in social psychology: Essential readings*. New York: Psychology Press.

Berle, D. (2007). Graded exposure therapy for longstanding disgust-related cockroach avoidance in an older male. *Clinical Case Studies, 6*, 339–347.

Berman, A. L., Jobes, D. A., & Silverman, M. M. (2006). An integrative-eclectic approach to treatment. In A. L. Berman, D. A. Jobes, & M. M. Silverman, *Adolescent suicide: Assessment and intervention* (2nd ed.). Washington, DC: American Psychological Association.

Bernstein, D. M., Loftus, G. R., & Meltzoff, A. N. (2005). Object identification in preschool children and adults. *Developmental Science, 8*, 151–161.

Berntsen, D., & Rubin, D. C. (2004). Cultural life scripts structure recall from autobiographical memory. *Memory and Cognition, 32*, 427–442.

Berntsen, D., & Thomsen, D. K. (2005). Personal memories for remote historical events: Accuracy and clarity of flashbulb memories related to World War II. *Journal of Experimental Psychology: General, 134*, 242–257.

Berridge, K. C. (2004). Motivation concepts in behavioral neuroscience. *Physiology and Behavior, 81*, 179–209.

Berrios, G. E. (1996). *The history of mental symptoms: Descriptive psychopathology since the 19th century*. Cambridge: Cambridge University Press.

Berthoud, H. R. (2002). Multiple neural systems controlling food intake and body weight. *Neuroscience and Biobehavioral Reviews, 26*, 393–428.

Beven, Y., Gillis, C., & Lee, K. (2007). "I take the good with the bad, and I moisturize": Defying middle age in the new millennium. *Menopause, 14*, 734–741.

Bhardwaj, R. D., Curtis, M. A., Spalding, K. L., Buchholz, B. A., Fink, D., Bjork-Eriksson, T., Nordborg, C., Gage, F. H., Druid, H., Eriksson, P. S., & Frisen, J. (2006). Neocortical neurogenesis in humans is restricted to development. *Proceedings of the National Academy of Sciences, 103*, 12564–12568.

Bhugra, D., & Mastrogianni, A. (2004). Globalization and mental disorders. *Journal of Counseling & Values, 35*(2), 83–93.

Biddle, L., Donovan, J., Hawton, K., Kapur, N., and Gunnell, D. (2008). Suicide and the internet. *British Medical Journal 336*, 800–802.

Bielski, Z. (2011). Meet the man behind Ashley Madison.com. Retrieved April 25, 2011, www.theglobeandmail.com/life/relationships/love/infidelity/meet-the-man-behind-ashleymadisoncom/article1352744/.

Binet, A., & Simon, T. (1916). *The development of intelligence in children (The Binet-Simon Scale)*. Baltimore: Williams & Wilkins.

Binstock, R., & George, L. K. (Eds.). (1996). *Handbook of aging and the social sciences* (4th ed.). San Diego: Academic Press.

Birren, J. E. (Ed.). (1996). *Encyclopedia of gerontology: Age, aging and the aged*. San Diego: Academic Press.

Bittles, A. H., Bower, C., & Hussain, R. (2007). The four ages of Down syndrome. *European Journal of Public Health, 17*, 121–225.

Bjorklund, D. F., & Ellis, B. J. (2005). *Evolutionary psychology and child development: An emerging synthesis*. New York: Guilford Press.

Bjornstad, R. (2006). Learned helplessness, discouraged workers, and multiple unemployment equilibria. *The Journal of Socio-Economics, 35*, 458–475.

Blair, C. A., Thompson, L. F., & Wuensch, K. L. (2005). Electronic helping behavior: The virtual presence of others makes a difference. *Basic and Applied Social Psychology, 27*, 171–178.

Blakeslee, S. (1992, August 11). Finding a new messenger for the brain's signals to the body. *The New York Times*, p. C3.

Blankstein, U., Chen, J. Y. W., Mincic, A. M., McGrath, P. A., & Davis, K. D. (2009). The complex minds of teenagers: Neuroanatomy of personality differs between sexes. *Neuropsychologia, 47*, 599–603.

Blass, T. (1996). Attribution of responsibility and trust in the Milgram obedience experiment. *Journal of Applied Social Psychology, 26*, 1529–1535.

Blass, T. (Ed.) (2000). *Obedience to authority: Current perspectives on the Milgram Paradigm*. Mahwah, NJ: Erlbaum.

Blass, T. (2004). *The man who shocked the world: The life and legacy of Stanley Milgram*. New York: Basic Books.

Blatter, K., & Cajochen, C. (2007). Circadian rhythms in cognitive performance: Methodological constraints, protocols, theoretical underpinnings. *Physiology & Behavior*, 90, 196–208.

Blennow, K., & Vanmechelen, E. (2003). CSF markers for pathogenic processes in Alzheimer's disease: Diagnostic implications and use in clinical neurochemistry. *Brain Research Bulletin, 61*, 235–242.

Bloch, M., Rotenberg, N., Koren, D., & Ehud, K. (2006, January). Risk factors for early postpartum depressive symptoms. *General Hospital Psychiatry, 28*(1), 3–8.

Block, R. I., O'Leary, D. S., Ehrhardt, J. C., Augustinack, J. C., Ghoneim, M. M., Arndt, S., & Hall, J. A. (2000). Effects of frequent marijuana use on brain tissue volume and composition. *Neuroreport 11*, 491–496.

Bloom, P. N., McBride, C. M., & Pollak, K. I. (2006). Recruiting teen smokers in shopping malls to a smoking-cessation program using the foot-in-the-door technique. *Journal of Applied Social Psychology, 36*, 1129–1144.

Blum, D. (2002). *Love at goon park: Harry Harlow and the science of affection*. Cambridge, MA: Perseus.

Boahen, K. (2005, May). Neuromorphic micro-chips. *Scientific American*, 56–64.

Bode, C., de Ridder, D. T., Kuijer, R. G., & Bensing, J. M. (2007). Effects of an intervention promoting proactive coping competencies in middle and late adulthood. *Gerontologist, 47*, 42–51.

Bodin, G. (2006). Review of harvesting free association. *Psychoanalytic Quarterly, 75*, 629–632.

Bogart, R. K., McDaniel, R. J., Dunn, W. J., Hunter, C., Peterson, A. L., & Write, E. E. (2007). Efficacy of group cognitive behavior therapy for the treatment of masticatory myofascial pain. *Military Medicine, 172*, 169–174.

Bohart, A. C. (2006). Understanding person-centered therapy: A review of Paul Wilkins' Person-centered therapy in focus. *Person-Centered and Experiential Psychotherapies, 5*, 138–143.

Cartwright, R., Agargum, M. Y., & Kirkby, J. (2006). Relation of dreams to waking concerns. *Psychiatry Research, 141*, 261–270.

Carver, C., & Scheier, M. (2002). Coping processes and adjustment to chronic illness. In A. Christensen and M. Antoni (Eds.), *Chronic physical disorders: Behavioral medicine's perspective.* Malden: Blackwell Publishers.

Case, R., & Okamoto, Y. (1996). The role of central conceptual structures in the development of children's thought. *Monographs of the Society for Research in Child Development, 61*, v–265.

Casey, S. D., Cooper-Brown, L. J., & Wacher, D. P. (2006). The use of descriptive analysis to identify and manipulate schedules of reinforcement in the treatment of food refusal. *Journal of Behavioral Education, 15*, 41–52.

Cashon, C. H., & Cohen, L. B. (2004). Beyond U-shaped development in infants' processing of faces: An information-processing account. *Journal of Cognition and Development, 5*, 59–80.

Cassells, J. V. S. (2007). The virtuous roles of truth and justice in integral dialogue: Research, theory, and model practice of the evolution of collective consciousness. *Dissertation Abstracts International Section A: Humanities and Social Sciences, 67*(10-A), 4005.

Cattell, R. B. (1965). *The scientific analysis of personality.* Chicago: Aldine.

Cattell, R. B. (1998). Where is intelligence? Some answers from the triadic theory. In J. J. McArdle & R. W. Woodcock (Eds.), *Human cognitive abilities in theory and practice* (pp. 29–38). Mahwah, NJ: Lawrence Erlbaum.

Cattell, R. B., Cattell, A. K., & Catell, H. E. P. (1993). *Sixteen personality factor questionnaire* (16PF) (5th ed.). San Antonio, TX: Harcourt Brace.

Cattell, R. B., Cattell, A. K., & Cattell, H. E. P. (2000). *The sixteen personality factor™ (16PF®) questionnaire.* Champaign, IL: Institute for Personality and Ability Testing.

Cauce, A. M. (2007). Bringing community psychology home: The leadership, community and values initiative. *American Journal of Community Psychology, 39*, 1–11.

Cavallini, E., Pagnin, A., and Vecchi, T. (2003). Aging and everyday memory: The beneficial effect of memory training. *Archives of Gerontology & Geriatrics, 37*, 241–257.

Cavenett, T., & Nixon, R. D. V. (2006). The effect of arousal on memory for emotionally-relevant information: A study of skydivers. *Behaviour Research and Therapy, 44*, 1461–1469.

CBC (Canadian Broadcasting Corporation) News. (2003, February 12). Hell to pay. The police task force. *The Fifth Estate.* Retrieved from www.cbc.ca/fifth/martin/investigation.html.

CBC (Canadian Broadcasting Corporation) News. (2007). Luck of the draw: By the numbers. *The Fifth Estate.* Retrieved April 4, 2011 from www.cbc.ca/fifth/luckofthedraw/.

CBC (Canadian Broadcasting Corporation) News. (2008). Alcohol: By the numbers. Retrieved March 8, 2011 from www.cbc.ca/news/canada/story/2008/10/10/f-alcohol-numbers.html.

CDC (Centers for Disease Control and Prevention). (2000). Cigarette smoking among adults—United States. *Morbidity and Mortality Weekly Report* [serial online] 2002;51 (29):642–645 [accessed 2009 Oct. 12].

CDC (Centers for Disease Control). (2004, June 11). Suicide and attempted suicide. *MMWR, 53*, 471.

Chamberlain, K., & Zika, S. (1990). The minor events approach to stress: Support for the use of daily hassles. *British Journal of Psychology, 81*, 469–481.

Chambless, D. L., Crits-Christoph, P., Wampold, B. E., Norcross, J. C., Lambert, M. J., Bohart, A. C., Beutler, L. E., & Johannsen, B. E. (2006). What should be validated? In J. C. Norcross, L. E. Beutler, & R. F. Levant (Eds.) *Evidence-based practices in mental health: Debate and dialogue on the fundamental questions.* Washington, DC: American Psychological Association.

Chan, M., Rogers, K. H., Parisotto, K. L., & Biesanz, J. C. (2011). Forming first impressions: The role of gender and normative accuracy in personality perception. *Journal of Research in Personality, 45*, 117–120.

Chandra, P. (2007). Review of Language, mind, and brain: Some psychological and neurological constraints on theories of grammar. *Cognitive Systems Research, 8*, 53–56.

Chandran, S., & Menon, G. (2004). When a day means more than a year: Effects of temporal framing on judgments of health risk. *Journal of Consumer Research, 31*, 375–389.

Chang, J., & Sue, S. (2005). Culturally sensitive research: Where have we gone wrong and what do we need to do now? In M. G. Constantine, *Strategies for building multicultural competence in mental health and educational settings.* Hoboken, NJ: John Wiley & Sons.

Chanon, V., & Boettiger, C. (2009). Addiction and cognitive control. *The Praeger international collection on addictions, Vol 2: Psychobiological profiles* (pp. 273–285). Santa Barbara, CA: Praeger/ABC-CLIO.

Chapelot, D., Marmonier, C., Aubert, R., Gausseres, N., & Louis-Sylvestre, J. (2004). A role for glucose and insulin preprandial profiles to differentiate meals and snacks. *Physiology and Behavior, 80*, 721–731.

Chaplin, W. F., Phillips, J. B., Brown, J. D., Clanton, N. R., and Stein, J. L. (2000). Handshaking, gender, personality and first impressions. *Journal of Personality and Social Psychology 79*(1), 110–117.

Chapman, L. J., & Chapman, J. P. (1973). *Disordered thought in schizophrenia.* New York: Appleton-Century-Crofts.

Chechil, R. A. (2003). Mathematical tools for hazard function analysis. *Journal of Mathematical Psychology, 47*, 478–494.

Chen, A., Zhou, Y., & Gong, H. (2004). Firing rates and dynamic correlated activities of ganglion cells both contribute to retinal information processing. *Brain Research, 1017*, 13–20.

Cheng, C., & Cheung, M. L. (2005). Cognitive processes underlying coping flexibility: Differentiation and integration. *Journal of Personality, 73*, 859–886.

Cheston, S. E. (2002). A new paradigm for teaching counseling theory and practice. *Counselor Education & Supervision, 39*, 254–269.

Cho, A. (2000). Gene therapy could aid hearing. *ScienceNOW, 518*, 1.

Cho, S., Holyoak, K. J., & Cannon, T. D. (2007). Analogical reasoning in working memory: Resources shared among relational integration, interference resolution, and maintenance. *Memory & Cognition, 35*, 1445–1455.

Choi, Y. S., Gray, H., & Ambady, N. (2004). Glimpses of others: Unintended communication and unintended perception. In J. Bargh, J. Uleman, & R. Hassin (Eds.), *Unintended thought* (2nd ed.). New York: Oxford University Press.

Chomsky, N. (1968). *Language and mind.* New York: Harcourt Brace Jovanovich.

Chomsky, N. (1978). On the biological basis of language capacities. In G. A. Miller & E. Lennenberg (Eds.), *Psychology and biology of language and thought.* New York: Academic Press.

Chomsky, N. (1991). Linguistics and cognitive science: Problems and mysteries. In A. Kasher (Ed.), *The Chomskyan turn.* Cambridge, MA: Blackwell.

Chou, K. (2005). Everyday competence and depressive symptoms: Social support and sense of control as mediators or moderators? *Aging and Mental Health, 9*, 177–183.

Choy, Y., Fyer, A. J. & Lipsitz, J. D. (2007). Treatment of specific phobia in adults. *Clinical Psychology Review, 27*, 266–286.

Christ, S. E., Steiner, R. D., & Grange, D. K. (2006). Inhibitory control in children with phenylketonuria. *Developmental Neuropsychology, 30*, 845–864.

Chronicle, E. P., MacGregor, J. N., & Ormerod, T. C. (2004). What makes an insight problem? The roles of heuristics, goal conception, and solution recoding in knowledge-lean problems. *Journal of Experimental Psychology: Learning, Memory, and Cognition, 30*, 14–27.

Chrysikou, E. G. (2006). When a shoe becomes a hammer: Problem solving as goal-derived, ad hoc categorization. *Dissertation Abstracts International: Section B: The Sciences and Engineering, 67*(1-B), 569.

Cialdini, R. B. (2006). *Influence: The psychology of persuasion.* New York: Collins.

Cialdini, R. B., & Sagarin, B. J. (2005). Principles of interpersonal influence. In T. C. Brock & M. C. Green (Eds.), *Persuasion: Psychological insights and perspectives* (2nd ed.). Thousand Oaks, CA: Sage Publications.

CIHI (Canadian Institute for Health Information). (2011). Psychologists. Canada's health care providers, 1997 to 2006. A reference guide. Retrieved from http://secure.cihi.ca/cihiweb/dispPage.jsp?cw_page=hpdb_psych_e#.

Clark, D. A. (2004). *Cognitive-behavioral therapy for OCD.* New York: Guilford.

Clark, D. A. (2007). Obsessions and compulsions. In N. Kazantzis, & L. L'Abate, *Handbook of homework assignments in psychotherapy: Research, practice, prevention.* New York: Springer Science + Business Media.

Clarke-Stewart, K. A., Vandell, D. L., McCartney, K., Owen, M. T., & Booth C. (2000). Effects of parental separation and divorce on very young children. *Journal of Family Psychology, 14*, 304–326.

Clarkin, J. F., & Lenzenweger, M. F. (Eds.) (2004). *Major theories of personality disorders* (2nd ed.). New York: Guilford.

Clay D. L. (2000). Commentary: Rethinking our interventions in pediatric chronic pain and treatment research. *Journal of Pediatric Psychology, 25*, 53–55.

Clayton, R., Segress, M., & Caudill, C. (2008). Prevention of substance abuse. *The American Psychiatric Publishing textbook of substance abuse treatment* (4th ed.) (pp. 681–688). Arlington, VA: American Psychiatric Publishing, Inc.

Cleary, A. M. (2006). Relating familiarity-based recognition and the tip-of-the-tongue phenomenon: Detecting a word's recency in the absence of access to the word. *Memory & Cognition, 34*, 804–816.

Clements, A., M., Rimrodt, S. L., & Abel, J. R. (2006). Sex differences in cerebral laterality of language and visuospatial processing. *Brain and Language, 98*, 150–158.

Clemons, T. L. (2006). Underachieving gifted students: A social cognitive model. *Dissertation Abstracts International Section A: Humanities and Social Sciences, 66*(9-A), 3208.

Cloud, J. (2000, June 5). The lure of ecstasy. *Time*, pp. 60–68.

Coan, J. A., Schaefer, H. S., & Davidson, R. J. (2006). Lending a hand: Social regulation of the neural response to threat. *Psychological Science, 17*, 1032–1039.

Coates, S. L., Butler, L. T., & Berry, D. C. (2006). Implicit memory and consumer choice: The mediating role of brand familiarity. *Applied Cognitive Psychology, 20*, 1101–1116.

Cobos, P., Sanchez, M., Garcia, C., Vera, M. N., & Vila, J. (2002). Revisiting the James versus Cannon debate on emotion: Startle and autonomic modulation in patients with spinal cord injuries. *Biological Psychology, 61*, 251–269.

Cochran, S. D. (2000). Emerging issues in research on lesbians' and gay men's mental health: Does sexual orientation really matter? *American Psychologist, 56*, 33–41.

Coffman, S. J., Martell, C. R., Dimidjian, S., Gallop, R., & Holon, S. D. (2007). Extreme nonresponse in cognitive therapy: Can behavioral activation succeed where cognitive therapy fails? *Journal of Consulting Clinical Psychology, 75*, 531–545.

Cohen, B. H. (2002). *Explaining psychological statistics* (2nd ed.). New York: Wiley.

Cohen, P., Slomkowski, C., & Robins, L. N. (Eds.). (1999). *Historical and geographical influences on psychopathology*. Mahwah, NJ: Erlbaum.

Cohen, S. (2004, November). Social relationships and health. *American Psychologist*, 676–684.

Cohen, S., Doyle, W. J., Turner, R., Alper, C. M., & Skoner, D. P. (2003). Sociability and susceptibility to the common cold. *Psychological Science, 14*, 389–395.

Cohen, S., Hamrick, N., & Rodriguez, M. (2002). Reactivity and vulnerability to stress-associated risk for upper respiratory illness. *Psychosomatic Medicine, 64*, 302–310.

Cohen, S., Kamarck, T., & Mermelstein, R. (1983). A Global Measure of Perceived Stress. *Journal of Health and Social Behavior, 24*, Appendix A.

Coleman, E. (2002). Masturbation as a means of achieving sexual health. *Journal of Psychology and Human Sexuality, 14*, 5–16.

Coles, R. (1997). *The moral intelligence of children*. New York: Random House.

Collins, A. M., & Loftus, E. F. (1975). A spreading-activation theory of semantic processing. *Psychological Review, 82*, 407–428.

Collins, A. M., & Quillian, M. R. (1969). Retrieval times from semantic memory. *Journal of Verbal Learning and Verbal Behavior, 8*, 240–247.

Collins, S. L., & Izenwasser, S. (2004). Chronic nicotine differentially alters cocaine-induced locomotor activity in adolescent vs. adult male and female rats. *Neuropharmacology, 46*, 349–362.

Colom, R., Jung, R. E., & Haier, R. J. (2006). Finding the g-factor in brain structure using the method of correlated vectors. *Intelligence, 34*, 561–570.

Coltheart, M., Langdon, R., & McKay, R. (2007). Schizophrenia and monothematic delusions. *Schizophrenia Bulletin, 33*, 642–647.

Coltraine, S., & Messineo, M. (2000). The perpetuation of subtle prejudice: Race and gender imagery in 1990s television advertising. *Sex Roles, 42*, 363–389.

Colwell, M. J., & Lindsey, E. W. (2005). Preschool children's pretend and physical play and sex of play partner: Connections to peer competence. *Sex Roles, 52*, 497–509.

Combrink-Graham, L., & McKenna, S. B. (2006). Families with children with disrupted attachments. In L. Combrink-Graham, *Children in family contexts: Perspectives on treatment*. New York: Guilford Press.

Combs, D., & Mueser, K. (2007). Schizophrenia. *Adult psychopathology and diagnosis* (5th ed.) (pp. 234–285). Hoboken, NJ: John Wiley & Sons Inc.

Combs, D., Basso, M., Wanner, J., & Ledet, S. (2008). Schizophrenia. *Handbook of psychological assessment, case conceptualization, and treatment: Adults* (Vol. 1) (pp. 352–402). Hoboken, NJ: John Wiley & Sons Inc.

Compagni, A., & Manderscheid, R. W. (2006). A neuroscientist-consumer alliance to transform mental health care. *Journal of Behavioral Health Services & Research, 33*, 265–274.

Compas, B. E., & Wagner, B. M. (1991). Psychosocial stress during adolescence: Intrapersonal and interpersonal processes. Adolescent stress: Causes and consequences. In M. E. Colten, & S. Gore, Eds., *Adolescent stress: Causes and consequences. Social institutions and social change*. Hawthorne, NY: Aldine de Gruyter.

Compton, W., Conway, K., Stinson, F., & Grant, B. (2006, December). Changes in the prevalence of major depression and comorbid substance use disorders in the United States between 1991–1992 and 2001–2002. *American Journal of Psychiatry, 163*(12), 2141–2147.

Comuzzie, A. G., & Allison, D. B. (1998, May 29). The search for human obesity genes. *Science, 280*, 1374–1377.

Conduit, R., Crewther, S. G., & Coleman, G. (2004). Spontaneous eyelid movements (ELMS) during sleep are related to dream recall on awakening. *Journal of Sleep Research, 13*, 137–144.

Conference Board of Canada (2007). How Canada performs: Suicides. Retrieved March 6, 2012, from www.conferenceboard.ca/hcp/details/society/suicides.aspx.

Conner, M., Povey, R., Sparks, P., James, R., & Shepherd, R. (2003). Moderating role of attitudinal ambivalence within the theory of planned behaviour. *British Journal of Social Psychology, 42*, 75–94.

Connolly, A. C. (2007). Concepts and their features: Can cognitive science make good on the promises of concept empiricism? *Dissertation Abstracts International: Section B—The Sciences and Engineering, 67*(7-B), 4125.

Consumer Reports (1995). Mental health: Does therapy help?

Conte, H. R., Plutchik, R., & Draguns, J. G. (2004). The measurement of ego defenses in clinical research. In U. Hentschel, et al. (Eds.). *Defense mechanisms: Theoretical research and clinical perspectives*. Oxford, England: Elsevier Science.

Conway, M. A. (Ed.) (2002). *Levels of processing 30 years on special issue of memory*. Hove: Psychology Press.

Cooke, J. R., & Ancoli-Israel, S. (2006). Sleep and its disorders in older adults. *Psychiatric Clinics of North America, 29*, 1077–1093.

Cooklin, A. (2000). Therapy, the family and others. In H. Maxwell, *Clinical psychotherapy for health professionals*. Philadelphia: Whurr Publishers.

Cooper, J. (2007). *Cognitive dissonance: Fifty years of a classic theory*. Thousand Oaks, CA: Sage Publications.

Cooper, J., Mirabile, R., & Scher, S. J. (2005). Actions and attitudes: The theory of cognitive dissonance. In T. C. Brock & M. C. Green (Eds.), *Persuasion: Psychological insights and perspectives* (2nd ed.). Thousand Oaks, CA: Sage Publications.

Copolov, D. L., Seal, M. L., Maruff, P., Ulusoy, R., Wong, M. T. H., TochonDanguy, H. J., & Egan, G. F. (2003). Cortical activation associated with the human experience of auditory hallucinations and perception of human speech in schizophrenia: A PET correlation study. *Psychiatry Research: Neuroimaging, 123*, 139–152.

Corcoran, J., & Pillai, V. (2009, March). A review of the research on solution-focused therapy. *British Journal of Social Work, 39*(2), 234–242.

Cordnoldi, C., De Beni, R., & Helstrup, T. (2007). Memory sensitivity in autobiographical memory. In S. Magnussen, & T. Helstrup, *Everyday memory*. New York: Psychology Press.

Coren, S., & Ward, L. M. (1989). *Sensation and perception* (3rd ed.). San Diego, CA: Harcourt Brace Jovanovich.

Cornelius, M. D., Taylor, P. M., Geva, D., & Day, N. L. (1995). Prenatal tobacco and marijuana use among adolescents: Effects on offspring gestational age, growth, and morphology. *Pediatrics, 95*, 57–68.

Cornell, C. B. (2006). A graduated scale for determining mental age. *Dissertation Abstracts International: Section B—The Sciences and Engineering. 66*(9-B), 5121.

Costa, P. T., & McCrae, R. R. (2008). The NEO inventories. In R. P. Archer & S. R. Smith *Personality Assessment*. New York: Routledge/Taylor & Francis Group.

Costa, P. T., Jr., & Widiger, T. A. (Eds.). (2002). *Personality disorders and the five-factor model of personality* (2nd ed.). Washington, DC: American Psychological Association.

Cotton, P. (1993, July 7). Psychiatrists set to approve DSM-IV. *Journal of the American Medical Association, 270*, 13–15.

Couturier, J., & Lock, J. (2006). Eating disorders: Anorexia nervosa, bulimia nervosa, and binge eating disorder. In T. G. Plante, *Mental disorders of the new millennium: Biology and function* (Vol 3.). Westport, CT: Praeger Publishers/Greenwood Publishing.

Coventry, K. R., Venn, S. F., Smith, G. D., & Morley, A. M. (2003). Spatial problem solving and functional relations. *European Journal of Cognitive Psychology, 15*, 71–99.

Cowan, N., Towse, J. N., Hamilton, Z., Saults, J. S., Elliott, E. M., Lacey, J. F., Moreno, M. V., & Hitch, G. J. (2003). Children's working-memory processes: A response-timing analysis. *Journal of Experimental Psychology: General, 132*, 113–132.

Cowen, V. S. (2010). Functional fitness improvements after a worksite-based yoga initiative. *Journal of Bodywork & Movement Therapies, 14*, 50–54.

Cowley, G. (2000, January 31). Alzheimer's: Unlocking the mystery. *Time*, pp. 46–54.

Coyne, J. D. (1976). Toward an interactional description of depression. *Psychiatry, 39*, 28–40.

CPA (Canadian Psychological Association). (2000). *Canadian code of ethics for psychologists* (3rd ed.). Ottawa, ON: Canadian Psychological Association.

CPA (Canadian Psychological Association). (2010). A career in psychology. Retrieved from www.cpa.ca/students/career/.

Craik, F. I. M. (1990). Levels of processing. In M. E. Eysenck (Ed.), *The Blackwell dictionary of cognitive psychology*. London: Blackwell.

Cramer, P. (2007). Longitudinal study of defense mechanisms: Late childhood to late adolescence. *Journal of Personality, 75*, 1–23.

Creasey, G. L. (2005). *Research methods in lifespan development* (6th ed.). Boston: Allyn & Bacon.

Crews, F. (1996). The verdict on Freud. *Psychological Science, 7*, 63–68.

Crocker, J., & Park, L. E. (2004). The costly pursuit of self-esteem. *Psychological Bulletin, 130*, 392–414.

Cropley, A. (2006). In praise of convergent thinking. *Creativity Research Journal, 18*, 391–404.

Crosnoe, R., & Elder, G. H., Jr. (2002). Successful adaptation in the later years: A life course approach to aging. *Social Psychology Quarterly, 65*, 309–328.

Crum, A. J., & Langer, E. J. (2007). Mind-set matters: Exercise and the placebo effect. *Psychological Science, 18*, 165–171.

Cruz, A., & Green, B. G. (2000). Thermal stimulation of taste. *Nature, 403*, 889–892.

Cummings, A., Ceponiene, R., & Koyama, A. (2006). Auditory semantic networks for words and natural sounds. *Brain Research, 1115*, 92–107.

Cwikel, J., Behar, L., & Rabson-Hare, J. (2000). A comparison of a vote count and a meta-analysis review of intervention research with adult cancer patients. *Research on Social Work Practice, 10*, 139–158.

Czopp, A. M., & Monteith, M. J. (2006). Thinking Well of African Americans: Measuring Complimentary Stereotypes and Negative Prejudice. *Basic and Applied Social Psychology, 28*, 233–250.

D

D'Amico, E., Chinman, M., Stern, S., & Wandersman, A. (2009). Community prevention handbook on adolescent substance abuse prevention and treatment: Evidence-based practices. *Adolescent substance abuse: Evidence-based approaches to prevention and treatment* (pp. 213–249). New York: Springer Science + Business Media.

D'Arcy, R. C. N., Bolster, R. B., & Ryner, L. (2007). A site directed fMRI approach for evaluating functional status in the anterolateral temporal lobes. *Neuroscience Research, 57*, 120–128.

D'Eramo, K., & Francis, G. (2004). Cognitive-Behavioral Psychotherapy. *Anxiety disorders in children and adolescents* (2nd ed.) (pp. 305–328). New York: Guilford Press.

Daftary, F., & Meri, J. W. (2002). *Culture and memory in medieval Islam*. London: I. B. Tauris.

Dai, D. Y., & Wang, X. (2007). The role of need for cognition and reader beliefs in text comprehension and interest development. *Contemporary Educational Psychology, 32*, 332–347.

Daines, B. (2006). Violations of agreed and implicit sexual and emotional boundaries in couple relationships—some thoughts arising from Levine's "A clinical perspective on couple infidelity." *Sexual and Relationship Therapy, 21*, 45–53.

Daitz, B. (2002, December 3). A DOCTOR'S JOURNAL; In Pain Clinic, Fruit, Candy And Relief. *NY Times*.

Dal Cin, S., Gilson, B., Zanna, M. P., Shumate, R., & Fong, G. T. (2007). Smoking in movies, implicit associations of smoking with the self, and intentions to smoke. *Psychological Science, 18*, 559–563.

Dale, J. W., & von Schantz, M. (2007). *From genes to genomes: Concepts and applications of DNA technology*. New York: John Wiley & Sons.

Dalla Barba, G., & Decaix, C. (2009). "Do you remember what you did on March 13, 1985?" A case study of confabulatory hypermnesia. *Cortex 45* (5): 566.

Dalsgaro, O. J., Hansen, N. G., Soes-Petersen, U., Evald, T., Hoegholm, A., Barber, J., & Vestbo, J. (2004). A multicenter, randomized, double-blind, placebo-controlled, 6-month trial of bupropion hydrochloride sustained-release tablets as an aid to smoking cessation in hospital employees. *Nicotine and Tobacco Research, 6*, 55–61.

Damasio, H., Grabowski, T., Frank, R., Galaburda, A. M., & Damasio, A. R. (1994). The return of Phineas Gage: Clues about the brain from the skill of a famous patient. *Science, 264*, 1102–1105.

Damon, W. (1999, August). The moral development of children. *Scientific American*, 72–78.

Darley, J. M., & Latané, B. (1968). Bystanders intervention in emergencies: Diffusion of responsibility. *Journal of Personality and Social Psychology, 8*, 377–383.

Darwin, C. J., Turvey, M. T., & Crowder, R. G. (1972). An auditory analogue of the Sperling partial-report procedure: Evidence for brief auditory storage. *Cognitive Psychology, 3*, 255–267.

daSilva, T. L., Ravindran, L. N., Ravindran, A. V. (2009). Yoga in the treatment of mood and anxiety disorders: A review. *Asian Journal of Psychiatry, 2*, 6–16.

Davidson, J. E., Deuser, R., & Sternberg, R. J. (1994). The role of metacognition in problem solving. In J. Metcalfe & A. P. Shimamura (Eds.), *Metacognition: Knowing about knowing*. Cambridge, MA: MIT.

Davidson, P. S. R., & Glisky, E. L. (2002). Is flash-bulb memory a special instance of source memory? Evidence from older adults. *Memory, 10*, 99–111.

Davis, P. (2007). *Shakespeare Thinking*. London: Continuum.

Davis-Marchand, H. (2009). Psychology works fact sheet; physical activity. Retrieved March 21, 2012 from www.cpa.ca/psychologyfactsheets/physicalactivity/.

Day, A. L., & Livingstone, H. A. (2003). Gender differences in perceptions of stressors and utilization of social support among university students. *Canadian Journal of Behavioural Science/Revue, 35*, 73–83.

Day, R. D., & Lamb, M. E. (2004). *Conceptualizing and measuring father involvement*. Mahwah, NJ: Lawrence Erlbaum Associates.

De Beni, R., Pazzaglia, F., & Gardini, S. (2007). The generation and maintenance of visual mental images: Evidence from image type and aging. *Brain and Cognition, 63*, 271–278.

de Groot, A. (1966). Perception and Memory versus Thought: Some Old Ideas and Recent Findings. In B. Kleinmuntz (Ed.), *Problem Solving: Research, Method, and Theory* (pp. 19–50). New York: John Wiley.

de Groot, A. (1978). *Thought and choice in chess*. Paris: Mouton de Gruyter.

de Maat, S., de Jonghe, F., Schoevers, R., & Dekker, J. (2009, February). The effectiveness of long-term psychoanalytic therapy: A systematic review of empirical studies. *Harvard Review of Psychiatry, 17*(1), 1–23.

De Mello, M. F., De Jesus Mari, J., Bacaltchuk, J., Verdeli, H., & Neugebauer, R. (2005). A systematic review of research findings on the efficacy of interpersonal therapy for depressive disorders. *European Archives of Psychiatry and Clinical Neuroscience, 255*, 75–82.

Dean, C., & Dresbach, T. (2006). Neuroligins and neurexins: Linking cell adhesion, synapse formation and cognitive function. *International Journal of Psychiatry in Clinical Practice, 10* (Suppl), 5–11.

Dean-Borenstein, M. T. (2007). The long-term psychosocial effects of trauma on survivors of human-caused extreme stress situations. *Dissertation Abstracts International: Section B—The Sciences and Engineering, 67*(11-B), 6733.

Deary, I. J., & Der, G. (2005). Reaction time, age, and cognitive ability: Longitudinal findings from age 16 to 63 years in representative population samples. *Aging, Neuropsychology, & Cognition, 12*, 187–215.

DeCoster, V. A. (2003). Predicting emotions in everyday social interactions: A test and comparison of affect control and social interactional theories. *Journal of Human Behavior in the Social Environment, 6,* 53–73.

Dediu, D., & Ladd, D. R. (2007). From the Cover: Linguistic tone is related to the population frequency of the adaptive haplogroups of two brain size genes, ASPM and Microcephalin. *Proceedings of the National Academy of Sciences, 104,* 10944–10949.

del Rosal, E., Alonso, L., & Moreno, R. (2006). Simulation of habituation to simple and multiple stimuli. *Behavioural Processes, 73,* 272–277.

DeLamater, J. D., & Sill, M. (2005). Sexual desire in later life. *Journal of Sex Research, 42,* 138–149.

Delgado, M. R., Labouliere, C. D., & Phelps, E. A. (2006). Fear of losing money? Aversive conditioning with secondary reinforcers. *Social Cognitive and Affective Neuroscience, 1, Special issue: Genetic, Comparative and Cognitive Studies of Social Behavior,* 250–259.

Delinsky, S. S., Latner, J. D., & Wilson, G. T. (2006). Binge eating and weight loss in a self-help behavior modification program. *Obesity, 14,* 1244–1249.

Demaree, H. A., & Everhart, D. E. (2004). Healthy high-hostiles: Reduced para-sympathetic activity and decreased sympathovagal flexibility during negative emotional processing. *Personality and Individual Differences, 36,* 457–469.

Denmark, G. L., & Fernandez, L. C. (1993). Historical development of the psychology of women. In F. L. Denmark & M. A. Paludi (Eds.), *A handbook of issues and theories.* Westport, CT: Greenwood Press.

Dennis, I. (2007). Halo effects in grading student projects. *Journal of Applied Psychology, 92,* 1169–1176.

Denollet, J. (2005). DS14: standard assessment of negative affectivity, social inhibition, and Type D personality. *Psychosomatic Medicine, 67,* 89–97.

Denollet J., & Brutsaert, D. L. (1998). Personality, disease severity, and the risk of long-term cardiac events in patients with a decreased ejection fraction after myocardial infarction. *Circulation, 97,* 167–173.

Deouell, L. Y., Parnes, A., & Pickard, N. (2006). Spatial location is accurately tracked by human auditory sensory memory: Evidence from the mismatch negativity. *European Journal of Neuroscience, 24,* 1488–1494.

Deregowski, J. B. (1973). Illusion and culture. In R. L. Gregory & G. H. Combrich (Eds.), *Illusion in nature and art* (pp. 161–192). New York: Scribner.

Derryberry, W. P. (2006). Review of social motivation: conscious and unconscious processes. *Journal of Moral Education, 35,* 276–278.

DeRubeis, R., Hollon, S., & Shelton, R. (2003, May 23). Presentation, American Psychiatric Association meeting, Philadelphia.

Deshpande, S., Basil, M. D., & Basil, D. Z. (2009). Factors influencing healthy eating habits among college students: An application of the health belief model. *Health Marketing Quarterly, 26,* 145–164.

Detoledo-Morrell, L., Stoub, T. R., & Wang, C. (2007). Hippocampal atrophy and disconnection in incipient and mild Alzheimer's disease. *Progressive Brain Research, 163C,* 741–823.

Detterman, D. K., Gabriel, L. T., & Ruthsatz, J. M. (2000). Intelligence and mental retardation. In R. J. Sternberg, et al. (Eds.), *Handbook of intelligence.* New York: Cambridge University Press.

DiCano, P., & Everitt, B. J. (2002). Reinstatement and spontaneous recovery of cocaine-seeking following extinction and different durations of withdrawal. *Behavioural Pharmacology, 13,* 397–406.

Dickerson, S. S., Kemeny, M. E., Aziz, N., Kim, K. H., & Fahey, J. L. (2004). Immunological effects of induced shame and guilt. *Psychosomatic Medicine, 66,* 124–131.

Dickstein, L. S. "Death concerns: Measurement and correlates." *Psychological Reports, 1972, 30,* 563–571.

Diener, E., & Biswas-Diener, R. (2002). Will money increase subjective well-being? *Social Indicators Research, 57,* 119–169.

Diener, E., & Biswas-Diener, R. (2008). *Happiness: Unlocking the mysteries of psychological wealth.* Malden: Blackwell Publishing.

Diener, E., & Clifton, D. (2002). Life satisfaction and religiosity in broad probability samples. *Psychological Inquiry, 13,* 206–209.

Diener, E., & Seligman, M. E. P. (2002). Very happy people. *Psychological Science, 18,* 81–84.

Diener, E., & Seligman, M. E. P. (2004). Beyond money: Toward an economy of well-being. *Psychological Science in the Public Interest, 5,* 1–31.

Diener, E., Lucas, R. E., & Oishi, S. (2002). Subjective well-being: The science of happiness and life satisfaction. In C. R. Snyder & S. J. Lopez (Eds.), *Handbook of positive psychology* (pp. 463–473). London: Oxford University Press.

Diener, E., Lucas, R. E., & Scollon, C. N. (2006). Beyond the hedonic treadmill: Revising the adaptation theory of well-being. *American Psychologist, 61,* 305–314.

DiGiovanna, A. G. (1994). *Human aging: Biological perspectives.* New York: McGraw-Hill.

Dillard, J. P., & Shen, L. (2007). Self-report measures of discrete emotions. In R. A. Reynolds, R. Woods, & J. D. Baker, *Handbook of research on electronic surveys and measurements.* Hershey, PA: Idea Group Reference/IGI Global, 2007.

DiLorenzo, P. M., & Yougentob, S. L. (2003). Olfaction and taste. In M. Gallagher & R. J. Nelson, *Handbook of psychology: Biological psychology* (Vol. 3). New York: Wiley.

Dinges, D. F., Pack, F., Wiliams, K., Gillen, K. A., Powell, J. W., Ott, G. E., Aptowicz, C., & Pack, A. I. (1997). Cumulative sleepiness, mood disturbance, and psychomotor vigilance performance decrements during a week of sleep restricted to 4–5 hours per night. *Sleep, 20,* 267–273.

Dion, K., Berscheid, E., & Walster, E. (1972, December). What is beautiful is good. *Journal of Personality and Social Psychology, 24*(3), 285–290.

Dixon, L., & Goldman, H. (2003, December). Forty years of progress in community mental health: The role of evidence-based practices. *Australian and New Zealand Journal of Psychiatry, 37*(6), 668–673.

Dixon, R. A., & Cohen, A. L. (2003). Cognitive development in adulthood. In R. M. Lerner, M. A. Easterbrooks, et al. (Eds.), *Handbook of psychology: Developmental psychology* (Vol. 6) (pp. 443–461). New York: Wiley.

Dixon, R. A., Rust, T. B., & Feltmate, S. E. (2007). Memory and aging: Selected research directions and application issues. *Canadian Psychology Psychologie Canadienne, 48,* 67–76.

Do, V. T. (2006). Asian American men and the media: The relationship between ethnic identity, self-esteem, and the endorsement of stereotypes. *Dissertation Abstracts International: Section B—The Sciences and Engineering, 67*(6-B), 3446.

Dobbins, A. C., Jeo, R. M., Fiser, J., & Allman, J. M. (1998, July 24). Distance modulation of neural activity in the visual cortex. *Science, 281,* 552–555.

Dodge, K. A. (2004). The nature-nurture debate and public policy. *Merrill-Palmer Quarterly, 50,* 418–427.

Dodgen, C. (2005). Nicotine and Addiction. *Nicotine dependence: Understanding and applying the most effective treatment interventions* (pp. 65–80). Washington, DC: American Psychological Association.

Dohrenwend, B. P., Turner, J. B., Turse, N. A., Adams, B. G., Koenen, K. C., & Marshall, R. (2006, August 18). The psychological risks of Vietnam for U.S. veterans: A revisit with new data and methods. *Science, 313,* 979–982.

Dolan, P., & White, M. P. (2007). How can measures of subjective well-being be used to inform public policy? *Perspectives on Psychological Science, 2,* 71–85.

Dolbier, C. L., Smith, S. E., & Steinhardt, M. A. (2007). Relationships of protective factors to stress and symptoms of illness. *American Journal of Health Behavior, 31,* 423–433.

Dollinger, S. J. (2003). Need for uniqueness, need for cognition and creativity. *Journal of Creative Behavior, 37,* 99–116.

Domhoff, G. W. (1996). *Finding meaning in dreams: A quantitative approach.* New York: Plenum Press.

Dortch, S. (1996, October). Our aching heads. *American Demographics,* pp. 4–8.

Dougall, A. L., & Baum, A. (2004). Psychoneuroimmunology and trauma. In P. P. Schnurr and B. L. Green (Eds.), *Trauma and health: Physical health consequences of exposure to extreme stress* (pp. 129–155). Washington, DC: American Psychological Association.

Douglas Brown, R., Goldstein, E., & Bjorklund, D. F. (2000). The history and zeitgeist of the repressed-false-memory debate: Scientific and sociological perspectives on suggestibility and childhood memory. Mahwah, NJ: Lawrence Erlbaum Associates Publishers.

Dovidio, J. F., & Gaertner, S. L. (2006). A multilevel perspective on prejudice: Crossing disciplinary boundaries. In P. A. M. Van Lange, *Bridging social psychology: Benefits of transdisciplinary approaches.* Mahwah, NJ: Lawrence Erlbaum Associates.

Dovidio, J. F., Gaertner, S. L., & Kawakami, K. (2003). Intergroup contact: The past, present, and the future. *Group Processes and Intergroup Relations, 6,* 5–20.

Doyle, K. A. (2002). Rational Emotive Behavior Therapy and its application to women's groups. In W. Dryden, & M. Neenan (Eds.), *Rational emotive behaviour group therapy*. London: Whurr Publishers.

Drewes, A. A. (2005). Play in selected cultures: Diversity and universality. In E. Gil and A. A. Drewes, *Cultural issues in play therapy* (pp. 26–71). New York: Guilford Press.

Drob, S. (2005). The mystical symbol: Some comments on Ankor, Giegerich, Scholem, and Jung. *Journal of Jungian Theory & Practice, 7*, 25–29.

Druss, B. (2005, September). A new front in the tobacco wars. *General Hospital Psychiatry, 27*(5), 319–320.

Dubovsky, S. (1999, February 25). Tuning in to manic depression. *HealthNews, 5*, 8.

Duffy, M., Gillig, S. E., Tureen, R. M., & Ybarra, M. A. (2002). A critical look at the DSM-IV. *Journal of Individual Psychology, 58*, 363–373.

Dugas, M. J., Savard, P., Turcotte, J., Gaudet, A., Brillon, P., Ladouceur, R., Leblanc, R., & Gervais, N. J. (2010). A randomized clinical trial of cognitive-behavioral therapy and applied relaxation for adults with generalized anxiety disorder. *Behavior Therapy, 41*, 46–58.

Dukakis, K., and Tye, L. (2006, September 18). I feel good, I feel fine. *Newsweek*, pp. 62–63.

Duke, M., & Nowicki, S., Jr. (1979). *Abnormal psychology: Perspectives on being different*. Monterey, CA: Brooks/Cole.

Dumas, T. M., Lawford, H., Tieu, T., & Pratt, M. W. (2009). Positive parenting in adolescence and its relation to low point narration and identity status in emerging adulthood: A longitudinal analysis. *Developmental Psychology, 45*, 1531–1544.

Duncker, K. (1945). On problem solving. *Psychological Monographs, 58* (5, whole no. 270).

E

Eaker, E. D., Sullivan, L. M., Kelly-Hayes, M., D'Agostino, R. B., Sr., & Benjamin, E. J. (2004). Anger and hostility predict the development of atrial fibrillation in men in the Framingham Offspring Study. *Circulation, 109*, 1267–1271.

Ebbinghaus, H. (1885/1913). *Memory: A contribution to experimental psychology* (H. A. Roger & C. E. Bussenius, Trans.). New York: Columbia University Press.

Eberhard, K. M., Cutting, J. C., & Bock, K. (2005). Making syntax of sense: Number agreement in sentence production. *Psychological Review, 112*, 531–559.

Eberhardt, J. L., Goff, P. A., Purdie, V. J., & Davies, P. G. (2004). Seeing black: Race, crime, and visual processing. *Journal of Personality and Social Psychology, 87*, 876–893.

Ebstein, R. P., Benjamin, J., & Belmaker, R. H. (2003). Behavioral genetics, genomics, and personality. In R. Plomin & J. C. DeFries (Eds.), *Behavioral genetics in the postgenomic era* (pp. 365–388). Washington, DC: American Psychological Association.

Ecenbarger, W. (1993, April 1). America's new merchants of death. *The Reader's Digest, 50.*

Eckardt, M. H. (2005). Karen Horney: A portrait: The 120th anniversary, Karen Horney, September 16, 1885. *American Journal of Psychoanalysis, 65*, 95–101.

Edinger, J. D., Wohlgemuth, W. K., Radtke, R. A., Marsh, G. R., & Quillian, R. E. (2001). Cognitive behavioral therapy for treatment of chronic primary insomnia: A randomized controlled trial. *Journal of the American Medical Association, 285*, 1856–1864.

Edwards, R. R., & Fillingim, R. B. (2007). Self-reported pain sensitivity: Lack of correlation with pain threshold and tolerance. *European Journal of Pain, 11*, 594–598.

Eichenbaum, H. (2004). Toward an information processing framework for memory representation by the hippocampus. In M. S. Gazzaniga (Ed.), *Cognitive neurosciences* (3rd ed.) (pp. 679–690). Cambridge, MA: MIT.

Eizenberg, M. M., & Zaslavsky, O. (2004). Students' verification strategies for combinatorial problems. *Mathematical Thinking and Learning, 6*, 15–36.

Ekman, P. (1972). Universals and cultural differences in facial expressions of emotion. In J. Cole (Ed.), *Darwin and facial expression: A century of research in review* (pp. 169–222). New York: Academic Press.

Ekman, P. (1994a). All emotions are basic. In P. Ekman & R. J. Davidson (Eds.), *The nature of emotion: Fundamental questions*. New York: Oxford University Press.

Ekman, P. (1994b). Strong evidence for universals in facial expressions: A reply to Russell's mistaken critique. *Psychological Bulletin, 115*, 268–287.

Ekman, P. (2003). Sixteen enjoyable emotions. *Emotion Researcher, 18*, 6–7.

Ekman, P., & O'Sullivan, M. (1991). Facial expression: Methods, means, and moues. In R. S. Feldman & B. Rimé (Eds.), *Fundamentals of nonverbal behavior*. Cambridge: Cambridge University Press.

Ekman, P., Davidson, R. J., & Friesen, W. V. (1990). Emotional expression and brain physiology: II. The Duchenne smile. *Journal of Personality and Social Psychology, 58*, 342–353.

Ekman, P., Levenson, R. W., & Friesen, W. V. (1983, September 16). Autonomic nervous system activity distinguishes among emotions. *Science, 223*, 1208–1210.

Elfhag, K., Tynelius, P., & Rasmussen, F. (2007). Sugar-sweetened and artificially sweetened soft drinks in association to restrained, external and emotional eating. *Physiology & Behavior, 91*, 191–195.

El-Hai, J. (2005). *The lobotomist: A maverick medical genius and his tragic quest to rid the world of mental illness*. New York: Wiley.

Elliott, J., Berman, H., & Kim, S. (2002). Critical ethnography of Korean Canadian women's menopause experience. *Health Care for Women International, 23*, 377–388.

El-Mallakh, R. S., & Abraham, H. D. (2007). MDMA (Ecstasy). *Annals of Clinical Psychiatry, 19*, 45–52.

Emick, J., & Welsh, M. (2005). Association between formal operational thought and executive function as measured by the Tower of Hanoi-Revised. *Learning and Individual Differences, 15*, 177–188.

Engler, J., & Goleman, D. (1992). *The consumer's guide to psychotherapy*. New York: Simon & Schuster.

Eranti, S. V., & McLoughlin, D. M. (2003). Electroconvulsive therapy: State of the art. *British Journal of Psychiatry, 182*, 8–9.

Erikson, E. H. (1963). *Childhood and society*. New York: Norton.

Ervik, S., Abdelnoor, M., & Heier, M. S. (2006). Health-related quality of life in narcolepsy. *Acta Neurologica Scandinavica, 114*, 198–204.

Etchegary, H. (2004). Psychological aspects of predictive genetic-test decision: What do we know so far? *Analyses of Social Issues and Public Policy, 4*, 13–31.

Evans, A. M. (2007). Transference in the nurse-patient relationship. Journal of Psychiatric and Mental Health Nursing, 14, 189–195.

Evans, J. B. T. (2004). Informal reasoning: Theory and method. *Canadian Journal of Experimental Psychology, 58*, 69–74.

Evans, J. B. T., & Feeney, A. (2004). The role of prior belief in reasoning. In J. P. Leighton (Ed.), *Nature of reasoning*. New York: Cambridge University Press.

Evcik, D., Kavuncu, V., Cakir, T., Subasi, V., & Yaman, M. (2007). Laser therapy in the treatment of carpal tunnel syndrome: A randomized controlled trial. *Photomedical Laser Surgery, 25*, 34–39.

Everly, G. S., Jr., & Lating, J. M. (2007). Psychotherapy: A cognitive perspective. In A. Monat, R. S. Lazarus, & G. Reevy, *The Praeger handbook on stress and coping* (Vol. 2). Westport, CT: Praeger Publishers/Greenwood Publishing.

Eysenck, H. (1990). Biological dimensions of personality. In L. A. Pervin (Ed.) *Handbook of Personality: Theory and Research*. (p. 246). New York: Guilford Press.

Eysenck, H. (1991). Dimensions of personality: The biosocial approach to personality. *Explorations in temperament: International perspectives on theory and measurement* (pp. 87–103). New York: Plenum Press.

Eysenck, H. (1995). *Eysenck on extraversion*. New York: Wiley.

Ezzati, M., Henley, S. J., Thun, M. J., & Lopez, A. D. (2005). Role of smoking in global and regional cardiovascular mortality. *Circulation, 112*, 489–497.

F

Fagan, J. F., & Holland, C. R. (2002). Equal opportunity and racial differences in IQ. *Intelligence, 30*, 361–387.

Fagan, J. F., & Holland, C. R. (2007). Racial equality in intelligence: Predictions from a theory of intelligence as processing. *Intelligence, 35*, 319–334.

Fallon, A. (2006). Informed consent in the practice of group psychotherapy. *International Journal of Group Psychotherapy, 56*, 431–453.

Fanselow, M. S., & Poulos, A. M. (2005). The neuroscience of mammalian associative learning. *Annual Review of Psychology, 56*, 207–234.

Farmer, R., & Chapman, A. (2008). Changing behavior by changing the environment. *Behavioral interventions in cognitive behavior therapy: Practical guidance for putting theory into action* (pp. 105–139). Washington, DC: American Psychological Association.

Favazza, A. (1996). *Bodies under Siege: Self-Mutilation and Body Modification in Culture and Psychiatry* (2d ed.). Baltimore: The Johns Hopkins University Press.

Fazio, R., & Olson, M. (2003). Implicit measures in social cognition research: Their meaning and uses. *Annual Review of Psychology, 54*, 297–327.

Fearing, V. G., & Clark, J. (Eds.). (2000). *Individuals in context: A practical guide to client-centered practice.* Chicago: Slack Publishing.

Fee, E., Brown, T. M., Lazarus, J., & Theerman, P. (2002). Exploring acupuncture: Ancient ideas, modern techniques. *American Journal of Public Health, 92*, 1592.

Feinel, W., & Penfield, W. (1954). Localization of discharge in temporal lobe automatism. *Archives of Neurology & Psychiatry, 72*(5), 605–630.

Feldhusen, J. F., (2006). The role of the knowledge base in creative thinking. In J. C. Kaufman, & J. Baer, *Creativity and reason in cognitive development.* New York: Cambridge University Press.

Feldman, D. H. (2003). Cognitive development in childhood. In R. M. Lerner, M. A. Easterbrooks, et al. (Eds.), *Handbook of psychology: Developmental psychology* (Vol. 6) (pp. 195–210). New York: Wiley.

Feldman, D. H. (2004). Piaget's stages: The unfinished symphony of cognitive development. *New Ideas in Psychology, 22*, 175–231.

Feldman, R. S. (2003). *P.O.W.E.R. learning* (2nd ed.). New York: McGraw-Hill.

Feldman, R. S. (2009). *P.O.W.E.R. Learning* (4th ed.). New York: McGraw-Hill.

Feldman, R. S. (Ed.). (1993). *Applications of nonverbal behavioral theories and research.* Hillsdale, NJ: Erlbaum.

Feldt, L. S. (2005). Estimating the reliability of a test battery composite or a test score based on weighted item scoring. *Measurement & Evaluation in Counseling & Development, 37*, 184–191.

Fernander, A., Shavers, V., & Hammons, G. (2007, October). A biopsychosocial approach to examining tobacco-related health disparities among racially classified social groups. *Addiction, 102*(2), 43–57.

Festinger, L. (1957). *A theory of cognitive dissonance.* Stanford, CA: Stanford University Press.

Festinger, L., & Carlsmith, J. M. (1959). Cognitive consequences of forced compliance. *Journal of Abnormal and Social Psychology, 58*, 203–210.

Feuerstein, M. (2007). *Handbook of cancer survivorship.* New York: Springer Science + Business Media.

Fichtenberg, C. M., & Glantz, S. A. (2006). Association of the California tobacco control program with declines in cigarette consumption and mortality from heart disease. In K. E. Warner, *Tobacco control policy.* San Francisco: Jossey-Bass.

Fields, R. (2008, March). White Matter. *Scientific American, 298*(3), 54–61.

Fields, R. D. (2004, April). The other half of the brain. *Scientific American,* pp. 55–61.

Fields-Meyer, T. (1995, September 25). Having their say. *People,* pp. 50–60.

Fine, L. (1994). Personal communication.

Fine, R., & Fine, L. (2003). *Basic chess endings.* New York: Random House.

Fingelkurts, A., Fingelkurts, A. A., & Kallio, S. (2007). Hypnosis induces a changed composition of brain oscillations in EEG: A case study. *Contemporary Hypnosis, 24*, 3–18.

Fink, M. (2000). Electroshock revisited. *American Scientist, 88*, 162–167.

Finke, R. A. (1995). Creative insight and preinventive forms. In R. J. Sternberg & J. E. Davidson (Eds.), *The nature of insight.* Cambridge, MA: MIT.

Finkler, K. (2004). Traditional healers in Mexico: The effectiveness of spiritual practices. In U. P. Gielen, J. M. Fish, & J. G. Draguns (Eds.), *Handbook of culture, therapy, and healing.* Mahwah, NJ: Lawrence Erlbaum Associates.

Finlay, F. O., Jones, R., & Coleman, J. (2002). Is puberty getting earlier? The views of doctors and teachers. *Child Care, Health and Development, 28*, 205–209.

Finley, C. L., & Cowley, B. J. (2005). The effects of a consistent sleep schedule on time taken to achieve sleep. *Clinical Case Studies, 4*, 304–311.

Finney, M. L., Stoney, C. M., & Engebretson, T. O. (2002). Hostility and anger expression in African American and European American men is associated with cardiovascular and lipid reactivity. *Psychophysiology, 39*, 340–349.

First, M. B., Frances, A., Pincus, H. A. (2002). *DSM-IV-TR Handbook of Differential Diagnosis.* Washington, DC: American Psychiatric Publishing.

Fishbach, A., Dhar, R., & Zhang, Y. (2006). Subgoals as substitutes or complements: The role of goal accessibility. *Journal of Personality and Social Psychology, 91*, 232–242.

Fisher, C. B. (2003). *Decoding the ethics code: A practical guide for psychologists.* Thousand Oaks, CA: Sage.

Fisher, C. B., Hoagwood, K., Boyce, C., Duster, T., Frank, D. A., Grisso, T., Levine, R. J., Macklin, R., Spencer, M. B., Takanishi, R., Trimble, J. E., & Zayas, L. H. (2002). Research ethics for mental health science involving ethnic minority children and youths. *American Psychologist, 57*, 1024–1040.

Fisk, J. E., Bury, A. S., & Holden, R. (2006). Reasoning about complex probabilistic concepts in childhood. *Scandinavian Journal of Psychology, 47*, 497–504.

Fitch, K. L., & Sanders, R. E. (2005). *Handbook of language and social interaction.* Mahwah, NJ: Lawrence Erlbaum Associates.

Flam, F. (1991, June 14). Queasy riders. *Science, 252*, 1488.

Flavell, S. W., Cowan, C. W., Kim, T., Greer, P. L., Lin, Y., Paradis, S., Griffith, E. C., Hu, L. S., Chen, C., & Greenberg, M. E. (2006, February 17). Activity-dependent regulation of MEF2 transcription factors suppresses excitatory synapse number. *Science, 311*, 1008–1010.

Fleeson, W. (2004). Moving personality beyond the person-situation debate: The challenge and the opportunity of within-person variability. *Current Directions in Psychological Science, 13*, 83–87.

Fogel, S., & Smith, C. (2006). Learning-dependent changes in sleep spindles and Stage 2 sleep. *Journal of Sleep Research, 15*, 250–255.

Folkman, S., & Moskowitz, J. T. (2000). Stress, positive emotion, and coping. *Current Directions in Psychological Science, 9*, 115–118.

Folkman, S., & Moskowitz, J. T. (2004). Coping: Pitfalls and promise. *Annual Review of Psychology, 55*, 745–774.

Forlenza, M. J., & Baum, A. (2004). Psychoneuroimmunology. In T. J. Boll & R. G. Frank (Eds.), *Handbook of clinical health psychology: Models and perspectives in health psychology* (Vol. 3). Washington, DC: American Psychological Association.

Forquer, L. M., & Johnson, C. M. (2007). Continuous white noise to reduce sleep latency and night walking in college students. *Sleep and Hypnosis, 9*(2), 60–66.

Fortier-Brochu, E., Beaulieu-Bonneau, S., Ivers, H., & Morin, C. M. (2010). Relations between sleep, fatigue, and health-related quality of life in individuals with insomnia. *Journal of Psychosomatic Research, 69*, 475–483.

Foulds, J., Gandhi, K. K., & Steinberg, M. B. (2006). Factors associated with quitting smoking at a tobacco dependence treatment clinic. *American Journal of Health Behavior, 30*, 400–412.

Fountas, K. N., & Smith, J. R. (2007). Historical evolution of stereotactic amygdalotomy for the management of severe aggression. *Journal of Neurosurgery, 106*, 716–723.

Fountoulakis, K. N., Vieta, E., Sanchez-Moreno, J., Kaprinis, S. G., Goikolea, J. M., & Kaprinis, G. S. (2005). Treatment guidelines for bipolar disorder: A critical review. *Journal of Affective Disorders, 86*, 1–10.

Foussias, G., Mann, S., Zakzanis, K. K., van Reekum, R., & Remington, G. (2009). Motivational deficits as the central link to functioning in schizophrenia: A pilot study. *Journal of Schizophrenia Research, 115*, 333–337.

Fox, C. R. (2006). The availability heuristic in the classroom: How soliciting more criticism can boost your course ratings. *Judgment and Decision Making, 1*, 86–90.

Fox, S., & Spector, P. E. (2000). Relations of emotional intelligence, practical intelligence, general intelligence, and trait affectivity with interview outcomes: It's not all just "G." *Journal of Organizational Behavior, 21*, 203–220.

Fraley, R. C., & Shaver, P. R. (1998). Airport separations: A naturalistic study of adult attachment dynamics in separating couples. *Journal of Personality and Social Psychology, 75*, 1198–1212, http://faculty.sjcny.edu/~treboux/documents/airportseparations.pdf.

Francis, G., & Beidel, D. (1995). Cognitive-behavioral psychotherapy. *Anxiety disorders in children and adolescents* (pp. 321–340). New York: Guilford Press.

Frank, L. R. (2002). Electroshock: A crime against the spirit. *Ethical Human Sciences and Services, 4*, 63–71.

Frankenburg, W. K., Dodds, J., Archer, P., et al. (1992). The Denver II: a major revision and restandardization of the Denver Developmental Screening Test. *Pediatrics, 89*, 91–97.

Franko, D., and Striegel-Moore, R. (2002). The role of body dissatisfaction as a risk factor for depression in adolescent girls: Are the differences Black and White? *Journal of Psychosomatic Research, 53,* 975–983.

Franzek, E., & Beckmann, H. (1996). Gene-environment interaction in schizophrenia: Season-of-birth effect reveals etiologically different subgroups. *Psychopathology, 29,* 14–26.

Fraser, J., & Solovey, A. (2007). *Second-order change in psychotherapy: The golden thread that unifies effective treatments.* Washington, DC: American Psychological Association.

Frasure-Smith, N., Lesperance, F., & Talajic, M. (2000). The prognostic importance of depression, anxiety, anger, and social support following myocardial infarction: Opportunities for improving survival. In P. M McCabe, N. Schneiderman, T. M. Field, & A. R. Wellens (Eds.), *Stress, coping, and cardiovascular disease.* Mahwah, NJ: Erlbaum.

Frederickson, B. L., & Branigan, C. (2005). Positive emotions broaden the scope of attention and thought-action repertoires. *Cognition & Emotion, 19,* 313–332.

Freedman, D. S. (1995). The importance of body fat distribution in early life. *American Journal of the Medical Sciences, 310,* S72–S76.

Freedman, J. L. (2002). *Media violence and its effect on aggression: Assessing the scientific evidence.* Toronto, ON: University of Toronto Press.

Freedman, J., & Fraser, S. C. (1966). Compliance without pressure: The foot-in-the-door technique. *Journal of Personality and Social Psychology, 4,* 195–202.

Freeman, A., Mahoney, M., DeVito, P., & Martin, D. (2004). *Cognition and psychotherapy* (2nd ed.). New York: Springer Publishing Co.

Fregni, F., & Pascual-Leone, A. (2007). Technology insight: Noninvasive brain stimulation in neurology-perspectives on the therapeutic potential of rTMS and tDCS. *Nature Clinical Practice Neurology, 3,* 383–393.

Frensch, P. A., & Rünger, D. (2003). Implicit learning. *Current Directions in Psychological Science, 12,* 13–18.

Freud, S. (1900). *The interpretation of dreams.* New York: Basic Books.

Freud, S. (1920). *Beyond the pleasure principle: A study of death instinct in human aggression* (J. Strachey, Trans.). New York: Bantam Books.

Freud, S. (1922/1959). *Group psychology and the analysis of the ego.* London: Hogarth.

Friborg, O., Barlaug, D., Martinussen, M., Rosenvinge, J. H., & Hjemdal, O. (2005). Resilience in relation to personality and intelligence. *International Journal of Methods in Psychiatric Research, 14,* 29–42.

Friedberg, R. D. (2006). A cognitive-behavioral approach to family therapy. *Journal of Contemporary Psychotherapy, 36,* 159–165.

Friedman, J. N. W., Oltmanns, T. F., & Turkheimer, E. (2007). Interpersonal perception and personality disorders: Utilization of a thin slice approach. *Journal of Research in Personality, 41,* 667–688.

Frijda, N. H. (2005). Emotion experience. *Cognition and Emotion, 19,* 473–497.

Frings, L., Wagner, K., Unterrainer, J., Spreer, J., Halsband, U., & Schulze-Bonhage, A. (2006). Gender-related differences in lateralization of hippocampal activation and cognitive strategy. *Neuroreport, 17,* 417–421.

Friscolanti, M., Gulli, C., & Patriquin, M. (2011). Russell Williams's Final Victim: His Wife. Retrieved April 2011, www2.macleans.ca/2011/04/11/her-only-crime-was-trusting-him/.

Frohman, E. M., Racke, M. K., & Raine, C. S. (2006). Multiple Sclerosis – The plaque and its pathogenesis. *New England Journal of Medicine, 354,* 942–955.

Frost, R. O., & Steketee, G. (Eds.). (2002). *Cognitive approaches to obsessions and compulsions: Theory, assessment, and treatment.* New York: Pergamon Press.

Fu, G., Xu, F., Cameron, C., & Lee, K. (2007). Cross-cultural differences in children's choice, categorization and evaluation of truth and lies. *Developmental Psychology, 43,* 278–293.

Funder, D. C. (1991). Global traits: A Neo-Allportian approach to personality. *Psychological Science, 2,* 31–39.

Furnham, A., & Crump, J. (2005). Personality traits, types, and disorders: An examination of the relationship between three self-report measures. *European Journal of Personality, 19,* 167–184.

Furumoto, L., & Scarborough, E. (2002). Placing women in the history of psychology: The first American women psychologists. In W. E. Pickren (Ed.), *Evolving perspectives on the history of psychology* (pp. 527–543). Washington, DC: American Psychological Association.

G

Gaab, J., Rohleder, N., Nater, U. M., & Ehlert, U. (2005). Psychological determinants of the cortisol stress response: The role of anticipatory cognitive appraisal. *Psychoneuroendocrinology, 30,* 599–610.

Gabbard, G. (2009). Psychoanalysis and psychodynamic psychotherapy. *Essentials of personality disorders* (pp. 185–207). Arlington, VA: American Psychiatric Publishing, Inc.

Galanter, E. (1962). Contemporary psychophysics. In R. Brown, E. Galanter, E. Hess, & G. Maroler (Eds.), *New directions in psychology* (pp. 87–157). New York: Holt.

Galatzer-Levy, R. M., & Cohler, B. J. (1997). *Essential psychoanalysis: A contemporary introduction.* New York: Basic Books.

Galavotti, C., Saltzman, L. E., Sauter, S. L., & Sumartojo, E. (1997, February). Behavioral science activities at the Center for Disease Control and Prevention: A selected overview of exemplary programs. *American Psychologist, 52,* 154–166.

Gami, A. S., Howard, D. E., Olson, E. J., Somers, V. K. (2005). Day-night pattern of sudden death in obstructive sleep apnea. *New England Journal of Medicine, 353,* 1206–1214.

Gangwisch, J., Heymsfield, S., Boden-Albala, B., Kreier, F., Pickering, T., Zammit, G., et al. (2008, August). Sleep duration associated with mortality in elderly, but not middle-aged adults in a large US sample. *Sleep: Journal of Sleep and Sleep Disorders Research, 31*(8), 1087–1096.

Ganong, L. H., & Coleman, M. (1999). *Changing families, changing responsibilities: Family obligations following divorce and remarriage.* Mahwah, NJ: Erlbaum.

Garb, H. N., Wood, J. M., Lilenfeld, S. O., & Nezworski, M. T. (2005). Roots of the Rorschach controversy. *Clinical Psychology Review, 25,* 97–118.

Garcia, S. M., Weaver, K., Moskowitz, G. B., & Darley, J. M. (2002). Crowded minds: The implicit bystander effect. *Journal of Personality and Social Psychology, 83,* 843–853.

Garcia-Palacios, A., Hoffman, H., & Carlin, A. (2002). Virtual reality in the treatment of spider phobia: A controlled study. *Behavior Research & Therapy, 40,* 983–993.

Gardner, E. P., & Kandel, E. R. (2000). Touch. In E. R. Kandel, J. H. Schwartz, & T. M. Jessell (Eds.), *Principles of neural science* (4th ed.). New York: McGraw-Hill.

Gardner, H. (1999). *Intelligence reframed: Multiple intelligences for the 21st century.* New York: Basic Books.

Gardner, H. (2005). Scientific psychology: Should we bury it or praise it? In R. J. Sternberg (Ed.), *Unity in psychology: Possibility or pipe dream?* (pp. 77–90). Washington, DC: American Psychological Association.

Gardner, H. (2006). *Multiple Intelligences: New Horizons.* Basic Books.

Garwick, G. B. (2007). Intelligence-related terms in mental retardation, learning disability, and gifted/talented professional usage, 1983–2001: The 1992 mental retardation redefinition as natural experiment. *Dissertation Abstracts International Section A: Humanities and Social Sciences, 67*(9-A), 3296.

Garwood, C. L., & Potts, L. A. (2007). Emerging pharmacotherapies for smoking cessation. *American Journal of Health Systems Pharmacology, 64,* 1693–1698.

Garza-Guerrero, C. (2000). Idealization and mourning in love relationships: Normal and pathological spectra. *Psychoanalytic Quarterly, 69,* 121–150.

Gatchel, R. J. & Weisberg, J. N. (2000). *Personality characteristics of patients with pain.* Washington, DC: APA Books.

Gatchel, R. J., & Oordt, M. S. (2003). Obesity. In R. J. Gathchel & M. S. Oordt, *Clinical health psychology and primary care: Practical advice and clinical guidance for successful collaboration* (pp. 149–167). Washington, DC: American Psychological Association.

Gawryluk, J., Mazerolle, E., Brewer, K., Beyea, S., & D'Arcy, R. (2011). Investigation of fMRI activation in the internal capsule. *BMC Neuroscience, 12*(56), 1–7.

Gazzaniga, M. S. (1998, July). The split brain revisited. *Scientific American,* pp. 50–55.

Gazzaniga, M. S., Ivry, R. B., & Mangun, G. R. (2002). *Cognitive neuroscience: The biology of the mind* (2nd ed.). New York: W. W. Norton.

Ge, X., Kim, I. J., Brody, G. H., Conger, R. D., Simons, R. L., Gibbons, F. X., & Cutrona, C. E. (2003). It's about timing and change: Pubertal transition effects on symptoms of major depression among African American youths. *Developmental Psychology, 39,* 430–439.

Gegenfurtner, K. R. (2003). Color vision. *Annual Review of Neuroscience, 26,* 181–206.

Gelernter, J., & Stein, M. (2009). Heritability and genetics of anxiety disorders. *Oxford handbook of anxiety and related disorders* (pp. 87–96). New York: Oxford University Press.

Gelfand, M. M. (2000). Sexuality among older women. *Journal of Women's Health and Gender Based Medicine, 9*(Suppl. 1), S15–S20.

Gelman, R., & Baillargeon, R. (1983). A review of some Piagetian concepts. In J. H. Flavell & E. M. Markman (Eds.), *Handbook of child psychology: Cognitive development* (Vol. 3) (4th ed.). New York: Wiley.

Gelman, R., & Kit-Fong Au, T. (Eds.). (1996). *Perceptual and cognitive development.* New York: Academic Press.

George, S., & Moselhy, H. (2005). Cocaine-induced trichotillomania. *Addiction, 100,* 255–256.

Geraerts, E., Schooler, J., Merckelbach, H., Jelicic, M., Hauer, B., & Ambadar, Z. (2007, July). The reality of recovered memories: Corroborating continuous and discontinuous memories of childhood sexual abuse. *Psychological Science, 18*(7), 564–568.

Gershkoff-Stowe, L., Connell, B., & Smith, L. (2006). Priming overgeneralizations in two- and four-year-old children. *Journal of Child Language, 33,* 461–486.

Gershoff, A. D., & Johar, G. V. (2006). Do You Know Me? Consumer Calibration of Friends' Knowledge. *J. Consumer Research, 32*(4) 496–503.

Giacobbi, P. R., Jr., Lynn, T. K., Wetherington, J. M., Jenkins, J., Bodendorf, M., & Langley, B. (2004). Stress and coping during the transition to university for first-year female athletes. *Sports Psychologist, 18,* 1–20.

Gibb, K., Tunbridge, D., Chua, A., & Frederickson, N. (2007). Pathways to inclusion: Moving from special school to mainstream. *Educational Psychology in Practice, 23,* 109–127.

Gibbons, R. D., Brown, C. H., Hur, K., Marcus, S. M., Bhamik, D. K., Erkens, J. A., Herrings, R. M. C., & Mann, J. J. (2007). Early evidence on the effects of regulators' suicidally warnings on SSRI prescriptions and suicide in children and adolescents. *American Journal of Psychiatry, 164,* 1356–1363.

Gibbs, N. (2005, August 8). Being 13. *Time,* pp. 41–55.

Gibbs, W. W. (2002, August.) From mouth to mind. *Scientific American,* p. 26.

Gilbert, D. T., McNulty, S. E., Guiliano, T. A., & Benson, J. E. (1992). Blurry words and fuzzy deeds: The attribution of obscure behavior. *Journal of Personality and Social Psychology, 62,* 18–25.

Gilbert, D. T., Miller, A. G., & Ross, L. (1998). Speeding with Ned: A personal view of the correspondence bias. In J. M. Darley & J. Cooper (Eds.), *Attribution and social interaction: The legacy of Edward E. Jones.* Washington, DC: American Psychological Association.

Gilboa, A., Winocur, G., & Rosenbaum, R. S. (2006). Hippocampal contributions to recollection in retrograde and anterograde amnesia. *Hippocampus, 16,* 966–980.

Gilligan, C. (1996). The centrality of relationships in psychological development: A puzzle, some evidence, and a theory. In G. G. Noam & K. W. Fischer (Eds.), *Development and vulnerability in close relationships.* Hillsdale, NJ: Erlbaum.

Gilligan, C. (2004). Recovering psyche: reflections on life-history and history. *The Annual of Psychoanalysis, 32,* 131–147.

Gilovich, T., Griffin, D., & Kahneman, D. (Eds.). (2002). *Heuristics and biases: The psychology of intuitive judgment.* Cambridge, England: Cambridge University Press.

Gladwell, M. (2004, September 20). Annals of psychology: Personality, plus how corporations figure out who you are. *The New Yorker,* pp. 42–45.

Gladwin, T. (1964). Culture and logical process. In N. Goodenough (Ed.), *Explorations in cultural anthropology: Essays in honor of George Peter Murdoch.* New York: McGraw-Hill.

Glickler, J. (2006). Advancing in advancement: A self-efficacy study of development practitioners in higher education. *Dissertation Abstracts International: Section B: The Sciences and Engineering, 67*(2-B), 1190.

Glicksohn, J., & Nahari, G. (2007). Interacting personality traits? Smoking as a test case. *European Journal of Personality, 21,* 225–234.

Glisky, E. L. (2007). Changes in cognitive function in human aging. In D. R. Riddle, *Brain aging: Models, methods, and mechanisms.* Boca Raton, FL: CRC Press.

Goffin, R. D. & Boyd, A. C. (2009). Faking and personality assessment in personnel selection: Advancing models of faking. *Canadian Psychology, 50,* 151–160.

Goffin, R. D., Jelley, R. B., & Wagner, S. H. (2003). Is halo helpful? Effects of inducing halo on performance rating accuracy. *Social Behavior and Personality, 31,* 625–636.

Goin, M. K. (2005). A current perspective on the psychotherapies. *Psychiatric Services, 56,* 255–257.

Goldstein, I. (2000). Female sexual arousal disorder: New insights. *International Journal of Impotence Research, 12*(Suppl. 4), S152–S157.

Goldstein, S. N. (2006). The exploration of spirituality and identity status in adolescence. *Dissertation Abstracts International: Section B: The Sciences and Engineering, 67*(6-B), 3481.

Goldstone, R. L., & Kersten, A. (2003). Concepts and categorization. In A. F. Healy & R. W. Proctor (Eds.), *Handbook of psychology: Experimental psychology* (Vol. 4) (pp. 599–621). New York: Wiley.

Golimbet, V. E., Alfimova, M. V., Gritsenko, I. K., & Ebstein, R. P. (2007). Relationship between dopamine system genes and extraversion and novelty seeking. *Neuroscience Behavior and Physiology, 37,* 601–606.

Gontkovsky, S. T. (2005). Neurobiological bases and neuropsychological correlates of aggression and violence. In J. P. Morgan (Ed.), *Psychology of aggression.* Hauppauge, NY: Nova Science Publishers.

Gontkovsky, S. T., & Beatty, W. W. (2006). Practical methods for the clinical assessment of information processing speed. *International Journal of Neuroscience, 116,* 1317–1325.

Good, M. & Adams, G. R. (2008). Linking academic social environments, ego-identity formation, ego virtues, and academic success. *Adolescence, 34,* 221–237.

Goode, E. (1999, April 13). If things taste bad, "phantoms" may be at work. *The New York Times,* pp. D1–D2.

Goodman, W. K., Rudorfer, M. V., & Maser, J. D. (2000). *Obsessive-compulsive disorder: Contemporary issues in treatment.* Mahwah, NJ: Lawrence Erlbaum Associates.

Goodwin, R. D., & Hamilton, S. P. (2003). Lifetime comorbidity of antisocial personality disorder and anxiety disorders among adults in the community. *Psychiatry Research, 117,* 159–166.

Goodwin, R., Costa, P., & Adonu, J. (2004). Social support and its consequences: "Positive" and "deficiency" values and their implications for support and self-esteem. *British Journal of Social Psychology, 43,* 465–474.

Gooren, L. (2006). The biology of human psychosexual differentiation. *Hormones and Behavior, 50,* 589–601.

Gorfine, T., & Zisapel, N. (2009, February). Late evening brain activation patterns and their relation to the internal biological time, melatonin, and homeostatic sleep debt. *Human Brain Mapping, 30*(2), 541–552.

Goslin, D.A. (Ed.). (1969). *Handbook of socialization theory and research.* Chicago: Rand McNally.

Gotlib, I. H., Krasnoperova, E., Yue, D. N., & Joorman, J. (2004). Attentional biases for negative interpersonal stimuli in clinical depression. *Journal of Abnormal Psychology, 113,* 127–135.

Gottesman, I. I. (1991). *Schizophrenia Genesis.* New York: Henry Holt and Company, LLC.

Gottesman, I. I. (1997, June 6). Twin: En route to QTLs for cognition. *Science, 276,* 1522–1523.

Gottesman, I. I., & Hanson, D. R. (2005). Human development: Biological and genetic processes. *Annual Review of Psychology, 56,* 263–286.

Gottfredson, L. S. (2004). Schools and the g factor. *Wilson Quarterly,* 35–45.

Gottfredson, L. S., & Deary, I. J. (2004). Intelligence predicts health and longevity, but why? *Current Directions in Psychological Science, 13,* 1–4.

Gottlieb, D. A. (2004). Acquisition with partial and continuous reinforcement in pigeon autoshaping. *Learning and Behavior, 32,* 321–334.

Gottlieb, D. A. (2006). Effects of partial reinforcement and time between reinforced trials on terminal response rate in pigeon autoshaping. *Behavioural Processes, 72,* 6–13.

Gould, E., Reeves, A. J., Graziano, M. S. A., & Gross, C. G. (1999, October 15). Neurogenesis in the neocortex of adult primates. *Science,* 548–552.

Gould, R. L. (1978). *Transformations.* New York: Simon & Schuster.

Govindarajan, A., Kelleher, R. J., & Tonegawa, S. (2006). A clustered plasticity model of long-term memory engrams. *Nature Reviews Neuroscience, 7,* 575–583.

Grann, J. D. (2007). Confidence in knowledge past: An empirical basis for a differential decay theory of very long-term memory monitoring. *Dissertation Abstracts International Section A: Humanities and Social Sciences, 67,* 2462.

Gray, G. C. (2006). The regulation of corporate violations: punishment, compliance, and the blurring of responsibility. *British Journal of Criminology, 46*, 875–892.

Green, B. G., & George, P. (2004). 'Thermal Taste' Predicts Higher Responsiveness to Chemical Taste and Flavor. *Chemical Senses, 29*, 617–628.

Green, G., & Osborne, J. (1985, January). Does vicarious instigation provide support for observational learning theories? A critical review. *Psychological Bulletin, 97*(1), 3–17.

Greenberg, R. M., & Kellner, C. H. (2005). Electroconvulsive therapy: A selected review. *American Journal of Geriatric Psychiatry, 13*, 268–281.

Greene, J. D., Sommerville, R. B., Nystrom, L. E., Darley, J. M., & Cohen, J. D. (2001, September 14). An fMRI investigation of emotional engagement in moral judgment. *Science, 293*, 2105–2108.

Greenspan, S. (2006). Functional concepts in mental retardation: Finding the natural essence of an artificial category. *Exceptionality, 14*, 205–224.

Greenwald, A. G., Nosek, B. A., & Banaji, M. R. (2003). Understanding and using the Implicit Association Test: 1. An improved scoring algorithm. *Journal of Personality and Social Psychology 85*, 197–216.

Greenwald, A. G., Nosek, B. A., & Sriram, N. (2006). Consequential validity of the implicit association test: Comment on Blanton and Jaccard. *American Psychologist, 61*, 56–61.

Greenwald, A. G., Spangenberg, E. R., Pratkanis, A. R., Eskenazi, J. 1991. Doubl-blind Tests of Subliminal Self-help Audiotapes. *Psychological Science, 2*, 119–122.

Greer, R. D., Dudek-Singer, J. & Gautreaux, G. (2006). Observational learning. *International Journal of Psychology, 41*, 486–499.

Greer, S. (1999). Mind–body research in psychooncology. *Advances in Mind-Body Medicine, 15*(4), 236–244.

Gregory, R. L. (1978). *The psychology of seeing* (3rd ed.). New York: McGraw-Hill.

Grigorenko, E. L. (2000). Heritability and intelligence. In R. J. Sternberg, et al. (Eds.), *Handbook of intelligence*. New York: Cambridge University Press.

Grigoriadis, S., & Ravitz, P. (2007). An approach to interpersonal psychotherapy for postpartum depression: Focusing on interpersonal changes. *Canadian Family Physician, 53*, 1469–1475.

Grilo, C M., Sanislow, C. A., Skodol, A. E., Gunderson, J. G., Stout, R. L., Shea, M. T., Zanarini, M. C., Bencer, D. S., Morey, L. C., Dyck, I. R., & McGlashan, T. H. (2003). Do eating disorders co-occur with personality disorders? Comparison groups matter. *International Journal of Eating Disorders, 33*, 155–164.

Gronholm, P., Rinne, J. O., Vorobyev, V., & Laine, M. (2005). Naming of newly learned objects: A PET activation study. *Brain Research and Cognitive Brain Research, 14*, 22–28.

Gross, D. M. (2006). *The secret history of emotion: From Aristotle's Rhetoric to modern brain science*. Chicago: University of Chicago Press.

Grossmann, T., Striano, T., & Friederici, A. D. (2007). Developmental changes in infants' processing of happy and angry facial expressions: A neurobehavioral study. *Brain and Cognition, 64*, 30–41.

Grunwald, T., Boutros, N. N., Pezer, N., von Oertzen, J., Fernandez, G., Schaller, C., & Elger, C. E. (2003). Neuronal substrates of sensory gating within the human brain. *Biological Psychiatry, 15*, 511–519.

Guilleminault, C., Kirisoglu, C., Bao, G., Arias, V., Chan, A., & Li, K. K. (2005). Adult chronic sleepwalking and its treatment based on polysomnography. *Brain, 128* (Pt. 5), 1062–1069.

Gurunjj, R., & Roethel-Wendorf, A. (2009). Stress and mental health. In S. Eshun, & R.A.R. Gurunjj, (Eds.) *Culture and mental health: Sociocultural influences, theory, and practice* (pp. 35–53). New York: Wiley-Blackwell.

Gwynn, M. I., & Spanos, N. P. (1996). Hypnotic responsiveness, nonhypnotic suggestibility, and responsiveness to social influence. In R. G. Kunzendorf, N. P. Spahos, & B. Wallace (Eds.), *Hypnosis and imagination*. Amityville, NY: Baywood.

H

Haberstick, B. C., Schmitz, S., Young, S. E., & Hewitt, J. K. (2005).Contributions of genes and environments to stability and change in externalizing and internalizing problems during elementary and middle school. *Behavior Genetics, 35*, 381–396.

Haberstick, B. C., Timberlake, D., & Ehringer, M. A. (2007). Genes, time to first cigarette and nicotine dependence in a general population sample of young adults. *Addiction, 102*, 655–665.

Hackam, D. G. (2007). Translating animal research into clinical benefit. *British Medical Journal, 334*, 163–164.

Halford, S. (2006). Collapsing the boundaries? Fatherhood, organization and home-working. *Gender, Work & Organization, 13*, 383–402.

Hall, R. E. (2002). The Bell Curve: Implications for the performance of black/white athletes. *Social Science Journal, 39*, 113–118.

Hallschmid, M., Benedict, C., Born, J., Fehm, H., & Kern, W. (2004). Manipulating central nervous mechanisms of food intake and body weight regulation by intranasal administration of neuropeptides in man. *Physiology and Behavior, 83*, 55–64.

Hamann, S. (2001). Cognitive and neural mechanisms of emotional memory. *Trends in Cognitive Sciences, 5*, 394–400.

Hamberg, K. (2005). Biology, Gender and Behaviour. A Critical Discussion of the Biological Models Used for Explaining Cognitive and Behavioural Gender Differences. *Psychology of gender identity* (pp. 127–144). Hauppauge, NY: Nova Biomedical Books.

Hambleton, R. K. (2006). Psychometric models, test designs and item types for the next generation of educational and psychological tests. In D. Bartram, & R. K. Hambleton, *Computer-based testing and the Internet: Issues and advances*. New York: John Wiley & Sons.

Hamer, D. H., Hu, S., Magnuson, V. L., Hu, N., & Pattatucci, A. M. L. (1993, July 16). A linkage between DNA markers on the X chromosome and male sexual orientation. *Science, 261*, 321–327.

Hamer, M., Taylor, A., & Steptoe, A. (2006). The effect of acute aerobic exercise on stress related blood pressure responses: A systematic review and meta-analysis. *Biological Psychology, 71*, 183–190.

Hamilton, A. C., & Martin, R. C. (2007). Semantic short-term memory deficits and resolution of interference: A case for inhibition? In D. S. Gorfein, & C. M. Macleod, *Inhibition in cognition*. Washington, DC: American Psychological Association.

Hamilton, W. L., Biener, L., & Brennan, R. T. (2007). Do local tobacco regulations influence perceived smoking norms? Evidence from adult and youth surveys in Massachusetts. *Health Education Research*, Health Education Research Advance Access published online on October 18, 2007, Health Education Research, doi:10.1093/her/cym054.

Hanley, S. J., & Abell, S. C. (2002). Maslow and relatedness: Creating an interpersonal model of self-actualization. *Journal of Humanistic Psychology, 42*, 37–56.

Hannon, E. E., & Johnson, S. P. (2005). Infants use meter to categorize rhythms and melodies: Implications for musical structure learning. *Cognitive Psychology, 50*, 354–377.

Hanson, M. & Chen, E. (2010). Daily stress, cortisol, and sleep: The moderating role of childhood psychosocial environments. *Health Psychology, 29*, 394–402.

Hardison, D. M. (2006). Review of Phonetics and phonology in language comprehension and production: Differences and similarities. *Studies in Second Language Acquisition, 28*, 138–140.

Hardy, L. T., (2007). Attachment theory and reactive attachment disorder: theoretical perspectives and treatment implications. *Journal of Child and Adolescent Psychiatric Nursing, 20*, 27–39.

Harlaar, N., Spinath, F. M., Dale, P. S., & Plomin, R. (2005). Genetic influences on early word recognition abilities and disabilities: A study of 7-year-old twins. *Journal of Child Psychology and Psychiatry, 46*, 373–384.

Harlow, H. F., & Zimmerman, R. R. (1959). Affectional responses in the infant monkey. *Science, 130*, 421–432.

Harlow, J. M. (1869). Recovery from the passage of an iron bar through the head. *Massachusetts Medical Society Publication, 2*, 329–347.

Harmon-Jones, E., & Winkielman, P. (2007). *Social neuroscience: Integrating biological and psychological explanations of social behavior*. New York: Guilford Press.

Harold, G. T., Fincham, F. D., Osborne, L. N., & Conger, R. D. (1997). Mom and dad are at it again: Adolescent perceptions of marital conflict and adolescent psychological distress. *Developmental Psychology, 33*, 333–350.

Harper, T. (1978, November 15). It's not true about people 65 or over. *Green Bay Press-Gazette* (Wisconsin), p. D-1.

Harris, G. (2009). Flavors banned from cigarettes to deter youths. *The New York Times*, Sept. 23, p. A1.

Hart, B., & Risley, T. R. (1997). Use of language by three-year-old children. Courtesy of Drs. Betty Hart and Todd Risley, University of Kansas.

Hartung, C. M., & Widiger, T. A. (1998). Gender differences in the diagnosis of mental disorders: Conclusions and controversies of the DSM-IV. *Psychological Bulletin, 123,* 260–278.

Harvey, J. H., Wenzel, A., Sprecher, S. (2004). *The handbook of sexuality in close relationships.* Mahwah, NJ: Lawrence Erlbaum.

Hauke, C. (2006). The unconscious: Personal and collective. In R. K. Papadopoulos, *The handbook of Jungian psychology: Theory, practice and applications.* New York: Routledge.

Hausenblas, H., & Downs, D. (2002). Relationship among sex, imagery and exercise dependence symptoms. *Psychology of Addictive Behaviors, 16,* 169–172.

Hauser, M. D., Chomsky, N., & Fitch, W. T. (2002, November, 22). The faculty for language: What is it, who has it, and how did it evolve? *Science, 298,* 1569–1579.

Havermans, R. C., Mulkens, S., Nederkoorn, C., & Jansen, A. (2007). The efficacy of cue exposure with response prevention in extinguishing drug and alcohol cue reactivity. *Behavioral Interventions, 22,* 121–135.

Hayflick, L. (2007). Biological aging is no longer an unsolved problem. *Annals of the New York Academy of Sciences, 1100,* 1–13

Hayslip, B., Neumann, C. S., Louden, L., & Chapman, B. (2006). Developmental stage theories. In J. C. Thomas, D. L. Segal, & M. Hersen (Eds.). *Comprehensive Handbook of Personality and Psychopathology, Vol. 1: Personality and Everyday Functioning.* Hoboken, NJ: John Wiley & Sons.

Health Canada. (2006). First Nations, Inuit and Aboriginal Health, Suicide Prevention. Retrieved March 21, 2012, from www.hc-sc.gc.ca/fniah-spnia/promotion/suicide/index-eng.php.

Health Canada. (2007). How much food you should eat. Retrieved March 21, 2012, from www.hc-sc.gc.ca/fn-an/food-guide-aliment/basics-base/quantit-eng.php.

Health Canada. (2010a). Alcohol: Health concerns. Retrieved March 8, 2011, from www.hc-sc.gc.ca/hc-ps/alc/index-eng.php.

Health Canada. (2010b). Canadian Tobacco Use Survey. Retrieved March 19, 2012, from www.hc-sc.gc.ca/hc-ps/tobac-tabac/research-recherche/stat/ctums-esutc_2010_graph-eng.php.

Health Canada. (2010c). Major findings from the Canadian alcohol and drug use monitoring survey. Retrieved March 8, 2011, from www.hc-sc.gc.ca/hc-ps/drugs-drogues/stat/index-eng.php.

Health Canada. (2010d). Medicinal use of marihuana. Retrieved March 8, 2011, from www.hc-sc.gc.ca/dhp-mps/marihuana/index-eng.php.

Health Canada. (2010e). Safe use of energy drinks. Retrieved March 8, 2011, from www.hc-sc.gc.ca/h-vs/alt_formats/pdf/iyh-vsv/food-aliment/boissons-energ-drinks-eng.pdf.

Heath, R. A. (2006). *The Praeger handbook of trans-sexuality: Changing gender to match mindset.* Westport, CT: Praeger Publishers/ Greenwood Publishing.

Hecht, J. M. (2007). *The happiness myth: Why what we think is right is wrong. A history of what really makes us happy.* New York: HarperSanFrancisco/ HarperCollins.

Hedgepeth, E. (2005). Different lenses, different vision. *School Administrator, 62,* 36–39.

Hedges, D. W., Brown, B. L., Shwalk, D. A., Godfrey, K., & Larcher, A. M. (2007). The efficacy of selective serotonin reuptake inhibitors in adult social anxiety disorder: A meta-analysis of double-blind, placebo-controlled trials. *Journal of Psychopharmacology, 21,* 102–111.

Hegarty, P. (2007). From genius inverts to gendered intelligence: Lewis Terman and the power of the norm. *History of Psychology, 10,* Special issue: Power matters: Knowledge politics in the history of psychology, 132–155.

Hegarty, P., & Massey, S. (2007). Anti-homosexual prejudice . . . as opposed to what? Queer theory and the social psychology of anti-homosexual attitudes. *Journal of Homosexuality, 52,* 47–71.

Heinrichs, R. W. (2005). The primacy of cognition in schizophrenia. *American Psychologist, 60,* 229–242.

Heller, S. (2005). *Freud A to Z.* New York: Wiley.

Helmuth, L. (2000, August 25). Synapses shout to overcome distance. *Science, 289,* 1273.

Henderson, J., Kesmodel, U., & Gray, R. (2007). Systematic review of the fetal effects of prenatal binge-drinking. *Journal of Epidemiology and Community Health, 61,* 1069–1073.

Henderson, N. D. (1982). Correlations in IQ for pairs of people with varying degrees of genetic relatedness and shared environment. *Annual Review of Psychology, 33,* 219–243.

Hendrick, C., & Hendrick, S. S. (2003). Romantic love: Measuring cupid's arrow. In S. J. Lopez & C. R. Snyder (Eds.), *Positive psychological assessment: A handbook of models and measures.* Washington, DC: American Psychological Association.

Hentschel, U., Smith, G., Draguns, J. G., & Elhers, W. (2004). *Defense mechanisms: Theoretical, research and clinical perspectives.* Oxford, England: Elsevier Science.

Herrán, A., Carrera, M., & Sierra-Biddle, D. (2006). Panic disorder and the onset of agoraphobia. *Psychiatry and Clinical Neurosciences, 60,* 395–396.

Herrnstein, R. J., & Murray, D. (1994). *The bell curve.* New York: Free Press.

Herzog, H. A. (2005). Dealing with the animal research controversy. In C. K. Akins & S. Panicker (Eds.), *Laboratory animals in research and teaching: Ethics, care, and methods.* Washington, DC: American Psychological Association.

Heshka, S., Anderson, J. W., Atkinson, R. L., Greenway, F. L., Hill, J. O., Phinney, S. D., Kolotkin, R. L., Miller-Kovach, K., & Pi-Sunyer, F. X. (2003). Weight loss with self-help compared with a structured commercial program: A randomized trial. *Journal of the American Medical Association, 289,* 1792–1798.

Hess, E. H., & Polt, J. M. (1960). Pupil size as related to interest value of visual stimuli. *Science, 132,* 249–350.

Hess, T. M., Hinson, J. T., & Statham, J. A. (2004). Explicit and implicit stereotype activation effects on memory: Do age and awareness moderate the impact of priming? *Psychology and Aging, 19,* 495–505.

Hettema, J. (2005). Genetics of Anxiety Disorders. *Psychiatric genetics* (pp. 141–165). Arlington, VA: American Psychiatric Publishing, Inc.

Heywood, S., & McCabe, M. P. (2006). Negative affect as a mediator between body dissatisfaction and extreme weight loss and muscle gain behaviors. *Journal of Health Psychology, 11,* 833–844.

Hiby, E. F., Rooney, N. J., & Bradshaw, J. W. S. (2004). Dog training methods: Their use, effectiveness and interaction with behaviour and welfare. *Animal Welfare, 13,* 63–69.

Hilarski, C. (2007). Antisocial personality disorder. In B. A. Thyer, & J. S. Wodarski, *Social work in mental health: An evidence-based approach.* Hoboken, NJ: John Wiley & Sons.

Hilgard, E. (1992). Disassociation and theories of hypnosis. In E. Fromm & M. E. Nash (Eds.), *Contemporary hypnosis research.* New York: Guilford.

Hill, J. O., Catenacci, V., & Wyatt, H. R. (2005). Obesity: Overview of an epidemic. *Psychiatric Clinics of North America, 28,* 1–23.

Hill, J. O., Wyatt, H. R., Reed, G. W., & Peters, J. C. (2003, February 7). Obesity and the environment: Where do we go from here? *Science, 299,* 853–855.

Hines, M. (2004). *Brain gender.* New York: Oxford University Press.

Hirschler, B. (2007, May 1). Doctors test gene therapy to treat blindness. *Reuters,* p. 9.

Hirsh, I. J., & Watson, C. S. (1996). Auditory psychophysics and perception. *Annual Review of Psychology, 47,* 461–484.

Hjertaas, T. (2004). Adler and Binswanger: Individual psychology and existentialism. *Journal of Individual Psychology, 60,* 396–407.

Ho, W. (2004). Using Kohonen neural network and principle component analysis to characterize divergent thinking. *Creativity Research Journal, 16,* 283–292.

Hobfoll, S. E., Freedy, J. R., Green B. L., & Solomon, S. D. (1996). Coping in reaction to extreme stress: The roles of resource loss and resource availability. In M. Zeidner & N. S. Endler (Eds.), *Handbook of coping: Theory, research, applications.* New York: Wiley.

Hobfoll, S. E., Hall, B. J., & Canetti-Nisim, D. (2007). Refining our understanding of traumatic growth in the face of terrorism: Moving from meaning cognitions to doing what is meaningful. *Applied Psychology: An International Review, 56,* 345–366.

Hobson, J. A. (1989). *Sleep.* New York: Henry Holt & Company, LLC.

Hobson, J. A. (2005). In bed with Mark Solms? What a nightmare! A reply to Domhoff (2005). *Dreaming, 15,* 21–29.

Hock, H. S., & Ploeger, A. (2006) Linking dynamical perceptual decisions at different levels of description in motion pattern formation: Psychophysics. *Perception & Psychophysics, 68,* 505–514.

Hoff, E. (2003). Language development in childhood. In R. M. Lerner, M. A. Easterbrooks, et al. (Eds.), *Handbook of psychology: Developmental psychology* (Vol. 6) (pp. 171–193). New York: Wiley.

Hoff, E. (2008). *Language development.* New York: Wadsworth.

Hofmann, S. G. (2007). Enhancing exposure-based therapy from a translational research perspective. *Behaviour Research and Therapy, 45*, 1987–2001.

Hogan, J., Davies, S., & Hogan, R. (2007). Generalizing personality-based validity evidence. In S. M. McPhail, *Alternative validation strategies: Developing new and leveraging existing validity evidence.* Hoboken, NJ: John Wiley & Sons.

Hogg, M. A. (2006). Social identity theory. In P. J. Burke, *Contemporary social psychological theories.* Stanford University Press.

Hogg, M. A., & Hains, S. C. (2001). Intergroup relations and group solidarity: Effects of group identification and social beliefs on depersonalized attraction. In M. A. Hogg & D. Abrams (Eds.), *Intergroup relations: Essential readings.* New York: Psychology Press.

Holden, C. (2003, January 17). Deconstructing schizophrenia. *Science, 299,* 333–335.

Holden, C. (2005, June 10). Sex and the suffering brain. *Science, 308,* 1574–1577.

Hollingworth, H. L. (1943/1990). *Leta Stetter Hollingworth: A biography.* Boston: Anker.

Hollon, S. D., Thase, M. E., & Markowitz, J. C. (2002). Treatment and prevention of depression. *Psychological Science in the Public Interest, 3,* 39–77.

Holmes, A., Yang, R. J., Lesch, K. P., Crawley, J. N., & Murphy, D. L. (2003). Mice lacking the Serotonin Transporter Exhibit 5-HT-sub(1A) receptor-mediated abnormalities in tests for anxiety-like behavior. *Neuropsychopharmacology, 28,* 2077–2088.

Holowka, S., & Pettito, L. A. (2002, August 30). Left hemisphere cerebral specialization for babies while babbling. *Science, 297,* 1515.

Holt, M., & Jahn, R. (2004, March, 26). Synaptic vesicles in the fast lane. *Science, 303,* 1986–1987.

Holtzman, D., & Kulish, N. (1996). Nevermore: The hymen and the loss of virginity. *Journal of the American Psychoanalytic Association, 44,* 303–332.

Hong, E., Milgram, R. M., & Gorsky, H. (1995). Original thinking as a predictor of creative performance in young children. *Roeper Review, 18,* 147–149.

Hongchun, W., & Ming, L. (2006). About the research on suggestibility and false memory. *Psychological Science (China), 29,* 905–908.

Horínek, D., Varjassyová, A., & Hort, J. (2007). Magnetic resonance analysis of amygdalar volume in Alzheimer's disease. *Current Opinion in Psychiatry, 20,* 273–277.

Horn, J. L. (2002). Selections of evidence, misleading assumptions, and over-simplifications: The political message of The Bell Curve. In J. M. Fish (Ed.), *Race and intelligence: Separating science from myth* (pp. 297–325). Mahwah, NJ: Erlbaum.

Horney, K. (1937). *Neurotic personality of our times.* New York: Norton.

Horton, K. D., Wilson, D. E., Vonk, J., Kirby, S. L., & Nielsen, T. (2005). Measuring automatic retrieval: A comparison of implicit memory, process dissociation, and speeded response procedures. *Acta Psychologica, 119,* 235–263.

Horwath, E., Weissman, M. M. (2000). The epidemiology and cross-national presentation of obsessive-compulsive disorder. *Psychiatric Clinics of North America, 23,* 493–507

Howe, C. J. (2002). The countering of overgeneralization. *Journal of Child Language, 29,* 875–895.

Howells, J. G., & Osborn, M. L. (1984). *A reference companion to the history of abnormal psychology.* Westport, CT: Greenwood Press.

Hrabosky, J. I., White, M. A., Masheb, R. M., & Grilo, C. M. (2007). Physical activity and its correlates in treatment-seeking obese patients with binge eating disorder. *International Journal of Eating Disorders, 40,* 72–76.

Hubel, D. H., & Wiesel, T. N. (2004). *Brain and visual perception: The story of a 25-year collaboration.* New York: Oxford University Press.

Huber, F., Beckmann, S. C., & Herrmann, A. (2004). Means-end analysis: Does the affective state influence information processing style? *Psychology and Marketing, 21,* 715–737.

Hudson, W. (1960). Pictorial depth perception in subcultural groups in Africa. *Journal of Social Psychology, 52,* 183–208.

Hudspeth, A. J. (2000). Hearing. In E. R. Kandel, J. H. Schwartz, & T. M. Jessell (Eds.), *Principles of neural science* (4th ed.). New York: McGraw-Hill.

Hui, L., Hua, F., Diandong, H., & Hong, Y. (2007, March). Effects of sleep and sleep deprivation on immunoglobulins and complement in humans. *Brain, Behavior, and Immunity, 21*(3), 308–310.

Huijie, T. (2006). The measurement and assessment of mental health: A longitudinal and cross-sectional research on undergraduates, adults and patients. *Psychological Science (China), 29,* 419–422.

Hull, C. L. (1943). *Principles of behavior.* New York: Appleton-Century-Crofts.

Humphrey, N., Curran, A., & Morris, E. (2007). Emotional intelligence and education: A critical review. *Educational Psychology, 27,* 235–254.

Humphreys, G. W., & Müller, H. (2000). A search asymmetry reversed by figure-ground assignment. *Psychological Science, 11,* 196–200.

Hunt, E. (2005). Information processing and intelligence: Where we are and where we are going. In R. J. Sternberg & J. E. Pretz, *Cognition and intelligence: Identifying the mechanisms of the mind.* New York: Cambridge University Press.

Hunt, J. S., Seifert, A. L., & Armenta, B. E. (2006). Stereotypes and prejudice as dynamic constructs: reminders about the nature of intergroup bias from the hurricane Katrina relief efforts. *Analyses of Social Issues and Public Policy (ASAP), 6,* 237–253.

Hunt, M. (1974). *Sexual behaviors in the 1970s.* New York: Dell.

Huprich, S. (2009). *Psychodynamic therapy: Conceptual and empirical foundations.* New York: Routledge/Taylor & Francis Group.

Hurdle, J. (2010, September 21). Social media can rule your life, college finds. *Reuters.* Retrieved November 17, 2010 from www.reuters.com/article.idUSN2115055220100921.

Huston, A. C., Donnerstein, E., Fairchild, H. H., Feshback, N. D., Katz, P., Murray, J. P., Rubinstein, E. A., Wilcox, B. L., & Zuckerman, D. (1992). Big world, small screen: The role of television in American society. Omaha, NE: University of Nebraska Press.

Hutchinson, S. L., Baldwin, C. K., & Oh, S-S. (2006). Adolescent coping: Exploring adolescents' leisure-based responses to stress. *Leisure Sciences, 28,* 115–131.

Hyde, J. S. & Grabe, S. (2008). Meta-analysis in the psychology of women. In F. L. Denmark & M. A. Paludi (Eds.), *Psychology of women: A handbook of issues and theories* (2nd ed.). Westport, CT: Praeger Publishers/ Greenwood Publishing Group.

Hyde, J., Mezulis, A., & Abramson, L. (2008, April). The ABCs of depression: Integrating affective, biological, and cognitive models to explain the emergence of the gender difference in depression. *Psychological Review, 115*(2), 291–313.

I

Iachini, T., & Giusberti, F. (2004). Metric properties of spatial images generated from locomotion: The effect of absolute size on mental scanning. *European Journal of Cognitive Psychology, 16,* 573–596.

ICMPA (International Center for Media and the Public Agenda). (2010). A day without media. Research Project, University of Maryland, Phillip Merrill College of Journalism. Retrieved November 17, 2010 from http://withoutmedia.wordpress.com/.

Ievers-Landis, C. E., Hoff, A. L., Brez, C., Cancilliere, M. K., McConnell, J., & Kerr, D. (2005). Situational analysis of dietary challenges of the treatment regimen for children and adolescents with phenylketonuria and their primary caregivers. *Journal of Developmental and Behavioral Pediatrics, 26,* 186–193.

Ikonomidou, C., Bittigau, P., Ishimaru, M. J., Wozniak, D. F., Koch, C., Genz, K., Price, M. T., Stefovska, V., Hörster, F., Tenkova, T., Dikranian, K., & Olney, J. W. (2000, February 11). Ethanol-induced apoptotic neurodegeneration and fetal alcohol syndrome. *Science, 287,* 1056–1060.

Ilies, R., Arvey, R. D., & Bouchard, T. J., Jr. (2006). Darwinism, behavioral genetics, and organizational behavior: A review and agenda for future research. *Journal of Organizational Behavior, 27,* Special issue: Darwinian Perspectives on Behavior in Organizations, 96–141.

Inhelder, B. and Piaget, J. (1958). *The Growth of Logical Thinking from Childhood to Adolescence.* New York: Basic Books.

Innocenti, G. M. (2007). Subcortical regulation of cortical development: Some effects of early, selective deprivations. *Progressive Brain Research, 164,* 23–37.

Irwin, R. R. (2006). Spiritual development in adulthood: Key concepts and models. In C. Hoare, *Handbook of adult development and learning.* New York: Oxford University Press.

Isay, R. A. (1994). *Being homosexual: Gay men and their development.* Lanham, MD: Jason Aronson.

Isbell, L. M., & Tyler, J. M. (2003). Teaching students about in-group favoritism and the minimal groups paradigm. *Teaching of Psychology, 30,* 127–130.

Ishikawa, S.-I., Okajima, I., Matsuoka, H., & Sakano, Y. (2007). Cognitive behavioural therapy for anxiety disorders in children and adolescents: A meta-analysis. *Child and Adolescent Mental Health, 12*(4), 164–172.

Iverson, L. (2000). *The science of marijuana.* Oxford, England: Oxford University Press.

Iverson, P., Kuhl, P. K., Reiko, A. Y., Diesch, E., Tohkura, Y., Ketterman, A., & Siebert, C. (2003). A perceptual interference account of acquisition difficulties for non-native phonemes. *Cognition, 87*, B47–B57.

Iverson, S. D., & Iversen, L. L. (2007). Dopamine: 50 years in perspective. *Trends in Neurosciences, 30*, 188–191.

Izard, C. E. (1990). Facial expressions and the regulation of emotions. *Journal of Personality and Social Psychology, 58*, 487–498.

Izard, C. E. (1994). Innate and universal facial expressions: Evidence from developmental and cross-cultural research. *Psychological Bulletin, 115*, 288–299.

Izard, C. E., & Abe, J. A. (2004). Developmental changes in facial expressions of emotions in the strange situation during the second year of life. *Emotion, 4*, 251–265.

J

Jacoby, L. L., Bishara, A. J., Hessels, S., & Hughes, A. (2007). Probabilistic retroactive interference: The role of accessibility bias in interference effects. *Journal of Experimental Psychology: General, 136*, 200–216.

Jaffé, A., Prasad, S. A., & Larcher, V. (2006). Gene therapy for children with cystic fibrosis—Who has the right to choose? *Journal of Medical Ethics, 32*, 361–364.

Jain, S., Mills, P. J., & Von Känel, R. (2007). Effects of perceived stress and uplifts on inflammation and coagulability. *Psychophysiology, 44*, 154–160.

James, W. (1890). *The principles of psychology.* New York: Holt.

Jamieson, G. A. (2007). *Hypnosis and conscious states: The cognitive neuroscience perspective.* New York: Oxford University Press.

Jamison, K. R. (1995). *An unquiet mind: A memoir of moods and madness.* New York: Knopf.

Jang, S. J., You, S. H., & Ahn, S. H. (2007). Neurorehabilitation-induced cortical reorganization in brain injury: A 14-month longitudinal follow-up study. *NeuroRehabilitation, 22*, 117–122.

Janssen, D. (2007, May). First stirrings: Cultural notes on orgasm, ejaculation, and wet dreams. *Journal of Sex Research, 44*(2), 122–134.

Jaret, P. (1992, November/December). Mind over malady. *Health,* pp. 87–94.

Jarlais, D. C. D., Arasteh, K., & Perlis, T. (2007). The transition from injection to non-injection drug use: Long-term outcomes among heroin and cocaine users in New York City. *Addiction, 102*, 778–785.

Jelinek, G. A. (1997). Widow spider envenomation (latrodectism): A worldwide problem. *Wilderness and Environmental Medicine, 8*, 226-231.

Jenkins, S. R. (1994). Need for power and women's careers over 14 years: Structural power, job satisfaction, and motive change. *Journal of Personality and Social Psychology, 66*, 155–165.

Jensen, A. R. (2002). Galton's legacy to research on intelligence. *Journal of Biosocial Science, 34*, 145–172.

Jensen, A. R. (2003). Do age-group differences on mental tests imitate racial differences? *Intelligence, 31*, 107–121.

Jensen, A. R. (2005). Psychometric g and mental chronometry. *Cortex, 41*, 230–231.

Jequier, E. (2002). Pathways to obesity. *International Journal of Obesity and Related Metabolic Disorders, 26*, S12–S17.

Jetten, J., Hornsey, M. J., & Adarves-Yorno, I. (2006). When group members admit to being conformist: The role of relative intragroup status in conformity self-reports. *Personality and Social Psychology Bulletin, 32*, 162–173.

Joe, G. W., Flynn, P. M., & Broome, K. M. (2007). Patterns of drug use and expectations in methadone patients. *Addictive Behaviors, 32*, 1640–1656.

John, O., & Srivastava, S. (1999). The Big Five Trait taxonomy: History, measurement, and theoretical perspectives. *Handbook of personality: Theory and research* (2nd ed.) (pp. 102–138). New York: Guilford Press.

Johnson, H. D. (2004). Gender, grade and relationship differences in emotional closeness within adolescent friendships. *Adolescence, 39*, 243–255.

Johnson, J. G., Cohen, P., Smailes, E. M., Kasen, S., & Brook, J. S. (2002, March 29). Television viewing and aggressive behavior during adolescence and adulthood. *Science, 295*, 2468–2471.

Johnson, S. P. (2004). Development of perceptual completion in infancy. *Psychological Science, 15*, 769–775.

Johnson, S., Fulford, D., & Eisner, L. (2009). Psychosocial mechanisms in bipolar disorder. *Behavioral mechanisms and psychopathology: Advancing the explanation of its nature, cause, and treatment* (pp. 77–106). Washington, DC: American Psychological Association.

John-Steiner, V., & Mahn, H. (2003). Sociocultural contexts for teaching and learning. In W. M. Reynolds & G. E. Miller (Eds.), *Handbook of psychology: Educational psychology* (Vol. 7) (pp. 125–151). New York: Wiley.

Johnston, L. D., O'Malley, P. M., Bachman, J. G., & Schulenberg, J. E. (2007). *Monitoring the Future: National results on adolescent drug use: Overview of key findings, 2006.* (NIH Publication No. 07-6202). Bethesda, MD: National Institute on Drug Abuse.

Johnston, M. V. (2004). Clinical disorders of brain plasticity. *Brain and Development, 26*, 73–80.

Jokela, M., Elovainio, M., Kivimäki, M., Keltikangas-Järvinen, L. (2008). Temperament and migration patterns in Finland. *Psychological Science 19*(9): 831–837.

Jones, A. L. (2006). The contemporary psychoanalyst: Karen Horney's theory applied in today's culture. *PsycCRITIQUES, 51*, 127–134.

Jones, J. E., & Corp, E. S. (2003). Effect of naltrexone on food intake and body weight in Syrian hamsters depends on metabolic status. *Physiology and Behavior, 78*, 67–72.

Jones, R. K., Darroch, J. E., Singh, S. (2005). Religious differentials in the sexual and reproductive behaviors of young women in the United States. *Journal of Adolescent Health, 36*, 279–288.

Jonides, J., Lewis, R., Nee, D., Lustig, C., Berman, M., & Moore, K. (2008). The mind and brain of short-term memory. *Annual Review of Psychology, 59*, 193–224.

Jonides, J., Sylvester, C., Lacey, S., Wager, T., Nichols, T., & Awh, E. (2003). Modules of working memory. *Principles of learning and memory* (pp. 113–134). Cambridge, MA: Birkhäuser.

Jorgensen, G. (2006). Kohlberg and Gilligan: Duet or duel? *Journal of Moral Education, 35*, 179–196.

Juliano, L. M., & Griffiths, R. R. (2004). A critical review of caffeine withdrawal: Empirical validation of symptoms and signs, incidence, severity, and associated features. *Psychopharmacology, 176*, 1–29.

Julien, R. M. (2001). *A primer of drug action* (9th ed.). New York: Freeman.

Jung, C. G. (1961). *Freud and psychoanalysis.* New York: Pantheon.

Jung, J. (2002). *Psychology of alcohol and other drugs: A research perspective.* Thousand Oaks, CA: Sage.

Jussim, L. (1989). Teacher expectations: Self-fulfilling prophecies, perceptual biases, and accuracy. *Journal of Personality and Social Psychology, 57*(3), 469–480.

Juster, F. T., Ono, H., & Stafford, F. (2002). *Report on housework and division of labor.* Ann Arbor, MI: Institute for Social Research.

Jylha, M. (2004). Old age and loneliness: Cross-sectional and longitudinal analyses in the Tampere longitudinal study on aging. *Canadian Journal on Aging/La Revue canadienne du vieillissement, 23*, 157–168.

K

Kaasinen, V., & Rinne, J. O. (2002). Functional imaging studies of dopamine system and cognition in normal aging and Parkinson's disease. *Neuroscience & Biobehavioral Reviews, 26*, 785–793.

Kadzin, A. (1988). The token economy: A decade later. *Human operant conditioning and behavior modification* (pp. 119–137). Oxford, England: John Wiley & Sons.

Kahneman, D., Diener, E., & Schwarz, N. (1998). *Well-being: The foundations of hedonic psychology.* New York: Russell Sage Foundation.

Kalb, C. (2003, May 19). Taking a new look at pain. *Newsweek.* p. 32.

Kaller, C. P., Unterrainer, J. M., Rahm, B., & Halsband, U. (2004). The impact of problem structure on planning: Insights from the Tower of London task. *Cognitive Brain Research, 20*, 462–472.

Kallio, S., & Revonsuo, A. (2003). Hypnotic phenomena and altered states of consciousness: A multilevel framework of description and explanation. *Contemporary Hypnosis, 20*, 111–164.

Kaminer, Y. (2010). Problematic use of energy drinks by adolescents. *Child and Adolescent Psychiatric Clinics of North America, 19*(3), 643–650.

Kaminski, P., Chapman, B. P., Haynes, S. D., & Own, L. (2005). Body image, eating behaviors, and attitudes toward exercise among gay and straight men. *Eating Behaviors, 6*, 179–187.

Kandel, E. R., Schwartz, J. H., & Jessell, T. M. (Eds.) (2000). *Principles of neural science* (4th ed.). New York: McGraw-Hill.

Kane, M. J., & Engle, R. W. (2002). The role of prefrontal cortex in working-memory capacity, executive attention, and general fluid intelligence: An individual-differences perspective. *Psychonomic Bulletin and Review, 9*, 637–671.

Kanner, A. D., Coyne, J. C., Schaefer, C. & Lazarus, R. S. (1981). Comparison of two models of stress management: Daily hassles and uplifts versus major life events, *Journal of Behavioral Medicine, 4*, 1–39.

Kaplan, R. M., & Saccuzzo, D. P. (2001). *Psychological testing: Principles, applications, and issues* (5th ed.). Belmont, CA: Wadsworth/Thomson Learning.

Kassel, J. D., Evatt, D. P., Greenstein, J. E., Wardle, M. C., Yates, M. C., & Veilleux, J. C. (2007). The acute effects of nicotine on positive and negative affect in adolescent smokers. *Journal of Abnormal Psychology, 116*, 543–553.

Kato, T. (2007). Molecular genetics of bipolar disorder and depression. *Psychiatry and Clinical Neurosciences, 61*, 3–19.

Katsiyannis, A., Zhang, D., & Woodruff, N. (2005). Transition supports to students with mental retardation: An examination of data from the national longitudinal transition study 2. *Education and Training in Developmental Disabilities, 40*, 109–116.

Kaufman, A. S. & Lichtenberger, E.O. (1999). *Essentials of WAIS-III assessment.* Hoboken, NJ: John Wiley & Sons Inc.

Kaufman, A. S., & Lichtenberger, E. O. (2000). *Essentials of WISC-III and WPPSI-R assessment.* New York: Wiley.

Kaufman, J. C., & Baer, J. (2005). *Creativity across domains: Faces of the muse.* Mahwah, NJ: Lawrence Erlbaum Associates.

Kaufman, J. C., & Baer, J. (2006). *Creativity and reason in cognitive development.* New York: Cambridge University Press.

Keating, D. P., & Clark, L. V. (1980). Development of physical and social reasoning in adolescence. *Developmental Psychology, 16*, 23–30.

Keats, J., & Stam, H. J. (2009). "The disadvantaged psychological scene": Educational experiences of women in early Canadian psychology. *Canadian Psychology, 50*(4), 273-282.

Keck, P., & McElroy, S. (2007). Pharmacological treatments for bipolar disorder. *A guide to treatments that work* (3rd ed.) (pp. 323–350). New York: Oxford University Press.

Keillor, J. M., Barrett, A. M., Crucian, G. P., Kortenkamp, S., & Heilman, K. M. (2002). Emotional experience and perception in the absence of facial feedback. *Journal of the International Neuropsychological Society, 8*, 130–135.

Kelley, H. (1950). The warm-cold variable in first impressions of persons. *Journal of Personality and Social Psychology, 18*, 431–439.

Kellner, C., Pritchett, J., Beale, M., & Coffey, C. (1997). *Handbook of ECT.* Washington, DC: American Psychiatric Association.

Kelly, D., & Tangney, B. (2006). Using multiple intelligence informed resources in an adaptive system. *Intelligent Tutoring Systems*, 412–421.

Kelly, I. W., Rotton, J., & Culver, J. (1985, Winter). The moon was full and nothing happened. *Skeptical Inquirer, 11*, 129–133.

Kelly, J. B. (2000). Children's adjustment in conflicted marriage and divorce: A decade review of research. *Journal of the American Academy of Child & Adolescent Psychiatry, 39*, 963–973.

Keltikangas-Järvinen, L., Räikkönen, K., Ekelund, J., & Peltonen, L. (2004). Nature and nurture in novelty seeking. *Molecular Psychiatry, 9*, 308–311.

Keltner, N. L., & Grant, J. S. (2006). Smoke, smoke, smoke that cigarette. *Perspectives in Psychiatric Care, 42*, 256–261.

Kemeny, M. E. (2003). The psychobiology of stress. *Current Directions in Psychological Science, 12*, 124–129.

Kemeny, M. E. (2007). Psycho neuroimmunology. In H. S. Friedman, & R. C. Silver, *Foundations of health psychology.* New York: Oxford University Press.

Kempermann, G., & Gage, F. H. (1999, May). New nerve cells for the adult brain. *Scientific American*, pp. 48–53.

Kemps, E., & Tiggemann, M. (2007). Reducing the vividness and emotional impact of distressing autobiographical memories: The importance of modality-specific interference. *Memory, 15*, 412–422.

Kendler, K. S., Gatz, M., & Gardner, C. O. (2006). Personality and major depression. *Archives of General Psychiatry, 63*, 1113–1120.

Kenshalo, D. R. (1968). *The Skin Senses.* Springfield, IL: Charles C Thomas, Publisher, Ltd.

Kenway, L., & Wilson, M. A. (2001). Temporally structured replay of awake hippocampal ensemble activity during rapid eye movement sleep. *Neuron, 29*, 145–156.

Kess, J. F., & Miyamoto, T. (1994). *Japanese psycholinguistics.* Amsterdam, Netherlands: John Benjamins.

Kessler, R. C., Berglund, P., & Demler, O. (2005). Lifetime prevalence and age-of-onset distributions of DSM-IV disorders in the National Comorbidity Survey replication. *Archives of General Psychiatry, 62*, 593–602.

Kettenmann, H., & Ransom, B. R. (2005). *Neuroglia* (2nd ed.). New York: Oxford University Press.

Kihlstrom, J. F. (2005). Is hypnosis an altered state of consciousness or what? Comment. *Contemporary Hypnosis, 22*, 34–38.

Kihlstrom, J. F., Schacter, D. L., Cork, R. C., Hurt, C. A., & Behr, S. E. (1990). Implicit and explicit memory following surgical anesthesia. *Psychological Science, 1*, 303–306.

Kim, J., & Mueller, C. (1978). *Introduction to factor analysis: What it is and how to do it.* New York: Sage Publications.

Kim, S-E., Kim, J-W, & Kim, J-J. (2007). The neural mechanism of imagining facial affective expression. *Brain Research, 1145*, 128–137.

Kimbrel, N. A. (2007). A model of the development and maintenance of generalized social phobia. *Clinical Psychological Review, 8*, 69–75.

King, D. (2008). Doctoral graduates in Canada: Findings from the survey of earned Doctorates, 2004/2005. Culture, Tourism and the Centre for Education Statistics Division—Research papers. Statistics Canada Catalogue no. 81-595-M—No. 065.

Kirk, K. M., Bailey, J. M., & Martin, N. G. (2000). Etiology of male sexual orientation in an Australian twin sample. *Psychology, Evolution & Gender, 2*, 301–311.

Kirsch, I., & Braffman, W. (2001). Imaginative suggestibility and hypnotizability. *Current Directions in Psychological Science, 10*, 57–61.

Kirschenbaum, H. (2004). Carl Rogers's life and work: An assessment on the 100th anniversary of his birth. *Journal of Counseling and Development, 82*, 116–124.

Kirschenbaum, H., & Jourdan, A. (2005). The current status of Carl Rogers and the person-centered approach. *Psychotherapy: Theory, Research, Practice, Training, 42*, 37–51.

Kishore, R., & Dutt, K. (1986, March). Electrically induced aversion therapy in alcoholics. *Indian Journal of Clinical Psychology, 13*(1), 39–43.

Klein, R. (1999). The Hebb legacy. *Canadian Journal of Experimental Psychology, 53*(1). Retrieved from www.cpa.ca/cpasite/userfiles/documents/publications/cjep/special_eng.html.

Klein, S. M., Giovino, G. A., Barker, D. C., Tworek, C., Cummings, K. M., & O'Connor, R. J. (2008). Use of flavored cigarettes among older adolescent and adult smokers: United States, 2004–2005. *Nicotine &Tobacco Research, 10*:7, 1209–214.

Kleinman, A. (1996). How is culture important for DSM-IV? In J. E. Mezzich, A. Kleinman, H. Fabrega, Jr., & D. L. Parron (Eds.), *Culture and psychiatric diagnosis: A DSM-IV perspective* Washington, DC: American Psychiatric Press.

Kluger, J. (2001, April 2). Fear not! *Time*, pp. 51–62.

Kluger, J. (2006, December 4). Why we worry about the things we shouldn't and ignore the things we should. *Time*, pp. 64–71.

Knoblich, G., & Sebanz, N. (2006). The social nature of perception and action. *Current Directions in Psychological Science, 15*, 99–111.

Kobayashi, F., Schallert, D. L., & Ogren, H. A. (2003). Japanese and American folk vocabularies for emotions. *Journal of Social Psychology, 143*, 451–478.

Kocovski, N. L., Endler, N. S., Rector, N. A., & Flett, G. L. (2005). Ruminative coping and post-event processing in social anxiety. *Journal of Behaviour Research and Therapy, 43*, 971–984.

Kohlberg, L. (1984). *The psychology of moral development: Essays on moral development* (Vol. 2). San Francisco: Harper & Row.

Kohlberg, L., & Ryncarz, R. A. (1990). Beyond justice reasoning: Moral development and consideration of a seventh stage. In C. N. Alexander & E. J. Langer (Eds.), *Higher stages of human development: Perspectives on adult growth.* New York: Oxford University Press.

Kohler, C. G., Turner, T., Stolar, N. M., Bilker, W. B., Brensinger, C. M., Gur, R. E., & Gur, R. C. (2004). Differences in facial expressions of four universal emotions. *Psychiatry Research, 128,* 235–244.

Kolata, G. (2002, December 2). With no answers on risks, steroid users still say "yes." *The New York Times,* p. 1A.

Kolb, B., Gibb, R., & Robinson, T. E. (2003). Brain plasticity and behavior. *Current Directions in Psychological Science, 12,* 1–5.

Konig, R. (2005). Introduction: Plasticity, learning, and cognition. In R. Konig., P. Heil., E. Budinger & H. Scheich (Eds.), *The auditory cortex: A synthesis of human and animal research.* Mahwah, NJ: Lawrence Erlbaum Associates Publishers.

Koocher, G. P., Norcross, J. C., & Hill, S. S. (2005). *Psychologists' desk reference* (2nd ed.). New York: Oxford University Press.

Kopelman, M. D., & Fleminger, S. (2002). Experience and perspectives on the classification of organic mental disorders. *Psychopathology, 35,* 76–81.

Koper, R. J., & Jaasma, M. A. (2001). Interpersonal style: are human social orientations guided by generalized interpersonal needs? *Communications Reports, 14,* 117–129.

Kosslyn, S. M. (2005). Reflective thinking and mental imagery: A perspective on the development of Posttraumatic Stress Disorder. *Development and Psychopathology, 17,* 851–863.

Kosslyn, S. M., Cacioppo, J. T., Davidson, R. J., Hugdahl, K., Lovallo, W. R., Spiegel, D., & Rose, R. (2002). Bridging psychology and biology. *American Psychologist, 57,* 341–351.

Kotre, J., & Hall, E. (1990). *Seasons of life.* Boston: Little, Brown.

Kozulin, A., Gindis, B., Ageyev, V. S., & Miller, S. M. (2003). *Vygotsky's educational theory in cultural context.* New York: Cambridge University Press.

Krijn, M., Emmelkamp, P. M. G., Olafsson, R. P., & Biemond, R. (2004). Virtual reality exposure therapy of anxiety disorders: A review. *Clinical Psychology Review, 24,* 259–281.

Kring, A., & Earnst, K. (2003). Nonverbal Behavior in Schizophrenia. *Nonverbal behavior in clinical settings* (pp. 263–285). New York: Oxford University Press.

Kring, A., & Moran, E. (2008, September). Emotional response deficits in schizophrenia: Insights from affective science. *Schizophrenia Bulletin, 34*(5), 819–834.

Krueger, R. G., Hicks, B. M., & McGue, M. (2001). Altruism and antisocial behavior: Independent tendencies, unique personality correlates, distinct etiologies. *Psychological Science, 12,* 397–402.

Kübler-Ross, E. (1969). *On death and dying.* New York: Macmillan.

Kudler, H., Krupnick, J., Blank, A., Herman, J., & Horowitz, M. (2009). Psychodynamic therapy for adults. *Effective treatments for PTSD: Practice guidelines from the International Society for Traumatic Stress Studies* (2nd ed.) (pp. 346–369). New York: Guilford Press.

Kuppens, P., Ceulemans, E., Timmerman, M. E., Diener, E., & Kim-Prieto, C. (2006). Universal intracultural and intercultural dimensions of the recalled frequency of emotional experience. *Journal of Cross Cultural Psychology, 37,* 491–515.

Kuriyama, K., Stickgold, R., & Walker, M. P. (2004). Sleep-dependent learning and motor-skill complexity. *Learning and Memory, 11,* 705–713.

Kuther, T. L. (2003). *Your career in psychology: Psychology and the law.* New York: Wadsworth.

Kvavilashvili, L., & Fisher, L. (2007). Is time-based prospective remembering mediated by self-initiated rehearsals? Role of incidental cues, ongoing activity, age, and motivation. *Journal of Experimental Psychology: General, 136,* 112–132.

Kwon, P., & Laurenceau, J. P. (2002). A longitudinal study of the hopelessness theory of depression: Testing the dia-thesis-stress model within a differential reactivity and exposure framework [Special issue: Reprioritizing the role of science in a realistic version of the scientist-practitioner model]. *Journal of Clinical Psychology, 50,* 1305–1321.

L

Laas, I. (2006). Self-actualization and society: A new application for an old theory. *Journal of Humanistic Psychology, 46,* 77–91.

Lacerda, F., von Hofsten, C., & Heimann, M. (2001). *Emerging cognitive abilities in early infancy.* Mahwah, NJ: Lawrence Erlbaum Associates.

Laederach-Hofmann, K., & Messerli-Buergy, N. (2007). Chest pain, angina pectoris, panic disorder, and Syndrome X. In J. Jordan, B. Barde, & A. M. Zeiher, *Contributions toward evidence-based psychocardiology: A systematic review of the literature.* Washington, DC: American Psychological Association.

Lagacé-Séguin, D. G., & d'Entremont, M. L. (2006). The role of child negative affect in the relations between parenting styles and play. *Early Child Development and Care, 176,* 461–477.

Lahti, J., Räikkönen, K., Ekelund, J., Peltonen, L., Raitakari, O. T., & Keltikangas-Järvinen, L. (2005). Novelty seeking: Interaction between parental alcohol use and dopamine D4 receptor gene exon III polymorphism over 17 years. *Psychiatric Genetics, 15,* 133–139.

Laird, J. D., & Bressler, C. (1990). William James and the mechanisms of emotional experience. *Personality and Social Psychology Bulletin, 16,* 636–651.

Lal, S. (2002). Giving children security: Mamie Phipps Clark and the racialization of child psychology. *American Psychologist, 57,* 20–28.

Lalumière, M. L., Blanchard, R., & Zucker, K. J. (2000). Sexual orientation and handedness in men and women: A meta-analysis. *Psychological Bulletin, 126,* 575–592.

Lamal, P. A. (1979). College students' common beliefs about psychology. *Teaching of Psychology, 6,* 155–158.

Lamb, H. R., & Weinberger, L. E. (2005). One-year follow-up of persons discharged from a locked intermediate care facility. *Psychiatric Services, 56,* 198–201.

Lamb, M. E., & Garretson, M. E. (2003), The effects of interviewer gender and child gender on the informativeness of alleged child sexual abuse victims in forensic interviews. *Law and Human Behavior, 27,* 157–171.

Lana, R. E. (2002). The cognitive approach to language and thought [Special issue: Choice and chance in the formation of society: Behavior and cognition in social theory]. *Journal of Mind and Behavior, 23,* 51–57.

Lanctot, K. L., Herrmann, N. & Mazzotta, P. (2001). Role of serotonin in the behavioral and psychological symptoms of dementia. *Journal of Neuropsychiatry & Clinical Neurosciences, 13,* 5–21.

Lane, K. A., Banaji, M. R., Nosek, B. A., & Greenwald, A. G. (Eds.). (2007). Understanding and using the implicit association test: iv: what we know (so far) about the method. In B. Wittenbrink, & N. Schwarz, *Implicit measures of attitudes.* New York: Guilford Press.

Lane, S. D., Cherek, D. R., & Tcheremissine, O. V. (2007). Response preservation and adaptation in heavy marijuana-smoking adolescents. *Addictive Behaviors, 32,* 977–990.

Langan-Fox, J., & Grant, S. (2006). The Thematic Apperception Test: Toward a standard measure of the big three motives. *Journal of Personality Assessment, 87,* 277–291.

Langlois, J. H., Kalakanis, L., Rubenstein, A. J., Larson, A., Hallam, M. & Smoot, M. (2000). Maxims or myths of beauty? A meta-analytic and theoretical review. *Psychological Bulletin, 126,* 390–423.

Langreth, R. (2000, May 1). Every little bit helps: How even moderate exercise can have a big impact on your health. *The Wall Street Journal,* p. R5.

Lankov, A. (2004). The dawn of modern Korea: Changes for better or worse. *The Korea Times,* p. A1.

Lanza, S. T., & Collins, L. M. (2002). Pubertal timing and the onset of substance use in females during early adolescence. *Prevention Science, 3,* 69–82.

Laqueur, T. W. (2003). *Solitary sex: A cultural history of masturbation.* New York: Zone.

Larsen, R. J., & Buss, D. M. (2006). *Personality psychology: Domains of knowledge about human nature with PowerWeb* (2nd ed.). New York: McGraw-Hill.

Latané, B., & Darley, J. M. (1970). *The unresponsive bystander: Why doesn't he help?* New York: Appleton-Century-Crofts.

Latané, B., & Nida, S. (1981). Ten years of research on group size and helping. *Psychological Bulletin 89, 2,* 309–324.

Lavelli, M., & Fogel, A. (2005). Developmental changes in the relationship between the infant's attention and emotion during early face-to-face communication. *Developmental Psychology, 41,* 265–280.

Lazarus, R. S. (2000). Toward better research on stress and coping. *American Psychologist, 55,* 665–673.

Leckman, J. F., & King, R. A. (2007). A developmental perspective on the controversy surrounding the use of SSRIs to treat pediatric depression. *American Journal of Psychiatry, 164,* 1304–1306.

Lecrubier, Y. (2001). Prescribing patterns for depression and anxiety worldwide. *Journal of Clinical Psychiatry, 62*(13), 31–36.

Lee, D., Kleinman, J., and Kleinman, A. (2007). Rethinking depression: An ethnographic study of the experiences of depression among Chinese. *Harvard Review of Psychiatry, 15*, 1–8.

Lee, H. J., & Kwon, S. M. (2003). Two different types of obsession: Autogenous obsessions and reactive obsessions. *Behaviour Research & Therapy, 41*, 11–29.

Lee, H. J., Kwon, S. M., Kwon, J. S., & Telch, M. J. (2005). Testing the autogenous reactive model of obsessions. *Depress Anxiety, 21*, 118–129.

Lee, K., & Ashton, M. C. (2007). Factor analysis in personality research. In R. W. Robins, R. C. Fraley, & R. F. Krueger, *Handbook of research methods in personality psychology* (pp. 424–443). New York: Guilford Press.

Lee, S. H., Ahn, S. C., & Lee, Y. J. (2007). Effectiveness of a meditation-based stress management program as an adjunct to pharmacotherapy in patients with anxiety disorder. *Journal of Psychosomatic Research, 62*, 189–195.

Lee-Chai, A. Y., Bargh, J. A. (Eds.). (2001). *The use and abuse of power: Multiple perspectives on the causes of corruption.* Philadelphia: Psychology Press.

Lee-Chiong, T. L. (2006). *Sleep: A comprehensive handbook.* New York: Wiley-Liss.

Lefaucheur, J. P., Brugieres, P., Menard-Lefaucheur, I., Wendling, S., Pommier, M., & Bellivier, F. (2007). The value of navigation-guided rTMS for the treatment of depression: An illustrative case. *Neurophysiologic Clinics, 37*, 265–271.

Lehar, S. (2003). *The world in your head: A gestalt view of the mechanism of conscious experience.* Mahwah, NJ: Erlbaum.

Leib, J. R., Gollust, S. E., Hull, S. C., & Wilfond, B. S. (2005). Carrier screening panels for Ashkenazi Jews: is more better? *Genetic Medicine, 7*, 185–190.

Leibel, R. L., Rosenbaum, M., Hirsch, J. (1995, March 9). Changes in energy expenditure resulting from altered body. *New England Journal of Medicine, 332*, 621–628.

Leiblum, S. R. & Chivers, M. L. (2007). Normal and persistent genital arousal in women: New perspectives. *Journal of Sex & Marital Therapy, 33*, 357–373.

Leigh, J. H., Zinkhan, G. M. & Swaminathan, V. (2006). Dimensional relationships of recall and recognition measures with selected cognitive and affective aspects of print ads. *Journal of Advertising, 35*, 105–122.

Leitner, L. M. (2007). Diversity issues, postmodernism, and psychodynamic therapy. *PsycCRITIQUES, 52*, No pagination specified.

Lemay, E. P., Jr., Clark, M. S., & Feeney, B. C. (2007). Projection of responsiveness to needs and the construction of satisfying communal relationships. *Journal of Personality and Social Psychology, 92*, 834–853.

Lemonick, M. D. (2000, December 11). Downey's downfall. *Time*, p. 97.

Lengua, L. J., & Long, A. C. (2002). The role of emotionality and self-regulation in the appraisal-coping process: Tests of direct and moderating effects. *Journal of Applied Developmental Psychology, 23*, 471–493.

Lengua, L. J., & Kovacs, E. A. (2005). Bidirectional associations between temperament and parenting and the prediction of adjustment problems in middle childhood. *Journal of Applied Developmental Psychology, 26*, 21–38.

Lenzenweger, M. F., & Dworkin, R. H. (Eds.). (1998). *The origins and development of schizophrenia: Advances in experimental psychopathology.* Washington, DC: American Psychological Association.

Leo, R. J., & Latif, T. (2007). Repetitive transcranial magnetic stimulation (rTMS) in experimentally induced and chronic neuropathic pain: A review. *The Journal of Pain, 8*, 453–459.

Leong, F. T. I., & Blustein, D. L. (2000). Toward a global vision of counseling psychology. *Counseling Psychology, 28*, 5–9.

Leppanen, J. M., Moulson, M. C., Vogel-Farley, V. K. & Nelson, C. A. (2007). An ERP study of emotional face processing in the adult and infant brain. *Child Development, 78*, 232–245.

LeVay, S. (1993). *The sexual brain.* Cambridge, MA: MIT.

Levi, A., Chan, K. K., & Pence, D. (2006). Real men do not read labels: the effects of masculinity and involvement on college students' food decisions. *Journal of American College Health, 55*, 91–98.

Levin, B. E., (2006). Metabolic sensing neurons and the control of energy homeostasis. *Physiology & Behavior, 89*, 486–489.

Levin, R. J. (2007). Sexual activity, health and well-being—the beneficial roles of coitus and masturbation. *Sexual and Relationship Therapy, 22*, 135–148.

Levine, J. M., & Moreland, R. L. (2006). Small groups: An overview. In J. M. Levine & R. L. Moreland (Eds.), *Small groups.* New York: Psychology Press.

Levine, M., & Crowther, S. (2008, December). The responsive bystander: How social group membership and group size can encourage as well as inhibit bystander intervention. *Journal of Personality and Social Psychology, 95*(6), 1429–1439.

Levine, S. Z., & Rabinowitz, J. (2007). Revisiting the 5 dimensions of the Positive and Negative Syndrome Scale. *Journal of Clinical Psychopharmacology, 27*, 431–436.

Levinson, D. J. (1990). A theory of life structure development in adulthood. In C. N. Alexander & E. J. Langer (Eds.), *Higher stages of human development: Perspectives on adult growth.* New York: Oxford University Press.

Levy, B. (1996). Improving memory in old age through implicit self-stereotyping. *Journal of Personality and Social Psychology, 71*, 1092–1107.

Levy, B. R., & Myers, L. M. (2004). Preventive health behaviors influenced by self-perceptions of aging. *Preventive Medicine: An International Journal Devoted to Practice and Theory, 39*, 625–629.

Levy, B. R., Slade, M. D., Kunkel, S. R., & Kasl, S. V. (2002). Longevity increased by positive self-perceptions of aging. *Journal of Personality & Social Psychology, 83*, 261–270.

Levy, S. (2004, April 12). All eyes on Google. *Newsweek*, p. 40.

Lewandowski, S., Stritzke, W. G. K., Oberauer, K., & Morales, M. (2005). Memory for fact, fiction and misinformation: The Iraq War 2003. *Psychological Science, 16*, 190–195.

Li, J., Wang, L., & Fischer, K. W. (2004). The organization of Chinese shame concepts. *Cognition and Emotion, 18*, 767–797.

Li, T-K., Volkow, N. D., & Baler, R. D. (2007). The biological bases of nicotine and alcohol co-addiction. *Biological Psychiatry, 61*, 1–3.

Liang, K. A. (2007). Acculturation, ambivalent sexism, and attitudes toward women who engage in premarital sex among Chinese American young adults. *Dissertation Abstracts International: Section B: The Sciences and Engineering, 67*(10-B), 6065.

Lidz, J., & Gleitman, L. R. (2004). Argument structure and the child's contribution to language learning. *Trends in Cognitive Sciences, 8*, 157–161.

Lien, Y. W., Chu, R. L., Jen, C. H., & Wu, C. H. (2006). Do Chinese commit neither fundamental attribution error nor ultimate attribution error? *Chinese Journal of Psychology, 48*(2), 163–181.

Lilienfeld, S. O. (2007). Psychological treatments that cause harm. *Perspectives on Psychological Science, 2*, 53–58.

Lin, C-H., & Lin, H-M. (2007). What price do you ask for the 'extra one'? A social value orientation perspective. *Social Behavior and Personality, 35*, 9–18.

Lin, Y. Y., Chen, W. T., Liao, K. K., Yeh, T. C., Wu, Z. Z., & Ho, L. T. (2005). Hemispheric balance in coding speech and non-speech sounds in Chinese participants. *Neuroreport, 16*, 469–473.

Lindblad, F., Lindahl, M., & Theorell, T. (2006). Physiological stress reactions in 6th and 9th graders during test performance. *Stress and Health: Journal of the International Society for the Investigation of Stress, 22*, 189–195.

Lindorff, M. (2005). Determinants of received social support: Who gives what to managers? *Journal of Social and Personal Relationships, 22*, 323–337.

Lindsay, P. H., & Norman, D. A. (1977). *Human information processing* (2nd ed.). New York: Academic Press.

Lindsey, E., & Colwell, M. (2003). Preschoolers' emotional competence: Links to pretend and physical play. *Child Study Journal, 33*, 39–52.

Linehan, M. M., Cochran, B. N., & Kehrer, C. A. (2001b). Dialectical behavior therapy for borderline personality disorder. In D. H. Barlow (Ed.), *Clinical handbook of psychological disorders: A step-by-step treatment manual* (3rd ed.) (pp. 470–522). New York: Guilford Press.

Linehan, M. M., Cochran, B., & Kehrer, C. A. (2001a). Borderline personality disorder. In D.H. Barlow (Ed.), *Clinical handbook of psychological disorder* (3rd ed.). New York: Guilford Press.

Links, P. S., Eynan, R., & Heisel, M. J. (2007). Affective instability and suicidal ideation and behavior in patients with borderline personality disorder. *Journal of Personality Disorders, 21*, 72–86.

Linnen, A., Rot, M., Ellenbogen, M. A., & Young, S. N. (2009). Interpersonal functioning in adolescent offspring of parents with bipolar disorder. *Journal of Affective Disorders, 114*, 122–130.

Lippa, R. A. (2005). *Gender, nature, and nurture* (2nd ed.). Mahwah, NJ: Erlbaum.

Litowitz, B. E. (2007). Unconscious fantasy: A once and future concept. *Journal of the American Psychoanalytic Association, 55*, 199–228.

Little, A., Burt, D. M., & Perrett, D. I. (2006). What is good is beautiful: Face preference reflects desired personality. *Personality and Individual Differences, 41*, 1107–1118.

Liu, L., He, S-Z., & Wu, Y. (2007). An analysis of the characteristics of single parent families with different structures and their children. *Chinese Journal of Clinical Psychology, 15*, 68–70.

Lobato, M. I., Koff, W. J., & Manenti, C. (2006). Follow-up of sex reassignment surgery in transsexuals: A Brazilian cohort. *Archives of Sexual Behavior, 35*, 711–715.

Lobban, F., Barrowclough, C., & Jones, S. (2006). Does Expressed Emotion need to be understood within a more systemic framework? An examination of discrepancies in appraisals between patients diagnosed with schizophrenia and their relatives. *Social Psychiatry and Psychiatric Epidemiology, 41*, 50–55.

Locke, J. L. (2006). Parental selection of vocal behavior: Crying, cooking, babbling, and the evolution of language. *Human Nature, 17*, 155–168.

Loftus, E. F. (1993). Psychologists in the eyewitness world. *American Psychologist, 48*, 550–552.

Loftus, E. F. (2004). Memories of things unseen. *Current Directions in Psychological Science, 13*, 145–147.

Loftus, E. F., & Palmer, J. C. (1974). Reconstruction of automobile destruction: An example of the interface between language and memory. *Journal of Verbal Learning and Verbal Behavior, 13*, 585–589.

Loftus, E., & Cahill, L. (2007). Memory Distortion: From Misinformation to Rich False Memory. *The foundations of remembering: Essays in honor of Henry L. Roediger, III* (pp. 413–25). New York: Psychology Press.

Long, A., (1987, December). What is this thing called sleep? *National Geographic, 172*, 786–821.

Long, G. M., & Beaton, R. J. (1982). The case for peripheral persistence: Effects of target and background luminance on a partial-report task. *Journal of Experimental Psychology: Human Perception and Performance, 8*, 383–391.

López, S. R., & Guarnaccia, P. J. (2000). Cultural psychopathology: Uncovering the social world of mental illness. *Annual Review of Psychology, 51*, 571–598.

Lorenz, K. (1966). *On aggression*. New York: Harcourt Brace Jovanovich.

Lorenz, K. (1974). *Civilized man's eight deadly sins*. New York: Harcourt Brace Jovanovich.

Lothane, Z. (2005). Jung, A biography. *Journal of the American Psychoanalytic Association, 53*, 317–324.

Lowery, D., Fillingim, R. B., & Wright, R. A. (2003). Sex differences and incentive effects on perceptual and cardiovascular responses to cold pressor pain. *Psychosomatic Medicine, 65*, 284–291.

Lubinski, D., Benbow, C. P., Webb, R. M., & Bleske-Rechek, A. (2006). Tracking exceptional human capital over two decades. *Psychological Science, 17*, 194–199.

Lublin, H., Eberhard, J., & Levander, S. (2005). Current therapy issues and unmet clinical needs in the treatment of schizophrenia: A review of the new generation antipsychotics. *International Clinical Psychopharmacology, 20*, 183–198.

Luchins, A. S. (1946). Classroom experiments on mental set. *American Journal of Psychology, 59*, 295–298.

Lucki, I., & O'Leary, O. F. (2004). Distinguishing roles for norepinephrine and serotonin in the behavioral effects of antidepressant drugs. *Journal of Clinical Psychiatry, 65*, 11–24.

Luders, E., Narr, K. L., Zaidel, E., Thompson, P. M., & Toga, A. W. (2006). Gender effects on callosal thickness in scaled and unscaled space. *Neuroreport, 17*, 1103–1106.

Lutz, C. K. & Novak, M. A. (2005). Environmental enrichment for nonhuman primates: theory and application. *ILAR Journal, 46*, 178–91.

Lutz, W., Lambert, M. J., Harmon, S. C., Tschitsaz, A., Schurch, E., & Stulz, N. (2006). The probability of treatment success, failure and duration—What can be learned from empirical data to support decision making in clinical practice? *Clinical Psychology & Psychotherapy, 13*, 223–232.

Ly, D. H., Lockhart, D. J., Lerner, R. A., & Schultz, P. G. (2000, March 31). Mitotic mis-regulation and human aging. *Science, 287*, 2486–2492.

Lykken, D. T. (1995). *The antisocial personalities*. Mahwah, NJ: Erlbaum.

Lymberis, S. C., Parhar, P. K., Katsoulakis, E., & Formenti, S. C. (2004). Pharmacogenomics and breast cancer. *Pharmacogenomics, 5*, 31–55.

Lynn, S. J., Fassler, O., & Knox, J. (2005). Hypnosis and the altered state debate: Something more or nothing more? Comment. *Contemporary Hypnosis, 22*, 39–45.

Lynn, S. J., Kirsch, I., Barabasz, A., Cardena, E., & Patterson, D. (2000). Hypnosis as an empirically supported clinical intervention: The state of the evidence and a look to the future. *Int J Clin Exp Hypn, 48*(2), 239–259.

Lynn, S. J., Lock, T., Loftus, E. F., Krackow, E., & Lilienfeld, S. O. (2003). The remembrance of things past: Problematic memory recovery techniques in psychotherapy. In S. O. Lilienfeld, S. J. Lynn, & J. M. Lohr (Eds.). *Science and pseudoscience in clinical psychology*. New York: Guilford Press.

Lyubomirsky, S. (2010). *The how of happiness: A practical approach to getting the life you want*. London: Piatkus.

Lyubomirsky, S., Sousa, L., Dickerhoof, R. (2006). The costs and benefits of writing, talking, and thinking about life's triumphs and defeats. *Journal of Personality and Social Psychology, 90*(4), Apr 2006, 692–708.

M

Macaluso, E., & Driver, J. (2005). Multisensory spatial interactions: a window onto functional integration in the human brain *Trends in Neurosciences, 28*, Issue 5, 264–271.

MacCallum, E. P. (2006). Commission of inquiry into the wrongful conviction of David Milgaard. Retrieved from www.justice.gov.sk.ca/milgaard.

Mace, J. (2007). Involuntary memory: Concept and theory. *Involuntary memory* (pp. 1–19). Malden: Blackwell Publishing.

MacIntyre, T., Moran, A., & Jennings, D. J. (2002). Is controllability of imagery related to canoe-slalom performance? *Perceptual & Motor Skills, 94*, 1245–1250.

Mack, J. (2003). *The museum of the mind*. London: British Museum Publications.

Mackay, J., & Eriksen, M. (2002). *The tobacco atlas*. Geneva, Switzerland: World Health Organization.

Maclean's/CTV Poll. (1995, January 2). Looking inward: Examining the state of the Canadian mind. *Maclean's, 108*, 10–31. Additional data from Decima Research, Toronto, Ontario, provided by Maclean's.

MacLeod, C. M., Gopie, N., Hourihan, K. L., Neary, K. R., & Ozubko, J. D. (2010). The production effect: Delineation of a phenomenon. *Journal of Experimental Psychology: Learning, Memory, and Cognition, 36*(3), 671–685.

Macmillan, M. (1996). *Freud evaluated: The completed arc*. Cambridge, MA: MIT.

Madden, D. J. (2007). Aging and visual attention. *Current Directions in Psychological Science, 16*, 70–74.

Mader, S. S. (2000). *Biology*. New York: McGraw-Hill.

Madon, S., Willard, J., & Guyll, M. (2006). Self-fulfilling prophecy effects of mothers' beliefs on children's alcohol use: accumulation, dissipation, and stability over time. *Journal of Personality and Social Psychology, 90*, 911–926.

Magalhaes, A. C., Holmes, K. D., Dale, L. B., Comps-Agrar, L., Lee, D., Yaday, P. N., Drysdale, L., Poulter, M. O., Roth, B. L., Pin, J., Anisman, H., & Ferguson, S. G. (2010). CRF receptor 1 regulates anxiety behavior via sensitization of 5-HT2 receptor signaling. *Nature Neuroscience, 13*, 622-629.

Magida, A. J. (2006). *Opening the doors of wonder: Reflections on religious rites of passage*. Berkeley, CA: University of California Press.

Mahmood, M., & Black, J. (2005). Narcolepsy-cataplexy: How does recent understanding help in evaluation and treatment. *Current Treatment Options in Neurology, 7*, 363–371.

Maier, S. F., & Watkins, L. R. (2000). Learned helplessness. In A. E. Kazdin, *Encyclopedia of psychology* (Vol. 4). Washington, DC: American Psychological Association.

Majdandzic, M., & van den Boom, D. C. (2007). Multimethod longitudinal assessment of temperament in early childhood. *Journal of Personality, 75*, 121–167.

Majeres, R. L. (2007). Sex differences in phono-logical coding: Alphabet transformation speed. *Intelligence, 35*, 335–346.

Malle, B. F. (2004). *How the mind explains behavior: Folk explanations, meaning, and social interaction*. Cambridge, MA: MIT.

Malouff, J. M., Thorsteinsson, E. B., & Schutte, N. S. (2007). The efficacy of problem solving therapy in reducing mental and physical health problems: A meta-analysis. *Clinical Psychology Review, 27*, 46–57.

Mamassis, G., & Doganis, G. (2004). The effects of a mental training program on juniors pre-competitive anxiety, self-confidence, and tennis performance. *Journal of Applied Sport Psychology, 16*, 118–137.

Mancinelli, R., Binetti, R., & Ceccanti, M. (2007). Woman, alcohol and environment: Emerging risks for health. *Neuroscience & Biobehavioral Reviews, 31*, 246–253.

Mann, K. (2004). Pharmacotherapy of Alcohol Dependence A Review of the Clinical Data. *CNS Drugs, 18*(8), 485–504.

Mann, K., Ackermann, K., Croissant, B., Mundle, G., Nakovics, H., Diehl, A. (2005). Neuroimaging of gender differences in alcohol dependence: are women more vulnerable? *Alcoholism: Clinical & Experimental Research, 29*, 896–901.

Manning, M. A., & Hoyme, E. H. (2007). Fetal alcohol spectrum disorders: A practical clinical approach to diagnosis. *Neuroscience & Biobehavioral Reviews, 31*, 230–238.

Manor, J. K., & Gailliot, M. T. (2007). Altruism and egoism: Prosocial motivations for helping depend on relationship context. *European Journal of Social Psychology, 37*, 347–358.

Manstead, A. S. R., & Wagner, H. L. (2004). *Experience emotion.* Cambridge, England: Cambridge University Press.

Manstead, A. S. R., Frijda, N., & Fischer, A. H. (Eds.) (2003). *Feelings and emotions: The Amsterdam Symposium.* Cambridge, England: Cambridge University Press.

Marcaurelle, R., Bélanger, C., & Marchand, A. (2003). Marital relationship and the treatment of panic disorder with agoraphobia: A critical review. *Clinical Psychology Review, 23*, 247–276.

Marcaurelle, R., Bélanger, C., & Marchand, A. (2005). Marital predictors of symptom severity in panic disorder with agoraphobia. *Journal of Anxiety Disorders, 19*, 211–232.

Marcus-Newhall, A., Pedersen, W. C., & Carlson, M. (2000). Displaced aggression is alive and well: A meta-analytic review. *Journal of Personality and Social Psychology, 78*, 670–689.

Markowitz, J., & Patrick, K. (2008, June). Introduction. *Journal of Clinical Psychopharmacology, 28*(32), S37–S38.

Marks, I. M. (2004). The Nobel prize award in physiology to Ivan Petrovich Pavlov–1904. *Australian and New Zealand Journal of Psychiatry, 38*, 674–677.

Markus, H. R., & Hamedani, M. G. (2007). Sociocultural psychology: The dynamic interdependence among self systems and social systems. In S. Kitayama & D. Cohen (Eds.) *Handbook of cultural psychology.* New York: Guilford Press.

Markus, H. R., & Kitayama, S. (2003). Models of agency: Sociocultural diversity in the construction of action. In V. Murphy-Berman & J. J. Berman (Eds.), *Cross-cultural differences in perspectives on the self.* Lincoln, NE: University of Nebraska Press.

Marrie, R. A. (2004). Environmental risk factors in multiple sclerosis aetiology. *Lancet Neurology, 3*, 709–718.

Marshall, K., Laing, D. G., & Jinks, A. L. (2006). The capacity of humans to identify components in complex odor-taste mixtures. *Chemical Senses, 31*, 539–545.

Marshall, M. K. (2007). The critical factors of coaching practice leading to successful coaching outcomes. *Dissertation Abstracts International: Section B: The Sciences and Engineering, 67*(7-B), 4092.

Marshall, R. D., Bryant, R. A., Amsel, L., Suh, E. J., Cook, J. M., & Neria, Y. (2007). The psychology of ongoing threat: Relative risk appraisal, the September 11 attacks and terrorism-related fears. *American Psychologist, 62*, 304–316.

Martelle, S., Hanley, C., & Yoshino K. (2003, January 28). "Sopranos" scenario in slaying? *Los Angeles Times*, p. B1.

Martin, A. J., & Marsh, H. W. (2002). Fear of failure: Friend or foe? *Australian Psychologist, 38*, 31–38.

Martin, P. D., & Brantley, P. J. (2004). Stress, coping, and social support in health and behavior. In J. M. Raczynski & L. C. Leviton (Eds.), *Handbook of clinical health psychology: Disorders of behavior and health* (Vol. 2). Washington, DC: American Psychological Association.

Martin, R. C. (2005). Components of short-term memory and their relation to language processing. *Current Directions in Psychological Science, 14*, 204–208.

Martindale, C. (1981). *Cognition and consciousness.* Homewood, IL: Dorsey.

Mashour, G., Walker, E., & Martuza, R. (2005, June). Psychosurgery: Past, present, and future. *Brain Research Reviews, 48*(3), 409–419.

Maslow, A. H. (1970). *Motivation and personality.* New York: Harper & Row.

Maslow, A. H. (1987). *Motivation and personality* (3rd ed.). New York: Harper & Row.

Mast, F. W., & Kosslyn, S. M. (2002). Visual mental images can be ambiguous: Insights from individual differences in spatial transformation abilities. *Cognition, 86*, 57–70.

Masters, W. H., & Johnson, V. E. (1966). *Human sexual response.* Boston, MA: Little, Brown.

Masuda, M. (2003). Meta-analyses of love scales: Do various love scales measure the same psychological constructs? *Japanese Psychological Research, 45*, 25–37.

Mataix-Cols, D., & Bartres-Faz, D. (2002). Is the use of the wooden and computerized versions of the Tower of Hanoi Puzzle equivalent? *Applied Neuropsychology, 9*, 117–120.

Matsumoto, D. (2002). Methodological requirements to test a possible in-group advantage in judging emotions across cultures: Comment on Elfenbein and Ambady (2002) and evidence. *Psychological Bulletin, 128*, 236–242.

Matthews, G., & Funke, G. J. (2006). Worry and information-processing. In G. C. L. Davey & A. Wells, *Worry and its psychological disorders: Theory, assessment and treatment.* Hoboken, NJ: Wiley Publishing.

Maurer, D., Lewis, T. L., Brent, H. P., & Levin, A. V. (1999, October 1). Rapid improvement in the acuity of infants after visual input. *Science, 286*, 108–110.

Maxwell, J., Bohman, T., & Spence, R. (2004, May). Differences in Characteristics of Heroin Inhalers and Heroin Injectors at Admission to Treatment: A Preliminary Study Using a Large Database of Client Records. *Substance Use & Misuse, 39*(6), 993–1012.

Mayer, J. D., Salovey, P., & Caruso, D. R. (2004). Emotional intelligence: Theory, findings, and implications. *Psychological Inquiry, 15*, 197–215.

Maynard, A. E., & Martini, M. I. (2005). *Learning in cultural context: Family, peers, and school.* New York: Kluwer Academic/Plenum Publishers.

Mayseless, O., Bartholomew, K., Henderson, A., & Trinke, S. (2004). "I was more her mom than she was mine:" Role reversal in a community sample. *Family Relations, 53*, 78–86.

Mazard, A., Laou, L., Joliot, M., & Mellet, E. (2005). Neural impact of the semantic content of visual mental images and visual percepts. *Brain Research and Cognitive Brain Research, 24*, 423–435.

McAdams, D. (1989). *Intimacy: The need to be close.* New York: Doubleday.

McAdams, D. P., Diamond, A., de St. Aubin, E., & Mansfield, E. (1997). Stories of commitment: The psychosocial construction of generative lives. *Journal of Personality and Social Psychology, 72*, 678–694.

McCabe, C., & Rolls, E. T. (2007). Umami: A delicious flavor formed by convergence of taste and olfactory pathways in the human brain. *European Journal of Neuroscience, 25*, 1855–1864.

McCarthy, J. (2005). Individualism and collectivism: What do they have to do with counseling? *Journal of Multicultural Counseling and Development, 33*, 108–117.

McCleary, L., and Sanford, M. (2002). Parental expressed emotion in depressed adolescents: prediction of clinical course and relationship to comorbid disorders and social functioning. *Journal of child psychology and psychiatry and allied disciplines, 43*(5), 587–595.

McClelland, D. C. (1985). How motives, skills, and values determine what people do. *American Psychologist, 40*, 812–825.

McClelland, D. C. (1993). Intelligence is not the best predictor of job performance. *Current Directions in Psychological Research, 2*, 5–8.

McClelland, D. C., Atkinson, J. W., Clark, R. A., & Lowell, E. L. (1953). *The achievement motive.* New York: Appleton-Century-Crofts.

McClelland, L. E., & Pilcher, J. J. (2007). Assessing subjective sleepiness during a night of sleep deprivation: Examining the internal state and behavioral dimensions of sleepiness. *Behavioral Medicine, 33*, 17–26.

McClure, J., Sutton, R. M., Sibley, C. G. (2007). Listening to reporters or engineers? How instance-based messages about building design affect earthquake fatalism. *Journal of Applied Social Sciences, 37*, 1956–1973.

McCormick, C. G. (2003). Metacognition and learning. In W. M. Reynolds & G. E. Miller (Eds.), *Handbook of psychology: Educational psychology* (Vol. 7, pp. 79–102). New York: Wiley.

McCrae R. R., Terracciano A., & 78 Members of the Personality Profiles of Cultures Project. (2005b). Universal features of personality traits from the observer's perspective: Data from 50 cultures. *Journal of Personality and Social Psychology, 88*: 547–561.

McCrae, R. R., Terracciano, A., and 79 Members of the Personality Profiles of Cultures Project. (2005a). Personality profiles of cultures: Aggregate personality traits. *Journal of Personality and Social Psychology, 89*, 407–425.

McCrae, R. R., & Costa, P. T. (1986). Personality, coping, and coping effectiveness in an adult sample. *Journal of Personality, 54*, 385–405.

McCrae, R. R., & Costa, P. T. (1990). *Personality in adulthood.* New York: Guilford Press.

McDonald, C., & Murray, R. M. (2004). Can structural magnetic resonance imaging provide an alternative phenotype for genetic studies of schizophrenia? In M. S. Keshavan, J. L. Kennedy, & R. M. Murray (Eds.), *Neurodevelopment and schizophrenia.* New York: Cambridge University Press.

McDonald, H. E., & Hirt, E. R. (1997). When expectancy meets desire: Motivational effects in reconstructive memory. *Journal of Personality and Social Psychology, 72*, 5–23.

McDowell, D. M., & Spitz, H. I. (1999). *Substance abuse.* New York: Brunner/Mazel.

McEwen, B. S. (1998, January 15). Protective and damaging effects of stress mediators [Review article]. *New England Journal of Medicine, 338*, 171–179.

McGilvray, J. (Ed.). (2004). *The Cambridge companion to Chomsky.* Oxford, England: Cambridge University Press.

McGlynn, F. D., Smitherman, T. A., & Gothard, K. D. (2004). Comment on the status of systematic desensitization. *Behavior Modification, 28*, 194–205.

McGregor, K. K., & Capone, N. C. (2004). Genetic and environmental interactions in determining the early lexicon: Evidence from a set of tri-zygotic quadruplets. *Journal of Child Language, 31*, 311–337.

McGuire, W. J. (1997). Creative hypothesis generating in psychology: Some useful heuristics. *Annual Review of Psychology, 48*, 1–30.

McGuire, W. J., & Papageorgis, D. (1961). The relative efficacy of various types of prior belief-defense in producing immunity against persuasion. *Public Opinion Quarterly, 26*, 24–34.

McKeever, V. M., & Huff, M. E. (2003). A diathesis-stress model of post-traumatic stress disorder: Ecological, biological, and residual stress pathways. *Review of General Psychology, 7*, 237–250.

McKenzie-McLean, J. (2006, August 3). On the scent of a new detector. *The Press* (Christchurch, New Zealand), 7.

McKinley, M. J., Cairns, M. J., Denton, D. A., McLaughlin, T., & Williams, R. (1988). The token economy. *Handbook of behavior therapy in education* (pp. 469–487). New York: Plenum Press.

McLellan, A., & Childress, A. (1985). Aversive therapies for substance abuse: Do they work?. *Journal of Substance Abuse Treatment, 2*(3), 187–191.

McManus, C. (2004). *Right hand, left hand: The origins of asymmetry in brains, bodies, atoms and cultures.* Cambridge, MA: Harvard University Press.

McMullin, R. E. (2000). *The new handbook of cognitive therapy techniques.* New York: W.W. Norton.

McMurtray, A. M., Licht, E., Yeo, T., Krisztal, E., Saul, R. E., & Mendez, M. F. (2007). Positron emission tomography facilitates diagnosis of early-onset Alzheimer's disease. *European Neurology, 59*, 31–37.

McNamara, P. (2004). *An evolutionary psychology of sleep and dreams.* Westport, CT: Praeger Publishers/Greenwood Publishing Group.

Mead, M. (1949). *Male and female.* New York: Morrow.

Means, M. K., & Edinger, J. D. (2007). Graded exposure therapy for addressing claustrophobic reactions to continuous positive airway pressure: a case series report. *Behavioral Sleep Medicine, 5*, 105–116.

Medeiros, R., Prediger, R. D. S., Passos, G. F., Pandolfo, P., et al. (2007). Connecting TNF-Î± signaling pathways to iNOS expression in a mouse model of Alzheimer's disease: Relevance for the behavioral and synaptic deficits induced by amyloid Î2 protein. *Journal of Neuroscience, 27*, 5394–5404.

Mel, B. W. (2002, March 8). What the synapse tells the neuron. *Science, 295*, 1845–1846.

Mel'nikov, K. S. (1993, October–December). On some aspects of the mechanistic approach to the study of processes of forgetting. *Vestnik Moskovskogo Universiteta Seriya 14 Psikhologiya*, pp. 64–67.

Meltzer, H. Y. (2000). Genetics and etiology of schizophrenia and bipolar disorder. *Biological Psychiatry, 47*, 171–173.

Meltzoff, A. N. (1996). The human infant as imitative generalist: A 20-year progress report on infant imitation with implications for comparative psychology. In C. M. Heyes & B. G. Galef, Jr. (Eds.), *Social learning in animals: The roots of culture.* San Diego: Academic Press.

Melzack, R. (2005). The McGill Pain Questionnaire: From description to measurement. *Anesthesiology, 103*, 199–202.

Melzack, R., & Katz, J. (2004). *The gate control theory: Reaching for the brain.* Mahwah, NJ: Lawrence Erlbaum Associates.

Merikangas, K. R., Ames, M., Cui, L., Stang, P. E., Ustun, T. B., VonKorff, M., & Kessler, R. C. (2007). The impact of comorbidity of mental and physical conditions on role disability in the US adult household population. *Archives of General Psychiatry, 64*, 1180–1188.

Merskey, H. (1992). The manufacture of personalities: The production of MPD. *British Journal of of Psychiatry, 160*, 327–340.

Messer, S. B., & McWilliams, N. (2003). The impact of Sigmund Freud and *The Interpretation of Dreams*. In R. J. Sternberg (Ed.), *The anatomy of impact: What makes the great works of psychology great* (pp. 71–88). Washington, DC: American Psychological Association.

Meyer, R. G., & Osborne, Y. V. H. (1987). *Case studies in abnormal behavior* (2nd ed.). Boston: Allyn & Bacon.

Meyerowitz, J. (2004). *How sex changed: A history of transsexuality in the United States.* Cambridge, MA: Harvard University Press.

Meyers-Levy, J., & Zhu, R. (2007) The influence of ceiling height: The effect of priming on the type of processing that people use. *Journal of Consumer Research, 34*, 174–186.

Mialet, J. P., Pope, H. G., & Yurgelun, T. D. (1996). Impaired attention in depressive states: A non-specific deficit? *Psychological Medicine, 26*(5), 1009–1020.

Michael, R. T., Gagnon, J. H., Laumann, E. O., & Kolata, G. (1994). *Sex in America: A definitive survey.* Boston: Little, Brown.

Midanik, L. T., Tam, T. W., & Weisner, C. (2007). Concurrent and simultaneous drug and alcohol use: Results of the 2000 national alcohol survey. *Drug and Alcohol Dependence, 90*, 72–80.

Middlebrooks, J. C., Furukawa, S., Stecker, G. C., & Mickey, B. J. (2005). Distributed representation of sound-source location in the auditory cortex. In R. König, P. Heil, E. Budinger, & H. Scheich (Eds.), *Auditory cortex: A synthesis of human and animal research.* Mahwah, NJ: Lawrence Erlbaum Associates.

Mifflin, L. (1998, January 14). Study finds a decline in TV network violence. *The New York Times*, A14.

Miklowitz, D. J., & Thompson, M. C. (2003). Family variables and interventions in schizophrenia. In G. Sholevar & G. Pirooz (Eds.), *Textbook of family and couples therapy: Clinical applications* (pp. 585–617). Washington, DC: American Psychiatric Publishing.

Mikulincer, M., & Shaver, P. R. (2005). Attachment security, compassion, and altruism. *Current Directions in Psychological Science, 14*, 34–38.

Miletic, M. P. (2002). The introduction of a feminine psychology to psychoanalysis: Karen Horney's legacy [Special issue: Interpersonal psychoanalysis and feminism]. *Contemporary Psychoanalysis, 38*, 287–299.

Milgram, S. (1963, October). Behavioral Study of obedience. *The Journal of Abnormal and Social Psychology, 67*(4), 371–378.

Milgram, S. (1974). *Obedience to authority: An experimental view.* New York: Harper & Row.

Milgram, S. (2005). *Obedience to authority.* Pinter & Martin: New York.

Millar, M. (2002). Effects of guilt induction and guilt reduction on door-in-the-face. *Communication Research, 29*, 666–680.

Miller, G. A. (1956). The magical number seven, plus or minus two: Some limits on our capacity for processing information. *Psychology Review, 63*, 81–97.

Miller, G. F., & Penke, L. (2007). The evolution of human intelligence and the coefficient of additive genetic variance in human brain size. *Intelligence, 35*, 97–114.

Miller, J. G. (1984). Culture and the development of everyday social explanation. *Journal of Personality and Social Psychology, 46*, 961–978.

Miller, N. E., & Magruder, K. M. (Eds.). (1999). *Cost-effectiveness of psychotherapy: A guide for practitioners, researchers, and policymakers.* New York: Oxford University Press.

Miller-Jones, D. (1991). Informal reasoning in inner-city children. In J. F. Voss & D. N. Perkins (Eds.), *Informal reasoning and education.* Hillsdale, NJ: Lawrence Erlbaum.

Milling, L., Chau, P., & Mills-Baxter, M. (2006). A Review of Psychopathology. *Your practicum in psychology: A guide for maximizing knowledge and competence* (pp. 105–127). Washington, DC: American Psychological Association.

Millon, T., & Davis, R. O. (1996). *Disorders of personality: DSM-IV and beyond* (2nd ed.). New York: Wiley.

Millon, T., Davis, R., & Millon, C. (2000). *Personality disorders in modern life*. New York: Wiley.

Millon, T., Simonsen, E., Birket-Smith, M., & Davis, R. (1998). *Psychopathy: Antisocial, criminal, and violent behavior*. New York: Guilford Press.

Milner, B. (1966). Amnesia following operation on temporal lobes. In C. W. M. Whitty & P. Zangwill (Eds.), *Amnesia*. London: Butterworth.

Milner, B. (2005). The medial temporal-lobe amnesic syndrome. *Psychiatric Clinics of North America, 28*, 599–611.

Miltenberger, R. (2008). Behavior modification. *Handbook of clinical psychology: Children and adolescents* (Vol. 2) (pp. 626–652). Hoboken, NJ: John Wiley & Sons Inc.

Milton, J., & Wiseman, R. (1999). A meta-analysis of mass media ESP testing. *British Journal of Psychology, 90*, 235–240.

Milton, J., & Wiseman, R. (1999). Does psi exist? Lack of replication of an anomalous process of information transfer. *Psychological Bulletin, 125*, 387–391.

Miner-Rubino, K., Winter, D. G., & Stewart, A. J. (2004). Gender, social class, and the subjective experience of aging: Self-perceived personality change from early adulthood to late midlife. *Personality and Social Psychology Bulletin, 30*, 1599–1610.

Minuchin, S. (1999). Retelling, reimagining, and re-searching: A continuing conversation. *Journal of Marital and Family Therapy, 25*, 9–14.

Miquel, J. (2006). Integración de teorías del envejecimiento (parte I). Integration of theories of ageing. *Revista Espanola de Geriatria y Gerontologia, 41*, 55–63.

Mischel, W. (2004). Toward an integrative science of the person. *Annual Review of Psychology, 55*, 1–22.

Miserando, M. (1991). Memory and the seven dwarfs. *Teaching of Psychology, 18*, 169–171.

Mitte, K. (2005). Meta-analysis of cognitive-behavioral treatments for generalized anxiety disorder: A comparison with pharmacotherapy. *Psychological Bulletin, 131*, 785–795.

Moffitt, T. E., & Caspi, A. (2007). Evidence from behavioral genetics for environmental contributions to antisocial conduct. In J. E. Grusec, & P. D. Hastings, *Handbook of socialization: Theory and research*. New York: Guilford Press.

Moffitt, T. E., Caspi, A., & Rutter, M. (2006). Measured gene-environment interactions in psychopathology: Concepts, research strategies, and implications for research, intervention, and public understanding of genetics. *Perspectives on Psychological Science, 1*, 5–27.

Mohapel, P., Leanza, G., Kokaia, M., & Lindvall, O. (2005). Forebrain acetylcholine regulates adult hippo-campal neurogenesis and learning. *Neurobiology of Aging, 26*, 939–946.

Mokdad, A. H., Brewer, R. D., & Naimi, T. (2007). Binge drinking is a problem that cannot be ignored. *Preventive Medicine: An International Journal Devoted to Practice and Theory, 44*, 303–304.

Montgomery, C., Fisk, J. E., Newcombe, R., Wareing, M., & Murphy, P. N. (2005). Syllogistic reasoning performance in MDMA (Ecstasy) users. *Experimental and Clinical Psychopharmacology, 13*, 137–145.

Montgomery, S. (2006). Serotonin noradrenaline reuptake inhibitors: Logical evolution of antidepressant development. *International Journal of Psychiatry in Clinical Practice, 10*, 5–11.

Moody, H. R. (2000). *Aging: Concepts and controversies*. Thousand Oaks, CA: Sage.

Moore, D. G., Goodwin, J. E., & George, R. (2007). Infants perceive human point-light displays as solid forms. *Cognition, 104*, 377–396.

Moore, D., Aveyard, P., Connock, M., Wang, D., Fry-Smith, A., & Barton, P. (2009, April). Effectiveness and safety of nicotine replacement therapy assisted reduction to stop smoking: Systematic review and meta-analysis. *BMJ: British Medical Journal, 338*(7699), 9–9.

Moore, M. M. (2002). Behavioral observation. In M. W. Wiederman & B. E. Whitley (Eds.), *Handbook for conducting research on human sexuality*. Mahwah, NJ: Lawrence Erlbaum.

Mora-Giral, M., Raich-Escursell, R. M., Segues, C.V., Torras-Claras, A. J., & Huon, G. (2004). Bulimia symptoms and risk factors in university students. *Eating and Weight Disorders, 9*, 163–169.

Morley, K., Lynskey, M., Madden, P., Treloar, S., Heath, A., & Martin, N. (2007, September). Exploring the inter-relationship of smoking age-at-onset, cigarette consumption and smoking persistence: Genes or environment? *Psychological Medicine, 37*(9), 1357–1367.

Morone, N. E., & Greco, C. M. (2007). Mind-body interventions for chronic pain in older adults: A structured review. *Pain Medicine, 8*, 359–375.

Morris, J. F., Waldo, C. R., & Rothblum, E. D. (2001). A model of predictors and outcomes of outness among lesbian and bisexual women. *American Journal of Orthopsychiatry, 71*, 61–71.

Morrone, A. S., & Pintrich, P. R. (2006). Achievement motivation. In G. G. Bear & K. M. Minke, *Children's needs III: Development, prevention, and intervention*. Washington, DC: National Association of School Psychologists.

Morrow, J., & Wolff, R. (1991, May). Wired for a miracle. *Health*, 64–84.

Mosher, C. J., & Akins, S. (2007). *Drugs and drug policy: The control of consciousness alteration*. Thousand Oaks, CA: Sage Publications.

Moskowitz, G. B. (2004). *Social cognition: Understanding self and others*. New York: Guilford Press.

Motley, M. T. (1987, February). What I meant to say. *Psychology Today*, 25–28.

Muammar, O. M. (2007). An integration of two competing models to explain practical intelligence. *Dissertation Abstracts International: Section B: The Sciences and Engineering, 67*(7-B), 4128.

Munakata, Y. (2006). Information processing approaches to development. In D. Kuhn, R. S. Siegler, W. Damon, & R. M. Lerner, *Handbook of child psychology: Cognition, perception, and language* (Vol. 2) (6th ed.). Hoboken, NJ: John Wiley & Sons.

Murphy, G. J., Glickfield, L. L., Balsen, Z., & Isaacson, J. S. (2004). Sensory neuron signaling to the brain: Properties of transmitter release from olfactory nerve terminals. *Journal of Neuroscience, 24*, 3023–3030.

Murphy, G. L. (2005). The study of concepts inside and outside the laboratory: Medin versus Medin. In W. Ahn, R. L. Goldstone, B. C. Love, A. B. Markman, & P. Wolff (Eds.), *Categorization inside and outside the laboratory: Essays in honor of Douglas L. Medin*. Washington, DC: American Psychological Association.

Murphy, S., Monahan, J. L., Miller, L. C. (1998). Interference under the influence. *Personality and Social Psychology Bulletin, 24*, 517–528.

Murray, S. L., Holmes, J. G., & Griffin, D. W. (2004). The benefits of positive illusions: Idealization and the construction of satisfaction in close relationships. In H. T. Reis & C. E. Rusbult (Eds.), *Close relationships: Key readings*. Philadelphia: Taylor & Francis.

Mussolum, E. (2009). Disconnecting in the age of connection. *Digital Addiction*. Retrieved November 17, 2010 from www.twu.ca/sites/magazine/no-17/features/digital-addiction.html.

Myers, D. G. (2000). The funds, friends, and faith of happy people. *American Psychologist, 55*, 56–67.

Myers, D. G., & Diener, E. (1995, May). The pursuit of happiness: New research uncovers some anti-intuitive insights into how many people are happy—and why. *Scientific American*, pp. 70–72.

Myers, D., & Diener, E. (1995, January). Who is happy? *Psychological Science, 6*(1), 10–19.

Myers, L. L. (2007). Anorexia nervosa, bulimia nervosa, and binge eating disorder. In B. A. Thyer, & J. S. Wodarski. *Social work in mental health: An evidence-based approach*. Hoboken, NJ: John Wiley & Sons.

Myerson, J., Adams, D. R., Hale, S., & Jenkins, L. (2003). Analysis of group differences in processing speed: Brinley plots, Q-Q plots, and other conspiracies. *Psychonomic Bulletin and Review, 10*, 224–237.

Myrtek, M. (2007). Type a behavior and hostility as independent risk factors for coronary heart disease. In J. Jordan, B. Barde, & A. M. Zeiher, *Contributions toward evidence-based psychocardiology: A systematic review of the literature*. Washington, DC: American Psychological Association.

Mytinger, C. (2001). *Headhunting in the Solomon Islands: Around the Coral Sea*. Santa Barbara, CA: Narrative Press.

N

Nadeem, E., & Graham, S. (2005). Early puberty, peer victimization, and internalizing symptoms in ethnic minority adolescents. *Journal of Early Adolescence, 25*, 197–222.

Nagai, Y., Goldstein, L. H., Fenwick, P. B. C., & Trimble, M. R. (2004). Clinical efficacy of galvanic skin response biofeedback training in reducing seizures in adult epilepsy: A preliminary randomized controlled study. *Epilepsy and Behavior, 5*, 216–223.

Nagda, B. A., Tropp, L. R., & Paluck, E. L. (2006). Looking back as we look ahead: Integrating research, theory, and practice on intergroup relations. *Journal of Social Research, 62*, 439–451.

Nagel, K., & Jones, K. (1992, Spr). Sociological factors in the development of eating disorders. *Adolescence, 27*(105), 107–113.

Najman, J. M., Aird, R., Bor, W., O'Callaghan, M., Williams, G. M., & Shuttlewood, G. J. (2004). The generational transmission of socioeconomic inequalities in child cognitive development and emotional health. *Social Science and Medicine, 58*, 1147–1158.

Nakamura, Y. (2004). Isolation of p53-target genes and their functional analysis. *Cancer Science, 95*, 7–11.

Narrow, W. E., Rae, D. S., Robins, L. N., & Regier, D. A. (2002). Revised prevalence estimates of mental disorders in the United States: Using a clinical significance criterion to reconcile 2 surveys' estimates. *Archives of General Psychiatry, 59*, 115–123.

Nash, R. A., Wade, K. A., & Lindsay, D. S. (2009). Digitially manipulating memory: Effects of doctored videos and imagination in distorting beliefs and memories. *Memory and Cognition, 37*(4), 414–424.

National Institute on Drug Abuse. (2000). *Principles of drug addiction treatment: A research-based guide.* Washington, DC: National Institute on Drug Abuse.

Natvig, G. K., Albrektsen, G., & Ovarnstrøm, U. (2003a). Methods of teaching and class participation in relation to perceived social support and stress: Modifiable factors for improving health and well-being among students. *Educational Psychology, 23*, 261–274.

Natvig, G. K., Albrektsen, G., & Qvamstrøm, U. (2003b). Associations between psychsocial factors and happiness among school adolescents. *International Journal of Nursing Practice, 9*, 166–175.

Naveh-Benjamin, M., Guez, J., & Sorek, S. (2007). The effects of divided attention on encoding processes in memory: Mapping the locus of interference. *Canadian Journal of Experimental Psychology, 61*, 1–12.

Neitz, J., Neitz, M., & Kainz, P. M. (1996, November 1). Visual pigment gene structure and the severity of color vision defects. *Science, 274*, 801–804.

Nelson, G., Lavoie, F., & Mitchell, T. (2007). The history and theories of community psychology in Canada. *International Community Psychology,* Part 2, 13–36.

Nelson, W. M., III, & Finch, A. J., Jr. (2000). Managing anger in youth: A cognitive-behavioral intervention approach. In P. C. Kendall, *Child & adolescent therapy: Cognitive-behavioral procedures* (2nd ed.). New York: Guilford Press.

Nesdale, D., Maass, A., & Durkin, K. (2005). Group norms, threat, and children's racial prejudice. *Child Development, 76*, 652–663.

Nestler, E. J. (2001, June 22). Total recall—the memory of addiction. *Science, 292*, 2266–2267.

Neubauer, A. C., & Fink, A. (2005). Basic information processing and the psychophysiology of intelligence. In R. J. Sternberg & J. E. Pretz, *Cognition and intelligence: Identifying the mechanisms of the mind.* New York: Cambridge University Press.

Neuberg, S. (1989, March). The goal of forming accurate impressions during social interactions: Attenuating the impact of negative expectancies. *Journal of Personality and Social Psychology, 56*(3), 374–386.

Newby-Clark, I. R., & Ross, M. (2003). Conceiving the past and future. *Personality and Social Psychology Bulletin, 29*, 807–818.

Newell, A., & Simon, H. (1972). *Human problem solving.* Englewood Cliffs, NJ: Prentice Hall.

Newman, C. F., Leahy, R. L., Beck, A. T., Reilly-Harrington, N. A., & Gyulai, L. (2002). *Bipolar disorder: A cognitive therapy approach.* Washington, DC: American Psychological Association.

Newport, F., & Carroll, J. (2002, November 27). Battle of the bulge: Majority of Americans want to lose weight. *Gallup News Service,* 1–9.

Niccols, A. (2007). Fetal alcohol syndrome and the developing socio-emotional brain. *Brain Cognition, 65*, 135–142.

Nicholson, I. A. M. (2003). *Inventing personality: Gordon Allport and the science of selfhood.* Washington, DC: American Psychological Association.

Nickerson, R., & Adams, M. (1979), Long-term Memory for a Common Object, *Cognitive Psychology, 11*, 287–307.

Nielsen, S. L., Smart, D. W., Isakson, R. L., Worthen, V. E., Gregersen, A. T., & Lambert, M. J. (2004). The Consumer Reports effectiveness score: What did consumers report? *Journal of Counseling Psychology, 51*, 25–37.

Nigg, J. T., & Goldsmith, H. H. (1994). Genetics of personality disorders: Perspectives from personality and psychopathology research. *Psychological Bulletin, 115*, 346–380.

Nikles, C. D., II, Brecht, D. L., Klinger, E., & Bursell, A. L. (1998). The effects of current concern- and nonconcern-related waking suggestions on nocturnal dream content. *Journal of Personality and Social Psychology, 75*, 242–255.

Nimrod, G., & Kleiber, D. A. (2007). Reconsidering change and continuity in later life: Toward an innovation theory of successful aging. *International Journal of Human Development, 65*, 1–22.

Nisbett, R. (2003). *The geography of thought.* New York: Free Press.

Nisbett, R. E. (2007, December 9). All brains are the same color. *New York Times,* p. E11.

Nissle, S., & Bschor, T. (2002). Winning the jackpot and depression: Money cannot buy happiness. *International Journal of Psychiatry in Clinical Practice, 6*, 183–186.

Nittrouer, S., Lowenstein, J. H. (2007). Children's weighting strategies for word-final stop voicing are not explained by auditory sensitivities. *Journal of Speech, Language, and Hearing Research, 50*, 58–73.

Noble, H. B. (1999, March 12). New from the smoking wars: Success. *The New York Times,* pp. D1–D2.

Noice, T., & Noice, H. (2002, April). Very long-term recall and recognition of well-learned material. *Applied Cognitive Psychology, 16*(3), 259–272.

Noland, R. W. (1999). *Sigmund Freud revisited.* New York: Twayne Publishers.

Nolen-Hoeksema, S. (2007). *Abnormal psychology* (4th ed.). New York: McGraw-Hill.

Norcia, A. M., Pei, F., Bonneh, Y., Hou, C., Sampath, V., & Pettet, M. W. (2005). Development of sensitivity to texture and contour information in the human infant. *Journal of Cognitive Neuroscience, 17*, 569–579.

Norcross, J. C. (2002). Empirically supported therapy relationships. In J. C. Norcross, *Psychotherapy relationships that work: Therapist contributions and responsiveness to patients.* New York: Oxford University Press.

Norcross, J. C., Beutler, L. E., & Levant, R. F. (2006). *Evidence-based practices in mental health: Debate and dialogue on the fundamental questions.* Washington, DC: American Psychological Association.

Northwestern University (2009, May 20). Exposure to two languages carries far-reaching benefits. *ScienceDaily.* Retrieved August 11, 2009, from www.sciencedaily.com/releases/2009/05/090519172157.htm.

Norton, P. J., & Price, E. C. (2007). A meta-analytic review of adult cognitive-behavioral treatment outcome across the anxiety disorders. *Journal of Nervous and Mental Disease, 195*, 521–531.

Nowak, A., Vallacher, R., & Miller, M. (2003). Social influence and group dynamics. *Handbook of psychology: Personality and social psychology* (Vol. 5) (pp. 383–417). Hoboken, NJ: John Wiley & Sons Inc.

Ntinas, K. M. (2007). Behavior modification and the principle of normalization: Clash or synthesis? *Behavioral Interventions, 22*, 165–177.

Nucci, L. P. (2002). The development of moral reasoning. In U. Goswami (Ed.), Blackwell handbook of childhood cognitive development. *Blackwell Handbooks of developmental psychology* (pp. 303–325). Malden, MA: Blackwell.

Nunes, A., & Kramer, A. F. (2009). Experience-based mitigation of age-related performance declines: Evidence from air traffic control, *Journal of Experimental Psychology: Applied* (Vol. 15, No. 1), www.apa.org/journals/releases/xap15112.pdf.

Nurnberger, J. I., Jr., & Bierut, L. J. (2007, April). Seeking the connections: Alcoholism and our genes. *Scientific American,* pp. 46–53.

Nyberg, L., & Tulving, E. (1996). Classifying human long-term memory: Evidence from converging dissociations. *European Journal of Cognitive Psychology, 8*, 163–183.

O

O'Brien, K. M., & LeBow, M. D. (2007). Reducing maladaptive weight management practices: Developing a psychoeducational intervention program. *Eating Behaviors, 8*, 195–210.

O'Connor, D. B., & O'Connor, R. C. (2004). Perceived changes in food intake in response to stress: The role of conscientiousness. *Stress and Health: Journal of the International Society for the Investigation of Stress, 20*, 279–291.

O'Keefe, T., & Fox, K. (Eds.). (2003). *Finding the real me: True tales of sex and gender diversity.* San Francisco: Jossey-Bass.

O'Sullivan, L. F., Udell, W., Montrose, V. A., Antoniello, P., & Hoffman, S. (2010). A cognitive analysis of college students' explanations for engaging in unprotected sexual intercourse. *Archives of Sexual Behaviour, 39*, 1121–1131.

Oberauer, K. (2007). In search of the magic number. *Experimental Psychology, 54*, 245–246.

Oehman, A., & Mineka, S. (2003). The malicious serpent: Snakes as a prototypical stimulus for an evolved module of fear. *Current Directions in Psychological Science, 12*, 5–9.

Offer, D., Kaiz, M., Howard, K. I., & Bennett, E. S. (2000). The altering of reported experiences. *Journal of the American Academy of Child & Adolescent Psychiatry, 39*, 735–742.

Ogren, K., & Sandlund, M. (2007). Lobotomy at a state mental hospital in Sweden. A survey of patients operated on during the period 1947–1958. *Nordic Journal of Psychiatry, 61*, 355–362.

Ohira, T., Hozawa, A., Iribarren, C., Daviglus, M. L., Matthews, K. A., Gross, M. D., & Jacobs, D. R., Jr. (2007). Longitudinal association of serum carotenoids and tocopherols with hostility: The CARDIA study. *American Journal of Epidemiology, 18*, 235–241.

Olds, M. E., & Fobes, J. L. (1981). The central basis of motivation: Intracranial self-stimulation studies. *Annual Review of Psychology, 32*, 123–129.

Olijslagers, J. E., Werkman, T. R., & McCreary, A. C. (2006). Modulation of midbrain dopamine neurotransmission by serotonin, a versatile interaction between neurotransmitters and significance for antipsychotic drug action. *Current Neuropharmacology, 4*, 59–68.

Olivardia, R., & Pope, H. (2002). Body image disturbance in childhood and adolescence. In D. Castle & K. Phillips (Eds.), *Disorders of body image.* Petersfield: Wrightson Biomedical Publishing.

Olivares-Olivares, P., Rosa-Alcázar, A., & Olivares-Rodríguez, J. (2008, May). Does individual attention improve the effect of group treatment of adolescents with social phobia? *International Journal of Clinical and Health Psychology, 8*(2), 465–481.

Olson, D. (2006). Becoming responsible for who we are: The trouble with traits. Howard Gardner under fire: *The rebel psychologist faces his critics* (pp. 39–44). Chicago: Open Court Publishing.

Olson, D. H., & DeFrain, J. (2005). *Marriages and families: Intimacy, diversity, and strengths with PowerWeb.* New York: McGraw-Hill.

Oppenheimer, D. M. (2004). Spontaneous discounting of availability in frequency judgment tasks. *Psychological Science, 15*, 100–105.

Ornat, S. L., & Gallo, P. (2004). Acquisition, learning, or development of language? Skinner's "Verbal behavior" revisited. *Spanish Journal of Psychology, 7*, 161–170.

Oskamp, S. (Ed.). (2000) *Reducing prejudice and discrimination.* Mahwah, NJ: Erlbaum.

Ost, J. (2006). Recovered memories. *Investigative interviewing: Rights, research, regulation* (pp. 259–291). Devon: Willan Publishing.

Otake, K., Shimai, S., & Tanaka-Matsumi, J. (2006). Happy people become happier through kindness: A counting kindnesses intervention. *Journal of Happiness Studies, 7*, 361–375.

Overgaard, M., & Timmermans, B. (2010). How unconscious is subliminal perception? *Handbook of Phenomenology and Cognitive Science*, 501–518.

Owen, C., Tarantello, C., Jones, M., & Tennant, C. (1998). Lunar cycles and violent behaviour. *Australian and New Zealand Journal of Psychiatry, 32*, 496–499

P

Pachankis, J. E. & Goldfried, M. R. (2007). An integrative, principle-based approach to psychotherapy. In S. G. Hofmann & J. Weinberger (Eds.), *The art and science of psychotherapy.* New York: Routledge/Taylor & Francis Group.

Paddock, C. (2010, November 3). Bedtime texting, internet use, disturbs sleep and mood in teens. *Medical News Today.* Retrieved January 17, 2012, from www.medicalnewstoday.com/articles/206546.php.

Pagoto, S. L., Kozak, A. T., & Spates, C. R (2006). Systematic desensitization for an older woman with a severe specific phobia: an application of evidenced-based practice. *Clinical Gerontologist, 30*, 89–98.

Palladino, J. J. & Carducci, B. J. (1984). Students' Knowledge of Sleep and Dreams. *Teaching of Psychology, 11*, 3, 189–191.

Palma, B., Tiba, P., Machado, R., Tufik, S., & Suchecki, D. (2007, May). Immune outcomes of sleep disorders: The hypothalamic-pituitary-adrenal axis as a modulatory factor. *Revista Brasileira de Psiquiatria, 29*(1), S33–S38.

Pandit, S., Argyropoulos, S., & Nutt, D. (2001, March). Current status of anxiolytic drugs. *Primary Care Psychiatry, 7*(1), 1–5.

Pandya, M., Pozuelo, L., & Malone, D. (2007). Electroconvulsive therapy: What the internist needs to know. *Cleveland Clinic Journal of Medicine, 74*, 679–685.

Paniagua, F. A. (2000). *Diagnosis in a multicultural context: A casebook for mental health professionals.* Thousand Oaks, CA: Sage.

Paquette, D., Carbonneau, R., & Dubeau, D. (2003). Prevalence of father-child rough-and-tumble play and physical aggression in pre-school children. *European Journal of Psychology of Education, 18*, 171–189.

Paquier, P. F., & Mariën, P. (2005). A synthesis of the role of the cerebellum in cognition. *Aphasiology, 19*, 3–19.

Paradis, J. (2010). Bilingual children's acquisition of English verb morphology: Effects of language exposure, structure complexity, and task type. *Language Learning, 60*, 651–680.

Paris, J. (2000). Predispositions, personality traits, and posttraumatic stress disorder. *Harvard Review of Psychiatry, 8*, 175–183.

Park, C. L., & Grant, C. (2005). Determinants of positive and negative consequences of alcohol consumption in college students: Alcohol use, gender, and psychological characteristics. *Addictive Behaviors, 30*, 755–765.

Park, D. C. (2007). Eating disorders: A call to arms. *American Psychologist, 62*, 158.

Park, H., & Antonioni, D. (2007). Personality, reciprocity, and strength of conflict resolution strategy. *Journal of Research in Personality, 41*, 110–125.

Parke, R. D. (2004). Development in the family. *Annual Review of Psychology, 55*, 365–399.

Parker, E. S., Cahill, L., & McGaugh, J. L. (2006). A case of unusual autobiographical remembering. *Neurocase, 12*, 35–49.

Parker, J. D. A., Creque, R. E., Barnhart, D. L., Iron Harris, J., Majeski, S. A., Wood, L. A., Bond, B. J., & Hogan, M. J. (2004). Academic achievement in high school: Does emotional intelligence matter? *Personality and Individual Differences, 37*, 1321-1330.

Parker, J. D. A., Summerfeldt, L. J., Hogan, M. J., & Majeski, S. (2004). Emotional intelligence and academic success: Examining the transition from high school to university. *Personality and Individual Differences, 36*, 163-172.

Parker-Pope, T. (2003, April 22). The diet that works. *The Wall Street Journal*, R1, R5.

Parrott, A. C. (2002). Recreational Ecstasy/MDMA, the serotonin syndrome, and serotonergic neurotoxicity [Special issue: Serotonin]. *Pharmacology, Biochemistry & Behavior, 71*, 837–844.

Pary, R., Matuschka, P., Lewis, S., & Lippmann, S. (2006, February). Managing Bipolar Depression. *Psychiatry, 3*(2), 30–41.

Pascual, A., & Guéguen, N. (2005). Foot-in-the-door and door-in-the-face: A comparative meta-analytic study. *Psychological Reports, 96*, 122–128.

Pascual, A., & Guéguen, N. (2006). Door-in-the-face technique and monetary solicitation: An evaluation in a field setting. *Perceptual and Motor Skills, 103*, 974–978.

Pascual, M. A., & Rodriguez, M. A. (2006). Learning by operant conditioning as a nonlinear self-organized process. *Nonlinear Dynamics, Psychology, and Life Sciences, 10*, 341–364.

Paukert, A., Stagner, B., & Hope, K. (2004). The assessment of active listening skills in helpline volunteers. *Stress, Trauma, and Crisis: An International Journal, 7*, 61–76.

Paul, A. M. (2004). *Cult of personality: How personality tests are leading us to miseducate our children, mismanage our companies and misunderstand ourselves.* New York: Free Press.

Paulozzi, L. J. (2006). Opioid analgesic involvement in drug abuse deaths in American metropolitan areas. *American Journal of Public Health, 96*, 1755–1757.

Pavitt, C. (2007). Impression formation. In B. B. Whaley & W. Samter, *Explaining communication: Contemporary theories and exemplars.* Mahwah, NJ: Lawrence Erlbaum Associates.

Pavlov, I. P. (1927). *Conditioned reflexes.* London: Oxford University Press.

Payne, D. G. (1986). Hyperamnesia for pictures and words: Testing the recall level hypothesis. *Journal of Experimental Psychology: Learning, Memory, and Cognition, 12*, 16–29.

Pearce, J. M. S. (2007). Synaesthesia. *European Neurology, 57*, 120–124.

Pedersen, D. M. (2002). Intrinsic-extrinsic factors in sport motivation. *Perceptual & Motor Skills, 95*, 459–476.

Pedersen, P. B., Draguns, J. G., Lonner, W. J., & Trimble, J. E. (Eds.). (2002). *Counseling across cultures* (5th ed.). Thousand Oaks, CA: Sage.

Pellegrini, S., Muzio, R. N., Mustaca, A. E., & Papini, M. R. (2004). Successive negative contrast after partial reinforcement in the consummatory behavior of rats. *Learning and Motivation, 35*, 303–321.

Pelli, D. G., Burns, C. W., & Farell, B. (2006). Feature detection and letter identification. *Vision Research, 46*, 4646–4674.

Pellis, S. M. & Pellis, V. C. (2007). Rough-and-tumble play and the development of the social brain. *Current Directions in Psychological Science, 16*, 95–97.

Penfield W., & Steelman H. (1947). *The Treatment of Focal Epilepsy* by Cortical Excision. *Ann Surg. 126* (5):740–761.

Penley, J. A., Tomaka, J., & Wiebe, J. S. (2002). The association of coping to physical and psychological health outcomes: A meta-analytic review. *Journal of Behavioral Medicine, 25*, 551–603.

Penn, D. L., Corrigan, P. W., Bentall, R. P., Racenstein, J. M., & Newman, L. (1997). Social cognition in schizophrenia. *Psychological Bulletin, 121*, 114–132.

Penney, J. B., Jr. (2000). Neurochemistry. In B. S. Fogel, R. B. Schiffer, et al. (Eds.), *Synopsis of neuropsychiatry*. New York: Lippincott Williams & Wilkins.

Pennington, D. (2003). *Essential personality*. London: Arnold.

Penzel, F. (2000). *Obsessive-compulsive disorders: A complete guide to getting well and staying well*. New York: Oxford University Press.

Perez, R. M., DeBord, K. A., & Bieschke, K. J. (Eds). (2000). *Handbook of counseling and psychotherapy with lesbian, gay, and bisexual clients*. Washington, DC: American Psychological Association.

Perkins, K., Conklin, C., & Levine, M. (2008). *Cognitive-behavioral therapy for smoking cessation: A practical guidebook to the most effective treatments*. New York: Routledge/Taylor & Francis Group.

Perloff, R. M. (2003). *The dynamics of persuasion: Communication and attitudes in the 21st century* (2nd ed.). Mahwah, NJ: Erlbaum.

Pert, C. B. (2002). The wisdom of the receptors: Neuropeptides, the emotions, and body-mind. *Advances in Mind-Body Medicine, 18*, 30–35.

Pervin, L. A. (1990). "The Big Five Personality Factors and Dimensions of Sample Traits," Chapter 3. *Handbook of Personality: Theory and Research*. New York: Guilford Press.

Pesmen, C. (2006, March). Don't let pain get in your way. *Money*. p. 48.

Peters, E., Hess, T. M., Västfjäll, D., & Auman, C. (2007). Adult age differences in dual information processes. *Perspectives on Psychological Science, 2*, 1–23.

Peters, J., Suchan, B., Koster, O., & Daum, I. (2007). Domain-specific retrieval of source information in the medial temporal lobe. *European Journal of Neuroscience, 26*, 1333–1343.

Peterson, C. (2000). The future of optimism. *American Psychologist, 55*, 44–55.

Peterson, R. A., & Brown, S. P. (2005). On the use of beta coefficients in meta-analysis. *Journal of Applied Psychology, 90*, 175–181.

Petersson, K. M., Silva, C., Castro-Caldas, A., Ingvar, M., & Reis, A. (2007). Literacy: A cultural influence on functional left-right differences in the inferior parietal cortex. *European Journal of Neuroscience, 26*, 791–799.

Petraglia, J., Thygesen, K. L., Lecours, S., & Drapeau, M. (2009). Gender differences in self-reported defense mechanisms: A study using the new defense style questionnaire-60. *American Journal of Psychotherapy, 63*, 87–99.

Petrill, S. A. (2005). Introduction to this special issue: Genes, environment, and the development of reading skills. *Scientific Studies of Reading, 9*, 189–196.

Petrill, S. A., & Deater-Deckard, K. (2004). The heritability of general cognitive ability: A within-family adoption design. *Intelligence, 32*, 403–409.

Pettigrew, T. F. (2004). Justice deferred: A half century after Brown v. Board of Education. *American Psychologist, 59*, 521–529.

Pettigrew, T. F., & L. R. Tropp. (2006). A meta-analytic test of intergroup contact theory. *Journal of Personality and Social Psychology, 90*, 751–783.

Pettingale, K. W., Morris, T., Greer, S., & Haybittle, J. L. (1985). Mental attitudes to cancer: An additional prognostic factor. *Lancet*, 750.

Pettito, L. A. (1993). On the ontogenetic requirements for early language acquisition. In B. de Boysson-Bardies, S. de Schonen, P. W. Jusczyk, P. McNeilage, & J. Morton (Eds.), *Developmental neurocognition: Speech and face processing in the first year of life. NATO ASI series D: Behavioural and social sciences* (Vol. 69). Dordrecht: Kluwer Academic.

Petty, R., Cacioppo, J. T., Strathman, A. J., & Priester, J. R. (2005). To think or not to think: Exploring two routes to persuasion. In T. C. Brock & M. C. Green (Eds.), *Persuasion: Psychological insights and perspectives* (2nd ed.). Thousand Oaks, CA: Sage Publications.

Phelps, R. P. (2005). *Defending standardized testing*. Mahwah, NJ: Lawrence Erlbaum Associates.

Philip, P., Sagaspe, P., Moore, N., Taillard, J., Charles, A., Guilleminault, C., & Bioulac, B. (2005). Fatigue, sleep restriction and driving performance. *Accident Analysis and Prevention, 37*, 473–478.

Piaget, J. (1970). Piaget's theory. In P. H. Mussen (Ed.), *Carmichael's manual of child psychology* (3rd ed.) (Vol. I). New York: Wiley.

Picchioni, D., Goeltzenleucher, B., Green, D. N., Convento, M. J., Crittenden, R., Hallgren, M., & Hick, R. A. (2002). Nightmares as a coping mechanism for stress. *Dreaming: Journal of the Association for the Study of Dreams, 12*, 155–169.

Pickering, G. J., & Gordon, R. (2006). Perception of mouthfeel sensations elicited by red wine are associated with sensitivity to 6-N-propylthiouracil. *Journal of Sensory Studies, 21*, 249–265.

Piechowski, M. M. (2003). From William James to Maslow and Dabrowski: Excitability of character and self-actualization. In D. Ambrose, L. M. Cohen, et al. (Eds.), *Creative intelligence: Toward theoretic integration: Perspectives on creativity* (pp. 283–322). Cresskill, NJ: Hampton Press.

Pietarinen, A-V. (2006). The evolution of semantics and language-games for meaning. *Interaction Studies: Social Behaviour and Communication in Biological and Artificial Systems, 7*, 79–104.

Pillay, S. S., Gruber, S. A., Rogowska, J., Simpson, N., & Yurgelun-Todd, D. A. (2006). fMRI of fearful facial affect recognition in panic disorder: the cingulate gyrus-amygdala connection. *Journal of Affective Disorders, 94*, 173–181.

Pillay, S. S., Rogowska, J., Gruber, S. A., Simpson, N., & Yurgelun-Todd, D. A. (2007). Recognition of happy facial affect in panic disorder: an fMRI study. *Journal of Anxiety Disorders, 21*, 381–393.

Pincus, T., & Morley, S. (2001). Cognitive-processing bias in chronic pain: A review and integration. *Psychological Bulletin, 127*, 599–617.

Pinel, J. P. J., Assanand, S., & Lehman, D. R. (2000). Hunger, eating and ill health. *American Psychologist, 55*, 1105–1116.

Pinker, S. (2002). *The blank slate: The modern denial of human nature*. New York: Viking.

Pinker, S. (2004). *How the mind works*. New York: Gardner Books.

Pinker, S., & Jackendoff, R. (2005). The faculty of language: What's special about it? *Cognition, 96*, 201–236.

Pinquart, M., Duberstein, P. R., & Lyness J. M. (2006). Treatments for later-life depressive conditions: a meta-analytic comparison of pharmacotherapy and psychotherapy. *American Journal of Psychiatry, 163*, 1493–1501.

Piper, A. (1997). *Hoax and reality: The entire world of multiple personality disorder*. Northvale, NJ: Jason Aronson.

Pi-Sunyer, X. (2003). A clinical view of the obesity problem. *Science, 299*, 859–860.

Plomin, R. (2003a). 50 years of DNA: What it has meant to psychological science. *American Psychological Society, 16*, 7–8.

Plomin, R. (2003b). General cognitive ability. In R. Pomin, J. C. DeFries, et al. (Eds.), *Behavioral genetics in the postgenomic era*. Washington, DC: American Psychological Association.

Plomin, R., & Kovas, Y. (2005). Generalist genes and learning disabilities. *Psychological Bulletin, 131*, 592–617.

Plomin, R., & McGuffin, P. (2003). Psychopathology in the postgenomic era. *Annual Review of Psychology, 54*, 205–228.

Plomin, R., DeFries, J. C., Craig, I. W., & McGuffin, P. (2003). *Behavioral genetics in the postgenomic era*. Washington, DC: American Psychological Association.

Plous, S., & Herzog, H. A. (2000, October 27). Poll shows researchers favor lab animal protection. *Science, 290*, 711.

Plowright, C. M. S., Simonds, V. M., & Butler, M. A. (2006). How bumblebees first find flowers: Habituation of visual pattern preferences, spontaneous recovery, and dishabituation. *Learning and Motivation, 37*, 66–78.

Pogarsky, G., & Piquero, A. R. (2003). Can punishment encourage offending? Investigating the "resetting" effect. *Journal of Research in Crime and Delinquency, 40*, 95–120.

Pole, N. (2007).The psychophysiology of post-traumatic stress disorder: A meta-analysis. *Psychological Bulletin, 133*, 34–45.

Polivy, J., & Herman, C. P. (2002). Causes of eating disorders. *Annual Review of Psychology, 53*, 187–213.

Polivy, J., Herman, C. P., & Boivin, M. (2005). Eating disorders. In J. E. Maddux and B. A. Winstead, *Psychopathology: Foundations for a contemporary understanding* (pp. 229–254). Mahwah, NJ: Lawrence Erlbaum Associates.

Polk, N. (1997, March 30). *The trouble with school testing systems*. The New York Times, p. CN3.

Polonsky, D. C. (2006). Review of the big book of masturbation: From angst to zeal. *Journal of Sex & Marital Therapy, 32*, 75–78.

Ponterotto, J. G., Gretchen, D., & Chauhan, R. V. (2001). Cultural identity and multicultural assessment: Quantitative and qualitative tools for the clinician. In L. A. Suzuki, & J. G. Ponterotto (Eds.), *Handbook of multicultural assessment: Clinical, psychological, and educational applications* (2nd ed.). San Francisco: Jossey-Bass/Pfeiffer.

Poo, C. & Isaacson, J. S. (2007). An early critical period for long-term plasticity and structural modification of sensory synapses in olfactory cortex. *Journal of Neuroscience, 27*, 7553–7558.

Porkka-Heiskanen, T., Strecker, R. E., Thakkar, M., Bjorkum, A. A., Greene, R. W., & McCarley, R. W. (1997, May 23). Adensosine: A mediator of the sleep-inducing effects of prolonged wakefulness. *Science, 276*, 1265–1268.

Porte, H. S., & Hobson, J. A. (1996). Physical motion in dreams: One measure of three theories. *Journal of Abnormal Psychology, 105*, 329–335.

Porter, C. L., & Hsu, H. C. (2003). First-time mothers' perceptions of efficacy during the transition to motherhood: Links to infant temperament. *Journal of Family Psychology, 17*, 54–64.

Posner, M. I., & DiGirolamo, G. J. (2000). Cognitive neuroscience: Origins and promise. *Psychological Bulletin, 126*, 873–889.

Poteat, V. P., & Espelage, D. L. (2007). Predicting psychosocial consequences of homophobic victimization in middle school students. *Journal of Early Adolescence, 27*, 175–191.

Pottick, K. J., Kirk, S. A., Hsieh, D. K., & Tian, X. (2007). Judging mental disorder in youths: Effects of client, clinician, and contextual differences. *Journal of Consulting Clinical Psychology, 75*, 1–8.

Powell, L. H. (2006). Review of marital and sexual lifestyles in the U.S.: attitudes, behaviors, and relationships in social context. *Family Relations, 55*, 149.

Powers, K. D. (2006). An analysis of Kohlbergian moral development in relationship to biblical factors of morality in seminary students (Lawrence Kohlberg). *Dissertation Abstracts International: Section B: The Sciences and Engineering, 67*(6-B), 3485.

Pratkanis, A. R. (2007). Social influence analysis: An index of tactics. *The science of social influence: Advances and future progress*. New York: Psychology Press.

Pratt, H. D., Phillips, E. L., Greydanus, D. E., & Patel, D. R. (2003). Eating disorders in the adolescent population: Future directions [Special issue: Eating disorders in adolescents]. *Journal of Adolescent Research, 18*, 297–317.

Presbury, J., McKee, J., & Echterling, L. (2007). Person-centered approaches. *Counseling and psychotherapy with children and adolescents: Theory and practice for school and clinical settings* (4th ed.) (pp. 180–240). Hoboken, NJ: John Wiley & Sons Inc.

President's Council on Bioethics. (2003). *Beyond therapy: Biotechnology and the pursuit of happiness*. Washington, DC: Government Printing Office.

Pressley, M. P., & Harris., K. R. (2006). Cognitive strategies instruction: from basic research to classroom instruction. In P. A. Alexander, & P. H. Winne, *Handbook of educational psychology*. Mahwah, NJ: Erlbaum.

Pretzer, J. L., & Beck, A. T. (2005). A cognitive theory of personality disorders. In M. F. Lenzenweger & J. F. Clarkin (Eds.), *Major theories of personality disorder* (2nd ed.). New York: Guilford Press.

Prince, C.V. (2005). Homosexuality, transvestism and transsexuality: Reflections on their etymology and differentiation. *International Journal of Transgenderism, 8*, 15–18.

Prinz, J. J. (2007). Emotion: Competing theories and philosophical issues. In P. Thagard, *Philosophy of psychology and cognitive science*. Amsterdam: North Holland/ Elsevier.

Prislin, R., Brewer, M., & Wilson, D. J. (2002). Changing majority and minority positions within a group versus an aggregate. *Personality and Social Psychology Bulletin, 28*, 650–647.

Proffitt, D. R. (2006). Distance perception. *Current Directions in Psychological Science, 15*, 131–139.

Province of Manitoba. (2011). The inquiry regarding Thomas Sophonow. Jailhouse informants, their unreliability and the importance of complete crown disclosure pertaining to them. Retrieved from www.gov.mb.ca/justice/publications/sophonow/jailhouse/cheng.html.

Puca, R. M. (2005). The influence of the achievement motive on probability estimates in pre- and post-decisional action phases. *Journal of Research in Personality, 39*, 245–262.

Q

Quartana, P. J., & Burns, J. W. (2007). Painful consequences of anger suppression. *Emotion, 7*, 400–414.

Quas, J. A., Malloy, L. C., & Melinder, A. (2007). Developmental differences in the effects of repeated interviews and interviewer bias on young children's event memory and false reports. *Developmental Psychology, 43*, 823–837.

Quenot, J. P., Boichot, C., Petit, A., Falcon-Eicher, S., d'Athis, P., Bonnet, C., Wolf, J. E., Louis, P., & Brunotte, F. (2005). Usefulness of MRI in the follow-up of patients with repaired aortic coarctation and bicuspid aortic valve. *International Journal of Cardiology, 103*, 312–316.

Quinn, D. M., Kahng, S. K., & Crocker, J. (2004). Discreditable: Stigma effects of revealing a mental illness history on test performance. *Personality and Social Psychology Bulletin, 30*, 803–815.

Quintana, S. M., Aboud, F. E., Chao, R. K., (2006). Race, ethnicity, and culture in child development: Contemporary research and future directions. *Child Development, 77*, 1129–1141.

R

Rabin, J. (2004). Quantification of color vision with cone contrast sensitivity. *Visual Neuroscience, 21*, 483–485.

Rachman, S., & deSilva, P. (2004). *Panic disorders: The facts*. Oxford, England: Oxford University Press.

Rahman, Q., Kumari, V., & Wilson, G. D. (2003). Sexual orientation-related differences in pre-pulse inhibition of the human startle response. *Behavioral Neuroscience, 117*, 1096–1102.

Rajagopal, S. (2006). The placebo effect. *Psychiatric Bulletin, 30*, 185–188.

Ralston, A. (2004). *Between a rock and a hard place*. New York: Simon & Schuster.

Ramachandran, V. S., & Hubbard, E. M. (2001). Synesthesia—a window into perception, thought and language. *Journal of Consciousness Studies, 8*, 3–34.

Ramachandran, V. S., Hubbard, E. M., & Butcher, P. A. (2004). Synesthesia, cross-activation and the foundations of neuroepistemology. In G. A. Calvert, C. Spence, & B. E. Stein, *The handbook of multisensory processes*. Cambridge, MA: MIT Press.

Rambaud, C., & Guilleminault, C. (2004). "Back to sleep" and unexplained death in infants. *Journal of Sleep and Sleep Disorders, 27*, 1359–1366.

Ramus, F. (2006). Genes, brain, and cognition: A roadmap for the cognitive scientist. *Cognition, 101*, 247–269.

Ranganath, C., & Blumenfeld, R. (2005, August). Doubts about double dissociations between short- and long-term memory. *Trends in Cognitive Sciences, 9*(8), 374–380.

Raskin, N. J., & Rogers, C. R. (1989). Person-centered therapy. In R. J. Corsini, & D. Wedding (Eds.), *Current psychotherapies* (4th ed.). Itasca, IL: F. E. Peacock.

Rassin, E., & Muris, P. (2007). Abnormal and normal obsessions: A reconsideration. *Behaviour Research and Therapy, 45*, 1065–1070.

Rattazzi, M. C., LaFuci, G., & Brown, W. T. (2004). Prospects for gene therapy in the Fragile X Syndrome. *Mental Retardation and Developmental Disabilities Research Reviews, 10*, 75–81.

Ravindran, A. V., Matheson, K., Griffiths, J., Merali, Z., & Anisman, H. (2002). Stress, coping, uplifts, and quality of life in subtypes of depression: A conceptual framework and emerging data. *Journal of Affective Disorders, 71*, 121–130.

Ray, L. A., & Hutchison, K. E. (2007). Effects of naltrexone on alcohol sensitivity and genetic moderators of medication response: a double-blind placebo-controlled study. *Archives of General Psychiatry, 64*, 1069–1077.

Raz, A. (2007). Suggestibility and hypnotizability: Mind the gap. *American Journal of Clinical Hypnosis, 49*, 205–210.

Rechtschaffen, A., Bergmann, B., Everson, C., Gilliland, M., & Kushida, C. (2002, February). Sleep deprivation in the rat: X. Integration and discussion of the findings. *Sleep: Journal of Sleep and Sleep Disorders Research, 25*(1), 68–87.

Redding, G. M. (2002). A test of size-scaling and relative-size hypotheses for the moon illusion. *Perception and Psychophysics, 64,* 1281–1289.

Redding, G. M., & Hawley, E. (1993). Length illusion in fractional Müller-Lyer stimuli: An object-perception approach. *Perception, 22,* 819–828.

Redding, R. E., Herbert, J. D., Forman, E. M., & Guadiano, B. A. (2008). Popular self-help books for anxiety, depression, and trauma: How scientifically grounded and useful are they? *Professional Psychology: Research and Practice, 39*(3), 537–545.

Redish, A. D. (2004). Addiction as a computational process gone awry. *Science, 306,* 1944–1947.

Reed, S. K. (1996). *Cognition: Theory and applications* (4th ed.). Pacific Grove, CA: Brooks/Cole.

Reese, R. J., Conoley, C. W., & Brossart, D. F. (2002). Effectiveness of telephone counseling: A field-based investigation. *Journal of Counseling Psychology, 49,* 233–242.

Regan, P. C. (2006). Love. In R. D. McAnulty, & M. M. Burnette, *Sex and sexuality: Sexual function and dysfunction* (Vol. 2). Westport, CT: Praeger Publishers/Greenwood Publishing.

Reid, J. L. & Hammond, D. (2011). *Tobacco use in Canada: Patterns and trends, 2011 Edition.* Waterloo, ON: Propel Centre for Population Health Impact, University of Waterloo.

Reif, A., & Lesch, K. P. (2003). Toward a molecular architecture of personality. *Behavioural Brain Research, 139,* 1–20.

Reijonen, J. H., Pratt, H. D., Patel, D. R., & Greydanus, D. E. (2003). Eating disorders in the adolescent population: An overview [Special issue: Eating disorders in adolescents]. *Journal of Adolescent Research, 18,* 209–222.

Reilly, T., & Waterhouse, J. (2007). Altered sleep-wake cycles and food intake: The Ramadan model. *Physiology & Behavior, 90,* 219–228.

Reiss, S. & Havercamp, S. H. (2005). Motivation in a developmental context: Test of Maslow's theory of self-actualization. *Journal of Humanistic Psychology, 45,* 41–53.

Reissig, C. J., Strain, E. C., & Griffiths, R. R. (2009). Caffeinated energy drinks—growing problem. *Drug and Alcohol Dependence, 99,* 1–10.

Reitman, J. S. (1965). *Cognition and thought.* New York: Wiley.

Rende, R. (2007). Thinking inside and outside the (black) box: Behavioral genetics and human development. *Human Development, 49,* 343–346.

Repp, B. H., & Knoblich, G. (2007). Action can affect auditory perception. *Psychological Science, 18,* 6–7.

Reynolds, C. R., & Ramsay, M. C. (2003). Bias in psychological assessment: An empirical review and recommendations. In J. R. Graham & J. A. Naglieri (Eds.), *Handbook of psychology: Assessment psychology* (Vol. 10) (pp. 67–93). New York: Wiley.

Reynolds, R. I., & Takooshian, H. (1988, January). Where were you August 8, 1985? *Bulletin of the Psychonomic Society, 26,* 23–25.

Ricciuti, H. N. (1993). Nutrition and mental development. *Current Directions in Psychological Science, 2,* 43–46.

Rice, L., & Greenberg, L. (1992). Humanistic approaches to psychotherapy. *History of psychotherapy: A century of change* (pp. 197–224). Washington, DC: American Psychological Association.

Rice, M. L., Tomblin, J. B., Hoffman, L., Richman, W. A., & Marquis, J. (2004). Grammatical tense deficits in children with SLI and nonspecific language impairment: Relationships with non-verbal IQ over time. *Journal of Speech, Language, and Hearing Research, 47,* 816–834.

Rich, E. L., & Shapiro, M. L. (2007). Prelimbic/ infralimbic inactivation impairs memory for multiple task switches, but not flexible selection of familiar tasks. *Journal of Neuroscience, 27,* 4747–4755.

Richard, D. C. S., & Lauterbach, D. (Eds). (2006). *Handbook of exposure therapies.* New York: Academic Press.

Richard, M. (2005). Effective treatment of eating disorders in Europe: Treatment outcome and its predictors. *European Eating Disorders Review, 13,* 169–179.

Richardson, A. S., Bergen, H. A., Martin, G., Roeger, L., & Allison, S. (2005). Perceived academic performance as an indicator of risk of attempted suicide in young adolescents. *Archives of Suicide Research, 9,* 163–176.

Richgels, D. J. (2004). Paying attention to language. *Reading Research Quarterly, 39,* 470–477.

Rieber, R. W., & Robinson, D. K. (2006). Review of the essential Vygotsky. *Journal of the History of the Behavioral Sciences, 42,* 178–180.

Rieder, R. O., Kaufmann, C. A., & Knowles, J. A. (1996). Genetics. In R. E. Hales & S. C. Yudofsky (Eds.), *The American Psychiatric Press synopsis of psychiatry.* Washington, DC: American Psychiatric Press.

Rigby, L., & Waite, S. (2007). Group therapy for self-esteem, using creative approaches and metaphor as clinical tools. *Behavioural and Cognitive Psychotherapy, 35,* 361–364.

Rinn, W. E. (1984). The neuropsychology of facial expression: A review of neurological and psychological mechanisms for producing facial expressions. *Psychological Bulletin, 95,* 52–77.

Rinn, W. E. (1991). Neuropsychology of facial expression. In R. S. Feldman & B. Rimé (Eds.), *Fundamentals of non-verbal behavior.* Cambridge: Cambridge University Press.

Riolo, F. (2007). Ricordare, ripetere e rielaborare: Un lascito di Freud alia psicoanalisi futura. Remembering, repeating, and working through: Freud's legacy to the psychoanalysis of the future. *Rivista di Psicoanalisi, 53,* 439–446.

Robins, R. W. (2005, October 7). The nature of personality: Genes, culture, and national character. *Science, 310,* 62–63.

Robinson, D. N. (2007). Theoretical psychology: What is it and who needs it? *Theory & Psychology, 17,* 187–198.

Robinson, D. S. (2007). Antidepressant drugs: Early onset of therapeutic effect. *Primary Psychiatry, 14,* 23–24.

Rock, A. (1999, January). Quitting time for smokers. *Money,* pp. 139–141.

Rodd, Z. A., Bell, R. L., Sable, H. J. K., Murphy, J. M., & McBride, W. J. (2004). Recent advances in animal models of alcohol craving and relapse. *Pharmacology, Biochemistry and Behavior, 79,* 439–450.

Roediger, H. L., III, & McDermott, K. B. (2000). Tricks of memory. *Current Directions in Psychological Science, 9,* 123–127.

Roediger, H., Balota, D., & Watson, J. (2001). Spreading activation and arousal of false memories. *The nature of remembering: Essays in honor of Robert G. Crowder* (pp. 95–115). Washington, DC: American Psychological Association.

Roesch, S. C., Adams, L., Hines, A., Palmores, A., Vyas, P., Tran, C., Pekin, S., & Vaughn, A. A. (2005). Coping with prostate cancer: A meta-analytic review. *Journal of Behavioral Medicine, 28,* 281–293.

Rogers, C. R. (1951). *Client-centered therapy.* Boston: Houghton-Mifflin.

Rogers, C. R. (1971). A theory of personality. In S. Maddi (Ed.), *Perspectives on personality.* Boston: Little, Brown.

Roid, G., Nellis, L. & McLellan, M. (2003). Assessment with the Leiter International Performance Scale—Revised and the S-BIT. In R.S. McCallum & R. Steve (Eds.), *Handbook of nonverbal assessment.* New York: Kluwer Academic/Plenum Publishers.

Roisman, G. I., Collins, W. A. Sroufe, L. A., & Egeland, B. (2005). Predictors of young adults' representations of and behavior in their current romantic relationship: Prospective tests of the prototype hypothesis. *Attachment and Human Development, 7,* 105–121.

Roizen, N. J., & Patterson, D. (2003). Down's syndrome. *Lancet, 361,* 1281–1289.

Romeu, P. F. (2006). Memories of the terrorist attacks of September 11, 2001: A study of the consistency and phenomenal characteristics of flashbulb memories. *The Spanish Journal of Psychology, 9,* 52–60.

Room, R., Babor, T., & Rehm, J. (2005, February). Alcohol and public health. *Lancet, 365*(9458), 519–530.

Rorschach, H. (1924). *Psychodiagnosis: A diagnostic test based on perception.* New York: Grune & Stratton.

Rosen, H. (2000). The creative evolution of the theoretical foundations for cognitive therapy. *Journal of Cognitive Psychotherapy, 14, Special issue: Creativity in the context of cognitive therapy,* 123–134.

Rosenbloom, T., & Wolf, Y. (2002). Sensation seeking and detection of risky road signals: A developmental perspective. *Accident Analysis and Prevention, 34,* 569–580.

Rosenhan, D. L. (1973). On being sane in insane places. *Science, 179,* 250–258.

Rosenman, R. H., Brand, R. J., Jenkins, C. D., Friedman, M., Straus, R., & Wurm, M. (1994). Coronary heart disease in the Western Collaborative Group Study: Final follow-up experience of 8 1/2 years. In A. Steptoe, & J. Wardle, Eds., *Psychosocial processes and health: A reader.* New York: Cambridge University Press.

Rosenstein, D. S., & Horowitz, H. A. (1996). Adolescent attachment and psychopathology. *Journal of Consulting and Clinical Psychology, 64,* 244–253.

Rosenthal, J. S. (2006). *Struck by lightning: The curious world of probabilities.* Toronto, ON: HarperCollings Publishing, Ltd.

Rosenthal, R. (2002). Covert communication in classrooms, clinics, courtrooms and cubicles. *American Psychologist, 57,* 838–849.

Rosenthal, R. (2003). Covert communication in laboratories, classrooms, and the truly real world. *Current Directions in Psychological Science, 12,* 151–154.

Rosov, A. (1993). Striving for superiority as a fundamental drive. *Psikhologicheskiy Zhurnal, 14*(6), 133–141.

Ross, H. E. (2000). Sensation and perception. In D. S. Gupta, S. Deepa, & R. M. Gupta, et al. (Eds.), *Psychology for psychiatrists* (pp. 20–40). London: Whurr Publishers.

Ross, J. (2006). Sleep on a problem . . . It works like a dream. *The Psychologist, 19,* 738–740.

Ross, L. (1977). The intuitive psychologist and his shortcomings: Distortions in the attribution process. In L. Berkowitz (Ed.), *Advances in experimental social psychology* (Vol. 10) (pp. 173–240). Orlando, FL: Academic Press.

Rossell, S. L., Bullmore, E. T., Williams, S. C. R., & David, A. S. (2002). Sex differences in functional brain activation during a lexical visual field task. *Brain and Language, 80,* 97–105.

Rossier J, Dahourou D., McCrae, R. R. (2005). Structural and mean level analyses of the Five-Factor Model and locus of control: Further evidence from Africa. *Journal of Cross-Cultural Psychology, 36,* 227–246.

Roughton, R. E. (2002). Rethinking homosexuality: What it teaches us about psychoanalysis. *Journal of the American Psychoanalytic Association, 50,* 733–763.

Routtenberg, A., & Lindy, J. (1965). Effects of the availability of rewarding septal and hypothalamic stimulation on bar pressing for food under conditions of deprivation. *Journal of Comparative and Physiological Psychology, 60,* 158–161.

Rowe, J. B., Toni, I., Josephs, O., Frackowiak, R. S. J., & Passingham, R. E. (2000, June 2). The prefrontal cortex: Response selection or maintenance within working memory? *Science, 288,* 1656–1660.

Rowley, S. J., Sellers, R. M., Chavous, T. M., & Smith, M. A. (1998). The relationship between racial identity and self-esteem in African American college and high school students. *Journal of Personality and Social Psychology, 74,* 715–724.

Royal Canadian Mounted Police. (2008). Lottery fraud. *Gazette magazine, 70*(1). Retrieved April 4, 2011 from www.rcmp-grc.gc.ca/gazette/vol70n1/lot-eng.htm.

Royzman, E. B., Cassidy, K. W., & Baron, J. (2003). "I know, you know": Epistemic egocentrism in children and adults. *Review of General Psychology, 7,* 38–65.

Rozencwajg, P., Cherfi, M., Ferrandez, A. M., Lautrey, J., Lemoine, C., & Loarer, E. (2005). Age-related differences in the strategies used by middle aged adults to solve a block design task. *International Journal of Aging and Human Development, 60,* 159–182.

Rubichi, S., Ricci, F., Padovani, R., & Scaglietti, L. (2005). Hypnotic susceptibility, baseline attentional functioning, and the Stroop task. *Consciousness and Cognition: An International Journal, 14,* 296–303.

Rubin, D. C. (1999). *Remembering our past: Studies in autobiographical memory.* New York: Cambridge University Press.

Rubin, D. C., Schrauf, R. W., Gulgoz, S., & Naka, M. (2007). Cross-cultural variability of component processes in autobiographical remembering: Japan, Turkey, and the USA. *Memory, 15,* 536–547.

Rudman, L. A. & Ashmore, R. D. (2007). Discrimination and the Implicit Association Test. *Group Processes & Intergroup Relations, 10,* 359–372.

Runco, M. A. (2006). Introduction to the special issue: divergent thinking. *Creativity Research Journal, 18,* 249–250.

Runco, M. A., & Sakamoto, S. O. (1993). Reaching creatively gifted students through their learning styles. In R. M. Milgram, R. S. Dunn, & G. E. Price (Eds.), *Teaching and counseling gifted and talented adolescents: An international learning style perspective.* Westport, CT: Praeger/Greenwood.

Rusche, B. (2003). The 3Rs and animal welfare–conflict or the way forward? *ALTEX, 20,* (Suppl. 1), 63–76.

Ruscher, J. B., Fiske, S. T., & Schnake, S. B. (2000). The motivated tactician's juggling act: Compatible vs. incompatible impression goals. *British Journal of Social Psychology, 39,* 241–256.

Russell, J. A., & Sato, K. (1995). Comparing emotion words between languages. *Journal of Cross Cultural Psychology, 26,* 384–391.

Rustin, M. (2006). Infant observation research: What have we learned so far? *Infant Observation, 9,* 35–52.

Rutter, M. (2006). *Genes and behavior: Nature-nurture interplay explained.* Malden, MA: Blackwell Publishing.

Rymer, R. (1994). *Genie: A scientific tragedy.* New York: Penguin.

S

Saarni, C. (1999). *Developing emotional competence.* New York: Guilford.

Sabbagh, K. (2009). *Remembering our childhood: How memory betrays us.* New York: Oxford University Press.

Sachs-Ericsson, N., Joiner, T., Plant, E. A., & Blazer, D. G. (2005). The influence of depression on cognitive decline in community-dwelling elderly persons. *American Journal of Geriatric Psychiatry, 13,* 402–408.

Sackeim, H. A., Haskett, R. F., Mulsant, B. H., Thase, M. E., Mann, J. J., Pettinati, H. M., Greenberg, R. M., Crowe, R. R., Cooper, T. B., & Prudic, J. (2001). Continuation pharmaco-therapy in the prevention of relapse following electroconvulsive therapy: A randomized controlled trial. *Journal of the American Medical Association, 285,* 1299–1307.

Sacks, F., Bray, G., Carey, V. et al. (2009). Comparison of weight-loss diets with different compositions of fat, protein, and carbohydrates. *New England Journal of Medicine, 360,* 9, 859–873.

Saczynski, J., Willis, S., and Schaie, K. (2002). Strategy use in reasoning training with older adults. *Aging, Neuropsychology, & Cognition, 9,* 48–60.

Saggino, A., Perfetti, B., & Spitoni, G. (2006). Fluid intelligence and executive functions: New perspectives. In L. V. Wesley, *Intelligence: New research.* Hauppauge, NY: Nova Science Publishers.

Sagi, A., Van Ijzendoorn, M. H., & Koren-Kari, N. (1991). Primary appraisal of the strange situation: A cross cultural analysis of preseparation episodes. *Developmental Psychology, 27,* 4, 587–596.

Sahin, N. T., Pinker, S., & Halgren, E. (2006). Abstract grammatical processing of nouns and verbs in Broca's area: Evidence from fMRI. *Cortex, 42,* 540–562.

Sakai, K. L. (2005, November 4). Language acquisition and brain development. *Science, 310,* 815–817.

Salgado, D. M., Quinlin, K. J., & Zlotnick, C. (2007). The relationship of lifetime polysubstance dependence to trauma exposure, symptomatology, and psychosocial functioning in incarcerated women with comorbid PTSD and substance use disorder. *Journal of Trauma Dissociation, 8,* 9–26.

Salmela-Aro, K., & Nurmi, J-E. (2007). Self-esteem during university studies predicts career characteristics 10 years later. *Journal of Vocational Behavior, 70,* 463–477.

Salsman, N. L. (2006). Interpersonal change as an outcome of Time-Limited Interpersonal Therapy. *Dissertation Abstracts International: Section B—The Sciences and Engineering, 66*(9-B), 5103.

Salzman, L. (1964). Psychoanalysis in evolution. *Comprehensive Psychiatry, 5*(6), 364–373.

Samantaray, S. K., Srivastava, M., & Mishra, P. K. (2002). Fostering self concept and self actualization as bases for empowering women in national development: A challenge for the new millennium. *Social Science International, 18,* 58–63.

Samoilov, V., & Zayas, V. (2007). Ivan Petrovich Pavlov (1849–1936). *Journal of the History of the Neurosciences, 16,* 74–89.

Sampson, M., McCubbin, R., & Tyrer, P. (2006). *Personality disorder and community mental health teams: A practitioner's guide.* New York: John Wiley & Sons Ltd.

Sampson, S. M., Solvason, H., B., Husain, M. M. (2007). Envisioning transcranial magnetic stimulation (TMS) as a clinical treatment option for depression. *Psychiatric Annals, 37,* Special issue: Neuromodulation: Patients with depression may benefit from treatment with vagus nerve and transcranial magnetic stimulation, 189–196.

Sams, M., Hari, R., Rif, J., & Knuutila, J. (1993). The human auditory memory trace persists about 10 sec: Neuromagnetic evidence. *Journal of Cognitive Neuroscience, 5,* 363–370.

Samuel, D. B., & Widiger, T. A. (2006). Differentiating normal and abnormal personality from the perspective of the DSM. S. Strack, *Differentiating normal and abnormal personality* (2nd ed.). New York: Springer Publishing.

Sandoval, J., Frisby, C. L., Geisinger, K. F., Scheuneman, J. D., & Grenier, J. R. (Eds.). (1998). *Test interpretation and diversity: Achieving equity in assessment*. Washington, DC: American Psychological Association.

Santel, S., Baving, L., Krauel, K., Munte, T. F. & Rotte, M. (2006). Hunger and satiety in anorexia nervosa: fMRI during cognitive processing of food pictures. *Brain Research, 1114*, 138–148.

Saper, C. B., Lu, J., Chou, T. C., & Gooley, J. (2005). The hypothalamic integrator for circadian rhythms. *Trends in Neuroscience, 28*, 152–157.

Sapolsky, R. M. (2003). Gene therapy for psychiatric disorders. *American Journal of Psychiatry, 160*, 208–220.

Sargent, J. D., Stoolmiller, M., Worth, K. A., Cal, C. S., Wills, T. A., Gibbons, F. X., Gerrard, M., & Tanski, S. (2007). Exposure to smoking depictions in movies: Its association with established adolescent smoking. *Archives of Pediatric Adolescent Medicine, 161*, 849–856.

Satel, S. (2006). Is caffeine addictive?—A review of the literature. *American Journal of Drug and Alcohol Abuse, 32*, 493–502.

Saucier, D. A., & Cain, M. E. (2006). The foundations of attitudes about animal research. *Ethics & Behavior, 16*, 117–133.

Savas, H. A., Yumru, M., & Kaya, M. C. (2007). Atypical antipsychotics as "mood stabilizers": A retrospective chart review. *Progress in Neuro-Psychopharmacology & Biological Psychiatry, 31*, 1064–1067.

Savazzi, S., Fabri, M., Rubboli, G., Paggi, A., Tassinari, C. A., Marzi, C. A. (2007). Interhemispheric transfer following callosotomy in humans: Role of the superior colliculus, *Neuropsychologia, 45*, 2417–2427.

Sawa, A., & Snyder, S. H. (2002, April 26). Schizophrenia: Diverse approaches to a complex disease. *Science, 296*, 692–695.

Sayette, M. A. (1993). An appraisal disruption model of alcohol's effects on stress responses in social drinkers. *Psychological Bulletin, 114*, 459–476.

Saywitz, K., & Goodman, G. (1990). Unpublished study reported in Goleman, D. (1990, November 6). Doubts rise on children as witnesses. *The New York Times*, pp. C-1, C-6.

Scarr, S., & Weinberg, R. A. (1976). IQ test performance of black children adopted by White families. *American Psychologist, 31*, 726–739.

Scaturo, D. J. (2004). Fundamental clinical dilemmas in contemporary group psychotherapy. *Group Analysis, 37*, 201–217.

Scelfo, J. (2007, February 26). Men & depression: Facing darkness. *Newsweek*, pp. 43–50.

Schachter, S., & Singer, J. E. (1962). Cognitive, social, and physiological determinants of emotional state. *Psychological Review, 69*, 379–399.

Schacter, D. L., & Badgaiyan, R. D. (2001). Neuroimaging of priming: New perspectives on implicit and explicit memory. *Current Directions in Psychological Science, 10*, 1–4.

Schacter, D. L., Dobbins, I. G., & Schnyer, D. M. (2004). Specificity of priming: A cognitive neuroscience perspective. *Nature Reviews Neuroscience, 5*, 853–862.

Schacter, D. L., Wagner, A. D., & Buckner, R. L. (2000). Memory systems of 1999. In E. Tulving, F. I. Craik, I. M. Fergus, et al. (Eds.), *The Oxford handbook of memory*. New York: Oxford University Press.

Schaefer, R. T. (2000). *Sociology: A brief introduction* (3rd ed.). Boston: McGraw-Hill.

Schaie, K. W. (2005). *Developmental influences on adult intelligence: The Seattle Longitudinal Study*. New York: Oxford University Press.

Schaller, M., & Crandall, C. S. (Eds.) (2004). *The psychological foundations of culture*. Mahwah, NJ: Lawrence Erlbaum Associates.

Schechter, T., Finkelstein, Y., Koren, G. (2005). Pregnant "DES daughters" and their offspring. *Canadian Family Physician, 51*, 493–494.

Scheele, B., & DuBois, F. (2006). Catharsis as a moral form of entertainment. In J. Bryant, & P. Vorderer, *Psychology of entertainment*. Mahwah, NJ: Lawrence Erlbaum Associates Publishers.

Scheier, M. F., Carver, C. S., & Bridges, M. W. (1994). Distinguishing optimism from neuroticism (and trait anxiety, self-mastery, and self-esteem): A revision of the Life Orientation Test. *Journal of Personality and Social Psychology, 67*, 1063–1078.

Schepers, P., & van den Berg, P. T. (2007). Social factors of work-environment creativity. *Journal of Business and Psychology, 21*, 407–428.

Schieber, F. (2006). Vision and aging. In J. E. Birren, & K. W. Schaire, *Handbook of the psychology of aging* (6th ed.). Amsterdam, Netherlands: Elsevier.

Schiffer, A. A., Pedersen, S. S., Widdershoven, J. W., Hendriks, E. H., Winter, J. B., & Denollet, J. (2005). The distressed (type D) personality is independently associated with impaired health status and increased depressive symptoms in chronic heart failure. *European Journal of Cardiovascular Prevention and Rehabilitation, 12*, 341–346.

Schmidt, J. P. (2006). The discovery of neurotransmitters: A fascinating story and a scientific object lesson. *PsycCRITIQUES, 61*, 101–115.

Schmidt, N. B., Kotov, R., & Joiner, T. E., Jr. (2004). *Taxometrics: Toward a new diagnostic scheme for psychopathology*. Washington, DC: American Psychological Association.

Schmitt, D. P., Allik, J., & Mccrae, R. R. (2007). The geographic distribution of big five personality traits: patterns and profiles of human self-description across 56 nations. *Journal of Cross-Cultural Psychology, 38*, 173–212.

Schneider, D. J. (2003). *The psychology of stereotyping*. New York: Guilford Press.

Schneider, D., & Logan, G. (2009, January). Selecting a response in task switching: Testing a model of compound cue retrieval. *Journal of Experimental Psychology: Learning, Memory, and Cognition, 35*(1), 122–136.

Schredl, M., & Piel, E. (2005). Gender differences in dreaming: Are they stable over time? *Personality and Individual Differences, 39*, 309–316.

Schretlen, D., Pearlson, G. D., Anthony, J. C., Aylward, E. H., Augustine, A. M., Davis, A., & Barta, P. (2000). Elucidating the contributions of processing speed, executive ability, and frontal lobe volume to normal age-related differences in fluid intelligence. *Journal of the International Neuropsychological Society, 6*, 52–61.

Schutt, R. K. (2001). *Investigating the social world: The process and practice of research*. Thousand Oaks, CA: Sage.

Schwartz, B. L. (2001). The relation of tip-of-the-tongue states and retrieval time. *Memory & Cognition, 29*, 117–126.

Schwartz, B. L. (2002). The phenomenology of naturally-occurring tip-of-the-tongue states: A diary study. In S. P. Shohov (Ed.), *Advances in psychology research* (Vol. 8) (pp. 73–84). Huntington, NY: Nova.

Schwartz, J. M., & Begley, S. (2002). *The mind and the brain: Neuroplasticity and the power of mental force*. (2002). New York: Regan Books/ Harper Collins.

Scullin, M. H., Kanaya, T., & Ceci, S. J. (2002). Measurement of individual differences in children's suggestibility across situations. *Journal of Experimental Psychology: Applied, 8*, 233–246.

Sebel, P. S., Bonke, B., & Winograd, E. (Eds.). (1993). *Memory and awareness in anesthesia*. Englewood Cliffs, NJ: Prentice Hall.

Segall, M. H., Campbell, D. T., & Herskovits, M. J. (1966). *The influence of culture on visual perception*. New York: Bobbs-Merrill.

Segerstrom, S. C., & Miller, G. E. (2004). Psychological stress and the human immune system: A meta-analytic study of 30 years of inquiry. *Psychological Bulletin, 130*, 601–630.

Seibt, B., & Förster, J. (2005). Stereotype threat and performance: How self-stereotypes influence processing by inducing regulatory foci. *Journal of Personality and Social Psychology, 87*, 38–56.

Seli, H. (2007). 'Self' in self-worth protection: The relationship of possible selves to achievement motives and self-worth protective strategies. *Dissertation Abstracts International Section A: Humanities and Social Sciences, 67*(9-A), 3302.

Seligman, M. E. (1975). *Helplessness: On depression, development, and death*. San Francisco: Freeman.

Seligman, M. E. (1995, December). The effectiveness of psychotherapy: The Consumer Reports study. *American Psychologist, 50*, 965–974.

Seligman, M. E. (1996, October). Science as an ally of practice. *American Psychologist, 51*, 1072–1079.

Seligman, M. E. (2007). *What you can change . . . and what you can't: The complete guide to successful self-improvement*. New York: Vintage.

Seligman, M. E. P. and Maier, S. F. (1967). Failure to escape traumatic shock. *Journal of Experimental Psychology, 74*, 1–9.

Selkoe, D. J. (1997, January 31). Alzheimer's disease: Genotypes, phenotype, and treatments. *Science, 275*, 630–631.

Sellbom, M., & Ben-Porath, Y. S. (2006). The Minnesota Multiphasic Personality Inventory-2. In R. P. Archer, *Forensic uses of clinical assessment instruments* (pp. 19–55). Mahwah, NJ: Lawrence Erlbaum Associates.

Selove, R. (2007). The glass is half full: Current knowledge about pediatric cancer and sickle cell anemia. *PsycCRITIQUES, 52*, 88–99.

Selye, H. (1976). *The stress of life*. New York: McGraw-Hill.

Selye, H. (1993). History of the stress concept. In L. Goldberger & S. Breznitz (Eds.), *Handbook of stress: Theoretical and clinical aspects* (2nd ed.). New York: Free Press.

Semykina, A., & Linz, S. J. (2007). Gender differences in personality and earnings: Evidence from Russia. *Journal of Economic Psychology, 28,* 387–410.

Serpell, R. (2000). Intelligence and culture. In R. Sternberg (Ed.), *Handbook of intelligence.* Cambridge, England: Cambridge University Press.

Serrano, E., & Warnock, J. (2007, October). Depressive disorders related to female reproductive transitions. *Journal of Pharmacy Practice, 20*(5), 385–391.

Seymour, B. (2006). Carry on eating: Neural pathways mediating conditioned potentiation of feeding. *Journal of Neuroscience, 26,* 1061–1062.

Shafer, V. L. & Garrido-Nag, K. (2007). The neurodevelopmental bases of language. In E. Hoff & M. Shatz, *Blackwell handbook of language development.* Malden, MA: Blackwell Publishing. 21–45.

Shao, R., & Skarlicki, D. P. (2009). The role of mindfulness in predicting individual performance. *Canadian Journal of Behavioural Science, 41,* 195–201.

Shapiro, L. R. (2006). Remembering September 11th: The role of retention interval and rehearsal on flashbulb and event memory. *Memory, 14,* 129–147.

Sharif, Z., Bradford, D., Stroup, S., & Lieberman, J. (2007). Pharmacological treatment of schizophrenia. *A guide to treatments that work* (3rd ed.) (pp. 203–241). New York: Oxford University Press.

Sharma, H. S., Sjoquist, P. O., & Ali, S. F. (2007). Drugs of abuse-induced hyperthermia, blood-brain barrier dysfunction and neurotoxicity: Neuroprotective effects of a new antioxidant compound h-290/51. *Current Pharmaceutical Design, 13,* 1903–1923.

Shaver, P., Schwartz, J., Kirson, D., & O'Connor, C. (1987). Emotion knowledge: Further exploration of a prototype approach. *Journal of Personality and Social Psychology, 52,* 1061–1086.

Sheehan, S. (1982). *Is there no place on earth for me?* New York, NY: Houghton Mifflin.

Sheline, Y. I., Gado, M. H., & Kraemer, H. C. (2004). Untreated depression and hippocampal volume loss. *American Journal of Psychiatry, 161*(7), 1309–1310.

Shepard, R. N., Metzler, J., Bisiach, E., Luzzati, C., Kosslyn, S. M., Thompson, W. L., Kim, I., & Alpert, N. M. (2000). Part IV: Imagery. In M. S. Gazzaniga et al. (Eds.), *Cognitive neuro-science: A reader.* Malden, MA: Blackwell.

Shi, P., Huang, J. F., & Zhang, Y. P. (2005). Bitter and sweet/umami taste receptors with differently evolutionary pathways. *Yi Chuan Xue Bao, 32,* 346–353.

Shier, D, Butler, J., Lewis, R. (2000) *Hole's Human Anatomy and Physiology* 8th ed., New York: McGraw-Hill.

Shiffman, S. (2007). Use of more nicotine lozenges leads to better success in quitting smoking. *Addiction, 102,* 809–814.

Shimono, K., & Wade N. J. (2002). Monocular alignment in different depth planes. *Vision Research, 42,* 1127–1135.

Shinn, M., Gottlieb, J., Wett, J. L., Bahl, A., Cohen, A., & Baron, E. D. (2007). Predictors of homelessness among older adults in New York city: disability, economic, human and social capital and stressful events. *Journal of Health Psychology, 12,* 696–708.

Shorey, G. (2000). Bystander non-intervention and the Somalia incident. *Canadian Military Journal,* Retrieved May 9, 2011, www.journal.dnd.ca/vol1/no4/doc/19-28-eng.pdf.

Shurkin, J. N. (1992). *Terman's kids: The ground-breaking study of how the gifted grow up.* Boston: Little, Brown.

Shweder, R.A. & Haidt, J. (1994). The future of moral psychology: Truth, intuition, and the pluralist way. In B. Puka (Ed), *Reaching out: Caring, altruism, and prosocial behavior.* New York: Garland Publishing.

Sidman, M. (2006). The distinction between positive and negative reinforcement: Some additional considerations. *Behavior Analyst, 29,* 135–139.

Siegel, J. M. (2003, November). Why we sleep. *Scientific American,* 92–97.

Siegel, L., & Davis, L. (2008). Somatic disorders. In R. J. Morris, & T. R. Kratochwill, Eds., *The practice of child therapy* (4th ed.) (pp. 249–298). Mahwah, NJ: Lawrence Erlbaum Associates.

Siegel, R. (2005). Psychophysiological Disorders: Embracing Pain. *Mindfulness and psychotherapy* (pp. 173–196). New York: Guilford Press.

Siegel, R. K. (1989). *Intoxication: Life in Pursuit of Artificial Paradise.* New York: Pocket.

Siemer, M., Mauss I., & Gross, J. J. (2007). Same situation—Different emotions: How appraisals shape our emotions. *Emotion, 7,* 592–600.

Sifrit, K. J. (2006). The effects of aging and cognitive decrements on simulated driving performance. *Dissertation Abstracts International: Section B: The Sciences and Engineering, 67,* 2863.

Sigman, M. (1995). Nutrition and child development: More food for thought. *Current Directions in Psychological Science, 4,* 52–55.

Silverstein, M. L. (2007). Rorschach test findings at the beginning of treatment and 2 years later, with a 30-year follow-up. *Journal of Personality Assessment, 88,* 131–143.

Simons, W., & Dierick, M. (2005). Transcranial magnetic stimulation as a therapeutic tool in psychiatry. *World Journal of Biological Psychiatry, 6,* 6–25.

Simonton, D. K. (2003). Scientific creativity as constrained stochastic behavior: the integration of product, person, and process perspectives. *Psychological Bulletin, 129,* 475–494.

Skeptics Dictionary. (2011). *Full moon and lunar effects.* Retrieved April 6, 2011, from www.skepdic.com/fullmoon.html.

Skinner, B. F. (1957). *Verbal behavior.* New York: Appleton-Century-Crofts.

Skinner, B. F. (1975). The steep and thorny road to a science of behavior. *American Psychologist, 30,* 42–49.

Sloan, E. P., Hauri, P., Bootzin, R., Morin, C., et al. (1993). The nuts and bolts of behavioral therapy for insomnia. *Journal of Psychosomatic Research, 37* (Suppl.), 19–37.

Smetana, J. B. (2007). Strategies for understanding archetypes and the collective unconscious of an organization. *Dissertation Abstracts International Section A: Humanities and Social Sciences, 67*(12-A), 4714.

Smith, B. H., Barkley, R. A., & Shapiro, C. J. (2006). Attention-Deficit/Hyperactivity Disorder. In E. J. Mash & R. A. Barkley, *Treatment of childhood disorders* (3rd. ed). New York: Guilford Press.

Smith, C. (2006). Symposium V—Sleep and learning: New developments. *Brain and Cognition, 60, Special issue: Methods and Learning in Functional MRI,* 331–332.

Smith, C. A., & Lazarus, R. S. (2001). Appraisal components, core relational themes, and the emotions. In W. G. Parrott (Ed.), *Emotions in social psychology: Essential readings* (pp. 94–114). Philadelphia: Psychology Press.

Smith, C. D., Chebrolu, J., Wekstein, D. R., Schmitt, F. A., & Markesbery, W. R. (2007). Age and gender effects on human brain anatomy: a voxel-based morphometric study in healthy elderly. *Neurobiology of Aging, 28,* 1057–1087.

Smith, D. (October 2001). Can't get your 40 winks? Here's what the sleep experts advise. *Monitor on Psychology, 37.*

Smith, E. R., & Semin, G. R. (2007). Situated social cognition. *Current Directions in Psychological Science, 16,* 132–135.

Smith, M. B. (2003). Moral foundations in research with human participants. In A. E. Kazdin (Ed.), *Methodological issues & strategies in clinical research* (3rd ed.). Washington, DC: American Psychological Association.

Smith, R. A., & Weber, A. L. (2005). Applying social psychology in everyday life. In F. W. Schneider, J. A. Gruman, & L. M. Coutts, *Applied social psychology: Understanding and addressing social and practical.* Thousand Oaks, CA: Sage Publications.

Smith, W. B. (2007). Karen Horney and psychotherapy in the 21st century. *Clinical Social Work Journal, 35,* 57–66.

Snyder, D. J., Fast, K., & Bartoshuk, L. M. (2004). Valid comparisons of suprathreshold sensations. *Journal of Consciousness Studies, 11,* 96–112.

Snyder, J., Cramer, A., & Afrank, J. (2005). The contributions of ineffective discipline and parental hostile attributions of child misbehavior to the development of conduct problems at home and school. *Developmental Psychology, 41,* 30–41.

Snyder, M. (2002). Applications of Carl Rogers' theory and practice to couple and family therapy: A response to Harlene Anderson and David Bott. *Journal of Family Therapy, 24,* 317–325.

Society for Personality Assessment. (2005). The status of Rorschach in clinical and forensic practice: An official statement by the board of trustees of the Society for Personality Assessment. *Journal of Personality Assessment, 85,* 219–237.

Sohr-Preston, S.L. & Scaramella, L. V. (2006). Implications of timing of maternal depressive symptoms for early cognitive and language development. *Clinical Child Care and Family Review, 9*, 65–83.

Sorbring, E., Deater-Deckard, K., & Palmerus, K. (2006). Girls' and boys' perception of mothers' intentions of using physical punishment and reasoning as discipline methods. *European Journal of Developmental Psychology, 3*, 142–162.

Sori, C. F. (Ed.). (2006). *Engaging children in family therapy: Creative approaches to integrating theory and research in clinical practice.* New York: Routledge/ Taylor & Francis Group.

Soussignan, R. (2002). Duchenne smile, emotional experience, and automatic reactivity: A test of the facial feedback hypothesis. *Emotion, 2*, 52–74.

Spackman, M. P., Fujiki, M., & Brinton, B. (2006). Understanding emotions in context: The effects of language impairment on children's ability to infer emotional reactions. *International Journal of Language & Communication Disorders, 41*, 173–188.

Spangler, W. D. (1992). Validity of questionnaire and TAT measures of need for achievement: Two meta-analyses. *Psychological Bulletin, 112*, 140–154.

Spanos, N. P., Barner, T. X., & Lang, G. (2005). Cognition and self-control: Cognitive control of painful sensory input. *Integrative Physiological & Behavioral Science, 40*, 119–128.

Spanos, N. P., Burgess, C. A., Wallace-Capretta, S., & Ouaida, N. (1996). Simulation, surreptitious observation and modification of hypnotizability: Two tests of the compliance hypothesis. *Contemporary Hypnosis, 13*(3), 161–176.

Spearman, C. (1927). *The abilities of man.* London: Macmillan.

Speirs Neumeister, K. L., & Finch, H. (2006). Perfectionism in high-ability students: Relational precursors and influences on achievement motivation. *Gifted Child Quarterly, 50*, 238–251.

Spence, M. J., & DeCasper, A. J. (1982, March). *Human fetuses perceive maternal speech.* Paper presented at the meeting of the International Conference on Infant Studies, Austin, TX.

Spencer, S. J., Fein, S., Zanna, M. P., & Olson, J. M. (Eds.) (2003). *Motivated social perception: The Ontario Symposium* (Vol. 9). Mahwah, NJ: Erlbaum.

Sperry, R. (1982). Some effects of disconnecting the cerebral hemispheres. *Science, 217*, 1223–1226.

Spiegel, D. (1993). Social support: How friends, family, and groups can help. In D. Goleman & J. Gurin (Eds.), *Mind-body medicine.* Yonkers, NY: Consumer Reports Books.

Spiegel, D. (1996). Hypnosis. In R. E. Hales & S. C. Yudofsky (Eds.), *The American Psychiatric Press synopsis of psychiatry.* Washington, DC: American Psychiatric Press.

Spiegel, D. (Ed.). (1999). *Efficacy and cost-effectiveness of psychotherapy.* New York: American Psychiatric Press.

Spiller, L. D., & Wymer, W. W., Jr. (2001). Physicians' perceptions and use of commercial drug information sources: An examination of pharmaceutical marketing to physicians. *Health Marketing Quarterly, 19*, 91–106.

Spinella, M., & Lester, D. (2006). Can money buy happiness? *Psychological Reports, 99*, 992.

Spitz, H. H. (1987). Problem-solving processes in special populations. In J. G. Borkowski & J. D. Day (Eds.), *Cognition in special children: Comparative approaches to retardation, learning disabilities, and giftedness.* Norwood, NJ: Ablex.

Sprecher, S., & Regan, P. C. (2002). Liking some things (in some people) more than others: Partner preferences in romantic relationships and friendships. *Journal of Social and Personal Relationships, 19*, 436–481.

Sprenkle, D. H., & Moon, S. M. (Eds.). (1996). *Research methods in family therapy.* New York: Guilford Press.

Springen, K. (2004, August 9) Anxiety: Sweet and elusive sleep. *Newsweek,* p. 21.

St. Dennis, C., Hendryx, M., Henriksen, A. L., Setter, S. M., & Singer, B. (2006). Postdischarge treatment costs following closure of a state geropsychiatric ward: Comparison of 2 levels of community care. *Primary Care Companion Journal of Clinical Psychiatry, 8*, 279–284.

Staddon, J. E. R., & Cerutti, D. T. (2003). Operant conditioning. *Annual Review of Psychology, 54*, 115–144.

Staley, J. K., & Sanacora, G., & Tamagnan, G. (2006). Sex differences in diencephalon serotonin transporter availability in major depression. *Biological Psychiatry, 59*, 40–47.

Stankov, L. (2003). Complexity in human intelligence. In R. J. Sternberg, J. Lautrey, et al. (Eds.), *Models of intelligence: International perspectives* (pp. 27–42). Washington, DC: American Psychological Association.

Stanojevic, S., Mitic, K., & Vujic, V. (2007). Exposure to acute physical and psychological stress alters the response of rat macrophages to corticosterone, neuropeptide Y and beta-endorphin. *International Journal on the Biology of Stress, 10*, 65–73.

Stanton, A. L., Danoff-Burg, S., Cameron, C. L., Bishop, M., Collins, C. A., Kirk, S. B., Sworowski, L. A., & Twillman, R. (2000). Emotionally expressive coping predicts psychological and physical adjustment to breast cancer. *Journal of Consulting and Clinical Psychology, 68*, 875–882.

Stapel, D. A., & Semin, G. R. (2007). The magic spell of language: Linguistic categories and their perceptual consequences. *Journal of Personality and Social Psychology, 93*, 23–33.

Starcevic, V., Berle, D., Milicevic, D., Hannan, A., Pamplugh, C., & Eslick, G. D. (2007). Pathological worry, anxiety disorders and the impact of co-occurrence with depressive and other anxiety disorders. *Journal of Anxiety Disorders, 21*, 1016–1027.

Statistics Canada (2004). Adult obesity in Canada: Measured height and weight. Retrieved April 20, 2011 from www.statcan.gc.ca/pub/82-620-m/2005001/ article/adults-adultes/8060-eng.htm.

Statistics Canada (2006). Persons in same-sex unions by broad age groups and sex. Retrieved April 26, 2011, http://www12.statcan.ca/census-recensement/2006/dp-pd/hlt/97-553/pages/page.cfm?Lang=E&Geo=PR& Code=01&Table=3&Data=Count&Age=1&StartRec=1&Sort=2&Display =Page.

Statistics Canada (2008a). Leading causes of death in Canada, Retrieved March 5, 2012, from www.statcan.gc.ca/pub/84-215-x/2011001/hl-fs-eng.htm.

Statistics Canada (2008b). Trends in teenage behaviour and condom use. Michelle Rotterman, Retrieved April 25, 2011, www.statcan.gc.ca/pub/82-003-x/2008003/article/10664-eng.pdf.

Statistics Canada. (2010). Study: Chronic pain in the age group 12 to 44. The Daily, December 15, 2010. Retrieved from www.statcan.gc.ca/daily-quotidien/101215/dq101215b-eng.htm.

Steblay, N., Dysart, J., Fulero, S., & Lindsay, R. C. L. (2003). Eyewitness accuracy rates in police showup and lineup presentations: A meta-analytic comparison. *Law & Human Behavior, 27*, 523–540.

Steele, C. M., & Josephs, R. A. (1990). Alcohol myopia: Its prized and dangerous effects. *American Psychologist, 45*, 921–933.

Steele, J. D., Christmas, D., Eljamel, M. S., & Matthews, K. (2007). Anterior cingulotomy for major depression: clinical outcome and relationship to lesion characteristics. *Biological Psychiatry, 12*, 127–134.

Stegerwald, F., & Janson, G. R. (2003). Conversion therapy: Ethical considerations in family counseling. *Family Journal—Counseling and Therapy for Couples and Families, 11*, 55–59.

Steiger, A. (2007). Neurochemical regulation of sleep. *Journal of Psychiatric Research, 41*, 537–552.

Stein, L. A. R., & Graham, J. R. (2005). Ability of substance abusers to escape detection on the Minnesota Multiphasic Personality Inventory-Adolescent (MMPI-A) in a juvenile correctional facility. *Assessment, 12*, 28–39.

Steiner, B., Wolf, S., & Kempermann, G. (2006). Adult neurogenesis and neurodegenerative disease. *Regenerative Medicine, 1*, 15–28.

Stemler, S. E., & Sternberg, R. J. (2006). Using situational judgment tests to measure practical intelligence. In J. A. Weekley, & R. E. Ployhart, *Situational judgment tests: Theory, measurement, and application.* Mahwah, NJ: Erlbaum.

Stenbacka, L., & Vanni, S. (2007). fMRI of peripheral visual field representation. *Clinical Neurophysiology, 108*, 1303–1314.

Stenklev, N. C., & Laukli, E. (2004). Cortical cognitive potentials in elderly persons. *Journal of the American Academy of Audiology, 15*, 401–413.

Stephens, M., & Townsend, A. (1997, June). Stress of parent care: Positive and negative effects of women's other roles. *Psychology and Aging, 12*(2), 376–386.

Stephenson, R. H., & Banet-Weiser, S. (2007). Super-sized kids: Obesity, children, moral panic, and the media. In J. A. Bryant, *The children's television community.* Mahwah, NJ: Lawrence Erlbaum Associates.

Stern, R. M., & Koch, K. L. (1996). Motion sickness and differential susceptibility. *Current Directions in Psychological Science, 5*, 115–120.

Sternberg, R. J. (1990). *Metaphors of mind: Conceptions of the nature of intelligence.* New York: Cambridge University Press.

Sternberg, R. J. (1998). *Successful intelligence: How practical and creative intelligence determine success in life.* New York: Plume.

Sternberg, R. J. (2000). Intelligence and wisdom. In R. J. Sternberg et al. (Eds.), *Handbook of intelligence.* New York: Cambridge University Press.

Sternberg, R. J. (2001). What is the common thread of creativity? Its dialectical relation to intelligence and wisdom. *American Psychologist, 56,* 360–362.

Sternberg, R. J. (2002a). Individual differences in cognitive development. In U. Goswami (Ed.), Blackwell handbook of childhood cognitive development. *Blackwell handbooks of developmental psychology* (pp. 600–619). Malden, MA: Blackwell.

Sternberg, R. J. (2002b). *Why smart people can be so stupid.* New Haven, CT: Yale University Press.

Sternberg, R. J. (2004). A triangular theory of love. In H. T. Reis & C. E. Rusbult (Eds.), *Close relationships: Key readings.* Philadelphia, PA: Taylor & Francis.

Sternberg, R. J. (2006). A duplex theory of love. In R. J. Sternberg, Ed., *The new psychology of love.* New Haven, CT: Yale University Press.

Sternberg, R. J., & Beall, A. E. (1991). How can we know what love is? An epistemological analysis. In G. J. O. Fletcher & F. D. Fincham (Eds.), *Cognition in close relationships.* Hillsdale, NJ: Erlbaum.

Sternberg, R. J., & Grigorenko, E. L. (2005). Cultural explorations of the nature of intelligence. In A. F. Healy (Ed.), *Experimental cognitive psychology and its applications.* Washington, DC: American Psychological Association.

Sternberg, R. J., & Hedlund, J. (2002). Practical intelligence, "g," and work psychology. *Human Performance, 15,* 143–160.

Sternberg, R. J., & Jarvin, L. (2003). Alfred Binet's contributions as a paradigm for impact in psychology. In R. J. Sternberg (Ed.), *The anatomy of impact: What makes the great works of psychology great* (pp. 89–107). Washington, DC: American Psychological Association.

Sternberg, R. J., & O'Hara, L. A. (2000). Intelligence and creativity. In R. Sternberg et al. (Eds.), *Handbook of intelligence.* New York: Cambridge University Press.

Sternberg, R. J., & Pretz, J. E. (2005). *Cognition and intelligence: Identifying the mechanisms of the mind.* New York: Cambridge University Press, 2005.

Sternberg, R. J., Grigorenko, E. L., & Kidd, K. K. (2005). Intelligence, race, and genetics. *American Psychologist, 60,* 46–59.

Sternberg, R. J., Hojjat, M., & Barnes, M. L. (2001). Empirical aspects of a theory of love as a story. *European Journal of Personality, 15,* 1–20.

Stettler, N., Stallings, V. A., Troxel, A. B., Zhao. J., Z., Schinnar, R., Nelson, S. E., Ziegler, E. E., Strom, B. L. (2005). Weight gain in the first week of life and overweight in adulthood. *Circulation, 111,* 1897–1903.

Stevens, G., & Gardner, S. (1982). *The women of psychology: Pioneers and innovators* (Vol. 1). Cambridge, MA: Schenkman.

Stevens, P. & Harper, D. J. (2007). Professional accounts of electroconvulsive therapy: A discourse analysis. *Social Science & Medicine, 64,* 1475–1486.

Stevenson, H. W., Lee, S., & Mu, X. (2000). Successful achievement in mathematics: China and the United States. In C. F. M. van Lieshout & P. G. Heymans (Eds.), *Developing talent across the life span.* New York: Psychology Press.

Stevenson, R. J., & Case, T. I. (2005). Olfactory imagery: A review. *Psychonomic Bulletin and Review, 12,* 244–264.

Stickgold, R. A., Winkelman, J. W., & Wehrwein, P. (2004, January 19). You will start to feel very sleepy . . . *Newsweek,* pp. 58–60.

Stickgold, R., Hobson, J. A., Fosse, R., & Fosse, M. (2001, November 2). Sleep, learning, and dreams: Off-line memory reprocessing. *Science, 294,* pp. 1052–1057.

Stimson, G., Grant, M., Choquet, M., & Garrison, P. (2007). *Drinking in context: Patterns, interventions, and partnerships.* New York: Routledge/Taylor & Francis Group.

Stockton, R., Morran, D. K., & Krieger, K. M. (2004). An overview of current research and best practices for training beginning group leaders. In J. L. DeLucia-Waack, D. A. Gerrity, C. R. Kalodner, & M. T. Riva (Eds.), *Handbook of group counseling and psychotherapy.* Thousand Oaks, CA: Sage Publications.

Stompe, T., Ortwein-Swoboda, G., Ritter, K., & Schanda, H. (2003). Old wine in new bottles? Stability and plasticity of the contents of schizophrenic delusions. *Psychopathology, 36,* 6–12.

Stouffer, E. M., & White, N. M. (2006). Neural circuits mediating latent learning and conditioning for salt in the rat. *Neurobiology of Learning and Memory, 86,* 91–99.

Strange, D., Clifasefi, S., & Garry, M. (2007). False memories. In M. Garry, & H. Hayne, *Do justice and let the sky fall: Elizabeth Loftus and her contributions to science, law, and academic freedom.* Mahwah, NJ: Lawrence Erlbaum Associates.

Strathern, A., & Stewart, P. J. (2003). *Landscape, memory and history: Anthropological perspectives.* London: Pluto Press.

Strauss, E. (1998, May 8). Writing, speech separated in split brain. *Science, 280,* 287.

Strayer, D. L., & Drews, F. A. (2007). Cell-phone-induced driver distraction. *Current Directions in Psychological Science, 16,* 128–131.

Striano, T., & Vaish, A. (2006). Seven- to 9-month-old infants use facial expressions to interpret others' actions. *British Journal of Developmental Psychology, 24,* 753–760.

Striegel-Moore, R., & Bulik, C. M. (2007). Risk factors for eating disorders. *American Psychologist, 62,* 181–198.

Strong, T., & Tomm, K. (2007). Family therapy as re-coordinating and moving on together. *Journal of Systemic Therapies, 26,* 42–54.

Stronski, S. M., Ireland, M., & Michaud, P. (2000). Protective correlates of stages in adolescent substance use: A Swiss national study. *Journal of Adolescent Health, 26,* 420–427.

Stroup, T., Kraus, J., & Marder, S. (2006). Pharmacotherapies. *The American Psychiatric Publishing Textbook of Schizophrenia* (pp. 303–325). Arlington, VA: American Psychiatric Publishing, Inc.

Strupp, H. H. (1996, October). The tripartite model and the Consumer Reports study. *American Psychologist, 51,* 1017–1024.

Strupp, H. H., & Binder, J. L. (1992). Current developments in psychotherapy. *The Independent Practitioner, 12,* 119–124.

Suh, E. M. (2002). Culture, identity consistency, and subjective well-being. *Journal of Personality & Social Psychology, 83,* 1378–1391.

Suhail, K., & Chaudhry, H. R. (2004). Predictors of subjective well-being in an Eastern Muslim culture. *Journal of Social and Clinical Psychology, 23,* 359–376.

Suizzo, M-A., & Bornstein, M. H. (2006). French and European American child-mother play: Culture and gender considerations. *International Journal of Behavioral Development, 30,* 498–508.

Summerfeldt, L. J., Kloosterman, P. H., Antony, M. M., McCabe, R. E., & Parker, J. D. A. (2011).Emotional intelligence in social phobia and other anxiety disorders. *Journal of Psychopathology and Behavioural Assessment, 33,* 69–78.

Sun, T., Patoine, C., Abu-Khalil, A., Visvader, J., Sum, E., Cherry, T. J., Orkink, S. H., Geschwind, D. H., & Walsh, C. A. (2005, June 17). Early asymmetry of gene transcriptions in embryonic human left and right cerebral cortex. *Science, 308,* 1794–1796.

Surette, R. (2002). Self-reported copycat crime among a population of serious and violent juvenile offenders. *Crime & Delinquency, 48,* 46–69.

Sutin, A. R., & Robins, R. W. (2007). Phenomenology of autobiographical memories: The Memory Experiences Questionnaire. *Memory, 15,* 390–411.

Svartdal, F. (2003). Extinction after partial reinforcement: Predicted vs. judged persistence. *Scandinavian Journal of Psychology, 44,* 55–64.

Swain, P. I. (2006). *New developments in eating disorders research.* Hauppauge, NY: Nova Science Publishers.

Swann, W. B., Jr., Chang-Schneider, C., & Larsen McClarty, K. (2007). Do people's self-views matter? Self-concept and self-esteem in everyday life. *American Psychologist, 62,* 84–94.

Swanson, H. L., Harris, K. R., & Graham, S. (Eds.). (2003). *Handbook of learning disabilities.* New York: Guilford Press.

Swithers, S. E. & Davidson, T. L. (2008). A Role for Sweet Taste: Calorie Predictive Relations in Energy Regulation by Rats. *Behavioral Neuroscience, 122,* 1.

Szasz, T. (1994). *Cruel compassion: Psychiatric control of society's unwanted.* New York: Wiley.

T

Tajfel, H., & Turner, J. C. (2004). The social identity theory of intergroup behavior. In J. T. Jost & J. Sidanius (Eds.), *Political psychology: Key readings.* New York: Psychology Press.

Takahashi, M., Nakata, A., Haratani, T., Ogawa, Y., & Arito, H. (2004). Post-lunch nap as a worksite intervention to promote alertness on the job. *Ergonomics, 47,* 1003–1013.

Takahashi, T., & Washington, W. (1991, January). A group-centered object relations approach to group psychotherapy with severely disturbed patients. *International Journal of Group Psychotherapy, 41*(1), 79–96.

Takizawa, T., Kondo, T., & Sakihara, S. (2007). Stress buffering effects of social support on depressive symptoms in middle age: Reciprocity and community mental health: Corrigendum. *Psychiatry and Clinical Neurosciences, 61*, 336–337.

Talukdar, S., & Shastri, J. (2006). Contributory and adverse factors in social development of young children. *Psychological Studies, 51*, 294–303.

Tanner, J. M. (1978). *Foetus into man: Physical growth from conception to maturity*. Cambridge, MA: Harvard University Press.

Tanner, J. M. (1990). *Foetus into man: Physical growth from conception to maturity* (rev. ed.). Cambridge, MA: Harvard University Press.

Taras, H., & Potts-Dema, W. (2005). Chronic health conditions and student performance at school. *Journal of School Health, 75*, 255–266.

Taylor, F., & Bryant, R. A. (2007). The tendency to suppress, inhibiting thoughts, and dream rebound. *Behaviour Research and Therapy, 45*, 163–168.

Taylor, S. E., Kemeny, M. E., Reed, G. M., Bower, J. E., & Gruenewald, T. L. (2000). Psychological resources, positive illusions, and health. *American Psychologist, 55*, 99–109.

Teff, K. L., Petrova, M., & Havel, P. J. (2007). 48-h Glucose infusion in humans: Effect on hormonal responses, hunger and food intake. *Physiology & Behavior, 90*, 733–743.

Tellegen, A., Lykken, D. T., Bouchard, T. J., Jr., Wilcox, K. J., Segal, N. L., & Rich, S. (1988). Personality similarity in twins reared apart and together. *Journal of Personality and Social Psychology, 54*, 1031–1039.

Templer, D. I., & Arkawa, H. (2006). Association of race and color with mean IQ across nations. *Psychological Reports, 99*, 191–196.

Tenenbaum, H. R., & Ruck, M. D. (2007). Are teachers' expectations different for racial minority than for European American students? A meta-analysis. *Journal of Educational Psychology, 99*, 253–273.

Tenopyr, M. L. (2002). Theory versus reality: Evaluation of 'g' in the workplace. *Human Performance, 15*, 107–122.

Teodorov, E., Salzgerber, S. A., Felicio, L. F., Varolli, F. M. F., & Bernardi, M. M. (2002). Effects of perinatal picrotoxin and sexual experience on heterosexual and homosexual behavior in male rats. *Neurotoxicology and Teratology, 24*, 235–245.

Tervaniemi, M., Jacobsen, T., & Röttger, S. (2006). Selective tuning of cortical sound-feature processing by language experience. *European Journal of Neuroscience, 23*, 2538–2541.

Thatcher, D. L., & Clark, D. B., (2006). Adolescent alcohol abuse and dependence: Development, diagnosis, treatment and outcomes. *Current Psychiatry Reviews, 2*, 159–177.

The Turtle Lodge. Makoose Ka Win & The Vision Quest, Retrieved May 26, 2011, www.theturtlelodge.org/visionquest.html.

Thompson, J. (2000, June 18). "I was certain, but I was wrong." *The New York Times*, p. E14.

Thompson, P. M., Hayaski, K. M., Simon, S. L., Geaga, J. A., Hong, M. S., Sui, Y., Lee, J. Y., Toga, A. W., Ling, W., & London, E. D. (2004, June 30). Structural abnormalities in the brains of human subjects who use methamphetamine. *The Journal of Neuroscience, 24*(26), 6028–6036.

Thornton, A., & Young-DeMarco, L. (2001). Four decades of trends in attitudes toward family issues in the United States: The 1960s through the 1990s. *Journal of Marriage and the Family, 63*, 1009–1017.

Thrash, T. M., & Elliot, A. J. (2002). Implicit and self-attributed achievement motives: Concordance and predictive validity. *Journal of Personality, 70*, 729–755.

Titone, D. A. (2002). Memories bound: The neuroscience of dreams. *Trends in Cognitive Science, 6*, 4–5.

Tolman, E. C., & Honzik, C. H. (1930). Introduction and removal of reward and maze performance in rats. *University of California Publications in Psychology, 4*, 257–275.

Toth, J. P., & Daniels, K. A. (2002). Effects of prior experience on judgments of normative word frequency: Automatic bias and correction. *Journal of Memory and Language, 46*, 845–874.

Tov, W., & Diener, E. (2007). Culture and subjective well-being. In S. Kitayama (Ed.), *Handbook of cultural psychology* (pp. 691–713). New York: Guilford Press.

Tracy, J. L., & Robins, R. W. (2004). Show your pride: Evidence for a discrete emotion expression. *Psychological Science, 15*, 194–197.

Travis, F. (2006). From I to I: Concepts of self on a object-referral/self-referral continuum. In A. P. Prescott, *The concept of self in psychology*. Hauppauge, NY: Nova Science Publishers.

Treas, J. (2004). Sex and Family: Changes and Challenges. *The blackwell companion to the sociology of families* (pp. 397–415). Malden: Blackwell Publishing.

Tremblay, A. (2004). Dietary fat and body weight set point. *Nutrition Review, 62*(7 Pt 2), S75–S77.

Tropp, L. R., & Bianchi, R. A. (2006). Valuing diversity and interest in intergroup contact. *Journal of Social Issues, 62*, 533–551.

Tropp, L. R., & Pettigrew, T. F. (2005). Differential relationships between intergroup contact and affective and cognitive dimensions of prejudice. *Personality and Social Psychology Bulletin, 31*, 1145–1158.

Tropp, L. R., Stout, A. M., Boatswain, C., Wright, S. C., & Pettigrew, T. F. (2006). Trust and acceptance inresponse to references to group membership: Minority and majority perspectives on cross-group interactions. *Journal of Applied Social Psychology, 36*, 769–794.

Troyer, A. K., Häfliger, A., & Cadieux, M. J. (2006). Name and face learning in older adults: Effects of level of processing, self-generation, and intention to learn. *Journals of Gerontology: Series B: Psychological Sciences and Social Sciences, 61*, P67–P74.

Trull, T. J, Solhan, M.B., and Watson, D. (2008). Affective instability: Measuring a core feature of borderline personality disorder with ecological momentary assessment. *Journal of Abnormal Psychology, 117*(3): 647–661.

Trull, T. J., & Widiger, T. A. (2003). Personality disorders. In. G. Stricker, T. A. Widiger, et al. (Eds.), *Handbook of psychology: Clinical psychology* (Vol. 8) (pp. 149–172). New York: Wiley.

Trull, T. J., Stepp, S. D., & Durrett, C. A. (2003). Research on borderline personality disorder: An update. *Current Opinion in Psychiatry, 16*, 77–82.

Tryon, W. W. (2005). Possible mechanisms for why desensitization and exposure therapy work. *Clinical Psychology Review, 25*, 67–95.

Tsai, K. J., Tsai, Y. C., & Shen, C. K. (2007). GCSF rescues the memory impairment of animal models of Alzheimer's disease. *Journal of Experimental Medicine, 11*, 1273–1289.

Tsaousis, I., Nikolaou, I., & Serdaris, N. (2007). Do the core self-evaluations moderate the relationship between subjective well-being and physical and psychological health? *Personality and Individual Differences, 42*, 1441–1452.

Tse, W. S., & Bond, A. J. (2004). The impact of depression on social skills: A review. *Journal of Nervous and Mental Disease, 192*(4), 260–268.

Tseng, W. S. (2003). *Clinician's guide to cultural psychiatry*. San Diego: Elsevier Publishing.

Tudor, K. (2008). Person-centred therapy, a cognitive behaviour therapy. *Against and for CBT: Towards a constructive dialogue?* (pp. 118–136). Ross-on-Wye: PCCS Books.

Tuerlinckx, F., De Boeck, P., & Lens, W. (2002). Measuring needs with the Thematic Apperception Test: A psychometric study. *Journal of Personality and Social Psychology, 82*, 448–461.

Tugay, N., Akbayrak, T., Demirturk, F., Karakaya, I. C., Kocaacar, O., Tugay, U., Karakay, M. G., & Demirturk, F. (2007). Effectiveness of transcutaneous electrical nerve stimulation and interferential current in primary dysmenorrhea. *Pain Medicine, 8*, 295–300.

Tulving, E. (2000). Concepts of memory. In E. Tulving, F. I. M. Craik, et al. (Eds.). *The Oxford handbook of memory*. New York: Oxford University Press.

Tulving, E. (2002). Episodic memory and common sense: How far apart? In A. Baddeley & J. P. Aggleton (Eds.), *Episodic memory: New directions in research* (pp. 269–287). London: Oxford University Press.

Tulving, E., & Psotka, J. (1971). Retroactive inhibition in free recall: Inaccessibility of information available in the memory store. *Journal of Experimental Psychology, 87*, 1–8.

Tulving, E., & Thompson, D. M. (1983). Encoding specificity and retrieval processes in episodic memory. *Psychological Review, 80*, 352–373.

Turk, D. C. (1994). Perspectives on chronic pain: The role of psychological factors. *Current Directions in Psychological Science, 3*, 45–49.

Turkewitz, G. (1993). The origins of differential hemispheric strategies for information processing in the relationships between voice and face perception. In B. de Boysson-Bardies, S. de Schonen, P. W. Jusczyk, P. McNeilage, & J. Morton (Eds.), *Developmental neurocognition: Speech and face processing in the first year of life. NATO ASI series D: Behavioural and social sciences* (Vol. 69). Dordrecht: Kluwer Academic.

Turnbull, C. (1961). *Some observations regarding the experiences and behavior of the BaMbuti Pygmies*. Urbana-Champaign, IL: University of Illinois Press.

Turner, W. J. (1995). Homosexuality, Type 1: An Xq28 phenomenon. *Archives of Sexual Behavior, 24*, 109–134.

Turtle, J., Lindsay, R. C. L., & Wells, G. L. (2003). Best practice recommendations for eyewitness identification procedures. *Canadian Journal of Police and Security Services, 1*, 5–18.

Tuszynski, M. H. (2007). Nerve growth factor gene therapy in Alzheimer disease. *Alzheimer's Disease and Associated Disorders, 21*, 179–1898.

Tversky, A., & Kahneman, D. (1973, September). Availability: A heuristic for judging frequency and probability. *Cognitive Psychology, 5*(2), 207–232.

Tversky, A., & Kahneman, D. (1987). Rational choice and the framing of decisions. In R. Hogarth & M. Reder (Eds.), *Rational choice: The contrast between economics and psychology*. Chicago: University of Chicago Press.

U

U.S. Bureau of the Census. (2000). *Census 2000*. Retrieved from American Fact Finder http://factfinder.census.gov/servlet/BasicFactsServlet.

Ubell, E. (1993, January 10). Could you use more sleep? *Parade*, 16–18.

Ulmer, M. (2011). Yoga craze hits Leafs. Mapleleaf.com. Retrieved March 22, 2012, from http://mapleleafs.nhl.com/club/news.htm?id=596472.

Umphress, E. E., Smith-Crowe, K., & Brief, A. P. (2007). When birds of a feather flock together and when they do not: Status composition, social dominance orientation, and organizational attractiveness. *Journal of Applied Psychology, 92*, 396–409.

Underwood, A. (2003, April 7). Shining a light on pain. *Newsweek*, p. 31.

Underwood, A. (2005, October 3). The Good Heart. *Newsweek*, p. 49.

Unsworth, N., & Engle, R. W. (2005). Individual differences in working memory capacity and learning: Evidence from the serial reaction time task. *Memory and Cognition, 33*, 213–220.

Updegraff, K. A., Helms, H. M., McHale, S. M., Crouter, A. C., Thayer, S. M., & Sales, L. H. (2004). Who's the boss? Patterns of perceived control in adolescents' friendships. *Journal of Youth & Adolescence, 33*, 403–420.

Uttl, B., Graf, P., & Cosentino, S. (2003). Implicit memory for new associations: Types of conceptual representations. In J. S. Bowers & C. J. Marsolek (Eds.), *Rethinking implicit memory* (pp. 302–323). London: Oxford University Press.

Uylings, H. B. M. (2006). Development of the human cortex and the concept of 'critical' or 'sensitive' periods. *Language Learning, 56*, 59–90.

V

Vagg, R., & Chapman, S. (2005, May). Nicotine analogues: A review of tobacco industry research interests. *Addiction, 100*(5), 701–712.

Vaillant, G. E., & Vaillant, C. O. (1990). Natural history of male psychological health: XII. A 46-year study of predictors of successful aging at age 65. *American Journal of Psychiatry, 147*, 31–37.

Valencia, R. R., & Suzuki, L. A. (2003). *Intelligence testing and minority students: Foundations, performance factors, and assessment issues*. Thousand Oaks, CA: Sage.

Valente, S. M. (1991). Electroconvulsive therapy. *Archives of Psychiatric Nursing, 5*, 223–228.

Van Ameringen, M. V., Mancini, C., Patterson, B., & Boyle, M. H. (2008). Post-Traumatic Stress Disorder in Canada. *CNS Neuroscience & Therapeutics, 14*, 3, 171–181.

Van Beekum, S. (2005). The therapist as a new object. *Transactional Analysis Journal, 35*, 187–191.

van den Brink, W., & van Ree, J. (2003, December). Pharmacological treatments for heroin and cocaine addiction. *European Neuropsychopharmacology, 13*(6), 476–487.

Van den Wildenberg, W. P. M., & Van der Molen, M. W. (2004). Developmental trends in simple and selective inhibition of compatible and incompatible responses. *Journal of Experimental Child Psychology, 87*, 201–220.

van der Helm, P. A. (2006). Review of perceptual dynamics: Theoretical foundations and philosophical implications of gestalt psychology. *Philosophical Psychology, 19*, 274–279.

van Hooren, S. A. H., Valentijn, A. M., & Bosma, H. (2007). Cognitive functioning in healthy older adults aged 64–81: a cohort study into the effects of age, sex, and education. *Aging, Neuropsychology, and Cognition, 14*, 40–54.

Van Overwalle, F., & Siebler, F. (2005). A Connectionist model of attitude formation and change. *Personality and Social Psychology Review, 9*, 231–274.

Vanasse, A., Niyonsenga, T., & Courteau, J. (2004). Smoking cessation within the context of family medicine: Which smokers take action? *Preventive Medicine: An International Journal Devoted to Practice and Theory, 38*, 330–337.

Vandervert, L. R., Schimpf, P. H., & Liu, H. (2007). How working memory and the cerebellum collaborate to produce creativity and innovation. *Creativity Research Journal, 19*, 1–18.

Varma, S. (2007). A computational model of Tower of Hanoi problem solving. *Dissertation Abstracts International: Section B: The Sciences and Engineering, 67*(8-B), 4736.

Vaughn, L. A., & Weary, G. (2002). Roles of the availability of explanations, feelings of ease, and dysphoria in judgments about the future. *Journal of Science and Clinical Psychology, 21*, 686–704.

Veasey, S., Rosen, R., Barzansky, B., Rosen, I., & Owens, J. (2002). Sleep loss and fatigue in residency training: A reappraisal. *Journal of the American Medical Association, 288*, 1116–1124.

Veltman, M. W. M., & Browne, K. D. (2001). Three decades of child mal-treatment research: Implications for the school years. *Trauma Violence and Abuse, 2*, 215–239.

Veniegas, R. C. (2000). Biological research on women's sexual orientations: Evaluating the scientific evidence. *Journal of Social Issues, 56*, 267–282.

Venning, A., Kettler, L., Eliott, J., & Wilson, A. (2009, March). The effectiveness of cognitive–behavioural therapy with hopeful elements to prevent the development of depression in young people: A systematic review. *International Journal of Evidence-Based Healthcare, 7*(1), 15–33.

Verdejo, A., Toribio, I., & Orozco, C. (2005). Neuropsychological functioning in methadone maintenance patients versus abstinent heroin abusers. *Drug and Alcohol Dependence, 78*, 283–288.

Verfaellie, M., & Keane, M. M. (2002). Impaired and preserved memory processes in amnesia. In L. R. Squire & D. L. Schacter (Eds.), *Neuropsychology of memory* (3rd ed.). New York: Guilford Press.

Viding, E., Blair, R. J., Moffitt, T. E., & Plomin, R. (2005). Evidence for substantial genetic risk for psychopathy in 7-year-olds. *Journal of Child Psychology and Psychiatry, 46*, 592–597.

Vieira, E. M., & Freire, J. C. (2006). Alteridade e Psicologia Humanista: Uma leitura ética da abordagem centrada na pessoa. Alterity and humanistic psychology: An ethical reading of the Person-Centered Approach. *Estudos de Psicologia, 23*, 425–432.

Villablanca, J., de Andrés, I., & Garzón, M. (2003, September). Debating how rapid eye movement sleep is regulated (and by what). *Journal of Sleep Research, 12*(3), 259–262.

Villemure, C., Slotnick, B. M., & Bushnell, M. C. (2003). Effects of odors on pain perception: Deciphering the roles of emotion and attention. *Pain, 106*, 101–108.

Vitiello, A. L., Bonello, R. P., & Pollard, H. P. (2007). The effectiveness of ENAR(R) for the treatment of chronic neck pain in Australian adults: A preliminary single-blind, randomised controlled trial. *Chiropractic Osteopathology, 9*, 9.

Vleioras, G., & Bosma, H. A. (2005). Are identity styles important for psychological well-being? *Journal of Adolescence, 28*, 397–409.

Voicu, H., & Schmajuk, N. (2002). Latent learning, shortcuts and detours: A computational model. *Behavioural Processes, 59*, 67–86.

Volterra, V., Caselli, M. C., Capirci, O., Tonucci, F., & Vicari, S. (2003). Early linguistic abilities of Italian children with Williams syndrome [Special issue: Williams syndrome]. *Developmental Neuropsychology, 23*, 33–58.

Voruganti, L. P., Awad, A. G., Parker, B., Forrest, C., Usmani, Y., Fernando, M. L. D., & Senthilal, S. (2007). Cognition, functioning and quality of life in schizophrenia treatment: Results of a one-year randomized controlled trial of olanzapine and quetiapine. *Schizophrenia Research, 96*, 146–155.

Vygotsky, L. S. (1926/1997). *Educational psychology*. Delray Beach, FL: St. Lucie Press.

W

Waber, R. L., Shiv, B., Carmon, Z., & Ariely, D. (2008), Commercial Features of Placebo and Therapeutic Efficiency. *Journal of the American Medical Association, 299*, 1016–1017.

Wadden, T. A., Crerand, C. E., & Brock, J. (2005). Behavioral treatment of obesity. *Psychiatric Clinics of North America, 28*, 151–170.

Wade, K. A., Sharman, S. J., & Garry, M. (2007). False claims about false memory research. *Consciousness and Cognition: An International Journal, 16*, 18–28.

Wagner, E. F., & Atkins, J. H. (2000). Smoking among teenage girls. *Journal of Child & Adolescent Substance Abuse, 9*, 93–110.

Wagner, H. J., Bollard, C. M., Vigouroux, S., Huls, M. H., Anderson, R., Prentice, H. G., Brenner, M. K., Heslop, H. E., & Rooney, C. M. (2004). A strategy for treatment of Epstein Barr virus- positive Hodgkin's disease by targeting interleukin 12 to the tumor environment using tumor antigen-specific T cells. *Cancer Gene Therapy, 2*, 81–91.

Wagner, R. K. (2002). Smart people doing dumb things: The case of managerial incompetence. In R. J. Sternberg (Ed.), *Why smart people can be so stupid* (pp. 42–63). New Haven, CT: Yale University Press.

Walker, W. R., Skowronski, J. J., & Thompson, C. P. (2003). Consolidation of long-term memory: Evidence and alternatives. *Review of General Psychology, 7*, 203–210.

Wallerstein, J. S., Lewis, J., Blakeslee, S., & Lewis, J. (2000). *The unexpected legacy of divorce.* New York: Hyperion.

Walsh, B. T., Kaplan, A. S., Attia, E., Olmstead, M., Parides, M., Carter, J. C., Pike, K. M., Devlin, M. J., Woodside, B., Robert, C. A., & Rockert, W. (2006). Fluoxetine after weight restoration in anorexia nervosa: A randomized controlled trial. *JAMA: Journal of the American Medical Association, 295*, 2605–2612.

Wang, A., & Clark, D. A. (2002). Haunting thoughts: The problem of obsessive mental intrusions [Special issue: Intrusions in cognitive behavioral therapy]. *Journal of Cognitive Psychotherapy, 16*, 193–208.

Wang, P. S., Aguilar-Gaxiola, S., Alonso, J., Angermeyer, M. C., Borges, G., Bromet, E. J., Bruffaerts, R., deGirolamo, G., deGraaf, R., Gureje, O., Haro, J. M., Karam, E. G., Kessler, R. C., Kovess, V., Lane, M. C., Lee, S., Levinson, D., Ono, Y., Petukhova, M., Posada-Villa, J., Seedat, S., & Wells, J. E. (2007, September 8). Use of mental health services for anxiety, mood, and substance disorders in 17 countries in the WHO world mental health surveys. *Lancet, 370*, 841–850.

Wang, Q. (2004). The emergence of cultural self-constructs: autobiographical memory and self-description in European American and Chinese children. *Developmental Psychology, 40*, 3–15.

Wang, Q., & Conway, M. A. (2006). Autobiographical memory, self, and culture. In L-G. Nilsson & N. Ohta, *Memory and society: Psychological perspectives.* New York: Psychology Press.

Wang, Q., & Ross, M. (2007). Culture and memory. *Handbook of cultural psychology* (pp. 645–667). New York: Guilford Press.

Wang, X., Lu, T., Snider, R. K., & Liang, L. (2005). Sustained firing in auditory cortex evoked by preferred stimuli. *Nature, 435*, 341–346.

Ward, L. M. (2004). Wading through the stereotypes: Positive and negative associations between media use and Black adolescents' conceptions of self. *Developmental Psychology, 40*, 284–294.

Ward, W. C., Kogan, N., & Pankove, E. (1972). Incentive effects in children's creativity. *Child Development, 43*, 669–677.

Ward-Baker, P. D. (2007). The remarkable oldest old: A new vision of aging. *Dissertation Abstracts International Section A: Humanities and Social Sciences, 67*(8-A), 3115.

Warden, C. A., Wu, W-Y., & Tsai, D. (2006). Online shopping interface components: relative importance as peripheral and central cues. *CyberPsychology & Behavior, 9*, 285–296.

Warriner, A.B., & Humphreys, K. (2008). Learning to fail: Reoccurring tip-of-the-tongue states. *The Quarterly Journal of Experimental Psychology, 61*(4), 535–542.

Waslenki, D. (2008). A century of learning, a century of caring. University of Toronto Department of Psychiatry. Retrieved March 15, 2012, www.utpsychiatry.ca/wp-content/uploads/2010/12/AnnualReport2007-08-Centenary.pdf.

Wass, T. S., Mattson, S. N., & Riley, E. P. (2004). Neuroanatomical and neurobehavioral effects of heavy prenatal alcohol exposure. In J. Brick (Ed.), *Handbook of the medical consequences of alcohol and drug abuse.* (pp. 139–169). New York: Haworth Press.

Watson, D., Hubbard, B., & Wiese, D. (2000). Self-other agreement in personality and affectivity: The role of acquaintanceship, trait visibility, and assumed similarity. *Journal of Personality and Social Psychology, 78*, 546–558.

Watson, J. & Rayner, R. (1920). Conditioned emotional responses. *Journal of Experimental Psychology, 3*, 1–14.

Watson, M., Haviland, J. S., Greer, S., Davidson, J., & Bliss, J. M. (1999). Influence of psychological response on survival in breast cancer: a population-based cohort study. *Lancet, 354*, 1331–1336.

Weber, R., Ritterfeld, U., & Kostygina, A. (2006). Aggression and violence as effects of playing violent video games? In P. Vorderer & J. Bryant, *Playing video games: Motives, responses, and consequences.* Mahwah, NJ: Lawrence Erlbaum Associates.

Wechsler, H., Davenport, A., Dowdall, G., Moeykens, B., & Castillo, S. (1994). Health and behavioral consequences of binge drinking in college. A national survey of students at 140 campuses. *Journal of the American Medical Association, 272*, 1672–1677.

Wechsler, H., Kuo, M., Lee, H., & Dowdall, G. W. (2000). *Environmental correlates of underage alcohol use and related problems of college students.* Cambridge, MA: Harvard School of Public Health.

Wechsler, H., Lee, J. E., Nelson, T. F., & Kuo, M. (2002). Underage college students' drinking behavior, access to alcohol, and the influence of deterrence policies. *Journal of American College Health, 50*, 223–236.

Wegener, D. T., Petty, R. E., Smoak, N. D., & Fabrigar, L. R. (2004). Multiple routes to resisting attitude change. In E. S. Knowles & J. A. Linn (Eds.), *Resistance and persuasion.* Mahwah, NJ: Lawrence Erlbaum Associates.

Weinberg, M. S., Williams, C. J., & Pryor, D. W. (1991, February 27). *Personal communication.* Indiana University, Bloomington.

Weiner, I. B. (2004). Rorschach Inkblot method. In M. E. Maruish (Ed.), *Use of psychological testing for treatment planning and outcomes assessment: Instruments for adults* (Vol. 3) (3rd ed.). Mahwah, NJ: Lawrence Erlbaum Associates.

Weinstein, M., Glei, D. A., Yamazaki, A., & Ming-Cheng, C. (2004). The role of intergenerational relations in the association between life stressors and depressive symptoms. *Research on Aging, 26*, 511–530.

Weis, R., Crockett, T. E., & Vieth, S. (2004). Using MMPI-A profiles to predict success in a military-style residential treatment program for adolescents with academic and conduct problems. *Psychology in the Schools, 41*, 563–574.

Weissman, M., Bland, R. C., Canino, G. J., Faravelli, C., Greenwald, S., Hwu, H. G., Joyce, P. R., Karam, E. G., Lee, C. K., Lellouch, J., Lepine, J. P., Newman, S. C., Rubio-Stipec, M., Wells, J. E., Wickramarante, P. J., Wittchen, H., & Yeh, E. K. (1997, July 24–31). Cross-national epidemiology of major depression and bipolar disorder. *Journal of the American Medical Association, 276*, 293–299.

Weissman, M., Markowitz, J., & Klerman, G. L. (2007). *Clinician's quick guide to interpersonal psychotherapy.* New York: Oxford University Press.

Weisz, A., & Black, B. (2002). Gender and moral reasoning: African American youth respond to dating dilemmas. *Journal of Human Behavior in the Social Environment, 5*, 35–52.

Welkowitz, L. A., Struening, E. L., Pittman, J., Guardino, M., & Welkowitz, J. (2000). Obsessive-compulsive disorder and comorbid anxiety problems in a national anxiety screening sample. *Journal of Anxiety Disorders, 14*, 471–482.

Wells, G. L., Olson, E. A., & Charman, S. D. (2002). The confidence of eyewitnesses in their identifications from lineups. *Current Directions in Psychological Science, 11*, 151–154.

Wen, C. P., Wai, J. P. M., Tsai, M. K., et al. (2011). Minimum amount of physical activity for reduced mortality and extended life expectancy: a prospective cohort study. *The Lancet, 378*, 9798, 1244–1253.

Wenzel, A., Zetocha, K., & Ferraro, R. F. (2007). Depth of processing and recall of threat material in fearful and nonfearful individuals. *Anxiety, Stress & Coping: An International Journal, 20*, 223–237.

Werblin, F., & Roska, B. (2007, April). The movies in our eyes. *Scientific American*, 73–77.

Werker, J. F., & Tees, R. C. (2005). Speech perception as a window for understanding plasticity and commitment in language systems of the brain. *Developmental Psychobiology, 46*, 233–234.

Wertheimer, M. (1923). Untersuchungen zur Lehre von der Gestalt, II. *Psychologische Forschung, 5*, 301–350. In R. Beardsley and M. Wertheimer (Eds.) (1958), *Readings in perception.* New York: Van Nostrand.

West, D. S., Harvey-Berino, J., & Raczynski, J. M. (2004). Behavioral aspects of obesity, dietary intake, and chronic disease. In J. M. Raczynski and L. C. Leviton (Eds.), *Handbook of clinical health psychology: Disorders of behavior and health* (Vol. 2) (pp. 9–41). Washington, DC: American Psychological Association.

West, J. R., & Blake, C. A. (2005). Fetal alcohol syndrome: An assessment of the field. *Experimental Biological Medicine, 6*, 354–356.

Westen, D., Novotny, C. M., & Thompson-Brenner, H. (2004). The empirical status of empirically supported psychotherapies: Assumptions, findings, and reporting in controlled clinical trials. *Psychological Bulletin, 130*, 631–663.

Westerterp, K. R. (2006). Perception, passive overfeeding and energy metabolism. *Physiology & Behavior, 89*, 62–65.

Westmacott, R. & Hunsley, J. (2010). Reasons for terminating psychotherapy: a general population study. *Journal of Clinical Psychology, 66*(9), 965–977.

Wetter, D. W., Fiore, M. C., Gritz, E. R., Lando, H. A., Stitzer, M. L., Hasselblad, V., & Baker, T. B. (1998). The Agency for Health Care Policy and Research. Smoking cessation clinical practice guideline: Findings and implications for psychologists. *American Psychologist, 53*, 657–669.

Whalley, M. G. & Brooks, G. B. (2009). Enhancement of suggestibility and imaginative ability with nitrous oxide. *Psychopharmacology, 203*, 745–752.

Whiffen, V., & Demidenko, N. (2006). Mood Disturbance Across the Life Span. *Handbook of girls' and women's psychological health: Gender and well-being across the lifespan* (pp. 51–59). New York: Oxford University Press.

Whitbourne, S. K. (2000). The normal aging process. In S. K. Whitbourne & S. Krauss (Eds.), *Psychopathology in later adulthood*. New York: Wiley.

Whitbourne, S. K., Zuschlag, M. K., Elliot, L. B., & Waterman, A. S. (1992). Psychosocial development in adulthood: A 22-year sequential study. *Journal of Personality and Social Psychology, 63*, 260–271.

White, C. A., & Macleod, U. (2002). ABC of psychological medicine: Cancer. *British Medical Journal, 325*, 377–380.

White, L. (2007). Linguistic theory, universal grammar, and second language acquisition. In B. Van Patten, & J. Williams, *Theories in second language acquisition: An introduction*. Mahwah, NJ: Lawrence Erlbaum Associates.

White, L. (2012). Reducing stress in school-age girls through mindful yoga. *Journal of Pediatric Health Care, 26*, 1, 45–56.

Whitfield, J. B., Zhu, G., Madden, P. A., Neale, M. C., Heath, A. C., & Martin, N. G. (2004). The genetics of alcohol intake and of alcohol dependence. *Alcoholism: Clinical and Experimental Research, 28*, 1153–1160.

Whitton, E. (2003). *Humanistic approach to psychotherapy*. Philadelphia: Whurr Publishers.

WHO World Mental Health Survey Consortium. (2004). Prevalence, severity, and unmet need for treatment of mental disorders in the World Health Organization World Mental Health Surveys. *Journal of the American Medical Association, 291*, 2581–2590.

Wickelgren, E. A. (2004). Perspective distortion of trajectory forms and perceptual constancy in visual event identification. *Perception and Psychophysics, 66*, 629–641.

Wickelgren, I. (2006, May 26). A vision for the blind. *Science, 312*, 1124–1126.

Wickens, C. D. (1984). *Engineering psychology and human performance*. Columbus, OH: Merrill.

Widiger, T. A., & Clark, L. A. (2000). Toward DSM-V and the classification of psychopathology. *Psychological Bulletin, 126*, 946–963.

Widiger, T., & Mullins-Sweatt, S. (2008). Classification. *Handbook of clinical psychology: Adults* (Vol. 1) (pp. 341–370). Hoboken, NJ: John Wiley & Sons Inc.

Widmeyer, W. N., & Loy, J. W. (1988). When you're hot, you're hot! Warm-cold effects in first impressions of persons and teaching effectiveness. *Journal of Educational Psychology, 80*, 118–121.

Wielgosz, A. T., & Nolan, R. P. (2000). Biobehavioral factors in the context of ischemic cardiovascular disease. *Journal of Psychosomatic Research, 48*, 339–345.

Wiggins, J. S. (2003). *Paradigms of personality assessment*. New York: Guilford Press.

Wildavsky, B. (2000, September 4). A blow to bilingual education. *U.S. News & World Report*, 22–28.

Willander, J., & Larsson, M. (2006). Smell your way back to childhood: Autobiographical odor memory. *Psychonomic Bulletin & Review, 13*, 240–244.

Willems, R. M., & Hagoort, P. (2007). Neural evidence for the interplay between language, gesture, and action: a review. *Brain Language, 101*, 278–289.

Williams, J. E., Paton, C. C., Siegler, I. C., Eigenbrodt, M. L., Nieto, F. J., & Tyroler, H. A. (2000). Anger proneness predicts coronary heart disease risk: Prospective analysis from the Atherosclerosis Risk in Communities (ARIC) Study. *Circulation, 101*, 2034–2039.

Willis, G. L. (2005). The therapeutic effects of dopamine replacement therapy and its psychiatric side effects are mediated by pineal function. *Behavioural Brain Research, 160*, 148–160.

Willis, S. L., & Schaie, K. W. (1994). In C. B. Fisher & R. M. Lerner (Eds.), *Applied developmental psychology*. New York: McGraw-Hill.

Wilmshurst, L. (2009). *Abnormal child psychology: A developmental perspective*. New York: Routledge/Taylor & Francis Group.

Wiloughby, T. & Hamza, C. A. (2011). A longitudinal examination of the bidirectional associations among perceived parenting behaviours, adolescent disclosure, and problem behaviour across the high school years. *Journal of Youth and Adolescence, 40*, 463–478.

Wilson, M. A. (2002). Hippocampal memory formation, plasticity and the role of sleep. *Neurobiology of Learning & Memory, 78*, 565–569.

Wilson, T. G., Grilo, C. M., & Vitousek, K. M. (2007). Psychological treatment of eating disorders. *American Psychologist, 62, Special issue: Eating disorders*, 199–216.

Winik, L. W. (2006, October 1). The true cost of depression. *Parade, 7*.

Winner, E. (2003). Creativity and talent. In M. H. Bornstein & L. Davidson (Eds.), *Well-being: Positive development across the life course* (pp. 371–380). Mahwah, NJ: Lawrence Erlbaum.

Winsler, A., Madigan, A. L., & Aquilino, S. A. (2005). Correspondence between maternal and paternal parenting styles in early childhood. *Early Childhood Research Quarterly, 20*, 1–12.

Winson, J. (1990, November). The meaning of dreams. *Scientific American*, pp. 86–96.

Winstead, B. A., & Sanchez, A. (2005). Gender and psychopathology. In J. E. Maddux & B. A. Winstead, *Psychopathology: Foundations for a contemporary understanding*. Mahwah, NJ: Lawrence Erlbaum Associates.

Winston, A. S. (2004). *Defining difference: Race and racism in the history of psychology*. Washington, DC: American Psychological Association.

Winston, J. S., O'Doherty, J., & Kilner, J. M. (2006). Brain systems for assessing facial attractiveness. *Neuropsychologia, 45*, 195–206.

Winter, D. G. (2007). The role of motivation, responsibility, and integrative complexity in crisis escalation: Comparative studies of war and peace crises. *Journal of Personality and Social Psychology, 92*, 920–937.

Wiseman, R., Greening, E., & Smith, M. D. (2003). Belief in the paranormal and suggestion in the séance room. *British Journal of Psychology, 94*, 285–297.

Witt, C. M., Jena, S., & Brinkhaus, B. (2006). Acupuncture for patients with chronic neck pain. *Pain, 125*, 98–106.

Wittenbrink, B, & Schwarz, N. (Eds.). (2007). *Implicit measures of attitudes*. New York: Guilford Press.

Wixted, J. (2005, February). A theory about why we forget what we once knew. *Current Directions in Psychological Science, 14*(1), 6–9.

Wixted, J. T., & Carpenter, S. K. (2007). The Wickelgren Power Law and the Ebbinghaus Savings Function. *Psychological Science, 18*, 133–134.

Wolf, M., van Doorn, G. S., Leimar, O., & Weissing, F. J. (2007). Life-history trade-offs favour the evolution of animal personalities. *Nature 447*, 581–584.

Wolfe, M. S. (2006). Shutting down Alzheimer's. *Scientific American, 294*, 72–79.

Wolff, N. (2002). Risk, response, and mental health policy: learning from the experience of the United Kingdom. *Journal of Health Politic and Policy Law, 27*, 801–802.

Wolitzky, D. L. (2006). Psychodynamic theories. In J. C. Thomas, D. L. Segal, & M. Hersen, *Comprehensive handbook of personality and psychopathology: Personality and everyday functioning* (Vol. 1). Hoboken, NJ: John Wiley & Sons.

Wood, J. M., Nezworski, M. T., Lilienfeld, S. O., & Garb, H. N. (2003). *What's wrong with the Rorschach? Science confronts the controversial inkblot test*. New York: Wiley.

Woodruff, S. I., Conway, T. L., & Edwards, C. C. (2007). Sociodemographic and smoking-related psychosocial predictors of smoking behavior change among high school smokers. *Addictive Behaviors, 33*, 354–358.

Woods, S. C., & Seeley, R. J. (2002). Hunger and energy homeostasis. In H. Pashler & R. Gallistel (Eds.). *Steven's handbook of experimental psychology: Learning, motivation, and emotion* (3rd ed.) (Vol. 3) (pp. 633–668). New York: Wiley.

Woods, S. C., Schwartz, M. W., Baskin, D. G., & Seeley, R. J. (2000). Food intake and the regulation of body weight. *Annual Review of Psychology, 51*, 255–277.

Woods, S. C., Seeley, R. J., Porte, D., Jr., & Schwartz, M. W. (1998, May 29). Signals that regulate food intake and energy homeostasis. *Science, 280*, 1378–1383.

World Health Organization (2011), What is Depression? Retrieved May 24, 2012, www.who.int/mental_health/management/depression/definition/en/.

Wren, A. M., & Bloom, S. R. (2007). Gut hormones and appetite control. *Gastroenterology, 132*, 2116–2130.

Wright, K. (September 2002). Times of our lives. *Scientific American*, pp. 59–65.

Wrosch, C., Bauer, I., & Scheier, M. F. (2005). Regret and quality of life across the adult life span: The influence of disengagement and available future goals. *Psychology and Aging, 20*, 657–670.

Wrzesniewski, K., & Chylinska, J. (2007). Assessment of coping styles and strategies with school-related stress. *School Psychology International, 28*, 179–194.

Wu, L-T., Schlenger, W. E., & Galvin, D. M. (2006). Concurrent use of methamphetamine, MDMA, LSD, ketamine, GHB, and flunitrazepam among American youths. *Drug and Alcohol Dependence, 84*, 102–113.

Wuethrich, B. (2001, March 16). Does alcohol damage female brains more? *Science, 291*, 2077–2079.

Wurtz, R. H., & Kandel, E. R. (2000). Central visual pathways. In E. R. Kandel, J. H. Schwartz, & T. M. Jessell (Eds.), *Principles of neural science* (4th ed.). New York: McGraw-Hill.

Wynn, K. (1995). Infants possess a system of numerical knowledge. *Current Directions in Psychological Science, 4*, 172–177.

Wynn, K. (2000). Findings of addition and subtraction in infants are robust and consistent: Reply to Wakeley, Rivera, and Langer. *Child Development, 71*, 1535–1536.

Wynn, K., Bloom, P., & Chiang, W. C. (2002). Enumeration of collective entities by 5-month-old infants. *Cognition, 83*, B55–B62.

Wyra, M., Lawson, M. J. & Hungi, N. (2007). The mnemonic keyword method: The effects of bidirectional retrieval training and of ability to image on foreign language vocabulary recall. *Learning and Instruction, 17*(3) 360–371.

Y

Yao, S-Q., Zhour, Y-H., & Jiang, L. (2006). The intelligence scale for Chinese adults: item analysis, reliability and validity. *Chinese Journal of Clinical Psychology, 14*, 441–445.

Yeomans, M. R., Tepper, B. J., & Ritezschel, J. (2007). Human hedonic responses to sweetness: Role of taste genetics and anatomy. *Physiology & Behavior, 91*, 264–273.

Yesilyaprak, B., Kisac, I., & Sanlier, N. (2007). Stress symptoms and nutritional status among survivors of the Marmara region earthquakes in Turkey. *Journal of Loss & Trauma, 12*, 1–8.

Young, M. M., Saewyc, E., Boak, A., Jahrig, J., Anderson, B., Doiron, Y., Taylor, S., Pica, L., Laprise, P., & Clark, H. (Student Drug Use Surveys Working Group). (2011). *Cross-Canada report on student alcohol and drug use: Technical report*. Ottawa, ON: Canadian Centre on Substance Abuse.

Young, M. W. (2000, March). The tick-tock of the biological clock. *Scientific American*, pp. 64–71.

Z

Zaitsu, W. (2007). The effect of fear on eyewitness' retrieval in recognition memory. *Japanese Journal of Psychology, 77*, 504–511.

Zajonc, R. B. (2001). Mere exposure: A gateway to the subliminal. *Current Directions in Psychological Science, 10*, 224–228.

Zalsman, G., & Apter, A. (2002). Serotonergic metabolism and violence/aggression. In J. Glicksohn (Ed.), *The neurobiology of criminal behavior: Neurobiological foundation of aberrant behaviors* (pp. 231–250). Dordrecht: Kluwer Academic.

Zaragoza, M. S., Belli, R. F., & Payment, K. E. (2007). Misinformation effects and the suggestibility of eyewitness memory. In M. Garry, & H. Hayne, *Do justice and let the sky fall: Elizabeth Loftus and her contributions to science, law, and academic freedom*. Mahwah, NJ: Lawrence Erlbaum Associates.

Zarate, C., & Manji, H. (2009). Potential novel treatments for bipolar depression. *Bipolar depression: Molecular neurobiology, clinical diagnosis and pharmacotherapy* (pp. 191–209). Cambridge: Birkhäuser.

Zebrowitz, L. A., & Montepare, J. M. (2005, June 10). Appearance DOES matter. *Science, 308*, 1565–1566.

Zeidner, M., Matthews, G., & Roberts, R. D. (2004). Emotional intelligence in the work-place: A critical review. *Applied Psychology: An International Review, 53*, 371–399.

Zeigler, D. W., Wang, C. C., Yoast, R. A., Dickinson, B. D., McCaffree, M. A., Robinowitz, C. B., & Sterling, M. L. (2005). The neurocognitive effects of alcohol on adolescents and college students. *Preventive Medicine: An International Journal Devoted to Practice and Theory, 40*, 23–32.

Zelkowitz, P., Paris, J., Guzder, J., Feldman, R., Roy, C., & Rosval, L. (2007). A five-year follow-up of patients with borderline pathology of childhood. *Journal of Personality Disorders, 21*, 664–674.

Zhang, F., Chen, Y., Heiman, M., & Dimarchi, R. (2005). Leptin: Structure, function and biology. *Vitamins and Hormones: Advances in Research and Applications, 71*, 345–372.

Zhou, Z., Liu, Q., & Davis, R. L. (2005). Complex regulation of spiral ganglion neuron firing patterns by neurotrophin-3. *Journal of Neuroscience, 25*, 7558–7566.

Zians, J. (2007). A comparison of trait anger and depression on several variables: Attribution style, dominance, submissiveness, "need for power," efficacy and dependency. *Dissertation Abstracts International: Section B: The Sciences and Engineering, 67*(7-B), 4124.

Ziegler, R., Diehl, M., & Ruther, A. (2002). Multiple source characteristics and persuasion: Source inconsistency as a determinant of message scrutiny. *Personality and Social Psychology Bulletin, 28*, 496–508.

Zigler, E. F., Finn-Stevenson, M., & Hall, N. W. (2002). The first three years and beyond: Brain development and social policy. In E. F. Zigler, M. Finn-Stevenson, & N. W. Hall, *Current perspectives in psychology*. New Haven, CT: Yale University Press.

Zimbardo, P. G. (1973). On the ethics of intervention in human psychological research: With special reference to the Stanford Prison Experiment. *Cognition, 2*, 243–256.

Zimbardo, P. G. (2004). Does psychology make a significant difference in our lives? *American Psychologist, 59*, 339–351.

Zimbardo, P. G. (2007). *The Lucifer effect: Understanding how good people turn evil*. New York: Random House.

Zimbardo, P. G., Maslach, C., & Haney, C. (2000). Reflections on the Stanford Prison Experiment: Genesis, transformations, consequences. In T. Blass (Ed.), *Obedience to Authority: Current Perspectives on the Milgram Paradigm*. Mahwah, NJ: Lawrence Erlbaum Associates.

Zimmermann, U. S., Blomeyer, D., & Laucht, M. (2007). How gene- and stress-behavior interactions can promote adolescent alcohol use: The roles of predrinking allostatic load and childhood behavior disorders. *Pharmacology, Biochemistry and Behavior, 86, Special issue: Adolescents, drug abuse and mental disorders*, 246–262.

Zito, J. M. (1993). *Psychotherapeutic drug manual* (3rd ed., rev.). New York: Wiley.

Zuckerman, M. (1978). The search for high sensation. *Psychology Today*, pp. 30–46.

Zuckerman, M. (2002). Genetics of sensation seeking. In J. Benjamin, R. P. Ebstein, et al. (Eds.), *Molecular genetics and the human personality* (pp. 193–210). Washington, DC: American Psychiatric Publishing.

Zuckerman, M., & Kuhlman, D. M. (2000). Personality and risk-taking: Common biosocial factors [Special issue: Personality processes and problem behavior]. *Journal of Personality, 68*, 999–1029.

Zung, W. W. K. 1965. A self-rating depression scale. *Archives of General Psychiatry, 12*, 63–70.

PHOTO CREDITS

Page iii: (from top) © BananaStock/PictureQuest, © Image Source/Getty Images, © Bettmann/Corbis, © Getty Images/Stockbyte, © Stockbyte; **v:** (top) © Matthius Engelien/Alamy, (bottom) © Brand X Pictures/JupiterImages; **vi:** © Anderson Ross/Getty Images; **vii:** Image Source/Alamy; **viii:** © Richard Hutchings/Digital Light Source; **ix:** © Ron Yue/Alamy

Chapter 1

Pages 2-3: © Pixellover RM 9/Alamy; **4:** (from left) © Reuters/Corbis, Karenr/Dreamstime.com/GetStock.com, Iculig/Shutterstock; **5:** (bottom) © AJPhoto/Photo Researchers; **6:** (top row, from second from left) © David Sanger/Getty Images, Yuri_arcurs/Dreamstime.com/GetStock.com, © White Packard/Getty Images, (bottom row, from left) © Royalty-Free/Corbis, Ariel Skelley/Blend Images/Photolibrary/Getty Images, doglikehorse/Shutterstock; **7:** (left) Library of Congress Prints and Photographs Division [LC-USZ62-72266], (right) Stockbyte/Punchstock; **8:** David Suzuki Foundation, www.davidsuzuki.org; **9:** (from second from left) © David Sanger/Getty Images, Yuri_arcurs/Dreamstime.com/GetStock.com, © White Packard/Getty Images, © Royalty-Free/Corbis, Ariel Skelley/Blend Images/Photolibrary/Getty Images, doglikehorse/Shutterstock; **10:** Kingjon/Dreamstime.com/GetStock.com; **11:** Lisa F. Young/Shutterstock; **12:** (from left) © Bettman/Corbis, © Corbis Images, Courtesy, Wellesley College Archives. Photographed by Notman, © Pixtal/SuperStock, © Bettman/Corbis, © The Granger Collection; **13:** (from left) Penfield Archive, Montreal Neurological Institute, McGill University, © Nina Leen/Time Life Pictures/Getty Images, © The Granger Collection, Courtesy, Elizabeth Loftus, © The Granger Collection, © SSPL/The Image Works; **14:** © Photo Researchers; **15:** Reuters/Corbis, **16:** © Comstock/PunchStock; **18:** Karenr/Dreamstime.com/GetStock.com; **19:** REUTERS/Department of National Defence/Master Corporal Miranda Langguth/Landov; **21:** (from top) © Spencer Grant/PhotoEdit, © Hill Street Studios/Getty Images, © Louise Psihoyos/Science Faction; **23:** Dynamic Graphics Group/PunchStock; **24:** (left, and far right bottom) © moodboard/Corbis, (top row, and bottom centre) Courtesy of Lafayette Instrument Company, Inc.; **25:** © Dennis Wise/Digital Vision/Getty Images; **26:** Iculig/Shutterstock; **27:** (right) Dejan750/GetStock.com; **28:** (from second from left) © David Sanger/Getty Images, Yuri_arcurs/Dreamstime.com/GetStock.com, © White Packard/Getty Images, © Royalty-Free/Corbis, Ariel Skelley/Blend Images/Photolibrary/Getty Images, doglikehorse/Shutterstock

Chapter 2

Pages 30-31: HO-COC-Mike Ridewood/CP Photo; **32:** (top, from left) © Jamie McCarthy/Getty Images, Thomas Kienzle/AP Photo/CP Photo, © Christopher Stubbs/Alamy, (centre) © Craig Zuckerman/Visuals Unlimited, (bottom) © UpperCut Images/Getty Images; **33:** © Dennis Kunkel/Visuals Unlimited; **38:** (top) © Jamie McCarthy/Getty Images, (bottom) Thomas Kienzle/AP Photo/CP Photo; **39:** © Mark Andersen/Getty Images; **40:** © Larry Williams/Blend Images/Getty Images; **41:** (top) PunchStock/Image Source, (bottom) © Doug Menuez/Getty Images; **42:** CP PICTURE ARCHIVE; **43:** © Radius Images/Alamy; **44:** (top left) © Hank Morgan/Photo Researchers, (bottom left) © Volker Steger/Peter Arnold, (centre) © Bryan Christie Design, (top right) © Roger Ressmeyer/Corbis Images, (bottom right) SOVEREIGN, ISM/SCIENCE PHOTO LIBRARY; **45:** © Dana Neely/Getty Images, **48:** © Royalty-Free/Corbis; **49:** (top) Courtesy, Trustees of the British Museum, Natural History; **50:** © Christopher Stubbs/Alamy; **52:** © RubberBall Productions; **54:** © StockByte/PictureQuest

Chapter 3

Pages 58-59: © Carlos Ebert/Flickr/Getty Images; **60:** (from left) AP Photo/Anja Niedringhaus, © AP Photo/The Green Bay News Chronicle, Boyd Fellows, © Anthony Bradshaw/Getty Images, (bottom) © Matthew Leete/Photodisc/Getty Images; **61:** (top) AP Photo/Anja Niedringhaus, (bottom) © R. C. James; **63:** © AP Photo/The Green Bay News Chronicle, Boyd Fellows; **66:** © Cary Wolinsky/Stock Boston; **67:** © Jeff Greenberg/Stock Boston; **68:** © John G. Ross/Photo Researchers;

70: (both) © BioPhoto Associates/Photo Researchers; **71:** Dynamic Graphics/JupiterImages; **72:** © Omikron/Photo Researchers; **73:** © Lars Niki; **74:** © Corbis; **75:** © Corbis; **76:** © Tyler Edwards/Getty Images; **77:** (top) Dynamic Graphics Group/PunchStock, (bottom) NASA; **78:** (top) © Reed Kaestner/Royalty-Free/Corbis, (centre) Taden/Dreamstime.com/GetStock.com, (bottom) © Omikron/Photo Researchers; **79:** © Anthony Bradshaw/Getty Images; **80:** © Chase Jarvis/Getty Images; **81:** © Liu Yang/Redlink/Royalty-Free/Corbis

Chapter 4

Pages 86-87: © Gabriela Medina/Blend Images/Getty Images; **88:** (from left) © Nick Norman/Getty Images, © AP Photo, Midland Daily News, Erin Painter, © Wolfgang Kaehler/Alamy, (bottom) © Photodisc/Getty Images; **89:** © The McGraw-Hill Companies, Inc./Photo by David Planchet; **90:** © Rob Melnychuk/Getty Images; **92:** (top) © Nick Norman/Getty Images, (bottom) Ingram Publishing; **93:** (from left) © Brand X Pictures/PunchStock, DAJ/Getty Images, Flying Colours Ltd./Getty Images, © Stockbyte/Getty Images, © Brand X Pictures/PunchStock, © Purestock/PunchStock; **94:** © Thinkstock; **96:** © CMCD/Getty Images; **97:** © AP Photo, Midland Daily News, Erin Painter; **98:** © Liquidlibrary/PictureQuest; **99:** Dynamic Graphics Group/PunchStock; **101:** © Wolfgang Kaehler/Alamy; **102:** (top) © iStockPhoto.com/ALEAIMAGE, (bottom) © PhotoDisc Collection/Getty Images; **103:** (from left) © Stockbyte/PunchStock, © Jonnie Miles/Getty Images, © Per-Anders Pettersson/Getty Images; **105:** © iStockPhoto.com/Jail Free

Chapter 5

Pages 110-111: © kpzfoto/Alamy; **112:** (top row, from left) © Tim Hall/Getty Images, Brand X Pictures, © Gary Salter/Corbis, (bottom) Norman Chan/Shutterstock; **113:** AISPIX by Image Source/Shutterstock; **114:** © Photodisc, © iStockPhoto.com/Mark Coffey, © iStockPhoto.com/Leonid Nyshko; **115:** (top) nullplus/iStockphoto.com; **116:** (top) © Scott T. Baxter/Getty Images, (bottom) Bloomberg via Getty Images; **117:** © Brand X Pictures/PunchStock; **118:** © Nina Leen/Time Life Pictures/Getty Images; **119:** (top) © Tim Hall/Getty Images, (bottom) © Getty Images/Photodisc; **120:** (from left) © BananaStock/PunchStock, © Ryan McVay/Getty Images, © Amy Etra/PhotoEdit, © Royalty-Free/Corbis; **121:** © Tony Freeman/PhotoEdit; **122:** Brand X Pictures; **123:** (top) © Beau Lark/Corbis, (bottom, from left) Rachwalski/Dreamstime.com/GetStock.com, Montenegro1/Dreamstime.com/GetStock.com, Tan510jomast/Dreamstime.com/GetStock.com, Perkmeup/Dreamstime.com/GetStock.com; **125:** (left) Getty Images, (right) Veer; **127:** © Ariel Skelley/Corbis; **128:** (block of cheese) © Digital Vision, (rat) © Punchstock/BananaStock; **129:** (top) Courtesy of Albert Bandura, (bottom) © Gary Salter/Corbis; **130:** Kingjon/Dreamstime.com/GetStock.com

Chapter 6

Pages 134-135: wavebreakmedia ltd/Shutterstock; **136:** (from left) © Paul Avis/Stone/Getty Images, © Purestock/Getty Images, Chris O'Meara/AP Photo/CP Photo; **137:** (top left) Martinmark/Dreamstime.com/GetStock.com, (from top right) rangizzz/Shutterstock, D. Hurst/Alamy, © McGraw-Hill Companies, Inc./Gary He, Photographer, © Ron Yue/Alamy; **138:** (top) © Paul Avis/Stone/Getty Images, (bottom) © C Squared Studios/Getty Images; **140:** Robwilson39/Dreamstime.com/GetStock.com; **142:** © Kathy McLaughlin/The Image Works; **143:** © iStockPhoto.com/Rayasick; **144:** © Greatstock Photographic Library/Alamy; **146:** © Purestock/Getty Images; **147:** (top) © Amos Morgan/Getty Images, (bottom) Chris O'Meara/AP Photo/CP Photo; **150:** Siede Preis/Getty Images; **151:** (top) © Monkey Business Images, Ltd./Punchstock, (bottom) © Joseph Nettis/Photo Researchers; **156:** Paul Thompson, UCLA Laboratory of Neuroimaging, 2003

Chapter 7

Pages 160-161: photobywayne/Alamy; **162:** (from left) REUTERS/Hans Deryk /Landov, © Aflo Foto Agency/Alamy, © Bob Daemmrich/The Image Works; **163:** (top) REUTERS/Hans Deryk /Landov, (bottom left) © Bettman/Corbis, © Jonathan Brady/epa/Corbis; **164:** © David Young-

Wolff/Alamy; **166:** Sampete/Dreamstime.com/GetStock.com; **167:** (top left) © Hoby Finn/Getty Images, (top right) © Stockbyte/PunchStock, (bottom) © Photodisc/Getty Images; **168:** Sampete/Dreamstime.com/GetStock.com; **169:** © iStockPhoto.com/Diane Diederich; **171:** (top) © Ryan McVay/Getty Images; **172:** © Rob Crandall/Stock Connection Blue/Alamy; **174:** © Aflo Foto Agency/Alamy; **175:** © Image Source Black/Alamy; **176:** © David Hiser/Still Media; **177:** © Bob Daemmrich/The Image Works; **179:** (from top left) REUTERS/Jonathan Drake / Landov, Canadian Space Agency, © Chris Cheadle/Alamy, Adrian Wyld/TCPI/The Canadian Press, (from top right) REUTERS /Rick Wilking / Landov, © jeremy sutton-hibbert/Alamy, THE CANADIAN PRESS/Paul Chiasson, David Suzuki Foundation, www.davidsuzuki.org; **180:** © Andersen Ross/Digital Vision/Getty Images; **181:** © Doug Menuez/Getty Images; **185:** © AP Photo/Gregory Bull; **186:** Design Pics/Monkey Business

Chapter 8

Pages 190-191: © Corey Rich/Aurora Photos/Corbis; **192:** (top row, from left) © AP Photo/Gautam Singh, © AP Photo/Eugenio Savio, © Galen Rowell/Corbis, (bottom) CP Photo by Boris Spremo; **193:** (top) © Chase Swift/Corbis, (bottom) © Reuters/Corbis; **195:** (top) © Photodisc/Getty Images, (bottom) Kingjon/Dreamstime.com/GetStock.com; **196:** (from top, clockwise) © iStockPhoto/com/Photogl, © Brand X Pictures/PunchStock, © Brand X Pictures, © Brooke Fasani/Corbis, © Digital Vision, (bottom) © AP Photo/Gautam Singh; **197:** Photo by Cpl. Jasper Schwartz, Army News Montreal 10 (LS2008-2800d), Department of National Defence. Reproduced with the permission of the Minister of Public Works and Government Services Canada, 2012; **198:** (top) REUTERS/Chris Wattie, (bottom left) © AP Photo/Volker Wiciok; **199:** © Doable/amanaimages/Corbis; **200:** Elena Schweitzer/Shutterstock; **201:** (top) Marifa/Dreamstime.com/GetStock.com, (bottom) © Ellen B. Senisi/The Image Works; **202:** (top) © AP Photo/Eugenio Savio; **205:** (top) © Bettmann/CORBIS, (bottom) © Amos Morgan/Getty Images; **206:** © ballyscanlon/Digital Vision/Getty Images; **207:** © mauritius images GmbH/Alamy; **208:** © Cornstock Images; **209:** © Stockbyte/Getty Images; **210:** © Galen Rowell/Corbis; **213:** (all) © Matsumoto & Ekman, 1988.

Chapter 9

Pages 216-217: © Image Source/Getty Images; **218:** (from left) © Paul Barton/Corbis, © Masterfile Royalty-Free, © Reuters NewMedia Inc./Corbis Images; **219:** REUTERS/Christinne Muschi /Landov; **221:** (top) © PhotoAlto/Alix Minde/Getty Images, (bottom) Nexus7/Dreamstime.com/GetStock.com; **223:** © PhotoAlto/PunchStock; **224:** © Paul Barton/Corbis; **225:** © Masterfile Royalty-Free; **226:** William Vandivert, Scientific American, November 1955, Vol. 193, Issue 5, p. 31-35; **227:** © CMCD/Getty Images; **230:** (top) From the film OBEDIENCE © 1965 by Stanley Milgram and distributed by Penn. State Media Sales. Permission granted by Alexandra Milgram, (bottom) PeJo29/Dreamstime.com/GetStock.com; **232:** Robert Ginn/Photolibrary/Getty Images; **233:** Bakalusha/Dreamstime.com/GetStock.com; **236:** Rorem/Dreamstime.com/GetStock.com; **239:** © Reuters NewMedia Inc./Corbis Images

Chapter 10

Pages 242-243: Courtesy of Barbara Bond; **244:** (top row, from left) © Ethno Images, Inc./Alamy, Rob Melnychuk/Getty Images, © Deborah Davis/PhotoEdit, (bottom) © Peter Byron; **245:** © Getty Images/Digital Vision; **246:** © Dave King/Dorling Kindersley/Getty Images; **247:** © D.W. Fawcett/Photo Researchers; **248:** (left) © Lennart Nilsson/Albert Bonniers Forlag AB/A Child is Born/Dell Publishing, (right) © Petit Format/Science Source/Photo Researchers; **249:** © Brand X Pictures/Punchstock; **250:** © Picture Partners/Alamy, **251:** (all) From Meltzhoff, A.N. (1988). Imitation of Televised Models by Infants. Child Development, 59, 1221-1229. Photo courtesy of A.N. Meltzhoff & M. Hanak; **253:** (bottom) © Courtesy Helen A. LeRoy, Harlow Primate Laboratory, University of Wisconsin; **254:** (top, both) Photos by John Oates © 2012 The Open University, www.open.ac.uk, (bottom) © Ethno Images, Inc./Alamy; **255:** © Gunter Marx/Alamy; **256:** (left) ©

FotoKIA/Index Stock/Photolibrary, (right) David Ellis/Digital Vision/Getty Images; **257:** © David Tipling/Alamy; **258:** © Flying Colours Ltd./Getty Images; **259:** (top row, from left) Stockbyte/Getty Images, © Laurence Mouton/PhotoAlto/PictureQuest, © Corbis, © Royalty-Free/Corbis, (bottom) © Laura Dwight/Peter Arnold; **262:** (top) © Syracuse Newspapers/Gary Walts/Image Works, (bottom) Kingjon/Dreamstime.com/GetStock.com; **263:** © Stockbyte/Getty Images; **265:** © Corbis Images/JupiterImages; **266:** (from left) © iStockPhoto.com/Tarinoel, © BananaStock/PunchStock, Ariel Skelly/Getty Images, © Jon Feingersh/Blend Images/Getty Images; **267:** (from left) Mel Curis/Getty Images, © Blue Moon Stock/Alamy Images, © Cornstock Images/Jupiter Images/Alamy, Ryan McVay/Getty Images; **268:** Courtesy of Barbara Bond; **269:** Rob Melnychuk/Getty Images; **270:** © Granger Wootz/Blend Images/Corbis; **271:** © Jose Luis Pelaez Inc./Blend Images/Corbis; **272:** (top) © Randy Faris/Corbis, (right) © Zave Smith/UpperCut Images/Getty Images, (bottom) © Jose Luis Pelaez Inc./Blend Images/Getty Images; **273:** (top) © Harry Scull, Jr./Buffalo News, (bottom) © Dennis Wise/Digital Vision/Getty Images; **274:** © Deborah Davis/PhotoEdit;

Chapter 11

Pages 280-281: © Werner Dieterich/Photographer's Choice/Getty Images; **282:** (top row, from left) Digital Vision/Photolibrary/Getty Images, © BananaStock/PunchStock, © Michael Newman/PhotoEdit, (bottom) © Photodisc; **285:** Digital Vision/Photolibrary/Getty Images; **287:** © Warner Bros./Courtesy Everett Collection; **288:** Karen Horney papers, 1899-1999 (inclusive), 1899-1974 (bulk). Manuscripts & Archives, Yale University, MSSA#010556; **292:** PeJo29/Dreamstime.com/GetStock.com; **293:** © Michael Newman/PhotoEdit; **294:** © BananaStock/PunchStock; **297:** (bottom) © Corbis; **298:** (bottom) Gibsonff/Dreamstime.com/GetStock.com

Chapter 12

Pages 302-303: © Martin Barraud/Getty Images; **304:** (from left) © Rino Gropuzzo/age fotostock, © Kevin Winter/Getty Images for Nickelodeon, © The McGraw-Hill Companies, Inc./Luke David, Photographer; **308:** (from top) © PhotoAlto/PictureQuest, © Photodisc/Getty Images, © Royalty-Free/Corbis, © Alamy Images, © Rino Gropuzzo/age fotostock; **310:** © Kevin Winter/Getty Images for Nickelodeon; **313:** (both) Courtesy Ian H. Gotlib, Ph.D.; **314:** © Chad Baker/Ryan McVay/Getty Images; **322:** © Cornstock Images/PictureQuest; **323:** Graphiapl/Dreamstime.com/GetStock.com; **325:** © HBO/The Kobal Collection; **327:** © Colin Young-Wolff/PhotoEdit; **328:** © Photodisc/PunchStock; **329:** © Michael Newman/PhotoEdit; **332:** © Jon Bradley/Getty Images; **334:** (top) © The McGraw-Hill Companies, Inc./Luke David, Photographer, (bottom) © Doug Menuez/Getty Images

Chapter 13

Pages 338-339: Tyler Olson/Shutterstock; **340:** (from left) © Nick Daly/Getty Images, © AP Photo/Mark Humphrey, THE CANADIAN PRESS/Paul Chiasson; **341:** © J.J. Guillen/epa/Corbis; **342:** © Barry Lewis/Corbis; **345:** (top) © Ned Frisk Photography/Brand X/Corbis, (bottom) © Dr. David Phillips/Visuals Unlimited; **346:** PeJo29/Dreamstime.com/GetStock.com; **347:** (top) © Nick Daly/Getty Images, (bottom) © Dennis Wise/Digital Vision/Getty Images; **348:** © AP Photo/Mark Humphrey; **349:** (bottom) THE CANADIAN PRESS/Paul Chiasson; **351:** Vancouver Board of Parks and Recreation © 2012; **353:** Eat Well and Be Active Poster. Health Canada, 2011. Reproduced with the permission of the Minister of Health, 2012; **354:** The Canadian Press Images/Larry MacDougal

TEXT CREDITS

Chapter 1

Page 5: Adapted from Lamal, 1979; *12-13: Professional Psychology in Canada*, K.S. Dobson, D. June, G. Dobson (1993). Hogrefe & Huber; **13:** Service Canada, *Job Futures Quebec - Occupation Search: Psychologists.* http://www.servicecanada.gc.ca/eng/qc/job_futures/statistics/4151.shtml. Reproduced by permission of the Minister of Public Works and

Government Services Canada, 2012; **17:** © The New Yorker Collection 1998 Roz Chast from Cartoonbank.com. All rights reserved. **20:** Santrock & Mitterer, *Psychology*, 3rd Cdn Ed. "Scatter Plots Showing Positive and Negative Correlations." Figure 2.3, p. 53. Copyright © 2006 by McGraw-Hill Ryerson. Reprinted with permission.; **21:** Based on a study by Kaplan & Manuck; **22:** © The New Yorker Collection 2004 Mike Twohy from Cartoonbank.com. All rights reserved; **24:** Fogel, S.M., Smith, C.T., & Kote, K.A. (2007). Dissociable learning-dependent changes in REM and non-REM sleep in declarative and procedural memory systems. *Behavioural Brain Research*, 180, 48-61; **25:** © The New Yorker Collection 1993 Donald Reilly from Cartoonbank.com. All rights reserved.

Chapter 2

Page 33: From K. Van De Graaff, *Human Anatomy* 5th ed, 2000. Copyright © 2000 The McGraw-Hill Companies. Reprinted with permission.; **34:** Stevens, 1979; **35:** *Human Biology*, 6th ed., by S. Mader. Copyright © 2000 by The McGraw-Hill Companies, Inc. Reprinted with permission; **36:** From S. S. Mader, *Biology*, 2000. Copyright © 2000 The McGraw-Hill Companies. Reprinted with permission; **41:** From Michael Passer and Ronald Smith, *Psychology: Frontiers and Applications*, 2001. Copyright © 2001 The McGraw-Hill Companies. Reprinted with permission; **45:** From George Johnson and Thomas Emmel, *The Living World*, 2nd ed., 2000. Copyright © 2000 The McGraw-Hill Companies. Reprinted with permission. **46:** (top) From Rod Seeley, Trent Stephens and Philip Tate, *Anatomy & Physiology*, 5th ed, 2000. Copyright © 2000 The McGraw-Hill Companies. Reprinted with permission; **49:** (bottom) From Damasion, H., Grabowski, T., Frank, R., Galaburda, A.M., Damasio, A.R.: The return of Phinea Gage: Clues about the brain from the skull of a famous patient. *Science*, 264:1102-1102, 1994. Department of Neurology and Image Analysis Facility, University of Iowa; **51:** Adapted from *Brain and Cognition*, Vol. 41, No. 3, B.E. Morton, "Assymetry Questionnaire Outcomes Correlate with Several Hemisphericity Measures," p. 372-374. Copyright © 2003 with permission from Elsevier; **52:** From Robert Brooker, Eric Widmaier, Linda Graham and Peter Stiling, *Biology*, Copyright © 2008 by The McGraw-Hill Companies. Reprinted by permission; **54:** From Robert Brooker, Eric Widmaier, Linda Graham and Peter Stiling, *Biology*, 1st ed, 2008. Copyright © 2008 The McGraw-Hill Companies. Reprinted with permission.

Chapter 3

Page 63: Adapted from Galanter, 1962; **65:** From Stanley Coren and Lawrence M. Ward. *Sensation & Perception*, 3rd ed. (1989), p. 329. Reprinted with permission of John Wiley & Sons, Inc.; **66:** © The New Yorker Collection 2006 Paul Noth from Cartoonbank.com; **68:** (top right illustrations) Coren & Ward, 1989, p. 5; **69:** From Fig. 1 of W. Hudson "Pictorial Depth Perception in Sub-Cultural Groups in Africa." *Journal of Social Psychology, 52*, 183-208. Reprinted by permission of Heldref Publications, via Copyright Clearance Center; **70:** From Camille B. Wortman, Elizabeth F. Loftus, and Charles Weaver, *Psychology*, 5th ed. p. 113. Copyright © 1999 by The McGraw-Hill Companies, Inc. Reprinted with permission; **71:** Stock Disk; **72:** From David Shier, Jackie Butler, and Ricki Lewis, *Human Anatomy and Physiology* 7th ed., 2000. Copyright © 2000 The McGraw-Hill Companies. Reprinted with permission; **73:** From Sylvia Mader, *Biology* 7th ed. Copyright © 2000 The McGraw-Hill Companies. Reprinted with permission; **76:** *Biology*, by Brooker, et al. Copyright © 2008 The McGraw-Hill Companies. Reprinted by permission; **79:** Reprinted by permission of Dr. Linda Bartoshuk; **80:** Kenshalo, *The Skin Senses*, 1968. Courtesy of Charles C. Thomas, Publisher, Ltd., Springfield, Illinois; **82:** From Macalusoa, E. and Jon Driver, J., Multisensory spatial interactions: a window onto functional integration in the human brain. *Trends in Neurosciences*, Volume 28, Issue 5, May 2005, p. 264-271

Chapter 4

Page 88: Young, 2000; **90:** From *Sleep*, by J. Allen Hobson, p. 16. Copyright © 1989 by J. Allen Hobson. Reprinted by permission of Henry Holt & Company, LLC; **91:** (top) From *Teaching of Psychology*, by J. J. Palladino and B. J. Carducci. Copyright 1984 by Taylor & Francis

Informa Ltd. Journals. Reproduced with permission of Taylor & Francis Informa UK Ltd. Journals via Copyright Clearance Center, (Figure 4.3) From Ernest Hartmann, *The Biology of Dreaming* (1967), p. 6. Courtesy of Charles C. Thomas Publisher, Ltd., Springfield, Illinois; **92:** Statistics Canada, General Social Survey, 2005. Chart 2: More time working means less sleep. www.statcan.gc.ca/pub/11-008-x/2008001/c-g/10553/5214730-eng.htm; **93:** Schneigler & Domhoff, 2002; **99:** From Brefczynski-Lewis, J.A., Lutz, A., Schaefer, H.D., Levinson, D.B. and Davidsoni, R.J. Neural correlates of attentional expertise in long-term meditation practioners. *PNAS*, Vol. 104, no. 17, p. 11483-11488; **100:** From Sylvia S. Mader, *Human Biology*, 6th ed., p. 250. Copyright © 2000 by The McGraw-Hill Companies, Inc. Reprinted with permission; **101:** Adapted from Young, et al., *Student Drug Use Surveys Working Group*, 2011. Cross-Canada report on student alcohol and drug use: Technical report. Ottawa, ON: Canadian Centre on Substance Abuse; **102:** *New York Times* graphic "Levels of caffeine in various foods" from Blakeslee, S. (1991, August 7). The secrets of caffeine: America's favorite drug. *New York Times*. Copyright © 1991 by The New York Times Co. Reprinted with permission; **104:** Health Canada. Canadian Alcohol and Drug Use Monitoring Survey (CADUMS) 2009. Table 6. http://www.hc-sc.gc.ca/hc-ps/drugs-drogues/stat/_2009/tables-tableaux-eng.php#t6 (accessed January 23, 2012). Reproduced with the permission of the Minister of Public Works and Government Services Canada, 2012; **106:** Adapted from Young, et al. *Student Drug Use Surveys Working Group*, 2011. Cross-Canada report on student alcohol and drug use: Technical report. Table 24, p18. Ottawa, ON: Canadian Centre on Substance Abuse

Chapter 5

Page 128: (top) © The New Yorker Collection 1995 Gahan Wilson from Cartoonbank.com. All rights reserved, (maze) Tolman & Honzik, 1930.

Chapter 6

Page 138: Atkinson & Shifrin, 1968; **140:** © The New Yorker Collection 1994 Roz Chast from Cartoonbank.com. All rights reserved; **141:** Adapted from Baddeley, Chincotta, & Adlam, 2001; **143:** From Collins, A. M., & Loftus, E. F. (1975). A spreading-activation theory of semantic processing. *Psychological Review, 82*, 407-428. Published by The American Psychological Association, adapted with permission; **149:** Reprinted from *Journal of Verbal Learning and Verbal Behavior*, Vol. 13, Loftus, E. F., & Palmer, J. C., "Reconstruction of automobile destruction: An example of the interface between language and memory," p. 585-589. Copyright 1974, with permission from Elsevier; **151:** Data from Table 2 (p. 266) from Bahrick, H. P., Hall, L. K., & Berger, S. A. (1996). Accuracy and distortion in memory for high school grades. *Psychological Science, 7*, 265-269. Reprinted by permission of Blackwell Publishing; **152:** From *Essentials of Psychology*, 8th ed., by Robert Feldman. Copyright © 2009 by The McGraw-Hill Companies, Inc. Reprinted by permission; **153:** Ebbinghaus, 1885, 1913; **157:** From Kent Van De Graaff, *Human Anatomy*, updated 5th ed. Copyright © 2000 by The McGraw-Hill Companies, Inc. Reprinted with permission.

Chapter 7

Page 166: Bourne et al., *Cognitive Processes*, "Three Major Categories of Problems," p. 233, © 1979 Prentice-Hall, Inc. Reproduced by permission of Pearson Education, Inc.; **170:** © The New Yorker Collection 2005 Leo Cullum from Cartoonbooks.com. All rights reserved; **177:** © The New Yorker Collection 1983 W.B. Park from Cartoonbank.com. All rights reserved; **179:** Adapted from *Multiple Intelligences: New Horizons* by H. Gardner. © 2006 by Howard Gardner; **183:** Simulated items similar to those in the Wechsler Adult Intelligence Scale--Third Edition (WAIS-III). Copyright © 1997 by NCS Pearson, Inc. Reproduced with permission. All rights reserved; **187:** Reprinted, with permission, from the *Annual Review of Psychology, Volume 33* © 1982 by Annual Reviews www.annualreviews.org and Norman D. Henderson, Professor Emeritus.

Chapter 8

Page 194: "Do you seek out sensation?" questionnaire from Marvin Zuckerman, "The Search for High Sensation," *Psychology Today*,

February 1978, pp. 30-46; **196:** After Maslow, 1970; **202:** From Santel, S., Baving, L., Krauel, K., Muente, T.F. Hunger and Satiety in Anorexia Nervosa; fMRI during cognitive processing of food pictures. *Brain Research.* Vol. 1114, (1)9, Oct. 2006, p. 138-148, **207:** © The New York Collection 1997 Robert Mankoff, Cartoonbank.com. All rights reserved; **209:** Adapted from Figure 1 (p. 1067) from Shaver, P., Schwartz, J., Kirson, D., & O'Connor, C. (1987). Emotion knowledge: Further exploration of a prototype approach. *Journal of Personality and Social Psychology, 52,* 1061-1086. Published by The American Psychological Association, adapted with permission; **213:** © The New York Collection 2000 Gahan Wilson from Cartoonbank.com. All rights reserved.

Chapter 9

Page 220: From "Social Neuroscience: Principles of Psychophysiological Arousal and Response" by J.T. Cacioppo, G.G. Berntson, & S.L. Crites, Jr. (1996). *Social Psychology: Handbook of Basic Principles* edited by E.T. Higgins & A.W. Kruglanski. Copyright © 1996 by Guilford Publications, Inc. Reprinted by permssion from Guilford Press; **223:** Adapted from C.A. Anderson, D.S. Krull, & B. Weiner "Explanations: Processes and Consequences." *Social Psychology: Handbook of Basic Principles* edited by E.T. Higgins & A.W. Kruglanski, p. 274. Copyright © 1996 by Guilford Publications, Inc. Reprinted by permission from Guilford Press; **226:** William Vandivert, *Scientific American,* November 1955, Vol. 193, Issue 5, p. 31-35; **235:** "Defining Aggression: An Exercise for Classroom Discussion" by L.T. Benjamin, Jr. *Teaching of Psychology*, 12(1), 40-42. © 1985. Reprinted by permission of Taylor & Francis Group, http://www.informaworld.com; **238:** Bibb Latane & John M. Darley. *The Unresponsive Bystander: Why Doesn't He Help?* 1st ed., © 1970. Reproduced in print and electronic formats by permission of Pearson Education, Inc. Upper Saddle River, New Jersey.

Chapter 10

Pages 252-253: Frankenburg et al, 1992; **252:** Adapted from Figure 5 from W.J. Robbins, *Growth.* Copyright © 1928 Yale University Press. Used by permission of Yale University Press; **260:** Schickedanz et al., *Understanding Children & Adolescents,* Fig. 13.1, p. 440, "Tests of the Principle of Conservation Chart," © 2001 Judith Schickedanz, David Schickedanc, and Peggy Forsyth. Reproduced by permission of Pearson Education, Inc.; **263:** Based on Tanner, 1978; **265:** D. Goslin (ed.), *Handbook of Socialization and Research.* © 1969 by Rand McNally; **266:** © The New Yorker Collection 1993 Roz Chast from Cartoonbank.com. All rights reserved; **268:** The Conference Board of Canada, "How Canada Performs: Society: Suicide Rates, 2007 to Present", (Accessed: April 30, 2012) www.conferenceboard.ca/hcp/details/society/suicides.aspx; **274:** Schaie, K.W. (2005). Longitudinal studies. In *Developmental influences on adult intelligence: The Seattle Longitudinal Study,* Figure 5.7a (p. 127). Copyright © 2005 by Oxford University Press, Inc. By permission of Oxford University Press, Inc. www.oup.co.uk; **276:** © The New Yorker Collection 1993 Roz Chast from Cartoonbank.com. All rights reserved; **277:** Dickstein, L. S. "Death concerns: Measurement and correlates." *Psychological Reports,* 1972, 30, 563-571. © *Psychological Reports* 1972. Reproduced by permission of Ammons Scientific, Ltd. and Copyright Clearance Center.

Chapter 11

Page 289: From "Biological dimensions of personality" by H.J. Eyesenck (1990). L.A. Pervin (Editor) *Handbook of Personality: Theory and Research,* p. 246. Copyright © 1990 by Guilford Publications, Inc. Reprinted by permission of Guilford Press; **290:** From "The Big Five Personality Factors and Dimensions of Sample Traits," Chapter 3. L.A. Pervin (Editor) *Handbook of Personality: Theory and Research,* p. 246. Copyright © 1990 by Guilford Publications, Inc. Reprinted by permission of Guilford Press; **293:** From A. Tellegan, D.T. Lykken, T.J. Bouchard Jr., K.J. Wilcox, N.L. Segal, and S. Rich (1988). "Personality Similarity in Twins Reared Apart and Together." *Journal of Personality*

and Social Psychology, 54, 1031-1039. Published by The American Psychological Association, reprinted with permission.

Chapter 12

Page 306: © Reprinted with permission from the *Diagnostic and Statistical Manual of Mental Disorders,* Text Revision, Copyright 2000; **307:** © The New Yorker Collection 2000 Arnie Levin from Cartoonbank.com. All rights reserved; **308:** *Abnormal Psychology,* 4th ed., by S. Nolen-Hoeksema. Copyright © 2007 by The McGraw-Hill Companies, Inc. Reprinted by permission; **309:** From *Anxiety Disorders and Phobias,* by Aaron Beck. Copyright © 1985 by Basic Books. Reprinted by permission of Basic Books, a member of Perseus Books Group; **312:** Adapted from W.W.K. Zung (1965). A self-rating depression scale. Archives of *General Psychiatry, 12,* 63-70, Table 3 (p. 65). Copyright © 1965, American Medical Association. Reprinted with permission; **315:** Table "The closer the genetic links between two people, the greater the likelihood…" from *Schizophrenia Genesis,* by Irving I. Gottesman. Copyright © 1991 by Irving I. Gottesman. Reprinted by arrangement with Henry Holt and Company, LLC; **319:** Government of Canada. The Human Face of Mental Health and Mental Illness in Canada. 2006. p. 3, Figure 1.1. http://www.phac-aspc.gc.ca/publicat/human-humain06. Public Health Agency of Canada, 2006. Reproduced by permission of the Minister of Public Works and Government Services Canada, 2012; **320:** From Benton, S.A., et al. (2003). "Changes in counseling center client problems across 13 years." *Professional Psychology: Research and Practice, 34,* 66-72. Published by The American Psychological Association, reprinted with permission; **321:** "Lifting the Cloud" from *Shock: The Healing Power of Electroconvulsive Therapy* by Kitty Dukakis and Larry Tye, Copyright © 2006 by Kitty Dukakis & Larry Tye. Used by permission of Avery Publishing, an imprint of Penguin Group (USA) Inc.; **326:** © The New Yorker Collection 2007 Michael Maslin from Cartoonbank.com. All rights reserved; **328:** From *Meditation* by Herbert Benson, M.D., Benson-Henry Institute for Mind Body Medicine. Reprinted with permission from Dr. Herbert Benson; **332:** © The New Yorker Collection 2005 Tom Cheney from Cartoonbank.com. All rights reserved; **333:** Westmacott, R. and Hunsley, J. (2010), Reasons for terminating psychotherapy: a general population study. J. Clin. Psychol., 66: 965–977. doi: 10.1002/jclp.20702, p. 971, Table 1. Reproduced by permission of Wiley Periodicals

Chapter 13

Page 342: With kind permission from Springer Science+Business Media: *Journal of Behavioral Medicine,* "Comparison of two models of stress management: Daily hassles and uplifts versus major life events," 4, no. 1, p. 1-39, A. D. Kanner, J.C. Coyne, C. Schaefer, and R.S. Lazarus, data from Table III. Original copyright (C) 1981 by Plenum Publishing Corporation; **343:** From *The Stress of Life,* by Hans Seyle. Copyright © 1976 by The McGraw-Hill Companies, Inc. Reprinted by permission; **344:** Sheldon Cohen, Tom Kamarck, and Robin Mermelstein, "A Global Measure of Perceived Stress." From *Journal of Health and Social Behavior,* Vol. 24, No. 4 (December 1983), Appendix A. Reprinted by permission from the American Sociological Association; **345:** Adapted from Baum, 1994; **348:** From: Coan, J., Schaefer, H., Davidson, R. "Lending a Hand: Social Regulation of the Neural Response to Threat." *Psychological Science,* Volume 17, Issue 12, p. 1032-1039. Fig. 3, Published online: 13 Dec. 2006. © 2009 Association for Psychological Science; **350:** Reprinted from *The Lancet,* vol. 325, no. 8431. K. Pettingale, T. Morris, S. Greer, and J. Haybittle, "Mental attitudes to cancer: An additional prognostic factor," p. 750, Copyright 1985, with permission from Elsevier via Copyright Clearance Center; **352:** Canadian Tobacco Use Monitoring Survey (CTUMS). Health Canada (2010). Current Smoking "Prevalence by Age, Canada, 1985-2010". http://www.hc-sc.gc.ca/hc-ps/tobac-tabac/research-recherche/stat/ctums-esutc_2010-eng.php. Reproduced with permission of the Minister of Health, 2012; **354:** Myers, 2000, p. 57, drawn from *Social Indicators of Well-being: Americans' Perceptions of Life Quality,* pp. 207 and 306, by F. M. Andrews and S. B. Withey, 1976. New York, Plenum. Copyright 1976 by Plenum.

A

abnormal behaviour, **304**
  definition and diagnosis, 304–307
  descriptions, 306
  in *DSM*, 305–307
  perspectives, 304–305, 305*f*, 311
absolute threshold, **62**
accommodation, 70, **258**
acetylcholine (ACh), 37*f*, 38
achievement, need for, 197–198
achievement tests, **182**–183
action potential, 34*f*, **35**, 35*f*
activation-synthesis theory, **94**–95, 94*f*
activity theory of aging, **276**
acupuncture, 80, 270
adaptation, **63**
addiction to alcohol, 105–106
addictive drugs, **100**
adolescence, **263**
  coming of age, 269
  moral and cognitive development, 264–265
  physical development, 263–264, 263*f*
  psychosocial development, 266–268
  social development, 265–269
  suicides, 268–269, 268*f*
adrenal glands, 54*f*
adulthood
  aging and, 273–276
  development, 269–276
  health in, 270–271
  roles of men and women, 272–273
  social development, 271–273
afferent neurons, **40**
affiliation, need for, 197, 198
afterimage, 74–75
aggression, 235–237, **236**
  approaches to, 236–237
  media and, 130
aggressive cues, 236
aging, 273–276
  death and, 276
  memory and, 275
  social world, 275–276
  thinking and, 274–275, 274*f*
agoraphobia, 308*f*
agreeableness, 289, 290*f*
alarm and mobilization, 343, 343*f*
alcohol
  addiction, 105–106
  binge drinking, 104
  effects, 103*f*, 105*f*
  influence on fetus, 249–250, 249*f*
  problem, identification, 107–108
  usage by students, 101f, 104, 104*f*
  use disorder, 318
alcoholics, 105–106
algorithm, **163**
all-or-none law, **34**
altered states of consciousness, 88, 99
altruism, **238**–239
Alzheimer's disease, **155**–156, 156, 275
Ambien, 106
amnesia, **156**, 317
amphetamines, 101*f*, 102, 103*f*
amygdala, 157
analytical intelligence, **177**
androgens, **204**
anger management, 237
animal brain, **46**–47, 46*f*
animals
  classical conditioning, 113–114
  latent learning, 127–128, 128*f*
  operant conditioning, 118
  use in research, 26–27
anorexia nervosa, **201**–202, 202, 203
anterograde amnesia, **156**
antianxiety drugs, **323**–324
antidepressant drugs, **323**

antipsychotic drugs, 322
anti-social personality disorder, **316**–317
anvil, 75–76, 76*f*
anxiety disorders, 285, 307–311, **308**
aptitude tests, **182**–183
archetypes, **286**
arousal approaches to motivation, **193**–194
arrangement problems, 165, 166*f*
assimilation, **258**
association areas, **49**
assumed-similarity bias, **224**
attachment, 252–255, **253**
attention-deficit hyperactivity disorder (ADHD),
    318
attitudes, **218**
  behaviour and, 220–221
  communicator, 218
  of patients, and cancer survival, 350*f*
  persuasion and, 218–221
attribution and social cognition, 223–225
  processes, 223–224, 223*f*
attribution theory, **223**
atypical antipsychotics, 323
auditory canal, 75, 76*f*
authoritarian parents, **255**–256, 256*f*
authoritative parents, **255**–256, 256*f*
autobiographical memories, **150**–151, 151*f*
autonomic division, 39*f*, **40**
autonomic nervous system, functions, 41*f*
autonomy-versus-shame-and-doubt stage, **257**, 266*f*
availability heuristic, 164
aversive conditioning, **327**
avoidant coping, 346
axon, **33**–34, 33*f*

B

babble, **173**
Babinski reflex, 250
balance, 75, 77
barbiturates, 106
basic emotions, 209, 211–212, 212*f*
basilar membrane, **76**
behaviour
  abnormal, 304–307
  attitudes and, 220–221
  control or change of, 4–5
  modern perspectives, 5–8
  modification, 126–127
  observable, 9, 9*f*
  personality and, 291
  prosocial, 239
  social, 233–239
  Type A/B/D patterns, 348–349
behaviour modification, **126**–127
behavioural approaches to therapy, 327–329
behavioural assessment, **299**
behavioural genetics, 11, **42**–43
behavioural neuroscience, 10
behavioural neuroscientists, 32
behavioural perspective, **6**–7, 6*f*
  abnormal behaviour, 305, 305*f*, 311
  key issues, 9*f*
behavioural treatment approaches, **327**
Benzedrine, 102
benzodiazepines, 106
binge drinking, 104
binocular disparity, 66–67
biofeedback, **53**–54, 81
biological and evolutionary approaches to
    personality, **293**–294, 295*f*
biological approach to behaviour, 5–6
biologically based addictions, 100
biomedical perspective of abnormal behaviour,
    304–305, 305*f*, 310
biomedical therapy, **322**–325
biopsychologists, 32
bipolar cells, 72
bipolar disorder, **312**

bisexuals, 206–208
blind spot, 72, 73
blindness, 73–75
borderline pathology of childhood, 317
borderline personality disorder, **317**
bottom-up processing, 64–**65**
brain
  anorexia and, 202
  biofeedback, 53–54
  central core, 45–46
  cerebral cortex, 45*f*, 47–49, 48*f*
  depression and, 313*f*
  effect of drugs on, 100
  emotions and, 211
  hearing and, 76–77
  hemispheres, 50–51, 52–53
  imaging techniques, 43–45
  lateralization, 50–52
  limbic system, 46–47, 46*f*
  meditation and, 99
  memory consolidation, 157*f*
  men vs. women, 51–52
  in nervous system, 39*f*
  old and new, 46*f*
  pain and, 80, 81
  regenerative powers, 49–50
  scanning techniques, 44*f*
  senses interaction and, 81, 82
  split, 52*f*
  stress and, 348*f*
  structures of, 45*f*
  vision and, 70, 71–72
Broca's area, **47**
bulimia, **202**–203
bystander effect, **237**

C

caffeine, 101, 102*f*
camera, 70, 71*f*
Canada's Food Guide, 352
cancer, 349–350, 350*f*
cannabis. *see* marijuana
Cannon-Bard theory of emotion, 210*f*, **211**
cardinal trait, 289
case study, **19**, 21*f*
cataclysmic events, **341**
catatonic schizophrenia, 314*f*
catharsis, **236**
cell body, 33*f*
central core, **45**–46
central nervous system (CNS), 39*f*, **40**–42, 40*f*
central route processing, **219**–220, 219*f*
central traits, **222**, 289
cerebellum, **45**–46, 45*f*
cerebral cortex, 45f, **47**, 48*f*
  lobes and sections, 47–48
  motor area, 48
  sensory area, 48–49
change or control of behaviour, 4–5
children and childhood. *see also* infancy
  attachment in, 252–255
  cognitive development, 257–263
  development, 250–263
  from infancy, 251–252
  language learning, 173–174
  memory and, 149–150, 262
  mental programs, 261–262
  parenting styles, 255–256
  physical development, to age two, 252–253*f*
  principles of conservation, 260*f*
  psychosocial development, 256–257
  relationship with caregivers, 252–255
  relationship with peers, 255
  in single-parent families, 272
chlorpromazine, 323
chromosomes, **247**
chunk, **139**–140
circadian rhythms, 88*f*, **89**

classical conditioning, **113**, 114*f*
  description, 113–114
  extinction of, 116
  generalization and discrimination, 116–117
  human behaviour and, 115–116
  treatments, 327–329
  vs. operant conditioning, 125, 125*f*
client-centred therapy, **331**
clinical neuropsychology, 11
clinical psychology, 10
close relationship, **233**
cocaine, 101*f*, 102–104, 103*f*
cochlea, **76**, 76*f*
cognitive appraisal, 330, **345**
cognitive approaches to motivation, **195**
cognitive approaches to therapy, 330
cognitive development, **258**
  adolescence, 264–265
  children, 257–263
  Piaget's theory, 258–261, 259*f*
  Vygotsky's socio-cultural view, 262–263
cognitive dissonance, **221**, 221*f*
cognitive learning theory, **127**–131
cognitive maps, 128
cognitive perspective, 6*f*, **7**
  abnormal behaviour, 305, 305*f*, 311
  key issues, 9*f*
cognitive psychology, 10
cognitive restructuring, 81
cognitive therapy, 330
cognitive treatment approaches, **330**
cognitive-behavioural approach, **330**
cohort, definition, 246
collective unconscious, **286**
collectivism, **239**
collectivistic orientation, 225
colour blindness, 73–74
colour vision, 73–75
coming of age, 269
common traits, 289
community psychology, 334–335
companionate love, **234**, 234*f*
compliance, 227–230, **228**
compulsion, **310**
concepts, 162–**163**
concrete operational stage, 259*f*, **260**, 261
concussion, 31
conditional positive regard, 295
conditioned response (CR), **114**–116, 114*f*
conditioned stimulus (CS), **114**–116, 114*f*
condoms, 205, 206
cones, 70–72, 72*f*, 74
confirmation bias, **169**
conformity, **226**–227
confounding variables, **23**
conscience, 284
conscientiousness, 289, 290*f*
consciousness, **88**
  altered states of, 99
  drugs and, 100
  hypnosis and, 97–98
  meditation and, 98–99
  vs. unconsciousness, 9, 9*f*, 295*f*
conservation, principles, 259–260, 260*f*
constructive processes, 148–151
contingency contracting, 329
continuous reinforcement schedule, **121**–122
control group, 22–23
control or change of behaviour, 4–5
conventional morality, 264, 265*f*
convergent thinking, **170**
coping, **345**
coping with stress, 345–348
  learned helplessness, 347
  social support, 347–348
  strategies, 346–347
cornea, 70
coronary heart disease, psychological aspects,
  348–349

corpus callosum, 45*f*
correlation coefficient, 19
correlational research, **19**–21, 21*f*
counselling psychology, 10
courtroom and memory, 148–150
creative intelligence, **177**
creativity, **169**–171
cross-cultural psychology, 11
cross-sectional research, 246
crystallized intelligence, **176**, 180*f*, 274
cue-dependent forgetting, **154**–155
culture
  altered states of consciousness, 99
  attachment in children, 254
  attribution and, 225
  coming of age, 269
  emotions and, 209, 212–214
  IQ and, 186–187
  memory and, 151
  perception and, 68–69
  psychological disorders and, 320–321
  psychotherapy and, 333–334
culture-fair IQ test, 186

D

daily hassles, **341**–342
dark adaptation, 71
death, and aging, 276
debriefing, **26**
decay, **154**
declarative memory, **142**, 143*f*
defence mechanisms, 285–286, 286*f*, 325
deindividuation, **227**
deinstitutionalization, **334**
dendrite, **33**, 33*f*
DEP-C, 4–5
dependent variable, **22**
depressants, 103*f*, 104–106
depression, 311–313, 313*f*
depth perception, 66–67, 67
description of behaviour, 4
descriptive research, 18–21, 21*f*
determinism, **7**, 291
  vs. free will, 9, 9*f*, 295*f*
developmental psychology, **244**
  adolescence, 263–269, 263*f*
  adulthood, 269–276
  aging and, 273–276
  cognitive, 257–261, 262–263
  conservation principles, 260*f*
  definition, 243
  head size relative to body size, 252*f*
  infancy and childhood, 250–263, 252–253*f*
  nature–nurture issue, 244–247
  newborns, 250–251
  physical, 252–253*f*, 263*f*
  prenatal development, 247–250
  psychosocial, 256–257
  reflexes, 250
  research techniques, 246–247
  senses, 250–251
  social behaviour, 252–263
  as subfield of psychology, 10
deviant behaviour, 304
devil's tuning fork, 69, 69
Dexedrine, 102
*Diagnostic and Statistical Manual of Mental
  Disorders, Fourth Edition, Text Revision (DSM-
  IV-TR)*, 305
  behaviour classification, 305–306
  schizophrenia, 314
  shortcomings, 306–307
  social and cultural factors, 320–321
difference threshold, **62**–63
diffusion of responsibility, **238**
discrimination, **231**, 232–233
  classical conditioning, 116–117
  operant conditioning, 124

discriminative stimulus, 124
disengagement theory of aging, **275**–276
disorganized schizophrenia, 314*f*
dispositional causes of behaviour, **224**
dissociative amnesia, **317**
dissociative disorders, 317–318
dissociative fugue, **317**
dissociative identity disorder, **318**
divergent thinking, **170**
divorce, 271–272
door-in-the-face technique, **228**
dopamine (DA), 37*f*, 38
double standard, **205**
double-blind procedure, 25
Down syndrome, 185, 249
dreams, 93–95
  meaning and interpretation, 93–94, 326
  REM sleep and, 92
  subjects of, 93*f*
  theories of, 94*f*
dreams-for-survival theory, **94**, 94*f*
drive, **193**
drive-reduction approaches to motivation, **193**
drug therapy, **322**–324
drugs. *see also* specific drugs
  abuse and problems, 107–108
  addiction, 100
  brain and, 100
  depressants, 103*f*, 104–106
  effects, 100, 103*f*
  influence on fetus, 249, 249*f*
  narcotics, 103*f*, 106–107
  psychological disorders, 322–324, 322*f*
  stimulants, 101–104, 103*f*
  usage, 100–101, 101*f*
DSM. *see Diagnostic and Statistical Manual of
  Mental Disorders*
dysomnias, 95–96

E

ear, 75–77, 76*f*
eardrum, **75**–76, 76*f*
eating
  disorders, 201–204, 318
  health and, 352–353
  needs and motivation, 198–204
  obesity and, 201
  social factors, 200–201, 203
  weight loss, 203
Ebbinghaus's forgetting curve, 153*f*
echoic memory, 138–139
Ecstasy, 101*f*, 103*f*, 107
efferent neurons, **40**
ego, 283, 283*f*, **284**, 287
egocentric thought, **259**
ego-integrity-versus-despair stage, **267**, 267*f*
egoism, 238
elaborative rehearsal, 140
Electra complex, **285**
electroconvulsive therapy (ECT), **324**
electroencephalogram (EEG), 43–44, 44*f*
electromagnetic spectrum, 70*f*
embryo, 247, 248
emotional intelligence, **178**–180, 180*f*
emotion-focused coping, 345–346
emotions, **208**, 213*f*
  basic, 209, 211–212, 212*f*
  brain and, 211
  cultural differences, 212–214
  facial expressions, 213–214
  functions of, 208
  hierarchy and range, 209, 209*f*
  roots, 209–212
  theories, 210–212, 210*f*
  understanding of, 208–214
empathy-altruism hypothesis, **239**
encoding, 137, 154
endocrine glands, 54*f*

endocrine system, **54**–55
endorphins, 37*f*, 38–39
energy drinks, 101–102
engram, 156
environment, influence, 249–250, 249*f*, 294. *see also*
    nature–nurture issue
episodic buffer, 141
episodic memory, **142**–143, 143*f*
Erickson's theory of psychosocial development,
    256–257, 266–268
estrogens, **204**
ethics of research, 26
evolutionary approaches to personality, **293**–294,
    295*f*
evolutionary perspective, 6*f*, 8, 9*f*
evolutionary psychology, 11
excitatory message, **36**–37
exercise and sport, 353
exercise bulimia, 202
exhaustion, 343*f*, 344
expectations, and perception, 63–64
experiment, **21**
    key elements, 23
    steps, 21–24, 24*f*
experimental bias, 24–26
experimental group, **22**–23
experimental manipulation, **21**–22
experimental psychology, 10
experimental research, 21–24, 21*f*
experimenter expectations, 24–25
explaining behaviour, 4
explicit memory, **146**–147
exposure, **328**–329
extinction, **116**, 122
extramarital sex, **206**
extrasensory perception (ESP), 83
extraversion, **289**, 289*f*, 290*f*
extrinsic motivation, **195**
eye. *see* vision
eyewitness testimonies, 148–150, 149*f*
Eysenck's three dimensions of personality, 289*f*

F

face blindness, 59
Face Scale, *354*
facial-affect program, **213**
facial-feedback hypothesis, **213**–214
factor analysis, 289
false memory, 150
familial retardation, **185**
family therapy, **332**
fat tissue, 54*f*
fathers, attachment of children, 254–255
fatuous love, 234*f*
fears, hierarchy of, 328
feature detection, **73**
fetal alcohol syndrome, **185**, 249–250
fetus, **247**–249, 248
fixations, **284**
fixed-interval schedule, **122**–123, 123*f*
fixed-ratio schedule, **122**, 123*f*
flashbulb memories, **147**
fluid intelligence, **176**, 180*f*, 274
food, perception of, 78, 81
foot-in-the-door technique, **228**
forebrain, 45*f*, 47–48
forgetting
    aging and, 275
    Ebbinghaus's curve, 153*f*
    memory and, 152–157
formal operational stage, 259*f*, **260**–261
fovea, 70
free association, **326**
free will, **7**
    vs. determinism, 9, 9*f*, 295*f*
frequency theory of hearing, **77**
Freud, Sigmund, and personality, 283–287, 283*f*
frontal lobes, 47

frustration, 236–237
functional fixedness, **168**
functional magnetic resonance imaging (fMRI),
    44, 44*f*
functionalism, **14**
fundamental attribution error, **224**

G

g (or g-factor), **176**
gag reflex, 250
Gage injury model, *49*
gamma-amino butyric acid (GABA), 37*f*
ganglion cells, 72
gate-control theory of pain, **80**
gene therapy, 42, 325
general adaptation syndrome (GAS), **343**–344, 343*f*
generalization
    classical conditioning, 116–117
    operant conditioning, 124
generalized anxiety disorder, **309**–310, 309*f*
generativity-versus-stagnation stage, 267, 267*f*
genes, 42, 247
genetic preprogramming theories of aging, **273**–274
genetics
    behavioural, 11, **42**–43
    characteristics influenced by, 245*f*
    counselling, 43
    influence on personality, 293–294, 293*f*
    nature–nurture issue, 9, 9*f*, 244–247, 295*f*
    prenatal development, 247, 248–249
    schizophrenia and, 315*f*, 316
Gestalt diagrams, 65
Gestalt laws of organization, **65**–66
gestalt psychology, **14**
g-factor of intelligence, 176
glands, 54–55
glial cells, 33
glutamate, 37*f*
graded exposure, 328
grammar, **172**–173
group, **225**–230
    compliance, 227–230
    conformity, 226–227
    stereotypes and, 231–232
group polarization, **225**
group therapy, **332**
group think, **225**
gustation, 77–78

H

habituation, 112, 251
hair cells, **76**
hallucinogens, 103*f*, **106**, 106–107
halo effect, **224**
hammer, 75–76, 76*f*
happiness, 354–355
hassles and stress, 341–342, 342*f*
health psychology, **340**
    definition, 10, 340
    eating and, 352–353
    happiness and, 354–355
    hostility and, 348–349
    promotion, 352–355
    sport and exercise, 353
    stress and, 342–343
    yoga and meditation, 353–354
hearing, 75–77
heart, 53–54, 54*f*
helping, 237–239, 238*f*
hemisphere, **50**–51, 52–53, 73*f*
heredity. *see* genetics
heritability, **187**–188, 187*f*
heroin, 103*f*, 106
heterosexuality, **206**, 207
heuristics, **163**–164, 166–167
hierarchy of fears, 328
hindbrain, 45–46, 45*f*

hippocampus, 156–157
homosexuals, **206**–208
hormone, **54**–55
horn effect, **224**
hostility, 348–349
humanistic approaches to personality, **294**–296, 295*f*
humanistic perspective, 6*f*, 7–8, 9*f*
humanistic therapy, **330**–331
hunger
    biological factors, 199–200
    needs and motivation, 198–204
hyperthymesia, 135
hypnosis, **97**–98
hypothalamus, 45*f*, **46**, 54*f*, 199
hypothesis, **17**, 22

I

iconic memory, 138–139
id, **283**–284, 283*f*
identical twins, 207, **246**, 293–294
identification, **285**
identity, 266
identity-versus-identity confusion, 267*f*
identity-versus-role-confusion stage, **266**–267
ill-defined problem, 165
illness, psychological aspects, 348–352
imitation, 129–130, 251
immune system, and stress, 340, 345
implicit memory, **146**–147
impression formation, 222–223
imprinting, 251
incentive approaches to motivation, **194**–195
independent variable, 22, **22**, 24
individual differences *vs.* universal principles, 9–10,
    9*f*
individualist orientation, 225
inducing structure problems, 165, 166*f*
industry-versus-inferiority stage, 257, 266*f*
infancy. *see also* children and childhood
    development, 250–263
    to middle childhood, 251–252
    newborns, 250–251
    physical development, to age two, 252–253*f*
    relationship with caregivers, 252–255
    vision in, 250–251
inferiority complex, **288**
information processing, **261**–262
information-processing approach to intelligence,
    177–178, 180*f*
informed consent, 26
inhalants, 101*f*
inhibitory message, **36**–37
initiative-versus-guilt stage, 257, 266*f*
inner ear, 76, 76*f*
inoculation theory, 229
insomnia, 95, 96, 106
instincts, **192**, 236
integration, 185
intellectual disabilities, **184**–185
intellectually gifted, **185**–186
intelligence, **176**. *see also* intelligence quotient (IQ)
    achievement and aptitude tests, 182–183
    aging and, 274–275
    approaches to, 180*f*
    distribution, 182*f*
    emotional, 178–180, 180*f*
    fluid and crystallized, 176, 180*f*
    g-factor, 176
    group differences, 186
    information-processing approach, 177–178, 180*f*
    intellectually gifted, 185–186
    mental retardation, 184–185
    multiple intelligence theory, 178, 179*f*, 180*f*
    nature, nurture, and IQ, 186–188
    overview, 175–176
    tests, 180–184
    theories of, 176–180
    triarchic theory, 177, 180*f*

variation in ability, 184–186
WAIS-III, 182, 183*f*
intelligence quotient (IQ), **181**, 182*f*
    culture and, 186–188
    heritability, 187–188, 187*f*
    tests, 181–182
intelligence tests, 180–184
interactionist approach to language, **175**
interference, **154–155**
internal mental processes *vs.* observable behaviour, 9, 9*f*
Internet surveys, 19, 298
interneurons, **40**
interpersonal attraction, **233**
interpersonal therapy (IPT), **331–332**
intimacy-versus-isolation stage, **267**, 267*f*
intrinsic motivation, **195**
introspection, **14**
IQ. *see* intelligence quotient (IQ)
iris, 70

J

James-Lange theory of emotion, 210–**211**, 210*f*
just-noticeable difference, 62–63

K

keyword technique, 136
kidneys, 54*f*
Kohlberg's theory of moral development, 264–265

L

language, 171–175
    acquisition theories, 174–175
    brain and, 51–52
    development, 173–174
    grammar, 172–173
language-acquisition device, **174**
latent content of dreams, **94**
latent learning, **127–129**, 128*f*
lateralization, **50–52**
learned helplessness, 313, **347**
learning, **112–113**
    animals and, 113–114, 127–128, 128*f*
    cognitive approaches, 127–131
    of language in children, 173–174
    latent, 127–129, 128*f*
    model, 129–130
    observational, 129–130, 236–237, 291, 329
    personality and, 290–292, 295*f*
learning-theory approach to language, **174**
lens of eye, 70
leptin, 201
levels-of-processing theory, **145**
life review, **276**
light adaptation, 71
light therapy, 81
liking, 233–234
limbic system, **46–47**, 46*f*
linear perspective, 67, 67
lithium, 323
liver, 54*f*
lobes, **47**
longitudinal research, **246**
long-term memory, **138**, 138*f*
    autobiographical memories, 150–151
    children and, 262
    constructive processes, 148–151
    courtroom and, 148–150
    culture and, 151
    explicit memory, 146–147
    flashbulb memories, 147
    implicit memory, 146–147
    levels-of-processing theory, 145
    modules, 142–143
    recall of, 144–151
    retrieval cues, 144–145

semantic networks, 143
short-term memory transfer to, 140
subcategories, 143*f*
workings of, 141–142
lottery tickets, 124, 161
love, 234–235, 234*f*
low-ball technique, **228**
LSD (lysergic acid diethylamide), 103*f*, 107
lunar effect, 171
Lunesta, 106

M

magnetic resonance imaging (MRI), 44, 44*f*
mainstreaming, 185
major depression, **311–312**
maladaptive behaviour, 304
mania, **312**
manifest content of dreams, **94**
marijuana, 101*f*, 103*f*, 106–107, 106*f*
marital sex, 205–206
marriage, 271–272
Maslow's hierarchy of needs, 195–196, 196*f*
masturbation, **204–205**
maturation, 245
MDMA. *see* Ecstasy
means-ends analysis, **166–167**
medication, for pain, 81
meditation, **98**–99, 99
    health and, 353–354
medulla, 45*f*
memory, **137**. *see also* long-term memory
    aging and, 275
    children and, 149–150, 262
    consolidation, 157*f*
    culture and, 151
    dysfunctions, 155–156
    false, 150
    forgetting and, 152–157
    foundations of, 137–144
    improvement strategies, 136
    modules, 142
    neuroscience of, 156–157
    overview, 135–136
    proactive interference, 155, 155*f*
    processes, 137*f*
    rehearsal, 140
    repressed, 150
    retroactive interference, 155, 155*f*
    semantic networks, 143–144
    sensory memory, 138–139
    short-term memory, 139–141
    three-system approach, 138, 138*f*
    traces, 154
    traumatic events, 153
    working, 140–141, 141*f*
men
    brain lateralization, 51–52
    morality, 265
    physical development in adolescence, 263*f*
    roles in adulthood, 272–273
    sex organs, 204*f*
menarche, 263–264
menopause, 270–271
mental age, 181
mental health, self-perception in Canada, 319*f*
mental images, **162**
mental retardation, **184–185**
mental set, **168**, 169*f*
meta-analysis, 24
metabolism, **200**
metacognition, **262**
methadone, 106
methamphetamine, 102
midbrain, 45*f*, 46
middle ear, 75–76, 76*f*
mindful meditation, 98–99
Minnesota Multiphasic Personality Inventory-2 (MMPI-2), **296–297**

minority groups, 186–188, 232
model, for learning, 129–130
modifiability *vs.* stability, 295*f*
money and happiness, 355
monoamines, 92
monocular cues, 67
mood disorders, **311–313**
mood stabilizers, **323**
moral development, 264–265, 265*f*
morpheme, **172**
morphine, 103*f*, 106
mother
    attachment of children, 253–254
    influences on fetus, 249–250, 249*f*
motion, sense of, 75
motion parallax, 67
motivation, **192**
    achievement and, 197–198
    affiliation and power and, 197, 198
    approaches to, 192–197
    arousal approaches, 193–194
    cognitive approaches, 195
    drive-reduction approaches, 193
    human needs and, 197–208
    hunger and eating, 198–204
    incentive approaches, 194–195
    instinct and, 192
    Maslow's hierarchy of needs, 195–196
    sexual, 204–208
motor area, **48**
motor (efferent) neurons, **40**
Müller-Lyer illusion, 67–68, 68
myelin sheath, 33*f*, **34**
myelination, 34
Myers-Briggs Type Indicator, **298**

N

narcissistic personality disorder, **317**
narcolepsy, 96
narcotics, 103*f*, **106–107**
nativist approach to language, **174–175**
naturalistic observation, **18**, 21*f*
nature–nurture issue, 9, 9*f*, **244–247**, 295*f*
need for achievement, **197–198**
need for affiliation, 197, **198**
need for cognition, 220
need for positive regard, 295*f*
need for power, 197, **198**
needs
    affiliation and power, 197, 198
    hierarchy, 196*f*
    hunger and eating, 198–204
    motivation and, 197–208
negative after-potential, 35
negative correlations, 20, 20*f*
negative punishment, 119–120, 120*f*
negative reinforcement, 118–120, 120*f*
negative reinforcer, 118–**119**
neo-Freudian psychoanalysts, **286**, 287–288
nerve cells. *see* neurons
nerve stimulation, for pain, 81
nervous system, structure and parts, 39–43, 39*f*
neurogenesis, 50
neurons, **33**
    communication, 33–34
    firing of electrical impulses, 34–35, 35*f*
    gap bridging between, 35–37
    motor and sensory, 40
    in nervous system, 39
    neurotransmitters, 35–39
    perception and, 61
    renewal, 50
    structure, 33–34, 33*f*
    vision and, 71–73
neuroplasticity, **50**
neuroscience perspective, 5–6, 6*f*, 9*f*
    memory and, 156–157
neuroscientists, 32

neuroticism, 289, 289f, 290f
neurotransmitters, **35**–39
  effect of drugs, 100
  how they work, 36f
  psychological disorders drugs and, 323
  types, 37f
neutral stimulus (NS), **113**–116, 114f
new brain, 45f, 47–49, 48f
newborns, 250–251
nicotine, 102, 350–351. *see also* smoking
nightmares, 96
noise, 62
norm of reciprocity, 228–229
norms, **184**, 226, 296
not-so-free sample, 228–**229**

O

obedience, **229**–230
obesity, **199**, 201
object permanence, **258**–259
observable behaviour *vs.* internal mental processes,
  9, 9f
observational learning, **129**–130, 291, 329
  aggression and, 236–237
obsession, **310**
obsessive-compulsive disorder, **310**
occipital lobes, **47**
Oedipal conflict, **285**
old brain, 45–46
olfactory cells, 78
openness, 289, 290f
operant conditioning, **117**
  behaviour analysis and modification, 126–127
  description, 117
  discrimination, 124
  how it works, 118–125
  positive and negative reinforcers, 118–120
  punishment in, 118–121
  schedules of reinforcement, 121–124
  shaping in, 124–125
  techniques, 329
  vs. classical conditioning, 125, 125f
operational definition, 17
opponent-process theory of colour vision, **74**
optic chiasm, 72
optic nerve, **72**
organic mental disorders, 319
others, understanding of, 222, 223f
otoliths, **77**
ovaries, 54f
overgeneralization, **174**
overlearning, 136
ovulation, **204**

P

pain
  management, 81
  mechanisms of, 78–80
pancreas, 54f
panic attacks, 309
panic disorder, **309**
paranoid schizophrenia, 314f
parasomnias, 95–97
parasympathetic division, 39f, **41**–42, 41f
parathyroids, 54f
parenting, styles of, 255–256, 256f
parietal lobes, **47**
partial reinforcement schedule, **121**–122
participant expectations, 25
participants, choice of, 22–23
passionate love, **234**, 234f
penis envy, 285
perception, **61**
  culture and, 68–69
  of depth, 66–67
  examples of, *61*, 64–69
  Gestalt laws of organization, 65

perceptual constancy, 66
perceptual sets, 64
  subliminal, 83
  top-down and bottom-up processing, 64–65
  visual illusions, 67–68
  vs. sensation, 60, 61
perceptual constancy, **66**, 66
perceptual set, **64**
peripheral nervous system, 39f, **40**–42, 40f
peripheral route processing, **219**–220, 219f
peripheral vision, 71
permissive parents, **255**–256, 256f
personal stressors, **341**
personality, **282**
  behavioural assessment, 299
  biological and evolutionary approaches, 293–294,
    295f
  collective unconscious, 287
  defence mechanisms, 285–286, 286f
  disorders, 316–317
  Eysenck's three dimensions, 289f
  feminist perspective, 288
  Freud and, 283–287, 283f
  genetic influences, 293–294, 293f
  humanistic approaches, 294–296, 295f
  learning approaches, 290–292, 295f
  need for positive regard, 295f
  neo-Freudian psychoanalysts, 287–288
  projective methods, 297–298
  psychoanalytic theory and, 283–287
  psychodynamic approaches, 282–288, 295f
  psychology, 10
  psychosexual stages, 284–285, 284f
  self-actualization, 294–295
  self-efficacy, 291–292
  self-esteem, 292
  self-report measures, 296–297
  tests, 296–298
  trait approaches, 288–290, 290f, 295f
personality disorders, **316**–317
personally distressful behaviour, 304
person-centred therapy, **331**
persuasion, 83, 218–221, 219f, 229
PhD programs, 12
phenylketonuria (PKU), 248
phobias, 115, **308**–309, 308f
phonemes, **172**
phonology, **172**
photographic memory, 135
phrenology, 43
Piaget's theory of cognitive development, 258–261,
  259f
pineal gland, 54f
pituitary gland, 45f, 54f, **55**
place theory of hearing, **76**–77
placebo, **22**, 25
pleasure principle, 283–284
pons, 45, 45f
positive correlations, 19–20, 20f
positive punishment, 119–120, 120f
positive regard, 295, 295f, 331
positive reinforcement, 118–120, 120f
positive reinforcer, 118–**119**
positron emission tomography (PET), 44, 44f
postconventional morality, 264, 265f
post-traumatic stress disorder (PTSD), 341
power, need for, 197, 198
practical intelligence, **177**
preconventional morality, 264, 265f
predicting behaviour, 4
predisposition model to schizophrenia, 315–316
prefrontal lobotomy, 324
prejudice, **231**–233
premarital sex, 205
prenatal development
  environmental influences, 249–250, 249f
  genetics, 247, 248–249
preoperational stage, **259**, 259f
pressure, 79

primacy effect, 141
primary drives, 193
primary reinforcer, 118
priming, **146**
principle of conservation, **259**–260, 260f
principlism, **238**
proactive interference, **155**, 155f
problem
  categories of, 165, 166f
  creativity and, 169–171
  evaluating solutions, 167
  generating solutions, 166–167
  obstacles to solving, 167–169
  steps to solving, 164–167
  understanding and diagnosing, 165, 167f
problem-focused coping, 345–346
procedural memory, **142**, 143f
progesterone, **204**
projective personality test, **298**
propranolol, 153
prosocial behaviour, **237**–239
prosopagnosia, 59
prototypes, **163**
psychedelic drugs. *see* hallucinogens
psychoactive drugs, **100**
psychoactive substance-use disorder, 318
psychoanalysis, **326**
psychoanalytic perspective of abnormal behaviour,
  305, 305f
psychoanalytic theory, **283**–287
psychodynamic approaches to personality, 282–288,
  283, 295f
psychodynamic approaches to therapy, 325–327
psychodynamic perspective, **6**, 6f, 9f
psychodynamic therapy, **325**, 326–327
psychological disorders
  anxiety, 285, 307–311
  behavioural approaches, 327–329
  biomedical therapy, 322–325
  categories, 306f, 307–321
  cognitive approaches, 330
  dissociative, 317–318
  drug treatments, 322f
  group and family therapy, 332
  humanistic therapy, 330–331
  interpersonal therapy, 331–332
  mood, 311–313
  personality, 316–317
  perspectives, 304–305, 305f
  prevalence, 319–320
  psychotherapies, 325–327
  schizophrenia, 313–316
  social and cultural contexts, 320–321
  symptoms, 335
  treatment, 321–335, 322f
psychological tests, **296**
psychologically based addictions, 100
psychologists
  careers, 12–13
  education, 12
  portrait of, 11
  women as, 11, 15, 16
  work and workplace, 11–14, 13f
psychology, **4**
  future of, 16
  goals, 4–5
  historical views, 13–14
  key issues, 8–10, 9f
  milestones in, 12–13f
  perspectives of, 5–8, 6f
  roots of, 14
  subfields, 10–11
psychoneuroimmonology (PNI), **340**, 344–345
psychophysics, **61**
psychophysiological disorders, **343**
psychosexual stages, **284**–285, 284f
psychosocial development, **257**
  adolescents, 266–268
  children, 256–257

stages of, 257, 266–267f
psychosurgery, **324**
psychotherapy, **322**
    evaluation, 332–335
    reasons for stopping, 333f
    for treatment of disorders, 325–327
psychoticism, 289, 289f
PsyD programs, 12
puberty, **263**–264
punishment, 118–121, **119**, 120f
pupil, 70

R

random assignment to condition, **23**
random sample, **18**
rapid eye movement (REM) sleep, 89, 90f, **91**–92, 91f
rapid eye movement (REM) sleep behaviour disorder, 87, 97
reality principle, **284**
reasoning. *see* thinking
rebound effect, 92
recall, **145**
recency effect, 141
receptor cells, 72f
reciprocal altruism, **239**
reciprocal determinism, **291**
recognition, **145**
reflex, **40**
reflexes development, 250
rehearsal, **140**
reinforcement, **118**, 120f
    punishment and, 118–124
    schedules, 121–124, 123f
reinforcer, **118**–119
relative size, 67
relaxation, for pain, 81
relaxation response, 328f
reliability of tests, **183**–184, 296
REM. *see* rapid eye movement (REM) sleep
replication, **24**
representative sample, **18**
representativeness heuristic, 164
repressed memories, 150
repression, **285**
research challenges, 24–27
    ethics, 26
    validity assessment, 25–26, 27
research process
    descriptive, 18–21
    experimental, 21–24
    hypotheses, 17
    methods, 17–24
    scientific method, 16, 16f
    strategies, 21f
    theories, 17
residual schizophrenia, 314f
resistance, **326**, 343–344, 343f
resting state, **34**
reticular formation, 45f, **46**
retina, 66–67, **70**–72
retinal disparity, 66–67
retrieval, 137
retrieval cues, 144–145
retroactive interference, **155**, 155f
retrograde amnesia, **156**
reuptake, **37**
rods, **70**–72, 72f
Rohypnol, 106
romantic love, **234**
rooting reflex, 250
Rorschach test, **298**–299
rote memorization, 145

S

salivation, 113–114, 114f, 116
sample, in survey research, 18

scaffolding, 262
Schacter-Singer theory of emotion, 210f, **211**–212
schedules of reinforcement, 121–124
schemas, **148**, 222, 223, 258
schizophrenia, 313–316, **314**
    characteristics, 314–315
    risk of developing, 315f
    types and subtypes, 314f, 315
scientific method, **16**, 16f
seasonal affective disorder (SAD), **89**
secondary drives, 193, 197
secondary reinforcer, 118
secondary traits, 289
securely attached children, 253–254
sedatives, 103f, 106
selective serotonin reuptake inhibitors (SSRIs), 323
self-actualization, **196**, 294–295
self-concepts, 294–295
self-efficacy, **291**–292
self-esteem, **292**
self-fulfilling prophecy, 231
self-help books, 318
self-report measures, **296**
self-serving bias, **224**
semantic memory, **142**, 143f
semantic networks, **143**–144
semantics, 172
semicircular canals, 77
senility, 275
sensation, **61**, 61
    absolute thresold, 62
    difference threshold, 62–63
    sensory adaptation, 63–64
    vs. perception, 60, 61
senses. *see also* perception; sensation; vision
    development in newborn, 250–251
    hearing, 75–77
    interaction among, 81–82, 82
    overview, 60–62
    pain, 78–81
    skin, 78–80
    smell and taste, 77–78
    thresholds and, 62–63
    touch/pressure/temperature, 78–80
sensitive periods, 248
sensorimotor stage, **258**, 259f
sensory adaptation, 63–64
sensory area, **48**–49
sensory memory, **138**–139, 138f
sensory (afferent) neurons, **40**
sensory stimuli, **82**
sequential research, **246**, 247
serial position effect, 141–142
serotonin, 37f, 38
sex organs, 204f
sexual disorders, 318–319
sexual motivation
    heterosexuality, 206
    homosexuality and bisexuality, 206–208
    marital sex, 205–206
    masturbation, 204–205
    premarital sex, 205
    transsexualism, 208
sexual orientation, 207
shaping, in operant conditioning, 124–**125**
short-term memory, **138**, 138f, 139, 139–141, 262
sickle-cell anemia, 248
significant outcome, **24**
single-parent families, 272
situational causes of behaviour, **224**
skin, 78–81, 80f
sleep
    amount of, 92–93, 92f
    apnea, 96
    circadian rhythms, 88f, 89
    cycle, 91f
    deprivation, 92–93
    disturbances, 95–97
    electronics and, 93

    problems, 95
    reason for, 92–93
    REM sleep, 89, 90f, 91–92, 91f
    REM sleep behaviour disorder, 87, 97
    spindles, 90
    stages of, 89–91, 90f, 91f
    talking, 96
sleepwalking, 96
small intestine, 54f
smell, 77–78
smoking
    cognitive dissonance and, 221, 221f
    prevalence, 352f
    promotion, international, 351–352
    psychological aspects, 350–352
    quitting, 351
    reason for, 350–351
social behaviour
    development, 252–263
    late adulthood, 275–276
    liking and loving, 233–235
    positive and negative, 233–239
social cognition, **222**
    attribution and, 223–225
    impression formation, 222–223
    personality and, 291–292
    understanding others, 222, 223f
social cognitive approaches to personality, **291**
social development
    adolescents, 265–269
    adulthood, 271–273
social identity theory, 231–232
social influence, **225**–230
    compliance, 227–230
    conformity, 226–227
social media, life without, 3
social phobia, 308f
social psychology, **218**
    aggression, 235–237
    attitudes, 218–221
    attribution, 223–225
    compliance, 227–230
    conformity, 226–227
    discrimination, 232–233
    helping others, 237–239
    liking and loving, 233–235
    persuasion, 218–221
    prejudice, 231–233
    social cognition, 222–225
    social influence and groups, 225–230
    stereotypes, 231
    as subfield of psychology, 11
social roles, conformity to, 227
social support, for coping with stress, **347**–348
social supporter, **227**
socio-cultural perspective, 6f, **8**, 9f
somatic division, 39f, **40**
sound, 75–77
sound localization, 75
source traits, 289
spermarche, 264
spinal cord, 39f, **40**, 45f
split brain, 52f
spontaneous recovery, **116**
spontaneous remission, **333**
sport and exercise, 353
stability vs. modifiability, 295f
stage 1-4 sleep, 89–91, **90**, 90f, 91f
Stanford-Binet Intelligence Scale, 182
startle reflex, 250
status, **226**
stereotype, **231**–232, 233
steroids, 101f
stimulants, **101**–104, 103f
stimulation. *see* motivation
stimulus, **61**. *see also* perception; sensation
stimulus control training, 124
stimulus discrimination, **117**
stimulus generalization, **116**–117, 124

stirrup, 75–76, 76f
stomach, 54f
storage, 137
stress, **340**
    brain and, 348f
    consequences, 344–345, 345f
    coping with, 345–348
    cost of, 342–343
    general adaptation syndrome, 343–344
    personal aspect of, 340–341
    psychoneuroimmonology, 344–345
    PTSD, 341
    reduction, 53
    stressors, 340–345
stressors, 340–345
    categorization, 341–342
    hassles and uplifts, 342f
stroke, 32
structuralism, **14**
subjective well-being, **354**–355
subliminal perception, 83
subliminal persuasion, 83
substance P, 80
sucking reflex, 250
suicides, adolescents, 268–269, 268f
superego, 283, 283f, **284**
suprachiasmatic nuclei (SCN), 89
survey research, **18**–19, 21f
sympathetic division, 39f, **41**–42, 41f
synapse, **35**, 36f
synesthesia, 81
syntax, **172**
systematic desensitization, **327**–328

T

taste, 77–78
taste buds, 78
Tay-Sachs disease, 248
telegraphic speech, **173**
temperament, **256**
temperature, 79
temporal lobes, **47**
teratogen, **249**
terminal buttons, **33**, 33f
test standardization, **296**
testes, 54f
tetrahydrocannabinol (THC), 106
texture gradient, 67
thalamus, 45f, **46**, 211
that's-not-all technique, **228**
Thematic Apperception Test (TAT), 197–198, **298**
theories, 17
theory of multiple intelligences, **178**, 179f, 180f
thinking, **162**–171
    aging and, 274–275, 274f
    algorithms and heuristics, 163–164
    concepts, 162–163
    mental images, 162

problem solving, 164–170
    three-candle problem, 168f
thyroid, 54f
tip-of-the-tongue phenomenon, **144**
token system, 329
tolerance, **100**
top-down processing, 64–**65**
touch, 79
Tower of Hanoi puzzle, 164–165, 165f
trait theory, **288**, 295f
    Big Five, 289–290, 290f
    factors and dimensions of, 290f
    personality and, 288–290
    principal, 289
transcranial magnetic stimulation (TMS), 44–45, 44f, **324**
transduction, **61**
transference, **326**
transformation problems, 165, 165f, 166f
transgenderism, 208
transsexuals, **208**
traumatic memories, 153
treatment, 22
triarchic theory of intelligence, 177, 180f
trichromatic theory of colour vision, **74**
trust-versus-mistrust stage, **257**, 266f
twins, 207, 246, 293–294
Type A behaviour pattern, 348–349
Type B behaviour pattern, **348**
Type D behaviour, 349

U

umami, 78
unconditional positive regard, **295**, 331
unconditioned response (UCR), **113**–116, 114f
unconditioned stimulus (UCS), **113**–116, 114f
unconscious, **283**–287, 283f
    components of personality, 283–284
    defence mechanisms, 285–286
    psychosexual stages, 284–285, 284f
    vs. consciousness, 9, 9f, 295f
unconscious wish fulfillment theory, **93**–94, 94f
undifferentiated schizophrenia, 314f
uninvolved parents, **255**–256, 256f
universal grammar, **174**
universal principles vs. individual differences, 9–10, 9f
uplifts and stress, 342, 342f

V

validity of tests, **184**, 296
Valium, 106
variable-interval schedule, 122, **123**–124, 123f
variable-ratio schedule, 122, 123f
variables, 19
    confounding, 23
    dependent and independent, 22

operationalization, 22
verbal store, 141
violence in media, 130–131
visceral experience, 210
visible spectrum, 69, 70f
vision
    brain and, 70, 71–72
    camera, 70, 71f
    colour and blindness, 73–75
    hemispheric differences, 73f
    newborns, 250–251
    overview, 69–70
    process, 70–73
    retina and, 70–71
    stimuli principles, 65
visual illusions, **67**–69, 68
visual store, 141
Vygotsky's socio-cultural view of cognitive development, 262–263

W

waking consciousness, 88
wear-and-tear theories of aging, **273**–274
Weber's law, **62**–63
Wechsler Intelligence Scale (WAIS-III), 182, 183f
weight set point, **199**–200, 201
well-being
    happiness and, 354–355
    psychological aspects, 348–352
well-defined problem, 165
wellness, promotion, 352–355
Wernicke's area, **47**
white noise generator, 95
withdrawal, **100**
women
    alcohol and, 104–105
    brain lateralization, 51–52
    cancer survival, 349–350, 350f
    depression, 313
    morality, 265
    in personality studies, 288
    physical development in adolescence, 263f
    as psychologists, 11, 15, 16
    roles in adulthood, 272
    sex organs, 204f
working memory, 140–**141**, 141f

X

Xanax, 106

Y

yoga, 353–354

Z

zone of proximal development (ZPD), **262**
zygote, **247**